F. Paul

KINDRED
SPIRITS
2

2,400 Reviews of Whiskey,
Brandy, Vodka, Tequila, Rum, Gin,
and Liqueurs from
F. Paul Pacult's Spirit Journal 2000-2007

F. Paul Pacult
Editor, *F. Paul Pacult's Spirit Journal*

ISBN 978-0-9801238-3-8

Library of Congress Control Number: 2008921480
COOKING/Beverages/Wine & Spirits
COOKING/Beverages/Bartending

Designed by www.Zenarts.biz
Cover photograph and photograph of F. Paul Pacult by Michael Gold

Printed in the United States of America.

1.0

Dedicated to friends and mentors, present and departed:

Rodney and Charlotte Strong;
Peter and Roberta Morrell;
Gary Regan; Bonnie Jenkins;
my partners in Beverage Alcohol Resource, LLC,
Dale DeGroff, Doug Frost, Steve Olson, Andy Seymour,
and David Wondrich, for taking the leap with me;

and all the world's distillers, large and artisanal.

Other books by F. Paul Pacult

✦✦ *Kindred Spirits: The Spirit Journal Guide to the World's Distilled Spirits and Fortified Wines* (Hyperion, 1997)

✦✦ *The Beer Essentials: The Spirit Journal Guide to Over 650 of the World's Beers* (Hyperion, 1997)

✦✦ *American Still Life: The Jim Beam Story and the Making of the World's #1 Bourbon* (John Wiley & Sons, 2003)

✦✦ *A Double Scotch: How Chivas Regal and The Glenlivet Became Global Icons* (John Wiley & Sons, 2005)

CONTENTS

ACKNOWLEDGMENTS

1 INTRODUCTION
Why After Ten Years a New *Kindred Spirits* • Nuts and Bolts of KS2 and
What Lies Ahead • How the KS2 Reviews and Ratings are Arrived At •
The Evaluation Regimen • So, Off We Go

8 RUDIMENTARY SPIRITS KNOWLEDGE
Spirits Production: Fermentation, Distillation, Wood Maturation

12 GIN & GENEVER—WORLD
26 VODKA—WORLD
104 RUM, CACHAÇA & GUARO—WORLD
167 TEQUILA, SOTOL, MEZCAL & OTHER AGAVE BASED SPIRITS—MEXICO—WORLD
214 WHISKEY—IRELAND
223 DISTILLERY ISSUE SINGLE MALT SCOTCH WHISKY—SCOTLAND
284 MERCHANT ISSUE SINGLE MALT, SINGLE GRAIN & BLENDED
MALT WHISKY—SCOTLAND
342 BLENDED, SINGLE GRAIN & BLENDED MALT WHISKY—SCOTLAND
358 WHISKEY—USA
395 WHISKY—CANADA
402 WHISKEY—WORLD
406 COGNAC—FRANCE
457 ARMAGNAC—FRANCE
506 CALVADOS—FRANCE
518 GRAPPA, EAU-DE-VIE, PISCO, ARAK, MARC, SLIVOVITZ & BRANDY—WORLD
550 BRANDY—USA
561 BRANDY—SPAIN
566 LIQUEURS, SCHNAPPS & VERMOUTHS—WORLD

634 APPENDIX A: CONSUMERS' FAQS
637 APPENDIX B: F. PAUL PACULT'S 111 BEST WHISKEYS, BRANDIES,
LIQUEURS, AND WHITE SPIRITS IN THE WORLD
641 APPENDIX C: ABOUT *F. PAUL PACULT'S SPIRIT JOURNAL*

643 BIBLIOGRAPHY

INTRODUCTION

WHY AFTER TEN YEARS A NEW *KINDRED SPIRITS*

In the decade that has followed the publishing of my first book *Kindred Spirits: The Spirit Journal Guide to the World's Distilled Spirits and Fortified Wines*, I have been astonished by the number of consumers who have told me that they still use KS as a buying guide for distilled spirits. "But it's obsolete. Some of the spirits reviewed are no longer in the marketplace," I tell them. These kind people have typically followed up their claim of continued use with a question regarding the availability of the next edition. My wife and partner Sue Woodley and I have heard the question "When will the updated version of *Kindred Spirits* be out?" more times than we care to count.

Allow me to introduce you to F. Paul Pacult's *Kindred Spirits 2*. In the Spirit Journal offices, located in New York State's Hudson Valley, we describe the book simply as KS2. This updated edition of *Kindred Spirits* covers all of my detailed reviews and ratings on brandies, whiskeys, liqueurs, and white spirits dating from 2000 through 2007. These many hundreds of detailed evaluations have appeared in editions of our advertising-free, subscription-only quarterly newsletter, *F. Paul Pacult's Spirit Journal*. Although abridged versions of some of the reviews have appeared in *Wine Enthusiast Magazine's* Spirits Buying Guide, where I am Spirits Tasting Director, KS2 contains every review in its original unabridged, full-strength, unfiltered, bare-knuckle form.

Since the publishing of the original *Kindred Spirits* in 1997, the distilled spirits category of alcoholic beverages has experienced dramatic changes and unprecedented growth in North America and around the globe. Similar to how fine wine leapt ahead in our nation's consciousness in the 1980s and how handcrafted beers became celebrated in the early 1990s, spirits turned a corner in the middle 1990s. The explosion of popularity in spirits over the last ten years has happened—and continues to accelerate—due to three distinct yet interdependent reasons.

First, the coming of age of the consuming public's collective palate has helped cultivate a healthy and fertile environment of sensory adventure. Never before in history have so many legal-age women and men searched for more profound spirits experiences and challenges in all distillate categories.

Second, the public's burgeoning interest has been aggressively met by the distilling industry with the release of hundreds of new and sometimes cutting-edge spirits in all categories. The current plethora of spirits, most good, some abominable, that is available in North America (at present, over 4,000) keeps perpetuating the grassroots interest. Consumers demand, producers supply; producers supply even more and consumers sample more.

Third, the public's acute fascination with high-end spirits has been fueled, in part, by the vibrancy of the New Golden Era of Cocktails, which in many quarters has been propagated by the emphasis on fresh ingredients and top drawer spirits. This third point is key because the trend towards better quality has kept raising the standards for consumers and at the same time has honed their palates.

Additionally, the last decade of cocktail fever has introduced younger drinkers to the glories of fine spirits through creative mixology. This phenomenon has erased the generational boundaries concerning spirits that were rampant during the 40-year period of 1945 to 1985, an era where bland, predictable, and safe products dominated the worldwide marketplace. Nowadays, card-carrying members of the Greatest Generation (1926-present), the Baby Boomer Generation (1946-present), Generation X (1966-present), and Generation Y (1986-present) are all enjoying, or at least beginning to enjoy as in the case of Gen-Y-ers, the uplifting delights of better spirits and the innovative cocktails that they make.

There's no longer any question about the attraction of brandies, whiskeys, white spirits, and liqueurs. In 2006, according to statistics offered by the Distilled Spirits Council of the United States (DISCUS) in their annual report, spirits revenues in the US rose by a healthy 6.3% from 2005 totals, producing revenues of $17 billion. Not surprisingly, the areas of major growth were in the premium (up 5.1%), high-end (up 6.5%), and super-premium sectors (up a rollicking 17.5%). Spirits accounted for 32.8% of all beverage alcohol sales, an increase of 0.7% from 2005. The numbers merely affirm what any savvy consumer already knows: Spirits are hotter than asphalt in July.

Game on.

NUTS AND BOLTS OF KS2 AND WHAT LIES AHEAD

It has been my job as well as my personal mission to chronicle product evaluations for all categories of distilled spirits in the quarterly editions of *F. Paul Pacult's Spirit Journal* since the winter of 1991 when the *Spirit Journal* debuted. This compilation of roughly 2,400 reviews and ratings is taken directly from the pages of *Spirit Journals* spanning from March 2000 (Volume 10, Issue 1) through the December issue of 2007 (Volume 17, Issue 4). That period of time makes certain that KS2 is in line with what's in the marketplace until at least 2010.

If you're concerned that pre-2000 items aren't going to be present and accounted for in KS2, don't be. The most important items are. Through the *Spirit Journal Retaste Program*, which was established over three years ago, hundreds of spirits that were reviewed prior to 2000 have been given another formal evaluation in order to update my impressions of them. So, yes, longstanding spirits like Tanqueray London Dry Gin, Delamain Pale & Dry Grande Champagne Cognac, Glenfiddich 12 Year Old Special Reserve Single Malt Whisky, and George Dickel Special Barrel Reserve Tennessee Whiskey that appeared in the original *Kindred Spirits*, receive a critical makeover. The ratings that appear after each review are the most recent scores.

Is every spirit that's currently available in the US marketplace reviewed in KS2?
No. I taste as much as I possibly can. Considering how my office time has dwindled over the past half decade due to increased commitments to consulting and public appearances, now with well over 4,800 distillates out there and that total increasing each year, it would be

almost impossible to get a hold of them all. Suffice it to say that KS2 is as comprehensive a collection of spirits reviews as you're likely to find.

Are all the KS2 reviewed products available?
The vast majority of the 2,400+ reviewed spirits are still available in retail stores. However, there may be a few pre-2003 products that have been pulled from the marketplace.

Do any products reviewed in the original *Kindred Spirits* reappear in KS2?
Yes, quite a few. This is due directly to the *Spirit Journal Retasting Program* begun in 2003 wherein I re-evaluate spirits reviewed in the 1990s. Some products have been altered; others haven't been tampered with. About 20% receive a new rating, higher or lower. So that three star single malt you loved from *Kindred Spirits* could be upgraded in KS2.

What is different in KS2 from its forerunner aside from the deletion of Fortified Wines, meaning Sherry, Port, and Madeira?
While I remain an ardent admirer of all three, especially sherry, I no longer feel it appropriate, as I did in 1997, to lump them together with beverages that were distilled. KS2 is distilled spirits only. No wines of any style. No beers.

Also, I would never claim that these reviews and scores are the last word on any one product. They are merely my take on these particular distilled beverages over a specified period. That is all. I will allow myself to make one ironclad claim. After painstakingly evaluating between 9,000 and 11,000 spirits in the identical twenty to thirty minute format over the last twenty years, KS2 readers have my personal assurance that my process is unbiased and comprehensive to the admitted point of obsession. It is this personal guarantee of fairness that, I hope, gives each reader the confidence to make safe purchasing decisions based on this book's content. As opposed to advertising-friendly publications that live with the possibility of an advertiser pulling their print ads unless a glowing review of a particular product is published, the advertising-free nature of *F. Paul Pacult's Spirit Journal* has allowed me the freedom to speak my mind without fear of retribution. I believe that this is the pivotal point that underpins the veracity of this compilation.

How the KS2 Reviews and Ratings are Arrived At

Over the years, I've come to adore a handful of sublime distillates, meaning those that I've rated five stars. These are my benchmarks. To counter that reality, I've likewise managed to abhor another handful of distasteful distillates whose ratings have registered a solitary star. These are my bottom feeders and should be avoided. The overwhelming majority has fallen into the safety of the two to four star range.

But promises and claims aren't enough, in my estimation. When I place my trust in the opinion of a theater, book, car, music or movie critic, I like to know their method, when possible. So, I'm going to briefly describe how I render whether or not a spirit is recommendable or not. In my view, I owe a sacred responsibility both to the distiller and the consumer to go about my business in a professional and uncompromising manner, unimpeded by distraction.

Here, then, are some of my voluntarily imposed mandatory rules when conducting formal evaluations:

1) *Proper environment*

The environment for evaluation purposes must be quiet, clean, and appropriate to the task at hand. My formal reviews are conducted solely in my office at the Spirit Journal HQ and never outside that space. I utilize the same thin crystal glasses for all spirit categories, a combination of stemmed copitas, small wineglasses, 6-ounce Riedel Vinum Port glasses, and other top-notch glassware that I wash myself by hand without the use of detergent. The glasses are air-dried because sometimes even cotton towels and/or paper towels can leave residue.

2) *Spitting, numbers, timing*

I use opaque plastic beer cups for spittoons because I rarely swallow a sample. As a matter of policy, **I never sample more than eight spirits in any one session.** I usually taste early in the morning, normally from 8:30 am to noon. I am a morning person, so that suits me best. I never have tea (I don't drink coffee), fruit juice or anything to eat before formal tastings. **An unadulterated, fresh palate is essential.** If I begin to experience palate fatigue, I stop for the day. I also make every attempt to taste products from the same category in one session.

3) *Inputting*

I write the review on my computer in **real time** to convey my most immediate thoughts and impressions. I sometimes return to a product if I feel that there's a possibility that I've been overly harsh or euphoric. That said, it is the rare occasion that I alter a rating after sampling a product a second time. My first impressions ring true and accurate the vast majority of the time.

4) *Absence of price*

In my evaluations, **suggested retail price is not an issue**. I judge only the sensory characteristics and how they match up against the standards of the category. Neither do I care about the bottle nor packaging.

5) *Ratings*

What my critiques come down to are these two salient points: Is this product something that stacks up well in relation to the established, contemporary standards of the specific category? And, most important of all, would I recommend this product to a friend or colleague?

I employ a **one to five star rating system**, with one being the lowest score and five the highest. Here's what they signify:

★ tells you that that particular product's **quality is well below the established standard** for the category. One star products are often undrinkable, unbalanced, and obviously are deemed as being **Not Recommended**.

★★ indicate an item that is only **average or fair** when judged against its peers and is, therefore, **Not Recommended**. These spirits may be drinkable and without severe failings, but in the end they are uninspiring and lacking any special merit. I would not tell a friend to buy them.

★★★ mean that the character profile of this item is **better than average** and exceeds what would be considered as the norm for product quality of this category. Three star products are <u>**Recommended**</u>. I would positively advise a friend to hunt them down.

★★★★ indicate that the product under scrutiny is starting to get into pretty heady territory. These products **far exceed what is thought to be average/fair**. Four stars point to a product of authentic quality and distinct personality. These high quality items come <u>**Highly Recommended**</u>. I would, with gusto, counsel all my friends to buy these products.

★★★★★ indicate a **watershed, landmark product** whose seamless quality is as ideal as an item within that category can get. These are the benchmark products that can be thought of as defining a spirits category due to their harmonious natures in which all the chemical components— alcohol, acids, base materials, wood use, if any—are perfectly integrated through outstanding distillation, maturation, filtration, blending and/or other production techniques. They receive my <u>**Highest Recommendation**</u>. At this degree of excellence, I tell anyone who'll listen, strangers in the street, my parking attendant, the UPS man, anyone, to do whatever needs to be done in order to get a bottle of these rare and exquisite spirits.

It is my belief that the world's distillers have gotten better across the board over the last decade. Shared experience, advanced technology and improved filtration and maturation management have combined to make finer spirits in all categories, especially tequila and rum. Consequently, I find myself recommending a slightly higher percentage of products nowadays, not because I'm getting sentimental but because the quality is noticeably better.

6) *Alcohol by volume, or abv.*
As part of every review, the abv is cited for informational purposes. Typically when you come across a whiskey or a brandy abv that's wildly different from the standard 40% to 43% level, such as 59.2%, 63.3%, or 49.9%, it frequently signals a "cask strength" spirit. This means that the spirit was drawn from the barrel and bottled without dilution down to a lower range.

7) *Listed suggested retail prices and unlisted importers.*
As part of each review, you'll find the suggested retail price as ascertained <u>**at the time of the review**</u>. In other words, a cognac review from 2001 will have posted the price that it was at the time of the review. It's probable that the price in 2008 will be higher by a few dollars. The idea is to offer a price range more than a specific price. Also, no importers are listed because they have a habit of changing often.

THE EVALUATION REGIMEN THAT I EMPLOY

I take 20-30 minutes for every formal product evaluation. That is one reason why I am an admittedly deliberate critic. Some of my peers can whiz through a line-up of twenty items in an hour. I just can't move that quickly. As stated earlier, my obligation to KS2 readers and to the world's distillers, many of whom I know, is to supply them with the clearest, most accurate, and thorough sensory data that I'm able to so that they can make astute buying and/or production decisions in the real world.

I pour at least one ounce but never more than two ounces of the product in question. I employ the same glasses, flight after flight, meticulously and naturally cleaned after each use. I always have mineral water close at hand for thorough palate rinsing between items. The four-sense system I've used for the past two decades goes as follows:

Sight: First, but not the most important stage, is looking at the spirit under a bright lamp for 10 to 30 seconds. At this point, I'm gauging the color (brown, yellow, red, green, blue and their various shades), the clarity (is it opaque or translucent?), and the overall cleanliness (do I see any sediment and if so, what does it appear to be?). Most of all, does it own an appealing appearance? This stage rarely consumes more than one minute.

Smell: Next comes the pivotal phase of the whole exercise, the one that, for me, makes up at least 50% to 60% of the final score. Smell is our most primitive sense and is the only sense that triggers the feeling of déjà vu. Smell directs and impacts the sense of taste by up to 90%. When I have a sinus problem due to allergies or a cold, I cannot and will not conduct formal evaluations. Smell is the most crucial of all the senses for people in my line of work.

I smell every item in three stages. I take a series of gentle sniffs right after the pour, holding the glass just beneath my nose, lips parted to help circumvent the rush of alcohol. I allow it to sit undisturbed for another three minutes and at the five minute mark take deeper, longer inhalations. It often takes a spirit several minutes to adjust to its new environment. Then, at the ten minute mark, I take a parting whiff just in case I missed anything in the first two nosing passes. In all, I spend from 5 to 15 minutes total smelling each spirit. In some instances, I will return to the smelling phase after the tasting phase to double-check an observation or to erase a doubt.

Taste: Immediately following the smelling stage, I take a small sip and let the liquid rest at the tip of my tongue for a few seconds, then spit it out. This is the palate entry stage. This initial impression should remind me at least a little of what was occurring in the smell. Sometimes it doesn't. Smell and taste are usually in harmony, but on occasion show little resemblance. After another minute, I take a larger sip and let that amount rest on the tongue for a quarter to a half a minute. This allows the whole of the tongue to be saturated. This midpalate phase makes or breaks the mouth experience. And it's here where the rating begins to firm up. I spend up to 10 minutes tasting several times. Some spirits, like cask strength whiskeys, need another round of sniffing and tasting when mineral water is added. A rigid format such as this trains your 10,000 taste buds to work together.

Touch: The feel of a spirit is the final piece of information that I need to render a final decision. Is the spirit oily, thin, syrupy, raw, biting, silky smooth? Any or all of these attributes can affect the score by as much as a star.

Savor: By "savor" I simply mean to sit back and enjoy—or not—the entire experience of all the senses over a few moments. The key is to ponder the following three questions: Do I like this product? If I do like it, to what degree of enthusiasm do I like it? If I don't care for it, to what degree do I dislike it?

This entire process requires usually 20 to 30 minutes, give or take five minutes. There is no magic to it. One needn't be a chemist, a wizard, or a MENSA candidate to do it well.

Success in spirits analysis requires, above all, **repetition, strict adherence to a comfortable and thorough format, and keen observation**. Practice helps to build the mental library that is absolutely necessary for critical analysis. Without such a storehouse of reference data, accurate and reliable analysis won't happen.

SO, OFF WE GO...

Distilled spirits—brandies, whiskeys, white spirits, and liqueurs—are genuinely beautiful creations that should always be treated with the utmost respect and care, not just for oneself, but for everyone within our sphere of influence. I know you've heard it ad infinitum, but moderation and restraint ARE absolutely necessary for the proper enjoyment of these ancient elixirs. Appreciation of fine spirits comes with the price tag of personal responsibility. We taste and savor; we don't guzzle and potentially harm anyone. Spirits enjoyment is all about the celebration of community and it is our obligation to give these fine beverages the respect they deserve.

Since around 11th century A.D., when distillation was first taught at the Salerno School of Medicine in Italy by Benedictine monks, the products of distillation have restored the inner reserves of countless millions when life has dealt difficult hands. They have toasted millions of marriages, births, graduations, the closing of business deals, the buying of new houses, and other myriad conquests, solemn occasions, and victories. Spirits have been a vital thread in the history of western civilization for a millennium. Over the last ten centuries, technology, hygiene, the quality of base materials, and production technique have all markedly improved. Now, we find ourselves in a period of Spirits Renaissance. Aren't we the fortunate ones?

When you get the chance, visit our web site at www.spiritjournal.com

I would also like to thank Zenon Slawinski and Karin Huggens of Zenarts.biz for their expertise and patience in creating the KS2 layout and design.

Last and most vital: everything that I do, from speaking to groups of consumers to training industry personnel to writing columns and books to endless research travel, could not happen without the 24/7/365 dedication, administrative skill, sage advice and supreme assistance of my wife, soul-mate, and life-long partner, Sue Woodley. Those of you who are fortunate enough to know her are hip to the fact that Sue is the "Spirit" in, of and about Spirit Journal, Inc. and *F. Paul Pacult's Spirit Journal*. Sue also happens to be my all-time favorite person.

Salut. Na Zdrovye. Saúde, Kampai. Prosit. Salud. Skal. Proost. Santé. Iechyd dda. Na Zdrowie. Con-cin. Sláinte. To health.

RUDIMENTARY SPIRITS KNOWLEDGE

SPIRITS PRODUCTION: FERMENTATION, DISTILLATION, WOOD MATURATION

Fermentation is a natural biochemical process that creates alcohol and carbon dioxide and is triggered whenever sugary liquids come into contact with either airborne or purposely injected yeasts. Because fruit juices are innately sugary, wines can, under the right circumstances, virtually make themselves. A bit of human intervention, as the world has observed for the past thousand years as wines have dramatically improved, helps.

With beer, the procedure is a bit more complicated, in that the starches in the grains must first be converted to sugar through dampening which stimulates partial germination. Once the grain starches have changed over to sugars, the resultant soupy mash starts to transform with the introduction of yeast cells. Thus, beer really does need an assist from mankind in order to happen. Via fermentation, fruit juices become wines and grain mashes become beers. Simple.

Distillation, the word, is derived from destillare, the Latin verb meaning "to drip down". At its most fundamental, distillation is a purification process that utilizes concentrated heat to boil fermented liquids, such as beer and wine, for the express purpose of separating the alcohol from the water and base materials. Alcohol boils at precisely 173.1 degrees Fahrenheit while water boils at 212 degrees Fahrenheit, so the alcohol turns gaseous before the water turns to steam.

This procedure works best when carried out in a kettle or any variety of mechanical contraptions, in which intense heat can be generated and sustained and in which vapors can be captured. These kettles are referred to as "pot stills".

As the alcohol changes from liquid into vapor, it rises in the pot still's chambers and is guided through channels whereupon it cools and condenses (drips down) back into clear liquid form. The intense heat of distillation strips away impurities in fermented liquids, thereby leaving behind the liquid's essence, or, as the Christian monks were inclined to describe it, the "spirit" or "water of life". With each round of distillation, the liquid gets less contaminated and the percentage of alcohol is elevated.

The concept of pot still distillation is direct in its simplicity.

Here's how it works, step-by-step:

1) The distiller pumps fermented liquid (beer or wine) into the chamber of the pot still.
2) The pot still is heated, gradually bringing the alcohol to the boil whereupon it vaporizes.
3) The vapors ascend into the upper region of the pot still chamber and flow through a "swan neck" pipe at the top of the pot still. (The pipe is referred to as such for its resemblance to its namesake.)

4) The vapors move from the swan neck through to cooled coils where they condense, turning back into liquid form (spirits), purer, clearer and higher in alcohol than when they started.

5) The distiller carefully selects the middle part of the distillation run, the best portion or so-called "heart"(similar to the best cuts of meats, like the center cuts, tenderloins, filets, etc.) and separates that prime segment from the rest of the run.

6) The lesser, more impure parts of the distillation run, the "heads" and the "tails" are often put through another distillation to purify them to the desired degree.

7) Many single-batch spirits are distilled again in other smaller pot stills to elevate levels of purity and alcohol.

Maturation in wood. The concept of using wooden barrels for storage and the shipping of wares hit stride with the Romans by the 3rd century A.D. They constructed barrels out of palm wood in order to transport common goods, like olive oil, olives, dried fruit, wine, nails, herbs and gold coins, across the Roman Empire via ocean-going vessels.

Roman commercial shippers and merchants began replacing their amphorae with wood barrels that could be easily rolled and stacked onto ships. Wood barrels had one more virtue that shippers liked: in the event of a ship sinking, wood barrels floated. Amphorae sank like rocks. So, for durability, ease of movement, stacking, and floating, wood barrels became indispensable.

What European merchants found in the ensuing centuries was that wine and spirits changed for the better when stored in wood barrels. They mellowed; they darkened; they became far more drinkable with wood contact due to the influence of acids found in wood, in particular lignin and tannin.

Wood also allowed the encased liquid to breathe, due to the fact that wood is porous. The moderate contact with air softened the spirits, making them more drinkable. Over the centuries, winemakers and distillers moved to oak because they found that oak has the ideal level of porosity that lets spirits and wines mature gradually and evenly.

WHITE SPIRITS

GIN & GENEVER—WORLD

Gin's name comes from the French term for juniper, genièvre. Juniper berries or oil of juniper are derived from among the 60 to 70 species of the aromatic evergreen trees or shrubs of the Juniperus genus of the cypress family. The fragrant, cedary/piney smelling berries from juniper shrubs are the ones most frequently used in the flavoring of gin. Other key botanicals, which distillers may or may not use, include roots such as angelica, orris root, and ginger; seeds and pods like coriander, caraway, aniseed, and cardamom; dried fruit peels like orange, lime, tangerine, and lemon peels; barks such as cassia bark; spices, most notably, cumin, nutmeg, and rosemary; plants/flowers like fennel, liquorice, and rose petals; nuts like almonds; non-juniper berries such as cubeb and grains of paradise; and vegetables such as cucumber.

In order to achieve the desired house style, time after time, each distiller employs by his/her own closely guarded recipe of botanical ratios. Some distillers infuse the oils of botanicals into their neutral grain spirits while others steep mixtures of whole, fresh botanicals into them during a second stage of distillation. On all accounts, distillation is the production phase where botanicals are introduced. The key lies in making certain that the properties that you want accented are and the ones you want muted remain in the background supporting roles. Angelica root, for example, is a botanical that is employed more as a unifying factor than as a flavoring agent on its own. Because of the delicate balance of the botanicals, gin is an extremely difficult spirit to produce well on a consistent basis.

The contemporary fundamental styles of gin are **Genever** (Holland), **London Dry** (universal), and **Plymouth** (only from Plymouth, England). An old, sweet style, known as **Old Tom**, no longer exists. The most prevalent style is London Dry. In my world, gin is the best of the white spirits for cocktails and my favorite overall white spirit. No white spirit exhibits the elegance of many gins, period.

Aviation Gin Batch Distilled (USA); 42% abv, $28.
Very minor sediment spotted; otherwise clear and pure. The initial aromatic burst is minty and mouthwash-like, with heavy emphasis on spring garden, flowers, jasmine, and pine; the bouquet noticeably diminishes after aeration, emitting earthy/mineral-like and fruity scents of slate/stone, wax, and orange zest. The palate entry is very citrusy and tart; the midpalate stage displays minor botanical impact but major grain and citrus fruit influence as the flavor profile turns astringent and bitter. Concludes zesty, acidic, fresh, and clean. A floral/citrusy style that's 180 degrees apart from London Dry.
2007 Rating: ★★★/Recommended

Back River Gin (USA); 43% abv, $28.

Limpid, silvery color; flawless clarity. Smells richly and vibrantly of juniper berries, cedar sap, and blueberries; the engaging freshness marches on with purpose after aeration as the bouquet takes a left, turning a touch riper and sweeter, yet is still markedly brambly and viny; the aroma's unlike any other gin in the world and better than a whole slew of them. Entry is keenly tart, fruit skin acidic (meaning, heavily tannic from the blueberries), and mouth-puckering; the dry, bittersweet taste profile at midpalate highlights more of the non-blueberry botanicals, especially the juniper and a particular cooking spice (Allspice? Marjoram? Can't quite pin it down). Finishes ultra-clean, amazingly tart and acidic, yet eye-poppingly fresh. A gin that pushes the white spirit envelope in a way that's creative and sophisticated.
2007 Rating: ★★★★/Highly Recommended

Bafferts Gin (England); 40% abv, $30.

Rain water clear; some whitish sediment spotted beneath the evaluation lamp immediately after the pour, but it quickly dissipated; not a problem. The opening nosing pass detects a tangy prickliness that's spirit generated; in the second whiff the coriander jumps into the lead as far as the aromatics go and holds that position until the later phase of the third pass whereupon the orange and juniper come to the forefront; by the final sniffing, some eight and a half minutes on, the aroma turns bean- or kernel-like; a totally dry, if slightly reluctant bouquet that requires some effort; is it the addition of so relatively few botanicals that's created this hesitant bouquet? In the mouth, the taste is desert dry at palate entry; then at midpalate it turns spirity and bittersweet in a grainy, cocoa bean-like manner. The suave aftertaste is medium long, intensely kernel-like, bitter, and a touch dark chocolaty. Definitely a Third Millennium gin that relies more on the grain spirit than the botanicals and is therefore a gin/vodka hybrid; the midpalate and the finish push this gin into recommended territory.
2001 Rating: ★★★/Recommended

Bardenay London Style Dry Gin (USA); 47.1% abv, $19.

Excellent clarity. In the first nosing passes, the cedary perfume of juniper is unmistakable and totally dominant; further aeration allows for a few other botanicals to peek through the enveloping haze of juniper, namely coriander, citrus, and fennel. The palate entry is sweet upfront, then quickly and sternly prickly on the tongue; the midpalate stage features major sappy/piney gulps of juniper and little else except for harsh, aggressive spirit. Concludes fiery, piny, intense, and too powerful for its—or the drinker's—own good. The overriding reason why I do not recommend this gin is this: while the distillers have the abv right at 47.1% for the style, the breakdown occurs with the imbalance between alcohol and botanicals. The charm of the botanicals, however they are mixed in, is obliterated by the vigorous thrust of the alcohol, causing 4-alarm spirity heat. This forces me to conclude that the base spirit was not very good to begin with. Drink Bardenay next to Beefeater or Tanqueray, both classic London Dry gins, and you'll understand what great base spirit does for gin. The platform is the spirit, not the botanicals. That said, there is definitely some promise here.
2006 Rating: ★★/Not Recommended

Beefeater London Dry Gin (England); 47% abv, $19.

Impeccably pure and silvery bright, almost pewter-like in appearance. In the initial whiffs, the juniper berry presence is perfectly supported by desert dry notes of dried orange peel and black pepper; following the usual seven minute extended period of air contact, the bouquet turns floral and earthy, spicy and crisp, all while never losing its juniper focus; a textbook London Dry Gin bouquet. The palate entry is sharp and crisp as a razor, lovely and balanced in its botanical usage and dry; at the midpalate point there's a burst of citrus juiciness that counters the earthiness of the juniper and angelica root. Finishes in a compelling rush of sweetish juniper madness that I find incredibly attractive. *See also Wet by Beefeater.*
2007 Rating: ★★★★/Highly Recommended

Blackwood's Vintage Dry Gin (Scotland); 40% abv, $36.

Some cork bits are spotted floating, but nothing of any concern; displays a pale green/gray sheen. The first two minutes of sniffing stay focused on spicy, vegetal, and biscuity notes that are moderately appealing in their collective banality; further aeration time doesn't stimulate anything more from this narrow bouquet that refuses to express itself with anything more than a whisper. The palate entry shows far more character than the lackluster aroma as creamy notes of grain mash, heather, stone, and green vegetable take charge; the midpalate stage is semisweet, clean, slightly chalky/minerally, and gently juniper/cedar-like. This gin's best moment occurs while in the throat as textured flavors of juniper, angelica, and distant honey come together in an impressive display of harmony. Admirers of Hendrick's Gin will like this new offering.
2007 Rating: ★★★/Recommended

Bluecoat American Dry Gin (USA); 47% abv, $25.

Silvery gray in appearance; ideal clarity. The opening aroma is strangely rubbery and keenly textile-like; following another seven minutes of aeration, my hope was that this would begin to smell like gin by displaying, at the minimum, a trace of juniper, but that hope was dashed on the trash heap of reality as the horrible burnt rubber odor gets stronger; without any doubt in my mind, the worst gin bouquet I've ever encountered. The palate entry uncovers hints of juniper berry, angelica and citrus, then the flavor drops off the table in midpalate leaving behind a manufactured taste of glue in the woeful finish. A new entry for my Bottom Feeder List, this one-car accident doesn't in the least resemble gin at any level. Beyond horrible. Makes me yearn for early retirement.
2007 Rating: ★/Not Recommended

Bombay Original Dry Gin (England); 43% abv, $18.

Flawlessly pure and silvery clean. First sniffs detect ample amounts of juniper, cedar, Christmas tree sap-like fragrance; coriander and orris root earthiness comes alive after further aeration, creating a peppery perfume that's zesty and mildly citrusy. Entry is silky, smooth, moderately sweet, and keenly pine-like; the midpalate stage is elegant, floral, sweet, and a touch sap-like. Finishes clean as a whistle, citrusy, and spicy. Not in the league of Beefeater and Tanqueray, but significantly better than its timid, weak-kneed kin, if nicely dressed in blue, Bombay Sapphire.
2007 Rating: ★★★/Recommended

Bombay Sapphire London Dry Gin (England); 47% abv, $26.
Limpid and flawlessly clean in appearance. The opening sniffs are met with hot, spirity aromas that provide a little bit too much burn in the nasal cavity for my liking; after additional time in the glass, the aroma's focal point remains the alcohol, with background traces of citrus and moss; but where's the juniper? What's happened to this gin's aromatic profile, which resembles nothing even close to London Dry? The palate entry is unacceptably hot, raw, and harsh and the midpalate is thin and timid. In its defense, Sapphire is drinkable, but touting this as a London Dry is laughable. The pretty bottle isn't enough.
2007 Rating: ★★/Not Recommended

Boodles British Gin London Dry Gin (England); 45.2% abv, $20.
Crystal clear, clean and pure. The opening sniffings detect more sage, nutmeg and cassia bark impact than juniper, thereby making the bouquet invitingly herbal and woodsy; seven more minutes allow for the juniper to hesitantly peek out from behind the assertive spice and herb flavorings; not your grandmother's style of gin, dear Muggins. The palate entry is round, semisweet and moderately oily; at midpalate the taste flow goes in the direction of the herbs, especially rosemary and coriander, even pepper. Finishes elegantly, firmly and squeaky clean. A gin that should be revisited by a lot of people.
2004 Rating: ★★★★/Highly Recommended

Boomsma Junge Genever (Holland); 40% abv, $15.
Translucent, but with noticeable particles floating about. The opening nose is fresh, spirity, and slightly oily; in the second sniffing, the spirit picks up the pace offering near-prickly waves of distillate as the botanicals take the low road; the penultimate whiff, following six minutes of exposure to air, finds more pronounced hints of orris, angelica, and cassia; the final nosing pass adds simple traces of juniper and black pepper; the best feature of this otherwise ordinary genever aroma is the freshness factor. The palate entry is fuller than I expected as the rich juniper/orris tastes impress the taste buds; the midpalate stage offers more subtle botanical tastes, especially the juniper. The aftertaste is medium long, concentrated, and bean-like. The mouth phases rescued this genever and placed it squarely into recommended territory.
2000 Rating: ★★★/Recommended

Boomsma Oude Genever (Holland); 40% abv, $16.
The pale appearance is of flax or hay and it shows very minor suspended debris. This aroma is far fruitier/grainier than the initial offering of its sibling, the Junge; with time in the glass, the aroma turns into a full-fledged bouquet, emitting graceful notes of fresh flowers, subtle spice, and restrained botanicals; the third sniffing offers an expanding aromatic landscape as scents of orris and lemon zest get added to the mix; the grain dominates the fourth and final pass, after a full eight minutes of aeration; while the Junge's bouquet relied almost solely on its appealing immaturity, this older, more mature bouquet offers levels of aroma that deepen with exposure to air; very nice. The palate entry flavor reminds me of fabric, especially cotton, and is stunningly neutral; by the midpalate stage I'm happy to report that flavors of cocoa bean, angelica, cassia, and juniper come to life. The finish is medium long, more sweet than dry, lightly botanical, and quite pleasing.
2000 Rating: ★★★/Recommended

Broker's London Dry Gin (England); 47% abv, $20.

Touted on the label as "The Gin for Gentlemen"—that type of "reaching" marketing ploy instantly alienates me and don't even get me started about the completely cheesy twist-cap that's shaped in the form of a black bowler hat—godalmighty; the look of Broker's in the copita is ideally pure and clear. The opening nosing passes are found to be totally enthralling as exotic, yet classical scents of lemon zest, coriander and orris root delight the olfactory sense; further aeration time stimulates deeper aromatic notes, especially juniper berry and cassia bark; a dynamite bouquet. In the mouth, it sits well on the tongue and, thankfully, is the proper level of alcohol for gin, 94 proof; by the midpalate stage the lovely, firmly structured and focused flavor profile features lemon zest and coriander, all buttressed by a fine oily texture that's buttery and creamy. Finishes long, semisweet, tangy and luscious. A superbly made London Dry Gin that deserves a very close look by any admirer of that style.
2003 Rating: ★★★★/Highly Recommended

Bulldog London Dry Gin (England); 40% abv, $30.

Crystalline appearance; unblemished purity. First nosings play up the juniper as well as the assertive, prickly spirit (don't mind prickliness at all); later sniffs pick up citrus and floral notes that are enticing and appropriate; a solid London Dry bouquet that while lacking smoothness/creaminess is pleasantly forceful. Entry is surprisingly creamy (wasn't expecting that since the aroma gave away no hints of cream), juniper heavy, and curiously chalky; the taste profile at midpalate is herbal, piney, and citrusy. Hey, I like this gin a lot, mostly for its juniper-driven London Dry authenticity and creamy flavor phase. Can't help but wonder how splendid it would be at 47% abv.
2007 Rating: ★★★★/Highly Recommended

Cadenhead's Old Raj Dry Gin (Scotland); 55% abv, $50.

The slightly pale straw tint, rare in a gin, is due to the addition of saffron—impeccable purity and clarity. The first nosing pass offers a mildly fruity/spicy scent that doesn't for a nanosecond speak of the elevated alcohol level; the second and third sniffings, following ample aeration time, see the development of biscuity, rich aromas that feature atypical, but alluring and garden-like fragrances of flowers, orris root, and angelica; the fourth and final whiff stays the aromatic course plotted in the early passes, spotlighting the earthier, softer botanicals rather than the more pungent juniper and bitter citrus; the balance and harmony of this gentlemanly bouquet is of classical proportions. The palate entry is sweet and fruity, featuring for the first time the juniper berries; the midpalate is long, silky smooth, fruity, dry, and remarkably supple, even succulent. The finish brings the citrus more into play as the sweetness of the entry and midpalate gives way to a delightful tartness. What's so impressive about this breathtaking gin is that from start to finish the 110 proof acts only as a sublime foundation for the botanicals rather than as a star performer; as delicious and comely as I could ever imagine British gin to be.
2001 Rating: ★★★★★/Highest Recommendation

Cascade Mountain Hand Crafted American Gin (USA); 47.5% abv, $27.

Clear, but with the faintest tint of pale yellow; superb purity. This entry shows a sturdy background aroma of juniper berry; after seven more minutes in the copita, I was hoping for an aromatic expansion, but that failed to materialize. The palate entry displays an intense oiliness and an almost spritzy juniper taste and feel; at midpalate the spirit turns hot and rash, burning the tongue slightly. Finishes hot, harsh and grossly unappealing. Avoid altogether; a travesty in the mouth.

2004 Rating: ★/Not Recommended

Citadelle Gin (France); 44% abv, $25.

Clear as rainwater. The first waves of aroma bring with them scents of fresh flowers, jasmine, honeysuckle, and cardamom; exposure to air stimulates deeper, more herbal notes including anise, grains of paradise, and cinnamon; this tantalizing bouquet is like a springtime garden. At the palate entry, the off-dry juniper presence is clearly evident; at midpalate the taste profile turns creamy, rich, and flowery once again. Ends up off-dry, high on juniper essence, and elegant. The only gin in the world that can compete with the great Tanqueray Special Dry in terms of luscious richness and texture.

2005 Rating: ★★★★★/Highest Recommendation

Damrak Lucas Bols Amsterdam Original Gin (Holland); 41.8% abv, $30.

Distilled five times; perfectly clear and sediment free. The aroma is fresh, feathery light, and reminiscent of dried orange peel in the initial nosing; the moderately tart, squeaky clean fragrance highlights both citrus peel and orris root in the middle stages; the fourth and last sniffing adds both angelica (predominantly) and coriander to the aromatic mix; where are the juniper berries? The palate entry is where the juniper berries have hidden up until now as they storm the tongue with traditional gin flavor; the midpalate stage is piquant, dry-to-bitter, and flush with zesty, fruit peel and berry tastes. The tart finish features juniper, orange peel, and angelica. The quintuple distillation somewhat takes the brass out of the aroma but not out of the flavor and aftertaste. Lean and atypical for what I've come to expect from Holland in terms of gin making.

2001 Rating: ★★★★/Highly Recommended

Desert Juniper Hand Crafted American Gin (USA); 41% abv, $27.

Shows a very pale straw color and great purity. Oddly, there's hardly any aroma and frankly what odor is there is more like plain old unflavored neutral grain spirit, in other words, vodka; further exposure to air over the span of seven minutes does nothing to release any additional scents. The palate entry is more vodka-like than gin-like but owns a pleasant oiliness; at midpalate I detect barely any botanical presence, except for perhaps a trace of cassia bark and very reined-in juniper. Concludes as dully as it started; this is more a vodka than a gin, to be blunt. The use of the word gin on the label is a trifle misleading; as a drinkable vodka/gin hybrid, it's mediocre, so don't bother with it.

2004 Rating: ★★/Not Recommended

DH Krahn Gin (USA); 40% abv, $27.

Excellent silvery clarity; flawlessly pure. In the initial nosing passes after the pour there are intriguing, if woodsy scents of rubber pencil eraser, angelica, and orris; the foresty/bark-like aroma gets even more woodsy and peppery with extra time in the glass; the juniper evidence is faint while other botanical influences, especially of the wood/bark and leafy herb

leanings, are clear. The palate entry is significantly sweeter and oilier than the bouquet would lead one to believe and, therefore, this gin shows some good substance early-on in the mouth; at the midpalate stage the taste retreats a bit as the juniper emerges and overshadows other botanicals. A hike in abv of 3% to 4% would make this domestic gin even better.
2006 Rating: ★★★/Recommended

Dirty Olive Olive-Flavored Gin (USA); 35% abv, $22.
This product needs to be vigorously shaken in a shaker with some ice prior to using; the appearance shows a peculiar yellow/gray tint the likes of which I've never seen; some minor sediment seen, but not problematic. The aroma right after the pour is quite neutral, then with a couple of minutes in the glass slender scents of resin, juniper, and soft grain spirit emerge; the third and fourth nosing passes reveal little more in the way of aromatic thrust or expansion. In the mouth, the intensely overwhelming taste of salty brine/green olive unleashes itself at palate entry (even following the serving instructions) and dominates all through the midpalate. The finish is nothing but salt, green olive and brine with no evidence of gin presence; on its own or on-the-rocks. It's a nightmare, I'm sorry to say; to be fair, though, the clearly stated suggestion by the producer is for this gin to be employed in mixed drinks such as the Dirty Olive Gin Martini; I tried it as per the instructions and found it undrinkable. I like the concept very much, but the tongue-numbing saltiness and lack of subtlety, at least for my taste (and I love olives of all kinds), obliterates what should have been a nifty idea.
2001 Rating: ★/Not Recommended

G'Vine Gin de France Small Batch Gin (France); 40% abv, $38.
Excellent purity; silvery/gray transparent appearance. The floral botanicals come racing out from the glass in huge height-of-summer waves in the opening whiffs; six more minutes of air contact assist in bringing out other botanicals, most notably, lemon peel, cassia, cubeb berries and piny juniper. The palate entry focuses squarely on orange blossom and orange peel in a comely display of citrus and licorice; by the midpalate stage the taste profile expands enough to highlight the spice elements, especially nutmeg and coriander, in a satisfying mouth experience. Ends up lean, moderately oily, bark-like and floral. Has the making of something very special with some fine-tuning. If it were mine, I'd elevate the alcohol level to 42% to 44% and tone down the floral aspects one notch while building up the juniper and cubeb.
2007 Rating: ★★★★/Highly Recommended

Gilbey's London Dry Gin (USA); 40% abv, $9.
Unquestionable clarity; extremely pale silver/yellow tint, and flawless translucence. The opening whiffs pick up lots of telltale citrus zest; aeration brings out the juniper berry, in particular; not a deep London Dry bouquet. The palate entry focuses totally on the juniper, and then at midpalate the lemon zest is unmistakable and adds a note of keen acidity. Finishes on the citrusy side of the street and a little bit fiery.
2005 Rating: ★★/Not Recommended

Gordon's London Dry Gin (USA); 40% abv, $12/liter.

The appearance is blemish-free and mineral water clear. The first sniffings pick up toasty notes of charcoal and minerals more than botanicals; later inhalations following aeration stir glimpses of fabric, hemp, and butter. The palate entry is firm, moderately sweet, and nearly plump; at midpalate the taste profile turns a bit drier, if a touch fruity. Ends up uncomplicated, with no significant spirity fire or rawness, and grainy sweet.

2005 Rating: ★★/Not Recommended

Greenall's Original London Dry Gin (England); 40% abv, $17.

Properly crystalline and clean. The opening sniffings following the pour pick up lightly spiced, lean aromas that address the citrus peel botanical element; further exposure to air adds bittersweet notes of cassia bark and juniper berries. The palate entry emits minerally, slightly metallic tastes of slate, mica and pewter; at midpalate there's a botanical sweetness that tries to overcome the mineral/rock-like flavor but fails to do so. Ends a bit raw and seemingly unfinished. There simply isn't enough botanical substance at its core to overcome the low alcohol. Drinkable and mixable, but commonplace and indistinctive.

2004 Rating: ★★/Not Recommended

Hamptons Gin (USA); 47% abv, $30.

The rainwater appearance is marred by a multitude of floating bits, most that look like cork fragments; regrettably unappealing visually. The opening aroma shows a juicy zestiness that's compelling and inviting; the middle stage nosings highlight the citrus perfume that leans far away from the customary juniper berry/angelica thrust of the traditional gin style; the final sniffing offers citrus/lemon rind with undertones of coriander; a hip, vivacious gin bouquet that lacks grip. The palate entry is initially dry, then turns way too harsh and raw; the midpalate phase is totally dry and smacks of metal, sand, coriander and orris root. The finish is bitter, rough, and shockingly unsophisticated. Surprisingly poor after the showing in 2000 of Hamptons Vodka (★★★★); just goes to show how much more difficult gin-making is to that of vodka due to the botanicals. Back to the drawing board pronto for this one.

2001 Rating: ★/Not Recommended

Hendrick's Gin (Scotland); 44% abv, $30.

Properly clear, but I note more minuscule sediment than I like to see in any gin. The aroma is alive and vivid right from the start as wave after wave of botanical/floral perfume invades the olfactory sense; the driving forces out of the gate are flowery/spring garden-like notes as well as coriander, juniper, and cucumber; with additional time in the glass, the bouquet becomes more focused on the cucumber and spring garden floral aspects. The palate entry is moderately oily, semisweet, and gently herbal/earthy; the midpalate stage turns firm in its spirity oiliness and vegetal/earthy leaning. The juniper re-emerges keenly in the aftertaste, acting as the sweetish foil for the dry, minerally underlying flavor. I am aware that this gin is a favorite with many upper-echelon bartenders because they feel that it has excellent mixing virtues and capabilities. That said, it is a unique and feminine style of gin that I like very much, but still haven't come to love as much as classic London Dry.

2006 Rating: ★★★/Recommended

Juniper Green London Dry Gin Organic/Kosher (England); 43% abv, $31.

The distillers used only organically grown grain and botanicals and demineralized water; clear, pure. The initial two minutes of nosing highlights the angelica and the coriander more than the juniper or the grain; seven more minutes of aeration allows the juniper to marshal its forces, making a bigger splash toward the end of the nosing phase; neither a profound nor an enchanting gin bouquet, but one that offers reasonable charm. In the mouth, this gin displays more depth and structure than in the meandering aroma; the palate entry is semisweet and grainy; by the midpalate point there's a real sense of traditional London Dry Gin in its flavor layering and its round, supple texture. The aftertaste is medium-long, grainy sweet and warming.

2003 Rating: ★★★/Recommended

Magellan Gin The Original Natural Blue Gin (France); 44% abv, $27.

The transparent, attractive, pale aquamarine tint comes from the infusion of iris root and flower and is exceptionally pretty; excellent purity. The opening nosing passes feature the spice elements, mainly clove with supporting traces of cassia bark, grains of paradise and nutmeg; with several more minutes in the glass a moderately sweet and fruity bouquet develops, one that highlights orange zest, coriander and juniper berries; while I acknowledge that the bouquet is relatively complex, its lack of lushness didn't sweep me off my feet (think Citadelle, Tanqueray, Van Gogh, Beefeater for great textural depth). The palate entry is bittersweet and acceptably prickly on the tongue; by the midpalate stage the cocoa and bean-like taste focuses on the earthy/root/bark botanicals, especially the cassia, juniper and licorice. It finishes cleanly, bittersweet and long. One of the more bitter and intensely bean-like gins I've sampled over the years; should have been better.

2003 Rating: ★★★/Recommended

Martin Miller's Reformed London Dry Gin (England); 40% abv, $28.

Impeccably transparent and clean. The opening whiffs following the pour are treated to a tidal wave of woodsy scents including freshly ground black pepper and cassia bark; after another six minutes in the sampling copita, the intriguing, if nuanced, bouquet expands to add subtle fragrances of licorice, juniper berry and bitter orange peel, but make no mistake, the combination of black pepper and cassia bark rule; light, nimble and proper, the bouquet, in my opinion, could use a more pronounced jolt of juniper. At the palate entry, the prevailing early-on flavors boast the orange peel as a refreshingly bitter taste washes over the tongue; at the midpalate stage the juniper dominates, effectively vanquishing its flavor peers. In the finish, Miller's turns pleasantly floral and fruity. Far from a classic, Miller's nonetheless offers gin admirers a style that's quite long on fruity/floral taste and aftertaste, even if it is a bit lacking on the texture front.

2003 Rating: ★★★/Recommended

Martin Miller's Westbourne Strength Reformed London Dry Gin (England/Iceland); 45.2% abv, $35.

The appearance is properly bright and clean. In the initial whiffs after the pour the aroma bursts from the glass with the leading elements being lime peel and cassia bark; six more minutes of aeration time allows the bouquet to deepen as traces of juniper, angelica, and coriander

enter the aromatic arena, making for interesting and pleasing sniffing. The palate entry features off-dry licorice and orris root flavors that are snappy and zesty on the tip of the tongue; the midpalate stage offers a mellow creaminess that is accented by the juniper, tropical fruit, and a lead pencil-like hint of nutmeg. Finishes gracefully off-dry, textured, moderately creamy, and savory. Well done.
2005 Rating: ★★★/Highly Recommended

Mercury London Dry Gin (England); 47% abv, $30.
Another new gin with a less than thrilling appearance as scads of grayish/white particles are seen clearly under the evaluation lamp—HELLLLLOOO, has anyone ever heard of filtering prior to bottling? The nose after the pour is polite and light in the juniper department; the fresh and lithe aromatic personality continues in the middle stage passes as notes of earthy angelica and licorice mingle nicely with the juniper; the last whiff, following over seven minutes of time in the glass, reveals an almost flowery scent that reminds me of rose petal or carnation; a decent, middle-of-the-road gin bouquet that doesn't hammer you with any one botanical. The dry, moderately creamy palate entry features two botanicals, earthy cassia bark and orris root while the midpalate stage highlights the citrus rind, especially orange. The aftertaste is pleasantly dry, bordering on being bitter, and a good summation of the aroma and taste. A nicely made new entry into the top-end gin sweepstakes.
2001 Rating: ★★★/Recommended

Military Dry Gin (Scotland); 43% abv, $22.
Made in Scotland. Pristine, clear appearance. The opening round of sniffing produces fresh, more-grainy-than-botanical aromas; air contact of another six to seven minutes has insignificant impact on the bouquet except to add a clearly evident scent of citrus rind to the basic grain mash perfume. The palate entry shows a moderately plump, sweet, grainy taste with little virtue or depth other than being a rudimentary gin flavor; the midpalate point sees scant improvement; the "feel" is acceptable, but neither silky nor oily. The finish is its best phase, offering by far the most flavor impact in the forms of ripe juniper berries, coriander and spice. I anticipated sampling a much better gin than this wholly ordinary, lackluster and uninspiring effort, especially from a Scottish distiller; drinkable, but a missed opportunity.
2003 Rating: ★★/Not Recommended

Monarch Gin London Dry (United Kingdom); 40% abv, $7.
Crystalline appearance; excellent cleanliness. The first nosing passes pick up far more in the way of grassy/root-like botanical notes than juniper; elements of seeds, grain, fiber, and chalk enter the aromatic picture after aeration, with the juniper component as a mere distant echo. The palate entry is intensely grainy, nearly bitter, and not as juniper-like as I think it should be, but then there's an oily sturdiness in the midpalate that elevates the taste phase. Finishes tight, chalky, mildly floral, and a bit too heated in the throat. Needs to have the juniper element raised as well as some angelica added to pull the botanical components together.
2007 Rating: ★★/Not Recommended

No. 209 Gin (USA); 46% abv, $40.

Pristine perfection in appearance. The first sniffs are treated to generous notes of citrus zest, especially lemon peel; later swirlings and inhalations instigate earthier, root-like scents, in particular, juniper berry, orris root, licorice, coriander and angelica. The palate entry is bittersweet, intensely grainy and speckled with licorice and orris root; at midpalate the viscosity comes alive, underpinning the marginally sweeter (from palate entry) flavor that turns delightfully herbal. Finish is decidedly herbal/leafy/seed-like and, finally, bittersweet. Enough changes in direction to keep the taste buds fully alert for the entire ride. An adult gin with an adventurous attitude. Nicely rendered.
2006 Rating: ★★★★/Highly Recommended

Origine London Distilled Handcrafted Dry Gin (England); 40% abv, $26.

Shows a hazy appearance negatively affected by minuscule bits of sediment. The zesty, citrusy aroma after the pour offers a pleasing presence in the glass that highlights lemon peel, angelica, and coriander; it's following the seven additional minutes of air contact that the juniper makes an entrance along with scents of orris root, bark, cotton fiber, and lanolin. The palate entry is bean-like, bitter, and intensely herbal; the awkward midpalate stage features the citrus peel oil and a harshness that detracts from the taste profile. Finishes with flashes of juniper, citrus, and coriander, as well as a bit of heat. The ratio of the botanicals is off and I'd also raise the abv to 47%.
2006 Rating: ★★/Not Recommended

Players Extreme Bumpy Gin (USA); 40% abv, $14.

Properly clear and clean. The unspectacular opening bouquet is simple, adequately junipery and delicate; hints of citrus zest and angelica appear after seven further minutes of aeration. The mouth presence is far more expressive than the bouquet as zesty, piquant tastes of citrus peel and juniper berry impress the taste buds; by the midpalate point there's evidence of oily texture and orris root. The finish is firm, off-dry and lemony. After the meek aroma, the lively flavor profile surprised me; though it is definitely a basic Gin 101 without the slightest bit of depth or profundity whatsoever, I did like it enough in its fundamental, no-frills, citrus-heavy form to give it three stars; it isn't profound but for the money it isn't bad.
2003 Rating: ★★★/Recommended

Plymouth English Gin (England); 41.2% abv, $23.

Superb rain water-like clarity. The opening whiffs pick up delicate notes of juniper berry oil, citrus, orris, coriander, and caraway seed; extra time in the glass allows for the aroma to gather itself into a full-bodied, refreshing yet sleek bouquet of spicy distinction. The flavor at palate entry is mildly peppery, floral, and fruity; at midpalate the flavor profile focuses more on oils and juniper. A masterpiece of precision and *gravitas*. So complex. So authentic. So cutting-edge. Unique and great.
2006 Rating: ★★★★★/Highest Recommendation

Quintessential London Dry Gin (England); 40% abv, $28.

Absolutely impeccable clarity and purity. My first aromatic impression in the first two

minutes of inhaling is of a florist shop, so fresh, vivid, and floral is the redesigned bouquet; later sniffings detect delicate, more herbal/botanical notes of lemon peel, juniper berries, coriander, and orris root; a lovely aroma. The palate entry displays a fine, off-dry, bean-like quality that I like; at midpalate the flavor profile features lavender and off-dry grain. Finishes smooth, airtight, and flowery.
2005 Rating: ★★★/Recommended

Reval Dry Gin (Estonia); 40% abv, $13.

Clear, with white bits of sediment spotted floating about. The nose is mildly herbal/botanical and oddly fish-like, as in crab cakes in the first two nosing passes; contact with air seems to accelerate the fishiness/tankiness in the later sniffings as the botanicals, slight to begin with, are pushed further into the background. The weak-kneed taste profile cries out for a more balanced employment of botanicals as the entry continues with the fish problem; the midpalate displays a bit more sophistication and balance. The finish is long, warming, juniper-like and proper.
2001 Rating: ★★/Not Recommended

Rogue Spirits Spruce Gin (USA); 45% abv, $35.

Transparent, but shows some beading in the core plus minuscule debris. Smells of pine cleaning fluid, car wax, and textiles in the opening round of sniffing; with further aeration, the aroma takes on a wet wool blanket aroma that's unappealing and inappropriate; over the span of ten minutes there's nary of hint of juniper, coriander or citrus peel—just an old sneaker that stinks to high heaven. The awkward entry is waxy and cedary, off-balance and clumsy; the taste profile by midpalate is nothing short of disgusting and doesn't resemble any type of gin (London Dry, Plymouth, Genever) that I'm aware of. So bad that it absolutely gets a spot on my next SJ Bottom-Feeder List of the Worst Spirits Available. I mean, this doesn't remotely remind me of gin.
2007 Rating: ★/Not Recommended

Sarticious Gin (USA); 47% abv, $27.

I'm sorry to report that the appearance after the pour is dicey, at best, with way too much debris seen floating around; it eventually settles down after about five minutes. The initial whiffs offer zesty scents of orange peel, coriander, and fresh herbs; later inhalations following aeration detect subtle aromas, including cucumber, cilantro, parsley, orris, and thyme. The palate entry is woolly-textured, off-dry, and intensely herbal; at midpalate the flavor turns sweet, cucumber-like, licorice, and salad greens-like. Finishes well, with an oily texture and an orange peel prominence. Reminded me more, in terms of style, of Hendrick's Gin from Scotland than any typical London Dry Gin. A worthy attempt that with some tweaking can, I believe, even be better.
2005 Rating: ★★★/Recommended

Seagram's Distiller's Reserve Gin (USA); 51% abv, $15.

Translucent, but with a slight gunmetal/silver tint; superb clarity. The opening inhalations offer mineral-like scents of slate, limestone, chalk, and granite; by the later stages, after aeration, hints of lemon peel, white pepper, and juniper emerge from behind the veil of alcohol. The palate entry is surprisingly fruity (plums?), sappy and corn sweet; the midpalate stage features traces of orange, angelica, orris, and pine. Ends powerful but not stinging, rich but not unctuous, and spicy but not especially prickly. An intriguing concept (51% abv) that works.

2006 Rating: ★★★/Recommended

South Premium Gin (New Zealand); 48.2% abv, $33.

Crystalline appearance; flawless purity. The alluring opening scent is stunningly baked, bean- or, more precisely, pod-like; further air contact releases earthy aromas including moss, slate, charcoal, and mint. The palate entry is bittersweet, intensely grainy, and robust on the tongue; at midpalate the juniper at last peeks out from the behind the luxurious curtain of wet earth, roots (angelica, orris) and green vegetation. Concludes on a sweet, juniper note and also with a welcome touch of warmth in the throat. Dazzling, delicious, elemental, and definitely one of the new gins to watch.

2005 Rating: ★★★★/Highly Recommended

Stretton's London Dry Gin (South Africa); 43% abv, $13.

Distilled from sugar cane in South Africa. Crystalline appearance; excellent purity. The first nosings after the pour encounter pleasant notes of juniper and lemon peel, wrapped in a semisweet core flavor; in the later sniffs, more of an herbal/seed-like aroma emerges as the juniper recedes. The palate entry is sweet, moderately junipery, and thick in texture; the midpalate displays a bit too much of the sugar cane spirit base as the botanicals get overshadowed by the sweetness. Concludes caney, clumsy, and heavy-handed. Drinkable, but nowhere near what London Dry Gin should be. Raise the abv to 47% is my suggestion.

2006 Rating: ★★/Not Recommended

Tanqueray London Dry Gin (England); 47.3% abv, $22.

Flawless purity; silvery hue. The piny/cedary juniper breaks loose from the copita, filling the room with sap-like fragrance; aeration only serves to deepen the juniper presence while bringing into the picture subtle notes of citrus and minerals; in my twenty years of spirits evaluation experience, this remains the quintessential London Dry gin bouquet. The palate entry is creamy, elegant, smooth as silk yet substantial and bracing; at the midpalate stage a flurry of lemon/orange peel adds the ideal touch of astringency to the velvety texture. Finishes round, full, and comfortable as an old jacket. A distilling masterpiece; gin's benchmark. The finest gin of any variety ever produced and one of my Top Ten distillates of all time.

2007 Rating: ★★★★★/Highest Recommendation)

Tanqueray No. Ten Batch Distilled Gin (England); 47.3% abv, $22.

Crystalline appearance. The first sniffings are treated to a citric acid/citrus peel bonanza that's simultaneously powerful and graceful; this whopper of a bouquet evolves quickly in the glass during aeration offering singular and totally harmonious notes of pineapple, grapefruit, allspice, pine sap/Christmas tree, and beeswax. The palate entry highlights the orange/lemon peel and the angelica components while the midpalate stage features more of the juniper and earthy cassia. Concludes zestily and savory. If old standard Tanqueray London Dry didn't exist, this would be my all-time fave.

2007 Rating: ★★★★/Highest Recommendation

Vincent van Gogh Gin (Holland); 47% abv, $25.

Impeccable clarity. There is no early evidence of juniper, but lots of earthy/stony/minerally scents from roots and seeds; further aeration brings out an enticing dash of juniper/cedar, but air contact solidifies the earthy, dry notes and adds hints of lemon grass and orange peel. It's in the mouth where this rock solid, Dutch-style gin takes flight as the citrus presence comes on strong and clean at entry, then recedes, allowing the root and seed elements to take charge at midpalate along with an oily texture that's outstanding. Finishes long, medium-weighted, and off-dry. Redefines Dutch gin in a contemporary manner that's classic and immensely appealing for those drinkers searching for a non-London Dry style.
2007 Rating: ★★★★★/Highest Recommendation

Wet by Beefeater Gin (England); 35% abv, $24.

Beefeater base with a delicate infusion of pear flavor; superb clarity and purity. The initial nosing passes detect the telltale, semisweet botanical London Dry thumbprint of Beefeater but with a subtle fruity enhancement; time in the copita serves only to bring out the pear component a smidgen more, except that it reminds me more of banana than pear. The palate entry is nicely textured, semisweet and elegant; it isn't until the midpalate that I can actually isolate the pear/banana element from the rest of the botanicals. The finish is long, fruity in a slightly bitter pear peel way and full on the tongue. While I don't prefer this line extension to its wonderful parent, Beefeater London Dry Gin (★★★★), I commend Beefeater for trying something different and a little bit daring.
2003 Rating: ★★★/Recommended

Zuidam Dry Gin (Holland); 44.5% abv, $30.

Limpid, clear, flawless in appearance. I love this aroma right from the pour; the beginning stages highlight the dried citrus zest/rind, then following six minutes of aeration the bouquet turns more steely, linear, spicy and earthy; the palate entry is tart, sublimely orangey and borderline sour; at midpalate the angelica, juniper and cardamom take charge, mingling perfectly with the orange rind. Closes out like silk on the tongue with flashes of orange zest and juniper; a first-class effort. Buy it if you admire citrus-laden gin.
2004 Rating: ★★★★★/Highest Recommendation

Zuidam Genever Gin (Holland); 40% abv, $30.

The blue/silver appearance is blemish-free. The initial whiffs after the pour detect intense, dried-leaf, herbal, pod-like and pleasing aromas; seven minutes later, the aroma has become a bouquet, emitting leafy/earthy/peppery scents that remind me of wet forest/damp vegetation. The palate entry is off-dry, concentrated and very earthy/botanical/leafy; at midpalate the flavor profile turns more spice-driven and licorice-like. Finishes dry, toasted and I almost want to say a little like very immature malt whisky.
2004 Rating: ★★★/Highly Recommended

Vodka—World

The word "vodka" is derived from the Russian and Polish *zhizenennia voda*, which translates to "water of life". Any vodka's character is generated mainly from two sources: one, the base material and, two, the material used in the filtering process. The majority of modern vodkas are produced from grains, such as wheat, rye, corn, or barley, and grasses, specifically, sugar cane. These vodkas tend to be light, smooth and as neutral as vodka gets. Potato vodkas are typically heavier in texture and sweeter in taste than those made from grain. Vodkas produced from fruits, like apples or grapes, are tart and mildly fruity. In the last half decade, a minor movement has taken hold, both in Europe and the US, in using wine grapes as a base material. In the state of Vermont, one distiller even employs maple syrup as a foundation.

How vodkas are filtered also affects their character. Charcoal filtering, the most prevalent, imparts a hint of sweet smokiness, almost a sooty quality. Quartz crystals lend a stony, mineral-like kind of taste while cloth or fiber panel filtering gives off an aroma of parchment or cotton fabric. The most typical kinds of flavored vodkas employ fruit essences, namely, lemon/lime/citrus, orange, raspberry, strawberry, peach, blackcurrant, pineapple, tangerine, pear, and cranberry. Other contemporary flavorings include vanilla, coffee, cinnamon, chili pepper, grass, and chocolate.

Though vodka currently accounts for 28% of all spirits sold, it is my least favorite white spirit category due primarily to its hollow-by-nature character. That said, it constitutes a key component to the success of spirits in the last decade and for that fact alone it must be viewed with respect.

2 Rooz Eucalyptus Gum Leaf Flavored Vodka (Australia); 45% abv, $30.
Rivals the flawless purity of the Neutral version; superb clarity. The first whiffs are assaulted by potent and aggressive piny/eucalyptus cleaning fluid odors; further time in the glass doesn't see that much of the cleaning fluid character blow off; I mean, I certainly don't mind a deft touch of eucalyptus, but this unnecessarily goes way past the STOP sign. The palate entry is over-manufactured, oily in the worse sense of the term, and heavily menthol-like. The finish is the best part of the experience, in that the cool menthol takes charge, but it's too late to salvage this distilled train wreck. Turn down the volume of the eucalyptus on the next batch and I'll try it again. Further, in what cocktails could one possibly use this vodka?
2007 Rating: ★/Not Recommended

2 Rooz Lemon Myrtle Leaf Flavored Vodka (Australia); 45% abv, $30.
Ideal purity. The vividly exotic scent of lemon peel oil and flowers entice the olfactory sense in the initial whiffs; following further aeration the aroma settles into a floor wax or

furniture wax vein that's not as compelling as the first scent. The palate entry tastes of lemon floor wax; the midpalate is even worse as there's no sense whatsoever of fresh lemon essence; the flavoring beats you into submission. What am I, a crash dummy? This is nothing more than clumsy production by somebody who doesn't have a clue about flavor subtlety or nuance. Avoid like herpes.

2007 Rating: ★/Not Recommended

2 Rooz Neutral Vodka (Australia); 45% abv, $30.

Impeccable clarity. The first nosing pass comes up with scents of charcoal, chalk, and gum; six more minutes in the glass reveals nothing more in the way of aromatics, except for the vigor of the spirit. The palate entry is nicely full-bodied, acidic and sharp, and moderately oily; at the midpalate stage the spirit stings the sides of the tongue and the taste profile displays just enough grapiness to confirm the label data. Finishes ramped up on the piquant spirit, but that's all right. Like most things Australian, this unflavored vodka is straight up and honest, without any frills.

2007 Rating: ★★★/Recommended

2 Rooz Peppermint Flavored Vodka (Australia); 45% abv, $30.

Clean spirit. I smell this crude, jet fuel-smelling monstrosity and I think that some wise ass is playing a joke on me. Someone actually wants me to evaluate this Titanic of vodkas? Okay, I'll play along then. The opening nosing passes are bludgeoned by over-the-top scents of *faux* mint and floor wax; aeration time does lower the intensity enough to allow one to appreciate the finer points of this pig swill. The palate entry is mouthwash-like and a bit like peppermint candy, so well, gee, there's a rating star right there, by gosh; the midpalate is hopelessly awkward and insipid, over-flavored, and pitifully cleaning fluid-like. Let's not even talk about the finish. Why put you through that? It's enough that I had to endure it.

2007 Rating: ★/Not Recommended

267 Infusions Cranberry Vodka (USA); 21% abv, $25.

Cranberries in bottle. The soft pastel rose/red cherry color is attractive and bright; very good purity. The aroma after the pour is gently fruity and berry-like, even a bit floral and spring garden-like; additional aeration brings out appealing notes of spice, acidity, and dried fruit; the bouquet is remarkably true to the source and as fresh as one could hope for. The palate entry is way too lean and thin due to the lack of alcohol by volume (abv), but there is some nice cranberry presence early-on; the midpalate stage, like the entry, would benefit greatly by having the abv at a minimum of 35% rather than the insubstantial and, therefore, detrimental 21%; while I see enormous potential here, the abv deficiency undercuts all that's positive.

2006 Rating: ★★/Not Recommended

267 Infusions Lemon Vodka (USA); 21% abv, $25.

Lemon slices in bottle. Properly cloudy for an infusion; lemon pulp bits are floating everywhere after the pour. The smell out of the gate is fresh, stunningly citrusy/lemony, stimulating, and totally authentic; several more minutes in the glass simply add deeper scents of fresh lemon pulp and oil; a mesmerizing and luscious bouquet. The palate entry is lip-puckeringly sour, citrusy and juicy; the midpalate comes off merely as water with lemon

rather than as infused vodka and there lies the damage and the disappointment.
2006 Rating: ★★/Not Recommended

267 Infusions Olive & Pearl Onion Vodka (USA); 21% abv, $25.

Pearl onions and green olives in bottle. Clear, but with a soft yellow/gray tint; good purity. The briny smell of green olives mingles perfectly with the onion scent providing a lovely first impression; following a few more minutes of air contact, the olive brine grows deeper and more seductive; well done in the aroma department. The palate entry offers ample olive and onion taste impact, but at midpalate the flavor profile heads south as the lack of enough alcohol foundation comes back to haunt the in-mouth phases.
2006 Rating: ★★/Not Recommended

267 Infusions Orange Vodka (USA); 21% abv, $25.

Has the look of cloudy, orange-tinged water, but that's totally fine since it's an infusion. The first sniffs unfortunately uncover a weak aroma that comes off as water with a little orange juice added; I didn't even bother with further aeration time. The palate entry is as timid and skimpy as the bouquet; ditto the midpalate. The worst of the 267 vodkas.
2006 Rating: ★/Not Recommended

3 Vodka (USA); 40% abv, $25.

Grain and soy base materials. The examination lamp exposes minor floating debris but nothing that takes away from the rating; otherwise crystal clear. The aroma in the opening sniffing stages is reticent and shy, with just the bare minimum scent of dry cereal grain present and accounted for; aeration and swirling do little to encourage more in the way of aromatics and, thus, the final couple of nosing passes unearth nothing new. In the mouth the entry at first is salty, then it turns unpleasantly bitter and astringent on the tongue; the midpalate point is no better as the baked, industrial taste goes sour and keenly astringent. The finish is tanky and sulfury. Terrible to the point of being undrinkable.
2001 Rating: ★/Not Recommended

42 Below Feijoa Flavored Vodka (New Zealand); 40% abv, $34.

A feijoa (pronounced, fay-YO-eh) is a type of southern hemisphere tree that bears a green-colored fruit that bears a passing taste resemblance to pineapple. Impeccably transparent and pure appearance. The opening whiffs detect a highly distinctive, almost synthetic aroma that reminds me most of new plastic vinyl; sorry to say that additional time in the glass doesn't help this linoleum-like perfume to blow off; basically, it's an unappealing bouquet. The plastic vinyl character just won't go away, even as the evaluation moves on into the entry and midpalate stages; the only noticeable change is the emergence of a rubbery flavor, à la a new Michelin tire (specifically, off-road, 16 inch—just kidding); not my cup of vodka, period; I went back to it 20 minutes later and found no development, at all. My wife, Sue, the SJ managing editor tried it and was kinder to it, but she did say as she walked out of my office, sniffing and tasting, "Why would anyone want to drink this?"
2003 Rating: ★/Not Recommended

42 Below Manuka Honey Vodka (New Zealand); 42% abv, $30.

The appearance has a very pale beige/burnished gold tint to it; some sediment. The opening whiffs are confronted by highly pungent odors of old sneakers, rotting bark and vegetation, and burning rubber, all of which do no more than hint of wild honey; aeration doesn't help the smelly situation all that much as reeking aromas of wet cardboard, stale closet, mildew, and locker room provide the less than thrilling bouquet highlights. The palate entry mirrors the entire nosing phase; things get worse at midpalate as the flavor profile reflects the taste of honey at its worst. Ends up flat, disagreeable, and basically atrocious. My suggestion: Get the bees drunk on this slop then ship them to an uninhabited South Pacific isle.

2005 Rating: ★/Not Recommended

42 Below Passionfruit Flavored Vodka (New Zealand); 40% abv, $34.

Clear as rain water. The first few minutes of nosing provide a pleasurably fruity/ripe experience that's elegant and restrained; aeration allows the bouquet to evolve into a splendidly ambrosial/fruit salad fragrance that's more semisweet than sweet; lovely. The palate entry is bittersweet and juicy; by the midpalate stage the flavor profile accents as much of the grainy/beany spirit as it does the passionfruit infusion. The aftertaste is long and more beany than fruity. Very nice, but I still prefer the unflavored bottling the most.

2003 Rating: ★★★/Recommended

42 Below Vodka (New Zealand); 42% abv, $22.

Crystal clear and pure. Smells curiously of wet cement or damp stones in the initial minutes of sniffing; about half way into the eight minute extended aeration period the aroma shifts gears, offering toasty, ash-like, smoky scents of tobacco leaf, roasted cereal grains, pencil eraser, and vegetable oil; following a bit of puzzlement, I ended up liking this bouquet. The palate entry shows an oily, medium-to-heavy bodied texture and tastes of charcoal and mildly sweet grain (made from maize?); the midpalate displays well-structured flavors of lead pencil, off-dry grain, and licorice. Finishes full in the mouth, acceptably fiery, and off-dry. Extremely nice.

2002 Rating: ★★★★/Highly Recommended

44o North Huckleberry Flavored Vodka (USA); 35% abv, $29.

Made from Idaho-grown Russet and Burbank potatoes and flavored with huckleberry, a deep blue relative of the blueberry. Impeccably flawless and clear appearance. The first delightful waves of sweet, ripe aroma say without hesitation "berry", but not exactly blueberry or blackberry or raspberry as much as "deep colored berry candy"; another six minutes in the glass urges the aroma to turn more plummy and jam-like, moving past the candy stage; there's a delicacy to the aroma that I favorably responded to. The flavor at entry is sweet and intensely ripe, and then at midpalate the taste becomes preserves-like and a touch more bitter than sweet, making the flavoring seem more authentic. Ends up fruity and properly bittersweet. Very nice job here of matching vodka and flavoring.

2005 Rating: ★★★★/Highly Recommended

Absolut Vodka (Sweden); 40% abv, $18.

Spotless and limpid. The aroma is vaguely grainy, fresh, and pleasing in the initial sniffs after the pour; further aeration brings out a mildly oily scent. The palate entry is simple, fundamentally sound, and intensely dry and grainy; by the midpalate point a shy, kernel-like bittersweet taste enters the picture, then fades all-too-quickly. Ends up meek and ethereal. Never has this drinkable, but ultimately lackluster vodka impressed me, including now; and I'll reiterate that while as an unflavored vodka it is deficient when compared to, say, Stolichnaya, Absolut Vodka does make an excellent base for flavored vodkas; that is its real strength; it is the quintessential two star vodka.

2004 Rating: ★★/Not Recommended

Absolut 100 Vodka (Sweden); 50% abv, $30.

Silvery pure and impeccably clean. The initial nosing is greeted by pleasantly zesty and pungent waves of grain spirit, then the aroma settles down after further aeration, offering mildly fiery notes of toasted grain, chalk, and textile. Entry is warming and intensely grainy; the midpalate stage is surprisingly sweet. Concludes on an aggressive, but hardly off-putting note of sweet grain spirit. I like this offering significantly more than Absolut's wildly popular 80-proof which has always come off to me as anemic, hollow, and too ethereal for its own good.

2007 Rating: ★★★★/Highly Recommended

Absolut Citron Vodka (Sweden); 40% abv, $18.

Dazzlingly clear and unblemished. Citron sings with fresh, vibrant, lemon zest right from the opening bell; aeration serves to illustrate how beautifully balanced the flavoring is as the aroma displays ample citrus peel/zest, acidity, and ripeness; the prototypical citrus-flavored vodka bouquet. The palate entry is so clean and effortless that you just want to consume more immediately; at midpalate there's a rush of lemon zest and oil; finishes with grace, vibrancy, and elegance. A first-class vodka in which the distillers reached the ideal degree of flavor balance, without submerging the vodka presence.

2004 Rating: ★★★★/Highly Recommended

Absolut Kurant Vodka (Sweden); 40% abv, $20.

Unblemished appearance, limpid and clean. The tart, bitter blackcurrant bouquet is stunning and luscious right from the beginning whiffs; another six minutes in the glass serve to deepen the blackcurrant concentration to the brink of the bouquet becoming cassis-like; this is a stupendously luscious and engaging bouquet. The crisp, tart palate entry is razor sharp and clean; at midpalate there's an oily quality to the texture that underscores the racy, zesty, blackcurrant flavor. Ends up ripe, fruity. Absolut Kurant is the godfather, the trailblazer, the unequivocal prototype for all berry-flavored vodkas.

2004 Rating: ★★★★★/Highest Recommendation

Absolut Mandarin Vodka (Sweden); 40% abv, $17.

Properly limpid, but with more suspended particles than I'd like to see in a product with the name Absolut. The nose leaps from the sampling glass right from the pour in sweet/sour waves of ripe orange (actually, to me, more like clementine orange than mandarin) and orange hard candy; the second and third nosing passes offer little in the way of derivation from the initial impression; the fourth and last whiff shows authentic staying power as the orange perfume is every bit as vivid and alluring as in the very first inhalation; it's a lovely bouquet. The mouth presence remains true to the cracking good bouquet as both the palate entry and the midpalate burst with ripe, sweet, juicy orange flavor. The finish is long, citrusy acidic, and pleasing on all counts; easily the equal of rival Stolichnaya Ohranj (rated ★★★★) though as is Absolut's thumbprint trait, Mandarin is lighter than the beefier Ohranj; both are terrific products and make outstanding mixers.

2000 Rating: ★★★★/Highly Recommended

Absolut Pears Pear Flavored Vodka (Sweden); 40% abv, $19.

Limpid, clean, pure. The pear flavoring comes off very inviting in the first sniffs as the aroma leans more to ripe pear flesh than pear juice and that's largely the attraction of it; further aeration sees the aroma add a slightly bitter note of pear peel, but the overall aromatic effect is sound, genuine, and compelling. The palate entry is clean, ripe, fruity, and keenly pear-like; at the midpalate stage the taste profile turns softly sweet in a ripe way that's startlingly authentic. Finishes elegantly and with a last minute thrust of pear that's remarkably vivid, crisp, and true. Another outstanding flavoring job here from Absolut.

2007 Rating: ★★★★★/Highest Recommendation

Absolut Peppar Vodka (Sweden); 40% abv, $20.

Clear and pure. The zesty, piquant, intensely peppery opening bouquet immediately stimulates the olfactory sense with prickly darts of black pepper and hot red chili pepper seed aroma; aeration only intensifies the peppery fragrance as it fills and tickles the nasal cavity. The palate entry is mildly hot and spicy, giving off deep tastes of dried red chili pepper; at midpalate there's a brief respite but at the finish the chili pepper heat returns, pleasantly zapping the taste buds. Concludes peppery and clean.

2004 Rating: ★★★/Recommended

Absolut Raspberri Raspberry Vodka (Sweden); 40% abv, $20.

Clear and clean. The opening perfume is extremely raspberry-like, but not as much in "just-picked-off-the-vine" way as in a jam/preserves manner; aeration serves to tone down the jammy intensity a little as the bouquet turns seed-like by the end of the nosing round. The palate entry is fruity, mildly sweet, ripe, and pleasant; at midpalate there's a slight embers-on-the-tongue warmth that accompanies the ripe raspberry flavor. End comfortably fruity and acidic/astringent. A very good and recommendable but not remarkable Absolut flavored vodka. Kurant remains the benchmark for Absolut.

2005 Rating: ★★★/Recommended

Absolut Vanilia Vanilla Vodka (Sweden); 40% abv, $18.

Crystal clear and pure. The initial nosing passes immediately following the pour offer a stunningly true and intensely bean-like aroma that's assertive and properly bitter; with further time in the copita the aroma softens, retreating slightly, but in the meantime the fragrance turns plumper, sweeter and even nicer; superb bouquet development. The palate entry is squeaky clean, acidic and bittersweet; by the midpalate stage the flavor profile is displaying focused, well-knit tastes of vanilla bean and cocoa bean. The aftertaste is long, semisweet

and intensely vanilla-like. Another flavored vodka triumph for Absolut who started the ball rolling in 1979 with the introduction of Absolut Peppar. Bravo again.
2003 Rating: ★★★★/Highly Recommended

Admiral Vodka (Ukraine); 40% abv, $20.

Silvery transparent and pure. The nose immediately following the pour is crisp, lightly grainy, mildly perfumed (citrus peel), a bit salty, and spirity; with air contact the citrus peel/zest element accelerates noticeably in the third whiff, but by the last nosing pass it vanishes leaving behind a concentrated fragrance of ground black pepper; this is a vivid vodka nose that runs the aroma gamut; very nice. The taste at palate entry is full-bodied, dry, and pleasingly grainy; at the midpalate point the flavor turns moderately sweet in a grain mash manner but ultimately it's the fleshy texture that I admire the most. The finish is bittersweet, very long, and intensely grainy. Very good job here.
2002 Rating: ★★★★/Highly Recommended

Alchemy Czekoladowa Chocolate Infused Polish Vodka (Poland); 40% abv, $29.

The vibrant tawny color is of orange pekoe tea; outstanding purity. The first nosing finds exaggerated beaniness and bittersweet Cocoa Crisp-like fragrance; aeration serves to expand the cocoa theme by adding layers of dark chocolate, bitterness, cake frosting, and malted grain. The palate entry is a touch hot, concentrated, properly beany, and medium-weighted; the midpalate turns down the bean volume a bit, leaving behind a pleasant, semisweet dark chocolate bar quality. Ends on a bittersweet, dark cocoa note. Not as intense or genuine as the cutting-edge Vincent van Gogh Dutch Chocolate (★★★★★), but a worthy and nicely made flavored vodka all the same.
2006 Rating: ★★★/Recommended

Alchemy Imbirowa Ginger Infused Polish Vodka (Poland); 40% abv, $29.

Superb clarity; silvery appearance. The opening whiffs detect very delicate notes of earthy/rooty ginger; extended time in the glass has little effect on the bouquet. The palate entry is marked by a strong ginger root flavor that's more earthy/bark-like/botanical than spicy; the midpalate is sprightly, nearly prickly and warming, and correctly spicy/gingery, even earthy/soil-like. Finishes up quietly as the ginger taste fades in the throat. Well-made and even borderline elegant, but how would this be served, I wonder?
2006 Rating: ★★★/Recommended

Alchemy Wisniowa Wild Cherry Infused Polish Vodka (Poland); 40% abv, $29.

The gorgeous merlot-like, ruby port, crimson red color is flawlessly clean. In the first sniffs after the pour, the aroma displays viny/brambly notes that are more garden-like than fruity; aeration pushes the buttons on this bouquet as the scents of tart, slightly under-ripe cherry and black pepper collide. The palate entry is syrupy and cloyingly sweet; the midpalate is chunky, awkward, and totally improper for a flavored vodka, ringing true more as a heavy-handed liqueur. My suggestion: avoid.
2006 Rating: ★/Not Recommended

Amazon Rainforest Vodka (Brazil); 40% abv, $25.

Made from sugarcane. Clear, better than average clarity. The first sniffings detect dull notes of burnt paper and charcoal; over six more minutes of aeration accomplish nothing in terms of aromatic expansion. The palate entry is sweet and toasty; at midpalate a moderate oiliness acts as a nice foundation for the toasty, sweet, almost smoky/sooty taste. Concludes sweet and oily. A vodka with a "save the rainforest" theme and a bonfire-like personality.

2004 Rating: ★★★/Recommended

Armadale Vodka (Scotland); 40% abv, $30.

Made at Girvan Distillery in Ayrshire, Scotland from wheat and barley. Impeccably clean and pure. The wheat component is immediately apparent as the early-stage bouquet reminds me of wheat crackers; aeration time of another six minutes allows for a dry stony/mineral-like aroma to develop, mingling gracefully with the biscuity underpinning scent. The palate entry is surprisingly semisweet and, as such, is lip-smacking delicious; at midpalate the taste profile shows flashes of spirity heat that ride on top of the barley/wheat semisweetness, acting as something of a distraction. Finishes well and decidedly oily. Very good but I thought that the hot/raw midpalate pulled the rug out from under the palate entry, which was terrific.

2004 Rating: ★★★/Recommended

Balinoff Vodka (France); 40% abv, $14.

The silvery clear appearance is spotless and pure. Opening sniffings after the 2-ounce pour offer muted aromas of textile/fiber, cardboard, and slate; six more minutes of air contact release more pleasant and customary scents of grain mash, corn husk, and rainwater. Far more enjoyable in the mouth, Balinoff's entry taste is dry and moderately grainy, an altogether amiable front flavor; by midpalate the satiny texture underscores the intense graininess and dryness. Finishes stone dry, slate-like, and only mildly grainy. The highlight is the flavor phase.

2005 Rating: ★★★/Recommended

Bardenay Vodka Small Batch Cane Sugar Vodka (USA); 40% abv, $19.

Crystalline appearance; no sediment. The first nosing picks up a clear bean-like/fruit stone-like aroma that's acutely bitter, but not in the least unpleasant; aeration stimulates earthy scents, most prominently, straw/hay and minerals, ending up with a dried grass/ wicker basket aroma. The palate entry is smooth, intensely bean-like (cocoa, vanilla, especially), caney, and bittersweet; the midpalate is moderately oily and even buttery. Ends bittersweet and round.

2006 Rating: ★★★/Recommended

Beluha Special Vodka (Russia); 40% abv, $20/liter.

Clear as rain water; very good purity. The opening two nosing passes find a totally proper, slightly sweet neutral grain spirit aroma of grain mash and alcohol; time in the sampling glass has little effect on the olfactory part of the evaluation as the aroma stays the straight and narrow course found right after the pour. At the palate entry a different phase obviously dawns as the initial tastes are stiffly concentrated and intensely sweet, almost sugary; the sweet-a-thon continues at midpalate as the grain component is unfortunately overshadowed by the sugar additive. The aftertaste while not terrible is nonetheless cloying and candied. Nothing noteworthy here.

2002 Rating: ★★/Not Recommended

Belvedere Vodka (Poland); 40% abv, $30.
Superb clarity. The first whiffs detect a bittersweet to semisweet grainy aroma that's focused if lean; aeration time of another six minutes fails to stimulate further aromatic growth or dimension; it's a one-note, "okay" vodka nose. The palate entry is intensely kernel-like and beany and, therefore, bittersweet; at midpalate the flavor profile stays the bean/kernel course but adds a trace of tar or creosote. Finishes a bit too hot and raw for my taste. Some SJ readers have not understood how I could not like super-premium unflavored Belvedere enough to recommend it. I can't understand, on the other hand, how people could be so blinded by a price tag that alludes to higher quality and then doesn't deliver. This is mediocre unflavored vodka that, like unflavored Absolut (★★), serves best as a platform for flavoring. The point in unflavored Absolut's favor, though, is that it is $10 less per bottle.

2004 Rating: ★★/Not Recommended

Belvedere Cytrus Citrus Flavored Vodka (Poland); 40% abv, $33.
Like its orange sibling, Cytrus displays an overall clean appearance, with just a dash of grayish sediment. Initially, the aroma is reined in and polite, showing just a whisper of lemon peel zestiness; another seven minutes of exposure to air stimulates more of the lime juice component as the lemon retreats to the background. The palate entry likewise features more of the lime essence than lemon as the flavor goes keenly citrusy, acidic, razor-sharp, and refreshing; at midpalate the off-dry flavor remains focused on the lime juice/pulp, with just a complementary trace of lemon. It concludes cleanly, long, and astringent. Again as with the orange, the flavoring is done with a deft, careful hand and not once through the entire evaluation do you feel overwhelmed by the flavor; as it always should be but seldom is, the flavoring is a supplement to the vodka, not the other way around. Excellent job here.

2004 Rating: ★★★/Highly Recommended

Belvedere Pomarańcza Orange Flavored Vodka (Poland); 40% abv, $33.
Very good clarity, with some widely dispersed and inconsequential sediment seen. The initial nosings pick up delightfully fruity, delicate, and semisweet aromas of orange rind and pulp; six more minutes of air contact have no impact upon the bouquet which remains lithe, understated, and pulpy. The palate entry taste is fine, almost feminine, and appropriately astringent; at the midpalate this feline, pulpy taste profile carries on with a sense of balance and grace. Ends in a strong, zesty manner as the orange peel oils take charge. What's so winning about this clean, refreshing vodka is its sense of minimalism until the aftertaste, where the orange zest element rises to the surface; unfussy and delicious.

2004 Rating: ★★★/Highly Recommended

Beryozka Vodka (Russia); 40% abv, $11.
Triple distilled whole wheat and rye mashes at Tulaspirit distillery. Absolutely crystal clear with some very minor bits of sediment spotted. The opening bouquet is fresh with a touch of dill; aeration brings out further scents including slate, minerals, dry grain, and

lead pencil; not a deep bouquet but serviceable and nicely grainy. The palate entry is mildly prickly on the tongue and offers tastes of dry-roasted cereal grain and black pepper; the midpalate shows a bit of background herbs and botanicals that don't overshadow the base graininess. The aftertaste is medium long, off-dry, moderately rich in texture, and lead-like.
2002 Rating: ★★★/Recommended

Black Diamond Vodka (USA); 40% abv, $n/a.

Crystalline, but shows moderate sediment under the exam lamp. The initial nosing passes following the pour offer understated aromas of chalk and grain mash; additional time in the glass doesn't accomplish much in the way of stimulation and, as a result, only meek scents of scallion and metal get added to the bouquet assessment. The palate entry is sweet and properly grainy; by the midpalate stage the flavor menu expands to include cocoa butter and sesame oil. The aftertaste is long, oily, concentrated, and semisweet. Forget the aroma and proceed directly to the taste where all the action is; the sweet, buttery flavor profile and oily texture rack up the three stars.
2002 Rating: ★★★/Recommended

Blavod Black Vodka (England); 40% abv, $25.

I can't honestly say that I like the appearance of this stuff which is, in truth, more of a blood red/blackberry jam hue than what I'd consider to be a serious opaque black. The nose is mildly grainy and fabric-like in the first passes; after the aeration period of six minutes, the bouquet drops off the table altogether. The palate entry is pleasantly grainy and husk-like in its off-dry demeanor; at midpalate the taste turns more customary in its base graininess and spiritiness. Concludes mildly and off-dry. A borderline two/three rating star vodka; aside from the gimmicky "look", the vodka itself is more pedestrian than I'd have liked; it would have been nice to have the gimmick backed up by a more intense vodka; as it is, I just think, "All right, so?"
2005 Rating: ★★/Not Recommended

Blue Ice Potato Vodka (USA); 40% abv. $20.

Made from Russet potatoes grown in Idaho. Silvery clear and clean. The aroma after the pour is a bit shy, showing barely discernible and dry scents of spirit off the still and potato; air contact over the course of several minutes does nothing to coax out more fragrance(s); okay, be that way. In the mouth this vodka comes alive at palate entry in the flavor forms of sweet grain and licorice; the midpalate walks the fence between being potato sweet and astringent, but it works in that there's a sense of true balance. The aftertaste is long, off-dry, and slightly bitter. Big gains in the taste give it enough to be recommended.
2001 Rating: ★★★/Recommended

Blue Sky Icy Vodka (USA); 43% abv, $30.

Another "vodka" distilled from grapes. Thank you, Ciroc. Now, it's an epidemic. Reasonably good clarity; minor floating debris spotted beneath the examination lamp. The opening aromas are soft, plump, ripe and fruity, meaning kind of like eau-de-vie or marc; later sniffs discover nothing new here as the fruit/gum scent fades significantly with aeration, leaving behind a sickly sour grape candy smell. The palate entry is barely drinkable as the taste of sap and grape must limp along on the tongue; the midpalate stage is a hollow mess as the awkward, astringent grape acid taste assaults the taste buds. The finish reflects the latter stage of the aroma and the horrible midpalate. A clinic in how to make a vodka without a single redeeming characteristic.

2006 Rating: ★/Not Recommended

Boru Vodka (Ireland); 40% abv, $20.

Impeccable purity; clear as mineral water. The initial whiffs detect pleasantly dry grainy and stone-like aromas; aeration stimulates subtle notes of grass, grain kernel, beans, and granite. Entry is clean, off-dry, and intensely grainy; the taste profile at midpalate reflects the stony/mineral quality more than the graininess. Ends on a tangy, spirity note that's welcome and grainy sweet. Comes off more composed and focused than its previous incarnation.

2007 Rating: ★★★★/Highly Recommended

Boru Crazzberry Vodka (Ireland); 35% abv, $18.

Ideally clear and flawless in appearance. The zesty, ripe berry aroma jumps from the glass in the first two minutes of sniffing; aeration calms the aroma down a bit at the seventh minute as the cranberry part of the flavoring equation takes charge, presenting the olfactory sense with a cranberry jelly thrust that's quite appealing. The palate entry is soft, piquant, acidic and tart, then at midpalate the cranberry once again rushes to the forefront. Ends up nicely tart, yet ripe and engaging.

2004 Rating: ★★★/Recommended

Brilliant Vodka (Scotland); 40% abv, $20.

Admirably clear and clean. Not much happening in the nose during the first two whiffs; with time in the glass, the bouquet reluctantly opens up in the third sniffing, but just barely; following over eight minutes of exposure to air, I'm exasperated by the fourth nosing pass as the aroma imparts hardly anything in terms of aromatic expression; this lackluster nose takes the concept of "neutral grain spirits" to new regions. The palate entry is meek, neutered, and distilled into submission; the midpalate makes an attempt at redemption as, at last, some evidence of character is noted in the tastes of charcoal and toasty grain. The finish is short, basically weak, and mildly sooty. In this case, the form does not live up to the name; the promotional materials actually boast about "five times distilled" and "three times filtered"; what it doesn't say is that all that processing has completely stripped this vodka of any virtues whatsoever. For a good chuckle taste this faceless gelding next to a real vodka, say, Stolichnaya or Original Polish.

2001 Rating: ★/Not Recommended

Burnett's Blueberry Flavored Vodka (USA); 35% abv, $8.

Limpid as rainwater; flawless purity. The first aromatic go-round offers a juicy, neither ripe nor sweet blueberry perfume; additional time in the glass stimulates only a metallic, coin-like scent that's neutral. The palate entry, a clear departure from the lackluster aroma, is intensely fruity and ripe, with full candied blueberry taste; at the midpalate point the blueberry flavoring shifts into fifth gear as the flavor overachieves to the point of being overbearing. Not the best effort from this brand.

2007 Rating: ★★/Not Recommended

Burnett's Cherry Flavored Vodka (USA); 35% abv, $8.

Clear and impeccably clean. The aroma out of the box is tremendously ripe and alluring in its true-to-the-fruit-source manner; time in the glass sees the aroma change to a more cherry preserves leaning than fresh-picked. The palate entry is properly sweet, ripe, and cherry-like; at midpalate the taste profile becomes more Maraschino cherry in nature than just-off-the-tree. Finishes well and vibrantly fruity. A stunning bargain, when considering the quality and judicious employment of the flavoring.

2005 Rating: ★★★★/Highly Recommended

Burnett's Citrus Flavored Vodka (USA); 35% abv, $10.

Impeccable clarity. The nose at opening is properly juicy and lemony, then in the second pass there's significant diminishment in the freshness as the aroma turns a bit stilted and sap-like; the third and fourth whiffs turn up little in the way of aromatic expansion or deepening and regrettably the citrus scent comes off as being manufactured rather than fresh; this sour nose showed some real promise after the pour, but faltered soon after that. The palate entry is dry and almost metallic or, perhaps better, stone-like (minerally) in its bearing when it should be tart and fruity; the midpalate shows more flair in the fruit department, then fades in the finish as the minerally taste overtakes the fruit. The lemon element is lost in the maze of awkward metal/minerally aromas and tastes.

2001 Rating: ★/Not Recommended

Burnett's Coconut Flavored Vodka (USA); 35% abv, $9.

Properly transparent and clean. The initial nosing passes are awkward as the olfactory sense is assaulted by horribly aggressive and remarkably inaccurate aromas of what is supposed to be coconut but more resemble nail polish remover or worse, rancid butter; the aromatic disaster continues even after several minutes of aeration as the smell becomes more like a wet dog than a flavored vodka; one of the worst spirit aromas I've come across in the past few years. So unappealing in the mouth is it at entry that it's like licking asphalt or a burnt tire so I refuse to continue with the evaluation. Whither quality control?

2002 Rating: ★/Not Recommended

Burnett's Cranberry Flavored Vodka (USA); 35% abv, $12.

Translucent and properly pure. Whoa, the cranberry burst in the opening nosings makes my head snap back as the cranberry fruit runs rampant, filling my head with thoughts of Thanksgiving and autumn; seven minutes of aeration does nothing to turn the volume down on this irrepressibly fruity and ripe bouquet. The palate entry features, well, truckloads of ripe, slightly metallic cranberry taste and nothing else; at midpalate the cranberry flavor calms down a bit, becoming more semisweet than sweet. Finishes fairly well and fruity. The explosion of aroma and taste surprisingly didn't put me off because neither is cloying or syrupy; for the money, hard to beat, providing that you're not expecting flavored vodka genius.

2004 Rating: ★★★/Recommended

Burnett's Lime Flavored Vodka (USA); 35% abv, $12.

Clean and clear. The ripe, freshly cut lime perfume wafts up from the sampling glass in moderately strong waves; after aeration the lime perfume actually lessens to the point where the tartness/acid elements take over, nicely countering the lime zest/lime pulp intensity. In the mouth, the lime flavoring is remarkably clean, acidic, tart and fresh from entry through midpalate. Concludes clean, tart and ripe. Good job here.

2004 Rating: ★★★/Recommended

Burnett's Mango Flavored Vodka (USA); 35% abv, $8.

Absolutely clear and blemish-free appearance. The first whiffs pick up a pleasant mango flesh/pulp freshness; over time, the aroma becomes slightly spicy and even green melon-like. The taste at palate entry is off-dry, suitably fruity, and mango-like; at midpalate the mango flavor is less pronounced as the acidity turns stronger. Ends up nicely ripe and mellow.

2005 Rating: ★★★/Recommended

Burnett's Orange Flavored Vodka (USA); 35% abv, $10.

Excellent purity. I like the simple, fruity opening aroma after the pour which comes off more as orange soda pop than fresh oranges but it's still acceptable; the middle stage passes see the aroma turn a bit more candied as the juiciness begins to diminish; the fourth and last sniffing finds the orange component holding up admirably; this is hardly a landmark orange vodka bouquet and won't ever be confused with Absolut Mandarin or Stoli Ohranj, but to its credit it remains vibrant and zesty throughout the entire ten minute aromatic examination. The palate entry is orangey but light and uncomplicated; the midpalate is simple, orangey, and moderately sweet. The aftertaste is medium long, nicely juicy, and off-dry. For the money, a decent deal.

2001 Rating: ★★/Not Recommended

Burnett's Peach Flavored Vodka (USA); 35% abv, $9.

Superb clarity. The opening whiffs pick up ripe scents of white peaches; aeration keeps the aroma focused on the fruit source and while some people might be looking for more depth of aroma, I find this fancifully carefree bouquet true and pleasing. The palate entry is nicely peachy, without hitting you over the head with the flavoring; the midpalate stage isn't quite as natural as the bouquet, but it's still agreeable enough to be recommendable. Ends up fresh, ripe and fruity.

2006 Rating: ★★★/Recommended

Burnett's Raspberry Flavored Vodka (USA); 35% abv, $10.

Ideal purity. While the argument can be made that this bouquet travels the tutti-frutti/candied path rather than that of fresh-picked fruit one can't deny that the scent is true to raspberry and full of vigor throughout the second and third nosings; by the fourth and final sniffing, following over eight minutes of aeration, the fragrance of raspberry preserves is the dominant feature; a rousing, almost bawdy perfume that leaves no doubt as to what fruit is the source. The palate entry is charged and unabashed in its straightforward manner; the midpalate is a bit more reserved and calm as the tart/dry raspberry essence is evident. The finish is very extended, tart/sweet and overtly true to the fruit source. While anything but subtle, I found myself liking the unbridled enthusiasm of this flavored vodka; you get your money's worth with it and for that I warmly recommend it as a solid summertime mixer.

2001 Rating: ★★★/Recommended

Burnett's Sour Apple Flavored Vodka (USA); 35% abv, $9.
Silvery transparent and pure. A crisp, tart, unripened apple fragrance leaps from the glass following the pour; with time in the glass, the apple scent turns a bit more ripe, banana-like, and cotton fabric-like, a peculiar direction considering how intensely apple-like and delightfully acidic it is at the start. This vodka unravels at the palate entry as the taste turns weirdly manufactured and diesel fuel-like, offering no resemblance to apple whatsoever; by midpalate things only degenerate further as the flavor goes completely off the fruit chart. The aftertaste is of fabric, metal, and cardboard (from the filtration?). Undrinkable and painfully inadequate when placed next to other sour apple spirits; I wouldn't even use it as a mixer.
2002 Rating: ★/Not Recommended

Burnett's Watermelon Flavored Vodka (USA); 35% abv, $8.
Like its siblings, ideally transparent and sediment-free. The first aromatic burst has genuine fresh watermelon written all over it, then with time in the glass and further exposure to air, the bouquet deteriorates badly, becoming skunky and sour. The palate entry can't shake the skunkiness, which to me is like watermelon that's turning brown and fermentable; the midpalate recovers slightly, but not enough to salvage this vodka disaster. Finishes poorly, smelling musty and fusty.
2005 Rating: ★/Not Recommended

Business Class Cranberry Vodka (Ukraine); 40% abv, $19/liter.
Unblemished colorless appearance. There are delicate aromas of red fruit and cranberry in the opening round of nosing; further aeration only sees the fruit element diminish; pleasant, though, while it was there. The palate entry reflects the delicacy of the fruit in the first sniffings; at midpalate the taste of cranberry is faint but alluring all the same in its freshness. Finishes elegant, clean, semisweet, ripe, and with a whisper of cranberry fruit. Nice to see for a change a vodka distiller not overplaying his/her hand with the added flavoring.
2005 Rating: ★★★/Recommended

Business Class Platinum Vodka (Ukraine); 40% abv, $19/liter.
Flawlessly pure, silvery and bright. The initial sniffings pick up stone dry aromas of minerals (quartz) and stone; later whiffs detect deeper traces of grain and charcoal. The palate entry is totally dry, mildly grainy, and squeaky clean; at midpalate there are additional mineral-like flavors of chalk and quartz, with a welcome spirity, low-key, embers-like burn in the throat. Concludes smooth, chalky, showing for the first time in the entire evaluation a note of grainy sweetness.
2005 Rating: ★★★/Recommended

Business Class White Gold Vodka (Ukraine); 40% abv, $18/liter.
Clear and impeccably clean. Displays a gently off-dry to sweet grainy perfume in the first nosings after the pour; swirling and additional aeration stimulate further scents, including gum and glue. The palate entry is pleasingly sweet and intensely grainy; the midpalate stage stays the sweet grain course and offers a nicely firm and silky texture. Ends up extended and beany sweet. Admittedly one dimensional, but good all around.
2005 Rating: ★★★/Recommended

Charbay Vodka (USA); 40% abv, $27.

A genuine small batch domestic vodka with a 525 case release. Crystal clear, but with some minor degree of dark sediment noted. The opening nosing passes take note of subtle toasty, charcoal aromas that entice but don't overpower the olfactory sense; additional time in the glass stimulates other scents, primarily off-dry grain mash and palm oil; a teasing, come-hither type of bouquet that's both inviting and compelling. The palate entry is rock solid, off-dry to sweet and properly oily; by the midpalate juncture the sweet graininess (midwestern corn?) dominates the other flavor contributors, namely toastiness, ash and smoke. The aftertaste is long, bittersweet and delectably oily. This vodka is fashioned more in the plump/sweet style of Holland than either eastern Europe (thick, hearty) or Scandinavia (light, flowery); a revelation on the scale of Pearl Vodka from Canada (★★★★★); is North America set to become the next super-premium vodka mecca? Maybe it's already happening; an authentic classic from Miles Karakasevic and family; wow.

2002 Rating: ★★★★★/Highest Recommendation

Charbay Green Tea Vodka (USA); 35% abv, $35.

The attractive appearance is a honey/green tint that borders on gold and is ideally pure. The opening nosing passes discover seductive fragrances of ripe green melon, sage, and lightly honeyed green tea; later whiffs pick up jasmine, honeysuckle, even grapy aromas that, though disparate, work well together with the early scents in the formation of an overall bouquet impression. The palate entry is exotic, gently tea-like and even a touch honeyed; the midpalate profile accents the delicate sweetness and herbaceousness that border on being spicy. The finish is long, lazy, and luxurious. Yet another creative innovation by the distilling wizards at Domaine Charbay.

2005 Rating: ★★★/Highly Recommended

Charbay Key Lime Vodka (USA); 40% abv, $40.

The yellow/greenish hue is terribly attractive; absolutely pure. The key lime aroma blasts from the glass, reminding me more of Roses Lime Juice than actual fresh key limes due to a syrupy sweet aromatic quality; by the middle stages the aroma has shifted down into third gear, allowing for a proper bordering-on-bitter, tart ripeness to dominate that's far more in line with the perfume of fresh key limes; the last nosing pass stays the course as the nearly bitter perfume features robust, tangy key lime scents in abundance. The palate entry is sour, acceptably bitter, and concentrated; the midpalate stage focuses more on the fruity quality of key lime than the rank-and-file acidity. The finish is long, citric, tart, and quite tasty. This vodka has vodka daiquiri written all over it.

2001 Rating: ★★★/Recommended

Charbay Meyer Lemon Vodka (USA); 40% abv, $40.

The very pale flax/straw/green tint is barely discernable; pure. The opening perfume is very nuanced and citric, but not the least bitter; the middle stage nosings enter deeper aromatic territory as the scents of lemon pulp and zest entice the olfactory sense to probe further; the final nosing, after over eight minutes of exposure to air, reveals oily, slightly sulphury odors that go a long way in resembling burning rubber rather than lemon of any variety. The palate entry is unripe, green, and top-heavy with citric acid; the midpalate stage is rubbery, sour not quite to the point of being unpleasantly bitter but within a hair of it. The finish is long, dismally bitter, and awkward and harsh in the throat. One of distiller Miles Karakasevic's experiments that simply goes down in flames; this vodka is so out of whack that I don't see any application at all, straight or mixed.

2001 Rating: ★/Not Recommended

Charbay Pomegranate Flavored Vodka (USA); 35% abv, $36.

The rose pink color is eye-catching; perfect purity. The opening sniffs detect floral/stemmy/garden-like scents of vines, undergrowth, carnations, bark, pomace, and spice; with aeration, the bouquet turns fruitier and less astringent as the direction clearly goes towards ripe fruit, pulp, red pepper, and rind and away from the earthiness of the initial inhalations. The palate entry is acidic, astringent, and tart; the midpalate phase highlights the peppery/zesty side of pomegranate that is missing from other pomegranate-flavored spirits. Finishes more tart than ripe; more biting and sap-like than juicy. As with all Charbay spirits, the level of production skill is of the highest rank.

2006 Rating: ★★★★/Highly Recommended

Charbay Ruby Red Grapefruit Vodka (USA); 40% abv, $40.

This vodka has the yellow/gold look of a fino sherry; perfect purity. The opening bouquet is a dead-ringer for ruby red grapefruit; with aeration, the bouquet expands in the middle stage nosings to include scents of mustard seed and dill; the final pass sees the aroma return to what brought it to the dance, RUBY RED GRAPEFRUIT! The palate entry dances on the tongue as the grapefruit ripeness thankfully overcomes a bit too much bitterness; the midpalate is surprisingly soft, juicy, and ripe. The aftertaste echoes the midpalate to the nth degree in the delicacy department. As an ardent lover of ruby red grapefruit from Texas, I can say that this idiosyncratic vodka is true to the fruit source; once again, how one uses such an unusual animal is the question I'm left with.

2001 Rating: ★★★/Recommended

Chopin Potato Vodka (Poland); 40% abv, $30.

Unquestionable purity. The first two minutes of sniffing unearths a soft, slightly sour, and vegetal aroma; six more minutes in the copita serve to add minor scents of ash and unsmoked cigarette. The bittersweet palate entry taste flashes on cocoa bean and sap; at midpalate the taste profile enlarges itself by adding toasty, sooty flavors of tobacco leaf, wood smoke, wood resin, and vanilla. Ends up more semisweet than bittersweet, succulent, and roughly spirity.

2004 Rating: ★★★/Recommended

Christiania Ultra Premium Vodka (Norway); 40% abv, $35.

Distilled six times; clear as rain water, but displays a considerable amount of whitish, unappetizing floating debris; filtering problem is my guess. Right from the initial nosing pass following the pour there's nary a hint of aroma from this vodka that self-consciously bills itself as "the world's smoothest"; ten minutes of air contact and swirling in the glass stimulate only the barest minimum of spiritiness by the fourth sniffing; "smooth" is fine but "vacant" is another matter; obviously the aroma has been stripped naked by all the distillations. The palate entry is almost totally neutral except for a tactile oiliness; then at midpalate a pleasing taste of bittersweet potato arrives to somewhat save the day. The finish is austere, clean, and short. This vodka ended up being drinkable but I question the wisdom of over-distilling a product to the point of being little more than neutral/neutered spirit.

2001 Rating: ★★/Not Recommended

Ciroc Snap Frost Vodka (France); 40% abv, $30.
Made from 100% grapes cultivated in France's Gaillac region (just northeast of the city of Toulouse); distilled five times. Clear as rain water; absolutely pure. It owns one of the most peculiar early-on bouquets I've come across in the last five years; the only way to describe it is to liken it to the smell of turkey dressing; the bouquet shows scents of herbs (big-time sage), oil, bread and, well, to my sense of smell, dressing; aeration cements the oil/sage/dough effect; let's be clear about this: I like it, but it's so atypical that I'm not sure most vodka lovers will understand it. The palate entry is sweet, ripe and grapy, a complete 180° turn from the odd bouquet; the midpalate stage highlights the sweet, fruity ripeness to the point where it starts to remind me a bit of grappa. The finish is delightfully sweet, polished and elegant. Even with the oddball bouquet, I hand this spirit four stars due mostly to the fabulous flavor and aftertaste phases which are stellar and world-class.

2002 Rating: ★★★★/Highly Recommended

Citadelle Vodka (France); 40% abv, $23.
100% Beauce wheat; distilled five times; impeccable purity. The initial nosing passes pick up concentrated aromas of grain, moss and wet earth; additional aeration time doesn't expand the bouquet. The palate entry is grainy, off-dry and piquant; at the midpalate point the grain cracker, off-dry to semisweet taste deepens slightly. The aftertaste is long, clean and agreeably grainy. Very nice, elegant, understated.

2003 Rating: ★★★/Recommended

Citadelle Apple Vodka (France); 35% abv, $23.
100% Beauce wheat; distilled five times. Properly transparent, but with some white sediment seen. The opening nosings are greeted by crisp, fresh scents of ripe apple and especially apple peel; over time, the aroma turns into a bouquet as the fresh apple fragrance evolves into an apple sauce/apple candy aroma by the seven minute mark; a very nice bouquet at first, then it fades a tad too much. In the mouth, the initial impression is a little confusing because I'm not quite certain that it's apple I'm tasting; by the midpalate the peel-like flavor seems slightly burnt as in over-baked apple pie or apple strudel. The burnt/toasted/peel taste continues well into the finish. A flavored vodka that, while certainly drinkable, is bested by a European competitor, namely Vincent van Gogh Wild Appel from Holland (★★★).

2003 Rating: ★★/Not Recommended

Citadelle Raspberry Vodka (France); 35% abv, $23.
100% Beauce wheat; distilled five times; excellent purity. The vibrant, ambrosial bouquet jumps from the copita right from the beginning, emitting succulent, ripe aromas of raspberry and a trace of red currant; the focused bouquet only deepens with aeration; the raspberry intensity is accurate and enthralling. The palate entry is dry and acidic; then

at midpalate the flavor explodes in tart raspberry splendor, sweet/sour, juicy and true. The aftertaste is medium-long, more tart than sweet and very enjoyable. Not a profound flavored vodka, but a very good one; ideal for numerous mixed drink recipes.

2003 Rating: ★★★/Recommended

Cold River Vodka (USA); 40% abv, $35.

Silvery clear and crystalline; sediment-free and pure. Smells enticingly of black pepper, charcoal, and limestone in the initial sniffs; further air contact brings out the spirit as well as a sweetness that's focused and stony/minerally; this bouquet is tight, austere, yet lovely and elegant. Entry is sweet and lightly spiced, then the flavor profile goes into overdrive at midpalate as the luscious tastes of caramel corn, charcoal, quartz, and cocoa bean make for the best North American unflavored vodka drinking since Skyy 90, Pearl, Charbay, and Shaker's. Concludes smooth as silk yet complex and layered. A coming superstar.

2007 Rating: ★★★★★/Highest Recommendation

Colorado Premium Vodka (USA); 40% abv, $20.

Silvery clear, but with some fabric-like sediment floating about. The first nosing is all about stone dry grain and minerals, especially slate, shale, and granite; further aeration doesn't stimulate much else in the aromatic sense; a clean, solid, totally dry, and stone-like vodka bouquet. The palate entry is medium-full, dry, and grainy; the midpalate stage displays a smooth oiliness that turns pleasantly vigorous and nearly prickly in the throat. Finishes long, stony/shale-like, and expectedly piquant.

2006 Rating: ★★★/Recommended

Crater Lake Hand Crafted American Vodka (USA); 40% abv, $27.

Crystal clear and pure. The first whiffs pick up precious little in the way of aromatic thrust; even after seven minutes of aeration, the aroma remains distant except for a slight corny/buttered popcorn trace. The palate entry is silky smooth and oily; at midpalate there's a sooty/ashy core flavor that might be a remnant of charcoal filtering; ends smoothly and with a spit of spirity fire at the very conclusion. Not a great vodka, but one that's nicely balanced, completely dry and very silky.

2004 Rating: ★★★/Recommended

Cristall Limited Edition Vodka (USA); 40% abv, $16.

The clarity is vivid and silvery blue; impeccable purity. The first whiffs pick up kernel- and seed-like scents that are dry and attractive; aeration stimulates deeper pod-like, almost peppery aromas that are more vegetal and spicy than either grain- or bean-like; a composed bouquet that while lacking some layering is seamless. The palate entry is nicely peppery and spicy, with underpinning tastes of rye and breakfast cereal; the midpalate is snappy, pleasantly prickly/spirity and dry/bitter. Concludes dry, clean, and moderately oily.

2006 Rating: ★★★/Recommended

Cristall Premium Vodka (Russia); 40% abv, $25.

Clear and clean to the eye. The opening aroma is tight, trim, and fully integrated; five to eight minutes of aeration sees this terrifically zesty vodka perfume blossom into a profound vodka bouquet, featuring lovely scents of charcoal and minerals; stately, composed, multilayered, and deep. The palate entry is lusciously oily, stone dry, and textured like velvet; the midpalate offers evolved flavors of minerals, bittersweet grain, and cocoa. The finish is long, muscular, and concentrated. About as good as vodka can get; a spirit that is full of character and traditional bounty; zowie, it's good!

2002 Rating: ★★★★/Highest Recommendation

Cristall Lemon Twist Lemon Flavored Vodka (Russia); 40% abv, $22.

Translucent and impeccably pure, totally free of suspended particles. The lemon juice scent teases the olfactory sense in the first couple of sniffings following the pour; further aeration of six minutes sees the lemon element turn more zest-like and slightly bitter in the later whiffs; at no time does the lemon component leap out of the glass; it's controlled, poised. The palate entry is clean, tart, citrusy, and zesty; the midpalate is tart, acidic, and remarkably clean and fresh. The aftertaste is whistle clean, a touch pulpy, and utterly delicious. A new lemon flavored vodka star that's perfect for your next crowd pleasing Lemon Drop cocktail; a zesty winner that comes on the heels of the fabulous unflavored Cristall.

2002 Rating: ★★★/Highly Recommended

Danzka Citron Lemon Flavored Vodka (Denmark); 40% abv, $17.

Translucent and silver and pure. The first nosings discover fresh though indistinct citrus aromas; time in the glass doesn't help to define the bouquet, though I know from past experience with this vodka that the flavoring is lemon. In the palate entry phase, the lemon component becomes more apparent as a pleasingly tart/bittersweet taste refreshes the taste buds; at midpalate a flavor of lemon hard candy takes charge, lasting well into the clean, acidic finish. A solidly made lemon vodka that's not a prototype, but is very good nonetheless.

2004 Rating: ★★/Recommended

Dirty Olive Olive-Flavored Vodka (USA); 35% abv, $22.

Shake very well in a shaker filled with ice before using. The yellow/slate hue isn't attractive but it's unique; excellent purity. The opening bouquet shows some genuine grain spirit zest; the middle stage nosing passes pick up faint traces of brine/green olive; the final sniffing goes flat. The palate entry hammers the tongue with high octane levels of salt; the midpalate phase, in which I felt my tongue swelling to eight times its normal size, displays nothing but concentrated saltiness. Ditto the aftertaste. I tried Dirty Olive Vodka in a Bloody Mary made with fresh ingredients and it faired slightly better in that arena, but even so the off-the-charts saltiness is, to me, very off-putting. I wanted to embrace this concoction because I love olives and it seemed on paper to be a terrific idea so I'm disappointed that I ended up disliking it so ardently.

2001 Rating: ★/Not Recommended

DiVine Vodka (USA); 40% abv, $33.

Another entry in the made-from-grapes vodka sweepstakes. Excellent clarity; flawless purity. After the pour, the first burst of aroma carries faint scents of grape seed and red fruit; additional time in the glass doesn't produce aromatic expansion or deepening, except for a marginal stemminess. The palate entry showcases a clean, viny/vegetal taste that's dry

and medium-weighted; in the midpalate stage a surprising (to the good) structural oiliness dominates the mouth phase as the fruit/grape seed diminish in impact. Concludes firm, medium-bodied, dry, and even a tad bittersweet.
2007 Rating: ★★★/Recommended

Dué Genuine Vodka (Italy); 40% abv, $30.
Impeccable clarity. The aroma right after the pour is prickly, pungent and smoky; in the middle stage nosings the spirity prickliness backs off, leaving the road clear for the resiny grain and charcoal scents; the final whiff, after nine minutes in the glass, finds a round, supple, and toasted bouquet; in the mouth a spirity bite greets the tongue at entry, then the flavor turns more mellow and grainy sweet at midpalate. It finishes off very well, even sophisticated on the tongue and in the throat, no heat to speak of. While not creamy like the world's best vodkas, Dué offers plenty of charm in its smoky/grainy way; a solid workman-like vodka which is frequently the best kind; boffo, mes amis.
2001 Rating: ★★★★/Highly Recommended

Dué Original Chardonnay Flavored Vodka (Italy); 40% abv, $30.
As near ideal clarity and purity as one could hope for. The opening nosing passes pick up a definite wine-like perfume but to equate it to chardonnay would not be accurate; to me, it's far more like orangey Muscat; later whiffs following plenty of aeration time build on the perfumy wine/muscat theme and indeed offer further muscat-like scents of honeysuckle, jasmine, and fresh flowers; the bouquet reminds me more of grappa than wine flavored vodka. The palate entry is tart at first then it turns intensely winy; the midpalate point is stunningly grappa-like as the wine component streaks to the forefront of the taste experience leaving the grain spirit in the dust. The finish is clean, wine-like, and unique. While clearly a grappa knock-off, I can say unequivocally that this is a smashingly savory spirit; but the question begs to be asked, how do you use it?
2001 Rating: ★★★★/Highly Recommended

Dué Original Merlot Flavored Vodka (Italy); 40% abv, $30.
Limpid, but lots of floating debris spotted under the lamp. The initial nosing passes reveal ripe berry-like and jammy aromas; aeration serves merely to bolster the findings of the first passes, adding nothing new; it's not as enticing a bouquet as the chardonnay flavored version. The palate entry is sweet, ripe, red berry-like, almost jammy but not quite; the midpalate candy sweet and pleasant. The aftertaste is long, tutti-frutti, and clean. Nice.
2001 Rating: ★★★/Recommended

Dwor Artusa Polish Vodka (Poland); 40% abv, $26.
Pure and clear. In the first sniffings, there are zesty, bone-dry scents of minerals, slate, and lead, with a bit of spirity piquancy in the nostrils; by the tail end of six more aeration minutes, the bouquet reminds my memory bank of fruit stones, the kind of nutty/organic smell you get when you crack open a peach pit. The palate entry offers off-dry to moderately sweet tastes of grain and metal; in the midpalate stage the flavor profile leans more towards the grain than the minerals/metals, thereby providing a sound, if lean taste experience.

Finishes crisp, medium-weighted, and sinewy. Not a chunky Eastern European vodka in the oily/pungent tradition, but a good one that goes its own way.
2005 Rating: ★★★/Recommended

Effen Vodka (Holland); 40% abv, $30.
Perfect purity. The initial nosing passes after the pour reveal an agile, zesty and mildly spicy aroma that's focused squarely on the cereal grain; aeration time of an additional six minutes maintains the aromatic course laid out in the first sniffings; the bouquet registers on the leaner, drier side of neutral grain spirits and as such is in direct opposition to creamier, sweeter, plumper Dutch vodkas like the fine Vincent van Gogh (★★★★★). In the mouth, Effen turns abruptly at palate entry into a moderately sweet, almost smoky vodka that's different from the aroma; at midpalate a flash of black licorice tempts the taste buds, then recedes totally allowing the sweet, nearly smoky/pipe tobacco leaf taste to dominate. Effen finishes quietly and quickly with just a brief nod to the sweet core taste. An intriguingly clean new vodka statement from northern Holland.
2003 Rating: ★★★★/Highly Recommended

Emerald Vodka (Canada); 40% abv, $20.
Suitably clear, with minor sediment noted. The first nosings find a starchy, cotton fiber, desert dry aroma that's quite appealing; later nosing passes following aeration only heighten and reinforce the very dry, starch- and seed-like bouquet. Squeaky clean and dry at palate entry; by midpalate there's a faint bittersweet note that fades quickly, leaving the astringent, pod-like flavor. Ends up oily in texture and taste which is a huge positive for my palate. Not a great unflavored Canadian vodka (as Pearl Vodka is) because there's little in the way of character depth or layers; that said, it is a very good vodka that comes on strong when you want it most, in the taste and aftertaste.
2004 Rating: ★★★/Recommended

Exclusiv Vodka (Moldova); 40% abv, $20/liter.
Ideal clarity; pewter color. The opening aroma is mildly grainy and, well, wholly neutral; things pick up somewhat after another seven minutes of air contact as light spice and ripe yellow fruit get added to the aromatic menu; this is a rather nondescript bouquet. Entry is meek and softly sweet in a grainy/corny manner; the taste profile at midpalate moves ahead better than anticipated as flavors of charcoal, maple, and sugar syrup meet the challenge left by the bouquet and the palate entry. Finishes well in a sweet grain manner that's neither cloying nor icky-sticky.
2007 Rating: ★★★/Recommended

Finlandia Cranberry Infused Vodka (Finland); 40% abv, $15.
The silvery limpid appearance is blemish-free. The nose in the first couple of minutes is tart and dry, yet perfumed and berry-like; the following six minutes of undisturbed aeration seriously stir the intense cranberry aroma to a heightened stage in which the bouquet is fresh and ripe, but neither candied nor jammy. The palate entry is more ripe than flat-out sweet and is very authentic; by midpalate the taste is harmonious, in concert with the alcohol base, and delightfully sweet; the finish is a bit more pedestrian, but is doable.
2004 Rating: ★★★/Recommended

Finlandia Grapefruit Flavored Vodka (Finland); 40% abv, $18.
Limpid as rainwater; impeccably clean. Holy moly! The fresh, citrusy, acidic, juicy, just-squeezed-in-your-eye grapefruit scent is unbelievably attractive and true to the source; further aeration reinforces the first positive impressions. The palate entry is engagingly grapefruit-like, juicy, tart, and ripe; by the midpalate stage the flavor profile is more like an infusion, so real and authentic is the grapefruit flavor. What a gift to creative mixologists. Finishes as seductively and right-on-the-money as it started. One of the best flavored vodkas I've recently tried.
2007 Rating: ★★★★/Highest Recommendation

Finlandia Lime Vodka (Finland); 40% abv, $16.
Limpid and absolutely pure, with nary a speck of floating debris. The tart, juicy lime essence is incredibly fresh, as though someone just sliced a lime in half and squeezed it into the vodka; another seven minutes of air contact merely reinforces the acute freshness and the tart fruit aromatic profile; an outstanding citrus fruit bouquet. The palate entry is properly acidic and tart, more in a lime peel manner than fruit flesh or juice; but then at midpalate the juiciness takes charge as the flavor turns bittersweet and intensely key lime-like, almost like good lime flavored hard candy. The finish is clean, tart, and elegant.
2002 Rating: ★★★/Highly Recommended

Finlandia Mango Infused Vodka (Finland); 40% abv, $15.
The appearance is translucent and pure. The opening bouquet is strikingly clean, fruity, ripe, and true to the infusion source; aeration serves to intensify the luscious, off-dry, and dead-on-target mango perfume; an outstanding fruit infusion bouquet of the highest rank. The palate entry is tart, but concentrated and accurate; the midpalate is sophisticated, sublimely silky, properly fruity, moderately sweet and ripe, and totally engaging. The finish is long, concentrated, wonderfully mango-like, and firm. By astutely leaving the alcohol level at 40% (most flavored vodkas are 35%), Finlandia has given this beauty the spirit foundation that's frequently lacking in so many other flavored vodkas; bravo because it's a real vodka with authentic in-the-mouth presence, not a wobbly vodka/liqueur hybrid.
2005 Rating: ★★★/Highly Recommended

FireFly Muscadine Wine Flavored Vodka (USA); 40% abv, $17.
Perfect clarity. The husky opening aroma is thick with a pear-like ripeness and the musty smell of grape skins; aeration forces out a keen and proper grapiness that's gum-like and citrusy; a mildly appealing bouquet that's gently sweet and fruity. The fruity burst of flavor at palate entry is pleasing and simple; the midpalate features a razor-edged acidity that keeps the fruit ripeness in check. Concludes viney, winey, acidic, and clean.
2006 Rating: ★★★/Recommended

French Alps Vodka (France); 40% abv, $25.
A wheat vodka; as clear and clean as rain water; particle-free. The opening nosing picks up very delicate traces of grain that are rather sweet; the second nosing doesn't find much in the way of aromatic deepening or expansion as the graininess remains the sole contributor; following six minutes of aeration, the bouquet stays the grainy course; the fourth and last

sniffing is a replay of the second and third passes; overall, it's still a mediocre vodka bouquet. The palate entry is firm, mildly sweet, and intensely grainy; the midpalate point displays the identical sweet, concentrated, and spirity flavor experience of the previous version; I like this taste very much. The aftertaste is medium long, pleasingly sweet in a mash-like manner, and even a tad bean-like.

2000 Rating: ★★★/Recommended

Fris Skandia Apple Vodka (Denmark); 40% abv, $15.

Perfectly clean. There's no mistaking what flavor has been added to this vodka as the tart green apple perfume rises from the glass and fills my office in the first couple of sniffing minutes; the period of aeration merely deepens the pleasingly crisp apple scent. The palate entry is delightfully tart and acidic to launch the taste experience; then at midpalate the flavor turns softly sweet and ripe, almost as fresh as just-picked green apples. The aftertaste returns to the squeaky clean, astringent tendency found in the palate entry and ends in a cleansing manner. I have yet to see the real point of teaming apple and vodka, but I have to admit that Fris gets me wondering (for a nanosecond) if it isn't such a bad concept; as savory as Vincent van Gogh Wild Appel (★★★) from Holland; fine, I guess, for the witless goofballs among us who actually get animated when they think of sickly, stupid, ersatz cocktails like apple martinis.

2003 Rating: ★★★/Recommended

Fris Skandia Lime Flavored Vodka (Denmark); 40% abv, $15.

Perfectly clean. The initial nosing pass right after the pour picks up a mild perfume of lime/citrus; the second and third passes see little in the way of expansion on that theme, except for the addition of a ripe sweetness; by the final sniffing, the lime essence is bursting from the sampling glass in fresh, juicy aromas; what began as a limp aroma, concluded as a bright, fresh, and vivacious bouquet. The palate entry is squarely focused on the lime as a slight bitterness greets the tongue; the midpalate is slightly sweeter and ripe, but is still quite tart, reflecting the lime essence. The finish is tart, long, and very lime-like. A nice marriage of spirit and fruit essence and a capable, stylish mixer for a whole roster of cocktails.

2001 Rating: ★★★/Recommended

General John Stark Vodka (USA); 40% abv, $28.

An unusual vodka made from state of New Hampshire apples. Visually, this is an intriguing distillate, in that you so clearly see the wavy images of oils floating about; clean and clear. The nose after the pour is slightly burnt, fabric-like, and smoky; later whiffs pick up delicate scents that are fruity and ripe but not necessarily sweet. The palate entry is strangely alluring in a viscous manner, but difficult to pin down in terms of taste likenesses; the midpalate is fruit peel-like and nicely astringent on the tongue. The aftertaste is dry, cleansing. Don't even think "apple brandy" because this unique spirit is nowhere near an applejack or eau-de-vie. It absolutely comes off as a vodka.

2005 Rating: ★★★/Recommended

Goldenbarr Chocolate Flavored Vodka (Ukraine); 40% abv, $22.

Transparent with a slight tint of silver/brown; excellent purity. The aroma right after the pour is pleasantly sweet more in a milk chocolate way than a dark chocolate or cocoa manner; further aeration stimulates other more subtle scents, especially white chocolate and butter cream; a satisfying, correctly chocolaty bouquet that while not stretching one's imagination does accomplish its goal. The palate entry is delightfully chocolaty and candy bar-like; the midpalate stage is more subtle and mildly sweet as the chocolate intensity winds down. The finish is round, gently sweet, and endlessly polite. A good flavored vodka.

2002 Rating: ★★★/Recommended

Grey Goose Vodka (France); 40% abv, $30.

Perfect clarity; translucent. Smells of rain, minerals, and semisweet grain in the first sniffs; following aeration, I pick up distant hints of orange zest or lemon zest, but citrus zest of some sort. Entry is sweet and sugary; the taste profile at midpalate takes on heavy notes of glycerin, cane sugar, and charcoal; basically, GG's become too sweet for its own good since my first review in 1997. Finishes with a sugar rush that's simply out of order and balance. Drinkable, but a mere shadow of the product that burst on the scene in the late 1990s.

2007 Rating: ★★/Not Recommended

Grey Goose l'Orange Vodka (France); 40% abv, $30.

Absolutely pure and clear as rain water. The initial nosing pass picks up a lovely, tart orange pulp scent; the second pass reveals a shift in tack to orange zest/peel from the fruity pulp perfume; the steadfastness of this aroma in terms of strength is admirable and alluring in the third sniffing after six minutes of aeration; in the fourth and final whiff a bit of diminishment is noted, but overall the bouquet remains vibrant, citric, and orangy, very true to the fruit; a good flavored vodka nose. The dry, almost nondescript palate entry is followed by a ripe orange, medium-bodied midpalate flavor that flashes a bit of cocoa in the throat. The finish is long, acceptably hot, oily, and more spirity than orange-like. A solid orange vodka entry that scores well for its oily texture.

2000 Rating: ★★★★/Highly Recommended

Grey Goose La Poire Pear Flavored Vodka (France); 40% abv. $30.

Clear and clean in appearance. Smells gently of ripe pears and fruit peel; aeration sees the pear quality fade to the background, leaving behind mere nuances of fruit peel and grain. Entry is meekly pear-like and a bit dull; the hollow midpalate stage features stony/minerally tastes that completely overshadow any sense of pears. Concludes tart, even bitter. Can't hold a pear-flavored candle to Absolut Pears (★★★★★). Whoever came up with this one should be looking for a job in another industry.

2007 Rating: ★/Not Recommended

Grey Goose La Vanille Vanilla Flavored Vodka (France); 40% abv. $30.

Superb purity and silvery hue. Smells mildly of vanilla bean/vanilla extract in the first aromatic passes; even after another seven minutes of air contact, the aroma has no conviction behind it in its vanilla fragrance and therefore the vanilla character falls flat and flabby, even a bit candied. Entry taste offers more in the way of genuine vanilla focus as the flavor comes off properly bittersweet and spicy; the taste profile at midpalate picks up the pace in the vanilla reflection department and comes off balanced, appropriately bitter and tasty. After a rocky beginning, this vodka stepped up to the plate in the mouth and hit a double to drive in a run.

2007 Rating: ★★★/Recommended

Grey Goose le Citron Vodka (France); 40% abv, $30.
Absolutely crystal clear and pure. The opening whiffs are greeted by the snappy, citrusy perfume of lemon peel; five minutes of aeration allows the zest-like piquancy to soften out as the bouquet becomes ripe, moderately sweet, and as sublime as lemon meringue pie; a wonderfully vivacious bouquet that ranks with the best of the category. The palate entry is fresh, citrusy, and intensely lemony; the midpalate phase is lip-puckeringly zesty and cleansing. It finishes tart and long. Right in line with the terrific Grey Goose l'Orange.

2002 Rating: ★★★★/Highly Recommended

Gvori Vodka (Poland); 40% abv, $20.
Clear as rain water. The initial nosing pass unearths a toasted/charred/sooty aroma that's beguiling, mildly sweet and concentrated on the grain; the middle stage nosings add an oiliness that perfectly complements the smoke; by the last pass, following nearly nine minutes of time in the glass, the aromatic potency hasn't lost a step and indeed adds a further scent of dark-roasted coffee bean; one hell of a robust but elegant vodka bouquet. The coffee bean feature found at the tail end of the nosing stage continues on at palate entry in the form of a cocoa/coffee taste that's absolutely lip-smacking delicious; the midpalate is bold, beautifully textured, and offers hearty but silky flavors of vanilla, coffee bean, and cocoa. The aftertaste is medium long, intensely bean-like, sweet, and warming in the throat. Superbly satisfying simply on its own, chilled.

2001 Rating: ★★★★★/Highest Recommendation

Hamptons Vodka (USA); 40% abv, $30.
Properly transparent, but with noticeable white bits floating about; so much for the quadruple filtration. The nose at opening is pleasantly rich and fresh, even sweet in a grainy rather than candied manner; the middle stage nosing passes feature serious notes of charcoal and ash; the final nosing bash, following slightly over ten minutes of aeration, goes grainy sweet and very pleasantly round and full; a very compelling, endowed, and inviting vodka bouquet. Quite remarkably sweet at palate entry as the corn really becomes fully engaged on the tongue; the midpalate is stellar, clean, mildly oily, very full-bodied, and intensely sweet to the taste. The finish is long, luxurious, and cereal sweet. While not as multilayered or complex as European vodkas, in particular, those of Russia, Holland, and Poland, this is nonetheless an American Beauty that deserves lots of attention both from vodka fanatics and from mixed drink freaks.

2000 Rating: ★★★★/Highly Recommended

Hangar One Vodka (USA); 40% abv, $30.
Clear as rain water; as pure and clean as one could hope for. The bouquet right after the pour is intensely grainy and gently sweet; aeration leads to perfumy hints of licorice,

linseed oil, and paraffin; a seductive, come-hither type of vodka bouquet that can only be achieved in small batch distilling. The palate entry is piquant, zesty, and intensely spirity; by the midpalate point rich, sweet, and kernel-like flavors of cocoa bean, corn mash, and—am I dreaming?—grape pomace/grappa make willing prisoners of my taste buds; what kind of vodka is this? The finish is medium-long, grainy sweet, and slightly…well…grapy. Love it, but at least to my palate it comes off almost as a cross between grain vodka and grape-must grappa; maybe I've been doing this for too long now.

2002 Rating: ★★★★/Highly Recommended

Hangar One Citron Buddha's Hand Vodka (USA); 40% abv, $36.

Impeccably clear and clean. The opening nosing passes in the initial three minutes after the pour reveal stunningly fresh and "just picked" aromas of lemon and a trace of lime; aeration for another five minutes unleashes more of the snappy grated lemon peel, or zest, which enchants the sense of smell; neither punchy nor pungent, this perfume is delicately balanced to be laser beam direct but soft; lovely, truly lovely. What the bouquet lacks in fruit concentration is more than made up for in the astonishing bitter-citrus, fourth gear taste at palate entry; the midpalate offers more of an oily taste experience of the citron than the fruit-laden entry. The finish is as though I just bit into the peel of a citron, so intense and real is it. Devilishly good.

2002 Rating: ★★★★/Highly Recommended

Hangar One Fraser River Raspberry Infused Vodka (USA); 40% abv, $36.

The pale brick pink color is attractive; excellent purity. What scent in yonder glass breaks? the bouquet rushes out from the sampling copita and enchants the olfactory sense immediately, offering concentrated and moderately sweet notes of fresh-picked raspberries; with time, the bouquet takes on a more candied or, better, a densely preserves-like personality. "Surprise, surprise" bleats my pea brain as the entry flavor is accurately lean, astringent, and authentically fruity; at midpalate the flavor turns vinous, leafy, off-dry to bitter, just as raspberries off the vine can be. Ends on a bittersweet note that closes the circle on yet another prize from Jorg Rupf, genius distiller of northern California's East Bay.

2005 Rating: ★★★★★/Highest Recommendation

Hangar One Kaffir Lime Vodka (USA); 40% abv, $36.

Translucent, with minor sediment. The acute citrus/lime intensity of the bouquet right from the first sniffing steps out of the glass and slaps you in the face, forehand then backhand; the exhilaration continues as this incredible bouquet adjusts to the air contact by turning more to the juicy lime pulp and turning away from the more bitter peel; one of the two or three most spectacular flavored white spirits bouquets I know of. The keen limey tartness at the palate entry makes my face twist; the flavor at midpalate is intriguingly sweet and sour (smacks of Rose's Lime Juice). The aftertaste is intense, but manageably citrusy/limey and tart. For the ultimate Vodka Gimlet.

2002 Rating: ★★★★★/Highest Recommendation

Hangar One Mandarin Blossom Tangerine Vodka (USA); 40% abv, $36.

Limpid and pure. The opening nosing sensation of orange pulp and juice radiates from the sampling copita with startling impact; subsequent inhalations over the next five minutes serve to bolster the original sense of wonder and delight; perhaps more than anything else it's the freshness, the immediate perfume as though I were holding a tangerine in my hand that is so impressive to the olfactory sense. The palate entry seems a bit dumb at first, then the citrusy/zesty flavor detonates on the tongue, releasing wave after wave of intense and sublimely bittersweet tangerine taste; by the midpalate stage the concentrated, juicy tangerine flavor reaches its peak, receding into the throat in the soft, elegant aftertaste. A classic spirit that just happens to be a flavored vodka.

2002 Rating: ★★★★/Highest Recommendation

Heavy Water Vodka (Sweden); 40% abv, $32.

Flawless purity. There's a pleasant though hardly expressive or dynamic grainy presence in the first round of sniffing; aeration serves to bring out a nice oily, cottony scent that's off-dry, rounded and attractive in an understated, typically Swedish manner. The palate entry is friskily vibrant, grainy and off-dry to moderately sweet; the midpalate features the medium-weighted, moderately oily spirit that's keenly fresh and delightfully grainy/spirity. Finishes well as it cleanses the palate in well-defined tastes of grain and oil. Not a blockbuster, not a bruiser; just a sophisticated spirit that puts a premium on elegance.

2006 Rating: ★★★★/Highly Recommended

Herb's Cilantro Herb Infused Vodka (USA); 40% abv, $29.

Impeccably pure and crystalline appearance. As the name states in bold lettering on the frosted bottle, the heavenly scent of fresh cilantro (is there any better on the planet, maybe except for garlic?) bursts forth from the copita, impressing the olfactory sense; time in the glass takes its toll over seven minutes as the cilantro rush diminishes, leaving behind a totally seductive if not mesmerizing bouquet of muddled cilantro. The palate entry could be criticized as a one-note song, boasting cilantro only, but it is likewise reined in, more subtle than blaring, and strangely attractive as a vodka flavoring; the midpalate stage plays down the cilantro aspect even more and just gets deeply leafy and herbal. Not sure of the applications, but that's not my calling. I just like this vodka a whole lot for what it is.

2007 Rating: ★★★★/Highly Recommended

Herb's Dill Leaf Herb Infused Vodka (USA); 40% abv, $29.

Crystal clear and flawlessly clean. The initial whiffs detect soft waves of pickle brine and fresh dill cuttings and nothing more, but that's quite enough to impress; later sniffings pick up far more herbal/earthy/leafy scents that steer away from brine and more towards summer garden as the bouquet also becomes delightfully peppery; wow, what an aromatic trip. The palate entry is dill-dill-dill and fresh-fresh-fresh; by the midpalate stage the taste profile is delicately sweet and ethereally earthy, almost viny/leafy; jeez, I love the authenticity and the daring of this vodka.

2007 Rating: ★★★★★/Highest Recommendation

Herb's Fennel Herb Infused Vodka (USA); 40% abv, $29.

Like its siblings, perfectly pure and unblemished. The garden-like scent of fennel is medium-strong and true in the first inhalations; after another seven minutes of air contact, the fennel impact lessens slightly but remains firm and pleasantly herbal. The palate entry is genuine, moderately herbal and deep, and pleasingly bittersweet; the midpalate stage is deeper than the entry and is, thereby, far more gripping. Ends up spicy, tangy, earthy and, well, herbal.

2007 Rating: ★★★/Recommended

Herb's Rosemary Herb Infused Vodka (USA); 40% abv, $29.

Superb purity. The opening whiffs pick up ample oily, pine nut-like, cedary, rosemary scent that's right on the money in authenticity; with aeration, the rosemary aspect picks up marked depth and potency, coming on strong in potent aromatic waves that stimulate the sense of smell. The palate entry is keenly rosemary bitter and real; the midpalate stage highlights the sap-like intensity of rosemary and ends up being semisweet in the finish. Concentrated and aggressive, but a mixologist's supreme challenge.

2007 Rating: ★★★★/Highly Recommended

High Spirits American Vodka (USA); 40% abv, $28.

Appearance-wise, obvious problems with the filtration process have left behind unappealing chunks of sediment that ruin the look of this vodka. The aroma after the pour is understated, earthy and slightly perfume-like; aeration serves to introduce tantalizing, if faint scents of yellow fruit (peach, cantaloupe), sand, tilled soil and green vegetation; a totally different and intriguing direction for vodka bouquets. The palate entry offers immediate bittersweet tastes of licorice, molasses and bean (most like vanilla); the midpalate stage highlights the beaniness and a subtle trace of nutmeg. Finishes delicious, medium-weighted, a tad fiery and vibrant. Had the appearance not been so off-putting due to the blocks of debris, I would have given it four stars. Look into it since the sample bottle may have been irregular.

2006 Rating: ★★★/Recommended

High Spirits Prickly Pear Flavored Vodka (USA); 35% abv, $28.

The rose/pink tint is alluring and clean overall. The sweet/sour aroma at the start of the nosing process is pleasant, vividly fruity and unique; aeration takes the aroma into leaner, more astringent territory as the bouquet develops with increased air contact displaying the acidic nature of prickly pears; I really like this earthy/vegetal/garden-like bouquet. The palate entry shows a meeker side as the prickly pear flavor loses much of its fruitiness and leans heavily on the natural acids; the midpalate stage offers a delicate, cleansing taste experience that's long on astringency and tartness. The aftertaste is short, refreshing and understated. Would make an interesting mixer providing that the right fruit element is there to bolster the acidity.

2006 Rating: ★★★/Recommended

Idol Vodka (France); 40% abv, $40.

A grape-based vodka from France; clean and clear appearance. The initial nasal impact is firmly structured and a tad baked, but with no evidence (unlike rival Ciroc) of its base material; following the seven minute period of additional air contact, the aroma opens up, adding charming scents of burnt match/sulphur, cigar ash, linseed oil, and peanuts. The palate entry is very smooth and off-dry; by the midpalate phase the flavor profile expands to include paraffin, creamery butter, and vegetable oil. Finishes elegantly, creamy smooth, integrated, and oily textured. A far cry from the grapy/citrusy Ciroc and is in fact more vodka-like in the traditional sense. Though vastly different in style, they are equal in terms of quality.

2005 Rating: ★★★★/Highly Recommended

Ikon Vodka (Russia); 40% abv, $15.

Flavorings of seed of flax, distilled glycerine, and vanilla. Limpid and pure. The nose at opening is fresh and seed-like; the second and third sniffings have a faint vanilla bean-like scent; the fourth and last whiff, after ten minutes of aeration, highlights the grain mash; a middle-of-the-road vodka bouquet. The palate entry is beany, toasty, sweet, and mildly oily; it's in the midpalate stage that the vanilla flavoring, in particular, shows its face. The finish is intensely bean-like off-dry, and vanilla-driven. Hardly a great vodka, but a well-crafted one that exposes its best side in the concentrated taste phase.

2001 Rating: ★★★/Recommended

Imperia Vodka (Russia); 40% abv, $35.

Crystalline clarity and superb purity. The first burst of aroma is grainy and dry cereal-like; the later sniffings detect semisweet, moderately creamy, and lush scents that evoke thoughts of old-fashioned egg cream soda, brown butter, and vanilla bean. The palate entry is lean and focused, with bittersweet notes of vanilla extract, unsalted butter, and grain husk/grain mash; at midpalate the astringency of the beaniness/graininess is pleasingly refreshing. The finish is more semisweet than bittersweet and convinces me that this is a well-crafted, medium-bodied unflavored vodka of presence, elegance, and refinement. It would have garnered a fifth rating star had the palate entry exhibited greater fullness. A borderline four star/five star vodka and, as usual, unless I'm completely convinced, I go with the lower score.

2005 Rating: ★★★★/Highly Recommended

Jazz Vodka (Poland); 40% abv, $15.

Touted as "Vintage Vodka", meaning that it's produced according to a centuries-old formula, though that's up for debate. Clear and clean; the early nosings pick up intensely grain-like aromas, almost like toasted morning cereal; aeration bolsters the concentrated, dry graininess but adds pungent supplemental scents of burning rubber, charcoal, baked beans and cigarette ash; a strangely alluring and satisfying bouquet that I keep going back to. The palate entry is sweet, grainy and a bit muted after the robust aroma; the midpalate stage is semisweet, oily and concentrated. The finish is long, sweet and grainy. I'd have given this vodka a fourth rating star had it maintained the pedal-to-the-metal character of the bouquet, but as it is you get your money's worth.

2002 Rating: ★★★/Recommended

Jean-Marc XO Vodka (France); 40% abv, $50.

Limpid, silvery, pure. The first inhalations offer traces of caraway seed and unprocessed cotton fabric; aeration stimulates atypically odd and bittersweet aromas of unsweetened, shredded coconut meat, plastic seat cover, citrus rind, and pine; this is a peculiar vodka bouquet that keeps ringing my coconut chime. The palate entry is pleasantly bittersweet, ashy, and absolutely coconut-like, then in midpalate the coconut fades, leaving behind the ash/soot/charcoal, beeswax, and oil characters that dominate all the way into the finish. I liked this vodka, but I can't seem to shake the coconut meat/citrus oil quality. And the price tag? I acknowledge that super-premium vodkas are flying off shelves, but do even image-conscious consumers really think that any unflavored vodka is worth more than $30?
2005 Rating: ★★★/Recommended

Jewel of Russia Classic Vodka (Russia); 40% abv, $29.

Clear and relatively pure. Scents of lightly toasted grain, almost like Wheat Thins, are noted in the first three minutes of inhalations; another six minutes in the glass does very little to stimulate further aromatic depth. The palate entry is stunningly silky and grainy sweet, with a slightly toasted background flavor; at midpalate the taste profile turns sap-like and creamy, with undercurrents of burning matches and seared beefsteak. Finishes creamy and rich, ideally sweet and poised. Had the bouquet shown more finesse, it would have earned a fifth rating star.
2004 Rating: ★★★★/Highly Recommended

Jewel of Russia Ultra Vodka (Russia); 40% abv, $66.

Silvery limpid; shows some sediment but not enough for concern. The delicate perfume is softly grainy in the first passes; seven more minutes of air contact stir nuances of white pepper, wheat crackers and cigarette tobacco. The palate entry is fine and elegant yet a touch hot; at midpalate the dry flavor turns silky in texture and minerally and stone-like in taste. Concludes bean- and kernel-like, bittersweet and a touch soy curd-like. A subtle, understated vodka with lots of layers and grip; a solid four star vodka.
2004 Rating: ★★★★/Highly Recommended

Kapitanska Captain's Polish Vodka (Poland); 40% abv, $20.

Shows excellent clarity; colorless. The initial whiffs detect subtle, if organic and earthy notes of flowers, spring garden, spring forest; following six minutes of air contact, the bouquet emits a grainy sweetness that is also moderately oily. The palate entry is oily, nicely viscous, and grainy; the midpalate stage shows more weight in the texture and an unabashed sweetness that's totally attributable to the grain mash. The aftertaste is sweet, if a bit metallic in the late phase. Might have earned a fourth rating star had the finish displayed more finesse and less bite.
2005 Rating: ★★★/Recommended

Ketel One Vodka (Holland); 40% abv, $28.

Clear as rainwater clean and pure. First nosings don't pick up much, to be frank; where's the grain? Seven more minutes of exposure to air plus a bit of swirling don't accomplish much as the aroma remains a virtual nonentity. What's this, Swedish? Entry is admittedly clean and neutral, but considering that it's distilled in pot stills it is lacking grain definition; the midpalate stage offers an attractive oiliness and a trace of graininess that rescue the bouquet and the entry. Finishes elegantly and a touch sweet. Very good for its impeccably clean character, but my feeling is that there isn't as much character as when I first formally reviewed KO in 1998.

2007 Rating: ★★★/Recommended

Ketel One Citroen Vodka (Holland); 40% abv, $19.

Limpid and silvery/pale yellow-flaxen hue; inconsequential suspended debris noted. The citrus infusion is immediately evident in the first whiff after the pour; with time in the glass, the lemony scent becomes more pulpy and juicy than peel-like in the second and third sniffings; by the fourth and final nosing pass after eight minutes of exposure to air, the bouquet remains remarkably vibrant and fresh, even zesty. The palate entry is richly, tartly lemony; the midpalate stage is intensely citrusy and slightly sweet. The finish is very long, bone dry, and more peel-like than the midpalate phase. A delicious. one-note flavored vodka that leaves a devilishly refreshing taste in the mouth; excellent.

2000 Rating: ★★★★/Highly Recommended

Kirkland Vodka (France); 40% abv, $30.

Shows more than a few bits of sediment that shouldn't be there; otherwise silvery in color. The initial inhalations don't pick up much in the way of aromatics except for a fiber-like scent; seven more minutes in the glass fail to stimulate anything much past the lame addition of cardboard/parchment; truly neutral. The palate entry, by contrast to the ethereal aroma, offers a substantial opening flavor of semisweet grain, fructose, and spice; the midpalate stage sees the silky, medium-bodied texture become a major factor in concert with the intensely grainy flavor. Finishes assertively, with a lick of fire in the throat. Came back a long way from the anemic bouquet.

2007 Rating: ★★★/Recommended

Koenig Distillery Idaho Potato Pot Still Vodka (USA); 40% abv, $20.

Superb purity. The unmistakable potato aroma leaps from the copita in the first whiffs; further aeration stimulates additional fragrances including pork rind, bacon fat, fried potato skins, and soil; a wham-bang bouquet that's potent, inviting, and idiosyncratic. The palate entry is concentrated, honeyed, and rich; the midpalate stage highlights the oiliness of the potato and the batch distilling process. Finishes fat, assertive, a touch hot in the throat, and expressive. A genuine mouthful.

2007 Rating: ★★★★/Highly Recommended

Krakus Exclusive Polish Vodka (Poland); 40% abv, $26.

Superb silvery clear appearance; unblemished purity. The first few inhalations pick up very little in the way of vodka fragrance; time in the glass allows for some meek, perhaps understated aromas of soft grain and parchment to peek through; skip the bouquet. The palate entry tells a totally different story to the aroma's as punchy, piquant, and sweet tastes of wheat and vanilla bean impress the taste buds; by the midpalate stage the flavor unfolds completely in waves of delectably sweet, bean-like, and oily grain. The finish is long, thick, and appealingly sugar cane-like sweet. This is a big-hearted vodka fully in the tradition of Eastern Europe.

2005 Rating: ★★★★/Highly Recommended

Kremlyovskaya Chocolate Flavored Vodka (Russia); 40% abv, $19.

Triple distilled; this vodka possesses ideal clarity. The highly unusual nose combines scents of milk chocolate and cocoa butter at the pour; in the middle stage sniffing, the aroma turns sweet yet nut-like in its bearing; by the fourth and final nosing pass after slightly more than ten minutes of air contact, the aroma goes more in the bittersweet direction of baking chocolate; I can't quite make up my mind as to whether or not I like this oddball vodka bouquet. Tasting it makes up my mind: I like it despite its weird, liqueur-like presence on the tongue; the palate entry is dry; then at midpalate the taste turns slightly sweet in a milk chocolate manner, but wait a minute; in the finish the taste reverts back to being stone dry and slightly bitter. Even though this peculiar vodka is all over the map, there's something about it that I like; I just can't for the life of me figure out how I'd employ it; nonetheless, A for effort, and as such I'm recommending it with the caveat that the purchaser had better be in for a surprise.

2000 Rating: ★★★/Recommended

Kremlyovskaya Limonnaya Lemon Flavored Vodka (Russia); 40% abv, $19.

Triple distilled; clear; the minor suspended particles noted under the evaluation lamp don't pose a problem. The opening nose hits you with a sweet, almost candy-like fragrance of ripe lemon; the second pass sees some diminishment in aromatic depth as the lemon scent goes more in the way of ripe lemon pulp rather than sweet hard candy; the third nosing displays no change; the fourth and last whiff picks up more lemon rind than previously noted; it's an average citrus vodka bouquet. The palate entry is fresh and lively; then the midpalate turns a touch harsh, but not overly so as the lemon flavor goes sour and acidic. The aftertaste shows way too much harshness in the throat, however, which assures non-recommended status. I sampled this vodka along side the previously reviewed Stolichnaya Limonnaya (★★★★) and the Absolut Citron (★★★★) and the Kremlyovskaya showed neither the finesse nor the integration of flavor with spirit of either of its formidable rivals; drinkable, to be sure, but ordinary.

2000 Rating: ★★/Not Recommended

Krolewska Vodka (Poland); 40% abv, $24.

A grain vodka; translucent and silvery bright; only very minor bits of floating particles. The initial nosing pass doesn't offer very much in the way of aromatic expression; ditto the middle stage nosings; after giving this aroma a full ten minutes to come out and play, the fourth and last nosing pass at last finds some faint traces of fragrance, namely an oily, dull, mashy odor that's superficial and plodding. The flavor redeems the limp noodle aroma in fine fashion as the palate entry makes the tongue tingle with smoky, grainy, charcoal-like tastes; the sweet, thick-textured midpalate is charred, tobacco leaf smoky, and intensely grainy. The finish is long, rich, toasty, and sweet. This vodka came from way behind to make it a more than decent race; if judged on the aroma alone it would have gotten only one star; advise: go past the nose and just start drinking.

2000 Rating: ★★★/Recommended

Krzeska Herb Flavored Small Batch Vodka (Poland); 40% abv, $100.

The amber/green/yellow hay color is pretty and pure. The nosing passes after the pour encounter robust and intensely herbal scents of parsley, sage, and rosemary; extra time in the glass stimulates deeper aromas including green chili pepper, rutabaga, pine needle, and tarragon. The palate entry offers intense tastes of tarragon, scallion, and rosemary; the midpalate adds tastes of palm oil, butter mixed with sage, and steamed green vegetables. Concludes on a concentrated herbal/vegetal note that's clean.

2006 Rating: ★★★/Recommended

Kutskova The Noble Russian Vodka (Russia); 40% abv, $25.

Silvery clear but with some sediment floating about. The initial nosing passes detect mildly sweet, even fruity scents of grain; time in the glass affords it some room to expand aromatically and it does so by offering late fragrances of vanilla bean and red berry; a curious bouquet, in that, just when it appears that there's not much happening you discover another hidden aroma lurking in the background. While the aroma benignly charmed me with its fey nature, the taste phase started out with a bang at entry as huge, viscous, toasted, and concentrated flavors of grain and molten spirit entertain the taste buds; the midpalate shows moderate heat, spirity oil, and a thick texture as the heavy-duty grain presence seizes the spotlight. The finish is long, bittersweet, grainy, and oily. Typically Russian.

2001 Rating: ★★★★/Highly Recommended

Level Vodka (Sweden); 40% abv, $29.

The appearance is crystal clear and sediment-free. The aroma is bittersweet, concentrated, oily/fatty, and kernel-like in the first two inhalations after the pour; six more minutes of exposure to air see the bean and oil/fat qualities blow off, leaving behind a totally dry, totally clean fragrance of dry cereal. The palate entry is rich and grainy sweet; at midpalate the taste is enhanced greatly by an oily, viscous texture that's husky and buttery at the same time. The flavor intensity fades slightly in the finish as the bittersweet grain element returns, bumping the oily/fatty component down the ladder. Obviously, a masterful move by Absolut, who gave it their level best, to enter the super-premium vodka subcategory which is exploding; a superb unflavored vodka that's going to turn lots of heads.

2004 Rating: ★★★★/Highly Recommended

Levsha Vodka (Russia); 40% abv, $11.

Triple distilled whole wheat and rye mashes at Tulaspirit distillery. Clear as rain water; completely sediment free. Owns the prototypical Russian vodka bouquet that displays equal parts grain, herbs (especially dill), and a dash of spice (black pepper); strikingly similar in aromatic profile to its sibling Beryozka. The palate entry features sweet grain and a pleasantly oily texture; at the midpalate point, flavors of charcoal, tobacco smoke, and lead pencil get added to the strong grain foundational flavor. The aftertaste is oily, medium long, and as herbal as it is grainy.

2002 Rating: ★★★/Recommended

Liquid Ice Organic Grain Vodka (USA); 40% abv, $37.

Made from organically grown wheat, oats, corn, rye and barley. Quadruple distilled and filtered three times through lava rock (I'm serious, really). Admirably clear and relatively sediment-free. This unflavored vodka owns an extremely nice opening bouquet that's intensely grainy, a touch cocoa-like and comes off being bittersweet; later nosing passes reveal a toasted cereal, sooty and almost cigar ash-like scent that I find lovely, compelling and atypical; love this bouquet and I wonder if it's, to my amazement and chagrin, the bloody lava rock that's making it so intriguing. In the mouth, the initial taste is bittersweet and dark cocoa-like; at midpalate there's a minerally, smoky sweetness that's got my vote of confidence. The aftertaste is long, sweet, coffee bean-like and a touch ashy. For all my cynical misgivings about the lava filtration, I hereby admit that I eat my sarcasm and drink this terrific domestic vodka.

2003 Rating: ★★★★/Highly Recommended

Lysholm Linie Aquavit (Norway); 41.5% abv, $25.

Potato spirit flavored with herbs and spices that's been aged in sherry casks. The pretty hay/straw color is bright and pure. The first couple minutes of nosing exposes exotic and compelling aromas of bark, wood chips and fennel; further aeration releases more spirity/heady and dry to off-dry scents of spice and honey; this is a complex, teasing kind of bouquet that never seems to shift into passing gear, but is stately, firm and directed. The palate entry taste reminds me most of caraway seeded rye bread; by the midpalate stage the flavor profile adds mild sweetness, soft spice and that persistent caraway seed. The aftertaste is moderately oily to the feel and off-dry to the taste. Very herbal; technically a flavored vodka; I flat out love this spirit for two reasons: it's elegant and it's intensely flavorful without being overbearing; ideal balance between spirit and flavorings and aging vessel.

2003 Rating: ★★★★★/Highest Recommendation

Mazama Infused Pepper Flavored Vodka (USA); 40% abv, $27.

Mazama is the wan, pale straw/lemon juice color of a young muscadet; total purity. Ooh, I like this zesty, piquant, intensely, jalapeño/serrano pepper-like bouquet right from the first nanosecond; time in the copita adds complexity and greenness as the core aroma highlights what I believe to be hot serrano peppers; what a blast. The palate entry is all sweet green pepper; then midway through the midpalate the hot peppers kick in with a burst of heat that warms but doesn't char the taste buds. Finishes calmly and warm, but not overly piquant. After tasting and admiring this brazen hussy of a vodka, I am left thinking but one thought, BLOODY MARY TIME!

2004 Rating: ★★★★/Highly Recommended

Metore's Russian Heritage Grain Vodka (USA); 40% abv, $28.

The silvery/gray color is pure and sediment-free. The first nosing passes detect dry, toasty, and intense grain aromas that are almost fabric-like; in later moments of inhaling I notice a flattening out of the bouquet as the ash/smoke recedes completely into the background, leaving a muted grain odor that's not substantial enough on its own to impress. The palate entry shows positive early signs of licorice-like bittersweetness; then that switches over at midpalate to the same kind of grainy neutrality and dullness found in the latter stages of the nosing. Concludes average, if somewhat muted and faded. Quality vodka engages the senses with multiple layers. This one, while perfectly drinkable, fails to intrigue the taste buds due primarily to it being superficial and fey.

2005 Rating: ★★/Not Recommended

Millennium Vodka (Poland); 40% abv, $20.

Pure and clear. Sports a clean, off-dry, nicely grainy opening scent; following seven more minutes of aeration, the bouquet turns pleasantly but not dynamically expressive as the sweet spiciness of the grain kicks in in second gear. The palate entry is very sweet and medium-bodied which, considering the sweetness, helps to maintain the balance; the midpalate flavor is focused on the intense grainy sweetness, but little else. The aftertaste shows a bit more in the way of expansion as the taste goes slightly honeyed and Graham cracker-like. Certainly good enough to recommend solely as a mixing vodka, but lacking in the finesse required for a vodka that's served neat.

2005 Rating: ★★★/Recommended

Mishka Vodka (Israel); 40% abv, $20.

Excellent purity and transparency. The opening aroma shows plenty of charm and dry graininess; later sniffings after further air contact discover scents of chalk/limestone and wheat. The palate entry is elegant, smooth, and dry to off-dry; at midpalate there's a quick flash of spirity warmth, then a grainy dryness that cleanses the palate well. Ends up off-dry, minerally, and admirably clean and lean.

2005 Rating: ★★★/Recommended

Mishka Citron Vodka (Israel); 40% abv, $20.

Handsome, pure appearance. The seductive hint of lemon peel gets my attention immediately; further exposure to air stimulates the aroma a bit as the lemon perfume becomes more juicy/pulpy as the minutes pass. The palate entry is intensely lemony and tart; at midpalate the flavor profile turns alluringly bitter and true to the fruit source. Concludes on an astringent, concentrated lemon juice note. Can see myriad cocktail/mixed drink applications.

2005 Rating: ★★★/Recommended

Mishka Jaffa Orange Vodka (Israel); 40% abv, $20.

Silvery clear and pure. The first inhalations detect delicate traces of fresh orange pulp and peel; aeration doesn't particularly affect the bouquet. The palate entry borders on being sour and is very acidic and orange zest-like; at midpalate the taste profile continues the astringent, orange peel lean. Finishes very bitter and zesty and a tad too harsh and raw in the throat. The use of the orange flavoring is not overdone, but there isn't a sense of balance between the grain spirit and the fruit.

2005 Rating: ★★/Not Recommended

Modern Spirits Black Truffle Flavored Vodka (USA); 35% abv, $50.

The appearance shows a pale straw/hay tint almost like pond water; good purity. The opening whiffs pick up the mushroomy/earthy scents that I had hoped would be present, but with much greater concentration and definition that I expected; aeration time heightens the truffle intensity as the musty/fusty bouquet takes flight. The palate entry is remarkably truffle-like and as a result is keenly earthy, dry soil-like and herbal; at midpalate the taste profile while one-dimensional delivers the goods as promised in a mildly bitter and mineral-like manner that's quite enchanting. Truffle aficionados (which I am not) should definitely

check out this one-of-a-kind vodka that I suggest you enjoy along with meals impacted by truffles. Chill to about 45 degrees Fahrenheit and serve neat in a small-bowled wine glass.
2006 Rating: ★★★★/Highly Recommended

Modern Spirits Candied Ginger Flavored Vodka (USA); 35% abv, $40.

Like some of its siblings, this infused vodka exhibits a pale silver/gray tint and excellent purity. I love ginger, first off, so inhaling this vodka was a treat since it's acutely ginger-like in an elegant, clean and understated way; more time in the glass allows the aromatic frame to become more pronounced, herbal, rooty and vigorous especially in the forefront. The palate entry is semisweet, properly gingery and medium zesty while not being prickly or overheated; the midpalate is monotonal, to be sure, but it's likewise appealingly earthy/rooty/spicy with even a quick dash of spirity warmth as the midpalate evolves into the aftertaste. I'd serve this infused vodka chilled and neat with spicy Chinese.
2006 Rating: ★★★★/Highly Recommended

Modern Spirits Celery Peppercorn Flavored Vodka (USA); 35% abv, $40.

Owns a pale silver/gun metal hue that's impeccably clean and transparent. Right from the initial burst of aroma this vodka makes good on its label claim of being flavored with celery and peppercorn as the fragrance of fresh celery leaf and mildly spicy pepper mingle with grace and suitability; as time goes on it's the bitter peppercorn element that grows in concentration, leaving the celery in the background. The palate entry is surprisingly delicate in its vegetal/spice display; at midpalate the pepper once again distinguishes itself while the celery taste serves as more a support player to the bitter zestiness of the peppercorn. Finishes in an oily (the vodka base is, by all accounts, a quality spirit), peppery, nicely spicy manner. Mixologists can try this in a Bloody Mary. Chill. Very well made.
2006 Rating: ★★★★/Highly Recommended

Modern Spirits Chocolate Orange Flavored Vodka (USA); 35% abv, $40.

The rich auburn/henna color is like an old copper penny; superb purity. The first round of sniffs are nearly overloaded by the aggressive intensity of the dark chocolate/cocoa perfume, which negates any trace of orange; seven more minutes in the glass serve this aroma well as the extra time calms the severely bittersweet dark chocolate component, thereby allowing the orange flesh flavoring to peek out from between the thick veils of cocoa. The palate entry juggles the cocoa/orange tag-team with some finesse as the chocolate element rounds off into a more gently sweet influence; at midpalate the orange makes a stronger statement, balancing the keen sweetness/beaniness of the dark chocolate. A nifty post-prandial vodka that should be served with things like crème brulée or chocolate mousse. Chill.
2006 Rating: ★★★★/Highly Recommended

Modern Spirits Grapefruit Honey Flavored Vodka (USA); 35% abv, $40.

Ideally translucent and flawless clean. The fruity/citrusy aroma begins tart and juicy then turns milder and less acidic right in the first two minutes of sniffing; aeration lets the grapefruit regroup and come out swinging in the latter stages of nosing; this is a deftly crafted bouquet that's true to the sources, classy and compelling. The palate entry features the ripeness of the grapefruit immediately then evolves at midpalate into a delicately sweet/sour taste profile in

which both flavor infusions stand out yet complement each other with grace. Finishes with more of the grapefruit influence showing and is therefore tart and fresh. Chill.
2006 Rating: ★★★★★/Highest Recommendation

Modern Spirits Pear Lavender Flavored Vodka (USA); 35% abv, $40.

There's a slight pale gold/silver tone to this appearance; excellent purity. The first whiffs pick up the lilting, garden-like aroma of the lavender but not much of the pear, which of course is the more ethereal of the two; seven more minutes doesn't bring all that much alteration to the aroma phase as the picked and dried lavender scents prevail with very faint evidence of pear. The palate entry is fruity and ripe, more in an indistinct yellow fruit way than obvious pear; the midpalate taste profile is medium-weighted, mildly oily in texture and even a touch buttery. The aftertaste features the dried lavender. Chill.
2006 Rating: ★★★/Recommended

Modern Spirits Rose Petal Flavored Vodka (USA); 35% abv, $40.

The harvest gold/metallic/burnished orange color isn't as pretty as it is different; perfect purity. All I could think of as I sniffed the aroma right after the pour is "florist shop" as the sweetish odor of at-their-prime roses wafts from the sampling glass; aeration doesn't strongly affect this intensely floral bouquet as the rose petal aromatic dominance is unrelenting. The palate entry is, well, rose-like and moderately sweet and glycerine-like; at midpalate the texture turns oily and buttery while the flavor profile remains firmly entrenched in roses. Finishes oily. While admittedly one-dimensional, the infusion is done so well that it's hard not to admire the skill of the distiller. Major points for the authenticity found in the bouquet and the entry. Chill.
2006 Rating: ★★★★/Highly Recommended

Modern Spirits Tea Flavored Vodka (USA); 35% abv, $40.

The medium amber/light bronze color is pretty and unblemished. The opening aroma is soft-voiced and only distantly tea-like; it's through aeration that the real bouquet comes about as luscious scents of mild English Breakfast and vegetal/leafy green teas emerge and make themselves known. The palate entry is elegant and mildly sweet with an underpinning of pleasing tea leaf bitterness; at midpalate the taste profile features more black tea astringency and pungency. Finishes delicately, leafy and a bit spiced. Chill.
2006 Rating: ★★★★/Highly Recommended

Monarch Vodka Extra Dry/Double Charcoal Filtered (USA); 40% abv, $6.

Clear and clean. Offers solid grainy aromas that remind me of grain mash, cardboard, and breakfast cereal; the bouquet flattens out after further air contact, emitting only a touch of ashy charcoal. The palate entry features a smoky sweetness that flies in the face of the label description as "Extra Dry", but I don't mind because the initial flavor impact is pleasant; the midpalate is more of the same ashy/charcoal, Vodka 101 taste profile. Medium-bodied, moderately oily, properly grainy, clean and good for the price.
2007 Rating: ★★★/Recommended

Mother Russia Premium Vodka With Natural Flavors and Honey (Russia); 40% abv, $18.

Impeccable appearance; debris-free. Owns a lovely grainy/wheat-like opening aroma that's firm and medium oily; seven more minutes of air contact do little to expand or deepen the aromatic stage; it's not an unappealing aroma, just static. The palate entry is velvety, acceptably hot, and sweetly grainy; the midpalate stage features a minerally/slatey flavor that highlights the earthy core taste. Concludes stoutly, robust, and concentrated solely on the grain aspect.

2006 Rating: ★★★/Recommended

Moya Dorogoya Vodka (Russia); 40% abv, $24.

Limpid and pure appearance. The initial couple of nosing passes are pleasantly composed, grainy, spirity, and understated; following seven minutes of aeration, the grain element gently takes charge over the alcohol; mildly pleasing. The palate entry is soft, oily, and poised on the tongue, showing a deft touch of sugary sweetness; by the midpalate point, though, the sweetness becomes the dominant taste feature as the grain, oil, and the spirit all take back seats. The finish is firm, less sweet than the flavor phase, and elegant. A solid Russian vodka that's well suited either as a neat drink on-the-rocks or as a mixer.

2002 Rating: ★★★/Recommended

O2 945 Sparkling Super Premium Vodka (United Kingdom); 47% abv, $35.

Very clean and clear; timid, lazy, big-bubbled effervescence; just looks like club soda. At least in this bouquet as opposed to its sibling, there's greater evidence of grain; deeper inhalations and more time in the glass provide a mildly pleasant sniffing experience as the aroma goes slightly sour and even doughy; didn't mind this aroma at all. The palate entry is a bit salty on the tongue and intensely grainy; by midpalate the taste profile crumbles under the weight of the ungainly marriage of carbonation and grain neutral spirit. These two components simply don't go together, if this is any indication. Drinkable, but uninteresting.

2007 Rating: ★★/Not Recommended

O2 Sparkling Premium Vodka (United Kingdom); 40% abv, $30.

Perfect purity; mild-to-medium vigorous effervescence. Smells of cracked grain, textiles, and metal/carbon dioxide; after six minutes of further air contact, the metallic gassy odor recedes slightly, leaving behind dry grain and corrugated cardboard fragrances. The palate entry is a bit harsh, parchment-like, chalky, and gravelly dry; at the midpalate point the taste profile stays the course of chalk, gravel, etc. I'm sorry, maybe I'm being thick, but I don't see the point of this (being kind, here) mediocre product. If I want something sparkling, I'll order champagne, American sparkling wine, Spanish cava, or Italian prosecco. Is the world ready for carbonated vodka? Not my world.

2007 Rating: ★/Not Recommended

Old Russian Vodka (Russia); 40% abv, $10.

Superb purity. The opening nosing passes pick up interconnected scents of wheat cracker and pine; subsequent whiffs discover minor aromatic additions of grass, autumn leaves, and mineral/coal. The palate entry shows a sophisticated taste of moderately sweet grain and beeswax; the midpalate is elegantly sweet, medium-bodied and creamy textured, and

mineral-like, with a welcome and warm taste of spirit. The finish is subdued, understated, and bittersweet. Going somewhat against the stereotype, this unflavored Russian vodka exhibits a cultured personality and a pleasing sense of distilled spirit.
2005 Rating: ★★★★/Highly Recommended

Oliphant Vodka (Holland); 40% abv, $14.

Clear and pure as rain water. The nose shows a solidly fragrant core in the first sniffings after the pour; with aeration the aroma lifts off in the later stages in the form of charcoal, tar, burnt toast and moderately sweet grain; a dandy, intensely grainy bouquet that expands and develops nicely with time in the glass. The palate entry is stone dry and mineral-like; then at midpalate the taste profile explodes on the tongue in sturdy flavors of sweet grain, slate, minerals, and charcoal. The finish is long, off-dry to sweet, and toasty. Another well-made vodka from the distilling city of Schiedam in the Netherlands.
2002 Rating: ★★★/Recommended

OP Natural Flavored Spirit with Aquavit (Sweden); 35% abv, $25.

Absolutely crystal clear and pure. The citrusy/peel-like nose hits you immediately at the pour; the second nosing pass displays some muted spice in the background (nutmeg? ginger?); by the third whiff, following seven minutes of air contact, the citrus/spice dance seems in fine form and synchronization; nothing new to report in the fourth and final sniffing. Pleasantly light, clean, acidic/orangy, and fruited at palate entry; then at midpalate the spice kicks into gear and dominates. The aftertaste is clean, medium long, and more citrusy then spicy.
2000 Rating: ★★★/Recommended

Opulent Vodka (USA); 40% abv, $25.

Translucent and clear as rainwater. Right upfront there's a pleasing graininess that's dry, crisp, and kernel-like that I favorably respond to; the laser beam-like aroma continues after aeration but becomes even more delightful as scents of peanut and white pepper enter the mix. Entry is lean, clean, and sweeter than the nose had promised; at midpalate the grain element is sweet but neither cloying or sappy. Finishes elegantly, smoothly, and silkily. A dandy unflavored vodka that runs with the best of the countless super-premiums. This one deserves a wide audience.
2007 Rating: ★★★★/Highly Recommended

Orange V Orange Flavored Vodka (USA); 38% abv, $25.

Impeccably clean and sediment-free. The bouquet right from the first whiff is remarkably fruity and ripe; aeration time of another six minutes accentuates the easy, friendly, gently sweet orange soda pop fruitiness of the aroma; not a profound bouquet, not even close, but an amiable one whose best face is its ripeness. The palate entry taste goes off the charts in making a deep impression as it blasts out O-R-A-N-G-E; by midpalate my taste buds are screaming for mercy as the monster orange flavoring component becomes an unnecessary tidal wave of intensely fruity, pulpy orange; geez, I got the picture on this one, mates, so you don't have to hammer it home quite that ostentatiously and brazenly. Finishes as brassy and overbaked as the midpalate. The appearance and the rudimentary, but moderately pleasing, aroma account for something, but there's no excuse for being so heavy-handed in the flavor and aftertaste stages; ever hear about the concept of *subtlety*? This is an example of what's frequently so wrong with flavored white spirits: flagrant overkill; don't even think of buying this slobbering bow-wow.

2004 Rating: ★/Not Recommended

Origine Vodka (France); 40% abv, $26.

Excellent clarity. The initial inhalations detect subtle herbal scents that include soft lavender, grain mash, and wheat; later nasal passes pick out barely discernable citrus zest, hemp, and cracker-like notes. The palate entry is off-dry to semisweet in a grainy manner; at midpalate the taste profile goes citrusy and semisweet, displaying enough astringency to keep the flavor crackling dry and delightfully clean. The finish is engaging, pleasantly grainy sweet, and exceedingly drinkable. A very nice vodka with a polished, even gentle personality that emphasizes understatement and elegance.

2005 Rating: ★★★★/Highly Recommended

Origine Citrus Flavored Vodka (France); 40% abv, $26.

Owns a strange cloudiness that shouldn't be present under the examination lamp; seems unstable. The aroma is really strange and bears scant resemblance to anything having to do with lemons and limes; what it smells like, very strangely, is new carpeting; further exposure to air does nothing to lessen the synthetic aroma. The mildly pleasing, if peculiar, palate entry is curiously candy-like yet void of real citrus flavor, except for a distant backnote of mandarin orange peel; the midpalate is more directed to citrus peel astringency and is therefore quite pleasing. Finishes so-so in the throat as it displays some lemon peel zestiness. Falls short in the appearance, the aroma and the finish departments.

2006 Rating: ★★/Not Recommended

Origine Orange Flavored Vodka (France); 40% abv, $26.

Clean, pure, and pristine in appearance. The first nosings detect soft, perfumed and orangey scents that are a touch leather- and fabric-like; the orange fragrance advances with aeration, charming the olfactory sense with its delicate pulpiness. The palate entry is oily, peel-like, orangey, and mildly bittersweet; the midpalate stage is lovely, elegant, gently bittersweet, and very much like orange candy. Concludes soft, tart, and bittersweet.

2006 Rating: ★★★/Recommended

Origine Pomegranate Flavored Vodka (France); 40% abv, $26.

Pure and clean with just the faintest hint of pink coloring. Right off the bat the nose offers astringent if just-ripe scents of pomegranate that ring with authenticity; as the liquid remains longer in the copita, the aroma gets riper and slightly sweeter but never cloying, just fresh. The palate entry highlights the core flavor of pomegranate by not overcompensating and, therefore, the flavoring comes off well and balanced, if slightly understated; the midpalate shows more length and presence, especially of nicely astringent fruitiness. Finishes medium-long and moderately sweet and ripe. Good job.

2007 Rating: ★★★★/Highly Recommended

p.i.n.k. Caffeine & Guarana Infused Vodka (Holland/USA); 40% abv, $40.

Clear as rainwater, with just the slightest, faintest hint of pink; the frosted bottle has pastel pink coloring in it, so I have to think that's the connection, kind of like Bombay Sapphire not, in fact, being blue. The opening nosing passes pick up off-dry, seductively delicate aromas of yellow fruit and wet earth; further aeration heightens the come-hither aspect of the just-ripened fruit bouquet, elevated by a deft touch of vanilla; I like this slinky bouquet a lot. The palate entry is almost liqueur-like in its accelerated fruitiness and coffee bean-like character; the midpalate stage features bittersweet tastes such as cocoa and coffee bean and, as a result, the flavor profile steers away from the fruit and more in the direction of minerally beans. Ends up bittersweet and beany. Well executed.

2007 Rating: ★★★★/Highly Recommended

Palm Vodka (USA); 40% abv, $27.

Pristine in appearance; flawless clarity. This blend of potato and grain spirits exhibits a potato sweetness as well as a grainy, dry cereal-like leaning in the opening nosings; down the aromatic road following seven more minutes of air contact, though, the aroma turns lead-like, stonily dry, and featureless. The palate entry is clean, a touch biscuity, semisweet, and quite pleasing; the midpalate is minerally, sweetly potato-like yet with a background note of wheat cracker. Concludes well, lean, and delectable.

2006 Rating: ★★★/Recommended

Palm Key Lime Vodka (USA); 40% abv, $27.

Excellent appearance; bright, unblemished, and pure. The disappointment comes right in the first sniffing which detects nothing but an embarrassingly timid aroma that's vaguely lime-like and hardly anywhere near the crisply tart aromatics of real key lime; additional exposure to air brings out astringent lime peel but that's about all; a missed opportunity. The palate entry does display ample key lime authenticity in a somewhat reduced capacity; the midpalate is the best feature of the experience as the tart, properly astringent, and distinct taste of key lime comes through. Ends up tangy, limey/citrusy, and oily. The sound midpalate and seriously pleasant finish propel this vodka forward into recommended territory.

2006 Rating: ★★★/Recommended

Parliament Vodka (Russia); 40% abv, $20.

Clear as rain water; no sediment whatsoever. The initial couple of sniffings after the pour detect very little other than delicate scents of grain mash and lanolin; aeration brings out a fried potato with salt and pepper quality that confounds me completely; that's not to say that this earthy, fried perfume isn't pleasant when, in fact, I like it; it's just unusual. The palate entry is dry and concentrated on grain mash; the midpalate phase displays rich flavors of bittersweet grain, black pepper, and birch root. The aftertaste is mellow, more sweet than dry, and very polite, considering it's from Russia. The oddball bouquet actually adds to the pleasure of it.

2002 Rating: ★★★★/Highly Recommended

Peachka Peach Flavored Vodka (USA); 35% abv, $9.

The godawful name alone gives me cause for concern. Ideal clarity and purity. As I suspected, the opening aroma clubs the olfactory sense with sweet, manufactured, liqueur-like peach perfume; seven minutes of aeration do nothing to rein in this sappy, cloying bouquet. The unbridled sweet-a-thon continues in the palate entry as the thick, gummy texture covers the tongue like honey; at midpalate there's a flash of recovery as the taste profile settles down slightly, emitting flavors of ripe, but canned, peaches. The finish is sugary sweet and sap-like. Calling this bull-in-china-shop spirit a vodka is misleading because it's, in actuality, a liqueur and should be identified as such; so bad that it makes me want to go out and beat up three or four peaches.

2003 Rating: ★/Not Recommended

Pearl Vodka (Canada); 40% abv, $25/liter.

Impeccably pure and clear. The dry winter wheat aroma is both polite and bountiful in a dry morning cereal manner in the opening nosing; the second and third passes detect an understated aromatic richness that highlights the wheat; the final nosing reinforces the earlier impressions as the strength stays the course, not wilting in the face of aeration; this is not a big, street-brawling bouquet, but a quietly opulent, grain-driven perfume that's stately and defined. The satiny, even mildly oily, texture at palate entry is a class act; the midpalate stage features warm, slightly roasted, but delicate tastes of steamed rice, Wheat Thins crackers, and sweet grain. The finish is smooth and surprisingly flavorful in a concentrated grainy way. A fine North American vodka.

2001 Rating: ★★★★★/Highest Recommendation

Pearl Lo Coco Coconut Flavored Vodka (Canada); 35% abv, $25.

Clear and pure. The coconut flavoring is evident right from the first whiff, but it seems manufactured rather than fresh; seven more minutes in the copita do nothing to improve the fruity/sweaty aroma that hints of canned coconut. The palate entry is as metallic as it is faux-coconut-like; at midpalate the coconut sweetness is more expressive, but it still seems anything but fresh. Ends up relatively sweet and coconut-like. There's something flat, vague and unauthentic about this flavored vodka; it's a borderline two/three star vodka; tasted next to Vincent van Gogh Coconut (★★★★★), Pearl Lo Coco faded from sight instantly; to say that I'm disappointed is saying little after I rated the unflavored Pearl Vodka (★★★★★) and have crowed about it for three years.

2004 Rating: ★★/Not Recommended

Peconicka Vodka The Classic Vodka from the Hamptons (USA); 40% abv, $23.

A unique marriage of 80% grain spirits and 20% potato spirits. Excellent clarity and purity. The initial nosing pass registers nothing, the big zero, on the aroma radar screen (please, Higher Power, not another stripped down, over-distilled/over-filtered vodka, please, please, please); the middle stage passes see no improvement in the bouquet department except for a weak-kneed trace of dull grain; the fourth and final (hurray) sniffing detects meager notes of grainy sweetness and flower garden; don't get me started about the new gutless trend in vodka, for crying out loud. Thankfully, the flavor at palate entry shows a pulse, at least, as moderately pleasant tastes of sweet grain and clove/nutmeg make themselves evident;

the midpalate is warm, inviting, and relatively round and supple. The aftertaste is sweet, grainy, and acceptably spirity. What began as yet another *cojone*-less vodka ended up being drinkable, if banal.

2001 Rating: ★★/Not Recommended

Perfect Vodka (France); 40% abv, $35/liter.

The clarity is impeccable. At first, I have a bit of trouble recognizing any defining fragrance—there's just not a lot there in the initial sniffings; another six minutes in the glass fails to register anything further on the aromatic front, except for an extremely faint scent of cotton. The palate entry is pleasantly smooth, off-dry, and snack cracker-like; the midpalate displays medium weight, moderate oiliness, and a chewy quality that's more grainy/cereal-likethan buttery/oily. Concludes bittersweet, a bit licorice-like, and nicely balanced.

2006 Rating: ★★★/Recommended

Pinky Vodka With Natural Flavors (Sweden); 40% abv, $33.

The appearance of this flavored vodka actually is a pink shade that's more silvery than rose petal-like; excellent clarity. The first burst of aroma blares out spring/summer flower garden as expressive scents of roses, orange blossom, honeysuckle, violets, honey, and cucumber entice and entertain the olfactory sense; additional time in the glass brings out a spiciness (chinchona, anise) that nicely complements the floral mélange that adds cactus flower at the very end of the phase. The palate entry is medium sweet, intensely floral, and lip-smackingly tangy; at the midpalate juncture the taste profile turns sweeter as a light-fingered hint of honey enters the picture. Concludes classy, understated, and luscious. Great job here.

2007 Rating: ★★★★/Highly Recommended

Pinnacle Vodka (France); 40% abv, $14.

Crystal clear and pure. The first nosings offer tight, focused scents of roasted grain and toasted marshmallow; additional minutes of aeration stimulate further aromas of peanut butter and ash. The palate entry is toasty/ashy and clean; by midpalate the taste profile turns semisweet, intensely grainy, and a tad hot on the tongue. Ends hot, sap-sweet and grainy.

2005 Rating: ★★★/Recommended

Players Extreme Vodka (USA); 40% abv, $14.

Admirable clarity. The initial nosing passes detect subtle notes of grain kernel and sweet breakfast cereal; six more minutes in the glass reveal scents akin to Brazil nuts and honey wheat toast. The palate entry is grainy sweet and bare bones; by the midpalate phase the sweet grain becomes almost dark chocolate-like in its bitterness. The aftertaste is long, bitter and intensely grainy. A very good product for the reasonable price.

2003 Rating: ★★★/Recommended

Players Extreme Caramel Infused Vodka (England); 35% abv, $18.

Ideal clarity; perfectly pure. The first nosing reminds me very much of the light caramel candies that used to come cellophane-wrapped in small cubes; the rich, mildly sweet caramel/butterscotch perfume strengthens with aeration. The palate entry is sweet but lean; at midpalate the caramel flavoring is all that there is in terms of taste presence; I understand completely why this is so because caramel is such a distinctive flavor. Ends up slightly awkward and bittersweet. I'm recommending this vodka because I think it's well-made and true to the flavor source, but even though I like caramel I have a difficult time envisioning applications for it.

2005 Rating: ★★★/Recommended

Players Extreme Cherry Infused Vodka (USA); 35% abv, $14.

Clear and clean. The initial nosing passes leave no room for error in guessing which fruit this is since the ripe red cherry perfume fills the nasal cavity; time in the glass sees a portion of the cherry intensity diminish, but not much; this is a brawling, in-yer-face, Cherry Herring-like bouquet whose watchword will never be subtlety. The A-type personality of the cherry flavor assaults the taste buds immediately upon palate entry; by the midpalate point the onslaught continues as the bitter, stone-like cherry flavor takes no prisoners. The finish is as raucous and demanding as the entry and midpalate. I'm exhausted just sampling it; if the cherry concentration would be toned down, this vodka could fly; as it is, it's simply too overwrought; when I want this level of cherry intensity I go to Cherry Herring, a liqueur.

2003 Rating: ★/Not Recommended

Players Extreme Green Apple Infused Vodka (USA); 35% abv, $14.

Pure as spring water. The tart green apple perfume jumps from the sampling glass immediately following the pour; the apple intensity calms down with aeration and actually turns into a delightful aroma that's equal parts ripeness and tartness. The palate entry is pleasingly tart and crisp; then at midpalate there's a nice oiliness that's picked up that complements the fruit rather well. The aftertaste is brief, tart and properly apple-like.

2003 Rating: ★★★/Recommended

Players Extreme Lemon Infused Vodka (USA); 35% abv, $14.

Clean and pure. The lemon juice perfume is strong but manageable in the first couple of sniffings; aeration over another seven minutes doesn't alter the potency or direction of this bouquet one iota. No subtlety in the palate entry as the initial flavor impact screams LEMON; not much change by the midpalate. Ditto the aftertaste. Turn down the flavor volume, please.

2003 Rating: ★/Not Recommended

Players Extreme Mandtango Infused Vodka (USA); 35% abv, $14.

Crystalline in appearance. The exotic and second gear aroma after the pour is inviting, citrusy and mild; further aeration sees the aroma lean towards citric acid, acute tartness and astringency; I like this refreshing, snappy bouquet. The palate entry is keenly tart, almost lip-puckeringly so; then by midpalate the taste profile accents the orange and mango fruit elements nicely. The finish is tart, crisp and long. An excellent mixer for many tropical cocktails and punches.

2003 Rating: ★★★/Recommended

Potocki Wodka (Poland); 40% abv, $35.

The limpid, rainwater appearance is crystal clear and blemish free. The bouquet at first is subtle and alluring, with distant, but potent aromatic notes of buttered popcorn and escarole broth; aeration stimulates the aroma to the point of hinting of peanut butter, rye toast, and damp cobblestone; a multilayered bouquet that begs for a half hour of sniffing and evaluation rather than the usual ten minutes. The silky palate entry is slightly sweet, concentrated, and grainy; at midpalate the flavor turns drier, lightly spiced, and more breakfast cereal-like, almost becoming fruity (as in dried fruit). The aftertaste is long, off-dry, and spicy. Well-crafted and quality-driven.

2004 Rating: ★★★★/Highly Recommended

Pravda Vodka (Poland); 40% abv, $30.

Clear, but shows some whitish sediment. Smells pleasantly of flowery/grainy spirit fresh off the continuous still; aeration brings a note of hearty, rye-based spice. The palate entry is bittersweet and a touch oily/charcoally; at midpalate the charcoal/ash quality shifts into high gear, leaving behind the spice/grain/rye flavor. Finishes well in an oily/sooty manner. Very drinkable and an excellent mixer for minimalist cocktails such as vodka martinis, gimlets, vodka and tonics.

2004 Rating: ★★★/Recommended

Precis Vodka (Sweden); 40% abv, $35.

100% corn; single distilled and unfiltered (a rarity in an era when multiple distillation and filtration through everything including precious gems, old tee shirts and ticket stubs from Eminem concerts are worn as badges of honor). As pristine and transparent as fresh rainwater. The opening nosing passes in the first two minutes after the pour detect the unmistakably soft sweetness of corn; further air contact over another seven minutes serves to deepen the bouquet only minimally as a husk-like underpinning aroma is the sole addition. The palate entry is sweet on the tongue and delightfully viscous; by midpalate the integrated, sweet corniness becomes kernel-like. It finishes smoothly, warmly in the throat. An understated but elegant unflavored vodka that comes off extremely well when it is allowed some time to develop in the glass; don't rush it; sit and savor it.

2003 Rating: ★★★★/Highly Recommended

President Vodka (Lithuania); 40% abv, $13.

Excellent clarity. The aroma after the pour is fatty/lanolin-like and a tad mushroomy; time in the glass catapults the lanolin forward on the aromatic pecking order as little other perfume is discerned even after eight minutes of sniffing; I don't mind the fatty/buttery smell of lanolin, but this bouquet is a one-note song. It's unabashedly sweet, but not cloyingly so, at palate entry; the midpalate flavor is sweet grain and nothing else; I can't help but wonder if the primary grain is maize due to the all-out sweetness. The aftertaste is, well, pleasantly sweet. Good enough to warrant three stars but skeptics and serious vodka mavens might view it as boring.

2002 Rating: ★★★/Recommended

Puriste No. 1 Premium Vodka (Austria); 40.2% abv, $40.

Impeccable purity. The soft grainy notes are dry and cracker-like in the first sniffings; an additional seven minutes add delicate and completely dry scents of beeswax and hemp/fiber; an austere bouquet that's not terribly expressive, but compelling in its reluctance. I can immediately tell that this distillate is masterfully made as the clean, sleek, wonderfully smooth palate entry shines and charms; the midpalate stage bolsters the entry findings as the purity of the spirit woos the taste buds in soft waves of intensely grainy flavor. One of the best, most seamless, swankest unflavored vodkas I've sampled in the last two or three years. World-class.

2007 Rating: ★★★★★/Highest Recommendation

Quadro Ultra Premium Vodka (Russia); 40% abv, $30.

Good purity and blue/silver transparence. I detect an intriguing ashy/wood smoke/charcoal quality at the aromatic edge of this vodka nose that I like as a tease; another six minutes of undisturbed air time stimulate scents of kernel, dry grain, and a faint bit of white pepper. The palate entry is lush, no, make that fat and buttery and mildly grainy sweet; the midpalate is full-bodied to the point of being voluptuous, intensely oily, moderately sweet and grainy. Ends on a sweet, biscuity note. Big-hearted, fat, and chewy.

2006 Rating: ★★★★/Highly Recommended

Rain Vodka (USA); 40% abv, $18.

Unquestionable purity. The sweet corn aroma right after the pour is enticing, clean, and soft as a whisper; air contact stimulates the very appetizing corny/caramel-like sweetness in the later sniffings. The palate entry is far more bittersweet than the fat aroma, but just as seductive and disarming; at midpalate there's a focused lead pencil taste that brings the grainy sweetness into check. Finishes sweet, warming, and a tad prickly.

2005 Rating: ★★★★/Highly Recommended

Red Bull Vodka (USA); 40% abv, $15.

Crystalline; pure. The first nosing run-throughs following the pour find a clean, grainy, almost peppery bouquet; aeration totaling another six minutes doesn't bring out any other aromatic qualities; it's a simple, clean, and brisk vodka aroma. The robust, tightly-knit sweetness noted at the palate entry reminded me a bit of Stolichnaya, which is a compliment to an American vodka; at the midpalate RB displays a firm structure, slightly oily texture, and sweet grainy, fresh-off-the-still flavor. Lingering, sweet aftertaste. Even though RB is something of a one-note song (read: sweet corny grain), its texture, firmness, and presence in the mouth definitely make it a recommendable product; nice to see a US unflavored vodka that echoes the Russian style.

2002 Rating: ★★★/Recommended

Regalia Royal Vodka (Russia); 40% abv, $100/liter.

The promotional material claims that this vodka was matured for six months in vats lined with white gold. I'm not kidding. Better than average purity. Smells of glass, sand, and grain; aeration time of another six minutes doesn't have any notable impact. The palate entry is sweet, waxy, and quite delicious; at the midpalate phase there's a thrust of minerals, cereal

(wheat especially), and a leanness that's crisp, acidic, and very refreshing. Not the type of monster you expect from the jolly land of Tolstoy, Rasputin, and the gulag.
2006 Rating: ★★★★/Highly Recommended

Regalia Vodka (Russia); 40% abv, $30/liter.
Excellent purity. The initial nosings after the pour offer generously proportioned scents of breakfast cereal, slate, charcoal, and wet grass; nothing more to add following additional air contact. The palate entry is supple, charcoal/smoky sweet, thick in texture and altogether delightful; the midpalate phase highlights the wood smoke/ashy sweetness to the hilt. Finishes robustly and with panache.
2006 Rating: ★★★★/Highly Recommended

Reval Classic Vodka (Estonia); 40% abv, $12.
Clear, pure and appealing to the eye. The initial nosing passes right after the pour find lovely, toasted grain aromas present; further aeration brings with it a significant deepening of the totally dry and very fetching roasted grain/toasty perfume; while not a blockbuster, wall-to-wall bouquet, an extremely comely and sensuous one that's dry, toasty, and nutty; gorgeous. In the mouth the palate entry shows a touch of vanilla sweetness at the start; then the flavor at midpalate turns grainy dry once again and only a bit toasty. The aftertaste is long and the feel is silky and remarkably smooth. An incredible buy and a vodka that's completely true to eastern European vodka profiles; excellent job here and a buy by-the-case proposition.
2001 Rating: ★★★★/Highly Recommended

Reyka Vodka (Iceland); 40% abv, $23.
Excellent clarity; crystalline appearance. In the first round of inhalations, there's a noticeable sootiness to the aroma; later whiffs following seven minutes of further air contact encounter enticing, completely dry notes of palm oil, unsalted butter, grain mash, and stone/slate. The palate entry brings together the soot/ash and mineral/slate in a bone dry opening flavor; at midpalate the mineral taste turns delightfully oily and textured as a touch of bittersweet graininess enters late and influences the entire aftertaste stage. Clean, medium-weighted, nicely made.
2005 Rating: ★★★★/Highly Recommended

Roberto Cavalli Vodka (Italy); 40% abv, $60.
Overall a very good, very clean appearance. The opening inhalations offer off-dry to slightly bitter smells of toasty grain, parchment and cardboard; additional minutes in the glass do little more than accentuate the spirity core aroma, which is pleasing and fine but I would have liked a bit more depth and expansion. The palate entry is directed, clean, grainy and off-dry; the midpalate stage is notable for its well-mannered, integrated demeanor as the graininess gains ground on the spirits influence. Finishes gracefully, if somewhat meekly. That said, if I'm going to drop $60 on a vodka (which at least in my next 75 incarnations, I would never do), I'll go with the drop-dead gorgeous tasting Stoli elit. For this price I'd like to get a pair of designer cufflinks, as well.
2006 Rating: ★★★/Recommended

Romance Vodka (Mexico); 40% abv, $20.

Silvery clear; minor floating debris. The opening nosing passes within the initial two minute span after the pour reveal a dry, delicate, mildly creamy, and altogether pleasant bouquet that's well-formed early-on; time in the glass allows for additional nuances of wet grass, new leather, and fresh-off-the-still flowery spirit; a sophisticated, come-hither bouquet that is coy but enchanting. The palate entry is totally stone dry and mineral-like; at the midpalate point the flavor turns slightly grainy sweet but the taste like the aroma is delicate and graceful. Finishes with a moderately sweet charcoal flurry that captivates the tongue. Hey, if this taste treat is any indication maybe Mexico's distillers should start producing grain spirits as well as tequila; boffo.

2002 Rating: ★★★★/Highly Recommended

Roth Vodka (USA); 40% abv, $30.

Displays ideal, unblemished appearance. The first nosing offers delicate, yet defined scents of grape must, light esters, keen acid and flowers; aeration time of another seven minutes gives the aroma the opportunity to evolve into a full-blown spirits bouquet that emits lacy, garden-like perfumes of citrus rind, ripe grapes, cotton fabric and carnations. The palate entry is tight, integrated, semisweet and pleasingly ripe; by midpalate there's a rush of acidity that cleanses the palate, leading to a crackerjack finish that's firmly structured, bittersweet to semisweet, fruity and leanly muscular. While I roll my eyes at the grape vodka, no-dearie-it's-not-an-eau-de-vie concept, I like this entry a lot.

2006 Rating: ★★★★/Highly Recommended

Rus Bogorodskaya Authentic Russian Vodka (Russia); 40% abv, $16.

Admirable clarity; impeccably pure. In the first couple of passes, there's a limp hint of grain and that's it; six minutes later, air contact has managed to stir only meek scents of peanut shells and dry earth. The palate entry is thickly textured, off-dry and grainy to the taste; at midpalate the flavor profile remains dry to off-dry, the feel stays ropy, and the core flavor of lightly toasted grain stays the course. Concludes metallic (like licking old coins), off-dry and faintly nutty/kernel-like. If this vodka had shown more in the bouquet and the aftertaste I would have given it a third rating star.

2004 Rating: ★★/Not Recommended

Russia Vodka (Russia); 40% abv, $30.

Quadruple distilled whole wheat and rye mashes at Tulaspirit distillery. Clear, but with minor black bits showing up under the examination lamp; nothing to be concerned about. This nose at the pour showcases the aromatic thumbprint of seemingly all Tulaspirit vodkas, a touch of dill, a pinch of black pepper, and a dash of off-dry grain mash; eight more minutes of air contact releases notes of licorice and rubber eraser. The palate entry is very smooth (mellower than its twin-like siblings Beryozka or Levsha) and herbal; the midpalate point highlights delectably silky and oily tastes of black pepper, linseed oil, charcoal, and pipe tobacco. The aftertaste is long, very satiny, and a touch hot; definitely the top of the class of the Tulaspirit family.

2002 Rating: ★★★★/Highly Recommended

Russian Standard Original Vodka (Russia); 40% abv, $30.

Clean as rainwater; silvery blue color. Nose is nondescript in the first whiffs after the pour; allowing it to settle for seven more minutes, the aroma emerges just slightly, emitting dry notes of parchment, stone, and lead. Entry is sweet and a touch flabby in texture due to a lack of palpable acidity; the midpalate profile is better, but still a little too paunchy for my liking as the grainy sweetness fails in the balance department because of the acid deficit. Finishes as it starts with no glaring flaws, but with a blander personality than I expect from a Russian vodka. Drinkable, but boring and just another blank face in the vodka horde.
2007 Rating: ★★/Not Recommended

Russov Vodka (Ukraine); 40% abv, $12.

Flawless clarity; silvery appearance. Notes of cracked grain kernels and breakfast cereal highlight the opening nosings; six more minutes in the glass stimulate earthy aromas of straw, flax/fiber, and hemp/rope. The palate entry lands on the sweeter side of the dry/sweet scale as the grain concentration takes charge of the taste; the midpalate phase features medium to heavy-bodied texture and sweet grain/Graham cracker flavors that propel the flavor phase forward into the aftertaste, which is plump, semisweet, and downright tasty. Russov makes many a $30-$60 per bottle vodka look appropriately ridiculous.
2007 Rating: ★★★★/Highly Recommended

Sahuaro Vodka (Mexico); 40% abv, $25.

Absolutely crystal clear and flawless. In the first couple of passes, the aroma is pleasingly oily, mildly sweet, and bean-like; six more minutes of air contact do little to bolster the bean/kernel quality as the bouquet becomes intensely cereal-like, as in, dry breakfast cereal. The palate entry is more bittersweet and beany than sweet and the oily texture works for me; at midpalate the intensity of the grain kernel flavor accelerates. Finishes sweetly and quietly. Another savory vodka from Mexico, though Romance Vodka (★★★★) is still the best from Mexico.
2004 Rating: ★★★/Recommended

Seagram's Black Cherry Flavored Vodka (USA); 35% abv, $13.

Clear and clean as rainwater. The first whiffs sense a burst of fresh, sour cherry perfume; additional aeration time steals the freshness and stimulates more of a manufactured aroma that reminds me of the chocolate covered cherry candies I used to devour as a youngster, but now don't especially care for. The palate entry is clean, semisweet, and candied; at midpalate the taste profile is all about "constructed, clinical" flavoring that bears little resemblance to fresh fruit or fruit essence. Concludes sweet. Certainly drinkable and mixable, but not even close to the best cherry/berry flavored vodkas out there.
2005 Rating: ★★/Not Recommended

Seagram's Extra Smooth Vodka (USA); 40% abv, $13.

Ideally clear and pure. The first couple of whiffs detect toasted/smoky notes of tobacco leaf, cigar ash and charcoal; further time in the glass allows a kernel-like scent of cocoa bean. As advertised, smooth on the tongue at palate entry; then it turns a bit prickly and hot by midpalate, all the time featuring very toasty/smoky notes. The finish is ashy, charcoal-like and slightly oily (which I welcomed). Not the most refined or sophisticated of frontline vodkas, but considering the volume of production, pretty darn good.

2003 Rating: ★★★/Recommended

Seagram's Orange Flavored Vodka (USA); 35% abv, $13.

Perfect clarity; excellent purity. The initial nosing passes detect moderately true scents of orange pulp; time in the glass does nothing to enhance the fruit profile, leaving the impression once again of a "manufactured" aroma rather than an authentic true-to-the-source bouquet. The palate entry is mildly pleasing and striving to be orangey; the midpalate supplies this vodka's best moment as the orange flavoring seems the freshest, though it is still leagues behind a host of other orange flavored vodkas in terms of genuineness. Finishes sweet, metallic, and peel-like. Drinkable, ordinary. When there are so many good to very good orange flavored vodkas available, why bother with mediocrity?

2005 Rating: ★★/Not Recommended

Seagram's Platinum Select Vodka (USA); 50% abv, $15.

Limpid, bluish/silver and perfectly pure. The opening whiffs detect firm notes of dry breakfast cereal and egg cream; following six more minutes of air exposure, the aroma turns a touch cocoa/chocolate-like and beany. The palate entry is alluringly oily, bittersweet and vanilla bean-like; at midpalate the alcohol comes into play as it provides a smoldering, almost prickly, warmth on the tongue as toasty, roasted grain tastes impress the taste buds. Concludes more sweet than bittersweet as the beany quality fades, leaving the sweet grain to take centerstage. The spirit intensity keeps the heat on "medium high" which might not play well with non-aficionados; for the money, the purchaser is getting a lot.

2004 Rating: ★★★/Recommended

Shakers Vodka (USA); 40% abv, $33.

Crystal clear and pure. The opening whiffs after the pour offer attractive, bittersweet vanilla extract, Wheat Thin cracker, and cocoa bean-like aromas; air contact serves to deepen the alluring bean-like core aromas but doesn't expand the fragrance beyond that point. The palate entry is beany, bittersweet, and intensely vanilla extract-like; by the midpalate juncture the vanilla bean/Wheat Thin cracker concentration shifts into fourth gear as the bittersweet, almost honey- or molasses-like taste profile soars on the tongue. It finishes semisweet, intense and as close to a flavored vodka as one could get without flavoring. Another stunning North American vodka achievement.

2003 Rating: ★★★★/Highest Recommendation

Shakers Rose Flavored Vodka (USA); 32.5% abv, $33.

The beguilingly rosy pink, pastel hue enchants the eye; impeccably pure; one of the prettiest spirits I've ever seen. The opening whiffs pick up a concentrated, intensely floral aroma that describes one solitary thing, uncut red roses; aeration time only serves to deepen the floral perfume, but does add traces of dew, rosewater, and berries; an utterly sensational flavored vodka bouquet of the first rank. The palate entry is delicate, floral, perfumed, and off-dry; at midpalate the taste exhibits a definite grainy sweetness that beautifully enhances

the rich rose-petal flavor. Finishes like a whisper, gently floral, rosy, and clean. A landmark in American distilling, but I can't help asking "What does one do with it?"
2004 Rating: ★★★★★/Highest Recommendation

Shakers Rye Vodka (USA); 40% abv, $33.

Clean, silvery clear appearance. The first stage aroma is vividly grainy and reminiscent of rye bread; aeration, to my surprise, reins in the bouquet as deeper, more ponderous scents, most notably, gun metal, rubber pencil eraser, and rye crackers, take the helm. The palate entry is mashy/grainy sweet and totally compelling; at midpalate the sweetness of the grain overrides all other taste elements. Ends up sweet, biscuity, and kernel-like. A supremely well crafted spirit, make no mistake, but I place the original wheat-based version ahead of it because of its remarkable intensity.
2004 Rating: ★★★★/Highly Recommended

Shakespeare Vodka (Poland); 40% abv, $30.

100% Polish rye, quadruple distillation. Crystal clear; impeccable purity. The initial nosing pass unveils a rich, nearly chocolaty bouquet that's dry and inviting; the middle stage inhalations find significant aromatic expansion as the bouquet adds developed scents of vanilla bean and spice paste; by the fourth and final whiff, after eight minutes of aeration, the bouquet is as fresh and firm as in the first go-round, offering bean-like and mildly spicy (more coriander than cinnamon or nutmeg) aromas that delight the olfactory sense. The palate entry is smooth, intense, stone dry, and similar to rye bread; the midpalate phase is highlighted by the silky texture and medium-body. The aftertaste is long, beany, vanilla-like, and mildly spicy.
2001 Rating: ★★★★/Highly Recommended

Shustoff Luxury Vodka (Ukraine); 40% abv, $30/liter.

Ideally clear; flawless appearance. The opening inhalations after the pour offer proper, if standard issue scents of grain and dry-roasted peanuts; seven more minutes of air contact introduce uninspiring and totally dry aromas of cardboard, textile-synthetic fibers, and palm oil; neither an improper nor bad bouquet, just uninteresting and commonplace. The immediate palate entry flavors are far more alluring than the entire ten minutes of aroma sniffing as lively, vivid, off-dry tastes of wheat and resin impress the taste buds; by midpalate the taste profile expands to include bittersweet cocoa and prickly (a plus) cereal spirit. Concludes in a rascal-like manner, offering moderately hot tastes on the tongue. I was glad to see a little bit of sass come into the picture at the taste stage.
2004 Rating: ★★★/Recommended

Shustov No. 28 Vodka (Russia); 40% abv, $20.

Very good clarity; flawlessly clean. The buoyant, animated aroma is grainy sweet and inviting right from the pour; aeration brings out a fruity/doughy ripeness in the bouquet that's almost like fruit pastry, meaning that the aroma turns bakery-like in the latter stages. The palate entry is soft, even delicate in its bearing; the midpalate stage features high levels of bittersweet grain kernel flavor, laced with clean acidity and ample viscosity. Ends gracefully, tight, and bean-like. Very nice job here.
2006 Rating: ★★★★/Highly Recommended

Siberian Tiger Vodka (Hungary); 40% abv, $25.

Rainwater clear; excellent purity. The opening nosing pass picks up a fruity, strikingly pear-like fragrance that's totally atypical, but intriguing nonetheless; aeration doesn't stimulate further development and as a result the second and third whiffs merely echo the first pass; the final sniffing stays the ripe pear-like course; a one note aroma, but inviting and friendly all the same. The palate entry is grainy sweet and firmly structured; then at midpalate the taste adds touches of charcoal and beans. The finish is fruity, off-dry to sweet, and packed with grainy oiliness. While there's not an abundance of complexity here, the overall impression is of a simple, but well-made vodka, one that is easily recommendable.
2001 Rating: ★★★/Recommended

Siku Glacier Ice Vodka (Holland); 40% abv, $40.

For the What-It's-Worth Dept: Made from glacier ice from Greenland's Qalerallit Sermia Glacier. Superb clarity. The first nosing passes reveal delicate scents of wheat and oatmeal; additional aeration time discovers earthy, mossy notes that are mildly sweet; an understated, but elegant bouquet. The palate entry is engagingly sweet and biscuity; the midpalate point is notable for its firm viscosity and grainy sweetness. Ends gracefully, with a touch of grain kernel tang.
2007 Rating: ★★★/Recommended

Single Single Malt Vodka (Italy); 40% abv, $35.

Flawless purity. The opening whiffs pick up moderately evolved scents of dry grain and sour mash; I was hoping that this bouquet would become a bit more expressive after the additional aeration period, but that didn't happen as the impressions of the first two minutes are the impressions of the final pass. The palate entry shows a bit more in the way of personality as the taste goes oily and semi-dry; at midpalate there's a touch of lanolin that firms up the flavor profile as the grain advances and becomes more intense. Finishes dry and vegetal.
2007 Rating: ★★★/Recommended

SKYY Vodka (USA); 40% abv, $18.

The clear-as-rainwater appearance shines beneath the evaluation lamp; superb purity. The grain takes a backseat in the early stages of the sniffing as bittersweet bean- and kernel-like scents dominate; later whiffs merely confirm the intense bean/cocoa quality. The palate entry mirrors the bouquet to a tee as the concentrated cocoa bean element leaves no doubt as to who's in charge; at midpalate the kernel-like intensity turns smooth and viscous on the tongue. Ends bittersweet and oily.
2004 Rating: ★★★/Recommended

SKYY 90 Vodka (USA); 45% abv, $35.

Properly clear and impeccably pure. Right out of the box the aroma is assertive, concentrated, dry, and grainy; further aeration uncovers a pleasingly piquant aromatic burst of grainy spirit that comes off as minerals/granite/slate; a powerhouse of a vodka bouquet that I find irresistible. The palate entry has plenty of grainy/spirity giddy-up and adds a note of sweetness; by the midpalate stage the spirit warmth fades, leaving behind the biscuity/wheat cracker taste of the grain; and then there's the velvety texture. Ends up as assertively

as when it began. A straightforward, down-the-hatch, ba-dah-bing type of unflavored vodka that isn't afraid to show its muscle or its swagger. Now we're talking.
2005 Rating: ★★★★★/Highest Recommendation

SKYY Berry Vodka (USA); 35% abv, $16.
Impeccable purity. The intense berry freshness in the opening nasal blast is delightful and stimulating; air contact deepens the blackberry/boysenberry concentration to the point of jamminess; this splendid bouquet leaves no room for doubt as to what it is. The ripe, freshly picked taste at palate entry is tart and inviting; the midpalate point is lush, ripe and only marginally sweet. The finish is fruity, ripe, sweet/sour and long. The SKYY Spirits distillers hit the mark with this elegant flavored vodka.
2003 Rating: ★★★★/Highly Recommended

SKYY Citrus Flavored Vodka (USA); 35% abv, $14.
The appearance owns the slightest tint of flax/hay; good clarity. The opening nose is very orange and tangerine-like (essences of lemon, lime, and grapefruit are also employed); in the middle stage sniffings, the tangerine and grapefruit dominate as the vodka aerates; the fourth and final whiff, following seven minutes of air contact, finds that the tangerine component takes the helm all by itself; a fresh, invigorating, but simple bouquet. The palate entry is tart and slightly acidic; the midpalate juncture shows considerable charm as the sweet citrus essences meld into one flavor with no one element coming to the forefront. The finish is medium long, tart, and more grapefruit-like than anything else. Refreshing, perfect for fruit/tropical mixed drinks and punches; entirely recommendable.
2000 Rating: ★★★/Recommended

SKYY Melon Flavored Vodka (USA); 35% abv, $17.
Pure and translucent in appearance. The melon scent in the opening bouquet is firm, fresh and pleasantly green melon-like; with time in the glass, however, the aroma profile changes from green melon to ripe cantaloupe/orange melon and fades slightly. The palate entry is soft, melony, alluring and ripe; at midpalate the taste disappointingly turns metallic/industrial, losing the melon focus. Finishes tinny/coppery to the taste. What happened to this vodka in the latter stages of the bouquet and the taste?
2004 Rating: ★★/Not Recommended

SKYY Orange Vodka (USA); 35% abv, $17.
Standard issue spring water clarity. The first nosings unearth fresh, rind-like scents of orange; time in the glass sees the aroma change slightly from the rind to the pulp; a very good (Valencia?) orange scent that's true to the source. The palate entry is keenly tart and acidic, with a pleasant bittersweet leaning that works well; at midpalate the flavor fades slightly, but not enough to be of concern; the aftertaste returns to the zesty, rind-like quality first noticed in the early stages of the nosing. Finishes tart, and properly fruity.
2005 Rating: ★★★/Recommended

SKYY Spiced Vodka (USA); 35% abv, $16.
Absolutely pure. The spice aroma in the initial passes highlights the clove component to the near-exclusion of nutmeg and cinnamon; exposure to air unleashes the nutmeg as the

clove fades; an odd spiced bouquet, in that, with neutral vodka as the base the spices don't get the opportunity to fully develop in the same way that they tend to do when rum is the base spirit. In the palate entry, cinnamon makes its first appearance; by the midpalate point the cinnamon/nutmeg tandem comes together and actually support the clove plus there's an interesting distant touch of apple. The aftertaste is dominated by the cinnamon. I completely understand why the SKYY Spirits people would want to take a crack at a spiced vodka, but this attempt just barely makes it across the finish line; though a good try, rum, in my opinion, is a more suitable spirits vehicle than vodka.
2003 Rating: ★★/Not Recommended

SKYY Vanilla Vodka (USA); 35% abv, $16.

Clear and pure, with noticeable oils seen floating in the core. The pronounced vanilla bean fragrance in the opening nosing passes is assertive, attractive and semisweet; air contact wears down the vanilla presence and it becomes plump and fatty in the final whiffs. The palate entry owns a vanilla bean core, to be sure, but there's a distracting oiliness to it that takes away from the initial enjoyment; by the midpalate stage the vanilla focus seems thrown off by a mineral/chalky quality that derails the vanilla element. The aftertaste is mellow, fat and makes an effort to redeem the awkward taste. When viewed in the context of its rivals this is a surprisingly mediocre venture by the normally solid SKYY Spirits distillers; wha' happened?
2003 Rating: ★★/Not Recommended

Smirnoff Triple Distilled Vodka (USA); 40% abv, $11.

Clear as rainwater and pure. The aroma in the first whiffs is very tar-like/charcoal-like, which I don't mind at all—it just seems heavily filtered; after about six minutes down the aeration road, the presence of dry cereal grain makes an appearance and an impression. The palate entry is where this vodka completely falls apart as a crude and astringent harshness grabs the taste buds and throttles them; by midpalate the taste profile is so ultra-bitter that it's undrinkable. Couldn't finish it fast enough. This ubiquitous loser makes the case in spades for premium and super-premium vodkas; pure crapola.
2004 Rating: ★/Not Recommended

Smirnoff Orange Twist Vodka (USA); 35% abv, $12.

Properly clear, bright, and sediment-free. The first nosing pass reveals an intensely orangy/citrusy aroma that leaps from the sampling glass; subsequent sniffings after some aeration time see the aroma go very much in the direction of fresh orange peel rather than pulp as the bouquet loses some of the early-on acidity; the last pass confirms the second and third nosings as the bouquet bears a striking resemblance to the yellowish inside skin of an orange; a good bouquet that's relatively true to the fruit source. The taste at palate entry is citrusy but not in the least bitter or acidic; the midpalate stage offers a moderately sweet, orange skin flavor that's crisp and clean. The aftertaste is very citrusy, crackling, and bordering on being bitter. A good mixing vodka.
2001 Rating: ★★★/Recommended

Smirnoff Raspberry Twist Vodka (USA); 35% abv, $12.

Clean, absolutely clear and pure. The ripe raspberry essence charges from the glass after the pour in waves of ripe, sweet, juicy perfume; the middle stage passes are a little less aggressive as the raspberry flavoring settles down in a round, ripe bouquet; the final pass sees a further muting of the berry intensity. The palate entry is notable in that its volume seems significantly turned down from the pungently fruity bouquet; the midpalate stage is pleasingly ripe, correctly acidic, and fruity, but not preserve-like or jammy. The finish is clean, harmonious, and fresh. An excellent mixer.

2001 Rating: ★★★/Recommended

Smirnoff Strawberry Twist Vodka (USA); 35% abv, $13.

Crystalline and clean. The aggressive plume of strawberry jam scent almost lifts me out of the chair in the first wave of sniffing; further air contact doesn't in the least diminish the intensity of the moderately sweet strawberry preserves aromatic tsunami. The bittersweet, juicy palate entry isn't subtle about the flavoring, but that's okay because it's neither syrupy nor cloying; at midpalate the taste profile settles down a bit as the flavor turns astringent and stunningly steely/metallic. Finishes on a disappointing steely/metal coin note that suddenly and sadly eclipses the robust fruit component. This vodka had a lock on a recommendation until it flattened out completely in the less than enchanting midpalate stage; what happened to this vodka that had "promise" written all over it?

2005 Rating: ★★/Not Recommended

Smirnoff Twist of Lime Vodka Recipe No. 21 (USA); 35% abv, $13.

Superbly clear and clean appearance, as with all Smirnoff vodkas. The delightfully tart juiciness of the opening sniff leaves no doubt as to the flavoring agent; the freshness of the later bouquet is so buoyant and citrusy that it's almost as though there's a slice of lime in the glass; remarkably genuine and fresh. The palate entry is clean, lean, keenly astringent, and tightly focused on lime peel rather than juice or pulp; at midpalate there's more evidence of fresh squeezed lime juice as the taste profile gathers more in the way of palate-cleansing acidity. Finishes a tad flat and raw after showing so well all the way through sight/smell/taste. Even with that minor final misstep, this is the best of the Smirnoff Twist line.

2006 Rating: ★★★★/Highly Recommended

Smirnoff Watermelon Twist Vodka (USA); 35% abv, $13.

The appearance is limpid and blemish-free. The opening aroma is watermelon-like only in that it's reminiscent of slightly turned, a day-too-old watermelon; things only get worse aromatically as aeration takes its toll and the regrettable bouquet turns more like smelly old watermelon rind straight out of the trash bin; are they serious? The palate entry is wobbly and vaguely similar to watermelon hard candy, but hardly evocative of fresh watermelon; by midpalate the taste has gone totally off the rails and smacks of rotting fruit. The sole positive thing about the finish is that it is the finish. A putrid mess and a vigorous nominee for the SJ Bottom-Feeder list.

2005 Rating: ★/Not Recommended

Snow Queen Vodka (Kazakhstan); 40% abv, $29.

Crystalline as spring water; unblemished purity. The initial sniffs pick up delicate notes of quartz crystals, minerals, earth, and cotton; further aeration sees the bouquet diminish a bit too rapidly, except for the grain. The palate entry is surprisingly sweet and assertive, considering how soft the aroma is; the midpalate taste is properly grainy, sweet, and is minerally enough to offset the sweetness. Concludes grainy, semisweet, and clean.
2007 Rating: ★★★/Recommended

Spudka Vodka (USA); 41% abv, $18.

Potato vodka. Clean as a whistle. The opening sniffings pick up delicate, mineral-like scents of lead pencil, wet slate and black pepper; aeration lasting another six minutes releases a comely, almost fruity (blackcurrants?) aroma that overtakes the mineral-like perfume; an understated, but firm bouquet. The palate entry is round, fatty and very textured; at the midpalate juncture there're bittersweet tastes of cocoa, stone/slate and charcoal. The finish features the ash-like charcoal and is extended on the tongue. Very nice, indeed, and a good mixer in just about any vodka-based cocktail.
2003 Rating: ★★★/Recommended

Square One Organic Rye Vodka (USA); 40% abv, $35.

Produced from 100% certified organic rye. Shows quite a lot of floating debris. The engaging first sniff encounters sweet, ripe, tropical fruit-like aromas of papaya, mango and/or guava as well as floral scents of orchids, roses, honeysuckle; additional aeration time brings out the grainy, mildly spicy core fragrance of rye; a stunningly attractive bouquet that is unlike any other unflavored vodka perfume. The palate entry is dry to off-dry, intensely grainy, and alluringly oily; the midpalate phase offers a welcome dash of prickly heat along with baked tastes of crackers, dry breakfast cereal, and bread. Finishes warm, grainy, spicy, and rich.
2006 Rating: ★★★★/Highly Recommended

Staraya Moskva Vodka (Russia); 40% abv, $13.

Crystalline, but with more sediment than I like to see. The opening shows a strong, assertive aroma of wheat cracker, wheat bread, ointment, and fusel oil; aeration doesn't do much except heighten the oil/ointment smell. The palate entry is rough, spirity, and more raw on the tongue than is suitable nowadays; the bitter tasting midpalate is the best feature of this otherwise underwhelming vodka. Finishes up raw, harsh, and prickly in the throat. I could see where some hard-line vodka traditionalists might be attracted to such an Ivan the Terrible style. The problem is, the world has now moved on to more sophisticated vodkas that exhibit finesse as well as rippling power. This is more a stylistic choice. Nyet for me.
2006 Rating: ★★/Not Recommended

Status Original Vodka with Ginseng (Ukraine); 38% abv, $30.

Transparent and flawlessly pure. The mellow aroma out of the gate is softly spicy/root-like and not the least bit grainy; more of the spirit base becomes apparent after the aeration period, mingling nicely with the rooty/earthy ginseng. The palate entry is firmly structured, dry and lead-like; at the midpalate juncture the taste turns intriguingly spicy, peppery, and oily, with just a slight hint of bittersweet flavor. Ends astringent, metallic, and downright bitter, which in the end takes a rating star away.

2007 Rating: ★★/Not Recommended

Stolichnaya Vodka (Russia); 40% abv, $22.
Impeccable purity; pewter tint. A burst of snack cracker (Wheat Thins) greets the olfactory sense with vigor and staying power in the opening nosing; additional aeration stimulates deeper notes that include metal/nickel/minerals and eve a dash of tobacco smoke; I have always liked this non-nonsense bouquet—it says "vodka" to me. Entry is beefy, firm, big-textured, and drier than I recalled; the midpalate stage turns markedly sweeter as the grain element comes to the forefront as well as a charcoal/soot aspect which nicely balances the grain. Sturdy, sweet, sap-like finish. This vodka just simply works for me on multiple levels.

2007 Rating: ★★★★/Highly Recommended

Stolichnaya Blueberi Blueberry Flavored Vodka (Russia); 35% abv, $20.
Flawless clarity. The blueberry muffin perfume right out of the gate is alluring and more fruity than candied, for which I am grateful; further air contact makes the fruit component seem more genuine and ripe and just-picked; a really good job here of capturing the delicacy of blueberry. The palate entry is delightfully fruity, berry-like, and fresh; the midpalate stage reflects the careful merging of the fruit essence with the neutral grain spirit. A more than worthy addition to the already fine Stoli flavored portfolio.

2006 Rating: ★★★★/Highly Recommended

Stolichnaya elit Vodka (Russia); 40% abv, $60.
The sparkling clean appearance is perfectly flawless. The first aromatic bursts are dry, clean, and grainy, with delicate background notes of parchment and litchi; the second and third nosing passes offer semisweet, mildly smoky/ashy scents of charcoal and smoldering embers. The palate entry is firm, moderately oily, bittersweet, and intensely reminiscent of Wheat Thin crackers; the midpalate stage is where this vodka displays the full array of its powers and virtues as near-succulent, concentrated, and spicy grain flavors mingle adroitly with the smoky, sap- and resin-sweet, birch-charcoal filtering influence. Concludes sweetly and almost candy-like. World-class elit is Stolichnaya's way of throwing down the gauntlet to its main competitors (Absolut, in particular) in the ever-escalating price realm of luxury vodka.

2005 Rating: ★★★★★/Highest Recommendation

Stolichnaya Citros Citrus Flavored Vodka (Russia); 35% abv, $22.
One must assume that Stoli Citros, flavored with lemon and lime, is replacing Stolichnaya Limonnaya, which was flavored with just lemon. Clear as rain water; the opening whiffs provide ample evidence of the presence of both lemon and lime riding in tandem; further minutes in the glass do nothing to expand on the fundamental aromatic theme as the aroma, in fact, fades noticeably by the fifth extra minute. I liked this flavored vodka much more in the mouth than in the nose as right off the crack of the bat at palate entry the marriage of grain spirit to flavors is seamless and attractive; the midpalate point is especially savory as the lemon/lime duo comes off as crisp and tart, showing off more genuine citrus zest and pulp features than ersatz candied citrus flavoring. The aftertaste

accents the tartness of the citrus without being astringent or harsh. As usual, a sterling flavoring job by the Stolichnaya distillers.

2003 Rating: ★★★★/Highly Recommended

Stolichnaya Cranberi Cranberry Flavored Vodka (Russia); 35% abv, $22.

Admirable clarity. The first inhalation after the pour stamps the impression of ripe, fresh CRANBERRY on my somewhat stunned olfactory sense; no mistaking this flavor, pal; thankfully, with further time in the glass, the rip-snortin' cranberry jubilee settles down into a rather respectable fruity bouquet that says cranberry and a little bit of strawberry preserves. The palate entry is surprisingly polite and subtle as the lovely, ripe cranberry essence emerges at the end of the first taste wave; by the midpalate point the flavor profile becomes downright graceful as the cranberry taste turns ideally ripe, sweet and juicy, but neither cloying nor domineering. The luscious aftertaste is long, ripe and properly acidic. The three star bouquet is lifted into four star territory by virtue of marvelously balanced and delicious taste and finish profiles; a natural for Cosmopolitans.

2003 Rating: ★★★★/Highly Recommended

Ston Vodka (Estonia); 40% abv, $21.

Absolutely flawless in appearance. The first sniffing detects a subtle, underlying semisweet graininess that's alluringly soft; a further six minutes in the glass stimulate delicate scents of beans, damp straw, and moss. The palate entry displays a really nice oiliness and viscosity that underpins the grainy, wheat-like sweetness; at midpalate there's a firmness to the texture that I have to ascribe to the spirity oiliness and the taste profile remains subtle as bittersweet flavors of fruit pit, beans, and spicy grain (is rye the grain employed?). The finish is whistle clean, satiny, and slightly oily. A whisper of a vodka.

2003 Rating: ★★★★/Highly Recommended

Strom Vodka (Finland); 40% abv, $25.

Made from potatoes. Transparent and relatively clean, with just a touch of inconsequential sediment seen floating about. The opening sniffing finds me a bit confused as the first aromas remind me of ink, clams, clam sauce, ocean spray, seaside sand, fish, and brine; air contact does little to alter, expand, or improve the unpleasant aroma. The palate entry taste bears no resemblance to the awful, fishy bouquet, going potato sweet and a touch honeyed; the midpalate stage echoes the entry flavor. Ends up semisweet, still a bit fishy/briny, and very odd. The pleasant palate entry and midpalate saved this vodka from one star purgatory. That said, I wouldn't bother with it in view of scores of other much better unflavored vodkas out there.

2005 Rating: ★★/Not Recommended

Svedka Vodka (Sweden); 40% abv, $12.

Good clarity except for insignificant, minor debris; no worries here. The compelling nose at opening and pouring is intensely grainy and mash-like plus it's almost chalky, which I favorably respond to; the bone dry chalkiness especially continues to unfold in the second pass with air contact; the third sniffing, following eight minutes of aeration, adds a barely perceptible trace of nutmeg-like spice in the background; the final nosing pass highlights the grain mash and chalk; I very much liked this aromatic and dry bouquet; true to Swedish

distilling tradition. The texture and taste are light and very approachable at palate entry; the flavor is of toasted grain, mostly like Wheat Thins crackers at midpalate. The finish is long, toasty, and grainy. An outstanding value that runs rings around standard, unflavored Absolut on two fronts, pure drinking pleasure and suggested retail price.
2000 Rating: ★★★★/Highly Recommended

Svedka Apple Flavored Vodka (Sweden); 40% abv, $23.
Brilliant and clear; unblemished purity. Owns a crisply acidic green apple perfume in the first whiffs after the pour; after another six minutes in the glass, the aroma turns peel-like and very tart; obviously, the blender understood the importance of retaining the natural acidity of the fruit in order to maintain the fruit's integrity. The palate entry displays a mild sweetness that's more ripe than candied; the midpalate stage is the strong point of the experience as the taste profile accurately mirrors fresh green apple flavor and is delightfully razor-edged. Finishes tart, piquant, and lean. Not an ounce of fat/oil on this winner.
2006 Rating: ★★★★/Highly Recommended

Svedka Clementine Orange Flavored Vodka (Sweden); 35% abv, $13.
Pristine and unblemished appearance. The opening bouquet is low-key to the point where I know without question that it's orange, but it's elusive and coy; time in the copita brings out a touch more in the way of astringent orange zest and pulp, making it desirable and a bit of an aromatic temptress. The palate entry is clean, acidic, bittersweet and straightforward; by the midpalate there's ample expansion in the orange peel department as a pleasantly acidic and refreshing orange pulp taste takes control. Ends cleanly and understated, fresh and clean. Understated, composed, lean, and a winner, especially for the money.
2004 Rating: ★★★/Recommended

Svedka Raspberry Flavored Vodka (Sweden); 35% abv, $13.
Excellent clarity; completely sediment-free. The lovely, seductive perfume of ripe raspberries fills the office upon pouring Svedka Raspberry into the sampling copita; six minutes of air contact stimulate more than ample ambrosial, berry-like, properly fruity aromas; what's attractive about this bouquet is the fact that it holds onto the natural fruit acidity/astringency aspect, therefore, allowing it to largely remain true to the fruit source. The palate entry is tart and lean; by midpalate the tartness begins to turn peel-like and seed-like, never going the sweet, hard candy route traveled by so many other raspberry flavored vodkas. Ends extremely tart and appropriately bitter. One of the two or three best less-than-$15 berry flavored voddies out there; make homemade Cosmos? Get Svedka Raspberry.
2004 Rating: ★★★/Recommended

Svedka Vanilla Flavored Vodka (Sweden); 35% abv, $13.
Absolutely pure and blemish-free. The beany vanilla bean aroma wastes no time in leaping from the sampling glass; aeration time encourages the vanilla essence to turn more plump, fatty, and biscuity than bittersweet or extract-like; it's a friendly, undemanding bouquet. The palate entry is bittersweet and intensely beany; while the midpalate stage is all about the buttery/oily side of processed vanilla essence. Concludes without a bang, going a bit soft in the finish. While not in the same quality league as the more expensive Stoli Vanil (★★★★★),

Absolut Vanilia (★★★★) or Vincent van Gogh Vanilla (★★★★★), Svedka's strong suit is that it offers exceptional value; in today's over-priced, over-hyped vodka universe, that's something to crow about.
2004 Rating: ★★★/Recommended

Svensk Lake Vattern Vodka (Sweden); 40% abv, $23.
Silvery appearance; unblemished purity. The smoky, bean-like aroma is vivid, beautifully bitter and bark-like; love it; while aeration doesn't enhance the existing bouquet, it does serve to round off the bitterness, leaving behind a gently bark-like perfume that's clean and focused. The palate entry is root- and bark-like, herbal, and moderately oily; at the midpalate stage the flavor profile leans back towards refreshing bitterness and a minerally quality that brings to mind slate/friable soil/desert. Ends up dry yet oily and smooth. A dandy value that drinks better than several super-premium unflavored vodkas selling for $30 or more.
2006 Rating: ★★★★/Highly Recommended

Svensk Lake Vattern Smultron Wild Strawberry Flavored Vodka (Sweden); 40% abv, $24.
Absolute clarity; pure and clean. In the initial sniffs, the grain quality of the spirit actually competes with the subtle strawberry fragrance for dominance; aeration time serves to bring out the strawberry scent a bit more, though it's still very delicate and is more an essence than a keen fruitiness. The palate entry offers the nuance of fresh, ripe strawberry and is delightfully tart; the midpalate also displays the skill of the distiller, in that, the flavoring is an accentuation more than a dominant force. Finishes elegant, savory, ripe, and clean. Three winners out of three for this exciting new line of vodkas from Sweden.
2006 Rating: ★★★★/Highly Recommended

Svensk Lake Vattern Vanilj Vanilla Flavored Vodka (Sweden); 40% abv, $24.
The pale yellow/buff/cream soda/egg white color is pretty and pure. The use of the vanilla flavoring is measured and, to my mind, nearly perfect in its melding with the base spirit; time in the glass brings out more of the vanilla beanniness and bittersweet nature of the flavoring agent; a lovely bouquet. The palate entry is mildly vanilla-like and quite beany; at midpalate there are subtle tastes of cocoa, milk chocolate, and cream that pair up beautifully to the vanilla core flavor. Finishes well as the vanilla turns slightly sweet and a bit extract-like more than beany. Luscious.
2006 Rating: ★★★★/Highly Recommended

Svovoda Vodka (Russia); 40% abv, $10.
Looks like mineral water, clear, but with some black/gray sediment evident; not to be considered problematic. Owns the typical Russian aromatic traits of off-dry grain mash, light dried herbs, and smoke and charcoal; aeration only serves to deepen the existing smells, except to add a trace of lead pencil. Very pleasant at palate entry as sweet grainy, almost candied tastes impress the taste buds; the midpalate shows a trace of spirity fire as well as light touches of sweet grain and coconut oil. The finish is long, embers-warm, intensely sweet, and charcoal-like. What I like the most about this vodka is its brazenly sweet taste profile; incredible bargain all the way.
2002 Rating: ★★★★/Highly Recommended

Swan's Neck French Grape Vodka (France); 40% abv, $45.

Limpid, flawlessly clean appearance. The initial sniffings detect obvious grapy/musty notes that leave no doubt as to the base material; after another seven minutes of air contact, the grapiness turns more red fruit-like (strawberries? red cherries?), almost to the point of resembling a fortified (port) or aromatized (vermouth) wine and, thus, veering off the spirits track. The palate entry is fruity and overripe; at the midpalate the acid deficiency comes into play as the flavor profile becomes fat and flabby, lacking crispness and therefore structure. Vodka, at its finest, is smooth and crisp. This vodka has the right idea, but now it needs to be bumped up in the acid department to gain shape. It's too fat as it is.

2007 Rating: ★★/Not Recommended

Swan's Neck Lemon Zest French Grape Vodka (France); 35% abv, $45.

Excellent clarity; completely unblemished. The lemon candy perfume clubs you over the head in the first whiffs; allowing it another seven minutes in the glass, the aroma settles down and exhibits a pleasing blend of lemon peel and grainy spirit. The palate entry is concentrated in its zestiness, but not overbearing; in the midpalate the lemon flavor turns very lean and peel-like. Concludes fresh, lemony, and correctly acidic.

2007 Rating: ★★★/Recommended

Symphony Vodka (Czech Republic); 40% abv, $20.

Distilled from potatoes. Impeccable cleanliness and purity. The initial sniffings find friendly scents of uncooked white potato and light spice; further time in the glass leads to additional, pleasingly off-dry aromas of yam, butter, and multi-grain cereal. The taste profile in the entry flavor is off-dry to semisweet, succulent, and moderately oily; at midpalate the oiliness comes to the forefront and then a keen peppery quality takes charge, leading to the off-dry, medium-long aftertaste. The delectable combination of tight, oily texture and off-dry taste make for exquisite drinking.

2004 Rating: ★★★★/Highly Recommended

T & W American Luxury Vodka (USA); 40% abv, $26.

Distilled from rye. Looks correctly pure and flawless. The initial whiffs pick up a distinctly glue-like aroma that I have to believe is the cockeyed rye mash—yikes; further time in the copita adds unappealing fragrances of floor wax, nail polish, and vinyl as well as an incongruous scent of nuts; okay, I give up; cut to the taste. The palate entry is marginally better and more appropriate than the direct-from-the-paint-factory aroma as it gives off tastes of candle wax and mild grain; the midpalate unfortunately implodes, going nowhere as the flavor turns abrasive and industrial. Let's not even mention the flat finish that tastes like paint thinner. Not another word from moi.

2006 Rating: ★/Not Recommended

Teton Glacier Potato Vodka (USA); 40% abv, $25.

Transparent as rainwater; minor but evident floating debris. The opening aromas include a bittersweet vegetal scent and a fiber-like hint of hemp/rope; following aeration there's a keen fragrance of charcoal/tar. The palate entry is sweet and nicer than I remembered from my first evaluation in 1998; the texture becomes an issue in the midpalate as the feel becomes smooth and thick while the taste profile turns sharp, smoky, and bitter. The bitterness accelerates in the finish. I had hoped for a better score, but this vodka simply doesn't cut it for me. There's no subtlety and the midpalate/finish bitterness factor detracts from gains made in the later stage nosing and palate entry.

2006 Rating: ★★/Not Recommended

Thor's Hammer Vodka (Sweden); 40% abv, $25.

Whistle clean and pure. In the tradition of Scandinavian vodkas, this nose is agile, grain-driven, and delicate in the first sniffing after the pour; the middle stage passes reveal a totally dry, minerally/stony aroma that's wonderfully clean; the fourth and final nosing finds the bouquet drifting into the sunset as the aromatic potency lessens with longer air contact; a typical, well-made, Nordic-style vodka bouquet that's light as a feather to the point of being ethereal. Slightly more expressive in the mouth, Thor's starts out dry and grainy at palate entry, then turns moderately sweet, almost fruity, at midpalate. The aftertaste is long, sweet, minerally, and more intensely grainy than the midpalate. A solid, nicely crafted vodka that's easily recommendable.

2001 Rating: ★★★/Recommended

Three Olives Vodka (England); 40% abv, $20.

Perfect clarity. The opening nosing passes detect subtle but firm odors of sweet grain and fresh, damp vegetation; another six minutes of air contact introduce aromas including marshmallow and fiber. The palate entry is supremely silky, textured, substantial, and grainy sweet; at midpalate the addition of charcoal/ash makes the overall flavor phase seductive and sophisticated. Concludes on a sweet grain, sap-like note that's generous and smooth. This is a classy unflavored vodka that deserves a huge audience.

2004 Rating: ★★★★/Highly Recommended

Three Olives Berry Flavored Vodka (England); 35% abv, $20.

Pure and completely unblemished. The ripe, inviting perfume in the first nosings leaps from the glass in potent waves of fresh-picked raspberry and blackberry; wow, what a rush of intense, true-to-the-source aroma right out of the gate; additional minutes of aeration assist the bouquet in becoming more jammy, more restrained as the berry acidity overtakes the fruity ripeness. The palate entry is berry sweet/ripe and concentrated; by the midpalate point the fresh flavor intensity starts to fade. In the finish the flavor leans towards the berry preserves side of the spectrum.

2006 Rating: ★★★/Recommended

Three Olives Cherry Flavored Vodka (England); 35% abv, $20.

Perfect clarity. The lovely bouquet in the initial nosing passes displays a round, gently sweet ripeness of red cherries that is alluring and proper; time in the glass finds the bouquet turning more cherry stone-like as it goes from keen ripeness to pit-like bitterness; another winning flavored bouquet from Three Olives. The palate entry is ripe, concentrated and accurately fruity; by the midpalate stage the taste profile is sweeter than the bouquet and

the palate entry but not so sweet that the fruit perspective is diluted or lost. The aftertaste is pleasantly jammy and lip-smacking. A solid, properly reflective flavored vodka that pleases.
2003 Rating: ★★★/Recommended

Three Olives Chocolate Vodka (England); 35% abv, $20.

Pure and absolutely crystalline. In the first sniffings the chocolate/cocoa presence is subtle and off-dry; aeration time of another six minutes doesn't stir much more in the way of aromatic expression. The palate entry displays the bean-like, cocoa-like flavor thrust that hits the mark; at midpalate the taste turns more processed dark chocolate-like than raw cocoa-like as it shows a touch of sugary sweetness. Concludes moderately sweet, mildly chocolatey, and appealing. Very recommendable, indeed; chocolate is clearly one of the more difficult flavors to get right, but Three Olives does a good job at keeping the flavoring low-key and therefore approachable.
2005 Rating: ★★★/Recommended

Three Olives Citrus Flavored Vodka (England); 35% abv, $20.

Shows absolutely no sediment at all; perfect purity. The fresh, breezy, mildly ripe yet zesty smell of citrus peel (both lemon and lime) hits the mark early-on; later sniffings highlight the citrus zest rather than the acid or the fruit. The palate entry is suitably bitter/tart, but with a strong fruit pulp underpinning; at midpalate the taste profile turns sweeter as some of the bitter peel quality is softened in favor of the sweetness. Finishes citrusy sweet and only moderately tart. Enhanced sourness would have given it the real possibility of being a four star vodka.
2006 Rating: ★★★/Recommended

Three Olives Grape Flavored Vodka (England); 35% abv, $20.

Impeccable purity. Oy, we may have a slight problem here in the overly ambitious, intensely grapy, but ultimately juicy, baseball card bubble gum-like opening aroma; aeration doesn't do much except heighten the grape candy concentration—a bouquet that's trying too hard to be grapy (any of you Midwestern American subscribers remember Nehi Grape Soda from the 1960s?) and it ends up being more candied than fruity. The palate entry is more serious and focused than the aimless bouquet, coming off sweet, slightly sugary, but drinkable and light; the midpalate is slightly better even than the entry as the grape flavor settles down, becoming more realistic and true-to-the-source. Aftertaste is short, sweet, grapy and carefree. Drinkable certainly, but not as good as I've come to expect from Three Olives.
2006 Rating: ★★/Not Recommended

Three Olives Green Apple Vodka (England); 35% abv, $20.

Clean, pure and clear. The delicate apple-like opening aroma leans more to apple skin than pulp or juice; with time, the aroma shifts direction in the way of fruit pulp and seed and away from skin; since it's not sweet or ripe, some people may not like this bouquet, but I did because it doesn't come off as being "manufactured" or ersatz. The palate entry is ripe and sweet, with just a background trace of tartness; by midpalate the flavor trail leads to sweetened apple sauce, or candied apple. Ends politely sweet. I like this vodka which, like all Three Olives vodkas, is well made, but it would have garnered a fourth rating star had the flavor and finish phases shown more appley tartness.
2005 Rating: ★★★/Recommended

Three Olives Orange Vodka (England); 35% abv, $20.

The appearance is properly clean and clear. The first couple minutes of sniffing reveal lovely, elegant, and subtle hints of fresh orange pulp and juice; aeration goes a long way to enrich the juice part of the equation while all the while remaining more a nuance than a burst of aroma; it's an astute and sophisticated distilling/flavoring decision to tempt rather than to bludgeon; way to go. The palate entry is pleasantly sweet and juicy; at midpalate the taste highlights the sweetish fruit, downplaying the acidic side. Concludes more astringent and tart than the midpalate phase, therefore, restoring the balance and earning it a fourth rating star.

2005 Rating: ★★★★/Highly Recommended

Three Olives Raspberry Flavored Vodka (England); 35% abv, $20.

Absolute purity. The perfumed scent of fresh-picked raspberries is enticing and true-to-the-source; with further aeration the raspberry aroma turns jammy and bittersweet; a very good, nicely balanced bouquet. The palate entry is tart and fruity; then at midpalate the taste develops a ripe sweetness that goes a touch too sugary and syrupy for my taste. The aftertaste is long, candied and semisweet. The bouquet begins the experience in good form and I'm thinking that I may have a four sr product here and then the flavor profile descends into a manufactured, sugary state that undercuts much of the delectable ripe fruitiness enjoyed in the fragrance; this vodka is passable, to be sure, if you like sweeter than normal flavoring; the best raspberry flavored vodkas (Stolichnaya Rahberi, Vincent van Gogh Raspberry) to me are the ones that remain decidedly tart and crisp…like the original fruit source itself; I wanted to score this higher but felt let down by the midpalate and finish.

2003 Rating: ★★/Not Recommended

Three Olives Vanilla Flavored Vodka (England); 35% abv, $20.

Clear and clean. The first couple of sniffings detect lovely, round, softly sweet and supple scents of vanilla bean; seven additional minutes in the glass bring out deeper, more profound vanilla qualities, qualities that add hints of cocoa and caramel; got to hand it to the Three Olives distillers in the UK who really get the bouquets down on their flavored vodkas. The palate entry taste is acutely bittersweet and intense; at the midpalate the flavor profile shifts slightly to a sweeter, almost honeyed or even sherried taste that reminds me of vanilla cake frosting. The aftertaste is long, properly sweet, and delicious.

2003 Rating: ★★★★/Highly Recommended

Tito's Handmade Vodka (USA); 40% abv, $20.

Clear as rainwater. Opening whiffs detect subtle traces of charcoal and roasted grain; aeration brings out sweeter aromas of sweet grain mash and pipe tobacco. Entry is smoky, charred, almost woody; the midpalate point is oily, moderately viscous, semisweet, and robust in the mouth. Ends on an oily, bacon-like note that's delicious and full-bodied. A genuine no-nonsense, 100% corn, well-made American pot still vodka that deserves every accolade.

2007 Rating: ★★★★/Highly Recommended

Touch Vodka Honey & Grain Vodka (USA); 40% abv, $40.

Ideal, flawless clarity. The initial whiffs detect delicately scented aromas of honey and parchment; additional exposure to air deepens the honey factor significantly, adding more gentle sweetness and perfume. The palate entry is pleasingly sweet and lush in texture as the honey core flavor dominates the phase; the midpalate stage is marked by a toasty/bakery shop flavor of buttered and toasted honey wheat bread. Concludes silkily, moderately sweet, and assertive.

2006 Rating: ★★★★/Highly Recommended

Tovtry Golden Fields Vodka with Natural Flavors (Ukraine); 40% abv, $20.

Transparent and clean. The aroma in the opening stages is pure and moderately grainy; aeration time spanning another seven minutes affords scents of spice and rye to emerge, not in an assertive manner but delicately. The palate entry is dry, grainy and concentrated; by the midpalate stage there's a mild oiliness to the texture and a semisweet flavor of grain mash. The taste in the finish goes dry once again and moderately grainy with just a trace of rye spice. I sensed the presence of a substantial, potentially wonderful vodka lying just beneath the surface; it is very good at the moment, very agreeable on the palate, but I think it could be even better if the rye flavoring was accentuated to a greater degree.

2003 Rating: ★★★/Recommended

Tovtry Old Fortress Vodka with Natural Flavors (Ukraine); 40% abv, $20.

Rainwater clear and 100% pure. The opening sniffings offer very meek, understated aromas of roasted grain, toasted bread and lead pencil; aeration does nothing to expand the bouquet beyond what already is noted; it's pleasant but timid. The palate entry is off-dry, similar in timidity to its siblings, mildly oily and mash-like; by the midpalate point there's a trace of spicy flavor, but it's so hidden in the background by the grain thrust that it's a virtual non-factor. The finish is off-dry, pleasant and far more "unflavored" than "flavored" in scope. All three of these Ukrainian vodkas are nicely made, but the supposed differences are paper thin and I am forced to wonder why they are even mentioned in the first place.

2003 Rating: ★★★/Recommended

Tovtry Ternopil Vodka with Natural Flavors (Ukraine); 40% abv, $20.

Good clarity and relatively pure, some sediment spotted. The initial nosing passes in the first two minutes are a tad mute and non-descript; another seven minutes in the copita slightly pry open the aroma as distant hints of berries, toasted bread and spearmint make fleeting appearances; not much to grip onto here in the bouquet. Subtlety, almost to a fault, seems to be the rule here as the palate entry shows very little flavor other than a limp graininess; the pleasant midpalate flavor profile at last displays some defining characteristics in the ethereal forms of under-ripe red berries and very elusive mint. The aftertaste is long, mostly grain mash-like and off-dry. Once again, the flavoring is so nuanced that it's almost negligible; absolutely enjoyable, but to call it "flavored" is to confuse the issue—and the purchaser—because it tastes like a better than average unflavored vodka, that's all.

2003 Rating: ★★★/Recommended

Trump Vodka (Holland); 40% abv, $33.

The Vodka from The Donald. Clear appearance; superb clarity. The first nosings after the pour reveal dry, earthy scents of grain and paraffin; following the seven minute aeration period, the bouquet offers tantalizing nuances of kid leather, jasmine, flowers, moss, and soot. The palate entry displays far better than average grain focus and viscosity; at the midpalate juncture the taste profile turns off-dry, intensely breakfast cereal-like, and biscuity. Finishes elegantly, oily/creamy, and snack cracker-like. You're NOT fired.

2007 Rating: ★★★★/Highly Recommended

Turi Vodka (Estonia); 40% abv, $30.

Quadruple distilled rye grain mash; clear, but with considerable floating particles seen under the exam lamp. The bouquet starts out mildly spicy in the first couple of whiffs after the pour; aeration positively affects this vodka as deeper scents of rye bread, black pepper, and dried herbs make for interesting sniffing in the later nosing stages. On the palate Turi is light-to-medium in body, not oily at all, and bittersweet in a grainy/flowery fresh-off-the-still manner. The finish is long, lean, floral, and delightfully sweet. As opposed to the bruising, viscous, and oily vodkas of neighboring Russia, this Estonian spirit is lithe, fresh, and clean on the tongue; nice stylish, almost feminine aroma and taste profile.

2002 Rating: ★★★★/Highly Recommended

U.K. 5 Organic Grain Vodka (Germany); 40% abv, $31.

Distilled in Germany, but bottled in Great Britain; no data was given to us regarding base materials, distillation or filtration. Clear and clean. The opening bouquet is very fruity and gum-like, hardly grainy at all; seven additional minutes of exposure to air makes the fruitiness come off as being mildly pineapple-like; pleasantly fruity and off-dry at palate entry; the midpalate highlights the pineapple/cottony candy quality and nothing else; no depth to it. The aftertaste is medium-long, sweet and Juicy Fruit-like. I almost liked it enough to give it a third rating star, but its undeniable flaws are that it is basically one-dimensional, pedestrian, and indistinct.

2003 Rating: ★★/Not Recommended

U'Luvka Vodka Polish Grain Vodka (United Kingdom); 40% abv, $50.

Transparent, silvery, unblemished. The nose after the pour offers firm, concentrated scents of cereal grain and grain snack wafer; aeration releases pleasant smells of palm oil, parchment, and nuts. The palate entry is full, semidry, and intensely grainy; in the midpalate stage the taste profile turns more oily and waxy, all the time maintaining a high degree of grain kernel. Concludes dry, clean, and elegant.

2007 Rating: ★★★★/Highly Recommended

Universum Vodka (Poland); 40% abv, $20.

Flawless clarity. Displays aromatic notes of grainy sweetness up front in the first pass; subsequent sniffings detect off-dry to semisweet notes of parchment, grain mash, and rye bread toast. The palate entry offers only partially defined flavors of refined sugar, spice, and honey; the midpalate profile stays the semisweet/grainy route and, while drinkable, comes off a bit coarse and jaded in the finish, enough to drop it from three to two stars.

2005 Rating: ★★/Not Recommended

UV Vodka (USA); 40% abv, $12.

Clear and impeccably clean. The first whiffs are treated to uncomplicated dry breakfast cereal, parchment, and cotton/fiber scents; the aroma expands measurably after aeration bringing on board bone dry odors of shale, minerals, cardboard, and beans; a solid, no-nonsense, grainy vodka bouquet. The palate entry introduces a taste that's sweeter than the bouquet, but just as focused on the grain/fiber/paper character; the midpalate taste profile adds bittersweet flavors of cocoa, coffee bean, sugar, and sap. Concludes with a slight kick and a welcome note of spirity warmth. A fantastic bargain.
2005 Rating: ★★★★/Highly Recommended

V One Vodka (Poland); 40% abv, $26.

Superb clarity. The opening nosing passes pick up subtle and dry scents of black pepper, moss, and mushrooms; the earthy/spicy personality of this bouquet continues on without great fanfare or expansion in the later sniffing stages. The palate entry is keenly spicy and sharply sweet; in the midpalate the spirit presence is strong as the clean, but meaty texture takes command, buttressing the surface tastes of oil, intensely sweet grain (wheat, in this case), and even a touch of honey/sugar cane. The aftertaste is elegant yet sweet and hefty. V One to get.
2005 Rating: ★★★★/Highly Recommended

V2 Energy Vodka with Taurine and Caffeine (Holland); 40% abv, $35.

Limpid and superbly pure. The opening smell is of moderately sweet grain mash and parchment; very distant elements of spice and earth send out signals after aeration; just not a lot happening in the aroma, period. Entry is pleasantly and moderately sweet and grainy; the flavor profile at midpalate grows in grain intensity as well as sweetness. While drinkable and probably fine for many people, it finishes too grainy/sugary sweet for my liking.
2007 Rating: ★★/Not Recommended

Vampire Vodka (England); 40% abv, $20.

The appearance is, what a surprise, blood red! Oh, those wacky, unpredictable, devil-may-care blood suckers! Not much to report in the initial nosings, except for a reasonably pleasing grain presence; in later sniffings, the grain accelerates, becoming a dry, breakfast cereal-like bouquet of minor consequence. The palate entry is actually quite nice as the grain mash taste remains clean and dry to off-dry; the midpalate shows a nice, zesty spirity quality that moves past the graininess, providing for an appealing aftertaste that warms the throat.
2005 Rating: ★★★/Recommended

Van Gogh Vodka: *See Vincent van Gogh*

Vermont Gold 100% Maple Sap Vodka (USA); 40% abv, $44.

Perfect, limpid, and unblemished in appearance. The initial aromatic blast takes the olfactory sense by surprise due to its gracefully presented and fresh sugar maple candy charm and sweetness; seven further minutes of air contact serve to bolster the first impressions; this is a unique and seductive vodka bouquet unlike anything I've encountered. The palate entry is toasty, maple sweet, and full-bodied; at midpalate the toastiness found in the entry gives way to full-out lip-smacking tastes of sugar maple candy, dark honey, sap, resin, and malt. Finishes divinely sweet and sap-like. A new gold standard for non-grain vodkas. Worth every bloody cent.

2005 Rating: ★★★★★/Highest Recommendation

Vermont White 100% Milk Sugar Vodka (USA); 40% abv, $38.

Impeccably clear, translucent, and pure in appearance. In the first nosings I detect subtle notes of chalk and paper; additional aeration time of six minutes adds only soft whispers of cream, powdered milk, and refined sugar. The palate entry is bittersweet and tightly structured—there's no flab or fat in the opening taste profile; by midpalate the bittersweet aspect develops into a fully sweet, honey-like presence that underlies the other more superficial flavors of honey and powdered milk. Concludes pleasingly sweet and silky. Excellent distilling job here.

2005 Rating: ★★★★/Highly Recommended

Vertical Vodka (France); 40% abv, $35.

This vodka is produced in Grenoble, France at the same distillery that produces one of my all-time fave spirits, Chartreuse. Impeccably clear and clean in appearance; the opening nosing picks up dry, lightly smoked aromas of toasted grain and leather; seven more minutes of air contact releases foundation scents of minerals, slate, and parchment. The palate entry is smooth, stone dry, and just a bit grainy; while at midpalate there's an acceptably prickly rush of spirit at center tongue that lasts well into the warming, smoldering aftertaste which features toasted grain and charcoal-like, almost tobacco-like, flavors.

2003 Rating: ★★★/Recommended

Viking Fjord Vodka (Norway); 40% abv, $21.

100% potatoes. Absolutely pure and clear; not much is available in the way of an opening aroma; more time in the glass fails to stimulate the timid bouquet. The palate entry is as meek as the bouquet; it's not bad tasting, it's just ethereal; by midpalate the flavor begins to showcase a bit of grainy, off-dry taste but that's about as far as it dares to go. The finish is where the flavor develops on the tongue and in the throat, but by then, frankly, I don't really care. The idea of having an aroma and a flavor is to afford a multistage sensory experience; though drinkable and certainly mixable, this lame, reluctant vodka fails to deliver the goods; this is an age when unflavored vodkas are featuring distinct characters and virtues; this one takes the definition of vodka as "tasteless, odorless" too seriously; pass on it.

2003 Rating: ★/Not Recommended

Vincent van Gogh Vodka (Holland); 40% abv, $30.

Clear as rain water. The bouquet is direct and focused right from the pour with nuances of charcoal, oil, and dried herbs; the second pass offers further deepening of the aroma as the charcoal turns just a tad sweet; the penultimate nosing pass adds delicate touches of smoke, tobacco leaf, and linseed oil; the final sniffing brings the various elements together for a harmonious finale that hasn't lost one iota of strength or charm; let's face it, how many vodkas can be said to have lovely bouquets? Vincent does by the bushel full. On the palate it owns a silky, mildly oily though not overly voluptuous texture and grainy sweet flavor; and, to my liking, Vincent displays a brief flash of fire on the back of the tongue. The evolved, organic, mashy sweetness comes to the fore in the finish as does the grip and guts of the texture. Vincent is a totally different concept of vodka from the Russians', the Poles', and the Swedes' in that there's unabashed sweetness and spectacular textural smoothness; yet another white spirits gem from the Dirkzwager Distillery, located in Schiedam, Holland and master distiller John DeLange.

2000 Rating: ★★★★★/Highest Recommendation

Vincent van Gogh Acai-Blueberry Flavored Vodka (Holland); 35% abv, $25.

The transparent lavender color is beguiling and ideally clean. Out of the gate, it smells of ripe blueberries, brambles, and blackberries; an additional seven minutes of air contact releases delightfully tart fragrances of ripe blueberry, blackberry, and black cherry, with intriguing side notes of cocoa bean, cotton fiber, textile, and green vegetation. Entry is mildly sweet first, then turns refreshingly tart and acidic by the midpalate phase; all the while, the flavor of ripe and bittersweet berries leads the charge. Ends clean, ripe, appealingly tart, and fresh-tasting.

2007 Rating: ★★★★/Highly Recommended

Vincent van Gogh Black Cherry Vodka (Holland); 35% abv, $30.

Clean as a whistle appearance. Smells stunningly of black cherries that you'd pick straight off the trees, ripe but tart, juicy, and fresh; the aroma responds to further aeration by becoming even more deeply cherry-like, almost jammy. The palate entry directs the taste buds to the natural acidity of the fruit as the flavor goes very sour at first, then at midpalate becomes noticeably sweeter as the fruit pulp and juice elements move to the forefront. Finishes juicy, medium-weighted, and moderately sweet. Another flavor clinic from VVG's guiding light, Dave van de Velde.

2006 Rating: ★★★★/Highly Recommended

Vincent van Gogh Citroen Vodka (Holland); 40% abv, $30.

Limpid, translucent, and impeccably pure in appearance. The opening nosing pass offers succulent, sweet and ripe scents of key limes and lemons, a fabulously alluring initial burst; with air contact the aroma becomes more focused on the ripeness/tartness of lime/lemon, with a leaning to the lemon; following seven minutes of exposure to air, the aroma turns into a full-fledged lemony bouquet that's both firm and graceful; the fourth and last sniffing sees hardly any diminishment of potency, even after nearly ten minutes of time in the glass; a well-knit, elegant citrus perfume that ranks with the best of the subcategory. The palate entry is mildly lemony, elegant, understated, yet purposefully directed and firm; the midpalate stage features a ripe lemon flavor that's more akin to pulp than to zest. The finish is long, lovely, intensely lemony/citrusy, and delicious. Hands-down, runs with the best of the flavored vodkas.

2000 Rating: ★★★★/Highly Recommended

Vincent van Gogh Coconut Flavored Vodka (Holland); 35% abv, $30.

Impeccable purity and silvery blue. The coconut essence in the first whiffs is so astonishingly real and authentic that it makes you think there are actual coconut slivers in the

glass; further time in the glass deepens the richness/oiliness of the coconut meat fragrance. The palate entry is dry to off-dry and delectably creamy/oily; at midpalate the coconut meat flavor reaches its peak freshness and soft bitterness level. Ends up semisweet, viscous on the tongue, and creamy. Unlike most coconut flavored spirits, VVG tastes completely genuine and not in the least manufactured; its only serious rival is Cruzan Coconut Flavored Rum (★★★★), which is marginally sweeter and plumper; another state-of-the-art flavored vodka from the flavor wizards, David van de Velde and the distilling team at Dirkzwager Distillery in Schiedam, Holland.
2004 Rating: ★★★★★/Highest Recommendation

Vincent van Gogh Double Expresso Double Caffeine Coffee Flavored Vodka (Holland); 35% abv, $30.
Resembles cola in its nut brown, deeply tawny color. The beany/nutty first perfume leapfrogs from the glass; this supple bouquet really responds to extended aeration by deepening vertically as the coffee bean-like quality grows in strength and expand horizontally as scents of cocoa, road tar, roasted chestnut, and wood smoke get added to the aroma menu. In the palate entry, the bitter espresso flavor is spot on by not being too sweet or too bitter, but in a comfortable place in between; the midpalate is surprisingly mellow even though there's plenty of rich espresso character to go around. Finishes smoked and tar-like, with the coffee taking a back seat. A must-have for caffeine freaks.
2006 Rating: ★★★★/Highly Recommended

Vincent van Gogh Dutch Chocolate Flavored Vodka (Holland); 35% abv, $30.
Limpid as mineral water; perfect clarity. The first couple of nosing passes are deeply impressed by the depth of bittersweet dark chocolate/cocoa authenticity; another five to seven minutes in the glass bring out a concentrated, accentuated bean or, better, pod-like character that's as close to espresso as it is to cocoa powder; an amazing, fifth-gear nosing experience that's clearly the prototype of the subcategory. The palate entry is intensely bean-like and bittersweet, as in X-TREME COCOA; the midpalate stage is lip-smacking delicious as well-knit, tight, but wholly integrated flavors of cocoa butter, cocoa powder, and dark roasted coffee bean take the taste buds on a stimulating ride. The finish is bittersweet and long. A distinctly different direction for chocolate vodkas, one that's not for everybody but therein lies its beauty and singularity; bravo, importer Luctor…again.
2002 Rating: ★★★★★/Highest Recommendation

Vincent van Gogh Espresso Vodka (Holland); 35% abv, $30.
Like all Van Gogh vodkas and gins, the appearance is impeccably clean, bright, and appealing. The first inhalation takes in a fresh, concentrated, kernel-like, properly bitter coffee bean perfume that's right on target in terms of intensity and authenticity; over the next few minutes of air contact, the aroma expands modestly to include cocoa and charred almond, but stays the espresso course in style and focus. The palate entry is, well, totally like top quality espresso in its bearing; at midpalate the taste profile displays the ideal amounts of bitterness, pod-like genuineness, and real-deal espresso bite and elegance. Finishes with just the right balance of bitterness, beaniness, and coffee jolt. As I've said so many times before, David van de Velde of Luctor International and his talented Holland-based distilling team

are the best in the flavored vodka business, period. This is yet another state-of-the-art line extension. Wow.

2005 Rating: ★★★★★/Highest Recommendation

Vincent van Gogh Mango Vodka (Holland); 35% abv, $30.

Limpid, unblemished clarity. The just-picked mango freshness in the initial whiffs after the pour simply confirm the total commitment to authenticity sought by the Dirkzwager Distillery in Schiedam, Holland; aeration time brings out even deeper levels of fruitiness and tart mango flesh/pulp perfume; amazingly genuine. The taste profile in the entry phase is ripe and sweet, then by midpalate the flavor turns tart, acidic, yet completely true to the source. Finishes sweet, lean, and savory. All sorts of cocktail possibilities come to mind. Van Gogh founder David van de Velde's unique vision continues to be the touchstone for all other flavored vodka wannabes as well as a pleasure for savvy spirits critics.

2005 Rating: ★★★★/Highly Recommended

Vincent van Gogh Melon Vodka (Holland); 35% abv, $30.

Limpid, pure, silvery. Right from the very first sniff, there's no doubting what flavor essence is utilized as the lovely, balanced, pleasantly ripe fragrance of melon appears; another seven minutes in the copita simply draws out more of the concentrated melon ripeness and freshness; as with all Van Gogh flavored vodkas, the key aromatic element is the underlying balance and subtlety. The palate entry is plump, viscous, and reeks of ripe melon; the midpalate displays a lovely oiliness and viscosity that underpins the flavor of freshly harvested and cut melon. Concludes sweetly and mildly. Another flavored vodka triumph for the immensely talented distillers at Dirkzwager Distillery in Schiedam, Holland.

2004 Rating: ★★★★/Highly Recommended

Vincent van Gogh Mojito Mint Vodka Mint Flavored Vodka (Holland); 35% abv, $30.

Sparklingly clear and pure. The spry mint aroma in the first whiff is underpinned by a citrus rind/citrus juiciness that accentuates the freshness of the mint beautifully; further on down the aromatic line, the mint comes to the forefront and the lime/citrus recedes, making for fresh, invigorating, and stunningly vivid nosing. The palate entry is crisp, intensely minty, and sweet at the back end; the midpalate flavor thrust is all semisweet peppermint with a hint of balancing citrus/lime. Ends up moderately fiery in the throat (from the concentrated mintiness) yet smooth and generous. So well-crafted that it squeaks with tightness.

2006 Rating: ★★★★★/Highest Recommendation

Vincent van Gogh Oranje Vodka (Holland); 40% abv, $30.

As clear and clean as one could hope for. The opening aroma is slightly sweet and ripe, more in a fruity manner than a citric acid manner; in the second nosing pass, the aroma settles down into a pulpy fragrance; the third pass, following seven minutes of air contact, sees the bouquet subside measurably as the scent becomes more zest-like than fruity; the fourth and last sniffing finds the nose losing its pacing, but there's still some pleasing remnants of orange pulp. The palate entry shows bits of tart orange pulp; the midpalate stage is fuller, a touch chocolaty, and seed-like. The aftertaste is long, spirity,

mildly oily, and more seed-like than orangy. Easily recommendable but not as sophisticated as the Absolut Mandarin, Stoli Ohranj, or Grey Goose.
2000 Rating: ★★★/Recommended

Vincent van Gogh Pineapple Vodka (Holland); 35% abv, $30.

Rain water clear and impeccably pure. The opening bouquet is intensely pineapple-like, as in freshly cut pineapple, not canned or juice; later nosings reveal nothing new; but know that the pineapple perfume is as true-to-the-fruit as is possible. The palate entry is sweet and fruity; by the midpalate stage it's the viscous texture that I love as much as the intense pineapple fruit flavor. It finishes sweet and fruity. Obviously a cocktail ingredient, though I can see it on-the-rocks with a pineapple wheel; as usual, Van Gogh through the vision of David van de Velde excels.
2002 Rating: ★★★★/Highly Recommended

Vincent van Gogh Pomegranate Flavored Vodka (Holland); 35% abv, $25.

Pretty cherry juice/rose color; superb purity. Smells of genuine pomegranate, slightly berry-like and acutely brambly; aeration maintains the strength of the ripe, but not overly ripe pomegranate. Entry displays a crispness that was not there in the previous incarnation and is therefore far more refreshing and true to the fruit; the midpalate offers succulent tastes of pomegranate beads plus a distant citrus note (lemon zest?). A substantial improvement over the first attempt because the sugary veil of sweetness has been removed, allowing the natural acidity of the pomegranate (which is a difficult flavor to deal with) to lead the charge.
2007 Rating: ★★★★/Highly Recommended

Vincent van Gogh Raspberry Flavored Vodka (Holland); 35% abv, $30.

Superbly clean and limpid. The stunning fresh raspberry perfume following the pour leaps from the glass like a pole-vaulter; time in the glass makes the bouquet all the more concentrated as the aromatic focus shifts more to raspberry preserves than fresh-picked fruit; a lush, sweet, and ripe bouquet. The taste at palate entry is true to the fruit and crisply acidic; the midpalate juncture shows off the breadth of the fruit reflection, from pulpy juice to tart raspberry jam. The aftertaste is very long, ambrosial, and juicy. A really fine flavored vodka effort from David van de Velde and his Dutch team.
2002 Rating: ★★★★/Highly Recommended

Vincent van Gogh Vanilla Flavored Vodka (Holland); 35% abv, $30.

Absolutely pure and clean. The aroma after the pour is intensely vanilla bean-like and strangely but pleasingly a little like carob, even maple; aeration affects the bouquet very little as the bittersweet vanilla bean/vanilla extract perfume remains firmly in control; I do notice, though, a deft hint of chocolate covered cherries hiding in the background. The palate entry reminds me of French vanilla ice cream, so luscious and creamy is the initial taste burst; by the midpalate stage the vanilla extract intensity settles down into a plump, buttery, moderately sweet flavor profile that's very bean-like. The finish is extended, firm, and reminds me of egg cream soda. A new vanilla vodka star that easily matches the acknowledged flavor pinnacle reached earlier by Stolichnaya Vanil; now, there are two.
2002 Rating: ★★★★★/Highest Recommendation

Vincent van Gogh Wild Appel Vodka (Holland); 35% abv, $30.

Absolutely clear. The first whiff after opening offers dazzling and balanced aromas of spiced apple and vanilla; the middle stage nosing passes, after several minutes of exposure to air, deliver richer, fruitier aromas plus the added element of the clean spirit; the final pass sees the vanilla and spice outpoint the apple or the spirit; as delicate and polite a vodka perfume as you can find. In the mouth the crisp spirit emerges at entry and becomes dominant by midpalate forcing the apple and spice to become supporting players. The aftertaste is clean, austere, and spirity. Very good, but I felt slightly let down by the taste after the delicacy of the bouquet lifted my expectations perhaps a bit too lofty; the only vodka with which to make Apple Martinis.

2001 Rating: ★★★/Recommended

Vodka Fourteen Vodka Made From Organic Grain (USA); 40% abv, $35.

Wonderfully clear and pristine. Shows a solid, grainy, cracker-like aroma right from the beginning; more time in the glass brings out mildly pleasing notes of nuts, parchment and palm oil. The palate entry is smooth, a little toasty and very refreshing; the midpalate stage highlights the deep grain taste along with touches of smoke and spice. Aftertaste is long, lean and properly grainy/spirity, with a dash of prickliness on the tongue.

2006 Rating: ★★★/Recommended

Vox Green Apple Flavored Vodka (Holland); 40% abv, $30.

Clear and impeccably clean. The initial whiffs uncover a firm, assertive, ripe apple perfume; following six minutes in the glass the bouquet turns down the aromatic volume as the aroma becomes delicate, juicy, and just moderately sweet. The palate entry is more sweet that tart and hence more like candied apple than fresh apple; at midpalate the taste turns layered, viscous, and apple butter sweet and creamy. Finishes sweet, candied, and full-bodied. Borderline three star/four star. As usual when I hesitate, I chose the lower rating. I need to be fully convinced before bestowing an additional star.

2005 Rating: ★★★/Recommended

Vox Raspberry Flavored Vodka (Holland); 40% abv, $30.

Absolutely pure and clean in appearance. The opening nosings are greeted by understated, subtle, some could say distant, aromas of raspberries still on the vine; like all products evaluated in the SJ, Vox Raspberry was allowed an additional six minutes of aeration time at which point the bouquet evolved slightly to include a note of raspberry preserves; it's a reluctant bouquet, really. The palate entry displays a medium-full, velvety texture and a firm taste of raspberry juice, not so much the fruit flesh; the midpalate provides this vodka's finest hour as the flavor deepens and showcases the natural tartness and berry nuances of fresh raspberry. The finish is fruity, mildly sweet and ripe. While I certainly like and recommend this flavored vodka, I can't help but feel that it was holding back as though it was reined in; what would it be like if it was allowed to cut loose, I wonder.

2003 Rating: ★★★/Recommended

Wasabé Vodka Vodka Blended with Sake (USA); 35% abv, $40/liter.
Bright, clean, translucent. The initial waves of aroma are properly grainy and cracker-like; additional air contact brings about more of a gentle fruitiness in the underlying stratum of fragrance; my only gripe with the bouquet is that there's not a lot of depth. The palate entry is warm, dry, and grainy; the midpalate stage shows a tad more finesse as the mildly fruity sake element emerges on the tongue. Concludes well as the sake aspect becomes more of a factor in the throat. Easily recommendable, but not in the same league as Wokka Saki, which I rated ★★★★★. The difference here is that the sake is less integrated into the vodka and therefore is less seamless and focused.
2006 Rating: ★★★/Recommended

White Birch Vodka (Russia); 40% abv, $18.
Perfect purity; no evidence of oils. The first nosing pass is greeted with an aroma that's in a muted stage of development; further inhalations up to seven minutes after the first find the bouquet still disappointingly neutral and closed off. The palate entry, on the other hand, displays lots of typical vodka character in the forms of off-dry flavors of sap, bark, and unrefined sugar; the midpalate stage highlights the sap and wood bark as the flavor profile grows in the mouth, culminating in a firm, medium-bodied, semisweet aftertaste that is graceful and refined. Just skip past the aroma and proceed directly to sipping.
2005 Rating: ★★★★/Highly Recommended

White Gold Vodka (Russia); 40% abv, $24/liter.
Rainwater clear and pure. Smells of chalk/limestone and grain kernels in the initial sniffings; six more minutes of air contact do nothing to expand on the dry earth aromatic theme; a simple, unexceptional bouquet. The palate entry is intensely grainy, medium oily, and wheat cracker-like; at the midpalate point a huge rush of sweet, smoky charcoal overtakes the graininess, setting up the ashy/sooty/wood smoke finish.
2007 Rating: ★★★/Recommended

Wodka Gorbatschow Vodka (Germany); 40% abv, $11.
Limpid, with superb clarity. The bean-, almost curd-like aroma is punchy, semisweet, and firm in the initial two minutes of sniffing, then inexplicably following six more minutes of undisturbed air contact the bouquet flatlines, becoming just a standard issue grain spirits scent; it's a shame that the nose couldn't hold on to its upfront charm. The palate entry is grainy sweet and a touch lead pencil-like; at midpalate the flavor profile is unabashedly sweet, minerally, and grain mash-like. Finishes semisweet and slightly oily. The flavor phase recovered some of the momentum lost in the latter stages of the bouquet, certainly enough for a recommendation.
2005 Rating: ★★★/Recommended

Wokka Saki Vodka With Sake Added (United Kingdom); 40% abv, $40.
Clean as a whistle, appearance-wise. The opening sniffings detect incredibly vibrant, ripe, and alluring scents of peaches and nectarines (there is "Asian fruit" flavoring added according to a technical sheet); with time in the glass, the aroma softens to a whisper as the fruity perfume recedes; a stunningly elegant and supple bouquet. The palate entry is sweet, ripe, oily, and

textured; at midpalate the taste profile turns equally grainy and fruity, with the 80-proof alcohol serving well as a base for the nimble flavorings. Ends up well in a satiny, oily manner, showing just a trace of peach/nectarine flavor. Clearly, the distiller understands that violins and cellos are far more attractive and compelling in flavored spirits than are trumpets and tubas.
2005 Rating: ★★★★★/Highest Recommendation

Wyborowa Single Estate Vodka (Poland); 40% abv, $30.

Produced from 100% rye that's cultivated on one estate. The silvery clear appearance is flawless; in the opening nosing passes my olfactory sense is charmed by the spicy, tar and asphalt-like, mineral-like aroma; another six minutes of air contact stimulate meatier, bread-like, more buttery scents, including almond paste and traditional rye bread. The palate entry is clean, spicy, stone-like and off-dry; at midpalate the taste profile highlights the intensely spicy/peppery quality of the rye. Closes in a flurry of minerals, dry, dried spice (black pepper) and off-dry cereal. Intriguing, savory and complex.
2004 Rating: ★★★★/Highly Recommended

Xellent Swiss Vodka (Switzerland); 40% abv, $34.

The standard issue mineral water sparkle is ideally clean and limpid. The initial whiffs pick up herbal/summer garden odors, with faint hints of jasmine and moss; the aromatic intrigue continues in the latter passes as additional scents of tea leaves, minerals, and wet stone all vie for attention; a fascinating, multi-layered bouquet that adds something new with each inhalation. The palate entry is clean, semisweet, grainy, and biscuity; the midpalate is moderately toasted, nutty, concentrated, and remarkably mineral-like. Concludes as dynamically as it begins. A vodka tour de force that never for a moment slumps or strays; it's always moving forward, challenging and enlightening; one of only three or four over-$30 super-premium vodkas that is actually worth the price tag; wow.
2005 Rating: ★★★★★/Highest Recommendation

X-Rated Vodka (France); 40% abv, $40.

Made from wheat and roseberry grain, distilled seven times, charcoal filtered. Excellent limpid appearance; an initial haze dissipates quickly. First inhalations pick up pointed and minerally scents of limestone, granite, and soil; aeration serves this vodka perfume well as extra time stimulates more grainy/viny odors of dried grain kernels, dry breakfast cereal, wheat bread, and bran muffin. The palate entry is off-dry, concentrated, and oily; the midpalate teems with oily/grainy richness and off-dry tastes of wheat crackers. Ends on a predictably oily note with a flash of spirity heat. Stately and elegant.
2006 Rating: ★★★★/Highly Recommended

Yazi Ginger Flavored Vodka (USA); 35% abv, $20.

Pure and clean. The first inhalations leave no doubt as to the snappy, ginger root leaning of this flavored vodka; aeration time stirs other aromas including cola nut, steel wool, and thistle; an overall pleasant bouquet, providing you like ginger. The palate entry is very sweet and texturally thick; then at midpalate a mild background spicy/peppery warmth emerges but doesn't overshadow the ginger influence. Concludes moderately peppery, zesty, ginger beer-like, and rooty. I like the quality of it but I can't help but stumble when I ponder the paucity of application possibilities.

2005 Rating: ★★★/Recommended

Yemets Russian Vodka (Russia); 40% abv, $12.

Silvery transparent, but too much sediment. In the initial nosing passes I'm really forced to hunt down any traces of aroma and I find a limp slightly metallic odor; after another six minutes, the aroma goes nowhere and I cry, "Uncle". The palate entry at least displays some character in the form of sweet wheat-like grain; at midpalate the flavor profile goes a bit lead pencil-like and roasted but holds the course on the grainy sweetness. Ends well, sweet and grainy. It's drinkable, but it's hollow and pedestrian in the core.

2004 Rating: ★★/Not Recommended

Yemets Vodka With Natural Flavors (Russia); 40% abv, $15.

Ideally clear and pure. Now the bad news, it's nowheresville, I mean nada/nothing/zippo in the opening nosing pass; aeration does nothing to encourage or stimulate the aroma, so the middle stage sniffings are a waste of time; finally, in the last pass after almost ten full minutes in the glass, there are subtle nuances of soft grain and palm oil; it's a shame that the nose isn't more expressive because what aromas finally faintly develop are nice. The palate entry is bitterly sooty/ashy and very pronounced from first contact with the tongue; the midpalate phase brims with off dry-to-sweet tastes of pipe tobacco, charcoal, palm oil, grain resin, and soot. The finish is long, expressive, and even aggressive in a prickly spirit manner. Do I like it, da; is it up to the classical Russian vodka standards, nyet; is it a good value, da; is it better than ordinary and therefore worthy of three stars? da.

2001 Rating: ★★★/Recommended

Yes Vodka (Holland); 40% abv, $30.

Admirable purity and silvery appearance. The first inhalation is greeted with a prickly wave of spirity heat that's more of a wake-up call than a nasty nose hair scorcher; further aeration settles this aroma down dramatically as the olfactory sense is then treated to pleasantly sweet, plump, mildly baked, and grainy scents of oatmeal, tar, tobacco leaf, and vines. The palate entry is sap-like, bitter, yet firm and sturdy; the midpalate stage features the hearty, toasted and dry grain underpinning flavor to the max. Concludes too minerally/metallic, which lopped off a rating star.

2006 Rating: ★★★/Recommended

Zodiac Vodka (USA); 40% abv, $27.

Silvery and translucent; inconsequential sediment seen, no problem. The initial whiffs pick up crisp scents of wet straw and earth; further aeration doesn't influence the aroma that much except to bring out some mild vegetal sweetness. Far more impact is discerned in the mouth as the taste at entry is focused, moderately oily, and semisweet; the midpalate stage is long, oily, and mineral-like. I'm curious as to why the bouquet seemed meek and stingy this time around because it doesn't accurately forecast what happens in the mouth since the vegetal/minerally taste is generous, oily to almost being fat, and delightful. I really wanted to bestow a fourth rating star but the aroma let this vodka down.

2006 Rating: ★★★/Recommended

Zone Banana Vodka (Italy); 25% abv, $16.

Clean and limpid; like just about every banana flavored spirit I've tried over the years. The opening aroma comes off like cardboard banana; the middle stage nosings do nothing to redeem the initial whiff as the manufactured odor just gets worse; the fourth and final sniffing stays the industrial, artificial course. In the mouth, this terrible stuff makes me wonder why anyone attempts to concoct any alcoholic beverage with a fruit as subtle as banana; it never works. Don't bother with this awkward, sickly goop; go for the savory Zone Tangerine or the mellow Peach.

2000 Rating: ★/Not Recommended

Zone Lemon Vodka (Italy); 25% abv, $16.

Clear with some suspended particles that are so minuscule no average consumer would spot them. This opening aroma is strangely spicy, almost like cumin or curry spices more than lemon; with air contact, the aroma stays the odd cumin/coriander course; the penultimate pass reveals a touch more in the way of lemon peel; nothing new in the last nosing pass. The palate entry begins the mouth experience in the same cumin-like manner; the midpalate is really weird in that it doesn't own a true lemony taste that's fresh; it tastes manufactured. The finish is nowhere on the pleasure scale. Skip this one.

2000 Rating: ★/Not Recommended

Zone Melon Vodka (Italy); 25% abv, $16.

The pale yellow/flax tint is clear and clean. The opening nose is all melon, most precisely ripe cantaloupe at first; the middle stage nosing passes see more of a honeydew influence in a sweet, ripe manner; the fourth and last pass gives more of the same; a pleasant, ripe, sweet aroma that is true to the label. The palate entry is sweet and moderately fruity; then the midpalate turns a bit acidic as the spirit element finally shows itself. The finish is medium long, melony, and acceptably sweet. Drinkable, amiable, and average.

2000 Rating: ★★/Not Recommended

Zone Peach Vodka (Italy); 25% abv, $16.

Crystal clear and free of debris. The first nosing pass perks up the nasal cavity as a burst of fresh peachy ripeness enchants the nose; the middle stage sniffings show equal parts spirit and fruit essence; the fourth and last pass focuses on the peach perfume, which I must admit is extremely pleasant and inviting; the most pronounced bouquet of all the Zones. The palate entry is more acidic than sweet or ripe; the midpalate phase is not as enthralling as the bouquet as the flavor falls slightly flat on the tongue. The aftertaste is fresh, ripe, sweet, and clean. I'm recommending this strange libation on the considerable strength of its aroma and finish.

2000 Rating: ★★★/Recommended

Zone Tangerine Vodka (Italy); 25% abv, $16.

Clear and particle free. This aroma is an actual bouquet, one with more than a little charm; the second whiff offers ripe, acidic, citrus perfume that's alluring and ethereal at the same time; the third and fourth passes unearth nothing new in terms of expansion or deepening. The palate entry is tart and definitely true to the fruit source; by the midpalate stage the tangerine flavor dances with the spirit quite nicely. The aftertaste is more tart than sweet and displays a trace of spiritiness at the back of the tongue. I liked this mild, flavored vodka enough to give it a third star.

2000 Rating: ★★★/Recommended

Zygo Peach Flavored Vodka (USA); 35% abv, $30.

Clear and very pale straw-hued. The ripe peach character makes itself known, pleasantly so, immediately in the first few minutes of sniffing; over the ensuing six minutes of further aeration time, the aroma becomes about as seductive as one could imagine for a flavored vodka as the ripe, juicy peach/nectarine perfume convinces the olfactory sense that this spirit is something special. The palate entry is ripe but not in the least candied or overly sweet, just juicy; by the midpalate point the flavor profile includes peach skin and peach nectar. The aftertaste is balanced, acidic, ripe and, from my standpoint, superb. A well executed job of melding flavor essence with neutral spirit.

2003 Rating: ★★★★/Highly Recommended

ZYR Russian Vodka (Russia); 40% abv, $32.

Distilled five times and filtered nine times, according to the promotional materials forwarded by the importer; combination of wheat and rye grains. Clear as spring water, but with very minor floating detritus seen. The opening sniff following the pour is greeted by firm, assertive aromas of grain mash, wheat biscuit and distant dried herbs; six more minutes of air contact stirs additional aromas, including wet pavement/wet slate, minerals and seedless rye bread; the bouquet is sleek, sophisticated and, even with the nine filtrations, is anything but stripped-down; it most assuredly is not cut from the typical Russian mold. The palate entry, however, reflects its Russian heritage as the dry to off-dry taste of grain mash blankets the tongue in richly textured waves; the midpalate surges forward in potent but silky flavors of concentrated grain/breakfast cereal and black peppercorn. The aftertaste is herbal, mildly sweet and entirely focused. Another outstanding vodka entry from the Russian Federation that just goes to reaffirm their long-established reputation as supreme grain distillers.

2002 Rating: ★★★★★/Highest Recommendation

Rum, Cachaça & Guaro—World

Rum is made from a mash of either sugarcane juice or molasses. The mash is first fermented then distilled. The majority of rums in most nations are bottled devoid of color and is neither matured nor stored in oak barrels. Puerto Rico is an exception, where by law, all rums must be aged in barrels for a minimum of one year. In most rum-producing locations, a relatively small percentage of rum production is matured in oak barrels for longer than one year. The French-speaking Caribbean area rum nations, like Martinique and Guadeloupe, prefer to employ freshly pressed sugarcane juice while those countries with long-held British (think Barbados, Jamaica, Bermuda) or Spanish connections (Puerto Rico, Dominican Republic) tend to use molasses, an easily attainable sugar refining by-product that is thick, gooey and dark brown.

Rums distilled from pressed sugarcane juice are called *rhum agricole* in French. They are routinely grassy, earthy and even herbal in character and as such are delightfully distinct, even idiosyncratic from distillery to distillery. Those made from molasses offer a stunningly wide menu of aromas, textures and tastes. The British style is typically robust, deeply flavored and intense while the Spanish style is, as a rule, lighter and more elegant.

Rum is another one of my "keep-an-eye-on-it" categories right now due to the fact that rhum agricoles have made the category exciting once again, as well as to a slew of good to very good flavored rums that make mixology a joy. Rum is raising its market value by going uptown in style and quality. Good things are afoot.

Produced only from sugarcane juice, **cachaça** is bottled in a range of from 38% to 51% alcohol by volume. Next to beer, cachaça is Brazil's most consumed alcoholic beverage, averaging about 350 million gallons per year, or roughly two gallons per Brazilian citizen. There are as many as 30,000 small distillers of cachaça scattered around South America's largest country in addition to the mammoth industrial distillers.

Cachaça comes in three fundamental classifications: unaged, aged and yellow. Unaged cachaças usually spend a year in wood barrels while aged cachaças spend from two to twelve years in barrels. Yellow cachaças are young spirits that have caramel or wood extracts added to them to make them appear older. Brazilians prefer to employ native woods for their cooperage, including imburana, freijo, cedar, jequitiba, and cherry. These native woods impart unique, sometimes resiny flavors to the spirits, making them exotic and delicious.

Guaro is a rum-like distillate produced in Costa Rica from fermented sugarcane juice that is at best a niche product of one particular locality.

1 Barrel Belize Travellers Refined Old Rum (Belize); 40% abv, $15.
The harvested wheat/gold color is a touch flat; excellent clarity. In the initial sniffing, the aroma comes across as big, fat, friendly, and gently molasses sweet; aeration doesn't particularly

alter the original impressions other than to add some delightful cocoa and tobacco notes; there's nothing fancy or profound here aromatically, but it's an altogether pleasing Rum 101 bouquet. The palate entry is surprisingly bittersweet and nearly dry; by the midpalate stage the flavor turns tobacco-like, almost smoky, yet appealingly sweet and, well, rummy. Finishes with all the simple, no-frills charm that it began with. A terrific bargain to boot.

2007 Rating: ★★★/Recommended

10 Cane Rum (Trinidad); 40% abv, $35.

Sugar cane juice based. The straw/lemon juice tint is very pale; good to very good purity. The first sniffings pick up intensely vegetal/grainy aromas of cooked brown rice and broccoli, then following another seven minutes of air contact the aromatics explode in the nasal cavity in the appealingly vinegary forms of brown sugar, raw cane, brine, soy sauce, and vanilla bean; this is a one-off rum bouquet that alone is worth the asking price. The palate entry screams sugar cane/unrefined cane in its bittersweet demeanor; by the midpalate phase the taste profile becomes more sophisticated, silky, honey sweet, even lightly spiced. Concludes nicely bittersweet, a bit cocoa-like, and beany, but fades just a bit too quickly to be given a fifth star.

2005 Rating: ★★★★/Highly Recommended

267 Infusions Mango Rum (Barbados); 21% abv, $25.

The pale gray/tan appearance shows some fruity sediment, which is to be expected since there are chunks of mango in the bottle. The first burst of aroma is intensely fruity and ripe and wholly authentic; in this case, further air contact really doesn't expand or detract what's already present and accounted for, which is monotonal. The palate entry is soft, tropical fruity, and pleasantly simple; the midpalate stage is MANGO, MANGO, MANGO. Ends up fresh, if anorexic and watery thin. The fruit component totally overwhelms the alcohol, leaving this libation wispy and timid. Bring the abv up to at least 27% (the acknowledged starting point for flavored/infused rums) and I'd bet odds that this would be recommendable. The flavor is there; the alcohol that carries the flavor forward isn't.

2006 Rating: ★★/Not Recommended

267 Infusions Pineapple Rum (Barbados); 21% abv, $25.

The lemon juice/yellow appearance is filled with bits of pineapple. The first nosing pass detects a muted but evident fresh pineapple perfume; with further time in the glass the aroma fades quickly. The palate entry is feeble and offers just a hint of pineapple; the watered down and anemic midpalate is completely hollow and unacceptable. Same comments as above regarding the lack of alcoholic substance, but in this instance the fruit element is vacant. The distiller/blender/importer should closely examine Cruzan Pineapple Flavored Rum to see how it's done between rum and pineapple.

2006 Rating: ★/Not Recommended

Agua Luca Cachaça (Brazil); 40% abv, $30.

Crystal clear and impeccably pure. In the first whiffs, the earthy/soil-like aroma of cane grass is evident and compelling; additional exposure to air brings out peppery, almost sooty/ash-like aromas that seem underpinned by the cane and creosote base aromas. The palate

entry is zesty, semisweet, herbal, and tar-like; the midpalate taste offers deeply herbal/vegetal flavors of grass/vegetation, textile/fiber and light smoke. Ends up off-dry and piquant.
2006 Rating: ★★★/Recommended

Angostura 1919 8 Year Old Rum (Trinidad & Tobago); 40% abv, $30.
Pretty amber hue; very minor floating particles seen. The nose starts out sophisticated and mildly spicy in the first couple of sniffings within three minutes of the pour; with aeration the aroma turns into an elegant bouquet that features scents of marshmallow, light caramel, and oak-influenced vanilla; a poised and stately bouquet. At the palate entry a focused, dry brown sugar, marzipan taste greets the taste buds; the midpalate phase highlights chewy, lush flavors of chocolate cake frosting, honey, nougat, and almond butter. The finish is long, creamy/buttery, and satiny.
2002 Rating: ★★★★/Highly Recommended

Angostura 3 Year Old White Rum (Trinidad & Tobago); 40% abv, $13.
Sparkling clear and clean. The initial two nosings uncover intriguing scents of wet vegetation, carob, and brown sugar; over time the aroma fades significantly in the glass, offering faint, chalky fragrances of unprocessed sugarcane and nutmeg; a peculiar bouquet with little staying power. The palate entry is pleasing sweet but not in the least cloying; then at midpalate the flavor turns focused on the bittersweet molasses in the forms of honeyed, almost biscuity/cake batter flavors. The aftertaste is moderately rich, nicely textured, medium sweet, and easy in the throat. A solidly made white rum whose three years of aging shows up especially in the midpalate and lush finish; nice job.
2002 Rating: ★★★/Recommended

Angostura 5 Year Old Dark Rum (Trinidad & Tobago); 40% abv, $17.
New copper penny color. The opening two nosing passes highlight luxurious, biscuity, and raisiny scents that go a long way to enchant the olfactory sense; with air contact the aroma turns sweeter and more candied as powerful, bittersweet scents of dark chocolate and caramel vie for dominance; a lovely, multilayered dark rum bouquet. At the palate entry the flavor is intensely sweet and sugary; the midpalate sees the sweetness level almost go off the chart as the evidence of caramel outweighs any other flavor component to the point of overkill. The finish is thick and cloying. What began well in the appearance and aroma turned blatantly manufactured and over-manipulated; drinkable for sweet-tooth fanatics but ordinary.
2002 Rating: ★★/Not Recommended

Angostura 5 Year Old Gold Rum (Trinidad & Tobago); 40% abv, $17.
Handsome, autumnal harvest gold hue; some black detritus spotted. The initial nosing passes in the first three minutes after the pour reveal a comely, holiday spice aroma profile that's snappy and pleasant; time in the glass sees the aroma develop and deepen as traces of oak, palm oil, and honey enter the picture; a good, able bouquet that's firm, persistent, and delightfully spicy. At palate entry there's a flowery/garden-like surge on the tongue that quickly vanishes leaving me a tad perplexed as to what it was; the midpalate phase features rich and dry flavors of brown sugar and oak resin. The aftertaste is dry and flashes a burst of spirity heat.
2002 Rating: ★★★/Recommended

Appleton Estate 21 Year Old Rum (Jamaica); 43% abv, $129.

The lovely appearance sports a coppery/tawny hue and perfect purity. The alluring aroma is floral, as in dried violets, in the initial passes then it turns bean-like and pleasantly nutty after about five minutes; additional aeration unearths nothing more in the bouquet's development. The palate entry is acutely astringent; at the midpalate point a flavor character of baked nuts comes on strongly in bitter tastes of oak and molasses. The aftertaste is long, desert dry, sugary, and sap-like. What I appreciated most about this gray-beard rum is its stateliness and its poise. Also, considering its age, it was not overly woody as many very old rums happen to be; delicious in an old-guard style.

2002 Rating: ★★★★/Highly Recommended

Appleton Estate Extra Rum (Jamaica); 43% abv, $35.

The bright bronze color dazzles the eye. The bouquet offers early-on scents of bacon fat and walnut butter that are tightly-knit and mature; later whiffs offer perfectly melded and balanced aromas of buttered corn-on-the-cob, oak resin, and marzipan; nothing short of a world-class distilled spirit bouquet that's both vigorous and evolved; an aroma in ideal pitch. The taste at palate entry is dusty dry and buttery; while at midpalate the flavor goes full-throttle with buttery/creamy, brown sugar, rancio-like tastes. The aftertaste is savory and bittersweet. A classic example of the most highly skilled blending of sugarcane-based spirit and oak barrels; an authentic "Cognac of the Caribbean".

2002 Rating: ★★★★★/Highest Recommendation

Appleton Estate Reserve Rum (Jamaica); 40% abv, $27.

The color is a spectacular burnished orange/copper hue that beams under the examination light; perfect purity; one of the most eye-catching rums you'll ever see. The initial whiffs detect tight, lean notes of molasses and walnut; additional aeration time releases bigger, spicier scents of nutmeg, tree bark (cassia-like), and spiced apple. The palate entry displays a wonderfully warm and spicy stateliness and elegance; at the midpalate juncture the taste profile turns cocoa- and vanilla-like, and remarkably creamy, even lip-smackingly honeyed. Concludes expressively, creamy, and oh-so delicious. I'd bathe in this one. Another Appleton Estate triumph that solidifies their status as one of the five top rum producers in the Caribbean region.

2007 Rating: ★★★★★/Highest Recommendation

Appleton Estate Special Rum (Jamaica); 40% abv, $13.

The amber/honey color is attractive and pure. In the opening nosings the bouquet is delicate and mildly sugary; with time in the glass the aroma takes on background notes that include palm oil, unimposing oak, and almond butter. The taste phase remains constant from palate entry through to the midpalate as flavors of brown sugar and oaky vanilla impress the taste buds. The aftertaste is sweet, supple, and moderately creamy. This nicely blended gold rum shows more than its share of tantalizing, understated molasses character.

2002 Rating: ★★★/Recommended

Appleton Estate V/X Rum (Jamaica); 40% abv, $20.

The pretty harvest gold hue dances in the light. In the first two nosing passes I detect gentle scents of light spice (nutmeg?) and brown sugar; later sniffings, following a minimum of six minutes of air contact, reveal solid aromas of molasses and buttered toast; the degree of aromatic deepening is significant over the span of five minutes. The palate entry is notable for its delicious, rich, and toasty flavor; the midpalate stage features elegant flavors of toasted honey-wheat bread, honey, and refined sugar. Finish is more bittersweet than sweet. A true connoisseur's rum; LUSCIOUS.

2002 Rating: ★★★★/Highly Recommended

Armazem Vieira Esmeralda Aged Artesian Cachaça Solera 4 Year Old (Brazil); 40% abv, $32.

The pale straw/hay/green hue is very faint; quite a bit of whitish sediment seen floating about beneath the unblinking eye of the examination lamp. The initial nosing passes pick up pungent, but oddly alluring scents of pickle brine, clam sauce, and green Spanish olive; aeration sets the stage for sour-leaning scents of fried egg, meringue, and increased pickle brine; I personally don't mind a sour bouquet, but it might not be to everyone's liking. It's sweeter tasting at palate entry than I figured it would be; at midpalate I respond favorably to the oiliness of the texture and the nuance of sugar cane sweetness at the taste's core. Concludes mildly sweet and almost biscuity, if rather fey.

2005 Rating: ★★★/Recommended

Armazem Vieira Onix Aged Artesian Cachaça Solera 16 Year Old (Brazil); 40% abv, $85.

Strangely to me, this appearance is nearly equal in pale yellow/green/silver color to its younger siblings Esmeralda and the Rubi; familiar debris problem. The aroma is subdued and is more peppery and eggy than sake sour or briny/seaweed; another seven minutes of air contact accomplishes virtually nothing to deepen or expand the bouquet; I move on. Tastes totally different from how it smells; the palate entry is intensely spirity, even heady in its alcohol rush, thereby leaving behind an early taste profile; the flavor makes a solid comeback in the midpalate stage as heightened tastes of prickly pear, white pepper, and refined sugar make entrances. Then it ends up meekly and only mildly sweet. Too uneven for its own good. I think it's tired, meaning too old. Go for the younger ones.

2005 Rating: ★★/Not Recommended

Armazem Vieira Rubi Aged Artesian Cachaça Solera 8 Year Old (Brazil); 40% abv, $45.

The pale straw/green color is seriously marred by clouds of unappealing gray/white floating debris that is far more evident here than in the Esmeralda; this filtering problem could and should be fixed for the finicky, hygiene-fixated North American audience. The aroma in the first two minutes of inhalation says "eggs over easy", green olive brine, and white pepper; further aeration time sees the brininess turn into a seaweed- and sake-like scent that also reminds me a little of escarole soup. The palate entry is pleasingly sweet and nearly biscuit-like; the midpalate stage shows even more charm as the flavor profile turns focused, laser-like, lean, and sugar cane sweet. Finishes on a sweet note that hits the right balance between the sugar cane, resiny wood, and eggy sourness. Rebounds well from a dubious beginning.

2005 Rating: ★★★/Recommended

Bacardi 1873 Extra Dry Rum (Puerto Rico); 40% abv, $n/a.

Pale amber color; perfect purity; the initial nosing pass immediately after the pour detects soft scents of sugar cane, brown butter, and roasted almond; the second sniffing serves to reinforce the first impression and adds a deft touch of cocoa; the third whiff, following seven minutes of air contact, picks up a fragrant cake frosting aroma that's very alluring; the fourth and last pass sees little diminishment as the primary themes of butter, sugar cane, and nuts remain firm; dry and delectable. The palate entry is dry, a bit weedy, but inviting and reserved; the midpalate stage introduces tastes of marshmallow, light caramel, and seed oil. The finish is long, mild, and vanilla-like. Very pleasant and certainly recommendable.

2000 Rating: ★★★/Recommended

Bacardi Big Apple Original Apple Rum (Puerto Rico); 35% abv, $15.

Limpid and flawlessly pure. The first burst of scent is strongly tart, authentically appley, and very apple peel-like; later sniffings serve to reinforce the original findings; a solidly good, tart, and real apple bouquet. The palate entry is astringent, cleansing, and delectably sweet/sour; the midpalate stage is nicely acidic, crisply apple-like, and engaging. Finishes pure, briskly tart, and just a touch ripe and sweet. Good job of balancing the fruit, acid, and alcohol components.

2005 Rating: ★★★/Recommended

Bacardi Coco Original Coconut Rum (Puerto Rico); 35% abv, $13.

Perfectly transparent and clean. The initial sniffings indicate a relaxed, balanced approach to the coconut flavoring; aeration allows even more delightful, low-key and unsweetened coconut perfume to waft up from the copita; a lovely, elegant bouquet. The palate entry is moderately sweet and pleasingly coconut-like; by the midpalate phase the coconut flavor turns drier and crisper, not to say it's acidic. The finish is long, dry to off-dry and savory. A terrific addition to any piña colada recipe.

2003 Rating: ★★★/Recommended

Bacardi Millennium 8 Year Old Rum Sherry Cask Finish (Puerto Rico); 40% abv, $700.

Only 3,000 decanters available worldwide; sherry wood finished. The color is a warm harvest gold/honey tone; excellent clarity. The opening bouquet is stately in its bearing, even brandy-like; by the second pass as Millennium mingles with air, the aroma turns slightly sweet, peppery, and even a touch wine-like; the third nosing pass after seven minutes of aeration finds the sherry influence growing in the background, beneath the surface layer of sugar cane spirit; the final whiff is a harmonious, if understated, display of sweetness, sherry cask, and cane spirit; very nice, indeed, if a bit restrained. The palate entry immediately sends the message that the mouth presence is heftier than the bouquet as the opening flavor is dry and oaky; by the midpalate, however, the taste opens up like a strutting peacock in multiple layers of sugar cane, caramel, old oak/vanillin, mild oloroso sherry, and honey. The finish is very extended, sweet but not cloying, and satisfyingly round. Not the blockbuster one might expect for the price, but a superb rum that shows authentic flashes of brilliance.

2000 Rating: ★★★★/Highly Recommended

Bacardi Original Orange Rum (Puerto Rico); 35% abv, $13.

Clear as mountain spring water and reasonably pure. The orange thrust is evident right from the first sniffing after the pour; the middle stage nosing passes focus more on orange peel than pulp/flesh, but by the fourth and final whiff the bouquet turns juicy and zesty; a delightfully fruit perfume. It's fresh and fruity at palate entry; the midpalate is juicy and slightly bitter and acidic (which I like). The finish is long, bittersweet, and tangy. The cocktail possibilities boggle the creative mind. I have to tip my hat to the Bacardi people for always striving to offer newer and more intriguing expressions of rum.

2001 Rating: ★★★/Recommended

Bacardi Razz Original Raspberry Rum (Puerto Rico); 35% abv, $13.

Pure and clear as rainwater. The zesty opening bouquet is fruity and pleasantly raspberry-like, almost soft in its bearing; further time in the glass reveals nothing new. The palate entry is very tart and fruity in an unripe way; at the midpalate the taste turns very tart, almost sour, but stays the raspberry course. The aftertaste is medium-long, sour, and angular. I appreciate the fact that this rum isn't overly sweet, if fact, it's hardly sweet at all; good mixer for lots of drinks.

2003 Rating: ★★★/Recommended

Bacardi Reserva Limitada (Puerto Rico); 40% abv, $50.

Only available at Casa Bacardi Visitor Center, PR. The harvest gold/honey color is bright and clean. In the opening whiffs there are assertive notes of brown sugar and molasses, then in the later inhalations after aeration the aroma turns drier, more tobacco-like, and honeyed as it evolves with air contact. The palate entry is intensely sweet and sugary; at midpalate the taste profile reminds me quite a lot of vanilla/spice cake or the cheese cream frosting found on carrot cake, plus there's a cola nut quality that comes on at the tail end of the midpalate. Finishes polished, unreservedly sweet, and sugary. Elegant and easily recommendable, but I hoped for greater depth and layering than is present.

2006 Rating: ★★★/Recommended

Bacardi Select Puerto Rican Rum (Puerto Rico); 40% abv, $18.

Very pretty topaz/hazel brown hue, displaying flawless purity. The opening whiffs pick up heavy duty, toasty aromas of dark caramel, molasses, and hard candy; seven more minutes of air contact encourage a resiny cane sugar quality to emerge and challenge the molasses fragrance for dominance; a pleasing, if simplistic rum bouquet that promises not to burn up too many brain cells. The palate entry is cloyingly sweet and sap-like as it coats the tongue like varnish; the midpalate stage offers only a concentrated, one-note, sugary taste profile that's more than likely very drinkable for sweet-freaks but hardly suitable for more perceptive imbibers. It concludes syrupy and sweet, with a trace of cola nut. Not in the least horrible, but about as Basic Dark (read: caramel added) Rum 101 as it can get; a mixer rum that's ideal for when you're concocting pina coladas by the batch for the gang.

2004 Rating: ★★/Not Recommended

Bacardi Superior Rum (Puerto Rico); 40% abv, $13.

Absolutely spotless clarity; silvery color. Smells of caramelized fruit, brown sugar, and bubble gum in the initial whiffs; aeration settles down the sweetness into a more focused ripe fruit/fruit compote scent that's accentuated by bittersweet molasses. Intensely sweet and sugary at entry, almost to the point of being a liqueur as much as a molasses-based rum; the midpalate is sugary sweet and cloying. Ridiculously and annoyingly oversweet. This rum doesn't deserve its number one standing in US spirits sales. When you want light rum, buy Cruzan Light.

2007 Rating: ★/Not Recommended

Bacardi Vaníla Original Vanilla Rum (Puerto Rico); 35% abv, $13.

Clear and ideally pure. The opening nosing passes reflect a strong, bean-like vanilla aroma; aeration does little to expand on that primary theme. The palate entry is intensely sweet, perhaps more bittersweet; the midpalate displays a deep vanilla bean flavor that is now totally bittersweet. The aftertaste is long, totally focused on the vanilla. Drinkable and best used in cocktails, but so heavy on the vanilla that on its own the entry flavor, in particular, is overbearing.

2003 Rating: ★★/Not Recommended

Bardenay Rum (USA); 40% abv, $10.

The pale hay color is bright and impeccably clean. In the initial nosings after the pour the aroma is mute and for all intents and purposes shut down; six more minutes of air contact do little to coax out any sort of rum-reminiscent bouquet beyond a distant buttery quality; just skip the aroma, period. The palate entry at least displays some delicate caney sweet tastes that are akin to light toffee, light caramel, and nougat; honey enters the scene at midpalate. Concludes sweet, a bit too confectioner's sugar-like, but agreeably average.

2006 Rating: ★★/Not Recommended

Batacha Cristal Rum (Mexico); 38% abv, $6.

Silvery and clear, showing only slight sediment. The opening sniffings detect delectable aromas of lead pencil, vanilla bean, and minerals/shale; aeration builds up the beaniness while downplaying the lead pencil and minerals/shale; in fact, the bean quality turns into an unbuttered popcorn scent by the very end of the aromatic appraisal. The palate entry is dry, pleasingly brown sugar-like, and intensely bittersweet; the midpalate phase showcases the vanilla extract to the limit. Concludes bittersweet, concentrated, and assertive. Can't believe the price, considering the quality.

2005 Rating: ★★★/Recommended

Beachcomber Apple Flavored Rum (USA); 27.5% abv, $9.

Clear and ideally flawless. The opening whiffs detect a reluctant, bitter scent of apple peel; further time in the glass doesn't assist much in coaxing out any kind of deeper aroma and I move on. The palate entry is the complete opposite of the limp bouquet as pleasantly ripe but almost borderline sugary tastes of apple greet the taste buds; by midpalate the sweetness calms down to the point where the ripe apple taste (kind of like apple struedel) becomes more acceptable. The finish is very sweet and too sugary; very simple. If the sugar was toned

down by two levels, I could easily envision giving it the third star and a recommendation; to be good, apple flavored spirits need a delicate balance of sweetness and acidity. Close but no cigar.
2003 Rating: ★★/Not Recommended

Beachcomber Coconut Flavored Rum (USA); 27.5% abv, $9.

Clean as a whistle and pure. The nose after the pour is fresh, mildly sweet, and properly coconut-like; further aeration doesn't really affect the bouquet one iota as it remains constant and pleasing throughout the entire nosing phase. The palate entry is gently sweet and coconut-true; at midpalate the flavor is pillowy sweet and has a marshmallow-like quality that's attractive in its simplicity. The aftertaste stays the course set out at palate entry. While not in the same league as Cruzan Coconut (★★★★), it is the equal of Captain Morgan Parrot Bay (★★★) and that's saying a lot. A very good job here that also represents good value.
2003 Rating: ★★★/Recommended

Beachcomber Pineapple Flavored Rum (USA); 27.5% abv, $9.

Properly pure and clean. The initial nosing passes pick up a delicate, fresh pineapple ripeness that's appealing; aeration adds supplementary scents of cotton candy, marshmallow, and refined sugar while the pineapple element remains in the background. The palate entry is sweet but not cloying and displays a bit more sugar than pineapple component; the midpalate point is intensely sweet and sugary as the sweetness overtakes any pineapple core flavor, leaving this rum awkward and out of tune. In the aftertaste there's just a flash of pineapple as again the sugar throws a blanket over what's supposed to be the headlining element. Should be renamed Beachcomber Sugar Flavored Rum; basically, it's cheap crap.
2003 Rating: ★/Not Recommended

Beachcomber Spiced Rum (USA); 27.5% abv, $9.

The autumnal gold fino sherry-like appearance is impeccably clean. The first couple of inhalations pick up one thing and one thing only, fat scents of refined sugar; so where's the zesty spice?; several more minutes in the glass do nothing, nada, zippo to expand the one-note bouquet; I mean, c'mon, spiced rums should have some evidence of cinnamon or nutmeg or pepper in the aroma. The palate entry displays some weak tastes of spice, but it's all wrapped up in a sugary/honey-like foundation flavor; by midpalate the taste profile drops off the chart. Don't even get me going about the non-existent finish. Captain Morgan Private Stock (★★★★) and Foursquare (★★★) are light years ahead of this pathetic entry; goes for the lowest common denominator and finds it in spades.
2003 Rating: ★/Not Recommended

Beleza Pura Super Premium Cachaça (Brazil); 40% abv, $28.

Perfect purity; clean and clear of any debris. The first whiffs detect beans, then raw grassy, sugar cane; aeration time for this spirit means fast evolution as the bouquet changes virtually every minute, finally ending up in aromatic waves of burning tires, black pepper, rope/hemp, steamed asparagus, celery salt, and tar; with every sniffing, there seems to be another two or three new dimensions; an amazing nosing experience. Tastes strongly of ash/soot/burning rubber at palate entry; at midpalate a sly sweetness comes into play as a foundation for the smokiness/tar. Finishes semisweet and smooth. Had the palate entry been more nuanced and less feral, I would have given a fourth rating star. As it is, however, this is a solid cachaça with a no-nonsense, love me/hate me personality that shows more than a few degrees of sophistication in the midpalate and aftertaste.

2005 Rating: ★★★/Recommended

Braddah Kimo's Mo'Bettah Gold Rum (Hawaii); 40% abv, $13.

The pale gold/dusty yellow color is clear and clean, just a mite dullish. Owns the near-identical aromatic profile of its silver sibling, meaning burning tires, chili peppers, and cat pee; once again, aeration doesn't make a dent in the armor shield of burning dung. The palate entry isn't quite as hideous as that of the silver as the actual taste of sugar cane/brown sugar comes through to rescue the taste; the midpalate stage has a smoky/tobacco-like leaning that works all the way through to the finish when the taste turns gently sweet and just a bit honeyed. Can't say that this rum is recommendable because it's not, but it is an improvement over the gum-numbing, pest-ridding silver.

2005 Rating: ★★/Not Recommended

Braddah Kimo's Mo'Bettah Silvah Rum (Hawaii); 40% abv, $12.

Excellent purity. In the first nosing pass, my olfactory sense is assaulted by horribly gross aromas of cat's piss/cat box, burning tires, and crushed red pepper—hey, this is great; further aeration does nothing to quell the aromatic mugging of my sniffing apparatus as the aroma runs amok with jalapeño pepper and urine-like scents; rivals the bouquets of several mescals that I've reviled. The palate entry is no less than awful as the taste regrettably mirrors the bouquet in terms of the over-the-top peppery/urinal-like aspect; the midpalate is a meager improvement as a whisper of sugar cane does reluctantly emerge. The aftertaste does nothing to redeem the embarrassing aroma and flavor. The distiller might defensively say, "It's stylistic." I say, "I've evaluated spirits since 1989 and I can distinguish trash and distilling ineptitude when I encounter them." An appalling mess that offers no resemblance to rum as we know it on Earth. Mars, maybe, but not Earth. Should never have left the island.

2005 Rating: ★/Not Recommended

Brinley Gold Vanilla Rum (St. Kitts); 36% abv, $20.

The mahogany/molasses/nut brown color is pretty and especially cola-like; very good purity. The opening aroma is as advertised, very vanilla extract-like; further time allows the aroma to settle in as additional bittersweet scents, most notably, brown sugar, old dark honey, and dark cocoa, make for intriguing sniffing. The palate entry is ultrasweet and regrettably syrupy as the viscous texture covers the tongue like three coats of paint; by midpalate there's a semblance of reined-in flavor as very toasty/roasted tastes of nuts, maple and vanilla extract vie for attention through the wet blanket of texture. Finishes thick, cloying, syrupy and intensely vanilla-like. An overblown, ridiculously top-heavy flavoring job that pushes this from the rum category into the liqueur category and even then doesn't cut it due to its complete lack of grace and balance. I can't imagine what gets into distillers who think that they have to bludgeon consumers with flavorings in order for them to "get it". Don't go near it unless you think force-feeding is the best method of eating. Personal message to Brinley

distiller: buy the whole line of Cruzan Estate flavored rums and study how it should and, more importantly, can be done, with restraint and an eye on balance.
2004 Rating: ★/Not Recommended

British Royal Navy Imperial Rum (Jamaica); 54.3% abv, $6,000/4.54 liter demijohn.
The deep color is mahogany with ruby core highlights; impeccable purity. Immediately after the pour, exotic scents of rubber tire, lanolin, and black pepper greet the olfactory sense; with time in the glass, the aroma slowly begins to unfold in the second whiff, offering mature, rind-like scents of bacon fat and poppy seed; in the third sniffing, the fat/oil component takes charge, providing a substantial aromatic phase; in the fourth and last nosing pass, following nearly ten minutes of aeration, indistinct notes of herbs (ginger? cardamom?), cocoa butter, molasses, and steamed asparagus get added to the peculiar aromatic stew. The palate entry is unctuous, layered, intensely honeyed, and molasses-like; the midpalate stage is opulent, cocoa-like, buttery, and shows traces of rancio. The aftertaste is long and is laden with ripe and sweet tastes of dried fruit, almond butter, and oak resin. Most of all, I liked the ethereal touch of rancio on the tongue; an interesting gorilla of a rum.
2000 Rating: ★★★★/Highly Recommended

BRN Sea Wynde Pot Still Rum (Jamaica/Guyana); 46% abv, $38.
This is the second release of BRN Sea Wynde, comprised from a slightly different formula than the first release. The harvest gold/light topaz appearance shines in the light of the examination lamp; superb purity; the initial whiffs detect seductive fragrances of paraffin, molasses and oak; an extra seven minutes in the sampling glass releases semisweet to flat-out sweet aromas of maple and brown sugar. This pot still rum really takes off, though, once in the mouth; the palate entry emits sweet, lightly baked tastes of maple and almond butter; by the midpalate point the flavor profile includes succulent tastes of cream, holiday spices (cinnamon, clove), oak resin that's approaching rancio-like proportions and top-grade honey. The aftertaste is long, luxurious, fruity, and utterly delicious. An outstanding, marginally sweeter/more biscuity upgrade from the very good original offering. At this price if you don't purchase at least three bottles of this instant classic, you're a fool.
2003 Rating: ★★★★★/Highest Recommendation

Brugal Añejo Gran Reserva Familiar Rum (Dominican Republic); 40% abv, $15.
The lovely bronze/amber/auburn color is bright and blemish-free. Right from the start, the bouquet says "stately maturity" as mildly toasty aromas of marshmallow, light toffee, caramel, and milk chocolate make for compelling sniffing; further aeration stimulates moderately spicy background notes of nutmeg and cinnamon. The palate entry is integrated, moderately oily, chocolatey, and gently sweet; at midpalate the taste profile expands to include honey, molasses, and egg cream. Finishes up elegantly and sweet. A splendid oak-aged rum expression that stands just below the absolute five star best.
2005 Rating: ★★★★/Highly Recommended

Cabana Boy Citrus Flavored Rum (USA); 35% abv, $14.
Spring water pure. The initial nosings find a zesty lemon peel odor that's somewhere between sweet and dry; time in the glass doesn't encourage much expansion or deepening, in

fact, the scents comes off manufactured, even industrial as aeration continues. In the mouth the entry is tart and citrusy; then at midpalate an explosion of fruity sweetness blankets the taste buds. The finish is long, citrusy, but sweet. Once again, more a liqueur in nature than a flavored rum. If the distiller had left more tartness in the blend I probably would have given it a third star and a recommendation; as it is, it's drinkable but way too sweet to be considered anything other than average.

2001 Rating: ★★/Not Recommended

Cabana Boy Orange Flavored Rum (USA); 35% abv, $14.

Crystal clear; the opening scent is more of orange peel/zest than orange juice/pulp. Aeration doesn't encourage much more in the way of deeper or broader aromatic expression. On the palate, the entry taste is intensely sweet and the texture is annoyingly syrupy; the midpalate is dizzyingly sweet and cloying. The finish is orangey sweet and medium long; alright, already! I get the point that this is an orange-flavored spirit; that fact doesn't have to be jack-hammered home; disgusting.

2001 Rating: ★/Not Recommended

Cabana Boy Pineapple/Coconut Flavored Rum (USA); 35% abv, $14.

Pure, particle free appearance. The nose owns a dull, sickly pineapple candy-like aroma in the first two nosing passes and suffers from being overly sweet; after time in the glass the coconut component becomes more evident and that adds a slight bit of charm to the experience in the later stages. In the mouth the flavor seems a bit strained and metallic at palate entry; then at midpalate the pineapple and coconut elements blend pretty nicely. The aftertaste is long, nicely melded, not cloying, and adds a subtle note of vanilla extract at the tail end. The best application here is the obvious one: make it the base for a piña colada.

2001 Rating: ★★★/Recommended

Cabana Boy Raspberry Flavored Rum (USA); 35% abv, $14.

Clean and limpid appearance. The initial two nosing passes detect an aggressively sweet and ripe perfume of raspberry preserves; though true to the fruit, the bouquet clubs the olfactory sense into submission with unnecessary force through to the final pass eight minutes after the pour. The palate entry is numbingly sweet and concentrated; the midpalate sees a minor lessening of the raspberry jam intensity but it's nonetheless still in fourth gear. The finish is strangely creamy and jammy, brimming with near over-the-top raspberry taste. More a liqueur than a rum.

2001 Rating: ★★/Not Recommended

Cabana Boy Vanilla Spice Flavored Rum (USA); 35% abv, $14.

Clear as rain water. The initial whiffs make no bones about the flavor source as high-flying aromas of vanilla bean and vanilla extract leap from the glass; by the last two sniffings supplementary scents of wet stone and nougat get added to the bouquet. The palate entry is lop-sided and awkward as the taste buds are forced to succumb to the heavyweight vanilla taste. The finish is a bit less intense. Drinkable and average; if the volume was turned down on the vanilla flavoring, this item would be recommendable.

2001 Rating: ★★/Not Recommended

Cabana Boy Wild Cherry Flavored Rum (USA); 35% abv, $14.
Clean and clear. The opening whiffs offer dry cherry fruit and cherry stone aromas that remind me of lesser kirschs; after several minutes of air contact the bouquet takes on a sweet, overly ripe perfume that comes off more as the fragrance of a liqueur than a flavored rum; no subtlety here. In the mouth the cherry flavor at entry is surprisingly tasty as the taste calls to mind chocolate cherries; the midpalate is a sweet, thick cherry bonanza but there's actually enough acidity and spirit backbone to pull it back out of the "cloying" category. The finish is rich, intensely cherry flavored, and candied. Think of it as a cherry liqueur and you'll save yourself a lot of confusion; drinkable but ordinary.
2001 Rating: ★★/Not Recommended

Cabana Cachaça Double Distilled Cachaça (Brazil); 40% abv, $35.
Unblemished clarity. The first inhalations pick up smells of concrete/sand, minerals, slate/granite, and grass; further aeration doesn't help with much aromatic expansion as the mineral/slate aspect moves in to dominate. The palate entry is pleasantly grassy and keenly vegetal; the midpalate stage is oily, full-bodied, and very, very minerally. Ends up zesty, intensely grassy (as it should be) and long in the throat. One of the smoother cachaças I've reviewed.
2007 Rating: ★★★/Recommended

Cachaça da Roça (Brazil); 40% abv, $14/liter.
Pristine as rainwater. The initial whiffs pick up cocoa-like scents that are likewise moderately fruity (red fruits, especially); aeration time of another seven minutes doesn't stimulate further aromatic expansion or deepening as the aroma remains properly and nicely fruity and chocolatey. The palate entry is a bit tanky/metallic for me, but does display a glimmer of sugar cane grassiness; by the midpalate stage the flavor recovers its sugar cane base material character to fully express itself in waves of refined sugar, sugar beets, and grass. Ends well enough for a recommendation.
2007 Rating: ★★★/Recommended

Cane Louisiana Rum Aged Five Years (USA); 40% abv, $34.
Pale gold color of sauternes; superb clarity. Starts out with pleasantly spicy (cinnamon) and minty aromas, backed up by moderately aggressive spirit; additional aeration corrals the zesty, piquant quality, making the aroma baked, spice cake-like, and slightly sweet and grassy. The palate entry is caney sweet but neither cloying nor sloppy, meaning there's a focus to the sweetness; the midpalate shows sound and ample acidity, which balances the cane sweetness, making the taste slightly bitter and cocoa bean-like. Finishes medium-long, bittersweet, bean/kernel-like, and tangy. Gets the job done.
2007 Rating: ★★★/Recommended

Canne Royale Extra Old Rum (Grenada); 40% abv, $25.
Pale amber/dusty yellow color; good purity. The initial nosings immediately pick up the sweetly fragrant aromas of vanilla bean and brown sugar; exposure to air over another five minutes sees the aroma turn slightly deeper as more profound scents of marzipan, light toffee and chocolate cake frosting make for intriguing and delightful sniffing. The palate entry is toasty, mildly sweet and medium-weighted; the midpalate goes much sweeter as tastes of

sugar cookies, brown sugar, honey and vanilla bean combine beautifully. The aftertaste is long, more bittersweet than sweet and elegant. A classy extra old rum that's long on balance and stately presence in the mouth. Bravo, great job here.

2002 Rating: ★★★★/Highly Recommended

Cannes Brulées Banane Banana Flavored Rum (Grenada); 30% abv, $20.

Clear and clean in appearance. Acknowledging that banana is frequently a difficult and delicate aroma as a beverage alcohol flavoring, I have to pull out all the nosing stops to locate any banana presence in the first inhalations; even after six minutes of additional aeration, evidence of banana is faint, at best. I decide to bag the nosing and proceed directly to tasting whereupon I encounter a surprisingly dry, squeaky clean, some might say tight palate entry; by midpalate a softly fruity, but crisply dry core flavor emerges as dried banana chips, not necessarily fresh banana. Concludes clean, refreshing, yet merely suggesting banana. If my scoring system allowed two and a half stars, that's what I'd give this understated rum. It is borderline recommendable. While the virtues of cleanness, dryness, and flavor subtlety are admirable, they end up being offset by the fact that I—and anyone—expect a more developed banana taste, not just the weakest of hints. Note to distiller: A good start, but turn up the volume a notch or two on the banana flavoring and it will earn a third star and a recommendation.

2005 Rating: ★★/Not Recommended

Cannes Brulées Light Classic Premium Red Rum (Grenada); 30% abv, $19.

The straw/silver color is hardly "Red", so the product name confuses me (not that that's difficult); superb clarity. In the initial inhalations after the pour, firm, moderately sweet aromas of refined sugar and cake frosting show a medium range appeal; in later whiffs not all that much expansion or deepening is detected, though the sugary/beany bouquet is still charming. The palate entry is sweet, satiny, and caney, but cheerily superficial; the midpalate flavor profile reinforces the palate entry impression, adding nothing new. Ends up silky smooth, appropriately sweet, completely likeable and recommendable, but not necessarily a hidden treasure for serious rum fanatics.

2005 Rating: ★★★/Recommended

Captain Morgan Original Spiced Rum (Puerto Rico); 35% abv, $14.

The butterscotch/oatmeal color is light and clear of sediment or particles. The no-nonsense bouquet opens up with a scattershot aroma that includes marshmallow, light toffee and light honey; further time in the glass clearly is not necessary for this rudimentary, but eminently pleasurable aroma that, in reality, is only moderately spicy (cinnamon, nutmeg standout) and nearly creamy. The palate entry is sweet, amiable, and molasses-centric, then at midpalate there's an overwhelming spiced honey flavor that gently guides you to the creamy, cake frosting finish. I'm fully aware that the most serious rum mavens among you will never forgive me for saying so, but I liked this affable spiced rum twelve years ago and I still like it. A groundbreaking brand.

2004 Rating: ★★★/Recommended

Captain Morgan Tattoo Puerto Rican Rum with Spices & Other Natural Flavors (Puerto Rico); 35% abv, $15.

Dark brown, the color of cola; did someone say "severe caramel coloring"? Smells faintly of aniseed, cinchona, ginger, and tree bark in the first aromatic go-round; an additional period of air contact does little to alter the aroma, except for allowing the scent of ginger to become the dominant feature. The palate entry is off-dry, fruity, sap-like, and mildly spiced; at midpalate the bittersweet taste profile centers on the core flavors of ginger, cola nut, and bark becoming almost a root beer- or Campari-like flavored rum. Finishes overly sweet. A poor line extension choice in view of the massively popular Original, Private Reserve, and Parrot Bay. Why the stumble now?

2005 Rating: ★★/Not Recommended

Captain Morgan's Parrot Bay Puerto Rican Rum with Natural Coconut Flavor (Puerto Rico); 21% abv, $13.

Clear and limpid as rain water. The fruity, sweet bouquet wastes no time with preliminaries as it foists plump aromas of sweetened coconut and bubble gum sugar into the olfactory sense; aeration is meaningless in this case. The decidedly sweet (but not cloying) palate entry taste is ALL COCONUT with nary a trace of rum; the midpalate is rich, creamy, properly sweet, and (dare I say it?), scrumptious. It ends as it began with the carefully sweet coconut flavor ruling the roost. Is Parrot Bay a rum or is it a liqueur? Doesn't matter all that much because it fills the bill in matters of aroma and taste; what more could one ask? Unpretentious Parrot Bay doesn't try to be something it's not and for that I recommend it.

2004 Rating: ★★★/Recommended

Chantal Comte Distillerie Depaz L'Arbre du Voyageur VSOP Rhum Vieux Agricole (Martinique); 45% abv, $90.

The attractive bronze/honey brown hue displays unblemished purity. The first nosing passes encounter moderately sweet and understated scents of sugar cane, carnations, and cotton candy; aeration time of another seven minutes helps to loosen the bouquet so that more pronounced aromas, such as gun metal, honey, and spice, take form. The palate entry is fresh, spicy (nutmeg), and mildly sweet; the midpalate taste features core flavors of sap/maple, brown sugar, and nutmeg. The aftertaste is long, moderately sweet, and honeyed. While very good and certainly recommendable, in comparison to the less expensive rhums from the La Favorite and Neisson distilleries, Chantal Comte VSOP is not as profound or as good a value.

2005 Rating: ★★★/Recommended

Chantal Comte Distillerie Depaz Plantation de la Montagne Pelée XO Rhum Vieux Agricole (Martinique); 45% abv, $120.

The copper color is brilliant; flawlessly clean. The opening whiffs pick up seductive scents of cigar box, paraffin, and brown butter; later sniffings detect a whole world of enticing scents, including black pepper, cinnamon, honey, sherry, onion, and marshmallow. The palate entry is silky, semisweet, intensely honeyed, and clean; the midpalate flavor profile exhibits delightful array of aromas, most notably, vanilla extract, cinnamon, brown sugar,

and orange zest. The aftertaste is long, concentrated, semisweet, oaky, and satiny. This is more like what Martinique rhum agricole should be like. Delicious.
2005 Rating: ★★★★/Highly Recommended

Charbay Rum (USA); 40% abv, $34.

Made from triple-distilled Hawaiian and Caribbean sugar cane syrup; absolute crystalline clarity. The opening nosing passes pick up piquant aromas that are a strange but extremely compelling cross between rum (grassy, syrupy, smoky) from sugar cane juice and (vegetal, intensely herbal, briny) 100% agave tequila; aeration allows the bean-like, kernel-like, grassy sugar cane to outdistance the saline/herbal quality, resulting in a mildly floral, definitely dry and bittersweet bouquet. The palate entry is keenly bittersweet, brown sugar-like and intensely cocoa bean-like; at midpalate the bean concentration settles down, clearing the way for the luscious sugar cane/molasses taste to dominate. Ends up beany and very cocoa-like. As complex, delicious and unique as Charbay Vodka and a must-have for serious rum mavens.
2004 Rating: ★★★★★/Highest Recommendation

Charbay Tahitian Vanilla Bean Rum (USA); 35% abv, $34.

The pale yellow color reminds me of new vintage muscadet from France's Loire Valley; excellent purity. The early sniffings detect the plump, oily presence of fatty vanilla extract; time in the copita adds aromatic hints of cocoa butter, egg cream, and vanilla. The palate entry is a touch sharp, but creamy and buttery; at midpalate the cream thins out as the vanilla bean element takes a leaner, more sinewy taste/texture profile. Finishes bittersweet, clean, and properly vanilla-like, without being sappy or cloying. An excellent flavored rum.
2004 Rating: ★★★★/Highly Recommended

Chauffe Coeur Blanc Rhum Agricole (Martinique); 54% abv, $28.

The appearance displays a barely detectable silvery/straw hue; perfect clarity. The piquant aroma right from the start leaps from the copita in pointed, buttery waves of milk chocolate, honeysuckle, and cream soda; seven minutes down the sniffing road the bouquet offers even deeper layers of unsweetened coconut, raw vanilla bean, raw cocoa bean, cane, walnut, paraffin, you know, this can go on and on. The palate entry is sumptuously sweet and oily; by the midpalate stage the flavor profile definitely includes the spirit presence more as a smoldering foundation for the honeyed taste than as a flavor itself. Finishes regally, sweet, caney/grassy, textured, and chewy. A state-of-the-art rhum agricole that defines the subcategory.
2005 Rating: ★★★★★/Highest Recommendation

Chauffe Coeur Brun Rhum Agricole (Martinique); 47% abv, $34.

The drop-dead gorgeous appearance is a bright burnished gold/amber/brandy-like color; unblemished purity. The first nasal go-round brims with toffee scents layered with even deeper aromas of dry oloroso sherry and fresh first-year honey; another seven minutes of exposure to air stimulates off-dry, grainy aromas that feature dark caramel, grassy cane, winter holiday spices, and marzipan; a fantastic, gold standard rhum agricole bouquet. The palate entry is as silky, zesty, and spiced as a rhum agricole can be; by midpalate the flavor profile lusciously highlights pipe tobacco, toffee, cocoa butter, and honey. Concludes bittersweet,

cocoa-like, and sherried. The ideal five star companion to the august Chauffe Coeur Blanc. A Martinique classic.
2005 Rating: ★★★★★/Highest Recommendation

Ciclón Bacardi Premium Gold Rum Infused with Imported Blue Agave Tequila & Natural Lime Juice (USA); 35% abv, $14.

A hybrid, aimed at the twenty-something market, made from 90% gold Puerto Rican rum, lime juice, and 10% 100% agave tequila. The amber color is pure; the initial sniffings are dominated completely by the tart perfume of fresh-squeezed lime juice, with nary a trace of rum or tequila presence; aeration only serves to heighten the lime juice intensity, leaving no room for any other aromatic contributions even after ten minutes in the glass. The palate entry is dry and herbal; by the midpalate it's obvious that the gold rum is employed merely as a base for the tequila and lime juice as they are firmly in control of the flavor phase; in fact, after tasting Ciclón, I'd have guessed that the tequila percentage was higher than 10%. It's in the finish in the throat that the gold rum makes its first distinct appearance, finally eclipsing the tequila. I'm all for experimentation and I see nothing blasphemous about combining different spirits; Ciclón works for me as it presents young drinkers with a different experience where all the mixing is done for them.
2002 Spirit Journal Rating: ★★★/Recommended

Cigana Aged Cachaça (Brazil); 40% abv; $16.

Pale amber in color; excellent purity, no sediment. The initial nosing passes detect strong, vegetal aromas of fennel, paper cup and palm oil; later sniffings after six more minutes of aeration detect little more than slightly salty, green leaf vegetable, kale-like, root-like aromas. The palate entry shows a bit of mildly pleasing smokiness; by the midpalate point, however, a stale, almost cardboard-like taste takes charge, overshadowing all other taste factors. The decent aftertaste is brief, bittersweet, and fennel-like. Better than the unaged version and probably okay in mixed drink situations.
2003 Rating: ★★/Not Recommended

Cigana Cachaça (Brazil); 40% abv; $14.

Transparent and clean as mineral water. The opening nosing passes are assaulted by aromas of sweat, oil and burning rubber; further time in the glass does nothing to improve the situation, even minimally; a rank, fishy, sweaty aroma with no redeeming value whatsoever. The palate entry is mildly sweet, vegetal and slightly syrup-like; by the midpalate juncture the taste improves enough to be categorized as "barely drinkable" as very herbal, vegetal flavors of celery, Brussels sprouts, tuna fish and cigarette smoke make for distinctive drinking. Finishes as tasty as something scraped off the bottom of your shoe. Am I allowed to give no stars?
2003 Rating: ★/Not Recommended

Clarke's Court Old Grog Rum (Grenada); 40% abv, $24.

The color is a pale amber; perfect purity. The opening nosing comes across a bit of holiday spice (nutmeg) and vegetation (juniper/carnation petals); with time in the glass, the aroma doesn't seem to want to expand beyond the spice and damp plant-like scents, or perhaps it cannot; the last sniffing, following a full nine minutes of aeration, displays no sign of developing further and consequently is a bust for something labeled as "Extra Old". The palate entry is pleasantly, though hardly profoundly, sweet and resiny; the midpalate stage offers a deft touch of vanilla/oakiness but just a smidgen while the flavor goes almost fruity—huh?—que es esto? The finish is sweet, nearly plump, and again mysteriously fruity. An oddball, ultimately deficient, though drinkable rum that can't make up its mind as to what level it's supposed to be—Dark? Extra old? A confused, overpriced rum.

2001 Rating: ★★/Not Recommended

Clarke's Court Original White Rum (Grenada); 69% abv, $22.
Immaculate clarity and purely transparent. The cocoa bean/brown sugar bouquet skyrockets out of the sampling copita as though it's the Fourth of July; the middle stage passes see a slight settling down of the aroma as the cocoa bean/vanilla scent takes charge; the fourth sniffing remains potent, firm, and intensely bean-like; I'm amazed that the alcohol (69%) doesn't wallop my olfactory sense at any stage of the ten minute nosing process. The palate entry is concentrated and intensely sweet; it isn't until the first moments of the midpalate phase that the alcohol stings the tongue; the flavors are definitely overshadowed by the alcohol at first but then offer tastes of cocoa bean, bittersweet chocolate, brown sugar, and vanilla extract. The aftertaste is strong and very bean-like. I don't gravitate toward spirits of this stratospheric strength, but within its categorical context I thought this rum brought home the bacon.

2001 Rating: ★★★/Recommended

Clarke's Court Special Dark Rum (Grenada); 40% abv, $14.
The appearance is light amber/honey/topaz and is very clean. The nose is subdued and distant in the first pass, offering paper-thin scents of honey and dried herbs; with time in the glass, the aroma shows little interest in exposing itself any further in the middle stage sniffings, remaining at arm's length; the fourth and final whiff, following eight minutes, surrenders no new aromatic ground ; fine, be that way, I'll just move on. The flavor is pleasantly sweet at palate entry; then it turns a bit like lead pencil/metal at midpalate. The aftertaste is medium long, mildly sweet, a dash caramel-like, and moderately pleasing. Drinkable, but wholly commonplace.

2001 Rating: ★★/Not Recommended

Clarke's Court Superior Light Rum (Grenada); 40% abv, $14.
Perfect clarity. The opening nose reeks with pod-like scents of cocoa bean and vanilla extract; the middle stage whiffs commit to bittersweet, dark cocoa in a major way as hardly any sweetness shows through; the final sniffing, following eight minutes of air contact, displays a slight decline in intensity, but stays the bittersweet, dark cocoa course as the aroma nearly turns smoky; it took me a while to figure out what this bouquet was up to, but once I did it garnered some heavy points to the positive. The palate entry continues the severely bittersweet character on the tongue as the dark cocoa/lead pencil feature delights the taste buds; the midpalate phase is marginally sweeter and less demanding as the taste goes a touch buttery and very rich in texture, almost oily/fatty, in fact. The aftertaste is long, buttery, dark chocolate bittersweet to sweet, and incredibly alluring. The concentrated bittersweet nature of this light rum doesn't make it for everyone, but for those rum drinkers who prefer a challenge it's ideal; an oily feast.

2001 Rating: ★★★★/Highly Recommended

Cockspur 12 Bajan Crafted Rum (Barbados); 40% abv, $35.

This is a gorgeous looking rum, dressed in a copper/tawny cloak that's brilliant and gleaming under the examination lamp; impeccable clarity. The aroma immediately shows layering as bittersweet molasses lies atop a subtle layer of dried red fruits, oak, and nuts; with time in the glass, the bouquet develops a lovely, integrated personality that gives equal time to the alcohol, the wood, and the molasses in gracefully semisweet to bittersweet waves. The palate entry is so influenced by the oak (borders on being too much) that it's actually off-dry, bittersweet, and beany; by the midpalate stage the taste profile adds touches of marzipan, dark caramel, vanilla extract, and nougat. Finishes well and cocoa-like.
2007 Rating: ★★★/Recommended

Cockspur Fine Rum (Barbados); 40% abv, $20.

The pale amber color is a bit dull; fine purity. The opening aroma is cane sugar sweet and simple, all right but lacking depth; aeration does this rum scent a lot of good as a keen spiciness (cinnamon, vanilla) comes to the forefront, giving the bouquet a firm, final thrust; no frills, just dead-on sugar and molasses fragrance. The palate entry is caney sweet and marshmallow-like; the midpalate stage is pleasingly candied fruit-like and very much like confectioner's sugar. Ends up predictably sweet and too one-dimensional. Easy and drinkable, to be sure, but way too by-the-numbers for me in the end. Takes simplicity to its limit.
2007 Rating: ★★/Not Recommended

Cohiba 5 Year Old Very Old Rum (Dominican Republic); 40% abv, $12.

Owns a very pretty, autumnal honey gold hue; excellent purity. Displays scents of chalk, molasses, brown sugar, and marshmallow in the first two nosing passes; later sniffings following five to eight minutes of total time in the glass reveal deeper scents of tar and nougat. The palate entry is dry then in a nanosecond turns bittersweet and sap-like; the midpalate stage features tastes of vanilla extract, oak resin, and intense and acceptably prickly spirits "heat". The aftertaste is bittersweet and long; tongue-tingling and darned tasty. Though five years old, this Cohiba makes for an exciting and deeply flavorful mixer in a wide array of rum cocktails, old and new; think: deeply flavored Daiquiri.
2002 Rating: ★★★/Recommended

Cohiba 8 Year Old Very Old Rum (Dominican Republic); 40% abv, $18.

Very brandy-like to the eye in its amber/bronze robe of color. The early nosings pick up genuinely lovely and evolved fragrances of tea leaves, molasses, and distant spice; a bit of swirling and aeration stimulates deeper scents of dark caramel, black pepper, and milk chocolate; a big league, no-nonsense old rum perfume. In the mouth it offers tastes of almond butter, bourbon whiskey (from the barrels?) and honey at entry then it turns creamy sweet and sugary at midpalate. Delightfully oily in the finish; composed and elegant.
2002 Rating: ★★★★/Highly Recommended

Coral Cachaça (Brazil); 40% abv, $20/liter.

The limpid, silvery appearance is crystal clear and pure. The early aroma owns some mineral-like qualities, almost like lead or granite, then with aeration the bouquet opens up emitting alluring scents of unprocessed sugar cane, brown sugar, green vegetation and leather. The palate entry is sweet and lip-smacking; at midpalate the taste turns slightly vegetal (asparagus?) but remains sweet, succulent and true to the cane. Concludes well in soft bursts of spirit, sugar, and oil. Very pleasant and a sound base for caipirinhas.

2004 Rating: ★★★/Recommended

Coruba Jamaican Rum (Jamaica); 40% abv, $17.

Deep tawny/russet color. The opening aroma is snappy, spicy, and fabric-like initially, then it fades after only three minutes in the glass; further aeration releases a minor scent of marshmallow; the hollow bouquet doesn't get this rum off to a great start. The palate entry is sugary sweet with core flavors of honey, molasses, caramel, and brown sugar; by midpalate the taste is a bit too over-caramelized and manufactured, making it border on being cloying. The finish highlights a taste of burnt toast. To be sure, it's both drinkable and mixable but, I wonder, why be so overtly heavy-handed with the caramel additive? Is it really necessary? Not in my mind.

2002 Rating: ★★/Not Recommended

Coyopa 10 Year Old Rum (Barbados); 40% abv, $50.

This rum is produced by the highly regarded Barbados distiller, R.L. Seale (Doorly's XO, Foursquare Spiced). The bright new copper penny color is dazzling under the lamp; perfect purity. The initial nosing passes within the first two minutes after the pour detect zesty surface scents of spice (cinnamon), oaky vanilla, and cocoa; after another eight minutes of air contact the aroma adds subtle off-dry scents of black tea leaves, molasses, honey, and bittersweet chocolate. It's in the mouth, though, that this comely, medium-bodied rum really earns its rating stars as the sap and maple-like entry tastes bring the taste buds to full attention; by midpalate the flavor explodes in taste waves of butter cream, brown sugar, honey, and chocolate covered cherries. The impressive flavor display continues on in the finish as assertive but melded tastes of marshmallow and dark chocolate dominate. This, to me, is sipping rum territory. I would not use this rum in cocktails.

2002 Rating: ★★★★/Highly Recommended

Cruzan Black Cherry Rum (US Virgin Islands); 27.5% abv, $12.

Crystalline appearance; flawless purity. The cherry scent leaps from the glass in a strikingly kirsch-like manner, meaning acidic, sharp, and intensely cherry-like: a great start; over aeration time, the cherry aspect grows plumper and riper as the acid recedes, allowing for the full frontal fruitiness, which is dead-on and beguiling. At entry, the taste is delicate, ripe cherry-like, forward, but elegant and integrated; the taste splendor continues into the midpalate phase as the creamy texture coats the tongue in rich, vibrant, and genuine black cherry flavor. Just a touch metallic in the finish, but otherwise a smashing flavored rum.

2007 Rating: ★★★★/Highly Recommended

Cruzan Black Strap Rum Navy Tradition (US Virgin Islands); 40% abv, $13.

Made from the thickest, darkest type of molasses. The opaque, dense appearance is the brown/black color of black coffee or cola or Pedro Ximenez sherry. The first whiffs pick up exceedingly toasty/roasted aromas of molasses, black coffee, and road tar; seven minutes of further aeration bring to the fore bittersweet scents of oatmeal stout ale, licorice, very dark

cocoa, pipe tobacco, and brown sugar. The palate entry is long, more sweet than bittersweet, and dark chocolate-like; at midpalate the flavor profile becomes even more intense and dense as tastes of bacon fat, oak resin, and brown sugar become creamy. Finishes well with the brown sugar and bacon fat leading the way. A good addition to the superb Cruzan rum line.
2004 Rating: ★★★/Recommended

Cruzan Estate Dark Rum - 2 Years Old (US Virgin Islands); 40% abv, $11.

Mild, amber/light topaz hue; ideal purity. The nose after opening is largely absent except for a distant autumnal touch of burning leaves; the middle stage passes stick with the burning leaves, but fail to expand beyond that even after more than five minutes of aeration; the last sniffing throws in soft traces of spice, dark chocolate, nut shells, and ashes; a bouquet that gives away too little of itself. The mouth phase is different right from the palate entry as the taste offers complex, ashy, and sweet flavors of molasses, dark honey, and brown sugar; the midpalate features the molasses as the texture thickens and blankets the tongue. The finish is long, more bitter than sweet, and ashy. A seriously up-and-down dark rum whose best face appears at the first taste, then it retreats into itself once again. Drinkable to be sure, but commonplace by the standards of the category. Funnily, the two years in American oak benefited the Light more than this Dark; go figure.
2001 Rating: ★★/Not Recommended

Cruzan Estate Diamond Rum - 5 Years Old (US Virgin Islands); 40% abv, $17.

Matured in charred, previously used, oak Bourbon barrels for from five to ten years. The color is an opulent topaz/honey brown; perfect purity; the opening whiff is loaded with buttery/resiny notes that address the maturity of this rum; the second and third sniffings reveal further deepening in the aromatic forms of dark chocolate, black coffee, cigar smoke, Christmas pudding, and oak resin; the final pass finds the biscuity bouquet in mild decline and offering parting scents of sugar cookies and oily oak; a succulent cornucopia of old rum perfumes; love it. The palate entry is rich, almost thick, and oaky sweet; the bittersweet, take-no-prisoners midpalate stage offers melded tastes of old resiny oak, burnt butter, brown sugar, and even a dash of spice; I relish this old rum's oily texture perhaps most of all. The aftertaste is medium long, concentrated, unabashedly bittersweet, and oily. A brassy, old school rum that isn't afraid to put up its dukes. Make mine a Cruzan Diamond double, bartender.
2001 Rating: ★★★★/Highly Recommended

Cruzan Estate Light Rum - 2 Years Old (US Virgin Islands); 40% abv, $11.

The very pale flax/straw hue distinguishes Cruzan Light from other "light" rums that are always crystal clear; impeccable purity. The initial nosing pass offers delicate, bittersweet scents of tar and dark cocoa; in the middle stage sniffings underlying aromas of almond and cocoa butter, bacon fat, and brown butter make for intriguing inhalations; the last whiff turns up the volume on the toasty cocoa butter and cocoa bean; a sturdy, bittersweet bouquet that's rimmed with cocoa. The dry, oily palate entry highlights the pod-like (cocoa bean or coffee bean) quality that's found in the aroma; the bitter, slightly harsh midpalate tastes feature the peculiar, but workable combination of brown butter, soot, and molasses. The finish is long, sooty, and intensely bitter; an improvement, by two rating stars, over the clumsy and cloying original Cruzan Light that I sampled in 1992.
2001 Rating: ★★★/Recommended

Cruzan Estate Single Barrel Rum Barrel No. 85110 (US Virgin Islands); 40% abv, $30.

A burnished orange hue, with impeccable purity. The initial nosing pass shows a muted, reluctant aroma; after several minutes of exposure to air, the middle stage passes offer slightly more in the way of aromatic depth as mellow, dry scents of wood and resin test the patience of the olfactory sense; following ten minutes of aeration, this bouquet remains as elusive and hesitant as ever; nothing to grip on to. Far more expressive in the mouth than in the nose, this rum kick-starts itself at palate entry as lean, but sweet tastes of brown sugar and cotton candy greet the taste buds; the midpalate is a tad harsh and raw on the tongue, but still savory as the sweetness delights the palate. The finish is brief, mildly sweet, and lean in texture. Uneven to distraction; my least favorite of the Cruzan single barrels.

2001 Rating: ★★/Not Recommended

Cruzan Estate Single Barrel Rum Barrel No. 85180 (US Virgin Islands); 40% abv, $30.

Tasted alongside Barrel 85110. Definitely the darker of the two, this gorgeous beauty displays a deep bronze/topaz sheen that reflects the light; absolute purity. The opening whiff picks up mature, if delicate, fragrances of nut butter and mild oak; with time in the glass the middle stage passes detect a sophisticated bouquet that's gradually opening up, offering added scents of baked pear, pie crust, and brown sugar; the fourth sniffing finds moderate lessening of potency, but still a solid, elegant, and mature bouquet. The palate entry is mildly sweet, medium textured, and rich in brown sugar flavor; the midpalate displays married flavors of sweet oak, nut butter, and brown sugar. The finish is medium long, moderately sweet, and polite in its bearing. A very nice rum but frankly I'll take the dazzling 5 Year Old Cruzan Diamond.

2001 Rating: ★★★/Recommended

Cruzan Junkanu! Citrus Rum (US Virgin Islands); 35% abv, $14.

Clear and clean as rain water. The wonderfully piquant bouquet of citrus pulp features lemon first, then orange pulp; aeration adds more subtle hints of lime and grapefruit; an ambrosial, tart and citrusy bouquet of the first order. The palate entry is tart, intensely citrusy, and authentically acidic; by the midpalate stage the acidity subsides leaving behind juicy, tart flavors of orange and lemon. Jankanu finishes properly acidic and mouth-puckering, with the orange/lemon duo still leading the way. Another graceful winner from the world's foremost flavored rum producer, Cruzan; I also like the fact that the abv is 35% rather than 27%, giving this rum a rock solid structure; BRAVO!

2003 Rating: ★★★★/Highly Recommended

Cruzan Mango Rum (US Virgin Islands); 27% abv, $12.

Perfect clarity. Like all Cruzan flavored rums the opening whiffs detect subtle, skillfully balanced scents, this time of barely ripe mango; with time in the glass, the aroma turns into an ambrosial bouquet that highlights the mango but offers lesser aromatic roles to pear and papaya; a lovely, understated bouquet of the first rank. The palate entry is tart, even bitter; then at midpalate the flavor profile becomes gently ripe and succulent, totally true to the mango essence. The aftertaste is long, sweet and fresh.

2003 Rating: ★★★★/Highly Recommended

Cruzan Raspberry Rum (US Virgin Islands); 27.5% abv, $12.

Clear and clean as a whistle. The raspberry aroma after the pour is true-to-the-source, ripe, and fresh; aeration gives the aroma the chance to turn more preserves-like than fresh-picked fruit-like. The palate entry is sweet, yet tart and pleasantly fruity; by the midpalate stage the flavor profile turns savory, fruity, and decidedly sweet/tart. Concludes elegantly and ripe. Another how-to lesson on rum flavoring by the wizards at Cruzan.

2005 Rating: ★★★/Recommended

Cruzan Vanilla Flavored Rum (US Virgin Islands); 27.5% abv, $12.

Perfectly clear and free from sediment. The initial inhalations immediately following the pour are confronted with aggressive vanilla perfume, then after eight minutes of air contact in the glass the aroma smoothes out into a fat, buttery vanilla-thon that's more like vanilla frosting or, better, egg cream than vanilla bean or extract. In the mouth, it's rich, thick, and properly vanilla-like, but there's no sense of the rum base spirit whatsoever. The aftertaste is short, sweet, eggy, and fine. Yet another hit from Cruzan.

2002 Rating: ★★★/Recommended

Cuba Libre 15 Year Old El Dorado Demerara Rum (Guyana); 40% abv, $55.

The brandy-like appearance is the burnished/bronze color of an XO cognac; flawless purity; a seriously attractive high-end spirit. In the opening salvo of aroma there are fresh vegetal/grassy notes that belie the time spent in oak; further air contact stimulates scents of textile/fiber, peanut, beeswax, and underlying honeyed sweetness; a medium-complex bouquet that demands its proper amount of concentration and time. The palate entry is surprisingly soft, mellow, and marshmallow sweet; the midpalate stage features luscious, if delicate, flavors that include light honey, cola nut, and cream. Elegant, poised, and succulent.

2006 Rating: ★★★★/Highly Recommended

Cuba Libre 21 Year Old El Dorado Demerara Rum (Guyana); 40% abv, $100.

The coppery color enchants the eye; perfect clarity. The first nosing passes detect very little except for brown butter and fiber-like scents; an additional seven minutes of air exposure bring out more serious aromas, most notably, oak, winter holiday spice, and vanilla cake frosting. The palate entry is supple, not overly sweet, and moderately honeyed; the midpalate stage highlights include the buttery/creamy texture and pointed tastes of cocoa, reed/fiber, ash, and beans. Like the 15 Year Old, classy and world-class.

2006 Rating: ★★★★/Highly Recommended

Cuba Libre 5 Year Old El Dorado Demerara Rum (Guyana); 40% abv, $25.

The amber/topaz color is pretty and impeccably pure. The initial burst of aroma is delightfully fruity (baked cherry/cherry glaze) and nutty (chestnut); following another seven minutes in the glass, the bouquet turns vanilla-like and winter holiday spicy; really loved this bouquet. The palate entry is engagingly sweet (marshmallow) in a moderate and composed manner; the midpalate stage offers long, honeyed flavors that generously coat the tongue and throat, with nary a hint of acidic edge or spirit-induced heat. Ends up plump and properly sweet.

2006 Rating: ★★★★/Highly Recommended

Cuba Libre Dark El Dorado Demerara Rum (Guyana); 40% abv, $18/liter.
The chestnut/mahogany color is pretty and clean. The first whiffs are confronted with greater concentrated/nougat-like sweetness than with the White; aeration time of another six minutes serves only to deepen the candy bar sweetness, thereby losing some of the rum charm as the bouquet turns leathery and men's club woody. The heightened sweetness factor is immediately apparent in the palate entry as the tip of the tongue is swathed in sugary notes; the midpalate stage thankfully regains this rum's composure by going leaner and more bittersweet than sweet. Concludes honeyed, bittersweet, and very pleasant. The midpalate phase rescued this rum.
2006 Rating: ★★★/Recommended

Cuba Libre White El Dorado Demerara Rum (Guyana); 40% abv, $18/liter.
Excellent clarity. The opening sniffs detect ashy, tarred cinders/asphalt, and molasses; seven minutes later, the sweetness element accelerates, leaving the smoke and road tar behind. The palate entry is bittersweet, a tad chalk-like, and warming; the midpalate phase hits stride as the taste profile offers a highly pleasing bitterness that's halfway to becoming laser-like sweet. Finishes mellow, cocoa sweet, and lusciously medium-weighted in texture. What all molasses-based white rum should be.
2006 Rating: ★★★★/Highly Recommended

D'aristi 10 Year Old Special Reserve Rum (Mexico); 40% abv, $50.
A very pretty, brandy-like topaz/bronze color; excellent purity. The opening whiff finds settled, calm, and mature scents of butterscotch, honey, and sweetened morning cereal; the second and third sniffings, following ample aeration time, sees the aroma turn nutty (especially walnut), caramel-like, and intensely sweet; the final aromatic go-round, after nearly nine minutes of exposure to air, adds bittersweet chocolate to the mix; this bouquet is a deceptive bruiser because at first it doesn't seem like it's going to be overly sweet, but as it quietly sits in the glass it builds up steam and ends up being too concentrated for me. In the mouth, it begins intensely caramel-like at the palate entry, then flavorwise it turns to heavy brown sugar, molasses, and honey at midpalate with, to my surprise, very little evidence of wood which makes me think that it was most likely aged in large wood vats. The aftertaste is sweet, syrupy, and basically over-the-top in terms of cloying sweetness. A classic case of a distiller not understanding what "balance" means in view of international standards; barely drinkable, to me.
2001 Rating: ★/Not Recommended

D'aristi Añejo Rum (Mexico); 40% abv, $39.
The topaz/amber hue is attractive and reminiscent of amontillado sherry; superbly clean and pure. This nose opens up with dry, roasted/toasty aromas of pecan butter, toffee, and brown sugar; the middle stage sniffings detect cigarette smoke, tobacco leaf, and dark honey; the final nosing pass, following seven minutes of time in the glass, reveals compelling fragrances of coffee bean and molasses; in contrast to the Special White this bouquet is very dry, ashy, nut-like and kernel-like; I keep thinking "buttered popcorn" in my aromatic overview. The palate entry is a no-holds-barred caramel/honey extravaganza; the midpalate is a bit more coy as more subtle, drier tastes of ash, brown sugar, and very dark caramel make nice with the

taste buds. The finish is focused, semi-sweet, and intense. Better than the flabby, fleshy Special White and with its semi-sweet approach I can see it in several rum-based cocktails; nothing better than ordinary, however.

2001 Rating: ★★/Not Recommended

D'aristi Special White Rum (Mexico); 40% abv, $35.

Clear as rain water and perfect in its purity. The opening nosing pass is impressive in its sweet vanilla extract intensity and concentration; it's almost more like a vanilla flavored vodka, so cake frosting-like is it; the middle stage whiffs serve only to bolster the entrenched vanilla aroma, leaving little space for any other aromatic components; the fourth and last nosing pass sees the sweet vanillarama continue at full force; a one-note song aromatically. The palate entry begins dry and vegetal; then at midpalate the sugar cane/vanilla assault on the taste buds commences. The aftertaste is heavy duty vanilla and sweetness. Certainly drinkable for vanilla lovers, but so top-heavy with pasty/sugary vanilla that I can't quite see this rum behaving properly in cocktails; it's almost a flavored rum. In my humble opinion; a "be careful or it'll swallow the furniture" spirit.

2001 Rating: ★/Not Recommended

DC Distillers Choice Gold Rum The Spirit of Hawaii Pot Distilled from 100% Hawaiian Molasses (USA); 40% abv, $20.

Harvest gold/amber color; blemish free. The tart first nosings are akin to candied apple and refined sugar; aeration does little to expand the narrow focus of the bouquet as muted scents of cardboard, plastic, and molasses fail to win me over. The palate entry is meek, mildly sweet, and light-weighted; the midpalate point displays a limp sweetness that regrettably is the flavor highlight. Aftertaste is simplistic, hollow, and timidly sweet. There's no direction to this rum and even less character. A miserable spirit, period.

2006 Rating: ★/Not Recommended

DC Distillers Choice Silver Rum The Spirit of Hawaii Pot Distilled from 100% Hawaiian Molasses (USA); 40% abv, $20.

Pristine appearance. The atypically fruity/musty initial aroma reminds me strikingly of fruit-based eau-de-vie far more than molasses-based rum; aeration stimulates additional weird and unexpected scents including rubber band, plastic, unhardened concrete, wet sand, damp earth, mushrooms/lichen/mold and that ol' staff favorite, dried cat pee. The palate entry is a mildly pleasant improvement over the unabashedly wrong bouquet as the taste thankfully doesn't fully mirror the aroma, giving off a moderate sense of fruitcake, dried fruit, and refined sugar; the midpalate taste is strangely similar to prune eau-de-vie, off-dry, raisiny yet oddly, not that bad. The finish is fruity, lazily floral, and mushroomy. I wanted to like this peculiar spirit that bears little resemblance to white rum, at least as I've come to understand it. Inappropriate aroma aside, the entry, midpalate and aftertaste together pulled this rum up from one star status.

2006 Rating: ★★/Not Recommended

Depaz Blue Cane Rhum Agricole (Martinique); 45% abv, $42.

The appearance sports a light amber/dusty gold color; impeccable purity. The enthralling opening aroma reminds me at times of grainy/almost briny Scotch whisky as much as it does grassy/vegetal/herbal rhum agricole; six more minutes of aeration open up a stunningly deep box of fragrances that include nutmeg, oak, wet grass, rubber pencil eraser, white pepper, and carnations; a compellingly complex and multilayered bouquet that always seems to offer something new with each sniff. The palate entry taste is not as expansive or broad as the aroma, but, in fact, trims the flavor possibilities down to herbs, caney sweetness, and flower garden; the midpalate features elements of smoke, tobacco leaf, black pepper, cinnamon, vanilla bean, nut paste, and honey. In a word, stupendous.

2006 Rating: ★★★★★/Highest Recommendation

Destileria Porfidio Single Cane Rum (Mexico); 45% abv, $30.

Clear and pure as rainwater. Distilled in pot stills and made from sugar cane juice as opposed to molasses, from which the majority of rums are produced. The opening aroma owns a distinct, bitter aroma of green olive; aeration time of another seven minutes introduces added, if atypical, aromas such as sea air, green peppercorn, and steamed green vegetables (broccoli, especially); intriguing and roguish, but not your standard issue pot still rum bouquet. The palate entry is bitter going on semisweet and curiously vegetal/grassy (sugar cane is a variety of grass, after all) rather than sugary; by the midpalate point the taste profile does offer some bittersweet and oily cane-like flavor. Ends grassy and green. While I don't think that this is anywhere near being a great rum, I give the Porfidio people ten out of ten for attempting something truly different with sugar cane and I look forward to their future pot still rums.

2004 Rating 2004: ★★★/Recommended

Diplomático Reserva (Venezuela); 40% abv, $18.

The saddle brown/chestnut color is dazzling and flawless in its purity. The initial whiffs pick up very subtle, if a tad muted, hints of peanut butter, black tea, and cinnamon; later inhalations detect even deeper, more accessible layers of honey, old leather, palm oil, old oak, and molasses. The palate entry explodes with succulent tastes of oak, vanilla cream, and honey; the midpalate expands the taste profile by offering Christmas cake, cookie spices, raisins, dates, and dark chocolate. Ends up balanced, correctly sweet, and elegant. I'd have bestowed a fifth rating star had the bouquet displayed greater early development. Very close to oak-aged, molasses-base rum perfection. Hey, for $18, this is nothing short of a fabulous deal.

2006 Rating: ★★★★/Highly Recommended

Diplomático Reserva Añejo (Venezuela); 40% abv, $15.

The honey/amber color is brilliant under the examination lamp; superb purity. The upfront nose displays robust notes of caramel, molasses, and oaky vanilla; following another seven minutes of aeration, the bouquet adds more subtle and baked traces of nutmeg, rubber, and cinnamon. The palate entry is toasty, brown sugar sweet, and slightly honeyed; the midpalate stage offers greater complexity as the flavor profile turns more candied, marzipan-like, and even treacle-like. Finishes silky smooth, concentrated, and sweet.

2006 Rating: ★★★/Recommended

Diplomático Reserva Exclusiva (Venezuela); 40% abv, $30.

The burnished orange/coppery appearance is bright and brandy-like; excellent clarity. The opening sniff detects expressive fragrances of orange zest, brown sugar, and cinnamon;

following another seven minutes in the copita, the aroma turns into a bouquet that emits composed and integrated scents of roasted chestnut, dried tobacco leaf, maple, and egg cream. The palate entry is curiously medicinal in a near quinine-like manner; the midpalate is much more pleasing than the odd entry as the taste profile includes bittersweet flavors of old oak, wood resin, molasses, and tree sap. Concludes intensely sap- and maple-like as it turns syrupy.

2006 Rating: ★★★/Recommended

Dogfish Head Brown Honey Rum (USA); 40% abv, $25.
Right now available only in the states of New Jersey, Delaware, and Maryland. An American potstill produced rum that's flavored with wildflower honey. The color is a soft, slightly pale amber/gold; a little bit more floating debris seen floating about than I'd like to see. Smells of honey right from the crack of the bat and holds that posture through the entire ten minute nosing phase, adding subtle traces of cheese and wood in the final sniffings. The palate entry is honey sweet and mildly agreeable; in the midpalate stage evidence of wood emerges in the form of resin, which balances the honey sweetness in a complementary manner. Finishes more resiny than honeyed. An oddball that has a certain rudimentary charm.

2005 Rating: ★★★/Recommended

Don Lorenzo Banana Flavored Rum (Bahamas); 30% abv, $13.
The neon gold, strikingly urine-like color can only be achieved through artificial coloring which the label confirms; sediment free. The banana-like aroma right after the pour is off-dry, subdued, and understated; with time in the glass the banana perfume becomes more akin to banana hard candy than to fresh fruit, but that's not to imply that it's unpleasant because, in actuality, it's mildly alluring. The palate entry is delightfully fruity and correctly ripe and sweet; by the midpalate stage the flavor is medium-rich, a bit honeyed, and very pleasant on the tongue. The aftertaste is moderately sweet, intensely banana-like, and very extended. Like its Coconut sibling, the flavoring doesn't completely overshadow the rum and as such affords far more pleasure and potential; makes a killer banana daiquiri.

2002 Rating: ★★★/Recommended

Don Lorenzo Coconut Flavored Rum (Bahamas); 30% abv, $13.
Exhibits an extremely pale flax/silver tint and excellent purity; no artificial coloring listed on the label. The properly sweet coconut meat nose at opening is carefree and welcoming; exposure to air over the span of an additional three to five minutes finds the coconut essence turning a tad sweeter and even a bit marshmallow-like. The palate entry seems a little unsure of itself as to whether it wants to be dry or sweet; then at midpalate the taste goes in the pleasant direction of sweetened, shredded coconut meat. The aftertaste is solid, correctly alcoholic, serenely coconut-like, and delightfully sweet. A good piña colada rum that doesn't go overboard with the coconut flavoring; nice job here.

2002 Rating: ★★★/Recommended

Don Lorenzo Dark Reserve Rum of the Bahamas (Bahamas); 40% abv, $15.
Attractive, new copper penny hue; absolute purity. This nose is far more aggressive and candied in the opening sniffing than either the Light Reserve or the Gold Reserve; the

middle stage whiffs offer scents of sugar cookies, mild spice, and semisweet toffee; the last run-through finds more developed aromas of honey and brown sugar; a decidedly bigger bouquet than those of its siblings but one that still shows restraint and a sense of balance. The palate entry is soft, marshmallowy sweet, and plump; the midpalate phase shows more of the spice and is nicely textured. The finish is medium long, semi-sweet, and vanilla wafer-like. A nimble dark.

2001 Rating: ★★★/Recommended

Don Lorenzo Gold Reserve Rum of the Bahamas (Bahamas); 40% abv, $13.

The pale amber hue is clean and pure. The opening nosing offers biscuity, vanilla wafer scents that are very inviting and soft, almost pillowy; the second and third sniffings add rum spirit, delicate holiday spices, and mellow honey; the fourth and last nosing pass finds soft vanilla bean; the overall impression of the bouquet is positive due mainly to its laid-back demeanor and sweet softness. The palate entry is fuzzy-warm, with supple, harmonious tastes of vanilla and spice; the midpalate owns an almost lazy approach to flavor as biscuity tastes of cookie batter, brown sugar, and honey enchant the taste buds. The aftertaste is medium long, undemanding, and mildly sweet. What's so delightful about this rum is that it doesn't feign being profound; it's simply a nice, easily quaffable, down-to-earth rum.

2001 Rating: ★★★/Recommended

Don Lorenzo Light Reserve Rum of the Bahamas (Bahamas); 40% abv, $13.

Clear white/silver and impeccably pure. The nose at opening displays semi-dry nuances of cane and marshmallow; the middle stage sniffings see the marshmallow aroma bumped up in prominence over the cane; the fourth and final nosing pass, following six minutes of aeration, adds subtle scents of vanilla bean and coconut. The palate entry is sure-footed, correctly sweet, and marshmallowy; the midpalate point shows a bit of fiery spirit on the tongue along with toasty flavors of vanilla bean and coconut. The finish is long, thick, and creamy, with a pleasant background hint of coconut. An easy-drinking, sweetish white rum that's recommendable.

2001 Rating: ★★★/Recommended

Don Lorenzo Mango Flavored Rum (Bahamas); 22.5% abv, $13.

The artificial color is orangy/honey/bright bronze and free from floating particles. The ripe mango fruit essence flows from the glass in huge, friendly waves in the initial two minutes of nosing; further aeration seems unnecessary as the concentrated ambrosial bouquet remains firm, very sweet, and unyielding in the later sniffings. The palate entry is not as sweet as I thought it would be in light of the chunky-sweet bouquet; by the midpalate point the ripe, if slightly manufactured, flavor of mango continues to dominate. The aftertaste flashes a bit of pineapple; drinkable and perfectly fine for mixing in punches. My biggest criticism is that at a feeble 45 proof there's no sense whatsoever that this is indeed a rum; on the positive side, it is neither cloying nor clumsy.

2002 Rating: ★★/Not Recommended

Don Perfil Añejo Rum (Mexico); 38% abv, $12.

Owns a very pretty, old copper penny color that's very much like an aged tawny porto; excellent purity. The out-of-the-gate aroma is very minerally/stony, with background notes of fruit; aeration encourages a pine-like, cigar tobacco scent that doesn't quite balance or suitably mingle with the shale/granite odor. The palate entry is sweet yet lean; the midpalate phase displays this rum's best, if meager, virtues in a sap-like taste that turn resiny in the finish. Drinkable, but wholly ordinary.

2005 Rating: ★★/Not Recommended

Don Perfil Cristal Rum (Mexico); 38% abv, $7.

Properly translucent and clean. Like its sister, Batacha Cristal, Don Perfil Cristal begins with the flurry of toasty, beany, lead-like scents, then after aeration the bouquet focuses on the bean character except in this case it seems more like cocoa bean than vanilla. The palate entry is rich, cocoa-like, and sweet; the midpalate stage offers tastes of vanilla extract, cola, and molasses. Ends up bittersweet and intensely flavorful.

2005 Rating: ★★★/Recommended

Doorly's XO Fine Old Barbados Rum (Barbados); 40% abv, $29.

Given a second round of maturation in old oloroso sherry casks from Spain. Very pretty as it sits in the sampling copita; brilliant topaz and absolutely pure. The opening nosings pick up flush scents of spice, oaky vanilla, and dark toffee; six more minutes of aeration go a long way in stimulating succulent aromas of tar, black raisins (perhaps an influence of the oloroso sherry butts?), and roasted almonds; this is a major league oak-aged rum bouquet with at least three layers of aromas. In the mouth this is a stately rum right from palate entry where it shows a semisweet side; the midpalate point displays toasty flavors of almond paste, spice, nougat, and dark honey. The finish is elegant, long, and semisweet. One of Barbados's classiest older rums.

2002 Rating: ★★★★/Highly Recommended

El Dorado Special Reserve 15 Year Old Demerara Rum (Guyana); 40% abv, $30.

Exceptionally pretty topaz/bronze hue; impeccable purity. The opening nosing pass is regal and shows deft touches of light caramel, light honey, and molasses; six more minutes of air contact releases lovely, exotic scents of tea leaves, tobacco, and old oak; a complex, multilayered and exquisite aged rum bouquet. The palate entry is dry to off-dry, focused, and mildly honeyed; the midpalate point is stately, medium-bodied and tastes of tar, tobacco, old oak and molasses. The aftertaste is long, bittersweet, brandy-like, and tastes of dark caramel. A true, bittersweet sipping rum that deserves a place in every serious spirits collection.

2003 Rating: ★★★★/Highly Recommended

English Harbour 5 Year Old Aged Antigua Rum (Antigua); 40% abv, $26.

The burnt gold/amber color is pretty; zero sediment seen. The zesty upfront aroma sparkles with forward notes of bark, oak, and brown sugar; additional time in the copita brings out deeper scents of bacon fat, sautéed banana, and maple. The palate entry is creamy, toffee-like, and extremely silky and sensual; the midpalate stage offers seamless baked flavors of pastry, chocolate fudge, nougat, chestnut, and honey. Finishes harmoniously as the sweet flavor is gracefully melded to the texture. A perfect oak-aged molasses rum.

2006 Rating: ★★★★★/Highest Recommendation

Fazenda Mae de Ouro (Brazil); 40% abv, $28/liter.

Perfectly transparent and flawlessly clean. The first inhalations detect synthetic-like aromas that are clean, fiber- and hemp-like, and, to a lesser degree, vegetal; later sniffs following aeration encounter scents of ink, cardboard, guava, and nylon. The palate entry is disconcertingly aggressive and sugary sweet after the controlled bouquet; the midpalate stage is more settled down but still assertively and cloyingly sweet and cane-like to the point of exclusion. Ends up rowdy, intensely spirity, and caney sweet. It's nowhere near horrible, but it is rough around the edges. Try it in a caipirinha where it works.

2006 Rating: ★★/Not Recommended

Flor de Caña Centenario 12 Year Old Rum (Nicaragua); 40% abv, $27.

The lovely bronze/butterscotch color delights the eye; impeccable purity. The aroma after the pour offers succulent, dried fruit, and nut notes that enchant the olfactory sense; further exposure to air stimulates scents of oak, black raisins, cinnamon, prunes, vanilla bean, and a trace of honey. The palate entry is stately, poised, and semisweet; by the midpalate point the taste profile features lip-smacking flavors of nougat, almond butter, molasses, and sherry. Finishes as elegantly and fully as it started. One of the finest examples of extra aged rums one can find.

2004 Rating: ★★★★/Highly Recommended

Flor de Caña Centenario 21 Year Old Limited Edition Rum (Nicaragua); 40% abv, $60.

Very attractive and brandy-like topaz/copper color; impeccable purity. The initial two sniffings pick up delectably rich aromas of oaky vanilla, cigar ash, cocoa butter and oil; seven additional minutes resting in the copita greatly deepen and enhance the existing aromas as they clearly meld with extended air contact, making the aroma a lovely, stately, buttery bouquet of the first rank; I absolutely love it. The palate entry is opulent, viscous, caramel-like and moderately sweet; the midpalate point features toasty, tobacco-like tastes that are complemented by the thick, chewy texture. The aftertaste is long, riveting, candied/honeyed, mature, and sophisticated. One of the best rums I've come across in the last two years; elevates Flor de Caña to superstar status; outstanding.

2003 Rating: ★★★★★/Highest Recommendation

Flor de Caña Centenario Gold 18 Years Old (Nicaragua); 40% abv, $30.

Deep bronze/topaz in color; ideal purity. The first nosing passes encounter reed- and vegetation-like scents that are green; further exposure to air helps this aroma become a bouquet as the greenness blows off, leaving behind more classical and, therefore, appealing fragrances of oak, medium-sweet cane, escarole, pine cone, and new leather. The palate entry is long, lovely, and medium-sweet; the midpalate stage is where this rum makes its mark as finely layered tastes of cocoa butter, palm oil, oaky vanilla, light honey, and almond paste enthrall the taste buds. Concludes silky smooth, mildly sweet, and more honey-like and biscuity than in the midpalate stage. Flor de Caña's mystique continues.

2006 Rating: ★★★★/Highly Recommended

Foursquare Spiced Rum (Barbados); 35% abv, $18.

The harvest gold/amber color is pretty and free from any type of debris. The initial nosing pass unearths all kinds of intriguing scents from clove to nutmeg to cinnamon to honey; the second whiff focuses more on the spice than the sweetness, alluding to what one normally describes as "holiday spices", as in fruit cake, spiced cider, cookies, and the like; the penultimate sniffing adds a welcome dash of citrus rind to the aromatic mix; the final nosing pass, following a full twelve minutes of aeration, loses not one whit of potency or vibrancy and, indeed, seems to deepen into a round, almost biscuity fragrance; at the end, I really came around to the bouquet as a whole entity. The palate entry is soft, smooth, spicy sweet and most inviting; the midpalate develops a broader, more rum-like flavor and mouth presence as the spirit at last takes command, revealing itself to be the foundational component upon which the spices and other natural flavoring dance. The finish is sweet, yet zesty and spicy enough to be balanced and warming. A natural and completely viable marketplace rival of category leading Captain Morgan.

2000 Rating: ★★★/Recommended

Gosling's Family Reserve Old Rum (Bermuda); 40% abv, $70.
The lovely cherry wood/mahogany/old tawny color gives a textbook appearance for an old oak-aged rum; perfect purity. The enticing first aromas offer expressive notes of quinine, baked apple, and molasses; further aeration brings out tart-to-sour scents of brown sugar, dried red berry fruit, tree bark, and allspice; the bouquet changes dramatically within the ten minute nosing period, going from a baked aroma to an earthy/spicy/woodsy aroma. The palate entry is smooth, intensely oaky/resiny, yet semisweet; at midpalate the sweetness component picks up in the forms of honey and molasses. Concludes elegantly, satiny smooth in the throat, and properly bittersweet.

2005 Rating: ★★★★/Highly Recommended

Gosling's Gold Bermuda Rum (Bermuda); 40% abv, $18.
Pale orange/light copper hue; excellent clarity. The opening sniffings pick up moderately burnt/baked notes of caramelized sugar and burnt match; later inhalations detect deeper scents of saddle leather, light maple, and molasses. The palate entry is pleasingly sweet and intensely rum-like; at midpalate the sweetness diminishes slightly as a more bittersweet element takes command, emitting flavors of maple, molasses, vanilla bean, and cinnamon. Ends up shyly, but agreeably spicy.

2005 Rating: ★★★/Recommended

Grand 'kaz Original Amber Rum (Martinique); 40% abv, $29.
The honey gold appearance is cloudy; while relatively free of large sediment, it is nonetheless dull and milky; not a compelling appearance. The opening sniffs detect soft, earthy, almost viney/vegetal scents that are even a touch smoky; with further aeration the aroma takes on a grassy/caney odor that's dry, vegetal and pleasing, in that it's true to the base material. The palate entry is sharp and biting on the tongue, then keenly bittersweet and vanilla bean-like; at the midpalate stage the taste develops more of an authentic agricole personality as the flavors become bittersweet to semisweet, definitely caney, and a touch honeyed. Ends on a grassy/green note that's more dry than bittersweet. Nowhere near as exciting as the Martinique rhums of Neisson and La Favorite, but certainly recommendable.

2006 Rating: ★★★/Recommended

Grand Havana Rum Reserva Excelencia Batch No. 1106 (Grenada); 40% abv, $26.
Made by the talented distillers at Westerhall Distillery which produces one of my favorite rums, Westerhall Plantation (★★★★). Light, pale amber color, the warm, almost honey tone of a barrel-fermented chardonnay; excellent purity. The opening nosing pass offers stately, classic scents of brown sugar and molasses; aeration stimulates further fragrances including honey, light toffee, and maple; a well-integrated bouquet. The palate entry is deliciously sweet and honey-like but light and agile on the tongue; by the midpalate point the taste profile adds flavors of milk chocolate and caramel. The aftertaste is very long, medium-bodied, and moderately sweet. The best feature of this savory rum is the balance between the nimble sweetness and the cruiserweight texture.
2003 Rating: ★★★★/Highly Recommended

GRM Silver Small Batch 2 Year Old Aged Artesian Cachaça (Brazil); 41% abv, $67.
Attractive, gray/green/pale yellow color; good clarity. The opening aroma is most peculiar, giving off oddly metallic, if incongruous, scents of steel nails, aluminum foil, polythene plastic, and oatmeal; additional aeration doesn't help the situation much as the sickly sweet odor goes minty, rotting banana- and cat box-like. The palate entry is sweet, sap-like, and totally unappealing in its herbal/metallic nature; the midpalate stage is just as mousy and funky as the entry. Concludes in the same sickly sweet manner as it began. Horrible.
2005 Rating: ★/Not Recommended

Hang Loose Coconut Rum (USA); 20% abv, $15.
Exemplary pale straw/yellow, flawlessly clean appearance. The opening aroma is somewhat like sweetened coconut, but then does this weird, fuzzy, just-out-of-the-dryer fabric thing that is very synthetic and therefore stunningly unappealing; following aeration other fun aromas like plastic trash bin and rice pudding get involved, making this a completely forgettable aromatic experience of the lower ranks. Flavorwise, the entry is moderately appealing, emitting juicy, gummy sweet tastes of confectioner's sugar and sweetened coconut out of the can; at midpalate the sweet, manufactured, tinny/metallic coconut taste heads south faster than a chicken with firecrackers tied to its tail. A fumbling, bumbling nightmare that should never have been released to the marketplace.
2005 Rating: ★/Not Recommended

Hang Loose Kauai Dark Rum (USA); 40% abv, $15.
The topaz/harvest gold color shows an inconsequential bit of sediment; nothing to affect the rating. The initial aromatic blast is lacking in charm and substance and comes off as a simple just off-the-column still scent; aeration does nothing to help this aroma round off or deepen. The palate entry is mildly sweet and brown sugar-like; by midpalate the flavor turns a touch more woody and honeyed, but not enough to make it recommendable. Finishes mildly pleasant and sweet. Ordinary, drinkable, but nothing more.
2005 Rating: ★★/Not Recommended

Hang Loose Kauai Light Rum (USA); 40% abv, $15.
Impeccably pure and clean in its silvery translucence. In the first nosing passes, the stony/slate-like/seed-like aroma almost has me thinking "vodka" more than "rum", but then following the aeration period the bouquet turns properly pod- and cane-like, in fact, almost fruity in its bearing; I wasn't sure what was happening aromatically in the first couple of minutes but then I really came around to this atypical mineral and fruit aroma. The taste profile has molasses written all over it as the flavor starts out bittersweet and yeasty; by midpalate the rustic flavor becomes sour yet succulent in its tartness. Concludes on a bittersweet note. Has none of the über-polish of, say a Bacardi Silver, and that's precisely why I'm recommending it.
2005 Rating: ★★★/Recommended

Hang Loose Mango Rum (USA); 20% abv, $15.
Superb clarity and flawless appearance. The opening aroma offers solid, tart mango scent, then after another six minutes of aeration the aroma turns riper; it's not a deep or layered bouquet, but it does exhibit ample mango authenticity. Tastewise, Hang Loose Mango displays pleasant fruitiness, moderate sweetness, even a touch of coconut (is that supposed to be there?) in the entry and turns juicy at midpalate. Finishes sweet, ripe, friendly, and more than drinkable. Not a profound flavored rum, but a good one.
2005 Rating: ★★★/Recommended

Hang Loose Pineapple Rum (USA); 20% abv, $15.
Clear and clean. The nose after the pour is strange beyond belief, giving off remarkably sour and rancid odors of footlocker, solvent, curdled milk, and floor wax; several more minutes in the glass serve only to make matters worse; the aroma is so bad that I feel trepidation at tasting it; skip the bouquet. The flavor menu offers entry tastes of canned pineapple with the emphasis on the can; the midpalate stage fares slightly better as some mild pineapple chunk flavor shows up for work. Ends dismally in a semisweet, manufactured heap. I have found through my evaluations that pineapple is one of the most notoriously difficult flavors to get right. This spirit, which is as charming as a mid-cheek pimple on the night of your big date, proves my point. $15 is $15 too expensive.
2005 Rating: ★/Not Recommended

Havana Club Puerto Rican Rum (Puerto Rico); 40% abv, $20.
Flawlessly clean and clear. The nose after the pour is tanky, musty, and mushroomy; further air contact turns at least some of the funkiness into beanniness, meaning legumes, such as chickpeas, lentils, kidney beans rather than bittersweet beans, like coffee or cocoa bean; an odd, burnt, damp earth aroma to understate the situation. The palate entry is harsh, raw, and metallic; the midpalate leans to a moderately semisweetness, but ends up being dominated by the tanky, metallic flavor that's like licking a coin. As a silver rum, it's a disaster in the bottle.
2007 Rating: ★/Not Recommended

Inner Circle Green Spot Traditional Pot Still Rum (Australia); 57.2% abv, $24.
The rich copper/russet color is dazzling; absolutely pure. The initial sniffings detect muscular, high-octane aromas of spirit, molasses, bacon fat, and honey; aeration unleashes

additional, very complex scents of old oak, brown butter, and walnuts; this is a monster bouquet that's simultaneously intimidating and alluring. The spicy, biscuity, cake-like palate entry (undiluted) is sweet in a baked manner, almost like the taste of a spiked coffee cake; the midpalate is a raging inferno of concentrated molasses/brown sugar/oak tastes and four-alarm spirit. The finish is loaded with peppery spice, oaky vanilla, maple syrup/molasses, pipe tobacco, and honey. Inner Circle Green Spot might be too powerful for many drinkers, but when cut with spring water by one-third, it still provides a stunning rum experience of the first order and turns remarkably chocolaty. A beautiful and affordable beast.

2003 Rating: ★★★★★/Highest Recommendation

Kahlua Kuya Fusion Rum Flavored With Spices, Citrus and Other Flavors (USA); 35% abv, $13.

Pretty amber tone; ideal purity. The initial nosings pick up a pleasantly sweet and amiable aroma that's equal parts vanilla, cola nut, citrus, and cinnamon; six more minutes in the glass doesn't alter the first findings at all. The palate entry is soda pop-like, in that, it's very vanilla cola-like and sugary; by midpalate the citrus element kicks in adding, at least, something of a balance to the sugary sweetness. The finish resembles the midpalate. While adequately drinkable for young, unsophisticated consumers who were weaned on sugary colas, there's no sense of rum in Kuya which is my major objection to it; it could have been better and didn't have to be such a no-brainer.

2003 Rating: ★★/Not Recommended

Kingston Coconut Rum (West Indies); 24% abv, $9/liter.

Crystal clear and silvery pure. There's absolutely no debate as to what the flavoring is as detected in the first round of sniffing; it is sweetened, shredded coconut all the way; six more minutes in the glass don't really open up new areas of aromatic territory and, as such, leave me feeling slightly disappointed. The palate entry is coconut-like and more bittersweet than sweet; at midpalate the bittersweet taste includes a touch of cocoa. Finishes smoothly, sweet, and concentrated on the sweetened coconut. A one-note song that would be better, meaning recommendable, if the flavoring dial was turned to a lower setting; that said, it's drinkable and suitable for mixing.

2005 Rating: ★★/Not Recommended

La Favorite Coeur de Canne Rhum Agricole Blanc Appelation d'Origine Controlée (Martinique); 50% abv, $28/liter.

The crystalline appearance is silvery and flawless. The first whiffs are confronted with rich, spirity (though neither hot nor prickly), and grassy aromas that seem melded and harmonious; it's a wonder what another seven minutes do to the fragrance as the bouquet turns spicy/peppery, moderately oily, cucumber-like, and properly and delectably cane-like; love this cutting-edge agricole perfume. Oh man, this bittersweet, raw cocoa-like rhum deftly dances on the tongue at entry; the midpalate stage is sweeter than the entry and multilayered with tastes of marshmallow, refined sugar, vanilla cake frosting, and flan. Finishes divinely sweet, remarkably balanced (considering the lofty abv), grassy/floral, and even at the tail end fruity. Wow, what a classic! Yet another reason why rhum agricoles are poised to be the next wave in clear spirits.

2005 Rating: ★★★★★/Highest Recommendation

La Favorite Rhum Agricole Ambré Appelation d'Origine Controlée (Martinique); 50% abv, $36/liter.

The color is pale amber/dusty gold; blemish-free purity. The curious opening bouquet reminds me of beeswax, green peppers, and uncooked broccoli; further aeration time of six minutes helps the aroma to unfold as it offers distinct scents of toasted marshmallow, light toffee, yeasty sourdough, green olives, and brine; an entire universe of disparate, yet strangely agreeable aromas in one single glass. The palate entry is semisweet, honeyed, and even a bit sherry-like; at midpalate there's a spirity thrust that makes the tongue prickle amidst the tastes of spice, honey, sherry, caramel, and nougat. Concludes rich, oily, concentrated, and wonderfully creamy. Another Martinique rhum god.

2005 Rating: ★★★★★/Highest Recommendation

La Favorite Rhum Agricole Vieux Appelation d'Origine Controlée (Martinique); 40% abv, $48/liter.

Aged in French and American oak barrels for a minimum of three years. The brilliant bronze/tawny/deep amber color is an eyeful; ideal purity. My initial impressions of the nose are of dried red fruits and marzipan; later sniffings after aeration pick up deeper, more brandy-like aromas of oaky vanilla, rum cake, holiday fruitcake, black pepper, cigar tobacco, and a hint of nutmeg. The palate entry is long, sweet, and moderately oily; the midpalate boasts flavors of butter cream, dark chocolate, cream sherry, cola, citrus, and honey. Ends on a sweet caramel-like note that is opulent yet agile. Dark, oak-aged rum at its finest.

2005 Rating: ★★★★★/Highest Recommendation

Leblon White Cachaça Rum (Brazil); 40% abv, $30.

Very faint pale straw tint; flawless purity. Hearty scents of damp hay/wet grass and linseed oil fill the copita; further time in the glass brings out more vegetal/leathery/sap-like aromas that are not the least bit sweet; this bouquet oozes authenticity and a sense of place. It's in the palate entry that the first burst of sugarcane sweetness emerges and that's a welcome development; the midpalate is caney sweet and medium-bodied, with enough notes of oil and spice to make it easily recommendable. Finishes grassy, semisweet, and spirity. Nice job here.

2006 Rating: ★★★/Recommended

Malibu Caribbean Rum with Banana Flavor (Canada); 21% abv, $15.

Clear but with a slight pewter-like tint. First whiff displays muted banana, almost banana skin-like more than banana flesh-like; later sniffs detect softly pulpy, paper-like notes that are neither dry nor sweet, just neutral. At palate entry, there's a pleasing upfront ripeness that can be described as medium-sweet but only mildly banana-like; the banana flavoring picks up momentum at midpalate and carries the taste profile forward into the aftertaste, which is angular, if slightly metallic, but too *faux* banana-like for its own good. Drinkable, but the flavor tastes like, well, banana flavoring, not real-deal banana. I expected more from this brand.

2007 Rating: ★★/Not Recommended

Malibu Caribbean Rum with Natural Coconut Flavor (Canada); 21% abv, $14.

Limpid and impeccably clean. The nose after the pour emits weak-in-the-knees scents of distant coconut and gunmetal; seven minutes of aeration time is wasted on this rum/liqueur. The palate entry features a weird taste that's kind of like parchment and kind of like metal and kind of like shredded coconut; at midpalate the coconut taste makes a better showing as the flavor turns sweet; finishes soft and a touch plump. Nowhere on the label does it say "Liqueur" which I feel that it is at 21% abv. It ridiculously and inappropriately says "Caribbean Rum". Puh-leeeze. So be it. Malibu is a brainlessly pleasant quaff whose strong suit is its mixability. Captain Morgan's Parrot Bay (★★★) and Cruzan Coconut (★★★★) both run rings around Malibu.

2004 Rating: ★★/Not Recommended

Malibu Caribbean Rum with Natural Mango Flavor (Canada); 21% abv, $14.

Silvery clear and pure. The nose is intensely fruity and ripe in the first stages; exposure to air adds a subtle note of spice. The palate entry offers simple, off-dry to semisweet flavors of mango; at midpalate the flavor profile stays the course, remaining appropriately fruity, without being overly sweet or ripe. Concludes softly and gently sweet, with a slight hint of honey.

2004 Rating: ★★★/Recommended

Malibu Caribbean Rum with Natural Pineapple Flavor (Canada); 21% abv, $14.

Pure and translucent. The initial whiffs pick up the kind of canned and sweetened pineapple fragrance that's manufactured and unappealing; time in the glass unfortunately doesn't afford the chance for aromatic redemption. The palate entry is pleasantly fruity, moderately sweet and quite refreshing, if simple; at midpalate the taste profile plays a one-note chorus of canned pineapple. Ends quietly and semisweet. While drinkable and inoffensive, the pineapple flavoring never reaches beyond a tinny quality that doesn't resemble fresh fruit.

2004 Rating: ★★/Not Recommended

Malibu Passion Fruit Caribbean Rum (Canada); 21% abv, $14.

Limpid but with barely perceptible specks of debris floating about. In the opening nosing, there's no hesitation in deciding that the ripe and sweet flavoring component is passion fruit; for a concoction such as this, aeration plays a minor role in the nosing phase: it's passion fruit, now and forever, case closed. The palate entry is gently sweet, not syrupy at all, and properly passion fruit-like; the midpalate stage shows a light reining in of the flavor as the passion fruit turns mild, smooth, and pleasant, if simple. Ends up ripe, adequately sweet, and controlled. Considering the low alcohol level, the flavoring agent could have run amok but didn't. As it is, this is a better than average flavoring job.

2005 Rating: ★★★/Recommended

Marti Autentico Mojito Licor de Ron Cuban Style Rum with Natural Lime & Mint (West Indies); 40% abv, $14.

The pale green/gray tint is appealing and immaculate. The initial nosing pass reveals delicate scents of what comes across as key lime and gentle mint (spearmint?); the second and third sniffings, following several minutes of aeration, find the mint beginning to overshadow the lime in a polite manner; the final pass sees the reemergence of the lime component; a delicate and harmonious perfume that's devoid of any spirit influence. The palate entry features the mint; but then at midpalate a ripe, sweet (like Rose's) taste of lime takes the helm and dominates well into the finish which is brief, citrusy, and pleasantly bittersweet. A definite mixer designed to complement such beverages as cola, club soda, and juices; even though this rum-based libation is 80 proof (40% alcohol) the alcohol is hardly noticed; nice job here.

2001 Rating: ★★★/Recommended

Marti Coco Suave Licor de Ron Rum with Natural Coconut Flavor (USA); 41.4% abv, $13.

Clear, clean, unblemished appearance. The first aromatic impression is positive as scents of unsweetened coconut and vanilla extract delight the olfactory sense; with time in the glass, the fragrance deepens as the coconut presence turns more oily and essence-like; unlike some coconut flavored rums, this is not a frivolous spirit. The palate entry is intensely coconut-like and medium-bodied; the midpalate flavor profile highlights the sweetened coconut more than the vanilla, making it a perfect ingredient for pina coladas and other coconut-driven cocktails. The aftertaste is surprisingly elegant and reined-in. I like the fact that the alcohol level is more than the standard issue 30% to 35% for flavored rums. The alcohol gives this rum the heft and gravitas that many flavored rums are missing.

2005 Rating: ★★★★/Highly Recommended

Maui Dark Rum (Hawaii); 40% abv, $17.

The cola/black coffee/mahogany appearance is pretty. I can tell immediately that this hails from the same distiller as the Braddah rums from Maui as the disgustingly phenolic aromas of creosote, urinal, and pepper waft from the sampling glass, thereby destroying all plant life in my office; leaving this rum in the glass for several minutes to gain its footing is wasted time. The palate entry screams "caramel coloring" as the taste displays some very minor, dry, sugary appeal; the midpalate is dry and tastes of three day old black coffee. The finish is…well, who cares at this point? Miserable and rancid-tasting. I once lived on Maui for six months, but I refuse to have this hog swill spoil that idyllic memory. But, hey, other than that….

2005 Rating: ★/Not Recommended

Montecristo 12 Year Old Rum (Guatemala); 40% abv, $30.

Gorgeous medium amber/honey hue; ideal purity. The first two nosing passes pick up very little in the way of aromatic impact; aeration releases meager scents of sugar cane and apple; I'm not saying that the bouquet is a negative, it's just not that big a factor. The palate entry is rich, snappy, mildly hot, and spirity; by the midpalate juncture the flavors have exploded on the tongue in fat waves of light caramel, molasses, honey, charred oak, tobacco leaf, and vanilla. The finish is textured, warming, fat, and damn near chewy. A dynamite older rum that's loaded with elegance and substance and is easily one of the best rums I've tasted so far this year. A splendid cigar companion due to the charred oak presence.

2002 Rating: ★★★★/Highly Recommended

Montecristo Spiced Rum (Guatemala); 35% abv, $19.
Pretty honey/amber color; excellent purity. Smells of bubble gum, molasses, brown sugar, and cinnamon in the front-end sniffing; aeration tamps down the molasses and bubble gum and highlights the brown sugar and cinnamon combination that ends up being a touch herbal at the end. Entry is fat and sugary sweet, but with enough cinnamon bitterness to offset the sweetness; the midpalate point is punctuated by a plumpness and soft spiciness that I find myself liking more than the critical side of my brain believes I should. The finish makes my decision for my divided gray matter by coming off a touch abrasive and waxy, thereby pulling this rum into Not Recommended territory. This rum should have been better.
2007 Rating: ★★/Not Recommended

Montecristo White Rum (Guatemala); 40% abv, $15.
Slightly dull, pewter-like appearance; average clarity. Opening whiffs pick up strong notes of molasses, hemp/rope, and black pepper; additional time in the glass stimulates faint aromas of yeast/bakery and cocoa bean. Entry is pleasingly, if simply sweet and sugary; the midpalate phase offers little other than a mild reinforcement of the entry sweetness, but there's no depth here. Finishes short and sweet. Easy drinking, but wholly common and uninteresting.
2007 Rating: ★★/Not Recommended

Monymusk 8 Year Old Rum (Jamaica); 46% abv, $44.
The translucent, unblemished appearance boasts a wine-like pale straw yellow hue. The vibrant aroma leaps from the sampling glass in zesty, floral, and near-prickly waves in the initial nosing pass, then settles down slightly in the second sniffing as the spirit recedes, allowing the floral/vegetal perfume to advance to the forefront of the bouquet; by the third whiff, after six minutes of air contact, the aroma of ripe green pepper playfully mingles with subtler scents of sugar cane syrup, cucumber, cinnamon, and cocoa; in the fourth and final nosing pass the vegetal presence overshadows all other aromas; not the ending I'd hoped for, but clean and brisk nonetheless. The palate entry is lean, even austere in its dryness and narrow focus; then at midpalate the flavors explode like fireworks in a dizzying array of bittersweet tastes, from black pepper to cocoa bean to vanilla bean to simple syrup. The finish is intensely kernel-like and beany, with just a hint of bittersweetness. This uneven, but ultimately charming rum keeps you guessing from start to finish; the underlying virtues are solid enough for a recommendation.
2000 Rating: ★★★/Recommended

Mount Gay Barbados Sugar Cane Rum (Barbados); 40% abv, $19.
The honey/medium amber color is pretty and absolutely pure. The nose at opening is intensely sweet and candied; the second pass detects a touch of smoke and truckloads of sugar cane; the pleasant sweet-fest continues in the third sniffing as delicate touches of oil and mild spice appear; the final whiff offers nothing new and serves to reinforce the well-established candied, sugary bouquet. Very sweet and milky at palate entry; the midpalate stage is a symphony of sugary, chocolaty flavors that envelop the tongue in a friendly manner; what I responded to most favorably was the milky quality in the mouth. The finish is long, sweet, and honeyed. Another solidly made, wholly recommendable rum from the Mount Gay stable.
2000 Rating: ★★★/Recommended

Mount Gay Eclipse Barbados Rum (Barbados); 40% abv, $16.

The pretty amber/light honey color is pure. The soft sugary/molasses smell in the first whiffs is round, mellow, and gently sweet; further air contact releases aromas that include marshmallow, almond paste, and light toffee. The palate entry is slightly smoky and properly sweet; the midpalate phase highlights flavors of honey and vanilla extract. Finishes smooth, soft, and eminently drinkable. A well-made molasses-based rum that will always be an emblem of Barbados.

2005 Rating: ★★★/Recommended

Mount Gay Extra Old Barbados Rum (Barbados); 40% abv, $30.

The lovely bronze/burnished orange color impresses the eye; perfect purity. Lots going on here in the initial minutes of sniffing, including well-defined scents of treacle, spice, and late summer flower garden; further aeration brings out drier, meatier aromas of black pepper, cola nut, dried red fruit, and molasses. The palate entry is long and toffee-like; at midpalate there's a turn to honeyed, apple butter-like, and creamy flavors that add zesty spice in the aftertaste.

2005 Rating: ★★★★/Highly Recommended

Mount Gay Mango Flavored Rum (Barbados); 32% abv, $16.

Translucent and flawlessly pure. The first whiffs detect unexpected aromas of lead pencil, baking bread, baked pear, and, can this be right?, brown butter; in the later passes, buttery hints of mango finally make an appearance; I really like this peculiar bouquet for its intense off-dry cleanness. The mango core flavor is detected quite clearly in the palate entry, and then it makes a slightly bigger fruity splash at midpalate. Concludes mildly sweet and fruity. A classy fruit flavored rum that gains momentum with time.

2005 Rating: ★★★/Recommended

Mount Gay Special Reserve Barbados Rum (Barbados); 40% abv, $18.

The translucent, pale straw tint is clean, clear and pure. The opening sniffing detects a restrained, modest aroma of molasses; with time in the glass, the aroma gradually unfolds, revealing in the second nosing a mild vegetal quality (cucumber? wetland grasses?); following seven minutes of exposure to air, the aroma expands slightly in the third whiff in the form of oiliness, as in seed oil; the fourth and final whiff picks up little more in the way of aromatic expansion, but remains firm and mildly sweet. On the palate at entry, there's a keenly sweet and sugary taste that's welcoming and warm, but simplistic; the midpalate phase sees a bit of taste layering as moderate flavors of spice, molasses, and honey vie for dominance. The aftertaste is smooth, silky, and to-the-point. Drinkable, easy, and uncomplicated.

2000 Rating: ★★★/Recommended

Mount Gay Vanilla Flavored Rum (Barbados); 32% abv, $16.

Clean as a whistle and clear. The first sniffing encounters a fully endowed frontline aroma of vanilla bean; additional minutes in the glass only serve to bolster the pleasingly perfumed vanilla bouquet. The palate entry displays the adeptness of the blender as the moderately sweet vanilla bean flavor maintains its focus by not careening off into overly sweet or biscuity territory; at midpalate the taste actually turns crisp and properly acidic as

the flavor profile goes from moderately sweet to bittersweet and beany. Finishes in a satiny texture and a rich, vanilla bean taste. Really good blending here.
2005 Rating: ★★★★/Highly Recommended

Murray McDavid Guyana Rum 1990 Distilled at Enmore-Versailles Viognier Wine Cask Finish (Guyana); 46% abv, $76.

The brilliant wheat/honey color is warm and flawlessly clean. The initial sniffs detect a vividly spirity aroma that is flecked with subtle scents of salted butter, green vegetable, and apple peel; there's quite a lot of fruit presence in this rum during both aromatic passes; the second phase turns slightly sweeter and more complex, even peppery as the bouquet deepens. The palate entry is peppery/spicy, nougaty, and bittersweet; at the midpalate stage the taste profile offers multiple layers of flavor, including baked pear, white raisins, maple, and molasses. Ends up gracefully elegant and spiced, with subtle elements of ripe grapes/raisins.
2006 Rating: ★★★★/Highly Recommended

Murray McDavid Guyana Rum 1991 Distilled at Uitvlught-Port Morant Syrah Wine Cask Finish (Guyana); 46% abv, $71.

The intriguing color runs from salmon to pink to burnt orange to soft copper; some sediment seen from the small sample bottle, but that's something that tighter filtration can easily correct. The initial inhalations pick up clear influences from the syrah as the first scents out of the gate are winey, ripe, and very grape-like; as the bouquet opens up with the air contact, the spirit starts to emerge and balance nicely with the oak/syrah/fruit elements, creating a sophisticated rum perfume that's both powerful and elegant. The palate entry is satiny, medium-sweet, and pear-like; it's during the midpalate stage where this rum takes flight as fruit flavors of baked pear, pineapple, and grapes meld to honey sweet tastes of cane spirit; the combination works well. Concludes medium-sweet, very smooth, and cake-like.
2006 Rating: ★★★★★/Highest Recommendation

Murray McDavid Jamaica Rum 1992 Distilled at Hampden Port Cask Finish (Jamaica); 46% abv, $80.

The appearance flashes a rather dullish color of peach; excellent clarity. The aggressive opening aroma conveys uninviting and incongruous impressions of sautéed onion, rancid butter, and cigarette smoke—not an awe-inspiring beginning; additional aeration time unleashes feral scents of seaweed, tidal pond, smelly cheeses, vinyl, synthetic fibers, and black pepper. The palate entry is better than the off-base aroma as it offers zesty flavors of tobacco leaf, sea salt, and mildly sweet oak; the midpalate stage delivers a taste profile that includes disparate flavors of beeswax, lip salve, popcorn, palm oil, lanolin, and ruby port. Finishes strangely and inexplicably appealing with tastes of wax, tobacco, port, and seaweed, wrapped in an oily texture. Islay-meets-Jamaica-meets-Douro is the only way I can describe this curiously fascinating oddball that displays more personalities than Sybil.
2006 Rating: ★★★/Recommended

Murray McDavid Trinidad Rum 1993 Distilled at Caroni Madeira Cask Finish (Trinidad); 46% abv, $65.

The pale amber/light honey color is pretty and unblemished by sediment/debris. After the pour, the nose is directed, spicy, lean, and cream soda-like; there's not much in the way of aromatic expansion following further aeration time. The palate entry is lovely in its delicacy and focused, cocoa-like bittersweet taste; the midpalate edges more towards cane-like/molasses sweetness as well as oakiness, with a vanilla taste emerging at the finish as one of the primary influences. Ends up with flavors of prunes/dates, fudge, vanilla bean, and cocoa. Complex and compelling in the entry, midpalate, and aftertaste and would have garnered a fifth rating star had the bouquet been more defined.

2006 Rating: ★★★★/Highly Recommended

Myers's Rum Original Dark (Jamaica); 40% abv, $19.

The mocha/walnut brown color is lovely, deep, and sherry-like; absolute purity. The initial inhalations within the two minute mark after the pour expose a moderately spicy, black peppercorn perfume that fills the glass; six more minutes of aeration bring about notes that include flax/textiles/linen, cooked vegetables, and an underpinning scent of brown sugar. The palate entry provides a graceful platform flavor that is semisweet and intensely cocoa-like; at midpalate the taste leaps ahead into deeper cocoa/bittersweet chocolate territory before turning lean and keenly bittersweet, fatty/oily, and chocolaty in the finish (which is this rum's best phase). The lackluster, textile-ish aroma holds all sorts of problems for me, but ultimately the sleek fineness of the flavor and aftertaste stages make enough of an impact to allow me to recommend it. When looked upon in the same group as the Bacardi Select, there is no question that this is a better rum.

2004 Rating: ★★★/Recommended

N.O. New Orleans Extra Premium White Rum (USA); 40% abv, $11.

Limpid, but appearance suffers from too much floating debris. The opening two sniffings offer acrid aromas of diesel fuel, motor oil and turpentine with just the slightest hint of brown sugar; aeration helps the bouquet only marginally as the sharp bitterness turns more chocolaty and dark cocoa-like; the bouquet improves modestly with air contact. The palate entry flavors are intensely bittersweet and cocoa-like; at midpalate the taste actually becomes pleasantly biscuity, molasses-like, and honeyed. The aftertaste is concentrated and bittersweet to the point of making one's lips purse, kind of like high content cocoa dark chocolate. While obviously a rough- around-the-edges rum, the core flavor from entry through finish raise it to two star status.

2002 Rating: ★★/Not Recommended

Neisson Rhum Agricole Blanc Appelation d'Origine Controlée (Martinique); 50% abv, $30/liter.

Transparent, silvery, and impeccably clean. The frontline aroma is marvelously beany, grassy, and stalk-like; in the later sniffings the aroma turns more baked/burnt and charcoal-like, as sweetish flavors of dark caramel, chimney soot, and dark, old honey make for scrumptious inhaling. The palate entry is spectacularly honeyed, warm, and cocoa-like; at midpalate there's a grassy/weedy/cane-like taste that balances the honeyed sweetness in perfect style and grace. Concludes cocoa-like, intense yet smooth, and memorably sweet. A clinic on how to make outstanding white rum from sugar cane juice.

2005 Rating: ★★★★★/Highest Recommendation

Neisson Rhum Agricole Elevé Sous Bois Appelation d'Origine Controlée (Martinique); 50% abv, $41/liter.

The color is honey gold/sauternes yellow; flawlessly clean. In the first nosings there are fabric-like aromas of synthetic, cotton, and rayon; secondary sniffings pick up vegetal scents of peas and asparagus plus a waxy/floor polish background note. The palate entry is pointed, pleasantly spirity, and lightly toffee-like; the midpalate flavor profile features dead-on tastes of cane, honey, and vanilla bean. Ends on an off-dry note that offers smooth, biscuity, and grassy flavors deep in the throat. A picture of rhum agricole elegance and understatement.

2005 Rating: ★★★★/Highly Recommended

Neisson Rhum Agricole Réserve Spéciale Appelation d'Origine Controlée (Martinique); 42% abv, $65/liter.

Gloriously bright copper color; ideal purity. The first whiffs detect agile scents of white pepper, citrus, and saddle leather; following seven minutes of air contact the bouquet ratchets up the volume in the forms of old oak, sautéed almonds, candied walnuts, old library, and distant oloroso sherry. The palate entry is rich, nutty, oaky, and long; the midpalate bursts with woody, sherried, honeyed, vanilla extract flavors that keep multiplying and deepening. Finishes opulent, fathomless, honeyed, and elegant. Holy moly.

2005 Rating: ★★★★★/Highest Recommendation

Origine Caribbean Amber Estate Reserve Rum (British West Indies); 40% abv, $27.

A blend of rums from Demerara, Barbados, Jamaica, and Trinidad. The bright bronze/ burnished orange color is impeccably clean and free from sediment. The nose after the pour is largely closed down, emitting only timid scents of mild spice; aeration time doesn't release much more in the bouquet, except for distant pulses of oak and sugar cane. The palate entry is smooth, clean, more animated than the bouquet and nicely toasted and medium-sweet; the midpalate is pleasingly oily in texture and nougaty in flavor. Concludes bittersweet, intensely oaky, and molasses-like. The deficient aroma really hurt the rating.

2006 Rating: ★★★/Recommended

Origine Platiné Grand Reserve Caribbean Rum (Trinidad/Jamaica); 40% abv, $36.

Clear, silvery, and as pristine as rainwater. The first nosing passes are treated to intensely fruity (tropical fruits like pineapple, guava, mango) and spicy (baking spices such as nutmeg and vanilla bean) fragrances that have real depth to them; seven more minutes of air contact and swirling bring out intriguing scents of hemp, textile, horseradish, pepper, and mustard seed; there's a lot going on in this complex bouquet. The palate entry is fat, oily, focused, and lusciously bittersweet; by the midpalate stage the oily texture gives way to succulent tastes of cocoa butter, nut meat, cinnamon, and vanilla cake frosting. Finishes elegantly and profoundly, with ideal viscosity. An absolute cracker of a white Caribbean rum blend.

2007 Rating: ★★★★★/Highest Recommendation

Oronoco Rum (Brazil); 40% abv, $35/liter.

The pale yellow tone is clear and clean. At first whiff, there's a buttery topside aroma that dominates the initial two minutes of sniffing; aeration allows this bouquet to deepen to the extent that the final eight minutes of nosing include hefty and diversified scents of honey, sugar cane, cut grass, charcoal, light wood smoke, and buttermilk. The palate entry highlights the concentrated sweetness of the sugar cane juice; at the meandering midpalate stage the syrupy thickness of the texture nearly overshadows the grassy/cane-like taste to the point of exclusion. The aftertaste is long, luxurious, intensely grassy, and medium-sweet, all of which bring the focus back to where it should be: raw sugar cane juice, not its chunky by-products. Would have received a fourth star but for the top-heavy sweetness in the entry and midpalate.

2006 Rating: ★★★/Recommended

Pango Rhum Rhum Barbancourt Rum with Natural Fruit & Spice Flavors (Haiti); 35% abv, $17.

The amber/harvest gold appearance is pleasing and clean. The first whiffs detect canned pineapple and guava, with soft traces of baking spices; aeration doesn't really apply to this rum as it pretty much stays the course established in the opening nosing. The palate entry is sweet and very fruity; by the midpalate phase the taste profile is a savory fruit salad of ripe tastes that include pineapple, guava, banana, and citrus, as well as delicate pinches of clove, ginger, and cinnamon. A tasty alternative to the heavily spiced flavored rums from Captain Morgan and Foursquare.

2007 Rating: ★★★/Recommended

Papagayo Spiced Rum Made With Rum, Mead and Spices (Paraguay); 40% abv, $21.

A fully approved organic libation. The attractive topaz color is pure. The first couple of whiffs pick up atypical aromas of cigarette tobacco and smoke, dill and rubber tire; I'd really like to say that aeration affected the bouquet in a positive manner but it basically stayed the course detected in the opening minutes; while I wouldn't characterize it as unpleasant, it's not the most attractive rum aroma. Better in the mouth than in the nose at palate entry, the flavor displays an appealing brown sugar taste on the tongue; then at midpalate the rum turns decidedly vegetal, ashy/sooty and intensely herbal. The aftertaste sums up the experience with a flash of spirity heat, followed by tastes of brown sugar, tobacco and dried herbs. While I acknowledge that this review can read in a negative light, I still believe that there's enough quality and virtue here to recommend it for hardcore rum aficionados, but not for casual rum drinkers.

2003 Rating: ★★★/Recommended

Pirate's Choice Key Lime Rum (USA); 40% abv, $17.

Very pretty and clear; unblemished clarity. The tart scent of key lime is evident right from the first whiff; aeration doesn't change the aromatic profile. The palate entry is startlingly sweet and cloying well before the taste buds encounter any sense of key lime; in the midpalate the key lime flavoring is less overshadowed by the sugary sweetness, but that's not to say that this rum enjoys any sense of balance. Ends up citric acid-like, mildly key lime-like, and, of course, concentrated in its refined sugar sweetness. Through all its problems, I actually saw some potential here. If the unrelenting sweetness were to be turned down, the key lime flavoring would emerge even more, making it, I reckon, at least recommendable as a mixer.

2006 Rating: ★★/Not Recommended

Pirate's Choice Molasses Reef Dark Rum (USA); 35% abv, $17.

Pleasing, deep honey/nut brown appearance. The nose after the pour is unexpectedly fruity, juicy, gummy, and cotton candy-like; further time in the glass fails to deepen or expand this simple aroma, which is more liqueur-like than rum-like. The palate entry is strangely and unpleasantly chemical-like in its metallic bittersweetness; the taste profile sinks even lower at midpalate as industrial flavors of gunmetal, coins, and brown sugar dominate. Concludes as tinny and coin-like as it starts at entry. A mess that should never have been bottled.

2006 Rating: ★/Not Recommended

Plantation 1983 Old Reserve Rum (Jamaica); 45% abv, $30.

The topaz/dark honey color is a dazzler; absolute purity. The opening whiff is chockful of impressive aromas including molasses, bittersweet chocolate, maple, Brazil nut, and distant orange zest; the aroma settles down into being a focused yet expansive bouquet in the second sniffing, one in which nuts and dark chocolate abound; the third whiff adds subtle notes of tobacco leaf and spice; the fourth and last nosing pass sees all the components come together in a sweet, stately, and highly complex bouquet that's definitely one of my all-time favorite aged rum aromas. The palate entry is full, sweet, and tangy; the midpalate phase is long, mildly oily, molasses sweet, and even a touch prune-like. The finish is sweet, luxurious, a bit smoky, and oaky. A supremely satisfying aged rum of the first rank.

2000 Rating: ★★★★★/Highest Recommendation

Plantation 1986 Old Reserve Rum (Barbados); 45% abv, $25.

Rich amber/harvest gold in hue; ideal purity. The vegetal, earthy, idiosyncratic aroma after the pour reeks of brown sugar and sugar cane; aeration serves to reinforce the potent brown sugar quality of the bouquet in the second sniffing; hints of lanolin, oil, and pumpkin seed enter the aromatic equation in the penultimate whiff; by the last nosing pass, after nearly nine minutes of air contact, the nose shows its spirity side as the bouquet turns pleasantly prickly and peppery (as in black pepper). The palate entry is shockingly sweet in a cocoa butter-like manner; the intriguingly delicious midpalate stage is oily and full-bodied, with bittersweet flavors of dark chocolate and brown sugar; it's a serious mouthful. The aftertaste is long, very sugary sweet, but fat and oily. It's almost like a lotion that you want to rub onto your body.

2000 Rating: ★★★★/Highly Recommended

Plantation 1991 Old Reserve Rum (Trinidad); 45% abv, $20.

The amber/honey color is bright under the evaluation lamp; impeccable purity. The nose at opening is clean and mildly spicy; the second whiff offers a pleasant biscuit/cookie batter scent that harmonizes well with the controlled spiciness; with six minutes of aeration, the third sniffing sees the spice catapult to the forefront in moderately sweet waves that caress the olfactory sense rather than pummel it; in the final nosing pass following nearly ten minutes of air exposure, the polite notes of cinnamon/nutmeg continue leading the charge; more a feminine bouquet than a masculine one in that the elements are presented in more a perfume-like way than in an assertive or aggressive manner; very savory, indeed. On the tongue at palate entry there's a touch of courteous heat, then at midpalate the spice seriously

kicks into gear as the flavor turns very sweet. The finish shows a good balance as the spirit intervenes with the sugary sweetness, cutting it seemingly by half in the throat. Very tasty and well-mannered in the most positive sense.
2000 Rating: ★★★★/Highly Recommended

Plantation Grande Reserve Barbados Rum (Barbados); 40% abv, $15.
The bright copper color is warm and appealing to the eye; excellent purity. The first whiffs discover deep scents that include brown sugar, molasses, and vanilla bean; seven minutes of further air contact unleash layers of aroma that consist of succulent ripe tropical fruit (baked banana?), marzipan, refined sugar, and honey. The palate entry features off-dry flavors of sweet oak and maple; at midpalate there's a whole army of intriguing, bittersweet tastes including black pepper, molasses, dark chocolate, and palm oil. The finish is long, bittersweet, and woody. Every bit the match of the earlier expression; a truly lovely, sophisticated rum that's true to the tradition profile of Barbados.
2003 Rating: ★★★★/Highly Recommended

Plantation Old Reserve 1990 Guyana Rum (Guyana); 45% abv, $45.
Lovely topaz color; excellent purity. The first couple of nosing passes discover the unusual combination of earthy and biscuity aromas, such as cake batter, cocoa, lead, slate, and rubber, all bundled together; aeration really helps to sort out the fragrances into separate layers of spice (cinnamon, nutmeg) and cake on the surface and earth, wood and minerals underneath; a highly complex bouquet that makes you ponder and pause. The palate entry is bittersweet, brown sugar-like and maple-like; by the midpalate stage the off-dry to semisweet core taste turns intensely sap- and maple-like while lesser flavors of cocoa and marzipan dance around the foundation taste. The aftertaste is long, sappy and even a little oily. A thinking person's oak-aged rum.
2003 Rating: ★★★★/Highly Recommended

Plantation Old Reserve 1991 Barbados Rum (Barbados); 45% abv, $30.
Very pretty deep gold; ideal purity. All sorts of scents are flying around in the initial nosings after the pour, including almond butter, honey, and distant mint; exposure to air over another six minutes unleashes additional aromas such as oaky vanilla, red fruit, vegetable (kale? spinach?), and black pepper. The palate entry is mildly sweet and sugary; the taste profile takes off at midpalate emitting firm, lean, and well-developed flavors of oak, brown sugar, and cocoa. The aftertaste is long, semisweet, and extremely honeyed. Owns the graceful profile of Barbados along with a woody sweetness that's very pleasing.
2003 Rating: ★★★★/Highly Recommended

Plantation Old Reserve 1992 Venezuela Rum (Venezuela); 45% abv, $40.
Burnished/amber hue; excellent purity. The opening nosing pass owns aromatic elements of cinnamon, candied almonds, and honey; aeration of an additional six minutes heightens the cinnamon/holiday spice characteristic especially, though the honey likewise grows in intensity. The palate entry is pleasantly raisiny and mildly burnt; the midpalate phase adds notes of spirity warmth, sweet oak, and lead pencil. It finishes on a semisweet note.
2003 Rating: ★★★/Recommended

Plantation Old Reserve 1993 Trinidad Rum (Trinidad); 45% abv, $22.

Autumnal gold/amber/honey color; superb purity. The initial sniffings offer subtle, earthy, dry scents of tobacco leaf and brown sugar; seven further minutes of air contact release faint, bittersweet traces of cinnamon, nutmeg, and cocoa; the aromatics never overpower the olfactory sense as much as they entice it; a splendid rum bouquet of delicacy and nuance. The palate entry is smoky, semisweet, and slightly honeyed; by the midpalate point the taste profile adds delectable spice notes that include cinnamon and clove. The finish is long, semisweet, and pointed. Neither a luxurious nor a multilayered rum, but one whose elegance and understatement go a long way in charming the taste buds.

2003 Rating: ★★★/Highly Recommended

Plantation Old Reserve 8 Year Old Jamaica Rum (Jamaica); 45% abv, $32.

Harvest gold color; impeccable purity. This curious little bouquet starts out being outlandishly, seductively fruity, almost like baked banana or baked pear; time in the glass adds zesty, off-dry notes of pear drop, dried herbs, gum and banana-nut bread; yeah, it's off-beat and yeah, it's kind of funky, but I really liked this atypical bouquet. The palate entry is mineral-like and dry, almost lead pencil- or slate-like; at the midpalate stage there's a softly sweet taste of honey that counters the dry mineral-like opening flavor. The aftertaste is minerally, lean, and mildly honeyed.

2003 Rating: ★★★/Recommended

Players Extreme Banana Flavored Rum (USA); 21% abv, $14.

Clear as spring water. Right from the pour the dried banana perfume leaps from the glass; aeration sees the fragrance subside into a mildly pleasant, off-dry, ripe banana bouquet. The banana taste profile at palate entry is softly sweet and ripe; the midpalate stage offers a pleasantly round, off-dry to sweet flavor of ripe banana that doesn't blanket the tongue in excess like its out-of-control sibling, the Players Coconut. The aftertaste is mellow, sweet almost like banana pudding.

2003 Rating: ★★★/Recommended

Players Extreme Coconut Flavored Rum (USA); 21% abv, $14.

Crystalline and pure. Right from the pour the aggressive, sweet coconut perfume clubs the olfactory sense into submission; further time in the glass doesn't tame the wild sweet coconut beast as the aroma remains in fourth gear. In the palate entry the sweet coconut taste washes over the tongue like a tsunami; by the midpalate stage I've had enough of this overbearing, overly sweet flavored rum; too syrupy, too sweet, too much, it's a case of overkill. I suggest the Players people take a close look at Cruzan Coconut or Parrot Bay by Captain Morgan to see how it should be done.

2003 Rating: ★/Not Recommended

Players Extreme Mango Infused Rum (England); 21% abv, $18.

Clear as mineral water. The lightly scented, near-spicy aroma after the pour is delicate and restrained; additional time in the glass helps to stir more ripeness and soft, almost ethereal mango fruit; a temptress of a bouquet. The palate entry is lovely, softly sweet, and ripe, and just marginally fruity; at midpalate the mango presence comes more into evidence, providing

a well-managed flavor profile that's elegant and refined, yet authentic. Ends with a whisper of mango. I would have rated this well-made rum four stars had the alcohol been higher, thus giving it more substance and foundation; very nice and feminine, however, as it is.
2005 Rating: ★★★/Recommended

Players Extreme Rum (USA); 40% abv, $14.
Clear and pure. The weird nose after the opening has a burnt match/sulphury quality to it that's not quite off-putting but close; time in the glass can't shake the sooty, cigarette ash-like aroma. The flavor at palate entry is simple, mildly sweet, and sugary; by the midpalate point there's not much to report on other than the identical rudimentary taste found in the entry. The aftertaste is sweet, medium-long, and moderately pleasant. Boringly average.
2003 Rating: ★★/Not Recommended

Port Morant 10 Year Old Demerara Rum (Guyana); 46% abv, $51.
The golden yellow color is similar to the sunshine-like tint of an oaky chardonnay from California or Australia; some inconsequential debris is seen floating about. The luscious aroma starts right in with a toasted, vanilla bean-like fragrance that's beguiling and compelling; with time in the glass, the aroma becomes focused and dry in the second whiff; by the third nosing pass, following seven minutes of aeration, a cocoa bean/coffee bean/fruit stone scent becomes the dominant aromatic player; in the fourth and last sniffing, the predominant kernel/stone aroma is joined by a distant trace of dark chocolate/molasses, making for a delightful, complex, and completely bittersweet finale. The palate entry is surprisingly sweet and sugary; then at midpalate the taste goes fruity, sappy sweet, and strangely appealing. The aftertaste is long, sugar cane sweet, and lip-smackingly satisfying. An odd rum whose offbeat eccentricities are its best virtues.
2000 Rating: ★★★★/Highly Recommended

Port Morant 18 Year Old Demerara Rum (Guyana); 46% abv, $76.
The clean, particle-free, gloriously tawny/burnt/deep honey brown appearance reminds me strikingly of fine palo cortado sherry. The opening aroma after the pour is tinged with roasted nuts, dried fruit, and caramel scents; the second pass offers buttery, brandy-like notes of almond paste and nougat; the third sniffing adds roasted notes of walnut and molasses; the fourth and final whiff, following eight minutes of exposure to air, adds a seductive baked apple/apple pastry perfume that tops off the nosing phase in style. The palate entry shows a bit of frying butter oiliness and mild sweetness; then at midpalate the flavors shift to fourth gear, offering softly sweet, even chocolaty, tastes of candy bar, molasses, and dark caramel. The finish is luxuriously long, though not in the least syrupy or thick, and focused on the nutty/buttery/oily flavors. Remarkably brandy-like, but not complex enough to merit a fifth rating star.
2000 Rating: ★★★★/Highly Recommended

Port Morant Blackbeard's Reserve 1976 26 Year Old Demarara Rum (Guyana); 60% abv, $130.
The amazing color is like the deep tawny/mahogany hue of an oloroso sherry; impeccable purity. The opening bouquet offers a menu of enticing, stone dry aromas, ranging from

molasses to old oak to wet slate; another seven minutes in the glass stimulates stately and mature aromas of marzipan, nougat, brown sugar, cocoa, pipe tobacco, and dry oloroso sherry; a monumental bouquet of the first rank and not for the faint of heart drinker. The palate entry shows bits of tongue-on-stone dryness and bitterness mixed with background notes of molasses; the midpalate is firm, bitter, and luscious in a brown sugar, dark chocolate manner. The aftertaste is long, intensely bitter, and memorable. I suggest that you substantially cut it with spring water in order to draw out the natural sweetness.

2003 Rating: ★★★★/Highly Recommended

Port Morant Blackbeard's Reserve Demarara Rum 1976, 24 Years Old (Guyana); 60% abv, $120.

One of the prettiest rums I've ever seen; it beams with deep bronze/auburn/henna/burnt orange hues; the rim is bright yellow; absolute purity; an eye-catcher of the first rank. The opening nosing picks up subtle scents of licorice (highly unusual for a rum) and hard cheese (evidence of rancio? in rum? could be unprecedented); the bouquet turns more expressive by the third sniffing as sinewy, almost smoky aromas of lead pencil, linseed oil, old oak, and resin delight the olfactory sense; the final pass adds dry, oily, and black pepper scents; a multi-layered feast for the nose that depicts how brandy-like some rums can get. The palate entry screams onto the tongue in tsunamis of baked, almost burnt-to-char, flavors, including molasses and brown sugar; the midpalate is slightly more polite as toasty, oily tastes of oak resin, tobacco leaf, and sautéed asparagus make for interesting tasting. The finish is dry, loaded with lead pencil flavor, and ash. A smoky blockbuster by any measure, but one that's most certainly not for every palate, in particular, those that haven't been around the rum block more than a dozen times.

2001 Rating: ★★★★/Highly Recommended

Prichards Cranberry Rum (USA); 35% abv, $24.

The cherry/berry red tint makes it clear from the outset where this rum is heading; again, some very minor sediment spotted. To my surprise in the first whiffs, there's absolutely no evidence of fruit, but rather a firm, bean-like scent that's more grainy than either grassy or fruity; seven more minutes of aeration do nothing to release any other aromatic component; the bouquet exhibits scant customary rum charm and, further, it doesn't reflect what the label promises. The palate entry is awkwardly fruity and bittersweet as the molasses and the fruit seem to be competing rather than complementing each other; the midpalate taste is so intensely sour that it makes my lips pucker. Ends up flat tasting, unforgivably raw in the throat, and dull. An unfortunate misstep by this small, earnest distillery.

2005 Rating: ★/Not Recommended

Prichards Crystal Rum (USA); 40% abv, $20.

Limpid and silvery transparent; very minor, inconsequential sediment seen floating under the examination lamp. The frisky aroma after the pour reminds me strikingly of egg cream or, even better, old fashioned cream soda pop; following seven minutes of further air contact the bouquet turns as sweet, fruity, and snappy as baseball card bubble gum, vanilla Coke or cotton candy; it's a bouquet that's very retro, making me recall summers of my long past youth. The palate entry is sweet, intensely sugary, and beany; the midpalate flavor profile

features vanilla bean and molasses (from which it is produced). Concludes well and smooth. An extra-sweet white rum by design that might be too narrow in focus for some experienced rum drinkers. That said, it's well made.
2005 Rating: ★★★/Recommended

Prichards Fine Rum (USA); 40% abv, $30.
Bottled at barrel strength; displays a particularly fetching deep amber/honey hue that's impeccably clean. The delectable, teasing, atypical aroma opens up with subtle traces of black pepper, minerals (granite? marble?) and oak; the curiosity continues after seven more minutes of aeration as the bouquet adds hints of black licorice, lemon drop, and beeswax; a remarkable rum bouquet that keeps you interested and searching from start to finish. The palate entry's first impression is of black licorice that then vanishes and a fine, resiny oakiness takes over; by the midpalate juncture the black pepper/spice returns along with a bittersweet flavor that's almost nutty or nougat-like. The aftertaste is long, medium-weighted, and bittersweet; superb job here of distilling a rum that's unique, full of personality and challenge; BRAVO.
2003 Rating: ★★★★/Highly Recommended

Pusser's British Navy Rum (British Virgin Islands); 47.75% abv, $24.
The brilliant copper penny color is pretty, but displays minor sediment beneath the examination lamp. The opening nosing detects peculiar smells of olive brine, seaweed, wood polish, and shellfish; extra air contact does nothing to enhance the briny/solvent-like and weird aroma. Better in the mouth than in the nasal cavity; the palate entry is piney, cedar-like, and astringent; at midpalate there are flashes of molasses, coffee, and tobacco that aren't significant enough to drag this oddball rum up into recommended territory. Ends up poorly as highly astringent and manufactured tastes dominate the exit. This was originally labeled as "Admiral's Reserve" in 1993 and 1996. That designation no longer appears on the label, though the abv strength is the same. The detergent-like, cleaning liquid finish brings the rating back down to one star. A waste of a good glass bottle. No wonder the British Navy fell into disrepair.
2005 Rating: ★/Not Recommended

Redrum Rum (US Virgin Islands); 35% abv, $15.
The appearance is a soft pastel pink/faint copper hue; excellent purity. The initial nosing detects a spicy/peppery bouquet that's mildly fruity/sweet/ripe; by the second sniffing clearly evident notes of coconut and pineapple make their aromatic move; in the third whiff, following seven minutes of air exposure, the fruit turns quite ripe and sweet, but there's also a solid acid backbone presence to maintain balance; the fourth and final nosing pass sees a slight fading, but overall the bouquet remains fresh and fruitily alluring. The palate entry is sweet on the surface but tart underneath; the midpalate juncture is notable for the coconut and pineapple flavors harmonizing with the zesty spice. The aftertaste is long, more tart than sweet, and even a bit cinnamon-like. A fun rum for mixing.
2000 Rating: ★★★/Recommended

Rhum Clément Cuvée Homère Rhum Vieux Agricole Hors d'Age (from vintages 2000, 1996, and 1991) (Martinique); 44% abv, $85.
Orange/copper color; flawless purity. The initial aromatic thrust is all about sugarcane and

butter sautéed almonds; seven more minutes in the glass stimulate scents of black pepper and potent spirit that's wonderfully nutty and buttery. The palate entry is delicate, compellingly oily, and spicy; the midpalate stage showcases the oak and the sugarcane in just the right amounts and the sheer elegance is exciting. Finishes refined, world-class, and slightly honeyed. All the moving parts work in total harmony. A seamless, outstanding aged rhum agricole of the first rank.

2006 Rating: ★★★★★/Highest Recommendation

Rhum Clément Premiere Canne White Rum (Martinique/France); 40% abv, $25.

Crystal clear and very clean. In the first whiffs I detect grassy/beany notes of sugar cane, cola nut, vanilla bean, and fresh, flowery spirit just off the pot still; after another six minutes in the copita, the aroma narrows its focus on the grassiness; a one-dimensional bouquet, but compelling in its purity just the same. The palate entry is sensational, in that, the narrow aroma becomes a broad, expansive, and generous early taste that includes healthy doses of cocoa bean, bittersweet chocolate, black tea, and unrefined sugar; the midpalate acts as a reinforcement of the palate entry, adding a more pronounced element of fresh, raw spirit. Concludes gracefully in the throat, with subtle notes of sugary sweetness, zesty spirit, and vanilla. What white rums should be. Liked this incarnation more than their Clément Blanc from the early 1990s.

2005 Rating: ★★★★/Highly Recommended

Rhum Clément Vieux XO Rhum Agricole (Martinique); 44%; $170.

A blend of 1952, 1971, and 1976 vintage rhums. The medium amber color is more brownish than gold; superb clarity. The opening sniffs are greeted by intensely toasty smells of rope/hemp/fiber, buttered toast, and tobacco leaf; aeration time of another seven minutes stimulates strong and strangely harmonious scents of old oak, burning cigarette, paraffin, charcoal, very old and worn saddle leather, and honey. The palate entry highlights the toasty/charcoal core flavor while the midpalate stage focuses more on the brown sugar, honey, oaky vanilla, and holiday spice qualities that make this rhum so sensationally luscious and idiosyncratic. Finishes semisweet, with not-so-subtle tastes of marzipan, nougat, candied walnut, and dark honey. A wonder that is in an extra aged class all on its own.

2006 Rating: ★★★★★/Highest Recommendation

Rhum Clément VSOP Aged Rum (Martinique/France); 40% abv, $30.

The amber/autumn leaf gold/honey color is very pretty and pure and very immature brandy-like. The first sniffings pick up muted aromas of brown sugar and milk chocolate; aeration time of another six minutes does little in the way of stirring further aromatic development, except for traces of peanut and black pepper. The elegant yet assertive palate entry is firm, peppery, moderately sweet, and cane-like; at midpalate the flavor profile turns silky in texture, semisweet and cocoa-like to the taste, and eminently elegant and sophisticated in style. Finishes sweet, honeyed, medium-bodied, svelte, and utterly yummy.

2005 Rating: ★★★★/Highly Recommended

Rhum J.M. Blanc White Rhum Agricole (Martinique); 50% abv, $38/liter.

Silvery clear and flawlessly clean. The intensely grassy opening aroma is zesty and vegetal; six more minutes of aeration stimulate fragrances of cauliflower, broccoli, sugarcane,

and hemp/fiber/rope; an atypically textile-like and grassy rhum agricole bouquet. The palate entry is fruity sweet (plum, quince) and not in the least hot, considering the 100-proof status; the midpalate phase features tastes of beans, vanilla, sugarcane, and jellybeans. Ends up moderately sweet, utterly graceful, and invitingly warm. Masterfully distilled.
2006 Rating: ★★★★/Highly Recommended

Rhum J.M. élevé sous bois Rhum Agricole (Martinique); 50% abv, $43/liter.

The golden/straw color is pretty and clean. The first nosings pick up delicate yet round scents of butter cream and cake frosting; additional minutes in the glass do little to expand the basic plump and sweet aroma profile, except to add distant touches of spice and vegetation. The palate entry is properly sweet and caney; the midpalate phase is delightfully sweet in a confectionery manner and is almost candied. Finishes plump, sugary sweet, and pleasant in the mouth and throat.
2006 Rating: ★★★/Recommended

Rhum J.M. Réserve Spéciale Rhum Agicole (Martinique); 45% abv, $50.

The honey hue is pretty and shiny. The first nosing following the pour offers intensely grassy/vegetal notes that are more sweet than dry and more caney than processed; after another seven minutes of exposure to air, the bouquet adds delicate notes of Christmas spices and treacle. The palate entry is firmly structured, semisweet, properly caney/grassy, and just a bit spicy; by the midpalate stage the oak emerges as a taste frontrunner, eclipsing the spice and the cane and giving the taste profile a vanilla-like succulence. Concludes elegantly and sweetly. Good job here.
2007 Rating: ★★★★/Highly Recommended

Rhum J.M. Vieux 1997 Rhum Agricole (Martinique); 48.8% abv, $90.

The harvest gold/light honey color is slightly dull; minuscule sediment seen, but not a problem. The opening whiffs are confronted with assertive and welcoming scents of winter holiday spice and dried red fruits, in other words, fruitcake; aeration brings about more of a traditional rummy sweetness/oakiness that works well; what was missing from this rhum agricole was the vegetal/grassy agricole part that I now expect from the category. The palate entry is confectioner sweet and bubble gum-like, with nary a hint of grass or sugarcane; the midpalate stage is pleasing and mature, sweet and woody. Concludes sweet, sap-like, and a touch maple-like. Give me more grassy thrust and I'd gladly hand it a fourth rating star. While very good, J.M. 1997 reminds me more of a molasses-based rum than a sugarcane juice-based rhum.
2006 Rating: ★★★/Recommended

Rio Joe's Silver Cachaça (Brazil); 39% abv, $22.

Clean and translucent as rainwater. First whiffs detect potent, pungent smells of white grapes, fresh fruity spirit off the still, and sand; the fruit gives way after further aeration to a rubber hose/rubber band/rubber inner tube aroma that's inoffensive, but one-note in its approach. Entry is semisweet then baked and spicy (black pepper); the midpalate is pleasantly chewy in texture, mildly sweet and grass-like, and even honeyed. Finishes well and stable, with delectably sweet tastes that gently coat the throat. I didn't think that this spirit

was going to earn a recommendation after the nosings, but the taste profile and aftertaste gained lots of ground.
2007 Rating: ★★★/Recommended

Rochinha Single Barrel 12 Year Old Aged Artesian Cachaça (Brazil); 40% abv, $80.

The gold/green color is littered with floating gray/white detritus, which unfortunately makes this libation look unappealing. The initial nosings detect traces of creosote, paint thinner, anise, and green pepper; seven more minutes of aeration do little to mitigate the early unpleasantries. The palate entry highlights flavors of black pepper, stone, and egg whites; at midpalate the taste turns slightly sweet and toffee-like, becoming more acceptable. Ends up moderately sweet, almond-like, and candied. Rebounded from a miserable start to being drinkable. But I flinch when I look at the bottle price.
2005 Rating: ★★/Not Recommended

Rochinha Single Barrel 5 Year Old Aged Artesian Cachaça (Brazil); 40% abv, $38.

The yellow/greenish hue shows moderately good purity. The pickle brine/olive brine opening aroma is sour, cat pee-like, and bracing; after another seven minutes of air contact, the aroma becomes vinegar-like and ultra-sour. The palate entry is sweet/sour, baked, and intensely green olive-like; at midpalate a pinched sweetness enters the flavor profile, mirroring the base material. Finishes sweet/sour, pineapple-like, and long. The cat pee surface odor is a problem, but I detect some potential here, especially in the entry and midpalate.
2005 Rating: ★★/Not Recommended

Rockley Still 13 Year Old Rum (Barbados); 46% abv, $54.

Owns the pretty, light amber/light honey hue of an old sauternes or barsac; minor detritus noted. The opening whiff is very spicy and exotic; in the second pass, the aroma becomes somewhat muted as compared to the first pass, but distant notes of spice can still be detected; in the third sniffing, a peppery scent emerges and takes charge; in the fourth nosing pass, following ten minutes of aeration, an earthy, almost chalk-like quality is discerned; I don't care for this bouquet at all. The palate entry is muted and dry; then in an intense burst of flavor at midpalate an entire menu of atypical and intriguing tastes commandeer the taste buds, especially linseed oil, salt/brine, herb-infused honey, wax, and flower essences. This weird cacophony of flavors finishes with an herbal thrust that's both botanical and peppery. An amazingly peculiar beast that's worth a try at a bar that's willing to serve a tasting sample of it; not a favorite of mine, though; I find it too far outside the established boundaries for rum.
2000 Rating: ★★/Not Recommended

Rogue Dark Rum (USA); 40% abv, $27.

The bright white wine yellow color is pretty and very pure. The upfront scent is heavily spirity and fruity, very similar to fresh, raw spirit coming straight out of the pot still; aeration time of another seven minutes doesn't affect the aroma at all as it remains raw and fruity fresh. The palate entry is basic, refined sugar sweet, and that's about it; by the midpalate point the taste profile hasn't deepened and is therefore still painfully fundamental, unabashedly sugary, and simplistically raw. Though drinkable, this one-note song needs work in order to get a sense of greater depth and varied expression.
2007 Rating: ★★/Not Recommended

Rogue Hazelnut Spiced Rum (USA); 40% abv, $27.

Slightly deeper in color than its sibling; this is gold; flawless purity. The opening inhalations are assaulted by tanky, musty-fusty, fusel oil, synthetic carpet aromas that, I believe, are supposed to be nut-like when in reality they are old gym locker-like and horrible; aeration fails to help this pitiful excuse for a rum bouquet; one of the worst bouquets of any kind I've been exposed to lately. An even worse disaster in the mouth as metallic, manufactured flavors of nickel, flax, textile, plastic…well, you get the picture. How could anyone of even the most rudimentary distilling acumen possibly think that this septic tank muck is appealing and, much worse, ready for the marketplace? Fit only for consumption on the Planet Zenoo by the slap-happy Zenites. Man alive, just when you think you've seen everything.
2007 Rating: ★/Not Recommended

Ron Barceló Añejo Rum (Dominican Republic); 40% abv, $14.

The bronze/burnished gold appearance is impeccably pure. The initial burst of aroma is a touch moldy/earthy/mushroomy and that's of concern; unfortunately, the sweaty mustiness seems to gain strength with aeration; not a welcoming bouquet; even though there isn't a cork (screwcap) this seems "corked" by TCA. The palate entry offers the same fusty/grandma's attic-like qualities detected in the nosing stages; the midpalate is barely drinkable as the flavor of mushrooms and mold dominate. Didn't bother with the finish since I didn't want it in my mouth another time. I can only hope that this was a bad bottle.
2006 Rating: ★/Not Recommended

Ron Barceló Imperial Rum (Dominican Republic); 40% abv, $25.

Displays a bright copper penny color that's as pure as could be. The initial burst of aromatic joy offers tight scents of tobacco leaf and bacon fat; aeration stimulates deeper fragrances including walnut, lanolin, parchment, and brown sugar. The palate entry leans towards caramel sweetness, with touches of oaky vanilla, vanilla bean, and honey; the midpalate phase features pleasing tastes of nut paste, treacle, marzipan, and sap. Concludes semisweet, with traces of cola nut, cotton candy, and dark caramel.
2006 Rating: ★★★/Recommended

Ron Cubaney 7 Year Old Gran Reserva Rum (Dominican Republic); 38% abv, $12.

Pretty honey color; superb purity. The nose right after the pour shows juicy bits of light caramel and brown sugar; seven minutes in the glass does little to expand the original impressions, except with the addition of egg cream/vanilla. The palate entry is firm, off-dry and sugary sweet; the midpalate displays considerable finesse as the brown sugar taste goes chocolaty and savory. The aftertaste shows some oakiness, vanilla, and toffee. A very decent older rum.
2002 Rating: ★★★/Recommended

Ron Cubaney Banana Flavored Rum (Dominican Republic); 32% abv, $10.

Clear as rain water; minor sediment. In the first sniffings the banana scent reminds me more, I'm sorry to report, of shoe leather than actual fruit; aeration releases more of the banana perfume, but really only as over-ripened banana, not fresh banana; it's a manufactured, industrial bouquet; there's nothing fresh or genuine about it. It tastes better

than it smells as the sweet banana candy taste greets the taste buds at palate entry; by the midpalate point the banana flavor turns a bit creamier, almost like in banana cream pie, but it's still candied and overly sweet. The finish is this rum's high point as the banana flavor suddenly becomes appealing and tasty without being cloying. A missed opportunity.
2002 Rating: ★★/Not Recommended

Ron del Barrilito Three Star Puerto Rican Rum (Puerto Rico); 43% abv, $32.
The amber/topaz color is regrettably cloudy and murky and therefore disappointing. The opening nosing passes detect mature smells of men's club leather chairs, old books, and molasses; the added time in the glass helps to release more comely aromas including honey, unsmoked cigar, milk chocolate, and nougat. The palate entry is intensely sweet and a touch smoky; at the midpalate point the honey and molasses factors take the lead, bringing home the taste profile in a warm, comfortable, "clubby" finish that's old-fashioned and mature.
2007 Rating: ★★★/Recommended

Ron del Barrilito Two Star Puerto Rican Rum (Puerto Rico); 43% abv, $24.
The golden/deep straw color is vibrant and pretty; impeccable purity. Opening aromas are subtle and suggest yellow fruit pulp; later sniffs pick up nuances of toffee, milk chocolate, and vanilla bean: the understated personality of this bouquet is totally charming and even stately. Palate entry is balanced, nicely acidic, fresh, creamy, cane sweet, and warming on the tongue; later tastes accentuate cocoa bean/dark chocolate at midpalate that leads to a supremely confident and elegant aftertaste that's world-class all the way. State-of-the-art, sophisticated, molasses-based, properly oak-aged rum.
2007 Rating: ★★★★/Highly Recommended

Ron Diaz Gran Reserva Spiced Rum (Barbados); 35% abv, $15.
Pretty topaz/bronze/burnished orange color; excellent purity. Subdued spice scents greet the olfactory sense after the pour; following another seven minutes in the glass, the aroma opens up and offers pleasantly succulent and bakery-like aromas of dough, cinnamon, brown sugar, nutmeg, vanilla extract, and spice cake. Entry highlights the vanilla especially as the taste profile goes in a sweet, but not necessarily candied direction; the midpalate is smooth, intensely vanilla-like, brown sugar sweet, and mildly toasted. Ends on a sugared almond note that's alluring. Does what it does well.
2007 Rating: ★★★/Recommended

Ron Diaz Vanilla Rum (West Indies); 27.5% abv, $9.
Excellent purity. The opening aroma after the pour displays a buttery scent that's seductive and intensely bean-like; seven more minutes of air contact release nut- and kernel-like scents of fresh coconut shell, milk, and meat. The palate entry is nicely balanced between semisweetness and fruitiness; at midpalate the flavor kicks in fully with sweetened coconut milk. Concludes sweet, lip-smacking, and alluring. Nice job of not allowing the flavor profile to get overcome with sugary sweetness.
2005 Rating: ★★★/Recommended

Ron Diaz Wild Cherry Rum (West Indies); 27.5% abv, $9.

Clear and clean as rainwater. The cherry scent comes on strong and a tad cough medicine/ cough drop-like in the initial whiffs; the candied/cough drop aroma profile remains prominent even after seven more minutes of exposure to air; it's not that the bouquet is unpleasant, it's more that it's not genuinely fruity. The palate entry is nicely sweet and candied; at midpalate the flavor replays what was played in the entry. Finishes drinkable, simple, and candied. Ordinary/average and so use it strictly as a mixer.

2005 Rating: ★★/Not Recommended

Ron Matusalem Clasico Rum (Dominican Republic); 40% abv, $20.

Pretty autumnal gold/honey color; very good purity. The opening nosing passes emit very delicate scents of sugar cane and honey; exposure to air for another seven minutes does next to nothing in releasing further aromas other than a distant nuance of vanilla. The palate entry is biscuity/sugar cookie sweet, pleasant, and medium-bodied; by the midpalate point there's clear evidence of molasses, sugar cane, pine, and cocoa. The aftertaste is long, bordering on luxurious and mature.

2003 Rating: ★★★/Recommended

Ron Matusalem Gran Reserva Rum (Dominican Republic); 40% abv, $30.

Really attractive honey/light topaz hue; superb purity. The aroma is reluctant in the first pass, then it begins to build with a bit of swirling; later sniffings following seven more minutes of air contact reveal sturdy, subtle scents of vanilla bean, molasses, dark caramel, and honey. The palate entry is slightly maple-like and almost more bittersweet than flat-out sweet; the midpalate is the highlight feature of this evaluation as the mature flavor profile reaches its zenith in the forms of rich molasses and sugar maple tastes that are bittersweet and refined. The aftertaste is long, slightly lead pencil-like, bittersweet, and elegant.

2003 Rating: ★★★★/Highly Recommended

Ron Matusalem Platino Rum (Dominican Republic); 40% abv, $17.

Transparent as rainwater but shows some light, inconsequential sediment under the examination lamp; no worries about it. The first couple of passes offer assertive aromas of molasses and cocoa bean; an additional seven minutes of aeration time brings out the bittersweet vanilla bean in full measure. The palate entry is sweet, viscous, and intensely bean-like; by the midpalate point the flavor profile includes molasses, raw sugar, and the ever-present vanilla bean/vanilla extract. The finish is long, sugary sweet, and bean-like. A very concentrated silver that shouldn't only be used in mixed drinks; good enough to be served straight up.

2003 Rating: ★★★/Recommended

Ronrico Citrus Rum (Puerto Rico); 30% abv, $10.

Clear as rain water. The opening whiffs detect a pleasing citrusy/lemony scent that's properly tart; unfortunately, exposure to air serves only to heighten the sweetness of the aroma and in the process wipes out any of the alluring virtue. Too sweet at the palate entry; too sweet and manufactured at midpalate; too sweet in the aftertaste. A waste of a good bottle.

2003 Rating: ★/Not Recommended

Ronrico Pineapple/Coconut Rum (Puerto Rico); 30% abv, $10.

Ideally clear and pure. This bouquet doesn't club you into submission like the horrible Vanilla fiasco, but rather introduces the pineapple/coconut components gently; aeration doesn't really serve to expand or enhance the aromatic attributes; my final impression of the nose is that while it's pedestrian and bubble gum-like, there are some pleasant features to it suitable for mixing. After allowing some latitude for the bouquet, I can't say that I feel greatly rewarded by the taste profile; the entry is very sweet and sappy while the midpalate turns completely candied and unctuous. Bubble gum all the way through the finish. Flavored rum for the taste challenged.

2003 Rating: ★★/Not Recommended

Ronrico Vanilla Rum (Puerto Rico); 30% abv, $10.

Clear and pure. The opening bouquet is a pungent, unrestrained, wall-to-wall vanilla-o-rama that comes off as a manufactured—dare I say, artificial—aroma rather than as a fresh, vanilla bean scent; more time in the glass doesn't help the bouquet's numerous inherent flaws. The palate entry mirrors the artificiality found and loathed in the nose to midpalate, where a curiously metallic taste tops off this less than inspiring experience. The aftertaste is dismal; bolsters the old adage: ya gets what ya pays for. I won't even suggest going back to the drawing board; instead I recommend that the drawing board itself be scrapped.

2003 Rating: ★/Not Recommended

S Guaro (Costa Rica); 35% abv, $25.

Absolutely pure and flawless, appearance-wise. I note coffee bean-like, bittersweet, and clean odors in the first two minutes of sniffing; another six minutes of air contact sees the aroma turn slightly fruity, cane-like, and Bubble gum-like before fading completely by the final whiff. The palate entry is razor-edge clean, bittersweet, and mildly citrusy; the midpalate is sweeter than the entry and turns a touch berry-like. Concludes well, moderately bittersweet, smooth, and dark chocolate-like. There will doubtless be some skeptics who will say, "But this is just a rum, mate". In my mind, it's similar, but not quite what I believe to be a rum in the strictest sense. I see it more as a rum/vodka hybrid. I also view it as a superb mixer, with just a hint of sweetness.

2005 Rating: ★★★/Recommended

Sailor Jerry Original Spiced Navy Rum (Virgin Islands); 46% abv, $15.

The color is topaz/honey; very good purity. The opening nosing passes pick up heavy-handed scents of vanilla extract and egg cream; aeration time adds a spicy gum-like scent; basically the aroma reminds me of chewing gum. The palate entry is mildly spicy and even a bit pleasing in a sappy sweet kind of way; at midpalate the taste profile turns smoky, ash-like, industrial, and strangely medicinal. Concludes tasting like last night's cigarette butts. A BOMB and not worth a quarter of the asking price.

2004 Rating: ★/Not Recommended

Santa Teresa 1796 Ron Antiguo de Solera (Venezuela); 40% abv, $35.

A stupendously lovely rich bronze/deep honey hue; excellent purity. The first couple of whiffs pick up very toasty notes of caramel, almond butter, cotton candy, and very old oak;

the additional seven minutes in the copita release even deeper, more profound aromas of saddle leather, vanilla extract, marzipan, honey, oloroso sherry, molasses, and dark caramel. The palate entry is perfectly balanced and sweet; by midpalate the flavor profile is honeyed, slightly cocoa-like, buttery to the feel and utterly decadent. It finishes long, layered, creamy, and dark chocolate bittersweet. BRAVO!

2003 Rating: ★★★★★/Highest Recommendation

Santa Teresa Gran Reserva Ron Añejo Rum (Venezuela); 40% abv, $14.

Impeccable clarity; the honey/amber/harvest gold hue is lovely. The aroma after the pour is lightly spicy and delicately brown sugar-like; another six minutes of air contact stirs deeper, foundational scents of molasses, dark caramel, and lead/minerals; overall, this is a restrained and understated bouquet that promises good things in the mouth. The palate entry is properly sugar sweet, almost sap-like in its bearing; at midpalate there's a taste rush to marshmallow, confectioner's sugar, oaky vanilla, and light honey; the texture is medium-bodied. Finishes gracefully, with lip smacking tastes of bittersweet brown sugar and honey. The pedigree is present and accounted for; in a word, "elegant".

2005 Rating: ★★★★/Highly Recommended

St. Vincent SLR Sunset Light Rum (Grenada); 40% abv, $12.

The clear appearance is as clean as one could hope for. This nose shows an aggressive, cotton fabric side in the initial sniffing, then it settles down in the second and third passes as notes of honey and brown sugar take hold of the olfactory sense; after nearly seven minutes of aeration, the final nosing reveals fully developed, almost thickset scents of honey, almond butter, and brown sugar; a good, solidly made bouquet. The palate entry is sleek, slightly fat, quite sweet, and delectable; by the midpalate stage the taste is buttery and sugary, but not overly sweet. The finish is long, sweet, supple, and smooth. Well-made and pleasing in a daiquiri.

2001 Rating: ★★★/Recommended

St. Vincent Sunset 169 Proof Rum (Grenada); 84.5% abv, $19.

Clear as spring water. The nose right after the pour ripples with fresh-off-the-still alcohol and a peculiar odor of wet pavement; aeration heightens the alcohol potency in the glass to the point where I can barely insert my nose to inhale in the middle stages; gingerly approaching this powerhouse by the fourth and final nosing pass (whew, the ordeal is almost over), I detect the sour odor of undiluted spirit and that's about all; don't try this at home or, and I'm totally serious, near an open flame. As I'd expected, the palate entry itself is fine, majorly potent, but doable; the midpalate is where the alcoholic muscles are flexed as the mega-spirit all but obliterates any opportunity at enjoying any flavor and certainly not a single nuance. The bare knuckle finish is harsh, rude, and unrepentant. In line with its category, but frankly I'm left wondering, what's the point? My rum can beat up your rum?

2001 Rating: ★★/Not Recommended

St. Vincent Sunset Extra Gold Rum (Grenada); 40% abv, $15.

The medium amber hue doesn't capture the light very well and as a result seems a little dull; pure. The nose right after the pour is innocuous and simple, a clinical case of Gold

Rum 101; the lack of nuance and definition continues in the second and third sniffings as an anemic aroma of brown sugar barely limps from the glass; the aromatic feeb-a-thon rages on in the fourth and (gratefully) last nosing pass; there's no aromatic structure in this rum. The palate entry displays a dash more character as the taste offers a sweet, sugary thrust at the tip of the tongue; by midpalate the sweet, sugary flavors seem to be rallying. The aftertaste is medium long, tinny sweet, and sugary. The notable recovery in the mouth lifted this ordinary rum into two star territory, but by no means is it recommendable.
2001 Rating: ★★/Not Recommended

Starr African Ultra Superior Light Rum (Mauritius); 40% abv, $30.
    Translucent, silvery blue appearance; some sediment noted. In the first stages of nosing, the aroma is earthy, dry, clean, and bean- and cane-like; seven minutes down the aromatic road, the bouquet expands only slightly, emitting delicate, almost spicy scents of cocoa bean, vanilla bean, and brown sugar. The palate entry is bittersweet, concentrated, and beany; at midpalate the flavor profile becomes sweeter and more like vanilla extract. The bean intensity reaches its bittersweet zenith in the high-flying aftertaste. Chic, racy, and delicious.
2005 Rating: ★★★★/Highly Recommended

Tommy Bahama Golden Sun Rum (Barbados); 40% abv, $28.
    Produced at the R.L. Seale Distillery in Barbados. The ochre/deep amber hue dazzles the eye, especially the bronze core highlights; unblemished purity. The first inhalations pick up lots of baking spices, most notably, cinnamon, nutmeg, and vanilla bean that lie atop a solid molasses foundation; further aeration reveals expanding dry to off-dry aromas of coffee bean, cocoa, new saddle leather, and toasted marshmallow. The palate entry is alluringly semisweet, leather-like, and even a touch smoky; at the midpalate stage the taste profile fills out with mature flavors of oaky vanilla, brown butter, molasses, butterscotch, and almond paste. Concludes semisweet, medium-weighted in texture, and elegant. Served straight or as a cocktail ingredient? Either, really. The distilling prowess of Richard Seale comes to the fore in this very pretty rum.
2007 Rating: ★★★★/Highly Recommended

Tommy Bahama White Sand Rum (Barbados); 40% abv, $28.
    Produced at the R.L. Seale Distillery in Barbados. The appearance is silvery clear and impeccably clean. The initial aromatic bursts are delicate and gently semisweet in a confectioner's sugar manner; the additional seven minute air contact period offers added, if subtle, dimensions of unsalted butter, nutshell, and paraffin. The palate entry offers early off-dry and delectable tastes of butter cream and refined sugar; by the midpalate stage the flavor profile includes a nicely viscous texture and animated tastes of nutshell, nutmeg, and molasses. Finishes gracefully, elegant, and creamy. A substantial, well-made white rum that's poised and ready for scores of up-market cocktails.
2007 Rating: ★★★/Recommended

Tortuga Gold Rum (Cayman Islands); 40% abv, $15/liter.
    Blended and bottled in Jamaica. The pretty amber/light brown color looks very similar to a young brandy; clean, clear. The opening nosing comes across soft, marshmallow-like

scents that are seed-like and earthy; later sniffs pick up disintegrated, if desultory aromas of tobacco, tar, light honey, and spice. The palate entry is candy sweet and bitter on the back of the tongue; the midpalate improves on the entry taste by offering a more cohesive flavor experience whose components include molasses, cake batter, dried fruits, and winter holiday spices, especially cinnamon and nutmeg. Decent, drinkable, best as a mixer but wholly average and unexceptional.

2006 Rating: ★★/Not Recommended

Tortuga Light Rum (Cayman Islands); 40% abv, $15/liter.

Blended and bottled in Jamaica. Impeccably clean and clear. The first whiffs pick up restrained aromas of dark honey and grass; later nasal rounds encounter subtle and bittersweet, slightly earthy elements of chalk, molasses, and brown sugar. The palate entry is off-dry, clean and chalky; the midpalate is where this rum shines brightest as the flavor profile advances rapidly once on the tongue, emitting savory tastes of molasses, dark honey, cream sherry, cake frosting, and cocoa. Finishes bittersweet, sugar cane-like, long, and a touch light caramel-like. Excellent value.

2006 Rating: ★★★/Recommended

Trader Vic's Authentic Spiced Rum (West Indies); 35% abv, $10/liter.

The pale amber/light honey hue is pleasing to the eye. The initial nosing passes pick up elusive scents of egg cream, delicate spice, and brown sugar; disappointingly, seven more minutes of aeration do very little to expand on the base aromas. The palate entry is lean, mildly spicy, but synthetic and metallic; at midpalate the taste profile is astringent and lead-like, lacking in spice and certainly deficient in quality. Ends up tasting like an old penny. Best described by the words "garbage" and "distilling embarrassment."

2005 Rating: ★/Not Recommended

Trader Vic's Pineapple Rum (West Indies); 27.5% abv, $10.

Admirably pure and silvery clean. Starts out aromatically with a flurry of pineapple candy and bubble gum scents; after another six minutes of air contact, the pineapple element goes from being candied to being canned and processed; no evidence of actual fruit here. The palate entry is moderately sweet and candied; at midpalate the taste profile turns tinny/metallic and not at all akin to fresh pineapple. Ends up tasting coin-like and minerally. Pineapple is admittedly a hard flavoring to get right, but this sorrowful, but not horrible offering isn't even on the radar screen.

2005 Rating: ★/Not Recommended

Trapiche Del Valle Premium Aged Rum (Columbia); 40% abv, $15.

Pretty topaz/medium bronze color; ideal purity. The first couple minutes of sniffing unearths big-hearted scents of old oak cask, vanilla extract, and tobacco ash; further time in the glass unleashes additional aromas including butterscotch, light caramel, and lanolin. The palate entry is maple-like and bittersweet; the midpalate juncture displays touches of honey, mead, and cocoa. The finish is long, off-dry to semisweet and very caramel-like. Hardly a classic, but it owns and displays enough virtues to give it the recommendation nod.

2003 Rating: ★★★/Recommended

Trapiche Gold Rum (Columbia); 40% abv, $13.
Attractive, golden hay/light amber color; superb purity. The initial nosings detect odd, but alluring scents of dried herbs, licorice and phenols; time in the copita of another six minutes adds subtle notes of almond butter and oil as the herbal/woodsy scent expands. The palate entry isn't as intriguing as the bouquet as the intense herbal quality doesn't translate well from aroma to flavor; the midpalate is better as bittersweet, kernel-like flavors of tar and oil bail the flavor phase out. The aftertaste is very acidic/acetate, dry and zesty. I almost recommended it, but it just didn't have what it takes in the final analysis to make it over the top; atypical but drinkable.
2003 Rating: ★★/Not Recommended

Trapiche Silver Rum (Columbia); 40% abv, $13.
Absolute purity and clean transparence. The opening nosing passes encounter fine, bean-like scents that remind me pleasingly of beeswax, even slightly salty acetate; regrettably, seven more minutes in the glass produce no further attributes worth mentioning, just the intense and pleasant beaniness. The palate entry is sweet, almost cocoa-like, and viscous; by the midpalate point the molasses bitterness makes itself known as it swamps any sense of sweetness. The aftertaste is long, sweet, and bean-like. Drinkable, if dangerously one-dimensional and plain; it's all surface, not enough genuine depth.
2003 Rating: ★★/Not Recommended

Versailles 15 Year Old Demerara Rum (Guyana); 46% abv, $67.
The attractive color is the bright amber/light honey of a better fino sherry; ideal purity. The nose is appealing in the first go-round as reluctant scents of black pepper, brown sugar, and pears mix and mingle politely; by the second whiff, there's a strange and mildly off-putting aroma of paraffin; the third sniffing sees no further expansion or deepening and, in fact, turns slightly metallic/slate-like; by the fourth nosing pass, clearly aeration has helped this bouquet as the perfume of spice just barely overrides the sheet metal aroma; a very strange and atypical bouquet that comes off as being manufactured. The palate entry shows signs of licorice and aniseed—huh? this is rum?—the midpalate stage is spicy (allspice? nutmeg?) and prickly on the tongue. The aftertaste is oily, long, and intensely peppery. Not my cup of Demerara rum, but drinkable.
2000 Rating: ★★/Not Recommended

Voodoo (Redrum) Spiced Rum (US Virgin Islands); 35% abv, $15.
Pretty, light amber/dessert wine hue; excellent purity. In the opening sniffings I detect heavy amounts of brown sugar and pleasant spice, especially cinnamon, aromas; extra time in the glass means little to this rum; a subtle element of vanilla that peeks through the veil of spice in the final whiff. The palate entry is mildly spicy; at midpalate the vanilla component comes through nicely on the tongue, yet I still feel that this is a mundane spiced rum. Finishes short and dull. Drinkable and certainly mixable, but not in the league of either Foursquare or Captain Morgan Original.
2002 Rating: ★★/Not Recommended

Whaler's "Killer" Coconut Coconut-Flavored Rum (USA); 20% abv, $13.

Limpid, but with a painfully faint off-white, buff tint; acceptable purity. The initial nosing pass finds a blockbuster sweet coconut perfume that is more liqueur-like than rum-like; the second and third passes only add a touch of oiliness as the coconut scent continues to dominate; the last sniffing is just more of the same, sweet coconut in the extreme. The palate entry mirrors the bouquet on the coconut front; the midpalate is, well, nothing but coconut. The aftertaste…forget it. The lack of balance and subtlety astound me; flavored spirits are at their best when they leave room for nuance; like the Vanille, the distiller didn't know when to turn off the flavoring spigot and, consequently, has ended up with another ham-fisted rum that's fit only for coconut fanatics and people with no palate sensitivity at all.
2001 Rating: ★/Not Recommended

Whaler's Big Island Banana Rum (USA); 24% abv, $12.

Clear as glass, but showing some sediment. The opening nose is off-dry and very banana-like; with time in the glass the banana perfume starts to turn like banana taffy candy rather than fresh fruit, but it's perfectly fine. The palate entry is dry to off-dry, somewhat banana-like and a touch bean-like; the midpalate point shows more in the way of actual banana fruit. The finish is all right, mildly sweet and long. I don't mind it at all but I don't see too many applications for this flavored rum; how many memorable banana cocktails are there?
2003 Rating: ★★★/Recommended

Whaler's Original Great White Rum (USA); 40% abv, $13.

Clear and clean; impeccable purity. The aroma at opening is forward, bean-like and inviting; the middle stage passes concentrate on the intense beaniness which smacks of vanilla bean and cacao; the final whiff, after eight minutes of air contact, sees the beaniness soften and turn from bittersweet to bitter, almost like brown sugar; pretty much a one-note aromatic melody, but it's a song that's played skillfully; I like this no-nonsense bouquet quite a lot. The palate entry is moderately sweet and near-prickly; then the midpalate becomes intensely sweet and cocoa-like; the texture is oily and supple. The long, leisurely aftertaste turns up the volume on the brown sugar component, making for a bittersweet conclusion. This is not a profound or benchmark white rum, but so few are. Whaler's Great White is a well-crafted, focused white rum that shows singular charm from beginning to end. It is priced right and runs rings around most other white rums in the marketplace.
2001 Rating: ★★★★/Highly Recommended

Whaler's Pineapple Paradise Rum (USA); 24% abv, $12.

Clear as rainwater and pure. The delicate first aromas following the pour offer delicate traces of crushed pineapple fruit, very soft; additional time in the glass doesn't affect this bouquet as the pineapple element remains the same throughout. The palate entry is off-dry and true to the fruit source; by the midpalate stage the flavor profile refrains from turning juicy or ooey-gooey which I favorably respond to; it just stays the straight and narrow taste course of off-dry crushed pineapple. The aftertaste is lean, tart, and just a touch fruity. A good ingredient for piña coladas.
2003 Rating: ★★★/Recommended

Whaler's Rare Reserve Dark Rum with Natural Flavors (USA); 40% abv, $13.

The orange pekoe tea-like appearance shines under the evaluation lamp; excellent purity. The friendly bouquet opens up with atypical scents of rubber eraser, tar, and sesame oil; with time in the glass, the aroma expands only slightly in the second and third passes, adding curious odors of cassia bark (a common flavoring in gin) and honeywheat bread; by the fourth and last sniffing, nine minutes on, the first glimpse of sugarcane is detected but way in the distance; an oddball rum aroma, to say the least, and I can't help but wonder what the "natural flavors" are, caramel? sherry? food coloring? Whaler's Dark is more normal in the mouth as semisweet tastes of molasses and honey are evident in the palate entry; the midpalate is bittersweet, subdued, and oily. The finish is long, oily (as in nut oil), and mildly peppery. Most certainly drinkable, but neither complex nor elegant; I didn't get the impression that this is anything more than the base rum with caramel added; it's average but hollow.

2001 Rating: ★★/Not Recommended

Whaler's Spiced Rum (USA); 35% abv, $13.

The color is light amber/harvest gold; fine purity. Compelling scents of cinnamon and nutmeg leap from the sampling glass in the first nosing pass; with aeration, the spiciness settles down in the middle stage sniffings, showing aromas of nougat, candied nuts, and cocoa butter; in the final nosing, the piquant spice has all but been laid to rest while the other aromatic elements, especially the cocoa butter and nuts, combine with a new scent, citrus peel, to make for a pleasant ending. In the mouth, the flavor of chocolate cream greets the taste buds at palate entry; the mildly spicy midpalate tastes expand to include butter cream and nutmeg. The finish is long, a touch hot, and more bittersweet than spicy; a solid and recommendable spiced rum by all accounts.

2001 Rating: ★★★/Recommended

Whaler's Vanilla-Flavored Rum (USA); 35% abv, $13.

This attractive rum is the bronze/topaz color of a quality oloroso sherry; ideal purity. The sensuous opening bouquet reminds me very much of cream (vanilla flavored) soda or egg cream; the second and third nosings unearth faint traces of bittersweet chocolate and marzipan; following nine minutes of exposure to air, the final pass turns even more eggy/creamy. In the mouth, this very sweet rum tastes of vanilla cake frosting and little else; in fact, the vanilla flavoring is so prevalent that scant opportunity is available for any other flavor element to emerge by midpalate. The aftertaste borders on being syrupy sweet, cloying, and viscous. The heavy-handedness of the vanilla flavoring tips the balance of the rum, making the end result awkward, clumsy, and over the top; once past the opening moments of the aroma, it's downhill all the way.

2001 Rating: ★/Not Recommended

Ypioca Crystal Cachaça Aguardente de Cana (Brazil); 39% abv, $35/liter.

The silvery/pale lemon juice yellow color shows quite a bit of floating sediment, but not enough to sound alarms. The nose after bottle opening is vegetal and slightly briny; the middle stage passes unearth nuances of metal, dill, and saline solution; the last sniffing reveals nothing new in terms of expansion or evolution; overview is that of a dull, plodding aroma with little or no charm. On the palate, it offers more in the way of intrigue as the taste starts dry at entry then turns semi-dry and a bit sugary (as in cane, not refined sugar) at midpalate. The finish is the best part of the sensory evaluation as the flavor turns sweet and warming. An okay, entirely average cane-based spirit.

2001 Rating: ★★/Not Recommended

Ypioca Ouro (Gold) Cachaça Aguardente de Cana (Brazil); 39% abv, $37/liter.

The color is a marigold/honey tint; excellent purity. The initial nosing pass reveals lots of dill and dried herbs; the middle stage sniffings see the aroma's development clip along at a respectable pace as scents of tapioca, mild brine, and steamed white rice make a favorable impression; the final pass adds a zesty note of black pepper, which somehow is the ideal element to round out the brine; I like this bouquet very much. Noticeably sweet, almost succulent, at palate entry as the taste of caramel overrides all other flavors in the early stage; the midpalate is even sweeter than the entry as the toasty/smoky caramel flavor borders on becoming syrupy sweet. The aftertaste is long, sweet, and warming. A solidly made, recommendable cachaça, but I prefer the splendid Prata.

2001 Rating: ★★★/Recommended

Ypioca Prata (Silver) Cachaça Aguardente de Cana (Brazil); 39% abv, $37/liter.

Look-alike of the Crystal; the identical, painfully pale flax/silver hue; the big difference is at the purity level, with Prata appearing much tighter and cleaner. This nose is more expressive and active than that of the lumbering Crystal; the second and third nosing passes detect far more herbal presence in the forms of dill, tea leaves, and evergreen; the final whiff, after six minutes of aeration, is zesty, piquant but not prickly, and altogether inviting; this is what I think of when I'm talking cachaça aromatics. The intensity level is kicked up a notch or two at palate entry as the tastes of sweet charcoal and soot give a wake up call to the taste buds; the midpalate phase shows development of the sweet sugar cane as the flavor goes concentrated and pleasantly sweet. The finish is round, firm, clean tasting, and agreeably sweet.

2001 Rating: ★★★★/Highly Recommended

Zaya 12 Year Old Gran Reserva Rum (Guatemala); 40% abv, $45.

The color is a burnished orange/bronze/topaz very similar to oloroso sherry; some minor sediment spotted; not a negative aspect. The seductive nose after the pour is juicy, with ripe, fruity aromas of baked apple, baked pear; aeration time of another seven minutes rouses deeper scents of brown sugar, nutmeg, vanilla bean, cardamom, and dried orange peel. The palate entry is firm, bittersweet, and focused; the midpalate is long, more lean than plump, more bittersweet than sweet, more maple-like than sugary. The finish is long, moderately oily, and keenly bittersweet. Sophisticated, intensely cane-like, and in that league of ultra-premium aged rums that begins to resemble brandies.

2003 Rating: ★★★★/Highly Recommended

TEQUILA, SOTOL, MEZCAL & OTHER AGAVE BASED SPIRITS—MEXICO—WORLD

All tequila is produced in the five west-central Mexican states of Jalisco, Nayarit, Michoacán, Guanajuato, and Tamaulipas in governmentally demarcated areas that taken together cover over 26 million acres. Jalisco, which accounts for 98% of tequila production, is the epicenter of the tequila industry and is home to the town of Tequila as well as most of the distilleries. Tequila is legally made in two fundamental types: 100% Agave and mixto. Those bottled as "100% Agave" are comprised totally from the fermented and twice-distilled juice of but one kind of agave plant, the blue agave. The official botanical moniker of blue agave is Agave Tequiliana Weber azul, named after the German botanist, F. Weber, who classified agaves at the turn of the 20th century. It generally takes a minimum of six to eight years for an agave plant to grow to the point of being ready for harvest. One liter of agave spirit requires at least 15 pounds of agave fiber. From the farmers' standpoint, agave farming is a long-term enterprise and investment.

Herbaceous 100% agave tequilas are considered to be Mexico's elite offerings. They are defined by age as Blanco, or tequila that is bottled within 60 days of production and is generally unaged; Reposado (rested), which is tequila that has been matured in wood barrels from 60 days to one year; Añejo, or tequila that's been aged in oak barrels (maximum size is 600 liters) from one to three years; and Extra Añejo, or tequila that's been matured in small oak barrels for at least three years.

The lesser class of tequila, mixto (pronounced mees-toe) is a marriage of convenience between pure blue agave spirits and sugar cane-based spirits. The saving grace of mixtos is that, by law, blue agave distillate makes up the majority (51%) of the blend. Typically, smooth-tasting 100% agave tequilas are of significantly higher quality than mixtos and, therefore, cost more. Most mixtos are perfectly suitable for mixing in cocktails, though nowadays enlightened bartenders lean towards making particularly distinctive mixed drinks with the more flavorful 100% agave tequilas.

Also be aware of tequilas named Gold, Abocado, Suave or Joven. These are unaged tequilas to which colorants and flavorings, like caramel coloring, oak tree extracts, glycerine, or sugar syrup, have been added before bottling. They can be made from 100% agave but are normally mixtos.

Tequila is one of the most exciting distillates right now because of its ironclad link to its place of origin and its agricultural foundation. Made under some of the strictest governmental regulations of all, tequila is showing how world-class a spirit it can be and is. The coming decade will see it propelled forward even further.

Mezcal (aka, mescal) by contrast, is made from any of five agave varieties rather than one, as in the case of tequila. The workhorse variety in the making of mezcal is Agave angustifolia Haw, which is known to Mexican farmers as espadin. The five non-blue agave types are one pivotal reason for mezcal's marked taste difference from smoother, silkier tequila. Mezcal production originates in primitive factories called palenques that are located in the five south-central Mexican states of Oaxaca, Durango, San Luis Potasi, Guerrero, and Zacatecas. Alcohol-by-volume content of mezcal ranges from a low of 40% up to a high of 47.5% in more specialized bottlings.

Mezcals for decades were—and to large measure still are—distilled only once. This means that many natural chemical compounds and oils remain in the finished product. These are thought in some quarters to be negative traits that give off musky odors reminiscent of burning tires, rotting meat or creosote. Mezcal proponents argue that these biochemical remnants are what make mezcal so special and unique…and refreshingly different from tequila. The champions of mezcal claim that mezcal is more authentic than tequila because its chemical properties aren't stripped away through distillation. While for years I struggled to find virtues in mezcal, I have made a turn-around as mezcal has cleaned itself up in the last five years.

Another agave-based gem is **sotol**, produced in the northern Mexican state of Chihuahua. I think of sotol as midway between tequila and mezcal in character.

PLEASE NOTE that retail prices for tequila have soared from 2005 to 2007 and that listed prices from before 2005 will have accelerated dramatically, sometimes by as much as 50% to 75%.

100 Años Blanco Tequila (Mexico); 40% abv, $20.
Silvery in color; ideally clean. Smells of herbal agave and plastic/vinyl in the first whiffs; high notes of white and black pepper come across assertively in the later inhalations, backed by a bittersweet agave note that underpins the bouquet. Entry is far sweeter than I thought it would be and nicely warm, with vegetal tastes of raw asparagus and Brussels sprouts; the flavor profile goes to an even higher level of sugary sweetness at midpalate and that occurrence wipes out any of the vegetal/spicy/herbal qualities whatsoever. Finishes keenly sweet. Has to be a mixto with this level of sweetness. I don't see the words "100% Agave" anywhere on the label or in the promotional materials. Certainly drinkable, but the in-yer-face sweetness does not make it easy to mix unless you use lots of lime juice to cut it.
2007 Rating: ★★/Not Recommended

1800 Antigua Reserva Añejo 100% Agave Tequila (Mexico); 40% abv, $39.
The gorgeous honey brown/topaz color is an eye-catcher; superb purity. The first couple of whiffs reveal plump, toffee-caramel notes that ride the surface aroma that's underpinned by asparagus-like agave; later inhalations unearth nuances of fennel, white pepper, sage, and rosemary; there's a lot happening in this complex and engaging bouquet. The palate entry is vegetal, green and off-dry; at midpalate the flavor profile swings back the other way turning sweet/sour, fruity, and oaky; concludes on a bittersweet note that somehow closes the circle on the journey. A good buy when one considers how ridiculously high most añejos have

gone in price as tequila producers continue to gauge consumers to see how much they are willing to pay.
2004 Rating: ★★★★/Highly Recommended

1800 Colección 100% Agave Añejo Tequila (Mexico); 40% abv, $1,800.
A tequila that should be classified as Extra Aged. The topaz/honey brown color displays a bright wheat harvest gold core and ideal purity. Vibrant aromatic notes of asparagus, dill, and pickle brine are featured in the initial inhalations after the pour; following another seven minutes of aeration, the bouquet shows minerally (slate, limestone), plastic/acetate (vinyl), and fresh herb (tarragon, sage) scents, even mint in the final sniff; there's a lot of aromatic levels occurring here. The palate entry is mildly sweet in an oaky/woody, slightly smoky/pipe tobacco manner; at midpalate the off-dry taste thrust is squarely on the deep herbal/vegetal/spicy flavors that remind me vividly of white pepper, palm oil, loose leaf tobacco, and steamed asparagus. Ends dry and complex, but not especially long in the mouth. Disproves all the naysayers' claims that tequila can't/won't/shouldn't be matured for extended periods in oak barrels. Even if I think that it's ridiculously and conspicuously overpriced, that has nothing to do with the tequila itself, which is delicious, round, and elegant.
2006 Rating: ★★★★★/Highest Recommendation

1800 Edicion Gran Reserva del Nuevo Milenio Single Barrel Añejo Tequila 100% Blue Agave Barrel 020, Bottle No. 051 (Mexico); 40% abv, $18,000 per Barrel.
The rich amber/honey color reminds me most of amontillado sherry; ideal purity. The nose owns a fine opulence right from the initial nosing pass; by the second sniffing, it's slap-in-the-face evident that this edition of 1800 is trailblazing lofty new territory for the Cuervo distillery as brandy-like aromas of biscuits, butter, and fresh cut flowers override the vegetal agave base; the third nosing pass reveals the crisp, acidic backbone of oak that's the real story here in my eyes as the regal aromas, highlighted by the semisweet, almost cocoa-like agave, dance on the surface; the fourth and last whiff after ten minutes of aeration convinces me without a doubt that this stately, integrated, and totally harmonious spirit deserves to be in the tequila pantheon; truly fabulous. The palate entry is silky smooth, muscular, and oaky; by the midpalate stage a layer of rich texture buttresses the bevy of flavors starting with bittersweet chocolate, butter, and oak resin and finishing with brandy-like bacon fat and hard cheese. The finish is long, lingering, warming, and caramel-like. The Beckmann family has created an instant classic and a benchmark that runs with the best from El Tesoro and Herradura; this is a genuinely great distilled spirit.
2000 Rating: ★★★★★/Highest Recommendation

1800 Reposado 100% Agave Tequila (Mexico); 40% abv, $28.
The pale gold/gray color is pretty and impeccably pure. The first two minutes of inhaling focus on the presence of black pepper and steamed broccoli; six minutes later, the aroma turns into a bouquet as lovely, succulent scents of Brazil nuts, egg cream, and light oak resin make for happy sniffing. The palate entry keys on an oily flavor of bacon; at midpalate the pepper returns with added tastes of spinach, sage, and butter. Finishes elegantly yet zestily as the pepper comes to the forefront.
2004 Rating: ★★★★/Highly Recommended

1800 Silver 100% Agave Tequila (Mexico); 40% abv, $24.

Clear and relatively pure. Dry scents of worn leather and Brussels sprouts dominate the first two minutes of sniffing; six more minutes of exposure to air stimulate added vegetal aromas of green pepper and uncooked asparagus; I notice at the very end of the nosing phase an aroma of oil. The palate entry is firm, moderately oily, and dry; by midpalate there's a flavor expansion that features nuances of black pepper and chalk. Ends up totally dry with a touch of black peppercorn. Perfect for tequila sunrises.

2004 Rating: ★★★/Recommended

267 Infusions Chili Pepper Tequila (Mexico); 21% abv, $25.

Pale silver/straw/gray color; some pepper sediment, which is expected since there are three chili peppers floating in the bottle. The engaging aroma is zesty, keenly peppery, and pleasingly vegetal right after the pour; further exposure to air brings out the spiciness of the peppers even more, making it a decidedly piquant nosing experience. The palate entry has my taste buds singing mariachi as the pepper intensity makes for low-to-medium chili pepper heat; the midpalate offers a curious sweetness that rides beneath the pepperiness. The agave factor is all but lost due to the peppers and I feel strongly that this could be a four star product if the abv were raised to 32%-35%, which would give far more presence to the herbal agave, thereby making it better balanced and toothsome.

2006 Rating: ★★★/Recommended

267 Infusions Orange Tequila (Mexico); 21% abv, $25.

The dirty water look of this spirit leaves a lot to be desired, even allowing for the infusion. The smell makes up for the appearance as a tart orange peel scent blends well with an herbal agave perfume; time in the glass bumps up the peppery agave quality and lessens the orange character; overall, however, a very, very game attempt that works. Regrettably, the palate entry falls flat as yet again there's not enough alcohol foundation to support the ambitions of the infusion; the midpalate stage makes an attempt at redemption as the tequila flavor moves forward. Ends up paper thin. I'm giving this libation two stars because I see the seed of something better than good here and with a heightened abv, say, of up to at least 35%, this one has some obvious potential.

2006 Rating: ★★/Not Recommended

30-30 Añejo Tequila 100% Blue Agave (Mexico); 40% abv, $27.

Marginally deeper in yellow shade than the reposado; it's a pretty straw yellow that's free of debris. The opening nose is a bit anemic, emitting weak-kneed aromas of green pepper, wood, and agave; the second and third nosing passes, after three and six minutes respectively, see virtually nothing in the way of expansion or deepening; the fourth and last whiff detects nothing but the status quo, green pepper, dill-like agave, and mild oak resin; I keep thinking "what is this añejo waiting for?". In the mouth, this limp tequila shows a bit more life than in the static aroma as pleasing tastes of vegetal agave, dried herbs, and sweet oak greet the taste buds at palate entry; the midpalate stage, however, turns lackluster and wan. The aftertaste shows a bit more zip as the sweet oak carries the ball. While drinkably ordinary this añejo is too up-and-down in character to be recommended; go instead for the reposado.

2000 Rating: ★★/Not Recommended

30-30 Blanco Tequila 100% Blue Agave (Mexico); 40% abv, $18.
Limpid as spring water; totally free of suspended particles. The nose at opening is more vegetal than herbal but attractive and fresh; the middle stage passes witness moderate deepening of aroma, mostly in the area of vegetal agave perfume; the fourth and final sniffing offers little in the way of expansion as aeration seems to have no effect on this silver tequila. At palate entry, I immediately detect greater substance as the opening taste is sweet and clean; the midpalate stage is sweeter still, but with scant agave personality. The finish is sweet, very long, a touch hot, and basic. Drinkable, entirely average, and unexciting due to its deficient character.
2000 Rating: ★★/Not Recommended

30-30 Reposado Tequila 100% Blue Agave (Mexico); 40% abv, $19.
The pretty color is of pale white wine; absolute clarity and purity. This opening nose is more peppery than the blanco; unfortunately, aeration doesn't appear to agree with this reposado since in the middle stage nosings I detect a notable weakening of aromatic strength; in the fourth and final sniffing, however, there seems to be something of a comeback as the peppery quality returns and the aroma as a whole springs back to life in simple waves of black pepper, vegetable broth, and very mild dill. Better in the mouth than in the nose, this reposado starts out almost buttery at palate entry, then turns silky smooth at midpalate as flavors of sweet agave, sweet oak, and light caramel save the day. The aftertaste is a touch smoky, almost candy-like, and quite extended. To its credit, this reposado engineered a remarkable turnaround in the eleventh hour of the aroma stage and carried it through to the finish; as such, I recommend it, in particular, for margaritas and tequila sunrises.
2000 Rating: ★★★/Recommended

Alcatraz Añejo Tequila (Mexico); 40% abv, $90.
The opulent amber/honey gold color is attractive; medium level of floating detritus noted. The initial nosing pass detects brandy-like caramel and sweet oak notes with hardly any resemblance to agave; with air contact, the middle stage passes finally see some moderate dried herb, lanolin, oak resin, and vegetal/briny agave scents that result in a near-stately bouquet; in the fourth and final sniffing, following more than ten minutes of aeration, a detectable diminishment of strength is noted and the aroma goes strangely sappy and resin-like; a disappointingly uneven bouquet except for flashes of real quality after three to four minutes of aeration, but by the seven minute mark the aroma heads south; significantly rounder, more substantial, and firmer in the mouth than in the nasal cavity. The palate entry is tart and rich on the tip of the tongue; at midpalate the brandy-like old oak component takes the helm and guides the flavor phase into the finish which is long, oaky, caramel sweet, and designer-luscious. While I'm giving this tequila three stars and a recommendation due mainly to its succulent flavor and finish, there is a caveat and that is, this is one of the growing number of añejo tequilas that runs the risk of becoming more a brandy than an oak-aged tequila; I point this out not to criticize the brand, but to make clear what consumers are receiving for their $90; if someone is expecting lots of vibrant and fresh-off-the-still herbal/vegetal agave aroma and flavor, don't purchase this tequila and instead buy the terrific Alcatraz Silver; if, by chance, you relish heavy, oak-laden, sweet to the taste tequilas by all means give this a try.
2000 Rating: ★★★/Recommended

Alcatraz Gold Tequila (Mexico); 40% abv, $33.

The pale yellow/hay-like color is marred slightly by too much transparent floating debris. The nose at opening isn't nearly as expressive as the sibling silver; with aeration the middle stage nosing passes pick up more fragrance primarily in the forms of spirity oil and very delicate sweet oak; the fourth and last whiff, following eight minutes of air contact, reveals very little new data, except for a meager strengthening of the vegetal agave perfume. On the palate, the flavor begins dry and almost caramel-like at entry, then expands into a herbal sweet, oaky, and vanilla-like midpalate phase that's pleasant to my taste but might border on being too heavy-handed with the sweetness for others. The aftertaste is round, composed, very long, and less sweet than the midpalate. A solidly made, wholly recommendable gold, but the price tag weighs heavily against it when viewed against competing, equally appealing, but far less expensive tequila golds, namely Jose Cuervo and Cesar Monterrey.

2000 Rating: ★★★/Recommended

Alcatraz Silver Tequila 100% Blue Agave (Mexico); 40% abv, $27.

Limpid; medium amount of suspended particles noted under the evaluation lamp. The opening whiff finds a vibrant, fresh, and herbal agave bouquet that seems almost fully formed right off the crack of the bat; with aeration in the second and third nosing passes, the aroma turns peppery, sprightly, and even more herbal; in the final sniffing, after nearly nine minutes of air contact, there's a minor diminishment of strength but likewise a pleasant rounding off of the edges that makes for a very satisfying aromatic experience. The palate entry is dry and focused on the dried herb/agave component; at the midpalate stage the taste turns moderately sweet, ripe, firm, gripping, and full of agave herbaceousness and spice; one of the better silver/blanco midpalates to come my way in a while. The finish completes the circle as the flavor again goes dry, indeed almost bitter, but direct, lean, and true to the agave source; just as one wants their silver tequila to be. Bravo, very nice job here.

2000 Rating: ★★★★/Highly Recommended

Amate Añejo 100% Agave Tequila (Mexico); 40% abv, $47.

Deep yellow/light gold hue; unblemished and clean. The early stage aroma is keenly briny/salty/herbal; six more minutes in the copita urges additional scents to make appearances including dark honey and light toffee. The palate entry is pleasantly sweet and viscous while the midpalate features tastes of roasted agave, tobacco leaf, black pepper, and palm oil. Ends up clean and buttery.

2004 Rating: ★★★/Recommended

Amate Blanco 100% Agave Tequila (Mexico); 40% abv, $40.

Faint silver/pale yellow hue; perfect clarity. The heady, spirity, peppery opening aroma is a knock-out; further time in the glass allows the aromas to integrate; the later stage aroma highlights piquant agave pulp, green onion, licorice/fennel, and pickling brine; a fabulous silver agave perfume. The palate entry is sweet, distinctly herbal, and peppery; at midpalate the taste turns creamier than the entry and more oily. Concludes on a sweet, buttery note that's delicious and buxom.

2004 Rating: ★★★★/Highly Recommended

Amate Reposado 100% Agave Tequila (Mexico); 40% abv, $43.

The pale golden color is pure and slightly oily. The initial inhalations detect tobacco smoke and palm oil scents; six more minutes of aeration see the emergence of lanolin, caraway seed, lead pencil, and steamed asparagus; a lovely, multidimensional bouquet. The palate entry is sweet and vegetal; at midpalate the taste profile expands significantly, adding flavors of roasted green peppers, pipe tobacco, and cream. Finishes in a peppery, zesty manner.
2004 Rating: ★★★★/Highly Recommended

AsomBroso Añejo 100% Agave Tequila (Mexico); 40% abv, $250.

Owns a pretty, old sauternes/amber/autumnal gold hue; not as much sediment as the silver, but still shows a tad too much for what you're paying. At first, I am actually puzzled, if thrilled by the semisweet, delicate, honey-like opening sniffs; six more minutes in the copita serve to deepen the honey component as it expands to include vanilla, butter cream, and light toffee; the agave foundation is present but blanketed by the overlaying biscuity, spicy, vanilla wafer aromas; a highly complex spirit nose and like few tequila bouquets I've come across. The palate entry doesn't quite mirror the bouquet as the initial taste goes surprisingly dry to off-dry and oily; by the midpalate stage the flavor profile features diverse and sweeter tastes of malt, light toffee, oaky vanillin, palm oil, and milk chocolate. Finishes smoothly, elegantly, with just a touch of honeyed sweetness. Had the entire taste stage accented or even equaled the sensational bouquet, I'd have easily bestowed a fifth rating star; there was a noticeable letdown at the entry phase; that said, this is still a well-made, luscious añejo tequila that deserves a close look by affluent drinkers.
2004 Rating: ★★★★/Highly Recommended

AsomBroso El Platino (Silver) 100% Agave Tequila (Mexico); 40% abv, $50.

Translucent silver/egg white color; more sediment than I'd like to see. The opening nose crackles with zesty scents of fennel, licorice, anise, and dried herbs; aeration of another six minutes brings out seductive, off-dry aromatic elements of milk chocolate, agave juice, olive brine, rye bread, and green olive; one of the busiest silver tequila bouquets I've encountered of late. The palate entry is compellingly peppery and astringent; then at midpalate the taste profile turns slightly sweeter and fruitier as flavors of sweet pepper, black pepper, and ripe agave meld for a savory silver taste experience. Concludes toasty and mellow. A superb silver that displays lots of finesse, but is hardly short of punch; excellent job here.
2004 Rating: ★★★★/Highly Recommended

Cabo Wabo Añejo 100% Agave Tequila (Mexico); 40% abv, $72.

Displays the golden wheat-like color of an oak-aged chardonnay as well as several bits of sediment. The initial dry fragrance is all black peppercorn and oak resin; seven more minutes allow the aroma to add seductive, semisweet notes of baked banana, bacon fat, dried sage, dried thyme, brown rice, and broccoli in butter sauce; there seem to be at least three layers of aroma to this captivating bouquet. The palate entry is more bitter than the bouquet promised and, as such, surprised me with its bean-like quality; by the midpalate point the taste profile swings around significantly, featuring sweet, wood-influenced tastes of honey, milk chocolate, cream sherry, and vanilla cake frosting. Ends up wrapped in slightly smoky vanilla and cocoa flavors. A superb, mature añejo tequila and spirit that hands-down earns

and deserves its four stars. The reason it didn't pick up a fifth star was that the oak effect stripped away a little too much of the inherent herbal/briny/peppery agave virtues away from it; by contrast, the beauty of the Cabo Wabo Reposado is that you always are aware you're drinking tequila.
2004 Rating: ★★★★/Highly Recommended

Cabo Wabo Blanco 100% Agave Tequila (Mexico); 40% abv, $39.
Silvery and limpid, but with more pulpy sediment floating about than I'd like to see. The zesty bouquet starts right in offering piquant, vegetal aromas that include salty brine, fennel, and green peppercorn; after an aeration period of seven minutes, an arid, dried sage/southwestern USA/desert-like aroma takes command, with assistance from palm oil, burnt match, and metallic notes of lead/rust/nickel; a real aromatic, briny handful for a blanco. The palate entry is vegetal/herbal, but semisweet and oily; the midpalate phase is sweet, buttery, fatty, and intensely peppery; ends in an agave pulp-like way, highlighting the vegetal/"green" side of agave. A rustic, unbridled blanco; in a word, delicious.
2004 Rating: ★★★★/Highly Recommended

Cabo Wabo Reposado 100% Agave Tequila (Mexico); 40% abv, $50.
Pale gold in color and, like its sibling, the Blanco, displays sediment beneath the examination lamp. The fine, early aroma is off-dry and gently herbal, with a trace of honey backnote; allowing it another six minutes in the glass, the aroma blossoms into a harmonious, integrated bouquet that's peppery, herbal, waxy, and even floral, with a sensational parting wave of English toffee; a restrained, understated aromatic masterpiece for tequila. The palate entry is medium-bodied, oily, resiny, herbal, and semisweet; the midpalate displays exceedingly refined and balanced flavors of green pepper, red pepper, light toffee, and light honey. It finishes as gracefully and politely as it began, with subtle hints of fresh herbs (in particular, sage and thyme), toffee, and oil. A classic distilled spirit that deserves your immediate attention and one that should be served neat in a wide-mouthed Old-Fashioned glass; an outstanding achievement.
2004 Rating: ★★★★★/Highest Recommendation

Calendé Añejo Tequila (Mexico); 40% abv, $25.
The color is off-dry white wine, a light golden/yellow hue; perfect purity. The nose comes off musty and attic-like in the initial stages, almost as though there's a cork problem; the TCA flaw blows off following further aeration, leaving behind a moderately biscuity/doughy scent that's pleasant, if atypical. The palate entry is intensely vegetal, medium-bodied, and more sweet than either spicy or herbal; the midpalate stage is zesty, peppery, and keenly vegetal (asparagus, kale). Concludes ripe, gently sweet, and just a tad oaky. Oaky-dokey.
2006 Rating: ★★★/Recommended

Calendé Reposado Tequila (Mexico); 40% abv, $23.
The light lemon juice/pale straw color is pretty and clean. The first nosings pick up pleasing peppery notes, buttressed by strong herbal/botanical scents that include tree bark and fiber; after another six minutes in the glass, the bouquet opens up, adding mildly bitter/mineral-like fragrances of green olive, brine, granite, and sea salt. The palate entry is ripe,

smooth, and sweet; the midpalate phase features flavors of milk chocolate, butter cream, and light caramel. Finishes sweet, oaky, and medium-textured.

2006 Rating: ★★★/Recommended

Carmessi Reposado 100% Agave Tequila (Mexico); 40% abv, $30.

Very attractive straw/gold tint; excellent purity. The opening nosing passes are treated to a textbook reposado bouquet right from the start as fully developed and clean aromas of herbs, dill, and citrus rind; with aeration the herbal notes become more pronounced in the later sniffings along with more subtle hints of light brine, green olive, and light oak; a superb reposado bouquet by any measure. The palate entry offers lean, but not austere tastes of wood and semisweet agave; the midpalate point features focused, correctly astringent tastes of agave, green vegetables (steamed asparagus, in particular), and olives. The aftertaste is brief, lean, and dry. What I like about this reposado is that unlike so many others it's not sweet from caramel or over-processed agave; this is graceful, natural reposado drinking.

2002 Rating: ★★★★/Highly Recommended

Casa Noble Crystal Blanco 100% Blue Agave Tequila (Mexico); 40% abv, $40.

The limpid, clear appearance is clean and pure. The initial nosing pass offers a high degree of dill pickle/pickling brine; the second sniffing sees the aroma turn peppery and spicy; following six minutes of aeration, the aroma in the third pass expands to include scents of lead pencil and herb-like agave pulp; in the fourth and last whiff the disparate aromas come together in a harmonious and highly attractive finale which features the pepperiness more than any other aromatic component. The palate entry is lean and even austere, then the flavor gets meatier at midpalate as the agave sweetness dominates over the spiciness. The aftertaste is medium long, sweet, and mildly oily. A very solid, well-structured blanco that's more sweet than spicy or spirity.

2000 Rating: ★★★/Recommended

Casa Noble Gold 100% Blue Agave Tequila (Mexico); 40% abv, $45.

Pale straw yellow/lemon juice hue; ideal clarity. Interesting aromatic notes of caramel, nut butter, and cream greet the olfactory sense; the second pass finds the aroma needing a jump start as the caramel becomes something of a blanket under which any other scents are hidden; with air contact, a more typical dill/brine perfume starts to stir in the third sniffing; the fourth and last whiff finds more defined dill, but little else; this is ultimately a muted, dull aroma that hides behind the caramel. Slightly more expressive in the mouth than in the nose; the palate entry is candy/toffee sweet; the midpalate stage offers very mild pepper/spice/brine as once again the caramel sweetness, while pleasing in a simplistic way, offers nothing else a chance to show up. The finish is medium long, a bit more herbal than the midpalate and silky smooth in the throat. Long on superficial charm, short on real distilled agave substance or complexity; the Crystal is the better bet.

2000 Rating: ★★/Not Recommended

Casa Noble Reposado 100% Blue Agave Tequila (Mexico); 40% abv, $50.

Matured in French oak for a full year. The light amber/yellow shade is really gorgeous and pure. The nose is seductive and compelling right from the first nosing pass after the pour as mature scents of brine, forest herbs, and lead pencil enchant the olfactory sense; the second sniffing features more of the herbs and pepperiness than the lead pencil; with further exposure to air, the third whiff offers deepening yet graceful aromas of soft caramel, mild oak, herbal agave, and sea salt (I especially like the bouquet at this stage of five to seven minutes of aeration); with further time in the glass, the final sniffing sees the dill/brine element come to the forefront; a genuinely elegant and top-of-the-category bouquet. The intensely sweet taste at palate entry is more vegetal than oaky or caramelly; the midpalate stage is laden with sweet light toffee and candied nut flavors, which while tasty, don't necessarily match-up to the elegance of the aroma. The finish is long, toasty/caramelly, and resiny from the oak. Highly Recommended, but could have gone even further in the ratings department had the taste phase equaled the superb quality found in the bouquet.

2000 Rating: ★★★★/Highly Recommended

Casa Noble Special Reserve Extra Aged 100% Blue Agave Tequila (Mexico); 40% abv, $80.

Aged in French oak for five years; the brilliant amber tone is impeccably pure and clean. The nose at opening is rich, almost brandy-like, and oaky; with time in the glass, the aroma becomes a bouquet as the oak influence is joined by a mild vegetal component and a background pepperiness; the third sniffing pass reveals a soft brininess that complements the pillowy oakiness; in the fourth and final whiff, the delicate, perfumy scents of oak resin and vanilla, mature agave, and nut butter unite to form an atypically biscuity tequila bouquet; while I actually prefer the nose of the reposado, this one is very pleasing and well-structured. The palate entry is mildly sweet and oaky, but then the midpalate stage explodes with firm, meaty tastes of nut butter, pepper, and light caramel. The finish is long, spirity, and elegant. Very nice indeed.

2000 Rating: ★★★★/Highly Recommended

Casca Viejo Gold Tequila 100% Blue Agave (Mexico); 40% abv $13.

The appearance is quite pretty; the color is a soft lemon yellow and is perfectly clean and clear. Unfortunately, the opening aroma is, well, stinky and kippery, almost like smoked fish; with air contact, the aroma doesn't improve one iota in the middle stage nosings as smelly odors of sulphur, burnt matches, petroleum, and fish hardly charm the olfactory sense; by the fourth and last nosing pass, the aroma tanks completely as the industrial odors just seem to keep getting stronger; one of the worst tequila aromas I've come across. Not much better in the mouth as the burnt rubber, smoky features found in the aroma get translated to the taste right from the entry; the midpalate is dismal, tanky, steely, sickly sweet, totally medicinal, and obnoxiously rank. The aftertaste echoes the midpalate. Terrible and undrinkable, period; hey, let's party!

2000 Rating: ★/Not Recommended

Cazadores Reposado 100% Agave Tequila (Mexico); 40% abv, $33.

Pale straw/gold color; good clarity. The first couple of nosings detect proper, if restrained 100% agave notes of dill and black pepper; further aeration time of seven minutes does little to encourage any broader aromatic expansion. On the palate Cazadores is nimble, light and off-dry at entry; by the midpalate point there are flavor elements of cocoa bean and

asparagus. The finish is clean, light, off-dry and quite brief. An ethereal style of reposado that is somewhat short on sensory impact but long on finesse; a kind of Reposado Light.
2003 Rating: ★★★/Recommended

Certeza Añejo 100% Agave Tequila (Mexico); 40% abv, $60.
Pretty honey/wheat harvest amber; superb clarity. Initially, the aroma is toasty, honey wheat-like, leathery, and round in the first two minutes of inhalations; with time in the glass, the aroma turns buttery and vanilla-like, with slight traces of cinnamon, rubber pencil eraser, and nut paste. The palate entry offers pleasant, if pointed and lean bittersweet flavors of nougat and caramel; the midpalate sees the addition of spicy oak, cocoa, and fruit stone. Ends up spry, a little too bittersweet, and acceptably average, if seriously overpriced.
2006 Rating: ★★/Not Recommended

Certeza Blanco 100% Agave Tequila (Mexico); 40% abv, $40.
Crystalline, silvery appearance; ideally free of sediment. The pickle-like first aromas are particularly vegetal and too top-heavy with acetone (cleaning fluid) notes; the acetone factor picks up momentum with aeration, making for disappointing (intensely floor polish-like) sniffing since the primary scent is too reminiscent of lighter or cleaning fluid or, worst, cleaning wax; a miserable bouquet that overshoots the mark by three football fields. The palate entry is raw, harsh, and biting; the midpalate taste sensation is overly hot, searing, unbridled, and displeasing; the flavor phase is more of an assault than an evaluation. Concludes as savory to the taste as pine-scented cleanser. Nothing short of a $40 train wreck. Indeed, this El Puro Woofer would be a sidesplitting laugher at $15...but only if it wasn't your money.
2006 Rating: ★/Not Recommended

Certeza Reposado 100% Agave Tequila (Mexico); 40% abv, $45.
Pretty straw-gold color; impeccable purity. The first sniffs detect light and mildly appealing scents of pine sap, cedar, and clove; later whiffs pick up some of the rank acetone/cleaning fluid odors that worked against the Blanco; the bouquet degrades with air contact. The palate entry is green, acidic, waxy, and moderately vegetal/briny; the midpalate displays a tad more character as the taste offers some customary elements of pepper, green vegetable, and minerals, but no fennel, no dill, no herbs. Finishes with a big rush of pine/cedar. Average and unjustifiably pricey.
2006 Rating: ★★/Not Recommended

Cesar Monterrey Gold Reserva Tequila 51% Blue Agave/49% Green Agave (Mexico); 40% abv, $18.
Made from 51% blue agave and 49% green agave. The pale honey gold color is attractive and correct for the category; insignificant particles noted. The nose at opening sports a pleasant, zesty herbal/dill agave bouquet; in the middle stage nosings, I pick up more in the way of dried herbs and a trace of brine; in the fourth and final sniffing, after nine minutes of aeration, there's a slight diminishment in aromatic potency, but not enough to be viewed as a negative happening; overall, a solid, properly herbal gold bouquet. In the mouth, there's plenty of piquant, vibrant, vegetal agave flavor immediately upon palate entry; the midpalate shows a spit or two of fire on the tongue, which I like, and plenty of straightforward, fresh

agave taste that suddenly turns sweet in the long, vegetal aftertaste. A very good new entry into the gold tequila sweepstakes.
2000 Rating: ★★★/Recommended

Cesar Monterrey Añejo Reserva 100% Agave Tequila (Mexico); 40% abv, $75.
Like its siblings, this tequila suffers from an unappealing appearance because of lots of cork-like debris; this should not be happening in a tequila costing this much; no excuse is good enough. Making up for lost ground, the opening aroma is zesty, acutely peppery and briny; aeration allows the aroma the time and space to add scents of new oak, tobacco leaf and light honey. The palate entry is long, sweet, oaky, and slightly honeyed; the midpalate stage boasts an elegance and a sturdy agave sweetness that wins major points. Finishes in a honeyed, almost sherry-like manner that's highly charming. Recovered by a long way from a shaky start.
2006 Rating: ★★★★/Highly Recommended

Cesar Monterrey Blanco Reserva 100% Blue Agave Tequila (Mexico); 40% abv, $40.
There's too much floating cork in this otherwise clear and silvery tequila. Exhibits very nice briny/pickled aromas at the beginning nosing phase; aeration serves to accentuate the keenly peppery, latter-stage bouquet that is true-to-the-source and attractive. The palate entry shows a sweeter, agave juice side to this tequila which is pleasing; at midpalate the taste profile returns squarely to the black pepper/red pepper note that drives the flavor forward into the delightfully prickly and full-weighted finish. This is a well-made silver that's more than suitable for tequila-based drinks of all varieties. Neither elegant nor profound; just solid and better than average.
2006 Rating: ★★★/Recommended

Cesar Monterrey Reposado Reserva 100% Blue Agave Tequila (Mexico); 40% abv, $50.
Like its sibling, the Blanco, there's an unwelcome abundance of floating bits of cork in this pale yellow tequila; I do not want that when I'm paying $50, thank you. The first whiffs detect a strong pickled aroma that's quite nice, if dominant; later sniffings discover little aromatic expansion except for a trace of smokiness. The palate entry is very sweet and pleasantly oily; the midpalate features lesser flavors of black pepper, slate and mineral, with no evidence of typical agave brininess/vegetation. Finishes sweet, plump and one-dimensional. This reposado has the makings of something better than it is but for some reason it doesn't pull the components together into a harmonious statement. There's discord, a lack of finesse and an aimlessness that I detected when I first reviewed it in 2000 that hasn't been corrected.
2006 Rating: ★★/Not Recommended

Chinaco Añejo 100% Agave Tequila (Mexico); 40% abv, $57.
I am stunned and disappointed by the amount of raunchy sediment and floating debris which badly mar the otherwise pretty pale straw color; it looks to me as though the cork has seriously deteriorated; whatever the case, this appearance is wholly unacceptable for a super-premium product. The subtle bouquet out of the gate is lightly peppery and mildly herbal; aeration releases other aromas, including fennel, green onion, sherry, and oak resin.

The palate entry is lean, but oily/creamy and moderately sweet; at midpalate there's a gentle rush of green vegetable, sherry/honey, and herbal agave flavors. Ends sweetly. Chinaco and its mentor Robert Denton are widely viewed as the forerunners of the super-premium tequila movement. Though I'm sometimes willing to overlook sediment/filtration problems when the core product is far better than average, Chinaco tequilas do have a long history of abysmal filtration and cork failure. When a product is touted as super-premium, consumers expect a clean, appetizing product.

2004 Rating: ★★★/Recommended

Chinaco Blanco 100% Agave Tequila (Mexico); 40% abv, $45.

The very pale straw/yellow tint is as clear as rainwater. The first sniffings encounter very delicate scents of dill, sage, and olive brine; in later whiffs after further aeration, a fine creaminess is discerned. The palate entry is crisply astringent and vegetal; at midpalate a butteriness bordering on toffee/caramel delights the taste buds. Ends up clean, spirity, briny, and astringent.

2005 Rating: ★★★/Recommended

Chinaco Reposado 100% Agave Tequila (Mexico); 40% abv, $46.

The bright silvery/yellow hue resembles the color commonly seen in muscadet white wines from France; only fair purity. The initial nosings come upon interesting scents of chalk/slate, green vegetable, and grass; further exposure to air stimulates aromas of rubber, black pepper, green pepper, broccoli, and thyme. The palate entry is pleasantly peppery and off-dry; the midpalate features a satiny texture that's underpinned by the astringency of the vegetal taste. Concludes tightly wrapped, lean, and peppery. The Chinaco style is obviously one that highlights leanness and the vegetal and peppery aspects of distilled agave juice. While not multilayered like the 100% agave tequilas of El Tesoro, Herradura, Asombroso, Don Julio and others, Chinaco owns a nimble charm that's appealing.

2005 Rating: ★★★/Recommended

Chinaco Extra Añejo Lot 71 100% Agave Tequila (Mexico); 43% abv, $251.

Ecru/champagne/silvery color; good clarity. Zesty, piquant, intensely peppery (jalapeño) scents assert themselves early-on in the sniffing process; aeration stimulates deeper aromas, including dill pickle, relish, fiber/textile, oaky vanillin, salt, and brine. Entry is sublimely sweet yet salty and peppery, oily and smooth; the midpalate stage features wonderfully creamy, almost baked goods-like, oily, and tangy flavors that coat the palate and delight the soul. Ends up earthy, sweet, satiny, concentrated, and oily. A classic extra añejo that makes a strong case for aging some substantial tequilas for extended periods.

2007 Rating: ★★★★★/Highest Recommendation

Chinaco Negro Extra Añejo Tequila Lot 15 (Mexico); 43% abv, $270.

Pale gold color; perfect purity. The first nosing passes detect inviting, if delicately piquant, notes of green pepper, wax paper, and well-worn saddle leather; after another seven minutes of air contact, the bouquet turns more vegetal, peppery, citrusy, and pleasantly prickly in the nasal cavity. The palate entry is tightly wound, semisweet (I didn't expect that), and tangy; the midpalate point reeks with baking spices, cocoa, and oak-influenced

vanillin. Finishes like a champion in long, sweet tastes of cocoa and caramel and even a dash of tobacco. Wow.
2007 Rating: ★★★★/Highly Recommended

Chinaco Negro Extra Añejo Tequila Lot 17 (Mexico); 43% abv, $270.

The straw color is a little duller than I'd like to see; some debris is noted. The initial whiffs pick up light scents of caramel and new leather; further exposure to air stimulates more evolved aromas of green pepper, jalapeño pepper, and uncooked asparagus. The palate entry is fresh, vegetal, lightly salted, and green olive-like; by the midpalate juncture the bouquet becomes honey sweet, tangy, moderately salty, and properly vegetal/briny. Concludes with grace and a deft touch of pipe tobacco. Wow-wow.
2007 Rating: ★★★★★/Highest Recommendation

Climax Joven Tequila (Mexico); 40% abv, $20/liter.

The pale gray/hay tint is unblemished in its clarity. The first couple of whiffs are treated to a mildly herbaceous scent that includes pleasant notes of dill, parsley, and sage; after further exposure to air, the sage aspect takes the lead as additional fragrances of nickel/coin and white pepper join the aromatic mix; a solid bouquet that doesn't scrimp on the agave presence. The palate entry shows enough herbal/peppery agave thrust to impress; it's the midpalate stage that suffers severely from a lack of cohesion as the metallic/coin-like aspect takes charge, leaving the agave element in the dust. Concludes brassy and too bitterly astringent to warrant a recommendation. The makings were there for a good score until the implosion at midpalate.
2007 Rating: ★★/Not Recommended

Corazon de Agave Blanco 100% Agave Tequila (Mexico); 40% abv, $50.

Clear as rain water; good purity. The nose right after opening is zesty, vegetal, and fresh; the middle stage whiffs add nuances of black pepper, chili pepper, and steamed asparagus; the fourth and final sniffing offers a concentrated, herbal scent that sums up the aroma perfectly; a fine-tuned, fresh agave bouquet. The palate entry focuses on a herbal/peppery flavor, then at midpalate the taste takes off, emitting sweet, even succulent, clearly defined flavors of licorice, ripe agave, and oil. The aftertaste zeros in on the ripe, sap-sweet agave. The almost honey-like quality of the midpalate and finish mildly concerned me that it went too far to the sweet end of the scale, but the overall effect is very positive.
2001 Rating: ★★★/Recommended

Corazon de Agave Añejo Tequila 100% Agave (Mexico); 40% abv, $75.

Pretty dusty gold appearance reminds me of amontillado sherry. The sweetly pungent opening aroma is mildly briny and very dill-like; with aeration, this firm bouquet expands to add fragrances of sweet oak, honeysuckle, and spiced apple in the second and third sniffings; the last go-round sees the agave spirit at last emerge from behind the veil of moderate sweetness, ending the nosing phase of the evaluation with style and substance. The palate entry is extremely sour and tart; then at midpalate the taste turns sweeter and decidedly woody/resiny. Its aftertaste is lean, woody sweet, and caramelized. I prefer the distiller's succulent Corazon Reposado.
2001 Rating: ★★★/Recommended

Corazon de Agave Reposado 100% Agave Tequila (Mexico); 40% abv, $55.
The color is an extra virgin olive oil gold; impeccable purity. The seductive opening aromatic blast is slightly salty (Islay single malt?) and woody; the second and third sniffings, after three and six minutes of aeration respectively, find lovely fragrances of soft vanilla, mint, light toffee, and green tea; in the fourth and final inhalation a sweet brininess overshadows all other aromatic elements, save for the ripe agave; a multilayered bouquet of the first rank. Sweet, viscous at palate entry, then at midpalate the taste turns off-dry, intensely vegetal, and resiny/oily. The aftertaste is brief, sappy sweet, and a touch caramelly. Like the Blanco it is lip-smacking sweet, but tasty, even savory; drink on-the-rocks with a healthy twist of lime to counter the sweetness.
2001 Rating: ★★★★/Highly Recommended

Corralejo Añejo 100% Agave Tequila (Mexico); 40% abv, $62.
The engaging appearance is pale gold and unblemished. The opening inhalations find concentrated, intense aromas of lead pencil, steamed asparagus, and rubber eraser; aeration time of another seven minutes sees the raw aroma transform into a sensuous, toasty agave bouquet that features scents of palm oil, hot green pepper (jalapeño), oak resin, and stone/granite/mineral. While I liked the bouquet, this tequila saves its best moment for the flavor phase as the palate entry offers subtle, semisweet tastes of toffee and egg cream; by midpalate the taste profile includes vanilla, cocoa, margarine, peppercorn, and honey. It ends in a flurry of sweet, creamy tastes that highlight the toffee. A prime example of how oak casks can heavily and positively influence agave spirit; though reposado is usually my favorite tequila category, this beauty provides an extremely compelling case for añejo tequila.
2004 Rating: ★★★★/Highly Recommended

Corralejo Blanco 100% Agave Tequila (Mexico); 40% abv, $35.
Clear and clean as rainwater. The initial whiffs detect an alluring road tar/asphalt, licorice-like sweetness; seven more minutes in the copita serve to dry out and expand the bouquet by including smoky scents of cigarette ash and cigarette tobacco, all underpinned by a surprising vanilla bean bitterness that's as seductive as it is atypical. The palate entry is sweet, nearly maple-like, and viscous; by the midpalate point the sweetness turns intensely bitter, bean- and sap-like. It concludes sweet in the throat. Never mind that there's hardly any trace of the herbal/vegetal/peppery side of the agave base material; just enjoy the robust, smoky character of this unusual, idiosyncratic, mezcal-reminiscent blanco tequila.
2004 Rating: ★★★/Recommended

Corralejo Reposado Tequila (Mexico); 40% abv, $39.
Double distilled, matured in French Limousin oak barrels; the pale flax/lemon juice/muscadet-like hue is free of any debris whatsoever. The opening sniff detects a lovely, fresh, vegetal scent of agave that's slightly sour but very compelling; the middle stage nosings offer delicate, understated aromas of spring flowers, grass, and agave; there is minimal fading of the aromatic potency by the fourth pass, at which time soft odors of dill, lemon peel, and dried herbs come to the forefront. Right from the palate entry, the sweetness dial is turned to high as rich, hard candy-like flavors of lemon and oak take the taste buds by storm; the midpalate phase is slightly less intense as the flavors settle down on the tongue, allowing the agave base

flavor to emerge from behind the curtain of sweetness. The aftertaste is medium long, more vegetal and herbal than candy sweet, and mildly pleasant. The slight letdown in the finish takes away from the experience as a whole, but this sweet reposado is certainly recommendable.
2000 Rating: ★★★/Recommended

Corralejo Triple Distilled Reposado 100% Agave Tequila Bottle No. 20632 (Mexico); 40% abv, $42.
The pale straw/silver color reminds me of a muscadet (white wine) from France's western Loire Valley. Excellent purity; delicate fragrances of pine needle and green olive greet the olfactory sense in the first two minutes of sniffing; an additional six minute block of undisturbed air contact unleashes a classical, elegant, harmonious perfume that includes peppercorn, brine, fennel, lead pencil, and a faint hint of honey; I could go on smelling this graceful, ever-changing bouquet all day. The palate entry shows dry, astringent tastes of agave, hemp, and resin/oil; followed at midpalate by integrated flavors of light caramel, cream, metal, and milk chocolate. It ends sweet, soft, and pleasingly vegetal. A sophisticated, eminently drinkable, satiny tequila that I'd serve slightly chilled on its own in a wine glass only for people who comprehend fine spirits.
2004 Rating: ★★★★/Highly Recommended

Corzo Añejo 100% Agave Tequila (Mexico); 40% abv, $65.
The light straw yellow color is impeccably clean and appealingly bright. In the first nosings there are pleasantly assertive aromatic and earthy notes of fennel and pickle brine; additional time in the copita brings about dry and vegetal scents of cucumber, green pepper, and escarole; a delicate, non-woody bouquet. The palate entry is lithe, medium-dry, and peppery; at the midpalate point the taste profile adds flavors of semisweet oak, agave sugars, and herbs. Ends up more dry than sweet and keenly earthy/vegetal as the oak element vanishes.
2006 Rating: ★★★/Recommended

Corzo Reposado 100% Agave Tequila (Mexico); 40% abv, $50.
The pale gray/yellow color displays minor amounts of sediment. The first nosings detect zesty aromas that remind me of green chili peppers and asparagus; further air contact brings out touches of vanilla/oak, palm oil, lanolin, and almonds. The palate entry is sweetish, a bit candied and oaky; at midpalate the underpinning flavor becomes a delicious buttery taste that supports the top-level flavors of oak, light spice, and sautéed almonds. The aftertaste is particularly appealing as the sweet oak comes to the front, providing a lengthy, satiny finish that's elegant and understated. Wow.
2006 Rating: ★★★★/Highly Recommended

Corzo Silver 100% Agave Tequila (Mexico); 40% abv, $45.
The bluish/silvery appearance shows more floating debris than I like to see, considering the price. In the initial nosing passes, the lovely, earthy bouquet seems fully evolved, focusing mostly on vegetable matter aromas in the expressive forms of cucumber, agave pulp, fennel, and pine; aeration time serves to mold these fine scents together with added elements of spice (coriander), mint, and beeswax; this is a seductive silver tequila fragrance that's long on finesse and freshness. The palate entry is sleek and smooth, with just the right touch of agave

juice sweetness; at midpalate the flavor components meld into a single taste thrust that's medium-weighted, harmonious, semisweet, and lusciously prickly. Finishes on a heated note as the spirit races to the forefront ahead of the agave. Superb distilling here.
2006 Rating: ★★★★/Highly Recommended

Destileria Porfidio Blue Agave Spirit - Unwooded (South Africa); 40% abv, $30.
Limpid and pure. The first sniffings detect true blue agave herbal/peppery scents, though the road tar/asphalt quality makes me think more of mezcal than tequila; further time in the glass bolsters the keenly herbal agave pulpiness as well as introduces traces of dill and fennel to the aromatic mix. The palate entry is immediately sweet, then it turns smoky and ashy; by the midpalate stage the smokiness becomes slightly bitter, then it turns moderately sweet and black licorice-like. The finish mixes licorice sweetness with smoky/tarry bitterness. Do I prefer this South African agave spirit to most authentic 100% agave, unaged premium silver tequilas from Mexico, no; is it interesting? yes; is there agave spirit potential in SA? I believe that Porfidio BAS demonstrates that there may be; that said, do I want to be around when the Mexican distillers discuss the threat posed by RSA and Grassl and the fireworks start? No, señor, my passport is missing.
2003 Rating: ★★/Not Recommended

Don Alejo Blanco Tequila 100% Blue Agave (Mexico); 40% abv, $42.
As limpid and clean as rain water. The nose at opening is fresh, herbal, and peppery (fresh ground black pepper, to be more precise); the middle stage passes see the aroma go slightly chalk-like and minerally; by the fourth and final nosing pass, following nine minutes of air contact, the aroma turns industrial, throwing off scents of charcoal and weak agave; not the bouquet of a keeper. On palate, the charcoal quality detected in the last nosing whiff is clearly evident in the palate entry; by the midpalate stage the flavor displays a sickly sweet taste that's neither fresh nor appealing. The aftertaste is long, manufactured, and dead on arrival. Not my cup of silver tequila.
2000 Rating: ★/Not Recommended

Don Alejo Reposado Tequila 100% Blue Agave (Mexico); 40% abv, $42.
The color is strikingly similar to a pale yellow/flax/lemon juice-hued white wine from the muscadet district of France's westernmost Loire Valley. The opening aroma is dry, but reminds me of damp cotton; the middle stage nosing passes don't stray from that initial theme, except to add a scent of lanolin; following ten minutes of aeration, the last sniffing makes an attempt at an agave aroma but falls short, instead going manufactured and flannel-like. Entry is soft and flabby, lacking acidic definition or structure; ditto midpalate and finish. I don't know what went wrong in production, but this tequila possesses very little resemblance to even average tequila; not even good enough to be a mixer.
2000 Rating: ★/Not Recommended

Don Amado Reposado 100% Agave Mezcal (Mexico); 40% abv, $35.
The straw yellow/lemon juice color is much like white wine; minor amounts of suspended particles noted. The opening sniffing can best be described as strikingly resembling new rubber tires; the second and third nosings do little to alter the aromatic course as the

rubberfest continues unabated; finally and thankfully, by the last intake the bouquet deviates to Brussels sprouts and mild cigarette smoke; a bouquet that only a mother could love. The palate entry reminds me of paint thinner and licking ash trays after an all-night poker game; the midpalate provides no relief whatsoever from the slugfest of tobacco ashes and turpentine. The aftertaste is long, stunningly mean, raw, and bitter. Alright, already, I admit that it's very possible that I'll never get the point of mezcal, hard as I try.
2001 Rating: ★/Not Recommended

Don Amado Silver 100% Agave Mezcal (Mexico); 40% abv, $30.

Clear with but the faintest tint of pale straw; some floating debris noted. The pungent/oily aroma of crushed agave, which is reminiscent of fresh dill in this case, surges from the glass with authority in the initial nosing pass; in the middle stage sniffings, the aroma settles down into a more vegetal/green chili pepper mode that's assertive but not aggressive; by the final whiff, following over seven minutes of air contact, the bouquet shows almost soap-like elements of dried dill, desert flowers, and peppery agave; I took to this aroma in the middle stage nosings and kept liking it through to the last inhalation. The palate entry is extremely sour on the tongue; the midpalate flavors turn tar-like, sooty, oily, and, I hate to say it, detergent-like. The aftertaste is sour/bitter, filled ash tray-like, and rancid. What began so pleasant in the aroma turned awkward, savage, and alarmingly bitter tasting in the mouth and throat; I really wanted to like this mezcal; fit only for the blindly converted.
2001 Rating: ★/Not Recommended

Don Diego Santa Reposado 100% Agave Tequila (Mexico); 40% abv, $50.

This tequila is the pale yellow color of lemon juice; some debris seen floating around in the glass, but not enough for concern. The first whiffs are treated to keen aromas of vanilla bean, brown sugar, and some distant brine/dill; later inhalations pick up slightly lessened fragrances of wood char, cocoa butter, and pipe smoke. The palate entry is suspiciously chocolaty sweet…I mean, am I supposed to be tasting vegetal/herbal tequila or not? The midpalate is confectioner sweet and, while tasty because it's not cloying or syrupy, it confuses me. Concludes on an off-dry, not unpleasant note of cocoa/coffee beaniness that smacks more of a liqueur than an agave-based spirit. What's with this spate of sweetness? JEEEZ.
2006 Rating: ★★/Not Recommended

Don Eduardo Añejo 100% Agave Tequila (Mexico); 40% abv, $50.

Pale lemon juice yellow/straw color, with minor sediment issues. The delicate opening aroma offers lightly spiced and vegetal (steamed asparagus) scents that tease rather than bludgeon; further air contact releases additional odors including green pepper, cotton fiber, and a soft oaky sweetness. The palate entry is delicate, mildly sweet, and linear; at midpalate the taste profile remains rather static and delicate, with no clear sense of direction; that's not to say that it's unpleasant because that's not the case; it's just surprisingly meek for an añejo. Concludes softly, moderately sap-like, and vegetal.
2004 Rating: ★★★/Recommended

Don Eduardo Reposado 100% Agave Tequila (Mexico); 40% abv, $43.

The pale straw/flax color is correct and sediment-free. The delicate opening perfume is softly herbal and peppery; seven more minutes of aeration time opens up the aroma just enough so that the olfactory sense gets treated to wispy scents of steamed asparagus, cocoa bean, and light toffee; an understated, yet richly elegant bouquet. The flavor profile is luscious and firmly structured at palate entry, and then at midpalate explodes into a full-throttle tequila taste experience that features not-so-subtle flavors of dark chocolate, honey, tar, and uncooked vegetables. Concludes in an acceptably fiery manner that allows for the agave spirit to shine. Highly sophisticated yet borderline feral in the mouth, simply the finest Don Eduardo in the marketplace right now. A superbly satisfying reposado.
2005 Rating: ★★★★/Highly Recommended

Don Eduardo Triple Distilled Silver 100% Agave Tequila (Mexico); 40% abv, $45.

Clear silver appearance, with some sediment. The nose is fresh, vegetal, and pine-like; aeration time of another six minutes allows the pine/cedar scent to dominate the latter nosing phase. The palate entry is sweet and sap-like, almost honeyed; at midpalate the flavor profile turns bittersweet and bean-like; ends up well with a taste flashes of cocoa bean and linseed oil. A solidly made silver.
2004 Rating: ★★★/Recommended

Don Julio 1942 Añejo 100% Agave Tequila (Mexico); 38% abv, $100.

Pale gold/dusty yellow color; impeccable purity. The opening aroma is enchantingly sweet and ripe, with only a mild pungency; the middle stages detect lots of layers, including sweet agave, hard candy, ripe apple, butter cream, oak, and, dare I say it, malted milk; the final pass highlights the sweet agave and oak marriage; a sublime, evolved tequila bouquet that ranks with the finest ever. The palate entry is round, but compact and intense in terms of agave and sweet oak impact; the midpalate is long, oaky/vanilla sweet, and bordering on being brandy-like. The aftertaste is smooth, fully endowed, satiny, slightly caramel-like, rich, and clean.Even tops the terrific Reposado (★★★★); fabulously satisfying and a new tequila powerhouse.
2001 Rating: ★★★★/Highly Recommended

Don Julio Añejo 100% Blue Agave (Mexico); 40% abv, $60.

The yellow hay color is vibrant and bright; flawless purity. The initial whiffs detect strong evidence of dill, brine, and bitter green vegetables (kale and escarole, especially); after another seven minutes in the glass, the aroma turns inward becoming a little too muted to my liking. The palate entry is a tad sharp in its acidic attack, but then that smoothes out at midpalate as tastes of honey, saltwater taffy, and pickles take charge. Ends rambunctious, spirited, and pungent.
2007 Rating: ★★★/Recommended

Don Julio Blanco 100% Blue Agave (Mexico); 40% abv, $50.

Pure and pewter colored. The peppery/dill-like aroma jumps from the copita and compels my sense of smell to dive back into it; further air contact stimulates waxy scents of lanolin and palm oil, along with desert-like aromas of sand, minerals, slate, and succulent

plant blossoms; how blanco tequila should smell, unadorned, raw, yet supremely fetching. The palate entry is semi-dry, intensely sap-like, and even honeyed; at the midpalate stage the taste profile turns as much to the satiny texture as to the robust, herbal, mildly salty flavor. A blanco that deserves to be in every backbar in every tequila joint in the world. A clinic on blanco tequila.
2007 Rating: ★★★★★/Highest Recommendation

Don Julio Real Extra Añejo 100% Blue Agave Tequila (Mexico); 40% abv, $350.

The pale yellow/muscadet-like appearance is clean and sediment free. The opening aromas are delicate and remind me of dried yellow fruit, in particular, lemon, pineapple, and apricot; aeration releases a small measure of salt/brine/dill that compliments the dried fruit aspect. The palate entry is silky and as sweet as honey; by the midpalate stage the taste profile has added white pepper, beeswax, light caramel, and nougat. Concludes highlighting the nougat and caramel. Had the aroma been more generous and expressive, I'd have easily bestowed a fifth rating star.
2007 Rating: ★★★★/Highly Recommended

Don Julio Reposado 100% Blue Agave (Mexico); 40% abv, $55.

The soft pale straw color is unblemished and clean. The delicate scent after the pour has "dill and other leafy herbs" written all over it; over the aeration period, a slightly honeyed, Crackerjack-like aroma develops that's one part caramel and one part vegetation; an intriguing, if understated bouquet that keeps unfolding. The palate entry is mild, moderately vanilla-like, and semisweet; the midpalate stage is long, biscuity sweet, and only slightly dill-like. Pickle brine surfaces in the engaging finish. A stunningly poised and graceful reposado.
2007 Rating: ★★★★/Highly Recommended

Dos Lunas Reposado 100% Blue Agave (Mexico); 40% abv, $45.

The attractive yellow/hay color is flawlessly pure and bright. In the opening inhalations the aroma is assertive, doughy, and slightly salty; following additional aeration, the bouquet becomes highly herbal, giving off piquant scents of prickly pear, desert flower, and cocoa bean. The palate entry features sweet oak and salted butter tastes; the midpalate stage highlights the fatty quality as much in the texture as in the taste. Finishes mildly chili pepper-like and seed-like.
2006 Rating: ★★★/Recommended

Dos Lunas Silver 100% Blue Agave (Mexico); 40% abv, $40.

Clear as rainwater and silvery pewter in appearance. The first whiffs detect medium-strong elements of tar, tobacco, and hemp fiber; further air contact stimulates scents of minerals/slate/stone, matchstick, and metal; where'd the tar/tobacco leaf go? The palate entry is sweet, poised, and a bit tobacco- and white potato-like; the midpalate stage is sweet in a creamy/buttery/fatty manner, but very pleasant. Ends up clean, nicely acidic, and synthetic fiber-like. Greater depth would have demanded a fourth rating star.
2006 Rating: ★★★/Recommended

El Diamante del Cielo Añejo 100% Agave Tequila (Mexico); 40% abv, $60.
Lovely autumnal gold/honey amber hue; perfect clarity. This opening bouquet is nicely biscuity, oaky sweet, and mellow; it's only in the later stages of the second round of nosing that I detect briny, herbal, peppery scents. The palate entry is semisweet, sap-like, and oily/resiny; at midpalate the maple/honey sweetness takes over, overshadowing much of the agave character. The aftertaste mirrors the midpalate totally. For lovers of intensely oaky, brandy-like aged tequila; built more for sipping than for cocktails or shots.
2005 Rating: ★★★/Recommended

El Diamante del Cielo Blanco 100% Agave Tequila (Mexico); 40% abv, $45.
Silvery appearance; ideal purity. Owns the type of vegetal/herbal/woodsy/peppery opening bouquet that I most favorably respond to; in the glass over the span of seven more minutes, the aroma changes into more of a fiber/cottony bouquet that even has traces of parchment and palm oil; a distinctive bouquet that offers different moods of itself freely and generously. The palate entry echoes the latter stages of the nosing as the initial dry tastes remind me more of fiber than of herbs/spices/green vegetables; at midpalate the flavor profile turns sweeter and more peppery, bringing the focus back onto the agave. The finish shows touches of smoke and oil, with a sweet tail end.
2005 Rating: ★★★★/Highly Recommended

El Diamante del Cielo Reposado 100% Agave Tequila (Mexico); 40% abv, $50.
The pale gold color is pure and clean. The first whiffs pick up incredibly briny and olive-like aromas that leap from the glass; further aeration and a few swirls stir up slightly sweeter notes that are keenly peppery and pickle relish-like; a no-nonsense bouquet that leaves no room for wondering, "Gee, what is this stuff?" This is raring-to-go tequila, man, and nothing else. The palate entry is pleasantly sweet, straightforward and ripe, with a firm texture that's slightly oily; at midpalate there's a charge from the spirit that warms the throat. Ends up vegetal, sap-sweet, and a touch maple-like. Not a reposado that will be admired for its finesse or razzle-dazzle; just very, very good and genuine, old-fashioned type of tequila that gets straight to the point of what tequila should be.
2005 Rating: ★★★★/Highly Recommended

El Jimador Añejo 100% Agave Tequila (Mexico); 40% abv, $25.
The topaz/medium honey color is attractive; minuscule white bits seen floating about. The intriguing opening aromatic display shows polite features, especially scents of honey and sautéed-in-butter asparagus; mild, milky, and oaky aromas highlight the second and third sniffings; the fourth pass unearths traces of black and green pepper; hardly profound, but a solid, sweet bouquet. The palate entry is sappy sweet, full of oaky overtones; the midpalate is sweet, easy, and flecked with black pepper and blue agave tastes that nicely counter the sweetness. The finish is short, sweet, and sap-like. A well-made añejo that's not a brandy-like blockbuster but is more in keeping with mainstream older, oak-aged tequilas.
2001 Rating: ★★★/Recommended

El Jimador Blanco Tequila 100% Agave (Mexico); 40% abv, $20.
To the eye, as crystalline as icy cold mountain spring water; ideally clean and pure. The deep, alluring nose at opening offers supple, stately aromas of grass, hay, and herbs;

the second sniffing adds a dash of licorice; nothing new is exposed in the third whiff, but in the fourth nosing pass fine linseed oil and slate-like perfumes rise from the glass; I favorably responded to this blanco's oiliness. The palate entry is dry and then at the midpalate stage a rich agave/herbal/licorice flavor profile impresses the taste buds. The finish is oily, long, chalky/minerally, and dry. Solidly made and easily recommendable.

2000 Rating: ★★★/Recommended

El Jimador Reposado Tequila 100% Agave (Mexico); 40% abv, $22.

The color is pale gold and white wine-like, but is blemished by clouds of transparent floating particles. The initial nosing pass detects sour scents of mustard seed and dill; the second sniffing picks up subtle aromas of green olive and brine; the third whiff, following six minutes of air contact, sees the mustard/dill strengthen and deepen; the fourth and last nosing sees no change as the mustard/dill perfume continues to hold court; an odd bouquet. More likeable in the mouth than in the nose, this reposado starts out bittersweet in the palate entry, then turns zesty and peppery at midpalate as sweet tastes of candied almonds and very ripe agave sugars rule the day. The aftertaste is long, sweet in an herbal, almost medicinal manner, and piquant. I ended up liking this tequila enough because of the flavor and finish to recommend it, though I preferred the blanco by a hair.

2000 Rating: ★★★/Recommended

El Tesoro de Don Felipe Añejo 100% Agave Tequila (Mexico); 40% abv, $59.

Tidy, green/straw color; superb purity. The lively, elegant nose shows traces of mushrooms, dried herbs and lead pencil; six more minutes of aeration stir deeper scents, including mustard seed, oak, vanilla bean, and toffee. The palate entry is sublimely rich yet focused; at midpalate the taste profile offers succulent, brandy/cognac-like flavors of oak resin, almond butter, and tobacco leaf. Finishes semisweet, sherry-like and a smooth as a baby's bottom. A classic.

2004 Rating: ★★★★★/Highest Recommendation

El Tesoro de Don Felipe Añejo Paradiso 100% Agave Tequila (Mexico); 40% abv, $120.

The color is medium amber/honey/harvest gold; impeccable purity. The initial sniffings pick up decidedly woody scents of oak, resin, and sawdust; in later whiffs after another seven minutes in the glass, the nose turns concentrated and remarkably briny and dill pickle-like. The palate entry is briny and very much like sweet pickle relish; the midpalate stage turns softly sweet and herbal. Finishes gently sweet and elegant, but without the highly complementary cognac barrel impact of earlier bottlings from the late 1990s. The earlier Paradiso possessed all the stunning charm of the five star original rendering, complete with rich, wine-like cognac notes. While the new bottling is certainly recommendable, it is a mere shadow of the Paradiso seen just five years ago.

2005 Rating: ★★★/Recommended

El Tesoro de Don Felipe Platinum 100% Agave Tequila (Mexico); 40% abv, $30.

Crystalline and pure. My olfactory sense detects early-on, green vegetable notes of uncooked broccoli, snow peas and zucchini; an extra six minutes of air contact see the addition only of very light brine to the aromatic mix. The palate entry is pleasantly creamy

and focused; then at midpalate the complexion changes, becoming lead pencil-like, narrow and desert dry. Finishes tongue-on-stone dry and medium-bodied.
2004 Rating: ★★★/Recommended

El Tesoro de Don Felipe Reposado 100% Agave Tequila (Mexico); 40% abv, $40.
The green/silvery/gold tint is pretty and flawlessly clear. There are subtle notes of cocoa, white chocolate, and straw in the first whiffs after the pour; aeration stimulates additional aromas including tar, gum, parchment, and grass. The palate entry is as smooth as silk and intensely vegetal and tobacco-like; at midpalate the flavor profile highlights tastes of uncooked asparagus, sweet oak, light toffee, and skimmed milk. Finishes elegantly, skating rink smooth, and semisweet. A class act.
2005 Rating: ★★★★/Highly Recommended

Espolon Añejo 100% Agave Tequila (Mexico); 40% abv, $40.
Light topaz/harvest gold/honey hue; shows lots of sediment, which looks like a combination of cork fragments and smaller agave shreds. The nose is alluring right from the opening pass as zesty, evolved aromas of buttery oak, ripe agave, and walnuts charm the olfactory sense; the middle stage sniffings unearth a small, but nonetheless noticeable lessening of potency as the buttery oak assumes command and the agave and nuts move to the background; the fourth and last whiff adds a mild pepperiness which nicely complements the oakiness; a good, if unspectacular, bouquet. The palate entry is medium-bodied and oaky sweet; the midpalate is solid, oaky/buttery, leafy, and just a dash briny. The aftertaste maintains the focus on the buttery oak and pleasant, honey-like sweetness. A polite añejo that displays just enough multilayered character and stamina to be recommended.
2001 Rating: ★★★/Recommended

Espolon Reposado 100% Agave Tequila (Mexico); 40% abv, $35.
The pretty color is a harvest gold; excellent purity. The aroma right after the pour is mildly dill-like, a touch briny, spirity, warming, and pleasing; the middle stage nosing passes highlight the almondy side of reposado as the bouquet turns moderately buttery and round; the final sniffing offers sweet aromas of almond paste, ripe blue agave, and mild brine; a sound, slightly reluctant, but overall competent bouquet. The palate entry is smoky but lean; the midpalate phase is sweet, moderately smoky, lightly oaked, and medium-bodied. The nimble finish is smooth, silky, and only mildly smoky. Not a briny/vegetal reposado bruiser, but shows good oak/blue agave presence both in the bouquet and the late flavor/finish.
2001 Rating: ★★★/Recommended

Espolon Silver 100% Agave Tequila (Mexico); 40% abv, $30.
Clear as rainwater; lots of cork bits floating about. The opening nosing reveals an intriguing aroma that's fresh, flowery, and strangely citrusy in its bearing; aeration serves to heighten the flowery quality as the citrus/acidic element calms down slightly in the second and third whiffs; the final sniffing at last displays some moderate blue agave character in a dill-like manner; the freshness is admirable. The palate entry is sleek, lean, and mildly sour; the midpalate stage is where the agave does its best work as the flavor turns moderately sweet and the texture medium oily. The finish is clean, nearly austere, and totally dry. A svelte,

drinkable, but ultimately middle-of-the-road silver that focuses more on agave intensity than textured mouthfeel.

2001 Rating: ★★★/Recommended

Fina Estampa Blanco 100% Agave Tequila (Mexico); 40% abv, $35.
Crystal clear; perfectly pure. In the first sniffings, the gloriously intense peppery, herbal aroma knocks me out of the chair, then after further time in the copita, the aroma becomes a graceful bouquet that highlights ash, green olive, asparagus, and chili pepper; a dynamite bouquet that's all about freshness and the herbal core of agave. The palate entry is medium-weighted, peppery, and a touch mineral-like; at midpalate there are quick bursts of wet stone and light honey. The aftertaste is brief, wonderfully peppery, and stony/slate-like.

2005 Rating: ★★★★/Highly Recommended

Fina Estampa Reposado 100% Agave Tequila (Mexico); 40% abv, $43.
The very pretty pale gold/pale straw is flawlessly clean. The opening nosing passes detect all sorts of lovely aromas, including black pepper, sea brine, fennel, and mint; six more minutes of air contact have little impact on the bouquet except for the addition of dill. The palate entry is sweet, almost fruity/grainy, and ideally oily; at midpalate there's a velvety feel on the tongue that underpins the briny, off-dry, salty taste. Finishes elegantly, oily, and extremely pepper- and dill-like. A terrific new reposado is now on the block.

2004 Rating: ★★★★/Highly Recommended

Frida Kahlo Añejo 100% Agave Tequila (Mexico); 40% abv, $90.
The yellow/amber color is pretty, suitable for the category and unblemished by sediment. The first aromatic impressions are of brine, peanut butter, and lanolin; later sniffs after seven more minutes of air contact add soft, even delicate notes of oaky vanilla, hemp/fiber, almonds, and dried herbs. The palate entry is grassy and sweet in a vegetal/agave manner; the midpalate stage is a tad restrained, but oily/buttery and deeply herbal (sage, rosemary, thyme). Finishes sedate, mildly sweet, and more timid than I like for an añejo. Of the three Fridas, I'd gravitate towards the Reposado and/or the weirdly wonderful Blanco.

2006 Rating: ★★★/Recommended

Frida Kahlo Blanco 100% Agave Tequila (Mexico); 40% abv, $50.
The pale silvery/gray tint exhibits impeccable purity and flawless appearance. The startling first whiff encounters wildly exotic, even provocative, scents of vinegar, brine, and green chili peppers; as the aeration process lengthens into the seventh minute, the aroma becomes a genuine 100% agave bouquet, emitting irresistible scents of tar, tobacco leaf, and sea salt. At the palate entry, a wave of road tar washes across the tip of the tongue, followed by a smoky taste of ash; the midpalate highlights a sweeter side of agave juice that rides atop the tar/smoke/tobacco. Finishes semisweet and a bit industrial-tasting, which is why it didn't receive a fifth rating star; but it comes very close if for no other reason than it has intense and pungent mezcal-like qualities.

2006 Rating: ★★★★/Highly Recommended

Frida Kahlo Reposado 100% Agave Tequila (Mexico); 40% abv, $65.

The pale lemon juice yellow color shows some sediment, but not enough to be concerned about. The opening nosings pick up peculiar but appealing aromas of saddle leather, old vinyl, cream, and distant black pepper; further time in the glass stimulates intriguing, atypical scents of mustard seed, grass, and paint. The palate entry is sweet, almondy, and near-oily; the midpalate taste pulls out the stops on the oiliness, going all out, but with a keen pepperiness that's at once spicy and pleasantly sharp. Finishes on a parchment-like note of dryness and brittleness that's very nice and somehow appropriate for what's gone on before.

2006 Rating: ★★★★/Highly Recommended

Gecko Black Spirits 100% Blue Agave (Mexico); 50% abv, $35.

For your information this spirit has FD&C Yellow No. 5 and other food colorings added; jet black, opaque appearance; remarkably unappetizing to the eye. The nose at opening is pungent, spirity, and agave-like in a boiled asparagus manner; the second and third sniffings unearth little more in the way of aromatic deepening; the fourth and last whiff shows a distant trace of licorice; this aroma borders on having a near-liqueur demeanor and much to my surprise I find it mildly alluring. The feel of this stuff at palate entry is liqueur thick and nearly cordial sweet; the midpalate is candy/botanical sweet and resembles tequila only in passing as the spirit leaps to the helm. The aftertaste is unabashedly sweet and liqueur-like, but tasty. These spirits ride the fence as to whether they're to be categorized as tequilas or tequila liqueurs; whatever the case, I like this version quite a lot.

2001 Rating: ★★★/Recommended

Gecko Blue Spirits 100% Blue Agave (Mexico); 43% abv, $30.

The color is a neon, apothecary sea blue/green; excellent clarity. The odd but interesting aroma after opening displays definite blue agave character underneath an overlay of wood resin; the second and third whiffs offer nothing in the way of expansion; after seven minutes of time in the glass, the fourth and last sniffing sees the agave come to the forefront; an intriguing, if curiously manufactured bouquet that's short on blue agave freshness but pleasing all the same. The palate entry is tart and lean; the midpalate flavors suddenly burst with ripe agave and sugary sweetness. The aftertaste is long, sweet, and nearly syrupy. A strange hybrid that obviously owns a blue agave base, but what else is in it is anybody's guess; could be that the green food coloring, FD&C Green 3, contributes to the almost candy-like disposition.

2001 Rating: ★★/Not Recommended

Gran Centenario Añejo 100% Agave Tequila (Mexico); 40% abv, $58.

Attractive honey/deep amber color; impeccable purity. The initial nosings after the pour pick up nothing in the least demonstrative, aromawise; further time seems to stimulate mild, reluctant scents of cocoa bean, light toffee, and even steamed broccoli. The palate entry emits delicate tastes of candied almond and nougat; at midpalate the flavors include light-fingered touches of dried herbs, fennel, brine, and hard candy. Concludes well and a tad smoky/dry.

2004 Rating: ★★★/Recommended

Gran Centenario Leyenda Extra Añejo 100% Agave Tequila (Mexico); 40% abv, $250.
Old gold/deep straw color; very good clarity. The smell right out of the gate is exotic, acutely vegetal, piney, and peppery—in other words, lots happening early-on; more time in the glass brings out added aromas of old oak, hemp/flax, beeswax, and asparagus; a complex, forever unfolding bouquet that clearly demonstrates how well distilled agave juice can mature for long periods in oak. The palate entry is velvety smooth, sap-like, sweet but not in the least cloying, and finely textured; at the midpalate juncture the flavors settle in and integrate in an ideal display of maturity, grace, and vigor. Ends up lip-smacking sweet, fiber-like, oaky, honeyed, and a touch salty. A thrilling addition to the growing extra añejo category.
2007 Rating: ★★★★★/Highest Recommendation

Gran Centenario Plata 100% Agave Tequila (Mexico); 40% abv, $50.
I like the very pale yellow/silver hue; flawless purity. The first sniffings detect intriguing desert dry scents of lead/nickel and black pepper; seven more minutes bring out bread-like fragrances such as saltines, sesame crackers, and dough; an atypical silver/blanco/plata bouquet which is usually heavily herbal/vegetal. The palate entry is viscous and off-dry; at midpalate the flavor profile becomes smokier and more green vegetable-like, with background hints of corn husk and agave. Finishes piquant, peppery and moderately spirity.
2004 Rating: ★★★/Recommended

Gran Centenario Reposado 100% Agave Tequila (Mexico); 40% abv, $53.
Soft medium amber/light honey hue; ideal purity. The first couple of sniffs detect robust aromas of agave pulp, lemongrass, fennel and green vegetable; aeration stirs even more aromatic intrigue as the tantalizing bouquet expands to offer substantial notes of cocoa bean, olive brine, and oaky vanilla; a no-nonsense bouquet that's right on the money. The palate entry is firm and oily; at midpalate there's a subtle fruitiness that's fino sherry-like in its yeasty/dried fruit bearing. Finishes lovely, round and biscuity. The clear pick of the regular Gran Centenario litter.
2004 Rating: ★★★★/Highly Recommended

Gran Patron Platinum Silver Tequila 100% Agave 40% abv, $189.
Crystal clear and clean appearance. The first nosing passes detect subtle notes of road tar, white pepper and just-harvested green agave; further air exposure stimulates aromatic nuances of palm oil and sage; a clean, if delicate come-hither bouquet. The palate entry is off-dry, spicy, and vegetal; at midpalate the taste profile turns surprisingly astringent and lean, with a disappointing backnote of fiber/flax/synthetic. Ends up on the flax-like note. Drinkable, to be sure, but this silver tequila gets derailed in the flavor phase and doesn't have enough substance to recover. I suspect that the triple distillation has stripped this tequila of its character; and don't even get me started about the ridiculous bottle price; somebody clearly has delusions of grandeur and an over-inflated opinion of the quality of this mediocre tequila. Savvy, seasoned tequila lovers will quickly spot the folly of this endeavor.
2004 Rating: ★★/Not Recommended

Hacienda de Chihuahua Añejo Sotol (Mexico); 38% abv, $40.
The pale straw/gray color resembles muscadet white wine from the western stretches of the Loire Valley; ideal clarity. The first sniffs detect reluctant and barely perceptible scents of

sand/earth and salt; another seven minutes of air contact and swirling do little to build on the scant foundation and all I pick up is a soft newly tanned leather/kid glove smell. The palate entry is limp and sap-like; by the midpalate stage any hope for significant improvement is dashed on the rocks as the flavor profile remains timid and lacking in terms of real depth of taste. Ends meekly. While this vodka-like sotol doesn't taste bad, I feel let down by the fact that there simply isn't much of a sense of agave or oak, just a mildly pleasing sap-like taste. When I decide to drink an agave-based spirit, I want to taste the agave.
2006 Rating: ★★/Not Recommended

Hacienda de Chihuahua Plata Sotol (Mexico); 38% abv, $30.

Some very minor sediment is spotted that is not problematic; otherwise crystal clear. This zesty aroma is invitingly minty and "green" in a vegetal sense; aeration time of seven minutes expands the aromatic theme in a minor way as the mintiness morphs into a desert-like dryness that's equal parts vegetation and arid earth. The palate entry is clean, focused, and lean; the midpalate displays a delicate touch of agave sugar sweetness and supplemental tastes of steamed asparagus and anise. Concludes dry, vegetal, and earthy.
2006 Rating: ★★★/Recommended

Hacienda del Cristero Blanco 100% Agave Tequila (Mexico); 40% abv, $50.

Crystal clear and absolutely pure. The opening aroma is textbook blanco tequila, pure, slightly smoky, herbal, and dry; the middle stage sniffings add cucumber, chili pepper, lead pencil/rusting lead pipe, and cumin; following a full ten minutes in the glass, the concluding nosing pass addresses the herbal/brine question with gusto as wonderful scents of pepper and dill enchant the olfactory sense; a knock-out bouquet that doesn't for a nanosecond forget the agave. The palate entry is dry and prickly, then at midpalate the flavor explodes on the tongue in waves of peppery, herbal, and briny flavors. Fiery finish. What a ride.
2001 Rating: ★★★★/Highly Recommended

Hacienda Los Diaz Reposado 100% Agave Tequila (Mexico); 40% abv, $40.

Pale straw/silver/gray color; excellent clarity. Smells pleasantly of dill, pickle brine, flowers, and green pepper; seven more minutes of aeration add tangy notes of black pepper, fiber/flax, and tobacco leaf. Entry is earthy and moderately sweet; the midpalate offers slightly honeyed, brown sugar-like, and vegetal tastes that are nicely melded and work in unison all through the aftertaste, which is oily, concentrated, peppery, and integrated. Nice work.
2007 Rating: ★★★★/Highly Recommended

Herencia de Plata Añejo 100% Agave Tequila (Mexico); 40% abv, $36.

The rich, harvest gold hue dazzles the eye; excellent purity. The nose is not present and accounted for in the early inhalations; seven minutes of swirling and aeration help a bit as somewhat tired, lumpy scents of agave pulp, mint, and citric acid do little to stimulate the olfactory sense. The palate entry offers a flat and flabby sweet taste along with some pleasing almond and walnut flavors; at midpalate the taste profile goes candied and rubbery. Ends up pleasantly sweet and oaky. A disappointment after the terrific silver and reposado. No bouquet worth discussing, a fleshy texture and flabby taste lead to no cigar.
2004 Rating: ★★/Not Recommended

Herencia de Plata Reposado 100% Agave Tequila (Mexico); 40% abv, $37.

The attractive lemon juice yellow color is spotlessly clean. The first sniffs pick up scents of cream and oaky vanilla; the oak influence continues on after further aeration to the point of near-exclusion. The palate entry is creamy and nutty (almond paste); at midpalate the intense nuttiness and creaminess stay the course; it's almost like a tequila liqueur, it's so sweet, caramel-like, and creamy. Ends up thick, concentrated, honeyed, and sweet. I have to admit that the lack of typical agave/herbal presence bothered me at first, but the stunningly biscuity/creamy nature of this reposado is hard not to admire.

2004 Rating: ★★★★/Highly Recommended

Herencia de Plata Silver 100% Agave Tequila (Mexico); 40% abv, $36.

The translucent appearance is silvery pure and flawless. The acutely herbal and spicy aroma out of the starting gate is delightfully piquant and alluring; aeration time really serves this aroma well as additional, deeper fragrances of green olives, twine/hemp, and almonds meld beautifully with the herbs and spice; superb silver bouquet. The palate entry is focused, dry to off-dry, and bean-like; at midpalate bitter to semisweet but succulent tastes of citrus rind, broccoli, and tobacco leaf come on the scene. The finish is concentrated, full-bodied, and intensely herbal (thyme, allspice). A zesty beauty of a silver.

2004 Rating: ★★★★/Highly Recommended

Herradura Añejo 100% Agave Tequila Natural (Mexico); 40% abv, $65.

Straw/yellow gold color; ideal clarity. The initial sniffs pick up exotic spicy, tropical fruit notes that are completely set apart from those of the Silver or Reposado as they display round, marginally resiny, fibrous scents that are mature yet vigorous; aeration stimulates incredibly seductive aromas of caramel, butter cream, pastry dough, and nutmeg, plus a background hint of honeyed peanuts; wow. Entry is piquant/spicy and full-bodied; the midpalate doesn't give way to oaky sweetness, displaying just a trace vanillin that supports the more vibrant flavors of brine, salt, green vegetable, and green pepper. Finishes clean, a touch smoky, and delicately spiced. A textbook añejo that always has been a classic. Still is.

2007 Rating: ★★★★★/Highest Recommendation

Herradura Reposado 100% Agave Tequila Natural (Mexico); 40% abv, $60.

Ecru/flax/pale gold in color; impeccable purity. This aroma displays a slightly sweeter character than the Silver Blanco Suave, driven by 11 months in oak; additional time in the glass sees the aroma thrust diminish in sweetness a bit, but it's still firm, biscuity, and dill-like. Entry is delightfully off-dry, keenly acidic and therefore fresh, and just slightly spicy; the midpalate stage features long, oily tastes of wax, black pepper, and palm oil. Ends up sturdy, oily, textile-like, and a touch metallic. A leaner style of reposado that's long been viewed as a favorite.

2007 Rating: ★★★★/Highly Recommended

Herradura Seleccion Suprema Extra Añejo 100% Agave Tequila Natural (Mexico); 40% abv, $350.

Color is old gold/maize/old sauternes; unblemished clarity. The first couple of whiffs after the pour detect resiny notes that are kind of textile-like as well; an oaky sweetness emerges over time in the glass and that manifests in the aromatic form of malted milk or pastry dough. Entry is slightly fat with oaky creaminess, but it's not enough to overshadow the structural acidity that holds its together; the midpalate offers earthy tastes of egg cream, peppery spice, jalapeño pepper, dill leaf, and nutmeg. Ends on an off-dry note that's nicely peppery and woody.

2007 Rating: ★★★★/Highly Recommended

Herradura Silver Blanco Suave 100% Agave Tequila Natural (Mexico); 40% abv, $55.

Clear pewter; silver appearance; flawless purity. Vibrant herbal/earthy aromas of dill, green pepper, and mace are appealing right out of the gate; further aeration brings this already frisky bouquet to fever pitch as raw but sophisticated scents of hemp/fiber mingle freely with aromas of green pepper and tilled earth; wonderfully animated. Entry is intensely herbal and earthy, but keenly peppery and piquant; the midpalate is the picture of immature agave spirit greatness as the acidity maintains a high exposure rate, fueling the flavor push of brine, dill, soil, textile, and light spice. Concludes as peppery and forceful as it begins. What 100% agave blanco tequila should be. A world-class spirit.

2007 Rating: ★★★★★/Highest Recommendation

Honorable Aged Tequila (Mexico); 40% abv, $30.

Attractive pale honey/yellow straw color; good purity. Emits a nice, round, almost toasty opening bouquet; the second and third passes add only subtle notes of licorice, dried herbs, and dried flowers to the aromatic impression; the last sniffing, following ten minutes of aeration, adds a sweet oak touch that's pleasant; while you won't file this tequila aroma in your "profound" box, it is nuanced enough to be seriously likeable. More expressive in the mouth than in the nose; the palate entry begins with a piquant, tingling wake-up call to the taste buds; the midpalate phase is highlighted by a silky texture and a round, full-bodied flavor that includes tastes of herbs, dried flowers, soft spice, and sweet oak. The aftertaste is long, round, sweet, and satiny. The pick of the litter.

2000 Rating: ★★★★/Highly Recommended

Honorable Reposado Tequila (Mexico); 40% abv, $32.

Pale straw yellow/lemon juice hue; acceptable purity. The opening pass owns a very similar trace of delicate licorice to its silver sibling; the middle stage nosing passes offer a bit more in the way of aromatic dimension as soft scents of ground black pepper, oil, and vegetal agave make an attempt at complexity; the fourth and final sniffing sees the complementary addition of oaky vanillin, making for a mildly charming bouquet. The palate entry starts out dry; then at midpalate the taste turns strikingly sweet, pleasantly fresh, and almost prickly. The aftertaste is medium long, studded with ripe agave flavor, and full-bodied. This reposado comes on strong past the palate entry, making a solid bid for respectability; the result, a firm SJ recommendation.

2000 Rating: ★★★/Recommended

Honorable Silver Tequila (Mexico); 40% abv, $30.

Silvery clear in color, but displays more suspended particles than I'd like to see. The initial nosing pass picks up only a very faint trace of licorice; the second and third sniffings, following three and five minutes of aeration respectively, see little in the way of expansion or deepening; the last whiff, after slightly more than ten minutes of air contact reveal absolutely nothing new; one of the most neutral smelling tequila bouquets I've encountered in some time. The palate entry is remarkably sweet (licorice again) in nature, but pleasingly so; by the midpalate juncture, however, the flavor expands only to include very soft notes of light caramel and ultrasweet agave. The aftertaste continues the sweet rush. Ordinary and drinkable, but way too one-dimensional as the sweet character obliterates all other taste possibilities; the overly sweet constitution might fool the uninitiated, but hardly the seasoned tequila maven.

2000 Rating: ★★/Not Recommended

JB Wagoner's 100% Blue Agave Spirits (USA); 50% abv, $58.

Impeccable clarity; transparent. The first whiffs encounter sweet/sour scents of nail polish/acetate and flowery fresh-off-the-still spirits; later sniffings pick up vegetal, sour aromas of cucumber, lemongrass, cactus, spice, and citrus; fresh and vibrant. Shows some semblance of green agave at entry, but initially comes off as more a vodka than a tequila wannabe; at midpalate a pleasantly piquant smoky/charcoal sweetness takes command of the tasting phase, again similar in impact to a charcoal filtered vodka. Ends up sweet and vegetal. Recommendable more as a curiosity than as a domestic tequila copycat, which it isn't. I guarantee that you won't be thinking "margarita" when you taste this spirit. Little wonder why the Mexican Governmental jealously guards the name Tequila.

2005 Rating: ★★★/Recommended

Jose Cuervo Añejo 100% Blue Agave Tequila (Mexico); 40% abv, $35.

The color is harvest gold/topaz/honey and the purity level is optimum. The opening nosing pass reveals touches of dill/brine, agave, and hazelnut; the same aromatic line-up stays the course during the second whiff while the penultimate sniffing unearths subtle notes of oak vanillin and almond butter; in the fourth and last nosing, following eight minutes plus of air contact, a deft trace of ashy soot, as in a chimney, is detected and liked; a good, solid, multilayered nose. The palate entry is concentrated and oaky; then at midpalate the big-hearted taste goes sugary/caramelly sweet and sap-like. The aftertaste is very long, prone to caramel, and slightly oaky. A legitimate argument can be made by tequila purists that this añejo borders on being too sweet, but nevertheless it delivers a satisfying, graceful, and recommendable aroma/flavor/finish package.

2000 Rating: ★★★/Recommended

Jose Cuervo Black Medallion Oak Barrel Signature Blend Añejo Tequila (Mexico); 40% abv, $21.

The color is chestnut brown; purity is excellent. The opening whiffs pick up ashy/sooty and unabashedly sweet aromas of wood smoke and spice that, while not unpleasant, drown out the agave presence; even after six more minutes in the glass, the agave foundation is but a whisper amid the cacophony of the oak extract, vanilla, and dark caramel. The palate entry is concentrated and sweet, with no reference points of natural agave herbaceousness or pepperiness; the midpalate mirrors the manufactured sweetness of the entry. Finishes warm, woody/smoky sweet. I'm all for experimentation, but this effort, which is clearly geared to

young male drinkers à la Jack Daniel's No. 7, misses the mark mostly because of its lack of subtlety. It makes no bones about its predestined aim of being a mixer with cola. It doesn't taste bad. It just bears scant resemblance to tequila. That's my main problem.
2006 Rating: ★★/Not Recommended

Jose Cuervo Citrico Tequila Flavored with Lime and other Citrus Fruits (Mexico); 40% abv, $21.

Clear as rainwater; perfect clarity. The citrusy opening fragrance is intensely acidic (citric acid, big surprise) and rife with lime rind and tangerine juice and is, truth be told, quite pleasing; aeration heightens the lime peel perfume, lessens the tangerine as it turns positively zesty and inviting; beneath all the citrus lies an earthy, mineral-like agave base. The palate entry is alluringly astringent, bursting with authentic lime peel tartness; the midpalate is zesty, peel-like, and owns just enough agave thrust to make it clear as to what the foundation spirit is, even though this is a mixto base of agave and neutral spirits. Editor's note: 100% agave purists will be howling over the Cuervo flavored tequilas and I understand their argument, but the reality is this: taken on its own merit, this is a very good, clean, and well-made product. "Extension" products such as these will never be as charming or profound as real deal 100% agave tequilas. That agreed upon, look what flavored vodkas did for that category, beginning in the mid-1970s. If it works, it works.
2006 Rating: ★★★/Recommended

Jose Cuervo Clasico Plata Tequila (Mexico); 40% abv, $17.

Nowhere on the label do the words "100% agave" appear, so I have to conclude that this is a mixto tequila. Absolute clarity. The opening sniffings detect unbecoming, industrial scents of burnt rubber, sulphur and, most unappealingly, creosote; aeration lasting another six minutes does nothing but deepen the ABA (anything-but-agave) bouquet; there's nothing good to be said about this road tar-like stinko nose. While I'd like to tell you that the flavor phase improved this dire situation, I can't because it actually, unbelievably, made it worse as the road tar smell became the lick-the-bottom-of-your-shoes taste; I'm stunned that the Jose Cuervo distillery would even consider bottling this horrific mess that they laughingly call "tequila"; this mixto tequila nadir almost gives mezcal, not a favorite spirit in this publication, a good name; one word review: yeccchhh.
2003 Rating: ★/Not Recommended

Jose Cuervo Orañjo Tequila Flavored with Orange and other Citrus Fruits (Mexico); 40% abv, $21.

As pristine, transparent, and immaculate as spirits get. The aroma is subtle at the opening stage as the delicate orange candy scent teases the olfactory sense; seven more minutes in the glass do little other than merely bolster the faint orange pulp aroma. The palate entry is as fey as the bouquet, offering only timid bittersweetness and astringency; the midpalate is a bit more expressive as the orange flavoring dominates any sense of agave. Decent, certainly drinkable, but entirely average. There's not enough bonding between the base spirit and the flavoring to make it anything other than two stars.
2006 Rating: ★★/Not Recommended

Jose Cuervo Tropiña Tequila Flavored with Pineapple and other Citrus Fruits (Mexico); 40% abv, $21.

As silvery limpid as its siblings; clear and clean. The pineapple fragrance overpowers the base spirit, rendering the first aromatic experience lopsided and therefore borderline pleasant/unpleasant; the aggressive canned pineapple assault continues following aeration making my nearly me scream, "All right already! I got it. It's pineapple." The palate entry is way off course as the flavoring hammers its point across like a carpenter with anger issues; the midpalate simply doesn't work as the core flavor clumsily becomes synthetic and totally manufactured. Ends in a heap of misery. This one should be lifted from the marketplace.
2006 Rating: ★/Not Recommended

Jose Cuervo Reserva de la Familia 2002 Barrel Select Añejo 100% Agave Tequila (Mexico); 40% abv, $110.

Aged in newly charred French and American oak barrels. The bronze/topaz color is like that of an amontillado sherry; perfect purity. The initial two nosing passes within two minutes after the pour unearth astringent and alluring aromas of jasmine, peppercorn, popcorn, and distant agave; eight minutes aeration allows more of the oak component to emerge, lending biscuity and resiny qualities to it; while not an overpowering bouquet in the least, it still is potent and multilayered in an understated way. The palate entry offers succulent tastes of sweet agave, oak char, maple, and resiny oil; the midpalate juncture features a rich taste of dark caramel, yet I would in no way consider this midpalate as sweet or candied. The finish is lush, elegant, bittersweet, and very extended. Heady drinking.
2002 Rating: ★★★★/Highly Recommended

Jose Cuervo Reserva de la Familia 2003 Barrel Select Añejo 100% Agave Tequila (Mexico); 40% abv, $110.

Very pretty light topaz/honey hue; impeccable purity; the opening nosing passes pick up incredibly zesty and harmonious aromas of dill, fennel, and pepper; time in the copita of another seven minutes sees the bouquet turn elegant, oaky, and herbal; a full-throttle but sophisticated aroma. The palate entry is semisweet, with deft traces of caramel and vanilla; by the midpalate point the flavors include marzipan, hard candy, dried herbs, green pepper, and vanilla. The finish is long, luxurious, and stately. A brandy-like tequila that's slightly better than the terrific Reserva de la Familia from 2002; wonderfully rich.
2003 Rating: ★★★★★/Highest Recommendation

Jose Cuervo Reserva de la Familia Platino 100% Agave Tequila (Mexico); 40% abv, $50.

Clear and clean as rainwater. The opening nosings offer piquant and totally dry scents of white pepper, rubber tire, and charcoal; aeration stimulates additional aromas, including stone/granite, minerals, prickly pear, leather, and cement. Entry is semisweet, peppery (jalapeño pepper especially) and nicely rich in texture; by midpalate the taste profile adds exotic flavors of anise, metal, clove, broccoli, and kale. Ends up clean, balanced, pleasantly warming in the throat, and off-dry.
2007 Rating: ★★★/Recommended

La Fogata Extra Aged Tequila Dona Carlota 100% Agave (Mexico); 40% abv, $45.
The very pale straw yellow tint is pretty and delicate. The nose right after opening is flat and muted; the middle stage nosing passes, allowing of course for air contact, unearth more in the way of deepening and expansion with soft, sweet aromas of dill, crushed flowers, and asparagus in the background; after ten minutes of aeration, this bouquet turns stately in an understated manner as firm, but delicate scents of ripe agave, dried herbs, and brine enchant the olfactory sense. Even better in the mouth than in the nose, La Fogata begins at palate entry with a dry taste of vegetal agave; the midpalate expands that theme quite well and introduces a peppery/dried herb flavor that's pleasant and round. The finish is very brief and dry. Not the most expressive or aggressive tequila, but don't let that fact deter you trying it; it's finest hour is in a classic margarita, along with fresh squeezed lime juice and a dash of Cointreau.
2000 Rating: ★★★/Recommended

La Reliquia Reposado 100% Agave Mezcal with Worm (Mexico); 40% abv, $30.
Attractive, bright, pale yellow hue; some minor lumps of sediment seen. The opening smell is strikingly reminiscent of the stale, rubbery air that's expelled from a deflating bicycle or automobile tire; additional air contact only adds aromas of oil slick and rubber pencil eraser; the perfect spirit bouquet for avid cyclists. The palate entry taste is ashy, smoky/ash tray-like, and off-dry; by midpalate there are bits of soy sauce and cocoa (an odder pair never existed) that make it absolutely drinkable. Thankfully ends up highlighting the cocoa element over the old tire air. Not recommendable, but drinkable for a mezcal.
2004 Rating: ★★/Not Recommended

Los Azulejos Reposado 100% Agave Tequila (Mexico); 40% abv, $33.
The pale yellow/straw color is flecked with inconsequential sediment. The initial nosing pass is rife with the aromas of dill and brine; aeration brings out further scents of salt, pickles, green vegetation, and, of course, agave. The palate entry is properly tart, acidic, and lean; the midpalate features a strong, firmly structured texture and flavors of sweet oak, sautéed asparagus, and vanilla. The aftertaste is long, sweet, and vegetal. A reposado whose sweet disposition is its finest asset.
2002 Rating: ★★★★/Highly Recommended

Los Azulejos Añejo 100% Agave Tequila (Mexico); 40% abv, $52.
The dusty honey color is remarkably clean and pure. The first burst of aroma offers scents of lead pencil, chalk, and granite, in other words, this bouquet is stunningly mineral-like in the initial moments; exposure to air for another seven minutes gives it the chance to expand aromatically as it includes rubber tire, cigarette ash, dried tobacco leaf, and dried leafy spices (allspice, sage). The palate entry highlights the sweeter side of the agave juice; the midpalate is more layered, offering tastes of minerals, fruit stone, oak, and a trace of mezcal-like ashy smoke. Ends on a vegetal/herbal flavor note that's similar to kale or escarole.
2006 Rating: ★★★/Recommended

Los Azulejos Silver 100% Agave Tequila (Mexico); 40% abv, $42.

Lovely and clear in appearance, with a slightly green tint; superb purity. The initial nosing passes detect rich and vibrant vegetal/herbal notes, especially green chili pepper and dill; seven more minutes of air contact release pleasing scents of rubber soles, beeswax, and slate/limestone. The palate entry is agave sweet, fully textured, and slightly peppery; the midpalate point rings with agave juice sweetness and lesser tastes of tobacco, asparagus, and sage. Concludes nicely with flavors of black pepper, ash, and green vegetables. A worthy younger companion of the Reposado.

2006 Rating: ★★★/Recommended

Los Danzantes Mezcal Joven (Mexico); 40% abv, $60.

Clear as rainwater; impeccable purity. Smells predictably of rubber inner tube and pencil eraser in the opening sniffs; seven minutes of further air contact and a bit of swirling don't budge the rubber-hose-up-your-nose fragrance; it's not disagreeable, but it's unshakably rubbery and wet suit-like. Entry offers pleasantly oily, even creamy texture and pungent tastes of cigarette smoke and burning rubber; the midpalate is surprisingly sweet and relatively well-behaved in its manner as lively and peppery tastes keep the taste buds alert. Finishes in a flurry of smoke, tobacco juice, road tar, and burning rubber flavors. For mezcal freaks, it'll be love at first bite.

2007 Rating: ★★★★/Highly Recommended

Los Danzantes Reposado Mezcal (Mexico); 42% abv, $70.

The marigold color is compelling; excellent purity. The rubber tire, burnt matchstick, road tar/asphalt aroma is right in line with expectations; another seven minutes of air contact serves up more intriguing scents of limestone/shale, minerals, charcoal, and cigar ash. The palate entry is sweet and creosote-like, medicinal and ashy/sooty; the midpalate stage is long, burnt marshmallow sweet, and very pleasant in its rustic manner. Finishes rubber tire-like and sooty/smoky. I'll vouch for it, even though mezcal will never be a favored spirit of mine. The rating should tell you something.

2007 Rating: ★★★★/Highly Recommended

Margaritaville Oro Tequila (Mexico); 40% abv, $16.

The pale honey/burnished gold color has an odd orange glow to it; minor floating particles. The nose at opening is very dill-like and vegetal; the middle stage nosing passes see some expansion of aroma as dull herbal and caramel notes emerge in the background; the fourth and final sniffing, following slightly more than nine minutes of air exposure, finds no discernable deepening. The palate entry is sweet more in a candy way than in an agave manner; the midpalate is meek, weak, and overly sweet in a manufactured fashion. The finish is caramel-like, medium long, and too sweet. This drinkably banal tequila resembles just about all of Jimmy Buffet's (after whom this stuff was named) numbingly mindless songs; a perfect example of stupid name reflecting ordinary form.

2000 Rating: ★★/Not Recommended

Milagro Añejo Single Barrel 100% Agave Tequila (Mexico); 40% abv, $33.

This golden yellow hue is spoiled by clouds of cork-like sediment. Sound familiar? The nose at opening is yeasty, dusty, and briny, with just a slight note of pickle; further

aeration brings out a peppery, almost gum-like, biscuity perfume that's exceedingly pleasant. The sweet palate entry speaks of roasted peppers, pineapple, and asparagus; the midpalate juncture features luscious flavors of chocolate, bitter orange, and sugar cookies. The finish is sweet, sugary, and long. Excellent except for the sediment problem.
2002 Rating: ★★★★/Highly Recommended

Milagro Reposado 100% Agave Tequila (Mexico); 40% abv, $29.
The attractive straw/gold color is unfortunately marred by black, cork-like sediment. The initial nosing passes within the first two minutes after the pour discover sensuous aromas of sweet oak, milk chocolate, and brine; later sniffings unearth delightful scents of sweet green pepper, buttered popcorn, creamery butter, and dill-like agave. The palate entry is chocolate sweet and tangy; the midpalate point highlights flavors of milk chocolate candy bar, nougat, green vegetable, and oak. The finish is very sweet, almost like honey, and extended. A multilayered reposado that would have scored better had it not been for the poor appearance; even allowing that the SJ could have been sent a bad bottle, no spirit today should have sediment problems like this; I believe it's the cork.
2002 Rating: ★★★/Recommended

Milagro Select Barrel Reserve Añejo 100% Agave Tequila (Mexico); 40% abv, $90.
Aged for three years in oak barrels. The appearance is a shimmering amber/gold color; minor sediment seen. The opening whiffs detect the buttery/resiny/lightly baked presence of the oak barrels in spades; following another seven minutes of air contact, the woodiness blows off leaving behind drier, more vegetal layers of aroma, including green pepper, green olive, candle wax, and garden flowers. The palate entry accentuates the oak barrel sweetness to the hilt while the midpalate adds succulent notes of cream, caramel, and light honey. Concludes sweet, silky in texture, and classy. By one star's worth I prefer the sophisticated sass of the Reserve Reposado, but this añejo is so elegant, who's complaining?
2005 Rating: ★★★★/Highly Recommended

Milagro Select Barrel Reserve Reposado 100% Agave Tequila (Mexico); 40% abv, $70.
Aged for 10 months in new oak barrels. Pretty and proper straw yellow/greenish hue; as is so typical of agave-based spirits such as tequila and mezcal, some sediment seen floating about. Right from the initial sniffings, the aroma smells of wax paper and freshly ground black pepper; aeration stimulates more exotic scents, including asparagus, broccoli, brand new leather, and herbal butter. The palate entry is zesty, spicy, and yet semisweet; the midpalate reaches far beyond the entry tastes adding subtle, yet firm flavors of butter, steamed green vegetables, white rice, and light toffee. Finishes as satiny smooth as a baby's cheek and appealingly spicy. A tour de force in balance and harmony. Genuinely luscious reposado that sits right at the front of the pack.
2005 Rating: ★★★★★/Highest Recommendation

Milagro Silver 100% Agave Tequila (Mexico); 40% abv, $24.
Clear as mineral water but blemished by a little too much floating debris. The opening bouquet is snappy fresh and smoky, kind of like smoldering embers; time in the glass affords the bouquet the opportunity to exhibit more defined aromas, especially licorice, anise, dill, and boiled asparagus. On the palate the taste is fresh, lovely, appropriately zesty, peppery,

and vegetal with just a hint of sugary sweetness at the midpalate point. The aftertaste is long, laced with pepper, and refreshing. A very good silver, but fix the filtration problem.
2002 Rating: ★★★/Recommended

Nacional Silver Tequila 100% Blue Agave (Mexico); 40% abv, $40.
Limpid as rain water, but in need of better filtration as there's too much in the way of floating detritus. The nose at opening is focused, tart, and highly botanical in a dried bark, root-like way; the second pass adds a touch of pepperiness; the third whiff, following six minutes of aeration, throws in unusual, but pleasing scents of charcoal and tar; by the fourth and last sniffing, the aroma is on its way south, leaving behind the dry herbaceousness and charcoal; a different, intriguing bouquet. The palate entry is stone dry; then the flavor at midpalate zooms ahead in a toasted, almost smoky, charcoal flare up on the tongue. The aftertaste is all smoke, ash, soot, and sweet agave. Not a landmark silver, but an awfully good one that's very recommendable; love that smoky quality.
2000 Rating: ★★★/Recommended

Oro de Oaxaca 100% Agave Mezcal with Worm (Mexico); 40% abv, $20.
The pretty pale straw yellow hue catches the eye's attention; very good clarity. The opening aromatic salvo offers musty air-from-deflating-tire charm (?); time in the glass does little to bail this bouquet out of the stale soup as the overwhelming aroma quality remains the relentlessly rubbery/old tire smell; what is there to say about it already? The palate entry shows a bit of zestiness as the taste goes peppery and bittersweet; the midpalate displays tastes of road tar, cigarette ash, and distant brown sugar. Finishes a tad flat and off-dry. To its credit, the taste stage salvaged this mezcal from the one rating star heap by making up enough ground to redeem the overall experience.
2004 Rating: ★★/Not Recommended

Partida Añejo 100% Agave Tequila (Mexico); 40% abv, $60.
The harvest gold hue shows a bit of dark sediment. In the first inhalations, I pick up keenly crisp and spicy notes of black pepper and oak; seven more minutes in the glass stir up plumper aromas, including green pepper, vanilla, and cocoa butter. The palate entry is unbelievably elegant and gently sweet with tastes of fresh honey and vanilla; the midpalate stage adds seductive flavors of buttercream, steamed asparagus, and sweet oak. The aftertaste advances the honey sweetness without losing the vegetal/peppery agave core. The Partida tequilas are simply the finest line of tequilas that money can buy right now. The bar has been raised to lofty new heights.
2005 Rating: ★★★★★/Highest Recommendation

Partida Blanco 100% Agave Tequila (Mexico); 40% abv, $50.
Absolute clarity; silvery hue. The opening nosing passes pick up savory and curiously mezcal-like scents of rubber inner tube, pickle brine, and papaya; later sniffings detect green olive, vinyl, new saddle leather, and kale; easily one of the most distinctive blanco tequila bouquets I've come across in years and also one of the finest and truest to agave. The palate entry is silky smooth, off-dry, and lightly peppery; at midpalate the taste profile highlights the vegetal side of the flavor, then switches gears as it nears the finish, turning more elegant

and gently peppery and lightly honeyed. Remarkable quality and individuality.
2005 Rating: ★★★★★/Highest Recommendation

Partida Elegante Extra Añejo 100% Agave Tequila (Mexico); 40% abv, $350.
Topaz/medium amber color; superb purity. Smells of mint, light toffee, summer vegetation, and gum; additional air contact unleashes subtle scents of cookie batter/biscuits, tapioca, brown rice, and a deft touch of honey. Entry is medium sweet, near-succulent, medium-weighted; the flavor profile turns on the charm at midpalate as the taste turns more peppery, honeyed, oaky, slightly toasty, and spicy. Finishes elegantly, moderately sweet in an oaky not a sugary manner, and completely integrated. Seamless quality from stem to stern.
2007 Rating: ★★★★★/Highest Recommendation

Partida Reposado 100% Agave Tequila (Mexico); 40% abv, $55.
The pale gold/flat amber color is impeccably pure. The initial whiffs encounter reined-in, but stunningly elegant scents of sawdust, pine, and vegetal agave; aeration stimulates deeper aromas that include old leather, stamp glue, cigarette ash, and pimento; without any doubt, one of the two or three finest reposado bouquets in existence. The palate entry is delicate, piquant, and peppery, yet understated and refined; the midpalate stage is notable for its sweet, honey-like core flavor and its harmonious supplemental tastes of cocoa, milk chocolate, and chili pepper. The finish is long, gently sweet and the model of finesse. The Bentley of reposado tequilas and, in my mind, the new benchmark.
2005 Rating: ★★★★★/Highest Recommendation

Penca Azul Reposado 100% Agave Tequila (Mexico); 40% abv, $90.
The silver/flax tint is very pale; minor debris of an insignificant nature is spotted. The opening nose is piquant and intensely herbal in the first two passes; aeration adds hints of dill, brine, agave, and green pepper. The palate entry is lovely and sweet; the midpalate is honeyed, warm, and lean in texture. The aftertaste shows signs of smoke, pepper, peas, and a finishing sweetness that nicely concludes the evaluation. More austere than many reposados currently out there, but its focus is undiverted and admirable; a margarita tequila, no doubt.
2002 Rating: ★★★/Highly Recommended

Pepe Lopez Premium Gold Tequila (Mexico); 40% abv, $11.
The rich honey/vibrant amber hue is extremely pretty; excellent clarity and purity. The initial nosing pass immediately following the pour detects delicate, lean, and laudably focused aromas of herbal agave, very mild dill, and a touch of salty brine; the second and third nosing passes, after three and seven minutes respectively, reveal additional background scents of black pepper, hay, and damp vegetation; the fourth and final sniffing, after a full ten minutes of air contact, sees the herbal agave take charge of the proceedings as the other aromatic components fade away; a nice, undemanding, but multidimensional tequila bouquet. The palate entry is dry but basically nondescript; the flavor grows dramatically by the midpalate stage as medium-full tastes of sweet, ripe agave, dried herbs, and buttered asparagus delight the taste buds. The finish is slightly hot, intensely vegetal, toned down in the sweetness department, but firm. A well-crafted gold tequila; very attractively priced.
2000 Rating: ★★★/Recommended

Pueblo Viejo Añejo 100% Agave Tequila (Mexico); 40% abv, $45.

The attractive light gold/apple juice color is helped by the unblemished, sediment-free appearance. The aging of eighteen months in American oak really doesn't seem to have much impact in the initial whiffs after the pour as the aroma focuses squarely on the agave; air contact does stimulate further aromatic activity in the pleasing forms of light vanilla and red pepper. The palate entry is smoky and charred, with a backnote of sweetness; the midpalate point is candy sweet and oily. It finishes warmly, spirity, toffee sweet, and oaky. Very good.

2002 Rating: ★★★/Recommended

Pueblo Viejo Blanco 100% Agave Tequila (Mexico); 40% abv, $25.

Sparkling clear; shows a little more sediment than I'd like to see. The initial two passes in the nose are zesty, pleasantly piquant, but not heady or prickly; exposure to air over five to six minutes encourages further aromas to emerge beneath the basic vegetal/agave perfume including green pepper, pickling brine, and lead pencil; a well-made, properly fresh, and dynamic blanco bouquet. The palate entry is dry and peppery; then at midpalate there's an explosion of off-dry licorice/anise flavor that shows up on the back of the tongue. The finish is long, keenly dry, and refreshing. What silver tequila should be; crisp, herbal, and fresh—and all too often isn't; very nice job here and a terrific margarita tequila.

2002 Rating: ★★★★/Highly Recommended

Pueblo Viejo Reposado 100% Agave Tequila (Mexico); 40% abv, $30.

Pale flax/straw yellow hue; insignificant debris spotted. The minimum of nine months in wood really shows up right away in the opening two nosings conducted within two minutes of the pour; the piney, woodsy, and gently sweet scents liked in the first sniffings continue and deepen following five minutes of sitting in the glass; a delicate, refined reposado perfume. The palate entry is dry and crisp; the midpalate stage highlights succulent tastes of sweet oak, licorice, and oaky vanilla. The aftertaste is astringent, sinewy, and medium long. Lovely, elegant, and delightfully low-key.

2002 Rating: ★★★★/Highly Recommended

San Matias Gran Reserva Añejo Tequila (Mexico); 40% abv, $40.

Smashing gold color with green highlights; excellent purity. The initial couple of sniffings reveal little except for mild pine/cedar and uncooked asparagus; allowing it to rest for seven minutes doesn't help in terms of encouraging greater aromatic depth or expansion and as a result only distant notes of vanillin and black pepper get added to the nosing notes. The palate entry is peppery and moderately semisweet to sweet and even a touch oily; by the midpalate stage there's a nice trace of hard candy sweetness that lies on top of the pepper and oiliness but frankly overall it's a lackluster taste exhibition. The aftertaste is muted, mildly sweet in a vegetal/weedy manner, and long. Perfectly acceptable but too lacking in genuine depth to be viewed as a recommendable product.

2002 Rating: ★★/Not Recommended

San Matias Reposado Tequila (Mexico); 40% abv, $25.

Pale flax hue; moderate amount of sediment. The nose in the first stages is peppery and herbal; aeration does little except add a heady/spirity note to the green pepper and dried

herbs. The palate entry is dry to the point of being very lean; then at midpalate there's a bit of flavor in the atypical forms of cocoa and cane sugar. The aftertaste highlights the mildly prickly spirit. Run-of-the-mill; suitable for mixing.
2002 Rating: ★★/Not Recommended

Sauza Blanco Tequila (Mexico); 40% abv, $13.

Silvery clarity; superb purity. The peculiar first aroma after the pour doesn't at all reflect the base material, agave, and therefore gets off wrong-footed and clumsy; aeration only makes the situation more dire as unappealing and totally inappropriate scents of linoleum, plastic, and synthetic fiber vie for dominance; when it says "Tequila" on the label, that's what I expect, not floor polish. Now I'm sorry that I brought up the concept of floor polish because that's what this liquid disaster tastes like in the horrible palate entry; ditto the midpalate stage; ditto the finish. So atrocious that I can't even laugh at it. An embarrassment to Sauza and to the tequila industry.
2007 Rating: ★/Not Recommended

Sauza Conmemorativo Añejo Tequila (Mexico); 40% abv, $26.

The cornflower yellow color is attractive; absolute purity; a nice looking tequila. The initial whiffs detect textile/waxy notes upfront and a deeper note of butter/vegetable oil that seems to underpin the beeswax scent; further aeration brings out white pepper, allspice, and caraway seed fragrances, which while nice, aren't very tequila-like. The palate entry is mildly sweet and caramel-like, but without much of an agave personality; by the midpalate point the spice element recedes, leaving behind a fat and moderately flabby spirit that's drinkably average and uninspiring because there's no edge to it. Tequila needs some edge, otherwise it's mundane. I can only ask a single question after tasting this offering: Where has Sauza, a sterling tequila producer in the 1990s and a former favorite of mine, gone?
2007 Rating: ★★/Not Recommended

Sauza Extra Gold Tequila (Mexico); 40% abv, $26.

Pretty, pale straw/hay color; impeccable purity. The pleasing opening aromas remind me of lemon zest, green olive, and saltine crackers; after another seven minutes of air contact the bouquet turns a touch flat, losing the nice piquancy enjoyed in the first nosings. The palate entry is semisweet, nicely peppery, and vegetal; at the midpalate juncture the taste profile edges more towards the peppery quality as it sheds some of the sweetness and natural agave character (the vegetal aspect). Ends up a bit flabby and mildly disappointing.
2007 Rating: ★★/Not Recommended

Sauza Hornitos Reposado 100% Agave Tequila (Mexico); 40% abv, $38.

The pale straw color is bright and clean. The aroma after the pour is lean and paraffin-like; swirling and additional time in the glass stimulate more expressive aromas of black pepper, sea salt, and jalapeño pepper. The palate entry is tight, acidic, and keenly peppery; by the midpalate stage the flavor profile's sinewy character goes totally dry and spicy. Ends up very trim. Good enough to be recommended, especially as a mixing tequila, but hardly the robust, assertive 100% agave tequila that was my house tequila for many years.
2007 Rating: ★★★/Recommended

Sauza Tres Generaciones Añejo 100% Agave Tequila (Mexico); 40% abv, $38.
The deep yellow/light gold color is genuinely pretty; flawless purity. In the opening nosing passes, the aroma is biscuity and vanilla-like; the fragrance picks up momentum with further aeration, mostly in the aromatic forms of saltwater taffy, light caramel, and vanilla extract. The palate entry is decidedly sweet and caramel-like; by the midpalate stage the caramel wrests away control of the taste profile and runs with it. Concludes sweet (in an oaky manner), mildly green olive-like, and vegetal enough to interesting.
2007 Rating: ★★★/Recommended

Sauza Tres Generaciones Plata 100% Agave Tequila (Mexico); 40% abv, $36.
Clean and clear; pretty appearance. The opening inhalations detect only distant notes of kale and escarole, but no hint of agave herbaceousness, saltiness or brininess; additional time in the glass fails to stimulate much in the way of customary agave-based aromatics, except for a feeble note of green pepper; this aroma is a no-show. The palate entry is so neutral and gravel-like that I have a flashing thought that it's vodka, not tequila; the midpalate stage is equally nowhere and stone- and gravel-like. Where's the salt? Where's the dill pickle quality? More importantly, where is the distillery I once knew and loved as Sauza? If this is worth $36, I'm George Clooney.
2007 Rating: ★/Not Recommended

Sauza Tres Generaciones Reposada 100% Agave Tequila (Mexico); 40% abv, $38.
Pale straw/dusty yellow color; excellent purity. The reluctant aroma ekes out a miserly morsel of timid herbal agave in the opening minutes but nothing more; another seven minutes of aeration and vigorous swirling do little other than to stimulate mildly attractive scents of tree bark, pine, cedar, and nutmeg; once again, where's the agave? The palate entry is flat, but displays some vanilla from the wood, I suspect; at the midpalate stage the taste profile, meager and anemic as it is, offers some semblances of black pepper, granite, and allspice. Finishes a bit harsh, but with a little (very welcome) agave brininess.
2007 Rating: ★★/Not Recommended

Scorpion Añejo 100% Agave Mezcal with Scorpion Lot 30 (Mexico); 40% abv, $47.
Attractive golden honey color; absolute purity. The opening bouquet emits very strong and firm aromas of saddle leather and oak; aeration adds minimal scents of vinyl, grass, and distant honey. The palate entry offers sap-like tastes of maple and butterscotch; by the midpalate point a smoky taste profile comes into play as soft, almost plump flavors of sap, steamed green vegetables, and palm oil take charge. Concludes softly, warm in the throat, and agave-like. Well, well, well.
2004 Rating: ★★★/Recommended

Scorpion Mezcal Añejo 5 Years Old (Mexico); 40% abv, $180.
The medium amber/harvest gold color is attractive and pure. The first nosings pick up intriguing, if oddly compelling, notes of quinine, sulphur/burnt match, and furniture polish; additional time in the glass brings out deeper scents, especially onion, brine, olives, and damp earth. The palate entry is as sooty as cigarette ashes, sweet, and close to creamy; at

midpalate the taste profile turns peppery/zesty, oaky sweet, charcoal-like, and, on the whole, savory. Finishes bittersweet and caramel-like. Nice job.
2005 Rating: ★★★★/Highly Recommended

Scorpion Mezcal Añejo 7 Years Old (Mexico); 40% abv, $225.
The deep amber/burnished gold color is clean and free of debris. The first inhalations find typical mezcal scents such as rubber tire, India ink, and vinyl; after seven more minutes of air contact, the aroma adds only burned/baked aromas, mostly of burning rubber. The palate entry is surprisingly sweet and mild; at midpalate a robust ashy/sooty flavor takes charge of the flavor proceedings, elbowing out all other taste possibilities. Ends up on a moderately sweet, smoky note that's quite pleasant.
2005 Rating: ★★★/Recommended

Scorpion Reposado 100% Agave Mezcal with Scorpion Lot 37 (Mexico); 40% abv, $37.
The pale yellow color is the color of lemon juice; excellent purity (keeping in mind, of course, that the exoskeleton of a scorpion creepily lurks at the bottom). This aroma offers more in the way of real herbal/peppery/briny agave quality; seven more minutes in the glass produce a modest aromatic expansion, mostly in the forms of gum, wheat bread toast, and spice. The palate entry highlights a zesty, piquant green pepper taste that's enjoyable; the midpalate features softer, even delicate (you read that right) flavors of steamed asparagus, herbs, and bittersweet agave juice. Finishes gently. Well, well.
2004 Rating: ★★★/Recommended

Scorpion Silver 100% Agave Mezcal with Scorpion Lot 34 (Mexico); 40% abv, $35.
Pleasingly clear and clean. The opening aroma is peppery, clean, and dry; aeration time of another six minutes helps the aroma expand to include notes of saddle leather, herbal agave, and wood resin. The palate entry emits simple tastes of dried herbs and black peppercorn; by midpalate the flavor profile turns astringent and a bit prickly on the tongue. Ends up desert dry, warm, and resiny. So-so and consumable.
2004 Rating: ★★/Not Recommended

Siembra Azul Blanco 100% Agave Tequila (Mexico); 40% abv, $19.
Kosher. Ideal translucence and purity. The opening aroma is vividly vegetal (green leaf veggies) and precisely green chili pepper-like; additional aeration adds only minor minty/herbal qualities. The palate entry is agave juice sweet, sappy, and simple; the midpalate offers more complex tastes of sweet wood smoke, tobacco, and dried herbs, in particular, sage. Finishes snappy, sap-like, and zesty. While hardly profound, it has a rustic charm that is mildly appealing. I only wish that this blanco would have offered more dill/fennel/brine depth, traditional agave traits. Ultra-clean, like a vodka among tequilas.
2006 Rating: ★★★/Recommended

Siembra Azul Reposado 100% Agave Tequila (Mexico); 40% abv, $24.
Kosher. The pale straw yellow color is attractive and pure. The opening bouquet emits mild scents of oak, vanilla, and green olive; the second round of sniffing after aeration is treated to seductive scents of ash, soot, vanilla bean, dill, and pickle brine. The palate entry is

medium sweet, juicy, and sap-like; the midpalate is long, moderately oily, peppery, vegetal, and dill-like. Concludes very short and vanilla-like. Had the finish been more extended, a fourth star would have been bestowed.

2006 Rating: ★★★/Recommended

Siglo Treinta XXX Gold Tequila (Mexico); 40% abv, $15.

A mixto tequila, meaning a blend of 51% agave spirit and 49% sugar cane distillate. Honey gold color; excellent purity; the opening nosing passes immediately pick up on the sweet, pulpy and peppery aromas that are pleasing and true to the agave component of the blend; further sniffings after six more minutes reveal nuances of corn syrup, black pepper, green olives, and brine; for the money one heck of a good tequila bouquet. The palate entry is sweet, herbal, and botanical; the midpalate point is delightfully straightforward, unabashedly sweet and keenly peppery. The aftertaste is long, a touch honeyed and surprisingly rich. I'd use this fine mixto in a tequila sunrise sooner than I would in a margarita; an excellent bargain that doesn't for a moment feign being anything other than what it is, a well-made mixto tequila.

2003 Rating: ★★★/Recommended

Sol Rey Añejo 100% Agave Tequila (Mexico); 40% abv, $390.

Aged in wood for approximately six years. The deep honey/gold color is pretty and serious-looking; some sediment, nothing detrimental. The opening nosing passes after the pour offer understated nuances of anise, prickly pear, and barely discernable dill; after leaving it in the glass for another eight minutes, round, supple, and intriguing aromas of agave, sulphur, minerals, and licorice make for interesting sniffing. The palate entry is plump, oily, and green vegetable succulent; the midpalate is mildly sweet, not as woody/resiny as I expected, and dry to off-dry. The aftertaste is long, keenly vegetal/cactus-like, and dry. It owns a purity and a vivacity that I admire but I was hoping for greater depth, considering the time spent in wood.

2002 Rating: ★★★/Recommended

Tezon Añejo 100% Agave Tequila (Mexico); 40% abv, $70.

Pleasing amber/harvest gold color; superb clarity. The lively brine/pepper opening aroma after the pour is zesty and a little smoked; later sniffings detect kippers, green olives, steamed asparagus, light caramel, and even a fine trace of honey. The palate entry is delicately sweet and honeyed; at midpalate the oak influence comes on in the forms of vanilla and maple. Concludes classy, smooth, and gently sweet. Not a profound or broad-shouldered añejo, but a dandy all the same.

2005 Rating: ★★★/Recommended

Tezon Blanco 100% Agave Tequila (Mexico); 40% abv, $60.

Clear as rain water; slight evidence of sediment. The opening inhalations are deeply dill-like and even almost like pickle relish; further time in the copita produces little in the way of aromatic expansion, except to add some notes of cream and pepper. The palate entry is nicely creamy, more bittersweet than sweet, and a bit metallic/lead pencil-like; at midpalate the dry to off-dry taste profile increases in depth, adding sharply bittersweet flavors of black pepper,

minerals/shale, soot, and potash. Finishes smooth, creamy, metallic tasting, and peppery. Not as elegant as some blancos (for elegance, think: Cabo Wabo, AsomBroso, Herradura) but certainly better than average.
2005 Rating: ★★★/Recommended

Tezon Reposado 100% Agave Tequila (Mexico); 40% abv, $65.
The color is pale amber/slightly greenish/silver; excellent clarity. The first nosings are spiced and intensely peppery; evidence of dill and olive brine comes to the surface in the later sniffings. The palate entry is smooth and creamy, even a touch vanilla-like; the midpalate stage is accentuated by long tastes of black pepper, roasted agave, new leather, and pickling brine. Concludes satiny in texture, slightly smoky, and toffee sweet. More sophisticated and round than the Blanco; stylish and racy. The pick of the Tezon litter.
2005 Rating: ★★★★/Highly Recommended

Trago Añejo 100% Agave Tequila (Mexico); 40% abv, $60.
The color is pale gold/flax/Muscadet Loire Valley wine; unblemished clarity. The spicy zestiness of the opening aroma is truly engaging and, at least to my taste, dead-on what I want 100% agave to be: in other words, I want earthy agave character from the beginning; the green pepper-like spiciness adds equally inviting smells of newly tanned leather, malted milk, rubber pencil eraser, textile/fiber (palm fronds?), and delicate honey. Smooth as satin at entry as semisweet tastes of honey, orange peel, dry soil, and vanilla enchant the taste buds; the flavor profile at midpalate is sweeter than at entry, but not in the least cloying or sugary: just integrated, moderately briny/saline, and citrusy. Finishes svelte, moderately sweet, creamy yet sassy and highly spiced. Elegance with a distinct rambunctious attitude.
2007 Rating: ★★★★★/Highest Recommendation

Trago Reposado 100% Agave Tequila (Mexico); 40% abv, $50.
The pale straw/gray tint shines in the glass and reminds me of manzanilla sherry; excellent clarity. The aroma is fruity (pears, in particular), slightly baked/toasty, leathery, and dry; seven more minutes of air contact bring out nuances of chalk, pickle brine, dill, and butter cream; a complex and compelling bouquet. Entry is classy, moderately sweet in an oaky/vanilla manner, and still keenly toasty; the flavor profile at midpalate is creamy, concentrated, rich in texture, yet still peppery/spicy, earthy and fruity. Ends on notes of sweet oak, vanilla bean, honey, orange peel, and jalapeño pepper. Absolutely lovely, yet retains a definite touch of the wild.
2007 Rating: ★★★★★/Highest Recommendation

Trago Silver 100% Agave Tequila (Mexico); 40% abv, $46.
Mineral water clear and impeccably clean. The first whiffs detect high-flying peppery notes that are dry, intensely vegetal, and zesty; further time in the glass allows for deeper scents of minerals/quartz, limestone, and agave fiber; what I like so much about this aroma is that it smells like the Jalisco Highlands, gravelly, arid, and earthy. Herbal, vegetal, and off-dry at entry, the taste is slightly chalky/earth-like but balanced; at midpalate the flavor profile turns sweeter, more peppery and spicy, and agave plant-like. Concludes as earthy and gritty, peppery, and piquant as it started with the initial nosing. Reflects its place of origin to a tee.
2007 Rating: ★★★★/Highly Recommended

Tres Rios Añejo 100% Agave Tequila (Mexico); 40% abv, $50.

Pretty straw/pale gold color; flawless purity. Like its younger siblings, this añejo's early aromatic profile is governed by sulfur dioxide, which comes off like burnt matches and/or gunpowder, but beyond that is evidence of burning rubber and pickle brine; aeration only serves to heighten the sulfur aspect and in the process accentuate saline pickle brine even more. Entry is burnt/toasty and road tar-like; by midpalate the taste profile offers somewhat incongruous but doable flavors of vanilla, oak, honey, gunpowder, dill, green olive, and metal. Weird and hardly pretty, but oddly attractive in a roguish, outsider way.

2007 Rating: ★★★/Recommended

Tres Rios Reposado 100% Agave Tequila (Mexico); 40% abv, $45.

Pale straw/ecru/pewter color; superb clarity. Pickle brine and olive brine leap from the glass in the first nosings; aeration stimulates more of the sulfur/burnt match/gunpowder odor found in the silver version, but here the wood mitigates the worst properties of it, leaving behind still formidable aromas of brine barrel, used ashtray, and over-steamed asparagus. Entry is semisweet, tobacco-like, slightly honeyed, and even caramel-like; at midpalate the oak presence is clearly evident as the flavor softens into a near-plump taste experience that features notes of toffee, nougat, and peanut butter. Ends up nicely briny and medium-sweet. This type of arrested agave, mezcal-like funk I can live with and even admire to a point.

2007 Rating: ★★★/Recommended

Tres Rios Silver 100% Agave Tequila (Mexico); 40% abv, $40.

Flawlessly clean; rainwater clear. The immediate aromatic impact after the pour is road tar, nail polish, mushrooms, and vinyl flooring; additional aeration at last adds some spiciness (green peppercorns) and iron-rich green vegetables, such as spinach, kale to the tarry and quite strange burnt match/sulfur-like aroma; actually smells of gunpowder to me. Entry is vegetal, semisweet, and keenly sulphury/burnt; the taste profile at midpalate doesn't change all that much from the wild and wooly entry. Concludes off-dry, rubbery, and just slightly herbal/spicy/briny. The biggest drawback is the indefatigable aroma that smells of way too much sulfur dioxide and gunpowder character. I never mind some agave "funk", but this is beyond what's natural and more like a production problem.

2007 Rating: ★/Not Recommended

Two Fingers Berry Raspberry Flavored Tequila (Mexico); 35% abv, $12.

Excellent appearance in its unblemished purity. The blackberry/raspberry rush during the first nosing pass is pleasant and ripe; over time, the aroma turns more industrial/clinical in its fruitiness and therefore less natural and fresh. At palate entry the berry flavoring overshadows any sense of agave spirit, yet is mildly tasty and zesty; at midpalate there's a faint trace of agave as the berry flavoring recedes a bit. Concludes moderately ripe and fruity, gently sweet and candied. Not as bad as I thought it might be, though the tequila presence is virtually zilch.

2006 Rating: ★★/Not Recommended

Two Fingers Gold Tequila (Mexico); 40% abv, $13.

The pale straw yellow/flaxen color is pure. The opening aroma is very green and vegetal; six more minutes of air contact reveal distant notes of black pepper and reed/tall grass. The palate entry is semisweet and bean/legume-like; at midpalate the semisweetness really comes through as does a spirity harshness that rakes the taste buds. Ends up bittersweet and a bit raw. Drinkable for people who like their mixto tequila (an entirely legal blend of agave spirits and "other" spirits) on the rough-and-ready side.

2004 Rating: ★★/Not Recommended

Two Fingers Lime Lime Flavored Tequila (Mexico); 35% abv, $12.

Clean and clear to the eye. The initial whiffs take in a salty, limey scent that's halfway to becoming attractive; additional exposure to air is virtually meaningless as the sole difference is the meager advancing of the salt component on the lime, but that's about all. The palate entry is all about citric acid, lime flavoring, and overwhelming tartness; my hopes of encountering at least some agave spirit by midpalate end in disappointment as all that the midpalate offers is tart lime. Finishes bitter, limey, and dismal. Tequila is such a strong and distinctive taste on its own that I question the use of it as a flavoring base. Tequila ain't vodka, brothers and sisters. Of the two, I thought that this one might work. It didn't.

2006 Rating: ★/Not Recommended

Viuda de Romero Añejo Tequila 40% abv, $21.

This añejo is a mixto tequila, meaning one that's made with 51% blue agave distillate. Honey colored appearance but with more floating brackish debris than I think should be found in a $20+ tequila. The nose in the first two passes is pleasantly toasty and agave vegetal/herbal; with time in the glass the aroma picks up hints of black pepper and subtle oaky vanilla in the last sniffings. In the mouth the flavor at palate entry is mildly woody and slightly sweet; then at midpalate the taste profile goes bitter and resiny so that the herbal agave element enjoyed in the latter stages of the aroma vanishes under the weight of the woodiness. Bitter aftertaste. The flavor doesn't fulfill the promise found in the bouquet.

2001 Rating: ★★/Not Recommended

Viuda de Romero Blanco Tequila (Mexico); 40% abv, $18.

51% agave. Clean appearance. The nose at opening is like saddle leather; the middle stages offer odd scents of wet canvas, dirt, and cigarette smoke; the final sniffing sees the leather aroma reinstated as the primary aroma. The palate entry is smoky and sweet; then at midpalate a Major League oiliness, like creosote, takes charge. The aftertaste is sooty/ashy and oily sweet. A mixer.

2001 Rating: ★★/Not Recommended

Viuda de Romero Reposado Tequila (Mexico); 40% abv, $20.

51% agave. Pale honey hue; minor sediment spotted. The initial two nosing passes emit peculiar scents of shoe polish and cigarette ash; the final two whiffs offer nothing new. The palate entry is candy sweet (caramel additive?) while the midpalate phase is drinkably herbal sweet. The finish is long, honeyed, and biscuity. Best applied as a margarita base.

2001 Rating: ★★/Not Recommended

XQ Gran Reserva Añejo Tequila 100% Agave (Mexico); 40% abv, $75.

Matured for three years in three types of wood barrels. The harvest gold/medium amber hue is pretty except, unforgivably, for all the floating debris. Toasted, woody scents inhabit the opening nosing; the middle stage passes unearth tangy, resiny aromas that include wet cotton, linseed oil, asparagus, and cucumber; the fourth and last sniffing, following over nine minutes of aeration, turns very resiny. The palate entry is very sweet, almost candied; that overriding, one dimensional flavor continues through the midpalate. The finish is long, overly candy/oaky sweet, and manufactured tasting. Stick with the Plata.

2000 Rating: ★★/Not Recommended

XQ Plata Tequila 100% Agave (Mexico); 40% abv, $45.

Crystal clear and free of particles. The nose at opening is extremely pleasant in a piquant herbal manner; the second pass picks up a citrus rind-like characteristic that's very fresh and inviting; after seven minutes of aeration, the third sniffing discovers the seductive agave/ vegetal/briny scent that could be nothing but tequila; there's no fading of potency in the fourth and final nosing pass as the bouquet turns intensely peppery. The palate entry is soft, almost neutral; then the midpalate taste sensation goes zesty, snappy, and prickly as concentrated vegetal, lead pencil agave flavors dominate the taste buds. The aftertaste is a bit ashy/sooty, very extended, and oily, but good. You must like the dry, raw, vegetal quality of agave to call this winner your own; I would place this rambunctious silver at the head of the class for margaritas-with-attitude.

2000 Rating: ★★★★/Highly Recommended

XQ Reposado Tequila 100% Agave (Mexico); 40% abv, $50.

The pale straw yellow/mown hay color is marred by too much floating detritus. The initial nosing pass finds a very fresh, green pepper aroma that comes off a bit wax-like; the second sniffing detects softer background scents of pine nuts, sea salt, and brine; after six minutes of air contact, the bouquet adds a deft touch of leather to the aromatic mix; the fourth and final whiff offers a classic vegetal/waxy/briny agave perfume with just a fading hint of oak. In the mouth, this reposado comes off much sweeter than the Plata as oily, briny, intensely peppery flavors enchant the taste buds; the midpalate is especially nice as the rich agave base gets topped off by a sweet oak taste that impresses the palate. The aftertaste is long, oily/waxy, and mildly sweet. A solid reposado, but I prefer the Plata.

2000 Rating: ★★★/Recommended

WHISK(E)Y

WHISKEY—IRELAND

In researching my fourth book, *A Double Scotch*, it became apparent and, to my mind, virtually irrefutable through the research that the Irish were the first to boil beer to create the distillate we now call whiskey. The Gaels very likely were distilling their ales by the 12th century. (Note: when referring to the grain-based, wood-matured distillate of Ireland and the United States, whiskey is spelled with an "e". When referring to those produced in Scotland and Canada, the "e" is dropped and the spelling is whisky. There are a few exceptions in America, such as George Dickel, Maker's Mark.)

There are four basic types of Irish whiskey:

- *Single Malt Whiskey*. This type is made from 100% malted barley in a pot still in a single distillery and is known for its distinctive flavors.
- *Grain Whiskey*. Produced in column stills, grain whiskey is made from wheat or corn and is normally lighter than Single Malt or Pure Pot Still Whiskeys.
- *Blended Whiskey*. This variety is a combination of grain and single malt whiskeys.
- *Pure Pot Still Whiskey*. Made from 100% barley, which is both malted and unmalted, and distilled in a pot still. A variety that is unique to Ireland, pure pot still whiskey is very potent and robust.

All Irish whiskeys by law must be aged for a minimum of three years in barrels. A distinguishing characteristic of Irish whiskeys is that most are distilled three times to promote extra smoothness and drinkability. At present, there are three distilleries on the island, two in the Irish Republic (Cooley in County Louth and Midleton in County Cork) and one in Northern Ireland (Old Bushmills in County Antrim).

Also be aware of an unaged type of Irish grain-based spirit called *potcheen* or poitín (po-CHEEN), which is essentially under-matured, moonshine whiskey. A couple of potcheens are tasty.

The good news is that Irish whiskey is currently on the rebound as sales have increased markedly over the last decade. I consider a couple of Irish whiskeys, Midleton Very Rare and Bushmills 16 Year Old, as two of the finest whiskeys made anywhere in the world. They just need to open up more distilleries to get the ball rolling even faster.

Brennan's Authentic Blended Irish Whiskey (Ireland); 40% abv, $17.

The attractive harvest gold/amber color reminds me of fino sherry; absolutely free of debris. The nose at opening is pleasantly forthcoming and biscuity, showing very soft notes of wood and malt; the middle stages nosings reveal a snappy, vibrant, and piquant but not prickly aromatic zest that closely resembles bramble and fresh ground black pepper; the sassy aroma continues with gusto into the fourth and final sniffing but more in a sweet almost honeyed fashion; to say I liked this crackling bouquet is understating the situation. In the mouth, the taste opens up at palate entry with a bit of fire and considerable grainy sweetness; by the midpalate stage the overriding tastes are of malt and wood, with a touch too much harshness at the back of the tongue. The aftertaste is lean, sweet, resiny, and long. But for the fleeting phase of raw, spirity harshness just prior to the finish, I'd have given it four stars and Highly Recommended status; as it is, this is a deserving three star blended whiskey that should be given a thorough looking over by any whiskey lover.

2000 Rating: ★★★/Recommended

Bunratty Potcheen (Ireland); 45% abv, $42.

This interesting poitín (pronounced po-CHEEN) hails from the Bunratty Mead & Liqueur Company in County Clare. Clear as rain water, but with some minor suspended particles showing. The opening whiff picks up intriguing and highly aromatic notes of evergreen, cotton candy, and sweet grain (corn?) spirit; by the second pass, the air contact unleashes an herbal perfume that's mildly akin to anise/licorice or fruit pit; with more exposure to air, the bouquet develops the herbal theme further by adding soft spearmint to the mix; the fourth and final sniffing, after a full nine minutes of time in the glass, highlights the herbal/sweet grain themes, adding just for fun a very subtle note of soot. The palate entry is smooth for a poitín, moderately sweet, and very herbal; the midpalate stage goes totally dry and herbal/ashy on the tongue. The aftertaste is long, stony/minerally, and completely dry. Drinkably average.

2000 Rating: ★★/Not Recommended

Bushmills White Label Blended Irish Whiskey (Ireland); 40% abv, $20.

Owns a pale gold, unblemished appearance. The early-stage sniffings following the pour find gentle, delicate aromas of green vegetables, carnations, and grain mash; six more minutes of air contact bring up slightly sour notes of damp soil, glue, and marshmallow. Exceedingly pleasant, grainy sweet and genial at palate entry; at midpalate there's a rush of sweet maltiness/graininess that overrides all other flavor elements. Finishes clean, uncomplicated, and warm in the throat.

2004 Rating: ★★★/Recommended

Bushmills Black Bush Black Label Blended Irish Whiskey (Ireland); 40% abv, $28.

Possesses a high ratio of malt whiskey (85%, I believe) and is therefore deeper in color (rich amber) than the White Label; absolute purity. The malt whiskey leaps from the glass in the forms of breakfast cereal and light caramel notes; following seven minutes of exposure to air, Black Bush's bouquet shifts into passing gear as racy aromas of toffee, cotton candy, malt mash, and cream highlight a dazzling bouquet. The palate entry is deep, dark caramel-like and stunningly luscious; at midpalate the malt component takes charge as the overall flavor depth and scope come into full perspective; concludes as majestically as it begins. One of the greatest whiskeys from Ireland, bar none. A delicious tot that I enjoy time and again, at home and on the road. Brilliant.

2004 Rating: ★★★★/Highly Recommended

Bushmills 10 Year Old Green Label Single Malt Whiskey (Ireland); 40% abv, $34.

The golden/autumnal/grain harvest hue sparkles in the glass; perfect purity. The early stage aroma is fresh, malty, yeasty/beery and a touch honey-like; further aeration time brings out intriguing notes of nougat, milk chocolate, and oaky vanilla. The palate entry offers pleasantly fruity/grainy tastes that are more off-dry than sweet; at midpalate the flavor profile is all about the malt. It ends up semisweet, candied, and even a tad sherried. I've liked, but never loved, this simple, straightforward Irish single malt for more than a decade. Compared to other Bushmills single malts (16 Triple Wood, 21 Madeira Cask), the 10 is amiable but simple.

2004 Rating: ★★★/Recommended

Bushmills 12 Year Old Single Irish Malt Whiskey (Ireland); 40% abv, $n/a.

Available at the distillery only. The color is a light amber/harvest gold with green highlights; wonderful purity. The opening two minutes of sniffing reveals focused, dry aromas of oak, vanilla, and lichee nuts; more time in the glass adds succulent scents of almonds sautéed in butter, rich, toasty malt, light honey, light caramel, and pepper; what's so appealing about this bouquet is that all the while I'm inhaling, I'm fully aware of the sweet malt foundation, not so much in a profound way as in an unshakably solid base manner. The palate entry immediately displays the sweet malty virtue that is this whiskey's core; at midpalate the buttery/nutty quality kicks in making the flavor phase deliciously fat and textured. The aftertaste is buttery, malty, and lusciously sweet. Rivals the great Bushmills 16 Year Old (★★★★★) in terms of stature and runs rings around the 10 Year Old.

2002 Rating: ★★★★★/Highest Recommendation

Bushmills 16 Year Old Irish Single Malt Whiskey (Ireland); 40% abv, $60.

Topaz/medium amber color; flawless clarity. Aroma begins with heavily toasted notes of toasted wheat bread, oatmeal, and dried red fruits, in particular, black raisins; later sniffs pick up utterly delightful and comely scents of trail mix, roasted chestnut, bacon fat, sweet butter, sweet oak, ruby port, and prunes; an incredible textbook bouquet of the top rank. Entry is peppery, moderately sweet, and smoky; the midpalate features succulent tastes of chocolate covered cherry, honey, smoked nuts, and strawberry dipped in dark chocolate. Finishes elegantly and clean, with deft traces of smoke and cocoa. Along with Midleton Very Rare, the finest whiskey that Ireland has to offer.

2007 Rating: ★★★★★/Highest Recommendation

Bushmills 21 Year Old Madeira Wood Finish Single Irish Malt Whiskey (Ireland); 40% abv, $100.

The color is yellow gold/amber; excellent purity. The opening nosing passes detect soft, mellow, malty sweet aromas that are accented by subtle notes of oak resin and orange rind; further contact with air encourages supple, winey sweet notes to mingle and integrate with the underpinning malt and the wood scents; an understated bouquet that's moderately complex; this whiskey's majesty is experienced in the mouth more than the nose. The palate entry is sweetly malty, lightly toasty, and shows plenty of grip on the tongue; by the midpalate the madeira wood finish is what takes center stage as the flavor profile turns winey, mildly oily, supple, and elegant. The finish is long, malty, slightly fruity, biscuity, and even a touch smoky/caramelly at the very end. A superb Irish single malt.

2002 Rating: ★★★★/Highly Recommended

Clontarf Black Label Irish Whiskey (Ireland); 40% abv, $20.

Matured in bourbon barrels; standard issue but attractive golden amber/autumnal hue; excellent purity. The opening nosing pass discovers a fresh, toasty, intensely grainy bouquet that's quite evolved; the second and third inhalations add pleasing scents of brown butter and light butterscotch; in the fourth and last sniffing, after over nine minutes of aeration, the aroma remains sturdy, potent, and firm as the toastiness comes to the forefront ahead of the pepper, light toffee, and butterscotchy grain; a solid, serviceable, and moderately alluring bouquet. It's in the mouth where this whiskey goes suddenly flat, flabby, and dull; the palate entry is dry and only mildly grainy, but the midpalate phase is where most of the diminishment is noted as the zesty pepper, toast, and butterscotch qualities admired in the bouquet simply drop off the table. The aftertaste scrambles to make a recovery and in fact does score some redemption points. Weirdly up-and-down but the hole in the taste really detracts from the entire experience.

2001 Rating: ★★/Not Recommended

Clontarf Reserve Irish Blended Whiskey (Ireland); 40% abv, $25.

Pale gold/green color; superb clarity. The opening bouquet is delicate, fruity, and gently grainy; the additional seven minutes of air contact encourage earthy stirrings of green pepper, uncooked asparagus, light maple, decaying fall leaves, and confectioner's sugar; an ethereal bouquet admittedly, but one that has staying power and deceptively nuanced strength. The palate entry is sweet, mildly grainy, and peppery; at midpalate the flavor profile features lemongrass and grain. Concludes sweet, with barely perceptible toffee end notes. I sit squarely on the two star/three star fence with this one. I cautiously liked it overall, but there is a hollowness about it that is evident, in particular, at the midpalate and in the finish when it evaporates into nothingness. I sensed genuine potential here in the early stages, but then felt a sense of disappointment in the final half of the evaluation.

2005 Rating: ★★/Not Recommended

Clontarf Single Malt Irish Whiskey (Ireland); 40% abv, $30.

Bright golden/yellow/straw color; flawless purity. The first few minutes of sniffing pick up delectable scents of pork sausage, malted milk, and grass; aeration time of another six minutes bring up sour, lemony, yeasty/doughy notes that are balanced by the sweet grain. The palate entry is firm, nicely structured, silky in texture, moderately sweet; at midpalate there's a pleasing oiliness in the texture that underpins the sweet, grainy, lightly wooded taste profile. Ends up malty, breakfast cereal grainy, lightly honeyed, and zesty.

2005 Rating: ★★★/Recommended

Connemara Pure Pot Still Cooley Distillery Peated Irish Whiskey (Ireland); 60% abv, $60.

The bright yellow/straw color reminds me of a French sauvignon blanc; excellent purity. The initial nosings are immediately confronted with prickly, medicinal, but highly aromatic notes of brine, green olive, and vinegar; further aeration allows the bouquet to settle down and soften into a mildly sweet, moderately smoky/briny perfume that's a touch salty but ultimately composed, focused, yet plentiful. The palate entry is not as jolting (considering the lofty abv) as I had anticipated and is even somewhat beguiling and understated; the

midpalate is compact, lightly salty, moderately smoky and tobacco-like, and even a tad sweet; the texture is a winner as the alcohol supports lots of viscosity and natural oils. The aftertaste is long, lush, more sweet than briny or smoky, and very pleasant.
2003 Rating: ★★★/Highly Recommended

Finian's Five Provinces Blended Irish Whiskey (Ireland); 40% abv, $30/liter.

Superbly clear and pretty harvest gold/marigold color. In the first sniffings I detect dry grain, dry breakfast cereal notes that are pointed and nicely astringent; swirling and further aeration add subtle scents of black pepper and soy sauce. The palate entry is stone dry, intensely grainy, and focused; at the midpalate juncture the svelte taste profile offers lean elements of minerals, barley, snack crackers, and a delicate touch of honey. Finishes clean, dry, and without an ounce of oil or fat on it.
2007 Rating: ★★★/Recommended

Jameson 12 Year Old Blended Irish Whiskey (Ireland); 40% abv, $35.

Amber/honey color; flawless clarity. Owns a similar opening aroma to its no-age-statement sibling, in that it's smoked, oily/waxy, nutty, and intensely grainy; aeration adds a buttery succulence and a fruity ripeness that wasn't in the opening whiffs. Entry is toffee-like, grainy sweet, and honeyed; the midpalate stage is all butter, cream, smoked trout, roasted nuts, bacon fat, bacon rind, and spice. Concludes in a potent, grainy, and honeyed manner that's wonderfully fulfilling. A terrific whiskey from A to Z.
2007 Rating: ★★★★/Highly Recommended

Jameson 18 Year Old Master Selection Irish Whiskey No. 03895 (Ireland); 40% abv, $65.

The pretty, medium amber color is spoiled by twisters of sediment stirred up by the action of pouring. The uncomplicated opening aromas are of cotton fabric and wet hay; time in the glass doesn't deepen the fragrance, adding only very delicate, little cat's feet notes of damp grain, nectarine, and spearmint; hardly what I expected bouquet-wise for a whiskey that spent close to two decades in cask. The palate entry is properly sweet and deliciously grainy; it's at the midpalate, though, where the flavor profile does its best work as taut, more suitable tastes of oak resin, malted grains, pears, light honey, and toasted honey wheat bread make a clear, definitive statement, befitting a whiskey that costs more than $60. The aftertaste is predictably mild, softly sweet, and more grainy than woody. Had the appearance and the bouquet showed me more personality and appeal then I'd have gladly dealt out a fourth star; but as it is, uh-uh
2003 Rating: ★★★/Recommended

Jameson Blended Irish Whiskey (Ireland); 40% abv, $22.

Pale gold/flax color; superb purity. The charred paper smells of toasted walnuts and roasted chestnuts excite the olfactory sense; following another seven minutes of air contact, the aroma adds notes of paraffin, cardboard, parchment, dry grain, and herbs to the nuttiness. Entry is grainy sweet and moderately oily; the midpalate stage is loaded with grainy/breakfast cereal flavors and, at times, even comes off oatmeal-like. Ends well on an oily, satiny note. A solidly made, attractively priced Irish blend that keeps winning over more and more converts each year.
2007 Rating: ★★★/Recommended

Kilbeggan Blended Irish Whiskey (Ireland); 40% abv, $20.

Pale hue is the silvery/green color of oyster shell/fino sherry; excellent clarity. Smells faintly of a flower garden deep into the growing season, meaning muted, earthy, and vegetal; further time in the glass allows for deeper aromas, especially grain, malt, flax, and oak to emerge. Entry is nimble in its supreme lightness and gently sweet; the midpalate stage displays a bit more profundity in the grain depth and flavor length. Ends up delectably sweet, easy, smooth, and better than average. Though hardly complex and to some perhaps frightfully rudimentary, it deserves a recommendation for its lovely, no-brainer drinkability.

2007 Rating: ★★★/Recommended

Knappogue Castle 1951 36 Year Old Irish Whiskey/Bottled in 1987 (Ireland); 40% abv, $600.

This whiskey was aged in sherry casks for 36 years. The rich honey/medium amber color is eye-catching and pure. The sherry influence in the bouquet is evident immediately as the opening sniffs don't have to work too hard to discover succulent, vibrant, dried fruit aromas that have a honeyed edge; seven more minutes allow the bouquet to add seductive scents of oaky vanillin, marzipan, candied almond, and butter cream chocolates; an altogether enticing and mature bouquet. The palate entry shows an edgy, sharp, and astringent personality that I favorably respond to; this is not a plump, warm 'n fuzzy sherry-a-thon in the taste stage, thank the Life Force; by the midpalate phase the aggressive, crisp spirit keeps the taste buds fully engaged as the flavor profile shifts a bit to the moderately candied side of the ledger. Finishes refreshing, agile, and immaculately clean. Kudos to importer Mark Andrews for not providing yet another over-oaked, over-sherried, belching old fart of a whiskey, but rather a kind of nimble, lean, and hungry whiskey that's got lots of living to do.

2004 Rating: ★★★★/Highly Recommended

Knappogue Castle 1993 Single Malt Irish Whiskey (Ireland); 40% abv, $35.

Owns the pale yellow complexion of a sauvignon blanc. Enticing aromas of pine needles, sweet barley, and distant cinnamon set the stage in the initial nosing pass; in the second and third inhalations, following three and six minutes of aeration respectively, the pine needles bow out, leaving the spotlight for the barley and muted spice; in the final sniffing the spirit comes alive, contributing direction to this wandering bouquet. More substantial in the mouth than in the nose, the palate entry is moderately sweet and toffee-like; then at midpalate the sweet, grainy flavors get propelled forward by the spirit foundation. This fine whiskey finishes sublimely sweet, more like honey than candy, and with a considerable amount of pizzazz; worthy addition to the series.

2001 Rating: ★★★/ Recommended

Knappogue Castle 1994 Single Malt Irish Whiskey (Ireland); 40% abv, $34.

The pale yellow color is flawless and muscadet-like. The first aromatic impressions are faint, weedy, grass-like and apple-like; six more minutes do little to counter or deepen the first whiffs that feature green vegetation and apples; hello, anybody home?; The green palate entry after the uninteresting bouquet highlights grain and gum; at midpalate the core seems hollow as mildly stirring tastes of malt, chocolate covered strawberry and apples swim on the surface. Ends off-dry and timid; drinkable, but not in the league of KC 1991 (★★★

in 1999) and KC 1993 (★★★ in 2001) and miles away from the outstanding KC 1992 (★★★★ in 1999).

2004 Rating: ★★/Not Recommended

Knappogue Castle 1995 Single Malt Irish Whiskey (Ireland); 40% abv, $34.
Pale flax/ecru/champagne-like in color; impeccable clarity. First whiffs encounter delicate but unmistakable aromas of barley malt, asparagus, hollandaise, egg whites, and dry breakfast cereal; aeration adds spicy/tangy notes of white peppercorn, salt, phenols, new kid leather gloves, and mild esters. Entry is soft, citrusy-orangy, moderately baked and toasty; the taste profile at midpalate graduates in sweetness as an almond paste/nougat taste enters the fray and nicely offsets the dry maltiness and vegetal flavors. Shows solid presence and a hint of heathery floral character in the finish. After a stumble with the 1994 edition, Knappogue Castle is back on track.

2007 Rating: ★★★/Recommended

Michael Collins Blended Irish Whiskey (Ireland); 40% abv, $25.
Orangy/bronze/pale amber color; excellent purity. Initial inhalations pick up pleasantly grassy, waxy and vegetal aromas (waxed beans?); with aeration the aroma turns more expressive and focused on the grain component as the scent becomes nearly creamy but still green vegetable-like; different and interesting. Palate entry is tobacco-like, a touch smoky, and biscuity sweet; the flavor profile turns intensely grainy and almost sweet corn-like at midpalate. Finishes composed, grainy/doughy/yeasty, and slightly honeyed.

2007 Rating: ★★★/Recommended

Midleton 1998 Bottle No. 010917 Very Rare Blended Whiskey (Ireland); 40% abv, $100.
The honey/amber/harvest gold color is pure and highly translucent. The luscious aroma is apple-like and bountiful right from the pour; the second pass reveals a decadent maltiness that's multilayered and totally engaging; by the third sniffing, after over six minutes of aeration, the bouquet expands into an obvious two-track whiskey experience that's sweet/malty/toasty on the surface and rich/fruity/ripe underneath; the fourth and last whiff adds refined fragrances of honey, marzipan, and pine needle; an altogether sumptuous aroma that's simply one of the two or three best from Ireland. The palate entry shows a brief, fleeting glimpse of orange zest, then turns quickly into sweet malt and toffee at the midpalate stage; what's so intriguing about this palate phase is that while the whiskey is agile, it's also profoundly concentrated and complex. The finish is long, sweet, malty, and a touch spicy. Compares favorably with the glorious 1995; continues on as one of my all-time faves in the whiskey category.

2000 Rating: ★★★★★/Highest Recommendation

Midleton 26 Year Old Bottle No. 614/1000 Pure Pot Still Irish Whiskey with Port Pipe Finish (Ireland); 40% abv, $600.
The intriguingly atypical color is more tawny and coppery than amber and bronze; the appearance almost reminds me more of plum brandy than grain-based whiskey; some widely dispersed dark sediment is spotted. The opening nosing pass trail blazes new whiskey aroma territory for me as assertive scents of black tea leaves, caramelized onion, and green

peppercorns astound and perplex my olfactory sense; the middle stage sniffings, following several minutes of air contact, add seductive notes of baked pear, honey mustard, toasted oak (the bourbon barrels?), and soy sauce; the fourth and final whiff, after allowing this thoroughbred to breathe for ten full minutes, highlights the salty soy, spice (nutmeg), and sherry-port wood; a genuinely memorable bouquet that's nothing short of dazzling, unique, and daring. The palate entry is sweeter than the aroma, silky, and slightly peppery; it's at the midpalate point that the winy port wood influence is most evident. The finish is long, medium bodied, spicy, off dry-to-sweet, and immensely satisfying. Is it worth the $600 price tag in view of the fact that the regular vintage bottlings of Midleton Very Rare cost $100? I believe that it is when the rarity, extended maturity, and port pipe factors are considered; worth every penny.

2001 Rating: ★★★★/Highest Recommendation

Midleton Very Rare 2006 Blended Irish Whiskey (Ireland); 40% abv, $130.

Jonquil yellow/gold/marigold color; near flawless purity. Opening whiffs pick up distant smoked trout notes as well as lead pencil, ink, and worn leather; another seven minutes of air contact stimulates comely fragrances of dried fruit, especially apricot and nectarine, pastry, beeswax, toasted Brazil nut, and parchment. Entry is sublimely satiny, potent yet grainy sweet, and honeyed; the midpalate stage couldn't be any more sensual or perfect as the flavor profile runs the gamut of sweet grain to paraffin to salted butter to dry breakfast cereal to toffee to honey and even a trace of sherry. Finishes so elegant, so sophisticated, so, well, everything that I cannot put it down. One of the ten greatest spirits in the world.

2007 Rating: ★★★★/Highest Recommendation

Redbreast 12 Year Old Pure Pot Still Irish Whiskey (Ireland); 40% abv, $40.

Medium amber hue; some sediment spotted. The initial couple of sniffings within three minutes of the pour reveal dry to off-dry scents of butterscotch, maple, and oak; additional time in the glass allows for more and deeper aromas to emerge, most prominent are peanut butter, road tar, beans (as in, legumes), and dry breakfast cereal; a complete, complex bouquet that keeps unfolding with aeration. The palate entry tastes are full-bodied and significantly sweeter and oilier than the aroma; the midpalate stage displays a beany, oily, buttered popcorn flavor profile that's really delicious and robust. The aftertaste is long, warming, and oily, with a trace of sweet oak. Something of a cult legend in Ireland; a dandy example of pure pot still whiskey.

2002 Rating: ★★★★/Highly Recommended

The Knot 100 Proof Whiskey (Ireland); 50% abv, $24.

Bright, welcoming maize/old gold/saffron color; impeccable clarity. The curiously engaging aroma after the pour reminds me of butterscotch, burning rope/hemp, hazelnut, and old cigarette ashes; following another seven minutes of exposure to air, the aroma takes on seductively medicinal notes of herbs (anise), spices (vanilla, nutmeg, cinnamon), vegetables (fennel), and honey; this bouquet is an aromatic banquet. Entry is intensely herbal, almost candied, and semisweet; the midpalate stage is medicinal, a touch smoky, leafy/herbal, and honey-like. Finishes with a notable honey taste and a parting flavor that's a little Drambuie-like. I like this weirdly satisfying flavored whiskey a lot.

2007 Rating: ★★★★/Highly Recommended

Tullamore Dew 12 Year Old Blended Irish Whiskey (Ireland); 40% abv, $32.

A blend of whiskeys that are from twelve to fifteen years old and aged in both old bourbon and old oloroso sherry casks. Lightish amber/honey hue; impeccable purity. The first two minutes of nosing exposes a mildly toasty, cereal sweet, and invitingly warm and cozy bouquet; added aeration time releases scents of citrus, melon/cantaloupe, light honey, and taffy candy; a welcoming, ripe and fruity bouquet that's easy and charming. The palate entry is tart, a tad astringent, and off-dry; by the midpalate stage flavors of caramel apple, moderately sweet sherry, candied fruit, and sweet grain (maize?) please the taste buds. It finishes a bit raw, spirity, and semisweet. Certainly recommendable, but it doesn't possess enough stuffing and finesse to nudge it into four star territory.

2002 Rating: ★★★/Recommended

Tullamore Dew Blended Irish Whiskey (Ireland); 40% abv, $25.

Pale gold/flax color; superior clarity. Lovely scents of sweet grains, sugared breakfast cereal, and pine make for pleasing early sniffing; the nose fades a tad following aeration, but displays enough quality to gain a star. Entry is nimble, gently sweet, almost piney and honeyed; the midpalate stage carries on with style and smoothness as the taste profile remains steadfast and mildly sweet. Finishes with a honey-like thrust that's exhilarating and delightful.

2007 Rating: ★★★/Recommended

Tyrconnell Single Malt Irish Whiskey (Ireland); 40% abv, $30.

Deep straw/tarnished gold color; flawless purity. Toasty notes of roasted nuts and nougat greet the pleased olfactory sense; following another seven minutes of air contact, the aroma evolves into a bouquet that offers light toffee, candy bar, mild oak, and brown sugar notes. Entry is satiny smooth, honeyed, and near-lush in texture; the midpalate point brings in spicy notes, in particular, black pepper and clove. The malt component takes charge in the finish, bringing a keen graininess to the final moment of enjoyment.

2007 Rating: ★★★★/Highly Recommended

Distillery Issue Single Malt Scotch Whisky—Scotland

Whisky has been part of the social fabric of Scotland since, at the minimum, the 15th century. Since the invention of the continuous still in the 1820s-1830s, there have been two distinct varieties of raw whisky made in Scotland: single malt whisky, or whisky made in small individual batches only from malted barley at a single distillery using the traditional pot still method; and grain whisky, or whisky made in enormous volumes from corn or wheat via the continuous distillation process in tall, metal column stills. Typically, single malt whiskies display deeper character and individual tastes than grain whiskies. These two fundamental whisky types create the four classifications of Scotch:

- *Single Malt Whisky.* This is the 100% malted barley whisky of one distillery distilled in a pot still, labeled under the originating distillery name. Some single malt whiskies are labeled under the names of independent merchants who purchase barrels from single malt distilleries than bottle them under their own name.
- *Blended Malt Whisky* (a.k.a., vatted malt, pure malt). A 100% malted barley whisky that is produced from the malt whiskies of two or more malt distilleries and labeled under a brand name.
- *Blended Whisky.* A whisky that is comprised of a combination of any number of single malt and grain whiskies and labeled under a brand name rather than a distillery name.
- *Single Grain Whisky.* A 100% corn or wheat whisky distilled in column stills and used mostly for blending, but sometimes bottled on its own.

Also, when a Scotch whisky label declares an age, like "15 Years Old", that indicates that the youngest whisky used in the creation of that whisky was aged for no less than 15 years. There may be older whiskies in the final product. The raw spirits are placed in oak barrels for maturation and mellowing for a legal minimum of three years.

Scotch thoughts to help you understand this complex category:

1. I used to place special emphasis on single malt regions. Over the years, however, I've altered my opinion as to the true relevance of the "regions concept" and I now think that it's overblown. Each distillery stands on its own merits, not on the merits of whether it hails from Speyside, Lowlands or Islay. I no longer espouse regional styles. Here's a question for single malt snobs. Can you honestly claim that there's an Islay "style" when you taste Bruichladdich against Ardbeg? Or, Caol Ila against Lagavulin? Those with working gray matter will answer, "No". (One hopes.)

2. Also, I've segregated the single malts into two distinct parts: **Distillery Issue**, which means that these single malt whiskies were produced, labeled, and issued exclusively by the distillery of origin and **Merchant Issue**, which indicates that a merchant with no affiliation

to the originating distillery has bought an allotment of single malt either from a broker or direct from a distillery and has bottled the whisky under their own label, which typically cites the distillery. I mention this because there is frequently a difference in quality and character between Distillery Issue and Merchant Issue whiskies, sometimes better, other times worse.

3. **SMSW** = single malt Scotch whisky.

4. Scotland's distilling industry is the finest in the world at present, so enjoy the delights out of them. I do.

Aberlour 12 Year Old Sherry Cask Matured Speyside SMSW (Scotland); 40% abv, $34/liter.

The color is bronze/deep honey/topaz; there's some sediment spotted under the evaluation lamp. The big-hearted, assertive opening aroma is sweet, oloroso sherry-like, and intensely caramelly; by the second whiff, the sherry impact dominates in the form of dark caramel/marzipan; the penultimate sniffing, after seven minutes in the glass, adds hard cheese and even a deft touch of cognac-like rancio; the fourth and final inhalation sees minor diminishment in potency, but the sweet sherry remains in charge; a chunky, headstrong malt bouquet. The palate entry is sap-like and honeyed; the midpalate is thick, concentrated, honeyed, and candied. The aftertaste is long, toasty sweet, and lip smacking. A completely different if bawdy spin of the bottle from the polite 1990; please return your tray table and raise your seat to the upright position—TAKE OFF!!

2001 Rating: ★★★★/Highly Recommended

Aberlour 15 Year Old Double Cask Matured Speyside SMSW (Scotland); 40% abv, $47/liter.

Matured in both bourbon and sherry casks for fourteen years, then blended and aged a further year in oloroso sherry butts. Medium amber hue; near perfect clarity. The intriguing opening aroma hints of cocoa butter, guava, and poppy seed; the second and third sniffings add wonderfully perfumy and inviting scents of pineapple, lemon drop, and moderately sweet grain to the aromatic mix while the final whiff, following a full nine minutes, features the citrusy tang on the surface but underneath lies the solid, almost flowery bourbon barrel foundation. As terrific as it is in the nose, the taste is even better and more evolved; the palate entry arrives in fourth gear as rich tastes of candied apple, walnuts, and honey delight the taste buds; at midpalate the oloroso sherry becomes a primary flavor along with banana, sweet oak, vanilla, and toast. The finish is long, luxurious and honeyed. Rivals the great 21 Year Old in my view.

2001 Rating: ★★★★★/Highest Recommendation

Aberlour 1990 Vintage Speyside SMSW (Scotland); 40% abv, $30/liter.

Absolutely pure, golden honey/amber hue. In the first nosing pass lovely aromas of honeydew melon and toasted bread delight the olfactory sense; the second and third whiffs add firm, slightly oily notes of honey and candied almond; following nine minutes of aeration, the aroma becomes a bona fide bouquet in the fourth sniffing as gentlemanly, off-dry scents of yellow fruit (banana especially), grain, and light toffee combine to create a grand aromatic finale. The palate entry is succulent and fruity sweet; at the midpalate juncture the toastiness of the oak barrel becomes the major flavor player. The finish is medium long, woody/resiny/sweet and satisfying. A very, very good younger expression.

2001 Rating: ★★★★/Highly Recommended

Aberlour a'bunadh Speyside SMSW (Scotland); 59.6% abv, $60.

Pronounced a-BOON-arh; aged in oloroso sherry casks and not run through the chill-filtering process that most single malts are routinely subjected to. The medium amber color is slightly flat under the evaluation lamp; good purity. The nose is immediately toasty and malty in the first sniffing; hints of hard cheese lurk in the background of the second nosing pass; by the third whiff, following almost seven minutes of exposure to air, the piquant spirit comes alive, but doesn't overshadow the toasty malt; the fourth and final pass finally sees some of the sherry emerge, though hardly any at all, leaving the spirit and roasted malt all to themselves; a solid bouquet, but not as stirring as two other relatively recent Aberlour releases, to wit, the fabulous 15 and 18 Year Olds, released in 1997 (both ★★★★). The palate entry is sassy, oily, and spirity in equal parts; the midpalate stage is very oily and sleek and rife with bittersweet flavors of cocoa, soot, and fruit pit; much to its credit, the tangy spirit is quiet at midpalate but explodes in the aftertaste, making for a combustible but exceedingly pleasing finish. While the aroma seems surprisingly tame, the mouth experience offers whisky lovers a fast ride well worth taking.

2000 Rating: ★★★★/Highly Recommended

Ardbeg "Lord of the Isles" 25 Year Old Islay SMSW (Scotland); 46% abv, £100.

Only available in the United Kingdom. The attractive golden wheat/burnished yellow color shows impeccable purity. The opening bursts of aroma offer tidal waves of almond butter, cigar smoke, and medicine cabinet; seven more minutes resting in the glass allows for the emergence of succulent scents of chocolate orange, fresh peat, black pekoe tea leaves, bonfire, and kippers; a mammoth bouquet that stacks up with the best ever from Ardbeg, Lagavulin, and Laphroaig. The palate entry is serenely fudgy sweet and poised; at midpalate the flavor profile turns to smoky cocoa, bittersweet nougat, pipe tobacco, textbook peat-reek, and straight black tea. Concludes sweetly, fruity, mildly peaty, and elegant. Right up there with the magical, mystical Ardbeg Uigeadail (★★★★★).

2004 Rating: ★★★★★/Highest Recommendation

Ardbeg 1974 Provenance Very Old Islay SMSW (Scotland); 54% abv, $600.

Glorious, brilliant, gem-like topaz/light honey color; superb purity. The initial two nosing passes following the pour expose dynamic and vibrant aromas of peat, cigarette smoke, heather, citrus rind, and charcoal (from bourbon casks?); an extra few minutes of air contact stimulate "seasoned" aromas of black pepper, allspice, dill, and seaweed; a tremendously sophisticated though robust bouquet. The palate entry shows a flash of spirity heat that then abates, allowing peaty, smoky, yet sweet tastes to develop on the tongue; at midpalate there's a whole array of flavors layering on top of each other including oaky vanillin, light toffee, nougat, and peaty smoke. The finish is long, oily, intensely smoky, and luscious. A serious malt.

2002 Rating: ★★★★/Highly Recommended

Ardbeg 1977 Islay SMSW (Scotland); 46% abv, $100.

Amber/harvest gold color; excellent purity. The aroma kicks off the nosing part of the evaluation in true Ardbeg fashion, in other words with lots of charcoal, smoke, seaweed, peat reek, and iodine-like phenols; another seven minutes in the glass allows for a deeper layer of the bouquet to emerge, namely scents of ripe green pepper, black pepper, Brazil nuts, and tobacco leaf; a broad-shouldered, explosive, yet strangely sublime bouquet. The palate entry is positively polite as lightly smoked tastes of seaweed and oatmeal greet the taste buds; the midpalate point is far more aggressive in its briny, peaty, but semisweet smokiness. The aftertaste is almost honeyed and lip-smacking sweet. A memorable Islay malt ride that owns a foundational thread of steadiness and order that keeps the experience from getting out-of-hand.

2002 Rating: ★★★/Recommended

Ardbeg Airigh Nam Beist 1990 Non-Chill Filtered Islay SMSW (Scotland); 46% abv, $110.

From distillate that was placed in used bourbon oak barrels in 1990. The yellow/hay color is pale and bright; excellent clarity. In the first inhalations, the aroma is stunningly delicate and grainy sweet; additional time in the glass brings out more of the peat fire, cigar tobacco, seaweed, and ocean breeze; the bouquet is a complete Islay profile package. The palate entry is sap-like in its gentle sweetness and the alcohol nips gently at the sides of the tongue; by the midpalate stage my 10,000 taste buds are enchanted to the point of being mesmerized as lush, but pointed tastes of sea salt, gentle pipe smoke, peat, and pineapple converge. Finishes elegantly, yet with an underpinning smoky/saltiness that has Islay written all over it. Wonderful.

2007 Rating: ★★★★★/Highest Recommendation

Ardbeg 10 Year Old Islay SMSW (Scotland); 46% abv, $35.

Put up your tray tables and fasten your seatbelts. The appearance is a vivid straw yellow; complete purity. The opening nosing gives a jolt of what makes Ardbeg infamous and a cult malt, a mesmerizing peatiness that's borderline medicine chest and fresh cigar ashes; the middle stage sniffings are relatively tame by comparison as the intense peatiness settles down into an ashy/sooty but mellow and composed midstage bouquet; further aeration allows a dry mossy/vegetal aroma to mingle with the ash. The palate entry is dry and concentrated; then the midpalate phase turns surprisingly sweet, oily, and only moderately peaty/smoky. The finish is long, embers warm, ashy, and only a bit unruly. Though some ardent mavens might think this Ardbeg has been neutered in production, I believe that it's the most drinkable Ardbeg offering I've evaluated so far, beating even the terrific 17 Year Old and the 1974 (both ★★★); bravo.

2001 Rating: ★★★★/Highly Recommended

Ardbeg Uigeadail Islay SMSW (Scotland); 54.2% abv, $75.

Medium amber/umber color; superb purity. The concentrated, smoky/peaty early-on aroma is thrillingly compelling, rich without being unctuous and amazingly nutty; more time and a splash of spring water unleash all sorts of multiple layers of fragrance, from oloroso sherry to almonds sautéed in butter to vanilla fudge to toffee pudding to malted milk; a supremely decadent, cutting-edge and luscious Islay aroma. The palate entry is LARGE, sweetly smoky, and as succulent as dried fruit, especially peaches and pears; the midpalate stage displays plenty of oak presence, along with vanilla wafer, pears in brandy, road tar, cigar smoke, and iodine. Finishes bittersweet, chewy, and smoky. A tour de force of the first Islay rank and a classic in the making.

2004 Rating: ★★★★★/Highest Recommendation

Arran 10 Year Old Isle of Arran SMSW (Scotland); 46% abv, $49.

Eye-catching color of wheat field/amber; superb purity. The opening whiffs detect deep, dry, and kernel-like scents of malt/flax; the bouquet flattens out with aeration, going horizontal and therefore uninteresting; this aroma frankly didn't seem to have a lot going for it in the initial sniffs. The palate entry is concentrated, highly spirited, verrrry oaky, and slightly awkward due to a lack of grain or fruit; the midpalate stage fares better as the spirit settles down, allowing the sweet, nougat-like taste to emerge and dominate. Concludes a tad too warm and smoldering, and resiny. A drinkable misfire that displayed its problems in the nose and wasn't able to overcome them in the three tasting phases. Some good traits and not a total bust, but one to skip nonetheless.

2006 Rating: ★★/Not Recommended

Arran Calvados Finish Isle of Arran SMSW (Scotland); 62.1% abv, £45.

Only available in the United Kingdom. The bright golden/marigold color is blemish-free. The opening nose is grain-driven and moderately sap-like and sweet; aeration doesn't seem to stir much in the way of calvados/apple presence as the malted grain element dominates the entire aroma stage; firm, a bit hot, and malty at palate entry; after being reduced with mineral water; the midpalate phase shows a honeyed sweetness that's pleasing. Ends sweet, assertive, and marshmallow-like. I simply couldn't detect the calvados influence, either with or without the addition of water.

2004 Rating: ★★★/Recommended

Arran Cream Sherry Cask Finish Gonzalez Byass Isle of Arran SMSW (Scotland); 57.4% abv, $79.

Harvest gold/topaz color; ideal clarity. In the first inhalations following the pour, the zesty perfume of sherry wood is unmistakable and more dry and nutty than fruity or sweet; further exposure to air brings out a ripe, red fruitiness and a bread dough quality that skip along on top of the fully evident spirit. The palate entry is like baked pineapple, toasted oats, and meat-like (roast pork loin?); the midpalate stage is marked by a pleasing buttery/creamy taste that's more nut paste than fruit-like. Finishes semisweet, a little unsure of itself structure-wise, but firm, prickly, caramel-like, and oaky.

2006 Rating: ★★★/Recommended

Arran Isle of Arran SMSW (Scotland); 46% abv, £40

Only available in the United Kingdom. The bright, harvest-time golden hue is blemish-free and very alluring. The initial whiffs detect a mellow honey/baked bread bouquet; after six more minutes of air contact, the bouquet turns decidedly leathery, pork rind-like, sausage-like, and burnt. The roasted/burnt/toasty quality revealed in the late stages of the nosing are all present and accounted for in the satisfying palate entry; by midpalate the taste

profile turns bittersweet, honeyed, waxy, lead pencil-like, and muesli-like. Concludes lip-smackingly bittersweet, honeyed, spirited, yet composed.
2004 Rating: ★★★/Recommended

Arran Isle of Arran SMSW (Scotland); 43% abv, $49.
Very pale flax/yellow/white wine appearance; fine clarity. The aroma at opening is keenly fruity and malty; in the second pass the bouquet offers tame scents of sweet dry cereal and flowers, backed up by a mild scent of citrus; after six minutes of air contact, the grain begins to overtake the fruit element in the next to final nosing pass; following almost ten minutes of aeration, what's emitted is a gently sweet, slightly restrained perfume of dry cereal grain; this is a fey malt bouquet that's pleasing and moderately alluring, but hardly profound or compelling. In the mouth, the palate entry is simple, sweet and grainy; the midpalate phase echoes the entry, adding nothing new in terms of expansion or deepening. The finish is swift, slightly harsh, grainy, and forgettable. A simple, but wholly decent beginner malt, nothing more.
2000 Rating: ★★/Not Recommended

Arran Lepanto PX Brandy Cask Finish Isle of Arran SMSW (Scotland); 58.9% abv, $79.
Pale yellow/white wine appearance; flawless purity. My olfactory sense is treated to a prickly, piquant opening fragrance that's intensely spirity and a dash tropical fruit-like (pineapple, banana, guava, especially); following additional time in the copita, the aroma profile adds succulent scents of light English toffee, sautéed almonds, quince, melon, and fruitcake. The palate entry is sweet, piny, and spirity; the midpalate stage is notable for its feisty spirit, intense oakiness/resininess, and backdoor sweetness. Intriguing marriage of malt whisky matured in brandy cask. I like the concept.
2006 Rating: ★★★/Recommended

Arran Malt A. Hardy Napoleon Cognac Cask Finish Single Cask Island SMSW (Scotland); 57.8% abv, $80.
Straw yellow color; superb clarity. The beguiling initial aroma is delightfully fruity, with assertive smells of prunes, black raisins, and dates; further air contact brings out big buttery/oaky aromas that are fatty/oily and bacon-like; a wonderfully expressive bouquet. The palate entry is lean, intensely spirity, buttery, and focused; I add mineral water before proceeding with the midpalate evaluation because of the status of the spirit; at the midpalate point the taste profile, with necessary dilution, is creamy, caramel-like and nougaty, with background traces of honey and vanilla. Finishes rich, round, and semisweet.
2007 Rating: ★★★★/Highly Recommended

Arran Malt Single Cask SMSW (Scotland); 58.2% abv, $70.
The pretty amber color is pure and clean. The opening sniffs encounter a candy sweet, ripe red fruit (raspberry? strawberry?) bouquet that's stunningly ambrosial; following another seven minutes of exposure to air, the bouquet stays the fruity/estery course as a subtle, underpinning note of confectioner's sugar comes alive; unlike any single malt bouquet I've encountered. The palate entry flashes a bit of spirity fire but underlying that is a delicious honey-like, almost butter cream taste; the midpalate shines for its unabashed sherry and

cocoa-like sweetness. The aftertaste is sweet, malty and spirity; young (5 years old) and restless. This spunky malt is definitely worth a look, especially for admirers of sweeter malts.

2003 Rating: ★★★/Recommended

Arran Malt Port Cask Finished Single Cask Isle of Arran SMSW (Scotland); 58.5% abv, $79.

Aged first in old sherry casks, then "finished" in port pipes. The orange/pink/peach-like color is very attractive and atypical; clarity level is perfect. The opening whiffs pick up delectable scents of grapes, oranges, cotton, tar, and wood shavings; additional aeration time allows the bouquet enough space to add fragrances of holiday spices, white raisins, quince, fruitcake, chocolate covered cherries, robust spirit, and candied almond; I mean, there is no stopping this aroma. Add mineral water before tasting. The palate entry is wonderfully vivid in its fruitiness and ripeness; the midpalate stage highlights honey, sherry, baked red apple, Bosc pear, ruby port, and grape preserves flavors. Finishes up warm due to the aggressive spirit, but sweet, ripe, and jammy. To date, the quintessential Arran and a landmark achievement for this still young distillery.

2006 Rating: ★★★★★/Highest Recommendation

Arran Non-Chill Filtered Malt Whisky Isle of Arran SMSW (Scotland); 46% abv, $49.

The attractive pale golden/straw color is flawless. The opening bouquet is jaunty, vivid, malty, and deeply grainy; another seven minutes in the copita allow for the vigorous aromas to settle down, becoming more refined and delicate in the bearing; I note dried aromas of Christmas spice, dates, white raisins, and shoe polish. The frisky taste at palate entry is spirity and fresh, if a bit disorderly; the midpalate holds a flavor profile that's sassy, zesty, woody/resiny, dry and astringent, and immature. Finishes as rambunctiously as it begins, with unbridled tastes of resin, grain husk, and raw heady spirit. No age statement on the label leads me to believe that this is a very young whisky, at most four years old; its ungainly, take-no-prisoners nature makes me think that it would be far better with another two years, at the minimum, in oak; loads of potential, but too juvenile and under-developed.

2004 Rating: ★★/Not Recommended

Arran Port Finish Isle of Arran SMSW (Scotland); 57.4% abv, £45.

Only available in the United Kingdom. The brilliant, brick red/blood orange color immediately captures the eye; perfect purity. The zesty, winey aroma in the first passes displays touches of mead and peanut oil; time in the glass encourages the heady spirit to come out in force, but it never overshadows the base material component, which is off-dry, wine-like, Christmas pudding-like, burnt matchstick-like, and resiny. The palate entry offers a smooth silkiness and a creaminess that are compelling; by midpalate a ruby port-like aroma enters the equation as further scents, such as orange rind, light toffee, and black pepper, are added. Finishes semisweet, if a little too searing and feral, so make certain that you add some mineral water. If it were my distilling decision, as with the sherry cask, I'd reduce the spirit down to 46% at the distillery and then bottle it.

2004 Rating: ★★★/Recommended

Arran Single Bourbon Cask Isle of Arran SMSW (Scotland); 58.4% abv, $79.

The medium amber/honey color is pretty and clean. The first sniffings pick up predictable aromas of vanilla, maple, and honey; following seven more minutes of air exposure, the bouquet turns bread-like and baked, with notes of resin, paraffin, cowhide, hemp, and egg noodle. The palate entry is sweet, maple- and sap-like; at midpalate the alcohol kicks in, warming the tongue and offering sweet flavors of honey, toffee, and marzipan. Concludes well, with warm bursts of alcohol and parting tastes of honey and toffee.

2004 Rating: ★★★/Recommended

Arran Single Sherry Cask Isle of Arran SMSW (Scotland); 57.3% abv, $79.

The color is deep amber/honey/tawny and flawlessly pure. The first nosing seems surprisingly green and vegetal, with a background trace of sea salt; further time in the copita stirs additional scents, including wet sand, green olives, and linseed oil; not the bouquet I expected. The palate entry is more in line with the cask maturing as lightly honeyed, caramel-like, and marshmallow tastes treat the taste buds well; by midpalate the sherry influence is in full bloom as succulent flavors of dark caramel, black tea leaves, nougat, treacle, and marzipan thrill the palate. Finishes sweet, plucky, and heady. I think that Arran would do itself a favor—and its customers—by reducing this feral malt to 46% at the distillery; the high rating reflects the personality of this malt after it's been reduced with mineral water.

2004 Rating: ★★★★/Highly Recommended

Auchentoshan 17 Year Old Bordeaux Wine Cask Finished Lowlands SMSW (Scotland); 51% abv, $120.

The bronze color is bright and flawlessly clean. My first nosing pass picks up woodsy scents of pine needle, sap, and moss; later inhalations, after seven minutes of aeration, reveal deeper aromas of black tea, sawdust, lead pencil, and coffee grounds; an amazingly complex, multilayered bouquet. The palate entry is sharply spirity at first, then the taste turns sweet and cocoa-like; at midpalate a remarkable caramel-like and honeyed sweetness take charge of the flavor profile. The finish is like fresh honey, butter cream, and cocoa butter. A thrilling Lowlands masterpiece that unfolds gradually, showing tremendous grace the whole route.

2005 Rating: ★★★★★/Highest Recommendation

Auchentoshan 18 Year Old Oloroso Sherry Matured Lowlands SMSW (Scotland); 55.8% abv, $1,000.

The light amber/gold dust color is pretty, but there's more sediment than I'd like to see. The first burst of gently sweet perfume is rife with toffee and caramel top notes that are supported by underpinning fragrances of doughy/bread-like spirit; the miracle of additional aeration stimulates bakery spices, especially nutmeg, vanilla, and cinnamon that completely complement the toffee/doughy/pastry aromas. The palate entry is tightly structured, focused on the delicate sherry sweetness, and sublime on the tongue (the elevated abv isn't an issue); the midpalate stage displays all the nuanced splendor of the Lowlands' foremost distillery as the taste profile includes spice, baked bread, sherry, caramel, and nougat. Yet another sterling expression from this hallmark distillery. Classic.

2006 Rating: ★★★★★/Highest Recommendation

Auchentoshan 1962 41 Year Old Lowlands SMSW (Scotland); 40.2% abv, $2,000.

Medium brown/topaz color; excellent clarity. The first couple of minutes of sniffing find soft, leathery notes of light toffee and oaky vanilla; seven minutes later much of the air is let out of this bouquet as it retreats into a lightly smoked/burnt grain aroma; a bouquet of diminishing returns. The palate entry is nicely baked and oven toasty; by midpalate there are traces of cocoa, nut paste and oatmeal. Ends up meekly, tired and, to me as a long time lover of Auchentoshan, sad. Doesn't hold a candle to two other great old Auchie's, the 1957 40 Year Old (★★★★★ in 1998) and the fantastic 31 Year Old (★★★★★ in 1997); this fatigued, spent malt should not have been released, in my opinion.

2004 Rating: ★★/Not Recommended

Auchentoshan 1966 36 Year Old/Cask No. 1008 Lowlands SMSW (Scotland); 49.4% abv, $119.

Available exclusively through Sam's Wine & Spirits in Chicago. The soft wheat harvest gold is clean and pure. The intensely grainy, soy-like opening aroma is unlike any other Auchentoshan perfume I've encountered; I find the strong evidence of soy sauce almost disconcerting; additional time in the glass serves to add oddball but intriguing notes of chicken bouillon, almond paste, fried eggs, and butterscotch; weird but wonderful. The palate entry is dry, lead pencil-like, astringent, and focused; at midpalate there's a whole range of new flavor layers including honey, nougat, candied nuts, black tea leaves, and minerals. The finish is long, minerally, and dry. Not my favorite Auchentoshan, but a lovable, quirky, atypical Lowlands.

2003 Rating: ★★★/Recommended

Auchentoshan 1966 37 Year Old/Cask No. 1007 Lowlands SMSW (Scotland); 48.1% abv, $150.

Available exclusively through Park Avenue Liquors in New York City. Light honey/amber hue; flawless clarity. The initial nosing passes detect a slight resemblance to this malt's sibling but there's more evidence of green vegetation, roasted nuts, and kelp than the Cask 1008; seven further minutes of air exposure allow for baked/cooked aromas to emerge, especially egg noodles, black pepper, and nut butter. The palate entry is desert dry, slate-like, minerally, yet appealing; at midpalate the taste highlights the oak through a sap-like, mildly resiny flavor that's astringent and clean, but neither malty nor memorable. The aftertaste is very vegetal and slate-like. I preferred the Cask No. 1008 to this slightly awkward and off-balance expression.

2003 Rating: ★★/Not Recommended

Auchentoshan 1973 32 Year Old Sherry Cask Finished Lowlands SMSW (Scotland); 55.5% abv, $740.

Displays the look of an old copper penny; impeccably pure. In the initial whiffs, there are fragrances of old saddle leather, pork rind, black pepper, and sausages; further time in the glass releases aromas of pine, blue cheese, candle wax, and a hint of rancio. The palate entry is meaty in texture, meaty in flavor profile, and intensely spirity; after adding a dash of room temperature mineral water I find that at midpalate the taste turns agreeably chocolatey, smooth, silky, and buttery. The aftertaste is cocoa-like, creamy, and succulent.

2005 Rating: ★★★★/Highest Recommendation

Auchroisk 28 Year Old The Diageo Rare Malts Selection Speyside SMSW (Scotland); 56.8% abv, £n/a.

Only available in the United Kingdom. Gorgeous, bright harvest gold hue; unblemished clarity. The first stage whiffs pick up lots of deep and oily dark toffee/butterscotch notes; seven more minutes of air contact expand the aromatic horizons to include marzipan, nougat, buttered walnuts, and oloroso sherry; the bouquet borders on displaying rancio. The palate entry is chewy, thick, and maple sweet; the midpalate stage highlights intense toasted/baked flavors of honey wheat bread, cocoa, black coffee, oloroso sherry, and bacon fat (rancio element). Ends up chunky and dense. Voluptuous, harmonious, and true to the historical profile of the malts from this distillery that are labeled as "The Singleton"; the abv never gets in the way and actually provides the ideal platform for the myriad aromas and flavors.

2004 Rating: ★★★★/Highest Recommendation

Balvenie 12 Year Old DoubleWood Speyside SMSW (Scotland); 43% abv, $50.

Amber/topaz/brown color; unblemished clarity. The first nosing exposes tightly wrapped and dry scents of walnuts, grass, and dark toffee; the leafy/grassy element continues in the later stages after aeration as aromas of black tea and tobacco come to the forefront. Entry is divinely grainy/malty and vanilla bean/extract bittersweet; the midpalate is seductively silky, creamy, sherry sweet, pruny, and black raisin-like. Ends on a dark chocolate note that's chewy, medium-sweet, and totally satisfying. Easily one of the top five 12 year old single malts that Scotland has to offer.

2007 Rating: ★★★/Highly Recommended

Balvenie 15 Year Old Single Barrel Speyside SMSW Cask 70; Bottled 2006 (Scotland); 47.8% abv, $68.

Bronze/burnished orange color; superb purity. Pungent, peppery, waxy, and fiber-like aromas greet the olfactory sense in the initial inhalations; aeration is this malt's best friend as deeper aromas emerge after seven minutes, especially, oak resin, beeswax, white raisins, and white pepper. Entry is intensely oaky and toffee-like, with distant touches of salt and butterscotch; the midpalate is salty, smoky, mildly peaty, and grainy dry. The elevated abv doesn't really enter the picture until the aftertaste, which is cleansing, crisp, mildly sweet and oaky, and a touch austere.

2007 Rating: ★★★/Recommended

Balvenie 17 Year Old Islay Cask Speyside SMSW (Scotland); 43% abv, $60.

A 17 year old Speyside malt that was "finished" for six months in oak casks that were formerly used to age malts from Islay. Attractive golden/harvest grain hue; ideal clarity. There's no doubting the briny/iodine Islay surface impact right from the first two nosing passes, but there's likewise total certainty about the gently sweet Speyside underpinning; aeration time of five to eight minutes sees the Islay reek blow off, leaving the sturdy, sweetly oaky, and malty Balvenie signature bouquet in charge of the proceedings. In the mouth the Islay peatiness and the Speyside creaminess collide at palate entry; at the midpalate point the medicinal Islay influence overshadows the Speyside elegance as the flavors turn sweet yet peaty. The finish is a confusing mishmash of conflicting flavors. A noble effort that, to my taste, simply didn't come to a reasonably pleasurable conclusion; while Speyside and Islay

malts are often married in the case of countless blends, this experiment fails because the components fight each other rather than complement each other; drinkable, even intriguing, but ultimately disappointing.
2001 Rating: ★★/Not Recommended

Balvenie New Wood 17 Year Old Limited Release Speyside SMSW (Scotland); 43% abv, $90.

The bronze/amber color is attractive, bright, and flawlessly pure. An aromatic yellow fruit (banana, pear, quince) perfume leaps from the glass in toasted/honeyed waves; additional air contact expands on the yellow fruit theme by adding subtle hints of citrus zest and tobacco leaf. The palate entry offers a succulent, woody sweet flavor that's medium-bodied and creamy; the midpalate stage showcases the elegance of the taste profile as the flavor turns buttery rich, intensely oaky, and moderately maple-like. Ends in a gently sweet, grainy, and appealingly fruity manner. This savory malt is a one-time-only treat. Buy and enjoy.
2006 Rating: ★★★/Highly Recommended

Balvenie 25 Year Old Cask 13143, Bottle No. 153 Single Barrel Speyside SMSW (Scotland); 46.9% abv, $99.

The attractive new copper penny/burnished orange hue impresses the eye; absolute purity. The start-up aroma after the pour is laced with sweet fragrances of paraffin, rose petals, old oak, and honey; time in the glass reinforces the early impressions, but it's the harmonious interplay between the honey, oak, and yellow fruit scents that make this nosing phase so exceptional; a clinic in what Speyside aromatics are all about when a zenith is reached. The flavor begins dry and tightly-wound at the palate entry; then at midpalate an explosion of oaky/honey flavors blankets the tongue, backed up by a zesty ripe fruit flavor that tops off the taste phase with flair. The aftertaste is toasty, oaky, concentrated, and seemingly infinite in its staying power. Rivals the now legendary 1966 bottling in terms of grandeur and presence; a classic.
2001 Rating: ★★★★★/Highest Recommendation

Balvenie Thirty 30 Year Old Speyside SMSW (Scotland); 47.3% abv, $499.

Warm honey/wheat field/amber hue; perfect clarity. The bouquet is reluctant at first to emerge, giving off mere hints of mead and almonds; seven more minutes in the glass release an intriguing menu of scents, from pencil eraser to coffee grounds to pork to old leather; even after ten minutes in the glass, it seems like the bouquet is just revving up. The palate entry is intensely resiny, smoldering warm, and waxy on the tongue; at midpalate taste explosions of honey, oloroso sherry, dark caramel, hard cheese, malted milk, and Christmas pudding treat the taste buds to an extraordinary library of flavors. Ends in a stately manner, warm and cozy in the throat, and deliciously sweet and honeyed. Without any doubt, the best Balvenie I've so far reviewed.
2004 Rating: ★★★★★/Highest Recommendation

Balvenie 1971 Single Cask, Barrel 8935 Bottle No. 29 of 219 total bottles Speyside SMSW (Scotland); 47.1% abv, $599.

The harvest gold/amber hue is lighter than I thought it would be and it's gorgeous; flawless clarity. The first passes encounter lovely fruit fragrances, including pear, tangerine, and nectarine; later sniffs detect more substantial foundational aromas of oak, soft cheese, heather honey, and new leather; a smashingly seductive, if understated and elegant bouquet of the first rank. The palate entry is compelling in its concentration on the vanilla-like oak and brown butter; the midpalate stage highlights the toffee/caramel/honeyed side of the malt and oak marriage, making for exquisite sipping. The aftertaste was as warm and friendly as smoldering embers in your fireplace and as spicy sweet as Christmas holiday cake. A classic that makes a strong case for Scotch distillers to release more single cask gems.

2005 Rating: ★★★★★/Highest Recommendation

Ben Nevis 10 Year Old Western Highlands SMSW (Scotland); 46% abv, $29.

Attractive, amber/honey hue; more than acceptable purity. The aroma is forward, mildly sweet and grainy with just a trace of cooked vegetable in the first pass; in the second and third nosings the sweet perfume expands to include delicate hints of beeswax and lightly charred oak barrel; by the fourth and last sniffing, after more than eight minutes of air contact, the aroma retreats, leaving behind a pleasant red berry, moderately peppery bouquet. The palate entry is marked by a keen dryness on the tongue, then as the taste advances to midpalate a sharp, bitter flavor of wood resin blankets the taste buds. The extreme bitterness dominates the aftertaste completely. What began as a relatively alluring, if simple malt evaluation in the aroma concluded harshly and bitterly in the mouth and throat; take a pass on it.

2001 Rating: ★/Not Recommended

Ben Nevis 12 Year Old Western Highlands SMSW (Scotland); 43% abv, $40.

Pretty, even brilliant bronze color; some floating debris. The initial nosing run-through offers an evolved aroma that sports equal parts sweet oak and sweet malty grain; in the middle stage whiffs, following several minutes of aeration, assertive scents of marzipan, candied almond, and light vanilla extract breathe life into this bouquet; the final sniffing comes off a little softer and less aggressive as more supple aromas of nougat, white peppercorn, grainy spirit, and green apple supply an appetizing finish to this phase; nice. The palate entry is firm, oaky sweet, and a touch resiny; by the midpalate the taste displays some genuine grainy charm in the forms of caramel, dry cereal, and sweetish oak. The aftertaste is long, focused, lean, and acceptably sharp. I liked this earthy malt enough to grant a third star and hence a recommendation due primarily to its solid bouquet and dry mouth presence.

2001 Rating: ★★★/Recommended

Ben Nevis 21 Year Old Western Highlands SMSW (Scotland); 43% abv, $50.

Bright honey/topaz hue; the purest of the three distillery bottlings. This nose shows some glimpses of gracefulness in the opening pass; with time in the glass, round, mildly oily, and pleasantly grainy aromas develop in the second sniffing and in the third whiff a gentle prickliness gets added to the aromatic mix; the final pass notes some lessening of strength as the aroma turns a bit neutral and muted, though I can still pick up distant echoes of dry grain and oaky resin. The taste profile at palate entry is dry, a bit thin in texture, but inviting; the midpalate shows a sweeter side as the flavor goes woody and almost candied. The finish is properly long, oaky off dry-to-sweet, and austere. This drinkable, but ultimately disappointing malt loses too much in the aroma and by midpalate to make it anything more than ordinary...at best.

2001 Rating: ★★/Not Recommended

BenRiach 12 Year Old Speyside SMSW (Scotland); 46% abv, $63.
The pale straw color is like flax/fiber; excellent clarity. The first aromatic thrust is typical of this fine, if neglected Speyside distillery in its fifth-gear, delicately sweet maltiness; another seven minutes improve the bouquet by making it more assertive as the sweet grain turns into ripe yellow fruit, with the accent squarely on banana and pear. The crisp, dry palate entry offers finely measured tastes of dried banana chips and light oak-influenced vanilla; the midpalate flavor rounds off nicely as the woody/resiny core flavor overshadows the fruit component. The aftertaste is delightfully clean, lean, off-dry, and in line with the established, easy-drinking BenRiach character profile.
2005 Rating: ★★★/Recommended

BenRiach 16 Year Old Speyside SMSW (Scotland); 46% abv, $90.
A marginally deeper straw/yellow hue than the 12 Year Old and actually approaches a bright gold/green color; flawless purity. The initial nosing pass immediately detects green apple/yellow pear scents that enchant the olfactory sense with their deft agility and elegance; later sniffings encounter more fully evolved, huskier, if earthier aromas, especially candle wax, linseed oil, grass, mown hay, and barely discernible mint. The palate entry is off-dry and even a tad bitter due to the high level of acidity and also the concentrated, resiny touch of the oak; at midpalate a bittersweet taste profile is discovered as the acid recedes, leaving behind more of the vanilla/honey quality of the oak barrel as well as a sweetly malty flavor. The maltiness comes to the foreground in the graceful finish. If the entry hadn't gone so bitter and astringent, I would have bestowed a fourth star. I suggest that you immediately add a few splashes of mineral water to mitigate the acid presence.
2005 Rating: ★★★/Recommended

BenRiach 20 Year Old Speyside SMSW (Scotland); 46% abv, $139.
The pretty amber color is bright and unblemished. The opening whiffs pick up astringent, angular, woodsy/earthy, and mineral-like scents that remind me of autumn leaves decaying in the forest; the later inhalations reinforce the findings of the initial sniffings as the acidic astringency is still present, but no longer presiding as deeper aromas of dry malt, linseed oil, paraffin, and pine all emerge. The palate entry is whistle clean and balanced between acidity and malt sweetness; the midpalate displays even more nimble finesse as the flavor profile leaps forward, highlighting mature but vivid tastes of oak resin, new honey, vanilla, and light toffee. The finish is long, lean, and refreshing. Add mineral water right away.
2005 Rating: ★★★★/Highly Recommended

BenRiach Authenticas 21 Year Old Heavily Peated Speyside SMSW (Scotland); 46% abv, $54.
The pale yellow color is a bit dull, but superbly clean. The initial inhalations have no trouble locating the smoky, pipe tobacco-like peat reek as it leaps from the glass in potent waves; being an inland Speyside distillery the peatiness found here is far different from Islay peatiness which includes a saline quality born of the sea; this peatiness is sweeter, earthier, and far more smoky/ashy than medicinal or iodine-like. The dominant palate entry taste is of tobacco leaf/cigarette ashes, which may sound unappealing but is actually sweet and more than savory; the midpalate stage continues the smoke-a-thon, but adds subtle notes of honey

and caramel. Finishes prickly in spirit, warm in the throat, and alluringly lip-smacking sweet. Works for me.
2006 Rating: ★★★★/Highly Recommended

BenRiach Curiositas 10 Year Old Peated Malt Speyside SMSW (Scotland); 46% abv, $63.

The color is a sturdy autumnal gold/amber; excellent clarity. The opening aroma is pleasingly smoky and soot-like, not at all Speyside-like in its bearing; with further air contact, the bouquet opens up to include beefy aromas of creosote, olive brine, and cigarette ash; this bouquet is a kind of Islay/Speyside hybrid, call it a Speylay. The palate entry is warming, nougaty sweet, and sap-like; at midpalate the chunky flavor profile offers a well-integrated marriage of barley malt and sweet smokiness/peatiness. Finishes on a decidedly sweet, grainy note that for a moment dominates the smoky peat.
2005 Rating: ★★★★/Highly Recommended

BenRiach Dark Rum Wood Finish 15 Year Old Speyside SMSW (Scotland); 46% abv, $95.

Sturdy gold color; flawless clarity. Smells of marshmallow, white raisins, chalk, and sawdust immediately following the pour; aeration brings out gently ripe, delicately fruity and earthy scents that include hints of pineapple, apricot, and truffle; a polite, understated bouquet that's totally delightful. Entry is grainy/malty sweet and medium textured; the taste profile turns more intensely fruity at midpalate offering white peach, white chocolate, wet earth, and pastry dough. Concludes ripe, creamy, and lithe. A whisper of a Speyside malt that's deceptively complex and far-reaching in its scope.
2007 Rating: ★★★★/Highly Recommended

BenRiach Limited Release 40 Year Old Speyside SMSW (Scotland); 50% abv, $1,800.

Only 265 bottles worldwide/60 for the US. Harvest gold/topaz/autumnal color; impeccable purity. I'm stunned at the vibrant, assertive pruny/figgy opening aroma that's a dead-ringer for Christmas season fruitcake or mince pies; following additional air contact the fruit perfume adds notes of walnut, chestnut, nutmeg, and paraffin—the youthfulness of this bouquet is beguiling and admirable. Entry is vividly fruity/nutty and rife with full-fledged tastes of orange zest, cherries, black tea, and chocolate. Finishes with all the verve and panache of a whisky half its age. One of the two or three finest 40 year old or older malts I've ever reviewed.
2007 Rating: ★★★★★/Highest Recommendation

BenRiach Madeira Wood Finish 15 Year Old Speyside SMSW (Scotland); 46% abv, $95.

Marigold/yellow-gold color; sediment-free. The alcohol rush in the first nosing brings my nose hairs (I admit to three to four) to attention as the prickly spirit dominates the initial aromatic stage; after another seven minutes of aeration, the spirit blows off, leaving in its wake big, accessible smells of grain, malt, light caramel, light fudge, and almond butter; this is a dry, biscuity bouquet that's worth waiting a few minutes to let it settle down. Entry is BIG FLAVORED and spirity, with upfront tastes of marshmallow, butter cream, egg cream, dark chocolate, nougat, and vanilla bean. Breathtakingly luscious and marvelously broad in its dimension. A Speyside classic.
2007 Rating: ★★★★★/Highest Recommendation

BenRiach Pedro Ximenez Sherry Wood Finish 15 Year Old Speyside SMSW (Scotland); 46% abv, $95.

Late summer corn gold/deep amber/wheat field tan color; unblemished clarity. The opening aroma is concentrated in its ripe and ready winey-ness and pruniness; added air contact brings out large-boned, demonstrative aromas of dark chocolate, cocoa butter, cream sherry, dates, black raisins, and sweet barley malt. Entry tastes include honey wheat bread, prune Danish, and lots and lots of honey; by midpalate the taste profile reads with the volume akin to War and Peace as hardy flavors of marzipan, treacle, blackberry preserves, cherries covered in dark chocolate, and orange flavored chocolates bombard the taste buds like the Blitzkrieg. Might not be everybody's expansive, aggressive, and sweet malt style, but that's fine by me, neighbors, 'cause that leaves more for the rest of us sickos.

2007 Rating: ★★★★★/Highest Recommendation

BenRiach Tawny Port Wood Finish 15 Year Old Speyside SMSW (Scotland); 46% abv, $95.

The gold dust/topaz/old sauternes color dazzles the eye; perfect purity. The aroma after the pour is decidedly restrained after the mega-bouquets of the previous four BenRiachs, but what's here is obviously good quality and is crisp, more austere, and citrusy than the others; further air contact stimulates latent smells of oak, vanilla, nutmeg, and old leather. Entry is sensationally satiny, plummy sweet, and ripe; the taste profile at midpalate is deep-running, concentrated, cocoa bean-like, chocolaty, and honeyed. Ends masterfully in a velvet rush of sweet oakiness, cocoa, and cake frosting. Yet another gem from this heavenly series.

2007 Rating: ★★★★★/Highest Recommendation

Blair Athol 27 Year Old Central Highlands SMSW (Scotland); 54.7% abv, £n/a.

Only available in the United Kingdom. The inviting brilliant bronze color displays flawless purity and visual warmth. The first inhalations detect very prickly spirit (it is 109.4-proof, after all) that invades the nasal cavity and overcomes any other aromatic aspects; aeration and a touch of mineral water assist in calming the spirit and, thereby, allow the aroma to emit mildly pleasant scents of varnished wood, rice pudding, pipe tobacco, soy, and peanut oil. The palate entry features some fire on the tongue but then more moderate tastes of light caramel and milk chocolate; the midpalate stage offers more flavor scope as candied tastes of maple, brown sugar, and honey vie for dominance. Concludes semisweet, concentrated and very honey-like. Here's one where I found the alcohol fighting the other inherent grain characteristics from beginning to end; that said, the additional of mineral water at a 50-50 ratio helps considerably; there's just enough virtue for a recommendation.

2004 Rating: ★★★/Recommended

Bowmore "Darkest" Sherry Cask Islay SMSW (Scotland); 43% abv, $65.

The bay/bronze color seduces the eye; ideal, flawless clarity. The opening inhalation offers deep aromas of nutmeg, oloroso sherry, dark toffee and black pepper; further aeration time stirs up thrilling scents of chocolate covered-cherries, tobacco smoke (most like pipe tobacco), sea brine, paraffin, praline, and cedar box; a textbook Islay/sherry perfume. The palate entry is winey, concentrated and stunningly sherry-like; at midpalate the taste profile expands to include dark honey, butterscotch, old oak, vanilla extract, and cocoa bean. Concludes

delicately and as sweet as honey. I've called this thoroughbred the "Baby Black Bowmore" after the legendary one-time offering from Bowmore (★★★★★) that was distilled in 1964 and aged in 100% sherry casks for almost thirty years. Though precious few bottles of Black Bowmore exist, people still ask me if I really think that it's the finest single malt I've ever tasted. I always answer, "Black Bowmore is the most memorable single malt I've ever tasted." If you want a hint at what Black Bowmore was like, pick up a bottle of Darkest (which is around 15 years old though it's not stated on the label) and turn off the television, unplug the phone and the computer, turn down the lights, and let it seduce you inch by inch.
2004 Rating: ★★★★★/Highest Recommendation

Bowmore "Dawn" Port Cask Islay SMSW (Scotland); 51.5% abv, $60.

This Islay malt's auburn/henna color bewitches the eye. The peculiar, but not off-putting, smell of iodine mixed with red cherry juice greets the olfactory sense in the first sniffing after the pour; in the second pass the cherry fragrance turns a bit medicinal, as in children's cough syrup, while the third whiff finds aromatic bits and pieces of barley malt, quinine, and, to my dismay, sour grape juice; the final pass shows flashes of the port pipes but not nearly enough to redeem the bouquet as a whole. This whisky is far more fetching in the mouth than in the nasal cavity as the palate entry turns the volume up on Bowmore's inherent Islay charm, a salty, biscuity virtue that's unique on the island; the midpalate is sweet/sour and more juicy than malty. It finishes with sophistication. This Bowmore is inherently polite, urbane, composed, yet bold.
2001 Rating: ★★★/Recommended

Bowmore "Dusk" Bordeaux Wine Cask Islay SMSW (Scotland); 50% abv, $70.

This weird bottling owns a peculiar cherry juice/bronze/tawny color and ideal purity. The opening nosing pass picks up intense iodine and blackcurrant as this oddball borders on being more akin to cassis than to malt whisky; the atypical bouquet continues in its strange cassis-like/intensely briny direction in the second whiff; by the third sniffing the nose is turning positively liqueur-like as well as prickly due to the high alcohol level; nothing more to report after ten minutes of air contact other than the bouquet stays the course that was set out early in the first nosing pass; cherry/berry cough medicine-like. The palate entry is surprisingly tame, sweet, and fruity after the whip-and-chair nosing; the midpalate improves the situation as the rich, damn-near succulent fruitiness mingles well with the sea breeze and oakiness, salvaging the total mouth experience. The finish is medicinal, iodine-like, yet fruity and cassis-like enough to rescue this curious beast from a one star fate like its horrifically disagreeable Claret Bordeaux Cask finished predecessor also tasted in 2000 (★).
2000 Rating: ★★/Not Recommended

Bowmore "Enigma" 12 Year Old Islay SMSW (Scotland); 40% abv, $51/liter.

Available at Duty Free only. Appearance of rich amber/burnished gold; perfect clarity. The first nosing passes detect obvious brine, sea breeze, and green olive; further inhalations bolster the initial findings and add subtle scents of baked brandied banana, almond paste, and cubeb berry. The palate entry is vividly salty, yet invitingly sweet and honeyed; the midpalate stage is medium rich, pipe tobacco-like, nutty, nougaty, fresh pineapple-like, and sublimely ashy-sweet. Finishes as toned, svelte, smoky, and focused a young Bowmore as

I've evaluated in 10 years. Puts the anemic Bowmore Legend to shame, not that it needed Enigma for that.

2007 Rating: ★★★★/Highly Recommended

Bowmore "Voyage" Port Cask Islay SMSW (Scotland); 56% abv, $80.

The attractive reddish/russet hue is striking and impeccably pure. The opening nosing pass sees a fast start from aromas of iodine, sea breeze, grapefruit, and sausage spice; with aeration, the aroma settles down into a leaner, more focused bouquet that offers seductive scents of crushed flowers in a yearbook, spice, sea spray, and even a delicate touch of dill; after seven minutes of air contact, the bouquet adds pencil eraser and gum to the aromatic mix; the fourth and final blast adds a trace of mint; a highly volatile, spirity, and engaging nose that's irritating one minute and sublimely enchanting the next; not an Islay aroma that could be easily pigeonholed. Remarkably sweet at palate entry then turns sinewy and focused at midpalate as sappy, sweet flavors of oak, sea salt, distant wine, and pear drop. The finish is extended, oaky sweet, and intensely fruited. I had serious mixed feelings about this malt but ended up liking it enough to recommend that you buy it.

2000 Rating: ★★★/Recommended

Bowmore Claret Bordeaux Wine Cask Islay SMSW (Scotland); 56% abv, $90.

While no age statement is given on the label of this limited edition (12,000 bottles/480 to the US) of Bowmore, the fact is it was matured for twelve years in a combination of used bourbon and sherry barrels, then aged an additional 18 months in barrels that formerly held red Bordeaux. The color is an odd amber/reddish hue with bronze/orange core highlights; impeccable clarity. The opening whiff detects the oily/saline thumbprint of Islay on top of an overtly wine-like fragrance that borders on being too perfumy; the second nosing whiff offers as much ripe red fruit as it does customary Bowmore oiliness and elegance; after seven minutes of aeration, a peculiar chocolate covered cherry aroma suddenly races to the forefront, out-distancing all other elements in a most curious aromatic display for a Bowmore malt; the fourth and final sniffing witnesses the bouquet getting refocused on the malt and the briny ocean influence, with the red wine component receding. On the palate, this malt is a mess, bounding wildly in flavor from cherry-flavored cough syrup to red claret to single malt, but what's lost completely is the sense that it's from the Bowmore distillery; this is a malt without an identity, which is the cornerstone facet of the single malt concept. The aftertaste is syrupy, overly wine-like, too heavily medicinal, and, in a word, unpleasant. For all the very good to great bottlings from this venerable distillery, I can't help but wonder why this serious mistake, which does nothing to honor the Bowmore name, was released at all; just to get something into the marketplace in order to keep pace with the wood finish craze simply isn't a good enough reason.

2000 Rating: ★/Not Recommended

Bowmore 12 Year Old Islay SMSW (Scotland); 43% abv, $45.

The brilliant, tidy appearance shows a deep harvest gold color; perfect purity. The unabashedly briny opening bouquet is all peat, sea salt and salted focaccia (the traditional, thick Italian bread); time in the glass serves to bring out a refined sherry scent that adds a welcome fruity balance to the aroma's saline foundation; Bowmore fragrance at its most

juvenile and rambunctious. The palate entry is lean, surprisingly sweet and acutely resiny; at midpalate the taste profile settles down, reflecting the inherent sweet, fruity and malty grace that is the hallmark of this legendary distillery. Ends pine-like, resiny, moderately salty, fruity (yellow fruit, like yellow plum or banana) and semisweet. While not my favorite Bowmore, this frisky 12 year old clearly depicts an important stage of development that all the older, better Bowmores experience. In view of this distillery's historical importance and place among the greats, these facts alone make this malt worth trying.
2004 Rating: ★★★/Recommended

Bowmore Mariner 15 Year Old Islay SMSW (Scotland); 43% abv, $50.
The rich, amber/light brown color displays an unblemished purity that arrests the eye. Smelling this right after the significantly more raw and feisty 12 year old dramatically illustrates the power of three additional years of oak barrel maturation; the initial nosings reveal subtle, refined, even feline leanings as the aroma highlights more of the sweet oak and honey than the salt/brine; in reverse to the 12 year old, aeration stimulates the gentle sea salt component as the oak/fruit element recedes to the background. The palate entry is succulent, elegant and creamy sweet; at midpalate tastes of cocoa, coffee bean, butterscotch and caramel blossom on the tongue. Finishes sweet, viscous and maple-like. A prototypical 15 year old Islay malt that's still very vigorous, but shows an extraordinary amount of grace and harmony. Delicious and agile.
2004 Rating: ★★★★/Highly Recommended

Bowmore 17 Year Old Islay SMSW (Scotland); 43% abv, $85.
Available at Duty Free only. Impeccable in purity, harvest gold/medium amber in color. The first couple of passes pick up melded, harmonious aromas that balance dry cereal scents with those of oak and sea; after another six minutes of exposure to air, the brininess fades to the background as the vanilla/honey/sherry component comes to the fore. The palate entry is ideally balanced, off-dry and slightly briny while the midpalate phase is viscous, honey sweet, and moderately oaky/resiny. Ends on a sweet, oily note. I recall tasting this malt in 1994 when I happened to sample several 15 to 20 year old malts in a single flight. I thought at the time that the best malts were in that age range and while I've expanded my viewpoint up to 25 years old over the last decade, I still find myself enthralled with the likes of this Bowmore, Macallan 18, Glenmorangie 18, Lagavulin 16, Longmorn 15 and Highland Park 18.
2004 Rating: ★★★★/Highly Recommended

Bowmore 18 Year Old Islay SMSW (Scotland); 43% abv, $85.
Replaces the Bowmore 17 Year Old. The pretty topaz colored appearance displays minor sediment that in the end is inconsequential. In the opening whiffs, my olfactory mechanism picks up lorry loads of chocolate covered cherries, chocolate covered orange peel, honey, sherry, and that's just for openers; an additional seven minutes of aeration releases hugely pleasing aromas of marshmallow/S'mores, cocoa, black coffee, and dark fudge. All of the fragrances detected in the nosing phases are present in the entry and the midpalate from chocolate covered fruits to honey to sherry to fudge to black coffee. Ends up rollickingly luscious, sweet, and as generous as any Bowmore this side of Darkest.
2007 Rating: ★★★★★/Highest Recommendation

Bowmore 25 Year Old Islay SMSW (Scotland); 43% abv, $160.

This is a new recipe for the 25 year old, one that employs a higher ratio of sherry-influenced whisky; I scored the original recipe ★★★★★. Deep tawny, copper hue; superb purity. The initial sniffings are distinctively briny, salty and cotton candy sweet; aeration serves to broaden the aromatic scope as scents of pastry, baked pear and butterscotch are added to the profile. The palate entry is rich, almost jammy and peppered with salty/winey flavors that say Bowmore, but with greater emphasis on the sweetness; the midpalate explodes on the tongue with deep tastes of maple, honey, brown sugar, and toffee. The finish is long, nicely balanced between the sea salt and the sherry, and succulent. The change in taste-profile direction is due entirely to what type of whisky was available for bottling and sherry cask whisky was there and ready; the superior craftsmanship of Bowmore remains steady and true.

2002 Rating: ★★★★★/Highest Recommendation

Bowmore 1957 38 Year Old Islay SMSW (Scotland); 40.1% abv, $2,500.

The gorgeous light honey/ amber/goldenrod hue is impeccably pure and very eye-catching. The initial nosing pass after the pour is ripe, intensely fruited (baked pear especially), and mildly floral, almost more in Highland fashion than that of Islay; the moderate alcohol level is hardly apparent in the second sniffing as the floral quality begins to advance; the third whiff offers gentle aromatic waves of heather, leather, and light sea breeze; the fourth and last pass, following nine minutes in the glass, reveals a barely perceptible marzipan quality that's immensely charming; a good, stately bouquet. Dark chocolate and caramel tastes greet the tongue at palate entry; the midpalate offers a bit of sea salt, but hardly enough to notice except by the more seasoned taste buds. The finish is heavenly sweet in a cocoa-like way, with mere hints of salt, peat, and oak. Not the blockbuster I expected, but a sound, savory older malt.

2000 Rating: ★★★★/Highly Recommended

Bowmore 1964 Bourbon Cask Islay SMSW (Scotland); 43% abv, $2,200.

Bright, pretty honey/light topaz hue; superb clarity and cleanliness. In the first two minutes of sniffing the olfactory sense is treated to a friendly, round, grainy and supple bouquet that seems fully matured; more time in the copita helps out especially since the aroma turns a bit, dare I say it, corn-like, slightly salty and biscuity; the aromatic integration is so complete that no one quality leaps out. The inviting palate entry is honeyed and mildly sweet; at the midpalate point the flavor profile becomes more honey-like and grainy; it's luscious. The aftertaste is polite, moderately sweet, biscuity and long. My clear favorite of these three Bowmore limited editions from 1964; "integrated" is the best term to describe this Islay beauty.

2003 Rating: ★★★★★/Highest Recommendation

Bowmore 1964 Fino Sherry Cask Islay SMSW (Scotland); 49.4% abv, $2,200.

Attractive, light amber color; perfect purity. The elegant opening bouquet is evolved, mature, tart, even a tad yeasty; seven more minutes of air exposure produces an animated, lightly fruity (banana? guava?), slightly salty and resiny bouquet that reminds me of salt water taffy; there's a trace of spirity prickliness as well; lovely. The palate entry is off-dry,

salty/yeasty and mildly cracker-like; by the midpalate stage a peppery quality emerges on the tongue that complements the oak resin. It finishes more dry than off-dry and is different from any Bowmore I've ever tasted.
2003 Rating: ★★★★/Highly Recommended

Bowmore 1964 Oloroso Sherry Cask Islay SMSW (Scotland); 43.6% abv, $2,200.
The deep old copper penny/vintage armagnac color is gorgeous; excellent purity. The initial nosing passes offer assertive aromas that include hints of old oak, palo cortado sherry and wood resin; additional time in the copita adds firmly structured, oily scents of almond butter, sea salt and malt. The palate entry is oily, buttery and semisweet; by the midpalate there's a touch of tea leaves, tobacco smoke, mince pie, honey, molasses and sherry. The aftertaste features the delightfully oily texture and the honey-like oloroso sherry. More buxom than the Fino as one would expect; very nice indeed.
2003 Rating: ★★★★/Highly Recommended

Bowmore 1968 32 Year Old Islay SMSW (Scotland); 45.5% abv, $300.
Only 1,860 bottles were produced (132 for the US). Has the golden/light honey hue of an older montrachet. The initial nosing passes after the pour detect gently sweet, harmonious aromas (hey, it's a Bowmore, right?) of ripe green apples, coconut oil, and background peat reek; time in the glass stimulates subtle scents of old Bourbon casks, wet hay, and popcorn; a low-key, understated Islay bouquet. In the mouth this whisky starts working on all cylinders as the palate entry goes succulent, malty, and sweet; at the midpalate point the reemergence of light peat melds beautifully to the rich graininess providing for a finish that's stately, racy, and totally integrated and seamless. Another older dandy malt from the magicians at Bowmore.
2001 Rating: ★★★★/Highly Recommended

Bowmore 1968 37 Year Old Bourbon Wood Islay SMSW (Scotland); 43.4% abv, $1,000.
The bright amber/honey color beams in the copita; excellent purity. The curious aroma after the pour reminds me of the clear vinyl/plastic that my Aunt Harriett had covering every square inch of her furniture back in the 1950s…okay; unfortunately, seven more minutes of air contact do little to rescue this aromatic misstep, except to stimulate meager scents of red cherry and orange peel. The palate entry is better than the regrettably directionless bouquet, featuring an agreeably toasty, maple-like surface flavor; in the midpalate stage even more order is restored as the flavor profile expands to include butter, almond paste, bacon fat, and pork rind. Finishes long, spirity, warm as embers, and elegant. That weird aroma, though, still has me shaking my head.
2006 Rating: ★★★/Recommended

Bowmore 1971 34 Year Old Sherry Cask Islay SMSW (Scotland); 51% abv, $799.
The deep amber/nut brown appearance is bright and clean. In the initial inhalations, the aroma is piny, forest-like, earthy, and herbal, with just the slightest evidence of sea air; another seven minutes, swirling, and a touch of mineral water unleash fragrances of dried red fruit, raisins, marzipan, smoldering bonfire, and soft cheese. The palate entry carries the sweet, winy emblem of long maturation in sherry cask, but doesn't club my taste buds into submission; at the midpalate stage the taste profile turns more intensely cocoa-like, almost

dark chocolaty and sublimely bittersweet. The finish is creamy, cocoa butter-like, and sherry sweet. Sherry fanatics only need apply. No, it's not Black Bowmore or even Darkest, but this sherry cask expression is multi-dimensional and lip-smacking delicious.
2005 Rating: ★★★★/Highly Recommended

Bowmore 1989 16 Year Old Islay Non-Chill Filtered SMSW (Scotland); 51.8% abv, $95.
The pale yellow/green color is pretty and pure. Vibrant waves of sea air, green olive, and brine start the aromatic proceedings with flair; the later sniffings focus primarily on the saline/sea air element, giving only slight chance for distant scents of pineapple, vanilla bean, and dates; the addition of mineral water sees the bouquet turn creamy and marshmallow-like. The palate entry is honey sweet and moderately oaky; the midpalate stage stands out for the oily, velvety, and salted butter-like flavor profile that merely suggests the maritime breeze. The aftertaste is long, semisweet, and only slightly briny. Lovely, composed, curiously atypical of the customary Bowmore style. Very agreeable once mineral water is added.
2005 Rating: ★★★★/Highly Recommended

Bowmore 1990 16 Year Old Sherry Matured Non-Chill Filtered Islay SMSW (Scotland); 53.8% abv, $85.
The deep topaz color is lovely; flawless clarity. This aroma is off the charts in terms of assertive scents of lead pencil, iodine, sea salt, and inner tube; seven more minutes of exposure to air bring out salty sherry notes as well as hints of prunes, dates, black raisins, cigarette ash, and smoked trout. Aggressive in the palate entry, this taste profile is equal parts sherry and seaweed; the midpalate stage showcases more of the sherry influence than the maritime influence and the result is deliciously raucous, hearty, and far more unruly than most Bowmores, which are renowned for their island grace and power. No grace here; just flat out in-yer-puss Islay grit and electric strength. A tongue-tingling experience that's well worth the $85.
2006 Rating: ★★★★/Highly Recommended

Brora 20 Year Old Northern Highlands SMSW (Scotland); 58.1% abv, £n/a.
Only available in the United Kingdom. Owns a pure, unblemished golden wheat-like hue; very pretty malt. The opening whiffs detect intense, husk-like, grainy aromas that seem a bit industrial, at first whiff; the addition of mineral water and more aeration make a huge difference in the demeanor of this malt's bouquet as it immediately becomes more open and amicable, emitting concentrated, dense scents of just-harvested grain, brown rice, light smoke, and sweet malt. The palate entry is rich, sweet and candied while the near-creamy midpalate highlights the interplay between the malt, alcohol, and natural oils. Finishes acceptably warm on the tongue, honey sweet, a touch maple-like, and altogether beguiling. Still sexy and racy.
2004 Rating: ★★★★/Highly Recommended

Brora 30 Year Old The Diageo Special Releases Northern Highlands SMSW (Scotland); 55.7% abv, £175.
Only available in the United Kingdom. The ready-to-be-harvested golden wheat color is comely and perfectly clean. The initial inhalations come across substantial aromas of peat-

reek, medicine chest, red meat, kippers, and smoking cigar ash; what's so astonishing is the 180-degree transformation following aeration time and a reduction with mineral water as the previously heavily smoked meat aroma turns intensely malty, heathery, even biscuity. The palate entry is simultaneously peaty and malty while the midpalate stage tries to reach a compromise between the two competing flavor forces. This attempt fails and the whisky concludes semisweet, honeyed and resiny; I didn't like this edition nearly as much as the wonderful 20 Year Old Rare Malt Selection because it's evident that this malt is on the downward slope of its chemical life (its major components aren't in harmony) and likely has been declining for a minimum of five years; a mistake to release it; it should have been used for blending.

2004 Rating: ★★/Not Recommended

Bruichladdich 10 Year Old Islay SMSW (Scotland); 46% abv, $48.

Pronounced "BROOK laddie". The pale yellow/straw hue is typical of Bruichladdich; absolutely pure. The initial nosing passes reveal a soft malty sweetness that's accented by a dollop of sea salt; with time in the glass more floral, light peat, seaweed, and wine scents emerge to enhance the salty/malty core fragrance; a nimble, light-footed Islay bouquet whose freshness and vivacity serve it well. The palate entry is lightly peaty, grain mash sweet, and just a touch salty; the midpalate impression is meatier as tangy tastes of sea breeze, unsweetened coconut, and oak resin unite. The aftertaste shows a flash of spirity heat.

2002 Rating: ★★★/Recommended

Bruichladdich 15 Year Old Islay SMSW (Scotland); 46% abv, $65.

Attractive amber/honey gold hue; perfect purity. This aroma begins already much evolved in the glass as tantalizing scents of sweet barley malt and pineapple make for an intriguing opening bouquet; aeration over another five minutes stimulates further fragrances including deft touches of oloroso sherry, heather, and sea salt; I don't detect as much peat in this bouquet as in that of the 10 Year Old; seductive and lovely just the same. The palate entry shows enormous charm in the forms of sap-sweet malt and the trace of peat that was missing from the aroma; the midpalate focuses tightly on the oloroso sherry and dried flowers. The finish is warm, comforting, sweet, and zesty.

2002 Rating: ★★★★/Highly Recommended

Bruichladdich 15 Year Old Second Edition Islay SMSW (Scotland); 46% abv, $80.

Whisky was aged in bourbon casks for 15 years, then moved to premier grand cru classe sauternes casks for 25 weeks before bottling. The attractive autumnal gold color is absolutely pure and pristine. Opening sniffs detect lovely, rounded scents of honeydew melon, candle wax, and fiber; seven more minutes in the copita allow the bouquet to stretch a bit more, adding notes of sawdust, ginger, and pencil eraser. The palate entry is spirity to the point of nearly being prickly and is off-dry, delicately fruity, and pleasantly oily; by the midpalate stage the flavor profile leaves any fruit evidence behind and instead focuses on malt and the wood impact, giving off an astringent/hard-edged finish that is totally in line with the later stages of the nosing. Good enough to be recommended for whisky drinkers who prefer their malts lean, edgy, and slightly mean.

2005 Rating: ★★★/Recommended

Bruichladdich 1966 "Legacy Series One" 36 Year Old Islay SMSW (Scotland); 40.6% abv, $485.

Only 1,500 bottles worldwide; 100% American oak hogshead. Deep amber hue that borders on being bronze; as expected, perfect clarity and purity. The initial whiffs after the pour on this old malt pick up garden-like, almost woodsy and hay field scents that blow off in about three minutes; following a bit of swirling and seven more minutes, the bouquet starts displaying its fruity/cereal-like base aroma on top of which dance more ethereal scents including paraffin, minerals, and sweet oak. The palate entry is off-dry and resiny; the midpalate point is the highlight as toasty, semisweet tastes of raisins, cocoa, and oak impress the taste buds. The finish is surprisingly hot, but clean and honeyed. Excellent, multilayered, and more robust than I expected considering the moderate alcohol level.

2003 Rating: ★★★★/Highly Recommended

Bruichladdich 1970 31 Year Old Islay SMSW (Scotland); 44.2% abv, $283.

100% American oak hogshead, meaning 55 Imperial gallons or 255 liters; 4,200 bottles available worldwide. Rich amber/honey color; excellent purity. Right off the crack of the bat after the pour this nose jumps out fully evolved and developed; assertive yet elegant, the bouquet highlights compelling notes of mint (spearmint, especially), lemon drop candy, Juicy Fruit gum, apple strudel, spring orchard full of blossoms, and light toffee; I genuinely love this fruity, amiable bouquet. Composed, subtle yet layered and sweet at palate entry; by midpalate the flavors and texture evolve beautifully, becoming full-bodied, malty sweet, just slightly oily, and seriously luscious. The aftertaste closes the sensory circle with style and nuance rather than a brass band of chunky flavor. Supremely sophisticated and integrated; to date, the finest Laddie I've encountered; a complete malt whisky experience.

2003 Rating: ★★★★★/Highest Recommendation

Bruichladdich 1984 17 Year Old Islay SMSW (Scotland); 46% abv, $143.

Only 6,000 bottles available worldwide; 60% bourbon, 20% fino sherry, 20% oloroso sherry barrels. Pretty and pure amber/gold color; the opening nosing passes discover full, substantial aromas of toffee and honey; six more minutes of aeration release deeper scents including saddle leather, barely detectable sea salt, pine needle, and malt; there's a lot happening on a subtle level in this bouquet. Lovely, succulent, and maple-sweet at palate entry; the midpalate phase is where this malt explodes in sweet, honeyed (though not necessarily sherried) flavors that also show hints of peat and dried fruit. The aftertaste is long, focused on the honey, and very light peat. A winner from the start, but the true reward hits pay-dirt at the fabulous midpalate point.

2003 Rating: ★★★★/Highly Recommended

Bruichladdich 20 Year Old Islay SMSW (Scotland); 46% abv, $115.

Pretty golden yellow color; some sediment seen. The initial two nosing passes within three minutes of the pour unearth a generous array of succulent, ripe fruit scents, most notably, banana and nectarine; exposure to air for another five minutes encourages the fruit concentration to deepen; hardly any evidence of peat, oak, or malt in this vividly ambrosial malt bouquet. The palate entry is luscious, malty sweet, and shows a dash of vanilla/maple (must be the influence of the old, charred bourbon barrels); by the midpalate stage the spirity heat impacts the tongue before the tastes of oaky vanillin and sweet barley malt. Finishes in a delicious flourish of malt.

2002 Rating: ★★★★/Highly Recommended

Bruichladdich 20 Year Old Second Edition Islay SMSW (Scotland); 46% abv, $180.

Whisky was aged in bourbon casks for 20 years, then moved to casks that formerly matured red mourvedre wines from France. The honey/amber hue beams beneath the examination lamp; flawless purity. The first nosings detect earthy notes of just-polished hardwood floor, tobacco leaf, and pork rind; swirling in the glass and further aeration encourages scents of beef bouillon, old saddle leather, and black tea to emerge. The palate entry is off-dry, almost bitter, and yet simultaneously a bit fudge-like; the midpalate highlights the fudge/cocoa quality which is more bittersweet than sweet; nice, solid texture. The aftertaste is extended, bittersweet, and resiny. Like the 15 Year Old, this whisky displays enough depth and elegance to be recommended to malt lovers who treasure austerity and steely charactered whiskies, but there's a reticence, a distance to both of them that keeps them from earning a fourth rating star.

2005 Rating: ★★★/Recommended

Bruichladdich 3D "The Peat Proposal" Islay SMSW (Scotland); 46% abv, $70.

Bright marigold/harvest yellow/gold color; impeccable clarity. The initial whiffs can't help but detect the moderate truckloads of smoky/ashy peat that seem to come in waves; further aeration time stirs deeper phenolic, intensely medicinal aromas, including kippers, dried seaweed, iodine, and caramelized onion. The palate entry is svelte, medium-bodied, and bittersweet; at midpalate there are traces of charcoal, charred meat, pork sausage, dry malt, and burnt marshmallow; I love the taste stages even more than the aroma stages. Ends up salty, off-dry to bittersweet, concentrated, and smoky. Not as strapping peat-wise as Islay's south coast monsters (Ardbeg, Lagavulin, Laphroaig), but that's just fine. 3-D is a tasty, leathery, tobacco smoke-like, medium-peated malt that works admirably well in the middle range of Islay's peated whiskies.

2005 Rating: ★★★★/Highly Recommended

Bruichladdich 3D Second Edition "Moine Mhor" Islay SMSW (Scotland); 50% abv, $65.

3D-2 is a combination of three different peating levels, drawn from three different decades and from three varieties of sherry and bourbon casks, hence the designation 3D. The pale gold color and the unblemished purity really yell out "Islay". Right off the crack of the bat, the bouquet offers slinky scents of lapsang souchong tea, kippers, and smoldering bonfire; additional time in the glass introduces eye-popping, much punchier notes of cigar ash, seared beef roast, moss, and pungent iodine. The palate entry is amazingly sooty/ashy, yet oily and sweet; the midpalate displays remarkable finesse and seductive oiliness amidst the smoke and fire. The aftertaste is smoky, concentrated, delightfully sweet, even piney, with tidbit supporting role flavors of cigar box and seaweed. As superbly satisfying as the first 3D and one hell of a lot of fun.

2005 Rating: ★★★★/Highly Recommended

Bruichladdich Infinity Islay SMSW (Scotland); 55.5% abv, $75.

Very pale gold/straw color; ideal clarity. Notes of tar and nicotine lead the aroma parade after the pour, backed up by surprising floral scents (heather, honeysuckle); kippers, kippers and kippers in the second phase as the floral component fades away, leaving the door open for brine, seaweed, asphalt, and salty spirit. Entry flavors include bold spirit, bacon, pork roast, and smoke; the taste profile at midpalate is assertive, concentrated and spirity, offering flavors of almond, salted meat, dry malt, black pepper, and cocoa powder. Ends focused, vibrantly oaky, with clear evidence of vanilla cream, chocolate, and sherry.

2007 Rating: ★★★★/Highly Recommended

Bruichladdich Legacy II 37 Year Old 1965 Islay SMSW (Scotland); 41.8% abv, $470.

The color is medium amber, honey-like; impeccable clarity. The gorgeous, sumptuous aroma leaps from the glass, offering ripe, fruity notes of guava, light caramel, peach, and banana; an additional seven minutes allows the estery aroma to expand to include seductive scents of spice, vanilla, red apple, and maple; I love this totally integrated bouquet. The palate entry displays a honeyed richness that coats the tongue; at the oily midpalate semisweet tastes of pipe tobacco, marzipan, cocoa, and lanolin deeply impress the taste buds. Concludes a touch smoky, warm, and semisweet. The stature is equal to the splendid Bruichladdich Legacy I 36 Year Old released in 2003 (★★★★); bravo, Mister McEwan and team.

2004 Rating: ★★★★/Highly Recommended

Bruichladdich Links – Turnberry 14 Year Old Islay SMSW (Scotland); 46% abv, $75.

Dark flax/amber hue; flawless purity. I catch immediate aromatic notes of pineapple, papaya, and mango upfront; unexpectedly, aeration doesn't assist in stimulating further aromatic expansion as the bouquet goes flat and horizontal in the second stage. Entry is subdued, mildly nutty, grainy and malty, but without a clear direction; the taste profile at midpalate picks up some steam as flavors of vanilla, maple, and dry breakfast cereal take shape. Concludes light, lithe, and nuanced.

2007 Rating: ★★★/Recommended

Bruichladdich Rocks Islay SMSW (Scotland); 46% abv, $47.

The gold color has a slight rosy blush to it, making it exotic and very pretty; unblemished clarity. Smells delightfully of fruitcake, banana nut bread, and sweet malt in the first aromatic go-rounds; seven minutes of further exposure to air bring out devilishly toasty/roasted aromas of crispy pork rind, sweet oak, vanilla, red grapes, and blackberry jam; as inviting a bouquet as I've recently had from The Laddie. Entry is vividly sweet and grainy, yet nimble in its textural weight and acidic agility; gains momentum by midpalate as the taste profile suddenly bursts with red fruit presence (red currants, mostly) and oaky vanilla. Finishes clean as a whistle, chewy, and concentrated. Tight, composed, no body fat. This Laddie absolutely Rocks.

2007 Rating: ★★★★★/Highest Recommendation

Bruichladdich Valinch 1986 Cask 700, Bottle No. 82 Islay SMSW (Scotland); 53.5% abv, $n/a.

Only available at the distillery. Pretty, impeccably pure pale amber tint. The initial nosing passes pick up wonderfully nutty/malty aromas in the first two minutes after the pour; additional time in the glass encourages sweeter scents to emerge, most notably, pine nuts, light toffee, pipe tobacco, dried fruit, and almond paste; an ethereal bouquet whose lightness and fruitiness bedazzle the olfactory sense. The typical Islay saltiness/brininess makes its first appearance at palate entry; then at midpalate the taste turns deliciously caramel sweet and nougaty. The finish is concentrated, very sweet, and long. The great part is that you have to visit the distillery to get a bottle; what could be better?

2002 Rating: ★★★★/Highly Recommended

Bruichladdich Vintage 1973 Islay SMSW (Scotland); 40.2% abv, $285.

The appearance is clean and sports a harvest-time wheat field amber/gold hue. The initial nosing passes following the pour emit gently sweet, moderately nutty scents of banana bread and just-cracked walnuts; time in the copita affords the bouquet the opportunity to deepen slightly as it offers remarkably fresh notes of grass, hay, and light brine; a delicate bouquet that's quite typical of older Bruichladdichs. The litheness found in the nose doesn't prepare you for the alluring firmness and spirity punch of the palate entry; by midpalate there's all sorts of flavor activity going on, including a lovely honey/toffee quality that's succulent and a welcome touch of smoldering warmth on the tongue. Ends politely and moderately sweet and honeyed. While I like the agile nature of this vintage Islay malt, I prefer by quite a wide margin the magnificent Bruichladdich Vintage 1970 (★★★★★); tasted side-by-side, the multilayered, far more complex 1970 exhibits heaps more concentration, length, and character and is roughly the same price.

2004 Rating: ★★★/Recommended

Bruichladdich XVII 17 Year Old Islay SMSW (Scotland); 46% abv, $120.

100% bourbon barrels; the pale straw hue gleams under the lamp; impeccable purity. The opening sniffings in the first two minutes offer up concentrated grainy aromas, delicately touched by honey backnotes; seven more minutes in the glass allow the aroma to evolve into a full-fledged bouquet, notable for its biscuity, wafer-like and malty surface scents that lay atop fruity foundational aromas such as poached pear and baked apple in pastry; a rare Islay bouquet that's free of even the slightest trace of peat reek. The palate entry is firm, sugar cookie sweet and displays a welcome hint of oiliness; the midpalate is cereal/malty sweet and oily but hardly unctuous as the acidity level is clearly high enough to retain a lovely tartness/crispness. Finishes long, if a bit narrowly focused on the resiny acidity; a fully representative and true-to-the-style Laddie but one that I didn't take to as much as the new 15 and 20 Year Olds, not to mention the sleek, sexy Valinch 1986, all ★★★★.

2003 Rating: ★★★/Recommended

Bunnahabhain 18 Year Old Islay SMSW (Scotland); 43% abv, $90.

The very pretty light brown/medium amber color displays some minor sediment. The initial wave of aroma has in it intensely malty/cereal scents along with lesser traces of beeswax and dried herbs; aeration stimulates only trivial scents of cardboard and beans. The palate entry is off-dry, slightly salty, and intensely cereal-like; the midpalate stage highlights the medium sweet grain and oak teaming. Finishes off-dry to medium sweet, grainy/malty, though too one dimensional and narrowly focused to suit both the price and the age. Simply put, a drinkably average but wholly uninteresting single malt.

2006 Rating: ★★/Not Recommended

Bunnahabhain 25 Year Old Islay SMSW (Scotland); 43% abv, $260.

The deep amber/bronze color is terrifically attractive and flawless. This aroma offers toasted scents of walnuts, baked bread, and pork rind; later sniffs detect significantly deeper and broader aromas including old oak, herbs, dry earth, and soft brine. The palate entry is lip-smacking good as mildly salty tastes of salt water taffy, light toffee, and tea leaves win over the taste buds; the midpalate stage features flavors of sweet, toasted malt, brown butter, sultanas, and sweet oak. Finishes firmly, slightly oily, long, and even a tad smoky. Skip the timid 18 Year Old and proceed directly to this winner.

2006 Rating: ★★★★/Highly Recommended

Caol Ila 12 Year Old Islay SMSW (Scotland); 43% abv, $45.

The pale yellow hue boasts perfect clarity. The first sniffing leaves no doubt whatsoever about the place of origin as waves of sea salt, brine, and oily peat-reek greet the olfactory sense with aplomb and vigor; aeration accelerates the brininess, in particular, to the point where it turns medicinal and seductive. The palate entry phase features a surprisingly buttery/creamy leaning as the peat-reek takes on an oily face; at midpalate the flavor profile becomes concentrated, oily, malty sweet, and only moderately peaty. Ends on a sweet malty note that greatly complements the peaty underpinning. What I like about this youthful malt is how it builds from stage to stage, each phase being better than the last.

2005 Rating: ★★★★/Highly Recommended

Caol Ila 18 Year Old Islay SMSW (Scotland); 43% abv, $60.

Amber/burnished yellow/light honey color; superb purity. The opening aroma is slightly prickly in the nasal cavity; aeration smoothes the aroma out as moderately salty/kippery scents dominate the latter stages of the sniffing stage. The flavor profile at palate entry is integrated and sweet, and then at midpalate the presence of the peat takes shape in the form of smoky, woody, resiny tastes. Concludes with a flash of spirity fire on the tongue. I like this 18 year old expression, but prefer the animated 12 Year Old.

2005 Rating: ★★★/Recommended

Caol Ila Rare Edition 25 Year Old Islay SMSW (Scotland); 59.4% abv, $250.

Only 1704 bottles for the US. Burnished yellow/autumnal gold/auburn hue; ideal clarity. The opening nosing passes detect green olive, brine, pickling liquid; further air contact time of seven minutes brings out a barley malt sweetness that's touched with cedar; a beguiling and soft maritime bouquet. The palate entry is lean, but pipe tobacco sweet; at midpalate traces of unsweetened pineapple, mint, and barley malt are supported by pine/cedar/resin flavors that maintain a good balance between the sweetness of the grain and the resiny char of the bourbon barrel. Finishes like a sweet Vidalia onion, with a hint of mint. Delicious.

2005 Rating: ★★★★/Highly Recommended

Clynelish 14 Year Old Coastal (Northern) Highlands SMSW (Scotland); 46% abv, $40.
The honey/harvest gold color is pure and blemish-free. The aroma at the pour is large, biscuity, and grainy sweet; seven more minutes in the glass allow the aroma to deepen, becoming far more sugar biscuit-like and even a touch kippery/salty. While the bouquet is lovely, it's in the taste phase that this Northern Highlands thoroughbred takes flight as generous and malty sweet flavors thrill the taste buds at palate entry; by midpalate distinctive notes of black pepper, seaweed, oaky vanilla, honey, and dark caramel take the palate on a magic carpet ride through Clynelish's coastal home neighborhood. Finishes elegantly, sweetly, and malty, with just the slightest, barely discernable influence of the sea.
2005 Rating: ★★★★/Highly Recommended

Convalmore 24 Year Old Speyside SMSW (Scotland); 59.4% abv, £n/a.
Only available in the United Kingdom. The bright golden/yellow peach color enchants the eye; impeccable purity. The first sniffings pick up aromas of steamed white rice and green vegetables; strangely, the addition of mineral water hardly alters the aroma at all, leaving behind the hot moist air/steamy Chinese laundry/July-day-in-St. Louis quality. The palate entry reveals another side to this oddball malt as the taste profile begins on a nutty/kernel-like note; the midpalate is a domain unto itself as the nut quality found in the entry dissolves, leaving behind serious disparate flavor issues that include envelope glue, unspecified spice, malty sweetness, floor varnish, and intense oak. Finishes long, lean, waxy, and oaky. Just never got off the ground for me, with or without water.
2004 Rating: ★★/Not Recommended

Cragganmore 12 Year Old Speyside SMSW (Scotland); 40% abv, $39.
The harvest gold color is unblemished and brilliant. The sweet, grainy, malty, and deep bouquet comes flying out of the bottle at the pour, filling my office with the best aromatic evidence of Speyside; the succulent aroma develops further with aeration in the sweet forms of barley, cream, light caramel, and a trace of tropical fruit (is it banana or guava?). The palate entry is round, borderline plump, breakfast cereal sweet, and honeyed; at midpalate there's a flavor extension that reveals itself as manageable and slightly oily peat smoke. Sweetly concludes with the focus on the malt. Cragganmore is considered a master distiller's as well as a master blender's favorite. Along with Mortlach, Glenrothes, Longmorn, Macallan, and Aberlour, Cragganmore is a superlative representative distillery of Speyside's sweeter, woodier side. A "short list" malt to me and one that I order with enthusiastic regularity in bars, Cragganmore 12 brims with all that is Speyside.
2004 Rating: ★★★★/Highly Recommended

Cragganmore 29 Year Old The Diageo Special Releases Speyside SMSW (Scotland); 52.5% abv, $280.
The lovely amber/gold hue shows green highlights in the core as well as impeccable purity. The opening salvo of aromas includes toasty, off-dry, candied and honey notes as well as a plumpness which seduces me in a second; a splash of mineral water releases additional succulent fruity scents of pineapple, figs, dates, and pears; I love this plush style of Speyside bouquet. In the mouth Cragganmore 29 gets even sweeter, more honeyed, and clover-like yet is amiable, supple, and easy on the tongue and in the throat. Ends on a honey/sherry wood

note. Comfortable, succulent, and stylishly old-fashioned; will always be one of Speyside's top ten malt distilleries.

2004 Rating: ★★★★/Highly Recommended

Cragganmore Distiller's Edition 1992 Double Matured Port Cask Finished Speyside SMSW (Scotland); 40% abv, $65.

Deep brown/nut brown appearance. The aroma is closed initially, then after about five minutes succulent notes of red fruit (Santa Rosa plums, in particular), grapes and oaky wine emerge; another five minutes sees off-dry scents of dried red fruit and raisins top off the nosing stage in style. The palate entry is smooth, silky, medium sweet, and woody; the midpalate is honeyed, bittersweet, gum- and maple-like. Finishes in a flurry of litchi, caramel, and dark toffee. A gem from one of the ten best distilleries in Speyside.

2006 Rating: ★★★★/Highly Recommended

Cragganmore Rare Edition 10 Year Old Sherry Cask Speyside SMSW (Scotland); 60.1% abv, $150.

Only 2100 bottles for the US. The color is rusty and brilliant; superb clarity. The initial whiffs pick up scents of grapes, toffee, and sherry cask; later inhalations detect ripe tropical fruit, meringue, egg whites, and cocoa butter; a seductive siren of a bouquet. The palate entry focuses on the honey/sherry tag-team while the midpalate displays sublime butter cream, dark caramel, and peanut butter tastes that thrill the taste buds. Ends up maple-like, with a backnote of white chocolate. The finest Cragganmore I've tasted so far.

2005 Rating: ★★★★★/Highest Recommendation

Dalmore 12 Year Old Northern Highlands SMSW (Scotland); 43% abv, $25.

Solid bronze/medium amber color; slight traces of sediment seen. The opening whiffs detect firm, welcoming, and vibrant scents of toasted cereal grains and biscuit batter; seven more minutes of air contact stimulate deeper aromas of peanut butter, buttered popcorn, wheat toast, and lanolin; a bouquet that requires some extra time to unfold. The palate entry is sweet, maple-like, and sappy; the midpalate features oily, textured flavors of roasted nuts, brown butter, and nougat. Ends on a nutty, near honeyed note, with a trace of cigarette tobacco at the very end.

2005 Rating: ★★★/Recommended

Dalmore 1973 Vintage Gonzalez Byass 30 Year Old Sherry Cask Finish Northern Highlands SMSW (Scotland); 43% abv, $250.

Ever the underrated, underappreciated yet exemplary and sturdy Northern Highlands malt. In the opening whiffs, I detect vigorous, inviting notes of confectioner's sugar, lemon drops, and seaweed; aeration time unleashes additional intriguing, if atypical, scents of gum, banana extract, bread yeast, pineapple, and roasted grain. The palate entry is generous, tart, doughy, and a tad prickly; by midpalate there's a full-court-press of lemony/citrusy/yeasty flavor that's elegantly underpinned by tastes of oak resin, malt, and vanilla. Finishes sweeter than the entry, oily, deep and sensuous. Another gem from the ever-teasing mind of legendary master blender Richard Paterson.

2004 Rating: ★★★★/Highly Recommended

Dalmore 21 Year Old Northern Highlands SMSW (Scotland); 43% abv, $70.
The bright new copper/orange color dazzles the eye; very good purity. The first nosing picks up a wealth of intriguing aromas, including old leather, palm oil, and cigar tobacco; later sniffings encounter deeper layers of spice, caraway seed, black pepper, dry malt, and off-dry oak; a complex and superb bouquet. The palate entry is buttery, medium-bodied, and stunningly toffee-like; at midpalate the flavor profile goes mildly orangey/citrusy, creamy, and bittersweet. Finishes grandly as flavors of barley and maple take command.
2005 Rating: ★★★★/Highly Recommended

Dalmore Cigar Malt Northern Highlands SMSW (Scotland) 43% abv, $30.
The dark bronze/chestnut color still amazes me even after all the times I've enjoyed this stellar malt; clean and pure as a whistle. The first question about the aroma really is, where to begin?; the first stage appropriately highlights the lusciously smoky/tobacco-like side of Dalmore; after aeration, the bouquet features semisweet to sweet notes of honey, pipe tobacco, sherry, honey, and dark chocolate. The palate entry is silky smooth and caramel sweet; at midpalate the signature smokiness comes alive on the tongue in addition to sweet butter, toffee, honey, and sap. Finishes in a generous rush of smoke, charcoal, and ash. A malt whisky gem that, for the price, may just be the finest bargain in all of Scotch whisky, single malt or blended.
2005 Rating: ★★★★★/Highest Recommendation

Dalmore Stillman's Dram 28 Year Old Northern Highlands SMSW (Scotland); 45% abv, $120.
The orangey/bronze color shines; quite a lot of dark minuscule sediment seen under the examination lamp, though. Pleasantly soft scents of breakfast cereal and marshmallow float in the glass bowl; aeration time doesn't stir much more in the way of aromatics, except for very delicate hints of saddle leather and oats; I find the bouquet too timid and not enough of an active participant. The palate entry is oaky sweet and properly malty; at midpalate the flavor displays substantial and succulently sweet tastes of dark caramel, cream, and oloroso sherry. Concludes malty, toffee sweet, yet with an underlying bitterness that counters the candy-like core taste. Recommendable certainly as a malt whisky, but for the money I expect more from this great distillery.
2005 Rating: ★★★/Recommended

Dalwhinnie 15 Year Old Central Highlands SMSW (Scotland); 43% abv, $42.
Shows the golden sunshine hue of a sauternes; impeccable clarity. The opening aroma is more assertive than I remember as dry, almost peppery scents of barley husk, grainy oil, and cracked wheat wafer please my olfactory sense; seven more minutes in the copita bring out a mildly sweeter, slightly vanilla bean, brown rice-like side; it's concentrated and kernel-like by the nosing conclusion. The palate entry is pleasantly prickly, textured, and moderately sweet; at midpalate the taste profile turns stunningly sappy and resin-like. Finishes dry to off-dry and keenly resiny. I have always liked this malt for its resiny quality, which, at least to me, seems to come more from the malted barley than from the wood. Could be derived from both. Whatever the case, this Central Highlands malt has always delighted me.
2004 Rating: ★★★/Recommended

Dalwhinnie 29 Year Old Central Highlands SMSW (Scotland); 57.8% abv, $300.

The deep amber hue shows ideal clarity. The first couple of whiffs detect little in the way of distinctive aroma, other than a dull pine needle/graininess; reduction with H2O and a few more minutes in the copita serve this malt well as moderately rich scents of cucumber, heather, and mildly sweet malt emerge from behind the curtain of age. This malt performs its best when in the mouth; the palate entry is sinewy, creamy, even oily while the midpalate stage features delightfully cocoa-like tastes of milk chocolate, butter cream, linseed oil, and toffee. Finishes sweet, viscous, and long.

2004 Rating: ★★★/Recommended

Dalwhinnie Distiller's Edition 1990 Double Matured Oloroso Sherry Cask Finished Central Highlands SMSW (Scotland); 43% abv, $65.

The amber/harvest gold color is dazzling and flawless. The aroma has intriguing notes of marshmallow, cotton candy, and light toffee in the first sniffs; later whiffs pick up second wave aromas of candied almond and lanolin as the bouquet softens as it aerates. The palate entry is notable for its dry, malty, and slightly honeyed profile; at midpalate the taste turns richer and sweeter as the honey element intensifies, making the flavor almost bittersweet but long in the throat. Finishes concentrated on the malt and drier than in the midpalate stage. A dandy Central Highlands malt of distinction.

2006 Rating: ★★★★/Highly Recommended

Dewar's Aberfeldy 12 Year Old Central Highlands SMSW (Scotland); 40% abv, $40.

The color is old gold/sauternes-like, luminescent and flawlessly pure beneath the examination lamp. In the first nosing passes, I pick up lovely aromatic strands of baked yellow fruits (banana, pear, quince) and round, lightly toasted scents of malt; vibrant notes of new saddle leather get stimulated by further aeration and a few rounds of swirling and the yellow fruit follows suit, as well, making for a fresh, grainy bouquet experience. The palate entry offers wonderfully clean, crisp tastes of dry breakfast cereal in the form of lightly toasted barley malt; by the midpalate stage the dry to off-dry flavor profile expands to include oak-induced vanilla, light toffee, and nougat. Ends well on a woody note. As is the established Aberfeldy character, this vigorous yet polite malt is approachable and best served as a before-dinner appetite stimulant. Nice job here.

2007 Rating: ★★★/Recommended

Dewar's Aberfeldy 21 Year Old Central Highlands SMSW (Scotland); 40% abv, $170.

Topaz/medium-amber is the firm color; sterling clean appearance. The initial sniffings detect tart, yeasty aromas of barley malt and bread dough; an additional seven minute period of air contact bolsters the tart/sour aroma profile without adding anything deeper or more expansive. The palate entry is off-dry and a touch bittersweet in a caramel-like manner; at the midpalate stage the taste profile tends to the toasted cereal/toasted bread side of the scale and, to my surprise, doesn't offer much in the way of compelling single malt depth, considering its age. Finishes gracefully, dry, tart, crisp, and clean.

2007 Rating: ★★★/Recommended

Glen Elgin 32 Year Old Speyside SMSW (Scotland); 42.3% abv, £310.

Only available in the United Kingdom. Pretty, harvest gold/wheat field hue; absolute clarity. The unimpressive first sniffs pick up industrial aromas that bring to mind pine-scented cleaning fluid, bubble gum and inkwell; additional air contact plus dilution only accentuate the wax paper, candlestick, sour apple, and soap-like aromas; the Diageo guys must be kidding, I mean, c'mon, they can't be serious about this one. The palate entry, at least, shows some semblance of malt whisky in the mildly appealing forms of soft, if flabby, malt and baked pear; the midpalate stage is malty sweet but lackluster, over-the-hill, and weary. Finishes with a flash of industrial cleaner. Really, I'm serious now, Diageo sent this to me as a joke, right, huh, nudge-nudge, gotcha, nudge-nudge; may as well package this dishwater in the type of plastic squeeze-out container used for floor cleaners; calling Hans Blix, calling Hans Blix, I've finally found a WMD.
2004 Rating: ★/Not Recommended

Glen Garioch 10 Year Old Eastern Highlands SMSW (Scotland); 40% abv, $20.

Sauternes gold/amber hue; excellent purity. The initial sniffings are greeted by fresh, hay-like, malty aromas; aeration brings out deeper scents of honey, nougat, roasted almond, and heather. The palate entry is off-dry, clean, and resiny/oaky; the midpalate turns bittersweet as elegant tastes of honey, brown sugar, and oak dominate the flavor phase. The aftertaste is semisweet, candied, and honeyed, almost like candied walnuts. A nimble malt that's a superb before-dinner dram.
2002 Rating: ★★★/Recommended

Glen Garioch 1958 46 Year Old Eastern Highlands SMSW (Scotland); 43% abv, $2,600.

Only 43 bottles for the US (328 total for the world). The warm/autumnal harvest yellow/gold color is very appealing and is flawlessly pure. The first nosings pick up several layers of aroma, everything from spearmint to shale to wet cement to light toffee; seven more minutes of air contact stir up disparate yet strangely enmeshed scents including gum, white pears, cigarette ash, bay leaves, and pineapple. The palate entry is earthy/floral, herbal, and dry to off-dry; at midpalate the taste profile shows flavors of dry malt cereal, oak, vanilla bean, cocoa bean, and nougat. Ends up off-dry to bittersweet, balanced, intensely cereally, and admirably fresh and vivacious, considering the maturity.
2005 Rating: ★★★★/Highly Recommended

Glen Ord 28 Year Old Northern Highlands SMSW (Scotland); 58.3% abv, £180.

Only available in the United Kingdom. Attractive, golden/grain cracker color; perfect purity. The opening, undiluted sniffs detect lots of very pleasant grain mash, malty aromas that remind me somewhat of bran cereal mixed with honey and dried fruit; aeration and mineral water serve this malt well as the aroma turns mildly toasty, sherried, and heather honey-like. The palate entry is rich, concentrated and intensely honey-like; by midpalate the taste profile includes candied/fruity flavors of marzipan, dark toffee, and marmalade. Ends up hot (even with the water reduction), fruity, jammy, and semisweet. Like it, but don't love it; the spirit's density and vigor are impressive but so evident that they run the risk of trampling everything else of value.
2004 Rating: ★★★/Recommended

Glen Ord 30 Year Old Northern Highlands SMSW (Scotland); 58.7% abv, $275.
The pretty, bright gold hue shows some sediment, but not enough to be concerned about. The initial sniffs after the pour pick up spirity and grainy aromas that are forthright, if superficial; more time in the glass helps in bringing out moderately deeper aromas, including oak, palm oil, and tea. The palate entry displays a fiery core that's decorated with satellite flavors of moderately sweet grain and crackers; at midpalate the oak reemerges as a major taste element, moving past the grain; mineral water assists in stimulating pleasing tastes of light honey and light caramel. Finishes lean, assertive, and grainy.
2006 Rating: ★★★/Recommended

Glen Scotia 12 Year Old Campbeltown SMSW (Scotland); 43% abv, $66.
The appearance is gold/green/honey; superb purity. The strange aroma upfront is slightly seared/charred and nearly synthetic; further time in the copita allows it to gather itself as it then features maritime nuances of fish, seaweed, salt, and brine. The palate entry is more appealing than the aroma as the taste profile offers semisweet and salty flavors of kippers and saltwater taffy; the midpalate stage highlights the ocean influence as the taste turns more salty than sweet or grainy. Concludes tart, slightly medicinal. A good but hardly mindblowing malt that, to its severe disadvantage, shares a peninsula with another malt distillery by the name of Springbank.
2006 Rating: ★★★/Recommended

Glencadam 15 Year Old Eastern Highlands SMSW (Scotland); 40% abv, $70.
Pretty medium bronze hue; excellent purity. Displays spirity/warm aromas of toasted grain, burnt match, and holiday fruit cake in the initial inhalations; a few more minutes of swirling and aeration bring out roasted scents of baked pears, baked apple crisp, and burning candle; I like this fresh-out-of-the-oven, intensely grainy bouquet a lot. The palate entry is semisweet and lightly caramel-like; at midpalate there's more of a malty thrust as the taste profile turns a bit sour and astringent. Ends up sweet/sour, grainy, agile on the tongue, and medium-bodied. A very nice introductory Highlands malt.
2005 Rating: ★★★/Recommended

Glenfarclas 105 Speyside SMSW (Scotland); 60% abv, $75.
Deep bronze/copper/russet/tawny color; excellent purity; a stunningly lovely burnished appearance. The alluring, come-hither opening aroma offers scents of plum pudding/mince pie and dark caramel; seven more minutes of aeration time bring out roasted chestnut, beeswax, pork sausages, old saddle leather, and vanilla wafer; a tour de force bouquet that's surprisingly elegant as well as powerful. The taste at entry is heady, prickly, but sweet and sappy, almost candied; at midpalate man-sized doses of dark caramel, oloroso sherry, vanilla cream, and dark chocolate with a high cocoa content. Concludes as sizeable as it begins, with deep flavors of sweet oak, toffee, and butter cream. A remarkable heavyweight class single malt that fulfills expectations at each stage. Luscious, decadent single malt pleasure.
2005 Rating: ★★★★/Highly Recommended

Glenfarclas 17 Year Old Speyside SMSW (Scotland); 43% abv, $65.
The harvest gold/honey hue displays some sediment. Right out of the starting gate, the generous aroma emits muscle-bound scents of honey, oloroso sherry, and dark toffee;

aeration time serves to stimulate even broader, more oily aromas, most notably, nougat, roasted peanuts, brown butter, and very sharp cheddar. The palate entry treats the taste buds to mouth-filling flavors of sugar beet, chocolate/nut candy bar, maple, and oak; at midpalate the sweet/oaky taste profile expands to include marzipan and brandied cherries. Finishes beautifully, if a bit tight and suddenly reined-in. A true borderline four star/five star whisky. When I hesitate bestowing a fifth star, then I know it's a strong four star.
2005 Rating: ★★★★/Highly Recommended

Glenfiddich 12 Year Old Special Reserve Speyside SMSW (Scotland); 40% abv, $36.

The amber color is attractive and impeccably clean. The first nosing passes encounter scents of damp grain, wet cloth, and flax; aeration adds only ethereal notes of candle wax and distant yellow fruit. The palate entry is clean, lean, and mildly caramel-like; by the midpalate stage the taste profile takes on additional flavors like candied almond and walnut paste. Finishes light-bodied and moderately sweet in a dried apple/apricot manner. Good place to start for Scotch beginners.
2007 Rating: ★★★/Recommended

Glenfiddich 15 Year Old Solera Reserve Speyside SMSW (Scotland); 40% abv, $46.

The deep honey-like color is very pretty; superb clarity. The up-front aroma offers grainy/beany scents, with a backnote of paraffin; while I'd like to have a bit more aromatic substance here after aeration, the banana perfume is nice as is the subtle yeastiness. The palate entry tastes of baked banana and almond paste; the midpalate stage is notable for the deft touch of sweetness that's more dried fruit-like (white raisin) than honeyed and that's a plus. Ends up whistle clean, light-bodied, fresh.
2007 Rating: ★★★/Recommended

Glenfiddich 18 Year Old Ancient Reserve Speyside SMSW (Scotland); 43% abv, $62.

The bronze/honey color is immensely appealing and bright under the lamp; flawless purity. In the first couple of minutes after the pour, the nose emits tightly wound aromas of light caramel and unsweetened baker's chocolate; following another seven minutes of aeration, the bouquet turns slightly baked and caramelized, offering succulent fragrances of maple, old saddle leather, apricot pastry, and banana nut bread. The palate entry is supple, semisweet, and mildly honeyed; the midpalate stage features seriously delectable flavors of coconut, peach cobbler, and dark caramel. Concludes with beany notes of coffee and cocoa. A terrific malt.
2007 Rating: ★★★★/Highly Recommended

Glenfiddich 1937 Rare Collection Cask 843 Speyside SMSW (Scotland); 44% abv, $14,000.

Only 61 bottles are available worldwide and that IS the bottle price. Attractive medium amber color; superb purity. The initial nosing passes detect muffled scents of marzipan, dark caramel, and cheese; aeration doesn't release more, aromatically speaking, yet serves to deepen and broaden the existing aromas that suggest the presence of resiny/cheese-like rancio. The palate entry is dry to off-dry and mildly peaty/smoky; at midpalate there's an explosion of sweet oak, resiny, woody, tobacco leaf, and malty tastes that envelop the tongue. Finishes sweet, intense, woody/smoky. For only the most serious and moneyed of malt collectors.
2002 Rating: ★★★★/Highly Recommended

Glenfiddich 21 Year Old Gran Reserva Caribbean Rum Cask Speyside SMSW (Scotland); 40% abv, $120.

No longer able to sit on the sidelines, Glenfiddich now enters the wood-finish sweepstakes with this 21 year old malt that was "finished" in oak barrels that formerly held rum. The harvest gold color is eye-catching and immaculately pure. The opening aroma emits subtle, trademark Glenfiddich fragrances of cotton fiber, paraffin, and yellow fruit; aeration heightens the fruit element and brings in a slightly honeyed component. The palate entry is pleasingly lean, grainy sweet, honey-like, and floral; the midpalate stage keys more on the honey sweetness and oak and dispenses with the graininess and flowers. Finishes well and with medium concentration on the oak influence. Another worthy stable-mate for the Special Reserve, Glenfiddich's ubiquitous cash cow.

2007 Rating: ★★★★/Highly Recommended

Glenfiddich 30 Year Old Speyside SMSW (Scotland); 43% abv, $130.

Even though the color is medium amber/light honey, which seems light for such an elderly malt, the trademark Glenfiddich green tint is seen; excellent purity. The initial nosing pass offers dry, exotic, mature scents of almond butter and paraffin; the second sniffing finds added dashes of green and black pepper; in the third whiff, after six minutes of aeration, pleasing traces of lanolin, elderberry, and very mature oak are noted, filed, and admired for their subtlety; the fourth and last inhalation sees all the components meld into a single minded, overall dry, and crackling bouquet that has Speyside written all over it; savory, understated, significantly more complex than the 12 Year Old Special Reserve as one would expect. On the palate the entry nears being biscuity but ends up being more oaky and oily; the midpalate phase features calm, evolved tastes of lanolin, oak vanillin, and butterscotch. The aftertaste is leaner than I expected, but medium-long and woody. If I had to choose between the older Glenfiddichs, I'd most likely snatch the bulkier, meatier 18 Ancient Reserve, but this one is fine and elegant.

2000 Rating: ★★★★/Highly Recommended

Glenglassaugh 1960 44 Year Old Speyside SMSW (Scotland); 41.7% abv, $900.

The surprisingly light appearance displays a topaz/deep amber color and excellent purity. The nose is closed down throughout the first two minutes of inhalations; another seven minutes of aeration stir only rudimentary, if distant scents of malt and wood; just not a lot to show for the aroma, period. The palate entry completely counters the anemic bouquet by offering succulent, marshmallow-sweet tastes of candy, cream, marzipan, and butter; the midpalate stage goes even deeper as the oak impact becomes more apparent in the honeyed, sherried, vanilla and cocoa butter flavors that enchant the taste buds. Concludes smooth as buttah and cocoa-like. Just skip the aroma and dive right into the taste.

2006 Rating: ★★★★/Highly Recommended

Glengoyne 17 Year Old Central Highlands SMSW (Scotland); 43% abv, $75.

The autumnal gold/honey color is clean and pure. The plump aroma after the pour is round, fat, fruity, and malty; with six more minutes of aeration under its belt the bouquet adds alluring nuances of apple crisp, brown butter, and honey/sherry. The palate entry is whistle clean, grainy sweet, and slightly oaky; at midpalate the flavor profile deepens as tastes of marzipan, nougat, candied apple, and bacon fat get added to the flavor list. Concludes gracefully and balanced. An elegant malt whose trademark maltiness is most attractive in an age littered by malts that are too old, too brawny, or too unwhisky-like.

2005 Rating: ★★★/Highly Recommended

Glengoyne Scottish Oak Wood Finish Central Highlands SMSW (Scotland); 43% abv, $66.

Very pale gold/straw yellow; pure. The opening aroma is soft, malty and even a dash peppery; the bouquet deepens considerably after about the eighth minute in the glass, emitting succulent scents of light caramel, marshmallow and almond butter. The palate entry is tight, lean and gently sweet and malty; the midpalate stage shows lovely, moderately complex flavors of cocoa, black coffee, oak resin. and cake frosting. The aftertaste is long, grainy sweet and austere. Lean, mean and tasty.

2002 Rating: ★★/Recommended

Glenkinchie 10 Year Old Lowlands SMSW (Scotland); 43% abv, $38.

The appearance is clean, clear, and a pretty amber hue. The first couple of nosing passes unveil a malty, grainy, moderately sweet bouquet; aeration fails to stir any other notable aspects of this rudimentary, mildly appetizing bouquet. The palate entry is semisweet, weedy, and vegetal; in the midpalate the grain comes to the fore and repairs some of the damage done by the awkward entry. Ends on a grainy, husk-like note that's bittersweet. Always considered the idiot sister in comparison to the graceful malts from Lowlands distilleries such as Rosebank, Bladnoch, or the great Auchentoshan. I was prepared to give it the benefit of the doubt but then, that nasty, astringent, thumbprint flavor reared its ugly head in the midpalate and BINGO, one star. Want Lowlands? Go with any Auchentoshan.

2004 Rating: ★/Not Recommended

Glenkinchie Distiller's Edition 1991 Double Matured Amontillado Sherry Cask Finished Lowlands SMSW (Scotland); 43% abv, $65.

The amber/gold color is firm and clear. The aroma is muted at first, then grapy/fruity and like dried yellow fruit and gum after aeration; it's a bouquet of a slightly narrow focus, but pleasing all the same. The palate entry is stone dry, mineral-like, showing just a dash of woodiness; at midpalate the taste profile turns more concentrated, malty, oaky and lightly honeyed. Becomes sweeter in the aftertaste, going quite grainy with a bit of harshness in the fiery finish.

2006 Rating: ★★★/Recommended

Glenlivet: *See The Glenlivet*

Glenmorangie 10 Year Old Northern Highlands SMSW (Scotland); 43% abv, $35.

The pale straw/gold color shines brightly in the glass and is unblemished. The first sniffings detect delicate notes of candied apple, light toffee, and pear drops; further aeration adds nuances of rose petals, carnations, and lightly toasted malt; it's a fey aroma, with ethereal charms. The palate entry is grainy and moderately sweet; at midpalate there's a burst of red pepper that's backed by more composed tastes of pears, peaches, mushroom, old attic, and cigar tobacco. Ends cleanly and lithely. Have always liked this airy, bright and deceptively complex 10 year old.

2004 Rating: ★★★/Recommended

Glenmorangie 12 Year Old Madeira Wood Finish Northern Highlands SMSW (Scotland); 43% abv, $45.

The amber/gold/green appearance is pure and spotless. I prefer this fruity/candied opening aroma more than the Port Wood Finish's because it's deeper and more fleshy, meaning there's more grip; seven minutes of settling in the glass brings out toasty/rubber pencil eraser/slightly charred notes that are seductive and appealing. The palate entry is warm, smoldering, moderately smoky and pipe tobacco sweet; at midpalate the taste profile turns milky/creamy/buttery and decidedly toffee/fudge sweet. Ends up like chocolate covered cherries, chocolate fudge, and honey. I think this malt has improved over time and now runs with the exquisite sherry finishes, though this malt is meatier and huskier than the delicate, feline sherries.

2004 Rating: ★★★★/Highly Recommended

Glenmorangie 12 Year Old Port Wood Finish Northern Highlands SMSW (Scotland); 43% abv, $45.

The honey/topaz hue owns a pretty orange/russet core; impeccably pure. The initial whiffs find winey notes of ripe fruit and nuts; six more minutes in the copita serve to unleash moderately deeper but not profound scents, especially maple, vanilla, spice, and green apple. The palate entry is biscuity, sweet, and sap-like; at midpalate flavors range from vanilla to old oak to maple to nutmeg to cocoa. Concludes sweetly, porty, and racy.

2004 Rating: ★★★/Recommended

Glenmorangie 15 Year Old Northern Highlands SMSW (Scotland); 43% abv, $90.

The highly attractive honey brown/topaz/harvest gold color is dazzling, yet there shows up under the evaluation lamp small clouds of transparent particles; what gives? The opening nosing detects very little in the way of aroma other than a delicate maltiness; the second pass reveals precious little while the third sniffing at last picks up some peppery wood resin; the fourth and final whiff, following nine minutes of exposure to air, unearths deeper scents of marzipan, vanilla bean, and biscuit batter. The palate entry is creamy, almost buttery, and amazingly elegant; at the midpalate juncture a complex network of flavors, including caramel, apple butter, glycerin, and honey, transfixes the taste buds. The aftertaste features a startling fruitiness that's lusciously ripe and very extended. Yet another superior display of distilling mastery from Tain.

2000 Rating: ★★★★/Highly Recommended

Glenmorangie 18 Year Old Northern Highlands SMSW (Scotland); 43% abv, $99.

The brilliant autumnal gold/Tupelo honey hue is gorgeous and flawlessly clean. The opening nosing passes after the pour find several layers of aroma including honey, flowers (heather? jasmine?) and light toffee; seven minutes of additional exposure to air stimulate broad aromatic strokes of pine needle, caramel, nougat, marzipan, chocolate orange, and stewed apple; an amazing romp through the mystical land of barley malt and wood aroma.

The palate entry is dry as a bone then, to my delight, it runs bittersweet and pork rind-like; at midpalate the flavor profile combines tastes of burnt apple crisp, orange zest, fudge and candied nuts. Finishes as grandly and stately as it began. Continues to be one of the most luscious, satisfying and complex 18 year old malts in the marketplace.
2004 Rating: ★★★★/Highly Recommended

Glenmorangie 1977 Northern Highlands SMSW (Scotland); 43% abv, $200.

This malt was bottled at 21 years of age. The pale straw color is accented by blemish-free purity; the first sniffs detect an immediate rush of heather, green pepper, and sweet grain; seven minutes of further aeration allow the aroma to expand into a dry, softly peated bouquet that shows delicate hints of unsweetened coconut, banana cream, light toffee, and smoke. The palate entry is very resiny/woody right out of the gate; at midpalate there's a gentle sting of mature spirit on the tongue and lots of biscuity, sweet barley malt that rings with echoes of honey and vanilla. The finish is long, sweet, malty, and honeyed. A Northern Highlands malt whisky that is at the height of its powers; a brilliant job of cask selection, to be sure.
2003 Rating: ★★★★/Highly Recommended

Glenmorangie 1981 Sauternes Wood Finish Northern Highlands SMSW (Scotland); 46% abv, $300.

This 20 year old malt spent its last 2½ years of maturation in grand cru sauternes barrels. Striking harvest/honey gold color; ideal purity. The nose right off the crack of the bat is ambrosial and earthy as evolved scents of banana cream, pistachio, almond, and maple take the olfactory sense to higher planes of pleasure; aeration of another eight minutes only sees the bouquet reach phenomenal heights as the fruit component goes wild, offering rich aromas of baked pear, baked apple, maple syrup, and English toffee; a genuinely sensational bouquet. The palate entry is divinely rich, thick yet keenly balanced because of the acid presence; by the midpalate stage the flavors of honey, vanilla extract, banana cream, egg cream, and coconut are off the charts. Finishes warm, fruity, and grand. The 16 Men of Tain continue to dazzle us with their inventiveness and vision; I'm thrilled to be on this wood experiment adventure with them as a consumer.
2003 Rating: ★★★★★/Highest Recommendation

Glenmorangie 1987 Margaux Cask Finish Northern Highlands SMSW (Scotland); 46% abv, $399-499.

The auburn/copper color shows ruby highlights in the core; some sediment spotted under the examination lamp. The biscuity aroma after the pour seduces the olfactory sense in buttery, butterscotch-like waves that are luxurious and moderately baked/toasty; following seven minutes of additional air contact, the aroma transforms itself into a comely, stately bouquet that's long on red fruit/red berry scents and slightly resiny oak notes that are accented by black pepper and stone. The palate entry is delightfully fruity/wine-like and semisweet; at the midpalate stage the taste profile turns delectably sap- and vine-like, with subtle touches of maple and light caramel. Finishes gracefully and with a sap-like chewiness that's sensually pleasing, if not classical in nature. Another wood-finish gem from the 16 Men of Tain.
2007 Rating: ★★★★/Highly Recommended

Glenmorangie 21 Year Old Northern Highlands SMSW (Scotland); 43% abv, $400.
Comes packaged in a special crystal glass decanter handblown in Scotland. The pale amber color is tinged with yellow/green highlights; perfect purity. The sweet, soft, flowery nose after the pour is remarkably evolved and compelling; in the second pass, subtle hints of grass, hay, and wet earth are featured; by the third whiff, following eight minutes of aeration, the aroma exhibits just the slightest note of peat, backed by sweet malt; the final sniffing offers delicate, almost feminine scents of violets, malt, and heather. The elegance of this whisky is immediately apparent at palate entry as the polite flavors of malt and light oak enchant rather than bulldoze the taste buds; the midpalate point shows tastes that are mature and firm, yet delicate and harmonious. The finish is brief, to my surprise a touch smoky, and totally dry. A savory, agile, light-on-its-feet malt that's more José Carreras than Placido Domingo.
2000 Rating: ★★★★/Highly Recommended

Glenmorangie Burgundy Wood Finish Northern Highlands SMSW (Scotland); 43% abv, $55.
Atypical soft amber pear/peach color with orange/pink core; very good purity. The first whiffs pick up zesty, full notes of pork sausage, pork rind, green olive, and peanuts; by the end of the aeration term, notes of baked pears, sesame oil, and buttered popcorn highlight the bouquet, with background traces of dried herbs and fennel. At palate entry, there's a firm, moderately oily, semisweet taste of pear; at midpalate the pear presence expands on the tongue; medium viscosity. Ends up buttery, silky if a bit fey. A very good malt for aficionados of lighter, less dense malt styles.
2004 Rating: ★★★/Recommended

Glenmorangie Côte de Nuits Wood Finish Northern Highlands SMSW (Scotland); 43% abv, $300.
The whisky was distilled in 1975 and finished for an unspecified period in red Burgundy barrels; 2,000 bottles available worldwide, 480 for the US. The striking color rides the fence between bronze and copper, with a slight edge going to reddish copper; the opening aromas are amazingly biscuity, wine-like, and fatty, as in bacon fat; after several minutes in the sampling glass, the stunning bouquet offers scents of black raisins, burnt match, and linseed oil; perhaps the finest, most idiosyncratic and complete bouquet yet from the Glenmorangie "wood finish" program to date. The entry tastes of wine, oaky resin, roasted almonds, dried fruit, and malt blanket the taste buds; in the midpalate a flash of dark caramel-hard cheese-vanilla extract rancio elevates the flavor experience to the divine nectar category. The aftertaste is buttery, creamy, nutty, and oily. A perfect single malt whisky.
2001 Rating: ★★★★★/Highest Recommendation

Glenmorangie Fino Sherry Wood Finish Northern Highlands SMSW (Scotland); 43% abv, $90.
This fine malt was first matured in new American white oak casks for 13 years before being transferred to old sherry butts that formerly held fino sherry. The golden yellow/bright amber color is very attractive; very minor debris spotted. The nose in the initial pass is tangy and dry; the second pass reveals desirable touches of fino sherry yeastiness and oiliness; the

third sniffing offers delicate, even subtle, nuances of white wine, oak, and distant malt; the fourth and last whiff, which ends up totally dry and even lean, unearths traces of light toffee and almonds; a deft, agile bouquet that's a world apart in dryness/sweetness and texture from the regular Sherry Wood Finish bottling of Glenmorangie (★★★★). The palate entry is a dazzler as oily, nutty, and intensely malty flavors greet the taste buds in a marvelous display of panache; the midpalate point is mildly sweet, even a tad fiery (to my pleasure), and deliciously nutty; but it's the oily, satiny texture that I love so much. The aftertaste is long, almondy, only moderately malty sweet, and warming. Yet another sleek thoroughbred in the Glenmorangie stable.

2000 Rating: ★★★★/Highly Recommended

Glenmorangie Tain L'Hermitage Wood Finish Northern Highlands SMSW (Scotland); 46% abv, $200.

The brilliant orange/new copper penny color seduces the eye; perfect purity. In the first nosing passes after the pour, library aromas of hard wood and worn leather abound; after another seven minutes in the glass, the bouquet shifts into fifth gear as succulent notes of oak resin, nut loaf, light toffee, and citrus impress the olfactory sense with their harmonious display. The palate entry is focused, winey, and lusciously sweet; by the midpalate stage the taste profile has added somewhat bittersweet flavors of caramel, nougat, candy bar, and sap. Concludes elegantly, sweet, integrated, and tight as a snare drum. Runs with their best of the best offerings, like the 1981 Sauternes Wood Finish, the Côte de Nuits Wood Finish, and the First Growth Claret Wood Finish.

2005 Rating: ★★★★★/Highest Recommendation

Glenmorangie The Lasanta Extra Matured Range Sherry Cask Non-Chill Filtered Northern Highlands SMSW (Scotland); 46% abv, $65.

Butterscotch/gold/marigold hue; superb clarity. Right out of the gate, the stately aroma reminds me of butter cream candies; further air contact reveals deeper scents of melon, white raisins, dried yellow plums, and fudge. Entry is sublimely honey-sweet, ripe, and intensely fruity (especially dried white/yellow fruits, such as banana, pineapple, pear); the midpalate is long, luxurious, satiny, honeyed, eggy, fruity, and perfectly balanced. Concludes on vividly depicted high notes of sherry, apricot, white raisins, and light toffee. A winner.

2007 Rating: ★★★★/Highly Recommended

Glenmorangie The Nectar D'Or Extra Matured Range Sauternes Cask Non-Chill Filtered Northern Highlands SMSW (Scotland); 46% abv, $75.

18-carat gold/straw/maize color; flawless clarity. Dazzlingly smells of smoky, slightly burnt nectarine and/or apricot in the initial inhalations; additional exposure to air brings about buttery/creamy scents that are bakery reminiscent, toasty, nutty, and heavenly. Entry is chewy, viscous, concentrated, and intensely honeyed; the midpalate is long, waxy/oily, mildly spicy, grapy/jammy, nutty, and rub-my-body-with-it sensationally delicious and utterly decadent. Ends up more acidic and focused than the midpalate, but all the better as it finishes with panache and grace. The pick of the new litter.

2007 Rating: ★★★★★/Highest Recommendation

Glenmorangie The Quarter Century 25 Year Old Northern Highlands SMSW (Scotland); 43% abv, $850.

Dusty gold/old Burgundy yellow hue; unblemished purity. Smells of cookie/biscuit batter in the opening sniffs; seven more minutes of continued aeration stimulate somewhat reluctant scents of honeycomb, light toffee, and mild oak; not a great deal to grip onto here. This whisky saves its best shot for the entry as deep, rich, and succulent tastes of butter cream, light caramel, and honey rule the early roost; the midpalate offers lip-smacking viscosity, whipped egg white, creamy flavor and enough oak-influenced vanilla to capture the taste buds' attention for an extended period of joy. Finishes a bit too short and sap-like. The power and regal presence of the entry and midpalate aren't enough to alleviate my concerns about the brevity of the aftertaste and the hesitancy of the bouquet. Very good, but I'd still go with the more complete package offered by the Glenmorangie 18.

2007 Rating: ★★★/Recommended

Glenmorangie The Quinta Ruban Extra Matured Range Port Cask Non-Chill Filtered Northern Highlands SMSW (Scotland); 46% abv, $70.

Coral pink/rose-like color; ideal clarity. Emits delicate, mildly spicy, and grapy/juicy fragrances in the first aromatic go-round; additional time in the glass fails to open up any more aromatics. Entry is peppery, spicy, astringent, and tangy; the midpalate is moderately sweet, grapy, ripe, and succulently honeyed, no, almost sugary towards the finish. Ends up sweet and very likable. I'm never wild about port finishes but I like them. I always prefer sherry or Madeira as a fortified wine finish to a whisky.

2007 Rating: ★★★/Recommended

Glenrothes 1974 Speyside SMSW (Scotland); 43% abv, $95.

The rich amber/deep honey color is very attractive in the glass; very minor sediment seen. The opening nosing passes unearth typically deep, moderately smoky, and robust aromas of old oak and peat; eight minutes of further air contact add hearty, but refined notes of black pepper, road tar, maple, dark-roasted malt, and brown sugar; a fully engaged bouquet. The palate entry is sweet, honey-like, and very dark caramel-like; at midpalate the taste profile highlights more of the caramel and honey than other flavors and the velvety texture is state-of-the-art. The aftertaste features a peppery, cocoa-like, and sherry sweet taste that concludes the total experience extremely well. I've admired this heart of Speyside distillery for fifteen years but I believe that I've just sampled the finest malt whisky that it's yet released.

2003 Rating: ★★★★★/Highest Recommendation

Glenrothes 1987 12 Year Old Speyside SMSW (Scotland); 43% abv, $50.

The light honey/amber tint has Speyside plastered all over it; immaculate clarity. The first whiff hints at buttered walnuts, pine nuts, caramel, and bourbon casks; middle stage nosings reveal a keen dryness, almost a heathery quality that's stately and composed; seven minutes out of the bottle, this aroma transforms into a politely opulent bouquet whose primary virtues are serene scents of sautéed nuts, pine, mild oak, and a judicious touch of peaty smoke; a grand, poised bouquet that represents the best of Speyside greatness. The palate entry is dry, woody, and slightly resiny/sappy; the midpalate stage shows flavors of

oak that are approaching sweetness, malt, and a delicate nuttiness. The finish is elegant, dry, medium long, and supple. Another understated winner from this outstanding distillery.
2001 Rating: ★★★★/Highly Recommended

Glenrothes 1989 Speyside SMSW (Scotland); 40% abv, $50.

Pretty honey gold; ideal purity. The beckoning nose at opening doesn't speak of anything but buttery grain; with time in the glass, the aroma adds resiny oak, butterscotch, and linseed oil in the second run-through; in the third sniffing, delicate notes of black pepper and peat mingle with the malt and oak; the fourth and final pass, after ten minutes of aeration, detects no lessening of potency and adds light toffee; one of Speyside's more elegant and nuanced bouquets. The palate entry is resiny and dry; then at midpalate the flavors take on a sweeter lean, especially the vanilla and butterscotch tastes. The aftertaste is long, oaky sweet, and a touch caramelly; right in step with the other expressions that I've enjoyed over the years; bravo.
2001 Rating: ★★★★/Highly Recommended

Glenrothes Select Reserve Speyside SMSW (Scotland); 40% abv, $45.

The corn yellow color is pale and pretty; superb clarity. The opening sniffings detect lots of fruit, especially banana and apricot; seven minutes more in the glass afford it time to release its grainy scents that are mildly sweet if timid, even frail; a serious departure from what I normally expect from a Glenrothes bouquet. The palate entry is affably sweet and breakfast cereal grainy; at the midpalate stage the flavor profile showcases the sweet grain mash in the attractive, if simple forms of vanilla and toffee. Ends well on a mildly spicy, candied note. The lightest, least complex Glenrothes I've ever tasted and a far cry from the established style. I'm all for experimentation as evidenced by my full backing of Macallan's Fine Oak program, but the proof has to be in the bottle and at least on par with what's gone on before. Good enough to be recommended, to be sure because of the pedigree, but why emulate Glenfiddich 12 when you're Glenrothes? I can't help but ask.
2007 Rating: ★★★/Recommended

Glenury Royal 50 Year Old Eastern Highlands SMSW (Scotland); 42.8% abv, £950.

Only available in the United Kingdom. The deep bay/nut-brown/mahogany color speaks of the advanced age of this malt; superb clarity. The first whiffs detect distant aromas of coffee grounds, sour apple and cocoa; at this abv I choose not to reduce with water; aeration stimulates some latent fragrances, especially figs, dates, and raisins; not a memorable, earthshaking bouquet, but nice, mature, and fruity. This old geezer saves its best for the taste phase as the palate entry offers sap-like, rum-like tastes of maple, molasses, and brown sugar; the midpalate flashes traces of cinnamon, holiday spices, oloroso sherry, honey, and cigar box. Finishes thick, sweet, and intensely honeyed. Because of its maturity I really wanted to find myself screaming, "Bravo! Encore! Encore!" but in the end I came to the cold-hearted conclusion that I merely liked it; yes, it's a historical record of a long-closed (1985) Eastern Highlands distillery, but taking it on face value, it's only a very good, very old malt whisky and not a classic, very old malt whisky.
2004 Rating: ★★★/Recommended

Highland Park 12 Year Old Orkneys SMSW (Scotland); 43% abv, $40.

The yellow-gold/marigold color reminds me of an old vintage montrachet; absolute clarity. The opening nosing passes detect moderate salinity against an aromatic backdrop of oak, toasted cereal grain, and dried flowers; another seven minutes of exposure to air reveal even deeper (is that possible?) aromatic profile that's assertive yet welcoming, sweetish yet cereal dry, and oaky yet floral and a touch briny; the quintessential 12 year old malt bouquet. The palate entry is elegance itself as the integrated flavors greet the taste buds in taste waves of toasted walnut, dark caramel, toasted marshmallow, and barely perceptible seaweed; the midpalate stage takes all of these flavors deeper and adds honey. If the miraculous Highland Park 18 Year Old wasn't already my favorite distilled spirit of all time, this classic might well be.

2007 Rating: ★★★★/Highest Recommendation

Highland Park 15 Year Old Orkney Islands SMSW (Scotland); 43% abv, $55.

The wheat field/topaz color is pretty; unblemished purity. The first sniffings encounter lightly toasted malt notes that are off-dry and breakfast cereal-like; aeration time of another seven minutes releases more vigorous scents, including wood, sawdust, distant mint, and light caramel; for Highland Park, this is not the most expressive bouquet. It's in the mouth that this malt shifts into passing gear as the palate entry highlights the keen, husk-like, off-dry to semisweet maltiness; by the midpalate stage the taste profile goes much sweeter as a honey-like element enters the flavor equation, rounding out the grain/malt base component. Concludes in an assertive, spirity mode that underlines the honeyed sweetness. While my all-time favorite remains the HP 18, which incidentally is my choice as the best distilled spirit available at present, this noteworthy 15 displays the trademark HP finesse balanced beautifully by the grain/malt foundation and the clearly evident spirit.

2006 Rating: ★★★/Highly Recommended

Highland Park 18 Year Old Orkney Islands SMSW (Scotland); 43% abv, $79.

Maize/Indian corn gold color; flawless purity. Opening aromas remind me acutely of sea breeze, cigar smoke, old oak, and malted barley; seven more minutes of air contact release bigger, more complex scents, including light caramel, fudge, cocoa bean, paraffin, palm oil, burnt candle wick, and heather. Entry is the finest, most complete, most complex, most satisfying of any whiskey in the world; the midpalate soars to ridiculous heights on the wings of seamlessly melded oak, spirit, and grain; a masterpiece of precision, ideal maturation, and subtle grandeur in the mouth. Finishes with finesse, grace, and maritime power. One of a kind. The world's greatest distilled spirit at the present time. Buy whatever you can find.

2007 Rating: ★★★★/Highest Recommendation

Highland Park 1958 Orkney Islands SMSW (Scotland); 44% abv, $2,000.

Please note that I sampled this malt at the Highland Park Distillery in the Orkney Islands while barrel sampling in the aging warehouse, not at the SJ tasting facility. The amazing color is a profoundly deep copper/burnished orange hue, with bronze core highlights; ideal clarity. The opening bouquet is lush, ripe with incredible yellow fruit notes, and even a hint of toast; the second and third passes offer deep aromas of butterscotch, dark caramel, and cigar smoke; the last nosing pass after over ten minutes of air contact, adds notes of cigar box and marzipan. The palate entry is fiery and prickly, but smooth and agile, reminding me almost

of an eau-de-vie in its suppleness; by the midpalate point layers of flavor, including smoke, caramel, charcoal, and intensely sweet malt blanket the taste buds. The aftertaste is extended, satiny, warm like embers, and stately as only Highland Park can be. A real, rare treat of the first magnitude.
2000 Rating: ★★★★★/Highest Recommendation

Highland Park 25 Year Old Orkney Islands SMSW (Scotland); 48.1% abv, $230.

Amber/topaz/honey color; impeccable clarity. Immediately smells smoky/peaty out of the gate, along with nuances of sea salt, flowers, cookie batter, and light toffee; following seven more minutes of air contact, the elevated spirit makes itself known in spades as the aroma kicks up a couple of gears becoming woody, nutty (nougat), pastry-like, and buttery. Entry is oily, oaky, and richly peppery and salty; the midpalate is where all the components merge into a crescendo of elegant and potent maritime single malt flavors. Concludes spirity, near fiery, and with a parting taste of chocolate covered almonds. Along with HP 12, 18, and 30, the finest product line in all of whiskey.
2007 Rating: ★★★★★/Highest Recommendation

Highland Park 30 Year Old Orkneys SMSW (Scotland); 48.1% abv, $350.

The deep honey brown/bronze appearance is eye-catching and impeccably clean. The immediate aroma following the pour rings with subtle aromas of unsweetened coconut, bacon fat, and dark toffee; after seven minutes more in the copita, toastier, more roasted scents get added and they include honey wheat bread, dates, fruit pastry (apple crisp, in particular), toasted marshmallow, and oak. The palate entry is lusciously rich, even opulent in texture but still contains enough acidity to be fresh; the midpalate point features stunningly elegant, yet substantial flavors of bacon fat, dark honey, fudge, and bittersweet chocolate; a tour de force in the mouth that keeps unfolding for many minutes after the entry. The finish is long, toffee-like, and graceful. What can I say about this stellar Orkney Islands distillery that I haven't said many times before? The classiest act in distillery Scotland.
2005 Rating: ★★★★★/Highest Recommendation

Highland Park 38 Year Old Split Single Cask No. 10255 Distilled in 1967 Orkneys SMSW (Scotland); 55.5% abv, $2,000.

The color is deep straw/old gold; excellent clarity. The first nosings pick up intriguing traces of old fireplace and ash, but the spirit is aggressive and quickly drowns out the smoke/soot notes; swirling and further aeration stimulate more typical HPark scents of saltine cracker, honey, vanilla, and pine. The palate entry is strong, vibrant yet honey sweet and baked/glazed banana-like; I add some mineral water before proceeding to the midpalate stage; the midpalate is spirity, oaky, moderately briny, resiny, and keenly honeyed. Concludes warming, round, honey sweet, toffee-like, and focused.
2007 Rating: ★★★★/Highly Recommended

Inchmurrin 12 Year Old (Loch Lomond Distillery) Central Highlands SMSW (Scotland); 43% abv, $59.

Solid yellow straw color; flawless purity. The initial sniffs pick up loads of grainy/cereal-like character that's very flannel-like, but not much more than that; the cereal/fiber scent gives way to grassy and vegetal aromas, including peas, hay, and kale. The palate entry offers modest and timid tastes of dry breakfast cereal and grain crackers; the midpalate stage opens the flavor profile up a tad more by offering more succulent tastes of honey, caramel, and almond butter. Ends up slightly minty. Easy to drink, but lacks charm.

2006 Rating: ★★/Not Recommended

Inverarity "Ancestral" 14 Year Old Sherry Cask Speyside SMSW (Scotland); 40% abv, $60.

The very attractive, deep topaz/bronze tone is so typical of exclusive sherry cask aging; ideal purity. The aroma at opening is rich, marshmallow-like, and a tad nut-like; the second pass seems considerably sweeter than the first as the nuttiness turns into a toastiness; the third sniffing is full of ripe red fruit and dark caramel; the fourth and last whiff offers emerging rancio and a bit of wine and roses; a solid, sound sherry bouquet. The palate entry is sweet and oily; the midpalate stage is notable for its stately bearing, rich nuttiness, and sweet maltiness, all of which float upon the base flavor of sherry oak. The finish is long, pleasingly sweet, and oily. While easily recommendable due to its sweet, supple, if pedestrian, character, I didn't find in the final analysis an abundance of complexity to it considering that it was matured solely in sherry casks for 14 years; greater layering and depth of spirit would have earned it a fourth rating star quite easily; sweetness alone isn't enough.

2000 Rating: ★★★/Recommended

Isle of Jura "Superstition" Isle of Jura SMSW (Scotland); 45% abv, $38.

Honey/gold hue; excellent purity. Right away in the opening moments of inhalation I can tell that this aroma is a brawny, salty, lightly smoky departure from the typically polite and delicate Jura bouquet which usually features sweet grain; six more minutes of aeration see the aroma pick up hearty notes of peanut butter, baked apple and sea salt plus a deft touch of cigar tobacco. The taste at palate entry is robust, briny and sweet; by midpalate flavors of sweet cereal grain, buttered and salted popcorn, quince and nougat provide plenty of textural and taste depth. The aftertaste is long, buttery, oily and semisweet. A seriously distinct Jura that's leagues away from the Jura 16 (★★★★) in style.

2003 Rating: ★★★★/Highly Recommended

Isle of Jura 15 Year Old Isle of Jura SMSW (Scotland); 57.6% abv, £n/a.

Only available at the Isle of Jura Distillery. The lovely burnishes orange/dusty brown color offers excellent purity. The first nosings pick up ultra-toasty, amazingly tantalizing smells of wheat toast, nougat, roasted nuts, dried tropical fruit, roasted pork, and breakfast cereal; the later sniffings following seven minutes of aeration find generous scents of marzipan, treacle, baked banana, oak char, bacon fat, and the beginnings of rancio; an aromatic gem. The palate entry is fat, spiritedly zesty, and semisweet; at midpalate the flavor rush is directed towards dark caramel, aged tawny port, cheese, and old oak. Finishes with the flourish of spirit and toffee-like notes. Add water prior to tasting. Now the defining bottling of Isle of Jura, in my personal Scotch whisky book.

2005 Rating: ★★★★★/Highest Recommendation

Isle of Jura 16 Year Old Isle of Jura SMSW (Scotland); 40% abv, $44.

The pretty honey/topaz color is marred by too much floating debris; when I held up the clear glass bottle to the evaluation lamp the contents showed a virtual flotilla of whitish suspended particles. Looking on the bright side, the opening sniffing offers deliciously toasty and sweet aromas of malt and mild sea breeze (this is an island malt after all); with development in the glass the aroma becomes a true malt bouquet by the second pass, emitting succulent scents of marzipan, light toffee, mild salt, and cake batter; the sea breeze/brine element comes seriously alive by the third whiff as it takes the helm and changes the direction of the bouquet into brinier, deeper waters; the last pass is all about mild peat, sea salt, and sweet malt; this meaty, substantial bouquet really grew on me as it aerated and unfolded like layers of an onion. The palate entry is unabashedly sweet and back-slappingly expansive; the midpalate stage is friendly, intensely malty, toffee sweet and round, bordering on voluptuous; curiously the brininess so evident in the bouquet vanishes on the tongue. The aftertaste is medium-long, caramel sweet, and biscuity. A major league step up for Jura from the leaner, simpler, albeit cuddly and Highland-like, 10 year old (★★★★) bottling.

2000 Rating: ★★★★/Highly Recommended

Isle of Jura Twenty One 21 Year Old Isle of Jura SMSW (Scotland); 43% abv, $129.

The deep topaz/burnished orange color is lovely to look at and totally sediment free; gorgeous. The assertive aroma at the front end is concentrated, grainy dry, yet floral and lightly nutty, especially with notes of Brazil nut and walnut; another seven minutes of exposure to air stirs up vibrant scents of buttered honeywheat toast, sautéed almonds, cigar tobacco, and buttermilk. Much as I adore the bouquet, the taste is even more exciting; the palate entry is sap- and maple-like in its botanical sweetness; by the midpalate stage the roasted/toasty flavor profile runs from chocolate milk to nougat to milk chocolate to oatmeal-with-honey. Finishes with grace but more than ample late taste thrust. The new benchmark for this under-rated island malt distillery.

2006 Rating: ★★★★★/Highest Recommendation

Ladyburn 1973 Single Cask Bottle No. 89 Lowland SMSW Rare Whisky Collection (Scotland); 50.4% abv, $649.

Never one of my favorite malt distilleries, I was anxious to sample this rare and extremely expensive Lowlands offering; the facility was operational only from 1966-1976 as part of the Girvan grain distillery. Shows a pretty goldenrod/hay hue. Minor sediment noted; the opening nosings over two minutes detect peculiar, but pleasant scents of oatmeal, grape must and guava; aeration encourages even more fruitiness to emerge; not a complex bouquet, but appealing all the same. Much more developed and complex in the mouth as the palate entry starts with a bang of ripe, fruity, grainy tastes; by the midpalate point the flavor profile teems with rich, biscuity, cake-like flavors and a firm sweetness. The aftertaste is long, off-dry and warming. The best Ladyburn I've had; is it worth the hefty price tag? Only for the most avid collectors with very deep pockets.

2003 Rating: ★★★/Recommended

Lagavulin 12 Year Old Islay SMSW (Scotland); 57.8% abv, $250.

The pale yellow/lemon juice color is unblemished. The first whiffs pick up gently sweet notes of wine grapes, then following aeration the vigorous, youthful bouquet sports smoky, peaty scents of bonfire, sweet pipe tobacco, and kippers. The palate entry is firm, moderately oily, and lightly smoked; the midpalate stage offers racy flavors of toasted marshmallow, vanilla bean, honey, and dark, bittersweet chocolate. Finishes warm, spirity without being prickly, and sinewy. A sexy sophisticate that's long on style and charm.

2004 Rating: ★★★★/Highly Recommended

Lagavulin 16 Year Old Islay SMSW (Scotland); 43% abv, $55.

The deep bronze color is eye-catching; excellent purity. The opening aroma is rife with scents of soy sauce, olive brine, peat, and honey; seven more minutes unleash a whole other universe of mature aroma, one that features oloroso sherry, brewer's yeast, bread dough, barley malt, and cigar smoke; a memorable nosing experience. The entire flavor phase, from palate entry through midpalate, defines "classy Islay," that lovely maritime location that magically includes the innate intense peatiness of Islay malts and the masterly employment of oak barrels; a perfect marriage. Concludes sweetly, without sacrificing the tangy, astringent peatiness that is inherent. An elegant malt that artfully navigates the waters between Ardbeg and Laphroaig on one side and Bowmore and Caol Ila on the other. Gorgeous.

2004 Rating: ★★★★/Highly Recommended

Laphroaig 10 Year Old Cask Strength Islay SMSW (Scotland); 55.7% abv, $60.

This color is a deeper honey/topaz than the standard 10 Year Old; superb clarity. In the first inhalations, the peat-reek is sweet, floral, even honeyed and seashell-like; after another seven minutes of air contact, a yeasty/sourdough-like bakery tartness makes itself known prior to the bouquet rocking out in solid, maritime notes of seaweed, iodine, pine needle, sulphur/matchstick, and olive brine; a veritable aromatic feast. The palate entry is chock full of mint, sherry, pork rind, bacon fat, chimney soot, and rancio taste; by the midpalate phase the taste profile offers cocoa, coffee, pipe tobacco, chocolate covered orange, marzipan, and vanilla extract. Luscious; stupendously good. What's so exceptional about this malt is that while it is cask strength, the spirit never overshadows the acid, fruit, oak, or peat-reek. Wow.

2007 Rating: ★★★★/Highly Recommended

Laphroaig 10 Year Old Islay SMSW (Scotland); 43% abv, $50.

The golden color is brilliant and flawlessly pure. The initial sniffings after the pour immediately pick up new shoe leather, medicine chest/Band-Aid/iodine, smoked trout, and flowers; additional aeration time stimulates intense barley/grain/oatmeal and soft cheese notes that lie atop the mountain of peat-reek and dried seaweed. The palate entry is pleasantly smoky/ashy and grainy sweet; the midpalate stage offers many levels of flavor, from predictable olive brine, seaweed, iodine, and wood smoke to more exotic tastes of baked pear, toffee, and marshmallow. Concludes warm in the throat and toasty. While I'd choose the peaty likes of Lagavulin and/or Ardbeg over Laphroaig most of the time, I've come round to this venerable distillery.

2007 Rating: ★★★/Recommended

Laphroaig 15 Year Old Islay SMSW (Scotland); 43% abv, $66.
Old gold coin/bronze color; perfect purity. Smells appropriately of seaweed, shoe leather, cigarette smoke, and smoked fish; aeration brings out touches of oaky vanilla, pork rind, and bacon. Entry is amazingly sweet, caramel-like, and smoky; the midpalate features long, oily, cocoa bean flavors that gain in power with time, finally detonating in the throat in a sweet peat-reek bomb that coats the entire palate in smoke, vanilla, and cinnamon. Concludes oily, honeyed, and all Islay.
2007 Rating: ★★★★/Highly Recommended

Laphroaig 30 Year Old Islay SMSW (Scotland); 43% abv, $225.
The brilliant bronze color dazzles the eye; absolute purity. The initial couple of nosing passes after the pour are confronted by rich, composed, and mature scents of oak char, medium-sweet malt, mild sea salt, and spicy peat; later sniffings that follow six more minutes of air contact are treated to a quiet, serene sea air/seaweed perfume that hints at cigar tobacco and heather; this is one of the most elegant Islay bouquets this side of Bowmore 25 or 30. While the bouquet is genuinely lovely, languid, and elegant, the palate entry begins a memorable taste journey that, to me, is the finest ever for Laphroaig as mellow, perfectly melded flavors of soft peat, pipe smoke, and sweet malt greet the taste buds; the midpalate stage features succulent tastes of light toffee, caramel, and oak char. The finish is long, luxuriously sweet, slightly honeyed, and slow. What adult malt drinking is all about.
2002 Rating: ★★★★★/Highest Recommendation

Laphroaig Quarter Cask Double Cask Matured Non-Chill Filtered Islay SMSW (Scotland); 48% abv, $50.
This malt is matured first in standard size barrels, then transferred to casks a quarter of the size of modern barrels for the purpose of emulating how malt whiskies were aged in the 19th century when casks were typically smaller than today's barrels. The idea is to have more wood/whisky contact. The color is bright marigold/autumnal gold; ideal purity. The initial sniffs pick up astringent/acidic scents that are remarkably clean, apple peel-like, and peat-free; during the later inhalations, the aroma takes on a more sea breeze/mildly briny character that's far more in keeping with the customary Laphroaig aromatic profile. The palate entry is lean, earthy, moderately smoky, and lemony; at the midpalate stage there's a lovely oiliness that coats the tongue with flavors of ash, peat, sweet malt, and brine. Concludes sweet, pleasantly peaty, cigarette ash-like, and with an intriguing bite of green olive. Terrific job here of barrel management.
2007 Rating: ★★★★/Highly Recommended

Ledaig (Tobermory) 10 Year Old Isle of Mull SMSW (Scotland); 43% abv, $48.
The pale straw color is bright and unblemished. Oooh, I love the intensely malty and enticingly peaty opening aroma that emits pungent notes of filled ashtray, soot, sea breeze, and kippers; as this malt aerates, the bouquet turns even more piquant and peppery, offering deeper scents of oyster shell, sand, and brine; a genuine maritime aroma. The palate entry is dry initially then rapidly turns off-dry and salty/peaty, even a touch beeswax-like; at the midpalate point the taste profile explodes on the tongue in thrillingly salty/briny flavors of salted peanuts, smoked fish, paraffin, light toffee, and salted butter. Ledaig 10 is the finest,

most expressive Ledaig/Tobermory in the marketplace and one that all peat-reek admirers should purchase in multiple bottle volumes.

2007 Rating: ★★★★/Highly Recommended

Ledaig (Tobermory) Vintage 1972 Isle of Mull SMSW (Scotland); 48.5% abv, $340.
Lovely deep amber/brown leather color, with excellent clarity. The first whiffs pick up distinctive maritime/island traits, especially pickling brine and sea salt; aromatically expanding with more time in the copita, Ledaig 1972 displays intriguing notes of butter, cherry, oloroso sherry, marshmallow, and cotton candy in the latter stages of the sniffing phase. The taste menu starts at entry with moderately sweet notes that hint of sherry wood and caramel, then at midpalate the salty sea air kicks in, producing a sturdy, mature, and fully melded flavor that highlights kippers and oaky vanilla. Finishes moderately sweet in a stately, if restrained manner. I suggest you drink this malt neat. A very good island malt from Tobermory Distillery.

2005 Rating: ★★★/Recommended

Littlemill 12 Year Old Lowlands SMSW (Scotland); 43% abv, $61.
Brilliant and pretty harvest gold/deep amber color; unblemished purity. The opening whiffs pick up sweet scents of honeywheat toast and breakfast cereal; additional time in the copita stimulates added scents of peat moss/vegetation, baked pear, and baked pineapple. The palate entry features lovely and elegant taste of key lime, meringue, and toffee; the midpalate phase offers deeper flavors that include marshmallow, dark caramel, cocoa, cinnamon, marzipan, and maple. Finishes sweet, concentrated, and smooth.

2006 Rating: ★★★★/Highly Recommended

Longrow 10 Year Old Tokaji Wood Expression Campbeltown SMSW (Scotland); 55.6% abv, $112.
The attractive topaz color gleams under the light and is flawlessly pure. The exotic aroma right out of the gate oozes with ripe yellow fruit, including banana and pears; another seven minutes coax out deeper smells of baked banana bread, figs, toasty malt, and white grape preserves; an amazing tour de force of a bouquet that's unique and sensual. The palate entry is luxuriously rich, a touch salty, and as dense as fruit compote or jam; the midpalate stage features succulent and seamless flavors of dates, grapes, sautéed bananas, sweet malt, sea breeze, sweet oak, and honey. Ends up sweet, compelling, and idiosyncratic to the max. I place this instant classic right up there with the unforgettable Glenmorangie 1981 Sauternes Wood Finish. Worth every cent and more.

2006 Rating: ★★★★★/Highest Recommendation

Longrow 100 Proof 10 Year Old Campbeltown SMSW (Scotland); 50% abv, $130.
Flax/straw yellow hue; flawless clarity. Dry, earthy aromas of flowers, beans/kernels, and peanut oil greet the olfactory sense in the first whiffs; additional air contact releases added aromas of flax/textile, cloth, wool blanket, palm oil, and lanolin. The soft, grainy/malty sweetness of the entry threw me as I was expecting a drier, saltier opening—it's incredibly delicious out of the gate; the grainy sweetness builds at midpalate but leaves room for other, highly complementary tastes including pipe tobacco, blackberry jam, saltwater taffy, pipe

smoke, and palm oil. Concludes with enormous finesse, presence, medium-weight, and a sublimely sweet and oily end-taste. Campbeltown in a glass. There's something elementally genuine and untainted about this malt that thrills me to the core.
2007 Rating: ★★★★★/Highest Recommendation

Longrow 14 Year Old Campbeltown SMSW (Scotland); 46% abv, $123.
Yellow gold color; perfect purity. Smells remarkably of fried eggs, toast, and bacon out of the starting gate; the fried egg-like scent carries over following further aeration and is supplemented by salty fragrances of coal, bean paste, pork roast, pork sausage, and marjoram: a unique and strangely wonderful maritime bouquet. Lean to the touch, the entry taste is malty/grainy, off-dry, peanuty, and oily; at midpalate the sumptuousness of the oil is a major factor as the flavor sports tastes of seaweed, light peat, smoke, sweet malt, and pine. Finishes elegantly, on the lighter side of the textural spectrum, and lusciously oily and peanut-like.
2007 Rating: ★★★★/Highly Recommended

Longrow 1974 25 Year Old Campbeltown SMSW (Scotland); 46% abv, $525.
Remarkably yellow/green in color; superb purity. The opening aroma is gracefully saline and even prickly; the second nosing pass reveals further expansion of the saltiness, but the malt does emerge as a major aromatic component; the third sniffing sees the sweet maltiness take the lead, effectively out-running the saltiness; the final whiff cements the fruity maltiness in place as the predominant fragrance as a trace of grass lurks in the background; a complex, intriguing, and thoroughly sophisticated bouquet. Divinely malty sweet at palate entry, then the flavors grow more intense at midpalate in the forms of wet grass, sweet malt, yellow fruit, and cocoa; a supremely dazzling display of flavor balance and charm. The finish is very long, fruity/malty sweet, and a touch oily.
2000 Rating: ★★★★★/Highest Recommendation

Macallan 12 Year Old Speyside SMSW (Scotland); 43% abv, $45.
The deep amber/ochre color with bronze core highlights is a benchmark for sherry cask aged malts; perfect purity. Right from the start, the aroma is sweetish, winey, and oaky; with further time in the glass, the aroma expands to include marzipan, treacle, molasses, honey, vanilla bean, cinnamon, and cocoa butter; an amazing experience. The palate entry is textured, unabashedly sweet, creamy, and assertive; by the midpalate phase the flavor goes intensely nutty, buttery and bacon fat-like, with the beginnings of rancio. Mountains of concentration and sherry/honey flavors make this a very stylistic malt that to some newbee admirers might seem old-fashioned. One of Speyside Scotland's standard bearer 12 year olds.
2007 Rating: ★★★★/Highly Recommended

Macallan 10 Year Old Fine Oak Speyside SMSW (Scotland); 40% abv, $44.
The pale golden yellow color is pure and clean. The initial sniffs after the pour reveal supple, buttery, and piney aromas; six more minutes allow a pleasant fruitiness to come forth, backed up by traces of vanilla and cedar. The palate entry is honey sweet and silky; by midpalate the backbone flavors are clearly the sweet grain and vanilla bean. Concludes politely and warm in the throat. I admire the vitality and affable nature of this young malt; an extremely pleasant malt.
2004 Rating: ★★★★/Highly Recommended

Macallan 15 Year Old Fine Oak Speyside SMSW (Scotland); 43% abv, $65.

Deep gold/autumnal yellow color; impeccable purity. The first bursts of bouquet remind me of the dried yellow fruit (pineapple, apple, pear, peach) that you get in muesli or travel mix cereals; later on added scents of unsweetened coconut, honey, and light toffee beautifully complement the dried yellow fruit aroma profile. The palate entry is seductive, chewy, honeyed, and sweet; by midpalate the taste becomes fully integrated as the dried fruit, clover, and honey flavors lay in lovely fashion with the oily, creamy texture. Concludes sensuously, fully, and regally.

2004 Rating: ★★★★★/Highest Recommendation

Macallan 17 Year Old Fine Oak Speyside SMSW (Scotland); 43% abv, $120.

The color is like dark, late-harvested corn/maize; ideal clarity. The opening aroma is smoky (cigar box), clean, woody and delightfully direct, without any pretense or dancing around; touches of palm oil, brown butter, vanilla bean, and pork rind come wrapped in a seamless aromatic package that is simultaneously profound and inviting; a luscious Speyside bouquet that keeps unfolding long after the ten minute nosing phase. The palate entry is bittersweet and caramel-like, rich and creamy; at the midpalate juncture the taste profile turns sweeter, nuttier, and more fudge-like; an awesome midpalate experience. Finishes elegantly, yet very focused and integrated. I've been an ardent fan of the Fine Oak series right from the beginning and all I can say is, long may new expressions keep coming.

2007 Rating: ★★★★★/Highest Recommendation

Macallan 21 Year Old Fine Oak Speyside SMSW (Scotland); 43% abv, $220.

Beautifully rich honey/amber tone; ideal purity. The early bouquet is round, biscuity, and a touch spicy; subsequent sniffings after further aeration reveal an aroma deep in butterscotch, cream, vanilla, marzipan, and candied almond. The palate entry is lively and vividly spirity as the alcohol slightly pricks the tongue; the midpalate stage displays solid flavors of dried orange rind, white raisins, marmalade, and figs. Finishes elegantly and sweet.

2004 Rating: ★★★★★/Highest Recommendation

Macallan 30 Year Old Fine Oak Speyside SMSW (Scotland); 43% abv, $700.

Surprisingly light amber/maize/old gold coin color; ideal purity. Smells of chocolate covered orange, dry malt, and oak in the initial nosing passes; further aeration stimulates intensely grainy aromas that come off like grain kernels, dry breakfast cereal, lanolin, beeswax, and palm oil. Entry is utterly graceful, layered by sweet grain and oak barrel complexity that takes the forms of vanilla wafer, toffee, and fudge; the midpalate is crazily wonderful as the taste profile becomes a master of nuance, giving off wave after wave of totally integrated spirit, grain, wood, and acidity. Ends in a cascade of semisweet oaky flavor that borders on being honeyed. A perfect, understated Speyside single malt.

2007 Rating: ★★★★★/Highest Recommendation

Macallan 30 Year Old Speyside SMSW (Scotland); 43% abv, $350.

The stunning color is a brilliant copper/bronze, flecked with blood orange core highlights; what an eyeful. The nose at opening is surprisingly vibrant and energetic for such an oldster; the second pass offers even greater depth and definition of bouquet as succulent scents of red fruit, old oak in the form of vanilla extract, and mild oloroso sherry beguile the olfactory sense; the penultimate whiff, following nearly eight minutes of air contact, sees the addition of spicy notes plus a hint of cheese-like rancio in the background; the last sniffing offers deft touches of citrus rind and roasted nuts plus a trace of cigar box; this is a dynamic and soothing bouquet. The palate entry is smooth as silk, a touch honeyed, and strangely but pleasantly citrusy; the midpalate juncture features luscious tastes of spice, sherry oak, nuts, tobacco leaf, and cheese. The finish is medium long and shows a touch of molasses at the tail end. A superb example of an older malt that's still fresh, yet carries the stamp of maturity in style and grace.

2000 Rating: ★★★★/Highest Recommendation

Macallan 50 Year Old Speyside SMSW (Scotland); 43% abv, $3,500.

The deep topaz/brandy brown appearance is totally and shockingly ruined by a thick school of long, white, fabric-like tendrils and, worse, transparent chunks that float aimlessly and devastatingly in the core of this whisky; strikingly unappetizing, no matter the price, but in this case…. The opening sniffing detects chiseled scents of hard cheese, sherry oak, and raisins; the second whiff picks up further mature scents of toasted walnuts and creamy nougat; the penultimate nosing pass, following nearly eight minutes of exposure to air, adds nuances of dark caramel and tobacco smoke; the fourth and final aromatic run-through sees the fruity malt make a bid at dominance, but fades under the weight of the sherry/pruny sweetness; not as complex or grand a mature bouquet as one would hope, frankly. Massive and smoky at palate entry; the midpalate stage is intensely caramel-like, sherried, and so resiny as to be similar to dried tobacco leaves. The finish is long, intensely resiny though not the least rancio-like, and bittersweet. In looking past the fabulous wood box and crystal decanter that this malt comes packaged in to the whisky itself, I can state that ounce for ounce I vastly prefer the standard 18 Year Old bottling, the 25 Year Old, and the splendidly decadent 18 Year Old Gran Reserva, all of which received ★★★★★ ratings.

2000 Rating: ★★★/Recommended

Macallan Non-Chill Filtered Speyside SMSW (Scotland); 58.6% abv, $50.

The deep chestnut/oloroso sherry-like hue is stunning and quite lovely; very good clarity. This is the type of thick, sinewy, chewy malt whisky bouquet that brings me to my knees with thanks; there's lots of everything in there, including baked bananas, rancio, hard cheese, burnt matches, and charred hickory; aeration time for another six minutes accentuates the ripe, unabashedly sweet fruit aromas with sweet oak, oloroso sherry, fruit cake, dark chocolate, and dark caramel. On the palate, it's firm, not as hot as I thought it might be, and lip-smackingly luscious; at midpalate the intensity of the elevated alcohol overcomes the flavors to the degree of slightly burning the tongue; once spring water is added the taste profile readjusts itself and emits ambrosial flavors of Christmas pudding, honey, molasses, and dark caramel. The aftertaste is long, chewy and chunky. Did I like it? You bet; is it as decadent as the Gran Reserva? No. Should I add water? Absolutely.

2003 Rating: ★★★/Highly Recommended

Oban 14 Year Old Western Highlands SMSW (Scotland); 43% abv, $40.

The deep color reminds me of honey or, better, immature armagnac; absolute purity. The firm but not aggressive aroma speaks immediately of the combination of malt, wood,

and sea breeze since the mildly briny, lightly salted surface scent is buttressed by a biscuity, malty foundation; another six minutes affords the aroma time to muster all the grainy/malty sweetness possible, making the later bouquet a deliciously harmonious, even creamy marriage of maritime atmosphere and malted barley. The palate entry is chock full of biscuity, peaty, tobacco leaf tastes; the midpalate stage is sweet and a bit honeyed. Concludes strong, firm, slightly hot, pungent, and briny. The best-kept secret of Scotland's Western Highlands is Oban. A hearty, robust, in-yer-face malt that's always a crowd pleaser. Neither profound nor classical, but a straightforward, no-nonsense Highlands/seaside malt of notable gravity.
2004 Rating: ★★★/Recommended

Oban 1969 Rare Edition 32 Year Old Western Highlands SMSW (Scotland); 55.1% abv, $350.
Autumnal gold/wheat field/honey color; absolute purity. The hugely attractive opening whiff paints aromatic pictures of honey wheat toasted bread, light caramel, and gently sweet malt; another seven minutes of air contact unleashes highly attractive earthy/woodsy scents of pine, grass, sweet oak, and a distant trace of sea breeze; for a three decades old bouquet, it enchants with its vitality and keen freshness. The palate entry emits lightly toasted tastes of wheat bread, honey, fino sherry, and oaky vanillin; the midpalate is where the hint of lightly salty sea breeze enters the taste profile but beyond that there's also an astringent underpinning flavor of wood resin. The aftertaste is medium-long, moderately sweet, and composed. Vividly youthful despite its age and a total pleasure to drink.
2003 Rating: ★★★★/Highly Recommended

Port Charlotte PC5 Evolution (Distilled at Bruichladdich Distillery) Islay SMSW (Scotland); 63.5% abv, $110.
Shows a strong, bright amber/topaz hue; unblemished purity. The intensely peaty, cigar smoke-in-yer-puss opening aroma has my socks rolling up and down and, hey, wait a second, I'm not even wearing socks; an additional seven minutes of air contact revs up the peat machine even more as PC5 turns citrusy, grapefruit-like, Band-Aid-like, kippery, and yet amazing graceful at the same time. The palate entry rips into my taste buds as the spirit launches an assault on my tongue like a mini-D-Day, but, man, this medicinal stuff is simultaneously vicious and caressing, brutish and elegant; I add water before tasting again to put out the blaze on the cinder that used to be my tongue; the midpalate stage becomes wonderfully sweet and honeyed with the water, while remaining uncompromisingly smoky, ash-like, and sooty. Ends with a slap of spirity heat, but then why do I love this malt? An unbelievable journey through a peat-heated oven. Wow. Sign me up for more.
2007 Rating: ★★★★★/Highest Recommendation

Port Ellen 24 Year Old Islay SMSW (Scotland); 57.3% abv, £110.
Only available in the United Kingdom. Bright harvest gold/amber color; excellent purity. The intense aroma in the first whiffs is lean, dry, heathery, and focused; aeration and a few drops of mineral water encourage sweeter, earthier, grainier scents to emerge, including toasted malt, sweetened breakfast cereal, green grass, and dewy hay. It's in the mouth where this malt explodes with grainy/malty/chocolaty opulence in the entry phase; the midpalate emits lean, but muscular tastes of bread dough, sugar biscuits, toffee, fudge,

and tar; finishes smoky, toasted, nutty, and nougat-like. A sterling example of the kind of malts Port Ellen can produce.

2004 Rating: ★★★★/Highly Recommended

Scapa Vintage 1980 25 Year Old Orkney Islands SMSW (Scotland); 54% abv, $300.

The appearance is surprisingly light in color, a kind of corn gold/greenish amber hue that's perfectly sediment-free. In the first aromatic go-rounds, the bouquet is quite green, angular and lightly oaked, with no overt evidence of sea air; following aeration and some swirling, a floral/spring garden-like fragrance starts to emerge and it isn't until a few drops of mineral water are added that a keen, totally dry graininess takes control of the bouquet phase. The palate entry is minerally, dry, composed and even stately; at midpalate more of a flavor profile develops as a touch more water is mixed in, allowing the grain/malty elements the opportunity to mingle with oak, black pepper and grassy notes. Finishes lean, off-dry, intensely grainy/malty and buff.

2006 Rating: ★★★★/Highly Recommended

Singleton SMSW of Glendullan 12 Year Old Speyside SMSW (Scotland); 40% abv, $36.

Attractive deep amber/topaz color; excellent clarity. Smells of sugar cookies, orange zest, and baked pineapple; further air contact unleashes floral scents that are buttressed by deep, dry breakfast cereal and citrus-flavored hard candy aromas. Entry is malty sweet, nicely woody, and keenly toffee-like; at midpalate the flavor profile expands to include walnut butter, nougat, and honey. Finishes as affably and sweet as it began. Friendly, gently sweet quaffing.

2007 Rating: ★★★/Recommended

Speyside 12 Year Old Speyside SMSW (Scotland); 43% abv, $35.

Amber/honey gold in appearance; flawless purity. The ripe, fruity (pineapple, banana) opening bouquet is remarkably friendly, perfumey, and inviting; six more minutes of aeration add woody/leathery aromatic notes that complement rather than overshadow the fruit element; the only negative from my vantage point at least is how quickly the aromatic burst diminished after the initial whiffs. The palate entry is sweet, grainy, mashy, and caramel-like; by midpalate the taste profile expands marginally to include tastes of glycerine, heather honey, and almond paste. Concludes amiably, moderately sweet, and warming.

2004 Rating: ★★★/Recommended

Springbank 10 Year Old Campbeltown SMSW (Scotland); 46% abv, $70.

The color is flax/pale straw; flawless clarity. The first whiffs discover keenly malty notes right out of the gate, followed quickly by buttery/creamy scents that are round and just slightly peated; another seven minute span of air contact doesn't do much in deepening the bouquet, stimulating only subtle traces of paraffin/sealing wax and cereal. The fey character of the aroma is redeemed by the intensely malty and waxy palate entry, which is dry, elegant, and squeaky clean; by the midpalate stage the taste profile turns sweeter as the malt and oak barrel rush forward with flavors that include sea air and vanilla. Ends up lean and off-dry. Not my favorite Springbank by a long shot, but an expression that displays finesse and restraint.

2007 Rating: ★★★/Recommended

Springbank 100 Proof 10 Year Old Campbeltown SMSW (Scotland); 50% abv. $70.
Flax/straw yellow color; ideal purity. Smells of sea salt, hemp/rope and textile/fiber in the opening sniffs; the acute saltiness continues strongly after further aeration, but leaves room for other scents such as bean curd/tofu, sulfur, burning matches, palm oil, and browned margarine. The entry is aggressively malty, moderately spirity, and sweet in a smoky/peaty manner that's silky and highly appealing; the taste profile at midpalate accentuates the smoky sweetness by adding underpinning flavors of toffee, toasted marshmallow, leaf tobacco, and sweetened breakfast cereal. Ends on a smoky/sweet note that's lip smacking, savory, and lighter than expected.
2007 Rating: ★★★★/Highly Recommended

Springbank 12 Year Old Rum Cask Campbeltown SMSW (Scotland); 46% abv, $65.
White wine (chardonnay) yellow hue; excellent purity. The initial couple of inhalations after the pour find piquant, spiky, spirity aromas that have just a hint of sea breeze; nine more minutes of exposure to air stirs up sassy, herbal scents of anise/licorice, wet grass, and molasses. The palate entry is hot, searing the tongue at first, then it calms down and turns toasty and malty sweet; by the midpalate point the spirit element has calmed down, allowing for flavors of marshmallow, light peat, sweet malt, and toasty oak to emerge. It finishes sweet and oaky.
2002 Rating: ★★★★/Highly Recommended

Springbank 15 Year Old Campbeltown SMSW (Scotland); 46% abv, $116.
This whisky is remarkably pretty in its old gold/light topaz hue; superb purity. The first sniffs pick up layers of aroma, from barley malt to sea breeze to seaweed to heather; an additional aeration period of seven minutes really helps to bring out deeper layers of oaky vanilla, honey, sherry cask, scrambled egg, and minerals; a stunningly complex bouquet whose best virtue is its understatement. The palate entry is tantalizingly oily, buttery, and oaky sweet; by the midpalate stage the flavor profile expands to include assertive tastes of marzipan, marshmallow, baked pear/peach pastry, and bacon fat. Finishes with a fruit/grape thrust that's unbelievably luscious. A masterpiece.
2007 Rating: ★★★★★/Highest Recommendation

Springbank 32 Year Old Campbeltown SMSW (Scotland); 46% abv, $750.
The bright yellow/corn oil gold color is clear and brilliant beneath the examination lamp; impeccable clarity. The opening whiffs detect aromatic ripples of sweet oak, sawdust, and linseed oil; later nosing passes following further aeration find vibrant, resiny/oaky, leathery/cowhide-like aromas that mesh perfectly by the tenth minute. The palate entry is sublimely balanced, semisweet, lean, and outdoorsy; at midpalate the magic of Springbank becomes apparent as the flavor profile suggests tastes of pork sausage, bacon fat, almond oil, suet, and malted barley. Finishes dazzlingly clean, stately, balanced, and a touch warm on the tongue. Subtle, understated, great.
2005 Rating: ★★★★★/Highest Recommendation

Springbank 35 Year Old Campbeltown SMSW (Scotland); 43% abv, $600.
The color is bronze/topaz/amber and as pure as can be. The initial nosing pass offers nut-like perfumes of roasted walnuts and almond butter; the second sniffing reveals a rich

maltiness that's more bittersweet than sweet; in the third whiff, following seven minutes of air contact, a seductive. briny oiliness comes to the aromatic forefront and takes charge of the bouquet; the fourth and last nosing pass, after ten minutes of aeration time, sees the disparate elements come together in a harmonious, off-dry, lightly salted, aromatic display that's so typical of Springbank. The palate entry is warming, thick, sweet, intensely oaked, and malty; by the midpalate point the different levels of taste unite to become a rich, oaky, malty sweet program of flavor. The finish is medium long, sinewy, and marked by the sweet oak more than anything else. It's getting to the point where bottling after bottling Springbank appears to be Scotland's most accomplished and consistently brilliant distillery; this Limited Edition series has been a benchmark collection that while expensive on a per bottle basis is nothing short of spectacular.

2000 Rating: ★★★★/Highest Recommendation

Springbank 40 Year Old Campbeltown SMSW (Scotland); 46% abv, $950.
    Typical lightish green/yellow Springbank hue; excellent clarity. The initial nosing pass reveals roasted nuts and baked apple; in the second sniffing, the aroma gets serious about unfolding as wave upon wave of oiliness, nuttiness, and fruit waft up from the glass; in the third whiff, following six minutes of aeration, there's a sturdy brininess that flows under the surface scents of oil and nuts; the last nosing pass unearths a tide of dark chocolate and cola nut that dominate the bouquet; solid, but not the most expressive or elegant bouquet from Springbank. Intense and savory at palate entry as the oily taste takes charge early-on; the midpalate stage is far more balanced as flavors of mild salt, oaky rancio, sweet malt, and sherry cask meet in harmony at the back of the tongue. Oily, slightly smoky, but engagingly sweet and succulent aftertaste. The midpalate and finish stages are typical Springbank genius.

2000 Rating: ★★★/Highly Recommended

Springbank Marsala Wood Expression 9 Year Old Campbeltown SMSW (Scotland); 58% abv. $110.
    Old gold/amber/topaz hue; good clarity. High octane aromas of spirit, barley malt, saltine cracker, and bacon fat greet the olfactory sense in the initial nosings; much of the spirit thrust blows off after aeration, leaving behind nicely evolved fragrances of malt, peat, cigarette ashes, bacon, and sautéed sesame seeds. Entry is fruity sweet, jammy, and superbly ripe (obviously from the marsala wood influence), but balanced and only medium-weight in texture; at midpalate the flavor profile boasts comely, downright luscious tastes of over-ripe black grapes, plum preserves, cassis, mint, and vanilla cream. Concludes wonderfully sweet yet balanced since the high acidity keeps the sweet fruitiness in check. Another benchmark from Springbank.

2007 Rating: ★★★★/Highest Recommendation

Talisker 10 Year Old Skye SMSW (Scotland); 45.8% abv, $48.
    The bright appearance shows some unwanted sediment floating within the pretty amber color. The piquant nose offers immediate and stunning notes of sea salt, peat reek, and black pepper; aeration time encourages deeper aromas including malt and almond. The palate entry is malty sweet and nicely peppery, then at midpalate the peaty iodine character kicks in in spades, making for expressive and assertive drinking. Finishes well as it gives off fiery,

acutely peaty/tobacco-like flavors. Some people have said that I've never given this distillery a fair shake. Over the past few years, however, I've raved about a couple of stellar limited edition bottlings as well as some top-notch independent merchant offerings; I've even come around to this frontline bottling, though I'd still like to see it matured for another two to four years.

2004 Rating: ★★★/Recommended

Talisker 18 Year Old Isle of Skye SMSW (Scotland); 45.8% abv, $70.
The wheat harvest gold color is gorgeous and pure. The first two minutes of sniffing boast big-hearted aromas of maple sugar and caramel; further aeration stimulates marine notes of seaweed and light brine, but deeper notes of chili pepper, black pepper, honey, and vanilla top off the experience. The palate entry is honeyed and full; at midpalate the taste profile inches its way towards the smoke/tobacco/ash/tar side of the flavor scale, but is sweet. Concludes moderately oily, lightly salty, and firm on the tongue. A superb expression of this island distillery.

2005 Rating: ★★★★/Highly Recommended

Talisker 1981 Rare Edition 20 Year Old Isle of Skye SMSW (Scotland); 59.7% abv, $150.
A stunningly fetching bronze, topaz color; perfect purity. The initial sniffings reel me in as lightly toasted, lightly salted scents of sea breeze, malt and oak immediately impress deeply; six more minutes of sitting in the glass releases additional fragrances, including honey, fried bread, roasted almonds and oil (wood resin?); another highly complex and intricate bouquet from this great island distillery. The palate entry is warming, semisweet and almost fruity; by the midpalate juncture the taste takes a left turn and goes slightly briny, intensely oaky and flat-out sweet in a honeyed manner. The finish is hot-wired, lively to the point of being prickly on the tongue and luscious. While I prefer the outstanding 25 Year Old Rare Edition bottling more, this 20 Year Old shows why Talisker is held in such lofty esteem within the distilling community of Scotland.

2003 Rating: ★★★★/Highly Recommended

Talisker 25 Year Old Isle of Skye SMSW (Scotland); 59.9% abv, $200.
Gorgeous topaz/deep honey color with green highlights; perfect purity; a dazzling eyeful. The bouquet right after the pour leaps from the sampling glass in sumptuous waves of moderate peat, light toffee, honeywheat toast, and sea salt; an additional eight minutes in the glass encourages further aromatic development in the forms of soy sauce, sautéed mushrooms, oaky vanilla, dried heather, and even a fleeting trace of rancio. The palate entry is so ideally balanced between the right levels of alcohol, wood, malt, and sweetness that I'm virtually speechless; by the midpalate juncture the flavors turn far more focused and defined as luscious bittersweet-to-sweet tastes of candied almonds, honey, oloroso sherry, and dark chocolate totally enchant the taste buds. The finish is long, resiny sweet, honeyed, and most comforting of all, warming.

2002 Rating: ★★★★★/Highest Recommendation

Talisker Distiller's Edition 1992 Double Matured Amoroso Sherry Cask Finished Isle of Skye SMSW (Scotland); 45.8% abv, $65.
The rich brown/auburn color is lovely and unblemished. Right from the initial

inhalation, I note seaweed, smoke, peat, iodine, and medicine chest; aeration brings out added scents of kippers and pipe tobacco; this is a fantastically expressive and sophisticated bouquet from a maritime setting. The palate entry features the medicinal impact of salty sea air as the flavor is briny, intense and focused; the midpalate is oily in texture (a plus for me) and flecked with traces of anise, butterscotch and linseed oil. Finishes broad, vibrant, and long in tastes of salted butter, oil, and brine. Highly idiosyncratic and admittedly not for those malt admirers who prefer plump, sweet Speysides. But for lovers of emphatic, robust, seaside malts, this is pig heaven.

2006 Rating: ★★★★/Highest Recommendation

The Glenlivet 12 Year Old Speyside SMSW (Scotland); 40% abv, $32.

Honey/deep straw color; superb clarity. Off-dry malted barley and light toffee smells greet the olfactory sense after the pour along with flowery fragrances of heather, rose petal, and pine; further aeration stimulates a mild peppery, biscuity quality that's been one of my favorites for twenty years; the quintessential 12 year old Speyside bouquet. Entry features as much finesse and complexity as one could expect as sweet grain and candied apricot tastes delight the taste buds; the midpalate is remarkably mellow, grainy/malty, fruity (white raisins, apricots), and sophisticated. Ends on a buttery note. For all the hoopla over this "limited edition" wood-finished malt or that "rarest of the rare" cask strength single barrel monster, this whisky remains Speyside's benchmark malt.

2007 Rating: ★★★★/Highly Recommended

The Glenlivet 15 Year Old French Oak Reserve Speyside SMSW (Scotland); 40% abv, $50.

Pretty medium amber/soft orange highlights; ideal purity. First whiffs pick up off-dry to semisweet scents of fresh pineapple, cedar, and paraffin; later sniffings detect subtle notes of black tea leaves, baked pear, and sweet oak. The palate entry features a firm, moderately oily, and velvety texture; by midpalate integrated flavors of ripe peach, pear drops, and bran delight the taste buds. The finish is extended, semisweet, and coconut-like. Replaces the 12 Year Old French Oak Finish, which was also rated ★★★★.

2004 Rating: ★★★★/Highly Recommended

The Glenlivet 1959 Cellar Collection Speyside SMSW (Scotland); 42.28% abv, $700.

This malt was aged in oak for 40 years. The color is a rather youthful yellow/honey hue; the purity is superb. On the nose, this malt offers loads of ripe fruit aromas in the initial sniffings, then it opens up with some air contact, emitting very pleasing notes of wax, autumn leaves, light smoke, and dried violets. The palate entry is malty sweet, a bit peppery, and beeswax-like; the midpalate tastes of caramelized onion, honey, and sweet, flowery malt. The aftertaste displays a back door honey sweetness that ends up overshadowing the dried fruit and floral flavors; the texture is firm on the tongue. Yet another terrific bottling from this Glenlivet series born in old casks.

2002 Rating: ★★★★/Highly Recommended

The Glenlivet 1964 Cellar Collection Speyside SMSW (Scotland); 44.8% abv, $2,000.
The deep amber color shows a reddish/auburn core and impeccable purity. The aroma is vivid and energetic right from the first sniff, emitting luscious notes of light toffee, milk chocolate and cocoa bean; after another seven minutes of aeration, the aroma transforms into a plush bouquet that highlights dried red fruit, candied walnut, nougat, and faint vanilla bean. The palate entry is satiny smooth, yet smoldering and warm on the tongue; the midpalate stage features foundational tastes of mature oaky spirit that underpin surface flavors of cedar, resin, caramel and a tantalizing dash of plum eau-de-vie. Finishes firm, warm, and velvety. Brings to mind the sensational 1970 Cellar Collection bottling (★★★★★) that I raved about in 1998.
2004 Rating: ★★★★★/Highest Recommendation

The Glenlivet 1967 Cellar Collection Speyside SMSW (Scotland); 46% abv, $199.
Lovely amber/light topaz hue. The aroma after the pour brims with inviting, warm scents of butterscotch, nougat, palm oil, and oaky resin; after allowing it to aerate for a minimum of five minutes, I find luscious, expansive, and heady fragrances of walnut, dry malt, and almond butter that have taken over from the previous scents; a sensuous, multilayered bouquet that's more woody and resiny than fruity; I love it. In the mouth the palate entry is surprisingly sweet, much sweeter than the bouquet let on, and round; at the midpalate stage the texture turns silky and full and the flavors turn caramel sweet and even a touch honeyed. The finish lingers and is semisweet with a dash of acidic/resiny bitterness and heat in the very tail end of the mouth experience. This malt shows the deeper side of Glenlivet; smashingly good.
2001 Rating: ★★★★/Highly Recommended

The Glenlivet 1972 Cellar Collection Vintage Speyside SMSW (Scotland); 52.3% abv, $700.
In 1998 I evaluated another 1972 edition from The Glenlivet and scored it ★★★. This is a different bottling. The color is an oily medium amber/biscuit gold; superb clarity. The opening whiffs detect lots of oak, with lesser elements of mint and dried sage; further aeration time doesn't encourage much in the way of expansion, even after mineral water is judiciously added, except for the emergence of spice/black pepper. The palate entry is lean, off-dry, and oaky; at midpalate the taste profile is astringent, a bit pinched, and shows off intensely woody/oaky flavors that don't allow for the grain to develop properly. Finishes lean and angular. Not at all what I've come to admire about The Glenlivet and a departure from form that is disappointing.
2006 Rating: ★★/Not Recommended

The Glenlivet 1983 French Oak Finish Cellar Collection Speyside SMSW (Scotland); 46% abv, $125.
Autumnal topaz/wheat field color; absolute purity. The initial whiffs pick up appealingly biscuity, marshmallow-like, and grainy aromas that are semisweet in character; another seven minutes of exposure to air makes the bouquet even rounder as additional scents of oak, very light peat, tea leaves and creamery butter make for inspiring sniffing. The palate entry is firm (the 46% abv), moderately oily and off-dry; then at midpalate the flavor profile shifts into fourth gear as tastes of candied nuts, light caramel, vanilla, and pine nuts keep the taste

buds amply occupied. It finishes with a burst of vanilla and oak; lovely, sophisticated, and plumper than one expects Glenlivet to be.

2003 Rating: ★★★★/Highly Recommended

The Glenlivet Nàdurra 16 Year Old Non-Chill Filtered Speyside SMSW (Scotland); 57.2% abv, $60.

The brilliant golden hue is wine-like and pretty; unblemished purity. The first whiffs detect nuances of charred meat, deep vanilla bean, and pipe tobacco; further aeration time stimulates more grainy/floral scents as well as cocoa/dark chocolate; most impressive is the fact that the spirit never gets in the way of the inhalations. The palate entry is seductively sweet, oaky, and slightly spicy; at midpalate the taste profile cranks up the spirit warmth by a couple of notches as vivid flavors of malt, sweet oak, honey, nutmeg, and toffee dazzle the taste buds. Concludes warm, but not searing; sweet and succulent. A robust beauty from Scotland's most famous malt distillery.

2006 Rating: ★★★★/Highly Recommended

Tobermory 10 Year Old Isle of Mull SMSW (Scotland); 40% abv, $32.

The medium amber/harvest gold color is eye-catching and totally pure. What leaps out at me is the rich, but delicately sweet perfume of malted barley and mint; further exposure to air doesn't release much more in the way of aromatic expansion as the gentlemanly bouquet remains composed, gently sweet and generously malty. The palate entry is slightly salty and faintly peaty; at midpalate the grainy sweetness regains its footing, adding barely perceptible traces of green vegetable, mint, and black tea. Finishes with the tea out front. A more than decent introductory island malt of finesse and substance.

2006 Rating: ★★★/Recommended

Tomintoul 16 Year Old Speyside SMSW (Scotland); 40% abv, $50.

Pretty amber/light honey hue; excellent purity. The lovely, understated opening bouquet after the pour highlights the freshness of the malt in a gently sweet, almost honeyed way; aeration serves to deepen the delightful honey aspect and adds nuances of pine needle and sugar biscuits; an extremely appealing, low-key and seductive bouquet that beautifully illustrates Speyside's flowery, pleasantly sweet side. The palate entry is honey sweet and amiable; then at the midpalate stage the taste profile accelerates into a semi-rich honey, maple-like flavor that's approachable and easy. The finish is long, moderately sweet, and velvety. A solid introductory, medium-bodied, flowery/fruity Speyside malt.

2003 Rating: ★★★/Recommended

Tomintoul 27 Year Old Speyside SMSW (Scotland); 40% abv, $150.

The rich bronze/walnut color bedazzles the eye; perfect purity. The opening nosings detect little in the way of typical Speyside aromatics as the bouquet appears to be holding back; seven more minutes of exposure to air helps in exposing delicate aromas of marshmallow, cotton candy, light oak, marzipan, and almonds. Once in the mouth it's evident that this malt earns its spurs in the taste department; the palate entry is downright fruity/plummy/raisiny while the midpalate profile features deep, silky textures and mature tastes of dark caramel, coconut cream, oloroso sherry, and chocolate candy bar. Finishes full, sweet, oaky, and luscious. Give it more than a so-so bouquet and it's a five star whisky; as is, four will do handsomely and appropriately.

2004 Rating: ★★★★/Highly Recommended

Tormore 12 Year Old Speyside SMSW (Scotland); 40% abv, $40.
Attractive bronze/honey hue; excellent clarity. The initial whiffs find a one-note aroma of butter cream; another six minutes of air contact don't assist enormously in encouraging further aromatic growth; a lackluster, waxy bouquet that's disappointing considering that this distillery lies in the heart of Speyside. The palate entry offers pleasing, semisweet tastes of malt and breakfast cereal; the midpalate stage adds mildly alluring, estery flavors of raisins, plums, and grass. Concludes politely and moderately sweet. A simple, entry-level malt of modest virtue but gentle nature whose vast majority of production since 1960 has been included in such big-time blends as Long John and Ballantine's.

2004 Rating: ★★/Not Recommended

Tullibardine 1993 Central Highlands SMSW (Scotland); 40% abv, $50.
Very attractive, gleaming wheat field gold color; fair to good purity. The first nosings pick up grainy/grassy notes that are off-dry and slightly cardboard-like; another six minutes of aeration do next to nothing to stimulate additional aromatic breadth or depth; this is taking aromatic gentility to its limit, finally becoming a flaw. The palate entry, like the bouquet, is frustratingly meek and grassily off-dry; at midpalate the flavor profile offers faint tastes of barley malt, light caramel, and wood. Finishes as timidly as it begins. All the while, I felt that this malt was on the verge of breaking out, but it never did. Boringly drinkable and may be fine for unsophisticated malt drinkers. No major defects other than its hollow core.

2006 Rating: ★★/Not Recommended

MERCHANT ISSUE SINGLE MALT, SINGLE GRAIN & BLENDED MALT WHISKY—SCOTLAND

Blackadder Arran 5 Year Old Isle of Arran SMSW (Scotland); 57.4% abv, $45.

The color is a pale yellow/silver hue, a textbook appearance of an immature whisky; excellent purity. The first two sniffings after the pour confirm this whisky's youth as the fresh-off-the-still aromas talk of fresh flowers, freshly mown hay, and honeysuckle; further aeration does little to produce any aromatic sense of depth as the spirity, heady aromas of bread dough and yeast entertain the olfactory sense enough to charm but not enough to dazzle. The palate entry is intensely fruity, bold, and honeysuckle-like on the tongue; the midpalate point seems firmer in structure than the unruly entry tastes, offering calmer flavors of black pepper, grass, and wet vegetation. The finish is spirity/malty sweet and simple. A good, sweet malt if one wants to get the feel of a very young and vigorous malt with little polish or sophistication; ordinary for what it is and no more than that.

2002 Rating: ★★/Not Recommended

Blackadder Benrinnes 20 Year Old Speyside SMSW (Scotland); 59.3% abv, $110.

Pretty lemon yellow/gold color; very good clarity. The opening aromas are delightfully fresh and clean as scents of flowers, almond paste, light honey, and light wood resin make for exhilarating sniffing; further time in the glass for another five to six minutes expands the honey and wood elements especially; it's a green, unripe, but eminently fresh, breezy bouquet that has central Speyside written all over it. The palate entry is seductively creamy and a touch toasty; at the midpalate point there's a flash of spirity heat that lies atop the underpinning flavors of sherry, sweet malt, and oak. The aftertaste displays lots of heat but not enough to quash the honey and cream flavors that whisper the word "sherry aging" in my ear. By a long way, the finest, most complex Benrinnes I've encountered.

2002 Rating: ★★★/Highly Recommended

Blackadder Cragganmore 12 Year Old Speyside SMSW (Scotland); 59.8% abv, $54.

Straw yellow/gold hue; excellent purity. The opening sniffings find toasted, biscuity aromas that highlight the malt more than the spirit or the oak; aeration over the next seven minutes serves to expand the maltiness into a honeyed cereal bouquet that's both alluring and complex; a clinic on how Speyside malt should smell. The taste at palate entry is sweet, cereal-like, honeyed, and slightly sharp; the midpalate stage displays an array of typical Speyside flavors including light peat, honeywheat toast, light caramel, sweet oak, and almond oil; the oily texture shows itself amply in the finish. A dandy malt from one of Speyside's most respected distilleries.

2002 Rating: ★★★/Highly Recommended

Blackadder Longmorn 29 Year Old Speyside SMSW (Scotland); 45% abv, $124.

The gorgeous deep amber/topaz color is brandyesque; very minor sediment and overall superb purity. The opening nosing passes following the pour reveal defined scents of moderate peat, sweet malt, and what I would guess to be a preponderance of old bourbon barrels because of the light, char-like smokiness; another five to eight minutes of air contact deepens the oaky smoke into a vanilla extract mode that's luscious and graceful; a correct bouquet from this top-notch Speyside distillery. The palate entry disarms the taste buds immediately with succulent tastes of buttery cream, tar-like oak, and candied almonds; the midpalate point adds subtle background notes of spice, lanolin, and honey. The aftertaste is long, creamy, caramel-like, and sumptuous. A fully representative expression from this classic distillery which I consider to be one of Scotland's six best; bravo.

2002 Rating: ★★★★★/Highest Recommendation

Blackadder Mortlach 10 Year Old Speyside SMSW (Scotland); 43% abv, $30.

The pale amber color shows up a tad turbid beneath the examination lamp; no sediment seen however. The initial two nosing passes detect a subtle biscuity/cake batter fragrance that's yeasty, sweaty, and feinty; after several minutes in the glass the feinty/sweaty quality turns tobacco-like more in the manner of sweet pipe tobacco than either cigarette or cigar tobacco; it's a curious bouquet for Mortlach whose aroma profile is routinely more malty/oaky/nutty than spirity. At palate entry the taste is breakfast cereal sweet and slightly honeyed; the midpalate flavor phase features evolved tastes of dark caramel, candied almonds, roasted malt, and sherry oak. The finish is long, concentrated, and sweet. The mouth stages made up a lot of ground considering that the appearance and the bouquet were not up to normal Mortlach standards; a grand finale from one of Speyside's better distilleries.

2002 Rating: ★★★/Recommended

Blackadder Raw Cask Glen Grant 29 Year Old Speyside SMSW (Scotland); 57.3% abv, $159.

The auburn/topaz color is bright and gleaming under the lamp; widely dispersed large chunks of black sediment, though, are impossible not to see. The initial two nosing passes are confronted with a whole spectrum of intriguing scents including black pepper, cocoa, and butterscotch; five to seven minutes more allows the bouquet to settle down a bit, allowing further aromas to take hold, most notably pine nuts, toffee, and bacon fat; this is a broad-shouldered, concentrated, true winner-takes-all bouquet that displays the fatty/rancio side of Speyside that emerges on occasion, in particular, under very extended maturation. The serene palate entry is bittersweet like high cocoa-content dark chocolate; the midpalate point exhibits an entire menu of intense, mature flavors including bacon fat, oaky rancio, almond butter, nougat, and oil. The finish is sweet, coffee-like, and long. A buttery powerhouse that shows just how oaky Speyside can get when given the chance; lip-smacking, multilayered, and complex; finest Glen Grant I've tasted so far.

2002 Rating: ★★★★★/Highest Recommendation

Blackadder Rosebank 11 Year Old Lowlands SMSW (Scotland); 43% abv, $35.

Typical for Rosebank green/gray straw hue; very good clarity. The opening aroma is wonderfully flowery/heathery, soft, and polite; the later sniffing rounds after aeration stay the

floral course and add pleasing scents of moderately sweet malt and tea leaves. The palate entry is mildly malty sweet; at the midpalate juncture the taste turns intensely malty/grainy and considerably sweeter than at the entry. A concentrated, near lip-smacking Rosebank whose finishing touch of milk chocolate in the aftertaste makes for a lovely summation. As usual, Rosebank's malts aim to please with finesse and flowery panache.
2002 Rating: ★★★/Recommended

Cadenhead's Aberfeldy 25 Year Old Central Highlands SMSW (Scotland); 57% abv, $199.

Rich amber/dark honey color; bits of sediment seen. The opening aromatic salvos are tight, sap-like, and oily; aeration over an additional six minutes serves to release dry to bittersweet scents of sweet malt, oak resin, beeswax, and butterscotch. The palate entry taste is intensely caramelized, maple-like, and spirity; the midpalate focuses tightly on the oak resin and malt. The aftertaste is long, supple, and malty sweet. A solid, well-structured malt from the Central Highlands whose flavor thrust is not too overpowering; very nice.
2002 Rating: ★★★/Recommended

Cadenhead's Aberlour-Glenlivet 10 Year Old Speyside SMSW (Scotland); 63.8% abv, $89.

The pretty white wine yellow/light gold color is free from sediment. The potency of the spirit leaps from the glass in the first minutes of inhalations but interestingly it's neither prickly nor harsh, rather it's fruity; air contact for another seven minutes stimulates aromas of cotton fabric, heather, mint, and stone dry malt cereal. The palate entry tastes seem neutral and dry; then at midpalate stage the flavors explode on the tongue, most prominently, milk chocolate, intense malt, light caramel, and lanolin; the oily texture is a beaut. The finish is sweet, malty, fiery, heady, and focused. A volatile handful of immature spirit, but with Aberlour's trademark touch of class and complexity; absolutely dilute with cool, non-fizzy spring water to the tune of two ounces of whisky, one ounce H2O.
2002 Rating: ★★★★/Highly Recommended

Cadenhead's Auchentoshan 9 Year Old Lowlands SMSW (Scotland); 57.4% abv, $89.

Soft pale yellow/straw tint; quite a bit of floating sediment spotted. In the initial nosing passes first there's no aroma to speak of then after two minutes a fey, flowery bouquet emerges; with time in the glass a typical floral Lowlands aroma develops that shows traces of malt and sweet marzipan. To my shock the palate entry is potent, resoundingly sweet and almost syrupy in texture; the midpalate taste is punchy, flowery, malty, and overly sweet to the point of me wondering about the oak casks, first-fill old bourbon, perhaps? The aftertaste is calm, long, slightly heated, and woody sweet, as in vanillin. I usually love Auchentoshans, but this merchant bottling is commonplace at best, off-balance at worst.
2002 Rating: ★★/Not Recommended

Cadenhead's Banff 25 Year Old Speyside SMSW (Scotland); 56.3% abv, $211.

Wheat field gold color; excellent purity. The opening whiffs detect herbal and biscuity scents beneath the prickly sting of alcohol; aeration leads to more pronounced aromas of grain husk, tobacco leaf, and leather. At the palate entry the alcohol singes the tip of my tongue, then offers laser beam-like flavors of peanuts and semisweet malt; the midpalate is sweet, cake batter-like, biscuity, and keenly oily. It finishes razor-sharp, raw, and malty. Even

with a mineral water reduction, this whisky is robust and extremely heady; a so-so malt from this rarely seen and now closed distillery; firewater.
2002 Rating: ★★/Not Recommended

Cadenhead's Ben Nevis 1986 Western Highlands SMSW (Scotland); 62.9% abv, $120.
Dullish, straw yellow color, but good purity. The undiluted nose is brisk, acceptably prickly, a little bit biscuit-like, and, to my surprise, floral; the diluted bouquet loses some steam but offers vegetal, garden-like scents that require some coaxing but are pleasant. Far more drinkable with mineral water added than at full-strength; delectable, oily flavors of linseed, mild brine, roasted malt, light caramel, and toffee. The aftertaste is roasted, caramel-like and texturally impressive. Over the years Ben Nevis malts have shown me very little in the way of structural consistency; oily and gripping in one version, flat and flabby in the next; this expression shows the best of BN's oily, tactile side.
2001 Rating: ★★★/Recommended

Cadenhead's Bladnoch 12 Year Old Lowlands SMSW (Scotland); 58% abv, $87.
Dullish straw yellow hue; some sediment spotted. The initial nosing passes speak of the gentleness and floral character so typical of the Lowland malts; further air contact serves to accentuate the herbal/floral aromatic thrust of this benign bouquet as it becomes as perfumed as a spring garden; subtle background notes of soy and yellow fruit are noted. The palate entry is hot at first, then it turns sweet and intensely malty; the midpalate is honey sweet and caramel-like. The aftertaste is long, sweet, and malty.
2002 Rating: ★★★/Recommended

Cadenhead's Blair Athol 1989 Central Highlands SMSW (Scotland); 58.1% abv, $103.
Flax/yellow hue; acceptable purity. Without dilution with mineral water the aroma is intensely fruity, especially tropical fruits like bananas and guavas, and grainy/malty in a sweet manner; after water is added the nose goes strikingly fabric-like and cottony, like a new cotton shirt; the aroma turns very soft, dry, grainy, and pillowy with dilution. On palate, the lower-proof taste is clean, dry, moderately oily, and oaky. The finish is sweet, more concentrated than the midpalate, and shows an oiliness that borders on being heavy. Few malts from this unexceptional distillery located near Pitlochry in the Central Highlands have made me swoon; this is one of the better bottlings I've come across.
2001 Rating: ★★★/Recommended

Cadenhead's Bowmore 16 Year Old Islay SMSW (Scotland); 59.4% abv, $115.
The deep amber color is gorgeous; insignificant sediment seen. The Islay profile nose jumps from the glass in assertive waves of sea salt, medium medicinal-strength peat, and dry breakfast cereal; exposure to air works in stimulating the brininess further as the sea salt element takes charge but not before a wood resin odor mostly of char and vanilla surges into the nasal cavity; a rollicking aromatic ride that only can be provided by an Islay malt. At palate entry the taste is aggressive and spirity but loaded with pregnant tastes of oak, tar, tobacco leaf, and peat; the midpalate stage features the tar and iodine-like peatiness more than anything else. The aftertaste is long, mildly sweet, and intensely oaky. Certainly recommendable but not my favorite Bowmore in that it's far more feral and unruly than I

think Bowmore should be; that said, I believe it's still an interesting variation for Bowmore mavens to experience.

2002 Rating: ★★★/Recommended

Cadenhead's Bruichladdich 14 Year Old Islay SMSW (Scotland); 55.6% abv, $101.

Hay yellow tint; too much floating debris for my liking. The first two sniffings offer alluring scents of moderately sweet breakfast cereal and heather; six more minutes of exposure to air add aromas of mild brine, dill, and gentle phenols. The palate entry is moderately fiery but with enough malty oil and seaweed to make it acceptable; by the midpalate stage there's a fine toastiness that ends up being malty/nougaty sweet in the aftertaste. Benefits mightily from a few drops of mineral water and a quick swirl.

2002 Rating: ★★★/Recommended

Cadenhead's Caol Ila 1989 Islay SMSW (Scotland); 57.1% abv, $99.

The bright, burnt yellow/light amber tint is akin to an amontillado sherry; excellent purity. The dazzling, unadulterated bouquet leaps from the glass in salty, crisp waves of seaweed and soy sauce; with mineral water added, the bouquet tones down and takes on a creamy, vanilla wafer scent that doesn't block out the sea breeze or brine; smelling this beauty simply reminds me why avid whisky lovers admire the malts of Islay to the point of fanaticism; their definition and presence in the glass can be startling and even profound when they're at this level of excellence; a supremely satisfying bouquet. On the palate the smoke and embers flavor at entry is luscious, dry, and intensely oily; the midpalate offers refined, slightly sweet oak and vanilla flavors that complement the salty/kernel-like taste. The aftertaste is full bodied, oily, briny, and loaded with maritime character. A superb expression of this outstanding distillery that sits pondering the Paps of Jura; from Islay, only the malts of Lagavulin and Bowmore routinely match up against the sinewy, if overlooked, malts of the great Caol Ila.

2001 Rating: ★★★★★/Highest Recommendation

Cadenhead's Clynelish 12 Year Old Northern Highlands SMSW (Scotland); 60.2% abv, $99.

Yellow/amber hue; excellent purity. The opening nosing passes are met by flowery, slightly oily, moderately prickly scents that are dry to off-dry and more malty than woody; further exposure to air stimulates deeper aromas, most notably, citrus and rose petals; not a great bouquet, but a solid one that's concentrated and spirity. The palate entry is dry, mildly fiery, and heather-like; the midpalate stage is all about tobacco smoke/butts in an ash tray plus oil, peat, and charred bourbon oak barrels. Finishes intensely malty sweet, very oily, and, simply put, lip-smacking luscious. Dilute by two-to-one, whisky to water, then sit back and marvel.

2002 Rating: ★★★★/Highly Recommended

Cadenhead's Cragganmore 12 Year Old Speyside SMSW (Scotland); 59.2% abv, $98.

Plain Jane, rather dullish wheat field gold; good purity. This opening aroma starts off seductive and sherry-cask bittersweet; time in the glass finds the bouquet deepen significantly especially in the oily/resiny/green olive expression of the oak; I love this resin/leafy green style of malt bouquet. The palate entry is intensely spirity but the impact of the oak is immediately apparent; by the midpalate point the surface taste goes very leafy and green vegetable-like, but the core flavor is still resiny and oily. The finish is clean, oily, oaky, and bittersweet, as in nutty. I preferred the bouquet over the flavor.

2002 Rating: ★★★/Recommended

Cadenhead's Dalmore 1987 Northern Highlands SMSW (Scotland); 59.9% abv, $112.

Pristine medium amber color; superb purity. The bouquet, when undiluted, is warm, biscuity, sweet, and fruity/ripe, especially white grapes; the addition of mineral water brings out exotic scents of banana nut bread, nutmeg, allspice, butter, and walnuts; this is an entertaining bouquet with or without dilution; bravo. In the mouth the taste is toasty, sweet and ripe from palate entry through midpalate. Aftertaste is long, warming, oaky sweet, and almost smoky in a sooty way. One of the two best bottlings of Dalmore I've encountered and merely confirms my four star classification of this underappreciated distillery; find, purchase and savor.

2001 Rating: ★★★★★/Highest Recommendation

Cadenhead's Glen Craig 19 Year Old Speyside SMSW (Scotland); 59.5% abv, $89.

The deep amber color borders on being dark honey/brown; good purity. The nose is heavily caramelized and honey sweet in the first couple of sniffings after the pour; air contact and a half ounce of mineral water round out the rough edges as the final two nosing passes pick up dense aromas of sweet cereal, dark caramel, toffee, butterscotch, and oloroso sherry; a dense, lumbering bouquet that's short on finesse. Quite decent on the palate at entry as round, marzipan, cocoa, and carob tastes occupy (read: blanket) the taste buds; at the midpalate stage the flavors regrettably turn lead-like and metallic, quashing the confection and honeyed qualities found at the entry. The finish is clumsy, obese, overly wooded, and sappy sweet. I have an affinity for robust, chewy, sweet malts but this malt loses all sense of direction at midpalate and ultimately comes off as awkward, off-balance, and lame.

2002 Rating: ★/Not Recommended

Cadenhead's Glen Garioch 11 Year Old Eastern Highlands SMSW (Scotland); 56.6% abv, $89.

Pretty, absolutely pure, yellow straw color. Oh my, my, my, this lovely, seductive aroma starts out sweetly malty, slightly peppery, and intensely herbal; time in the sampling glass only serves to deepen this vixen's aromatic virtues as zesty, composed, nutty, and peppery scents of oak, malt, cigarette smoke, and garden herbs wash over the olfactory sense; a brilliant, beautifully structured, textbook Eastern Highlands bouquet that's simply the best I've come across from this distillery. The palate entry is buttery, rich, nutty, and sweet in a malty manner; the midpalate point explodes with generous, rich, honeyed flavors that include nougat, butterscotch, dark caramel, and bittersweet chocolate; all this flavor impact from an eleven year old? The aftertaste is long, dry, nutty, a tad buttery, and extremely satisfying. A tour de force from this distillery that favorably responds to the addition of spring water by becoming even more creamy/buttery and maple sweet; WOW.

2002 Rating: ★★★★★/Highest Recommendation

Cadenhead's Glen Grant 1989 Speyside SMSW (Scotland); 63.9% abv, $110.
Medium amber tint; superb purity. The extremely steep alcohol level is felt deep in the nasal cavity in the undiluted sniffing part of the evaluation; searching past the alcohol, I detect a fine, even graceful, maltiness that's moderately sweet; after dilution; a faint flowery/heathery scent emerges and overshadows the malt; not a memorable bouquet. The tastes of rich nougat, oaky vanilla, and savory light toffee enchant the taste buds right from the palate entry; the midpalate is warm, comforting, and floral sweet. The finish is long, simple, sweet, and clean. Like virtually all bottlings of this Rothes village-located distillery, it's straightforward, uncomplicated, and solidly made.
2001 Rating: ★★★/Recommended

Cadenhead's Glen Keith 15 Year Old Speyside SMSW (Scotland); 61.1% abv, $105.
Honey/amber hue; perfect purity. In the initial two sniffings within the three minute period following the pour reluctant aromas of almond butter, bourbon oak, and dry malt gradually make their way out of the glass; aeration (six more minutes) and the addition of mineral water much to my surprise assist very little in coaxing out much aroma besides a pedestrian maltiness; hmmm. The story of the taste phase is entirely different as the palate entry begins round, woody, and concentrated; by the midpalate stage opulent, mildly sweet tastes of malt, milk chocolate, and light caramel make for interesting quaffing. The finish is nutty, semisweet, and long. The flavor phase redeemed a lackluster bouquet to the point of a recommendation.
2002 Rating: ★★★/Recommended

Cadenhead's Glenallachie 11 Year Old Speyside SMSW (Scotland); 61.7% abv, $89.
Honey/amber color; excellent purity. The first two whiffs discover a biscuity, cereal-like, and garden herb bouquet that's tightly-knit yet approachable; mingling with air in the glass for an additional six minutes brings out light caramel and oak resin; not a classic multilayered Speyside bouquet but, nonetheless, it has enough charm and freshness to overcome its shortcomings. The biscuity quality noted in the bouquet is clearly evident at palate entry; at midpalate the flavors turn tight, astringent, and woody; the addition of a few drops of spring water doesn't rectify the taste phase situation. The aftertaste is resiny, tart, and lean. One of the most austere and ordinary offerings I've encountered from this overlooked distillery.
2002 Rating: ★★/Not Recommended

Cadenhead's Glenburgie-Glenlivet 16 Year Old Speyside SMSW (Scotland); 59.6% abv, $115.
Lovely, light amber/light honey brown color; superb purity. The first couple of sniffings detect lovely, controlled but not subtle aromas including marzipan, nougat, and toasted walnut; six more minutes of air contact brings out all sorts of intriguing scents, most notably, buttered popcorn, bacon fat, canola oil, dried red berry fruit, and light peaty smoke; there's a whole array of multilayered aromas occurring here. The palate entry is toasty, cereal sweet, honeyed, and even a touch sherry-like; by midpalate the taste profile expands to include tea leaves, salted butter, pipe tobacco, and light caramel. The finish is extended, malty sweet, oaky, and delicious.
2002 Rating: ★★★★/Highly Recommended

Cadenhead's Glencadam 18 Year Old Eastern Highlands SMSW (Scotland); 55.8% abv, $109.

The pleasing golden color of barley right before grain harvest; minor sediment. The opening nosing passes reveal compact, if meager, scents of dry malt and oak; aeration and the addition of spring water do nothing to stimulate further aromatic display; score so far: bouquet, zero. The palate entry is sharp, even with the abv reduction, and offers nasty tastes of lead pencil and asphalt; desperate, I keep hoping that it will open up into something worthwhile at midpalate but it flops spectacularly as terribly astringent and disturbingly raw flavors sear my tongue. Somebody at Cadenhead's must have been experiencing an LSD flashback when they okayed the release of this aggressive, undrinkable, totally out-of-whack mess; hey, wake up out there—this is nothing more than swill.

2002 Rating: ★/Not Recommended

Cadenhead's Glenglassaugh 1978 Speyside SMSW (Scotland); 48.8% abv, $148.

The incredible nut brown/deep topaz appearance is more like an old Spanish brandy from Jerez than a Speyside single malt; fine purity. The nose in undiluted form is thick, buttery, burnt, and emits a touch of sulphury burnt matches; with the addition of mineral water, the bouquet turns a bit rancio-like in its hard cheese incarnation; one can only wonder what type of barrels this buxom malt was matured in; my guess would be a combination of oloroso sherry casks and heavily charred bourbon barrels; it's not the type of bouquet that would charm anyone but for the most ardent fan of heavily oaked malt; I responded favorably to it despite the oak-a-thon. On the palate much of the blustery charm of the over-the-top, oaky/buttery bouquet is replaced by rancid flavors of tired oak barrels. The finish is a mere echo of the aroma. What began as an idiosyncratic, but good-hearted oddball ended as an overblown, vulgar floozy of a malt that should never have been released in the first place.

2001 Rating: ★/Not Recommended

Cadenhead's Glenlivet 12 Year Old Speyside SMSW (Scotland); 60.5% abv, $94.

Lovely, autumnal amber/honey color; very good purity. The opening sniffings come across as thumbprint Glenlivet: floral, mildly sweet, and elegant immediately; air contact brings out more polite virtues as lightly toasted, mildly peated aromas of dry cereal, oak, black tea, and tobacco leaf do nothing less than enchant the olfactory sense; as is so often the case with this great distillery, a clinic on what a Speyside bouquet should be like. All the fine qualities enjoyed in the aroma come across in the flavor phase right from the palate entry; by the midpalate point the flavors turn slightly buttery and smoky as a deft trace of peat appears. The finish is medium long, gentlemanly, malty sweet, and just a touch hot from the spirit. This excellent distillery never ceases to amaze and delight me.

2002 Rating: ★★★★/Highly Recommended

Cadenhead's Inverleven 1969 Central Highlands SMSW (Scotland); 50.9% abv, $278.

The deep amber/bronze/topaz color is truly beautiful in its brilliance; ideal purity. The undiluted nosing passes pick up crisp, vibrant, and acidic aromas of roasted almonds, cocoa, and dried fruit; following the addition of mineral water, the fruit element turns sour (unripe) and slightly green; the aroma was far more attractive and bristling prior to dilution; in this case, the water dulled the perfume. On palate the flavor at entry is narrow, dry, and intensely woody; then at midpalate the taste expands to include black pepper and linseed. A curious malt that straddles the fence at being too heavily oaked, not in the typical vanilla/buttery/creamy way but more in a stone dry, austere fashion; makes me wonder what type of oak this whisky was matured in as well as what size barrels; started out well, but unraveled with dilution.

2001 Rating: ★★/Not Recommended

Cadenhead's 15 Year Old Isle of Jura SMSW (Scotland); 57.7% abv, $105.

Very pale, early morning sunshine yellow; minor sediment. The early-on bouquet is ripe, fresh and malty, with just the barest hint of sea salt; exposure to air for another five minutes and a swirl or two encourages a distinct aromatic deepening, especially in the perfumy area of the sea salt; the end result is a genuinely fragrant island bouquet that's comely and gentle. The palate entry is medium-bodied, sweet in a cereal way, and richer than I'd expect from Jura; but who's complaining?; by the midpalate juncture a spirity heat overtakes the taste buds and I immediately add mineral water to cut the alcohol percentage—this helps put out the fire and the flavor turns malty and user-friendly. The aftertaste is sweet, just mildly salty, and almost biscuity, as in cookie batter. Another pleasant malt experience from this underrated island distillery.

2002 Rating: ★★★/Recommended

Cadenhead's Jura 1986 Isle of Jura SMSW (Scotland); 59.8% abv, $116.

The pale yellow/flax tint is clear and very clean. This peculiar bouquet opens up with piquant scents of barnyard, moss, and mushroom; mineral water definitely helps this rough-edged aroma transform into a graceful bouquet as the H20 rounds out the fragrance, bringing out scents of candied nuts, marzipan, and very sweet malt; an aromatic frog that was changed into a prince by the addition of water. As is so typical of Jura malts, the taste is far more akin to a Highland profile than that of an island as crackling, sweet, but medium-textured flavors of vanilla, caramel, and sweet oak take command at entry and wield their power well through the aftertaste. A malt that benefits remarkably from the marriage with pure mineral water.

2001 Rating: ★★★/Recommended

Cadenhead's Laphroaig 10 Year Old Islay SMSW (Scotland); 60.6% abv, $85.

Attractive amber/light honey color; some sediment seen. The opening aromatic salvo is not as peaty or medicinal as one might expect; in fact, I find the initial two whiffs only moderately smoky/peaty by Laphroaig standards; more time in the glass and a touch of mineral water stimulates pleasing notes of tobacco leaf and damp earth; not the street fighter bouquet I expected to wrestle with. In the mouth at palate entry the smokiness actually turns a touch sweet, almost like fruity pipe tobacco; at the midpalate stage the flavors of smoke, peat, sea salt, sweet malt, sweet oak (must be bourbon or Tennessee sour mash) meld beautifully into a stunning, chewy taste. The aftertaste is long, smoky, peaty, and sweet. As comely and powerful as a young, vigorous Laphroaig can get; bravo.

2002 Rating: ★★★★/Highly Recommended

Cadenhead's Linkwood 13 Year Old Speyside SMSW (Scotland); 58.6% abv, $104.

The old copper penny color is downright 20 year old aged tawny port-like; excellent purity. The opulent, sappy, mapley opening aromas are intensely oaky sweet in the first three minutes after the pour; with six more minutes of aeration the buxom, honeyed bouquet takes on a slight rancio quality, in that it turns remarkably concentrated, raisiny, and woody; not what one would normally expect from a Speyside distillery; an ambrosial banquet for those who prefer their malts raisiny and sweet; matured in 100% oloroso sherry butts for all 13 years? The palate entry is decadent and luxurious right from the start as tastes of maple, butterscotch, vanilla extract, and plum pudding trailblaze through my willing taste buds; the addition of mineral water makes the flavor experience accelerate especially in the midpalate where the oaky/rancio/nougat/sugar maple panorama of flavor goes off the charts. The aftertaste is rich but not overly sweet. Not a malt for everyone, that's for sure; reminds me of the Gran Reserva 18 Year Old from the Macallan (★★★★★); a quintessential after-dinner tot.

2002 Rating: ★★★★★/Highest Recommenation

Cadenhead's Littlemill 1989 Lowlands SMSW (Scotland); 61.6% abv, $107.

The pale yellow hue reminds me most of a dry, light-bodied wine, say, a muscadet, for instance; excellent purity. The full-strength nose is vividly alcoholic, displaying sour/unripe scents of fruits, most notably pineapple and green apple; with water added the aroma goes toasty and malty, but not for a moment fat or sassy; over time, the beguiling background scent of green olive charms the olfactory sense. On palate the taste is malty/biscuity, but searing on the tongue as the water cuts the alcoholic fire only minimally. The aftertaste is hot, aggressive, and basically begs for more water to be added. A tiger-by-the-tail malt that by my estimation should be cut by the ratio of three parts malt to two parts water.

2001 Rating: ★★★/Recommended

Cadenhead's Lochside 1981 Eastern Highlands SMSW (Scotland); 60.9% abv, $139.

A distillery that no longer exists; pretty, burnished yellow/honey color; perfect purity. This fiery nose sports a true Eastern Highland piquancy that's generated from the mingling of spirit and oak, a kind of weedy/vegetal aroma that's a cross between steamed white rice and dry morning cereal; with water added, the aroma turns floral, unbuttered popcorn-like, and resiny; a common malt aroma that displays little panache, with or without mineral water. The taste shows some admirable presence on the tongue especially at midpalate when the flavors turn mildly sweet and sap-like, with underlying notes of oak and malt. The finish is long, malty, sweet, and unexceptional.

2001 Rating: ★★/Not Recommended

Cadenhead's Longmorn-Glenlivet 14 Year Old Speyside SMSW (Scotland); 55.4% abv, $101.

Light straw/yellow hue; unblemished and pure. The initial two minutes of inhaling are punctuated with seductive peppery surface scents that float atop the more serious base aromas of oaky vanilla, toasty malt, and light caramel; with five minutes of aeration, the nose takes a peculiar turn by emitting atypical scents of glue, soft cheese, and boiled cabbage. The palate entry is intensely sweet and malty; at the midpalate point the maltiness turns chocolaty, bittersweet, oily, and resiny. The aftertaste shows similarity to pumpernickel bread, oatmeal, dark honey, and wood. An oddball expression from this normally classical distillery; after retasting it, I could see why the Longmorn people parted with this barrel, probably quite happy to.

2002 Rating: ★★/Not Recommended

Cadenhead's Macallan 12 Year Old Speyside SMSW (Scotland); 60.3% abv, $102.
Pretty medium amber/ light honey hue; sediment-free. The comely opening bouquet is toasty, slightly honeyed, and acutely buttery; a gorgeous beginning; exposure to air and a swirl or two unleashes further scents including heady, piercing spirit, medium-sweet malt, and a light touch of oak; after adding mineral water. The palate entry is deliciously rich, nutty/nougaty, and elegant in its restraint and composure; by the midpalate phase the flavors of candied nuts, light caramel, toffee, and oak become more lean and focused than buttery and expansive. The finish is long, keenly nougaty and luscious. Simply terrific.
2002 Rating: ★★★★/Highly Recommended

Cadenhead's Macallan 1989 Speyside SMSW (Scotland); 60.5% abv, $110.
The striking brandy/copper penny color shines in the glass; ideal purity. The nose, undiluted, is wine-like, almost grapy, clean, and a bit austere; after water is added, stately aromatic notes of light caramel, oak, and malt; the aroma's strength fades, however, after a mere five minutes in the glass. The palate entry shows a richness immediately as sherried, opulent, and sweet tastes blanket the taste buds in a medium-to-thick texture; the midpalate is malty/sherry oak sweet and delectable while the aftertaste turns plummy, even raisiny and sweet. This malt takes off once it's in the mouth; exhibits the kind of sheer elegance that can come from only a handful of malt distilleries, Macallan being one of them.
2001 Rating: ★★★★/Highly Recommended

Cadenhead's Pittyvaich-Glenlivet 16 Year Old Speyside SMSW (Scotland); 57.3% abv, $111.
Bright and pretty amber/honey hue; quite a lot of minuscule sediment though. The opening whiffs pick up dank aromas of wet pavement, mushrooms, and metal; further aeration does little to redeem this peculiar and very unmalt-like aroma that flashes scents of cardboard and fiberglass; phewwww. The palate entry tastes are oniony and husk-like; at midpalate there's a fleeting flavor of malt that's unfortunately quickly overwhelmed by pedestrian and atypically synthetic tastes of parchment and manmade fibers. The finish is bleak, flabby, and fatty. Falls in line with the weak character profile of this miserable distillery; thank goodness, it's moth-balled.
2002 Rating: ★/Not Recommended

Cadenhead's Rosebank 11 Year Old Lowlands SMSW (Scotland); 57.5% abv, $89.
Typical light straw/yellow tint; minor sediment spotted. The enticing opening aroma offers fragile scents of asparagus, malt, and green pepper in the first couple of passes; after five minutes of additional aeration the lean-to-austere bouquet expands to include fresh herbs, in particular, dill and thyme plus cardboard; moderately pleasant bouquet. The palate entry shows far better character than the nose as evolved, assertive tastes of sweet malt and light toffee delight the taste buds; the midpalate phase is especially sweet and biscuity. The aftertaste is firm, gently sweet, and malty. The mouth phase and satisfying finish save this malt from the ranks of the commonplace.
2002 Rating: ★★★/Recommended

Cadenhead's Royal Brackla 16 Year Old Speyside SMSW (Scotland); 52.3% abv, $115.
Very pale silvery/lemon juice yellow hue; some black floating debris seen. The initial two nosing passes reveal delicate, wispy scents of dry malt and green vegetables; aeration

and swirling do little to stimulate further aromatic expansion; the addition of mineral water only serves to mute the bouquet even more. The palate entry offers some moderately pleasant tastes, most prominently sweet malt and light toffee; at the midpalate juncture the malty sweetness deepens to include butterscotch and nuts. Finish is long and malty sweet. A lackluster aroma is redeemed in the mouth.
2002 Rating: ★★★/Recommended

Cadenhead's Tomatin 11 Year Old Speyside SMSW (Scotland); 58.1% abv, $89.

Attractive yellow/gold color; superb, ultra clean purity. The opening whiffs display a handsome, well-knit, mildly sweet and fruity aroma in the first three minutes following the pour; the aromatic integration continues in the final two nosing passes as the bouquet adds seductive scents of black pepper, tobacco leaf, and oak resin; one of the better bouquets I've come across from this normally underachieving malt distillery. The palate entry is deliciously sweet in a cookie batter/vanilla biscuit manner; the midpalate stage is vividly spirity, pleasantly oily, even succulent. The aftertaste highlights the oily malt and the light toffee taste. I've been slowly coming around to the malts of this distillery through various merchant bottlings.
2002 Rating: ★★★/Recommended

Caledonian Selection Bowmore 1992 10 Year Old Islay SMSW (Scotland); 55.8% abv, $76/decanter.

Has the golden straw look of an island youngster; excellent purity. The stiff sea breeze/briny nose comes right at you in the opening sniffings after the pour; aeration releases pungent notes of dill, fennel, and dry malt; not a totally attractive Bowmore bouquet because it lacks the usual sophistication and elegance of the distillery bottlings. The palate entry is marked with aggressive tastes of tobacco leaf, cigarette smoke, brine, and wood resin; by the midpalate stage there's a slight—and welcome—settling down of the flavor profile as calmer tastes of cocoa, vanilla, and maple make for sweet and pleasant sipping. The finish is raw, sweet, and aggressive. All the thumbprint characteristics of Bowmore are present but they're underdeveloped at this stage and, therefore, I can't recommend this offering due to its immaturity; though the potential is there, this malt simply isn't ready to be consumed yet; is this one of the inherent dangers of merchant bottlings? Yes.
2003 Rating: ★★/Not Recommended

Caledonian Selection Bruichladdich 1991 11 Year Old Islay SMSW (Scotland); 59.6% abv, $78/decanter.

Lemon juice/straw color; very good purity. Gives off a fresh, lightly briny, and almost flowery (rose petals?) bouquet in the first couple of whiffs after the pour; later sniffings following seven more minutes of aeration find traces of orange blossom, lemon drop candy, lightly roasted malt, cocoa, and sea breeze; this is a seductively alluring bouquet that's always at arm's length. The palate entry is delicate, buttery, and remarkably smooth; the midpalate stage features sound, solid and flowery flavors that are enhanced by hints of sweet malt, palm oil, bourbon cask, sulphur, and sea salt. The aftertaste is brief, nimble and malty. A very nice expression of pre-Jim McEwan Bruichladdich.
2003 Rating: ★★★/Recommended

Caledonian Selection Clynelish 1972 29 Year Old Northern Highlands SMSW (Scotland); 56.3% abv, $160/decanter.
Very pretty golden hue; some sediment seen. The initial nosing passes unearth dry, unfocused, slightly muted scents of malt, sesame and even in the distance, mustard seed; additional time in the glass releases scents of palm oil, lanolin, egg white, slight brine, and fresh almonds; not a typical malty Clynelish bouquet; significantly better in the mouth than in the nose. The palate entry is more in line with what I expect from this great distillery as the opening taste is deeply grainy/malty, sweet, and oily; by midpalate this whisky adds sensuous tastes of dark chocolate, sugar cookies, brown sugar, oak, and honey. It finishes medium-long, moderately sweet and succulent. I would have easily given a fourth star had it not been for the listless, wayward, undisciplined bouquet.
2003 Rating: ★★★/Recommended

Caledonian Selections Caperdonich 31 Year Old Speyside SMSW (Scotland); 72.3% abv, $135.
A really pretty amber/topaz color greets the eye; very minor sediment. The mature, fully evolved bouquet is composed, intensely oaky, moderately sweet, and cereal-like in the first couple of sniffings after the pour; five to eight minutes of aeration release further scented notes including glycerin, light caramel, and honey; a sophisticated, understated bouquet of charm and presence. The palate entry rings with sweet, oaky, caramel flavors; the midpalate point adds candied almond, toffee, and an atypical background taste of citrus rind. The finish is long, oaky sweet, mature, and luscious. The finest Caperdonich I've evaluated so far.
2002 Rating: ★★★★/Highly Recommended

Caledonian Selections Clynelish 1972 27 Year Old Northern Highlands SMSW (Scotland); 61.3% abv, $122.
Typically light amber in color for a Clynelish; excellent clarity. The pure, biscuity/doughy opening aroma reminds me instantly of why I've always rated this distillery as one of the best half-dozen in Scotland; the middle stages offer delicate touches of sea salt, heather, egg white, and dry malt; the fourth and last sniffing, after eight minutes of time in the copita glass, finds the doughiness receding and vigorous fruit and floral scents taking charge along with a dash of black pepper; bottling after bottling, I love the airy perfume of this distillery's malts; there's never an intrusion of alcohol, even at this elevated proof. The undiluted palate entry shows tastes of bittersweet chocolate, apple cobbler, and sweet malt; the midpalate, more exotic than the entry, is textured, appley, and fat, with hints of butterscotch and toffee. The finish is sweet, concentrated, and intensely malty, with just a splash of brininess. Yet another sensational malt from this underrated and underappreciated distillery.
2001 Rating: ★★★★★/Highest Recommendation

Caledonian Selections Glen Mhor 1977 23 Year Old Northern Highlands SMSW (Scotland); 59.3% abv, $110.
Very pretty medium amber/harvest gold hue; ideal purity. The opening aroma is terrifically friendly, open for business, and generous as delectable scents of linseed oil and cotton candy greet the olfactory sense; the middle passes add nice notes of cream and sweet cereal malt; the fourth and final sniffing, following over seven minutes of aeration, introduces

some mild spice and green pepper; a zesty, confident and pleasant bouquet. The palate entry is a touch heated but not enough to burn; the midpalate phase owns delightful flavors of pepper, light oak, off-dry malt, and sesame oil. The aftertaste turns on the heat to the point of light burning on the tongue, but also shows some length and malty sweetness. Never a favorite distillery of mine, however, this version does offer enough aromatic and taste pleasure to warrant a recommendation.

2001 Rating: ★★★/Recommended

Caledonian Selections Glenrothes 1967 32 Year Old Speyside SMSW (Scotland); 48.2% abv, $140.

Pale amber/light honey appearance; good purity. The nose after the pour is reluctant to show itself; with a few swirls and a couple of minutes in the glass, the aroma finally emerges in soft waves of dry grain and new oak; in the fourth and last whiff the aroma seems weary and decrepit; doubtless the worst, most lame Glenrothes bouquet I've ever come across but frankly I believe this whisky is simply too old for public consumption; it's beyond being a relic. The palate entry shows a bit more life in terms of flavor presence than the anemic aroma; the dusty/fusty midpalate is hard, brittle, overly spirity, and shows just a glimpse of its former glory. The aftertaste is ropy, medium-long, bitter, sooty, sulphury, and unpleasant. This one should never have gone into the bottle to begin with; it doesn't do justice to this outstanding Speyside distillery; it's a bad decision like this that spurs criticism of the merchant bottling concept both from distilleries and purists.

2001 Rating: ★/Not Recommended

Caledonian Selections Macduff 1973 27 Year Old Speyside SMSW (Scotland); 51.7% abv, $117.

The color is a brilliant gold; impeccable purity. The initial nosing pass discovers well-developed aromas of oak, light smoke, and dry malt; the second and third whiffs pick up banana, fennel, and spice; the final sniffing turns a bit like dried fruit as the malt disappears and the focus is lost; linear, pedestrian, and not in the least a complex or intriguing bouquet. Slightly better in the mouth than in the nose, the palate entry offers some chewy, malty surface flavors, but not much depth; the midpalate is mildly fruity, very oily (I like that), and intensely peppery/spicy. The finish is long, buttery, and oily. The hollow aroma really hurts this malt's overall performance, leaving it an ordinary, if pricey luxury.

2001 Rating: ★★/Not Recommended

Caledonian Selections Tomintoul 1976 23 Year Old Speyside SMSW (Scotland); 55.5% abv, $110.

Nice medium amber/gold hue; excellent purity. The opening aroma is moderately biscuity and saltine wafer-like; with time in the glass, this bouquet comes alive in the third pass as waves of marzipan, light toffee, sweet malt, and buttery oak meld well; the final sniffing sees the bouquet add flowers, grass, and coffee with milk; not a profound bouquet, but pleasant and expressive nonetheless. The palate entry is sweet, caramel-like, and moderately oily; the midpalate is particularly oily and textured, offering sweet cereal and creamy butter tastes. The aftertaste is long, a tad nutty/nougaty, and spirity. Nice job.

2001 Rating: ★★★/Recommended

Classic of Islay 15 Year Old Islay Blended Malt Scotch Whisky (Scotland); 46% abv, $82.

The flax/pale straw color is marred by being moderately cloudy/murky. The opening inhalations detect generous peat evidence in the forms of kippers and cigarette ash; with further air contact, the peatiness kicks in with bigger, semisweet gulps of dried seaweed, ashtray, cigar box, old leather, and iodine; there's no mistaking the origin of this blended malt. The palate entry offers large-as-life tastes of textbook peatiness in the forms of smoke, iodine, seaweed, and saltwater taffy; by the midpalate stage the flavor profile turns sweeter, caramelly, and more lip-smacking. This stuff is seriously tasty and that recovery in the nose and mouth redeems the unappealing appearance fully.

2007 Rating: ★★★★/Highly Recommended

Classic of Islay 21 Year Old Islay Blended Malt Scotch Whisky (Scotland); 46% abv, $128.

The appearance of this malt is clear, bright, and pale yellow/tarnished silver in color; flawless purity. Keen evidence of rubber tire/inner tube, pencil eraser, medicine cabinet, and creosote makes for intriguing sniffing right from the pour; what emerges after additional aeration is highly medicinal/hospital-like in aromatic nature, yet strangely beguiling and compelling all the same. The palate entry is pleasantly sweet and smoky simultaneously; at the midpalate point, the taste turns increasingly peppery/spicy as the smoke recedes. Ends vegetal, clean, and off-dry, as the peatiness returns in a rush of cigarette smoke. Islay in a glass.

2007 Rating: ★★★★/Highly Recommended

Classic of Islay 26 Year Old Islay Blended Malt Scotch Whisky (Scotland); 46% abv, $155.

Slightly foggy, but not nearly as bad as the 15 Year Old; marigold in color. The initial whiffs pick up floral notes of gorse, heather, and carnation, with scant presence of peat/sea breeze; what was flowery in the opening two minutes becomes waxy/paraffin-like, fruity, and almost coin-like following the additional seven minutes of air contact. The palate entry offers metallic tastes that coincide perfectly with the coin-like aroma; by the midpalate juncture flavors of dry grain, smoked fish, and barely perceptible honey balance the metallic foundational taste. Too long in the barrel. This whisky lost its edge several years ago.

2007 Rating: ★★/Not Recommended

Distillery Select Craiglodge 1998 Peated 8 Year Old Highlands SMSW (Scotland); 45% abv, $55.

The deep honey color is brown and oloroso sherry-like; some sediment spotted. The initial whiffs pick up awkwardly rubbery, sooty, putrid, barnyard scents that remind me of a pig farm; aeration only further accents the amazingly displeasing aroma that can only be described as rank; peat-reek traditionally is sweet, briny, and smoky, while this is like burning tires. The palate entry is marginally better than the horrible aroma, but not by much as the taste is of past-sell-by-date sickly sweet and moldy; the midpalate features the burning tire/melted rubber flavor that's awful. One of the worst whiskies from Scotland I've had in a while and a strong candidate for my Bottom-Feeder list.

2007 Rating: ★/Not Recommended

Distillery Select Croftengea 1997 Heavily Peated 9 Year Old Highlands SMSW (Scotland); 45% abv, $60.

Pale green/gold hue; excellent clarity. The first inhalations call to mind quinine, green pepper, licorice, and wheat; another seven minutes of exposure to air don't help this acrid, unpleasantly medicinal, textile/fiber-like bouquet; again, this sour mess doesn't reflect what one normally thinks of as peat-reek; this is more latrine-reek or cat's pee-reek. The palate entry is leathery, ashy, and iodine-like, if a bit vegetal, but not terrible; by the midpalate stage, there's a glimmer of customary peat presence in the forms of cigarette smoke, kippers, and olive brine. Ends up raunchy and sour.

2007 Rating: ★/Not Recommended

Dun Bheagan 8 Year Old Islands SMSW (Scotland); 43% abv, $30.

Lovely pale amber/flax hue; excellent purity. The opening nosing passes within three minutes of the pour discover svelte aromas of buttered toast, moderate peat smoke, and a subtle hint of heather; further aeration over another six minutes finds the emergence of semisweet malt, palm oil, cucumber, and cocoa bean; ends up developing into a deliciously inviting, mildly briny/peaty bouquet. The palate entry displays totally dry tastes of dry breakfast cereal and burnt toast; at the midpalate point piquant flavors of honey, orange blossom, tobacco leaf, heather, and light oak show their wares in medium-bodied style. It finishes politely in mildly sweet malty/fruity/heathery notes. As friendly as an old flannel shirt.

2002 Rating: ★★★/Recommended

Dun Bheagan 8 Year Old Islay SMSW (Scotland); 43% abv, $30.

Pretty medium amber/dusty gold color; quite a lot of sediment seen. One whiff of this vigorous peaty/tobacco-like aroma tells me exactly where it's from; the peat reek-a-thon continues with fervor into the later nosing passes as air contact lights the fire under the bouquet as it emits pungent, smoky, briny, and salty scents that tickle the nasal cavity; it's not a monster phenol-peat schnozz, but it certainly owns enough seaweed n' smoke to qualify as medium peated. The palate entry is almost gently sweet in a malty way; then at midpalate the peat smoke makes an appearance in earnest on the tongue. The finish is delightfully sweet and malty.

2002 Rating: ★★★/Recommended

Dun Bheagan 8 Year Old Speyside SMSW (Scotland); 43% abv, $30.

Standard issue amber/harvest gold hue; evidence of floating sediment spotted. The opening aroma comes across in the first couple of sniffings as being properly fruity/floral for Speyside, no surprises; time in the glass affords the aroma the chance to gather some steam which it does in the forms of mild barley, paraffin, feathery light peat smoke, and cantaloupe; a safe, wholly acceptable regional bouquet that doesn't rock the boat. In the mouth this malt is much sounder and more assertive than in the flaccid bouquet right from the lean, malty sweet, youthful but focused palate entry; the midpalate shows an even wider array of tastes including marzipan, sugar cookie, vanilla bean, and peppery oak. The aftertaste is long, sinewy, malty sweet, and almost lip-smacking.

2002 Rating: ★★★/Recommended

Dun Bheagan Caol Ila 1992 10 Year Old Rum Cask Finished Islay SMSW (Scotland); 43% abv, $56.

Pretty lemon juice/pale straw hue; some sediment spotted. The early bouquet offers some zesty, salty, mid-range peatiness, all of which combine into a perfumy, typically Islay aroma; time in the glass allows the bouquet the opportunity to introduce additional scents, most prominently, seaweed, soy sauce, and hot green peppers. The palate entry is surprisingly soft, plump, even oily; by midpalate the taste profile includes rich elements, such as cream and nut butter, that underpin the salty/peaty/briny surface flavors. Ends up frisky, piquant, spirity, and delicious. A gem from this underappreciated malt distillery.

2004 Rating: ★★★★/Highly Recommended

Dun Bheagan Clynelish 1983 20 Year Old Northern Highlands SMSW (Scotland); 53.4% abv, $95.

Pale yellow color; very good purity. The initial nosing passes detect a slightly citrusy, green apple-like, delightfully fruity aroma that charges out from the starting block seemingly fully evolved; following seven more minutes of aeration, the aroma transforms into a voluptuous, malty bouquet that's moderately sweet, leafy and vegetal, but composed, self-assured and sophisticated; loved this integrated, harmonious bouquet. The palate entry is intensely malty and creamy; then at midpalate the spirit is unleashed as the taste goes fiery on the tongue. The spirity heat dies down quickly right before the finish, which highlights the luscious, mouthwatering buttery creaminess and concentrated maltiness. Owns enough spirit to make one think "mineral water" well before the first sip is taken; the great Clynelish never ceases to amaze me.

2004 Rating: ★★★★/Highly Recommended

Duncan Taylor BenRiach 1968 Cask 2592 Speyside SMSW (Scotland); 48% abv, $240.

The bright, clean golden/lemon juice hue reminds me of Loire Valley chenin blanc; impeccable clarity. The vibrant, dry aroma wastes no time in impressing the olfactory sense with its briary/floral perfume; extra time in the glass really affords this aroma the room it needs to expand into a bona fide Speyside bouquet that presents the more delicate, heathery/flowery/fruity (grapes) side of the district with style and elegance. The palate entry is dry, minerally, and totally focused on the malt; the later flavor stages introduce tastes of maple, vanilla bean, coffee, and black pepper. Concludes gently and politely in a soft, warm wave of malty flavor. A distillery known mainly as a solid contributor to blended Scotches, BenRiach's malts, like this one, are overlooked Speyside gems.

2004 Rating: ★★★★/Highly Recommended

Duncan Taylor Bowmore 1982 22 Year Old Islay SMSW (Scotland); 58.9% abv, $180.

The medium bright honey color is flawlessly clean. Right from the pour, there's strong maritime evidence of sea breeze, seaweed, and pickling brine; allowed another seven minutes in the glass, the aroma expands to include high-toned fruit fragrances, including ripe red berry, green melon, and red grapes; the succulence of the fruit notes overshadows any coastal influence completely in the latter stages of nosing. The heady, fiery entry is more toasty warm than fierce, but don't underestimate the potency of the alcohol; at midpalate the fruit comes alive again and determines the taste profile through the ripe, berry-like aftertaste. The

addition of spring water brings out the wood and the malted barley in sweet notes. Delicious doesn't begin to tell the story on this ultra-classic Bowmore edition.
2006 Rating: ★★★★★/Highest Recommendation

Duncan Taylor Bruichladdich 1966 Islay SMSW (Scotland); 40.9% abv, $250.
Attractive harvest yellow/gold hue; good purity. The first whiffs detect subtle notes of green apple and pear; delicate elements of gum and polishing wax enter the aromatic picture after further air contact. The palate entry is tightly structured, oily, and moderately grainy; at midpalate, the taste profile turns semisweet to bittersweet as flavors of malt, oloroso sherry, marshmallow, and nougat take charge. Concludes pleasantly semisweet and mildly fruity.
2005 Rating: ★★★/Recommended

Duncan Taylor Bruichladdich 1969 Cask 2331 Islay SMSW (Scotland); 46.8% abv, $270.
The color is a fine bay/deep amber hue; excellent clarity. The early nose is charged with woody resin and intriguing notes of nougat and honey; can't help but wonder if Cask 2331 was a sherry butt, considering the dark color and the deep aroma; aeration time of another seven minutes adds more aromatic dimension in the forms of tobacco leaf, sea breeze, and blue cheese. The palate entry is uncharacteristically massive and concentrated for an older Laddie; at midpalate the flavor profile goes intense, sweet, and buttery/oily as mature tastes of dark honey, oloroso sherry, marzipan, coconut, cocoa, and dark toffee combine to make a lovely flavor experience. Ends sweetly. I doubt that I would have ever guessed that this oddball beauty was an old Bruichladdich, so delightfully out of Islay/Laddie character is it; find and buy.
2004 Rating: ★★★★/Highly Recommended

Duncan Taylor Bunnahabhain 1967 Cask 3326 Islay SMSW (Scotland); 40.2% abv, $260.
Displays a pleasing to the eye medium amber/harvest gold color and superb clarity. The opening nosing passes detect one thing only, strong, mildly salty sea breeze; six more minutes in the copita bring out halting traces of mild peat, smoke, and freshly mown hay. No surprises at palate entry as the taste is off-dry, grassy, moderately briny, and delicate; by midpalate the flavor profile shifts gears by going sweeter, more caramel-like, and malty. Ends up on the sweeter side of the scale. Not a fathomless depth of character, but in fairness it's totally within the traditional character of Bunnahabhain and even slightly better since I've learned to keep my expectations low with old Boonie.
2004 Rating: ★★★/Recommended

Duncan Taylor Bunnahabhain 38 Year Old Cask 3335 Islay SMSW (Scotland); 40.9% abv, $274.
The color is old hay/old gold; appearance is clean. The opening whiffs pick up earthy scents of wet straw, freshly tilled soil, and beeswax; additional time in the glass adds muted aromas of heather and seaweed. The palate entry is big, round, and generously sweet; at the midpalate point the flavor profile takes on more of the oak as biscuity tastes of vanilla, walnut, and toasted almond come into play. The flavor fades rapidly in the finish. An interesting expression from this oft-neglected Islay stalwart distillery.
2007 Rating: ★★★/Recommended

Duncan Taylor Glen Grant 1968 Cask 3882 Speyside SMSW (Scotland); 56.1% abv, $230.
Tasted first neat; the copper/chestnut color is nothing short of stunningly beautiful; some sediment seen. The higher alcohol content is immediately apparent in the early whiffs; so are unusual (for the distillery) scents of sulphur/burnt matches, saddle leather, and candied almond; seven more minutes of air contact contribute to slightly improving the bouquet, which now displays mature, more integrated aromas of intense oak resin, butterscotch, burnt toast, and toasted cereals. The palate entry is sweet, sugary, and intensely honeyed; the midpalate stage continues the oak-a-thon in the forms of honey, brown sugar, hard candy, and dark caramel. Finishes fiery on the tongue and concentrated. When room temperature mineral water is added, this malt comes alive and is biscuity, sherry-like, succulent, maple-like, and completely disarming; I've ended up rating this malt for you solely on the basis that one-half ounce of mineral/spring water will be added to every ounce of whisky; the properties do not come to full light without the help of mineral/spring water.
2004 Rating: ★★★★/Highly Recommended

Duncan Taylor Glen Grant 36 Year Old Cask 830 Speyside SMSW (Scotland); 54.10% abv, $280.
The gorgeous, if atypical, mahogany/old oak/cola color is strikingly similar to East India sherry; superb purity. In the first sniffs, the elevated spirit is aggressive and, as such, overshadows everything else going on aromatically; once some of the alcohol blows off during the additional aeration period, what's left behind are bakery notes of brown sugar, cocoa, treacle, as well as chocolate covered cherries and molasses. The palate entry is hearty, big textured, rich, and old sherry sweet; the midpalate point features creamy tastes of cocoa butter, dark caramel, and walnut paste. Finishes chunky, intensely nutty, and bakery treat-like. Not for everyone, but for admirers of outlandishly rich older malts, a bonanza.
2007 Rating: ★★★/Recommended

Duncan Taylor Glen Keith 1971 33 Year Old Speyside SMSW (Scotland); 50.8% abv, $234.
The old coppery/russet/nut-brown look of this old malt is of very old armagnac or, even brandy de Jerez; pristine and brilliant under the lamp. The astringent first nosings pick up lots of oak, acids, and rounded-off, on-the-decline spirit; additional aeration doesn't assist in any kind of aromatic expansion or deepening as the latter sniffs detect only weary spirit, old newspaper, and astringent oak. The palate entry is assertively spirity, mildly sweet, and even a tad grainy; the midpalate is whole lot more expressive as richly sweet, moderately honeyed tastes of marzipan and toffee impress the taste buds far more than the bouquet impressed the olfactory sense. Finishes well, stately, and surprisingly well-endowed. A splash of mineral water helps mightily in the flavor development. Acknowledging that this malt is well on its chemical downturn as is obvious by the lackluster, listless aroma, there remains enough substance for deep-pocketed mavens to enjoy. The mildly interested shouldn't bother with it.
2006 Rating: ★★★/Recommended

Duncan Taylor Glenrothes 1968 Cask 9970 Speyside SMSW (Scotland); 49% abv, $240.
The medium amber color has a greenish tint at the edge; excellent purity. The opening whiffs find woody, dusty, old library-like aromas of parchment, cardboard, and very distant malt; seven more minutes of aeration reveal mature, evolved scents that feature palm oil,

lanolin, old oak, wood resin, and faint vanilla bean; clearly a bouquet that's on the downside of its life cycle. While the bouquet may be fading, the palate entry offers a lip-smacking taste that's part maple and part oaky vanillin; by the midpalate the flavor profile shifts into the next gear, emitting semi-rich, woody, sherry/honey tastes that reflect the inherent greatness of this distillery's malts. Concludes sweet, unbowed, and cocoa-like; an old, proud lion whose prime has passed but which still retains an unmistakable air of dignity…and more than a little bite.

2004 Rating: ★★★/Recommended

Duncan Taylor Highland Park 1966 Orkney Islands SMSW (Scotland); 41.4% abv, $313.
Pleasing golden color; absolutely pure. The opening sniffings pick up lots of vinyl and prickly spirit; aeration time of another six minutes doesn't help the aromatic situation as the bouquet remains aggressive and mossy; not like any Highland Park I know. The palate entry is somewhat better as semisweet tastes of dried pineapple and mince pie come to the fore; at midpalate the taste profile owns the kind of HP maltiness/creaminess that I've come to enjoy, but the rest of the phase is simple and grainy with very little depth. Finishes fine and mildly sweet, if a dash flabby and hollow.

2004 Rating: ★★/Not Recommended

Duncan Taylor Linlithgow 1982 Lowlands SMSW (Scotland); 63% abv, $178.
This Lowlands distillery, now closed, is more commonly known as St. Magdalene. Very pale gold/pale amber color; good clarity. Even though the abv is very high, the initial nosings pick up mostly soft scents of sweet malt, almonds and olives; seven minutes more of aeration kick up added aromas of saddle leather and pork sausage. The palate entry does a good job in concealing the mammoth alcohol as toasted, toffee-like flavors override the spirit; at midpalate, however, the abv jumps in, setting my tongue on fire, but then there's a nice weed/grass-like taste that extinguishes the heat, leaving behind an assortment of flavors including fudge, dried figs, and sultanas. Intriguing right from the start.

2004 Rating: ★★★★/Highly Recommended

Duncan Taylor Longmorn 1973 Cask 8914 Speyside SMSW (Scotland); 47.6% abv, $227.
The brilliant yellow/straw color beams beneath the examination lamp. Flawless purity; the initial nosing blasts are treated to lively, vigorous aromas of damp earth, wet barley, wet concrete, and a deft touch of tobacco leaf-like peat; additional aeration serves to stimulate deeper, zestier scents, including black pepper, barley malt, steamed asparagus, steamed white rice, and unused oak barrel stave; this is an intriguing bouquet that shows this great distillery's pungent side. The palate entry exhibits a bit more in the way of classical Speyside character as succulent, semisweet tastes of light caramel, toffee, nougat, and oak thrill the taste buds; this is followed by a mesmerizing midpalate that's sinewy, full-bodied, vanilla-like, honeyed, and incredibly delicious. Finishes gracefully, sweet in a honeyed manner, and vigorous. A worthy expression from this landmark distillery (one of my six favorites).

2004 Rating: ★★★★/Highly Recommended

Duncan Taylor Macallan 1968 Cask 5585 Speyside SMSW (Scotland); 53.6% abv, $295.
Shows a lovely medium amber/honey/harvest gold hue; unblemished clarity. In the first couple of whiffs after the pour, the heady aroma is dominated by the piquant, but not prickly

spirit; allowed another seven minutes of resting in the glass, the spiritiness blows off, leaving behind delicate, waif-like aromas of toffee, unsalted butter, and pear drops. The expressive palate entry features an intensely oily, minty flavor that I like quite a lot; by the midpalate stage the flavor turns inward, returning to the oak/malt core as a light creaminess enters the equation and, in the process, mitigates some of the oiliness. Finishes semisweet, viscous, and spirity. Preferred this to the cask 5590 by a significant margin as there simply was more grip and dimension in this cask version.

2004 Rating: ★★★★/Highly Recommended

Duncan Taylor Macallan 1968 Cask 5590 Speyside SMSW (Scotland); 52.1% abv, $295.

The attractive golden/late season wheat field color is light for such an elderly Macallan; superb purity. The start-up aroma is green, lean, clean, and astringent; aeration time of an additional six minutes softens the astringency by bringing in more of the oak, which imparts agile aromas of resin, grain, new leather, and vanillin; not the usual honey/sherry-a-thon that you expect from Macallan. The palate entry accentuates the lean, astringent virtues liked in the bouquet; then at midpalate the taste profile turns heathery and slightly peaty/smoky. Ends up maintaining the sinewy flavor. Not a memorable Macallan, but an interesting expression all the same; can't help but wonder if Cask 5590 was an old bourbon barrel or a new American oak barrel.

2004 Rating: ★★★/Recommended

Duncan Taylor Miltonduff 1966 Speyside SMSW (Scotland); 41% abv, $246.

Bright harvest gold/medium amber color; flawless purity. The first inhalations pick up concentrated grainy/malty notes; with further aeration, the aroma expands marginally to include fruity/flowery scents of jasmine, pear drops, and heather; not an overly expressive bouquet, but tight and focused. Right from the biscuity, fruity palate entry it's clear that the finest virtues of this malt lay imbedded in the flavor phase; the midpalate stage brims with ripe, fruity tastes, especially white raisins, plums, and nectarines. Concludes in a sweet, grainy manner, with deft touches of light caramel and honey. Doubtless, one of the better Miltonduff's I've come across.

2005 Rating: ★★★★/Highly Recommended

Duncan Taylor NC2 Range Alt-A-Bhainne 14 Year Old Speyside SMSW (Scotland); 46% abv, $54.

Yellow/gold/corn color; superb clarity. Assertive vegetal scents of pine cone, sap, and maple make for interesting early on sniffing; aeration changes the face of the bouquet into more of a grainy/dry breakfast cereal direction where the featured aspect is the clean, kernel-like barley malt; this bouquet is as refreshing and immaculate as Speyside can get. Entry is surprisingly sweet and biscuity, with touches of maple and vanilla; the taste profile at midpalate reverts to dryness and is vibrant, clean, austere, and wonderfully grainy/malty. Ends up off-dry. Shows the lovely and elegant side of inland single malt.

2007 Rating: ★★★★/Highly Recommended

Duncan Taylor NC2 Range Isle of Arran 10 Year Old Isle of Arran SMSW (Scotland); 46% abv, $54.

Gold/deep straw color; excellent clarity. Offers delicate out-of-the-gate aromas of newly

tanned leather, baked pineapple, and quince; with an extra seven minutes of air contact, the aroma opens up to include sugar maple, cinnamon, and honeysuckle blooms. Entry is concentrated on the graininess and is dry and lightly smoked; the flavor profile at midpalate is pleasantly and moderately sweet and even a touch peppery (green pepper), with a silky texture that's very appealing. Concludes a little thin, but still is dry, lightly spiced, and tasty.
2007 Rating: ★★★/Recommended

Duncan Taylor NC2 Range Mortlach 13 Year Old Speyside SMSW (Scotland); 46% abv, $76.

Pale gold/light straw yellow color; flawless clarity. After the pour, the initial aroma is vegetal, brambly, and green; following the additional aeration period, the bouquet comes alive, emitting classical inland malt scents of dry barley malt, heather, and white rice. This malt shines brightest in the mouth; the entry is firm, tight, medium-sweet, a touch sap-like, and toffee-like; the flavor profile revs up at midpalate, offering chewy, semisweet tastes of sweetened breakfast cereal, light honey, nougat, and dried yellow fruit (pineapple, banana). Finishes clean, crisp, and with an oily surety that's both engaging and classy.
2007 Rating: ★★★★/Highly Recommended

Duncan Taylor North British 28 Year Old Single Grain Whisky (Scotland); 54.3% abv, $175.

Bright gold/chardonnay color; excellent purity. Smells of leather, white pepper, and pungent spirit in the initial sniffs; another seven minutes of exposure to air bring out vivid scents of honeywheat toast, pine needle, and flax/textile/nylon. Entry is corny/sassafras sweet, piquant spirits-wise, and mushroom/truffle-like; the taste profile at midpalate is assertively spirity, corny sweet, and still a touch mushroomy/musty. Concludes with sweet/resiny notes of sap and cedar. I found this whisky uninspiring and banal. Not the best example of what grain whisky can be.
2007 Rating: ★★/Not Recommended

Duncan Taylor Rarest of the Rare Banff 30 Year Old 1975 Cask 3421 Speyside SMSW (Scotland); 43.5% abv, $254.

Flax/yellow gold color; superb purity. Faint aromas of malt/grain and paraffin barely reach the rim of the glass; further aeration fails miserably to stir anything new here aromatically; I move on. Entry is intensely peppery, clove-like and more vigorous than the wilted aroma; the taste profile at midpalate supplies much needed animation in the forms of black pepper, clove, tobacco leaf, kale, and cedar. Concludes very dry, ethereal, and austere. I've never liked the malts from this demolished (1985) outer Speyside distillery and tasting this, I rest my case. Has all the allure of an ingrown buttock hair.
2007 Rating: ★/Not Recommended

Duncan Taylor Rarest of the Rare Glencraig 30 Year Old 1974 Cask 2926 Speyside SMSW (Scotland); 42% abv, $246.

Pale straw/silver in color; impeccably clear of sediment. Opening sniffs detect painfully subtle nuances of grass, brine, and leather; further air contact releases bland, tired seeming notes of candle wax, metal/nickel, and plastic. Entry presents the taste buds with dull, flaccid tastes of lemon zest and stale malt; there's a bit more animation in the midpalate as the taste profile adds some malted milk balls, old honey, and black pepper. Finishes meekly. Just because it might be rare doesn't automatically mean that it's good. Maybe there was a reason why this limp noodle was rare. Nobody wanted it.

2007 Rating: ★★/Not Recommended

Duncan Taylor Rarest of the Rare Glenugie 1981 23 Year Old Sherry Cask Eastern Highlands SMSW (Scotland); 58% abv, $228.
Brilliant nut brown/burnished orange color; perfect purity. The nose in unadulterated state is malty, dry and woody, with background traces of hazelnut and fudge; the addition of mineral water tones down the oakiness while turning up the nuttiness and introducing linseed oil and beeswax scents. The palate entry is chewy, spirity (even with the mineral water dilution), caramel- and toffee-like; the midpalate stage is gloriously succulent as ripe, maple-like tastes of chocolate covered banana, Raisinettes, and fudge make the taste buds swoon. The aftertaste is extended, honey sweet, and lush in the throat. A sterling example of what long-term sherry cask aging can do. This malt was taken from the cask at precisely the right moment. Bravo.

2005 Rating: ★★★★★/Highest Recommendation

Duncan Taylor Rarest of the Rare Glenugie 22 Year Old 1981 Sherry Cask 5156 Eastern Highlands SMSW (Scotland); 58% abv, $216.
The ochre/deep honey/oloroso sherry brown color dazzles the eye; ideal clarity. Out of the gate it smells of prune Danish, dried cherries, cocoa bean, and marshmallow; further air contact stimulates the spirit as it becomes prickly in the nasal cavity but only in the best way of being lively, smoky, and vivid, meaning there's no burn whatsoever. Entry is lush, caramel sweet, chocolaty, and bean-like; at midpalate the taste takes off in luxurious, if bittersweet waves of cocoa butter, dark chocolate, brown sugar, and black raisins. Ends up supple, sweet but not cloying, and very compelling and complete. I didn't add mineral water. Didn't need to.

2007 Rating: ★★★★/Highly Recommended

Duncan Taylor Rarest of the Rare Glenury Royal 20 Year Old 1984 Cask 3049 Eastern Highlands SMSW (Scotland); 50% abv, $179.
Bright corn yellow/sauvignon blanc appearance; ideal clarity. Smells sturdily of keen, almost minty barley malt and cooking spices/seeds, especially thyme and poppy seed; aeration brings out a lemony scent that gets mixed nicely with additional aromas of pine needle/cedar and green vegetable. Entry is pleasantly and appropriately sharp (it is 100-proof) and a bit sap-like; the flavor aspects at midpalate that I find most appealing are the semisweet taste of pipe tobacco (just a tad of smoke), charcoal, and butter cream. Finishes off-dry, with lots of embers-like warmth in the throat. Extremely nice dram.

2007 Rating: ★★★★/Highly Recommended

Duncan Taylor Rarest of the Rare Linlithgow 21 Year Old 1982 Cask 2214 Lowlands SMSW (Scotland); 63.5% abv, $217.
Faint gold/straw yellow color; unblemished purity. The elevated spirit level makes itself known immediately upon the initial inhalation as tidal waves of alcohol surge from the

glass; following more time, the spirit diminishes enough to expose smells of toasty malt, fried eggs, dried apricot, and lemongrass. Due to the abv, I add mineral water at this point. Entry is chockfull of dried fruit (prunes, raisins, apricots, cherries) and milk chocolate tastes; at midpalate the flavor profile turns waxy/oily in the most pleasing way. Finishes bawdy, assertive, fruity sweet, and satisfying. A thrilling experience that's worth the price.

2007 Rating: ★★★★★/Highest Recommendation

Duncan Taylor Rarest of the Rare North Port 24 Year Old 1981 Cask 774 Eastern Highlands SMSW (Scotland); 58% abv, $226.

The pale oyster shell/silver color reminds me of Loire Valley muscadet; excellent purity. In the first whiffs, there's a hint of sulfur/long ago burnt match that I like along with distant dried yellow fruits (dried banana? pineapple?); another seven minutes of air contact stimulates garden-like aromas of wet soil, moss, and heather. Entry is aggressively spirity, but neither raw nor harsh; at midpalate the taste profile includes firm and spirity flavors of peach pastry, biscuits, brown sugar, and vanilla wafer. End on a toffee/fudge note. This is the only North Port, now demolished, that I've ever liked.

2007 Rating: ★★★★/Highly Recommended

Duncan Taylor Strathisla 1967 Cask 1534 Speyside SMSW (Scotland); 49% abv, $255.

The dazzling color is a bright honey/oatmeal hue; ideal purity. The first two minutes of sniffing reveal lovely, cheese-like, oaky aromas; extra time in the copita unleashes deeper aromas of old oak, baked bread, light peat, butter cream, and almond paste; a mature bouquet that while waning still offers plenty of depth and intrigue. The palate entry is round, chewy, and steeped in dark caramel/toffee and dark coffee tastes; by the midpalate point the taste shifts more to the oaky vanilla and honey and actually begins to flirt with rancio-like qualities, though the flirtation ultimate peters out before reaching its goal. Finishes semisweet, properly oily, and with a flash of heat. A good, clearly old but not great whisky from the western reaches of Speyside; would have been four stars a decade ago and, therefore, only for those fanatical imbibers who relish genuinely old single malts.

2004 Rating: ★★★/Recommended

Duncan Taylor Strathisla 35 Year Old Cask 7009 Speyside SMSW (Scotland); 45.10% abv, $240.

The bright, gleaming color is of flax/gold; purity level is the highest it can be. The vibrancy of the aroma is delightfully startling in the first nosing passes as the spirit rises to the occasion in waves of floral and yellow fruit fragrances; over the additional seven minute aeration period, the bouquet changes tack, going more resiny/woody and nutty than spirity as the alcohol calms down with air contact. The palate entry is clean, lean, yet biscuity and pastry-like; the midpalate point is punctuated by assertive tastes of honey, oak resin, nougat/ nut butter, and sweet cereal grain. Ends up engagingly sweet and composed. Well-integrated and comely.

2007 Rating: ★★★★/Highly Recommended

Duncan Taylor Strathmill 1975 Speyside SMSW (Scotland); 48.7% abv, $230.

The golden grain/light topaz color is lovely and free from sediment. The aroma right from the pour is fruity and winey and almost sour; another seven minutes of air contact brings out a linseed oil/candle wax scent that's alluring. The palate entry shows a solid, high-octane, spirity and almost fiery profile; at midpalate the alcohol heat burns out a bit, allowing nice toasty tastes of hazelnuts and figs to emerge. Finishes up cleanly, mildly hot, and oily.

2004 Rating: ★★★/Recommended

Duncan Taylor Tamdhu 1969 Speyside SMSW (Scotland); 40.2% abv, $279.

Standard issue medium amber color; good purity. In the first whiffs I can't help but notice a floor polish/shoe polish twang and little else; six more minutes of aeration do not go a long way in turning my opinion around. The palate entry is sweet and large; at midpalate the honey sweetness accelerates, adding chunky tastes of nut paste, pork and baked banana. Concludes sweet, agreeably fiery and intensely honeyed. This tasted more like Macallan than the supposed Macallan; go figure.

2004 Rating: ★★★★/Highly Recommended

Duncan Taylor Tamdhu 34 Year Old 1969 Cask 7313 Speyside SMSW (Scotland); 40.2% abv, $202.

Pale gold/straw color; very good clarity. Opening aroma is dull and a bit flat and flax/textile-like; following aeration, the aroma comes alive with fruit-driven scents of papaya, banana, tangerine peel, and gum. Entry reverts back to the dullness found in the first stage of the aroma; the flavor profile at midpalate turns up the charm slightly as it offers moderate grainy sweetness and a mildly interesting fruit element, but the flabby core of this malt is hollow, which is not uncommon for this distillery. Take a pass on it.

2007 Rating: ★★/Not Recommended

Duncan Taylor Tamnavulin 1967 37 Year Old Speyside SMSW (Scotland); 46.7% abv, $242.

The deep, bright bronze/burnished orange color sparkles under the examination lamp and is unblemished. The opening whiffs detect toasted notes of butterscotch, brown butter, nougat, cigar ash, and a healthy dose of mushroomy rancio; further air contact stirs up leathery, dusty scents that remind me of wood-paneled men's club fragrances; everything about the intriguing bouquet says "old", though not necessarily "tired". The palate entry oozes sweet, caramel/treacle notes of dark chocolate, coffee bean, and honey; the midpalate stage reinforces all the impressions of the entry and tosses in nougat and candy bar. Finishes intensely sweet and rich. I wouldn't add mineral water to this malt. Just enjoy it full strength for what it is: rich, creamy, ancient Speyside. Not for every malt-lovers taste due to the off-the-charts oak-induced sweetness, but still a winning old geezer.

2006 Rating: ★★★★/Highly Recommended

Duncan Taylor The Glenlivet 1968 Cask 2844 Speyside SMSW (Scotland); 43.1% abv, $255.

The color is bright yellow/gold; perfect purity. In the initial couple of sniffs, the aroma is ethereal, astringent, and spirity; given another six minutes in the glass, the fey bouquet

emits gentle, if reluctant scents of heather, new leather, and yeast; to be blunt, not the best Glenlivet bouquet I've come across in the last fifteen years. The palate entry is properly flowery (heather, again, with a trace of rose petal) and mildly fruity (green apple, pears); the midpalate is moderately sweet, malty, and floral, but there's a fundamental hollowness to this edition. Finishes malty sweet and polite. One of the finest qualities of The Glenlivet is that while its malts are normally delicate, they are equally complex and layered; this single cask version fails, in that, there's little complexity or depth and, as such, the flavors seem superficial; while I fully comprehend that it's the nature of the beast, here's an instance when a merchant bottling falls far short of the established distillery profile.
2004 Rating: ★★/Not Recommended

Duncan Taylor Tomatin 1965 Cask 20945 Speyside SMSW (Scotland); 52.7% abv, $227.
Beautiful harvest gold/medium amber color; flawless purity. Aromatic notes of rubber pencil eraser, marshmallow, and tropical fruit (canned unsweetened pineapple?) greet the olfactory sense after the pour; an astringent grain scent takes charge of the bouquet, overriding all other fragrances except for the spirit; a directionless, featureless aroma. The palate entry does a minor salvage job on behalf of the aroma as toasty, creamy flavors moderately please the taste buds; at midpalate the taste continues on in a creamy/unsalted butter-like manner and adds a minor touch of old oak, with the elevated spirit never dominating. Ends up warming, a trace smoky, and creamy. Though a recovery is made in the taste phase, too much ground was lost in the bouquet to really make up; true to form for this perennially underachieving distillery.
2004 Rating: ★★/Not Recommended

Hart Brothers Aultmore 8 Year Old Speyside SMSW (Scotland); 58.4% abv, $47.
The attractive gold/yellow hue shows perfect purity. The opening nose offers extremely toasty/roasted scents of nuts/nougat and toasted oak barrel (matured in used bourbon barrels, I bet); the second sniffing emits a buttery/almondy/fatty perfume that's reminiscent of butterscotch and frying bacon; the penultimate whiff, following seven minutes of exposure to air, smacks with sweet oak/walnut/coconut butter fragrances that excite the olfactory sense; the fourth and final nosing pass after almost ten full minutes of undiluted aeration reveals only a slight diminishment of potency, but that's mostly in the alcohol, not the aroma which hangs in there in high-flying buttery/oily fashion; I love this bouquet. The palate entry is firm, oily, dry, and caramel-like; the midpalate stage is marked by dry and lovely tastes of butterscotch, butter cream, toasted oak, and dry cereal. The aftertaste is long, intensely malty, oaky/vanilla-like, and lip-smacking delicious. Shows the dry, concentrated-on-malt-and-oak side of Speyside; doubtless, the most satisfying malt whisky from Aultmore I've tasted so far.
2000 Rating: ★★★★/Highly Recommended

Hart Brothers Balmenach 18 Year Old Eastern Highlands SMSW (Scotland); 43% abv, $83.
The fetching honey/amber color is slightly blemished by a more than acceptable amount of floating debris. The opening nose is disappointingly waxy and soapy; the second sniffing doesn't see the off odors dissipate as a scent of wet cardboard gets added to the list; by the

third whiff, following six minutes of air contact, the aroma finally introduces some maltiness which helps to ward off the soapiness, in particular; the fourth and final nosing pass is an odd and unappealing mixture of waxiness and maltiness; with these stale, musty odors, I have to wonder about the barrels that this whisky was aged in. The whisky improves in the mouth as the palate entry displays a mildly sweet maltiness that's far more pleasing than the mushroomy bouquet; the midpalate juncture shows a little more charm via toasty flavors of almonds and toffee. The finish is long, a bit lean, more dry than sweet, and moderately oaky. The pleasant flavor experience simply doesn't own enough depth of character to redeem the lackluster, weedy, fishy aroma.

2000 Rating: ★★/Not Recommended

Hart Brothers Balmenach 1972 30 Year Old Eastern Highlands SMSW (Scotland); 50.1% abv, $160.
Shows the medium brown/deep honey hue of a palo cortado sherry; excellent purity. Right out of the bottle the bouquet is angular, lean, dry, and fabric-like; seven minutes of further aeration encourages meatier, more complex aromas to develop, including roasted chestnut, lanolin, and marshmallow; not an expressive nose, but intriguing enough to keep you guessing and going back to it. The palate entry shows a different, more generous and engaging side of this malt as rich, chocolaty flavors greet the taste buds; at midpalate the flavor gets even more opulent and honeyed. The aftertaste is long, toffee sweet, and a bit sherried. The potency is never an issue with this nicely balanced malt and, as a result, for most experienced whisky people I'd suggest that you not add water; your choice, of course.

2003 Rating: ★★★/Recommended

Hart Brothers Bowmore 13 Year Old Islay SMSW (Scotland); 46% abv, $67.
Gold/yellow color; unblemished clarity. The first whiffs are confronted with heavy doses of iodine, medicine chest, seaweed, and peat; later sniffs after further aeration pick up leathery scents that are suddenly more tanned skin- and rubber-like than smoky/peaty; a weird change of direction in the bouquet. The palate entry is concentrated, chalk-like, smoky, and intensely peaty; by the midpalate stage the taste profile settles down a bit, offering more moderate flavors of tobacco ash, wood smoke, charcoal, and sweet grain. Compellingly rambunctious for normally staid Bowmore and therefore intriguing and worth the money.

2006 Rating: ★★★/Recommended

Hart Brothers Braes of Glenlivet 20 Year Old Madeira Cask Speyside SMSW (Scotland); 43% abv, $95.
The bright amber/light honey tint does show some minor floating particles. Considering that this malt was matured in old madeira casks, there's hardly any evidence of that fact in the opening pass as the aroma offers only mildly malty and moderately prickly scents; in the second nosing, weedy/leathery/feinty odors make an unwelcome entrance; the third sniffing, after seven minutes of time in the glass, sees little improvement as the weedy scent becomes more a sour yeastiness; following nearly nine minutes of aeration, the meek aroma displays traces of malt and yellow fruit, but, surprisingly, no oakiness; a disinterested, meandering bouquet. The palate entry is amazingly chocolaty and plummy (like malmsey madeira can sometimes be) as if the malt was deeply roasted; the midpalate stage is very sweet and almost

honeyed; the midpalate phase really gives away the madeira aging vessels. The finish is thick, prune-like, sweet, and long. The nose is a complete bust while the flavor and finish are acceptable, but uninspiring.

2000 Rating: ★★/Not Recommended

Hart Brothers Clynelish 15 Year Old Northern Highlands SMSW (Scotland); 54.1% abv, $92.

One of my six favorite malt distilleries; typical, trademark golden yellow hue; perfect purity. The initial nosing pass finds chewy, succulent aromas of black pepper, lead pencil, and sweet grain mash; the second whiff picks up a background note of oaky vanillin; the third sniffing adds savory scents of green vegetable (kale or escarole), distant brine, and bacon fat; in the fourth and last sniffing, after nearly ten minutes of air contact, the bacon fat fades while the sea salt/brine/vegetal elements kick further into gear; a fast-evolving bouquet that ends up strikingly vegetal; with the addition of mineral water one can see how oily this malt is. The palate entry is firmly structured, malty sweet, and oily to the touch; the midpalate stage offers defined flavor layers of black pepper, sweet oak, luscious malt, caramel, bacon fat, and oloroso sherry. The finish is long, oily, a bit sharp even with water added, and fatty/buttery.

2000 Rating: ★★★★/Highly Recommended

Hart Brothers Clynelish 1988 Finest Collection 14 Year Old Northern Highlands SMSW (Scotland); 53.3% abv, $90.

Chardonnay look-a-like, golden and clean. The aroma begins in an intensely grainy, dry breakfast cereal-like way in the first few minutes; additional time in the glass adds woodsy/open field notes of pine/cedar, heather, and wood resin; there's not a trace of sweetness in the lanky, angular bouquet. The palate entry is dry to off-dry and grainy; then at midpalate the taste leaps forward in semisweet waves of woody vanillin, cocoa, malt, and light toffee. It finishes in a flurry of woody/caramel-like tastes, buttressed by a smoldering, but not overt spirity warmth. A good, but not spectacular young expression from one of my favorite malt distilleries.

2003 Rating: ★★★/Recommended

Hart Brothers Craigellachie 15 Year Old Speyside SMSW (Scotland); 57.2% abv, $92.

The pale sunshine/yellow color is very pretty and wine-like; impeccable clarity. The opening sniff picks up full, round, malty, and oaky/vanilla scents; the second whiff sees the spirit come more into play as the aroma goes acceptably prickly; in the penultimate nosing pass, allowing for over six minutes of air contact, keen notes of caramel and toffee are detected; by the fourth and last go-round the blocky, potent, and sweet caramel/burnt wood/butter aroma leaves no question as to which component rules the roost with lots of exposure to air; even with the addition of mineral water. The palate entry is raw and searing; the midpalate point shows burnt wood/intensely smoky flavors that smother all traces of malt-related flavor. The aftertaste is unpleasantly resiny, weedy, astringent, and oily. A worse than usual bottling from this underachieving distillery; frankly, offering a bottling from a distillery that suffers from chronic inconsistency is a disservice.

2000 Rating: ★/Not Recommended

Hart Brothers Dalmore 12 Year Old Northern Highlands SMSW (Scotland); 55.1% abv, $71.

The golden yellow/amber color is very attractive; ideal purity. The nose at opening is chunky, concentrated, and intensely malty; the second sniffing picks up various and disparate intriguing scents including steamed rice, soy sauce, grass, and dried flowers (as if pressed in a book); by the third whiff, following six minutes of aeration, the steamed rice element becomes dominant, but I also notice background traces of candied almonds and peat smoke; the fourth and final nosing pass turns slightly cooked in an oatmeal manner; I'm not entirely sure whether I like this bouquet or not, but in its favor it most assuredly holds my attention. The palate entry is smooth, incredibly malty sweet, and is a bit raw on the tongue; the midpalate phase offers toned-down, mannered, and truly luscious tastes of dark chocolate, almond butter, nougat, and dark malt. The aftertaste is long, rich, sweet, and delicious. Once in the mouth with water added, this sweet, savory, and complex malt takes flight; excellent.

2000 Rating: ★★★★/Highly Recommended

Hart Brothers Glen Albyn 1978 22 Year Old Northern Highlands SMSW (Scotland); 43% abv, $84.

Attractive, autumnal, honey tint; perfect clarity. The initial sniffing detects soft, mildly sweet, malty aromatic notes; the second and third whiffs add subtle traces of lanolin, bacon fat, and almonds; in the fourth and last pass the components marry into an undemanding bouquet that's easy and straightforward, but totally superficial. The palate entry is acidic, lean, and only moderately sweet; the midpalate turns strangely and abruptly spirity, raw, and harsh on the tongue but offers some malty sweetness—wha' happened? The aftertaste—natch—is medium-long, concentrated, and oaky/buttery. Where was this flavor impact and textural opulence in the entry and midpalate stages where they should have been? Drinkable, but too little too late for me.

2001 Rating: ★★/Not Recommended

Hart Brothers Glen Grant 1969 31 Year Old Speyside SMSW (Scotland); 45.1% abv, $148.

The attractive bronze/harvest gold color is marred by too many bits of whitish sediment. The opening nose emits piquant, but surprisingly unevolved scents of orange rind, grapefruit, and oak resin; in the second and third sniffings the piquancy turns to spirity prickliness that tweaks the olfactory sense but unfortunately obliterates just about all other aromas in the process; the final blast, following nine minutes of exposure to air, turns softly fruity but is still lean and narrow; I expect a lot more in the aroma department from this normally solid distillery. In the mouth at palate entry, there is increased presence, mostly in the forms of apple, honey, and light toffee flavors. The finish is sweet, but rather lean and sinewy with touches of clove and brown sugar. Not what I'd consider a typical offering from this reliable malt producer; in fact, I'd say that this malt is at least a decade off its prime.

2001 Rating: ★★/Not Recommended

Hart Brothers Glen Grant 1972 29 Year Old Speyside SMSW (Scotland); 53.6% abv, $150.

I've always liked the malts from this distillery. The astonishingly gorgeous appearance displays a brilliant topaz/deep bronze hue; minor sediment spotted. The opening whiffs discover a multilayered nose of toasted nuts, baked pear, and dried red apple; more time in

the glass stimulates the aroma further to include seductive, oily scents of paraffin, old oak, and well-worn saddle leather. The palate entry offers sublime, mature, fully melded tastes of oloroso sherry, honey, and dark caramel; the midpalate stage is noteworthy for its fullness, moderate heat, and glycerin, toffee and sherry tastes. The aftertaste is long, bittersweet, woody, and oily. A huge Glen Grant that begs for spring water.
2003 Rating: ★★★★/Highly Recommended

Hart Brothers Glen Grant 26 Year Old Speyside SMSW (Scotland); 51.1% abv, $137.
The deep amber/bronze color is gorgeous and relatively free of suspended particles. The brisk aroma in the opening sniffing is chockful of nutty/oily/oaky/cheese-like scents; the second whiff adds wood resin and that magical and rare feature found in old cognacs, rancio; the resiny/prune-like aromatic notes in the third pass serve to bolster the case for rancio; by the fourth and final nosing pass, following a full nine minutes of aeration, it's clear that this is a very special aromatic experience, found in but a precious few spirits; DAZZLING. The palate entry is rich in toffee and controlled sweet tastes; by the midpalate stage the flavor expands to include marzipan, cream, candied almond, and oloroso sherry. The finish is sweet, extended, and focused. What's brilliant about this malt is that it's big but not voluptuous; it's more stately than anything.
2000 Rating: ★★★★★/Highest Recommendation

Hart Brothers Glenrothes 10 Year Old Speyside SMSW (Scotland); 46% abv, $66.
Very pale straw yellow hue; superb purity. The aroma at first blush is reluctant and in a muted stage; the bouquet benefits significantly from another seven minutes of air contact as it offers highly pleasant fragrances of flowers, light honey, and sweet grain. The palate entry is elegant, youthfully vigorous, grainy, and moderately sweet; at midpalate the taste turns more spirity and aggressive, but neither hot nor unpleasant, just immature, a little awkward and gawky, but vivacious, grainy sweet, and altogether charming in its enthusiasm. Ends up intensely grainy and fruity. A wholly representative younger expression of this wonderful distillery.
2006 Rating: ★★★/Recommended

Hart Brothers Glenrothes 10 Year Old Speyside SMSW (Scotland); 58.3% abv, $54.
The youthful, immature appearance is tinted light lemon yellow/flax; it shows some suspended particles also. The nose at opening is muscular, sweet, and vigorous; with aeration the aroma turns into a precocious bouquet, emitting zesty scents of pepper, raisins, apples, and flowers; the third sniffing is extraordinarily floral, especially hints of roses, juniper blossoms, and hay; in the fourth and last nosing pass, after almost nine minutes of exposure to air, the bouquet finally displays some sweet mashy malt and mild oakiness; a flashy, exuberant aroma that's still relatively young and brash. The palate entry reveals a slightly awkward and ungainly malt that's sweet and oaky, but unpolished; the midpalate juncture shows more integration as ripe, fruity, and grainy flavors vie for attention. The finish is medium long, remarkably fruity, and sweet. This malt offers the trademark lithe sweetness of the distillery but in an undeveloped stage; I personally would have waited for this malt to mature in cask for three to five more years before bottling it; however, the inherent quality of the malt deserves a recommendation.
2000 Rating: ★★★/Recommended

Hart Brothers Glenturret 1991 Finest Collection 10 Year Old Eastern Highlands SMSW (Scotland); 55.5% abv, $63.

Clear straw yellow glow and perfect purity. The first impressions are delightfully fruity and floral, with just the merest trace of off-dry malt; even after seven more minutes in the glass, the flower-fest continues in the nose with the additions of honeysuckle and light new oak; an agile, even fey bouquet from one of the better Eastern Highland malt distilleries. The palate entry comes upon a sweet, pleasantly thick, and robust malt that belies the bouquet; at the midpalate the zesty spirit takes charge and guides the woody/floral/grainy supplementary, lip-smacking flavors into the delectably sweet, slightly honeyed aftertaste. A vigorous, no-nonsense EH treat from a terrific distillery.

2003 Rating: ★★★★/Highly Recommended

Hart Brothers Glenturret 25 Year Old Eastern Highlands SMSW (Scotland); 53.8% abv, $130.

I like the rich amber wheat/honey color of this malt; shows less than ideal clarity, however, as much floating detritus is noted. The initial nosing pass shows a rather reluctant aroma; with time in the glass, the aroma starts to emerge in the second pass in forms of very dry, almost resiny grain and peppery scents; the third sniffing unearths a delicate note of peat; the fourth and last whiff, after eight minutes of aeration, highlights the interaction between the malt and the oak; a mildly pleasing bouquet of modest virtue. The palate entry is marked by an odd taste of clove; the midpalate goes bitterly sweet and spiced. The aftertaste is long, bitter, dry, and tastes a bit like caramel corn plus there's way too much fire on the tongue as the last impression. Not my cup of tea.

2000 Rating: ★★/Not Recommended

Hart Brothers Highland Park 10 Year Old Orkney Islands SMSW (Scotland); 57.6% abv, $54.

The immaturity of this malt is characterized beautifully by its green/yellow/lemon juice color; impeccable purity. The zesty bouquet leaps from the sampling glass in cheeky waves of feinty, just-off-the-still, green (raw) spirit; with aeration, the aroma turns into a bouquet, offering nutty/salty aromas that tweak the olfactory sense; the penultimate sniffing continues in a feinty/leathery vein, but adding a trace of yeastiness; the fourth and last nosing pass, after a full ten minutes of exposure to air, reveals wafer thin hints of dill and spice; not my favorite HP bouquet, yet I do admire its precociousness and zeal. The palate entry is raw, searing, and awkward, even with mineral water added to cut the alcohol; then in midpalate the flavor turns chocolaty, sweet, and ripe, with a fine textural note of oil. The finish is very briny, long, hot, and oily. Far from my favorite HP; in my opinion this malt was bottled at too immature an age; one wonders what's the point of offering a whisky that is so obviously in middle stage development? Don't even consider it.

2000 Rating: ★★/Not Recommended

Hart Brothers Highland Park 19 Year Old Orkney Islands SMSW (Scotland); 43% abv, $94.

The straw yellow/golden hue is pretty; slight amount of floating debris. The salty seaside/island influence is unmistakable right from the very first sniff after the pour; with time in the glass, the aroma expands to include traces of prickly spirit, seaweed, and mild peat; the third whiff offers further deepening of the gently briny nature of the bouquet; as with all HP bouquets, there's not a hint of bulldozing character but rather a subtle array of aromatic nuances that merely hint at fragrances rather than club you with them; superb. The palate entry is all HP as the flavor of salt water taffy greets the taste buds; the midpalate is sweet in a malty manner and laced with tastes of pepper, sherry, and vanilla extract. The finish is lean, medium long, more salty than sweet. A fine example of the splendor of HP at a perfect age and stage of evolution; a malt that whispers to be heard.

2000 Rating: ★★★★★/Highest Recommendation

Hart Brothers Highland Park 1975 25 Year Old Orkneys SMSW (Scotland); 43% abv, $150.

Bright, honey/amber/light topaz color; ideal purity. The island-sea breeze pedigree of this malt is unmistakable right from the first nosing pass; with time, the aroma expands in the second whiff in the form of stale bread and seaweed; the third and fourth sniffings keep hitting away at the seaweed/brine theme to the point where it's overkill; not my favorite HP aroma and nowhere near as seductive as the distillery bottling of the same age; a clear case of the taste rescuing the evaluation. The palate entry is textured, rich, mildly briny, and malty sweet; the midpalate displays a touch of peatiness plus sherry/vanilla and almond butter. The finish is extended, creamy/buttery, moderately oily, and sap-like. After a lackluster bouquet, the taste and finish elevated this malt up to HP standards; however, let it be known that I tasted this bottling next to the great 25 year old distillery bottling; the clear, unequivocal choice was the classic distillery version; so I'd take the $150 and put it toward the distillery bottling.

2001 Rating: ★★★/Recommended

Hart Brothers Inchgower 1976 Finest Collection 26 Year Old Speyside SMSW (Scotland); 49.9% abv, $142.

The pale gold hue shines beneath the evaluation lamp; superb clarity. The first couple of whiffs detect reluctant grain and forest floor notes; the bouquet opens up markedly following seven more minutes of aeration, offering off-dry scents of green olive, very light peat and sweet midsummer grass. The palate entry supplies a grainy/malty sweet taste that's medium to full-bodied; then at midpalate the taste profile takes off in delightfully sweet, almost honeyed/sherried flavors that last well into the long, off-dry finish. The big winner, for me, is the buttery/oily/silky texture that's akin to a cream sherry; gorgeous drinking; also, the abv is at a level where I was fine without water throughout the entire review process; nice job here.

2003 Rating: ★★★★/Highly Recommended

Hart Brothers Linkwood 1989 11 Year Old Sherry Cask Speyside SMSW (Scotland); 43% abv, $47.

The pale green/yellow hue is reminiscent of muscadet white wine; impeccable clarity. The youthful, vigorous aroma comes leaping from the glass right after the pour; the middle stage sniffings offer firm and frisky waves of light peat, cigarette smoke, unripened fruit, asparagus, and dry malt; the fourth and last whiff goes toasty and off-dry; this bouquet is rambunctious, precocious, and all over the lot, but I have to love its exuberance. The palate entry is silky smooth, malty sweet, and oily; really delicious early-on; the midpalate is even better as the oily texture makes a perfect foundation for the lovely, unbridled, but sophisticated flavors of pear drop, lemon zest, light peat, tobacco leaf, and succulent, sweet malt. A superb and completely representative bottling from this overlooked Speyside gem of a distillery. So, continuing the merchant bottling/distillery bottling debate, this merchant bottling does nothing to detract, quite the contrary, from the malts distributed by the distillery, so what to do? I suggest that malt lovers try merchant bottlings of a favorite distillery, then taste them alongside a fresh bottle from the distillery to ascertain any difference.

2001 Rating: ★★★★/Highly Recommended

Hart Brothers Loch Lomond 10 Year Old Central Highlands SMSW (Scotland); 43% abv, $47.

The color is gold/yellow; good purity. The initial nosing pass is pleasantly malty and toffee-like; the second sniffing sees the dry aroma go a bit phenolic and medicinal, showing minor hints of peat and kippers; by the penultimate whiff, following six minutes of air contact, the aroma starts to fade slightly and adds a scent of bread dough/yeast; the fourth and last nosing pass sees further incremental diminishment. The palate entry is very appealing in a moderately rich malty way; the midpalate phase is malty sweet, simple, a bit fiery, and even a tad sherried. The finish is light, biscuity sweet, and uncomplicated. A well-made malt that doesn't feign being profound and that's its best feature.

2000 Rating: ★★★/Recommended

Hart Brothers Longmorn 10 Year Old Speyside SMSW (Scotland); 58.2% abv, $54.

The immature, lemon juice/pale yellow hue is absolutely pure. The opening sniff shows very estery aromatic notes of orange peel, peaches, and apples; the fruit-fest continues in the second nosing as grapes get added to the line-up; little further is noted in the third whiff, following seven minutes of air contact; in the fourth nosing pass the malt finally appears in a cocoa bean, bittersweet, tar-like perfume; what's so interesting about this bouquet is that through ten minutes and four nosings the alcohol, which is considerably high, never interferes with the aromas. The palate entry is smooth at first then quickly turns prickly as bittersweet tastes of tar, dried fruit, and dark chocolate envelop the taste buds; by the midpalate point the fruit element gives way to heavy doses of peat smoke, tobacco leaf, and soot. The finish is long, intensely oily, dry, grainy, wood resiny, and off-putting because of the resin taste. The high points are the opening minutes of the bouquet and the palate entry; beyond that this youngster is rough and anything but ready; another glaring case of a malt being bottled at too young an age; Longmorn is at its supremely satisfying best when it's at least 14 years old; tasting it younger than that doesn't do the malt justice no matter what the bottlers claim.

2000 Rating: ★/Not Recommended

Hart Brothers Longmorn 1967 33 Year Old Speyside SMSW (Scotland); 45.9% abv, $185.

Pale, mousy amber/honey tint that's unfortunately showing tons of highly unappetizing sediment. The first couple of nosing passes detect uncharacteristic (for the distillery) scents of green apple, pineapple, and gum; aeration time in the glass lasting a full seven minutes

does virtually nothing to release further aromas of consequence; where's the grain, where's the wood? In the mouth, this old, if atypical, Longmorn shows a more pleasing face as moderately alluring off-dry tastes of malt and toffee impress the taste buds; by midpalate the flavors shift into higher gears, offering near-succulent flavors of honey and vanilla. Finishes with suppleness and mildly sweet tastes of honey, old oak, and milk chocolate. Gets off the ground rather late, but once it does it's amiable and nice, but hardly what one is used to from this landmark malt distillery; I coughed up a fur ball when I saw the suggested retail price.
2003 Rating: ★★★/Recommended

Hart Brothers Longmorn 25 Year Old Sherry Cask Speyside SMSW (Scotland); 55.5% abv, $130.
The deep topaz/dark honey/cola color immediately says one thing; sherry cask—it actually looks like an oloroso sherry—impeccable purity. The initial nosing right after the pour speaks of dark caramel, sweet black raisins, marzipan, and honey; the second pass adds intense wood resin and hard cheese; the penultimate pass, after seven minutes of aeration, adds lanolin, nougat, almonds, and toasted wheat bread; the fourth and last sniffing sees the wine-like sherry note come out in force as the fruit overcomes the woodiness; a complex, sweet bouquet with a distant touch of rancio. The palate entry reveals a deep, smoky, concentrated flavor; the addition of water brings out a creaminess that's one part smooth, salty butter and one part smoky bacon fat; in the midpalate the aftertaste is long, resiny, smoky, and bitter. Recommendable for its unique intensity, but not the glimpse of nirvana that I was hoping for; the moral of this story? Stick with the classic 15 Year Old distillery bottling.
2000 Rating: ★★★/Recommended

Hart Brothers Macallan 10 Year Old Speyside SMSW (Scotland); 58.2% abv, $54.
The brilliant golden yellow hue is spoiled by the floating debris. The nose at opening is tremendously compelling and seductive as rich, estery (fruity) notes reach out of the glass and pull you in; further time in the glass reveals scents of mild sherry, glycerin, vanilla bean, and peaches; the third sniffing adds delicate but green (immature) touches of oak, fresh flowers, and vegetation; the last whiff, following nine minutes of exposure to air, displays tart citrus rind notes and hay; this bouquet while fetching in the early stages loses its focus after about five minutes and begins to meander. The palate entry is intensely sweet and fruity as the mineral water brings out the esters in a marked manner; the midpalate stage offers succulent, almost jammy tastes of peaches, white raisins, and plums; the flavor is concentrated and remarkably fruity. The finish is full, less intense, fruity but tart, a dash resiny, and long. Far from my favorite Macallan, but with mineral water added prior to sipping, this floral/fruity bottling shows some of the trademark grace of this stellar distillery.
2000 Rating: ★★★/Recommended

Hart Brothers Macallan 1968 Finest Collection 34 Year Old Speyside SMSW (Scotland); 46.3% abv, $230.
The deep topaz/dark honey color enchants the eye; impeccable purity. The initial nosing pass detects nuances of grass/forest vegetation and pine; with aeration the bouquet expands, adding zesty and dry, if uncharacteristic for Macallan, notes of cedar, black pepper and hay; not your usual sherry-a-thon Mac aroma, mates. The palate entry is surprisingly lean, off-dry

and sap-like, though it's alluring and muscular; things get rolling by the midpalate as the flavor profile swings more in the traditional Mac way, offering luscious vanilla-laden, oloroso sherry, maple sweet tastes that beguile the taste buds completely. The aftertaste is medium-long, moderately sherried/honeyed, and lip-smacking good. I had my early-on doubts but those were wiped away by the stunning midpalate and the finish.

2003 Rating: ★★★★/Highly Recommended

Hart Brothers Mortlach 10 Year Old Speyside SMSW (Scotland); 58.8% abv, $54.
The color is an eye-fetching lemon yellow; shows a tad too much floating translucent debris for my comfort level. The heavenly opening nose shows succulent, round, exotic aromas of orange blossom, lead pencil, and coconut milk; the second sniffing detects added aromatic notes of spice, prickly spirit, and mint; the penultimate whiff adds piquant traces of lanolin and oil; the fourth and final romp sees the bouquet become quite narrow and directed in a vegetal/floral way with undertones of waxy oil; a peculiar nose that starts out with an abundance of scents then folds in on itself with aeration. Once in the mouth, the flavor at entry speaks of the typical Mortlach firmness and malty sweetness; the midpalate stage is marked by delightfully sweet tastes of ripe citrus, nut butter, and sweet malt; there's not much evidence of oak impact on this immature malt in the flavor phase. The finish is rather short, very malty, and suddenly dry. Uneven, but good enough to be recommended if one bears in mind that this is a very young malt.

2000 Rating: ★★★/Recommended

Hart Brothers Mortlach 17 Year Old Speyside SMSW (Scotland); 43% abv, $81.
Not diluted; a bit of a dull amber/light honey color; some minor particles spotted; the opening nosing pass reveals a parchment, damp cardboard, mushroomy, wet forest-like aroma that's off-putting; the situation does not improve in the second sniffing as the woodsy/musty odor lingers in the glass; the third whiff, following nearly seven minutes of air contact, actually sees the aroma grow more attic-like and stale; by the fourth and last nosing pass, this nose should be given the last rites—what gives here? Didn't anyone notice this ridiculously obvious flaw in the aroma? The palate entry is bland, only mildly malty, and sweet in a sickly way—hardly fresh; the midpalate point is marked by a rescue attempt by the flavor as it shows at least some malty/dry cereal/oaky polish that faintly resembles traditional Mortlach. The aftertaste is medium long, tobacco leafy, and dry. I've been an ardent admirer of Mortlach for more than a decade and this bottling is far from what I've come to expect from this distillery; this bottling could be the poster child for the controversy that swirls around merchant bottlings; absolutely atrocious.

2000 Rating: ★/Not Recommended

Hart Brothers Mortlach 24 Year Old Speyside SMSW (Scotland); 54.9% abv, $124.
Eye-catching amber/light honey hue; acceptable purity. The initial nosing pass offers peppery, piquant and spicy scents; after three minutes of aeration, scents of dry malt and lanolin get added; the third pass unearths a deep grassy/pasture-like perfume that overtakes all other aromas; the fourth and final sniffing, following eight minutes of exposure to air, sees the bouquet go the way of dry hard candy, almonds, and soft malt; not an expressive or (to my surprise) wood-influenced bouquet, but intriguing in its narrow cereal focus. The palate

entry, even with mineral water added, is sharp, spirity, but praline sweet; the midpalate point is succulent, focused, and delicious, emitting nutty/buttery tastes with lots of spirity underpinning. The finish is long, fruity, and mildly oaky. The addition of mineral water brings out the best in this high octane malt as it calms the spirit enough to allow the malt to shine through.
2000 Rating: ★★★★/Highly Recommended

Hart Brothers Port Ellen 13 Year Old Islay SMSW (Scotland); 43% abv, $70.

The pale lemon juice/straw hue is marred by scads of suspended particles. The initial nosing pass detects intensely briny/seaweedy phenolic scents that could only originate from the southern tip of Islay; the second sniffing offers even more concentrated notes of sea salt and kippers; in the penultimate whiff, after over six minutes in the glass, the medicinal astringency becomes more iodine-like than salty; the fourth and final pass sees no abatement of the sea breeze/salt water core aromas; a true Islay maritime bouquet. The palate entry is extremely vegetal and salty/peaty; by midpalate the peatiness becomes the dominant flavor as the sea influence diminishes. The finish is long, salty, smoky, typical of the distillery and very medicinal. Perfect for fans of the genre and for the adventurous at heart.
2000 Rating: ★★★/Recommended

Hart Brothers Port Ellen 22 Year Old Islay SMSW (Scotland); 43% abv, $104.

The amber/green color is very appealing and atypical; shows quite a bit of floating debris. As opposed to the vigorous, even unbridled, aroma of the 13 Year Old, this older version displays far more poise and depth of character, mostly in the form of toasty malt and subtle hints of peat and sea breeze; the second sniffing adds customary, but composed island notes of brine and iodine; the third whiff offers intriguing scents of bacon fat and baked apples; the fourth and final go-round sees the various aromatic components come together nicely in a mildly sweet, fruity, and slightly sour finale; I like this bouquet very much because it shows the best of Port Ellen. The palate entry is sweet and succulent; the midpalate turns sharply focused as laser-like tastes of sea salt, older peat, nougat, and dried fruit dazzle the taste buds. The aftertaste is long, candy sweet, malty, and just a little bit smoky and iodine-like. This is easily the finest example of Port Ellen that I've evaluated since I sampled a 1974 in a merchant bottling from the now-defunct Whyte & Whyte; a muscular, but chiseled Islay malt that shows the positive effect of properly judged aging; this malt is in its peak form right now; truly excellent and one of the gems of this collection.
2000 Rating: ★★★★/Highly Recommended

Hart Brothers Pulteney 10 Year Old Northern Highlands SMSW (Scotland); 57.7% abv, $55.

The attractive golden hue is regrettably blemished by unacceptable amounts of floating debris. The opening passes are confronted with a less than forthcoming bouquet and as a result few aromatic qualities are discerned early-on; several minutes of exposure to air help somewhat as meek, mildly sweet scents of malty cereal and oak emerge at a snail's pace. What punch this malt lacks in the bouquet is made up for with zest in the flavor as the palate entry displays a prickly, oily texture and sweet, toasty flavors of malt and cake batter; by the midpalate point the animated flavor profile includes marzipan, caramel, nougat, and hay.

The aftertaste is extended, oily, and oaky sweet. Though the appearance and the aroma leave much to be desired the flavor phase and the aftertaste offer more than sufficient poise and character to elevate this malt to recommendable status; a case of redemption.
2002 Rating: ★★★/Recommended

Hart Brothers Royal Brackla 18 Year Old Speyside SMSW (Scotland); 43% abv, $83.

The golden amber hue is quite pretty; very minor, insignificant particles seen floating about. The opening nose is very toasty and doughy; the second sniffing adds notes of vanilla/oakiness and almond butter; the third whiff, following seven minutes of air contact, contributes an opulent maltiness; the fourth and last nosing pass shows just a faint hint of peatiness as the nose turns dry; a sleek Speyside bouquet that's disarming and self-contained. The palate entry is caramel sweet and beguiling; the midpalate stage is even more compelling as toasted, malty, nutty, and buttery flavors lavish the taste buds both taste-wise and texturally. The finish is toffee sweet, fruity, malty, and luscious. Shows the succulent, sweet side of Speyside with an air of class and ease; a definite winner.
2000 Rating: ★★★★/Highly Recommended

Hart Brothers Strathisla 1967 33 Year Old Speyside SMSW (Scotland); 46.3% abv, $160.

Correct medium amber/honey hue; unblemished purity. The opening nosing pass finds two layers of aroma, a wafer-thin surface odor that's acidic and a deeper layer that's woody and fruity and sweet; the middle stage passes find the more substantial aromatic layer taking charge in gentle waves of dried fruit, prickly spirit, and dry oak; the last sniffing, after almost ten minutes of aeration, sees the spirit dominate; I'd have liked to have seen a bit more oak presence here. The palate entry is grapy sweet and ripe; the midpalate is full, round, remarkably fruity sweet, and a touch paste-like in texture. The aftertaste features the sweet, ripe fruit and old oak. A senior citizen malt that still has some zip left, but frankly has seen better days; amiably drinkable, but not the least bit profound or up to this distillery's younger, more assertive offerings.
2001 Rating: ★★★/Recommended

Hart Brothers Strathmill 25 Year Old Speyside SMSW (Scotland); 50.1% abv, $130.

The attractive straw yellow/gold hue is blemished by the floating detritus; should be cleaned up. The initial nosing pass shows a minty/green leaf quality that's unusual; the second whiff merely adds to that impression by tossing in nuances of heather, hay, and rose petals; the third sniffing sees the green leaf element grow in strength; the fourth and final run-through, following a full ten minutes of aeration, finds that notes of raisins and nectarine have been added to the aromatic list; this nose shows no signs of stopping. The palate entry is very green leaf-like, minty, and vegetal; in the midpalate stage the flavor turns mint candy sweet and simple, showing no evidence of oak, resin, or other mature signs. The finish is fresh, green, sweet, and easy. What this malt lacks in complexity, it makes up for in drinkability.
2000 Rating: ★★★/Recommended

Hart Brothers Teaninich 13 Year Old Northern Highlands SMSW (Scotland); 43% abv, $65.

Pretty, golden/amber color; way too many minuscule floating particles. The reluctant bouquet shows faint scents of cardboard and wet fabric in the first nosing pass after the pour; in the second pass the tempo picks up in terms of vigor as the spirit comes through as does some herbaceousness, mostly dill; the third sniffing detects some mild maltiness and wet straw; the fourth and final whiff, following eight minutes of exposure to air, adds green mint, green leaf, and white raisins to the aromatic mix; a pleasant, if distant, bouquet that never quite wants to fully emerge. The palate entry is fruity sweet and damn near sublime in its poise and lean feel; at the midpalate stage sweetly succulent and intensely fruity flavors of nectarine, orange peel, and honey delight the taste buds with their flair and slight prickliness. The finish is long, cocoa sweet, and genuinely luscious. A low-key, immensely charming malt.

2000 Rating: ★★★★/Highly Recommended

John Barr Excellence Single Cask 29 Year Old Highland SMSW (Scotland); 56.2% abv, $199.

The total allotment of this single cask malt is 258 bottles; the bottler does not disclose the name of the distillery. Pale yellow/green color; perfect clarity. The first whiffs are heady/spirity, ripe and grainy, and nearly vegetal; seven more minutes bring out thought-provoking notes of dried figs, pork sausage, sawdust, and sultanas. The palate entry (sans mineral water) is grainy sweet and honeyed; with a bit of mineral water the flavor, strangely, becomes hot and searingly assertive; in the midpalate phase the heat-burst cools off, leaving behind mildly toasty grain and oak flavors that are not fully merged. Finishes well, sweet, woody, and lightly spiced. This is one case in which water doesn't work well with the whisky and I'd enjoy it neat and unadulterated.

2004 Rating: ★★★/Recommended

John McDougall's Selection Bladnoch 15 Year Old Lowland Single Cask Scotch Whisky (Scotland); 55.8% abv, $120.

The appearance is bright, golden, and flawlessly clean. The initial nosing passes pick up earthy, if somewhat disquieting, smells of ceramic tile, cement, wet sand, and moldering vegetation; following an addition of mineral water plus further aeration, the aroma finally displays some minor malty notes that are semisweet and moderately pleasing. The palate entry is mildly sweet and very grainy; at midpalate the flavor profile includes bittersweet tastes of brown sugar, light honey, and light toffee. The aftertaste is green and vegetal then grainy sweet and breakfast cereal-like. Made a more than respectable comeback in the entry and midpalate after a bit of a dodgy early bouquet where all the components didn't seem to fit.

2006 Rating: ★★★/Recommended

Lombard Bunnahabhain 1979 Islay SMSW (Scotland); 50% abv, $170.

Attractive pine/amber/burnished gold hue is bright and flawlessly clean. The first aromas after the pour are deep (this is normally lightweight and agile Bunnahabhain?) and woody; it's only after six minutes of additional aeration that the typical brininess/seaweed scents emerge along with particularly seductive notes of brown butter, roasted asparagus, and scorched vegetation. The palate entry is firm, focused, meaty, and mildly salty/briny; at midpalate the taste structure is concentrated, oily/creamy, and round as flavors of buttered walnut, nougat, and fudge contribute to an engaging mouth experience. Concludes moderately salty/seaweedy and toasty. The finest Bunnahabhain I've encountered since, strangely enough, the

1979 Murray McDavid bottling (46% abv) reviewed in 2001 and rated ★★★★. Is this a mere coincidence? They are strikingly similar. What was going on at Bunnahabhain in 1979 that these malts are so bountifully delicious?

2005 Rating: ★★★★/Highly Recommended

Lombard Pebble Beach 12 Year Old Speyside SMSW (Scotland); 43% abv, $60.

The color is flax/corn yellow; flawless purity. The first whiffs are greeted by an indistinct, somewhat flat aroma that's neither here nor there, neither this nor that; aeration doesn't assist all that much with this strangely neutered bouquet; what gives? (Most assuredly not this aroma, mate). The palate entry is more animated than the papier maché nose as alluring tastes of grain mash, caramel, and nut paste entertain the taste buds; at the midpalate point the taste profile adds leather, oil, and pepper to the flavor mix, but there's a brittleness to the taste that leaves me cold. Concludes semisweet, metallic, and lean.

2007 Rating: ★★/Not Recommended

Lombard Teaninich 12 Year Old Northern Highlands SMSW (Scotland); 43% abv, $33.

Pretty harvest gold/deep amber color; excellent purity. The opening inhalations pick up all sorts of horsey/outdoorsy/paddock scents like saddle leather, cut grass, hay, turned earth, sweat, and summer garden; further aeration doesn't introduce much more in the way of aromatic expansion and the bouquet remains concentrated on the out-of-doors in summertime. The palate entry is tight, sweetly malty, toffee-like, and grainy; at midpalate the flavor turns toasty, slightly smoked, rich, creamy, and lush. Ends up fat, creamy, oily, and luscious. The taste entry, midpalate, and finish stages elevated this malt to four stars on the strength of its depth and multilayered character.

2005 Rating: ★★★★/Highly Recommended

Lonach Caperdonich 33 Year Old Speyside SMSW (Scotland); 42.3% abv, $149.

Deep straw/corn yellow; excellent purity. Smells leathery and waxy in the first aromatic go-round; more time in the glass fails to release any other aromatic elements and as such the bouquet remains very leather- and fiber-like. Entry is timid and grainy sweet, but displays a lack of acidity which makes it seem fat and flabby; the crispness deficit isn't as pronounced in the midpalate stage as the taste takes on more of a caramel/toffee lean. Finishes clean, a touch too fat, and leathery. In a nutshell: it lacks charm and comes off as too old.

2007 Rating: ★★/Not Recommended

Lonach Carsebridge 43 Year Old Single Grain Whisky (Scotland); 43% abv, $109.

Topaz/honey/deep amber color; unblemished purity. Opening whiffs pick up mature, woody/oaky scents that have pretty much been leeched of all the graininess; Spartan aromatic notes of lanolin and palm oil emerge after the aeration period; a weary, over-the-hill aroma. What this whisky lacks in aromatic punch, it makes up for in the mouth; entry is fat, sweet, and caramel-like; the taste profile at midpalate turns meaty/pork-like, with touches of honey, bacon fat, cream sherry, and cocoa butter. Ends up clean, semisweet, and chocolaty. Not the greatest single grain whisky I've had, but notable due to its vibrant flavor and finish phases.

2007 Rating: ★★★/Recommended

Lonach Glen Grant 31 Year Old Speyside SMSW (Scotland); 42.3% abv, $143.

Deep gold/old sauternes hue; flawless clarity. Smells of wet hay, paraffin, and very dry malt in the opening whiffs; seven more minutes of aeration don't do a lot to expand on what's already been discovered in the bouquet. Entry is delightfully sweet, toffee-like, and honeyed; at midpalate there's a far-reaching inland malt grainy/oaky sweetness that's damn near luscious in its depth. Concludes medium-rich, buttery, caramel sweet, and elegant. Speyside at its over 30 best. Had the aroma been more expressive, there'd have likely been a fifth rating star bestowed.

2007 Rating: ★★★★/Highly Recommended

Lonach Macduff 33 Year Old 1972 Speyside SMSW (Scotland); 40% abv, $169.

The 14-carat gold color is brilliant and impeccably clean. Curious opening scents include butterscotch, marshmallow, and starch; aeration provides the impetus for additional aromas to emerge, most notably, tropical fruits such as guava and banana. The palate entry is polite, lean, and oaky; at the midpalate point the taste profile turns more biscuity and cookie batter-like. Finishes cleanly and moderately sweet.

2007 Rating: ★★★/Recommended

Lonach Miltonduff 37 Year Old 1968 Speyside SMSW (Scotland); 40% abv, $173.

The amber/saffron/harvest gold color is pretty and flawlessly pure. The initial inhalations pick up piney/cedary scents that are dry and resiny; aeration introduces regrettable aromas of toolbox, nails/metal, and little more. The palate entry is mildly sweet and a bit flabby, lacking acid for structure, but otherwise moderately pleasing in a fruity kind of way; at the midpalate juncture the flavor profile comes alive (finally) as attractive tastes of light toffee, butter cream, and almond paste take center stage. The impressive display of bacon fat, butter, and toffee continue to build in the aftertaste. Such a valiant resurrection at midpalate and finish deserves a recommendation.

2007 Rating: ★★★/Recommended

Lonach The Glenlivet 34 Year Old 1971 Speyside SMSW (Scotland); 40% abv, $160.

Deep straw/18-carat gold color; excellent clarity. Not much happening in the first nosings after the pour except for some painfully faint heather and green wood notes; the additional seven minutes of air contact stimulate nothing, leaving me feeling cheated about the lackluster bouquet when I normally love any expression of The Glenlivet. The palate entry is flat tasting and synthetic fiber/flax-like; at the midpalate juncture the taste profile unravels totally in disagreeable waves of oak resin and pine. Concludes in a heap of over-the-hill flavors. A classic case of "just because it's old doesn't automatically mean that it's good".

2007 Rating: ★/Not Recommended

McGibbon's Provenance Caol Ila 19 Year Old Autumn Distillation Islay SMSW (Scotland); 43% abv, $100.

The golden straw-like color is marred by lots of unsightly floating debris; while I fully understand that this whisky was not chill-filtered for the honorable purpose of originality, I don't necessarily think that average imbibers, even keen whisky mavens, would care to see this much detritus in a bottle for which they've paid $100; a definite minus. The opening

couple of nosing passes pick up the trademark combined aromas of Caol Ila, a soft, medium salty, dry, and malty perfume that never fails to bewitch me; aeration serves to release further, even deeper notes, especially cigarette smoke and moderate peat reek. The palate entry is zesty and spirity without being raw; the midpalate stage features firm, round tastes of dry-to-bittersweet dark chocolate, roasted malt, and a trace of marzipan. The finish is long, dry, and oaky/resiny. Not the best version I've tasted from this esteemed, if horrendously overlooked, distillery but still very good.
2002 Rating: ★★★/Recommended

McGibbon's Provenance Dallas Dhu 19 Year Old Speyside SMSW (Scotland); 43% abv, $100.

Rich amber/dark honey color; some minuscule sediment spotted, but not enough to factor into the rating. The startling opening whiffs after the pour are greeted by a pungent aroma assertively laced with bacon fat, sautéed mushrooms, almond butter and/ or paste, and oaky vanilla extract; further air contact over the course of five to seven minutes unleashes a barrage of additional scents that include lead pencil, rubber tire, pork rind, and ground black pepper; a wood-driven bouquet that's oily and astringent in its base but delectably nutty and candied at the surface. The palate entry is remarkably focused, like a laser beam, and candied not in a sweet way but more in a bittersweet/nougaty manner; the midpalate is nutty, intensely oaky, vanilla-like, and oily. The aftertaste is long, bittersweet, and concentrated squarely on the oak. Looking for a high quality malt whose personality is impacted almost entirely by wood? Here it is.
2002 Rating: ★★★★/Highly Recommended

McGibbon's Provenance Dufftown 11 Year Old Winter Distillation Speyside SMSW (Scotland); 43% abv, $45.

Pretty gold/flax hue; more suspended particles than I'd like to see; what is that floating whitish/gray stuff, anyway? Shows a flowery, garden-like aroma that's fresh and youthful in the initial two passes; with time in the glass the bouquet turns fruity and malty in the later sniffings. The fruity character discovered in the nose continues into the taste phase at palate entry; by the midpalate point the flavors become drier and more focused on the malt component. It concludes pleasantly enough. Overall, it's simple, but competent malt drinking with no surprises.
2002 Rating: ★★★/Recommended

McGibbon's Provenance Port Ellen 19 Year Old Islay SMSW (Scotland); 62.5% abv, $109.

Medium amber/autumnal gold color; adequate clarity. The initial two nosings pick up plenty of medicinal, assertively phenolic aromas that holler out "peat, peat and more peat"; the bouquet improves dramatically with time in the glass as the piquant aromas turn round, briny/salty, intensely malty, and correctly smoky and toasty for the place of origin. The palate entry stings the tongue but offers malty sweet and sherry-influenced tastes; by the midpalate juncture the flavor phase highlights include caramel, sea salt, nougat, and sweet oak. The finish is long, prickly on the tongue, and delicious. A lovely expression of this quality distillery that's currently closed.
2002 Rating: ★★★★/Highly Recommended

Michel Couvreur 33 Year Old Very Sherried Unfiltered Single Cask SMSW (Scotland); 45% abv, $275.

The deep bronze/tawny/brown nut liqueur hue dazzles the eye; some slight sediment seen, but not enough to lose sleep over it. The opening inhalations detect extremely toasty notes of charred beef, charcoal, and butterscotch; later sniffings dredge up black tea leaves, burning electrical wire, and dark caramel; not the honeyed/bacon fat sherry-a-thon that one would expect and, as such, it's a slightly disappointing bouquet. The palate entry is narrowly focused, medium rich, moderately honeyed, and waxy; by midpalate the taste profile turns mildly buttery/creamy and nutty/nougat-like. Concludes sweet, concentrated, and composed. The best years of this malt whisky are behind it; since I evaluate spirits not on a price level but on a quality status, I give this whisky three stars; that said, $275 is a lot for a three star whisky when other heavily sherried malts exist for less than half that price.

2004 Rating: ★★★/Recommended

Michel Couvreur Pale Single-Single Aged Over 12 Years Unfiltered Single Cask SMSW (Scotland); 45% abv, $85.

One of the cloudiest, dullest single malt whiskies I've seen in years; the flat amber color shows lots of residual fog and sediment. The first whiffs don't uncover much in the way of aromatics; seven more minutes serve to produce little other than a faint trace of linseed oil; it will take a lot to bring this muffled malt back from the dead. The palate entry is grainy, off-dry, and moderately oily; by midpalate the mildly honeyed core flavor displays some elegance, but there's not enough finesse here to justify the hefty price. Finishes with a burnt toast flavor. If you want to experience what an unadulterated barrel sample is like, then buy this raw, unfinished whisky; clearly, at least to me, there is a potentially nice whisky here if it were cleaned up and made presentable; as it is I can't recommend it.

2004 Rating: ★★/Not Recommended

Murray McDavid Ardbeg 1991 9 Year Old Cask MM2999 Islay SMSW (Scotland); 46% abv, $80.

Pale yellow/green color; considerable amount of whitish sediment noted beneath the evaluation lamp. The opening nosing pass highlights brash, piquant aromas of seaweed, peat smoke, and cooked vegetables; the second sniffing offers fresh mown hay; the third whiff, after seven minutes of air contact, starts to focus tightly on the peat smoke as the salty breeze/seaweed element gets pushed to the background; the fourth and final inhalation plays on the green vegetable component, even adding a touch of sweet red pepper at the very end; the pungent, but gentlemanly Islay bouquet from the island's biggest peat gun. The palate entry is almost neutral; then as the taste advances to midpalate the flavors of sweet oak, peat reek, seaweed, and linseed oil explode on the tongue, making for an almost chocolaty experience in the finish. I've been a little gun shy of Ardbeg up to this point, but I believe that this bottling with its cocoa/chocolate aftertaste is a winner; bravo.

2001 Rating: ★★★★/Highly Recommended

Murray McDavid Bowmore 1989 10 Year Old Cask MM8631 Islay SMSW (Scotland); 46% abv, $70.

Pale straw yellow color; excellent purity. The medium-salty, politely briny and flowery opening aroma signals this whisky's maritime place of origin; but it's in the smashing second pass after the whisky has had some time to stretch its legs that the irrepressible freshness of the seaside maturation location comes clearly into view; in the third sniffing the perfumy fragrance of fresh cut flowers enters the equation, beautifully complementing the sea breeze element; in the fourth and last whiff, after over nine minutes of exposure to air, the aromas settle into being a true malt bouquet, one that ends up showing distant spice scents, savory malt, light oak, and flowers; a dandy Islay bouquet. The palate entry is lighter, more fey in nature than I routinely expect from Bowmore but it's scrumptious nevertheless; the midpalate is firm, tightly structured, sweet in a grainy manner, and moderately briny. The aftertaste is medium-long, sappy, lightly salty, and crisp. There's even a flash of raw spirit in the tail end.

2001 Rating: ★★★★/Highly Recommended

Murray McDavid Bunnahabhain 1979 17 Year Old Cask MM2080 Islay SMSW (Scotland); 46% abv, $90.

Lovely goldenrod/pale gold hue; impeccable purity. The nose right after opening is biscuity, warm, and slightly honeyed; in the second pass a racy spirit element picks up steam while in the third sniffing (seven minutes of air contact) savory aromatic morsels of lemon peel, gently sweet malt, and light toffee appear; the fourth and final blast brings the disparate components together for an ethereal, almost fruity bouquet that shows very little sea breeze/salinity and tons of fresh fruit and grain poise; the finest, most sophisticated aromatic display I've yet encountered from this Islay distillery. The palate entry is dry and toffee-like; the midpalate offers substantial weight and grip both which underscore the dry to off-dry flavors of honey, marzipan, and sweet, resiny oak. The finish is medium long, sap-like, off-dry-to-mildly sweet, and honeyed. Easily the foremost Bunnahabhain I've so far had the pleasure of reviewing.

2001 Rating: ★★★★/Highly Recommended

Murray McDavid Caperdonich 1968 Mission Series II Speyside SMSW (Scotland); 46% abv, $180.

The brilliant golden/straw hue is the color of a white graves; sediment free. In the first couple of minutes the aroma is assertive, vegetal, and damn near prickly in the nasal cavity; six more minutes of aeration go a long way in smoothing out this rambunctious bouquet which turns malty, biscuity, and leathery in the final stages. The palate entry is sweet, concentrated, honeyed, and caramel-like; the richness found in the entry continues on at midpalate as the taste profile goes in a creamy, fatty, and pleasantly oily direction. Finishes semisweet, malty, oily, and warm in the throat. A better than average malt from this underachieving Speyside distillery.

2004 Rating: ★★★/Recommended

Murray McDavid Clynelish 1972 Mission Range Northern Highlands SMSW (Scotland); 46% abv, $150.

Shows the golden yellow look of a Burgundian chardonnay; excellent purity. Displays early on the unmistakable seed-like (sesame), pod-like aroma so representative of this great distillery (one of my six five star malt distilleries); later on after seven additional minutes of air contact, the zesty aroma turns briny, lightly peated, grassy and vegetal; this distillery's malts repeatedly offer the best aromas, a subtle combination of their maritime (the brine) and Highlands (grass, sesame, mustard) location. This malt takes off once on the palate, starting with dry to off-dry tastes of malt, oak and sesame; at the midpalate stage the flavor profile takes flight as pronounced, assertive tastes of honey, apple butter and oak resin blend perfectly for a savory taste finale. The finish is oily, rich, somewhat prickly on the tongue, and delicious.

2003 Rating: ★★★★/Highly Recommended

Murray McDavid Dallas Dhu 1979 Mission Range Speyside SMSW (Scotland); 46% abv, $150.

Amber/harvest gold color; superb clarity. This opening bouquet is decidedly grassy and woodsy in the first couple of whiffs following the pour; aeration unleashes intriguing scents of pine cone, lanolin, milk chocolate, and oak resin. The palate entry is oily, buttery, fatty and utterly luscious; at midpalate the taste of oaky, creamy fat and rich, oily feel go off the charts; I love the way this sensuous malt feels in the mouth more than anything else. The aftertaste continues the cream-a-thon and comes off tasting like nougat or, better, white chocolate. One of the two best Dallas Dhus I've evaluated since 1989.

2003 Rating: ★★★★/Highly Recommended

Murray McDavid Glen Grant 1969 Mission Series II Speyside SMSW (Scotland); 46% abv, $180.

The honey/butterscotch color is seriously pretty; reasonable purity. The punchy early stage aroma reeks of malt, breakfast cereal (especially steaming porridge), and heather; a spell of aeration brings out appealing scents of pears, peaches, brown sugar, honey, and almond butter; a traditional hearty but polite Speyside bouquet of the sweet cereal leaning. The palate entry shows off firm and slightly oily light toffee, nougat tastes; by midpalate the flavor profile becomes further enhanced by a deep, sinewy texture and off-dry to medium sweet tastes of oaky vanilla, maple, marzipan, and oloroso sherry. Concludes with a rush of toffee/maple. I was very tempted to bestow a fourth rating star when upon going back for one last sip, I noted a sharpness in the aftertaste that kept the score right—and appropriately—where it should be.

2004 Rating: ★★★/Recommended

Murray McDavid Glenlivet 1974 Mission Range Speyside SMSW (Scotland); 46% abv, $150.

Striking yellow gold appearance; textbook purity. The initial sniffings reveal incredibly soft yellow fruit and flower scents, with a trace of pencil eraser; seven more minutes of air contact stir up delicate aromas of malt, wood chips, and wet earth; a gentlemanly bouquet, typical of Glenlivet. The true virtues of this malt are evident in the mouth, however, as the palate entry boasts a lovely oily texture and a taste of unsweetened breakfast cereal; at the midpalate point the ultra-dry flavor profile leans heavily to the malt aspect while the texture turns creamy and silky smooth. "Understatement" is the watchword for this bottling and, therefore, I can't imagine that it would appeal to admirers of sweeter, fatter Speysides or smoky, husky island malts.

2003 Rating: ★★★★/Highly Recommended

Murray McDavid Glenlossie 1975 Mission Series II Speyside SMSW (Scotland); 46% abv, $180.

The straw/gold appearance is blemish-free and attractive in a white wine manner. The opening sniffs detect a strongly vegetal, earthy aroma that's a bit reminiscent of beeswax; further time in the copita gives rise to mildly pleasant, feinty scents of rubber eraser, tobacco leaf, light peat, cork, and worn saddle leather. The palate entry shows a firmness and integration lacking in the underwhelming bouquet and is, therefore, a pleasant development; by the midpalate stage the taste profile displays a moderately toasty, malty, semisweet, if downward spiraling face. Ends up malty sweet, simple, and basic. The malts from this average distillery have rarely impressed me and this edition holds form; frankly, I'd demand more for my money than this tired, nearly feeble, but still drinkable malt whisky; for more than $150, being merely ordinary and old just doesn't cut it when so many other less expensive choices exist.

2004 Rating: ★★/Not Recommended

Murray McDavid Highland Park 1979 Mission Range Orkney SMSW (Scotland); 46% abv, $150.

Sports a fino sherry gold/straw color; absolutely ideal clarity. The initial scent is flecked with delicate notes of honey, oloroso sherry, and tobacco leaf; aeration time of another six minutes stirs up succulent aromas including ashes, oaky vanillin, poppy seed, and sweet malt. The palate entry is divine, buttery, slightly herbal, lightly peated, and oily; by the midpalate stage the oiliness takes control of the texture while the lightly peated tastes overshadows the honey, seeds, and wood; luscious. The aftertaste is long, sweet without being cloying, and shows nuances of tobacco smoke. A tour de force from the legendary Highland Park (another of my six favorite malt distilleries).

2003 Rating: ★★★★★/Highest Recommendation

Murray McDavid Highland Park 1988 11 Year Old Cask MM1298 Orkney SMSW (Scotland); 46% abv, $60.

Very pale straw yellow hue; immaculate purity (could this be an immaculate perception?). The opening nosing pass picks up subtle honey and vanilla notes while the second sniffing detects minor peat presence and green vegetables (kale? asparagus?); in the third whiff, after seven minutes of aeration, a sly hint of welcome spirity heat enters the aromatic picture and underpins the more ethereal scents of honey, vanilla, and steamed green vegetable; following ten minutes in the sampling glass, there's a slight diminishment in aromatic potency but not enough to become an issue; it's a softer side of HPark. In the mouth the taste of sweet, oily grain soars at the delectable and assertive palate entry; at midpalate the vivid taste of the foundational spirit, mildly smoky peat, and oily wood put on a fabulous show of the inherent depth, stately demeanor, and classical style of HPark, even at a relatively immature age. Brilliant.

2001 Rating: ★★★★/Highly Recommended

Murray McDavid Lagavulin 1979 Mission Range Islay SMSW (Scotland); 46% abv, $180.

White wine yellow/gold; superb clarity. The bouquet after the pour immediately asserts itself, emitting peaty, smoky, briny aromas that are off-dry to sweet in nature; exposure to

air for an additional six minutes expands the bouquet to include nutmeg, almond butter, and grass; this bouquet is not overly peaty. The palate entry is succulent, sweet, sherried, and scrumptious; by the midpalate point the texture turns seriously oily and the taste profile takes on a tobacco leaf, tobacco smoke, sea brine posture that's surprisingly sweet but gentlemanly. The aftertaste is long, peaty, sweet, and loaded with herbal elegance. Another winner from this wonderful distillery.
2003 Rating: ★★★★/Highly Recommended

Murray McDavid Laphroaig 1988 14 Year Old Islay SMSW (Scotland); 46% abv, $n/a.
Straw yellow/white wine, hazy appearance; tons of minuscule sediment. Displays considerable peatiness/sea breeze right from the first whiff; seven additional minutes of air contact release medicinal aromas of iodine, antiseptic, seaweed, light wood smoke, and kippers; not the most phenolic Laphroaig bouquet I've come across, but briny and peaty enough. Lovers of hearty Islay malts won't be disappointed with this concentrated and cigarette smoke-like palate entry; at midpalate the taste profile takes a sweeter direction and actually comes off mildly maple-like, corn sugar-like and honeyed; the bourbon cask really comes through at the midpalate. It finishes clean and just a tad briny. A particularly attractive bottling of the great Laphroaig.
2003 Rating: ★★★★/Highly Recommended

Murray McDavid Leapfrog 1987 (Laphroaig) 12 Year Old Cask MM2868 Islay SMSW (Scotland); 46% abv, $80.
Pretty, chardonnay yellow/gold hue; impressive purity. The initial nosing pass is moderately dry, offering acceptably medicinal scents of evergreen, cedar, resin, and peat reek; the middle stage whiffs focus more on an ashy/almost sooty perfume that's very tobacco-like and earthy, as in dirt; following over eight minutes of aeration, the bouquet remains a bit reluctant in the fourth and final pass, emitting exotic scents of lead pencil, black pepper, light peat, and sea salt; this is a pensive Islay bouquet, not a brawler. More intriguing and expressive in the mouth than in the nasal cavity, Leapfrog grabs the taste buds at palate entry; the midpalate taste features oil, light peat smoke, cigarette tobacco, sweet bourbon barrel, and caramel. The finish is long, oily, more sweet than salty or peaty, and satisfying. A tad inconsistent, but savory and, dare I say it, mellower than one would expect, considering the distillery.
2001 Rating: ★★★/Recommended

Murray McDavid Linkwood 1973 Mission Series II Speyside SMSW (Scotland); 46% abv, $180.
Pretty honey/harvest gold color; excellent purity. In the first passes, the aromas take a little time to rev up; following another seven minutes of air contact, the still mysteriously dormant bouquet begins to emit muted and muffled scents that include breakfast cereal, light toffee, and grapes; not like any Linkwood bouquet I've come across before, which are normally biscuity and semisweet. Things finally get started in the palate entry which is moderately oily, a bit sharp and astringent, and cereal-like; by the midpalate phase there's more integrated, bittersweet flavors of old wood, oak resin, boiled cabbage, tired peat, and deep-roasted malt. Concludes bitterly and hot in an astringent, resiny fashion that shows precious little of this distillery's usual panache and quality. Certainly drinkable with but

a small echo of quality, though hardly typical of what I've experienced in the past from Linkwood; keep on walking past this one.
2004 Rating: ★★/Not Recommended

Murray McDavid Lochside 1981 18 Year Old Cask MM9636 Eastern Highlands SMSW (Scotland); 46% abv, $90.
The color is a stellar medium amber/honey/fino sherry hue; superb purity. The initial nosing pass reveals a pungent, almost prickly aroma that comes scrappily out of the bottle; with a bit of air contact the aroma settles down somewhat into a dry to off-dry, mildly honeyed, light toffee, and resiny bouquet that's pleasantly aggressive; by the third sniffing a curiously charming caramel corn-like, candied but dry aroma enters the fray and blunts the spirity quality; in the fourth and final whiff traces of lanolin and brown butter arrive but the aromatic element that stands out in the end is the woody resin feature. The palate entry is lean and dry; then at midpalate the flavors of sweet oak, vanilla extract, honey, butter, and dried fruit both challenge and delight the taste buds. The finish is downright succulent, oaky sweet, pine-like, and extended. Hands down the finest expression of this distillery I've ever had.
2001 Rating: ★★★★/Highly Recommended

Murray McDavid Macallan 1973 25 Year Old Cask MM4755 Speyside SMSW (Scotland); 46% abv, $150.
Harvest gold/medium amber tint; very minor sediment spotted. The nose immediately after the pour is toasty, white wine-like, and vanilla-like; with time, the aroma opens up slightly in the second whiff, emitting evolving scents of pear and dark toffee; the third sniffing displays a touch of prickly/mildly heated spirit; in the fourth and final pass a notable calming takes place as softer scents of oak resin, muted peat, and honey-like sherry settle in for the long haul; not the usual ambrosial, multilayered aromatic exhibition from this esteemed distillery, but solid and sweet all the same. The palate entry is malty/grainy/cereal sweet and full-bodied; in the midpalate stage succulent flavor notes of honey, oloroso sherry, and oaky vanilla shine and are more of what one expects from an older Macallan. The finish is lip-smacking sweet and sherried; husky, very honey-like, and opulent.
2001 Rating: ★★★★/Highly Recommended

Murray McDavid Macallan 1990 10 Year Old Speyside SMSW (Scotland); 46% abv, $n/a.
The golden yellow color is slightly hazy (remember that Murray McDavids are not chill filtered); alarmingly large chunks of cork are found floating to the surface. The first couple of sniffing minutes are all Macallan, gently sweet, clearly sherried and honey-like; following seven more minutes of aeration the aroma turns delightfully biscuity, oaky vanilla, and marzipan-like, with background scents of wood resin and butterscotch; lots happening here aromatically. The palate entry is sweet, oaky, and a touch hot and prickly; strong, aggressive notes of bittersweet chocolate and cocoa appear at midpalate, eclipsing the oak. Finishes honey sweet, piquant, and spirity. No mistaking the luscious Macallan thumbprint, but the rambunctious nature of this malt makes me think that another couple of years in cask would have served it well.
2003 Rating: ★★★/Recommended

Murray McDavid Mortlach 1990 12 Year Old Speyside SMSW (Scotland); 46% abv, $n/a.
The topaz/honey color is slightly foggy; harmless bits of sediment are seen at the core. The bouquet comes out of the box swinging as assertive aromas of dry malt, light caramel, and old oak provide plenty of interest; further time in the glass adds scents of brown rice, cocoa, bacon fat, and oatmeal. The palate entry is politely sweet and sap-like; then at midpalate the taste profile turns more focused and intense as seductive flavors of Christmas spices, nougat, and pipe tobacco emerge. The aftertaste is medium-long, sappy sweet, and a bit maple-like. An elegant, four star malt.
2003 Rating: ★★★★/Highly Recommended

Murray McDavid Rosebank 1989 10 Year Old Cask MM523 Lowland SMSW (Scotland); 46% abv, $60.
Displays the thumbprint lemon juice/straw yellow tint so typical of Rosebank; superb purity. The gentle, flowery perfume glides effortlessly out of the sampling glass in the initial nosing pass; the middle stage passes add polite but well-formed scents of bread dough, distant spice, and sweet malt; following nearly ten full minutes of aeration, inviting aromas of yellow tropical fruit and rose hip round out the bouquet; a definitive Rosebank bouquet that's nothing short of elegant and disarming; I love its Lowland simplicity, soft sweetness, and directness. On the tongue at palate entry the taste of ripe melon delights the taste buds; at the midpalate phase the succulent tropical fruit, sweet malt, and light honey flavors provide all the courteous taste impact one could hope for from a Lowland malt classic. The finish is brief, but concentrated on the malt. This is Lowland single malt Scotch at its zenith; outstanding.
2001 Rating: ★★★★★/Highest Recommendation

Murray McDavid Royal Brackla 1975 17 Year Old Cask MM9805 Speyside SMSW (Scotland); 46% abv, $100.
Medium amber/autumnal gold color; some sediment noted. The initial nosing pass shows a prickly, spirity, and rambunctious aroma, then in the second sniffing things calm down as the aroma offers mildly sweet, malty, and lightly peated scents that effectively counter the prickliness; in the third whiff, a minor diminishment of potency is noted as the sweet graininess takes the reins; in the fourth and final pass, following ten minutes of exposure to air, fragrances of peanut oil, honey, and sweet oak dominate the bouquet. The palate entry is guardedly sweet and honeyed; but then the midpalate stage shows a tad more flavor vibrancy in the forms of oak, caramel, and honey. The aftertaste is very long, sap-like, and rich. A better than average malt that displays the sap-like, sweet side of Speyside.
2001 Rating: ★★★/Recommended

Murray McDavid Royal Brackla 1975 Mission Range Speyside SMSW (Scotland); 46% abv, $150.
Lovely deep amber/honey/sauternes gold color; impeccable clarity. The initial two nosing passes detect evidence of tea leaves, hay, and flowers; seven more minutes of exposure to air release additional and deeper scents of toffee, wet vegetation, cedar, and oak resin. The palate entry is dry and cereal-like; then at midpalate the taste expands to include almond butter, resin, dried fruit, and oil; the texture is very oily. It finishes squeaky clean and dry, with just a trace of malt.
2003 Rating: ★★★/Recommended

Murray McDavid Strathisla 1976 Mission Series II Speyside SMSW (Scotland); 46% abv, $180.

The light amber/wheat color displays ideal clarity. The first whiffs detect nut-like and nougaty scents mixed up with resiny traces of grain husk and oak; aeration fails to stimulate further aromatic levels and indeed the bouquet comes up lame after an additional seven minutes in the glass, offering only mildly malty, biscuity, if distant aromas; what gives here? The palate entry is sweet and biscuity, with pleasant traces of cocoa and vanilla bean; at midpalate the taste kicks it up several notches, featuring round, oaky, even buttery flavors of sherry, milk chocolate, and honey. Finishes well in a medium-rich, creamy fashion. The taste and finish stages brought this malt back from the land of the commonplace.

2004 Rating: ★★★/Recommended

Origine 10 Year Old Islay SMSW (Scotland); 40% abv, $42.

The appearance is harvest gold/light honey/amber and moderately pure. In the initial whiffs, the aroma gives off scents of grain mash, new leather, and distant oak; seven more minutes of air contact stir more seductive and customary fragrances of seaweed, sea air, and low-to-medium peatiness; a composed, even gentlemanly Islay perfume. The palate entry is astringent, smoky, and briny at first, then it suddenly turns semisweet and malty; the midpalate stage is husk-like, moderately oily, oaky sweet, and tobacco- and cocoa-like. Finishes gracefully yet vividly, focusing on the natural smokiness of Islay malts. This malt is not trying to be a jaw-clenching peat King Kong, leaning instead to the more elegant, smoky yet sweet side of Islay. Well done.

2006 Rating: ★★★★/Highly Recommended

Origine 12 Year Old (BenRiach) Speyside SMSW (Scotland); 40% abv, $34.

The bright amber hue beams under the examination lamp and exhibits ideal purity; a beautiful whisky. The first whiffs pick up off-dry, fundamentally sound, if uninspiring scents of malted barley and breakfast cereal; further aeration time doesn't stimulate the bouquet as much as I had hoped, leaving my olfactory sense smelling the same aromas it encountered in the initial passes. The palate entry is whistle clean, medium-bodied, and intensely grainy sweet; at the midpalate stage the flavor profile adds attractive tastes of nougat, almond paste, and toffee. The finish is pleasingly malty, sweet, and even a touch honeyed. A very sound, very drinkable mid-tier Speyside malt whose trademark maltiness is evident from start to finish.

2005 Rating: ★★★/Recommended

Scott's Selection Ardmore 1977 Sherry Wood Speyside SMSW (Scotland); 57.5% abv, $182.

The attractive golden color is blemish-free. The first nosings unearth delicate scents of sawdust and cigar box; aeration, frankly, does little to stir further aromas other than a caramel popcorn odor in the final sniff. The palate entry is mannered, semisweet, and mildly honeyed; at midpalate the flavor really takes shape, offering lightly toasted tastes of honey wheat bread, toasted marshmallow, sap, oloroso sherry, vanilla, and clover honey. Finishes well and stately, a touch sweet and honey-like, but composed. Admittedly, I've been ho-hum about Ardmore malts over the years, but this offering shows lots of character and flair, especially in the excellent taste and finish phases.

2004 Rating: ★★★★/Highly Recommended

Scott's Selection Auchentoshan 1983 Lowlands SMSW (Scotland); 52.4% abv, $145.

Green/gold color; very good clarity. The aroma in the opening phase is light, grassy, green tomato-like, and herbal; in the later sniffing stages, the aroma transforms into an assertive bouquet, emitting scents of tar, cellophane, pine, dry malt, and pork rind. At palate entry, the texture goes creamy and the taste turns prickly, and spicy/peppery; at midpalate a sweetish flavor of mead blankets the taste buds, becoming the dominant force. Ends up treacle-like, sweet, and even honeyed. Absolutely douse with mineral water to cut the fiery alcohol. Very good but not as elegant as I normally know the malts from this superb Lowlands distillery to be.

2005 Rating: ★★★/Recommended

Scott's Selection Bladnoch 1984 Lowlands SMSW (Scotland); 55.1% abv, $190.

Very attractive and vibrant pale yellow/gold; superb purity. The first nosings immediately pick up beguiling scents of carnation, rose petal, spring garden, mint, and cinnamon spiciness; further aeration adds nuances of white pepper, pine/fir tree needles, and a faint dollop of honey; one of the finest Lowlands bouquets I've encountered in a while; disarming and elegant. The taste at palate entry is buttery/creamy and moderately spicy, then at midpalate the flavor profile turns biscuity, doughy, and sherry cask sweet. Concludes in the throat as gracefully as it began in the nose.

2005 Rating: ★★★★/Highly Recommended

Scott's Selection Bruichladdich 1990 Islay SMSW (Scotland); 58.1% abv, $100.

Silvery/pale yellow hue; excellent purity. Displays soft and grassy aromatics early-on; aeration time serves to stimulate moderately deeper scents, including refined sugar, new honey, and lightly toasted oak cask. The palate entry is firm, acceptably fiery/spirity, and semisweet; at midpalate there's a rush of spirit, then that subsides allowing flavors of malt cereal, brown butter, almonds, and cocoa to emerge. Finishes up moderately sweet and malty, with background accents of green olive, escarole, and seaweed.

2005 Rating: ★★★/Recommended

Scott's Selection Bunnahabhain 1988 Islay SMSW (Scotland); 53.8% abv, $130.

Bright amber/light topaz color; ideal clarity. The slightly saline/briny and toasty/nutty aroma lures me in immediately; further air contact stimulates scents of forest floor/damp woods, white pepper, salted peanuts, and saltine crackers. At palate entry this malt tastes of malted milk/Horlicks, and then at midpalate there are waves of seaweed, linseed oil, green olive, and oak. Ends up semisweet, nutty, intensely malty, moderately salty, and pleasingly briny. Typical Bunnahabhain lightish, almost fey nature, but ample grip and taste definition. Definitely add a healthy dose of mineral water.

2005 Rating: ★★★/Recommended

Scott's Selection Caol Ila 1984 Islay SMSW (Scotland); 53.5% abv, $225.

Pale straw/flax color; perfect clarity. Aromas of rubber tire, pencil eraser, light smoke, and road tar are featured in the opening inhalations; vaguely floral and leathery notes enter the aromatic mix after the aeration period. Entry is like licking an ashtray, so delectably smoky and peaty is this bad boy right off the crack of the bat; at midpalate a rich barley malt sweetness counters the smoke/peat in elegant fashion. Ends on desirable Islay notes of kippers, cigarette ash, salty brine, cigar smoke, and sea breeze. When Caol Ila's flying high, it offers this type of comely style that's 50% power and 50% finesse.

2007 Rating: ★★★★/Highly Recommended

Scott's Selection Glen Grant 1967 Sherry Wood Speyside SMSW (Scotland); 55.1% abv, $240.

Bright amber/medium honey color; perfect clarity. The first few inhalations pick up reluctant odors of paraffin, roasted grain, and malted milk; regrettably, further aeration fails to extract anything more in the aroma; no worries, though. The palate entry is succulent, fruity, and sweet; at midpalate the fruit disappears and is replaced by a dark toffee/maple/ sap flavor that's more semisweet than outright sweet. Finishes maple-like and muscular. A sturdy, robust offering from this renowned distillery.

2004 Rating: ★★★★/Highly Recommended

Scott's Selection Glen Grant 1977 Speyside SMSW (Scotland); 55.4% abv, $182.

The deep amber/honey/topaz hue is picture perfect in terms of purity. In the first sniffings, there's a creamy, toffee-like aroma that's semisweet and alluring; seven more minutes of air contact bring out notes of milk chocolate, coffee with cream, and candied almonds. The palate entry offers sweet, sap- and maple-like tastes, then at midpalate the flavor profile turns honeyed/sherried and intensely spirity. Finishes in a heady flurry of nutmeg/cinnamon spice and caramel tastes. Absolutely rein in (and thereby improve) this prickly malt with a healthy dose of mineral water.

2005 Rating: ★★★/Recommended

Scott's Selection Glen Mohr 1978 Northern Highlands SMSW (Scotland); 56.6% abv, $145.

Pale gold/medium amber hue; some sediment noted. The first whiffs after the pour find amiable, direct, mashy/malty scents that delight, but don't challenge the olfactory sense; even after six minutes of further aeration and swirling in the glass, the bouquet remains grainy sweet and uncomplicated. The palate entry is plump and generously malty; by midpalate the flavor profile gives off tastes of honey and light toffee. Ends up as simply and blue collar as it began with fat, oily, buttery flavors. Delightful due to its sheer simplicity.

2005 Rating: ★★★/Recommended

Scott's Selection Glenlivet 1977 Speyside SMSW (Scotland); 53.1% abv, $175.

Fine medium amber/wheat field gold color; flawless purity. The opening nosing passes detect subtle traces of malted milk and honey; aeration unleashes deeper scents of vanilla extract, seared bourbon oak, maple, and ash. The palate entry is semisweet, light toffee-like, and warm in spirit; at midpalate there's a burst of heady spirit presence, then that subsides, leaving behind toasty, honey wheat bread flavors. Concludes with a fleeting dash of honey/ brown sugar, then turns malty and sweet.

2005 Rating: ★★★/Recommended

Scott's Selection Glenrothes 1973 Speyside SMSW (Scotland); 50.4% abv, $165.
Lovely amber/straw gold color; impeccable purity. The opening nose is toasty, vibrant, malty, and dry; seven more minutes release deeper aromas of milk chocolate candy bar, heather honey, vanilla frosting, and dates; a quintessential Glenrothes bouquet. The palate entry is decadently oily, creamy, spirity (but neither prickly nor hot), and buttery; at midpalate the flavor profile turns sweet, honeyed, cocoa-like, and concentrated. Concludes velvety, honeyed, fat, and simply downright voluptuous. Right up there with the finest expressions of this hallowed Speyside distillery that I've reviewed. I suggest a minimal addition of room temperature mineral water; a definitive Glenrothes.
2004 Rating: ★★★★★/Highest Recommendation

Scott's Selection Highland Park 1981 Orkney Islands SMSW (Scotland); 50.6% abv, $225.
White gold/chardonnay color; excellent purity. The pungency of the spirit overshadows any other aromatic element in the initial whiffs; following aeration, the spirit blows off, leaving behind subtle (read: disappointingly undemonstrative) notes of oak, malt, and pine/cedar. Entry is delightfully oily and malty; the flavor at midpalate goes intensely grainy and honey sweet. Concludes balanced, elegant, and lean. A less expansive expression from this landmark distillery, but savory all the same.
2007 Rating: ★★★/Recommended

Scott's Selection Highland Park 1985 Orkney Islands SMSW (Scotland); 53.5% abv, $200.
The pale golden color does show some unsettled sediment, but nothing that I'd complain or whinge about. The first couple of inhalations take in small, dry, and slightly saline measures of peat reek, seaweed (kelp), sawdust, and malt; following seven more minutes of air contact, the bouquet expands to include scents of almond butter, smoked salmon, damp moss, and black tea; this challenging, compelling bouquet changes with every whiff and is increasingly intriguing with aeration. The surprising palate entry is long, honey sweet, biscuity, and moderately oily; at midpalate the taste profile extends well past the virtues of the entry to include sea breeze, cigar tobacco, kippers, and sherry. Ends up delicately sherried, creamy, and sublime. I've run out of descriptors for the malts from Highland Park.
2004 Rating: ★★★★★/Highest Recommendation

Scott's Selection Interleven 1979 Speyside SMSW (Scotland); 58% abv, $215.
Pale straw gold hue; excellent purity. The first whiffs pick up scents of grain husk, paraffin, and grape seed oil; further aeration stirs additional aromas of bran, malt, and cardboard. The palate entry is vigorous (after the tepid bouquet), oily, malty, and sweet; at midpalate notes of butter, light toffee, and fudge accent the taste phase. Finishes sweet, oily, and cereal-like. It is much more manageable after the addition of mineral water, which brings out the textured oiliness.
2004 Rating: ★★★/Recommended

Scott's Selection Linlithgow (St. Magdelene) 1982 Lowlands SMSW (Scotland); 61.6% abv, $160.
Attractive gold/amber color; some debris spotted. The opening whiffs uncover juicy, bubble gum, red fruit-like, and piney aromas; another seven minutes of exposure to air add

scents of white raisins, mince pie, marmalade, and pears. The palate entry is pleasantly sweet and fruity, with a background note of sweet maltiness; the midpalate at last shows a touch of spirity fire that underpins the juiciness/fruitiness. Finishes agile, limber, acidic, semisweet, and properly astringent.
2005 Rating: ★★★/Recommended

Scott's Selection Littlemill 1984 Lowlands SMSW (Scotland); 62.1% abv, $190.

The bright golden color displays a touch of air bubbles after the pour; otherwise superb clarity. This grassy, green, and affable opening aroma has Lowlands written all over it; seven more minutes of aeration turns the aroma into a sweet, malty/breakfast cereal bouquet that's approachable and easy. The palate entry offers supple, ripe tastes of green apple, ripe pear, and figs; at midpalate the flavor profile highlights the apple element but adds a cedar/pine/resiny background flavor that complements the fruity greenness. Finishes resiny/piney. An accurate expression of this historically important Lowlands distillery.
2004 Rating: ★★★/Recommended

Scott's Selection Longmorn-Glenlivet 1967 Speyside SMSW (Scotland); 52.2% abv, $235.

The pretty topaz color is marred slightly by too much debris. The initial whiffs detect only meager scents of mint, green oak, and green vegetation; six more minutes in the glass do little to encourage any aromatic deepening or expansion; basically this aroma is a flat out bust, considering the pedigree of this great distillery. The palate entry demeanor is lean, stingy, and only mildly malty; at midpalate there's more of a show of maltiness, even creaminess, but in the finish the hot spirit overwhelms the gains made in the midpalate. Uncharacteristically awkward. Just doesn't work when viewed in the context of what this distillery has done in other bottlings. Take a pass.
2005 Rating: ★★/Not Recommended

Scott's Selection Longmorn-Glenlivet 1968 Speyside SMSW (Scotland); 61.3% abv, $230.

The auburn/tawny color is clean and pure and eye-catching. The first inhalations following the pour offer dense aromas of black tea leaves, lead pencil, minerals, and straw; allowing it to sit for another seven minutes, the aroma deepens to include concentrated scents of candle wax, green olives, and linseed oil. The palate entry displays all the characteristic traits of Longmorn, meaning deep flavor notes of caraway, bacon fat, matchstick, and vegetable oil; at midpalate and after the addition of mineral water, the bacon fat/oil element turns creamy, vanilla-like, rancio-like, and nutty. Finishes luxuriously sweet, oaky/vanilla-like, caramel-like, and honeyed. Not for girlie men or for the single malt uninitiated.
2004 Rating: ★★★★/Highly Recommended

Scott's Selection Longmorn-Glenlivet 1971 Speyside SMSW (Scotland); 53.5% abv, $185.

Solid amber/light honey hue; clear of any debris. The first whiffs pick up unusual (for this distillery) scents of paint, solvent, and pine/fir; the resiny cedar/pine-fest continues in the later stages after aeration, creating something of a conundrum for me since I don't recall ever encountering a Longmorn bouquet quite this solvent-like. The palate entry is sweet and honeyed at first, then it turns fiery; at midpalate the alcohol heat is thankfully a memory as more sophisticated tastes of berries, ripe pears, and piecrust make for pleasing quaffing.

Finishes well, semisweet, oaky/vanilla-like, and aggressive. I liked this edition more than the rough 1967 and though it has problems I feel that there's enough raw quality here to justify the price. Add mineral water to the ratio of 1:2 water to whisky.
2005 Rating: ★★★/Recommended

Scott's Selection Macallan 1973 Speyside SMSW (Scotland); 44% abv, $300.

The green/yellow gold hue shows too much unsightly sediment beneath the examination lamp. The first burst of aroma emits notes of citrus rind, green tomatoes, and grass; seven more minutes of aeration add apple butter, fir tree, and peach; not what I'd normally expect from a Macallan bouquet. The palate entry makes up for the aromatic deficiencies, as the first taste is creamy, vanilla-like, and oily; at midpalate there's a surge of caramel flavor that overtakes all other taste components. Finishes maple sweet, buttery/creamy, citrusy, and warm in the throat. The enormous improvements once it was on palate pull this curious bottling to cautious recommendation status. I suggest that only the most fervent Macallan nuts and collectors lay out the three hundred dollars.
2005 Rating: ★★★/Recommended

Scott's Selection Macallan 1974 Speyside SMSW (Scotland); 49.2% abv, $250.

The bright golden/yellow/light honey color is unblemished and brilliant. The softly perfumed aroma in the initial inhalations is elegant and delicately breakfast cereal sweet; aeration time of another seven minutes allows the aroma to define itself in the glass as mildly succulent, fruity, and just-ripe scents of peach and pear entice the olfactory sense; a model of aromatic restraint. The palate entry flavor is heather honey sweet and moderately oily in texture, providing plenty of grip; at midpalate the taste profile turns more serious and complex as flavors of butter cream, dark fudge, dark caramel, and brown sugar round out a marvelously satisfying flavor phase. Ends up firm, oily, creamy, and buttery. A far more attractive value than the 1973. I likewise suggest you enjoy this stellar Macallan neat, or with just a very few drops of mineral water. A Macallan to love.
2005 Rating: ★★★★/Highly Recommended

Scott's Selection Macallan 1985 Speyside SMSW (Scotland); 53% abv, $225.

Rich topaz/honey color; good clarity. The first nosings find nuanced and off-dry scents of nutmeg, sturdy malt/grain, and brown sugar; the grain/malt fragrance picks up strength in the second stage of nosing as well as a pleasing Christmas season spiciness (cinnamon, vanilla). Entry is generously bittersweet upfront, then the taste displays welcome heat and pleasant doses of oaky sweetness and marzipan; at midpalate the taste profile serves notice that sweet/black raisin/fig-like Speyside is in the house by offering large, chewy, spirity flavors that are medium-weighted and mildly oily. Ends up lip-smacking luscious, maple fudge-like, honeyed, and amazingly focused still on the malt base.
2007 Rating: ★★★★/Highly Recommended

Scott's Selection North of Scotland (Strathmore) 1964 Single Grain Whisky (Scotland); 43.2% abv, $185.

Medium topaz/amber color; very good clarity. The first nosings detect the biscuity presence of oatmeal, green herbs, and cowhide/tannery; further aeration brings into play

aromas of dried figs and pine-essence; decent and different, but not necessarily an all-time favorite Scotch whisky bouquet of mine. The palate entry is semidry, nutshell- and sawdust-like; the midpalate stage offers a semisweet, breakfast cereal burst, then in the finish the taste profile becomes a bit too harsh and astringent for my liking. There are some good qualities here, especially in the first nosing and the palate entry, but there isn't enough follow-through and grace in the latter stages of the nosing or the midpalate to make this whisky recommendable. If money is no object and you badly hanker to sample a Single Grain Whisky, go for it. Otherwise, pass.
2005 Rating: ★★/Not Recommended

Scott's Selection Royal Brackla 1976 Speyside SMSW (Scotland); 57.2% abv, $180.
The light pale gold hue is blemish-free and pretty in its sparkling clarity. The initial nosing passes pick up very oily, medicinal, olive brine, and peaty aromas, then following another seven minutes of air contact the iodine/medicine cabinet odors blows off, leaving behind green apple, green tomato, and fir tree scents that are weirdly appealing, if not classical. The entry taste is semisweet, almost fruity in its concentrated graininess, and fresh; by midpalate the flavor profile evolves into a sap- and maple-like, lean textured, suitably astringent, and refreshing taste experience. Concludes squeaky clean and astringent. Keeps you guessing; keeps you alert and waiting for the next turn.
2005 Rating: ★★★/Recommended

Scott's Selection The Glenlivet 1970 Speyside SMSW (Scotland); 52% abv, $207.
The darkest, deepest worn-copper penny/pekoe tea color I've ever seen for a The Glenlivet; superb purity. All sorts of intriguing scents are alive in the first whiffs, including old leather, cheese, oatmeal, and pork roast; the later sniffings pick up treacle and damp forest. The palate entry is stunningly dark caramel-like and lip-smacking sweet; by midpalate the taste profile expands to include butter cream cake frosting, vanilla, maple syrup, and heather honey. Concludes in a stately, semisweet manner. An opulent expression of Speyside's prototypical distillery.
2004 Rating: ★★★★/Highly Recommended

The MacTarnahan 15 Year Old Highlands SMSW (Scotland); 46% abv, $50.
Attractive, deep honey hue; superb purity. The opening nosing passes deliver supple, sweet aromas of malt, orange blossom, and sherry; further aeration releases additional scents that include light toffee, honey, cigar smoke, and caramel; a pleasing nose that's integrated and honey/sherry sweet. The palate entry is honey sweet, but firm and a bit heated from the 92 proof (46% alcohol by volume which has become my preferred proof); the midpalate is fruity sweet, intensely malty, and sherried on the tongue with just the slightest trace of peat smoke. It finishes lustily and spirity, showing background flavors of caramel and cigar tobacco. A delectable malt with a fine balance reached between spirit, oak, and malt; there's no label info as to which distillery made this whisky and a spokesman at MacTarnahan declined to say; Singleton of Auchroisk? Lochnagar?
2002 Rating: ★★★★/Highly Recommended

Whisky Galore 1989 Pulteney Northern Highlands SMSW (Scotland); 46% abv, $69.
Pale gold/straw color; very good clarity. The opening burst of aroma has traces of lemon drop and cotton; further exposure to air stirs some meek scents of malt and oak, but not

much more. The palate entry is grainy/breakfast cereal sweet and pleasing; the midpalate stage highlights the sweetness of the malt, yet offers enough astringency to balance the natural sweetness. Ends up affable, simple, yet very tasty and agreeable.

2006 Rating: ★★★/Recommended

Whisky Galore 1996 Ben Nevis Western Highlands SMSW (Scotland); 46% abv, $54.

The pale yellow/green color is pretty and ideally pure. The nose after the pour is remarkably floral and fabric-like; aeration brings out a mildly candied scent that features light caramel, nougat, and quince; a carefree, engaging bouquet. The palate entry stays the yellow fruit course especially, adding a malty sweetness that's very inviting and warm; the midpalate stage heightens the hard candy sweetness as the taste profile zeroes in on the malt. Concludes light, wholly amiable, and savory. A very pleasant expression from an underachieving West Coast distillery.

2006 Rating: ★★★/Recommended

Whisky Galore Bowmore 1987 16 Year Old Northern Highlands SMSW (Scotland); 46% abv, $74.

The lovely deep bronze color is clear and pure. My initial aromatic encounter discovers odd (for Bowmore) scents of rubber band and parchment; later sniffings seem more in line with the traditional Bowmore fragrance bio as elegant aromas of oaky vanilla, dark toffee, marzipan, and cherry wood abound in the final laps. The palate entry offers the type of caramel sweetness that makes Bowmore so revered around the world; at midpalate the taste profile stretches to include chocolate, black fruit (plums, black grapes), and honey. Delicious in the finish as flavors of chocolate candy bar and honey go a long way to impress the taste buds.

2005 Rating: ★★★★/Highly Recommended

Whisky Galore Bowmore 1991 Islay SMSW (Scotland); 46% abv, $74.

The color is bright topaz; excellent clarity. The opening nosing passes are treated to sweetly medicinal aromas of worn cowhide, cigarette ash, fruity pipe smoke, and sea breeze; the additional seven minutes of aeration time only bring out added scents of beeswax and clover. The lush palate entry is honeyed, sherry-like, and dried fruit-like; at midpalate the spirit jumps on board directing the fruit and honey towards a cherry cake-like taste that's utterly beguiling. Finishes sweetly, fruity, and mildly iodine-like.

2004 Rating: ★★★★/Highly Recommended

Whisky Galore Bruichladdich 1991 Islay SMSW (Scotland); 46% abv, $69.

The color is very pale silver/yellow/green and pure. The opening sniffings pick up a cherry tree orchard two days before harvest; another seven minutes of air contact add lightly salted pretzels and white raisins. The palate entry is full, focused and intensely oily/buttery; at midpalate the butter turns paste-like and nougaty. Concludes green, mildly sweet, and woody, with a final blast of sea salt. Delightfully atypical and luscious.

2004 Rating: ★★★★/Highly Recommended

Whisky Galore Clynelish 1990 13 Year Old Northern Highlands SMSW (Scotland); 46% abv, $58.

Typical for Clynelish golden/white wine-like color; superb clarity. Smells fetchingly of young, flowery, slightly sour, rambunctious spirit in the first couple of whiffs, with little evidence of wood impact; later sniffings encounter ripe, almost lemony scents of banana, buttered popcorn, freshly sawn wood, and a trace of saltiness. The palate entry greets the taste buds with a richly textured taste of creamy butter, canola oil, and seaweed; at midpalate the flavor profile explodes on the tongue in a blaze of sweet butter, honey, and light toffee tastes. Concludes on a sweet, grainy/malty/honey note that closes the circle in style.

2005 Rating: ★★★★/Highly Recommended

Whisky Galore Glendronach 1990 Speyside SMSW (Scotland); 46% abv, $68.

Pale straw yellow color; ideal clarity. The zesty, piquant aroma in the opening whiffs offers strong notes of bran flakes, malted milk, and tree sap; another seven minutes of aeration bring out solvent-like aromas of pine needle and gum. The palate entry is toffee- and caramel-like, indeed almost creamy and buttery; at midpalate the flavor profile features intensely spirity tastes of almond paste and apple butter. Concludes oily, waxy, and fiery on the tongue.

2004 Rating: ★★★/Recommended

Whisky Galore Glen Garioch 1988 Eastern Highlands SMSW (Scotland); 46% abv, $74.

The attractive harvested wheat/autumnal gold color is gorgeous and pure. Right from the first whiff, there's a muscular backbone aroma of malted milk (or, for our UK subscribers, Horlicks); an aeration period of six minutes adds nuances of coconut, fudge, mead, and toffee. The palate entry is warm, embers-like and bittersweet; at midpalate flavors of light toffee, light honey, and nougat are highlighted. Concludes as nicely and handsomely as it started. A solid, medium-bodied, unpretentious malt.

2004 Rating: ★★★/Recommended

Whisky Galore Glenlossie 1993 Speyside SMSW (Scotland); 46% abv, $68.

Medium bright yellow/lemon juice color; excellent purity. The "green" aroma in the initial sniffings highlights scents of pine cones, cedar, green tomatoes, and green vegetables; six more minutes of air contact introduce a heady, concentrated, and spirity aroma that smacks more of flowers and garden vegetation, like moss and dirt. The palate entry is far more focused and directed than the aroma as sweet, lightly toasted tastes delight the taste buds; at midpalate the texture turns creamy and rich while the sweet, cake-like flavor gets slightly overshadowed by the alcohol. Ends sweetly, piney, and once again "green" and resiny. The palate entry nearly pushed this ordinary malt into three star territory.

2004 Rating: ★★/Not Recommended

Whisky Galore Highland Park 1990 Orkney Islands SMSW (Scotland); 46% abv, $66.

The pale green/yellow color is brilliant beneath the evaluation lamp; superb clarity. The first inhalations pick up incredibly woody/resiny notes that hint of tar, sulphur, and creosote; seven minutes of further air contact bring out prickly scents of apple mint, shoe polish, and uncooked beet. The palate entry is disagreeably woody/oaky/resiny; at midpalate the taste profile is metallic, minerally, and slate-like. Finishes awkwardly, antiseptic-like, and intensely piney. Somebody got duped into buying this bad barrel; don't buy it expecting to taste anything remotely comparable to Highland Park.

2004 Rating: ★/Not Recommended

Whisky Galore Isle of Arran 10 Year Old SMSW (Scotland); 46% abv, $53.
Color of brilliant 18-carat gold; unblemished purity. The opening inhalations are greeted by sweet aromas of oak and honey; the aroma after further aeration emits none-too-subtle notes of cake frosting, vanilla, marshmallow, and nectarine. The palate entry is sweet and honeyed; by the midpalate stage the taste is like glazed peach or glazed pear, very fruity and simple in its splendor. Uncomplicated, neither profound nor complex, but fat, juicy, and sweet to the point of absolute recommendation. A very good entry malt.
2007 Rating: ★★★/Recommended

Whisky Galore Macallan 1990 Speyside SMSW (Scotland); 46% abv, $64.
The pretty color is corn gold/yellow and pure. The first nosings detect perfumed scents of rose, gorse, and heather; six more minutes give this malt a chance to gain aromatic momentum as it emits sinewy aromas of candle wax, linseed oil, and green olives. The palate entry is a bit sharp, then it turns off-dry and moderately malty; at midpalate the spirit starts to sting the tongue a little too much as taut flavors of milk chocolate, malt, and butter cream candies impress the taste buds. Finishes moderately oily in texture and off-dry in flavor. So-so and very unMacallan-like.
2004 Rating: ★★/Not Recommended

Whisky Galore Rosebank 1990 Sherry Cask Lowlands SMSW (Scotland); 46% abv, $78.
The rich color is amber/light topaz (from the sherry cask) and pure. The reluctant aroma is muted and surprisingly closed off during the first couple of minutes of sniffing; seven more minutes and swirling in the glass help minimally to open up this inexpressive aroma. The palate entry is firm, dry, and cereally, if somewhat nondescript; at midpalate the flavor profile turns to old leather and roast meat; very uncharacteristic for Rosebank. The finish shows a bit of flash and pepper, then fades.
2004 Rating: ★★/Not Recommended

Blended, Single Grain & Blended Malt Whisky—Scotland

Ambassador Deluxe 25 Year Old Blended Scotch Whisky (Scotland); 43% abv, $100.
The color is topaz; the clarity is impeccable. The first two minutes of sniffing detects a latent richness that gives flashing glimpses of potential bouquet pleasure; allowing seven more minutes of aeration time unfortunately doesn't seem to budge the aroma very much; as it is, rather meek aromas of dark caramel, old oak, and sweet grain make a vain attempt at a grand bouquet, but fall short. The palate entry shows more assertiveness than the reluctant bouquet, especially in the form of grain whisky; in the midpalate this whisky appears to, at last, awaken as opulent, textured, and semi-dry tastes of oak, cereal grain, oatmeal, and lanolin take the helm. The aftertaste is long, semi-dry, more woody than grainy. This whisky's primary flaw is that it takes too long for it to show some character; a whisky this expensive owes more to the purchaser; go with the Royal 12.
2003 Rating: ★★/Not Recommended

Ambassador Deluxe Scotch Blended Scotch Whisky (Scotland); 40% abv, $13.
The clean, flax/straw yellow color is appropriate and pure. The opening nosings detect scents of sweet cereal grain, maple, and light toffee; later passes treat the olfactory sense to generous portions of honey and marshmallow; an uncomplicated, take-me-as-I-am bouquet. Tastes of maple syrup, corn syrup, and sweet grain highlight the palate entry and midpalate stages. Finishes as unpretentiously as it begins, sweet, honest, and amiable. A good entry-level, no-frills, blended Scotch 101 that is best utilized as a mixer.
2005 Rating: ★★★/Recommended

Ambassador Royal Deluxe 12 Year Old Blended Scotch Whisky (Scotland); 43% abv, $20.
The pale amber hue is pretty; perfect purity. The initial nosing passes detect concentrated, nutty, and semisweet aromas; exposure to air over another five minutes sees the aroma develop into a bouquet that emits exceedingly pleasant notes of butterscotch, almond butter, and dry cereal grains. In the mouth, Royal 12 is firm, intensely grainy and lightly caramel-like at palate entry; at midpalate the taste profile leans decidedly to the caramel flavor. Finishes well, with succulent, sweet notes of nut butter, sweet oak, and caramel.
2003 Rating: ★★★/Recommended

Bailie Nicol Jarvie Very Old Reserve Blended Scotch Whisky (Scotland); 40% abv, $n/a.
Not available in the US. The malt of Glen Moray forms the heart of this blend; straw yellow in color; impeccable purity. The round, slightly toasty nose offers oodles of sweet malty scents upfront in the first two minutes of sniffing; air contact serves to release further aromatic pleasures, most notably, fine aromas of sugar biscuits, light honey, heather, and a hint of

maple. The palate entry is bittersweet and almost cocoa-like; then at midpalate touches of oaky vanillin and wood resin harness the growing sweetness. Finishes elegantly and mildly sweet, and biscuity. A lovely, subtly complex blend that I'd love to see in North America.
2003 Rating: ★★★★/Highly Recommended

Bell's Extra Special 8 Year Old Blended Scotch Whisky (Scotland); 40% abv, $n/a.

Not available in the US. Very fetching honey/amber hue; impeccable purity. The initial nosing pass offers soft, grainy notes of heather and moss; this bouquet is dry but pleasingly malty and displays this feature ably in the second sniffing; in the penultimate whiff, delicate notes of hay/grass come through; the fourth and final aromatic blast, after nine minutes of aeration, shows a bit of peatiness/smokiness as well as some seed-like resin; a solid, good bouquet that's firm and sinewy. The taste begins moderately sweet at palate entry; the midpalate stage flavor is more caramel and candy-like, with not-so-subtle tastes of stone dry oak resin; the texture is oily and medium-bodied. It finishes medium long and politely flowery, ripe, and sweet in the throat. Comes close to being complex.
2000 Rating: ★★★/Recommended

Campbeltown Loch 21 Year Old Blended Whisky (Scotland); 46% abv, $70.

The blended whisky from Springbank Distillery that includes Longrow and Springbank malts in the blend. Sports a clean golden/honey color. Not an expressive aroma in the start but with ten minutes in the glass the bouquet develops, emitting savory, if reined-in smells of red fruit, grain, and milk chocolate. The palate entry is seamlessly smooth and moderately toffee- and marshmallow-like; at midpalate the tasting turns more buxom and full, giving off semisweet to bittersweet flavors of caramel corn, chocolate-covered raisins, and honey. Finishes well and warming in the throat, with a fruity turn in the last phase. A very different blended Scotch that shows its Campbeltown pedigree.
2005 Rating: ★★★/Recommended

Chivas Brothers Royal Salute 50 Year Old Blended Whisky (Scotland); 40% abv, $10,000.

Autumnal gold/honey amber color; absolutely pure and clean. The initial bouquet wastes no time in impressing the olfactory sense as full, biscuity aromas of light toffee and caramel bloom in the glass; later scents of honey, nutmeg, and vanilla blend beautifully with the foundational aromas of toffee and caramel; a stately, comely bouquet of the first rank. In the mouth tastes of honey, marshmallow, and cotton candy ignite the flavor profile; by the midpalate point fruity elements, especially banana and guava, get added to the taste list but ultimately it's the backnote of unsweetened coconut that seduces me the most. Finishes well, not in a flurry of flavor but more in an unfolding. This masterpiece was tasted alongside Royal Salute 21 Year Old ($150) (★★★★★) which is far more plentiful and for the money one of the greatest bargains in distilled spirits.
2003 Rating: ★★★★★/Highest Recommendation

Chivas Regal 12 Year Old Blended Scotch Whisky (Scotland); 40% abv, $30.

Bright old gold/maize color; flawless clarity. First whiffs pick up dry grainy notes, in particular, malted barley and wheat, as well as background scents of dried flowers and parchment; seven more minutes aeration bring about deeper fragrances, including light toffee, almond paste, and yellow fruit. Entry is oily textured, buttery, clean, and semisweet; the midpalate stage is where this whisky turns dazzling as layered flavors of brown butter, cooking oil, barley malt, and oatmeal cookie are underpinned by the sturdy, slightly smoky single malt foundation created by the Strathisla Distillery malt whisky. Concludes smoky, satiny, and ultra-sophisticated. I've heard this blended Scotch stupidly described as an "old-fashioned" style. Nothing could be further from the reality. Chivas 12 is contemporary and simply and utterly delicious. The official clinic for how a 12 year old blended Scotch should appear, smell, taste, and satisfy.

2007 Rating: ★★★★/Highly Recommended

Chivas Regal 18 Year Old Blended Scotch Whisky (Scotland); 40% abv, $55.

Brilliant topaz/honey color; unblemished purity. Smells immediately of toasted honeywheat bread, bacon fat, honey, and orange rind; further time in the glass allows deeper scents to be generated, including black pepper, cinnamon, vanilla bean, and pipe tobacco. Entry is silky smooth, semisweet, concentrated, and honeyed; the midpalate stage is a tour de force of masterful blending by Master Blender Colin Scott; the taste profile is all grainy sweet, yet spicy/tangy, fruity, nutty (hazelnut), and floral. The oak element really emerges in the aftertaste, closing the circle on this sensational blended Scotch. Along with its primary rival Johnnie Walker Gold 18 Year Old, the finest blended Scotch in the world. Defines the art of blending as well as any Scotch in the world.

2007 Rating ★★★★★/Highest Recommendation

Clan MacGregor Blended Scotch Whisky (Scotland); 40% abv, $13.

Pretty topaz/hay/autumnal gold color; impeccable purity. Opening aroma is intensely grainy and snack cracker-like, with background notes of flowers and pine; further air contact time brings out the grain spirit in clear, uncomplicated scents of pine, flax/textile, and beeswax. Entry is pleasantly sweet and caramel-like (thankfully, not oversweet); the midpalate stage offers added sweet flavors of honey, pipe tobacco, and tar. Ends engagingly sweet and grainy. Gleefully high bang-for-buck ratio. Displays unusual substance for this price range.

2007 Rating: ★★★/Recommended

Cluny Blended Scotch Whisky (Scotland); 40% abv, $11.

Deep straw/maize color; as sediment-free and clean as one could want. Hard boiled eggs, sulfur, and burnt matches greet the disappointed olfactory sense; additional exposure to air only makes the egg/match/sulfur odor worse; reminds me of the metallic/old coin reek of a deserted mine. Entry offers a weak-kneed hint of grainy sweetness that's almost sad; shows a bit more character at midpalate in the flavor forms of breakfast cereal with sugar, light caramel, and honey.

2007 Rating: ★★/Not Recommended

Compass Box "The Peat Monster" Vatted Malt Whisky (Scotland); 46% abv, $50.

The malt distilleries of Ardmore (Speyside) and Caol Ila (Islay) are key contributors to this virile vatted malt. The pale flax/straw color displays far more sediment than I'd like to see for a bottling that costs $50. The opening nose is, as advertised, intensely smoky but not in a medicinal/seaside manner as much as in a pipe tobacco/wood smoke way; as the aeration minutes pile up, the bouquet takes a left turn and becomes creamy, concentrated, citrusy/lemony, mash-like, and very, very malty, losing a bit of its peat-reek to the cereal odor. The palate entry takes the brunt of the peat-reek intensity as hefty, dense, and heavily smoked flavors of charred barley and kippers; at midpalate the taste profile turns sweet, bonfire-like, and strikingly like smoky black tea (lapsang souchong especially) and honey. Ends up sweet, moderately smoky, ash-like, and even caramel-like. While the moniker makes one believe that this vatted malt might be over-the-top, in reality the peat smoke is contained, even elegant, in particular, at midpalate; another nifty bit of blending from the intrepid John Glaser, captain of Compass Box.

2004 Rating: ★★★★/Highly Recommended

Compass Box Asyla Scotch Whisky (Scotland); 43% abv, $38.

Pale yellow/lemon juice color. The opening two nosing passes within the three minute window after the pour expose unusual fragrances of pear drop, banana, and kiwi; allowing it to rest in the glass for another five minutes, the third and fourth sniffings unearth a muted sweetness of grain mash, sunflower seeds, distant orange zest, and off-the-still spirit; hardly a profound whisky bouquet but moderately intriguing all the same. There's much more grip and animation in the mouth at palate entry than the reluctant aroma would lead one to believe; by the midpalate stage a strikingly rich and oily texture acts as the foundation for tastes of vanilla and intensely sweet grain. The aftertaste is fruity sweet, a bit fey, and mildly grainy. Love that explosion on the tongue at palate entry and the savory midpalate.

2002 Rating: ★★★/Recommended

Compass Box Eleuthera Scotch Whisky (Scotland); 46% abv, $50.

Pale straw hue; embarrassingly way too much unsightly floating sediment, as in clouds of small twigs/forest floor debris; no excuse for that. The initial nosing passes immediately detect firmly established traces of seaweed, light peat, mint, fennel, and dried herbs; aeration and a round or two of swirling unleash further assertive scents of licorice, brine, and medium-peated, dry malt; compared to the fruity, borderline-timid bouquet of the Asyla, this is serious aromatic business. The palate entry stage is focused, concentrated, and fiery; by midpalate the three-alarm blaze calms down to one-alarm and this reduction in spirity heat allows the flavor package of peat, dry malt, and licorice to shine through. The aftertaste is embers-warm, peaty, briny, and delicious. The emphasis is squarely on maritime influence; superb drinking for the pre-anointed whisky crowd.

2002 Rating: ★★★★/Highly Recommended

Compass Box Hedonism Scotch Whisky (Scotland); 43% abv, $75.

Pretty gold/yellow tint; sediment free, praise the lord of whisky hygiene. Right from the beginning nosings I could tell that this bouquet of almonds, hay, and lanolin was something special and serene; aeration adds succulent fragrances of sweet grain, mild oakiness, and caramel. In the mouth, the flavor at entry is round, supple, grainy sweet, and acceptably hot; by the midpalate stage additional tastes of truffles, fried banana, butter, and oaky vanillin contribute mightily to the overall flavor experience. It finishes oily/sweet, almost buttery and immensely satisfying. Great job here from start to finish.

2002 Rating: ★★★★/Highly Recommended

Compass Box Orangerie Orange Flavored Whisky Limited Edition Holiday Release (Scotland); 40% abv, $35.

The golden color is unblemished and pure. In the initial inhalations after the pour, the aroma displays a spicy, citrusy/zesty, and rind-like bearing that's simultaneously fetching and curious; later sniffings encounter hints of orange candy, fresh herbs, forest-like spice (coriander? clove? cinnamon?), and the oily presence of grain whisky; as time wears on the pungent bouquet gently fades. The palate entry is nicely acidic, bone dry, and clean due clearly to the orange peel shavings; at midpalate the grain component becomes more evident as the taste profile turns mildly sweeter, sap-like, and more whisky-like. The finish is off-dry, citrusy, sappy, yet creamy. I think that this is a splendid concept that illustrates how blended Scotch whisky can be so much more than, well, just great old blended Scotch whisky. Hats off to John Glaser, a genuine pioneer extraordinaire.

2005 Rating: ★★★★/Highly Recommended

Compass Box The Spice Tree Malt Scotch Whisky (Scotland); 46% abv, $65.

Attractive harvest gold color; excellent purity. The opening aroma is mildly nutty and spicy; more air contact assists this bouquet to round out as it then offers notes of spice fruit, toasted bread, and sweet cereal grains; a bouquet that needs time and patience. The palate entry is fuller than I expected, sweeter than I expected, and nuttier than I expected; the midpalate stage is rich, oaky, generously, but not overly sweet, grainy, and moderately spicy. Concludes well as the taste turns the volume down on the grain and goes more with fruit/nut/spice. Very nice addition to John Glaser's handsome roster of whiskies.

2006 Rating: ★★★/Recommended

Cutty Sark Scots Whisky Blended Scotch Whisky (Scotland); 40% abv, $23.

The pale marigold color is bright and impeccably clean. The intensely grainy aroma in the first whiffs reveals a biscuity, Graham cracker-like scent that's a tad salty; further aeration time stimulates the alcohol that burns the nasal cavity a bit, but not before the breakfast cereal, slightly metallic bouquet makes an impression. The palate entry is lithe, ethereal, grainy sweet, and uncomplicated; the midpalate stage offers more substance than the entry as the taste profile becomes caramel-like and nougaty/nutty. Ends up sweet and a dash peppery.

2007 Rating: ★★/Not Recommended

Dewar's Signature Blended Whisky Bottle 56 (Scotland); 43% abv, $200.

Really fetching medium amber/autumnal gold color; unblemished purity. The initial nosing pass detects very biscuity, almost doughy (sugar cookie?) scents that I like very much; seven more minutes in the glass afford the aroma time to gather itself; the later sniffings uncover elegant aromas of lightly toasted bread, almond paste, and sweet malt, with teasing traces of peat and cigar smoke. The palate entry is dry, grainy, and lightly smoked; the midpalate is sap-like, alluringly sweet, woodsy, and honeyed. The finish is medium-long, gentlemanly, and toasty. The gently sweet, honey-like core malt of this bottling hails from the fine Central Highlands distillery Aberfeldy; the precision balance of this blend is what makes it so delicious; terrific job of blending magic.

2003 Rating: ★★★★/Highly Recommended

Dewar's Special Reserve 12 Year Old Blended Scotch Whisky (Scotland); 43% abv, $30.

Pretty amber/yellow color; perfect clarity. The aroma after the pour is biscuity, warm, and welcoming; given a little time in the sampling glass, the aroma starts to expand in the second sniffing, adding outdoorsy scents of wet hay and grass, with a background note of light toffee; by the third whiff, following almost eight minutes of aeration time, the aroma becomes compellingly malty/grainy, leathery and medium-sweet; in the fourth and final nosing pass, I detect a slight, if insignificant, diminishment in power, but there's still more than ample structural charm especially in the aromatic form of light toffee/caramel and sweet malt. At the palate entry the lovely sweetness of the malt is on full display; the midpalate stage is firm, grainy sweet, and slightly oily (which I like). The aftertaste is medium-long, cookie/biscuity sweet, and exceedingly alluring. Very nice job here and certainly more than recommendable; this mature bottling runs rings the size of Saturn's around its anemic sibling, the flaccid and unforgivably hollow Dewar's White Label.

2000 Rating: ★★★★/Highly Recommended

Dewar's White Label Blended Scotch Whisky (Scotland); 43% abv, $18.

Stellar amber color and fine purity; so far, so good. The nose in the first two sniffings over four minutes remains remarkably meek and vacuous; the third whiff finds a little more stuffing in the forms of achingly light peat, smoke, and even pears; the fourth and last pass, following nearly ten minutes of air contact, locates only lonely and unevolved scents of wet earth and, well, dirt; a miserable example of blended Scotch aromatics. The palate entry offers vapid, stale tastes of sweet corn and sweet malt; the midpalate stage is no better as stingy flavors of dough and oats fly by the taste buds faster than a speeding bullet. No aftertaste to address really; even though this is the initial formal evaluation of DWL in the SJ, I've been sampling this blend for over a decade, hoping that it will improve; it hasn't; it woefully answers the question, Why single malts?

2000 Rating: ★/Not Recommended

Duggan's Finest Blended Scotch Whisky (Scotland); 40% abv, $18.

The honey/amber hue is very eye-catching; impeccable purity. The first nosings pick up toasty, grainy, and dry cereal aromas; additional air contact brings out a near fruity scent that mixes nicely with the deep grain foundational scent. The palate entry is stunning rich, caramel sweet, and even nutty; the midpalate stage displays a fat/oily, toasted grain and sweet oak profile that is utterly delicious. Finishes as full and toasty as it begins. On the sweet end of the scale, a very good blended Scotch value.

2006 Rating: ★★★/Recommended

Duncan Taylor Auld Blend 38 Year Old Blended Malt Whisky (Scotland); 40% abv, $181.

Pretty auburn/topaz color; flawless purity. The biscuity, intensely grainy opening aroma is sharp (a positive), clean, and totally focused; additional time in the glass brings out fiber-like scents of hemp/cord, wheat kernel, crackers, and dry breakfast cereal; not an ounce of fat on this lean and ultra-svelte whisky bouquet. The palate entry is fuller and sweeter than the bouquet indicated it would be and that's welcome; the midpalate stage highlights the oak resin and sap flavors that remind me of baked bread with herbs/seeds, like rosemary and caraway. Ends up dry and keenly resiny/sappy.

2006 Rating: ★★★★/Highly Recommended

Duncan Taylor Auld Reekie 12 Year Old Islay Malt Scotch Whisky (Scotland); 46% abv, $70.

Yellow straw color; flawless purity. The initial sniffs pick up medicinal/iodine scents that aren't overly aggressive, just green veggie-like and peppery (ground black pepper); additional exposure to air elevates the keen pepperiness and adds desert dry notes of old parchment and gravel/sand/dry earth. The palate entry dry, woody, and like unsalted butter; the midpalate phase offers tastes of saltwater taffy, egg cream, fino sherry, and almond butter. Ends on a prickly, peaty note that's just right for the smoky theme.

2006 Rating: ★★★★/Highly Recommended

Duncan Taylor Big Smoke 40 Islay Malt Scotch Whisky (Scotland); 46% abv, $40.

Pale gray tint; ideal clarity. The intense cigar smoke aroma jets from the sampling glass and tickles the olfactory sense; seven more minutes of air contact drops the volume on the peat reek as the scent becomes spicy, mildly smoky/peaty, green pepper-like, and semisweet. The palate entry is oaky and sweet in a pipe tobacco smoke manner; the midpalate stage is lean to medium-weight, sappy and toffee sweet, and delightfully peaty/soot-like. Finishes gracefully, medium smoky, and warming.

2006 Rating: ★★★★/Highly Recommended

Famous Grouse 10 Year Old Blended Malt Whisky (Scotland); 40% abv, $30.

This is a blend of several malt whiskies from several malt distilleries, including The Macallan and Highland Park. Owns a lovely honey-colored appearance and impeccable purity. The lively, green forest aroma highlights the vegetal/floral side of malt whisky; seven more minutes of air contact add only slight traces of unsalted butter and green tomatoes. The palate entry is more serious and integrated than the aroma as tightly wound, caramel and cotton candy flavors impress the taste buds; at midpalate a honey/vanilla/maple profile emerges and carries the t-buds on a lovely flavor journey that's moderately oily and semisweet. Concludes long, candied, honeyed and off-dry.

2004 Rating: ★★★/Recommended

Famous Grouse 12 Year Old Blended Malt Whisky (Scotland); 40% abv, $35.

Two of the high-profile malts that are included in this malt blend are The Macallan and Highland Park; not bad for starters. The honey/amber color is brilliant and flawless under the examination lamp. The start-up whiffs encounter toasty, warm, medium-sweet scents of toffee and raisin/cinnamon bread; later sniffings offer baked apple crisp, toasted cereal, roasted almonds, and nougat. The palate entry is full of generously sweet, raisiny, and orange rind-like tastes; the midpalate is like a winter holiday banquet filled with tastes of spice (nutmeg, especially), sweet cereal, Danish pastry, and figs. The aftertaste is moderately sweet, vanilla-like, and medium-long. Makes a strong case for the bright future of Blended Malt Whisky.

2005 Rating: ★★★★/Highly Recommended

Famous Grouse 18 Year Old Blended Malt Whisky (Scotland); 40% abv, $55.

The honey color is rich and bronze-like; ideal clarity. The first sniffings encounter rich, bosomy aromas of fudge, dark caramel, and cocoa; the sweetness turns a shade more woody/

oaky and vanilla-like in the later stages as aeration stimulates lots of perfumy richness and texture. The palate entry is seriously toffee-like, honeyed, and big in the mouth; at midpalate the flavor profile gets downright assertive with the butterscotch, marshmallow, and honey intensity. The aftertaste is very long, very baked, chewy, and marzipan sweet. The sweetness foot never lets up on the pedal and, for that reason, I prefer the more balanced and composed 12 Year Old as an overall whisky experience. This whisky is easily recommendable, but it is decidedly heavy on the baked sweetness.

2005 Rating: ★★★/Recommended

Famous Grouse Finest Blended Scotch Whisky (Scotland); 40% abv, $20.
Strong medium amber/honey color; perfect purity. Pleasantly toasty and buttery in the first nosings; aeration time stimulates lightly peated scents of butterscotch, light toffee, and marzipan. The palate entry features gently sweet grain and caramel tastes that delight the taste buds; the midpalate sensation is round, slightly prickly, buttery, and caramel sweet. I think that there must have been a flavor adjustment in this blend since I first reviewed it in 1997 because it definitely seems more compact and deeper, particularly in the flavor zone. More sophisticated.

2006 Rating: ★★★/Recommended

Gordon Graham's Black Bottle Aged 10 Years Blended Scotch Whisky (Scotland); 43% abv, $39.
Very autumnal, harvest gold/marigold color; superbly clean appearance. Man alive, I love this first burst of peaty, iodine, ashy aroma that could only be in large part that of the malts of Islay; seven more minutes of air contact bring out more subtle, yet equally complex scents of hemp/rope, road tar, burnt toast, and seaweed; a nosing romp that's wild and memorable. The palate entry is medium-weight, smoky sweet, and oaky; by the midpalate stage there's a strong taste of brown butter that wonderfully suits the aroma. One of the best deals in Scotch whisky at present.

2006 Rating: ★★★★/Highly Recommended

Grand MacNish Blended Scotch Whisky (Scotland); 40% abv, $12.
Pale straw/old gold color; superb clarity. Toasty notes of snack cracker and dried fruit pastry abound in the opening sniffs; with aeration, the dried fruit pastry turns figgy and date-like. Entry is very sweet and syrupy as the dried fruit element becomes near-cloying; the midpalate stage fares better since the über-sweetness settles down, allowing the grain and wood components to mitigate a portion of the sweetness. At least it didn't reek of sulfur as so many of its price-point peers do.

2007 Rating: ★★/Not Recommended

Inverhouse Green Plaid Very Rare Blended Scotch Whisky (Scotland); 40% abv, $12.
Attractive 14-carat gold/hay color; some sediment seen floating about. Opening whiffs detect pleasing, if meek notes of biscuits and pine; with further time in the glass, the biscuity quality fades and the pine/wood/resin element takes over, but that's about it on the aromatic front. Entry offers rudimentary, flabby, and needlessly sugary tastes of maple and sap; the midpalate stage sees the taste profile regroup a bit by punching down the sugar and elevating

the grain. Concludes far sweeter than any respectable or representative blended Scotch should be. Any time that I'm faced with over-sweetness, the question arises about what might be being concealed. Cheap garbage.
2007 Rating: ★/Not Recommended

J&B Rare Blended Scotch Whisky (Scotland); 40% abv, $22.

Sauternes gold color; excellent clarity. The delicate opening aroma shows bits of spice (black pepper), breakfast cereal graininess, and dried meat in finely measured, if meager amounts; additional air contact doesn't change a thing on the aroma front, except to diminish slightly what apparitional features were already there. Entry is mildly sweet and grainy and, consequently, moderately pleasing strictly in a fundamental manner; to this Scotch's detriment, the midpalate fails to build on the promising entry and at this juncture the story ends. Delicate is fine and sometimes really appreciated, but ghost-like is another thing and in an international brand, unacceptable. Brings new meaning to the words "bland" and "neutered".
2007 Rating: ★/Not Recommended

John Barr Finest Old Blended Scotch Whisky (Scotland); 40% abv, $20.

Pleasant bright golden hue; ideal clarity. The opening set of sniffings detect somewhat reluctant scents of apple and pear; another six minutes of aeration does little to stir more in the way of aromatics, leaving me feeling a bit cheated because, for me, the greatest delight of Scotch whisky is the bouquet; this is limp noodle country. The palate entry is very mild, banal, and grainy sweet; by midpalate there are additional, more comely flavors of almond paste, light oak, and clover honey. Ends up amiable, inoffensive drinkable, and entirely average and mundane. This whisky's feminine lightness makes it a suitably ordinary, if uninspiring, entry-level blended Scotch but nothing more.
2004 Rating: ★★/Not Recommended

John Barr Premium Reserve 17 Year Old Blended Scotch Whisky (Scotland); 40% abv, $40.

The bright harvest gold/tawny/honey tint is eye-catching and blemish-free. The opening nosing passes uncover aromas of toffee, biscuit batter, and buttered corn; seven minutes on, the bouquet expands only slightly, offering moderately succulent, if slightly pinched scents of green tomatoes, green vegetables, mint, and cedar. The palate entry makes me think of mint, baked apple pastry, and tea leaves; the midpalate stage is smooth, biscuity, woody, grainy sweet, and very toffee-like. Concludes sweet, satiny on the tongue, smoldering/warming, and resiny.
2004 Rating: ★★★/Recommended

John Begg Blue Cap Blended Scotch Whisky (Scotland); 40% abv, $15.

Color is pale gold/straw; flawlessly clean. Interesting aromas of cooking oil, rope/hemp, and fried egg greet the olfactory sense after the pour; with more time in the glass, the cooking oil turns more like frying bacon and the rope/hemp transforms into wood resin; owns an acceptable level of sulfur/burnt match/hard boiled egg smell. Entry is delicately sweet and fruity; the midpalate stage offers more succulence in the forms of sweet grain, sugared breakfast cereal, and heather honey. Finishes light, nimble, and clean.
2007 Rating: ★★★/Recommended

Johnnie Walker Black Label 12 Year Old Blended Scotch Whisky (Scotland); 40% abv, $32.

The bright amber/honey color shows some copper/orange core tones and immaculate purity. The opening aromas are firm, evolved, mature and biscuity; seven minutes in the copita allow this lovely blend to accentuate the subtle, sea breeze-like, saltine-like virtues even more. The palate entry is clean, keenly peaty and oily; by midpalate the island/salty/baked bread influence of Talisker is undeniable and welcome. Finishes elegantly, refined and with a last kiss of dark caramel. I've always admired this urbane 12 year old blend and still think that it's one hell of a bargain. It's a whisky that I ask for quite a bit when in bars, especially when on the road. Sometimes a comfortable, familiar blended whisky provides a needed boost.

2004 Rating: ★★★/Recommended

Johnnie Walker Blue 1805 Blended Scotch Whisky (Scotland); 45% abv, $25,000.

Available via auction only; no retail availability. The deep amber/medium brown color shows golden highlights and flawless clarity in the core. The first nosing passes detect fruity/estery notes of red cherry, red plum as well as a firm dash of sweet oak; additional time in the copita serves to dry out the fruitiness as the oaky astringency and bean-like vanilla characteristics advance to the aromatic forefront. The palate entry is off-dry to semisweet, parchment-like, nutty and mildly toasty; at midpalate there's a settling down of the components into a seamless flavor profile that's suddenly sherry- and honey-like to a moderate degree. Finishes semisweet, medium sappy/piney and compellingly warming. Sophisticated and understated.

2006 Rating: ★★★★/Highly Recommended

Johnnie Walker Blue Anniversary Blended Scotch Whisky (Scotland); 60.70% abv, $3,500.

Limited availability at selected retailers. The brilliant bronze color beams under the examination lamp; ideal purity. The expressive aroma springs from the glass in elegant but purposeful waves of malted barley, breakfast cereal, oatmeal, and brown rice; aeration unleashes succulent scents of prunes, black raisins, chocolate covered cherry, dark toffee, dark honey, and double cream; a dazzling blended whisky bouquet of the top rank. The palate entry is smoldering, warm but not hot, semisweet, caramel-like, and woody; at midpalate the taste profile expands to include charcoal, oloroso sherry, dark honey, marzipan, candied walnut, and even a touch of rancio. The aftertaste provides an inviting warmth in the throat and loads of oily/buttery/creamy flavors that appear to last forever. A smashing whisky.

2006 Rating: ★★★★★/Highest Recommendation

Johnnie Walker Blue Label Blended Scotch Whisky (Scotland); 40% abv, $180.

The color is autumnal gold with deep yellow/straw highlights; shows impeccable clarity. My first sniffings detect a restrained, slow-to-develop bouquet that's malty and a tad spicy, to be sure, but altogether distant in the first two minutes; additional aeration bridges the gap between whisky bouquet and drinker as more pronounced aromas of ripe red fruit, heather, mild peat, and light honey serve to entice the olfactory sense. The palate entry is sophisticated, multilayered, sweet, honeyed, and intensely cereal-like; the midpalate stage

features succulent tastes of Speyside- and Eastern Highland-like honey/sherry, oaky vanilla, and dark caramel. Finishes well and sweet. I'm fully aware that my lack of fervor for this expensive, cult-prone blend confuses more than a few SJ readers, many of whom like it far more than I do. I like it, but hardly love it. If I were in the business of bestowing half stars within the parameters of my scoring system, this is one whisky that I'd score as ★★★1/2. I'm not in that business, however. So, it remains ★★★.
2004 Rating: ★★★/Recommended

Johnnie Walker Gold Label "The Centenary Blend" 18 Year Old Blended Scotch Whisky (Scotland); 40% abv, $65.
The warm, welcome, pure appearance is of honey and golden harvested wheat; a feast for the eyes. The aroma off the mark offers nuances of buttered toast and almond paste; seven more minutes stimulate deeper, more exotic scents, including dried fruit (banana, pineapple), black pepper and white chocolate. The palate entry is viscous, malty, mashy, and sweet; at midpalate the taste profile adds flavors of sweet oak, marzipan, vanilla cake frosting, spice, and baked pears. Concludes as elegantly and gracefully as it begin. The Clynelish core is what makes this blend so special. I've loved this blended whisky ever since I first tasted it in the mid-1990s. It's one I keep going back to, which tells me a lot. For my money, JWGold is one of the three or four best blended Scotch whiskies in existence. Tasted right next to JWBlue, the Gold really shines, exposing the JWBlue for what it is: just a very nice, ridiculously overpriced whisky.
2004 Rating: ★★★★★/Highest Recommendation

Johnnie Walker Green Label 15 Year Old Blended Malt Whisky (Scotland); 43% abv, $55.
Seriously pretty honey/burnt umber color; absolute purity. The frontline aromas after the pour prove to be an interesting mix of paraffin, toasted cereal, and dried tobacco leaf; seven more minutes resting in the copita serve to stimulate additional, if peripheral, fragrances of summer grass, vegetable oil, light toffee and oak. The palate entry is sound, off-dry, and a touch toffee/nougat-like; at midpalate the oiliness/oakiness noted in the latter stages of nosing come to the fore as tastes of sweet butter, margarine, and black pepper vie for flavor dominance. Finishes a tad on the honeyed side and chewy. I wasn't sure, truth be told, about this whisky early on, but the latter stages of the bouquet and then the concentrated midpalate and finish totally won me over.
2004 Rating: ★★★★/Highly Recommended

Johnnie Walker Red Label Blended Scotch Whisky (Scotland); 40% abv, $22.
Sound amber/golden wheat color; excellent purity. There's lots of light caramel, off-dry, honey wheat toast, salty/sea breeze character in the opening whiffs; the bouquet deepens marginally with aeration as the aroma shifts from the light caramel/sea salt leaning to a more grain husk/malt/light peat orientation in the later sniffing stages. The palate entry is noticeably oily and sinewy; while at midpalate the flavor turns moderately peaty, dry, and smoked. Ends up clean, off-dry, mildly pleasing but unmemorable. JWRed has grown on me over the years, but not enough even now for me to put it in the frontline blended class of, say, William Grant's (★★★), Bell's (★★★) or White Horse (★★★★).
2004 Rating: ★★/Not Recommended

Jon, Mark and Robbo's The Rich Spicy One Blended Malt Whisky (Scotland); 40% abv, $30.

A combination of five malt whiskies from the Tamdhu, Highland Park, Glenrothes and Bunnahabhain distilleries. The medium amber/bronze color is bright and pure. I like the nose on this whisky right from the first crack of the bat as tangy aromas of pork rind, bacon fat, cream and almond paste make for luscious early-on sniffing; aeration adds a toastiness that's equal parts tar, tobacco and oak. The palate entry is chewy, rich, honey sweet, and just a tad spicy in a peppery manner; at midpalate the flavor profile shows off an oily/buttery side that greatly complements the baked, honeyed sweetness. The aftertaste is long, oaky sweet, and even vanilla-like.

2006 Rating: ★★★★/Highly Recommended

Jon, Mark and Robbo's The Smokey Peaty One Blended Malt Whisky (Scotland); 40% abv, $30.

Eight malts from six malt distilleries go into the make-up of this blended malt: Caol Ila, Laphroaig, Bunnahabhain,Highland Park, Ledaig, and Bowmore. The autumnal gold/ medium amber hue is gleaming and clear. The salty, seaside perfume found in the initial whiffs is inviting, clean and moderately smoky; aeration time of another seven minutes adds ashes, tobacco leaf, medium peat, and kippers. The palate entry offers polite and easily manageable tastes of mild iodine, pipe smoke, and sweet oak; at midpalate the flavor profile features ample amounts of peatiness and smoke but not as much as I had expected from the label name; that's okay because this blended malt was obviously created with balance in mind. Finishes salty, smoky, and elegantly sweet and pruny. I'd hike up the abv to at least 43% and possibly 45% to give the peat/smoke element a sturdier platform on which to unfold.

2006 Rating: ★★★/Recommended

Jon, Mark and Robbo's The Smooth Sweeter One Malt Irish & Scotch Whisky (Ireland & Scotland); 40% abv, $30.

A malted whisky blend of Irish malt from the Cooley Distillery and Islay's Bunnahabhain Distillery. The greenish golden color is of straw; very good purity. In the opening sniffs there's an unspectacular perfume of drying grain with background notes of snack cracker and citrus; further exposure to air fails to unlock what I suspect are deeper aromatic levels. The palate entry is engagingly sweet in a cereal/snack cracker/bread-like kind of way; at midpalate the flavor profile expands considerably as toasted flavors of wood, light toffee, light honey, and mint go a long way in pleasing the taste buds. Finishes light and mildly sweet and grainy. Fulfills its moniker.

2006 Rating: ★★★/Recommended

King William IV VOP Blended Scotch Whisky (Scotland); 40% abv, $14.

Yellow jonquil/chardonnay gold color; excellent purity. First whiffs pick up very strong sulfur/burnt match/hard boiled egg notes that are too aggressive; another seven minutes of aeration only serve to heighten the rotten egg odor; no Scotch whisky, blended or not, should smell like this. Entry is meek, more dry than sweet, and only mildly grainy; the midpalate stage is its best phase as the eggy/sulfur quality dies down enough to allow the grain to emerge, but the damage has been done. Take a pass.

2007 Rating: ★/Not Recommended

McIvor Blended Scotch Whisky (Scotland); 40% abv, $13.

Pretty amber/golden hay/18-carat gold color; ideal purity. Opening nosings pick up engagingly pleasant, if tempered scents of biscuits/cookies, sweetened breakfast cereal, and honey; further aeration stimulates added aromas, especially baking spices (cinnamon, vanilla), pastry dough, and beeswax. Entry is toffee sweet, but neither cloying nor syrupy, and chewy on the tongue; the midpalate stage turns a drier corner, offering bittersweet tastes of candied nuts, milk chocolate, and egg cream. Finishes sweet, but with a spirity tang of lead pencil/metal coin that balances the grainy sweetness. Could sell for $18-$20 and not blink an eye.

2007 Rating: ★★★/ Recommended

Michel Couvreur Aged 12 years Unfiltered Vatted Malt Whisky (Scotland); 43% abv, $55.

The pretty, rich amber/honey/bronze color is spoiled by unsightly clouds of sediment, but I keep in mind that the label does say that this whisky is not filtered. The opening nose is rich, fat, and biscuity; time in the glass reveals mineral-like touches of lead pencil, stone, and slate that overtake the plumpness, offering a dry to off-dry aromatic profile that I like. The palate entry is peaty, smoky, and oily; by midpalate there's a thick-slice layer of bacon fat that underscores the smoke and oil to near-perfection. Ends up sweet, sap-like, and intensely oily. A stud of a vatted malt.

2004 Rating: ★★★★/Highly Recommended

Mitchell's 12 Year Old 60% Malt, 40% Grain Blended Scotch Whisky (Scotland); 43% abv, $60.

The pale yellow/white wine color is bright and unblemished. The opening inhalations find workshop aromas of sawdust, sawn wood, pine sap, and lanolin; further aeration brings out more of a kernel-like personality that features hints of wheat cracker, fiber, burning rope, and bonfire. While I wasn't crazy about the bouquet, the palate entry is inviting, warm, gently sweet, grainy, and a touch oaky; by the midpalate phase the lean-to-medium-weight taste profile focuses exclusively on the sweet grain and wood resin flavors. Finishes angular, lean, and compact.

2006 Rating: ★★★/Recommended

Old Smuggler Blended Scotch Whisky (Scotland); 40% abv, $22.

Straw/pale yellow hue; excellent clarity. The initial whiffs are greeted by soft, biscuity/sugar cookie scents; aeration serves this whisky well as additional, deeper aromas of cereal, honey, yeast, and light caramel disarm the olfactory sense; neither complex nor profound, but a solidly good and agreeable blended whisky bouquet. Fat and creamy at palate entry, then toffee/caramel sweet tasting at midpalate. Finishes up mildly spicy and oaky, then round and supple on the tongue. Sturdy, reliable, and still a terrific bargain that first became fashionable during Prohibition times in the US.

2005 Rating: ★★★/Recommended

Passport Blended Scotch Whisky (Scotland); 40% abv, $17.

The appearance is very pretty in its brilliant golden/marigold color and bright clarity. The first nosings detect only timid and underdeveloped scents of grain and new leather; aeration

merely stimulates equally fey, non-descript aromas that just lazily merge into a cheap whisky bouquet. Entry offers flabby, desultory flavors that start from nothing and go nowhere; the midpalate could be just about any type of cheap, cheesy grain spirit. Should be renamed "Passport to Nowhere". Any knucklehead that says, "Yeah, but it's good for mixing" should be incarcerated for the sole purpose of separating such ignorance from the rest of society.
2007 Rating: ★/Not Recommended

Pig's Nose 5 Year Old Blended Scotch Whisky (Scotland); 40% abv, $30.

Lovely medium amber/honey color; perfect purity. In the opening whiffs, there are pleasantly grainy/cereal-like aromas that are off-dry and nutty; another six minutes in the copita allows the bouquet to expand only minimally. The palate entry is moderately sweet, biscuity, pastry-like, and deeply grainy; at the midpalate phase the taste profile displays a bit of heat that lies underneath the breakfast cereal surface flavor. Finishes well in a dry mode that's both nutty and grainily wheat-like.
2006 Rating: ★★★/Recommended

Sheep Dip Blended Malt Scotch Whisky (Scotland); 40% abv, $35.

The attractive topaz/deep amber color shines beneath the evaluation lamp and boasts flawless clarity. The initial sniffings after the pour uncover a prickly wave of spirit on top of dry hints of oak and almond paste; seven more minutes of air contact don't accomplish much except for a deepening of the wood resin quality. The palate entry is harsh, awkward, and uninviting; by the midpalate stage I've thrown in the towel as the flavor profile turns flabby, unfocused, off-dry and disappointingly narrow in range. Stumbles across the finish line, all gawky, raw, and uninteresting. This new and improved version is correct on only one count, it's new.
2006 Rating: ★/Not Recommended

Teacher's Highland Cream Blended Scotch Whisky (Scotland); 43% abv, $20.

Pleasant amber harvest gold hue; excellent clarity. The nose is a bit closed off in the opening pass, then with a couple of minutes of air contact subtle notes of bittersweet chocolate, dark toffee, and bacon fat appear and swiftly impress the olfactory sense; the third sniffing adds nuances of heather and marzipan; following a solid nine minutes of aeration, the fourth and last whiff displays a compelling harmony that's uncommon in most blends. The palate entry is marked by sweet, almost wine- and sherry-like tastes (could it be the Glendronach malt influence?); the midpalate juncture offers poised, united, and chewy flavors of malt, light peat, light oak, pepper, and toffee. The aftertaste is medium long, creamy, and sherried enough to be likened to oloroso sherry; sinewy, peaty, and elegant. One of the best values in all of whisky.
2000 Rating: ★★★★/Highly Recommended

The Classic Cask 35 Year Old Blended Scotch Whisky (Scotland); 43% abv, $275.

The deep bronze/topaz color is truly gorgeous and absolutely clean and pure. This aroma leaves the starting gate in full gallop as roasted/toasty aromas of almonds, marzipan, and dark toffee nearly overwhelm the olfactory sense; in the second pass, the nose is laced with buxom notes of butterscotch and dark caramel; the take-no-prisoners approach continues in the third sniffing, following six minutes of aeration, as the roasted quality deepens into a candied almond, or perhaps walnut, aroma that reminds me of Christmas holiday baking; in the fourth and final whiff the toffee sweet/nougat-like aroma of candied nuts so clearly dominates that other elemental scents, such as malt/grain and/or wood, are simply left standing at the station; potent, intensely sweet, and nougaty to the max. The palate entry is incredibly savory and focused on a dark caramel sweetness; the midpalate stage sees the nougat quality return in force as well as a sweet cereal/malty taste that serves to bolster the honey-like, thick textured legacy of this old blend. The aftertaste is long, luxuriously sweet, even decadent. A brawling, big-shouldered, perhaps to some people, overly sweet and syrupy whisky, but frankly I favorably responded to the bold-faced, over-the-top approach; not a whisky that I'd drink everyday but every now and then when I yearn for a sappy sweet, malty blockbuster this baby will easily fulfill that wish.

2000 Rating: ★★★/Recommended

VAT 69 Gold Blended Scotch Whisky (Scotland); 40% abv, $13.

Color is 14-carat gold/marigold; superb clarity. Intensely eggy and sulfury in the initial aromatic go-round; the obligatory additional seven minutes of aeration accentuates the burnt match quality, leaving no room whatsoever for grain, spirit, or wood. Entry displays at least a glimpse of grainy sweetness and even wood vanillin; the midpalate stage improves the taste profile by introducing a moderately pleasing united front of spirit, wood, and grain that resembles a decent blended Scotch presence. Finishes grainy, resiny, woody, and mildly sweet. Tries at the end, I'll give it that, but ultimately is short of the recommendation mark.

2007 Rating: ★★/Not Recommended

Vintage Hallmark of St. James 25 Year Old Special Blended Whisky (Scotland); 43% abv, $65.

Pale amber hue; some brownish chunks of sediment (cork?) spotted. The initial two nosing passes pick up very biscuity/cookie batter and buttery notes; more exposure to air finds the biscuit quality turning toasty/roasted and quite charming; I also notice a distant dash of black pepper in the final whiff. The palate entry is dry and slightly nutty; then at midpalate an oily butteriness takes charge of the taste which relegates other flavors, especially nuts, semisweet cereal, and salt water taffy to supporting roles. The aftertaste is medium-long, off-dry to sweet, cereal-like, and woody. Funny how at least for me the wood aspect didn't arrive until the finish; a very respectable dram.

2002 Rating: ★★★/Recommended

Vintage Hallmark of St. James 25 Year Old Vatted Malt Whisky (Scotland); 46% abv, $65.

Truly pretty deep amber/topaz hue; lots (too much, actually) of brown/gray sediment seen floating about. The first two minutes of sniffing unearths several layers of early-on aromas, including firm spirit, toasty/peaty malt, oatmeal, honey, and lanolin; the assertive arom-a-thon continues and deepens as the whisky aerates, displaying off-dry scents of black pepper, cayenne, tobacco smoke, bacon fat, chili oil, rose petals, black leaf tea, and almond paste; there's so much happening here aromatically that it's almost impossible to write down all the impressions and nuances. The palate entry is firm, moderately peaty/smoky, and off-

dry; at the midpalate juncture assertive flavors of walnuts, dark caramel, honey, sweet malt, and tobacco make for an extraordinary taste phase. The finish is oily, honey sweet, slightly smoky, and lightly peaty. A broad-shouldered, take-no-prisoners vatted malt that's a treat from start to finish but is not recommended for Scotch whisky neophytes.
2002 Rating: ★★★★/Highly Recommended

White Horse Blended Scotch Whisky (Scotland); 40% abv, $17.

Bright topaz/amber color; flawless purity. I find quietly focused and firm scents of seaweed, green vegetable, straw, and grain kernel in the opening sniffs; after aeration, the bouquet turns seriously complex as added aromas of toasted almond, dried fruit, pastry, and oak join in the fun. Entry bursts with single malt character as the early tastes include light toffee, brown butter, almonds, and pine; the dry midpalate juncture explodes with sea air, subtle peatiness, butter cream, cooking oil, and bacon fat. Concludes firm, oily, concentrated, and peaty/smoky. All the world's dictionaries should place a photo of a White Horse bottle or label next to the words, "Blended Scotch Whisky". In this price range, it leads the pack by fifteen lengths at the wire.
2007 Rating: ★★★★/Highly Recommended

Wild Scotsman 15 Year Old Vatted Malt Whisky (Scotland); 46% abv, $90.

The wheat field golden color is pretty and perfectly pure. The first nosing offers intensely grainy, almost bean-like aromas that are stone dry, if brittle; further aeration serves to turn the aroma into a biscuity, but dry bouquet that's grainy, minerally, metallic and minimally floral down the stretch; while mildly pleasant in a basic kind of way, there's no depth to this bouquet. The palate entry plays on the biscuit/snack cracker quality in the mouth; at midpalate the taste profile goes metallic and very mineral-like. Finishes a touch hot, sap-like, and grainy. Drinkable but neither multilayered nor compelling.
2006 Rating: ★★/Not Recommended

William Grant's The Family Reserve Blended Scotch Whisky (Scotland); 40% abv, $19.

Pleasing old gold coin color; unblemished clarity. The nose is a bit muted in the first go-round after the pour; aeration stimulates scents of heather honey, oak, and dry breakfast cereal. This whisky shines in the mouth, so forget nosing it; entry is supple, floral, intensely grainy, and off-dry; the midpalate stage displays harmonious flavor components including black pepper, honey, light caramel, and wood resin. Ends in a gentlemanly fashion, with no single component dominating. While I think it would benefit from tinkering especially in the aromatics and the aftertaste, it's better than average for the price range.
2007 Rating: ★★★/Recommended

WHISKEY—USA

Straight Bourbon Whiskey

While Kentucky is the traditional home and epicenter of the bourbon industry, in truth, bourbon can be legally produced in any state in the Union. Virginia remains a significant distilling center for bourbon in America. Bourbon as a straight whiskey (a whiskey made from at least 51% of one grain) is an international icon and is acknowledged by experts to be America's hallmark distillate. The American whiskey industry is a tightly regulated business, whose rules must be adhered to. In order for a whiskey to become properly labeled as a straight bourbon whiskey, it must meet a set of standards. Those regulations include:

1) *Straight bourbon's grain mash must be made from at least 51% corn.*
2) *Straight bourbon must be matured in new, charred barrels for a minimum of two years.*
3) *Straight bourbon cannot be distilled at higher than 80% alcohol by volume, or 160-proof.*
4) *Straight bourbon whiskey can be reduced in alcoholic strength only with distilled water.*
5) *Straight bourbon whiskey must be bottled at least 40% alcohol by volume, or 80-proof.*
6) *As a straight whiskey, it is unlawful to add any color or flavor enhancements.*

Bourbon distillation usually involves an initial distillation in a column still and a second pass in a pot still-like kettle called a "doubler" or a "thumper" (because of the pounding noises these stills make during distillation). American distillers must by law employ unused barrels in which to age their whiskeys. Barrels must also be charred on the inside. Charring levels of one-to-four are the norm, with level four being the deepest char. The deeper char levels (three and four) impact the new spirit more than lighter char levels (one and two), imparting smells and tastes of caramel, maple or vanilla. Bourbon warehouses are known as "rickhouses" and populate north-central Kentucky by the scores. The aging period in Kentucky is generally much shorter than in cooler climates, like those of Ireland and Scotland. Spirits mature much faster in warm, humid conditions than in cool, damp climates and so can be bottled sooner.

Bourbon, at present, is one of the two or three most exciting spirits categories in the world. Up until only a decade ago, the best American whiskeys were kept for blending. That changed over the last ten years as now almost every distiller is issuing special bottlings of rare whiskeys at a record pace. Enjoy the ride while it lasts.

Also, **KSBW** = Kentucky straight bourbon whiskey.

"**Bottled-in-Bond**" means a whiskey that's been bottled at 100-proof, or 50% alcohol by volume under strict governmental restrictions.

Labeling weirdness. I always identify a spirit by what's printed on the label to make purchasing them easier. All reviews are listed alphabetically. Sometimes, however, the same producer will use slightly different names. This occurs in bourbon. For example, the brand W.L. Weller is sometimes identified as William Larue Weller. They are the same distiller; just a variation on the label.

Tennessee Sour Mash Whiskey is very close in production methods to straight bourbon except for a filtration process, called the Lincoln County process, in which the whiskey is dripped through maple charcoal chunks in huge vats. This happens after distillation and prior to the spirit being placed in new, charred barrels for a minimum of two years. Ten feet deep, the charcoal is so densely packed that it takes each drip many hours to make it to the bottom. The idea is to leach out any impurities not stripped away by distillation. The result is a smoky type of whiskey that is reminiscent of cigarette ashes or chimney soot. Because of the inclusion of the Lincoln County process step, law does not allow Tennessee sour mash whiskeys, to be identified as "bourbon". This is no hardship for the Tennessee distillers who prefer to be known as makers of fine Tennessee sour mash whiskey. After enjoying a rich history of distilling, only two distilleries still exist in Tennessee, Jack Daniel's and George Dickel.

Aside from being the first important type of American whiskey (George Washington was an avid distiller), **Rye Whiskey** is an admired variety among distillers. Once corn-based straight bourbon became "America's whiskey" in the mid-19th century rye whiskey faded in the deluge of available bourbons. After the repeal of Prohibition in 1933, a handful of rye whiskey brands reappeared, but again the category flagged against the unstoppable tide of bourbon. By the 1970s and 1980s rye whiskey was scarcely seen. Then, following the turn of the Third Millennium, more rye whiskeys started becoming available as word spread about this variety's pedigree, historical importance and status within the American distilling industry.

At present, there are more straight rye whiskeys in the marketplace that at any time since the early 20th century. Rye whiskey is a robust, spicy, and substantial variety that is an authentic treat for seasoned whiskey lovers.

North American Blended Whiskey

Following World War II, a genuine phenomenon occurred in the North American whiskey category, spurred by the CEO of Canada-based drinks giant Joseph E. Seagram, Sam Bronfman: inexpensive and ubiquitous blended American and blended Canadian whiskeys. Two Seagram brands ruled supreme from the late 1940s through to the mid-1970s, Seagram's 7 Crown from the US and Seagram's VO from Canada. These easy-drinking whiskeys are blends of 20% straight whiskey and 80% neutral grain spirits. Both are wood-aged. While they lack the depth of character and elegance of straight bourbon, Tennessee sour mash whiskey, and straight rye whiskey, they nonetheless serve a noble purpose as excellent mixers.

80 Strong KSBW (USA); 40% abv, $21.

The wheat field/amber color is pretty; excellent purity. The aroma in the first whiffs after the pour is mute and requires additional air contact before rousing; later sniffs detect distant notes of corn muffin and husk; basically, forget the bouquet. The palate entry is pleasantly sweet and uncomplicated; the midpalate stage features warming spirit, sweet corn, breakfast cereal, and paraffin. Ends as a one-note wonder, sweet and waxy, that's about it. The lack of depth works against this Bourbon 101. Frankly, I'd spend significantly less for good old Jim Beam White Label, which in terms of quality and complexity reaches far past this one.
2006 Rating: ★★/Not Recommended

Baker's 7 Year Old Small Batch Batch No. B-90-001 KSBW (USA); 53.5% abv, $35.

The pretty, brilliant bronze hue is blemish-free. The opening nosing passes detect concentrated, nut (litchi especially) and deep-roasted grain scents; following another seven minutes of aeration, Baker's aroma turns baked, buttery, oaky, and almost brandy-like. The palate entry is integrated, sweet, and slightly peppery; at midpalate there's a sweet oak/vanilla rush that backs off prior to the finish, leaving behind taste traces of spirity heat, vanilla extract, cake frosting, butter cream, and resin. Ends up semisweet, sublimely oaky and spirity. The most sophisticated whiskey of Beam's very popular Small Batch Bourbon Collection, Baker's continues to be a whiskey marvel to me, even after the tens of times that I've tasted it.
2005 Rating: ★★★★/Highly Recommended

Basil Hayden's 8 Year Old KSBW (USA); 40% abv, $32.

Medium amber color; superb clarity. The first nosing passes detect uninteresting, limp scents of wet cardboard and parchment; further exposure to air adds only meek, ripe and sweet grain and timid yellow fruit aromas. The palate entry is moderately spicy and nicely grainy, but then at midpalate the taste profile goes south, ending up seed-like, mildly grainy, and on the whole drinkable but average. I have always considered this whiskey to be the weak link in the Jim Beam Small Batch Collection chain and another formal evaluation thirteen years after the first one merely acts to confirm that viewpoint. Hardly in the same league as Baker's, Knob Creek, and Booker's. Sampled next to Booker's only accentuates this whiskey's shortcomings.
2005 Rating: ★★/Not Recommended

Bernheim Original Kentucky Straight Wheat Whiskey (USA); 45% abv, $40.

The amber/autumnal gold hue is pretty and flawlessly clean. The first nosing finds delicate, and floral wheat grain cracker-like scents; seven more minutes of aeration unleash deeper, mildly sweet aromas of sap, fresh vanilla bean, Graham crackers, and light honey. Graceful yet firmly structured on the tongue, Bernheim offers a fine balance of wood, moderately sweet grain, and acidity at palate entry; by midpalate the 90-proof alcohol base rises to the surface as it warms the throat and serves as the launching pad for off-dry flavors of charred oak, light toffee, and sap. Finishes elegantly, warm, and chiseled. If you're looking for a fat bruiser of a whiskey, this one will not provide enough plumpness to satisfy your wishes. But for those whiskey lovers who appreciate balance, elegance, and the pleasure of a true sipping whiskey, good for it.
2005 Rating: ★★★★/Highly Recommended

Black Maple Hill 11 Year Old Cask 300 KSBW (USA); 47.5% abv, $45.

No whiskeys made anywhere on Earth are as pretty as bourbon when it's right; well, cowboys and cowgirls, consider this right; bronze/tawny overall color with a copper core and perfect purity; a feast for the eyes. To my surprise, the initial sniffings come up a bit empty-handed; another seven minutes and a bit of swirling rouse subtle, nuanced aromas of nougat, flax, crushed almond, and linseed oil. The palate entry is astonishingly delicate and polite, sweet and pillowy; at midpalate the flavor does a slow burn on the tongue as ripe, fruity tastes of baked apple, road tar, grapefruit, and buttered popcorn make it all worth it. Ends zestily, banana-like, and prickly on the back of the tongue.

2004 Rating: ★★★★/Highly Recommended

Black Maple Hill 14 Year Old Cask 114 Single Barrel Bourbon (USA); 46.6% abv, $56.

The stunningly eye-catching topaz/bronze color is outstanding; does exhibit some dark sediment. The initial nosing pass shows an invitingly oily, stone dry, and slightly burnt aroma that I find exquisite and comely; with time in the glass, the aroma expands to include scents of black pepper, jalapeño chilies, and green vegetables in the middle stages; by the final sniffing, nine minutes into the nosing exam, the aroma becomes a full-fledged bourbon bouquet that's ribboned with sweet corn, charred oak, grainy spice, and wood resin. The palate entry is off-dry-to-bittersweet, resiny and full; the midpalate is corny sweet, caramel-like, and biscuity. The aftertaste is long, a bit citrusy tart, woody, and delightful. A luscious example of bourbon's drier, bittersweet side; a definite keeper.

2001 Rating: ★★★★/Highly Recommended

Black Maple Hill 14 Year Old Cask 147 KSBW (USA); 47.5% abv, $60.

The stunning appearance is bright copper/bronze, with orange core highlights; superb purity. The aroma comes out swinging in the first passes as the high-flying, Rubenesque corn perfume wafts up from the copita in huge, lapping waves; after another six minutes, the aroma settles down, offering pleasingly sweet fragrances of caramel corn, cotton candy, old oak, baked banana, honey, and brown sugar; there's enough aromatic activity going on here for about four different bourbons. The palate entry is warm, succulent, honey sweet, and viscous; by midpalate the sweetness gets toned down as the flavor profile adds a zesty note of spice. Concludes a touch resiny/woody, but lip-smackingly corny and sweet. A dandy.

2004 Rating: ★★★★/Highly Recommended

Black Maple Hill 16 Year Old Cask 121 Single Barrel KSBW (USA); 47.35% abv, $74.

The deep topaz/bronze hue is gorgeous, but flecked with minor amounts of dark sediment. The opening sniffing is concentrated, very peppery, and even mildly fruity; in the second and third passes, after three and five minutes of aeration respectively, the bouquet turns serenely intense and nutty, even slightly buttery; in the fourth and last whiff, a remarkably toasty/dark caramel perfume competes with the buttery element, making for a smashing finale; love it. The palate entry is considerably sweeter than the aroma as tastes of pine, resin, and oily grain greet the taste buds; in the midpalate stage the resiny/woody flavor leads the taste pack by several lengths. The finish is lean, off-dry, intensely resiny/woody, and moderately sweet. I think that this whiskey, after a brilliant beginning, turns a bit too resiny in the midpalate and aftertaste to deserve a fourth rating star; that said, this is nonetheless a sturdy, better than average bourbon whose significant charms abound in the bouquet.

2001 Rating: ★★★/Recommended

Black Maple Hill 16 Year Old Cask 127 Single Barrel KSBW (USA); 47.5% abv, $78.

Another coppery/henna/bay/russet feast for the eye; ideal clarity. This nose is more subdued early on than its younger sibling, the 14 Year Old, and shows bittersweet traces of brown sugar, molasses, and bubble gum; an additional six minutes of swirling and aeration turn an okay aroma into a beguiling, sophisticated bouquet that emits succulent scents of creamed corn, honey, cocoa bean, and dark toffee; a mesmerizing bouquet of the first rank. The palate entry is lush, oily, creamy, and more semisweet than flat-out sweet; by midpalate the flavor profile features lovely, even stately tastes of nougat, honey, brown sugar, marzipan, and old sweet oak; finishes round, chewy, creamy and succulent.

2004 Rating: ★★★★/Highly Recommended

Black Maple Hill 18 Year Old Cask R66 Kentucky Straight Rye Whiskey (USA); 47.5% abv, $86.

The stunning, new copper penny color owns a reddish/henna core color; impeccable purity. This opening bouquet offers lots of early-on complexity that ranges from burnt marshmallow to cigar box to whipping cream; seven more minutes of air contact release additional scents of cotton candy, candied almond, spicy grain, confectioner's sugar, and maple; unbelievably layered and intricate. The palate entry is long, prickly, fruity, and semisweet; at midpalate the oily, viscous taste profile surges forward, highlighting flavors of baked pear, apple crumble, toffee, and butter cream. Finishes as stately as it began. One of the two or three finest ryes I've evaluated; a true superstar American whiskey; douse it with water and I might have to hurt you.

2004 Rating: ★★★★★/Highest Recommendation

Black Maple Hill 20 Year Old Cask 08 Single Barrel KSBW (USA); 48.3% abv, $107.

Beautiful new copper penny/tawny color; insignificant dark sediment noted. The nose after the pour is prickly, potent, grainy, but dry and peppery; in the second and third sniffings, a spice component that accents the oak comes on the scene and overshadows the grain; the fourth and last pass highlights the scents of black pepper, moss, and seared oak; a complex, multilayered bouquet that shows some diminishment after eight to nine minutes of aeration. The palate entry is succulent, ripe, and honey sweet (I never would have guessed from the bouquet); the midpalate is corny sweet and also tastes of ripe apple, honey, brown sugar, and maple. The finish is very extended, oaky sweet, and intensely honeyed. The complexity detected in the middle stages of the aroma come to full blossom in the midpalate and finish; a decadent, potent bourbon that's in the prime of its life.

2001 Rating: ★★★★/Highly Recommended

Black Maple Hill 21 Year Old Cask 07 KSBW (USA); 47.5% abv, $108.

The topaz/copper/deep honey color totally enchants the eye; unblemished purity. The perfumed early aroma highlights touches of caramel, oak barrel char, and palm oil; further aeration yields a whopper of a mature, buttery bourbon bouquet that's been around the block but is still plenty fit and svelte; there's no fat whatsoever on this bouquet. The palate entry shows incredible firmness, oil/cream and grain/wood presence; at midpalate the taste shifts into overdrive as sweet, sap-like flavors of caramel corn, maple sugar, and roasted grain converge to make a sensational taste experience. Finishes sweet, intense, and caramel-like. Superb and thrilling from beginning to end.

2004 Rating: ★★★★★/Highest Recommendation

Blanton's Barrel 125 Warehouse H Rick 02 Single Barrel KSBW (USA); 46.5% abv, $50.
The pretty bronze/honey color shows some brownish/brackish sediment but it's inconsequential. The first nosing passes encounter scents of corn husk, buttered popcorn, and chicken fat; after another seven minutes of exposure to air the bouquet stays the course set out in the opening two minutes, except for the subtle addition of toasty oak. The palate entry is corn syrup sweet and textured; at midpalate succulent and delicious flavors of nougat, honey, and baked banana. Finishes with the flurry of oaky/corny flavors that are focused and concentrated, if slightly astringent. An overall very good bourbon but the lack of aromatic development and a slight slip at the tail end of the aftertaste relegate it to solid three star status; the entry and midpalate phases strongly deliver the goods.
2004 Rating: ★★★/Recommended

Blanton's Barrel 150 Warehouse H Rick 09 Single Barrel KSBW (USA); 46.5% abv, $50.
Golden maize/amber/topaz color; flawless clarity. Emits a pleasing aroma of cracked corn, creamed corn, and oatmeal; aeration adds meager scents of baking spice, new felt, and resiny oak. Entry is assertive, spicy, and oaky/sappy sweet; the midpalate offers tastes of textile/flax, new oak, spirit attack, and sap. Finishes resiny, full-weighted, chewy, and concentrated on the sap flavor.
2007 Rating: ★★★/Recommended

Booker's 7 Year 11 Month Batch No. B96-L-23 KSBW (USA); 63.40% abv, $50.
Solid copper/burnt orange color; flawless clarity. In the initial whiffs, there are subtle notes of cocoa, cigar tobacco, and paraffin; an additional seven minutes of airing out bring to the surface aromas of caramel corn, cotton candy, light toffee, oak, and tapioca; a multilayered bouquet of the first rank. The palate entry is abuzz with lip-smacking tastes of spice, buttered corn, bacon fat, and cream; the midpalate displays brawny traces of butterscotch, nougat, sap, maple, and vanilla. Finishes warm, spirity, and biscuity. Water it down by half to reduce the alcohol. A fitting legacy of a Big Man.
2005 Rating: ★★★★★/Highest Recommendation

Buffalo Trace KSBW (USA); 45% abv, $20.
I couldn't imagine a more representative bourbon color than this brilliant copper/orange glow; blemish-free clarity. The opening aroma displays elements of spice, brown butter, and old leather gloves; after seven minutes aeration, the fat/butter component comes to dominate along with a buttered popcorn perfume that's absolutely lovely. The palate entry is corny sweet and almost fruity; at midpalate the taste profile includes sweet oak, cinnamon, nutmeg, honey, tar, and beeswax. Ends up heady, spirity, and feisty. Continues to be without any doubt whatsoever one of the greatest values in the worldwide whiskey category. A supremely well-made and compelling whiskey whose virtues are apparent from start to finish.
2004 Rating: ★★★★/Highly Recommended

Buffalo Trace Distillery Experimental Collection French Oak Aged 10 Year Old Single Barrel KSBW (USA); 45% abv, $46/375 ml.
The bronze color owns a golden/burnished orange core and flawless purity. The biscuity aroma comes flying from the glass in rich waves of nougat, toffee, and bread dough; another

seven minutes of exposure to air stimulate deeper foundational fragrances, including white pepper, roasted chestnut, nut butter, and palm oil. The palate entry is tight, oily, buttery, satiny, and peppery; in the midpalate stage the taste profile explodes into levels of marzipan, chocolate covered almond, bacon fat/rancio, brown butter, and, well, this could go on forever. Finishes in a stately manner, with upfront tastes of honey and oak and underlying flavors of corn bread and rye. An American whiskey masterpiece.

2006 Rating: ★★★★★/Highest Recommendation

Buffalo Trace Distillery Experimental Collection Fire Pot Barrel 10 Year Old Single Barrel KSBW (USA); 45% abv, $46/375 ml.

Looks lighter, more golden/amber than its bronze/topaz siblings. Perfect purity. In the initial sniffs, there's a mineral-like, lead pencil scent that's neither woody nor grainy; seven more minutes bring out a resiny wood facet that's just slightly sweet, tobacco-like, and tangy. The palate entry is sweeter than I thought it would be and nearly plump; in the midpalate stage the flavors integrate beautifully, creating warm, chewy tastes of caramel, nougat, sugared walnuts, and honey. Concludes on a sweet, oaky note that at the very end returns to the granite/lead pencil place where it began in the first inhalation. A dandy whiskey that would have earned a fifth rating star had the bouquet been more expressive. That said, wow.

2006 Rating: ★★★★/Highly Recommended

Buffalo Trace Distillery Experimental Collection Twice Barreled 12 Year Old Single Barrel KSBW (USA); 45% abv, $46/375 ml.

The brilliant color is topaz/bronze; unblemished clarity. The opening whiffs detect spice cake-like scents that are pointed, appealing, and dry; extra time in the copita brings out perfumed fragrances of cherry wood, maple, and rye bread. The palate entry is lean and resiny, almost sap-like in its regal bearing; by the midpalate juncture the taste turns significantly sweeter and oakier as the profile shifts from lean/dry to medium-full/honeyed and layered. Ends on a distinctly maple-like note that's savory and succulent. While not as broad or generous in scope as the lush French Oak Single Barrel, this whiskey displays a chiseled physique that, in its own right, is dazzling, sinewy, and attractive.

2006 Rating: ★★★★/Highly Recommended

Buffalo Trace Distillery Experimental Collection Chardonnay Aged After 10 Years KSBW (USA); 45% abv, $47/375 ml.

Matured for ten years/six months in a new oak barrel then re-barreled in a used French oak chardonnay barrel for another eight years. Copper-colored, with burnished orange/rusty core highlights; perfect clarity. The initial whiffs pick up focused aromas of cookie batter, orange rind, and bacon fat; following the standard seven minute aeration period, the bouquet turns bakery/pastry sweet, nougaty, and dried fruit-like, especially dates. The palate entry concentrates on the oak more than the grain aspect, giving off very oily and resiny tastes; by the midpalate the taste profile turns ashy/sooty/smoky and very resiny/flax-like. Concludes a tad too oaky for me, even if the experience is genuinely worthwhile and recommendable.

2007 Rating: ★★★/Recommended

Buffalo Trace Distillery Experimental Collection Chardonnay Aged After 6 Years KSBW (USA); 45% abv, $47/375 ml.

Matured for six years/three months in a new oak barrel then re-barreled in a used French oak chardonnay barrel for an additional eight years. The color is bronze; flawless purity. The opening nosing passes detect very spirity aromas that are flecked with notes of almond paste and walnut; the bouquet settles down alcohol-wise after another seven minutes in the glass, emitting succulent and elegant aromas of chocolate covered orange peel and honey. The palate entry is oily, textured, honey sweet, and grapy; by the midpalate point the grapiness/oiliness takes charge, effectively eliminating the honey momentarily and introducing a deep woodiness. Finishes as gracefully as it performs throughout and with the reinstatement of the honey.

2007 Rating: ★★★★/Highly Recommended

Bulleit Bourbon Frontier Whiskey KSBW (USA); 45% abv, $25.

The alluring autumnal gold/deep amber hue is blemished somewhat by infinitesimal black sediment. The first burst of smells includes rye toast, snack crackers, and brown butter; further inhalations following seven more minutes of air contact keeps the aromatic direction on the drier end of the scale as the intense graininess takes command of the bouquet. The palate entry is remarkably savory, corny sweet, and nearly honey-like; at the midpalate stage the core flavor of sweet corn mash stays the course while no less attractive tastes of buttered popcorn, brown sugar, and nougat expand. Finishes with a spurt of fire and lots of long, corny/grainy tastes. I like this neglected, under-appreciated bourbon as much today as I did seven years ago in its initial SJ evaluation. Should be part of every serious whiskey-lovers' collection.

2006 Rating: ★★★★/Highly Recommended

Charbay Double-Barrel Release One Whiskey (USA); 64.7% abv, $325.

100% two-row European malted barley, grown in British Columbia; only 840 bottles of Release One are available; cask strength, unfiltered. The bright bronze color is attractive and pure. The initial nosing passes detect leather, leafy vegetation and damp earth; I keep waiting for aeration to deepen or expand this bouquet but even after nearly ten minutes all I pick up is leather and damp vegetation. The palate entry is eerily beer-like and hoppy (hops were added, according to the PR materials); even diluted, the midpalate grills the taste buds with searing spirit. Hot finish. A whiskey distiller like Booker Noe can excel with cask-strength, but not here.

2002 Rating: ★/Not Recommended

Distillers' Masterpiece 20 Year Old Port Cask Finished KSBW (USA); 43% abv, $300.

Extremely pretty bronze/topaz hue. The initial aromas are intensely nutty and floral, with a trace of background winy sweetness; with exposure to air the aroma expands to include mild, rounded scents of mint, oak char, and port; a dazzler. As tantalizing as the bouquet is, this bourbon's true brilliance lies in the taste phase from palate entry to aftertaste; at entry the taste is off-dry and enchantingly nutty, even nougaty; at midpalate the flavor profile soars into the stratosphere as succulent, but ultimately dry and resiny tastes of charred oak, tobacco leaf, minerals, and apple butter keep the taste buds totally occupied and satisfied.

The finish is long, ripe, grapy, and grainy sweet. As superlative and ground-breaking for bourbon as its cognac-finished sibling of two years ago; outstanding.
2001 Rating: ★★★★★/Highest Recommendation

Eagle Rare 10 Year Old Single Barrel KSBW (USA); 45% abv, $25.

The bright honey/topaz color shows sparkling bronze core features; impeccable purity. The early aromas include gentle grain, toasted honeywheat bread, and tobacco leaf; with aeration the aroma quickly transforms into a pedal-to-the-metal bourbon bouquet as evolved scents of ripe banana and charcoal tweak the olfactory sense in the middle stage whiffs; fragrances of lanolin, almond butter, melon, and oil accent the toastiness beautifully; it's a somewhat restrained, or better, understated aroma but I sense lots of power lying just beneath the surface. My, my, my, what have we here; in the mouth this oily, toasty beauty seduces the taste buds at palate entry with dry flavors of cereal grain and mild oak resin; the midpalate tastes explode on the tongue in unabashedly sweet and oily flavors of black raisins, grapefruit, charred oak, and candied almonds. The finish is long, corny sweet, moderately fiery, and lasciviously oily. Easily one of the most tactile yet assertive and expressive bourbons I've tasted in the last two years; fasten your seat belts.
2001 Rating: ★★★★/Highly Recommended

Eagle Rare 17 Year Old KSBW (USA); 45% abv, $55.

The bronze/burnished orange color is very attractive; unblemished clarity. In the opening two minutes of sniffing, the aroma is a bit closed down, giving off only a distant scent of saddle leather; following another six minutes of aeration, the aroma gradually unfolds, emitting delicately sweet scents of buttered popcorn, light toffee, maple, and lanolin. The palate entry features a sap-like flavor that counterbalances the sweet corn base taste; the midpalate is the best stage as the melded flavor components come together into a relatively seamless taste profile that's simultaneously sweet, oaky, maple-like, and grainy. Ends up semisweet, intensely oaky/resiny, pineapple-like, and elegant.
2006 Rating: ★★★★/Highly Recommended

Early Times Kentucky Whisky (USA) 40% abv, $18.

Author's Note: Many people think that Early Times is a bourbon, but technically it is not. This is because it is aged for at least 3 years in barrels that had formerly been used for maturing whiskey. By law, bourbon has to be matured in new, unused barrels. Makes a great bar bet piece of trivia. The orange/honey appearance is delightful; very minor, inconsequential sediment noted. The initial stages of the aroma seem a bit muted; more time in the copita allows for a soft, rose-petal and almond aroma to develop; the aroma suffers from timidity. The palate entry is meek, gum-like and a touch caramel-like; at midpalate there's more semisweet flavor expression as toasted marshmallow mingles with caramel candy. Ends up resiny and cheesy and just a few pennies short of being recommended. An uncomplicated whiskey of modest proportions whose agreeable flavor phase brought it close to being recommended.
2004 Rating: ★★/Not Recommended

Elijah Craig 18 Year Old Single Barrel KSBW (USA); 45% abv, $36.

The rust/orange/bronze appearance is dazzling and lovely; impeccable purity. The opening passes pick up evolved notes of baked pears, peach, and caramel corn; six more

minutes of air contact release even more succulent fragrances of hazelnut, newly tanned leather, baked pineapple, and nougat. The palate entry is long, luxuriously textured, nutty, and semisweet; by the midpalate juncture the taste profile adds deep flavors of vanilla extract, oak, honey, and sugar maple. Ends with finesse and presence. Sensational and one of the benchmark single barrel bourbons in the marketplace.
2007 Rating: ★★★★★/Highest Recommendation

Elmer T. Lee Single Barrel Sour Mash KSBW (USA); 45% abv, $25.

The gorgeous, bronze/copper hue is marred by way too much grayish to transparent sediment floating about; a $25 bourbon should not look like this. The opening nosing pass is lusciously buttery, toasty, rich, and decadent; the grain, especially sweet corn, emerges in the second sniffing while in the third pass the oak influence dominates in the form of buttery resin and walnut; after close to nine minutes of exposure to air, the butteriness harmonizes well with a spirity thrust in the fourth and last whiff; a big league bourbon bouquet that's aggressive, peppery, intensely spirity, mildly prickly and most of all buttery; impossible not to like. The palate entry is generously sweet and buttery; at midpalate the flavor of buttered sweet corn is unmistakable; this couldn't be anything other than straight bourbon. The aftertaste is long, languid, and pleasantly sweet. This style of broad-shouldered, big-hearted, sweet corn bourbon is a crowd pleaser, no doubt.
2001 Rating: ★★★/Recommended

Evan Williams 100 Proof Bottled-in-Bond KSBW (USA); 50% abv, $14.

The bay/auburn color beautifully captures the light; traces of inconsequential sediment spotted beneath the examination lamp. The opening aroma is assertive and extremely grainy/corn-like, with background touches of paraffin and walnut butter; further aeration time of six minutes stimulates scents that include green peppercorn, cotton candy, and dried fruit. The palate entry is crisp, properly prickly, and lean; by the midpalate point the flavor profile highlights the toasty charring of the barrel as vivid tastes of maple, vanilla bean, and dark caramel dominate this stage. Ends fiery, grainy, and lean. Not my favorite version of Evan Williams, in that, it's surprisingly rudimentary.
2004 Rating: ★★/Not Recommended

Evan Williams 1783 10 Year Old KSBW (USA); 43% abv, $11.

Pure, brilliant under the examination lamp, and the color of new honey. The opening nosing passes detect subtle, almost floral/fruity scents of banana, matted rose petals, field grasses, and marzipan; seven additional minutes of aeration release deeper, more fundamental aromas, especially oaky vanillin, brown butter, deep-fried pork rind, and buttered sweet corn; an amazing bouquet that's more stately and understated at this mature stage than assertive. The palate entry is semisweet, oaky, and honeyed; at midpalate there's a surge in toffee and light caramel tastes as well as a gentle bite of spirit, but the vanilla bean, honey, and wood flavors hang in there, merging with the toffee/caramel element. Finishes lean, off-dry, and regal. A, to my shock, neglected American beauty courtesy of the remarkable father-son distilling team at Heaven Hill.
2004 Rating: ★★★★★/Highest Recommendation

Evan Williams Vintage 1991 Single Barrel KSBW (USA); 43.4% abv, $22.

Tasted alongside the 1990 version; the brilliant, eye-catching topaz/bronze hue is gorgeous and slightly deeper than the 1990; superb purity. The nose displays chewy scents of dark caramel, sweet oak, char, and a bit of cigar ash at the start; with aeration the oaky tang gives way to a grainy/corny sweetness that's round and gripping yet the final aromatic impression is one of leanness, moderate sweetness, and dexterity; this is no sappy, overly oaky bourbon bouquet. In the mouth, the sleek demeanor continues but in flavor form as the palate entry offers agile tastes of light woodiness, sweet corn, yellow fruit, and a faint dash of spice; the midpalate is sweet, nearly buttery, and delectably soothing. The aftertaste is spicy, acidic, and leaner than the 1990 but not so lean as to be austere or skeletal. While the 1991 doesn't possess the overall fruity/woody/spicy charisma of the 1990, it nevertheless elegantly displays its own notable charm and style; still an unbeatable value and a worthy link in the Evan Williams Vintage chain.

2001 Rating: ★★★★/Highly Recommended

Evan Williams Vintage 1992 Single Barrel KSBW (USA); 43.3% abv, $24.

One of the great success stories of super-premium bourbon is the Evan Williams Vintage series, which began with the 1986. The tawny/amber hue is one of the most eye-catching in bourbon. My olfactory sense is overwhelmed by the rich, fruity, sweet corn aromas in the initial pass; with time in the glass the bouquet turns less assertive, adding seductive notes of spice (nutmeg?), toasty oak, marzipan, and marshmallow; by the final nut-like whiff I'm a true believer. The palate entry is resiny sweet, concentrated, buttery, and fat and that's just for openers; the midpalate displays firm, mildly oily, and moderately smoked tastes of barrel char, sweet corn, barley spice, and bacon fat; a meal in a glass. It finishes with some welcome heat/bite, loads of fat and oaky resin. The 1990 was one of the best super-premium bourbons ever; this supple thoroughbred ranks right up there with it; can this price be real?

2001 Rating: ★★★★★/Highest Recommendation

Evan Williams Vintage 1993 Barrel 001 Single Barrel KSBW (USA); 43.3% abv, $25.

Basically a nine year old bourbon. The medium amber color is bright and shows just slight bits of sediment; no worries about it from this viewpoint. The opening sniffs after the pour display the trademark gentle, fruit-like sweetness/graininess of Evan Williams; time in the glass affords the chance for the bouquet to deepen and grow complex as layers of aroma include milk chocolate, marshmallow, sugar cookies, and freshly mown hay. The palate entry is concentrated, sweet, mildly oaky/resiny, and medium-bodied; by midpalate there's an embers-glow warmth on the tongue, followed by sturdy, woody tastes of oaky vanillin and almond butter. The finish shows a minor touch of honey. The remarkable legend of EW Vintage Single Barrel continues with this luscious addition; one of the five or six whiskeys that I genuinely look forward to every time it's released as a new bottling; Craig and Parker Beam are wizards in the selection of these utterly sensational bourbons; continues to be one of the finest whiskey values in the world.

2003 Rating: ★★★★★/Highest Recommendation

Evan Williams Vintage 1994 Single Barrel KSBW (USA); 43.3% abv, $25.

The bright amber/bronze hue captures the light and doesn't let go; excellent purity. The mildly peppery and spicy aroma in the initial whiffs herald the coming of something special;

the impetus caused by further aeration releases unbridled, multilayered scents of bacon fat, oak resin, buttered corn, and toasted honeywheat bread; there's a lot happening here, all of it stirring and compelling. The palate entry is firm, assertive, moderately oily, and grainy sweet; by midpalate the flavor profile settles down, offering elegant, bittersweet, but harmonious flavors of tobacco leaf, light caramel, nougat, pine needle, and sautéed almonds. Concludes sweet, moderately oily in the throat, and luscious. To me, rivals the wonderful 1990 Vintage in power and elegance.

2004 Rating: ★★★★★/Highest Recommendation

Evans Williams Vintage 1995 Single Barrel KSBW (USA); 45% abv, $25.

The topaz hue shows impeccable purity. The deeply layered, delightfully vivacious aroma after the pour is loaded with savory scents, including pine nuts, acorn, firm spirit core, and oak; additional aeration time bestows a softness and flowery elegance that has my personal star-o-meter humming; the bouquet is never sweet or corny, but always ultra-sophisticated, delicate, and as lean and muscular as a boxer in his prime. Flavorwise, the palate entry is nuanced, slightly sweet, and even a touch spicy while the midpalate stage is tight, fat-free, yet supple, grainy, and direct. Concludes moderately sweet and delicious. I seriously like this sinewy, crisp as parchment bourbon and rank it with the best of the Vintage series.

2005 Rating: ★★★★★/Highest Recommendation

Evan Williams Vintage 1996 Single Barrel KSBW (USA); 43.3% abv, $25.

The topaz-like color is flawed by way too much gray-colored floating debris. The nose is curiously limp, almost timid in the first go-round; aeration helps out to some degree as more vibrant and defined scents of caramel corn and wheat toast finally emerge. The palate entry soars higher than the disappointing aroma as the taste buds are met by lusciously deep and full-weighted flavors of corn syrup, breakfast cereal, and oak; the midpalate is properly oily, buttery, corny, and honey sweet. Finishes in a flurry of sap-like tastes and a round, honeyed texture. Far from my favorite EW Vintage Single Barrel since the appearance and the nosing stages were unsatisfactory in light of past offerings, but still nice. The weakest in the series since the 1986 edition.

2006 Rating: ★★★/Recommended

Evan Williams Vintage 1997 Single Barrel KSBW (USA); 43% abv, $25.

I can't convey my disappointment with the sediment-filled appearance of this whiskey; large, gray chunks of who knows what are seen floating about beneath the unflinching light of the examination lamp. The first sniffs detect pleasing aromas of pineapple, oak, and saddle leather; seven more minutes of aeration bring about added scents of toasted marshmallow, honeywheat toast, and cherry. The palate entry is firm, spirity, properly oily, and leathery; at the midpalate juncture the biscuity/honeyed flavor profile begins to remind me of the glory days of this series, especially the 1992 and 1994 editions. Finishes oily, slightly sherried, honey-like, pear-like, luscious, and nutty. After stumbling a bit with the Vintage 1996, it appears that this annual whiskey offering may be back on the rails. A cleaner appearance would have given it a fifth rating star.

2007 Rating: ★★★★/Highly Recommended

Four Roses KSBW (USA); 40% abv, $18.

The light-catching color is a lightish honey/harvest gold; ideal purity. The opening nosing pass exposes a lush, vibrant, cornbread-like scent that's compelling and firm; the middle stage passes see the aroma expand, adding subtle notes of spice and marshmallow; the last sniffing, after more than eight minutes of time in the glass, features a spicy sweetness which is nothing short of beguiling. In the mouth, this fine bourbon begins crisp but sweet at the entry, then turns a touch leathery and caramelly at midpalate. The aftertaste is medium long, grainy/corny sweet, and exceedingly pleasant in the throat. An unabashedly sweet whiskey whose supple demeanor speaks to me of moderately toasted oak barrels and sweet sweet corn; stylistic, savory.

2001 Rating: ★★★/Recommended

Four Roses Barrel Strength Limited Edition Single Barrel KSBW (USA); 52.1% abv, $75.

Bright bronze/ochre color; superb clarity. Opening the aroma stage is the seductive and potent smell of spirit, not in a harsh or aggressive manner, but with presence; notes of cooking spice, bread, yeast, and breakfast cereal make for intriguing sniffing after added aeration time. This whiskey explodes on the palate at entry, giving off wave upon wave of deeply satisfying, corny, caramel, honey flavor; the midpalate is marshmallow sweet, with supplementary notes of burnt orange rind, paraffin/beeswax, and palm oil. An angular, austere style of bourbon that benefits and blossoms (becomes far rounder) considerably with the addition of room temperature mineral water.

2007 Rating: ★★★★/Highly Recommended

Four Roses Single Barrel Warehouse CS Barrel 48-SP KSBW (USA); 50% abv, $43.

New copper penny bright; impeccable purity. What strikes me about the opening aroma is the balance between the alcohol, the oak, and the grain, which all seem to be pulling the wagon in harmony; it isn't until aeration unleashes the spirit that I detect the feistiness of the 100-proof alcohol, but fortunately that doesn't overshadow the leathery, mildly sweet breakfast cereal, honeyed graininess. The splendor of the bouquet is confirmed in the entry as warm, smoldering flavors of light caramel, nougat/almond paste, and oaky vanillin impress the daylights out of my 10,000 taste buds; the midpalate stage features toasted cereal, toasted rye bread, popcorn, and fresh honey right out of the hive. Aftertaste is of chocolate covered walnuts and that ever-present honey. A masterpiece of seamless integration, bourbon profundity, and grace. If ever someone says to you that Americans can't make great whiskey, introduce them to this golden nugget.

2007 Rating: ★★★★★/Highest Recommendation

Four Roses Small Batch KSBW (USA); 45% abv, $36.

Deep golden/honey/bronze hue; excellent clarity. Succulent notes of dark chocolate and toffee are countered by intriguing, if unexpected scents of hemp/fiber/rope; baked, gently spicy and fruity elements emerge in the latter sniffing stages almost like spiced apple cobbler or rhubarb pie; a no-nonsense bouquet of authentic depth and quality. Entry tastes are toffee-like, biscuity, vanilla bean-like, and whistle clean; the taste profile intensity builds substantially from entry to midpalate as the flavors turn resiny/rancio-like, citrusy, and caramel corn concentrated. Finish-wise, a seductive maple-like flavor closes the circle on the taste stages in a way that's both stirring and classy. A clinic on what small batch straight bourbon can be. Already an esteemed member in my bourbon pantheon.

2007 Rating: ★★★★★/Highest Recommendation

George Dickel Barrel Select Tennessee Sour Mash Whiskey (USA); 43% abv, $43.

Brilliant, impeccably clean topaz/honey color. The initial whiffs pick up subtle notes of hazelnut, wax paper, and lime; another seven minutes of air contact release attractive scents of peanut butter, citrus peel, unsalted butter, and a delicate spiciness that's hidden way in the aromatic depths. The palate entry showcases the peanut quality found in the nose, but adds a delicate touch of charred oak; at midpalate the taste profile becomes more bacon fat-like and smoky, with nuances of palm oil, nut paste, and cream. Nicely done all the way.

2006 Rating: ★★★★/Highly Recommended

George Dickel No. 8 Tennessee Sour Mash Whiskey (USA); 40% abv, $15.

The harvest gold/wheat field hue is bright and clean. The first sniffs detect very little in the way of corn-based aroma except for a mild waxiness; further aeration brings out notable scents of lanolin, textile/fiber, and fireplace soot. The palate entry displays toasty flavors that wrap around core tastes of dried fruit and nuts; the midpalate stage reveals the waxy quality first detected in the early-stage inhalation. On the lean side of the ledger, but shows very good grainy mouthfeel.

2006 Rating: ★★★/Recommended

George Dickel Superior No. 12 Tennessee Sour Mash Whiskey (USA); 45% abv, $20.

Strong bronze/medium amber color; excellent clarity. In the first couple of minutes after the pour the aroma seems plump and almost grassy, then following six more minutes of exposure to air much more potent notes of tobacco ash, paraffin, sweet oak, and grain kernel enchant the olfactory sense. The palate entry offers pleasant and welcome spirity warmth on the tongue, in addition to well-mannered tastes of cigarette tobacco, light honey, and cereal grain; what changes the most at midpalate is the texture that turns creamy, but not fat, as the sooty taste charms the taste buds. Ends up buttery, delightfully spirity, and clean. My favorite Tennessee whiskey of all time, thus far.

2006 Rating: ★★★★/Highly Recommended

George T. Stagg 15 Year Old Uncut Unfiltered KSBW (USA); 70.7% abv, $45.

The new copper penny color seduces the eye; perfect purity, which I find surprising given that this bourbon is not filtered. The first few whiffs pick up potent, rippling scents of alcohol and rancio; given the luxury of another seven minutes in the glass, the aroma turns into an authentic bouquet as layers of fragrance enchant, but don't assault the olfactory sense; those ultra-dry scents include walnut butter, linseed oil, charred oak, mocha and minerals (lead? limestone?). Without dilution, the palate entry is hot, caramel-like and sweet; the midpalate point offers intense flavors of raisins and other dried fruit, oak, marzipan and that true touch of nobility, rancio. It finishes boldly, richly and with enough heat to keep your attention. With a spring water reduction, the whiskey improves, in that, all the wonderful qualities noted prior to the addition of water are more noticeable and not found hiding behind the tsunami of raging alcohol; a grand idea and experiment by the adventurous team at Buffalo

Trace; but I hasten to point out that while I truly admire this whiskey and others like it (Booker's Bourbon), it's most balanced when the alcohol level hovers between 43%—50% so add a generous splash of mineral or spring water to the venerable Mr. Stagg; why not bring it out at, say, 50% or 100 proof? Nevertheless, bravo to Mark Brown and intrepid distilling team.
2003 Rating: ★★★★/Highly Recommended

George T. Stagg 2006 Antique Collection KSBW (USA); 70.3% abv, $55.

This whiskey's topaz/bronze color dazzles the eye; perfect clarity. The first nosings unearth big-hearted, intense spirit notes that are surprisingly dry and cardboard/parchment-like; additional aeration reveals a biscuity/grainy smell that's dry and kernel-like; this is a bouquet that's not willing to give away too much. I add a half-ounce of room temperature mineral water before tasting. The palate entry is colossal in weight, honey sweet, moderately oaky, and maple sugar-like; by the midpalate stage the flavor profile adds pork rind, bacon fat, nougat, walnut paste, and chocolate covered cherry. Finishes grandly in huge taste waves of sweet oak, sweet corn, and dark fudge.
2007 Rating: ★★★★/Highly Recommended

George T. Stagg Limited Edition Uncut & Unfiltered Barrel Proof KSBW (USA); 71.35% abv, $45.

Due to the bracing cask strength, I first sampled GTStagg neat, then with spring water and I strongly urge most drinkers to add a good dose of water before taking this monster on. One of the prettiest, most fetching whiskeys you'll ever see; the new copper penny/russet color completely disarms the eye; perfect purity; neat, the aroma offers an entire array of surprisingly tame but firm fragrances, including bittersweet chocolate, egg cream, brown sugar, marshmallow, nougat, and dried red fruit; diluted with water, the aroma turns up the volume on the nougat/nut butter, as well as the dried red fruit, which now turns grapy/raisiny; a dynamic, richly perfumed, and imposing but not insurmountable bouquet that's majestic and bountiful; sampled only with dilution. The palate entry is deep, silky, oily, and intensely flavorful (the water brings out a luscious honey-like element); by midpalate the muscular and sherry/dark toffee taste profile begins to remind me of very old Grande Champagne cognac, in that, there's a lingering background trace of dusty/earthy/oily rancio. Concludes LARGE, but refined and engagingly sweet, with just a merest hint of spirity heat.
2004 Rating: ★★★★★/Highest Recommendation

George T. Stagg Limited Edition Uncut/Unfiltered Barrel Proof KSBW (USA); 70.6% abv, $55.

Released in October of 2005. The deep bronze/topaz hue is fabulous; quite a bit of sediment seen, but then it is unfiltered. The opening aromas are potent (what'd you expect?), leathery, and intensely woody; following another seven minutes of exposure to air, the aroma turns atypically sweet, as in brown sugar/molasses rather than sweet corn or maple, but I seriously like it; the bouquet becomes a candy store. Undiluted, the palate entry is startlingly sweet, yet elegant, oaky, and balanced; before midpalate I add water and the flavor profile jumps off the charts in bittersweet flavors of cocoa bean, vanilla extract, and corn husk.

Concludes fiery (even with the mineral water dilution), candy sweet, intensely oaky, and minerally/lead-like. Stagg is a genuine over-the-top experience that should be tried.
2006 Rating: ★★★★/Highly Recommended

Hancock's President's Reserve Single Barrel KSBW (USA); 44.45% abv, $50.
Maize/saffron color; unquestionable purity. Compelling aromas of toasted honeywheat bread, cinnamon, and breakfast cereal make for early sniffing fun; the aroma trails off a bit following further aeration, leaving me feeling disappointed, especially after the slam-dunk start. Entry is acutely sweet, more in a sap-like, maple manner than candied or honeyed; the midpalate stage features highly complementary elements including baking spices (nutmeg, cinnamon, vanilla bean), fudge, butterscotch, maple syrup, and light toffee. Concludes engagingly sweet, medium-weighted, satiny, and round. A dazzler that would have picked up a fifth star had the latter stage of the nosing not dropped off the table. As with its cousin, the Rock Hill Farms, the alcohol level is never an issue except to the positive.
2007 Rating: ★★★★/Highly Recommended

Henry McKenna 10 Year Old Single Barrel Bottled-in-Bond KSBW (USA); 50% abv, $28.
Burnished copper/medium amber color; superb purity. Smells of new car leather, breakfast cereal, and cornmeal in the opening sniffs; goes spicy/peppery and a bit hemp-like in the inhalations after additional exposure to air. Entry is nicely sweet, almost candied and intensely grainy; the midpalate stage is the real star of the evaluation as the taste profile expands to include a broad array of semisweet flavors, including caramel corn, toasted marshmallow, dried fruit, and chocolate covered cherry. Concludes oaky sweet and chewy.
2007 Rating: ★★★★/Highly Recommended

Hirsch Selection 20 Year Old American Whiskey (USA); 48% abv, $84.
Pretty amber/topaz/burnished gold color; very good clarity. Enticing smells of buttermilk biscuits, salted butter, and fudge; the additional seven minutes of air contact bring out roasted scents of almond paste, nougat, corn bread, oatmeal, and caramel corn. Entry is semisweet, spirity warm, corn-like, and dry breakfast cereal-like; the midpalate however, is the star of this evaluation as the flavor profile turns buttery, rounded, maple-like, and nutty. Ends up clean, biscuity and keenly spirity, but never hot or fiery. The reined-in spirit is properly managed, creating a firm foundation on which the grain and wood influences shine, in particular, at entry and midpalate.
2007 Rating: ★★★/Recommended

Hirsch Selection 21 Year Old Kentucky Straight Rye (USA); 46.5% abv, $133.
The dark wood appearance owns a mahogany/roan color and flawless purity. The opening inhalation discovers intensely baked, tar/asphalt odors that startle the olfactory sense with their concentration; aeration and swirling force vague nut- and carnival candy-like aromas to reluctantly emerge; a peculiar, even confusing bouquet. Much more pleasing in the mouth as the palate entry offers big-hearted, oily textured flavors of oak resin, sap, and maple; the midpalate point displays a smooth richness that is chocolaty/cocoa-like in its bittersweetness and bearing. Finishes on a maple note that's as astringent as it is semisweet. A strange, idiosyncratic creature that's oddly compelling, even luscious.
2006 Rating: ★★★/Highly Recommended

Hudson Baby Bourbon Whiskey Batch: Reserve Bottle No. 15 (USA); 46% abv, $40/375 ml.

Dazzling new copper penny/burnished orange color; excellent clarity. The first burst of aroma brims with surface level sweet corn and corn flake cereal aromas; additional time in the glass allows a more nuanced fragrance to emerge and that is mineral/lead/stone; in a perfect world, which mine certainly is not, I'd have liked to smell more of the barrel influence (in particular since this whiskey was matured in a miniscule 3-gallon cask) to counter that odd slate/granite quality. The palate entry offers an amiable taste of sweet corn which is quickly followed by an oaky/resiny flavor that's pleasingly vanilla-like; at the midpalate point the angular, astringent taste profile features the minerally/dry stone-like characteristic that I detected in the second nosing stage and thereby undercuts the delectable grain and oak notes enjoyed in the entry. Genuine potential here, no doubt, but needs longer in the cask, in my view, to round off the rougher edges.

2007 Rating: ★★/Not Recommended

Jack Daniel's Gentleman Jack Tennessee Sour Mash Whiskey (USA); 40% abv, $24.

A lighter honey/harvest gold color than I remember; superb purity. The opening inhalations within the two minute span following the pour offer round, succulent scents of fresh flowers, new oak, light caramel and butter; six more minutes in the copita allow the aroma to develop a bit further (though not as much as I'd like) as moderately toasty/smoky/sooty aromas of come together nicely (but not as richly as I recall from the past). The palate entry is seamless, off-dry and slightly nutty/oaky; at midpalate the taste veers to the fruity/grainy side of the flavor spectrum. Finishes slightly raw, then smoothes out, offering a last blast of cream. This is not the same whiskey that I first reviewed in 1993. Somehow along the way, it's been dumbed down by a notch or two to become more homogenized and less adventurous. While it's still better than average, I'm disappointed that suddenly a favorite whiskey is less than it used to be.

2004 Rating: ★★★/Recommended

Jack Daniel's Old No. 7 Tennessee Sour Mash Whiskey (USA); 43% abv, $19.

The light amber/light honey/topaz color is attractive and flawlessly clean. The toasty/lightly smoked aroma is pleasant, but superficial and woody/cheese-like in the first few whiffs; aeration time spanning another six minutes adds intriguing but soft notes of tar, pipe tobacco, and cowhide. The palate entry is smoky, tight and sinewy; at midpalate the flavor profile shows the problem I've always had with this whiskey, a core hollowness with no substantial taste. Ends delicately and semisweet.

2004 Rating: ★★/Not Recommended

Jack Daniel's Single Barrel Rick No. L-24 Barrel No. 4-0623 Bottled 2-26-04 Tennessee Whiskey (USA); 47% abv, $40.

The bronze/orange/burnished color displays very good clarity. The first few sniffings pick up lively, vivid scents of buckwheat and hemp; seven more minutes in the copita encourage spirity aromas of light toffee, nougat, and oak to emerge; a good but not a great bouquet. The palate entry is moderately sweet, lead pencil-like, and a touch chalky; at midpalate the

roasted/toasty grain mash flavor eventually gives way to tastes of baked pear, pie crust, and spice. Concludes very warm, toasted, and tobacco-like.
2004 Rating: ★★★/Recommended

Jefferson's Reserve Very Small Batch KSBW (USA); 45.1% abv, $50.
Dazzling bronze/ocher/malmsey Madeira-like appearance; impeccable clarity. Initial sniffs detect comely scents of clean, vibrant spirit, light toffee, and marshmallow; another seven minutes in the glass bring out baking spices (nutmeg, cinnamon, especially), Christmas season fruitcake, poppy seed, brown sugar, and an ethereal underlying aroma of honey; a delicate, ultra-sophisticated bourbon bouquet. Entry is lip-smackingly clean and vibrant, giving off oaky sweet tastes of vanilla, baked bread, and buttered popcorn; at midpalate the taste profile deepens as rich flavors of molasses, burnt sugar, oak resin, maple, and honey all vie for dominance. Finishes big in the mouth, properly spirity, semisweet, and assertive. Not for the meek.
2007 Rating: ★★★★/Highly Recommended

Jefferson's Very Small Batch KSBW (USA); 41.15% abv, $30.
Very pretty amber/topaz hue; some minor sediment noted. Smells seductively of baked pears, baked apple, and caramel corn in the opening aromatic stage; turns a bit leathery, waxy, almondy, and textile-like after further aeration, losing some of its early phase appeal. Entry is firm, chewy, buttery, and fat-like; the pleasing buttery/oily taste continues strong at midpalate. Ends up smooth, silky, creamy, oily, and semisweet. I responded favorably to the full-weighted texture and fatty feel. An unflashy bourbon of substance.
2007 Rating: ★★★/Recommended

Jim Beam Black 8 Year Old KSBW (USA); 43% abv, $18.
The color is like honey, an amber/autumnal gold hue; the purity is perfect. The opening nosing passes detect moderately sweet notes of light caramel, toffee and, way in the background, yellow fruit; seven more minutes of aeration time stimulate slightly baked, dry aromas of tobacco leaf, oak resin, and breakfast cereal. The palate entry is firm and well-defined, semisweet and mildly grainy; by the midpalate point there's a slight oiliness to the texture that I like very much while the taste becomes narrowly focused on the grain/wood interplay. It finishes elegantly, emitting sophisticated, long and more dry than sweet flavors of toasted grain and oak. While far better than average, I don't believe that the year longer in barrel compensates quite enough for the 2% loss in abv; the original 90-proof level, I believe, fit this Jim Beam slightly better; still a lovely mouthful, though.
2003 Rating: ★★★★/Highly Recommended

Jim Beam Kentucky Straight Rye Whiskey (USA); 40% abv, $13.
The pretty bronze/copper hue shows impeccable clarity. The opening aroma doesn't have the delightful stoutness of Jim Beam bourbons and therefore seems lacking and timid; further air contact serves to unleash mild notes of melon, nuts, and woody resin. The palate entry is mildly spiced and grainy sweet, but simple; at midpalate the flavor profile displays a bit more thrust and grainy presence, but not enough to make it recommendable. Finishes sweet, drinkable, and easy. A borderline two star/three star whiskey. As always when I hesitate,

however, I go with the lesser score. I need to be fully convinced before I categorically say, "Recommended". Just not up to the standard of the price category competition, specifically meaning Old Overholt and the splendid Wild Turkey.

2005 Rating: ★★/Not Recommended

Jim Beam (White Label) KSBW (USA); 40% abv, $15.

Attractive golden grain/topaz/honey color; impeccable purity. Nose emits focused, fruity, cornmeal aromas in the initial whiffs; aeration highlights the red fruit scent, but doesn't leave behind the oaky vanilla quality that underpins the entire aromatic phase; a lovely, sophisticated bourbon bouquet. Entry is clean, gently sweet, toffee-like, and reserved; the midpalate stage features succulent tastes of light caramel, honeywheat bread, caramel corn, and toasted almond. Concludes as fruity and corny as it begins. For the price, a better American whiskey you cannot find. Hint: Taste Jim Beam White Label head-to-head against Jack Daniel's Black Label and those consumers with more than 10 functioning brain cells will go "White" for the rest of their drinking days. This is simply the finest big volume, frontline American produced bourbon for the money.

2007 Rating: ★★★/Recommended

Knob Creek 9 Year Old Small Batch KSBW (USA); 50% abv, $25.

The bronze/honey color dazzles the eye; excellent purity. Smells of sweet corn, buttered popcorn, and pistachio nuts in the early stages; later whiffs pick up well-endowed scents of brown butter, oaky vanilla, beeswax, and linseed oil. The palate entry is full-bodied, warm but not hot, sweet and honeyed; at midpalate the grain presence takes charge as the taste profile turns drier, more intensely grainy/mashy, and breakfast cereal-like. Finishes with high-flying notes of nougat, almonds, candy bar, and oak. I've tasted this superb bourbon numerous times over the last 12 years, but this is only the third time that I've put it through a formal evaluation. Knob Creek has stood up exceedingly well since its introduction in the early 1990s and competently earns every rating star that's bestowed on it.

2005 Rating: ★★★★/Highly Recommended

Laird's Applejack (USA); 40% abv, $17.

Author's Note: Technically, this is a whiskey. Pleasant bronze appearance; very good purity. The aroma is curiously and disappointingly neutral through all ten minutes of sniffing. Tastes distantly and vaguely of fruit, not necessarily apple or pear. Ends blandly and with no personality whatsoever. A waste of good glass.

2005 Rating: ★/Not Recommended

Maker's Mark KSBW (USA); 45% abv, $22.

The brilliant amber/topaz color shines under the examination lamp; excellent purity. The initial blast of aroma is all buttered corn-on-the-cob mixed with sugar maple; aeration brings out deeper spice, especially vanilla and cinnamon, while not forgetting for a nanosecond the corn base. The palate entry showcases the sweet breakfast cereal grain against the pristine distillate; at the midpalate stage there's a defining moment for this whiskey wherein the corn leaps across the footlights and dominates so thoroughly that you just know that this could be nothing other than one of the best straight bourbons from Kentucky. Ends spirity and heated. One of America's benchmark spirits.

2007 Rating: ★★★★/Highly Recommended

Mattingly & Moore KSBW (USA); 40% abv, $12.

The color is harvest gold/amber; clarity is perfect. Very corny/grainy in the upfront nose after the pour; aeration affects the aroma by turning it metallic and coin-like, going away from the plump corniness of the opening whiffs. Entry is chewy, corn syrup sweet, and, in bourbon terms, simple and straightforward with little in the way of depth; the midpalate stage sees a significant elevation of the corn in the form of caramel corn candy, as well as a honeyed backnote taste that brings a pleasing smoothness. Finishes drier than the midpalate and entry and with a burst of vegetation and herbs. Nearly displays enough bourbon charm to garner a third star and a recommendation, but not quite.

2007 Rating: ★★/Not Recommended

McCarthy's 3 Year Old Clear Creek Distillery Oregon Single Malt Whiskey (USA); 40% abv, $40.

The medium amber/light honey hue is ideally clear and pure. The initial nosing pass unearths an immediate malty tang and moderate sweetness; after several minutes of air contact in the glass, the second and third sniffings develop an earthy, almost mossy scent that nicely counters the expanding malty/grainy sweetness; following nine minutes of aeration, the bouquet stays firm but polite, emitting increasingly drier cereal notes and delicate dashes of oaky vanillin, caramel corn, and peanut butter; this feminine bouquet brings to mind characteristics both of Scottish Lowland single malts or younger Irish malts. There's a burst, like a sprint of woody/resiny flavor at the palate entry; then at midpalate the dry, malty flavor highlighted by light toffee and peanut notes steals the show. The aftertaste is moderately sweet, slightly oily, and damn near succulent. A quantum leap forward for McCarthy's malt whiskey program; can't help but wonder what, say, two to three more years in cask would accomplish; this is getting interesting.

2001 Rating: ★★★/Recommended

McKendric Western Style Whiskey (USA); 45.2% abv, $37.

Mellowed with mesquite. Very pretty topaz/dark honey color; good purity. The opening nosing pass detects a menthol-like perfume; with aeration, the second whiff picks up notes of paraffin, honeysuckle, and mesquite; by the third sniffing, following six minutes of exposure to air, the aroma turns unpleasantly medicinal and sap-like; the fourth and last sniffing highlights the botanical/herbal/minty component to distraction; too medicinal and liqueur-like for my taste. The palate entry is intensely resiny and oily and toothpaste sweet; by the midpalate point the sickly, herbal, pasty, sappy/creosote-like flavor more closely resembles a whiskey liqueur than a categorical whiskey. The finish is awkward, herbal, sooty, and well, truth be uttered, dismal. Nothing more needs to be said other than "Do yourself a favor and move on."

2000 Rating: ★/Not Recommended

Michter's 10 Year Old Single Barrel Bourbon Whiskey (USA); 47.2% abv, $50.

Gorgeous bronze/burnished orange hue; superb clarity. The first two sniffings detect a delightfully floral, as in juniper and honeysuckle, surface perfume that clearly overrides deeper aromas of cedary oak and sweet grain mash but doesn't conceal them altogether; after seven minutes in the glass spicy/pastry-like scents of ginger, brown sugar, and vanilla extract take full command of the bouquet. Initial tastes find sweet, succulent flavors that are borderline fatty and smoky; by the midpalate stage the taste profile is smoky, resiny, semisweet and delicious. The aftertaste is long, focused, piney/woody/sappy, and moderately sweet. A beauty.

2002 Rating: ★★★★/Highly Recommended

Michter's 10 Year Old Straight Rye Whiskey (USA); 46.4% abv, $60.

Rich and deep brown/old honey color; perfect purity. The first aromas are strong, nutty, and mocha-like; further sniffings following aeration pick up deep-seeded scents of walnut, new leather, flax/fiber, and soft cheese. Wow. The sweet and honeyed flavor profile bursts onto the tongue in the entry stage, then turns drier, grape seed-like, and woodier at midpalate. Ends up vanilla sweet, succulent, and incredibly honeyed. A tour de force rye whiskey that delivers at every level.

2005 Rating: ★★★★★/Highest Recommendation

Michter's Single Barrel Barrel 4A-R2 Straight Rye Whiskey (USA); 42.4% abv, $30.

The pretty orange/honey appearance is ideally pure. The initial nosing passes detect soft, almost plump scents of spicy, zesty rye; aeration adds notes of black pepper, marmalade, and plum preserves. The firm, moderately oily palate entry makes the tongue tingle pleasantly; by midpalate the flavor profile accentuates this whiskey's youth (it's around three years old) and vivacity by featuring racy tastes of alcohol, spicy grain, and light caramel. Finishes as sprightly and carefree as it starts. A comely straight rye with attitude that embellishes the hallowed American whiskey legend of Michter's.

2004 Rating: ★★★★/Highly Recommended

Michter's US 1 Small Batch Bourbon Batch No. 6G-1 (USA); 45.7% abv, $33.

The rich bronze color sparkles under the lamp; perfect purity. The initial whiffs uncover dry notes of stone-milled grist and dried fruit; following the aeration stage, the bouquet offers peppery/spicy scents that accent the dry graininess. The palate entry is surprisingly sweet and corny, considering how dry the aroma is; the midpalate point is deep, corny sweet, sap-like, and a bit syrupy. Ends up well and balanced, with a backnote of dried red fruit (raisins, prunes). A handsome edition to this series.

2007 Rating: ★★★★/Highly Recommended

Michter's US 1 Small Batch Unblended American Whiskey (USA); 41.7% abv, $30.

Truly gorgeous, absolutely spotless bronze/tarnished copper. The aggressive bouquet opens up with a shotgun spread of intriguingly disparate and vegetal yet complementary aromas, including hazelnut, road tar/asphalt, fennel, steamed asparagus, and damp hay; the additional seven minutes of air contact serve to add metallic/botanical fragrances that suggest lead pipe, rust, unbuttered popcorn, dill, brine, and charred oak; it's an aromatic handful,

to be sure, but once I got sniffing I found I couldn't, or wouldn't, stop; good sign. In the mouth, US 1 is a full-throttle bargain, showing loads of rich, sap- and maple-like charm right up front; by the midpalate point the taste scorecard adds brown rice, soy, dark caramel, and bittersweet cocoa powder. It finishes softer than I expected, displaying a disconcerting taste of distant agave; a rip-snortin' whiskey gem that's an adventure every single time you try it.
2003 Rating: ★★★★/Highly Recommended

Old Charter 8 Year Old KSBW (USA); 40% abv, $12.

The honey/medium amber hue is pretty and flawless. In the first couple of nosing passes I note a delicate, biscuity, sugar cookie batter aroma that's standing off in the wings; another six minutes in the copita brings forward, if reluctantly, soft scents of ripe yellow fruit, gum, confectioner's sugar, and a distant hint of honey. The silky palate entry features the corn component in its finest grainy sweet attire; by the midpalate stage a pleasing viscosity serves to underpin the accessible flavors that include caramel corn, cocoa butter, oak resin, and honey. Finishes well in a sinewy smooth manner in the throat. An eminently drinkable and likeable bourbon right from its biscuity start.
2004 Rating: ★★★/Recommended

Old Crow KSBW (USA); 40% abv, $14.

Golden grain/honey color; excellent purity. Owns a floral, delicate opening aroma that's pleasant and refined; not much happens aroma-wise after further air contact. Tastes a little too raw and austere at entry; the midpalate stage shows a trace more character but no depth whatsoever; in other words, what scant quality is there, is superficial. Ends corny, a touch smoky, lean, and hollow. Can't possibly be the same recipe as when this brand was the leading bourbon in the US. Junk is the only word that pops into my brain for this lemon.
2007 Rating: ★/Not Recommended

Old Fitzgerald Very Special 12 Year Old KSBW (USA); 45% abv, $34.

Drop dead gorgeous henna/copper color; impeccable purity. Smells of old worn leather, popcorn, and breakfast cereal upfront in the first inhalations; more subtle notes of creamed corn, dark caramel, molasses, and fudge get added to the aromatic mix after further aeration. Entry is sweet corn-like, buttery, maple-like, and deep; the expansive and generous midpalate stage offers cooking oil, lanolin, caramel, dark fudge, cocoa, and brown sugar. A flourish of oaky vanilla comes out in the robust finish. Excellent bourbon of bona fide character and hearty grace.
2007 Rating: ★★★★/Highly Recommended

Old Fitzgerald's 1849 KSBW (USA); 45% abv, $16.

Solid ocher/deep topaz hue; ideal purity. Out of the gate, it smells faintly of toffee and egg cream; the additional seven minutes of air contact do little to urge more aromatics to show themselves, except for wax. Entry is full, assertive, dry to off-dry, and grainy; the midpalate point offers a vertical, tightly wrapped flavor profile that's caramel- and fudge-like, but likewise oaky/vanilla and marzipan-like. Finishes long, gently sweet, corny, and savory. A compact package from start to finish and affordable to boot.
2007 Rating: ★★★/Recommended

Old Forester KSBW (USA); 43% abv, $14.

The warm honey/amber color shows ideal purity. Right from the very beginning, I respond favorably to this fragrant, flowery, popcorn-like aroma; further time in the glass reveals underlying scents of sweet grain, ripe red plums, spice, and sweet corn bathed in butter; a fine bourbon perfume. The palate entry is hard, brittle, unwelcoming, and not in the least reminiscent of the fetching bouquet; at midpalate there's a slight reflection of the grainy aroma, but that's washed away in the torrent of oaky resin; ends up bitter and biting. I didn't care for this uneven, Jekyll and Hyde of a bourbon. One minute it's sweet, inviting, and succulent in the nose; the next minute it's scraping the skin off your tongue and upper palate. Some points have to be granted for the fine appearance and lovely aroma.

2004 Rating: ★★/Not Recommended

Old Forester 100 Proof Bottled-in-Bond KSBW (USA); 50% abv, $16.

The deep bronze/topaz/dark honey hue is bedazzling and flawless. The opening whiffs encounter finely melded notes of spice, sweet grain, and saddle leather; after seven minutes of additional aeration, nuances of brown rice, beef stock, heady spirit, oak, and pork rind vie for aromatic dominance; a forceful, but not aggressive bouquet. The palate entry is rich, creamy, and honey-like; at midpalate the corny/grainy sweetness turns spicy, zesty, and spirity as the proof kicks in and takes this whiskey to its next level. Ends assertively, bittersweet, and grainy. A superb, racy, and full-bodied example of why many bourbons should, in my opinion, be bottled at 100-proof. The corn foundation lends itself to bigger alcohol levels better than most other types of whiskey.

2004 Rating: ★★★/Recommended

Old Forester 2004 Birthday Bourbon KSBW (USA); 47% abv, $35.

The copper/burnished orange color is seriously attractive and flawless. The initial whiffs detect delicately sweet aromatic notes that remind me of the heart-shaped powdery hard candy that always appears in February; seven more minutes of exposure to air unleashes more substantial aromas of corn husk, pine, and oak; neither a "big" nor an assertive bouquet, but quietly appealing. The palate entry is concentrated, corn syrup-like, and nearly fruity, as in dried red fruit; by midpalate the spirit comes into play making the flavor turn astringent and slightly biting, thereby eliminating the gains made in the latter phase of the bouquet and the palate entry. Finishes rambunctiously, fruity (that red fruit element again), spirity, and a tad too raw for me to recommend. Its peak is at palate entry, then it unravels.

2004 Rating: ★★/Not Recommended

Old Forester 2005 Birthday Bourbon KSBW (USA); 48% abv, $35.

The spectacular bronze/copper hue is flawless in its clarity. The opening sniffings are treated to tightly wound, but totally focused aromas of honey, old oak and dried herbs; I can't believe what good things come out of aerating this bourbon for another seven minutes as the bouquet turns perfumed, lightly spiced, gently woody but, most of all, lovely and elegant in its dry, kernel-like, breakfast cereal way. The palate entry is every bit as composed and integrated as the bouquet as melded tastes of toffee, buttered popcorn, and marzipan are featured; at midpalate the bittersweet flavor profile includes butterscotch, corn-flavored hard candy, brown sugar, and dark honey. The oak influence comes out in the aftertaste

that is long, off-dry to semisweet and corny, but not the least bit hot. Easily the crowning achievement thus far of this fast-rising series from Brown-Forman and Master Distiller Chris Morris. A supple beauty of the top rank.
2006 Rating: ★★★★★/Highest Recommendation

Old Forester 2006 Birthday Bourbon KSBW (USA); 48% abv, $40.
The brilliant topaz color shines under the examination lamp; flawless purity; a visual gem. The tightness of the corn aroma in the opening whiffs is a joy to behold; following another seven minutes of aeration, the aroma expands to include sweet oak, charcoal, and palm oil. The palate entry hits the jackpot as assertive yet graceful tastes of honeysuckle, light honey, and hard candy (red fruit, like cherry, maybe?) light up the taste buds; at the midpalate point the flavor profile explodes in succulent waves of bacon fat, bacon rind, and caramel corn tastes that lead to the succulent, semisweet finishes that glide down the throat like satin on ice. Yet another blockbuster in the limited edition Old Forester Bourbon series that now is starting to rival Heaven Hill's Evan Williams Vintage Single Barrel series and Buffalo Trace's Antique Collection series in quality and consistency.
2007 Rating: ★★★★★/Highest Recommendation

Old Forester Bourbon Spring 1990 KSBW (USA); 46.5% abv, $35.
A bronze color, with black bits of sediment showing. The first few inhalations after the pour detect an easy, polite aroma that highlights sweet grain, bread crust, and a distant trace of vanilla; the aroma expands with exposure to air, affording the grain element to deepen and become almost buttery. The palate entry is firm, sinewy, and grainy sweet; the midpalate finds the flavor opening further to include dark caramel, honey, vanilla bean, and a deft touch of tobacco leaf; to its credit, the 93-proof spirit never interferes with the innate taste components. The aftertaste is warming, moderately sweet, caramel-like, and almost biscuity. Top-notch bourbon making.
2003 Rating: ★★★★/Highly Recommended

Old Forester Fall 1990 Birthday Bourbon KSBW (USA); 44.5% abv, $35.
The harvest gold/amber hue is very fetching and displays a minor amount of sediment under the examination lamp. Right from the opening whiff, this elegant bourbon bouquet offers gentlemanly scents of corn-on-the-cob, light spice, and light caramel; further aeration time of seven minutes encourages the aroma to go deeper, especially into the corn element and how it interacts with the oak; a genuinely lovely, if restrained bourbon bouquet. The palate entry flares slightly on the tip of the tongue; then settles down at midpalate as the taste profile turns lean, resiny, even a tad candied at the tail end. The finish is austere, medium sweet, and short-lived. The best part of the experience, at least for me, is the nosing since the flavor phase is very tightly wrapped.
2003 Rating: ★★★/Recommended

Old Grand Dad 114 KSBW (USA); 57% abv, $22.
Brilliant, light-catching copper/auburn/burnished orange color; perfect purity. Initial sniffs pick up crisp, defined aromas of buttered corn-on-the-cob, sawdust, freshly sawed pine, and a deft touch of cedar; the aroma loses the woodiness as the spirit charges into the

lead, adding backbone, spice (vanilla, nutmeg), and dried fruit (banana especially). Entry is vividly spirity and potent but neither harsh nor overpowering; the midpalate highlights corn meal, breakfast cereal, orange rind, dark chocolate, and toffee. Polished, sophisticated, yet powerful and assertive. A best kept secret.

2007 Rating: ★★★★/Highly Recommended

Old Grand Dad KSBW (USA); 43% abv, $17.

The color is a dullish topaz/amber tint; good clarity. First whiffs detect lazy (undirected) caramel corn and marshmallow scents; aeration brings out moderately complex, slightly fat aromas of nut paste, pastry dough, yeast, and dry breakfast cereal. Entry is firmer and more focused than the near-sloppy bouquet as developed and toothsome tastes of bacon fat and corn meal dominate the early phase; the midpalate is even better as the flavor profile features the oak as much as the grain, making for balanced and far better than average taste enjoyment. Ends with a dash of fire on the tongue. Works for me.

2007 Rating: ★★★/Recommended

Old Gristmill Authentic American 100% Corn Whisky (USA); 40% abv, $25.

This unaged distillate is produced in a pot still from 100% corn grown in the Hudson Valley. Displays a very pale yellow color; good clarity. The assertive, intensely floral aroma right out of the gate has "white dog" and "white lightening" written all over it, but without the routine nose hair singeing effect of the ultra-high alcohol that's frequently found in raw, unaged grain spirits; with six more minutes of air contact, the bouquet turns concentrated and wonderfully corny, as in unbuttered popcorn. The palate entry is semisweet (don't forget that this is ALL CORN), cocoa bean-like, and balanced; by the midpalate stage the taste profile goes very chocolaty and bittersweet. Concludes slightly syrupy and sap-like, but good overall. A must-have for collectors and for whiskey mavens who hanker to see what fresh grain spirit smells and tastes like.

2007 Rating: ★★★/Recommended

Old Overholt Kentucky Straight Rye Whiskey (USA); 40% abv, $17.

The appealing harvest gold/bronze hue is flawless in its purity. The first sniffings detect notes of black pepper and oak resin; aeration adds stone-dry scents of minerals, slate, and sage; a nifty rye bouquet. This rye does its best work in the mouth; the entry is lean, semisweet, intensely grainy, and satisfying; at midpalate there's not a whole lot of expansion, but what is nice is the way in which this whiskey lies on the tongue, sweet, grainy, medium plump, and spicy to the point of being zesty. Finishes spicier than anything else. A very solid, very good rye whiskey that deserves a larger audience.

2005 Rating: ★★★/Recommended

Old Pogue Master's Select KSBW (USA); 45.5% abv, $40.

Invitingly warm medium amber/pale bronze color; impeccable purity. The opening inhalation immediately following the pour delights the olfactory sense with alluring, sweet grain, and plum scents; with further air contact, the fruity element goes dry (like prunes) and the grain softens and dries out, emitting delicate aromas of paraffin, confectioner's sugar, and a trace of maple. The palate entry is silky smooth and tastes of light caramel, buttered sweet corn, and maple; concludes firm, warm on the tongue, and moderately oily. A new American small batch gem.

2004 Rating: ★★★★/Highly Recommended

Old Rip Van Winkle 10 Year Old Kentucky Straight Rye Whiskey (USA); 45% abv, $30.

Brown/honey/saffron color; excellent purity. Smells right out of the gate of buttered popcorn and well-crisped bacon; with aeration dawns a lovely floral (honeysuckle) scent that comes out of nowhere yet beautifully accents the corniness and meatiness, making the final stages of sniffing a delight. Entry is red fruit ripe and caramel sweet; the midpalate stage is pleasingly oily, fatty, chewy, and bittersweet from the oaky vanillin. Ends up sturdy, assertive, and generous, with top notes of dark toffee and fudge.

2007 Rating: ★★★★/Highly Recommended

Old Whiskey River 6 Year Old KSBW (USA); 43% abv, $28.

Pretty amber color; excellent purity. The seductively sweet smell of corn greets the olfactory sense in the first two nosing passes; further aeration stimulates scents of buttered popcorn, evergreen, yellow fruit, and mint. The palate entry is friendly, soft, and sweet; the midpalate stage is moderately intense, corn-like, and mildly spicy. It finishes well in an oaky, uncomplicated, slightly charred, and smoky manner.

2002 Rating: ★★★/Recommended

Origine 8 Year Old KSBW (USA); 40% abv, $25.

The luminescent bronze color is denigrated by more floating debris than should be present. The opening sniffings pick up light-weighted scents of slate/minerals and cornmeal; after six more minutes of swirling and aeration, the delicate aroma gives off slender fragrances of bubble gum, cotton candy, and forest greenery (ferns, moss). The palate entry comes to the rescue of the less-than-thrilling appearance and bouquet, by offering the taste buds more than a little textural grip and bittersweet grainy/mashy flavor; by midpalate there's enough flavor evidence of authentic bourbon to go around as the core tastes of oaky vanilla, sweet corn, brown butter, light caramel, and marzipan bring this whiskey up to the ranks of the recommended. The finish is medium-bodied, crisp, a touch apple-like, and silky smooth. A textbook case of the flavor and aftertaste stages salvaging the rating score.

2005 Rating: ★★★/Recommended

Pappy Van Winkle's Family Reserve 15 Year Old KSBW (USA); 53.5% abv, $45.

The bright bronze/burnished orange/bay hue delights the eye; impeccable clarity. The elegant, focused early-on aroma paints pictures of sweet corn dripping with butter, dark toffee, and hazelnuts; later inhalations pick up not-so-subtle notes of chocolate cake frosting, cocoa beans, and vanilla; a top-heavy aroma that's loaded with classic and traditional rich, potent corn whiskey scents. The palate entry is spicy, piquant, prickly, and raisiny; at midpalate the taste profile features lead pencil, slate, black pepper, brown butter, and deep-seared oak. Finishes with an ash-like, chewy, and oily aftertaste that's smashingly luscious. Eleven years after first evaluating this husky, take-no-prisoners bourbon, I love it even more and admire its uncompromising core virtues at a higher level of appreciation. American whiskey doesn't come any finer.

2005 Rating: ★★★★★/Highest Recommendation

Pappy Van Winkle's Family Reserve 20 Year Old KSBW (USA); 45.2% abv, $76.
Extremely pretty tawny/deep amber/reddish color; superb purity. Right off the pour I'm impressed with the inviting smell that features dough, sugar, maple, and candy; in fact, it reminds me of a bakery aroma; later whiffs pick up deeper scents of old oak, a touch of rancio, and dates, plums, and figs. The palate entry is fruity, gently sweet, and gentlemanly; the pruny midpalate stage shows tastes of caramel, oak resin and toffee. The aftertaste is extended, candied, and almost liqueur-like. A brawnier, more intense expression of 20 YO bourbon whiskey; yeah, I like it.
2002 Rating: ★★★/Highly Recommended

Pappy Van Winkle's Family Reserve 23 Year Old KSBW (USA); 47.8% abv, $200.
Beneath the examination lamp the radiant copper color shines like a new penny; good clarity. The initial aromatic burst is chockfull of pork sausage and sweet spice scents; with aeration, the aroma transforms into a stately, mature, fully integrated whiskey bouquet of the first rank, emitting seamless scents of dark coffee, marzipan, praline, caramel corn, and oaky vanillin; remarkably seductive. The palate entry is passing-gear sap-like and sweet, but elegant at the same time; by the midpalate stage the flavor components have melded so thoroughly that no one feature leaps out. Finishes warmly, like smoldering embers, on the tongue and tangy, sweet, and resiny. An American distilling masterpiece. *See also Van Winkle and Old Rip Van Winkle.*
2005 Rating: ★★★★/Highest Recommendation

Parker's Heritage Collection Cask Strength KSBW (USA); 61.3% abv, $80.
The copper/henna/auburn color dazzles the eye; impeccable purity. First whiffs pick up topical oaky/resiny scents, but beneath that lay deeper aromas of spice, banana, and green vegetation; another seven minutes of air contact reveal white pepper, lanolin, and parchment, though the green vegetation remains strong. Entry is amazingly drinkable considering the cask strength and comes off chewy and caramel-like; the midpalate stage is powerful, intensely spirity, weedy/vegetal, peppery, and oaky/resiny. Reduction in strength by the addition of spring water improves this whiskey by a long way as the spirit slightly recedes, leaving the space open to be filled by succulent tastes of fudge, dark chocolate/cocoa, tobacco leaf, and brown sugar. Five star rating stands for diluted state. A fitting tribute to Parker Beam, one of the premier distillers in American history.
2007 Rating: ★★★★/Highest Recommendation

Peter Jake's Private Keep 10 Year Old KSBW (USA); 45% abv, $33.
Bright topaz/honey color; superb purity. The initial passes detect fruity aromas, almost like baked apple plus a trace of pekoe tea; additional time in the glass stimulates further aromas to emerge, most prominently, corn husk, light caramel, and mildly prickly spirit. The palate entry is vibrant, spirity but neither harsh nor raw; the midpalate point features lovely flavors of sweet corn, toffee, and baked pear. The aftertaste is long, mildly oily, and semisweet. A very nice bourbon that shows a good combination of maturity and vigor.
2003 Rating: ★★★/Highly Recommended

Phillips Union Whiskey (USA); 40% abv, $25.

A blend of bourbon from Kentucky and Canadian whiskies. Amber/harvest gold color. Beneath the examination lamp there's evidence of both black and gray sediment/debris, though I doubt that anyone but the most fastidious drinker would notice. The initial aromatic burst is delightfully semisweet and butterscotch-like; later whiffs detect inviting scents of cinnamon/nutmeg, roasted almond, vanilla bean, maple, and oak barrel char; this is an authentic hybrid bouquet, one that fittingly honors and bears witness to both types of NA whiskey. The palate entry is very sugary in its exaggerated sweetness and therefore comes off awkwardly more like a whiskey liqueur than a blended whiskey; the midpalate stage goes all sappy sweet, maple- and brown sugar-like. Finishes on a mildly pleasing spicy note that doesn't offset the intense sweetness enough to warrant a recommendation. That said, I see some genuine potential here and I applaud Phillips Distilling Company for trying something different. I hope that they continue to refine what they've begun with this concept.

2006 Rating: ★★/Not Recommended

Phillips Union Cherry Flavored Whiskey (USA); 35% abv, $25.

Displays an unblemished attractiveness wrapped in light amber that is missing in the Phillips Union Whiskey. Whoa, the intense cherry perfume in the opening inhalation almost snaps my head back; additional time in the glass fails to turn down the volume on the all-out cherry-a-thon and, as such, the whiskey is completely set adrift. The palate entry taste is like sweet/sour cherry hard candy and nothing else; by the midpalate phase the cherry flavor is running amok, raping and pillaging my palate. Finishes on the single note that runs through the entire evaluation experience, cherry candy. When the awards for "Flavoring Prowess & Expertise in Spirits" are announced, guess who'll be absent from the nominee list?

2006 Rating: ★/Not Recommended

Phillips Union Vanilla Flavored Whiskey (USA); 35% abv, $25.

The autumnal gold color is flawlessly clean. In the first sniffs after the pour, the aroma bolts from the glass like a jailbreak, emitting toasted, heavily bean-like fragrances of unpopped popcorn, legumes, and bean sprouts; seven further minutes of aeration do little to expand on what's already been discerned in the bouquet; it's all beans/legumes. The palate entry blankets the taste buds in the bittersweet flavor of extreme vanilla bean and nothing else; by the midpalate phase the vanilla concentration breaks down somewhat, offering a more rounded, less intense vanilla experience, but still one that totally dominates the in-mouth stages by obliterating any sense of whiskey whatsoever. The aftertaste echoes fully what occurs in the entry and midpalate stages, leaving no room for balance or elegance. This unfortunately is flavoring in red zone rpms and, by extension, severe overkill.

2006 Rating: ★/Not Recommended

Rawhide 6 Year Old KSBW (USA); 40% abv, $13.

Pretty topaz hue; excellent purity. The perfume is spicy and flowery in the opening stages then it turns grainy sweet, but only mildly so; later nosings unearth little in the way deepening or expansion; a pleasant, but unexceptional bourbon bouquet; light and nimble on the tongue; the uncomplicated flavors include light toffee, buttered pecan, and sweet corn; what concerned me the most was the paper-thin texture. The finish is medium long, agreeable, and simple. By all means for the price one doesn't get hurt, however, for that amount of money I'd still buy Jim Beam 4 Year Old or Old Grand Dad, both of which display far deeper bourbon pedigree and flavor.

2001 Rating: ★★/Not Recommended

Ridgemont Reserve 1792 Barrel Select 8 Year Old Small Batch KSBW (USA); 46.85% abv, $28.

Very pretty bronze/dusty orange color, with very minor sediment. The first couple of sniffings detect attractive dry scents of leather and black pepper; another seven minutes of aeration encourage sweeter, woodier aromas to emerge. The palate entry is sap- and pine-like and moderately sweet; at midpalate a flash of cocoa, almost like hot chocolate powder makes an appearance, then recedes leaving the door open for sweet oak, vanilla, palm oil, and sap. Finishes lean, moderately sweet, grainy/corny, and very appealing.

2004 Rating: ★★★/Recommended

Rittenhouse 10 Year Old Bottled-in-Bond Straight Rye Whiskey (USA); 50% abv, $14.

The auburn/bay color is gorgeous; unblemished clarity. The first nosings pick up intensely woody aromas like teak chest, cherry wood, and oak; secondary whiffs following aeration offer more succulent, marshmallow, bakery, and lanolin scents. The fat, chewy palate entry oozes butter cream, dark caramel, and brown sugar tastes that coat the tongue; the midpalate stage focuses more on the grain aspect as the flavor profile becomes toasty/roasted and damn near fruity and honeyed. Ends honey sweet, bountifully textured, decadent, maple-like, and nothing short of nectar-like. If anyone can explain to me how a straight whiskey costing less than $15 can taste so downright delicious, I'm open for business. A fifth rating star would have definitely been granted had the bouquet given me more in terms of straight rye definition. Still, quibbling aside, Rittenhouse 10 is an unbelievable American whiskey gem and bargain.

2006 Rating: ★★★★/Highly Recommended

Rittenhouse 21 Year Old Bottled-in-Bond Straight Rye Whiskey (USA); 50% abv, $150.

The color is henna/sienna; the purity is flawless. The initial sniffs pick up intriguing scents of flax/wax/textile; seven more minutes of aeration bring grainy/bakery odors to the table, mostly in the forms of brown rice, raisin bread, and seeded rye bread; the spice element alone has "rye" written all over it. The palate entry is oaky sweet, minerally, and roasted; the midpalate stage offers sap-like, semisweet tastes of honey, cane syrup, cocoa, and tobacco leaf. Finishes with vitality and heft as the sweet notes turn honeyed and almost sherry-like. A classic blockbuster that defines straight rye whiskey for me.

2006 Rating: ★★★★★/Highest Recommendation

Rock Hill Farms Single Barrel KSBW (USA); 50% abv, $50.

Amber/topaz color; unblemished clarity. Seductive aromatic notes of toasted walnut, dried red fruits, and marzipan highlight the sensational opening sniffs; later whiffs feature keen and focused scents of black pepper, cinnamon, clove, coriander, cocoa, and marshmallow. Entry is zesty, fruity, candied, and almost sherry-like, but the fun's just beginning; the midpalate bursts with flavors of cocoa, dark chocolate, chocolate covered almond, coffee, tobacco, and dark caramel; this is a monster taste profile that's as long as it is deep, roasted, and satiny. Ends smooth, silky, toffee sweet, and honeyed. An overlooked superstar in the Buffalo Trace stable of bourbons.

2007 Rating: ★★★★★/Highest Recommendation

Russell's Reserve 10 Year Old KSBW (USA); 45% abv, $30.

The deep amber/polished bronze color is dazzling and perfectly pure. In the first whiffs I detect subtle notes of sawed wood, matchstick, and pine; later inhalations following a seven minute period of additional air contact uncover dry scents of grain and resin beneath the woody/piney aromatic surface. The palate entry displays a flash of corny sweetness upfront, then a whisper of butterscotch; the midpalate stage is full-bodied, sweet as corn-on-the-cob, moderately oily, clean, and maple-like. Concludes warmly in the throat, with sumptuous tastes of dark honey and marzipan. Another winner from this stalwart, incredibly reliable distillery (Wild Turkey).

2005 Rating: ★★★★/Highly Recommended

Russell's Reserve 10 Year Old KSBW (USA); 50.5% abv, $26.

The topaz/new copper penny color dazzles the eye; ideal purity. The initial nosing pass lights up the olfactory sense with resiny scents of new oak and sap; the second pass, after three minutes in the glass, adds seductive and dry hints of lead pencil, bark, and oil; the third sniffing, following seven minutes of aeration, sees the green/woody element turn softer and slightly sweeter, though hardly sappy or plump; the fourth and last whiff reveals atypical traces of raisins, plum, and sugar cane; a highly complex aroma that transforms into a full-throttle bourbon bouquet after about five minutes in the glass; a muscular aroma. The palate entry is tight, dry, and spirity; the midpalate phase is tightly-wound, almost austere, and intensely oaky. The finish is woody, resiny, and extended. A deeply opulent bourbon that on the surface is lean; but underneath lies that thumbprint Wild Turkey grainy richness that defines every WT whiskey.

2000 Rating: ★★★★/Highly Recommended

Sam Houston Very Small Batch 10 Year Old Batch 1 Bottle No. 39 KSBW (USA); 45% abv, $30.

Beautiful, bright, and impeccably clean amber color. The initial nosing pass reveals a sweet corn-like perfume that's very alluring; in the second pass, the rye element comes to the foreground as spicy, zesty aromas surpass the foundational corn sweetness; by the third sniffing, after almost eight minutes of air contact, the bouquet turns softer and is notably more oak-influenced; the last nosing reveals delicate scents of red fruit, rye bread, and oak resin; a good, solid, if unspectacular, bouquet. The palate entry is firm, sweet, and slightly oily; the midpalate point blossoms with rich, tangy flavors including nut meat, wood resin, corn mash, rye bread, and dry cereal. The aftertaste is long, sweet, opulently textured, and, most importantly, invites a second sip. A nice, well-crafted bourbon that's on par with its more stately sibling, the very fine Jefferson's Reserve KSB (★★★★); nice job of distilling here.

2000 Rating: ★★★★/Highly Recommended

Sam Houston Very Small Batch Batch 52 Bottle No. 480 KSBW (USA); 42.8% abv, $35.

Topaz/honey color; minor, inconsequential sediment seen. First smells are outdoorsy, leafy, green vegetation-like and even a tad reminiscent of steamed corn-on-the-cob; the aroma swings around 180 degrees following aeration and it turns mildly woody/oaky, grainy, and even mildly peppery (roasted green pepper). Entry is intensely dry, sawdust-like, woody/oak chippy, and buttery in the background; the midpalate brings the butteriness out to the forefront and leaves behind the dry sawdust quality. Concludes off-dry, oaky, and appealing texture-wise. While I recommend this solid, nuts-and-bolts bourbon, I feel that for some reason it didn't/couldn't hit its prescribed high note. Just seemed reined in.

2007 Rating: ★★★/Recommended

Sazerac 18 Year Old Kentucky Straight Rye Whiskey (USA); 45% abv, $55.

The bright copper color is eye-catching and superbly pure. The first nosing passes detect sumptuously full bodied and doughy/bready scents that enchant the olfactory sense; more time in the glass stirs up woodier scents that are dry, resiny, and clean. The palate entry is fresh, surprisingly fruity (red plum, in particular), and wonderfully creamy; the midpalate taste profile is sweeter than the entry's, rich in a fruity/ripe manner, and engagingly oaky. Concludes sap- and maple-like, oaky, and more bittersweet than flat-out confection sweet. Easily one of the best examples of fine straight rye whiskey.

2006 Rating: ★★★★/Highly Recommended

St. George Single Malt Pure Barley Spirit (USA); 43% abv, $50.

The light amber/dull gold appearance shows some insignificant but noticeable sediment. The subtle aroma right after opening is ripe, fruity (banana, guava), delicately nutty, and pleasant but not very whiskey-like; with time in the glass, the bouquet stays the course of being more like the perfume of an eau-de-vie than whiskey as distant nuances of berry fruit and cake frosting lurk behind the curtain of aromatic ripeness; a strange, but wholly agreeable animal. On the palate, there's a suppleness that I like, but the flavors are subdued, moderately sweet, and vague. The aftertaste is appealing, long, grainy sweet, and a little sap-like. Would I have automatically guessed that this was a whiskey? Not necessarily; would I drink it on a regular basis? No, because there's simply not enough definable character to make the experience interesting.

2001 Rating: ★★/Not Recommended

St. George Single Malt Whiskey Lot No. 2 (USA); 43% abv, $45.

Light amber/gold color; excellent purity. The nose shows floral, pine and light nut scents in the first passes; aeration brings out added aromas of vinyl, milk chocolate, and yellow grapes; a more intriguing bouquet than that displayed by Lot No. 1. The palate entry is sap-like and slightly bitter; the midpalate features aldehydic tastes of hay, grass, vegetation and some spice in the distance; finishes bitter, lean and simple; I'd like to say that I like this effort more than Lot No. 1 (★★)...but I can't.

2002 Rating: ★★/Not Recommended

Templeton Rye Batch 1 Barrel No. 58 Bottle No. 401 Bottled January 30, 2007 Single Barrel Rye Whiskey (USA); 40% abv, $35.

Deep straw/dusty gold appearance; flawless purity. First sniffs detect bits of pine, cement,

spice, and stone; added aeration doesn't stimulate much more in the way of expression or depth with the exception of the introduction of baked spiced apple at the very last moment. Entry is lean, angular, tight-fisted, and nicely grainy, but more dry than sweet; midpalate stage hosts a lot of spicy, grainy, breakfast cereal flavor that's suddenly sweeter and even mildly biscuity/doughy. Growing in the glass, Templeton turns on the full beacon of its charm in the sweet, sap-like finish. Without any doubt, this distiller understands rye whiskey and I keenly look forward to future offerings. Serious potential here.
2007 Rating: ★★★/Recommended

The Classic Cask 15 Year Old Kentucky Straight Rye Whiskey (USA); 45.4% abv, $55.

Bright, bronze/new copper penny color; ideal purity. The piquant nose starts off intensely spicy, spirity, and peppery; the middle stage nosings expose ripe, concentrated, and sweet grain scents that are not overshadowed by the alcohol; the aromatic finale offers tantalizing fragrances of pumpkin seed, black pepper, sweet grain, and tangy spice; a smashing bouquet from start to finish. In the mouth this whiskey begins in a sweet, grainy way then turns intensely peppery and succulent at midpalate offering almondy/buttery tastes that enchant the taste buds. The aftertaste is long, oaky, a touch resiny, vanilla-like, and warm. An immensely pleasing rye that shows why this subcategory should by all rights be bigger than it is at present.
2001 Rating: ★★★★/Highly Recommended

The Classic Cask 17 Year Old KSBW (USA); 45.4% abv, $60.

The rich topaz/Tupelo honey hue is a dazzler; excellent purity. The nose at opening is opulent, nougat-like, and intensely oaky; over time, the aroma blossoms into a full-fledged bourbon bouquet that emits resiny, vanilla extract-like scents that deeply impress the olfactory sense; the bouquet finishes as gracefully as it started with loads of nougat, dark toffee, cane sugar/molasses, buttered popcorn, and sweet corn scents; lots happening here and all of it delicious. In the mouth the posh features, most notably, the textural richness and resiny/oaky flavor, don't allow the alcohol to rev up on the tongue and, as a result, the flavor phase is lip-smacking sweet and maple-like. The finish is long, ropy, smoky, and concentrated. A muscular, generously endowed bourbon whose maturity has worked in its favor, though its heft might be off-putting to some whiskey drinkers.
2001 Rating: ★★★★/Highly Recommended

The Classic Cask Selection 20 Year Old Distilled in 1983 Batch GL-108 KSBW (USA); 45.4% abv, $65.

Auburn/bronze core color with an orange rim; ideal clarity. The rich toasty aromas in the initial inhalations offer dense notes of dark caramel and nougat; another seven minutes of air contact unleash measured but potent scents of old oak, barrel char, ashes, and maple. The palate entry flavor startles the taste buds as the taste phase begins strangely metallic, medicinal, ash-like, and way over-candied; by midpalate the taste recovers slightly as elements of oak and grain emerge but not with enough gusto to redeem the serious faults found in the entry. Finishes metallic (like licking a coin), ashtray-like, burnt, and off-balance. Prime example of a bourbon that was left in the barrel for too long; somebody wasn't paying attention here.
2004 Rating: ★/Not Recommended

The Classic Cask Selection 22 Year Old Distilled in 1981 Batch RW-108 Kentucky Straight Rye Whiskey (USA); 45% abv, $70.

The deep mahogany/nut brown color shows absolute purity. The opening nosing passes find distant, but elegant aromas of almond butter, linseed oil, figs, and dates; more time in the glass affords more luxurious scents to emerge and meld, most notably, honey, molasses, and nutmeg. The palate entry is long, sweet, woody, and caramel-like; at midpalate the flavor profile turns chewy in texture and sap-like in taste. Finishes maple-like, fudge-like, and intense. A superb older rye.

2004 Rating: ★★★★/Highly Recommended

Thomas H. Handy 2006 Antique Collection Sazerac Straight Rye Whiskey (USA); 66.35% abv, $55.

The vibrant burnished orange hue is attractive and unblemished. The opening inhalations are treated to intensely spicy notes of parsley, savory, and sage; following seven minutes of additional exposure to air, the aroma shifts into fourth gear as it offers gamey, quinine-resembling, botanical-driven notes that remind me slightly of Italian bitters like Campari; a curious bouquet, to say the least. Tasted undiluted, I found the lofty abv too much to handle on its own, so I reduced it with one-ounce of room temperature mineral water and then found the sweet palate entry to be akin to marzipan, nougat, and caramel; by the midpalate stage the candied sweetness gets toned down as the taste profile once again turns spicy (again, not snappy baking spices such as cinnamon or vanilla, but leafy cooking spices like allspice, sage, etc.). Finishes elegantly, semisweet, and bacon fat-like. A controversial rye that will turn some heads.

2007 Rating: ★★★/Recommended

Van Winkle Family Reserve Rye 13 Year Old Kentucky Straight Rye Whiskey (USA); 47.8% abv, $50.

Bright, gorgeous henna/auburn/ocher color; flawless purity; as pretty an American whiskey as exists. Smells of worn leather, parchment, and uncooked beans/legumes; aeration doesn't seem to release anything more aromawise as the bouquet stays the course with the leather, writing paper, and beans. Entry is incredibly concentrated, as well as bittersweet and honeyed; the midpalate flavor profile full-weighted, chewy, oaky/vanilla-like, and reeks with cooking spices, like allspice and coriander. I like this whiskey a whole lot, but I didn't feel that this generation matched the one I first evaluated almost a decade ago.

2007 Rating: ★★★★/Highly Recommended

Van Winkle Special Reserve 12 Year Old Lot "B" Kentucky Straight Rye Whiskey (USA); 45.2% abv, $47.

Amber/topaz hue; superb clarity. The first aromas remind me most of peanuts and peanut butter, then in the later stages after further air contact the bouquet turns more fiber/textile-like and even smacks of yellow fruits, such as banana and papaya. Entry is long, oily, remarkably substantial, directed, and maple sweet; the midpalate stage features tastes of light fudge, maple, chocolate covered orange, caramel, and honey; what's so winning about the entry/midpalate phases is the finesse of this whiskey; it's so silky. Finishes as elegantly and sturdily as it begins. If there had been more grip in the bouquet, it'd have gotten a fifth star.

2007 Rating: ★★★★/Highly Recommended

Wild Turkey 101 KSBW (USA); 50.5% abv, $19.

Marginally dull honey brown color; good purity. Smells of uncooked corn and baking spices (alternately nutmeg and cinnamon); further time in the glass uncovers a leathery, grain kernel, black pepper dryness that's atypically attractive and diverting. Entry is extremely peppery and aggressive spirits-wise, but firm, meaty, and attractively focused on the corn; the fiery midpalate is potent and delightfully corny and oaky sweet, with background tastes of honey, nut paste, nougat, and black tea. Ends on a bittersweet, oaky note. Lots of unbridled power here. Approach this brawler with caution.

2007 Rating: ★★★/Recommended

Wild Turkey Kentucky Spirit Single Barrel Warehouse E Rick 13 Barrel 22 KSBW (USA); 50.5% abv, $46.

Deep bronze/burnished orange color; perfect purity. Out of the gate, the aroma is off-dry, nutty, oaky, and even a touch spicy; later sniffs reveal elements of caramel corn, popcorn, brown butter, and bacon. Entry offers round, elegant, medium-sweet tastes of oak, cereal grain, and buttered almonds; the midpalate stage is fat, bacon-like, meaty, honeyed, and ideally oaky/smoky. Taste profile keeps exploding and unfolding well into the finish. A WT/Jimmy Russell masterpiece. As deserving an American whiskey of five stars as there is.

2007 Rating: ★★★★★/Highest Recommendation

Wild Turkey Kentucky Straight Rye Whiskey (USA); 50.5% abv, $24.

The shiny, new copper penny color is unblemished and nothing short of beautiful. The tight-as-a-drum aroma after the pour is acutely spicy, cereal grain sweet, and even a touch citrusy; following seven more minutes of aeration, the aroma takes flight as fruity/resiny scents enchant the olfactory sense in their grace and integration; a near-textbook rye bouquet. The flavor at entry is laser beam-focused, snug, and concentrated; at midpalate the flavor profile goes deeply cereal-like, almost honeyed/sherried, and intense. Concludes a tad fiery (it's 101-proof, don't forget), zesty, toffee sweet, and nougat-like. I've characterized this whiskey as one of America's best-kept-whiskey-secrets for fifteen years and still feel that it's one of Master Distiller Jimmy Russell's greatest, unspoken achievements.

2005 Rating: ★★★★/Highly Recommended

Wild Turkey Rare Breed Barrel Proof Batch WT-03RB KSBW (USA); 54.1% abv, $35.

Bright topaz/amber hue; superb clarity. First sniffs detect dry notes of linoleum, new leather, and hemp; additional air contact brings out woody resin, cotton fiber, and pine aromas. Entry features well-balanced spirity heat with sweet vanilla oakiness and sweet corn piquancy; the midpalate stage is so smooth, satiny, chewy, cedary/piny, spicy, and creamed corn-like that I feel instantly compelled to take another taste. The spirity fire appears in the aftertaste along with a seductive candied walnut flavor that's a knockout.

2007 Rating: ★★★★/Highly Recommended

Wild Turkey Tribute Master Distiller Jimmy Russell's 50th Anniversary 15 Year Old KSBW (USA); 50.5% abv, $90.

The brilliant copper penny/russet color shines in the copita; there is more lazily floating sediment than I'd like to see. The first couple minutes of nosing defines for me what great

bourbon perfume is all about as rich aromas of caramel corn, marzipan and dark toffee hit all the right notes; seven minutes later the depth aspect has enlarged two-fold, emitting succulent, sweet, singed aromas of baked apple, baked pear, smoldering leaves, sweet corn, and hard candy. The palate entry is lip-smackingly delicious, sweet but lithe and racy; at midpalate the heady, fiery spirit underpins the bittersweet flavors of burnt pastry, dried red fruit, burnt cherry crisp, tar, and maple. Ends up roasted, nutty, fruity, and divinely perfect. Yet another confirmation that Jimmy Russell is without a doubt one of the three or four finest distillers America has ever produced and an artist who in his seventies is still at the top of his game; fittingly named.
2004 Rating: ★★★★★/Highest Recommendation

W. L. Weller 19 Year Old Wheated KSBW (USA); 45% abv, $40.

The brilliant bronze/new copper penny color dazzles the eye; perfect clarity. The nose is buxom, oaky, and opulent immediately following the pour; with time in the glass, the aroma turns nutty and seed-like in the second sniffing; in the penultimate whiff, after seven minutes of exposure to air, traces of oak vanillin and dried red fruit are noted; the fourth and last pass reinforces the sweet oak and vanilla presences; a sweet, muscular bouquet for the stout of heart. The palate entry is bittersweet and heavily oaked, running perhaps a bit too thick and syrupy; the midpalate phase features layered, sappy sweet flavors that flat-out overwhelm the taste buds. The finish is oily, bittersweet, and long. A stylistic bourbon that will find an audience in whiskey lovers who relish street-brawling, furniture-chewing bourbon, but will not impress those who prefer more harmonious, gentlemanly bourbons; this bruiser shows enough of its pedigree to recommend it, but just barely; good, but simply doesn't hold a candle to the legendary 10 Year Old Centennial (★★★★★).
2000 Rating: ★★★/Recommended

W.L. Weller 12 Year Old KSBW (USA); 45% abv, $17.

The deep bronze color beautifully reflects the light; perfect purity. The initial nosing pass finds fully mature aromas of lanolin, almond oil, and creamed corn; in the middle stage sniffings, following several minutes of air contact, a toasty oaky/vanilla perfume takes the aromatic helm; the fourth and last whiff highlights the oily/grainy quality that's firm and pungent; a high-spirited, lusciously toasty, and animated bouquet that has top-notch bourbon written all over it. The dry, complex, and toasty palate entry is reminiscent of the Centennial 10 Year Old's grand entry; the midpalate flavor profile is heavily wheated (like Wheat Thins crackers), oily, layered, moderately sweet, and sap-like. The finish is long, sweet, oaky, and intensely grainy. Follows in the footprints of the legendary Centennial and delivers the goods, all for an unbelievable price.
2001 Rating: ★★★★★/Highest Recommendation

William Larue Weller 2006 Antique Collection KSBW (USA); 64.95% abv, $55.

The gleaming copper color of this whiskey is breathtakingly lovely and flawlessly clear. In the first whiffs, I detect strangely alluring, if amorphous notes of cardboard, Wheat Thins crackers, and oak; over the next seven minutes of air contact, the aroma transforms into a bouquet as it emits wonderfully odd, even incongruous, fragrances of parchment, allspice, hemp, savory, and bitter green leaf vegetable (kale, escarole?). The palate entry with the addition of mineral water is incredibly luxurious, deeply honeyed, almost sherried, and nutty; by the midpalate stage the taste profile has spun off the chart for caramel/toffee succulence, yet is not in the least oversweet or gummy. Finishes deep, full-bodied (that's an understatement), chocolaty, and cake frosting-like. The weirdly indecisive aroma took away the fifth rating star.

2007 Rating: ★★★★/Highly Recommended

William Larue Weller Limited Edition 12 Year Old Uncut Unfiltered Barrel Proof KSBW (USA); 60.95% abv, $55.
The henna/auburn/copper color is stunning in its brilliance and impeccable clarity. Right from the crack of the aromatic bat this fragrance is alive with scents of pepper, oak, caramel corn, and new leather; further aeration stimulates the bouquet by adding elegant (this is barrel strength?) scents of blackberry pastry, plums, light toffee, and pipe tobacco; an amazing aroma that never even for a second is hot, prickly or too potent. The palate entry is astoundingly rich, deeply honey-like, and gently warming (this is barrel strength?); the midpalate stage features tastes of marshmallow, caramel corn, sautéed almonds, nougat, figs, and dates. Finishes composed, calm, and deeply, flavorfully sweet. When mineral water is added, the taste components especially accelerate to classic status. Technically speaking, wow, wow, wowee.

2006 Rating: ★★★★★/Highest Recommendation

Woodford Reserve Distiller's Select KSBW (USA); 45.2% abv, $30.
The lovely bronze color shines in the light; absolute purity. The first few sniffs detect restrained, lightly roasted kernel/bean-like scents; additional undisturbed time in the copita opens up the bouquet as added aromas of saddle leather, tobacco leaf, and walnut eventually come to the fore. The palate entry is semisweet, candied, and creamy; by midpalate the taste profile includes pepper, welcome spirity heat, oak resin, and caramel corn. Ends gracefully and leanly, showing the delicate, ultra-sophisticated side of bourbon. A world-class whiskey.

2004 Rating: ★★★★/Highly Recommended

Woodford Reserve Master's Collection Four Grain KSBW (USA); 46.2% abv, $80.
The four grains are corn, malted barley, rye, and wheat. The beautiful topaz/brown color is impeccably pure and dazzling to the eye. The first whiff encounters a strong, multigrain bread aroma that's earthy, kernel-like, and totally dry; further nosings after another six minutes of aeration add odd but not unpleasant notes as new carpet fiber/synthetic, bran muffins, roasted nuts and muesli/dry breakfast cereal scents dominate the latter nosing phase. While I feel the aroma was only mildly intriguing, if not a touch flat, the palate entry has my taste buds dancing to the tunes of sweet grain bread like honey wheat, toasty, sweet oak, and light honey; the midpalate stage is round, elegant, mildly buttery/oily, and gently honeyed. Finishes well in an understated manner as the dryness found in the aroma returns to a degree in the pleasingly easy aftertaste. I look forward to future bottlings of this adventurous idea, hatched from the brain of Master Distiller Chris Morris.

2006 Rating: ★★★/Recommended

Woodford Reserve Master's Collection Sonoma-Cutrer Finish KSBW (USA); 43.2% abv, $90.

Brilliant copper coin/burnished orange/saffron color; flawless clarity. Initial whiffs pick up warm, inviting smells of buttered popcorn, flax/textile, beeswax, and hemp/rope; following another seven minutes of swirling and contact with air, the aroma leans more in the direction of flax/fiber/cloth than grain or wood and I can't help but wonder if the chardonnay oak influence has mitigated some of the foundational bourbon character, at least aromatically. Entry is dry to off-dry and toasty and grainy; the critical midpalate point is punctuated with an overlapping taste of wine/sherry that mingles well with the intense graininess that (to my relief) assertively comes back into the picture. Concludes in an angular manner as the parting taste turns acidic (again, the wine barrel?), grainy, and lean. My feeling is that the wine barrel has sissified this bourbon. Interesting, but, for me, it misses the mark.

2007 Rating: ★★/Not Recommended

Whisky—Canada

Canada's first licensed distillery opened in 1769. Column still distillation is the driving force, as is a philosophy that focuses on the art of blending. The acknowledged thumbprint character of almost all Canadian whiskies is their delightful drinkability. Canadian whiskies are typically made from a majority of corn and lesser portions of rye and barley. Canadian whiskies are matured in barrels for a legal minimum of three years. Interestingly, as opposed to the rigors of governmentally imposed production regulations south of the border in the US, Canada's whisky industry is largely self-regulated and is thus a significant departure from other whiskey making nations.

This liberal system has triumphed for a century and a half as Canadian whiskies have flourished globally and have come to be viewed as reliable and welcome libations. Two pivotal companies, Hiram Walker and Joseph E. Seagram, led the charge in the 19th century and their brands still dominate to this day. In recent years, however, smaller distilleries, like Forty Creek in Ontario and Glenora in Nova Scotia, have raised the bar in terms of offering more idiosyncratic whiskies.

Black Velvet Blended Canadian Whisky (Canada); 40% abv, $11.
The pale gold color shows perfect purity. The opening aroma is soft, a touch herbal, and properly grainy; aeration time of another six minutes adds simple scents of marshmallow and cedar. The palate entry is creamy at first, and then turns a little hard-edged in the acidity department; at midpalate there are muted tastes of roasted hazelnuts and cereal grains. Concludes flat, very lean and acidic, but drinkable. An acceptable mixing whisky.
2005 Rating: ★★/Not Recommended

Canadian Club 100 Proof 6 Year Old Blended Canadian Whisky (Canada); 50% abv, $18.
Harvest gold color; excellent purity. Opening nose hints surprisingly of a bit too much spirity harshness; the aroma collects itself during aeration and comes off far better and more sophisticated in the fruity, fruitcake-like second pass. Entry is raw and hot; I don't remember this type of heat and sweetness the last time I evaluated this whisky; the midpalate recovers a bit, offering succulent notes of honey, sherry, and chocolate covered orange slices. Ends sweet and fruity. What's happened to this formerly impressive Canadian whisky?
2007 Rating: ★★/Not Recommended

Canadian Club 6 Year Old Blended Canadian Whisky (Canada); 40% abv, $14.

The pale golden/straw yellow hue is ideally pure. The first whiff of intense grain spirits reminds me amazingly of Eastern European vodka more than what I've come to think of as Canadian whisky; by the later inhalations, following the seven minute aeration period, the bouquet offers scents of cream, wild flowers, and honey. The palate entry features the cream, both in the flavor sense and the texture sense; by midpalate the taste profile expands to include flavors of cocoa, milk chocolate, and buttercream. The aftertaste is sweet, long, and creamy. Neither profound nor distinctive, but displays enough character in its core and obvious potential as a mixing whisky to be recommended specifically for lovers of whisky cocktails. Sipping whisky aficionados need not apply.

2005 Rating: ★★★/Recommended

Canadian Club Classic 12 Year Old Blended Canadian Whisky (Canada); 40% abv, $20.

Unblemished honey/amber hue. The deep notes of butterscotch right out of the gate are lush and compelling; additional time in the glass brings out nougat, almond paste, and light vanilla. The palate entry features succulent and evolved flavors of almond paste, hard butter/caramel/nut candy, and oaky vanilla; the midpalate stage is woody, caramel-like, with hints of dried yellow fruit, white pepper, and spice. Finishes balanced, sweet, and oaky. A very solid Canadian whisky from start to finish.

2007 Rating: ★★★★/Highly Recommended

Canadian Club Reserve 10 Year Old Blended Canadian Whisky (Canada); 40% abv, $16.

Flawlessly clean harvest gold/topaz color. The aroma in the first couple of minutes is reluctant and oddly chalky; vigorous swirling and further air contact do little to stimulate more fragrance, other than a dullish parchment note. The palate entry is lean, even metallic (like coins); the midpalate shows more flair and grainy taste (breakfast cereal), but hardly enough to transport my taste buds to a state of bliss. Drinkable, yes; memorable, no. How can a 10 year old whisky of any category be so common and lackluster?

2007 Rating: ★★/Not Recommended

Canadian Club Sherry Cask Blended Canadian Whisky (Canada); 41.3% abv, $24.

The gorgeous color is a clean topaz/amber; superb clarity. The initial whiffs detect potent spirity notes that ride on top of more subtle marshmallow and toffee scents; additional aeration doesn't add that much in the way of aromatic expansion or deepening, except for the addition of walnut butter. The palate entry is robust, nutty, semisweet, and honeyed; by the midpalate stage the taste profile is nougaty, mildly cocoa-like, sherried (big surprise), and marzipan-like. Concludes with flavors of dried red fruits, sherry, and dark caramel. A sweetfest that's more a guilty pleasure than a connoisseur's moment.

2007 Rating: ★★★★/Highly Recommended

Canadian Heritage Century Reserve 21 Year Old Small Batch Canadian Whisky (Canada); 60% abv, $100.

Sampled unadulterated first, then with water added to reduce the alcohol. Matured in old bourbon barrels. Pale amber color. The bouquet after the pour is pleasantly heady, piquant, and spicy, with touches of vanilla wafer and mint; later nosings after aeration reveal traces of menthol and marshmallow; with water added, the bouquet turns slightly candied, but focused. In the mouth the entry flavor is rich, biscuity, and honeyed; at the midpalate point traces of dark caramel, vanilla extract, and brown sugar highlight this very sweet taste phase. The finish is extended, concentrated, honeyed, and grainy in a sweet manner. A plump, thick, and velvety whisky that is short on subtlety but long on ripe, sugary flavor; reduce with mineral water right away.

2001 Rating: ★★★★/Highly Recommended

Canadian Mist Blended Canadian Whisky (Canada); 40% abv, $10.

The harvest gold/topaz color is pure and lovely. The first few whiffs encounter sweet, maple-like aromas; later inhalations detect dark caramel, honey, and vanilla extract. The palate entry is sweet, corny and honey-like; at midpalate the sweetness accelerates into a cotton candy, nougat, candy bar effect that's surprisingly palatable and easy. Finishes caramel sweet but simple. Hardly a benchmark Canadian whisky but one that is perfect for whisky cocktails of all sorts; its biggest drawback is its high level of sweetness.

2004 Rating: ★★/Not Recommended

Crown Royal Fine Deluxe Blended Canadian Whisky (Canada); 40% abv, $24.

The attractive honey/amber cloak is clean as a whistle. The opening sniffs locate hints of pine tar, dark caramel, and maple syrup; aeration deepens the bouquet and adds subtle notes of brown sugar and honey. The palate entry features the light toffee flavor and the smooth as silk texture; by midpalate there's a mild explosion of dried fruit and chocolate cherry flavors. Quiet, mild conclusion. I've tasted this lovely low-key whisky several times in the last few months, wanting always to like it more than three stars. I always find that there's something almost unidentifiable that prevents me from taking that leap to the next step. I like it very much, but I still don't love it, no matter how hard I try.

2004 Rating: ★★★/Recommended

Crown Royal Special Reserve Blended Canadian Whisky (Canada); 40% abv, $40.

The brown/wood paneling color shows a touch of orange/bronze in the core and perfect purity; gorgeous to sit and look at. The first whiffs pick up stunningly deep aromas that include honey, sherry, dried fruit, spearmint, and nougat; that's just in the first two minutes of nosing; further aeration stimulates more exotic aromas such as English Breakfast tea, cocoa butter, and tropical fruit (papaya?). The palate entry caresses the taste buds, wrapping them in thick, chewy layers of dry flavors, especially bittersweet chocolate and black tea; at midpalate the flavor shifts into overdrive, offering racy tastes of brown sugar, honey-coated peanuts, melon, and sherry. Finishes as elegantly as it began in a sumptuous wave of nougat and candy bar. One of North America's ten best, most complex whiskeys. No doubt in my mind that it's a modern day classic and Canada's foremost whisky at present. Nothing short of incredible.

2004 Rating: ★★★★★/Highest Recommendation

Crown Royal XR Extra Rare Blended Canadian Whisky (Canada); 40% abv, $150.

The burnished orange/bronze color is bright; slight bits of sediment seen. The first nosing passes pick up rich, pastry/cake scents that are more fruity than spicy, bringing to mind banana bread or lemon/poppy seed cake; seven more minutes in the glass stimulate deeper fragrances of old oak, figs, dates, and prunes. The palate entry is creamy but not thick, engagingly nutty and tightly focused, acidic, and fresh; the midpalate stage offers long, expansive tastes of oak resin, paraffin, nougat, and walnut paste. Concludes elegantly, sinewy, and off-dry rather than sweet. This whisky has it all: grace, potent but not overwhelming flavor presence, and most of all, harmony.

2006 Rating: ★★★★★/Highest Recommendation

Dr. McGillicuddy's Fireball Cinnamon Flavored Whisky (Canada); 33% abv, $14.

Pretty, light bronze/amber hue; good purity. Right from the pour the bittersweet cinnamon fragrance dominates the aroma through all four nosing passes over a ten minute span; nothing more to report. The palate entry is sweet, concentrated on spice, and very candied; the midpalate is, well, cinnamony, from wall-to-wall and cloyingly sweet. The finish is moderately fiery, zesty, prickly, and sweet. I could see where this overly sweet concoction might hold some appeal for the very young drinking crowd; beyond that, I can't conceive of too many palatable applications.

2001 Rating: ★★/Not Recommended

Forty Creek Barrel Select Canadian Whisky (Canada); 40% abv, $20.

Pretty topaz/honey hue; some black/brown sediment noted under the evaluation lamp. The inviting nose at opening is liberally laced with sweet notes of oak resin, marzipan, and light caramel; the middle stage sniffings offer a broader, more robust, and buttery bouquet, one that concentrates on the creamy aspect of seasoned oak barrels; the final whiff finds slight diminishment in intensity but remains firm in its butterscotch, cream, and cake frosting mode; ultracandied, thick, and chunky. The palate entry is dry at first, then the butteriness makes it seem sweet and creamy by midpalate when the caramel/marzipan tag-team dominates the ring. The extended finish is rich, honeyed, and fatty. If it were my creation, I'd rechristen it "Butterscotch Select"; sweet and sticky to the point of not being everyone's cup of whisky, especially most Scotch whisky or Irish whiskey aficionados, but for enthusiasts of North American whiskeys, an intriguing, if borderline gummy dram.

2001 Rating: ★★★/Recommended

Forty Creek Three Grain Canadian Whisky (Canada); 40% abv, $20.

The trio of grains are malted barley, maize, and rye; the autumnal color is bronze/burnished orange; minor floating particles are noted. This opening aroma is considerably more interesting and complex than that of the fat 'n fuzzy Barrel Select; with time in the glass, this aroma transforms into a solid whisky bouquet by the third sniffing, offering dry, grainy notes of morning cereal, perfumy barley, and oak; the final nosing pass, after almost ten minutes of aeration, detects distant hints of rye bread, nut meat, and dried fruit (Christmas-style fruit cake?); there's no doubt that this bouquet is superior to the Barrel Select as a race horse is to a plow horse. The palate entry is dry and nutty; then the midpalate tastes explode on the tongue in waves of butterscotch, trail mix (nuts and fruit), and holiday spice; while the malted barley rules the nose, the rye reigns supreme in the flavor. The finish is long, dry to off-dry, and immensely satisfying. Lovers of sweeter Speyside single malts, like Macallan or Aberlour, would most likely appreciate this finely made whisky from the north country.

2001 Rating: ★★★/Highly Recommended

Glen Breton (Glenora) Canadian Single Malt Whisky (Canada); 43% abv, $80.
No age statement given. Produced from malted barley, yeast, and water, as are the single malts of Scotland. The pale straw yellow hue is pretty and gleaming beneath the examination light; perfect purity. The opening nosing passes detect lovely, ripe, and clean scents of spice, dried banana, untreated cotton fiber, and cinnamon/nutmeg; further exposure to air brings out additional delicate aromas, including ginger, egg cream, and just a barely discernable hint of honey. The palate entry offers a zesty, spirity warmth on the tip of the tongue; by midpalate the pleasing distillate tingle gives way to a round, medium-bodied taste profile that features honey coated cereal, sweet oak, and candied almond. Finishes elegantly, smoldering warm, and more resiny bittersweet than honey sweet. A world-class malt whisky from the Glenora Distillery in Nova Scotia.
2005 Rating: ★★★★/Highly Recommended

Gold Very Light Canadian Whisky A Blend (Canada); 40% abv, $8.
Attractive, straw/gold color; superb purity. The first sniffs pick up delicate, gently sweet, grainy aromas that are simple but mildly alluring; six more minutes of air contact stimulate more of the grainy, caramel-like sweetness, with a backdoor trace of almonds; an uncomplicated and perfectly acceptable bouquet. The palate entry makes no lofty statement and, as such, comes off being pleasingly sweet in a candy/sugary manner; the midpalate is sugary then leans more towards honey in the finish. The whole taste experience doesn't even hint at wood or fruit or oil; modest, unpretentious, and, to my shock, drinkable, therefore, recommendable only for whisky neophytes or for drinkers who are looking for a sweeter style of blended whisky to employ in cocktails; serious whisky mavens shouldn't even consider this rudimentary whisky in their wildest dreams.
2003 Rating: ★★/Not Recommended

Hirsch Selection 10 Year Old Canadian Rye Whisky (Canada); 43% abv, $38.
Pale gold/green color; superb clarity. The initial sniffings encounter faint traces of cedar/ evergreen and fresh garden herbs; later inhalations following a seven minute aeration period turn up little more than what was noted in the first whiffs, maybe except for a trace of oaky sweetness. The palate entry is sweet, oaky, and amiable; the midpalate stage is less sweet than the sibling 8 Year Old, showing a bit of resiny astringency that counters the caramel sweetness. Ends up with ample focus, some tasty mellowness, but ultimately not enough core character or innate finesse to be recommended.
2005 Rating: ★★/Not Recommended

Hirsch Selection 12 Year Old Canadian Rye Whisky (Canada); 43% abv, $44.
The identical pale gold/green color of the 10 Year Old; unblemished clarity. Smells of solvent/pine cleanser in the very first sniffings; shows a bit more typical whisky odor in the later whiffs as scents of cedar, maple sap, and green vegetation abound. The palate entry is engagingly sweet and full-bodied; by the midpalate stage the taste profile expands to include light toffee, oak resin, and unsweetened coconut. Finishes bittersweet, spirity warm, and biscuity/wafer-like.
2005 Rating: ★★★/Recommended

Hirsch Selection 8 Year Old Canadian Rye Whisky (Canada); 43% abv, $31.

Firm gold/harvest yellow color; better than average clarity. The first whiffs pick up toasty/roasted and moderately sweet notes of S'mores-at-campfire, violets, and marshmallow; six more minutes of air contact add scents of dried flowers, dried cooking herbs, light English toffee, and milk chocolate; this is not a profound bouquet, but is accommodating enough to be considered friendly. The palate entry is semi-rich and candy sweet; at midpalate the flavor profile is dominated by the candy sweetness and brown sugar/molasses with scant grain evidence. Concludes concentrated and sugary sweet. The SJ non-recommendation reads as follows: An uncomplicated, inoffensive, wholly unexceptional beginner Canadian rye whisky, but one that would be too simple, one-dimensional, and plump for savvier medium-acumen drinkers and/or connoisseurs.

2005 Rating: ★★/Not Recommended

Monarch Canadian Blended Whisky (Canada); 40% abv, $10.

The pale gold/corn yellow color is pretty; superb clarity. The opening nosings detect cooked corn, charcoal, and palm oil; simple notes of butterscotch and light toffee enter the aromatic picture following seven minutes of aeration. The palate entry is sappy, honeyed, and pleasantly sweet; the midpalate stage showcases maple, honey, and caramel. Ends up clean, focused, and maple sugar sweet.

2007 Rating: ★★★/Recommended

Pendleton 10 Year Old Blended Canadian Whisky (Canada); 40% abv, $26.

Lovely bronze/burnished orange color; impeccable purity. The opening whiffs detect mature, oily/buttery scents of almond butter and oleo margarine; seven more minutes of exposure to air introduce delicate traces of oak resin, pepper, palm oil, and oloroso sherry. The palate entry is succulent and honeyed; by the midpalate stage the flavor profile has gone BIG in oily texture and honey/sherry-like taste on the tongue. The aftertaste is long, honey sweet, and even a touch toffee-like. What put me over the top in terms of recommended/not recommended was the silky, oily texture and the sherry-like taste; hardly a great Canadian whisky in the league of Crown Royal Special Reserve, but a more than respectable one that deserves attention.

2003 Rating: ★★★/Recommended

Pendleton Director's Reserve 2005 20 Year Old Blended Canadian Whisky (Canada); 40% abv, $75.

Bronze/burnished orange hue; shows some initial haziness after the pour but that clears up after about two minutes. The first bursts of aroma offer earthy scents of wet forest, pine, and cedar; later nosing passes pick up additional supplemental scents of light caramel, light honey, and coffee with milk. The palate entry is richly sweet and sugary; by midpalate the honey character turns more like cream sherry/Pedro Ximenez sherry and dates. The finish is toffee sweet and fudge-like. The taste and aftertaste phases really pull the sled on this whisky after the understated bouquet. In fact, they pull it so ably and with such vigor that it deserves four stars.

2005 Rating: ★★★★/Highly Recommended

The Revelstoke Canadian Spiced Whisky (Canada); 40% abv, $17/liter.

Medium amber hue, some floating sediment. The opening nosing pass discovers a candy sweet, minty aroma; aeration doesn't help the mintiness blow off, in fact, it seems to stimulate it to the point where the bouquet is like that of a liqueur, not a whisky; following nine minutes of air contact the bouquet hasn't budged one inch from its original candy/honey/minty state. More pleasing in the mouth than in the nose; the palate entry is overly sweet, slightly woody, and minted; by the midpalate stage a taste of whisky finally shows itself, but by then the damage has been done. The aftertaste is disgustingly sweet.

2001 Rating: ★/Not Recommended

Windsor Canadian Blended Canadian Whisky (Canada); 40% abv, $9.

The topaz/honey hue is very attractive and ideally pure. Aroma-wise, this whisky is clean, tucked in, but dull in the first two minutes after the pour; seven minutes of further air contact produce virtually nothing in terms of expansion or deepening. The palate entry is pleasantly grainy, uncomplicated, and candy sweet; at midpalate there's a firm thrust of dark caramel/fudge but that's it. Ends up moderately tasty, very sweet, and candied. Nothing special here. An all-purpose mixing whisky.

2005 Rating: ★★/Not Recommended

WHISKEY—WORLD

Whiskey production isn't the sole province of Ireland, Scotland, the United States, and Canada. Fine grain-based whiskeys are produced in Japan, New Zealand, and India. While this section isn't as long as I'd like, I will be focusing on reviewing more international whiskeys over the next few years for the next *Kindred Spirits* edition.

Milford 10 Year Old Single Malt Whisky Distilled in 1991 Batch 1M32 (New Zealand); 43% abv, $38.

Displays a pretty amber hue; also sports more sediment that I'd like to see. The opening sniffs discover a tightly wound aroma that says several things: chalk, minerals, flowers, and cowhide; aeration stimulates scents that include gum, allspice, ginger, saddle leather, and pencil eraser. The palate entry is dry and astringent; at midpalate a flash of smoke/peat makes things momentarily interesting, but then the mineral-like taste returns. Finishes spicy/gingery and moderately grainy. Due to its wandering, inconsistent, loose-ends personality I almost didn't give it a third star, but I feel that there's enough innate quality here to give better than average drinking pleasure.

2004 Rating: ★★★/Recommended

Penderyn Madeira Finish, Non-Chill Filtered Single Malt Whisky (Wales); 46% abv, $70.

Aged first in once-used bourbon barrels, then finished in Madeira wood. Appearance-wise, this whisky is impeccably pure and the color of fresh honey and straw. The first nosing emits friendly, fruity scents of baked banana and spiced apple; more air contact stimulates the grain element which is dry, kernel- and cereal-like; I don't detect much in the way of wood influence in the bouquet other than a low-key spiciness. The palate entry is semisweet, oaky, concentrated, grainy, and smooth; the midpalate stage mirrors the entry but with more emphasis on the oak. Finishes elegantly, with a bittersweet dash of vanilla bean. A bit more complexity in the midpalate and aftertaste would have made it eligible for a fourth rating star. A sterling single malt debut from Wales that has me looking forward with keen anticipation to future releases.

2006 Rating: ★★★/Recommended

Suntory "Yamazaki" 12 Year Old Single Malt Whisky (Japan); 43% abv, $40.

Golden/amber/wheat field-in-August color; excellent purity. The first nosing passes display a toasted grain/dry cereal quality that's very alluring; another seven minutes stimulate deeper, more complex aromas, in particular, toasted wheat bread, nougat, and light toffee.

The palate entry is clean, lean, and off-dry; at midpalate the flavor goes on the offensive, offering delicate waves of nut butter, roasted barley, almond pastry, and toffee. Concludes gracefully and off-dry. While it's good enough to stand and compete on its own, there is an echo-like similarity to a second tier Speyside malt.

2004 Rating: ★★★/Recommended

Suntory "Yamazaki" 18 Year Old Single Malt Whisky (Japan); 43% abv, $100.

The attractive burnt orange/burnished appearance is attractive and superbly pure. The opening bouquet offers sap-like, resiny notes of cigar box and pipe tobacco; further aeration brings out complex aromas of buttered popcorn, old leather, and sausages. The palate entry is long, silky, and wonderfully sap- and maple-like; the midpalate is firm, sweet, grainy, nougaty, and creamy. Finishes fiery, spirited, intensely grainy, and sophisticated. For comparison's sake, I'd liken this to a robust Eastern Highlands malt such as Lochnagar; a delicious treat.

2004 Rating: ★★★★/Highly Recommended

BRANDY

Cognac—France

The French government has demarcated six grape growing areas that fan out in irregular concentric circles from the core cities of Cognac, Jarnac, and Segonzac. The bulls-eye district is **Grande Champagne**, whose friable, chalky soils produce grapes which when fermented and distilled turn into long-lived brandies of great distinction. Approximately 13,000 hectares (or 32,110 acres) in Grande Champagne are devoted to cultivating the grapes that make Cognac. Cradling Grande Champagne are the larger **Petite Champagne** district (16,000 hectares/39,520 acres under vine) and the compact **Borderies** district (4,000 hectares/9,880 acres). Encircling Grande Champagne, Petite Champagne, and Borderies is **Fins Bois**, a vast area of limestone soils that covers over 350,000 hectares, 33,000 of which are planted to vineyard. Around Fins Bois lies the even bigger Bons Bois (386,000 hectares). The least crucial in terms of quality impact is Bois à Terroir, which sits at ocean's edge on the Atlantic. The districts of major influence are Grande Champagne, Petite Champagne, Borderies, and Fins Bois. In all, a total of nearly 80,000 hectares/197,600 acres are under vine in the six districts.

One of the distinctions of cognac is the use of a copper pot still called the Charentais still. French law dictates that Charentais stills may not hold more than 690 gallons. Small pot stills, like these, are known, by tradition, to distill spirits of high quality and individuality. To achieve the cleanest spirits, the Cognaçais distill twice, but as decreed by law, at never higher than 72% alcohol. The lower the alcohol, the more character is left behind. Once the fresh spirits (referred to as eaux-de-vie) are drawn off the pot still, they are placed in French oak barrels (from oak harvested from the Limousin and Tronçais forests, usually) that hold from 75 to 125 gallons for maturation. Many of Cognac's cellars are subterranean and are, therefore, humid, dark, and steady in temperature.

Cognacs are classified by age and how much time they've spent in oak barrels. Here is the breakdown:

- *Cognac VS/Three Stars:* 2 year minimum in barrels.
- *Cognac VSOP:* 4 year minimum.
- *Cognac XO/Hors d'Age/Napoleon/Extra:* 6 year minimum.
- *Cognac Vintage:* Grapes must all come from the harvest year displayed on the label.

Last, I'd like to see more of an intrepid approach by the close-to-the-vest Cognaçais, meaning, more intriguing bottlings, such as cask strengths and vintages. These are slowly beginning to appear. Make no mistake: I love cognac and everything it stands for, but it's time to release brandies that are more exciting than the current predictable roster. The brandies exist; cut them loose and delight the daylights out of every brandy lover in the world.

A. Edmond Audry Exception Fine Champagne Cognac (France); 43% abv, $250.

The deep brown/copper penny hue reminds me of the color of a top quality amontillado sherry; perfect purity. This aroma's maturity and poise are evident right from the first whiff as delicate fragrances of old oak, dark toffee, and baked pears enchant the olfactory sense; the second pass unearths even more aromatic treasures in the forms of almond paste, nougat, and mild spice; in the third sniffing, after five minutes of air contact, I notice a very slight diminishment in strength, but the bouquet turns biscuity and buttery and emits the initial fatty/cheesy signals of rancio presence; after allowing it to sit for another five minutes I'm delighted by what is now clear evidence of the most coveted cognac virtue of all, the nuance of rancio, the gifted child of oxidation. The palate entry is opulent, lip-smacking, and sweet as tastes of butter cream, bittersweet chocolate, dark coffee, and bacon fat dazzle the taste buds; the midpalate point is rich, silky, and even a tad fiery as the spirit rears its head in a friendly way. The aftertaste is divinely cheesy/fatty, oaky, and sweet. The all-too-rare brandy that makes my evaluation day.

2000 Rating: ★★★★★/Highest Recommendation

A. Edmond Audry Lorfund Trois Etoiles Three Star VS Cognac (France); 40% abv, $40.

Sunshine yellow/hay color; excellent clarity. The nose in the initial pass is spirity, green (young), and mineral-like; with exposure to air, the aroma deepens as scents of lead pencil and black pepper take the lead; in the penultimate nosing after five to six minutes of aeration the aroma turns into a biscuity bouquet, one that's supported by the immature/underripe fruit/slate foundation; in the fourth and final aromatic run-through I detect an additional hard cider scent that's way in the background but clearly evident just the same; no question, however, that the mineral/lead/pepper teaming still rules. It's every bit as angular in the mouth as it is in the nasal cavity as the entry shows a green, taut, nearly awkward cognac that flashes signs of potential vanilla creaminess later on; the midpalate strives to be pleasant but it's just too ham-fisted and undeveloped to make it. The finish is lean, stringy, mildly toasty, and vegetal. I feel strongly that though released within the legal maturation limits, this cognac was rushed to market without adequate aging time in wood and, of course, ratings have to be bestowed on the present reality, not on potential.

2000 Rating: ★★/Not Recommended

A. Edmond Audry Mémorial Fine Champagne Cognac (France); 42% abv, $150.

Lovely burnished orange/copper color; impeccable clarity. The opening nosing detects fey traces of green pepper, green apple, and in keeping with the house style, lead pencil; with help from aeration, the aroma turns into a bouquet in the second pass as rich scents of spice and oak resin get added to the mix; the penultimate whiff, following over six minutes of air contact, sees the spice drop off and the bittersweet oakiness/fattiness take charge so that the bouquet approaches a rancio condition; in the fourth and last sniffing, the delicate, raisiny, dried fruit-like rancio is the featured attribute; a stellar bouquet. The palate entry is polite, semisweet, caramelly, and breathtakingly luscious; the midpalate phase highlights the bacon fat/rancio/oaky quality to the maximum, making for a very memorable taste phase. The finish is long, sweet, honeyed, satiny, and delicious. This is a true winner that's notable for equal parts finesse and power; graceful, superb!

2000 Rating: ★★★★★/Highest Recommendation

A. Edmond Audry Réserve Spéciale Fine Champagne Cognac (France); 40% abv, $80.

Very pretty bronze/burnished orange hue, but with minor floating debris. The opening aroma is oaky and mildly buttery; with air contact, the buttery quality turns fatty (read, bacon fat) and intensely woody and resiny which I like as long as it's controlled; by the third nosing pass, the oaky feature starts to turn vanilla bean-like and the bouquet becomes quite toasted/roasted; the fourth and final sniffing reveals further deepening of the vanilla/burnt almond features so as to become very nougaty and bittersweet; I like this dry, toasty bouquet very much. The palate entry is long, oily, and sweet at the end in a dark caramel manner; by the midpalate the caramel is joined by old oak in the taste pattern, making for a mature but lean flavor profile. The aftertaste shows hints of black tea, very old oak, and dark caramel. This cognac has lots going for it including the fair suggested retail price.
2000 Rating: ★★★★/Highly Recommended

A. Edmond Audry Très Ancienne Lot 43 Grande Champagne Cognac (France); 50% abv, $350.

Attractive, bronze/copper color; excellent purity. The high alcohol is obvious right from the initial sniffing as prickly, but controlled aromas of buckwheat, brown sugar, and oak vie for dominance; with aeration, the aroma develops into a bouquet by the second pass as succulent, bittersweet scents of lead pencil, vanilla bean, and caramel come together; in the third nosing pass nuances of black pepper and toasted almonds emerge, but do not dominate; following nearly ten minutes of aeration, the bouquet remains as pungent and firm as found in the first whiff; no clear signs of rancio are detected in this bouquet, though it offers other extremely pleasant qualities. The palate entry is buttery and spirity on the tongue; by midpalate the spirity fire gets more serious and threatens to vanquish all other flavors which include baked pear, spice, black pepper, and toffee. The finish is long, a bit lean, oaky, and prickly. While I very much admire this old cognac distilled in 1943, I prefer the sensational Exception and Mémorial due primarily to their exquisite balance.
2000 Rating: ★★★★/Highly Recommended

A. Edmond Audry XO Fine Champagne Cognac (France); 40% abv, $60.

Attractive amber/honey hue; ideal purity. The first nosing pass after the pour reminds me instantly of the Lorfund Trois Etoiles as the aroma is laced with lead pencil and black pepper, though this shows more oakiness and maturity; by the second go-round, there's a fine note of lanolin; the pepperiness accelerates in the third nosing actually surging past the lead pencil and oily lanolin scent; the fourth pass, following nearly eight minutes of air exposure, offers in-your-face aromas of wood resin, wet slate, black pepper, and dried herbs; this bold aroma is one that I like, not because it's elegant which it is not, but because there's so much vitality. The palate entry is semisweet as muscular and lean tastes of caramel and toffee greet the taste buds; the midpalate is slightly less forceful as the flavor of bacon fat overrides the caramel. The finish is long, fatty, bitter sweet, and moderately oily; interesting and certainly recommendable.
2000 Rating: ★★★/Recommended

A. Hardy Napoléon Cognac (France); 40% abv, $50.

This eye-catching appearance is highlighted by the bronze hue and copper core; flawless purity. The opening nosing passes detect seductive scents of vanilla, nutmeg, and sweet oak;

another seven minutes of air contact introduces saddle leather and palm oil to the compelling mix of fragrances. The palate entry is sweet, but not cloying, chocolatey, and fruity; at the midpalate juncture the sweetness becomes a serious factor in that suddenly, it explodes on the palate, drowning out all other taste aspects, which for some cognac lovers would be attractive. Finishes sweet, silky, and assertive, with summary tastes of chocolate covered cherries. A truly savory, robust Napoleon cognac; I would have scored it higher had it been more nuanced and less aggressive with the sweetness. I like it a lot, but I'd never love it.
2007 Rating: ★★★/Recommended

A. Hardy Noces d'Or 50 Year Old Grande Champagne Cognac (France); 40% abv, $150/bottle or $500/crystal decanter.

Deep amber/bronze in color; perfect purity. The opening nosings pick up distant, delicate fruity/viny aromas in the forms of red fruit and grapes; time in the glass allows the bouquet to stretch its legs a bit as more expressive aromas such as pine, honeysuckle, and oak come alive and give this bouquet some shape and animation. In the mouth, the divinely sweet flavors of dark caramel, honey, oloroso sherry, candied walnuts, and spiced pears make for intriguing and beguiling tasting from palate entry through midpalate. It closes beautifully as rich, warming tastes of tea, cedar, tobacco, and honey excite the taste buds. The inviting, assertive flavor and finish phases deeply impress.
2002 Rating: ★★★★/Highly Recommended

A. Hardy Noces de Diamant 60 Year Old Grande Champagne Cognac (France); 40% abv, $500/crystal decanter.

The color is bronze/topaz; admirably pure. For a 60 year old cognac the opening bouquet is stunningly vivacious, compelling, and firm as biscuity, spicy/botanical waves of black pepper, milk chocolate, and oaky vanilla vie for dominance; eight more minutes sees the bouquet turn fruity, ripe, mildly spirity, and leathery. The palate entry is firmly structured, candied, grapy, and appropriately woody/resiny. On the palate, it's rich, grapy, honeyed, marzipan-like, and nougaty. The aftertaste is ripe, sweet, and intensely caramel-like. I absolutely loved it from start to finish.
2002 Rating: ★★★★★/Highest Recommendation

A. Hardy Noces de Perle 30 Year Old Grande Champagne Cognac (France); 40% abv, $500/crystal decanter.

Bottled in a crystal decanter; lovely amber/honey hue, excellent purity. The initial nosing pass detects a mildly spicy bouquet that's ready to fly right from the start; aeration doesn't really deepen this nose as much as it sweetens it in comely notes of toffee, brown sugar, leather, and vanilla extract. The palate entry is treated to a sap-like, sugary, oaky sweet burst of sprightly taste on the tip of the tongue; the midpalate shows generous flavors of pineapple, guava, mint, caramel, and oak resin. The aftertaste is firm, semisweet, and more fruity than woody. Terrifically satisfying and full, yet racy.
2002 Rating: ★★★★/Highly Recommended

A. Hardy Perfection Grande Champagne Cognac (France); 41% abv, $6,000.

Made in part from pre-phylloxera (pre-1870s) cognacs. Very deep amber/nutbrown color; superb clarity. The initial nosings detect mature, even stately aromas, including tea leaves, cigar tobacco, and delicate touches of oaky rancio; aeration serves to release leathery and spicy notes. The palate entry is nougaty sweet, luscious, honeyed, and deep; by midpalate the flavor phase has reached a zenith, offering richly sweet tastes of rancio, sap, honey, brown sugar, sugar biscuits, and cocoa. It finishes voluptuously honeyed, almost like Pedro Ximenez or moscatel sherry. One of the greatest brandy experiences that anyone could possibly have. If it were art, it would be Rembrandt; a masterpiece and one of the world's spirits where the name says it all.

2002 Rating: ★★★★★/Highest Recommendation

A. Hardy Vanille Cognac & Vanilla (France); 40% abv, $26.

The orangy/burnished/coppery color is pretty; superb purity. The initial blast of aroma is exclusively and powerfully vanilla bean-like, leaving no room for any trace of cognac scent; with time in the glass, the vanilla turns downs the volume becoming more like egg cream and vanilla cake frosting rather than beany or extract-like. The palate entry is creamy and concentrated on the semisweet vanilla flavoring; by the midpalate juncture the flavor profile is devoted still totally to vanilla. Finishes, well, with a strong vanilla thrust. While this flavored cognac is certainly drinkable, the lack of flavor subtlety doesn't do it for me. I prefer to have a marriage of flavors, not just an exclusive taste menu of one. The cognac presence in this effort ends up being a non-presence.

2007 Rating: ★★/Not Recommended

ABK6 VS Cognac (France); 40% abv, $32.

The pleasing-to-the-eye harvest gold/wheat field amber color is flawless and clean. The first whiffs detect invitingly spicy and fruity aromas that are lean and estery, rather than plump or ripe; the second and third nosings after aeration reveal a genuine grapy/pineapple-like presence that, while simple, is compellingly straightforward and delicately sweet. The palate entry is pineapple-like, gently ripe, and sweet; the no-frills midpalate highlights the fruitiness and downplays any acidity or woodiness. Obviously a young, vigorous, fruity, and friendly cognac that would be best employed as a mixer.

2006 Rating: ★★★/Recommended

ABK6 VSOP Cognac (France); 40% abv, $40.

Pretty topaz hue; excellent clarity. There's far more evidence of wood in this opening aroma than in the mindlessly fruity but affable VS; unfortunately aeration doesn't expand the bouquet much beyond the oaky/woody horizon, leaving the aroma one-dimensional and uninteresting. The palate entry is clumsy, in that it's too woody/resiny; the midpalate flavor profile gets a bit of a lift from a light toffee taste that advances past the woodiness. Finishes oaky sweet, resiny, and drinkable, if hollow.

2006 Rating: ★★/Not Recommended

ABK6 XO Cognac (France); 40% abv, $85.

Attractive honey/amber color; unblemished clarity. At first, the nose is very reluctant to emerge except for distant scents of cedar and lanolin; time in the glass brings out subtle notes of coconut, tobacco, and baked pear. The palate entry is citrusy yet moderately sweet;

the midpalate stage offers a pleasant oak core flavor around which all the fruit and spice tastes orbit. Ends up caramel-like, sweet, mildly oaky, and silky in the throat.
2006 Rating: ★★★/Recommended

Alizé VS Cognac (France); 40% abv, $36.
The copper/burnished orange color is very pretty; excellent purity. The nose at opening is dry, raisiny, and dried fruit-like, with nuances of caramel, lead pencil, and baked pear; the second and third nosing passes see little in the way of expansion or deepening as the stone dry lead pencil scent emerges by a hair as the primary aromatic element; the final sniffing, following eight minutes in the glass, finds the dried fruit/fruit peel fragrance matching the lead pencil component for dominance; overall I like the nose even though it's quite narrow in its scope. The palate entry is dry and focuses on dried fruit; the midpalate, however, erupts suddenly in overly sweet, concentrated, maple, and caramel-like flavors that bulldoze the taste buds, taking them by surprise in view of the dry, agile aroma and palate entry. The finish clubs the palate into submission with too much sticky sweetness. Drinkable, but an entry level cognac.
2001 Rating: ★★/Not Recommended

Alizé VSOP Cognac (France); 40% abv, $53.
The topaz color is nothing short of dazzling; superb purity. The opening nosing passes offer fruity, but not quite ambrosial, aromas of banana, papaya, and nectarine; air contact over six more minutes helps to open up further off-dry scents of light toffee, tea leaves, and marshmallow. The palate opening is very sweet, round, and a touch acidic; the midpalate stage highlights succulent flavors of cocoa butter, toasted almond, dark caramel, and molasses. The finish is long, brown sugar sweet, intense, tea-like, and almost Martinique rhum agricole-like. Like its sibling VS, a well-made, chewy, and uncomplicated cognac.
2002 Rating: ★★★/Recommended

Brillet Cognac Très Rare Heritage Brut de Fut Grande Champagne Cognac (France); 50% abv, $300.
Aged for 50 years in oak, then bottled at cask strength. The gorgeous color is tawny amber and impeccably pure. The opening sniff evokes memories of many great cognacs, this one offering subtle traces of marzipan, walnuts, spice cake, and dried red fruit; in the second pass, gentle scents of baked pears gets added to the list; the penultimate nosing sees the bouquet grow in intensity as vibrant aromas of old oak and vanilla vie for dominance; the fourth and last whiff delights the olfactory sense in that not one iota of strength or charm is diminished or found to be waning; a seriously complex bouquet of the first rank that owns a substantial foundation of rancio and oak upon which the various layers of cake, fruit, spice, and spirit play. The palate entry totally disarms the taste buds as elegant, classical tastes of dark caramel and old oak greet the tip of the tongue; the midpalate taste phase is truly enchanting as opulent, vanilla-laden, buttery, even creamy flavors exist in harmony and grace. The aftertaste is infinitely long, deeply caramel-like, sweet, and spiced. A brilliant and inspired cognac that deserves every star.
2000 Rating: ★★★★★/Highest Recommendation

Brillet Sélection Petite Champagne Cognac (France); 40% abv, $35.

The bright, clean appearance shows a yellow/gold, autumnal color and exceptional purity. The opening nosing offers several layers of aroma, from pears to soft, old oak to beeswax; the second pass, following three minutes of air contact, adds a subtle hint of citrus peel; the third sniffing adds a touch of pleasantly prickly spirit; the fourth and final whiff sees the various components merge into a unified bouquet that's delicate yet firm. The palate entry is sleek and mildly sweet more in a fruity way than a woody manner; the midpalate stage sings with harmonious tastes of ripe red fruit, buttery oak, and firm spirit; it's an uncluttered, straightforward flavor experience that's elegant and assertive simultaneously. The aftertaste is long, svelte, and more fruity than oaky. The usually complex character of Petite Champagne seems crystallized in this swank beauty.

2000 Rating: ★★★/Highly Recommended

Brillet Très Vieille Réserve XO Grande Champagne Cognac (France); 40% abv, $100.

The harvest gold color is attractive, if unexceptional, and the purity level is superb. The opening whiff offers succulent, evolved aromas of toasted almonds and apple butter immediately; the second sniffing adds delicate aromas of old oak and hard cheese; the third pass brings everything together in a cautiously sweet, completely classy bouquet that's very advanced and developed; by the fourth and last nosing pass, the two decades of maturing in small oak barrels is clearly apparent in the roasted nut, dried fruit, and rancio aromas; a dazzler of a bouquet. The palate entry is mature, oaky, resiny, and ripe in flavor; at midpalate the multilayered flavors turn fuller, though never are they chunky, as rich and powerful tastes of nuts, cheese, and oak glide along in perfect harmony. The finish is long, oaky sweet, and a bit caramel-like. The only descriptor to use is "luscious".

2000 Rating: ★★★★/Highest Recommendation

Camus Borderies XO Cognac (France); 40% abv, $130.

Deep copper/russet hue; impeccable purity. In the opening sniffs the aroma is melony, peppery and a touch woody; additional air contact of seven full minutes doesn't, to my surprise, stimulate much more in the way of aromatic expansion or deepening. The palate entry is pleasantly floral, with a sturdy backnote taste of oak; by the midpalate point, the taste profile features a medium-bodied texture and a softly sweet, grapy ripeness that's more than adequately engaging. In the aftertaste, a splendid taste of pine nut tops off the flavor experience. While very good and certainly recommendable, more bouquet presence and substance would have assured a fourth rating star.

2003 Rating: ★★/Recommended

Camus Cuvée Cognac (France); 40% abv, $45.

Pretty, bright copper color; superb clarity. The initial whiffs pick up mildly sweet scents of ripe grapes and white raisins; seven further minutes of aeration stimulate additional scents that include unsweetened coconut, palm oil, and sweet oak; this is an understated bouquet that needs some time to open up. The palate entry is ripe and sweet; the midpalate highlights a keen candied nuttiness that's racy and integrated. The aftertaste is maple sweet and slightly honeyed. A slow-to-develop bouquet, but ultimately a solid from bottom to top frontline cognac.

2003 Rating: ★★/Recommended

Camus Elegance VS Cognac (France); 40% abv, $24.

Pale gold/flax/straw color; unblemished clarity. Initial whiffs pick up delectable and fresh yellow fruits, especially green apple and Bosc pear; aeration stimulates deeper scents including poppy seed, parchment, apricot, and new leather. Entry is surprisingly composed, honeyed, dry, and luscious for what I have to think is a young cognac; the taste profile at midpalate displays many delicious flavors, such as honey, vanilla bean, pork sausage, cinnamon, and nutmeg. Finishes with oodles of finesse, elegance, and component integration. The best VS out there at present. A superior value.

2007 Rating: ★★★★/Highly Recommended

Camus Elegance VSOP Cognac (France); 40% abv, $34.

Light amber/topaz hue; perfect purity. Opening nose is strikingly similar to the VS in terms of the clear evidence of yellow fruit; further air contact releases nuances of wood resin, white pepper, and toasted honeywheat bread. Entry taste is assertively oaky, off-dry, and spicy (baking spices like cinnamon, nutmeg); the midpalate flavor profile turns up the oak/wood volume even more and thereby drowns a bit of the fruit and spice elements. Aftertaste is off-dry, calmer than the midpalate and simultaneously leathery, pruny, with a hint of baked apple. The toasty/roasted meat quality is intriguing.

2007 Rating: ★★★/Recommended

Camus Elegance XO Cognac (France); 40% abv, $99.

Gorgeous auburn/old copper penny color; flawless purity. As in the VS and the VSOP, the yellow fruit comes through early on (green apple and pear) but there's also a mature toasted bread, buttery fragrance that underpins the bouquet; aeration brings out baked apple and pear pastry, cinnamon and nutmeg, and delicate notes of old, worn leather, pipe tobacco, cigar wrapper, and burnt sugar. Moderate sweetness greets the taste buds at entry, then the profile turns more serious at midpalate as flavors of vanilla, toffee, dried cherry, and lanolin vie for dominance. Finishes elegantly and tightly, as the buttery oak supports the baked fruit and spice tastes.

2007 Rating: ★★★★/Highly Recommended

Chateau de Ligneres 10 Year Old Pure Single Estate Cognac (France); 40% abv, $50.

The dazzling color shines like a new copper penny. The opening whiff after the pour displays a youngish cognac demeanor as the fruit comes forward quickly, eclipsing the wood; in the second and third nosing passes the raisiny fruit remains in charge but subtle notes of pear and carnations get added to the aromatic mix; by the last sniffing light touches of oak resin and fresh herbs (mint? rosemary?) appear and assist in balancing the acidity of the fruit. The concentration of raisiny sweetness at palate entry is admirable and almost chewy; at midpalate there's a dry rush of intense oak as the ripe fruit suddenly vanishes from the picture. The aftertaste is firm, resiny, and dry to off-dry.

2001 Rating: ★★★/Recommended

Chateau Montifaud Heritage Louis Vallet 27 Year Old Fine Petite Champagne Cognac (France); 40% abv, $200.

The attractive bronze/topaz hue is totally ruined by the stringy gray and black sediment;

not a pretty sight. The initial nosing passes detect aromas of mint, yellow fruit, and soft oak; following several minutes of aeration the bouquet doesn't develop much beyond the minty perfume. In the mouth there are signs of redemption as the entry taste comes off toasty and nutty; at the midpalate point the toastiness recedes, leaving behind a woody, nut-like flavor that's neither complex nor interesting. The finish is meek, acidic, lean, hot, and somehow fitting. Definitely the dud of the Montifaud litter. One hopes that this sample was drawn off a lone poor bottle.
2001 Rating: ★/Not Recommended

Chateau Montifaud Heritage Louis Vallet 45 Year Old Fine Petite Champagne Cognac (France); 40% abv, $240.
Very attractive copper penny color; minor sediment seen. The nose is slightly oloroso sherry-like in the opening sniffings after the pour; with time in the glass the bouquet evolves quickly as semisweet aromas of brandied pear, tobacco leaf, and oak char; this is ultimately a very resiny and oily bouquet that's lost much of its fruit impact. In the mouth the entry is astringent, lethargic, and bland; the midpalate juncture is notable for its high resin influence and its fruit deficiency. The aftertaste is concentrated, flabby, and intensely woody/resiny. It is my suspicion that this cognac is over the hill by at least five to eight years. It's drinkable if you like a more acidic/astringent style of cognac.
2001 Rating: ★★/Not Recommended

Chateau Montifaud Heritage Maurice Vallet 1904 Fine Petite Champagne Cognac (France); 42% abv, $1,000.
Cellared in 1904; less than 400 bottles available. Shows a deep mahogany/nutbrown color. The aroma immediately following the pour displays remarkably vivacity and muscularity for a century old spirit; aeration reveals lush, poised aromas of old oak, bittersweet chocolate, wet stone, and unlighted cigars. In the mouth the entry taste is of leather, dried fruit, lead pencil, and tobacco leaf; the midpalate point highlights dark caramel, oak resin, hard cheese, and minerals. The aftertaste is surprisingly long, minerally, dry, and leathery. I am mildly disappointed that there isn't any hint of rancio in this old cognac, but that's not to say that it isn't complex and multilayered because it most definitely is. What strikes me most is the leathery/minerally interplay; a delectable piece of history.
2001 Rating: ★★★★/Highly Recommended

Chateau Montifaud Napoleon Fine Petite Champagne Cognac (France); 40% abv, $62.
15 to 18 years old; the appearance is topaz/bronze; a serious, comely feast for the eyes. The initial nosing passes highlight deep roasted nut and nougat aromas that are dry to off-dry; time in the glass finds the aroma leaning more to the wood influence than to the fruit base as subtle fragrances of hard cheese and oil come to the forefront; a deceptively powerful bouquet that comes off as being fat at first then with aeration a clear definition occurs; lovely. The palate entry is intensely caramel-like and dry, almost bitter and even slightly spicy; at midpalate the hard cheese quality spotted in the later stages of the bouquet returns and makes a solid case for early-phase rancio presence. The aftertaste displays definite rancio earthiness/dustiness. One of the better niche Napoleons in the marketplace at present. Bravo.
2001 Rating: ★★★★/Highly Recommended

Chateau Montifaud Prestige Grande Champagne Premier Cru de Cognac (France); 40% abv, $40.

A VS level offering; pale-to-light honey/medium amber hue. The initial nosings detect a youthful, vibrant opening aroma that's brimming with vines/leaves, fresh spirit, and a light touch of toffee; time in the glass does wonders for this muscular bouquet as the oxygen unleashes deeper scents, even layers of mint, tobacco leaf, and ripe grapes; a limber, agile bouquet that pulls at the leash. In the mouth the entry flavors are surprisingly supple, sinewy, and toffee sweet; the midpalate shows traces of marshmallow and nougat. The finish is long, toffee sweet, and very textured. Clearly a youngster, but a composed, well-mannered youth of substance.

2001 Rating: ★★★/Recommended

Chateau Montifaud Reserve Speciale Michel Vallet Fine Petite Champagne Cognac (France); 40% abv, $65.

Gorgeous, brilliant bronze hue with a golden rim; minor sediment. The dry bouquet, reminiscent of holiday fruit cake, is lithe but tightly wound out of the starting gate; after a few minutes in the glass the aroma seems more prone to expand and relax as dry but succulent fragrances of spiced apple, baked pear, beeswax, and light toffee enchant the olfactory sense. The entry flavor is dry and astringent; then at midpalate there's an explosion of lip-smacking sweet toffee/caramel tastes that carry the flavor phase into the finish. The aftertaste is long, bittersweet, and genuinely lovely.

2001 Rating: ★★★★/Highly Recommended

Chateau Montifaud VSOP Fine Petite Champagne Cognac (France); 40% abv, $43.

A 10 year old VSOP; lovely autumnal gold/bright amber color. The opening nosing passes are treated to vigorous and fruity scents of peach, nectarine, apricot, and palm oil; air contact helps to release further aromas including pineapple, lanolin, and distant walnut; a composed, integrated, and genuinely supple bouquet. In the mouth there's early evidence of crisp acid at entry; the midpalate point offers defined flavors of coffee, tobacco leaf, and oak resin. The finish is clean, off-dry, almondy, and astringent. A handsome, oily VSOP.

2001 Rating: ★★★/Recommended

Chateau Montifaud VSOP Grande Champagne Premier Cru de Cognac (France); 40% abv, $45.

Matured for 10 years; harvest gold/amber color. The opening nosing phases feature atypical aromas of blackcurrant and loganberry; following several minutes of aeration the fruit component, mostly red berry, maintains a firm grasp on the bouquet; unusual yet seductive; a bouquet that relies on fruit-based finesse rather than prickly spirit or heavy oak. As classy and graceful in the mouth as it is in the nose, the flavor starts out off-dry and slightly dried/baked at entry, then turns succulent, full, and round at midpalate. The aftertaste is sinewy, fruity, and ripely sweet. A low-key, utterly charming VSOP that should have a place in every serious spirits collection.

2001 Rating: ★★★★/Highly Recommended

Chateau Montifaud XO Fine Petite Champagne Cognac (France); 40% abv, $86.

27 to 30 years old. The medium amber/copper penny hue has lots of harvest gold in it; quite beautiful. Lots of spirity, almost peppery piquancy greets the olfactory sense in the whiffs right after the pour; exposure to air deepens the fruit element significantly and adds vibrant aromas of nougat, almond butter, and light toffee; a polite bouquet. This thoroughbred shines especially bright in the mouth as keenly balanced and oily flavors of oak resin, slate, caramel, and dried apricot delight the taste buds at entry; at midpalate the taste turns maple-like and almost sappy in its concentrated sweetness. The finish is long, maple-like, and intensely fruity. A beauty.

2001 Rating: ★★★★/Highly Recommended

Chaumont VS Cognac (France); 40% abv, $20.

The appearance is pure and the tawny/harvest gold color reminds me of an amontillado sherry. The opening nosing reveals a sweet, yellow fruit aroma that turns peppery and zesty in the second pass; by the third nosing following six minutes of aeration the aroma becomes a true bouquet as not-so-subtle scents of gum, citrus rind, and new oak get added to the roster; the fourth and final sniffing stays the course of overriding, ripe, even perfumy yellow fruit outshining all other fragrances; a jolly good bouquet for less than twenty bucks. The amiable, fruity sweetness so liked in the nose disappears at palate entry as the initial taste bites the tip of the tongue in a high-powered, acidic wave; the midpalate sees things settle down flavor-wise as a resiny taste of new oak dominates; what's happened to the lovely fruitiness, I ask. The finish is brittle, acidic, intensely woody/resiny, and borders on being harsh. After a very rousing lift-off, this cognac turns angular and sharp in the mouth, dashing all the promise found in the bouquet. Drinkable and ordinary, to be sure, but ultimately disappointing.

2000 Rating: ★★/Not Recommended

Chaumont VSOP Cognac (France); 40% abv, $33.

The copper tone is bright and like a new penny; completely free of suspended particles. The nose right after the pour is clean, slightly resiny, and a little cheese-like; with more time in the glass, the nose develops a pleasant surface fragrance of dried red fruit while in the background a hint of caramel lurks; in the penultimate whiff, a firm note of paraffin joins the dried fruit and caramel; after nearly eight minutes of exposure to air, the fourth sniffing sees the paraffin become an equal partner to the fruit while the caramel recedes slightly. The palate entry is candy sweet in a caramel-like manner, then at midpalate a buttery taste enters and overtakes the candy flavor, making for a simplistic but agreeable taste experience. The aftertaste is long, oaky sweet, and a touch resiny. Though I felt that the finish somewhat let down the aroma and the taste, the overall impression is attractive and, for the price, a good value.

2000 Rating: ★★★/Recommended

Chaumont XO Cognac (France); 40% abv, $82.

Very pretty to look at; the rust color shines under the examination lamp; excellent purity. The first nosing pass unearths a zesty, almost peppery quality that's right upfront; after three minutes of aeration, the peppery aroma starts to become vegetal, almost herbal in its bearing; in the third pass, following six minutes of air contact, a bit of sophistication starts to emerge in the shape of soft, ripe, berry-like fruit; the fourth and last whiff sees the aroma finally resemble cognac as a mildly oaky/hard cheese scent advances to the forefront and wrestles away the wheel from the peppery/herbal smell. Sweet, in fact a bit overly so right from the palate entry; the midpalate offers some pleasing, controlled notes of sweet oak, wood resin, ripe grapes, and almond butter. The finish is sweet in a woody way and long. At least this cognac righted itself in the aeration process and ended up being a better than average quaff, one that actually exhibited good balance by the midpalate stage.

2000 Rating: ★★★/Recommended

Chocoviac Cognac with Natural Vanilla and Chocolate Flavors (France); 35% abv, $29.

Has the golden/amber look of cognac; flawless purity. The initial nosing pass features bittersweet scents of dark chocolate powder, cocoa butter, and vanilla extract; aeration time of another six minutes doesn't have any impact on the aroma profile. The palate entry is off-dry and moderately chocolatey; the midpalate is where the flavor explodes in waves of dark chocolate and cocoa, with the vanilla component as a background taste. The finish is lush, lovely, intensely cocoa-like, and perfectly sweet. Never is this flavored cognac cloying or syrupy. Just the right alcohol level, as well. For serious chocolate lovers.

2005 Rating: ★★★★/Highly Recommended

Clos du Colombier 1961 Grande Champagne Cognac (France); 40% abv, $270.

The deep color is topaz/dark honey. In the initial nosings immediately after the pour the bouquet shows atypical aromas of evergreen and cedar along with resiny old oak; with aeration more unusual scents appear including lead pencil and ground black pepper; the overall impression of the bouquet is highly favorable, especially the fully aerated stages in which the dry oak notes reign supreme. The palate entry is dry and intensely oaky; at midpalate a touch of honey mingles with the old oak and acid to present a stately flavor experience that highlights the interplay of the wood with the dried fruit. The aftertaste is very long, concentrated, almost completely dry and resiny. Stunningly lively and vivacious for a forty year old geezer of a cognac.

2001 Rating: ★★★★/Highly Recommended

Clos du Colombier 1973 Grande Champagne Cognac (France); 40% abv, $170.

The tawny color leans to bronze and is truly beautiful. This aroma is vigorous, dry, tobacco-like, and vegetal in the opening two sniffings; the accent is squarely on the oak as the cognac aerates in the glass, giving off slightly bitter and totally dry scents of roasted almond, beeswax, cigar box, and old oak; while it's not a welcoming or warming bouquet, it does provide one with a sense of adventure in that there's hardly any trace of customary Grande Champagne intense, expansive grapiness. In the mouth the flavors of bitter almond and bacon fat greet the taste buds at palate entry; the flavors gather themselves a bit more at midpalate to present a united front; tastes include marzipan, nougat, bittersweet cocoa, dark honey, and old oak though not necessarily rancio. The aftertaste is surprisingly sweet, caramelly, even honeyed. A grand old dame of a cognac that's harder, more brittle in nature than one would expect from Grande Champagne but it's thrilling and racy nonetheless.

2001 Rating: ★★★★★/Highest Recommendation

Courvoisier L'Esprit de Courvoisier Cognac (France); 40% abv, $5,000.

A regal "paradis" blend of very old cognacs, none of which were distilled later than 1929. The amber/harvest gold color is very pretty; absolute purity. The opening nose is a bit muted but by the second pass three minutes later it's clear that this is no ordinary cognac as deep aromatic waves of hard cheese, oak, nutmeg, beeswax, and vanilla extract wash over the olfactory sense; the third sniff, following seven minutes of air contact, reveal further layers of cheese-like rancio and dark toffee; the fourth and final whiff is buttery, remarkably delicate, and sweet; much more finesse-prone than powerful in the bouquet, but what a lovely ride. The palate entry sings with refinement and maturity, yet is vigorous and firmly structured; by the midpalate stage the flavors are soaring as streamlined, hardly decadent tastes of marmalade, spice cake, old oak, keen, not clumsy, rancio and spirit are ideally matched and blended, making for a wonderful cognac experience. The finish is medium long (this is the point where the age shows the most), moderately sweet, and fruity. A stately, aristocratic cognac that comes through in flying colors on all sensory accounts.

2000 Rating: ★★★★/Highest Recommendation

Courvoisier VS Cognac (France); 40% abv, $28.

The copper color is pretty and pure. The opening whiffs pick up hardly anything in the way of brandy scent; only vigorous swirling and another seven minutes in the copita stimulate enough fragrance to form some sort of waxy, spirity, unfocused bouquet. The overly sweet flavor at palate entry is way too manufactured and thickly layered; the midpalate stage is dismally chunky and syrupy sweet. Ends fat, chewy, overblown. Hardly a model of restraint, this cognac is so over-stuffed with caramel sweetness that it's a prime example of what's so wrong with contemporary VS Cognac.

2007 Rating: ★/Not Recommended

Courvoisier VSOP Cognac (France); 40% abv, $36.

Bronze and extremely fetching in color; flawless in clarity. Smells of caramel apples and toffee in the first go-rounds; falls back into itself with aeration and doesn't emit much in the way of what you'd expect from a VSOP Cognac. The palate entry is fat, syrupy, and cloying; the midpalate stage is a resiny, pruny, sticky mess that's overly sweet and viscous. Ends up tasting like something that's been stuck on the bottom of your shoe for twelve years. VSOP Garbage. Want terrific VSOP Cognac? Hunt down Chateau Montifaud, which blows all others out of the water.

2007 Rating: ★/Not Recommended

Croizet Age Inconnu XO Cognac (France); 40% abv, $50.

Lovely new copper penny color. The initial nosing passes encounter genuinely enticing, mature scents of marzipan, nougat, and very ripe grapes; air contact releases further overlapping and poised scents of old oak, hard cheese, and dried fruit in later sniffings. In the mouth this cognac is seductive, concentrated, more dry than sweet, and approachable at entry; the midpalate is the zenith of flavor as focused, layered, and mature tastes of oak-influenced vanilla, baked pears, paraffin, and dark caramel enchant the taste buds. The finish is long, candy sweet but with a bit a acidic bitterness that beautifully balances the sweetness. Well-made, elegant, and unbelievably affordable.

2001 Rating: ★★★/Highly Recommended

Croizet VS Cognac (France); 40% abv, $19.

Shiny, autumnal gold/amber hue. The friendly bouquet right after the pour emits ripe scents of pears, mint, and new oak; subsequent nosing passes after several minutes of air contact unearth richer, deeper aromas of chalk, ripe grapes, and peach cobbler; a bouquet that builds in strength and presence. As nice as the bouquet is, it's in the mouth that this cognac hits stride; the entry is sweet and intensely grapy; the midpalate point is layered, textured, and loaded with very sweet oaky/vanilla and caramel tastes. The aftertaste is lip-smacking sweet, concentrated, and caramelly. A tremendous mouthful of sweet, unbridled cognac for a remarkably reasonable price.

2001 Rating: ★★★/Recommended

Croizet VSOP Cognac (France); 40% abv, $26.

Shows a wonderful bronze/honey color. The opening nosing passes come across mature, melded, and idiosyncratic aromas of old Limousin oak, mustard seed, and ripe grapes; time in the glass gives this cognac a chance to stretch and relax as it emits off-dry and subtle scents of beeswax, caramel, and vanilla; I like the nose of the VS, to be sure, but this bouquet is considerably more advanced and composed. In the mouth the primary taste at palate entry is dark caramel; at the midpalate juncture multilayered flavors emerge including vanilla, honey, toffee, nougat, and resiny oak. The aftertaste is long, off-dry to sweet, and very honeyed. A world-class brandy that's on the sweeter side of the cognac scale, but displays tons of simple charm and presence.

2001 Rating: ★★★/Recommended

Croizet XO Golden Collection Cognac (France); 40% abv, $100.

Beautifully rich topaz color; ideal purity. The nose shows considerable oak and vanilla in the initial two minutes of sniffing; with aeration the bouquet develops fragrant scents of dried apple, unsweetened coconut, pineapple, and almond paste. The buttery palate entry is delightfully sweet and lip-smacking; by the midpalate stage, the creamy/buttery feel is in full bloom as the taste profile goes drier than the entry, emitting delicate and mature flavors of raisins and, in general, dried red fruits. The finish is long, oaky and semisweet.

2003 Rating: ★★★★/Highly Recommended

Daniel Bouju Empereur XO Grande Champagne Cognac (France); 40% abv, $78.

This appearance is more orangey and new copper penny-like than the Napoleon or the Royal Brut de Fut; unblemished clarity. The aroma in the initial nosing pass offers a completely dry, dried herb, almost floral scent that's simultaneously beguiling and confounding; the middle stage sniffings turn a corner on dryness and show a sweeter side, most like ripe yellow fruit, especially nectarine and pear; the fourth and last inhalation finds the ripe fruit element grow in concentration and adds a deft touch of oaky hard cheese in the distance; a stunningly multilayered, complex bouquet and one that illustrates what inherent qualities still separate cognac from all other types of brandy made in the world. The palate entry is succulent, smoky, and ripe-fruit sweet right out of the gate; the midpalate turns more pensive, concentrated, and soft cheese-like by virtue of the elevated level of rancio. The finish is long, dry to off-dry, fruity, and slightly bitter. A clinic for anyone anxious to find out what the elusive, mysterious characteristic termed "rancio" is all about.

2001 Rating: ★★★★★/Highest Recommendation

Daniel Bouju Extra Grande Champagne Cognac (France); 40% abv, $100.

The dark wood/tawny/mahogany color is gorgeous and absolutely pure. The aroma is mute and reluctant to show itself in the first nosing pass after the pour; then in the second sniffing, following two minutes of aeration, stirrings of very old oak and dried fruit emerge; in the third whiff musty, off-dry, nutty notes of forest floor, prune, and grandmother's attic waft from the copita glass; the fourth and final inhalation, following eight minutes of exposure to air, adds distant touches of dark toffee and tobacco leaf; an obviously complex, but slightly too fat bouquet that frankly didn't light my fire. The palate entry is voluptuous, resiny sweet, and pruny; the midpalate is lip-smacking oaky sweet and intensely nougat-like, with faint echoes of apple peel. The finish is long, sap-like, off-dry to sweet, nearly syrupy, and buttery. A big-hearted, bruising, and muscle-bound cognac, to be sure, but regrettably the evident lack of finesse bothered me.

2001 Rating: ★★★/Recommended

Daniel Bouju Fines Saveurs Grande Champagne Cognac (France); 40% abv, $40.

Pretty golden hay/barrel-fermented chardonnay color that's blemish-free. The initial nosing passes detect agile, lean aromas of ripe grapes and grape must; seven more minutes of air exposure allow for additional scents of nectarine, pear, and beeswax to develop; a feline, nimble bouquet that's all about the fruit with hardly any wood impact. The palate entry is engagingly fresh, tart, and acidic, with just a trace of grapy ripeness; at the midpalate stage the flavor gets more serious and profound as it reveals a foundation taste of rich grapy fruit that's not sweet yet still comes off as a bit honeyed, even nectar-like. The aftertaste features the leanness and subtlety of the palate entry. While some diehard cognac traditionalists might scoff at this revolutionary cognac for its near total lack of wood influence, I think the other way and perceive this as perhaps a new and contemporary expression that accents freshness and fruit.

2003 Rating: ★★★★/Highly Recommended

Daniel Bouju Napoleon Grande Champagne Cognac (France); 40% abv, $60.

The rich topaz/autumnal color is dazzling especially in light of the fact that Daniel Bouju refuses to employ caramel for color adjustment as most other distillers do within legal limits; impeccable purity. The opening nose is gentle, stately, yet firmly in charge as opulent scents of oak and raisins greet the olfactory sense; the middle stages, following a period of aeration, find the aroma transforming into a full-throttle bouquet, offering perfectly married fragrances of oaky resin, ripe grapes, marzipan, and background spice; the final sniffing sees none of the seductive potency gone as the last aromatic impression is one of sheer grace, elegance, and quiet power; a textbook Grande Champagne bouquet, in which all of the dots are connected. The palate entry is studded with a mild prickliness and a lip-smacking, oaky sweetness; the midpalate is leaner than I thought it would be and much drier than the palate entry as the resiny, slightly bitter oak influence takes the helm. The finish is so dry as to be austere and sinewy, but the finish is one of finesse and gravity; superbly crafted. I can't believe the retail price on this supple beauty. Buy two.

2001 Rating: ★★★★/Highly Recommended

Daniel Bouju Premiers Aromes Grande Champagne Cognac (France); 45% abv, $40.

Lovely wheat field golden hue with ideal purity. In the first couple of passes the grapiness/mustiness is so apparent that if I didn't know better I might think that I'm sniffing a stately grappa or marc; another eight minutes of aeration time sees the bouquet turn tight, astringent, almost citrusy, and musty; like no cognac I've inhaled before. The palate entry is even more marc-like than the aroma as it highlights the acidic intensity of the ugni blanc grape; yet at midpalate the flavor profile displays ugni blanc's sweeter, riper side that almost resembles bittersweet citrus as much as it does grapes. It finishes whistle clean and completely refreshing. Admirers of multilayered, rancio-kissed cognacs will not like this lithe, blithe cognac/marc. I, on the other hand, think that a new and exciting direction in cognac has just dawned.

2003 Rating: ★★★★/Highly Recommended

Daniel Bouju Royal Brut de Fût Grande Champagne Cognac (France); 60% abv, $65.

The tawny/deep bronze hue is remarkably beautiful and bright under the evaluation lamp; ideal purity. The opening bouquet seems fully evolved, dry, and sap-like; but then in the second pass with a bit of aeration wonderfully sensuous aromas of fruit cake and nuts thrill the olfactory sense; the third whiff, after over six minutes of air contact, adds nuances of plum pudding, Christmas spice, and prunes; the final nosing pass finds the various components coming together in a subtle, but confident and totally dry bouquet that has Grande Champagne plastered all over it. While I admire the bouquet, I passionately love the flavor and texture; the palate entry is intensely nutty and resiny, then at midpalate the taste explodes on the tongue in the aggressive forms of smoldering spirit, resiny/buttery oak, and marzipan; it's the detonation of fiery spirit and concentrated flavors on the tongue that make this flavor phase extraordinary. The aftertaste sees the dry flavors calm and become a tad more focused. An unforgettable brandy experience, one that absolutely isn't for everyone because of the intensity of the flavors at the midpalate. A memorable ride that I'll remember with fondness for a long time; buy three.

2001 Rating: ★★★★★/Highest Recommendation

Daniel Bouju Très Vieux Grande Champagne Cognac (France); 40% abv, $155.

The deep, cola/chestnut/nut brown color startles the eye; this is cognac and not cream sherry?; ideal purity. The opening sniffing picks up firm, totally dry scents of nut meat and tobacco leaf; the second and third passes offer burnt, but dry aromas of oaky resin, banana, and dried berries; the last whiff, following almost ten full minutes of aeration, sees the oak take complete charge, leaving the fruit components in the dust; simply put, it smells like very old, slightly diminished spirit that's on the downhill side of its life cycle. The palate entry is full-bodied, concentrated, nutty, and oaky in a mildly sweet but not cloying manner; the midpalate shows elements of cheese, raisins, prunes, and oaky vanillin. The classic rancio component comes alive in the aftertaste. A grand, nostalgic old style that's definitely worth the effort and the money. Deserves a place in any better cellar or brandy collection.

2001 Rating: ★★★★/Highly Recommended

Daniel Bouju XO 27 Grande Champagne Cognac (France); 42.7% abv, $200.
The incredible color is deep chestnut brown/mahogany/cherrywood and simply one of the more astonishing cognac appearances I've seen in the last couple of years. The first burst of aroma offers peculiar scents of cigar tobacco and grilled vegetables; aeration time of another seven minutes plus swirling do little of expand the odd aromatic theme beyond the additions of soy and, most curiously, a quinine-like sourness. The palate entry is rife with incongruous, if hard-edged tastes of charcoal, black coffee/chicory, and pine resin; the midpalate flavor profile is disappointingly industrial, creosote-like, and totally deficient in the customary Daniel Bouju finesse and profundity. The finish is as dismal as the rancid midpalate. Tasted two 50 ml samples. Both were identically horrible and out of character for this normally brilliant producer. Somebody was asleep at the wheel for releasing this unpleasant cognac that goes totally against the established house style and character profile. XO 27 adds nothing but a stain to the DB legacy. One question: Why?
2005 Rating: ★/Not Recommended

Delamain Extra de Grande Champagne Cognac (France); 40% abv, $319.
The bronze/topaz appearance is lovely and bright; ideal purity. The initial sniffings pick up subtle aromas of oak, bacon, and oak; additional aeration stimulates nuances of toffee, baked pear, baked banana, and honey; the model of aromatic understatement and elegance. The palate entry is perhaps the apex moment of this evaluation as harmonious, completely integrated tastes of honey, oak, grapes, and spice disarm the taste buds; by the midpalate stage the taste profile adds bacon fat, pork rind, and oaky vanillin. A masterpiece. What the Hope Diamond is to fine jewelry, Delamain Extra is to cognac. This is sheer blending genius and, in my mind, is what makes cognac so special.
2007 Rating: ★★★★★/Highest Recommendation

Delamain Pale & Dry XO Grande Champagne Cognac (France); 40% abv, $77.
Indeed, the butterscotch/amber hue is pale, but, oh, so visually fetching; some minor, inconsequential sediment noted. The early nosing passes detect nuances of old flowers, parchment, and black raisins; aeration time of another seven minutes encourages the addition of spice, old oak, and fabric (cotton more than wool) to the aromatic mix; not an assertive or aggressive bouquet, but firm nonetheless. The palate entry is gloriously rich, fruity, resiny, and clean; at midpalate there are seductive, multilayered tastes of maple, palm oil, sap, light toffee, marzipan, spice and almond butter. Ends luxuriously rich, concentrated, oily, viscous, sweet, and oaky. The fact that it's priced at less than $100 is remarkable.
2004 Rating: ★★★★/Highly Recommended

Delamain Réserve de la Famille Grande Champagne Cognac (France); 43% abv, $473.
Far more coppery/russet in color than the Delamain Extra and equally dazzling; impeccable purity. In the first nosing passes after the pour, the aroma offers subtle but firm scents of pepper, spirit, and wood; following seven further minutes of air contact, the bouquet adds traces of grapes, paraffin, and spice. The palate entry is honey sweet, woody, and even a touch bacon fat-like; the midpalate stage is memorable for the semisweet tastes of marzipan, English toffee, and egg cream. Finishes as elegantly as it begins. My favorite Delamain after the Extra.
2007 Rating: ★★★★★/Highest Recommendation

Delamain Très Vénérable Grande Champagne Cognac (France); 40% abv, $265.

The topaz/dark honey color is attractive, but does display some sediment. The opening salvo of aroma is chockfull of holiday spice, vanilla bean, and marzipan perfumes; an additional seven minutes of air contact stimulates supplemental scents of candied almond, honey, old sweet oak, and dark toffee, even a touch of maple; a terrifically complex and layered bouquet. The palate entry is fruity, especially dried red fruits like raisins and prunes, and spirity warm; the midpalate taste profile includes touches of honey, orange peel, baked pear, cinnamon, vanilla, cocoa, and rancio. Finishes as elegantly and assertively as it begins. A masterfully crafted cognac that says all you need to know about Grande Champagne and why it's THE FOREMOST cognac demarcated district.
2006 Rating: ★★★★/Highly Recommended

Delamain Vesper Grande Champagne Cognac (France); 40% abv, $125.

Dark amber/bay color, with some widely spaced sediment floating about. I find lots of wood in the initial whiffs, then with aeration a gentle grapiness, almost a hard candy-like scent comes to dominate in the latter sniffing stages. The palate entry is graceful, semisweet, and moderately candied; at midpalate there's a pleasing juiciness/fruitiness in the flavor profile that's more than a little alluring; I even note a delicate touch of honey in the tail end. Finishes ably, elegantly, and caramel-like. I've never found this Grande Champagne as compelling or profound as the other Delamain GC standard offerings (Pale & Dry, Très Vénérable, Réserve de la Famille) and that conviction remains. That said, Vesper GC is still a mighty fine mainstream cognac that offers more than its share of drinking pleasure.
2004 Rating: ★★★/Recommended

Deret VS Cognac (France); 40% abv, $46.

Attractive honey color; very good clarity. The first nosing pass picks up very clear notes of green melon, banana, sultana, and light spice; further aeration and a bit of swirling release other fruity elements, most notably, green grapes and pear; this is a buoyant, expressive, and appealingly fruity bouquet that grows in the glass. The palate entry offers a semisweet, baked pear, toffee-like opening taste, then at midpalate the flavor accents oaky resin far more than the fruit, thereby losing significant steam in the overall mouth phase. Concludes lean (read: flimsy) and too intensely resiny/woody. I was all set to give this cognac three stars until I encountered the drastic change of direction in the midpalate which unfortunately overlapped into the finish. Halfway through, Deret VS lost its best asset, the fruit component. Sorry, but no cigar for what ends up being a mediocrity.
2005 Rating: ★★/Not Recommended

Deret VSOP Cognac (France); 40% abv, $55.

I like the fetching autumnal amber hue and the blemish-free purity. My opening sniffs detect near-succulent notes of baked apple, pear and apple crumble, and marshmallow; seven more minutes of air contact diminish none of this cognac's innate aromatic vigor as perfumy scents of carnations, honeysuckle, raisins, and bananas in brandy delight the olfactory sense. The palate entry displays round, almost plump tastes of light caramel and nougat; the midpalate tastes include marzipan, honey, and candied pear. Ends up integrated and semisweet. This substantial Deret edition follows through with the promise found in the bouquet. Very nice job here.
2005 Rating: ★★★/Recommended

Deret XO Cognac (France); 40% abv, $120.

The bright amber/burnished gold color is nearly identical to the VSOP; excellent clarity. In the first two minutes of sniffing, the fruity/apple/pear thumbprint detected in the VS and VSOP is unmistakably present; later inhalations pick up pine, cedar, cardamom, and a tantalizing hint of brown butter. The palate entry is smooth, medium-deep, pleasantly oaky, and off-dry; the dusty semisweet midpalate flavors include dark caramel, walnut paste, oak, and palm oil. Finishes woody, semisweet, and nutty. In fairness, I happened to taste this perfectly recommendable XO right next to Martell XO Supreme, which bested it by one star because of its swank opulence, and the Daniel Bouju XO No. 27, whose highly idiosyncratic nature blew both of them off the table.

2005 Rating: ★★★/Recommended

Des Ribauds XO Coeur du Temps Fine Champagne Cognac (France); 40% abv, $95.

Attractive, rich deep amber/copper/orange hue; some inconsequential sediment spotted, not critical. In the first two minutes of inhaling I find spicy/peppery notes that are semi-dry and alluring; later sniffings pick up slightly deeper scents of toffee, citrus rind, and hazelnuts. The palate entry starts semisweet then immediately turns bittersweet and resiny; at midpalate the flavor profile focuses almost entirely on the oak, leaving the fruit way behind. I enjoyed the clean, lean, mean aftertaste. An ethereal, sinewy cognac with no fat on it.

2004 Rating: ★★★/Recommended

Exquis Heritage Réserve de la Famille Grande Champagne Cognac (France); 40% abv, $99.

Dazzling color is that of a new copper penny; inconsequential sediment seen. This nose begins in understated toffee-like scents that at first seem shy but by the eight minute mark display ample aromatic presence in the shapes of toasted oak and almond butter. The palate entry is creamy, big-hearted, and buttery; the midpalate point features lovely, round tastes of old oak, almond butter, and nougat. The aftertaste is long, thick, and caramel sweet; nicely balanced, supple, and moderately rich. A good buy.

2002 Rating: ★★★★/Highly Recommended

Exquis Napoleon Très Vieille Réserve Grande Fine Champagne Cognac (France); 40% abv, $50.

The color is bright amber/auburn; minor sediment seen. The initial two sniffings find savory, dry aromas of vivid spirit, slightly underripe grapes, and distant spice; further aeration time stimulates aromas of orange rind, vanilla bean, almonds, and toasty oak; a solid bouquet that displays some multilayering and moderate depth. The palate entry is sweet, a trifle caramelized, and heady; at the midpalate point the flavor of ripe grapes overrides all other taste elements except for the sweet oakiness. The finish is medium long, a little sap-like, and semisweet. Shows some focus and style.

2002 Rating: ★★★/Recommended

Exquis Réserve Grande Fine Champagne Cognac (France); 40% abv, $38.

Pretty amber/light bronze hue; excellent purity. The opening nosing passes are so fruity and ripe as to nearly be ambrosial; extra time in the glass encourages light scents of oaky vanillin and spice; not a profound cognac bouquet but a very admirable and uncomplicated one. The palate entry shows bittersweet tastes of dark chocolate and cocoa bean; the midpalate stage features spice (cinnamon?) and vanilla extract. The aftertaste is long, medium-bodied, and moderately sweet. Pleasantly affable and straightforward.

2002 Rating: ★★★/Recommended

Exquis XO Grande Champagne Cognac (France); 40% abv, $63.

The pretty bronze hue is bordering on copper; impeccable clarity. The opening stages of the bouquet are vigorous and animated as heady, spicy aromas of paraffin, sugar cookie, and vanilla wafer leap from the glass; five more minutes in the glass afford the chance for more fragrances to emerge in the forms of orange blossom, toffee, lightly charred oak, and ripe grapes; I really respond to the full-throttle energy of this bouquet. After the frisky bouquet excited my olfactory sense I fully expected the flavor phase to be punchy as well—WRONG —the palate entry is silky, sweet, and textured but more elegant than vibrant; by the midpalate juncture a racy, sophisticated flavor profile develops that's very rich, candy sweet, and almost nutty. It finishes in a buttery flourish in the throat. Sensuous and complex.

2002 Rating: ★★★★/Highly Recommended

François Voyer Extra 40 Year Old Grande Champagne Cognac (France); 42% abv, $275.

Brilliant new copper penny color; inconsequential black bits seen floating. This bouquet right after the opening is biscuity, fruity, off-dry, but distant, by that I mean it's present and accounted for but just slightly out of reach; aeration works miracles with this bouquet as it opens up significantly following eight more minutes in the glass; developed scents of nuts, hard candy, honey, spice (cinnamon), and oak rise to the occasion. The palate entry is polite, intensely fruity, off-dry, and lip-smacking; the midpalate point features delicious tastes of baked pear, nectarine, white raisins, and oaky vanilla. The aftertaste is long, smoldering hot, biscuity again, and semisweet. This is a luscious cognac that takes time to evolve, but when it does it most certainly is worth every moment of patience.

2002 Rating: ★★★★/Highly Recommended

François Voyer Napoleon 15 Year Old Grande Champagne Cognac (France); 40% abv, $75.

Absolutely lovely amber/topaz color; more floating debris than I'd like to see at this level. The bouquet rushes up from the copita in zesty, compelling waves of spice (nutmeg, coriander) and black raisins; seven more minutes of exposure to air stimulates deeper, more profound scents of marzipan, nougat, dark honey, and oak resin. The palate entry is so dry as to be austere; the midpalate displays a dash more fruit/grape fleshiness but it's the dominating presence of oaky resin that lasts and singes the tongue. The aftertaste is long, mineral dry, resiny, and not the least bit generous. Atypical to what I've come to know about Grande Champagne cognac, which usually is rich, sweeping in scope, yet concentrated; this offering swings to the extreme side of the scale that highlights a narrow corridor of tight, bitter flavor. Why give it three stars? I believe that it's important to experience all styles of top-notch spirits and this one shows definite elegance, especially in the latter stages of the aroma, in its ascetic character. A thinking person's cognac.

2002 Rating: ★★★/Recommended

François Voyer XO 25 Year Old Grande Champagne Cognac (France); 40% abv, $125.

Attractive, bronze hue that shows some black sediment. The opening nosing passes detect obvious traces of butterscotch and dark caramel; further time in the glass expands the bouquet to include scents of honey, bark, ripe grapes, and leather. The palate entry is pointed, tart, semisweet, and moderately honeyed; at the midpalate point, mature, fully evolved, dessert-like flavors of brown sugar, old oak, and cocoa take charge. It finishes with some spirity heat that warms the tongue, ripe red fruit, and honey wafer flavors. Intriguing and piquant.

2002 Rating: ★★★★/Highly Recommended

Frapin Château de Fontpinot XO Grande Champagne Cognac (France); 41% abv, $95.

Made from estate-grown grapes distilled into chateau-bottled Grande Champagne eaux-de-vie between 15 and 20 years old. The rich, copper/orange color shows henna/russet core highlights beneath the examination lamp; ideal clarity. The aroma of damp earth greets the olfactory sense in the first couple of whiffs, then after further aeration the aroma expands to include succulent fresh fruit notes along with flowers and spice. The palate entry is off-dry, caramel-like, and properly oaky; at midpalate the flavor profile deepens significantly, offering lip-smacking tastes of light toffee, almond butter, and vanilla extract. Finishes smooth, candied, and rich. Absolutely delicious.

2004 Rating: ★★★★/Highly Recommended

Frapin Cuvée VSOP Rare Grande Champagne Cognac (France); 40% abv, $57.

Almost identical to the VS, but marginally more bronze and burnished; excellent clarity. Baked pear, baked peach, and bakery-like scents charm the olfactory sense right away; additional exposure to air brings about nuances of dried fruit and vanilla that work well together. Entry is honey sweet, fruity, mildly toasty, and caramel-like; the midpalate point highlights the ripe fruit, which seems more tropical in nature than grapy or berry-like at this stage. Concludes elegantly, satiny in texture, mildly honeyed, and sophisticated. A substantial VSOP that has genuine pedigree.

2007 Rating: ★★★/Recommended

Frapin Extra Grande Champagne Cognac (France); 40% abv, $491.

Gloriously coppery/henna/auburn color; flawless clarity. Mature fragrances of dried peach, oak, wood resin, and vanilla extract delight the olfactory sense in the first inhalations; further aeration time stimulates roasted/toasted scents of almond, fruit compote, dried fruit pastry, and moss/earth. Entry is oily, silky, decadently fruity and spicy, yet clearly firmly grounded and mature; the midpalate stage highlights honey, vanilla, dark caramel, fudge, coffee bean, and old oak. Finishes with flair and grace, with racy flavors of dried banana, dried nectarine, and vanilla, vanilla, vanilla. Wow, what a beauty.

2007 Rating: ★★★★★/Highest Recommendation

Frapin VIP XO Grande Champagne Cognac (France); 40% abv, $159.

Comprised of old cognacs that are around 35 years old, VIP XO is one of the most beautiful cognacs I've ever seen; the rich chestnut/bronze color shines under the examination lamp; perfect purity. The opening salvo of aroma is assertive and vigorous as zesty notes of pine, oak and parchment get the attention of the olfactory sense; seven more minutes of aeration serve to enhance the oak by introducing a fine caramel/toffee component that perfectly complements the wood. The palate entry is fruity, almost jammy, and sweet; at midpalate the smooth, satiny, creamy texture provides one of the highlights along with supple, mature, and beguiling flavors of cocoa, chocolate cake frosting, butter cream, and walnut. Concludes as elegantly as it began. A great distilled spirit.

2004 Rating: ★★★★★/Highest Recommendation

Frapin VS Luxe Grande Champagne Cognac (France); 40% abv, $42.

Topaz/deep honey color; ideal purity. Smells of dried berries in the initial sniffs; the aroma turns toasty and orange marmalade-like after another seven minutes of air contact. Entry is solid structurally, with a deep foundation taste of ripe white grapes and oak; the midpalate stage features long, silky, honey-sweet tastes as well as an astringency that maintains this cognac's freshness. Ends toasty, moderately sweet and honeyed. One of the finest VS cognacs that one can buy.

2007 Rating: ★★★/Recommended

Gabriel & Andreu 1970 Grande Champagne Cognac (France); 43% abv, $175.

The bright, clean appearance is lovely as the bronze/new copper penny color dazzles the eye; very good purity. Scarily, a stale/tanky/metallic odor dominates the opening nosing pass of this thirty-one year old cognac; the middle stage nosings see a slight improvement as traces of tropical fruit and oak emerge, just barely, though; the fourth and last sniffing reverts to the stale, canned fruit demeanor of the 1971 bottling; there's no other way to say it, this cognac, like its ailing sibling the 1971, is aromatically unappetizing, period. The flavor shows some life at palate entry in the form of a sweet, almost biscuity flavor; the midpalate is even more pleasing as the oak resin, dried fruit, and caramel tastes emerge. Disappointingly, the finish falls off the table, offering little in the way of a savory last impression. Had the aftertaste showed more character and not vanished so quickly, I would have given this cognac two stars.

2001 Rating: ★/Not Recommended

Gabriel & Andreu 1971 Grande Champagne Cognac (France); 43% abv, $175.

Deeper bronze/topaz hue; some infinitesimal sediment spotted under the lamp. The initial nosing pass picks up semi-dry scents of paraffin and canned unsweetened pineapple; the second and third aromatic run-throughs shows a delicate touch of banana; the final whiff, after seven plus minutes of time in the glass, stays the metallic, semi-dry, if totally uninteresting, course of canned fruit and tin; what's going on here? Why am I getting a sinking feeling about this cognac when I haven't even tasted it? The palate entry is sweet, but shockingly limp and stale; the midpalate stage doesn't get any better as the tired oaky/vanilla extract flavor displays no dimension or depth. The aftertaste is thin, weedy, and completely without charm. A dead in the water Grande Champagne that doesn't in the least reflect the greatness of that district; a weary, wrung-out cognac with nothing left to give. Simply put, at any price point it should not be in the marketplace, let alone at such a hefty financial bite.

2001 Rating: ★/Not Recommended

Gabriel & Andreu 1973 Grande Champagne Cognac (France); 43% abv, $175.

The bronze color beams under the evaluation lamp; superb purity. The nose immediately after the bottle opening is somewhat muted and reluctant; curiously, the middle stage nosing passes reveal dry/tart, beeswax, and cotton fabric-like notes with scant evidence of fruit or oak—am I missing something?—following eight minutes of swirling and aeration, hardly any progress is noted with regard to this aroma's development; not an auspicious start. It's more expressive and assertive once in the mouth; the palate entry is warm, medium sweet, and definitely oaky; by midpalate the flavors kick up the intensity several notches as they go from mild to concentrated, round, chewy, resiny, vanilla-like, and embers warm. The finish is long, raisiny/fruity (finally), and sweet. Though recommended, a rating star was deducted for the lackluster showing in the bouquet. When the price tag is $175 you have to give me more at every level of sensory experience.

2001 Rating: ★★★/Recommended

Gautier 1775-2005 Edition Anniversaire 250 Ans Fine Champagne Cognac (France); 40% abv, $n/a.

The "Fine" designation, of course, indicates a combination of Grande and Petite Champagne eaux-de-vie. Fine light amber hue; perfect purity. The first aromatic burst says just-ripened apples and grapes, perhaps even pears; later whiffs pick up wispily delicate scents of dried yellow fruit and barely discernable oak; a teasing, even fey kind of bouquet. The palate entry is crisp, acidic, cleansing, and dry, if void of tastes that one would expect of a Fine Champagne cognac; the midpalate stage displays light-bodied, astringent tastes of distant oak and light caramel. Concludes so delicately as to seem timid. I don't mind if a cognac makes an attempt to achieve finesse, but for crying out loud give me something in terms of core aroma and flavor. This cognac is so polite that it's weak in the knees. Give me Superman, not his alter ego Clark Kent. Pass on it.

2005 Rating: ★★/Not Recommended

Gautier Madame France Cognac (France); 40% abv, $20/375 ml.

Pretty amber/toffee color; excellent purity and oiliness. The delightful aroma starts out in a green apple and pear mode; intensely fruity; aeration adds notes of wax, sunflower seed, and cherry; one of the more appealing bouquets of the Gautiers. The palate entry flavor is more tart/dry than the gently ambrosial/fruit salad bouquet; the midpalate is warming, mildly caramelized, and more nutty than fruity, with just the slightest evidence of oak. It finishes lean, off-dry, showing hints of honey and oak resin.

2002 Rating: ★★★/Recommended

Gautier VS Cognac (France); 40% abv, $16.

Attractive harvest gold/auburn hue; impeccable purity. The nose at opening is delicate, feline, and mildly spiced; air contact stimulates additional aromas, specifically pear drop, orange rind, and marzipan. At the palate entry the taste is sweet, simple, immature, and vigorous; by the midpalate stage a mildly heated/spirity taste sensation makes the tongue tingle and the lips burn slightly as easy, if superficial, flavors of ripe grapes, sharp new oak, and beeswax assert themselves. The aftertaste is moderately sharp, harmless. Drinkably ordinary.

2002 Rating: ★★/Not Recommended

Gautier VSOP Cognac (France); 40% abv, $31.

Pleasant, autumnal amber color; excellent purity. The bouquet after the pour is a touch distant and meek, emitting only soft aromatic signals such as light fruit and gum; exposure to air over another five to six minutes does little to urge more aromatic expression to emerge; frankly, one of my favorite pleasures is smelling a cognac, but this bouquet is so dismally flat and timid that that delight comes up nil. The palate entry displays some flavor impact, mostly in the forms of caramel and oak; by the midpalate stage mildly pleasing tastes of dried red fruit, oak, and prunes are noted. Finishes sweet, honeyed, and almost syrupy. Pedestrian and commonplace.

2002 Rating: ★★/Not Recommended

Gautier XO Gold & Blue Cognac (France); 40% abv, $69.

Spectacularly brilliant, light-catching bronze/rust orange color; absolute purity. This bouquet is leagues ahead of the paper-thin bouquets of the VS and VSOP as openings scents of honey, brown sugar, and old oak encourage extensive inhaling; aeration adds decadent aromas of dark caramel, the beginnings of cheese-like rancio, and baked pears. The palate entry is richly flavored with tastes of brown sugar, oaky resin, and vanilla; the midpalate is a touch smoky as flavors of tobacco leaf, rancio, and honey make for intriguing, if rambunctious, sampling. The aftertaste is extended, juicy, and candy sweet. A rip-snortin' cognac whose armagnac-like nature is its finest virtue.

2002 Rating: ★★★/Recommended

Hennessy Ellipse Cognac (France); 43.5% abv, $4,000.

The topaz/honey color is brilliant and pure beneath the examination lamp. The first inhalations after the pour offer appetizing scents of caramel apple, baked fruit pastry, dates, figs, and white raisins; following another seven minutes of air contact, the bouquet adds tropical fruit notes and distant hints of spice. The palate entry is rich, floral (rose petal, honeysuckle), and fruity, with supporting flavors of vanilla and cinnamon; the midpalate phase is where this historically important cognac takes flight as earthy/floral, yet delicate flavors of honey, marzipan, light toffee, and spice merge into a delightful experience. Concludes gently, elegantly, and with enough gusto to make one appreciate its pedigree and heritage. The enclosed press materials cite the presence of rancio, which I didn't detect. The undeniable stars of this expensive extravaganza are the gracefully integrated midpalate and finish.

2006 Rating: ★★★★/Highly Recommended

Hennessy Paradis Extra Cognac (France); 40% abv, $325.

This cognac is so pretty with its deep copper/russet hue that I can't stop admiring it; flawless clarity. The opening fragrance is assertive, piny, nutty, and fruity; the bouquet explodes after further aeration into multilayered scents of baked pear/apple pastry, walnut, roasted chestnut, and maple. The palate entry is firm, semisweet, oaky, and spicy; the midpalate stage is well-balanced, sweet but not cloying, oaky but not astringent, and compellingly baked, with finishing touches of rancio, hard cheese, and caramel. Finishes elegantly and lushly, with final parting tastes of pepper and brown sugar. A hugely impressive older cognac that brings together maturity and power.

2006 Rating: ★★★★/Highly Recommended

Hennessy Private Reserve Grande Champagne Cognac (France); 40% abv, $150.

The shining bronze/orange/copper color is simply beautiful; immaculate clarity. In the initial nosing passes, there's evidence of ripe tropical fruits, especially banana and guava; later sniffings find old oak, wood resin, and citrus rind. The palate entry is clean and mildly astringent; by midpalate a serene grapiness/dried red fruit flavor profile dominates the taste phase in the most positive sense. Finishes with ripe, chewy tastes of plums, sweet oak, vanilla extract, cream, and honey. Lovely, composed, and elegant.

2005 Rating: ★★★★/Highly Recommended

Hennessy Privilege VSOP Cognac (France); 40% abv, $40.

The nut-brown color is dark, rusty/russet-like, and pure. The nose after the pour is surprisingly sedate, emitting only fey scents of vines and green vegetation; ample additional exposure to air doesn't further the cause of the bouquet as its remains mildly, no, timidly friendly in a grapy/fruity way and altogether hollow. The palate entry is very sweet, nearly syrupy, and gives the impression of trying too hard to be complex when it isn't; the midpalate stage is the best phase as rounded flavors of dark toffee, nougat, and maple work nicely together. Finishes sweet, sap-like, and acceptably woody. While wholly drinkable and mixable, this big-house VSOP suffers the sin of over-manipulation.

2006 Rating: ★★/Not Recommended

Hennessy XO Cognac (France); 40% abv, $150.

The henna/bay/dark bronze/chestnut color is beautiful and luminous beneath the examination lamp; impeccable purity. The first sniffs detect reluctant scents of grapes and dates; further aeration doesn't take the bouquet to the next level as much as I hope, coming off as one-dimensional. The palate entry is aggressive on the tongue, almost chunky in its brazen sweetness and oakiness; the midpalate phase is a little more restrained in the sweetness department as the oak becomes more of a participant in the form of earthy astringency, thereby introducing a sense of balance. Ends up seriously sweet, sticky, and way too sugary. This cognac displays an inexcusable lack of grace and balance. It's far too sweet

2006 Rating: ★★/Not Recommended

Hine 1957 Grande Champagne Cognac (France); 40% abv, $250.

The lovely bronze/orange color displays flawless purity. The aroma out of the starting block is somewhat steely and minerally; further time in the glass affords this aroma the opportunity to gather steam and by the seventh minute it displays scents of oak, pepper, walnut, and crushed flowers. But it's in the palate entry that this grand old cognac comes alive as svelte, lean, and biscuity flavors impress the taste buds; at midpalate the flavor profile expands to include almond paste, dried apricot, nougat, and vanilla extract. Finishes gracefully, but with a sassy final kick of spirit that charms the taste buds no end. Not the monumental achievement that 1953 was, but a sterling example of how majestic and stately vintage cognac can be.

2004 Rating: ★★★★/Highly Recommended

Hine 1975 Grande Champagne Cognac (France); 40% abv, $200.

Highly attractive bronze/copper color; perfect purity. The early stage sniffings detect nicely balanced aromas of dates, slate, and oak; aeration time of another six minutes stimulates

added aromatic qualities, including papaya and cedar; not a stunning bouquet, but solid and pleasing. The palate entry features sweet tastes of light caramel and brown sugar; at midpalate the oak influence counters some of the fruity/candied sweetness, resulting in an off-dry, slightly resiny finish. Recommendable, but my least favorite of the Hine Vintage Cognacs.
2004 Rating: ★★★/Recommended

Hine 1981 Early Landed Grande Champagne Cognac (France); 40% abv, $150.

Beautiful, brilliant harvest gold color; impeccable clarity. In the initial whiffs following, the pour there's delicate evidence of flowers (carnations, honeysuckle) and yellow fruit (nectarines); aeration time of another seven minutes encourages more yellow fruit to emerge, in particular, yellow plums and banana; a highly sophisticated and ethereal bouquet of the first rank. The palate entry is notable for its unexpected trace of fire; at midpalate the spirity warmth fades, leaving behind succulent and lithe tastes of honey, egg cream, and light toffee. Finishes deliciously warm and elegant.
2004 Rating: ★★★★/Highly Recommended

Hine Rare VSOP Fine Champagne Cognac (France); 40% abv, $40.

The appearance is genuinely gorgeous, a bright bronze/burnt sienna color, with near-flawless purity. In the nose, there are mild, light aromas of tropical fruit and parchment; seven more minutes in the glass release ethereal, if languid, aromas of spice and spirit, but little else; this bouquet suffers from a lack of personality and vigor. The palate entry displays a nut-like opening taste; then at midpalate there's an expanding profile that includes oaky vanillin, young spirit, and pear drop; the body is medium-weight and the texture is silky. Concludes regrettably austere and thin. This cognac is deficient in the identity department. It could be any one of ten mediocre VSOPs currently available. Great looks may be enough in the cinema, but not in cognac.
2004 Rating: ★★/Not Recommended

Hine Triomphe Grande Champagne Cognac (France); 40% abv, $200.

The brilliant copper/tawny hue is marred badly by a disconcerting and unacceptable amount of floating gray debris; a seriously flawed appearance. The opening aromatics are lovely, a touch spicy, and mildly sweet in a tropical fruit manner; following seven minutes of further aeration the bouquet becomes deeper as the oak enters the equation, lending weight to the delicately sweet aroma that also features honey and beeswax. It's in the mouth that Triomphe triumphs; the palate entry is sinewy, sweet with overtones of marzipan and light caramel; at midpalate the taste profile highlights the oaky vanilla and honey elements. Concludes gracefully, composed, integrated, and semisweet. This must have been a bad bottle with regard to the debris. In all other phases, it still holds up well as a Hine icon. Oh, that classic mouth-feel and flavor phase.
2005 Rating: ★★★★/Highly Recommended

Hine XO (formerly Antique Très Rare) Fine Champagne Cognac (France); 40% abv, $100.

The beautiful tawny/copper color is unblemished by sediment. The first inhalations after the pour reveal sophisticated aromas of lanolin, cream, and light oaky resin; further minutes in the copita afford the bouquet the chance to stretch its legs, offering succulent, melded scents of pine nuts, light caramel (like English toffee), the early stages of rancio

and butter; a superb bouquet. The palate entry is creamy, medium-rich, and sweet; by the midpalate stage, the flavor profile expands to include sautéed almonds, bacon fat, and sweet oak. Ends in a lush, sweet style. Now as in 1996 when last I evaluated this beauty, I simply love its streamlined elegance. This is a lovely FC cognac that's harmonious and a delight to savor. Bravo.
2004 Rating: ★★★★/Highly Recommended

J. Calvet Karavan Spirit Cognac & Cinnamon (France); 40% abv, $40.

Bronze hued and flawlessly clean. As anyone might guess, snappy, zesty, crackling cinnamon rules the early aromatic stage; the cinnamon deepens with exposure to air emitting an intensely bittersweet scent that is compelling even in its one-dimensional aspect. The palate entry is lean, spicy/cinnamony, and bittersweet; at midpalate there's a bit of a drop-off in the entire flavor phase that leaves the spirit a touch flabby. Concludes well and spicy. The vanilla holds itself together better.
2005 Rating: ★★/Not Recommended

J. Calvet Karavan Spirit Cognac & Vanilla (France); 40% abv, $40.

The pale gold/marigold color is pretty and pure. Right from the first whiff vanilla dominates the aroma, leaving little room for any other scents; aeration does nothing but maintain and reinforce the strong vanilla perfume; a dream for vanilla fanatics. The palate entry is bittersweet to sweet and heavily weighted towards vanilla; at midpalate a bit of the cognac shows through the heavy curtain of vanilla, but that moment is fleeting. Ends up intensely vanilla-like and bittersweet. Even though the vanilla component totally dominates this one-note song, I liked it because there's a sense of style and agility in the spirit core. Must be a relatively young cognac.
2005 Rating: ★★★/Recommended

J. Dupont XO Grande Champagne Cognac (France); 40% abv, $144.

Very pretty bronze color with orange core highlights; excellent clarity. The opening whiffs detect mature aromas that include dried red fruits, butterscotch, and butter sautéed walnuts; in the later sniffings, the oak element surges to the forefront, eventually dominating the aroma phase and the lesser scents of tar, ash, and tobacco. The palate entry highlights the desert dry, resiny taste of wood; the midpalate stage offers off-dry supporting role flavors of nougat, roasted walnuts, and treacle. The finish is long, off-dry, intensely oaky, and vibrant. Had the wood element rounded off a bit more, I would have given a fourth star.
2005 Rating: ★★★/Recommended

Jacques Cardin Apple Flavored Cognac (France); 40% abv, $18.

Burnt orange color; superb purity. The apple flesh perfume is immediate and pointed in the first nosings after the pour; following additional aeration time, the aroma leans more to dried apple peel than apple flesh making for tarter, more austere aromatics. Entry tastes include apple butter, apple sauce, and spice; the midpalate stage features sweet, ripe apple with supplemental tastes of oak, almond butter, and paraffin. Ends on a high note as the apple peel flavor accents the cinnamon/nutmeg spiciness in a graceful manner.
2007 Rating: ★★★/Recommended

Jacques Cardin Jasmine Flavored Cognac (France); 40% abv, $18.

New copper new/auburn color; impeccable clarity. The very Asian-like, perfumed scent of jasmine dominates the opening whiffs; additional time in the glass changes little on the aromatic front, except for the jasmine turning gently sweeter and nearly grapy. Entry is decidedly floral and leafy, but off-dry; the taste profile by midpalate seems a little adrift and unfocused as the jasmine becomes all that you taste, leaving all sense of the cognac base behind. Finishes more liqueur-like than brandy-like in its flowery/grapy sweetness. Wasn't as intriguing as I'd hoped.

2007 Rating: ★★/Not Recommended

Jacques Cardin VSOP Cognac (France); 40% abv, $18.

Bronze/burnished orange color; ideal clarity. Offers pleasing first scents of white raisins, baked pineapple, and new leather; aeration stimulates additional aromatic notes including marshmallow, orange peel, and orange marmalade. Entry is tart yet bittersweet at the same time, emitting well-balanced tastes of citrus, sweet oak, and nougat; the midpalate is firm, nicely acidic and woody enough to warrant kudos, but what's lacking is genuine depth and layering in the mouth. Concludes off-dry and savory. Good value and pleasing as long as you aren't expecting greatness or profundity.

2007 Rating: ★★★/Recommended

Jean Duree VS Fine Cognac (France); 40% abv, $14.

The pleasing honey color displays excellent purity. The opening whiffs discover plump, slightly spiced aromas; six minutes of aeration stir mild scents of resin, marshmallow, and soft cheese. The palate entry is sweet, fruity, and lean; by midpalate the taste profile turns a tad hot and acidic, losing its fresh, fruity early character. Ends up way too woody/resiny. This cognac began well, then lost it at midpalate and spun out of control by the aftertaste; some good points early on, but not recommendable.

2004 Rating: ★★/Not Recommended

Jean Duree VSOP Fine Cognac (France); 40% abv, $16.

The bronze/copper color is extremely attractive and inviting; impeccable purity. The initial inhalations pick up notes of bacon and oak; seven more minutes of air contact stimulate reluctant, distant scents of chalk, black pepper, and dried red fruit. The palate entry is off-dry to semisweet and candied, if slightly muted; at midpalate the flavor closes in on itself, shutting out all possibility for depth of taste. The finish is roasted, toasty, and bittersweet; the center stages of the taste just implode, leaving behind remnants of taste from the entry. A weird experience that owns more deficiencies than positive traits.

2004 Rating: ★★/Not Recommended

Jean Fillioux XO Réserve Grande Champagne 1er Cru du Cognac (France); 44% abv, $85.

The brilliant new copper penny color is gorgeous; some floating particles seen. The opening whiffs pick up luscious aromas of holiday spice (nutmeg, cinnamon) and white raisins; seven more minutes of aeration introduces traces of hard cheese, oak/vanillin, dried fruit (apricot mostly), black pepper, and almond paste. At palate entry the texture is oily and velvety while the early-on taste features include nuts and butter cream; at midpalate the taste profile highlights the viscous texture and the nut butter/oaky/maple-like flavor. Finishes regally, without any alcohol heat and plenty of lip-smacking sautéed almond. In a word, scrumptious.

2004 Rating: ★★★★/Highly Recommended

Jules Gautret "Quest of Venture" VS Cognac (France); 40% abv, $20.

The medium amber/honey color is pretty and flawless. The early nosing passes pick up fruity, animated aromas that, while uncomplicated, are nonetheless friendly and compelling; this cognac stretches its legs with aeration, offering assertive, no-nonsense aromas of gum, yellow fruit (grapefruit, pineapple), and white raisins. The palate entry is fresh, grapy, and maple-sweet; at midpalate the flavor profile suffers from a two-alarm flash of raw spirity heat on the tongue and a surprising bit of dullness/flatness. But then it attempts to move past those obvious blemishes and finishes sweet, a tad lean, banana- and caramel-like. Wholly average, but drinkable and inoffensive. Had the midpalate and the aftertaste conducted themselves as well as the appearance, aroma, and palate entry it would have faired better and been recommended. Nice try; close, but no cigar.

2004 Rating: ★★/Not Recommended

Jules Gautret "Quest of Venture" VSOP Cognac (France); 40% abv, $25.

The color is a handsome, deep bay/bronze hue; impeccable purity; this is as fetching an appearance as you can get with grape brandy. The initial sniffings are confronted with a rather closed-off early innings aroma; strangely, aeration and swirling, which normally help arouse some fragrance elements, largely fail as meager, timid scents of limp vegetation and hard candy do nothing to salvage the aroma phase of the evaluation; what's weird is that the VS displayed a sound, direct aroma that was simple but engaged and engaging. The palate entry is pleasantly sap-like and sweet, if kind of cognac-by-the-numbers; at midpalate there are traces of oaky, vanilla-like character and eventually a round, even supple ripe grapiness that lasts well into the aftertaste. Decent and drinkably ordinary once you proceed past the muted bouquet.

2004 Rating: ★★/Not Recommended

Jules Gautret 10 Year Old Cognac (France); 40% abv, $39.

One thing must be said about these three Jules Gautrets, they are extremely attractive cognacs to look at; this older edition is a lovely, shiny burnished orange/copper color that loves direct light; excellent purity. The first stages of the bouquet emit aromas that exhibit minor, almost weary hints of black raisins and plums; another seven minutes in the copita serve to stimulate meek, off-dry scents of tobacco, oak, and fruit candy; what happened to this bouquet and that of the equally lackluster VSOP? The palate entry at least comes to the dance with proper shoes as it shows fruity opening tastes of baked banana, pear drops, and guava; at midpalate the flavor profile turns to the oak impact as the taste goes sap- and maple-like, displaying some body and textural presence. Finishes sappy sweet, moderately fruity, and pleasant enough for a third rating star and a recommendation.

2004 Rating: ★★★/Recommended

Landy Désir Cognac (France); 40% abv, $50.

The bottle is regrettably shaped like a buxom, large-bottomed woman dressed in a clingy red dress topped off by a red toreador hat. Packaging simply doesn't come any more crass than this. The harvest gold color is flawlessly pure. The fruitiness detected right off the crack of the bat reminds me very much of the VS; after further air contact, notes of caramel/toffee get added to the aromatic mix in very similar fashion to the VS. The palate entry features light bodied tastes of hard candy, especially nougat; by the midpalate stage the flavor profile takes on a bakery/pastry aspect as the fruit diminishes and the sweetness drives forward along with a mild woodiness. Concludes a little thin, a little too astringent for my liking.

2007 Rating: ★★/Not Recommended

Landy VS Cognac (France); 40% abv, $20.

The amber color is pretty and pure. The opening whiffs detect vibrant fruit, especially green apple and grapefruit; later sniffings unearth solid, candied aromas of light toffee and nougat. The palate entry is lean, acidic/astringent, and semisweet; at midpalate the fruit component re-emerges alongside a potent resiny oakiness that adds some character to this otherwise breezy, slightly awkward, and astringent youngster. Ends with an acidic bite that takes a rating star away from it. While drinkable and potentially charming, its ungainly, stumbling, and unfocused youth gets in the way of it being recommendable.

2007 Rating: ★★/Not Recommended

Landy VSOP Cognac (France); 40% abv, $30.

The rich topaz/honey color is highly attractive; unblemished purity. In the first inhalations, the aroma comes across as being integrated and like chocolate covered apricots or cherries; aeration stimulates even more concentrated confectionary-like scents, including refined sugar, caramel, and cocoa, without losing the fruit element. The palate entry is clean, toffee-like, and semisweet; the midpalate stage reveals a moderately baked quality that's appealing and wholly complementary to the fruit/candy. Finishes medium-weighted, a touch oily, oaky, and fruity.

2007 Rating: ★★★/Recommended

Landy XO No. 1 Cognac (France); 40% abv, $70.

A marriage of 50% Grande Champagne and 50% Borderies eaux-de-vie, some upwards of 35 years old. The color is a deep old copper penny hue; the purity level is high. In the first few inhalations after the pour lovely, evolved aromas of crushed flower petals, very slight citrus rind and oaky vanillin are perfectly integrated; further air contact serves to bring up a mildly creamy/buttery scent that seems to underpin the flowers, citrus zest, and oak; to be blunt, it's not an assertive or expressive bouquet and I would therefore suggest that you simply move right on to the taste which tells the story of this cognac. The palate entry is warm, inviting, velvety, and honeyed; the harmonious midpalate stage highlights succulent tastes of light toffee, candied almonds, and coffee with cream. Landy XO finishes elegantly, sweet, and without any heat or harshness. Smooth, silky, excellent drinking for the money. The flavor and finish stages are truly wonderful.

2003 Rating: ★★★★/Highly Recommended

Le Réviseur VS Fine Petite Champagne Single Estate Cognac (France); 40% abv, $31.

The golden hay/wheat field hue is very pretty and absolutely pristine. The initial nosing passes find succulent, biscuity aromas of fruit tart and sugar cookie batter; later sniffs encounter light touches of newly tanned leather, marzipan, cinnamon, and honeysuckle. The palate entry is softly sweet like cake frosting and supple; the midpalate stage offers a nicely acidic/crackling taste of yellow fruit that's impacted by a vanilla/spicy oak quality; together these uncomplicated components work well. Finishes measuredly sweet and honest in that it's not trying to be something it's not. This is a sound no-nonsense cognac at a good price.
2006 Rating: ★★★/Recommended

Le Réviseur VSOP Fine Petite Champagne Single Estate Cognac (France); 40% abv, $38.

Honey/topaz color; flawless purity. The zesty smells coming from the glass in the first sniffs tell me that this brandy is young but self-assured, piquant yet elegant, racy but sophisticated; the later whiffs pick up minor oak impact, but lots of caramel and toffee. Tastes of honey and chocolate at the entry, then at midpalate there's a rush of almond butter, brown sugar, and cocoa. Concludes well and graceful in a satiny texture that bolsters the oaky sweetness. This cognac is fun to drink. Very well done.
2006 Rating: ★★★★/Highly Recommended

Le Réviseur XO Fine Petite Champagne Single Estate Cognac (France); 40% abv, $50.

The copper kettle color is gorgeous; ideal clarity. The opening salvo of aroma is all about plums, red berries, and raisins; further aeration reveals a woody/candied side that's marked by old sweet oak, cherry preserves as well as poppy seed. The palate entry is sleek, racy, and woody sweet; the midpalate stage is accentuated by long, sinewy flavors of pipe tobacco, marzipan, dark caramel, fudge, and chocolate orange. Finishes stately yet vivacious. This cognac rocks from stem to stern. Go out and track it down.
2006 Rating: ★★★★★/Highest Recommendation

Leyrat VS Domaine de Chez Maillard Fine Cognac (France); 40% abv, $40.

The pretty harvest gold/marigold color is free of sediment. The first nosing is very fruity and pruny, maybe even fig-like; aeration actually serves to diminish the fruit component while allowing the spirit and light oak elements to emerge into an ethereal bouquet that while fresh is slightly skimpy. The palate entry highlights the delicacy of the sweet, caramel-like taste; by the midpalate stage, there's additional and genuinely enticing flavors including cocoa, toffee, and molasses. Ends up with a welcome burst of sweet, silky flavor. This fey, immature (that's obvious due to its still-grapy nature) cognac came from behind to end up being wholly palatable and better than average for a VS.
2006 Rating: ★★★/Recommended

Leyrat VSOP Domaine de Chez Maillard Premium Cognac (France); 40% abv, $52.

The straw yellow/green color is attractive and flawlessly clean. Like the VS, there's an initial perfume of sweet, ripe grapes, but in this case there's likewise a note of butter; with time in the glass, the bouquet deepens moderately, emitting more substantial fragrances of oaky vanilla, dates, raisins, and worn saddle leather. The palate entry is subtle in its sweetness and intensely ripe and milk chocolate-like; at the midpalate stage, the taste profile adds

delectable notes of apple butter, cream, and cocoa. Concludes concentrated, sweet, and moderately oaky.
2006 Rating: ★★★/Recommended

Leyrat XO Domaine de Chez Maillard Premium Cognac (France); 40% abv, $120.
Significantly darker, more bronze-like in color than the three previous Leyrats; so clear and clean that I can see the natural oils; lovely and eye-catching. The opening nosing passes detect more mature scents of palm oil, old leather, and dried herbs; more air contact stirs notes of slate, minerals, and limestone; long aeration isn't an asset to this cognac. The palate entry tastes of meringue, light toffee, egg cream, and vanilla bean; by the midpalate stage, the flavor profile expands to include marizpan, nougat, and candied nuts. Ends up sweet, satiny, and pleasing, but considering it's an XO, not profound.
2006 Rating: ★★★/Recommended

Leyrat XO Elite Domaine de Chez Maillard Cognac (France); 41% abv, $170.
As with its Leyrat mates, this is a very pretty autumnal gold to bronze-colored brandy; unblemished clarity. This aroma shows the most quietly potent subtlety of the bunch as I pick up tightly wrapped scents of new leather and dried fruit immediately after the pour; following another seven minutes span in the copita, the aroma transforms into a bouquet of elegance and finesse, emitting sophisticated fragrances of pine needle, oak, nuts, and lanolin; by a long way, the most complex bouquet of the Leyrats. Plump and enticingly sweet at the palate entry; at the midpalate stage, the taste profile is honeyed, creamy, multilayered, and smooth. Concludes as gracefully as it begins, with reined-in notes of brown butter, roasted walnuts, nougat, honey, and dark caramel. A seriously nice and well made XO cognac. Seek and buy.
2006 Rating: ★★★★/Highly Recommended

Leyrat XO Vieille Réserve Domaine de Chez Maillard Cognac (France); 40% abv, $94.
Light topaz/amber in color; very minor sediment seen under the examination lamp. Like its younger siblings, this XO is fruity aroma-wise after the pour, especially tropical fruit and white grapes; aeration time doesn't stimulate a whole lot more in the way of aroma even after seven additional minutes, maybe some low-key nuts, but that's about all. The palate entry features nice pineapple and grapefruit flavors that are tangy and fresh; by the midpalate the tropical fruit components are joined by sweeter flavors of light honey, butter cream, and chocolate cake frosting; no oak/wood influence to speak of. Finishes svelte, gently sweet, and satiny smooth.
2006 Rating: ★★★/Recommended

Lheraud 1950 Grande Champagne Cognac (France); 40% abv, $449.
The deep honey/bronze appearance is ruined completely by clouds of gray-white floating debris. The opening bouquet is delicate, shy, and emits polite scents of lanolin, almond oil, and light oak; time in the glass doesn't stimulate further deepening or expansion; it's a bouquet lacking in charm and presence. In the mouth there's considerably more stuffing displayed as the palate entry taste offers sweet, honeyed flavors that are more oak-driven than fruit-driven; the midpalate phase is meaty, plump, and razor-edged in acid. The finish is

chewy, sweet, oaky, and intensely caramelized. The concentrated and racy flavor and finish stages redeemed this dubious cognac to the point of a cautious recommendation.
2001 Rating: ★★★/Recommended

Lheraud 1965 Grande Champagne Cognac (France); 48% abv, $325.
Bright coppery bronze/honey hue; like its siblings, some floating bits noted. The opening bouquet in the first couple of passes is incredibly toasted, charred, smoky, and baked, almost like the interior of a brick oven; aeration only makes the roasted quality more concentrated, becoming almost baked grain and husk-like; a genuinely intriguing and individual bouquet that I like very much. The entry tastes are baked, bittersweet, and intensely caramelized; the midpalate phase is off-dry to semisweet, showing flavors of baked apple, roasted chestnut, road tar, cigar smoke, and palm oil. The aftertaste is long, resiny, bittersweet, and idiosyncratic. There isn't an ounce of fat or flab on this sleek middleweight. I love the sinewy, bittersweet virtues; yum.
2001 Rating: ★★★★/Highly Recommended

Lheraud 1970 Petite Champagne Cognac (France); 48% abv, $270.
The color is a vibrant bronze; more minute floating debris than I'd like to see beneath the examination lamp. The initial nosing passes following the pour ferret out off-dry scents of oak roasted almond, and dried fruit; more than six minutes in the glass rouses more subtle aromas, specifically, egg cream, light caramel, vanilla, and very ripe grapes; a moderately supple and elegant bouquet. Pleasantly peppery and chocolaty at palate entry; the midpalate is lean and sinewy as tastes of cocoa, tar, and tobacco leaf highlight the flavor phase. The finish borders on austere as a streak of astringency overtakes the candy and fruit flavors. Perfect for admirers of wiry, dry, and resiny cognacs.
2001 Rating: ★★★/Recommended

Lheraud Edouard III VS Fine Petite Champagne Cognac (France); 40% abv, $22.
Terrifically pretty bronze/orange hue; minor sediment spotted. The bouquet from the opening passes is piquant, spirity, citrusy, and vibrant; with aeration the heady bite blows off, leaving the door open for vigorous scents of tropical fruit (unsweetened pineapple and coconut, especially), grape vine leaf, very light toffee, and cocoa; I like this immature but focused fragrance. The palate entry is so stone dry that it's bitter; by the midpalate point the resiny bitterness is so dominant on the tongue that no other taste characteristics are allowed through. The aftertaste is lean, even austere due to the unrelenting astringency and outright bitterness. The gorgeous appearance and moderately comely qualities of the bouquet are totally swamped by the overly bitter and resiny taste and finish phases. Awkward, with no redeeming virtues.
2001 Rating: ★/Not Recommended

Louis Royer VSOP "Préférence" Cognac (France); 40% abv, $40.
Attractive burnished copper color; some sediment seen. Smells of candied apple and candied banana out of the gate; the super-sweet, sugary aroma doesn't abate at all in strength with air contact and thus remains overly candied. Entry is cloying, icky-sticky, and unnecessarily sweet—what could these people possibly be thinking; the midpalate stage is

undrinkable, so refined sugar/molasses-like is it. I identified this sickly sweet beast perfectly in my 1993 review and unfortunately the chuckleheads at Louis Royer still haven't gotten the message. A blatant embarrassment for the cognac category.

2007 Rating: ★/Not Recommended

Louis Royer VSOP Force 53 Fine Champagne Cognac (France); 53% abv, $45.

Brilliant medium amber/topaz color that's gorgeous under the examination lamp; unblemished clarity. First aromatic impressions are fruity, clean, ripe, and vividly spirity without being overwrought or stinging; considering that the abv is 53%, the bouquet is surprisingly harmonious and integrated, even after the additional aeration period of seven minutes; nuts, chocolate, fruitcake scents abound. Entry is punchy, ripe, too syrup-like, and full-weighted in texture; midpalate stage makes an attempt at a tony/racy flavor profile that's underpinned by the elevated (cask strength?) abv, but there are likewise nut, dried fruit, oak, and spice tastes that try to make it all work. Regrettably, it finishes way too varnish-like, harsh, and raw in the throat. There simply isn't enough balance, blending skill, or foundational quality here.

2007 Rating: ★★/Not Recommended

Louis Royer XO Cognac (France); 40% abv, $110.

Beautiful mahogany/chestnut/henna color; superb purity. Gives off the odor more of an oak-aged rum than a cognac as the scent is heavily woody in the initial sniffs; seven more minutes of exposure to air doesn't improve the aromatic situation one iota; basically it's a hollow shell of caramel blanketing some obscure spirit that's been obliterated by mismanagement. Entry is fat, sappy, flabby, glue-like, and ultra sweet; midpalate merely affirms the gooey, over-caramelized entry. I don't bother with the finish since there's no point.

2007 Rating: ★/Not Recommended

Louis XIII de Remy Martin Grande Champagne Cognac (France); 40% abv, $1,500.

The auburn/topaz color is dazzling and the purity level is the highest. The initial sniffings after the pour find layered, dry to off-dry aromas that include banana, guava, and linseed oil; another seven minutes of exposure to air exposes more fruit elements, most importantly, fig and prune as well as pastry dough, honey, and maple. Once in the mouth, LXIII displays the grandeur of Grande Champagne eau-de-vie in the length of the flavor and in the intense woodiness of the taste; by the midpalate stage there are additional layers of flavor, including figs, dates, prunes, dried apricot, and vanilla. Finishes elegantly, even stately, warm, smooth as silk, and more oaky than fruity succulent. Minor rancio. I want to rate this Grande Champagne five stars but I can't justify ranking it with my all-time favorite GC cognac blockbusters that include AE Dor Hors d'Age No. 9, Brillet Très Rare Heritage Brût de Fut, Jean Fillioux Très Vieux, A. Hardy Noces de Diamant, Daniel Bouju Empereur XO, Delamain Extra, and Frapin VIP XO. That said, it's a terrific cognac that's close to five stars.

2006 Rating: ★★★★/Highly Recommended

Maison Rouge VSOP Cognac (France); 40% abv, $20.

Standard issue topaz color; excellent clarity. The first nosing passes pick up very delicate scents of apple, grape, and pear; following another seven minutes of air contact, the aroma adds a hint of wood in the form of vanilla bean; a fundamental bouquet, but it's sound and pleasing. The palate entry is mellow, rounded, and mildly spiced; by the midpalate stage the taste profile gains in scope as the flavor of the wood underpins the grapiness/fruitiness nicely. Ends firmly and with an unexpected oiliness that works in its favor. Good job here and all for an attractive price.

2007 Rating: ★★★/Recommended

Maison Surrenne 1986 Distillerie Galtaud Borderies Cognac (France); 40.5% abv, $70.
Bottled in 2001 from a mere three casks. The beautiful amber/honey hue is flawless and brilliant beneath the examination lamp. The first set of whiffs are treated to lovely scents of peach cobbler, guava, and mint; another seven minutes of aeration entice seductive and understated aromas of coconut, lanolin, walnut, and buttery oak resin to come out and play, dazzling the olfactory sense. The palate entry displays a quick flash of spirity heat on the tongue then that recedes, leaving behind lush, fruity tastes of candied walnuts, marshmallow, and resin; the midpalate's texture is silky, sinewy, and firm while the flavor profile highlights white raisins, dried peaches and pineapple, and just the dawning evidence of mushroomy attic-like rancio. The finish smacks of maple, butterscotch, oak, and even a devilish trace of cream sherry. There's so much going on here that right after one layer is detected, there are three more waiting to be discovered. Makes a strong case for what I've felt for many years: that the Borderies district can, if dealt with by deft hands, provide cognacs that absolutely rival those of the far more revered and famous Grande Champagne.

2003 Rating: ★★★★★/Highest Recommendation

Maison Surrenne Ancienne Distillerie 1993 Harvest 100% Petite Champagne Cognac (France); 40.2% abv, $35.
Old sauternes/old gold color; excellent purity. First whiffs detect welcoming aromas of ripe banana, marshmallow, and peach/nectarine; aeration stimulates background scents of oaky vanillin, baked peach/nectarine, white grapes, and milk chocolate. Entry highlights the oak-influenced vanilla bean element to a peak experience; midpalate sees more spice development, mostly in the emergence of nutmeg. Finishes clean, gently spicy, and woody, and moderately baked/toasty. Very good buy for a 100% Petite Champagne.

2007 Rating: ★★★★/Highly Recommended

Maison Surrenne Ancienne Distillerie Lot 1989/4 Petite Champagne Cognac (France); 40.2% abv, $30.
Pretty amber/light honey color; excellent purity. The aroma wastes no time by being coy and immediately puts on a dazzling display that features beautifully melded scents of vanilla wafer, citrus zest, and light wood resin in the first two nosings; aeration urges other fragrances, most notably, spice, raisins, and toasted bread, to blend with the previously noted aromas in the third pass; by the fourth and final nosing, the various components are seamlessly folded into a delicate, semisweet, and mildly oaky aroma that's more spicy than anything; seductive and wonderful. This cognac is lithe, dry, and woody at the palate entry, then at midpalate it turns authentically complex, layered, and blissfully sweet and lip-smacking; truly delicious in the mouth. The aftertaste is long but in keeping with the lightness of the flavor phase, agile and lean. A clinic that shows how cognac can be nimble and profound simultaneously quite like no other regional brandy. Bravo.

2000 Rating: ★★★★/Highly Recommended

Maison Surrenne Ancienne Distillery 1992 Petite Champagne Cognac (France); 40.2% abv, $32.

Good amber/harvest gold color that's flawless. The first few passes pick up a gum-like, tropical fruit sweetness that's alluring; with further time in the glass the aroma expands to include marshmallow, cotton candy, candied almond, and a deft touch of aloe. The palate entry goes a bit flat after the generous, vivacious bouquet but does offer some early pleasure in the form of baked apple; by midpalate additional flavors appear, mostly baked pear, mild tobacco leaf, and sweet oaky vanilla. The finish is medium-long, off-dry, and guava-like. Certainly likeable and recommendable, but not as majestic as some other Maison Surrenne bottlings of the recent past (think: Tonneau No. 1 Petite Champagne and Cask 356 Grande Champagne, to name two ★★★★ offerings). A good value, however.

2003 Rating: ★★★/Recommended

Maison Surrenne Collector's Series Cask 356 Grande Champagne Cognac (France); 42.3% abv, $2,000.

Only 24 bottles released per year from this single cask; a marriage of cognacs that are at least a century old. The color here is brilliant new copper penny. The compelling and spicy aroma after the pour smells of black pepper, hot green chili pepper, and moss; several minutes in the sampling glass unleash further, deeper scents of palm oil, almond butter, and tea leaves; coy, sensual, and seductive. In the mouth this senior citizen still shows remarkable spirity zest and a dry, resiny, dried fruit flavor profile at entry; the midpalate taste is a rancio clinic, all soft blue cheese, vanilla extract, and mushroom flavors. The finish is mapley and semisweet. Unbelievably luscious.

2001 Rating: ★★★★★/Highest Recommendation

Maison Surrenne Collector's Series Tonneau No. 1 Petite Champagne Cognac (France); 41.9% abv, $270.

A mere 198 bottles available from a cask filled in 1922. The chestnut brown color shows a wonderfully attractive golden edge. A heavenly note of dark, bittersweet chocolate delights the olfactory sense during the first two nosing passes after the pour; aeration helps this golden oldie hit aromatic stride as seductive and understated scents of high cocoa content chocolate, pear drops, dark caramel, oaky vanilla extract, and honey make for thrilling inhalations; while no evidence of rancio is noted, this composed, confident bouquet doesn't really need it. The palate entry is focused, off-dry, and smacks of dark caramel; at the midpalate point the creamy, slightly bitter flavor and silky texture escort the taste buds to cognac nirvana. The finish is medium-long, intensely toffee-like, semisweet, and lip-smacking delicious. A classic whose rarity makes it all the more special.

2001 Rating: ★★★★★/Highest Recommendation

Maison Surrenne Distillerie Galtaud Lot 1984/02, Casks 2 & 3 Borderies Cognac (France); 40.4% abv, $70.

Brilliantly clean copper/amber color; handsome appearance. Right from the initial nosing pass I detect the Borderies trademark nuttiness; the second go-round adds a buttery quality that's more akin to almond butter than to dairy butter; the third nosing sees the addition of wood resin, marzipan, and nougat; in the last pass following over seven minutes of air contact the bouquet focuses on the wood, emitting a divine nut butter/bacon fat aroma that has my socks rolling up and down; a serene, composed, elegant bouquet that's in my current crop of favorites. On the palate, this cognac sings with grace but likewise with significant authority as the entry flavor is oaky sweet and deep in dried fruit; the midpalate stage is sweet in a ripe, fruity manner that has elements of dried apple and pear plus sensuous notes of spice and dough. The finish is medium long, sweet, and even a touch smoky. A genuinely lovely Borderies that ranks with the best I've tasted from this overlooked Cognac district.

2000 Rating: ★★★★★/Highest Recommendation

Maison Surrenne Legacy XO Lot 1972/9 Grande Champagne Cognac (France); 41.2% abv, $100.

The pretty bronze/amber hue is marked slightly by some floating debris. The nose is generous and friendly right from the pour as developed aromas of oak, ripe grapes, and roasted nuts greet the olfactory sense; the second pass doesn't see any further expansion or deepening, but in the third nosing after six minutes of exposure the aroma becomes a bouquet as an oily quality unites the disparate scents into a single aromatic sensation that's moderately sweet, mildly woody, and verging on being delicate; in the fourth pass, I notice a slight decline in strength, but nothing that I'd consider serious or detrimental; overall an alluring bouquet. This cognac is more substantial in the mouth than in the nose as sweet tastes of vanilla extract, caramel, and nougat impress the taste buds at palate entry; the midpalate phase shows some pleasant layering and depth of flavor and is very sweet. The aftertaste is extended, candy sweet, and even a bit chalky. Not an unctuous, powerhouse Grande Champagne at all, but more to my taste like a solid, chalky Petite Champagne. Very nice.

2000 Rating: ★★★★/Highly Recommended

Maison Surrenne Lot 1875 Cognac (France); 41.9% abv, $1,200.

The surprisingly youthful copper/honey amber color is severely blemished by unappetizing detritus that floats around like a school of transparent fish; if I'm paying $1,200 I don't want to find a swamp in the bottle. The nose at opening shows a fey touch of rancio in the form of hard cheese which by the second pass is replaced by old oak resin and dried fruit; the third nosing reveals hints of toffee and caramel, but little else; with aeration, the bouquet becomes less expressive by the fourth and last nosing pass as the caramel, toffee, and fruit disappear leaving behind a minerally/steely aroma that's clearly over the hill. A bit better in the mouth than in the nose as the palate entry introduces a touch of nougat; the midpalate is laced with flavors of tropical fruit, old barrels, and hard cheese. The finish is short and oaky. A relic that should have been employed for blending purposes rather than as a singular bottling which sadly only serves to showcase its slow disintegration. A questionable call on this one by the usually spot-on team at Germain-Robin.

2000 Rating: ★/Not Recommended

Maison Surrenne Lot 1946 Cognac (France); 41.9% abv, $400.

Intense, attractive, copper/burnished orange tint; some minor suspended particles noted. The nose at opening is prickly in the nasal cavity and shows signs of nectarine and plum; in the second pass, subtle hints of cherry and paraffin get added to the mix; following seven

minutes of aeration, the nose expands to include scents of spice and oak, but turns sedate and inexpressive overall as the spiritiness subsides; the fourth and final nosing run-through displays the cognac's maturity and poise as aromas of old oak, dried fruit, and spice become more muscular and pronounced; an uneven bouquet, but one that ends well. Better in the mouth, the flavor starts off with a buttery/fatty bang at palate entry, then turns elegant and nutty/oily at midpalate; I particularly like the oily texture and mouth-feel of this old cognac. The finish is long, spirity, oaky sweet, and composed. While I like it enough to give it four ratings stars, I don't find it as profound as I like to see fifty year old-plus cognacs be.
2000 Rating: ★★★★/Highly Recommended

Marceille VS Petite Fine Champagne Cognac (France); 40% abv, $15.

Autumnal gold; superb purity. The bouquet is simple and distant, exhibiting mildly toasty/biscuity aromas of baked pear, refined sugar, and nut meat. Palate entry is lean, acidic, hot; midpalate shows a sweeter, candied taste but skimpy texture. Finishes with vanilla wafer and toffee tastes and harsh on the tongue. There's simply not enough of anything here to think it even average.
2002 Rating: ★/Not Recommended

Marceille VSOP Petite Fine Champagne Cognac (France); 40% abv, $20.

Golden color, with clouds of sediment. Reluctant nose smells of gum, cotton fabric. In the mouth, it begins by tasting of butter, candied almonds, sugar; midpalate is pear-like and moderately spicy. Aftertaste is long, sap-like, gum-like; stunningly fundamental grape brandy 101 stuff. Can't get too hurt by cheapo price, but it still is charmless. Almost can't believe this amateurish stuff was made in Cognac.
2002 Rating: ★/Not Recommended

Marceille XO Petite Fine Champagne Cognac (France); 40% abv, $35.

Pretty bronze/deep amber appearance; good clarity. The aroma just simply can't seem to gather itself even after eight minutes of aeration. In the mouth, there's a tangy caramel/toffee/nougat quality by midpalate that's actually quite appealing and lasts well into the pleasingly sweet, honeyed aftertaste. Far better than its faceless siblings. At least, this version displays some genuine cognac personality and presence. Do I think it's great? No, but, for the money it's actually a good buy. I'd employ it as a mixer when brandy is called for in a cocktail recipe.
2002 Rating: ★★★/Recommended

Marthe Aquarelle 18 Year Old Grande Champagne Cognac (France); 40% abv, $77.

Lovely bright amber hue; very good purity. The first two nosing passes offer gently fruited aromas of pear, peach, and nectarine; with aeration, deeper scents of wood resin, sugar, light honey, and vanilla wafer enchant the olfactory sense. Elegantly sweet and fruity at palate entry; at midpalate the taste profile expands significantly to include banana, white grapes, sugar cookie, and oak. The finish is woody/resiny and drier than the midpalate. A tightly-knit, well-integrated GC whose bearing is at once regal and racy. A cognac at its peak.
2002 Rating: ★★★★/Highly Recommended

Marthe Fauve 23 Year Old Grande Champagne Cognac (France); 40% abv, $95.

Lovely copper hue; excellent purity. The opening aroma displays inviting scents of hard candy, brown sugar, vanilla bean, and chocolate cake frosting; more time in the glass allows for a deepening of the candy quality, as it takes on more of a honey/toffee character than hard candy, plus there's a last minute fruitiness that reminds me most of sour cherry. The palate entry is totally dry and slightly peppery; the midpalate stage is opulent, lush, and fully textured as assertive and exotic flavors of peach cobbler, poached pear, tea leaves, and dark caramel vie for dominance on the tongue. The aftertaste is warming, fruity, mildly oaky, and rounded. A singularly rich, lip-smacking GC.
2002 Rating: ★★★★/Highly Recommended

Marthe Sepia 30 Year Old Grande Champagne Cognac (France); 44% abv, $125.

Bronze-reddish orange color; supremely pure. The nose in the first moments after the pour shows what I've come to identify as the trademark gentle fruitiness of the brand in the forms of pears, peaches, and tropical fruits, especially banana and pineapple; eight more minutes in the glass stimulates further aromatic growth as the nose begins to exhibit some oakiness that seems to underpin the fruit. The palate entry is firm and bold, but neither aggressive nor hot; by the midpalate point, the flavor takes off like a guided missile as tastes of light rancio, oak, blue cheese, candied walnuts, and ripe grapes totally disarm the taste buds. The finish is lovely, sweet, slightly cocoa-like, oaky, and refined. At the height of its powers.
2002 Rating: ★★★★/Highly Recommended

Menuet Extra 25 Year Old Grande Champagne Cognac (France); 40% abv, $95.

The topaz/copper hue is stunningly beautiful under the examination lamp; perfect purity. The initial sniffings after the pour offer zesty, piquant, spicy aromas, laced with black pepper and nutmeg; further time in the glass sees the addition of egg cream, light caramel, and sweet oak aromas that complement the underlying spiciness. At palate entry, it's immediately clear that this cognac mouth-presence relies heavily on ideal balance between sweetness, acidity, wood, and spirit; by midpalate succulent, bittersweet flavors of dark caramel, cocoa, pecan, and vanilla extract provide a seamless flavor phase. The finish is intensely bittersweet, molasses-like, nutty, and immensely appealing. Luscious and entirely satisfying; a cognac in its prime period.
2002 Rating: ★★★★/Highly Recommended

Menuet Hors d'Age 50 Year Old Grande Champagne Cognac (France); 40% abv, $299.

So tawny/red that it looks like a 40 year old tawny port; quite a bit of dark sediment seen floating under the exam lamp; that should not happen at this level. The opening bouquet is a touch faded and distant, emitting mere echoes of once-ripe fruit, oak, and cheese-like rancio; aeration assists this weary bouquet a little bit by adding a touch of prunes/black plums; an exhausted bouquet, period. The palate entry alone displays far more character and sensory impact than the entire ten minute nosing stage, offering semisweet flavors of bittersweet chocolate, orange pekoe tea, and cocoa butter; the midpalate stage comes on strong with added tastes of toasted walnut, almond butter, bacon fat (partial rancio), brown sugar, and intensely sweet oak. The aftertaste is rich, almost syrupy, and decadent. The terrific taste and aftertaste stages fully redeemed the limp, lights on-nobody-home bouquet.
2002 Rating: ★★★★/Highly Recommended

Menuet XO Grande Champagne Cognac (France); 40% abv, $60.

The new copper penny color enchants the eye; ideal purity. The initial nosing passes pick up mildly woodsy scents of mushroom, earth, and candy; aeration adds fragrances of marshmallow, hard candy, dark toffee, and damp pavement. At the palate entry, there's, to my complete surprise, a slight corkiness to the initial taste; then at midpalate the flavor phase rights itself by offering honey-sweet, ripe fruit, and black peppery tastes; there's a spirity zestiness, almost a hotness, to the flavor phase that's a tad disquieting and aggressive. The aftertaste is long, moderately sweet, honeyed, and hot. For an XO, too raw; what's with the "corked" aroma?

2002 Rating: ★★/Not Recommended

Origine VS Private Reserve Cognac (France); 40% abv, $26.

The color is deep amber/honey; excellent purity. The reticent bouquet takes a while to get its engine turned over, emitting very little until the ninth or tenth minute of the sniffing period when it at last offers timid scents of raisins, faint oak, and sweetened coconut. The palate entry is pleasingly sweet and smooth, displaying tastes of mint, cedar, almond, and white raisins; by the midpalate the flavor profile ratchets up the intensity by adding more concentrated elements of buttercream and maple that go on to dominate well into the sweet, sap-like finish.

2005 Rating: ★★★/Recommended

Origine VSOP Rare Cognac (France); 40% abv, $36.

The bronze color flashes an orange core; superb clarity. Similar to its younger sibling, the VS, the early-stage aroma borders on being meek to the point of annoyance; more time in the glass stirs languid scents of pine, grass, and non-descript yellow fruit. The palate entry is flabbier than it should be and lightweight; by the midpalate stage, there's more of a sense of authentic cognac as the taste profile includes equal measures of oak/wood, dried fruit (prunes, in particular), and a nice caramel/toffee/nougat sweetness that lasts long into the aftertaste. The virtues, however, didn't stage enough of a fight to rescue this cognac from mediocrity. Skip this; buy the VS for its value.

2005 Rating: ★★/Not Recommended

Pages Vedrenne "Forgotten Casks" Vat 48 Rare Cognac (France); 43% abv, $238.

Mahogany/cola/auburn color; excellent clarity. Dark chocolate malt, old oak, and old wood-paneled library aromas make for mildly interesting early-on sniffing; like the Vat 54, the aroma just doesn't develop well in the glass and therefore subtracts from the whole experience because aroma is pivotal to total enjoyment. Entry is very sweet and intensely honeyed, yet the taste displays ample acidity to carry off the sweetness; at midpalate the flavor profile goes in a decidedly chocolate/cocoa direction that is mildly reminiscent of Pedro Ximenez sherry. Ends up buttery/creamy and pruny/raisiny sweet. The Brandy de Jerez-like sweetness will not be to every cognac lover's liking and therefore the audience potential is niche only.

2007 Rating: ★★★/Recommended

Pages Vedrenne "Forgotten Casks" Vat 49 Rare Cognac (France); 45% abv, $279.

Pretty chestnut brown/mahogany color; flawless clarity. Offers notes of egg cream, very old leather, and molasses in the opening round of sniffing; aeration releases baked/oven roasted scents of brown sugar, honeywheat toast, prune Danish, and figs. The flavor intensity at entry is highlighted by the honeyed, cream sherry-like flavor, in which brown sugar and cane syrup are in complete charge; the midpalate stage features a sugar-sweet taste that unfolds in the finish with waves of oak, honey, cocoa, and coffee. While lacking in acidity, the over-the-top vanilla cream nectar flavor challenges the Cognac Establishment like few other cognacs I know of. I'm giving this one an extra nod for its intrepid attitude, something that's sorely lacking in cognac these days.

2007 Rating: ★★★★/Highly Recommended

Pages Vedrenne "Forgotten Casks" Vat 54 Rare Cognac (France); 40% abv, $157.

Chestnut brown color; superb purity. The aroma upfront takes some patience and deep inhalations to gain some traction, but once the scent starts coming it's woody and leathery, with a soft hint of cocoa; even with another seven minutes of air contact, this aroma remains reluctant and muted by typical cognac standards; light touches of cola and egg cream are noted at the last moment. Entry tastes include cocoa butter, honey, treacle, marzipan, and nougat; by midpalate the taste profile leans towards fudge and cake frosting. Finishes intensely sweet and chocolaty. Highly stylistic and admittedly lush in the mouth, but for the steep price I want a more complete package, one that harmonizes appearance (winner), aroma (loser), taste (winner with caveat attached due to concentrated sweetness), and aftertaste (winner).

2007 Rating: ★★★/Recommended

Pages Vedrenne "Forgotten Casks" Vat 91001 Rare Cognac (France); 46% abv, $298.

Auburn/henna/cream sherry brown color; unblemished purity. Curiously weird first aromas are almost fennel- and licorice-like, as well as like paraffin and floor wax; additional air contact does little to counter the waxiness that comes to dominate the whole aromatic stage. Entry is drier and leaner than the Vats 48, 49, and 54 but there's an unwelcome metallic/tinny taste that undercuts the first sampling; the midpalate taste goes waywardly bitter and unpleasantly sharp, almost like coffee grounds. This may be the reason why this is a "Forgotten Cask". Should have been "Long Forgotten".

2007 Rating: ★/Not Recommended

Park VSOP Cognac (France); 40% abv, $57.

Pleasing to the eye amber/honey color with golden core notes; good purity. The upfront aroma is assertive and generous in its bearing and biscuity and fruity (baked pineapple) in its perfume; further time for air contact reveals a leaner face as the acid emerges, thereby enhancing the fruit component and making the bouquet seem enticingly fresh. The palate entry retains the acid backbone noted in the nose, which allows the light wood and fruit elements to charm the taste buds; the midpalate stage features lively, immature flavors of ripe grape, slightly awry acid levels, and touches of pineapple and mango. Though the taste stumbles a little in the midpalate, there's enough overall quality here for a guarded recommendation.

2006 Rating: ★★★/Recommended

Park XO Cognac Traditional Reserve (France); 40% abv, $98.

The honey/burnished orange color is very pretty and blemish free. In the first nosing passes, there's plenty of wood, maple, and honey to grab onto; seven minutes of additional aeration stimulate seductive aromas of soft cheese and very ripe fruit, mainly pear and quince, plus mature scents of vanilla and cinnamon. The palate entry highlights waxy flavors of palm oil, pork rind, and bacon fat; the midpalate shows a touch more oak impact as the taste profile turns maple-like and slightly spicy. Ends up honeyed, oaky, and pleasing in the mouth and throat.
2006 Rating: ★★★/Recommended

Paulet Very Rare Fine Champagne Cognac (France); 43% abv, $1,500.

The deep sorrel/chestnut brown color is drop-dead beautiful; ideal clarity. The incredibly lush first aromas are laden with dried yellow fruit (banana, pineapple), figs, dates, and marzipan; after another seven minutes of aeration, earthy scents of forest and drying leaves enter the picture along with underpinning aromas of old oak, nutmeg, and dried cherry and hard cheese. The palate entry is supremely balanced, semisweet, slightly toasty, and even chewy; the midpalate stage features succulent tastes of Brazil nut, mince meat, figs, bacon fat, and prunes. Finishes with equal dashes of finesse and heartiness. A mature, totally evolved brandy at its peak from this obscure (at least in North America) producer that was established in Jarnac in 1848 by the Lacroux family.
2006 Rating: ★★★★/Highest Recommendation

Philippe Latourelle VS Cognac (France); 40% abv, $22.

Matured for four years in French Limousin barrels. Pretty, bright medium amber color; ideal purity. The nose after the pour emits accelerated fruit notes of apricot, quince, white grapes, and pear; another six minutes in the copita serve to bring out fabric/linen and cotton-like scents that, while in theory may seem at odds with the fruit, actually work really well; the very end of the bouquet offers a garden-fresh floral perfume that won me over. The palate entry is astringent, tart, very woody, and clearly immature; the midpalate stage shows a little more finesse as the fruit easily gives way to the wood impact that's more caramel-/toffee-like, but still too astringent. Ends quickly in the throat in feather-light layers of candy, oak, and toffee. The pleasing bouquet went a long way with me on this very young, if gangly cognac, but not far enough to rescue the raw, intensely resiny, paper-thin taste and aftertaste.
2006 Rating: ★★/Not Recommended

Pierre Ferrand 1965 Bottle No. 00048 Grande Champagne Cognac (France); 41% abv, $175.

Vibrant in color as the bronze/copper/orange hue delights the eye; clean and pure. The first pass offers alluring notes of peach and pear as well as oaky vanilla; the second nosing unearths a rich, toasty woodiness that accents the vanilla; the third go-round sees the fruit recede and the wood take full control as the oak/vanilla element surges ahead; after eight minutes of air exposure, nothing new is discerned in the fourth and last nosing. The palate entry is sweet, though not candied, and opulent; the midpalate flavors include baked pear, caramel, brown sugar, and peach. The aftertaste is long, luxurious, and sweet in a woody rather than fruity manner. Very good indeed and much more akin to other Pierre Ferrand cognacs, especially the Selecion des Anges.
2000 Rating: ★★★★/Highly Recommended

Pierre Ferrand 1968 Bottle No. 00048 Grande Champagne Cognac (France); 41% abv, $175.

The pale golden amber color is tainted by a cloud of minuscule sediment. The nose at opening is very soft; the second and third passes reveal little more in the way of aromatic expansion; after nearly ten minutes of air contact, the fourth and last nosing offers only limp scents of tired oak resin, fruit, and cloth. The palate entry is dry, green, and lean; then at midpalate the taste turns wildly spirity to the point of being harsh and hot; the parting shot at midpalate is an iron-like/metallic taste that's horrible. The finish is long, resiny, oily (not in the positive sense), raw, and like razors in the throat. A complete disaster that's not in keeping with what the name Pierre Ferrand has come to represent; weedy, metallic, harsh, and embarrassing. One that shouldn't even be in the marketplace.

2000 Rating: ★/Not Recommended

Pierre Fougerat "Tresor de Famille" Grande Champagne Cognac (France); 44% abv, $500/crystal decanter.

Lovely, topaz/deep honey/palo cortado sherry color; impeccable purity. After the pour, the aroma exhibits loads of oaky, vanilla-like, mature richness; seven more minutes of air contact unleashes further aromatic layers, including lead pencil, dried yellow fruit, grapefruit, and brown sugar; this is a complex and understated bouquet. The palate entry is deliciously sweet, buttery, and vanilla wafer-like; at the midpalate stage the flavor profile expands to include plums, raisins, dark caramel, cocoa, and tea leaves. The aftertaste is long, peppery, minerally, and semisweet.

2003 Rating: ★★★★/Highly Recommended

Pionneau 1969 Cask Strength Cognac (France); 56.4% abv, $1,200.

Tawny/deep bronze in color; flawless purity. The opening nosings detect lots of wood impact in the oaky, seed-like, and piney perfume; after the additional aeration period of seven minutes, the vibrant, natural-strength spirit becomes clearly evident as the bouquet turns honeyed, caramel-like, and decadently oily and buttery. The palate entry is where this vintage cognac takes flight as tastes of dates, roasted almond, walnut paste, and baked pear delight the taste buds; at midpalate the flavor profile highlights the cheese-like and bacony/pork rind-like rancio. The aftertaste blankets the tongue in sumptuous coats of oil, rancio, and maple sugar. Nice to see what the Cognaçais can do with very old, single estate brandy.

2006 Rating: ★★★★★/Highest Recommendation

Planat Napoleon Cognac (France); 40% abv, $20.

Easily one of the prettiest cognacs I've seen in a while; the deep, new copper penny hue shines under the examination lamp; impeccable purity. The opening bouquet is mature, intensely fruity in a concentrated dried fruit manner; an extra seven minutes in the copita serves to unleash very pleasing but delicate scents of prune, black coffee, black raisin, and even a touch of cocoa. The palate entry is fruity, properly acidic and raisiny; at the midpalate point, the flavor falls a bit flat as no discernable expansion is noted from the fine-tuned entry. The finish is medium-long, semisweet, a touch sap-like, and nicely oaked. That hollow spot at the midpalate a stage when a cognac should be showing its best stuff, held this cognac back

in three star territory; up until that point, I was actually thinking it had a chance at four. Too bad, I hate to see wasted opportunities.
2003 Rating: ★★★/Recommended

Planat VSOP Cognac (France); 40% abv, $23.
Very pretty medium bronze/honey color; superb purity. My first impression is of ripe, red fruit on the nose, in that, there is a plummy, berry presence that's simple but pleasing; later passes pick up soft, juicy notes of resin, pineapple, and now tropical fruit; no aromatic depth to speak of, but an altogether delightful bouquet of directness and simplicity. The palate entry is sap-like and semisweet bordering on bittersweet; by the midpalate stage the flavors are well-developed and at their peak performance, displaying lovely tastes of sap, maple, oaky vanilla, and light toffee. The aftertaste is brief, semisweet, and comfortable as an old friend. Not profound by any means, but that's fine because sometimes it's nice not to be confronted with monumental complexity; sometimes it's pleasant just to relax with an easy cognac.
2003 Rating: ★★★/Recommended

Planat XO Cognac (France); 40% abv, $50.
The rich topaz color is attractive but not as stunning as the appearance of the Napoleon; perfect purity. The aroma in the first two minutes is slightly reluctant and closed off, showing faint echoes of ripe fruit but that's about all; six more minutes of aeration does breath some life into this bouquet as remarkably sappy/mapley scents lead the way over more subtle fragrances of gum, old oak, and prune. The palate entry is well-endowed and forward in bearing, mostly in the form of lovely ripe red fruit tastes; the midpalate stage features ripe, sweet tastes of red berry, white raisin, light honey, and caramel. The finish is long, sappy sweet, nicely textured, and elegant. Surprisingly for an XO, the bouquet is the weak point; the flavor and finish phases, though, display enough polish, layering and character to redeem the lollipop nose with ease. Just skip by the bouquet and proceed with sipping.
2003 Rating: ★★★/Recommended

Prince Hubert de Polignac Premier Grand Cru Grande Champagne Cognac (France); 40% abv, $35.
Very pretty indeed, copper/henna color; some sediment seen. The opening bouquet offers scents of cocoa butter, oak, and ripe grapes; eight more minutes in the glass finds the bouquet deepening as aromas of bell pepper, palm oil, citrus rind, and butter show signs of genuine substance. The palate entry is sweet, candied, and almost honeyed; by the midpalate juncture the honey quality turns more brown sugar-like and sappy. The finish is zesty, oaky, and sweet. Hardly brilliant, but the pick of this litter.
2002 Rating: ★★★/Recommended

Prince Hubert de Polignac VSOP Cognac (France); 40% abv, $25.
Pretty bronze/burnished orange color; some sediment seen. The opening nosing passes pick up lots of dried fruit notes, including raisins and prunes; aeration spanning an additional seven minutes expands the bouquet profile by adding zesty scents of black pepper, leather, and pear. Starts smoothly at the palate entry, then turns a bit too hot at midpalate as off-dry

flavors of dried red fruit, ripe grapes, and candied almonds seem baked, minerally, and overly spiced. Rounds out in the steely/slate-like finish. Certainly one to mix cocktails with.
2002 Rating: ★★/Not Recommended

Prince Hubert de Polignac XO Cognac (France); 40% abv, $50.

Attractive bronze/orange hue; bits of black sediment spotted. The nose after the pour is strikingly like cardboard or, better, expensive parchment for letter writing and shows no typical aromatic traces of grape brandy; several more minutes in the glass help the situation somewhat by releasing friendlier, more appropriate off-dry aromas that include oak and ripe grapes; I hasten to point out that even after aeration time, there remains a paper/cardboard background presence that's distracting to the overall aroma phase. The texture at palate entry is surprisingly thin for what's supposed to be an XO; the midpalate stage displays more flavor animation mostly in the forms of mild oaky vanilla, candied nuts, and brown sugar. The aftertaste is lean, dry, and a touch hot. Ordinary.
2002 Rating: ★★/Not Recommended

Prince Hubert de Polignac XO Royal Cognac (France); 40% abv, $90.

Beautiful new copper penny hue; pure and sediment free; very inviting appearance. The initial nosing passes detect a dank, stale aroma that reminds me most of damp towels on a hot, humid day; not the best beginning; aeration doesn't assist much in blowing off the stale odor, even after vigorous swirling in the glass; an off-putting, limp bouquet with zero personality. The palate entry is meek, slightly thin in feel, and dry; by the midpalate stage the taste expands a bit, showing moderate charm in the forms of roasted nut, vanilla, chocolate, and coffee flavors. The aftertaste is medium-long, thin, and off-dry. A pricey, older cognac bottled in a lovely decanter should deliver plenty of sensory satisfaction; this bitter lemon misses at every stage of evaluation, except for appearance.
2002 Rating: ★/Not Recommended

Prunier 20 Year Old Cognac (France); 40% abv, $95.

The pretty amber/honey color is spoiled by way too much gray-colored sediment (found in both samples). The bouquet at first is very shy and elusive; nearly eight minutes of air contact allows a smattering of aromas to peek out if not fully appear and they are peaches, pears, and old oak; I'd expect a 20 year old bouquet to offer a bit more presence. The palate entry redeems the lackluster bouquet by offering a solid, woody, caramel-like first flavor stage; by midpalate bittersweet, nearly astringent flavors of sap, palm oil, resin, and tart pear get added to the flavor mix. The aftertaste is medium-long, dry, and resiny. Borderline, but I'm willing to give it the benefit of the doubt.
2003 Rating: ★★★/Recommended

Prunier Family Reserve Grande Champagne Cognac (France); 40% abv, $70.

Very pretty new copper penny hue. Perfect purity; the opening sniffs detect soft scents of candy cane, mint, and vegetation; seven additional minutes of air contact stimulate dessert-like aromas of pear, nectarine, and apple crisp. The palate entry is very chocolaty and dairy-like, almost creamy; at midpalate creamy flavors of dark caramel, toffee, honey, and brown sugar shine brightest. The finish is candied, sweet, and long.
2003 Rating: ★★★/Recommended

Prunier VS Cognac (France); 40% abv, $20.

Good clarity; bright amber color. The first sniffs pick up a fusty, old attic smell, kind of like a corked wine or sour apple; not a great beginning; the bouquet doesn't respond well to aeration as the aroma can't seem to shake the musty/mushroom-like odor. The palate entry shows some pleasant sweetness, mostly as light caramel; the midpalate stage is fine, if rather standard as moderately alluring tastes of oak, ripe grapes, and grape must hold court. Regrettably the finish finds the fusty/wet earth again, leaving one completely disenchanted. I tried both bottles that were sent for sampling and both deserved the one star rating.

2003 Rating: ★/Not Recommended

Prunier XO Très Vieille Grande Champagne Cognac (France); 40% abv, $125.

Gorgeous bronze color; impeccable purity. The first couple of nosing minutes unearth lean, slightly reluctant aromas of old oak, saddle leather, and distant plums; seven more minutes of air exposure don't compel the bouquet to expand further, so I move on. The palate entry immediately charms the bejesus out of the taste buds as tightly-wound, focused, and gamey flavors of dark toffee, cocoa bean, and marzipan make up a lot of lost ground due to the largely absent bouquet; the midpalate is even better as the taste profile goes deeper, offering succulent, mature, and integrated flavors of bittersweet chocolate, caramel apple, and maple syrup; and is there a touch of rancio in the tail end? The finish is long, sweet, and hearty.

2003 Rating: ★★★★/Highly Recommended

Remy Martin Extra Fine Champagne Cognac (France); 40% abv, $300.

Tarnished copper/auburn/henna color that's drop-dead appealing; spectacular brightness and purity. After the pour, the first whiffs offer subtle traces of dried fruit (apricot, peach), black pepper, and oak; aeration brings out more potent, but off-dry scents of spirits, oak, spice, and marzipan. Entry is wonderfully elegant and integrated on all levels; the midpalate stage builds on the finesse-driven entry as the taste profile turns far more focused, especially on the oak and dried fruit fronts. Finishes as gracefully, chewy, and harmonious as it starts. While this is not what I consider to be a fathomlessly deep or complex Extra, it nonetheless shows a wealth of charm that's well worth the price. The midpalate and finish are particularly savory and sophisticated.

2007 Rating: ★★★★/Highly Recommended

Remy Martin VS Petite Champagne Grand Cru Cognac (France); 40% abv, $30.

Autumnal gold/topaz/amber hue; excellent purity. Smells of grape seeds, grape skins, vines, and light toffee; seven more minutes of exposure to air stimulates only a timid woodiness that's barely perceptible and adds nothing to the overall meek aromatic equation. Entry is sweet, sugary, caramelized, and without any true depth or character; midpalate stage shows a touch more substance in a sweet, vanilla extract, cake frosting manner, but it's not enough to win me over for a recommendation by any stretch. It's significantly better than the edition I evaluated back in 1992, though, which was wholly awkward in the mouth. This edition is drinkable, at least, even if it is pedestrian.

2007 Rating: ★★/Not Recommended

Remy Martin VSOP Fine Champagne Cognac (France); 40% abv, $40.

There's no denying the shimmering bronze/topaz beauty of this stalwart VSOP; unblemished clarity. I detect clear evidence of grape spirit, baked yellow fruit (pears, mostly), and light toffee in the initial sniffs after the pour; an additional seven minutes in the glass release toasty fragrances of roasted chestnut, pine, palm oil, and brown butter. Entry borders on being too sweet and caramel-like, but it recovers a bit at midpalate as the semisweet taste profile becomes more focused on the grape spirits and oak and less on the concentrated caramel. Is it anywhere near classical for cognac's VSOP category? No. Is it better than in 1992 when I first evaluated it? Yes. Would I buy it today? No. Not as long as I could still find the seriously savory VSOPs from Camus, A. Hardy, Frapin, Chaumont, Leyrat, Toulouse-Lautrec, Croizet, Deret, Park, and Planat.

2007 Rating: ★★/Not Recommended

Remy Martin XO Excellence Fine Champagne Cognac (France); 40% abv, $130.

This new release, made up of 85% Grande Champagne eau-de-vie, replaces the old Remy XO. The appearance is a luxurious topaz/deep amber hue. Stately and succulent notes of orange peel, marzipan, and sweet oak are well accounted for in the initial two sniffings; with time in the glass the bouquet expands featuring spirity, sassy scents of ripe yellow fruit, cigar smoke, and bacon fat; a stellar, shapely bouquet. In the mouth round, almost fat flavors of brown butter, honey, and dark caramel enchant the taste buds at palate entry; resiny oak and nougat are highlighted in the midpalate phase. The aftertaste is dry, resiny, and long on the tongue. While I liked the previous XO (★★★★), this version is more contemporary in style.

2001 Rating: ★★★★/Highly Recommended

Richard Hennessy Cognac (France); 40% abv, $1,800.

Without any doubt, one of the most attractive spirits in the world; the deep bronze/topaz hue thrills the eye; unblemished purity. The first nosing passes discover amazingly profound and complementary aromas of hazelnut, butterscotch, laurel, and allspice; aeration time of another seven minutes brings out even more seductive aromas, including spice cake, wet earth, pipe tobacco, and honey. The palate entry is a clinic on how cognac should taste early-on as succulent flavors of toasted honeywheat bread, blueberry, and light toffee lead the taste parade; the midpalate stage features top layer tastes of brown sugar, cocoa, and butterscotch and foundational flavors of litchi, oak, vanilla, rancio, nougat, and black plum. Concludes as regally as it begins, with elegance, strength, and sheer grace. One of my all-time favorite cognacs and still the finest expression of Hennessy.

2006 Rating: ★★★★★/Highest Recommendation

Roullet 26 58 Year Old (1926) Grande Champagne Cognac (France); 41% abv, $423.

The amber/honey hue is bright and comely; pure as can be. The opening whiff shows delicate yet sinewy aromas of oak, caramel, and baked pear; the second pass, after four minutes of air contact, finds a fuller bouquet, laced with scents of oak resin, dried fruit, holiday spices, and the first hints of rancio in soft cheese form; in the third sniffing, traces of orange blossom get added; in the fourth and final nosing pass, after a full ten minutes of aeration and moderate swirling, the bouquet is completely melded and harmonious. The palate entry is sublimely sweet, round, full-weighted, and caramel-like; the midpalate stage

offers finely married, even stately tastes of oak, vanilla extract, soft cheese, and prunes. The finish is regal, lip-smacking, toasted, almondy, and brimming with oaky richness. A classical old Grande Champagne that has many decades yet to go. Bravo.
2000 Rating: ★★★★★/Highest Recommendation

Roullet 29 52 Year Old (1929) Borderies Cognac (France); 41.5% abv, $378.
The remarkably vibrant, even brilliant color is of new copper pennies; clean. The nose is mute in the first go-round after the pour; with swirling and aeration, bountiful, developed fragrances of biscuit batter and pears emerge in full Borderies glory; the third sniffing, following seven minutes of air contact, expands the biscuity/yellow fruit theme discerned in the second pass and adds slate and spice; the fourth whiff sees the spice come more to the forefront and the biscuity feature tone down as the bouquet continues to deepen and evolve. The palate entry is smooth and sweet. The midpalate point is wonderfully rich, biscuity sweet, vanilla-like, and fruity. The aftertaste is long, full, sweet, and oaky; the finish shows the beginnings of rancio; balanced between spirit-oak-fruit-acid; well done.
2000 Rating: ★★★★/Highly Recommended

Roullet 45 51 Year Old (1945) Petite Champagne Cognac (France); 42.5% abv, $288.
The pretty color is of old copper pennies; slightly oily but ideally clear of detritus. The initial nosing pass is prickly in the nasal cavity as the spirit supercedes all other aromatic features; three minutes into the nosing evaluation, the spirit continues its dominance, though scents of caramel, prune, and oak begin to emerge; the third sniffing finds the spirit still cranking out its piquant fumes, but the wood and fruit seem to be gaining in strength and influence; by the fourth and final nosing pass following nine minutes of exposure, the aroma at last settles down into a bona fide bouquet as the spiritiness calms somewhat, leaving the door open to dried fruit, toasted almonds, old oak/vanillin, and dark toffee scents. On the tongue at palate entry, it's supple, rich, and honeyed; the midpalate stage offers deep, layered flavors and textures of honey, oak resin, hard cheese, prunes, and dark toffee. The aftertaste is long, opulent, textured, spunky, and a tad harsh in the throat. While I like this old cognac enough to recommend it, its major flaw is the in-your-face, relentless spirit which hasn't mellowed much over the decades.
2000 Rating: ★★★/Recommended

Roullet 50 48 Year Old (1950) Borderies Cognac (France); 41.5% abv, $261.
Deep amber/honey color; perfect purity. The nose is very soft after the pour, showing subtle traces of molasses, caramel, and old oak; with air contact, the aroma expands in the second sniffing, adding scents of dried fruit and plums; the third whiff highlights two key aromatic qualities, oak resin and caramel; following ten minutes of aeration, the fourth nosing pass offers further deepening especially by the oakiness; I'm not bowled over by this bouquet, but it's pleasant, undemanding, and almost purely superficial. The palate entry is rich, ripe, cheese-like, and succulent in a fruity way; the midpalate stage offers expansive, deep flavors of coffee, vanilla bean, dried fruit, marzipan, and dark caramel. The finish is long, sweet, focused, and texturally round and luxurious. While I'm not impressed by the somewhat flaccid bouquet, I do very much admire the mouth presence from entry to finish.
2000 Rating: ★★★★/Highly Recommended

Roullet XO Cognac (France); 40% abv, $90.

The lively appearance displays a medium amber/orange hue; some infinitesimal sediment noted, but nothing that would detract from the score or the drinking experience. The nose after the pour is off-dry and fruity, with just a touch of glycerine; the middle stage sniffings offer additional seductive scents of orange rind, beeswax, plum, and sweet oak; by the fourth and final whiff, nine minutes into the nosing stage, aromatic diminishment is evident as the bouquet turns soft, waxy, and moderately fruity. The palate entry is firm, fat, and sweet; in the midpalate the silky texture is the star as the sweetly ripe flavors of grapes, plums, and oaky vanilla meld beautifully. The aftertaste is moderately rich, ideally fruity, and off-dry. A superlative, off-dry to sweet XO.

2001 Rating: ★★★★/Highly Recommended

Tesseron Domaine de Saint Surin XO Petite Champagne Cognac (France); 41% abv, $65.

Amber in color; pure and clean. Opening sniffs pick up attractive scents of flowers (rose petals, honeysuckle) and mature spirit; an additional seven minute period of air contact releases delicate notes of oak, jasmine, spice (black pepper), and dried red fruits. The palate entry is lighter than I expected, but elegant, medium-sweet, fruity, and woody; by the midpalate stage the bittersweet flavor profile streamlines down to dried red fruit and oaky vanilla; if there's any disappointment in the entry and midpalate phases, it's in the general lack of depth. Concludes sweetly, almost honeyed, and silky, with a final burst of heat in the throat.

2006 Rating: ★★★/Recommended

Tesseron Exception Lot No. 29 XO Grande Champagne Cognac (France); 40% abv, $300.

Bronze/copper/topaz color; ideal purity. This aroma owns a similar nut paste/oak scent as the Lot No. 53; with further air exposure, the bouquet takes on an orangy/citrusy leaning as the smell turns fruitier the more it aerates; lovely and compelling. The palate entry is supple, fruity sweet, and ripe; the midpalate stage highlights melded flavors of light caramel, marzipan, and nougat. Ends up oaky sweet, lightly spiced, and satiny. Like this cognac very much but not as much as the slinkier, more expressive Lot No. 53.

2006 Rating: ★★★★/Highly Recommended

Tesseron Perfection Lot No. 53 XO Grande Champagne Cognac (France); 40% abv, $150.

The color on this beauty is a burnished orange/bronze; impeccable clarity. The first whiffs detect sturdy, if perfumed scents of sweet oak, vanilla bean, and nut paste; the additional six minutes of aeration serve this bouquet well as fruity notes of berries, dried fruit, plums, pears, and soft cheese vie for attention. The palate entry is serenely composed, succulent, sweet as ripe red fruit, and honeyed; by the midpalate stage the taste profile shifts into deeper strata as the flavors expand and lengthen to include caramel, rancio, and orange rind. Finishes as beautifully as it begins, with self-assured depth, finesse, power, and maturity.

2006 Rating: ★★★★★/Highest Recommendation

Tesseron Selection Lot No. 90 XO Grande Champagne Cognac (France); 40% abv, $40.

Eye-catching topaz/honey color; dazzling purity. The opening smells include pears, apples, and soda water; additional air contact releases delicate, fruity scents of banana in brandy, cotton candy, maple, and new oak. The palate entry is light, sweet, and grapy ripe; the midpalate is chewier in texture, more honeyed in taste than the entry phase and tropical fruit-like. Finishes satiny smooth, sugary/piney sweet, and medium-long. Nice job.

2006 Rating: ★★★/Recommended

Tesseron Tradition Lot No. 76 XO Grande Champagne Cognac (France); 40% abv, $75.
The pristine condition of this stunningly copper-colored brandy is inspiring; it's gorgeous. In the nose there are delicate fragrances of spice, sesame seed, light oak, and baked pears; seven more minutes in the glass bring out pineapple, light toffee, milk, and brown sugar. The palate entry is elegant, composed, and moderately sweet in more of an oaky than a fruity way; by the midpalate stage there's flavor evidence of ripe pear, white grapes, cake frosting, oloroso sherry, orange peel, and dark honey. Ends up sugary sweet, satiny textured, and long in the throat.

2006 Rating: ★★★★/Highly Recommended

Tiffon VS Fine Cognac (France); 40% abv, $18.
Very pretty new copper penny color; some minor infinitesimal black specs sighted. The initial nosing pass offers gentle yellow fruit aromas (white grapes, pears); the second and third whiffs introduce dry to off-dry touches of oaky vanilla and beeswax while the final sniffing directs the attention more to dry, mildly resiny wood than to ripe fruit; a self-contained, immature bouquet. The palate entry is slightly meek and very dry; then the flavors shift into passing gear at midpalate as tastes of butter, light oak, pine sap, and ripe white grapes delight the taste buds. The finish is medium long, moderately sweet, grapy, sap-like, and ripe. It's, in truth, a borderline two star/three star rating VS; what fails to earn it an SJ recommendation in the end is the timid bouquet and palate entry. I can't deny, though, that the graceful midpalate and maple syrup-like aftertaste made it a frightfully close call.

2001 Rating: ★★/Not Recommended

Tiffon VSOP Fine Champagne Cognac (France); 40% abv, $27.
The rich topaz/bronze hue is gorgeous; but it displays some unsightly floating debris. The nose right after the pour shows aromatic traces of vanilla extract and black raisins; the middle stage nosing passes continue to display the understated bouquet style of Tiffon as only faint odors of oak and white peppercorn emerge with exposure to air; by the fourth whiff, following almost nine minutes in the glass, a buoyant citrusy scent blithely comes along but impacts the aromatic phase very little; another relatively meek aroma. The taste offers very pleasant butteriness in the entry; then at midpalate turns moderately oaky and off-dry. The aftertaste is medium long, fruity, off-dry, and slightly resiny. It mirrors the younger, ganglier VS in almost every stage, but offers significantly more mature and evolved flavors, in particular at palate entry. Good value.

2001 Rating: ★★★/Recommended

Tiffon XO Fine Champagne Cognac (France); 40% abv, $55.
The appearance is topaz/bronze with yellow core highlights; this Tiffon entry, I'm happy to say, is ideally pure and free from sediment. The aroma opens up with prickly spirit and a scent of beeswax; the second and third whiffs add typically (at least for Tiffon) passive aromas

of oak resin, butter, and marzipan; the fourth and final sniffing displays—finally—some genuine cognac aromatic substance in the forms of deep oak resininess, maple, marzipan, and raisins. The palate entry is sound, gripping, and semisweet; the midpalate is concentrated, grapy, mildly prickly, caramel sweet, and a touch toasty. The finish falls off sooner than I'd have liked but is good and sap-like nevertheless. While I like it a lot, there's still not enough dimension, especially in the bouquet, to raise it up to four stars.

2001 Rating: ★★★/Recommended

Toulouse-Lautrec VS Grande Champagne Cognac (France); 40% abv, $35.

Pretty amber/honey color; perfect clarity. The opening aroma is fresh, amiable, fruity/grapy, and just slightly acidic; later sniffings following another seven minutes of air contact uncover more delicate traces of oak, black pepper, and tea leaves; better than average bouquet. The palate entry is semisweet, with firmly structured, melded tastes of light toffee, butter cream, and sap; at midpalate the taste profile displays squeaky clean, properly astringent, if paper thin notes of fruit acid, ripe grapes, baked pear, and pine. Finishes gracefully, toffee-sweet, and elegant. Very good buy.

2005 Rating: ★★★/Recommended

Toulouse-Lautrec VSOP Grande Champagne Cognac (France); 40% abv, $39.

Deep amber/harvest bronze hue; ideal purity. Leads off aromatically with a single-minded scent of paraffin; aeration stimulates deeper odors of white pepper, light toffee, and palm oil; neither a profound nor a generous bouquet, but pleasing all the same. The palate entry is round, caramel-like, and nicely acidic; the midpalate stage is more biscuity and batter-like than the entry, showing more of an oak resin leaning at the end. Concludes concentrated and much fuller than either the palate entry or the midpalate.

2005 Rating: ★★★/Recommended

Toulouse-Lautrec XO Grande Champagne Cognac (France); 40% abv, $85.

Bright, attractive burnished orange/bronze color; superb purity. Smells early-on of light caramel, candied walnuts, baked apple, and honey; seven more minutes of air contact do little to expand on the original aroma, except to add a note of vanilla. The palate entry is medium-weighted, sweet, honeyed, and a touch buttery; the midpalate stage is round, sweet like dried red fruit, and pleasantly oaky. Ends up clean, toffee-like, and smooth.

2005 Rating: ★★★★/Highly Recommended

ARMAGNAC—FRANCE

Armagnac is the brandy of France's bucolic southwest region known as Gascony, home to the Musketeers, foie gras, and green, rolling hills. Like its distant cousin cognac, armagnac is distilled grape wine and is aged in oak barrels. Armagnac boasts three brandy districts. **Bas Armagnac**, whose capital is Eauze, contributes 57% of all brandy production in Gascony from its sandy/silty soils. Bas Armagnacs are delicate, elegant, and fruity. **Tenarèze**, whose commercial center is the town of Condom, accounts for 40% of production and is noted for its clay/limestone soils which are responsible for robust, long-lived brandies. Last is **Haut Armagnac**, from which a mere 3% of production is contributed. Whereas a century ago vineyards could be seen around every turn in the lane, these three areas in 2007 total only 15,000 hectares/37,050 acres of vineyard land.

Distillation in Armagnac occurs mostly in November and December of the harvest year. As opposed to the small pot stills employed in Cognac in which brandies are double distilled, the Armagnaçais opt to use for 95% of their brandies more efficient column stills that run continuously in a single distillation process. The remainder is distilled in smaller pot stills. The single distillation method automatically means that the brandies of Armagnac are stouter in nature than those made in Cognac because less of the natural chemical compounds have been stripped away. Maturation happens in black oak in Armagnac for a legal minimum of two years. Armagnac also specializes in vintage releases, meaning bottlings produced from the grapes of one particular harvest. These brandies especially showcase the peculiarities and virtues of individual vintage years in ways that brandies that are blended can never do. While the overwhelming majority of cognac is exported around the world, most annual production of armagnac (65%) remains within France. The balance of 35% is exported to over 130 nations.

Classifications:

- *Armagnac VS:* 2 year minimum in barrels.
- *Armagnac VSOP:* 5 year minimum.
- *Armagnac XO:* 6 year minimum.
- *Armagnac Hors d'Age:* 10 year minimum.
- *Armagnac Vintage:* Grapes must all come from the harvest year displayed on the label.

Parting distressed thoughts: While I relish armagnac almost as much as single malt Scotch (just look at the reviews of Darroze), I feel that we're just getting to experience a mere handful, compared to what I know is available. The problem of lack of supply has largely to do with the Armagnaçais, who are stunningly disorganized in their approach to marketing the "Armagnac" brand in the world's largest marketplace, the United States. They continually shoot themselves in the foot by not putting together a sound marketing plan and then executing it. Sadly, the overwhelming majority of North American consumers haven't a clue about armagnac, many actually thinking that it's a type of cognac.

Try an armagnac or two that I've recommended for a spirits experience of the first rank, whether or not you like brandy. Do it for you.

A.B. Pollentes 1965 Coeur de Terre Bas Armagnac, Cask Strength/Unfiltered (France); 47% abv, $125.

By far the prettiest of the Pollentes armagnacs; the deep, old copper penny/topaz hue is tremendously appealing; impeccable purity. The aroma jumps from the glass upon pouring, emitting a delightful woody/resiny perfume in the SJ evaluation room; what strikes me most in the second sniff is the elegant and profound roasted walnut/toasted chestnut aroma that dominates; following eight minutes of air contact, the third nosing pass adds scents of paraffin, lead pencil, prunes, and spice; the last whiff contributes an oily quality that I like very much; a remarkably deep, complex, and savory bouquet that doesn't show a trace of slowing down, even at over 30 years of age. The palate entry is surprisingly dry and sedate; then by midpalate the flavors explode on the tongue in the forms of dark caramel, toffee, chocolate covered cherries, candied walnuts, prunes, and oak resin (that approaches being rancio-like). The aftertaste is luxuriously long, oaky sweet, and intensely nut-like. A buttery, over-the-top brandy bonanza that shows armagnac at its mature best.

2000 Rating: ★★★★★/Highest Recommendation

A.B. Pollentes 1973 Epices Bas Armagnac, Cask Strength/Unfiltered (France); 48.4% abv, $100.

Attractive bronze/deep amber color; excellent purity. The initial nosing pass shows a closed-off aroma; by the second sniffing, after three minutes of aeration, the first stirrings of aroma are found; following a full seven minutes of air contact, the aroma develops into a bouquet, offering scents of black pepper, allspice, licorice, mild caramel, and almonds; with three additional minutes of aeration, the bouquet's profundity and depth become apparent in the shape of nougat, almonds, dried fruit, paraffin, melted butter, and black pepper; this is not a generous, back-slapping bouquet, but one that's multilayered, elegant, and focused. Supremely luscious right from the palate entry as succulent, bittersweet tastes of toffee, toasted almond, and apple butter greet the bedazzled taste buds; the midpalate stage is even more glorious as toasty flavors of ripe grapes, buttery oak, and light caramel are never interfered with by the cask strength alcohol (48.4%)—if anything, they are totally complemented by it. The finish is a wonderful display of alcohol supporting inherent fruit and wood flavors. A near clinic in structure and balance.

2000 Rating: ★★★★/Highly Recommended

A.B. Pollentes 1986 Sable Fauve Bas Armagnac, Cask Strength/Unfiltered (France); 47.9% abv, $80.

Pale amber/honey/harvest gold hue and perfectly pure. The expressive aroma leaves the starting gate in a flash, offering round scents of caramel, ripe grapes, prunes, and brown sugar and asking the question: will this sprinter have enough left by the final nosing pass? the second sniffing sees toasted almonds and marzipan getting added to the aromatic mix; after six to seven minutes of air contact, the discernable trace of holiday spice is noted as a contributing fragrance; by the fourth and last whiff, the components come together in a dazzling bouquet that's simultaneously spirity (the stiff and still relatively immature 47.9% alcohol comes through) and complex (the multiple layers of aromatic qualities unite into one sweet, ripe, and resiny aroma). The palate entry is bittersweet and ripe on the tip of the tongue; by the time the flavor advances to the midpalate a fiery wall of spirit alights on the top of the tongue to the detriment of the armagnac. The finish is hot, raw, and caramel-like. Unfortunately, this armagnac shoots itself in the foot by virtue of its unbridled alcohol; it's simply too awkward, harsh, and off-balance in the mouth to recommend despite the alluring bouquet.

2000 Rating: ★★/Not Recommended

A.B. Pollentes Hors d'Age Bas Armagnac (France); 40% abv, $55.

Bright, pure amber/honey-tinted and oily appearance. The opening nosing reveals a firmly structured bouquet that features caramel-like traces of hard candy and nougat; the almond paste quality accelerates in the second sniffing as the brandy begins to expand with aeration; in the penultimate whiff milk chocolate and coffee bean notes get added to the increasingly complex aromatic dynamics; following ten minutes of air exposure, the fourth nosing unearths a beguilingly harmonious and multilayered bouquet that fills the nasal cavity with succulently sweet scents of caramel and sweet old oak; it's a dashing aroma that promises dazzling things in the flavor phase. The palate entry is sublimely sweet and toasty, but not in the least cloying or syrupy; the midpalate tastes are round, firm, and caramel-like. The aftertaste is long, silky, candy sweet, and just a touch resiny; there's nothing subtle or namby-pamby about this big-hearted number and that, dear readers, is its greatest virtue. Bar the door, Evangeline, we're popping open the Pollentes Hors d'Age tonight.

2000 Rating: ★★★★/Highly Recommended

Baron de Lustrac 1965 Domaine Notre Dame de Bouit 100% Folle Blanche Bas Armagnac (France); 42% abv, $155.

Gorgeous, brilliant, copper color; impeccable purity. The initial sniffings after the pour detect biscuity, vanilla wafer-like scents that are mature and melded; an additional seven minutes in the glass adds aromas of caraway and sunflower seeds plus nuances of black pepper and oak; a curious bouquet that's both atypical and compelling. The palate entry is fruity sweet, almost jammy; by the midpalate point the taste profile features finely-tuned, mature flavors of dark caramel, vanilla, and maple. The aftertaste is concentrated, honeyed, and very extended. I sense that this armagnac recently hit its peak maturity status, so if you want it, get it now and open it—I don't believe that it's going to get any better and, indeed, might begin slipping a bit.

2003 Rating: ★★★★/Highly Recommended

Baron de Lustrac 1970 Domaine de Courros 100% Folle Blanche Bas Armagnac (France); 42% abv, $105.

Pretty topaz/deep bronze color; perfect purity. The aroma immediately asserts itself, emitting off-dry to semisweet and zesty scents of pine needle, paraffin, and raisins; with aeration, the aroma settles down a bit as a lovely, elegant ripe grapiness takes hold. The palate entry is lush, bittersweet, and caramel-like; at the midpalate stage the flavor goes decadently chewy, with tastes of vanilla extract, sweet old oak, marzipan, honey, and dark toffee. The aftertaste is long, luxuriously sweet, and thick; a sweet, honeyed, mouthwatering armagnac treasure that's worth every single penny; FIND AND BUY!

2003 Rating: ★★★★★/Highest Recommendation

Baron de Lustrac 1972 Domaine de Lacaze Cepage Bacco Bas Armagnac (France); 42% abv, $130.

Looks like an old, worn copper penny; excellent purity. The aroma right from the start shows round, biscuity, and mature praline-like notes that are simultaneously nutty and sweet; aeration time of another six minutes affords the bouquet the chance to gain some momentum and focus on the lusciously bittersweet candied almond core aroma. The palate entry is firm and nicely viscous; at midpalate the candied almond/praline dominates to the point of exclusion. Concludes intensely bittersweet and nutty. While very good, well-crafted, and certainly recommendable, the narrow focus of the taste profile and finish prevented the earning of a fourth rating star.

2004 Rating: ★★★/Recommended

Baron de Lustrac 1973 Domaine de Courros 100% Folle Blanche Bas Armagnac (France); 42% abv, $90.

Very deep bronze/old copper penny hue; excellent purity. The opening nosing passes pick up stately, evolved smells of baked apple, sweet oak, and vanilla; swirling and seven additional minutes of air contact stimulates deeper scents, including honey, green melon, nectarine, and a trace of spice. On the palate, it's medium-rich, intensely honeyed, and fruity in a dried fruit manner (prunes?); the deep, multilayered midpalate that's succulently sweet and woody is its strong suit. Finishes caramel-sweet, lush and full-bodied, with just a hint of spirity heat. Not as majestic as the awesome 1970, but a superb armagnac in its own right.

2003 Rating: ★★★★/Highly Recommended

Baron de Lustrac 1977 Domaine d'Espelette 100% Bacco Bas Armagnac (France); 42% abv, $82.

Attractive bronze hue; perfect purity; black tea leaves and light toast jump-start the nosing phase; another six minutes of aeration has very little effect on this one-note bouquet; it's pleasant, to be sure, but wholly one dimensional in scope. The palate entry is mildly honeyed and vanilla wafer sweet; the midpalate stage is this armagnac's peak experience as elegant, round, and seductive tastes of marzipan, old oak and honey dazzle the taste buds. The finish is long, berry sweet, and ripe. After a limp and uninspiring bouquet and palate entry, this armagnac took flight in the midpalate. A juicy, grapy, fruity treat.

2003 Rating: ★★★/Recommended

Baron de Lustrac 1980 Domaine de la Croix Pelanne 100% Bacco Bas Armagnac (France); 42% abv, $77.

Fine, deep bronze/topaz color; absolute purity. The opening whiffs are confronted with that tea leaf/toasty aroma so emblematic of the bacco varietal; further aeration time lets the bouquet calm down a little as it emits strangely attractive scents of honey wheat toast, rubber pencil eraser, new tires, butterscotch, fried eggs-on-toast, and starch. The palate entry is scrumptious, sweet, concentrated, and intensely caramel-like; by midpalate there are traces of asparagus and green leaf vegetable that get overshadowed by the high-voltage caramel/honey flavor. The finish is bittersweet, eggy, and creamy. I think that this armagnac is a love-it-or-hate-it proposition: the rating divulges which side of the tracks I'm standing on.

2003 Rating: ★★★★/Highly Recommended

Baron de Sigognac 1955 Bas Armagnac (France); 40% abv, $285.

The attractive color is old copper kettle/topaz in nature and flawlessly clean. The first salvo of aroma is baked and tobacco-like; further aeration doesn't help to release much in the way of additional odors, except for a timid leafy/resiny quality that seems tired and flabby. The palate entry shows a bit more vitality than the lame bouquet in the forms of bacon fat and stewed fruits; the midpalate phase offers cigar tobacco, pine, and palm oil. Ends bittersweet, sappy/resiny, and overly wooded. A brandy that lost all of its freshness years ago.

2006 Rating: ★/Not Recommended

Baron de Sigognac 1965 Bas Armagnac (France); 40% abv, $180.

The deep new copper penny color dazzles the eye; unblemished purity. The opening whiffs detect distant scents of old leather and dried yellow fruit; extra air contact and swirling stimulate the dried fruit more than the leather aspect as the bouquet turns slightly baked and dried, kind of like dried apricot pastry or prune Danish. The palate entry is oaky/resiny and semisweet; at midpalate the taste profile becomes toasted/roasted, a bit smoky, and intensely woody. Concludes with robust, almost bitter flavors of sap and maple. As with the 1975 but worse, what minor fruit facets exist in the bouquet, vanish totally by the entry, therefore, leaving behind a brandy that is out of balance.

2006 Rating: ★★/Not Recommended

Baron de Sigognac 1975 Bas Armagnac (France); 40% abv, $95.

Lovely bronze/burnished orange hue; superb clarity. The aroma comes at you in the first sniffs with ripe scents of green apple, yellow grapes, and fresh pineapple; seven minutes of additional aeration stimulate semisweet wood elements, especially vanilla, Christmas spices, black pepper, and walnuts, that complement the fruit fragrances firmly yet with finesse. The palate entry dispenses with the fruit altogether and focuses instead on peppery wood and minerals, such as quartz, limestone, granite; the midpalate continues what was begun in the entry as the by now dry flavor profile leans heavily towards resiny oak and stone. Finishes moderately oily, earthy/slaty, and trim. The dramatic change in direction from bouquet to flavor/finish took me by surprise. I wouldn't have minded if some of the fruit component had remained throughout the in-mouth stages, making the entire experience more complete.

2006 Rating: ★★★/Recommended

Castarède 1964 Gers Armagnac (France); 40% abv, $160.

The dark mahogany/chestnut brown color is a dazzler; impeccable purity. The nose after the pour is dusty, very mature, and even a tad tired; further aeration doesn't affect the bouquet that borders on being limply sweet and raisiny. The palate entry shows far more character than the over-the-hill aroma as ripe flavors of dates, figs, raisins, and prunes vie for dominance. The aftertaste is long, intensely fruity, and ripe, if a bit flabby. There's no question but that this brandy has seen a better day, but there remains enough innate charm for it to be recommended to fanciers of older, sweeter brandies who don't mind a little corpulence.

2006 Rating: ★★★/Recommended

Castarède 1974 Gers Armagnac (France); 40% abv, $84.

Seriously lovely deep saddle leather brown color; ideal purity. The first sniffs pick up mature yet still vivid scents of oak, dried fruit, and cream; much to my surprise, the additional seven minutes of air contact do little to stretch the bouquet. The palate entry is round, succulent, rich, and even tobacco-like; at the midpalate stage the taste profile adds almond paste, caramel, and honey. Ends up elegant, more fat than lean, pleasingly rich, ripe and sweet, and intensely nutty.

2006 Rating: ★★★★/Highly Recommended

Castarède Réserve de la Famille Gers Armagnac (France); 40% abv, $56.

Very bright topaz/autumnal amber; superb clarity. Loads of nuts, old leather, and milk chocolate in the opening inhalations; the bouquet turns drier with added aeration time as the leather scent comes to dominate. The palate entry is long, sweet, toffee-like and medium fat; the midpalate displays a firm core flavor of oaky vanilla, with satellite tastes of caramel, nougat, and sautéed almonds. Finishes well as the texture grows in a creamy/buttery manner. The good aspect of this armagnac is that it kept improving at each stage.

2006 Rating: ★★★/Recommended

Castarède VSOP Gers Armagnac (France); 40% abv, $34.

Solid burnt orange/topaz color; good clarity. In the first nosing pass, I detect dry woody notes of old oak and pine needle; further aeration time brings out sweeter, if limp scents of marshmallow, light spice, and rubber pencil eraser. Medium dry at palate entry with intense resiny/woody tastes that are very lean (almost astringent) and nutty; at the midpalate stage the concentrated resiny characteristic becomes something of a problem as the taste turns flat and bitter in the throat. Finishes a touch too raw.

2006 Rating: ★★/Not Recommended

Chabot Napoleon Armagnac (France); 40% abv, $58.

The deep topaz/burnishes orange color is pretty, but shows minor debris floating about. The first minutes of nosing don't seem to accomplish much as the aroma remains in the background, except for a slight mintiness; later passes reveal still subdued but firmer scents of honey wheat toast, soft oak, and muesli. The palate entry is stunningly long, rich, and deep, as well as honeyed; by midpalate the flavor profile is full-blown, caramel-like, and toasty sweet. Finishes with a honeyed/sherried taste and moderate sweetness. While I prefer the superb XO, this sap-like Napoleon does display some stirring sensory fireworks in the mouth phase.

2005 Rating: ★★★/Recommended

Chabot VSOP Armagnac (France); 40% abv, $36.

Pleasing medium honey/topaz color; some inconsequential sediment. The opening burst of aroma is delightfully toffee-like yet dry; later whiffs pick up mild autumnal scents of dried leaves, herbs, and woods; not a legendary bouquet, but one that displays good structure and a clear direction on the dry end of the scale. The entry flavor has more maple/oaky sweetness than the aroma implied it would have; then at midpalate the taste profile turns drier, nicely acidic and cleansing, and slightly bittersweet/resiny in its leaning. Ends up dry and tight. Very nice, understated, and firm.

2005 Rating: ★★★/Recommended

Chabot XO Armagnac (France); 40% abv, $88.

Attractive harvest gold/honey hue; nearly flawless in its appearance. The initial scent reminds me of walnuts and nougat; further aeration and swirling encourage plumper, more candied/honeyed/minty aromas to emerge from behind the veil of walnuts/nuts/nougat, providing a sophisticated sniffing experience that is simultaneously earthy and mildly honeyed. The opening taste at entry is sensuous, sweet, and a little like brown sugar; at midpalate there's a seductive smokiness that takes on a pipe tobacco quality. Concludes moderately sweet, yet razor sharp and nicely acidic and winy. I seriously like this racy, fully integrated XO.

2005 Rating: ★★★★/Highly Recommended

Chabot 20 Year Old Armagnac (France); 40% abv, $135.

The baked color is bronze/rusty orange and blemish-free. Inhalations in the first two minutes after the pour unearth traditional armagnac scents including freshly sawn wood and smoldering fire; following six minutes of further air contact, the aroma transforms into a bouquet, emitting elegant yet punchy odors of butter, sautéed mushrooms, clove, and cigar tobacco. The taste profile hits the ground running at entry, showing off toasty/biscuity flavors of sugar cookie batter, maple, and brown sugar; at midpalate honey, cocoa bean, and nougat get added to the taste menu. Concludes sweet, with just a bit of spirity warmth on the tongue. Borders on being scrumptious. An armagnac near its lifecycle apex.

2005 Rating: ★★★★/Highly Recommended

Chabot 30 Year Old Armagnac (France); 40% abv, $399.

The copper/bronze/russet color dazzles the eye; excellent purity. Wonderful things are promised in the early nosings as baked aromas of cherry pastry, dark bread (pumpernickel?), and toffee thrill the olfactory sense; aeration then serves to underline the moderately sweet virtues found in the opening inhalations but doesn't advance the bouquet to the next level. The palate entry displays soft but plump flavors of toast-with-honey and oaky vanilla, then at midpalate there's a rush of dark caramel/toffee/honey that nearly overwhelms the taste buds. Ends up sap-like. Positively recommendable but declines in the glass as the minutes rush by. Very good, but reach for the more vibrant 20 Year Old.

2005 Rating: ★★★/Recommended

Chabot 1932 Armagnac (France); 40% abv, $1,120.

Like the 1936, big pieces of black sediment blemish an otherwise pretty rusty bronze appearance. The initial sniffs detect candle wax, brown butter, and toasted almond; following the seven minute aeration period, the bouquet offers distant notes of figs, dried fruit, and black raisins. The palate entry is delectably sweet and cocoa-like, even lip smacking delicious; at midpalate the taste profile expands rapidly as flavors of chocolate-covered cherries and strawberries mix harmoniously with almond butter and oil. Concludes with pizzazz, honey-like sweetness, and vitality. Puts the 1936, 1940, and 1948 to shame.

2005 Rating: ★★★★/Highly Recommended

Chabot 1936 Armagnac (France); 40% abv, $1,035.

The henna/rust color displays some alarmingly large chunks of black sediment. The first scents are void of fruit and focus more on oak resin and spirit; there's very little aromatic expansion after seven minutes more in the glass except for a flash of palm oil. The palate entry shows a totally different side of this armagnac as the first sip explodes on the tongue in sweet, chocolate-like flavors of cocoa butter, honey, and vanilla extract; at midpalate the taste includes hints of baked apple and tobacco leaf. Finishes sweet and honeyed.

2005 Rating: ★★★/Recommended

Chabot 1940 Armagnac (France); 40% abv, $960.

The nut-brown hue displays a cloud of infinitesimal sediment under the examination lamp. The first couple of whiffs after the pour pick up bittersweet notes of caramel and hard candy; unfortunately, the extra seven minutes of air exposure add only fabric/synthetic-like scents of nylon and a burst of saddle leather; again, an absence of fruit detracts from the overall sniffing phase. The palate entry is diametrically opposed to the lackluster bouquet as crisp, semisweet and firm tastes of butter cream, dark toffee, and nougat delight the taste buds; at midpalate the taste profile enlarges itself to include charred marshmallow, oaky vanilla, sherry, and cocoa. Ends up bittersweet, date-like, leathery, and nutty. After a rough start, this old geezer collected itself and put on a spirited display in the taste and aftertaste stages. Hardly the best 60 year old armagnac I've had, but one that's still alive and kicking.

2005 Rating: ★★★/Recommended

Chabot 1944 Armagnac (France); 40% abv, $870.

The deep, dark brown/chestnut/mahogany color is flawless and gorgeous. The initial sniffings discover earthy/woodsy scents of maple syrup, pine nuts, and forest floor; additional aeration reveals further aromatic layers, including traces of hard cheese (rancio), oak resin, vanilla, butter, grapes, and sautéed almonds. The palate entry is rich, deep, sweet, and caramel-like; at midpalate the sweetness narrows, allowing for aromas like bittersweet cocoa, oloroso sherry, grapes, and dark caramel to enter the mix. Finishes sweet, cocoa-like, raisiny, and plummy. A Bentley in a Mini-Cooper world.

2005 Rating: ★★★★★/Highest Recommendation

Chabot 1948 Armagnac (France); 40% abv, $780.

The pretty burnished copper coin color is marred slightly by bits of black sediment. The peculiar opening aroma offers fusty scents of old leather, old books in a library, and limestone; after an additional undisturbed aeration period of seven minutes, the bouquet adds odors of parchment, carnauba wax, and resin; the lack of fruit seriously plays against this bouquet. The palate entry is bittersweet, surprisingly harsh and ungainly, and rustic; at midpalate the taste phase recovers somewhat, displaying waxy, oaky sweet, and slightly caramelized/burnt flavors. Concludes on an upbeat note as the oaky sweetness takes charge. Inconsistent and obviously feeling its age, this armagnac loses its focus at the palate entry stage following an aroma analysis that baldly reveals a chemical downturn. The gains realized in the midpalate and finish just aren't marked enough to warrant a recommendation.

2005 Rating: ★★/Not Recommended

Chabot 1952 Armagnac (France); 40% abv, $690.

The auburn/henna color dazzles the eye; ideal clarity. The first two minutes of inhaling reveal sophisticated, fruity scents of orange rind and apple strudel; seven minutes further down the nosing path the aroma develops into a multilayered bouquet, one that offers semisweet aromas of almond paste, oak resin, dark toffee, coffee bean, and candle wax. The palate entry is semisweet, mildly candied, and coffee-like; at midpalate the flavor profile expands to include walnuts, palm oil, the beginnings of blue cheese-like rancio, almond paste, and caramel. Finishes oily and sedately. A winner that affirms the power of very good armagnac at 50 years old.

2005 Rating: ★★★★/Highly Recommended

Chabot 1956 Armagnac (France); 40% abv, $480.

The brilliant rust/burnt orange/iron ore hue is lovely and impeccably pure. The opening nosings pick up lush, harmonious scents of old saddle leather, soft oaky spice, and sap; another seven minutes bump up the sweet oak presence especially, but likewise add very subtle scents of beeswax and carnauba. The palate entry is savory, semisweet, and maple-like; at midpalate the sweet oak returns to dominate the major portion of the taste phase. Ends succulently sweet, intensely oaky, and firm.

2005 Rating: ★★★★/Highly Recommended

Chabot 1959 Armagnac (France); 40% abv, $325.

The prettiest of all the Chabot armagnacs that I've evaluated, a brilliant copper/henna color, with unblemished purity; a dazzling eyeful. The opening nosings pick up deep scents of old saddle leather, dark coffee, and black cherry; aeration stirs further aromatics in the forms of pipe tobacco, bittersweet chocolate, plums, and toffee; the fruit/acid/alcohol/wood balance is stunning. The palate entry is semisweet, coffee-like, and concentrated; at midpalate an entirely new layer of flavor opens up, offering decadent tastes of cocoa, marshmallow, sweet oak, and even the beginnings of rancio. Concludes as stately and elegant as it began. Doubtless, one of the two finest, most integrated, most lip-smacking Chabot vintages of all. An armagnac masterpiece.

2005 Rating: ★★★★★/Highest Recommendation

Chabot 1960 Armagnac (France); 40% abv, $260.

Another copper/rust/orange embers color with perfect purity. The first sniffings discover a deeply nutty/nut paste aroma that's off-dry and appealing; seven minutes more in the sampling glass don't add much to the nutty bouquet except for barely discernable traces of hard cheese and marzipan. The palate entry is raisiny sweet, with a slight toffee kick thrown in; at midpalate the taste profile adds deft flavors of toasted almond, oak, and black pepper, becoming more off-dry than sweet as a result. Finishes well and smoothly in the throat; mature and integrated.

2005 Rating: ★★★/Recommended

Chabot 1964 Armagnac (France); 40% abv, $212.

Very pretty bronze/rusty orange hue; excellent purity. The opening aroma shows nicely toasted/fruity notes of oak, pine, and pineapple/banana; following another seven minutes of airing, the aroma evolves into a genuine bouquet that offers deep, succulent notes of maple, caramel, and nut butter. The palate entry is rich, lip smacking sweet, and oily; at midpalate the taste profile turns cake frosting-like, sap-like, nougaty, and luscious. Concludes on a

surprisingly minty note that frankly undercuts the high-quality entry and mid-palate phases, knocking off one star in the process.
2005 Rating: ★★★/Recommended

Chabot 1972 Armagnac (France); 40% abv, $125.
The harvest gold/topaz hue is deep; minor sediment showing. The toasty nose is friendly and full right from the first deep whiff; later nosings following an aeration period of seven minutes detect lovely scents of dark toffee, marzipan, roasted nuts (chestnuts especially), and oaky resin. The palate entry is fat, mildly spirity and warm, and semisweet; at midpalate there's a rush of fruity/grapy flavor that overrides the wood and toffee, making for balanced imbibing. Finishes back towards the caramel/honey side of the taste scale. One of the better, more vigorous vintage-dated armagnacs from Chabot. Bravo.
2005 Rating: ★★★★/Highly Recommended

Chabot 1976 Armagnac (France); 40% abv, $108.
The color is new copper penny; impeccable purity. The first burst of aroma is semisweet and very woody, then the aroma mysteriously retreats after only about thirty seconds becoming mute; seven more minutes of aeration time stirs only faint odors of rubber pencil eraser, unsweetened gum, and white raisin, with just the frailest hint of toffee; a wasted opportunity for this in-and-out, inconsistent and, therefore, disappointing bouquet. The palate entry is pleasingly sweet and maple-like; at midpalate the low-key flavor impact develops a bit more grip in the form of the sweet toffee first noted at the tail end of the nosing phase. Finishes appealingly sweet and mildly maple-like. I rode the two star/three star fence on this one but reasoned that the flaws were enough to keep this armagnac corralled in the two star pen. As with the 1980, nice looks alone just don't cut it.
2005 Rating: ★★/Not Recommended

Chabot 1980 Armagnac (France); 40% abv, $108.
Bright bronze/burnished orange color; superb purity. The initial whiffs detect delicate (or are they simply muted?) notes of chalk/limestone and spice; aeration time of another seven minutes fails to stimulate much in the way of deeper aroma except for woody/resiny and old parchment backnotes. The palate entry is off-dry, mildly woody, and a touch honey-like; at midpalate this slow-developing armagnac finally at long last appears to come together as moderately deep flavors including light toffee, honey, and old oak make a last ditch effort for respectability. Concludes flat and dull. It just doesn't offer enough fundamental virtues to be recommended.
2005 Rating: ★★/Not Recommended

Chateau de Briat 1985 Baron de Pichon-Longueville Bas Armagnac (France); 46% abv, $90.
Grape make-up is 85% bacco, 5% folle blanche, 10% colombard; exceptionally attractive and bright honey/dark amber hue; perfect purity. The opening whiffs detect hardly anything as the aroma displays little except for lots of dumbness; another seven minutes in the copita plus some swirling lets loose moderately pleasing scents of ripe yellow fruit (is it banana or pear?), tea leaves, and distant oak resin; do yourself a favor and simply by-pass the aroma. Shows

greater presence in the mouth than in the nose; the entry is off-dry, lean, and oaky; by the midpalate juncture the taste is sweeter, more evolved, and slightly oily. The oak dominates the aftertaste as do flavors of cardboard and light toffee. A drinkable, resiny if slightly immature armagnac that might have benefited from another three to five years in barrel.
2003 Rating: ★★/Not Recommended

Chateau de Briat 1986 Baron de Pichon-Longueville Bas Armagnac (France); 46% abv, $110.
Very pretty topaz/bronze color; flawless purity. Smells of chocolate covered almonds, figs, and pine needles; further aeration stimulates medium-dry scents of oak, wood resins, and beeswax. The palate entry is worth the price of admission as the flavor shows a decidedly sweet, caramel-like face that reminds me seriously of fine British toffee; later tastes in the midpalate stage are slightly more honeyed, almost sherried in their succulent way; a dynamite midpalate experience. Closes with sturdy grace, assertive tastes of toffee, honey, creamy butter, and even a dash of rancio. Owns a vigor that couples nicely with its 20 years of maturity.
2006 Rating: ★★★★/Highly Recommended

Chateau de Briat Hors d'Age Baron de Pichon-Longueville Bas Armagnac (France); 44% abv, $65.
Harvest gold/honey color; unblemished clarity. The peculiar, but not unpleasant aroma after the pour is metallic, herbal, and mineral-like and, most strangely of all, like peanut shells; with more time in the glass, the bouquet takes on a waxy quality that hovers between dryness and sweetness. It's in the mouth where this armagnac showcases its finer virtues; the palate entry is sweet, fig-like, and even a little nutty; by the midpalate stage there's another dimension of flavor that focuses on the oak/resin qualities that meld well with the fruit/nut element. Finishes gracefully, if a touch hot, but overall pleasing and elegant in a buttery, dry manner.
2006 Rating: ★★★/Recommended

Chateau de Maniban Mauléon d'Armagnac Bas Armagnac (France); 40% abv, $34.
Attractive, bright amber/burnished orange hue; excellent clarity. The initial nosings detect a largely one-dimensional aroma that's dry to bitter and very lean; aeration doesn't unleash any further qualities except for orange peel and the bouquet, while not unpleasant, is running-in-place; there's no depth, no genuine scope to it. The palate entry is fruity, if lean and bordering on astringent; there's more substance in the midpalate as the taste profile tosses in a mild dose of oak to pair up nicely with the citrus fruitiness. Finishes with a flavor of baked apple and singed orange rind. Not my cup of armagnac due mostly to a lack of core substance.
2006 Rating: ★★/Not Recommended

Chateau de Pellehaut Reserve Tenarèze Armagnac (France); 46% abv, $35.
A blend of Tenarèze armagnacs made in the 1970s, 100% from ugni blanc grapes. The topaz color shows orange core highlights and excellent purity. The comely aroma is assertive and intensely fruity right off the crack of the bat; aeration time of an additional six minutes sees the bouquet feature tropical fruit, especially unsweetened pineapple and papaya, with just a hint of background spice. The entry taste is dry and resiny on the tongue; at midpalate

the flavor turns candied and concentrated. It finishes semi-dry, caramel-like, and bittersweet. A tasty and tightly-wrapped armagnac of narrow focus but true definition. Definitely worth your $35 if for nothing else than a genuine glimpse at armagnac Tenarèze-style.
2003 Rating: ★★★/Recommended

Chateau de Pellehaut Reserve Tenerèze Armagnac (France); 43% abv, $50.
Toasted golden brown/bronze color; terrible purity situation due to way too much sediment and unsightly debris. Out of the gate it smells of nuts, especially cashews, and unsalted butter; added breathing time stirs distant, vague scents of palm oil, very old oak, and spice. The palate entry is semisweet, intensely sugar cane-like, and woody enough to be slightly bitter; by the midpalate stage it's candy sweet, a touch brittle texture-wise, and owns a backdoor honey quality that enters the flavor equation in the warm, nutty, fatty, vanilla extract-like finish. Had not its appearance been so dicey, I'd have given this one a fourth rating star purely on the strength of its flavor profile.
2006 Rating: ★★★/Recommended

Chateau de Saint Aubin Réserve du Chateau Bas Armagnac (France); 40% abv, $89.
The bright bronze/honey hue excites the eye; absolute purity. The initial two nosing passes uncover firm, no-nonsense, tightly-knit scents of holiday spices, lemon rind, and sweet, vanilla-like oak; time in the sampling glass allows for measured expansion and deepening as fully evolved scents of white raisins, bittersweet dark chocolate, and wood resin take the olfactory sense on a thrilling ride; a masterpiece grape brandy bouquet of the first rank. At the palate entry succulent, semisweet tastes of butterscotch and nougat enchant the taste buds early-on; by the midpalate juncture, full-throttle flavors including marzipan, light caramel, resiny oak, and grape jam complete the in-mouth flavor phase with finesse and grace. The finish is long, honey sweet, and sinewy in texture. A flawless, brilliantly crafted armagnac that stands at the head of its class. BRAVO.
2002 Rating: ★★★★★/Highest Recommendation

Chateau du Busca 1975 Tenarèze Armagnac (France); 41% abv, $170.
Appearance is a dazzling, brilliant copper color; flawless clarity. In the initial inhalations, the fruit component dominates, mostly in the forms of dried cherry and baked banana; additional aeration brings a fine acidity to underpin the fruity ripeness; the very final sniff detects the lovely woody, slightly spicy scent of oak. The palate entry is elegant, off-dry to bittersweet, tannic, and focused on the dried fruit element; at midpalate the taste profile offers slightly restrained flavors of spice, honey wheat toast, raisins, and prunes. Finishes as smoothly and seamlessly as it starts. Superior distilling, barrel selection, and aging make this a winner.
2006 Rating: ★★★★/Highly Recommended

Chateau du Busca 1985 Tenarèze Armagnac (France); 43% abv, $129.
The color beams under the examination lamp in bright shades of bronze/burnished orange; absolute purity. The early aromatic emphasis is on toasty, vanilla-laden oak; further exposure to air stimulates more candied, smoky scents, especially toffee, marzipan, and coffee-flavored hard candy that as a team accent the wood/oak core aroma; a hugely complex

network of smells. The palate entry is stunningly sophisticated, semisweet, cola-like, toffee-like, and downright spectacular; at midpalate the richness level reaches stratospheric heights as the broad flavor profile offers totally integrated tastes of nougat, roasted chestnuts, dark chocolate, orange rind, and treacle. Finishes with a deft touch of budding rancio. Holy-moly, this one is an instant classic.

2006 Rating: ★★★★★/Highest Recommendation

Chateau du Busca Hors d'Age 15 Year Old Tenarèze Armagnac (France); 40% abv, $99.

The solid brown/topaz/sorrel color bewitches the eye; ideal clarity. The wonderfully zesty aroma is spiced with nutmeg, black pepper, lemon, and thyme in the opening two minutes; later inhalations following aeration highlight tightly wound notes of margarine, lanolin, dark caramel, buttery oak, and holiday fruitcake. The palate entry is rich, creamy, and honeyed; at midpalate there's a strong sense of older spirit in the overall woody/creamy flavor that smacks of rancio beginnings. Finishes semisweet, cocoa- and maple sugar-like, and intensely oaky. A musketeer's mouthful of robust, mature, and, most pleasing of all, gentlemanly brandy.

2006 Rating: ★★★★★/Highest Recommendation

Chateau du Busca Hors d'Age Cigare Tenarèze Armagnac (France); 40% abv, $75.

The color of this brandy is a brilliant reddish copper/henna hue; impeccable clarity. The initial aromas offer woody, nutty scents that meld beautifully over the span of two minutes; the extra aeration period of seven minutes sees the aroma become a more expressive and integrated bouquet as lovely fragrances of baked pear, mince meat, pine sap, and pipe tobacco make for thrilling sniffing. The palate entry tastes of dried red fruits, maple sugar, and pine; at midpalate the flavor profile is laced with succulent tastes of maple, pear in brandy, sap, oaky vanilla, and pipe smoke. The aftertaste is every bit as fulfilling and gratifying as the sensational late bouquet and midpalate. A defining Tenarèze moment.

2006 Rating: ★★★★★/Highest Recommendation

Chateau du Busca XO No. 1 Tenarèze Armagnac (France); 40% abv, $85.

The color looks like newly tanned leather, a burnished brown/topaz hue that's unblemished in its purity. In the first nosings, I pick up soft but sturdy aromas of dried yellow fruit, buttered almonds, and orange blossom; an additional six minutes of air exposure offers the chance for more floral scents to be appreciated, including jasmine and honeysuckle; an understated bouquet that hints rather than dictates. The palate entry is lusciously oily, semisweet, and buttery while the midpalate stage highlights the oak, cocoa, black tea, and walnut paste. Finishes gracefully, semisweet, and tightly structured. Elegance in a glass.

2006 Rating: ★★★★/Highly Recommended

Chateau du Tariquet 1982 Bas Armagnac (France); 47% abv, $80.

Brown/deep bronze/bay color; fair purity. The aroma in the initial sniffings emits mature scents of old leather, mince pie, prunes, and meringue; further air contact brings out mesmerizing odors of baked peach cobbler, melting beeswax, and vanilla cake frosting. The palate entry is rich, full-bodied, maple-like, and sweet; at midpalate the taste profile stays the course, adding traces of gum, confectioners' sugar, and honey. Concludes balanced,

gently sweet, and clean. Mature yet vibrant; sweet, yet impeccably clean and elegant.
2005 Rating: ★★★★/Highly Recommended

Chateau du Tariquet 1985 Bas Armagnac (France); 47% abv, $75.

Medium brown/burnished gold hue, but like its siblings shows some unsightly sediment. The first blast of aroma is all about butterscotch and brown butter; additional exposure to air stirs up eggy scents of egg cream, meringue, and toffee. The full palate entry is lush, deeply caramel-like, and buttery/creamy in both texture and flavor profile; the midpalate stage is decadent, dried fruit-like, jammy, and candied. Ends up as luscious and velvety as it began in sweet, pillowy waves of texture and taste. Genuinely lovely.
2005 Rating: ★★★★/Highly Recommended

Chateau du Tariquet 1988 Bas Armagnac (France); 47% abv, $70.

The pretty, bright bronze/copper/russet color is near-ruined by the amount of floating debris. The nose is relatively subdued in the opening round of sniffing. The palate entry is surprisingly minty, yet sweet and pruny; at the midpalate stage sherry and Tupelo honey flavors override the mintiness. Concludes with husky, deep tastes of oloroso sherry, honey, cocoa bean, and nougat. The timid bouquet holds it back early on, but then the taste and finish come on strong enough to substantially impress.
2005 Rating: ★★★★/Highly Recommended

Chateau du Tariquet 8 Year Old Folle Blanche Bas Armagnac (France); 45% abv, $45.

The color is gold/old yellow/wheat field; undesirable appearance in terms of purity, however. The first whiffs offer intriguing aromas of celery, cedar, and nougat; six more minutes of aeration stimulate deeper odors, including pine, mown hay, praline, and light, new honey. The palate entry taste is warm, off-dry, ashy, and sweet in a pipe tobacco manner; the taste profile at midpalate swings into high gear as semisweet flavors of light caramel, chocolate-nut candy bar, and brown butter make for very nice drinking. Finishes semisweet, sap-like, and tight.
2005 Rating: ★★★/Recommended

Chauffe Coeur Hors d'Age Armagnac (France); 40% abv, $45.

Old Madeira/mahogany/cola color; flawless clarity. First whiffs are treated to butterscotch and tobacco leaf notes that are deep and buttery/oily; additional air contact releases mature, cigar wrapper scents of prunes, figs, dates, and burning leaves, and tar. Rich right from the start and nutty to the max at entry; at midpalate the old-oak vanillin leaps to the forefront, then in a moment gets eclipsed by dark chocolate/cocoa bean, then that gets overshadowed by pipe tobacco and honey; there is evidence of cheese-like rancio and butter fat at the very tail end of midpalate that overlaps with the aftertaste. Finish is pruny, cheese-like, and textured. Wow and all this for only $45? Buy at least two bottles of this rogue.
2007 Rating: ★★★★★/Highest Recommendation

Chauffe Coeur VSOP Armagnac (France); 40% abv, $33.

Ochre/dark amber/chestnut brown color; impeccable purity. Right off the crack of the bat the aroma is waxy/paraffin-like, fiber/flax-like, concentrated in oak, and, to my giddy

delight, slightly burnt/charred; further aeration stimulates other layers of aroma, most notably, buttered almond, caramelized onion, and buttered popcorn; an aromatic tour de force. Entry is caramel-like, honeyed, rich, assertive, and luscious; the taste profile adds brown butter, treacle, nougat, marzipan, and baked pineapple at the midpalate. Finishes clean, intensely honeyed, oaky, slightly too resiny, and burnt. The equal of several top dog XO armagnacs costing two to three times as much. To buy it is to love it.
2007 Rating: ★★★★/Highly Recommended

Darroze 10 Year Old Age de Fruits Bas Armagnac (France); 43% abv, $60.

The color is medium amber/honey; it's pure and free from sediment. The initial two nosing passes engage delightfully fruity, almost pear-like, and spicy aromas that stay within the confines of the glass; aeration serves to stimulate biscuity, sappy sweet, and ripe aromas of pear and apple cobbler, light honey, and sugar cookies. At palate entry, the flavor is focused and dry immediately, offering mildly toasty and buttery tastes of toffee and honeywheat bread; the midpalate expands the taste profile to include resiny/sappy flavors of oak, vanilla extract, maple syrup, and butterscotch. The aftertaste is long, resiny sweet, lip-smacking, and toffee-like. A youthful, precocious brandy whose exuberance is infectious.
2002 Rating: ★★★/Recommended

Darroze 15 Year Old Age des Epices Bas Armagnac (France); 43% abv, $75.

Bright topaz/solid amber tint, with ribbons of oiliness apparent. The immediate impact of the aroma is firm, direct, and full of toasty, roasted scents, like walnuts, cashews, and baked apple; further exposure to air stimulates scents of lanolin, palm oil, pecan pie, and tobacco leaf; a smoky bouquet that beautifully displays armagnac's oily side, an appealing aspect rarely seen in other brandy categories. The palate entry is keenly buttery, bittersweet, and fatty; the midpalate turns concentrated, offering intense and slightly burnt/charred tastes of cocoa butter, roasted almonds, and charcoal. The finish is all about the tobacco and the oil; atypical and daringly audacious; love it.
2002 Rating: ★★★★/Highly Recommended

Darroze 1945 Domaine de Bataille Bas Armagnac (France); 42% abv, $359.

Light bronze/burnished orange tint; excellent purity. The early stagings of the bouquet are tight, focused, and tart, emitting only scant scents of dried herbs and fruit peel; air contact releases astringent, mineral-like aromas of tar, pavement, parchment, and oaky vanilla, but no fruit to speak of. The palate entry tastes are sap- and maple-like; the midpalate flavor profile is all about resin, wood, and minerals, but once again no fruit aspect to properly balance the astringency of the oak influence. The aftertaste is long, resiny, sappy, and lean. An austere, out-of-balance brandy that's lost its fruit component.
2002 Rating: ★/Not Recommended

Darroze 1956 Domaine de Gaube Bas Armagnac (France); 45.3% abv, $508.

Gorgeous, mature, mahogany/bronze/burnished orange color; absolute purity. The bouquet hits the ground running in the forms of burnt marshmallow (S'mores), marzipan, and nougat scents; seven more minutes of air contact serve to deepen the candy-like aroma by adding honey, mint, and dark caramel. The palate entry is succulent and candy sweet,

but neither cloying nor chunky; the midpalate stage features creamy, spirity tastes of sweet butter, double cream, oaky vanilla, cigar tobacco, and maple. The aftertaste highlights the buttery caramel and tobacco leaf. This is the complete old armagnac package from appearance to finish.
2003 Rating: ★★★★★/Highest Recommendation

Darroze 1959 Domaine de Gaube Bas Armagnac (France); 47.2% abv, $357.
Medium amber/honey color; excellent purity. This aroma shows up for work immediately, offering tart scents of tropical fruit and green apple; six more minutes of aeration stimulate an odd perfume, almost medicinal in its scope but distantly fruity at the same time; don't know what to make of this late bouquet. The taste packs a punch in the palate entry as biting spirit sears the tip of the tongue; by midpalate however, the flavor settles down and offers lean, bittersweet, and mesmerizing tastes of old oak, vanilla, coffee bean, tree sap/maple, butterscotch, honey, and even a fleeting moment of rancio. The aftertaste is deliciously sweet, maple-like and melded. The weird late aroma threw me completely, but the experience taken as a whole was utterly charming, if disjointed, and in the end won me over totally. It would have been a five star brandy had it not been for that strangely abrupt aromatic turn in the road.
2003 Rating: ★★★★/Highly Recommended

Darroze 1960 Domaine de Dupont Bas Armagnac (France); 44% abv, $289.
The copper color is terrifically bright and appealing; excellent purity. The opening sniffings are a bit green smelling and underdeveloped considering this brandy's age; aeration and swirling aid to a point as pinched scents of apple peel, spice, and brown sugar attempt to make a statement, but fall short. The palate entry is meek as reluctant flavors of old caramel and toffee peek out from behind the strong flavor of old oak; the midpalate shows some improvement as mildly succulent tastes of nougat, chocolate banana, and very old wood make the taste phase interesting. The aftertaste is mild, medium-long, sweet but tired. While this brandy possesses some good traits, those virtues are beginning to get overwhelmed with age and a lack of tightness.
2002 Rating: ★★/Not Recommended

Darroze 1961 Domaine de Aux Ducs Bas Armagnac (France); 40.5% abv, $289.
Color is a brilliant new copper penny hue; impeccably pure. The first two sniffings are treated to assertive, intensely fruity aromas that turn slightly baked in the second pass; aeration unleashes deeper notes of black raisins, pine nuts, and oaky resin; a lovely, elegant bouquet that's moderately sweet and fruit-forward. Tart at palate entry, with supplemental tastes of lead pencil and slate; by midpalate the fine hand of buttery/fatty rancio is felt at the back of the tongue in the flavors of bacon fat, honey, dark caramel, and dry oloroso sherry. The finish is long, fatty, resiny, and sublime. Fit for seasoned brandy mavens only. A perfect, harmonious brandy that's at the peak of its life cycle.
2002 Rating: ★★★★★/Highest Recommendation

Darroze 1965 Domaine d'Eauze Bas Armagnac (France); 44.1% abv, $240.
Medium topaz hue; excellent purity. In the immediate post-pour sniffs, the aroma already seems fired and ready, emitting firm, earthy notes of witch hazel, pine needle, and

leaf compost; following another six minutes of air contact, the dry earth-a-thon continues as potent, woodsy/dried fruit scents of white raisins, leather, and lumber take the lead. The palate entry is polite, pleasantly sweet, and even a bit honeyed; the midpalate point features a semisweet taste of old honey. The finish is long, delightfully sweet, and creamy. I had my doubts at the start, but this brandy came on very strong once in the mouth.

2003 Rating: ★★★/Highly Recommended

Darroze 1965 Domaine de Peyrot Bas Armagnac (France); 49.2% abv, $290.

When the appearance of Bas Armagnac is "on", there's nothing quite as visually stirring like it in all of distilled spirits; this is one of those special copper-colored ones that seduce the eye; unblemished clarity. Charting the aroma in the first pass is easy because it's so expressive and ideally melded as finely measured scents of wood, old fruit, marzipan, and blue cheese enchant my olfactory sense; the bouquet develops further in the later stages as balanced aromas of oak barrel perfectly complement the aged fruit and supple acidity; if only evaluations were always like this. The palate entry shows a lusciously sweet side of this armagnac that was not evident in the bouquet; the midpalate displays classic richness and finesse in the forms of succulent fruit, toasty oak, and dark caramel, even a touch of old honey. The aftertaste sums up the entire experience with grace, vibrancy, and potency. Yet another state-of-the-art B-A from the great house of Darroze. A grape brandy masterpiece from appearance to finish.

2005 Rating: ★★★★★/Highest Recommendation

Darroze 1967 Domaine de Dupont Bas Armagnac (France); 44% abv, $200.

Amber color; insignificant debris; oily. The early-on aroma is a tad meek in the first few minutes; some swirling in the glass and an extra five minutes help to release off-dry and ripe scents of apple, oak, and prunes; there's also some echoes of dried herbs and flowers lurking way in the background. Pleasant, mildly sweet at palate entry; the midpalate stage displays more in the way of depth as traces of caramel and candied fruit mildly impress the taste buds. It finishes delightfully sweet, moderately oaky, and medium-rich. After a slow start it picked up enough steam to exhibit some nice, but hardly profound, virtues.

2002 Rating: ★★★/Recommended

Darroze 1967 Domaine de Saint Aubin Bas Armagnac (France); 44% abv, $200.

The bronze/tawny color is extremely orangy; superb purity. The initial sniffings find fragrances of lead, black pepper, and tobacco leaf; with another six minutes of aeration, the bouquet turns bitter, steely, and metallic; in view of previously reviewed St Aubins, I'm shocked by the lack of aromatic depth. Shows more character at palate entry as semisweet tastes of marshmallow, cola and walnut make for pleasant early-in-the-process drinking; the midpalate stage is highlighted by round, chewy flavors of almond butter, bacon fat, and palm oil. The finish is oily, thick, and semisweet. There's enough of a substantial recovery in the flavor and aftertaste phases to rescue this odd St Aubin from the "ordinary" bin.

2002 Rating: ★★★/Recommended

Darroze 1968 Domaine de Rieston Bas Armagnac (France); 50% abv, $190.

The new copper penny/henna color is nothing short of spectacular; impeccable purity. Right off the crack of the aromatic bat, this bouquet has seductive rancio written all over it,

mostly in the form of bacon fat/lard; time in the glass allows for other aromas to emerge, most notably, dried herbs, minerals, dark toffee, lanolin, and moss; an utterly beguiling, multilayered bouquet that forces one to sit, sniff, and savor. On the palate the texture is medium-bodied and round upon entry while semisweet tastes of cocoa butter and dark chocolate blanket the taste buds; by midpalate a concentrated, maple syrup, resiny, fatty flavor takes charge of the palate. The aftertaste features no-nonsense tastes of brown sugar, old oak, and oloroso sherry. A beauty that fires on all cylinders from start to finish.
2002 Rating: ★★★★★/Highest Recommendation

Darroze 1970 Domaine de Gaube Bas Armagnac (France); 44% abv, $180.
The pretty topaz/honey color shows impeccable purity. In the initial sniffs, there are touches of nail polish remover and boiled cabbage that prick the olfactory sense to attention; later passes manage to detect better, more well-rounded, almost fat, aromas of almond and lanolin. There's a tremendous rush of fatty butter flavor at palate entry, then at midpalate the flavor profile opens up to include oak, black raisins, and dark caramel. The aftertaste is thick, long, coating, and sweet. A notable comeback in the mouth after a lackluster bouquet earns this late-blooming, lip-smacking beauty four stars.
2003 Rating: ★★★★/Highly Recommended

Darroze 1970 Domaine de Lusson Bas Armagnac (France); 43.5% abv, $170.
Medium amber/honey hue; good purity. The initial whiffs after the pour detect semisweet, mildly toasted scents of pastry fruit and nuts; later aromatic stages reveal sweet, ripe fragrances of wood sap, maple, light caramel, pear, and white raisins. The palate entry is nicely ripe and fruity while the midpalate stage turns mapley, candied, nutty, and mildly oaky, with supplemental flavors of vanilla extract and cinnamon. The aftertaste is sweet, ripe, oily, and toasted; focused, almost lean, and acceptably astringent.
2002 Rating: ★★★/Recommended

Darroze 1970 Domaine de Rieston Bas Armagnac (France); 43.5% abv, $168.
The bronze/orange color is bright and reasonably pure, with minor bits sediment showing. The nose after the pour displays refined scents of wood bark, black pepper, and old oak, which together I like very much; exposure to air for another seven minutes allows other earthy aromas, such as lead pencil, wet stone, and autumn leaves, to emerge and meld with the existing fragrances; a composed, stately bouquet. The semisweet to sweet palate entry flavors include marzipan, nougat, dark caramel, and honey; at midpalate creamy, buttery, fatty tastes of nut paste, vanilla extract, and oaky resin dominate. The aftertaste is surprisingly bitter and tannic, with a touch of spirity bite. I love the palate entry and midpalate as much as any of the Darroze's, but it's not the complete package that a couple of the others from Marc Darroze are.
2002 Rating: ★★★/Recommended

Darroze 1971 Domaine de Pinas Bas Armagnac (France); 48.5% abv, $165.
The color is a deep bronze/Tupelo honey hue; excellent purity. The opening sniffings find off-dry to bittersweet scents of guava, banana, and hard candy; the bouquet noticeably fades with aeration, leaving behind faint traces of apple, pear, fruit stone, and parchment.

The palate entry flavor is sweet and sappy; by the midpalate stage the flavor highlight is fruit and nut, with slightly buttery/fatty undertones. The finish is concentrated, sweet, fatty, and oily. Where did this fine taste and finish come from after the anemic, wallflower bouquet? Erratic, but recommendable based upon the splendid flavor and finish.

2002 Rating: ★★★/Recommended

Darroze 1972 Domaine de Coquillon Bas Armagnac (France); 45.3% abv, $153.
The topaz/honey appearance is clear and clean. In the first couple of whiffs, it's abundantly clear that oak, wood resin, and glue are going to be major contributing factors throughout the nosing phase; seven minutes on, the wood intensity becomes the dominant feature and takes on a budding characteristic of foresty/wood panel/resiny rancio; a first class bouquet of significant depth. The palate entry offers honeyed, lip-smacking tastes of dark caramel and brown sugar; the midpalate stage zips along riding on well-endowed, oily tastes of cocoa butter, cream sherry, dark chocolate, and molasses. The aftertaste is long, sap sweet, and chewy. the thirty+ years really work in the favor of this delectable temptress of a brandy whose dalliance with elusive rancio makes the entire trip worthwhile.

2003 Rating: ★★★★/Highly Recommended

Darroze 1973 Domaine de Coquillon Bas Armagnac (France); 48.9% abv, $180.
The dazzling appearance sports the brownish/worn look of an old copper penny; superb clarity. The first inhalations encounter potent scents of egg yolk, dark caramel, and baked pear; later sniffings are treated to rounded-off aromas of oaky vanilla, old parchment, paraffin, peanut butter, and cigarette tobacco; there's so much happening in this assertive, yet mature bouquet that I could go back to it all day. The palate entry is medium-bodied, off-dry to semisweet, and more woody than I would have expected from the results of nosing; the midpalate turns lean, resiny, and narrowly focused on the oak element that turns sweeter in the finish. Another idiosyncratic beauty from this amazing estate producer, whose genius is not lost on the savvy likes of negociant Darroze or US importer Henry Preiss.

2005 Rating: ★★★★/Highly Recommended

Darroze 1973 Domaine Le Bret Bas Armagnac (France); 49.8% abv, $146.
Bronze/orange/copper color; superb purity. The initial nosing passes detect lovely, toasty scents of ripe tropical fruit and toasted honey wheat bread; further minutes in the glass stimulate the exotic fragrances of dried fruit (pineapple? coconut?) that overcome the burnt, toasty profile of early on. The palate entry is engagingly sweet and sap-like; then at midpalate there's a pleasing, mildly oily coming together of dried fruit and oak. It finishes with a hint of spirity bite and prickliness which is welcome and controlled. Nowhere near being a classic blockbuster, but a very nice, medium-weight find.

2003 Rating: ★★★/Recommended

Darroze 1974 Domaine de Coquillon Bas Armagnac (France); 49.3% abv, $172.
Wow, the deep copper/henna/russet color is fabulously appealing; unblemished clarity. The vibrant aroma offers spicy/bakery odors of Brazil nut, banana bread, and baking spices, in particular, nutmeg; additional time in the copita unleashes deeper fragrances of fruit stone, old oak, worn leather, dried cherry, and dates. The palate entry emits flavors of nut paste and

butter sautéed almonds; the midpalate phase goes all oily, buttery, bacon fat-like, and meaty. The oak influence comes roaring back in the aftertaste in the form of budding rancio, soft cheese, and maple. Now this bottling is more like the Coquillon that I've come to admire.
2006 Rating: ★★★★/Highly Recommended

Darroze 1975 Domaine de Lassis Bas Armagnac (France); 41.6% abv, $163.

The attractive burnished gold/medium amber hue catches the eye with its brightness and purity. The initial nosing passes pick up herbal, mineral scents that are far more earthy/woodsy than fruity/grapy or oaky/resiny; more time in the glass allows for the mossy earthiness to round out and become more buttery, baked/burnt, and dark caramel-like; the last whiff reminds of baked prunes. The palate entry is stunningly buttery/creamy and downright luscious; the midpalate stage is nutty, candy bar- and nougat-like, and richly delicious. The aftertaste is extended, semisweet, and beautifully oily and textured.
2005 Rating: ★★★★/Highly Recommended

Darroze 1976 Domaine de Dupont Bas Armagnac (France); 46.5% abv, $112.

The dazzling bronze color is spectacular and clean. The initial nosings detect focused, lean aromas of intense caramel, spiced pear, and baked apple; as beguiling an opening armagnac bouquet as I've encountered of late; further exposure to air stirs off-dry scents of fine English toffee, saddle leather, paraffin, and the early makings of rancio; outstanding aromatically at every level. The palate entry highlights positively succulent flavors of apple pastry, dark caramel, honey, brown sugar, black pepper and raisins. The finish is long, sweeter than the midpalate and as sexy as brandy can get. A tour de force brandy that's robust and elegant simultaneously. A true classic from appearance to aftertaste.
2002 Rating: ★★★★★/Highest Recommendation

Darroze 1976 Domaine de Guillemouta Bas Armagnac (France); 46.9% abv, $127.

The topaz/bronze appearance is perfectly clean and bright. Zesty and prickly with spirit right from the start, this aroma bristles with vivid fragrances including cotton fabric, and pine; another seven minutes of air contact serves to heighten other aromas, namely plums, chocolate cake frosting, and spice; the bouquet transformed itself completely during the additional aeration period. The palate entry is astringent, acidic, and fruity; by the midpalate stage there's a surge of oak that underpins the latter stage candied tastes of light toffee and marzipan. The finish is strong, a tad prickly, nougat-like, and honey sweet. A very nice package which, though hardly perfect, is intriguingly different and idiosyncratic enough to warrant a purchase.
2003 Rating: ★★★★/Highly Recommended

Darroze 1977 Domaine de Dupont Bas Armagnac (France); 47.5% abv, $123.

Beautiful copper penny hue; flawless and pure. The first aromatic impressions include scents of mellow spirit, old oak, and straw; time in the glass allows the aroma to develop into a full-throttle bouquet that highlights scents of palm oil, buttered wheat toast, popcorn, and oak. The palate entry is leaner than I thought it would be and agile; by the midpalate stage the taste profile really blossoms as lovely, off-dry to semisweet, multilayered flavors of light caramel, maple, honey, and sweet oak combine for a dazzling experience. It finishes sweet, svelte, and zesty.

2003 Rating: ★★★★★/Highest Recommendation

Darroze 1978 Domaine Aux Ducs Bas Armagnac (France); 47.1% abv, $120.
Deep amber/topaz hue; excellent purity. The peppercorn-like opening aroma is sassy yet firm and a bit vegetal; further air contact encourages faint traces of wood resin and licorice/aniseed to emerge but that's about it on the fragrance front. The palate entry is luscious and chocolaty; at midpalate the flavor profile stays the sweet, dark chocolate course, adding subtle notes of butter, cream and oil. It finishes long, oily, intensely bean-like, and intriguing. All the worthwhile action unfolds in the mouth, not the bouquet.

2003 Rating: ★★★/Recommended

Darroze 1978 Domaine du Martin Bas Armagnac (France); 42.5% abv, $149.
The bronze/topaz color is lovely; sediment and haze free. The first nosing picks up a vibrant, prickly, spirity aroma that's zesty and citrusy; after another seven minutes of aeration, the bouquet introduces a whole new slate of aromas, including beeswax, lanolin, resin, and polish. The palate entry offers succulent tastes of candied apple, cotton candy, and caramel corn; the midpalate stage features buttery, oily, concentrated but silky smooth flavors that gently and regally coat the tongue. Concludes sweet, toffee-like, oaky, slightly smoky, and wonderfully luxurious. Had the bouquet shown more dimension and depth, it would be another five star beauty from Darroze. As it is, four star rating is correct and fair.

2006 Rating: ★★★★/Highly Recommended

Darroze 1979 Domaine au Durre Bas Armagnac (France); 45.1% abv, $116.
Autumnal honey gold; showing some sediment. The aroma is a bit reluctant and pinched at first, but then it breaks out after a couple of minutes, emitting dry, chewy scents of bacon fat, lanolin, and palm oil; benefiting only slightly from another six minutes of air exposure, the bouquet adds touches of citrus rind and wax to its aromatic arsenal. This brandy takes a turn for the better in the mouth as a nicely sweet, near cocoa-like taste greets the taste buds; by midpalate the cocoa taste expands to include almond butter, walnuts, and a devilish trace of oaky/buttery rancio. It finishes well, offering long, creamy tastes of candied nuts, nut paste/butter, and light caramel. I had my doubts in the middle of the sniffing phase but this brandy exceeded my expectations in the luscious, dairy-like palate and aftertaste.

2003 Rating: ★★★★/Highly Recommended

Darroze 1979 Domaine de Guillemouta Bas Armagnac (France); 47.5% abv, $105.
Lovely honey/amber tone; more sediment than I like to see from a house like Darroze. The first couple of whiffs showcase a buttery richness that's inviting and creamy; aeration adds seductive but dainty scents of roasted almond, palm oil, and oak; a highly complex, but approachable bouquet. The palate entry is semisweet, oaky and resiny, but not at all astringent; the midpalate is sap-like, sweet, nougaty, and medium-rich. The aftertaste is apple-like, ripe, and caramel-intense. I liked this elegant expression as much as the stunningly luscious 1981 (★★★★).

2002 Rating: ★★★★/Highly Recommended

Darroze 1979 Domaine de Martin Bas Armagnac (France); 42.5% abv, $108.

Bronze hue; excellent purity. In the first two minutes of sniffing, a compelling but faint aroma of spiced apple overrides any other fragrance; air contact accentuates the spice element along with nuances of marshmallow and hard candy; a pleasant, but hard to pin down bouquet; lip-smacking flavors. Full texture and toffee-like in the mouth at entry; the midpalate is even more robust, apple-like, and spicy, plus there are intriguing background tastes of maple, butterscotch, and the early makings of rancio. Finishes deep, honey-like, caramelly, and fruity. If the bouquet had been more focused and complex I'd have given this winner a fifth star; as it is, however, it's a very solid four star.

2002 Rating: ★★★★/Highly Recommended

Darroze 1979 Domaine de Rieston Bas Armagnac (France); 45.4% abv, $145.

This appearance is notable for its textbook brilliant copper color; impeccable purity. The first bursts of aroma are intensely waxy (remember wax paper?), tea-like, and fibery; the second round of inhalations are rife with nutshell, toasted almond, and hemp/rope aromas. The palate entry is nutty (mirroring the distinct bouquet) and mildly tobacco-like; the midpalate stage is keenly resiny and bittersweet with soft touches of early-budding rancio, oaky vanilla, cocoa bean, and walnut paste. Finishes well and semisweet.

2006 Rating: ★★★/Recommended

Darroze 1980 Domaine du Martin Bas Armagnac (France); 46% abv, $141.

The copper color is striking in its brilliance; minor, hazy sediment spotted. Right from the crack of the bat, the aroma is toasty and jammy at the same time; after some vigorous swirling, the aroma turns spirity, mildly prickly, and nicely grapy/pear-like. The palate entry is biscuity/bakery-like and rich without being heavy or overly sweet; the midpalate showcases the balance between the candy bar sweetness, the sweet oak, the alcohol, and the dried fruit ripeness. There's just a dash of rawness/heat in the finish that prevents it from being another five star classic. But, hey, this is an outstanding display of distilling/oak maturing skill.

2006 Rating: ★★★★/Highly Recommended

Darroze 1983 Domaine de Coquillon Bas Armagnac (France); 49.5% abv, $100.

The bronze/copper/auburn color enchants the eye; superb purity. The opening nosing passes pick up nut/nougaty scents; exposure to air for another six minutes releases plump, maple-like aromas of caramel, sap, baked apple, and toasted almond. The palate entry is sap-sweet, concentrated, candied, and toasty; the midpalate stage features resiny tastes of nougat, oak, and palm oil. The finish is oily, woody, medium-hot, and semisweet; shows a quick blast of immature heat in the aftertaste.

2002 Rating: ★★★/Recommended

Darroze 1984 Domaine de Dupont Bas Armagnac (France); 48.5% abv, $100.

Pretty light amber hue; the evaluation lamp picks up a moderate amount of barely perceptible debris. The nose after the pour is animated, potent, heady, and intensely nutty; air contact for another six minutes encourages remarkably woody, resiny, and nutty aromas to merge into a butterscotch treat that, while lacking fruit presence, is fully endowed and hearty. The maple-like palate entry taste disarms my taste buds upon contact; I love this type of

sticky, lip-smacking flavor; the midpalate phase features caramel, toasted walnut, pepper, and oak. The finish is long, sinewy, and mature considering that this armagnac isn't that old.
2002 Rating: ★★★★/Highly Recommended

Darroze 1985 Domaine de Jouatmaou Bas Armagnac (France); 51.3% abv, $103.
Attractive golden honey hue; admirable clarity and purity. The spicy/peppery bouquet leaps from the glass, not waiting to be coaxed; the second aromatic stage offers vivacious, biscuity scents of cookie batter, butterscotch, and walnut. The palate entry is semisweet, warming, and delightfully honeyed; at midpalate the taste expands to include deft touches of mint, light toffee, marshmallow, and oloroso sherry. It finishes as well as it began, in an assertive manner, offering long, lush tastes of honey, ripe grapes and tropical fruit. Lovely from top to bottom.
2003 Rating: ★★★★/Highly Recommended

Darroze 1986 Domaine de Coquillon Bas Armagnac (France); 52% abv, $99.
Orange/bronze in color, with ideal purity. The first whiffs are treated to fruity/spicy scents of yellow fruit and green peppercorn; over time, the aroma bears down on the wood resin, leather, and vanilla bean components, leaving the spice and fruitiness behind; this is a sensuous bouquet that's simultaneously sophisticated and bawdy. The palate entry is off-dry, beany, and clean; at midpalate the overriding flavor turns out to be lean and woody/oaky/leathery. The aftertaste shows a touch of oil; tightly wrapped and therefore narrower in focus than some other Coquillons (1988 & 1977), but nonetheless very good.
2003 Rating: ★★★/Recommended

Darroze 1986 Domaine de Rieston Bas Armagnac (France); 53% abv, $125.
The deep bronze/burnt orange color is lovely and flawlessly pure. The opening nose is textile- and flax-like, very fibery; after another six minutes of aeration, the aroma showcases its elevated alcohol and features scents of wood chips, sawdust, and distant tropical fruits; methinks that the hearty abv gets in the way of the bouquet on this one. The palate entry is smoky, pipe tobacco-like, and nicely prickly on the tongue; the midpalate stage is all about mega-oak influence in the multilayered forms of vanilla, maple, butterscotch, dark toffee, and nougat. Ends unbelievably rich, sweet, honeyed and lush. The spectacular in-mouth experiences from entry through finish raised this brandy from three to four rating stars, an unusual circumstance. Man, what a mouthful!
2006 Rating: ★★★★/Highly Recommended

Darroze 1987 Domaine Aux Ducs Bas Armagnac (France); 51.9% abv, $96.
Attractive medium amber/light honey color; perfect purity. In the first few minutes of nosing the aroma displays some peppery spice and a touch of celery; six more minutes of aeration time do little to stimulate further aromatic growth except to add fiber-like scents of flax or nylon; an odd, kind of synthetic resembling bouquet, to say the least. The elevated spirit level comes right at you in the palate entry, singeing the tongue slightly before calming at the midpalate point where vigorous tastes of light caramel, unsalted butter, and oak resin rule in unquestioned authority. The finish shows a bit of bittersweet cocoa; immature, hot,

and brawny, all of which, at least at this stage, make for awkward drinking. A tad too volatile, ungainly, and unsettled for my personal liking.
2003 Rating: ★★/Not Recommended

Darroze 1987 Domaine de Coquillon Bas Armagnac (France); 49.3% abv, $121.
The appearance is deep amber/flat bronze; excellent purity. The animated aroma after the pour shows off woody and grapy fragrances that work in harmony; later whiffs detect pine, figs, white raisins, and fresh oak. The palate entry features tastes of resin, black pepper, and butter; the dry midpalate stage is full bodied, oily, spirity in a minor way, and mildly honeyed. Concludes toasty/roasted, tobacco-like, and semisweet. Very good indeed, but not as distinctive or compelling as the 1972, 1977 or 1988 (all rated ★★★★).
2006 Rating: ★★★/Recommended

Darroze 1987 Domaine de Martin Bas Armagnac (France); 52.5% abv, $90.
Pretty pale bronze/burnished orange color; some sediment noted. The opening nosing passes pick up extremely ripe, generous—no, make that vigorous—and fruity scents in the first two minutes; the bouquet quiets down with aeration, becoming tart to off-dry, lean, grapy, and woody by the last minute of the nosing stage; I like this immature bouquet because as it evolves in the glass, it grows more complex. The palate entry is off-dry to bittersweet, resiny, and a touch minty; by the midpalate stage flavors of walnut, cocoa, and honey are balanced by a subtle mini-blast of spirit that makes the tongue tingle. The aftertaste sees this brandy return to being lean, steely, grapy, almost austere. There's some potential here and I'd like to give it another five to seven years in bottle before I try it again.
2002 Rating: ★★★/Recommended

Darroze 1988 Domaine de Coquillon Bas Armagnac (France); 47.7% abv, $93.
The rich copper/russet hue is flawlessly clean. The initial nosing pass picks up youthfully spirity, almost prickly scents of estery grapefruit, and green melon; aeration allows a keenly peppery, nearly chili-like perfume to overcome the fruitiness as the bouquet takes a severe left turn towards spice and vegetation, especially grass; it offers wildly divergent aromas over the course of ten minutes. The palate entry is warm, cottony, and bittersweet; by the midpalate stage a refined smokiness appears in the flavor, followed by a creamy nut-like taste in the finish that sums up the whole alluring experience. Young, but not in the least immature or unready.
2003 Rating: ★★★★/Highly Recommended

Darroze 1988 Domaine du Martin Bas Armagnac (France); 50.4% abv, $117.
The color of amber/honey is eye-catching and pure. The opening burst of aroma is jam-packed with ripe fruit (plums, grapes/raisins, dates) and toasted oak scents of chocolate bar and cocoa; following another six minutes of air contact, the fruit element edges out the oak impact by a hair, releasing immensely pleasing fragrances of baked pear, banana, pineapple, and kiwi; an utterly sensational bouquet. The palate entry is semisweet, intensely honeyed, and properly woody; in the midpalate stage the taste profile offers graceful and harmonious flavors that include fruit pastry, oaky vanilla, marshmallow, toffee, pine nuts, and marzipan. Finishes firm, long, full bodied, and caramel sweet. Magically, the lofty abv is never an issue. A fantastic brandy.
2006 Rating: ★★★★★/Highest Recommendation

Darroze 20 Year Old Age du Rancio Bas Armagnac (France); 43% abv, $90.

The brilliant, light-catching bronze/topaz hue is beautiful; absolute purity. The initial nosing passes detect rich, dry, and intensely nutty aromas of sautéed walnut, dried red fruit (prune?), and lanolin; further aeration spanning seven minutes finds a deepening of the core fatty/nutty/oily aromas but no expansion of note. The palate entry features the oily/mildly sweet taste of old oak/vanillin and a touch of almond paste; the midpalate taste focus is squarely on the honeyed old oak, hard cheese, dried fruit, and black raisin flavor mix, with an emphasis on the honey-like oak resin. A deft trace of rancio does appear in the svelte, efficient finish which doesn't overstay its welcome but does manage to highlight the glories of buttery/honeyed oak.

2002 Rating: ★★★★/Highly Recommended

Dartigalongue 1900 100 Year Old Bas Armagnac (France); 40% abv, $1,200.

The dazzling deep bronze/caramel color is gorgeous and blemish-free. The opening nosing pass is confronted with concentrated, deep aromas of oak and nougat; after another seven minutes of air contact, subtle nuances of hard cheese, lanolin, figs, and black raisins take charge; I'm impressed that the bouquet still possesses this much vitality. The palate entry regrettably is very resiny; at midpalate the wood resin quality overshadows any remaining sense of fruit/grape character and basically goes sour and astringent. Finishes sour and poorly. I was enormously disappointed once I got around to the acrid taste and finish phases, both of which completely let down the sterling appearance and nosing phases. As much as I admire everything that importer Paul Joseph does, this old, over-the-hill brandy simply unravels in the mouth. No other way to put it.

2004 Rating: ★/Not Recommended

Dartigalongue 1954 50 Year Old "Celebration Collection" Bas Armagnac (France); 41% abv, $417.

The mahogany/chestnut brown color is gorgeous; excellent clarity. The aroma after the pour offers integrated woody/cocoa notes; after seven minutes more of aeration, the bouquet emits very mature, intensely oaky scents that are a touch oily/resiny but basically off-dry; no trace of rancio here. At palate entry the dry to off-dry taste is chocolaty and cocoa-like; at midpalate there's a rush of oak that passes quickly, leaving behind lush flavors of prunes, walnut butter, and honey. Ends up sweet, concentrated, and oaky.

2004 Rating: ★★★★/Highly Recommended

Dartigalongue 1964 40 Year Old "Celebration Collection" Bas Armagnac (France); 42% abv, $239.

The bronze/topaz color is flawless. The aroma starts off woody and marshmallow-like; after seven minutes, toasty notes of burnt apple crisp, lanolin, candle wax, and coffee bean fight for placement. The palate entry is sweet like dried fruit or black raisins, maybe even oloroso sherry; at midpalate the taste profile turns deeply oily/resiny, with seductive hints of rancio and soft blue cheese. Ends up sweet, viscous, raisiny, and honey-like. A stately beauty.

2004 Rating: ★★★★/Highly Recommended

Dartigalongue 1974 30 Year Old "Celebration Collection" Bas Armagnac (France); 43% abv, $140.

The henna/old copper color is dazzling; some inconsequential sediment seen; no worries about it. In the first two minutes of sniffing, the aroma resembles traces of gum, pencil eraser, and dried apricot; following a six minute span of undisturbed aeration, the bouquet becomes earthy, chalky, and minerally. The palate entry shows deep vanilla and cocoa flavors that totally disarm the taste buds; at midpalate the flavor turns creamier and more buttery and oily as the oak resin and rich fruit vie for dominance. Concludes semisweet, biscuity, and maple-like.

2004 Rating: ★★★/Highly Recommended

Dartigalongue 1984 20 Year Old "Celebration Collection" Bas Armagnac (France); 45% abv, $88.

Fantastically bright auburn/sorrel color; perfect purity. The first inhalations detect meaty notes, almost like roast beef and bacon fat; aeration time of another six minutes introduces sap and maple to the bouquet. The palate entry focuses directly on the resin, sap, and maple qualities found in the latter stages of the nose; at midpalate the marzipan/nougat flavor dominates the taste phase. Ends up bittersweet and intensely nutty.

2004 Rating: ★★★/Recommended

Dartigalongue Hors d'Age Bas Armagnac (France); 40% abv, $42.

Deep amber/medium topaz hue. The opening bouquet is supple, grapy/appley, and even a touch peppery in the initial two passes; after several minutes of air contact the aroma turns mildly buttery and fatty, with a distant hint of old oak; a lovely, well-mannered, even slightly shy bouquet that has quality written all over it. The palate entry is viscous, buttery/ creamy, and large-boned; at the midpalate point the flavor bursts open on the tongue offering succulent tastes of ripe grapes and tropical fruit all floating on a foundational flavor of bacon fat and butter. The aftertaste is fruity, mildly sweet, and lip-smacking delicious. Clearly the house style concentrates on subtle richness and understatement; bountiful and luscious.

2001 Rating: ★★★/Highly Recommended

Dartigalongue XO Bas Armagnac (France); 40% abv, $32.

Clean, topaz/dark honey color. The deep, resiny aroma is alive with scents of marzipan, paraffin, and pineapple in the first couple of nosing passes; aeration releases further fragrances of coconut and palm oil over the final two sniffings; a sedate bouquet that's atypical in that there's little evidence of wood or ripe fruit; I like it very much though it's not a muscular type of armagnac perfume—perhaps that's why. In the mouth a sinewy, dry, almost smoky entry flavor makes the mouth pucker; the midpalate phase is where the flavor puts on an incredible display of understated power and sheer elegance as intensely grapy/raisiny tastes underpin the surface flavor of tropical fruit and vanilla. The finish is medium-long, poised, vanilla-like, and even honeyed. Not a bruiser, not a blockbuster, just a supremely confident, multilayered brandy whose calling card is its graceful demeanor.

2001 Rating: ★★★/Highly Recommended

De Montal 1969 Armagnac (France); 40% abv, $100.

The color is deep honey/nutbrown and pure. The initial nosing pass reveals all sorts of fruit layers, including banana, guava, cherries, and baked pear; aeration serves to stimulate balancing aromas of wood, resin, and maple; the entire aromatic experience is wonderfully vibrant and ambrosial as the fruit elements definitely lead the way but are supported nicely by the wood. The palate entry shows a sap-like opening flavor that's sweet and maple-like; by the midpalate stage notes of caramel, toffee, and nougat take the helm and guide this taste phase through the sweet, lip-smacking finish. A terrific middle aged armagnac.

2002 Rating: ★★★★/Highly Recommended

De Montal VS Armagnac (France); 40% abv, $33.

Deep straw/bronze color; perfect purity. Initial whiffs detect aggressive alcohol that over-rides all other scents, except for a baked banana fragrance; time in the glass improves the aroma considerably, allowing for fruity, ripe aromas of banana, nectarine, peach, and date to emerge. Entry is decidedly sweet and slightly smoky; the flavor at midpalate is more sugar sweet than honey sweet and is laden with chunky wood aspects that wipe out all fruit elements. Aftertaste is simple and one-dimensional. Certainly drinkable, but it can't hide its flaws of imbalance and youthful awkwardness behind the veil of vigorous spirit.

2007 Rating: ★★/Not Recommended

De Montal VSOP Armagnac (France); 40% abv, $42.

Burnished copper color; excellent purity. At first, there's a delicate yellow fruit perfume and then that turns grapy and slightly ash-like after a minute or two; light touches of oak, black pepper, and damp straw enter the picture following the seven minute aeration period; I had hoped for more aromatic depth from this VSOP, but didn't get it. Intensely sweet at entry, the flavor is off-balance due to the top-heaviness of the candied sweetness; the midpalate point is a flat-out sweet-a-thon that's cloying, ridiculously fat, and completely stupid. Finishes as a clunky, chunky mess. Zero finesse due to off-the-charts sweetness/ glycerin level. Not for me, thanks.

2007 Rating: ★/Not Recommended

De Montal XO Armagnac (France); 40% abv, $126.

Dark copper/henna color; ideal clarity; seriously attractive. Initial nosings detect fey aromas of oak, light spice, and raisins; with extra time, the spice note accelerates and, in the process, nicely accentuates the grapiness; there's also a pleasant leathery quality at the very end of the aromatic evaluation. Entry is borderline fat with bacon rind and butter cream, but likewise shows enough acidity to counter the hefty sweetness; the midpalate stage is marked by tobacco leaf, leather, light toffee, cinnamon, and oaky resin. Aftertaste is almost too heavy for its own good, but it nonetheless displays enough core depth to retain the recommendation. The de Montals represent an old-fashioned style of armagnac (think: Larressingle, Samalens) that's typically husky and sweet. Perhaps it's time to rethink that game plan.

2007 Rating: ★★★/Recommended

Delord 25 Year Old Bas Armagnac (France); 40% abv, $95.

The deep, old copper penny color is reminiscent of aged tawny porto; flawless purity. The potent spirit races from the copita in the initial aromatic burst, leaving behind dried aromas of raisins, prunes, and herbs; aeration serves to alter the aromatic direction as the bouquet turns biscuity, caramel-like, honeyed, cream sherry-like, and even dark chocolate-like, with more than a passing perfume of cheese-like rancio; wow. The palate entry is suggestive of bittersweet dark chocolate, cocoa butter, chocolate covered raisins, and dark honey; at midpalate the taste profile becomes fruitier than the entry and less bittersweet, making for a succulent aftertaste that's spectacularly satisfying. As good as twenty+ year old armagnac can get. A genuine classic.

2006 Rating: ★★★★★/Highest Recommendation

Delord Napoleon Bas Armagnac (France); 40% abv, $38.
The brilliant copper color charms the eye; superb purity. The opening sniffs detect atypical scents of brown sugar, oak-aged rum, and lanolin; time in the glass sees the aroma settle down into more of a customary armagnac perfume as sweet oak, prunes, cocoa, spice, and raisins come together. The palate entry is assertive, sweet but not overly so, and raisiny; at midpalate there's a flash of spirit, then that's ushered out by fat flavors of brown butter, cocoa butter, almond paste, nougat, and dark honey. Aftertaste is rich, long, and sweet. The earlier, very strange version that I evaluated in 1999 did not have the depth or richness that this edition owns.

2006 Rating: ★★★★/Highly Recommended

Delord XO Bas Armagnac (France); 40% abv, $55.
The burnished/tawny/bronze color is gorgeous; excellent clarity. The first inhalations come across laid back aromas of caramel, marshmallow, and cotton candy; aeration brings out the depth and key importance of the oak through scents of vanilla bean, dark honey, nougat, pipe tobacco, and rancio. The palate entry is fat, buttery, and creamy; at midpalate the taste profile soars as robust flavors take charge, most prominently, honey, dark toffee, and cocoa. Texture is heavy. Finishes on a honeyed note. An excellent armagnac. What holds me back from bestowing a fifth star is the super-intense sweetness, which just might push it into top-notch territory for some people but not for moi. A solid four star brandy.

2006 Rating: ★★★★/Highly Recommended

Domaine Boingnères 1973 Cépages Nobles Armagnac (France); 48% abv, $156.
Bright topaz/honey in hue; pure as can be. The initial nosing passes right after the pour unearth an unusual scent of black pepper upfront, then that blows off and is replaced by a distant fruity aroma; aeration goes just so far in stimulating the bouquet and the final two whiffs discover little new, just some seemingly weary dried fruit and nut scents; not my favorite bouquet from this crop of Boingnères. In the mouth the palate entry is treated to a concentrated butter taste that zaps the taste buds into instant submission; the midpalate stage features oily, buttery, and fat tastes of almond butter, creamery butter, and bacon. The finish is long, dry, almost bitter, and brimming with heavy, old oak flavor. Intriguing and certainly better than average, but not as awe-inspiring as its siblings.

2001 Rating: ★★★/Recommended

Domaine Boingnères 1977 Bacco Armagnac (France); 48% abv, $138.
The color is medium amber/honey; rather large chunks of black sediment settle in the well of the tasting glass. The opening nosing passes pick up a stately, reserved bouquet that offers tightly-knit, melded aromas of tropical fruit, light toffee, and brown butter; later passes

after several minutes in the glass reveal deeper foundational scents of rich oak, dried red fruit, oil, and walnut; a bouquet that shows how graceful armagnac can be, at least perfume-wise. It's downright succulent and lip-smacking sweet in the mouth, especially in the form of dark caramel; the midpalate stage is firm, structured, and round yet brimming with nutty and fruity tastes that all seem to be underpinned by oaky/cheesy rancio. The finish is long, fat, intensely toffee-like, nougaty, and tarry. A beautiful brandy that's ideally proportioned and elegant, but also loaded with multiple layers of flavors; top-notch and classy.

2001 Rating: ★★★★★/Highest Recommendation

Domaine Boingnères 1980 Cépages Nobles Armagnac (France); 49% abv, $105.

The brilliant bronze color enchants the eye; sediment free. The rousing bouquet leaps from the glass after the pour in heady waves of marzipan, nougat, baked pear, and woody resin, a rollicking ride to say the least; the aroma markedly calms with exposure to air and in the final two nosing passes following over five minutes of aeration the aroma almost seems to be coming from a different armagnac so elegant, poised, and subtle is it; the oak overtakes the fruit in the later aromatic stages. In the mouth it starts out dry and oaky at palate entry; then turns on the afterburners at midpalate offering huge, chunky flavors of sweet oak, ripe grapes, baked pears, dark toffee, and gorgeous honey; an incredible midpalate phase. The aftertaste is enormously enchanting, caramel-like, sweet but with plenty of acid. A distinctive, genial, and exuberant brandy that is simply too open, bighearted, plump, and friendly not to adore.

2001 Rating: ★★★★/Highly Recommended

Domaine Boingnères 1984 Folle Blanche Armagnac (France); 48% abv, $115.

Bright topaz/bronze hue; lots of black/brackish sediment noted under the examination lamp. The bouquet straight out of the gate is warm, inviting, assertive, intensely nutty, and seductively honeyed; several minutes of air contact allows the bouquet to settle in, allowing for savory fragrances of paraffin, walnut, blue cheese, and dried red fruit to waft up from the glass. In the mouth my taste buds swoon at palate entry over the deeply succulent, fruity, mature, and ripe flavors; the midpalate stage features round tastes of almond butter, roasted chestnuts, dark caramel, oaky rancio, and deep honey. The aftertaste is long, fat, and sweet.

2001 Rating: ★★★★/Highly Recommended

Domaine Boingnères 1985 Cépages Nobles Bas Armagnac (France); 48% abv, $160.

Gobsmackingly lovely bronze/honey color; impeccable purity. Smells of butterscotch and vinyl; the aromatic returns after seven minutes of further aeration are scant as they showcase intense and horizontal odors of old oak and little more; much to my surprise and disappointment this narrowly focused bouquet is astringent to the point of exclusivity and that simply is not enough. The palate entry is robust in a spirity way and offers resiny/woody flavors that don't meld well with the unbridled spirit; the midpalate stage redeems some of the losses sustained in the awkward aroma and biting entry as the taste profile finally modestly expands to include some toffee, ripe grapes, and pipe tobacco flavors. Finishes hot, resiny, and clumsily astringent. An armagnac from an esteemed producer that regrettably takes the "hearty" moniker of armagnac past the limit of credibility by not including any sense of balance whatsoever. No excuses on this one. It just doesn't work, period.

2006 Rating: ★/Not Recommended

Domaine Boingnères 1988 Folle Blanche Bas Armagnac (France); 48% abv, $105.

Made from 100% folle blanche; the brilliant bronze/orange color dazzles the eye; impeccable purity. The initial nosing passes pick up teasing scents of grapes, baked apple, and oak; seven more minutes in the glass adds semi-dry fragrances of gum, paraffin, palm oil, and unsweetened coconut; luscious and grapy, but pointed and focused at entry; by midpalate the creamy taste and sinewy feel of almond butter overrides the oak and the fruit. The aftertaste is long, creamy, nutty, spirity, and only slightly oaky. A heady, refined armagnac that, though young, harkens back to the enchanted time when folle blanche was the grape of choice in armagnac. Another classy, elegant winner from Boingneres. A superb way to spend just over one hundred dollars.

2003 Rating: ★★★★/Highly Recommended

Domaine d'Espérance 10 Year Old Bas Armagnac (France); 43% abv, $55.

The bright bronze/burnished orange color is eye-catching, but displays more unsightly sediment than I like to see. The initial burst of aroma is toasty/roasted and nutty; the additional aeration time releases bean-like scents of vanilla and cocoa. The palate entry is bittersweet and intensely beany; at the midpalate stage the taste profile develops an inviting oiliness/butteriness that can only evolve with oak barrel maturation. The aftertaste turns sharp and resiny, unfortunately costing it a fourth rating star.

2006 Rating: ★★★/Recommended

Domaine d'Espérance 1990 Bas Armagnac (France); 43% abv, $75.

The deep brown/topaz hue is blemished by too much debris. The opening inhalations encounter sap- and maple-like semisweet aromas; aeration time stimulates sturdily nutty scents of roasted chestnut and sautéed almonds, all wrapped up in a caramel blanket. The palate entry is more toffee-like than nutty; at midpalate the flavor menu includes cocoa, dark caramel, and honey. Finishes maple sugar sweet and almost decadently unctuous.

2006 Rating: ★★★★/Highly Recommended

Domaine d'Espérance 5 Year Old Bas Armagnac (France); 43% abv, $42.

The gleaming bronze/topaz color is appealing; good clarity. In the first nosings after the pour, there's strong evidence of the fresh, still youthful spirit in the spicy forms of black peppercorn and caraway seed; as is typical of such young brandy, the peppery aroma doesn't back down or round off all that much with further air contact and that's fine because the bouquet is delightfully pungent, almost prickly. The palate entry offers a more semisweet expression as tastes of palm oil, beeswax, and light toffee vie for dominance up front; by the midpalate stage there are intriguing, if astringent and bittersweet flavors of coffee bean, tobacco leaf, pine, and new oak. Finishes as vigorous, clean, and assertive as it begins. An example of how compelling young armagnacs can be when handled properly.

2006 Rating: ★★★/Recommended

Domaine du Miquer 1977 Bas Armagnac (France); 45% abv, $120.

The gorgeous copper penny color bedazzles the eye; quite a lot of black floating sediment, however. The aroma is generous and expansive from the beginning nosing passes, offering top-form scents of dried fruit, oaky resin, waxed paper/old parchment, and black pepper;

as this bouquet mingles with air the depth of the brandy comes to the surface via layered, concentrated fragrances of dried violets, dried yellow fruit, roasted chestnuts, and bacon fat; a serious, ever-changing armagnac bouquet to ponder over the course of an evening. The palate entry is so finely-tuned and instantaneously defined it's almost impossible to take in as the bitter lead pencil flavor grabs the attention of the taste buds; in the midpalate stage the flavor detonates on the tongue in the forms of old oak, rancio, soft cheese, almond butter, and bacon fat. The aftertaste is only medium-long, but chockfull of cheesy rancio and resiny oak flavors. An armagnac clinic and a rancio banquet for lovers of that rare brandy quality. Simply put, if you don't own this legendary brandy your life has a huge spirits hole in it.
2001 Rating: ★★★★★/Highest Recommendation

Domaine Grassa 1975 Bas Armagnac (France); 47% abv, $110.

Bright, pretty, greenish/amber hue. The assertive bouquet after the pour is rich and fruity then with short aeration the aroma strangely turns flat and acidic; further air contact mutes the aroma even more as it becomes dumb and closed off after only four minutes in the glass; it's as though all the life was sucked out of the bouquet by air contact; after about nine minutes, the bouquet bounces back in waves of oak and toffee; weird, man. In the mouth, this armagnac exhibits gorgeous flavors of caramel, nougat, resiny oak, bittersweet chocolate, and toffee. The aftertaste is long, intensely toffee-like, and a touch bitter. Though this armagnac contains some strikingly good moments, the reality is that it is too uneven as an overall experience to merit a recommendation. Too bad.
2001 Rating: ★★/Not Recommended

Domaine Grassa Réserve Bas Armagnac (France); 40% abv, $28.

Light amber, almost pale honey/green hue. The curious opening aromas emit softly sweet scents of marshmallow and cheese cake (huh? you read that correctly, cheese cake); with time in the glass (five to eight minutes) the bouquet takes on a toffee/caramel personality that also displays distant hints of ripe grapes, walnuts, and red plums; not your run-of-the-mill armagnac aroma; what makes it so much fun is its unpredictability and idiosyncratic nature. The palate entry flavors explode on the tip of the tongue with huge flavors of rancio, oak resin, blue cheese, grape preserves, and dark caramel; this incredible flavor feast deepens and continues at midpalate as cake frosting and bittersweet chocolate jump into the taste mix—truly unbelievable. The aftertaste is long, lush, satiny, and honey sweet. A wonderful brandy.
2001 Rating: ★★★★★/Highest Recommendation

Domaine Grassa VSOP Bas Armagnac (France); 40% abv, $35.

Attractive, light amber color. The intriguing opening nosings detect viny/foresty aromas that are quite vegetal; the last two passes after at least five minutes of aeration reveal soft traces of new oak, vanilla, and heady spirit; it's the bouquet of an immature, vigorous, if slightly awkward armagnac. In the mouth this velvety brandy seems much more integrated and mature as supple, fat tastes of sweet oak, honey, and brown sugar highlight the palate entry; the midpalate stage features concentrated grape jam and toffee tastes that are large and inviting. The aftertaste is long, sappy sweet, and rustic. While this armagnac could never be accused of being sophisticated or elegant, it's generosity, precociousness, and youthful enthusiasm are appreciated enough for it to be heartily recommended.
2001 Rating: ★★★/Recommended

Domaine Grassa XO Bas Armagnac (France); 40% abv, $65.

Topaz/medium honey color. The initial nosing passes pick up remarkably defined aromas of nougat and roasted chestnuts; air contact serves to unleash further aromatic delights in the forms of hard cheese and oak resin; this is a volatile, aggressive but ultimately pleasing bouquet that's unabashedly nutty, woody, and vibrant. The ferocity continues at palate entry as forward tastes of almond butter, nougat, sautéed nuts, oily oak, and caramel overtake the taste buds; the midpalate point sees the flavor phase settle down only minimally as the nut and oil tastes take command. The finish is long, oily, buttery, and oaky/resiny. A barn-burner of an armagnac that should not be poured near an open flame. Wow! What a breathtaking ride!

2001 Rating: ★★★★/Highly Recommended

Duc de Loussac VS Bas Armagnac (France); 40% abv, $25.

Lightish amber/harvest gold color; very minor sediment seen. The first couple of sniffs pick up rudimentary scents of wood and grapes; further minutes in the glass unleash aromas of peanuts, baked bread, and oak resin. The palate entry is dry to off-dry, slightly stunted, and oaky; at midpalate the flavors pick up steam as they develop into nicely rounded, semisweet tastes of light toffee, honey, caramel, peanut butter, and marshmallow. The aftertaste is long, a little narrow in scope, and semisweet. This fundamental, young armagnac requires a bit of patience before it gets moving. Once it is moving, it's simple but quite nice.

2003 Rating: ★★★/Recommended

Duc de Loussac VSOP Bas Armagnac (France); 40% abv, $30.

Bright, light-catching honey/amber hue; impeccable purity. In the initial inhalations following the pour, the nose displays a keen oakiness that's more on the dry side of the sweet/dry scale; seven further minutes of air contact really jump start the bouquet as well-developed aromas of nut paste, roasted almond, cola nut, and meringue take the lead. The palate entry is dusty, semisweet, and very caramel-like; at midpalate the dense candied flavor raises the ante and turns almost nougat and marzipan-like. The finish is sweet, raisiny, and toffee-like; I really wanted to see this brandy break through into four star territory but the intense, localized candy feature held it back due to the fact that it left no room for other complementary flavor elements.

2003 Rating: ★★★/Recommended

Duc de Loussac XO Bas Armagnac (France); 40% abv, $45.

Attractive, burnished orange/deep amber/nut brown color, with ideal clarity. The opening bouquet offers tight, semisweet, toffee-covered apple, and wood resin fragrances; eight more minutes in the glass introduce toasted almond/roasted chestnut and oil to the increasingly complex, if firm aromatic mix. The palate entry is taut, sweet in a honey nut manner, and moderately oily; at midpalate the taste profile eases up a bit on the tightness and in the process releases harmonious flavors of nut butter, nougat, palm oil, dark caramel, and distant citrus zest. The finish is long, pleasingly sour, oily, and engagingly nut-like. A beauty.

2003 Rating: ★★★★/Highly Recommended

Gélas 10 Year Old Bas Armagnac (France); 40% abv, $36.

The topaz appearance owns a slight bit of haziness and a good amount of sediment. The first nosing encounters delicate scents of apple, white grapes, and cotton candy; it's fair to state that further air contact time of seven minutes lights the fire under this bouquet as the later sniffs get treated to luxurious and lush smells of light caramel, English toffee, baked apple pastry, pineapple, and oak. The palate entry features oaky sweet tastes of nougat, milk chocolate, and chocolate-covered raisins; the midpalate stage is more candied than honeyed, with suddenly bittersweet flavors of treacle and marzipan strutting their stuff on the tongue. Finishes candied, nougaty, and vigorous. Even though there's an unevenness about the sensory experience, there are more than ample pleasing virtues to warrant a recommendation.

2006 Rating: ★★★/Recommended

Gélas 20 Year Old Bas Armagnac (France); 40% abv, $75.

This bronze brandy suffers from the same type of haze/sediment condition that the 10 does. The opening whiffs pick up fiber-like scents of cheesecloth and wool; once again, aeration allows the aroma time to gather itself into a lovely experience that highlights smells of leather, grapefruit, oak, and unsalted butter; my message here is take the time to enjoy it aromatically. The palate entry is lusciously maple-like and earthy/viny; the midpalate stage showcases the oak influence in the forms of cocoa, honey, and oaky vanilla. Ends up very sweet, thickly textured, toffee-like, and robust. This is a big-hearted armagnac that approaches being over-the-top in sweetness. That said, for people with a sweet-tooth, it's brandy heaven.

2006 Rating: ★★★★/Highly Recommended

Gélas 50 Year Old Bas Armagnac (France); 40% abv, $150.

The deep copper/chestnut/mahogany color is the prettiest and cleanest of the three Gélas samples. In the initial nosing passes following the pour, there's a fruity aroma that is tantalizingly near, yet just far enough away to not clearly identify; seven more minutes in the copita stir up woody/oaky aromas that are drier than they are sweeter as they offer subdued and hit-and-miss notes of marshmallow, dried orange, dried red fruit, minerals, and slate. The palate entry is deliciously sweet and oaky; the midpalate is obviously mature, oaky, rum-, mocha- and vinyl-like, but without any evidence of rancio whatsoever, which surprises me. Finishes intensely sweet and brown sugar-like, almost like a rum. Worth trying to see how armagnac reacts to serious oak-aging.

2006 Rating: ★★★/Recommended

Laberdolive 1942 Jaurrey Bas Armagnac (France); 43% abv, $695.

Lovely brown/tawny color; minor sediment doesn't affect anything in terms of scoring impression. The vibrant, scintillating opening nose is peppery and has an intriguing, if unusual, backnote of caraway seed; following eight more minutes in the glass, the bouquet opens up to add piquant, peppery notes of rye bread, oak, lard, and pear drop candy. The entire experience accelerates to the loftiest level once this armagnac reaches the taste stage; the palate entry is unbelievably rich, bittersweet to sweet, concentrated, and honeyed; by the midpalate juncture, racy waves of fatty rancio wash over the stunned taste buds in flavors of bacon fat, nut butter, oaky vanilla extract, and palm oil. The finish is sublimely honeyed/sherried, dried fruit-like, and incredibly warming and opulent. In short, a true armagnac masterpiece from World War II.

2002 Rating: ★★★★★/Highest Recommendation

Laberdolive 1946 Jaurrey Bas Armagnac (France); 43% abv, $540.

The color is brown to nutbrown to light cola; moderate sediment. The bouquet after the pour is reluctant to show itself, giving off only a distant scent of marshmallow; the additional eight minutes of aeration breath life into this bouquet as it starts to emit mature, elegant aromas of old oak, baked pear, baked apple, dark caramel, and bacon fat. The palate entry immediately flashes a taste of rancio in the form of almond butter; by the midpalate point other mature flavors including honey, tobacco, and brown sugar enhance the moderate rancio presence. The aftertaste is chewy, medium long, and semisweet. While very good indeed I detected a bit of weariness at the end of the midpalate and into the finish. An aging lion that still roars enough to be recommended and appreciated, but not necessarily idolized.

2002 Rating: ★★★/Recommended

Laberdolive 1962 Pillon Bas Armagnac (France); 44% abv, $360.

Lightish, medium amber/honey hue; clouds of minuscule sediment spotted. The opening nosing passes within two minutes after the pour reveal deep-seated aromas that are dry, moderately candied, and very oaky on the surface; be forewarned: this is a bouquet that requires more than normal time in the glass; I allowed it the full standard ten minutes I always give to spirits but I believe it could use fifteen, even twenty minutes; with swirling, the bouquet is freed, exposing totally dry aromas of orange pekoe tea, cedar, black pepper, and old oak. In the mouth, this armagnac finds its footing immediately by offering semisweet to sweet entry tastes of dark caramel, nougat, and bittersweet chocolate; at midpalate succulent flavors of marshmallow, candied almonds, dried apricot, and honey get added to the mix. In the finish the dried apricot and candied almond take the lead; huge depth and multiple layers in the taste and finish phases. Lip-smacking.

2002 Rating: ★★★★/Highly Recommended

Laberdolive 1964 Pillon Bas Armagnac (France); 44% abv, $340.

The color is brilliant bronze; some sediment but not enough to be concerned about it. For a very mature brandy the nose after the pour is vibrant, displaying finely melded, dry scents of cigarette smoke, oak resin, and linseed oil; time in the glass affords the chance for other dry to off-dry aromas to emerge, including prunes, well-worn leather, honey, and chocolate covered cherries; a lovely, two-layered bouquet whose finest asset is its subtle smokiness. The palate entry is all dark caramel and cocoa; at the midpalate point an opulent richness develops that is characterized in an oily texture and tastes of honey, bacon fat, vanilla extract, oloroso sherry, and molasses. The aftertaste is thick, long, honeyed/sherried, and pruny. This is a slightly reluctant giant armagnac which I feel never really shifts into fourth gear. But, oh, that divine transfer from second to third gear.

2002 Rating: ★★★★/Highly Recommended

Laberdolive 1970 Pillon Bas Armagnac (France); 44% abv, $265.

Rich golden brown/topaz color; large brown chunks of debris spoil the appearance— what a shame. The initial passes in the first couple of minutes offer heavenly aromas of pear, pineapple, nectarine, and tobacco; an extra eight minutes releases more buttery/dairy/fatty scents including egg cream, vanilla, and bacon fat; this is a huge, generous bouquet that displays at least three layers. The taste at palate entry is biscuity, spicy, and semisweet; at midpalate intense tastes of butterscotch, light caramel, marzipan, nougat, and cocoa bathe the taste buds in a thick blanket of texture. The aftertaste is long, tobacco-like, and mapley. The finishes shows the early makings of rancio; semisweet, lush, and decadent. It would have earned a fifth rating star but for the appalling degree of sediment—no excuses are good enough.

2002 Rating: ★★★★/Highly Recommended

Laberdolive 1972 Pillon Bas Armagnac (France); 44% abv, $225.

Pale amber/autumnal gold color; barely detectable white clouds of sediment do not blemish the appearance. The initial nosing passes pick up ethereal scents of spiced apple, pears, grapefruit, and light oak; further aeration of eight minutes releases deeper scents of light honey, unsalted butter, almonds, and superfine sugar. This armagnac takes flight in the mouth as lightly toasted tastes of almonds, light caramel, and honey charm the taste buds at palate entry; by midpalate the honey quality takes command of the palate and dominates well into the medium-bodied aftertaste, which is sweet but not syrupy or cloying. An armagnac that builds in the glass with air contact and one that, starting with the palate entry, ends up impressing the bejesus out of me. The sleeper in this line-up.

2002 Rating: ★★★★/Highly Recommended

Laberdolive 1973 Jaurrey Bas Armagnac (France); 43% abv, $225.

Very pretty medium amber/pale bronze color; very good purity. The opening nosing passes pick up subtle scents of grape preserves, marshmallow, and oak; additional time in the glass stirs up off-dry, mildly prickly, almost biscuity scents of sugar cookies, black pepper, distant mint, and maple syrup; a somewhat hesitant, demure bouquet that requires some work and patience. In the mouth, it's off-dry to semisweet and lean in texture; by midpalate the flavors develop into impactful taste impressions that include prunes, spices, and nuts. The finish is medium long, resiny (oak), baked apple-like, and off-dry. Not the most generous of the Laberdolives, but a solid armagnac that lives at the leaner, more austere side of the spectrum.

2002 Rating: ★★★/Recommended

Laberdolive 1979 Jaurrey Bas Armagnac (France); 46% abv, $150.

Medium amber/light honey color; very good clarity. The initial nosing passes detect astringent, almost phenolic (strangely Scotch-like) scents of wood smoke, linseed oil, and wet earth (but not necessarily peat); time in the glass exposes further atypical scents of unripened grapes, barely aged spirit, grape must, and oily oak; a peculiar animal, to say the least. In the mouth it's far more armagnac-like than in the pungent, hard-to-pin-down bouquet; the entry is sweetly honeyed and almost cream sherry-like in its bearing; by midpalate tastes of toasted nuts, tea leaves, and marzipan take over and lead the taste buds to a slightly hot, mildly prickly finish that's sappy sweet and long. It's uneven to a fault and, at times, clearly flawed even if there are some genuine virtues such as the palate entry and appearance; but they aren't enough to recommend it.

2002 Rating: ★★/Not Recommended

Laberdolive 1985 Jaurrey Bas Armagnac (France); 46% abv, $99.

Stunning, shining new copper penny/auburn color; impeccable purity—the deepest Laberdolive in color from 1972 to 1988; visually enchanting. The disarming appearance serves as but an overture for the sterling opening bouquet as opulent, bittersweet scents of old oak, toasted almonds, nougat, cigar smoke, and dark caramel bedazzle the olfactory sense; eight more minutes of air contact only deepens what is already a remarkably profound bouquet by adding holiday spices (cinnamon, nutmeg), baked pears, vanilla extract, brown sugar, and black raisins; a sensational, first rank armagnac aroma. Just when I think that this experience can't get any better, it does at palate entry in the forms of nougaty, butterscotch flavors that are more bittersweet than sweet; as the midpalate unfolds so do layers of bittersweet tastes, especially brown sugar, tobacco smoke, and oaky vanilla. The finish is all about smoke and roasted nuts. A pinnacle achievement and brandy-lover experience. A classic powerhouse.

2002 Rating: ★★★★★/Highest Recommendation

Laberdolive 1988 Jaurrey Bas Armagnac (France); 46% abv, $89.

Harvest gold/amber hue; too much white bitty sediment for my personal comfort level. The bouquet right after the pour is clearly youthful and vibrant, giving off lovely perfumes of pears, powdered sugar, and spiced peach; further aeration brings to life moderately deep scents of honey-wheat toast, vanilla, and egg cream. Right from the palate entry the fiery spirit singes the taste buds but then by midpalate the taste buds adjust to the spirity character enough to search past it to find semisweet tastes of light toffee, nougat, walnut, and honey. The aftertaste is long, warm but not hot, and maple syrup sweet. Vivacious and frisky, but never harsh or overly spirity because it retreats a step before the precipice.

2002 Rating: ★★★/Recommended

Larressingle VSOP Armagnac (France); 40% abv, $40.

Looks like maize or old gold in color; excellent purity. The spirit leaps out of the glass in the first sniffings, overshadowing much lesser aromatic notes of butterscotch, prune, and worn leather; seven more minutes of exposure to air help to settle the alcohol, allowing the more interesting scents, most notably, baked pineapple, hemp/rope, and prune Danish, to emerge. The palate entry is thick, viscous, buttery, and oily; by the midpalate point the taste profile is laden with sticky sweet honey and caramel flavors that prove too fat and flabby for me. Ends fat, oily, and sweet. An obsolete style that's well past its prime. Almost like a liqueur more than what is known as modern armagnac.

2007 Rating: ★★/Not Recommended

Larressingle XO Grande Reserve Armagnac (France); 43% abv, $80.

Lovely, burnt umber/honey color; excellent purity. The opening nosings detect concentrated, nutty scents followed by dry cardboard, parchment, and brown rice-like aromas. The palate entry is rich, honey-like, and sweet; the midpalate gushes with piquant taste of nuts, nougat, dark caramel, and dark honey. Ends a bit too mossy/earthy/mushroomy and sweet. Even though there's a bit of a letdown in the finish, this brandy offers plenty of virtues in the aroma and taste phases.

2004 Rating: ★★★/Recommended

Laubade Intemporel No. 5 Bas Armagnac (France); 40% abv, $150.

Blend of bacco 41%, ugni blanc 35.5%, colombard 13.5 %, and folle blanche 10%. The topaz/deep honey color is rich and bronzed; some sediment seen floating about. The opening aroma is assertively spicy (cinnamon especially) and wonderfully bakeshop fruity (spiced apple, baked pear); the aroma turns into a full-fledged, two-fisted armagnac bouquet after seven minutes of further aeration, emitting more layers that are very bakery driven in terms of the keen spiced fruit, oak, and pastry components; zesty, comely, and inviting; it's this type of aromatic fruit thrust that you rarely find in cognac. The palate entry is oily, acceptably resiny, and is loaded with maple, caramel, marzipan flavor; the bittersweet midpalate stage adds honey, vanilla extract, and beeswax, but flattens out slightly after the buzz of the entry. Finishes chewy, but elegant; a powerhouse dressed in velvet.

2007 Rating: ★★★★/Highly Recommended

Laubade VSOP Bas Armagnac (France); 40% abv, $32.

Six years old; medium amber/harvest gold; perfect purity. In the initial two nosings after the pour, delicate, if shy, aromas of brown butter and almonds greet the olfactory sense; aeration serves to deepen the already buttery fragrance into bacon fat. Palate entry is round, moderately rich, and semisweet; by the midpalate point the taste profile adds flavors of bittersweet chocolate and nougat. It finishes medium-long, bittersweet, and spicy. Solid from top to bottom.

2002 Rating: ★★★/Recommended

Laubade XO Bas Armagnac (France); 40% abv, $52.

Twelve years old. The color is bright bronze leaning to copper/rust; absolute purity. The opening nosing passes emit gentle but firm scents of black pepper, litchi nut, and burnt toast; the smokiness picked up in the first whiffs accelerates into a tobacco leaf/charred oak aroma, buttressed by an underlying bacon fat/old oak smell; it's significantly more complex than the VSOP. The palate entry is oily in texture and semisweet in taste; by midpalate a concentrated flavor of almond butter and nougat make for lip-smacking tasting. The aftertaste is brief, semisweet tart, and just a touch smoky.

2002 Rating: ★★★★/Highly Recommended

Laubade 1936 Bas Armagnac (France); 40% abv, $820.

The fathomless color is all brown/deep bronze, without a trace of red; perfect clarity. Right off the crack of the bat there are strong scents of wax paper and lanolin; aeration time doesn't stimulate a whole lot more in the way of aroma, except for a touch of kiwi; I would expect an older brandy such as this to offer more oak and spice. The palate entry is gentle, satiny, and fruity sweet rather than oaky sweet; the midpalate point showcases chocolate covered cherry, banana nut bread, candied almond, and cocoa. Finishes deliciously sweet, medium-weighted, elegant, and graceful. Had the aroma shown more dimension it would have easily earned a fifth rating star.

2007 Rating: ★★★★/Highly Recommended

Laubade 1941 Bas Armagnac (France); 40% abv, $460.

Deep copper/tawny in hue; flawless clarity. The initial nosing passes pick up semisweet aromas of oaky vanilla, sugar plum, and dark honey; after seven more minutes, the aroma leaps forward emitting toasty, roasted, almost smoky fragrances of campfire, charcoal, pipe tobacco, old oak, blue cheese, and rancio. The palate entry is elegant, refined, and supple; at midpalate mature, melded tastes of oak, marshmallow, honey, oloroso sherry, black tea, and coffee organize themselves into a sensational burst of flavor on the tongue. The aftertaste reinforces all the impressions detected at midpalate. A seamless six decade-old jewel.

2003 Rating: ★★★★★/Highest Recommendation

Laubade 1945 Bas Armagnac (France); 40% abv, $400.

The mahogany/bay color is lovely, except for lots of sediment. The opening aromas are pretty well shut down in the first two minutes of inhaling; additional time in the glass encourages scents of thyme, tarmac, and pepper. The palate entry is big-hearted, luscious, and bittersweet; the midpalate stage is chockfull of nougat, honey, and dark chocolate tastes that delight the taste buds. Concludes sweet, medium-bodied, sherried, and honeyed. A true pleasure from the end of the Second World War.

2005 Rating: ★★★★/Highly Recommended

Laubade 1947 Armagnac (France); 40% abv, $420.

The bright reddish/rust/henna color is stunning and gleaming; unblemished clarity. Right out of the gate, the aroma is all walnut, Brazil nut, nougat, and pecan—in other words, seriously nutty; aeration settles the aroma down, narrowing its focus to engaging scents of beeswax and dried fruits, in particular, peach, apricot, and quince. The palate entry shows much of the nuttiness that dominated the early nosings, especially in the form of walnut paste/walnut butter; by the midpalate point a drier, oilier taste of high cocoa content dark chocolate shines through as well as copious amounts of rancio. In the finish there's an unexpected background taste of gunmetal/coin that undercuts the rancio and drops this otherwise stupendous armagnac to four rating stars.

2007 Rating: ★★★★/Highly Recommended

Laubade 1952 Bas Armagnac (France); 40% abv, $300.

Brilliant copper/rust hue; impeccable clarity. The first couple of sniffings after the pour are treated to a burning embers aroma that has additional scents of marzipan and black pepper; with time in the glass, the aroma grows marginally to include old oak, mild butterscotch, and nutmeg. While the bouquet is lovely, it's in the mouth that this fantastic armagnac earns its spurs in the forms of luscious tastes of butter cream chocolate, cocoa, tea leaves, dark caramel, molasses, and honey; a semisweet to sweet taste tour de force of multilayered flavors that keep evolving long into the off-dry, honey, and molasses aftertaste. One of the two armagnac greats that I've tasted from the 1950s; utterly wonderful and decadent.

2002 Rating: ★★★★★/Highest Recommendation

Laubade 1953 Armagnac (France); 40% abv, $219.

The color takes bronze/tawny to the max; superb purity. The bouquet opens up with subtle scents of brown sugar and oak; aeration serves to cut loose an intense nut-like perfume

that's off-dry and oily. The palate entry is thick, honey-like, and maple syrup-like; at midpalate the taste profile displays a wonderful harmony between the acidity, the ripe fruit, the nut-like oil flavor, the honey, and the dark cocoa; luscious and balanced. The aftertaste is succulent, maple-like, sap-like, and honeyed. Shows style and substance in just the right amounts.
2003 Rating: ★★★★/Highly Recommended

Laubade 1954 Armagnac (France); 40% abv, $295.
Minor sediment flaws don't detract from the pretty bronze/bright topaz color. The initial nosing passes discover mature scents of black olive, burnt matches, and cigar box; another seven minutes of air contact release expressive, basically dry to off-dry notes of black pepper, minerals/slate and old, crumbling parchment. The palate entry features subtle tastes of marzipan, prunes, black raisins, and cake batter; at midpalate the taste profile turns flat-out sweet, maple-like and woody/oaky. Ends sweetly, medium rich, and a touch cola-like, though it lacks the vigor of the 1964 and 1974, there's still enough character here to hang an evening on.
2004 Rating: ★★★/Recommended

Laubade 1955 Armagnac (France); 40% abv, $300.
A beautiful old bronze/chestnut color; quite a lot of sediment seen. The first nosings detect notes of orchard fruit and beeswax; later sniffings pick up subtle traces of red apple, pears, and pipe tobacco. The palate entry is loaded with rich, nut-like/nougaty tastes that wrap around the tongue; at midpalate there's a rush of sweetened tobacco that quickly gives way to succulent flavors of dark caramel, honey, and oaky vanilla. Finishes rich but not unctuous and with a flurry of caramel, marzipan, and nougat notes. Very nice and vibrant for an oldster.
2005 Rating: ★★★★/Highly Recommended

Laubade 1957 Armagnac (France); 40% abv, $300.
The color is old copper penny/burnished orange; excellent clarity. The first nosings reveal enormous aromas of fudge, palm oil, and burnt toast; seven more minutes stimulate bittersweet notes of wood resin, figs, dates, and pecan/praline. The palate entry is peppery, leathery, and sweetened coconut-like; by the midpalate stage the taste profile has gone intensely nutty/nougaty, like peanut brittle, and just a touch maple-like. Full-bodied, concentrated in the finish, with a compelling flash of rancio. A 9 on the Rambunctious Rogue-Meter. Metrosexuals are advised to give a wide berth to this rascal.
2007 Rating: ★★★★/Highly Recommended

Laubade 1958 Armagnac (France); 44% abv, $255.
The dark copper/burnished orange color is dazzling and pure. The first aromas are spirity and oaky, with traces of worn saddle leather and cedar; after additional air contact, light scents of pineapple and almond make appearances. The palate entry is moderately rich, caramel-like, and chewy; at midpalate the taste displays off-dry to bittersweet flavors of nougat, bacon fat, and old oak. Ends up warming, nutty, and bittersweet.
2005 Rating: ★★★/Recommended

Laubade 1962 Bas Armagnac (France); 40% abv, $165.

The spectacular color is old copper penny/russet/tawny; ideal purity. The nose is immediately alive with vibrant aromas of cigar smoke, oak, tar, and fireplace ashes; air contact brings out a fleshy, tart red fruit fragrance that beautifully complements the tar/cigar/ash. The palate entry is tight, integrated, dry to off-dry, and oily in texture; at midpalate the flavor profile includes baked apple, toasted almonds, bacon fat, old oak, and a fleeting dash of rancio. The aftertaste is a genuine delight as long, luxurious flavors of ash, cigar tobacco, and bacon fat thrill the taste buds. An armagnac to be enjoyed slowly with a cigar. Lights my fire.

2002 Rating: ★★★★/Highly Recommended

Laubade 1964 Bas Armagnac (France); 40% abv, $175.

The color is of a shiny new copper penny; burnt orange core color; excellent purity. In the first whiffs, I notice autumnal dashes of faint spice, fall leaves, and hemp/rope; more time in the copita brings about husky notes of bacon fat, toffee, milk chocolate, vanilla, and oak resin. The palate entry is sinewy and sweet as dark caramel; at midpalate the cake frosting sweetness takes on a buttery/creamy leaning. Concludes intensely maple-like and sappy. So rich, unctuous, and decadent you just want to bathe in it.

2004 Rating: ★★★★/Highly Recommended

Laubade 1967 Bas Armagnac (France); 40% abv, $175.

The mahogany/nut brown color is pretty and flawlessly clean. The aroma after the pour offers butcher shop notes of roasted pork loin, bacon fat, sawdust, with a touch of smokiness thrown in; seven more minutes of aeration do little to open this bouquet up any further, but what's there is strong, round to the point of being fat, and luscious. The palate entry is cocoa sweet, intensely oaky, vanilla-like, and honeyed; by the midpalate stage the smoke noticed in the latter phase of the nose reappears in tandem with a chocolate covered apricot taste that is mesmerizing and delicious. A fabulously plump, but focused B-A from start to finish.

2007 Rating: ★★★★★/Highest Recommendation

Laubade 1969 Bas Armagnac (France); 40% abv, $120.

The striking color is a tawny/deep copper hue; very minor sediment. The opening couple of inhalations within three minutes of the pour reveal seductive, teasing, dried scents of baked apple, lead pencil, and black pepper; aeration releases further elemental aromas especially chalk, earthy, slate-like fragrances that are compelling and minerally; at the very tail end of the nosing phase a burnt/charcoal aroma emerges and intrigues. The palate entry introduces the taste buds to bittersweet flavors of maple, rancio, oak resin, and soft cheese; the midpalate stage features luscious toasted/roasted flavors of burnt toast, honey wheat bread, cocoa butter, and roasted chestnuts. The aftertaste is long, focused, bittersweet, concentrated, oily, and honeyed. A fabulously oily, creamy, and decadent armagnac that has clear and undeniable evidence of rancio.

2002 Rating: ★★★★★/Highest Recommendation

Laubade 1973 Bas Armagnac (France); 40% abv, $130.

The color is deep topaz/dirty copper; infinitesimal bits of sediment seen floating near the top and bigger, spongy pieces of cork noted at the bottom. Right from the crack of the

bat, this supple bouquet displays off-dry aromas of gum, coffee bean, and vanilla extract; six more minutes in the glass helps the bouquet to open up further as sinewy aromas of nut butter, dark caramel, and molasses entice the olfactory sense. The palate entry is succulent, candied, and sweet; the midpalate owns sweet flavors of dark caramel, honey, old sweet oak, and maple. It finishes semisweet, chocolaty, and luscious. I'd have bestowed a fifth star if hadn't been for the heavy and unpleasant sediment.
2003 Rating: ★★★★/Highly Recommended

Laubade 1974 Bas Armagnac (France); 40% abv, $130.

Bright auburn/sorrel/copper color; imperfect purity as there is evidence of minute black sediment. The first nosings detect dark fudge, vanilla extract, and dried herbs; following six more minutes of aeration. The aroma displays powerful, centered, and layered aromas of oak/pine, old saddle leather, and crème caramel candy; a gorgeous bouquet. The palate entry is long, deep, and bittersweet; at midpalate the flavor profile turns toasty/smoky, sap- and maple-like, and chewy. Finishes on a maple-like note that's semisweet and lip-smackingly delicious. Another treasure from Laubade.
2004 Rating: ★★★★/Highly Recommended

Laubade 1976 Bas Armagnac (France); 40% abv, $125.

The brilliant bronze appearance displays clouds of minuscule sediment. Mesmerizing fragrances of ripe tropical fruit and red grapes lazily waft up from the glass; seven more minutes of air contact stimulate late blossoming aromas of nougat, dark toffee, honey, and brown sugar. The palate entry taste showcases a sturdily structured brandy with appealing opening flavors of pine, cedar, barely ripened grapes, and sweet oak; at midpalate the flavor profile takes on a bittersweet dark chocolate surface taste while underneath a savory flavor of almond butter supports the entire taste phase. The aftertaste is long, piny/resiny, and sap-sweet; lusty. Robust but shows enough maturity and core integration to easily earn an SJ recommendation.
2003 Rating: ★★★/Recommended

Laubade 1978 Bas Armagnac (France); 40% abv, $135.

The chestnut/mahogany color flashes cherry red core highlights that completely dazzle the eye; ideal purity. In the initial inhalations there's subtle, but unmistakable evidence of chocolate covered red cherry and old saddle leather; swirling and additional aeration stimulate gently sweet/tart hints of grapefruit, kiwi, and dried apricot; a fruit lover's aromatic paradise. The palate entry goes from initially fruity to intensely honeyed/sherried and lush on the tongue; at midpalate the taste profile becomes oily/creamy and concentrated on caramel/toffee/maple. Ends up silky, semisweet, and nutty. A teasing, provocative and altogether stunning B-A that is worth twice the price.
2007 Rating: ★★★★★/Highest Recommendation

Laubade 1984 Bas Armagnac (France); 40% abv, $106.

Pristine new copper penny color. I find the initial whiffs after the pour to be bittersweet, intense, assertive and very nutty; further aeration time doesn't lessen the vigor of this youthful bouquet; indeed, the bittersweet concentration of oaky resin seems to accelerate, obliterating

the pleasant nuttiness. The palate entry is seriously sap- and maple-like; by midpalate the taste focus shifts from sap to the resiny/seed-like flavor of unseasoned oak, road tar, and black tea leaves. The finish is firm but so resiny and tea-like that it's just flat-out bitter, kind of like retsina from Greece. Okay for aficionados of aggressive young Bas Armagnac, but I'd prefer to see it rest in barrel for seven or eight more years. Though it shows potential, as it is it's too angular and off-center for me to go beyond two stars.
2003 Rating: ★★/Not Recommended

Laubade 1986 Bas Armagnac (France); 40% abv, $105.
The rich bronze/copper color displays some inconsequential sediment beneath the examination lamp. The aroma leaps from the glass in the first couple of minutes after the pour, giving off buttery/fat scents of roast pork and cream; following seven minutes of additional aeration, the bouquet adds only hints of spice and cake, but little more. The palate entry is assertive, moderately chewy, and nutty; the midpalate stage owns a keen astringency that undercuts much of the pleasing fat nuttiness found in the entry. Concludes uninteresting, totally dry, and only mildly nutty. Too uneven, off-balance, and narrow in scope to be recommended.
2005 Rating: ★★/Not Recommended

Loujan 12 Year Old Bas Armagnac (France); 42.7% abv, $80.
The pretty autumnal honey color is marred by way too much black, hair-like sediment. The opening aromas include walnut butter, nougat, and jasmine; further aeration stimulates distant aromatic notes of papaya, grape skins, and leather; an unremarkable bouquet. This armagnac lights a fire under itself in the mouth as rich, textured, sweet, honey-like flavors emerge at palate entry; the midpalate offers stately tastes of nougat, toasted almond, sweet oak, vanilla bean, and tobacco. The finish is long, sweet, sap-like, and maple-like. The exceedingly pleasant taste and aftertaste phases salvaged this otherwise rather dull and ordinary armagnac to the point where a recommendation was pulled out of the hat.
2003 Rating: ★★★/Recommended

Loujan 22 Year Old Bas Armagnac (France); 42.9% abv, $125.
Brilliant old copper penny color; scads of unappealing sediment; a disaster to the eye. In the first couple of whiffs there's lots of vegetation (brambles especially), oak resin, and heady spirit; another eight minutes of air contact positively affect this bouquet as luxurious, opulent but astringent scents of honey, nut candy, and dark toffee impress the olfactory sense. The palate entry is tart, lean, and brown sugar-like, reminiscent of Haitian rum; the midpalate explodes with dynamic, multilayered tastes of marzipan, brown sugar, honey, cocoa, and toasted almond. The aftertaste is long, bittersweet, and stunningly sap-like. A rollicking armagnac ride that's filled with hair-raising twists and turns. While hardly a classic, it's certainly good enough for a strong recommendation (borderline three/four stars) and would definitely have scored higher had the appearance been cleaned up.
2003 Rating: ★★★/Recommended

Marcel Trépout 1925 80 Year Old Armagnac (France); 40% abv, $833.
Easily one of the oldest armagnacs I've ever sampled. The appearance beams under the lamp in appealing shades of bright copper/burnished orange; superb purity; a dazzling

visual display. The first couple of nosing passes pick up surprising amounts of vibrant spirit, orange marmalade, hard cheese/rancio, and spice—this 80 year old bouquet rocks; further air contact brings out unbelievably toned and firm notes of banana-nut bread, white raisins, and honey. The palate entry coats the tongue in succulent flavors of caramel, butterscotch, and brown sugar; the midpalate phase is sinewy, vivid, and not in the least tired or on the downturn chemically as taut tastes of nut paste, sausage, cake frosting, cocoa, and dark caramel stun the taste buds. Concludes with grace, genuine mature presence, and woodiness. Worth every penny. A classic old-timer that doesn't in the least betray its age either in the nose or the mouth. Perfect integration.
2006 Rating: ★★★★★/Highest Recommendation

Marcel Trépout Apotheose 30 Year Old Armagnac (France); 40% abv, $110.
The bronze color is luminous and unblemished under the examination lamp. The initial nosings detect an aroma that's relatively toasty/roasted, if slightly reluctant/muted; another seven minutes of exposure to air brings out sturdy scents of walnut paste, apple butter, baked apple/pear pastry, black pepper, and pipe tobacco. The palate entry is confectioner sweet, maple-like, and deeply honeyed; the midpalate stage bolsters the entry findings and adds complementary notes of cocoa, coffee, dark caramel, and bacon fat. Ends tight, but generous, luxurious, decadent, and unabashedly sweet. A hearty, candy bar style of armagnac that might not be for all, but count me as an ardent admirer.
2006 Rating: ★★★★/Highly Recommended

Marcel Trépout Hors d'Age 20 Year Old Armagnac (France); 42% abv, $55.
The nut-brown/walnut color is attractive and flawlessly clean. The opening sniffs pick up vibrant notes of pineapple, quince, pear, and brown butter; swirling and an extra period of air contact stimulate deeper oak-influenced scents of palm oil, cigar tobacco, vanilla bean, and Christmas spices. The silky palate entry is oily, sleek, nutty, and pleasingly oaky; by the midpalate phase, the taste profile becomes more honeyed/sherried than oily/buttery, displaying an obvious integration of large and small virtues. Finishes elegantly, stately, and woody sweet and sublime.
2006 Rating: ★★★★/Highly Recommended

Marie Duffau Hors d'Age Bas Armagnac (France); 40% abv, $60.
The deep, mature bronze/bay/tawny color is lovely except for early clouds of sediment immediately following the pour; once settled, the appearance is grand. The first aromatic impressions are of off-dry to semisweet, deeply potent notes of vanilla extract, figs, and resin; aeration stimulates lighter scents of marzipan, caramel corn, prune cake, and Danish pastry. The palate entry offers rich, near-smoky flavors of cigar box, tobacco, and herbs; the midpalate stage is leaner, more focused, and more tobacco-like than the entry. Finishes bittersweet and with a taste of dates/figs. Handsome, concentrated, baked.
2005 Rating: ★★★★/Highly Recommended

Marie Duffau 1973 30 Year Old Bas Armagnac (France); 43% abv, $132.
Russet in color; some black debris seen floating in the core and at the surface. The opening nosing passes detect serious, deep scents of paraffin, linseed oil, corn oil, and salted butter; seven more minutes of air contact stir added aromas of grapes, baked pear, sautéed almond,

and dark toffee. The palate entry is semisweet, cocoa-like, and black tea-like; at midpalate the taste profile expands to add honey, brown sugar, and old oak. Ends up semisweet, candied, honeyed, nutty, and fine. A beauty.
2005 Rating: ★★★★/Highly Recommended

Marie Duffau Napoleon Bas Armagnac (France); 47% abv, $30.

The new copper penny/orange color beams under the examination lamp; immaculate. I smell toasted walnut and chestnut, and baked pear in the opening nosings; later sniffings pick up succulent notes of pineapple, caramel, black raisins, prunes, and old oak. The palate entry is creamy textured and semisweet; at the midpalate point the flavor profile turns integrated and very nutty/woody. Concludes oily, semisweet, and oakier than either fruity or nutty. In line in terms of quality with the MD Hors d'Age and MD 1973.
2005 Rating: ★★★★/Highly Recommended

Marquis de Montesquiou Napoleon Armagnac (France); 40% abv, $34.

The medium bronze/Tupelo honey color is highly attractive and blemish-free. The first whiffs pick up nutty, slightly toasted/roasted scents that are dry to off-dry; time in the glass sees the aroma open up into a muscular bouquet that offers husky smells of brown butter, roasted chestnuts, pine, cask resin, and butterscotch. The palate entry is toffee-like, full-textured, and semisweet; at the midpalate stage the flavor profile turns dusty, intensely oaky, bacon-like, fat/suet-like, and meaty, with background notes of baked and caramelized banana. Concludes semisweet, fat, thick, and nut butter-like. A swashbuckling, on-the-sweet-side, hunk of brandy from the land of the Musketeers.
2005 Rating: ★★★/Recommended

Marquis de Montesquiou XO Armagnac (France); 40% abv, $45.

Copper-colored and flawless from a purity standpoint. I find myself getting swallowed up by the opening aroma as it emits seductive scents of pork sausage, bacon fat, and candied walnut; aeration time brings out further aromatic attractions especially dried figs and dates, marzipan, nougat, dark coffee, and honey. The palate entry is unabashedly sweet and maple-like; at midpalate the assertive, chewy taste profile rings of candied nuts, caramel, maple, sap, mature oak, and brown sugar. Finishes concentrated, sweet, pruny, and huge. Another no-nonsense, succulent, ropy brandy from this producer. Might be too much for those brandy lovers whose preferences lean towards delicacy and nuance. This is the armagnac equivalent of The Rock.
2005 Rating: ★★★★/Highly Recommended

Marquis de Montesquiou 1965 Bas Armagnac (France); 46.4% abv, $130.

The henna/bay color is gorgeous and without blemish. The first sniffings pick up toasty scents of burnt match, broiled meat, roasted nuts; further aeration brings out saltier, sweeter, and less smoky scents of old leather/cowhide, bacon, and brown butter. The palate entry is semisweet, with tastes of candied apple, caramel, and honey; at midpalate the taste profile expands to include mead, honey, mince pie, and molasses. Finishes up salty, oaky, and with more than a little touch of mushroomy, intensely honeyed rancio. About as good as vintage armagnac gets.
2005 Rating: ★★★★★/Highest Recommendation

Marquis de Montesquiou 1971 Bas Armagnac (France); 44.9% abv, $100.
The brilliant copper/rust hue dazzles the eye; flawless clarity. I detect subtle traces of minerals/shale, dried red fruits, and white raisins in the opening inhalations; the extra seven minutes in the glass stimulate deeper aromas, including white chocolate, peanut butter, lemongrass, and wool. The palate entry is the model of balance as the alcohol, acidity, and fruit components merge seamlessly; at midpalate the taste profile highlights flavors of dried herbs, oaky vanillin, pork sausage, dark caramel, molasses, and hard cheese-like rancio. Concludes with semisweet notes of cocoa and honey. Luscious, exquisite, mature, and world-class.
2005 Rating: ★★★★★/Highest Recommendation

Marquis de Montesquiou 1976 Bas Armagnac (France); 41% abv, $100.
Bronze/burnished orange color; excellent purity. The first few inhalations after the pour reveal little in the way of aromatic thrust except for notes of bacon fat, lard, and coffee grounds; additional air contact introduces racy, totally dry aromas of saddle leather, unbuttered popcorn, flax/textiles, oak, and chicory. The palate entry is long, silky, semisweet, and toffee-like; at midpalate there's a rush of maple, vanilla extract, cola nut, sap, dark caramel, and pine. Ends up semisweet, medium-bodied, marshmallowy, honeyed, and cocoa-like. Less aggressive and meaty than the M de M Napoleon and the XO, but still a heady mouthful.
2005 Rating: ★★★★/Highly Recommended

Samalens Réserve Impériale XO Bas Armagnac (France); 40% abv, $87.
The color sits right on the fence between bronze and copper; clean. The opening nosing passes offer exotic aromas of sweetened coconut, light caramel, tropical fruits, and apple; time in the glass sees the bouquet turn slightly peppery and spicy. In the mouth the sweet, caramelly flavor at entry is irresistible; the midpalate stage offers deeply creamy/oily tastes of dairy butter, nut oil, sautéed almonds, and cake frosting. The finish is long, sweet, succulent, and caramel-like. This is a no nonsense, full-speed-ahead type of traditional armagnac that is justifiably popular; sap and maple-like and extremely easy to drink.
2001 Rating: ★★★★/Highly Recommended

Samalens 1952 Bas Armagnac (France); 40% abv, $395.
The brownish, tawny/umber hue is genuinely beautiful and impeccably pure. The roasted/toasted nut perfume that welcomes the olfactory sense in the opening two nosing passes after the pour is classical, deep, and deliciously oily; air contact over another five to six minutes serves to open up other levels of aroma, in particular, focused, dry to off-dry scents of mint, grape vine, walnuts, palm oil, and honey; one of the most composed and elegant armagnac bouquets in recent memory. The palate entry is rich without being unctuous, sap-like, semisweet, and sinewy in texture; by the midpalate phase, sensational, multilayered flavors abound on the tongue, especially white chocolate, walnuts, sweet oak, rancio, and dark caramel. The aftertaste is opulent, firmly structured, concentrated, and divinely honeyed. A vintage Bas Armagnac clinic. Heavenly.
2002 Rating: ★★★★★/Highest Recommendation

Sauval Napoleon Armagnac (France); 40% abv, $47.
The deep bronze appearance is very attractive; ideal purity. The initial aroma after the pour is strikingly similar to the VSOP sibling as sweet scents of honey, nectar, and vanilla

bean vie for dominance; another seven minutes of aeration greatly benefits this bouquet as toasty notes of tobacco leaf, baked apple, baked pear, and sweet oak come to the fore. The palate entry is sweet, apple crisp-like, and intensely honeyed; at midpalate there's a plumpness to the texture that's pleasing and tastewise it's almost dry cream sherry-like as the honey element zooms past every other flavor feature. Concentrated and sweet in the finish. The sweet/brown sugar/honey component just gets to be too much by the midpalate and finish, ruining any chance of a recommendation. Simply too off balance and lacking in acidity; it's almost a liqueur which is not a compliment.
2003 Rating: ★★/Not Recommended

Sauval VSOP Armagnac (France); 40% abv, $38.
Attractive medium honey hue and excellent purity. The opening nosing hints of vanilla bean (oakiness), tobacco leaf, and mild honey; aeration doesn't do much in urging more fruit presence as the wood impact takes over completely, edging out any other aromatic attribute. The palate entry is simple, candy sweet, and marshmallow-like; the midpalate highlights the sugary marshmallow flavor as though it was something to be proud of—it isn't—it's just sweetness without any depth or scope. The aftertaste is predictably sweet and un-profound. While drinkable, it's wholly commonplace and, as a result, uninteresting.
2003 Rating: ★★/Not Recommended

Sauval XO Armagnac (France); 40% abv, $55.
Pretty copper color with superb clarity. The first few inhalations don't really pick up much in the way of bouquet; the aroma does make a good showing, however, following seven minutes of aeration as succulent, nut-like scents of almonds, toasty oak, lanolin, light toffee, and paraffin entice the olfactory sense. The palate entry is unfortunately intensely sweet and honey-like; at midpalate the sweetness/honey/brown sugar characteristics obliterate any other flavor profile possibilities. The aftertaste sweetness clobbers the taste buds into submission, tasting more like a liqueur than a brandy. Designed for brandy lovers with a sweet tooth and while drinkable it is hardly worthy of a recommendation.
2003 Rating: ★★/Not Recommended

Sempé 1941 Armagnac (France); 40% abv, $730.
The old copper penny tint is both tawny and brilliant under the examination lamp; perfect purity; what an eyeful. In the first two whiffs the dry, dusty, lead pencil bouquet is firmly structured and remarkably vivid considering the age of the brandy; exposure to air and a swirl or two releases bewitching and multilayered scents of oak resin, almond butter, wet granite, cigar tobacco, and a touch of cedar; what a stunning aromatic package. The palate entry is honey sweet, biscuity, and very much like chocolate cake frosting; the midpalate phase highlights the chocolate as a definite presence of cheesy/woody rancio enters the picture. The finish is toasty, buttery, and honeyed. Simply a great armagnac which dates to the early days of the Second World War.
2002 Rating: ★★★★/Highest Recommendation

Sempé 1942 Armagnac (France); 40% abv, $700.
The color is deep copper/henna; minuscule clouds of black sediment spotted. The opening two sniffings unearth very mature, concentrated, and intensely woody aromas that are more dry than sweet; air contact brings out the tightly-wound oakiness even more in later

inhalations plus some secondary notes of lead pencil and slate. The palate entry is intensely buttery and a touch fusty/musty, as in very old oak barrels that might have turned a bit gamey/rotted over the decades; the midpalate stage confirms the mustiness discerned in the entry but likewise acknowledges the positive tastes of hard blue cheese and molasses. The aftertaste is long, dry to off-dry, and oaky. Recommended for hardcore armagnac fans only.
2002 Rating: ★★★/Recommended

Sempé 1961 Armagnac (France); 40% abv, $180.

Dazzling reddish/copper hue; impeccable purity. The bouquet after the pour offers lovely, dry, and nut-like/nougaty aromas; following six more minutes of aeration, delectable aromas of marshmallow, honey, and old oak/vanilla extract make for lusciously rewarding inhaling; I like this bouquet very much. The palate entry is politely buttery/creamy and very, very oily (resiny); by the midpalate point expressive and assertive tastes of fudge, cocoa bean, almond butter, and a faint trace of rancio delight the taste buds. The finish is a bit hot and heady spirit-wise but is long, honeyed, and sap-like. Delicious, buttery, and oily to the max. Get your whip and chair ready for when you open this one.
2002 Rating: ★★★★/Highly Recommended

Sempé 1965 Armagnac (France); 47% abv, $165.

Bronze/orange in color; infinitesimal floating particles seen; not a problem, however. The opening nosing passes within three minutes of the pour unearth vibrant, piquant aromas of black pepper, jalapeño pepper, and heady spirit (this armagnac owns the highest proof— 94—of these vintage Sempés); aeration stimulates the bouquet bringing out additional scents of baked pear, apple cobbler, resiny oak, and butterscotch. The palate entry is seductively buttery and oily, forcing me to lick my lips in delight so as not to miss a drop; at the midpalate stage the buttery/oily character becomes sweet and honeyed with background tastes of cocoa and double cream. The finish is chewy, sweet, chocolaty, and honey-like, even a tad oloroso sherry-like. What an incredible mouthful which for the money is almost unbeatable. Decadent and luscious. Does the extra 7% of alcohol help, one may wonder; well, it doesn't hurt.
2002 Rating: ★★★★★/Highest Recommendation

Sempé 1973 Armagnac (France); 40% abv, $100.

The light-catching bronze /orangy hue is fetching and pure. The vigor of the bouquet found in the opening couple of nosings is delightful as are the subtle scents of holiday spices and egg cream; six more minutes in the glass encourages further dry to off-dry aromas to appear, most notably almond oil, lead pencil, and white raisins; an understated bouquet that's more superficial than complex. The palate entry is so lusciously sweet, animated, and honeyed that it comes as something of a shock after the reserved, low key bouquet; at the midpalate point the astoundingly rich, sugary sweet, cake frosting-like taste profile borders on being too sweet, cloying, and intense. The aftertaste is concentrated, super-sweet, and honeyed, almost to a fault. Not mincing words here, I don't think that this armagnac exhibits enough charm in the bouquet to recommend it. If you happen to taste it don't for a nanosecond think that the taste phase mirrors the aroma because it most assuredly does not. A chunky, fat armagnac that's drinkable but dull.
2002 Rating: ★★/Not Recommended

Sempé 1975 Armagnac (France); 40% abv, $95.

Gorgeous medium amber/bronze hue; excellent purity. The initial two sniffings following the pour emit very understated scents of hay, dried yellow fruit, and paraffin; aeration brings out additional minerally fragrances including wet slate, wet pavement, and old oak; not the most animated or inviting Sempé bouquet. The palate entry is stone dry, mineral-like (like running one's tongue over a smooth rock which I'm certain that readers do at least twice a week) and peppery; by the midpalate stage a baked pear-like taste emerges followed immediately by flabby flavors of honey and caramel. The finish is sweet and medium long. Though it looks pretty, in matters of aroma, taste, and finish it's not in keeping with its classier, more substantial and older siblings.

2002 Rating: ★/Not Recommended

Sempé 1981 Armagnac (France); 40% abv, $80.

Attractive bronze/honey color; excellent purity. The opening nosing passes following the pour discover zesty scents of cinnamon, wet flannel, and carob; with six more minutes of aeration in the glass the bouquet remains dry and slightly backward, emitting only minerally, fabric-like scents that are devoid of oak or fruit. The palate entry is ambrosial and jammy and seems out of sync with the meek aroma; at midpalate the flavor of caramel is highlighted. The finish is long, toffee sweet, and a touch maple-like; while certainly drinkable. For the price I expect greater evidence of character depth, poise, and steady presence.

2002 Rating: ★★/Not Recommended

Vaghi 1976 Bas Armagnac (France); 40% abv, $69.

Attractive topaz/deep amber hue; flawless clarity. The initial nosings are intensely piny/cedary and woody/resiny with no fruit showing whatsoever; more time in the glass does improve the situation by introducing tobacco leaf, baked pineapple, and citrus. The palate entry is surprisingly sweet and honeyed after the resin-fest in the bouquet; the midpalate phase highlights a very sweet, caramel-like taste that overwhelm all other flavor aspects. The aftertaste is so sweet as to be clumsy and over-the-top. Not enough high points here to salvage a third rating star. Go for the unassuming, rustic but affable XO.

2006 Rating: ★★/Not Recommended

Vaghi 1986 Bas Armagnac (France); 40% abv, $58.

The brilliant bronze/orange color is pretty under the lamp; impeccable clarity. The opening whiffs detect vibrant spirit (almost prickly in the nasal cavity, even though it's only 80-proof/40% abv), oak, fiber/hemp/flax, and new leather; further aeration doesn't pry open more in the way of aroma, except for a subtle floral note that unfortunately can't compete with the fibery/ropy odor. The palate entry is stunningly different—and better—from the synthetic nose as well-defined tastes of baked fruit (apple, apricot) and light toffee charm the taste buds; the midpalate stage offers far more oak/wood influence in the forms of resin, vanilla extract, and honey. Ends up buttery, satiny, composed, and sweet. The in-mouth stages redeemed the less-than-thrilling aroma.

2006 Rating: ★★★/Recommended

Vaghi XO Bas Armagnac (France); 40% abv, $33.
The pale amber/bronze color is clean and pure. The first inhalations detect proper opening scents of spice and dried fruit; following additional time in the copita, the bouquet turns woody and nicely paraffin-like, with distant accents of pine nuts and cedar. The palate entry is agile, youthful, and engagingly sweet; the midpalate shows a bit more depth as the oakiness transforms into a pleasant vanilla extract taste. Ends up like chocolate covered cherries, fresh honey, confectioner's sugar, and vanilla cake frosting. Nothing profound; just unadulterated youthful exuberance and in-yer-face attitude, which for the price is positively worth it.
2006 Rating: ★★★/Recommended

Calvados—France

Calvados is the world's finest apple and pear brandy. It comes from Normandy in France's northwest corner, which has the perfect climate and precipitation, soil types and topography for fruit orchards. Calvados is defined as a distilled spirit made either from cider apples or a marriage of cider apples and perry pears. After harvesting in the autumn, apples are pressed and the juice is fermented into cider. The cider is then distilled and the resultant crystal clear spirits are placed in oak barrels ranging in size from 220 to 400 liters (50 to 105 gallons) or huge vats that can hold up to 6,000 liters (1,500 gallons).

The Calvados region is demarcated into three brandy-making districts. The largest is designated as "**Calvados**" in which the brandies are created out of apple cider in column stills from one distillation. The apple brandies labeled under this classification are generally good, but lacking in distinction. Brandies from the hallowed "**Calvados Pays d'Auge**" district, on the other hand, are to calvados what Grande Champagne, Petite Champagne and Borderies brandies are to cognac, the best of the best. These frequently exquisite and delicate brandies are double distilled in copper pot stills and, consequently, offer far more depth of character and the chance of long life than those labeled only as Calvados. Minimum aging in oak barrels or vats is two years in these two districts. Calvados Pays d'Auge brandies are for serious aficionados. The third district is **Domfrontais**, an official designation that was created only a decade ago. As opposed to Calvados and Calvados Pays d'Auge, at least 30% of the juice must come from pears. The combination of apple and pear makes Domfrontais brandies concentrated and fruitier than those from the apple dominant districts. Minimum maturation in oak for Domfrontais is three years.

Classifications:

- *Calvados Fine/Three Stars:* 2 year minimum in barrels.
- *Calvados Vieux/Réserve:* 3 year minimum.
- *Calvados VO/Vieille Réserve/VSOP:* 4 year minimum.
- *Calvados Extra/XO/Napoleon/Hors d'Age/Age Inconnu:* 6 year minimum.

Calvados deserves to be discovered in a huge way by consumers. It's one of the best-kept secrets in spirits.

Apreval 1974 Brut du Fut Pays d'Auge Calvados (France); 46.5% abv, $210.
    While I understand that this calvados is bottled directly from the cask, the lovely harvest gold color is marred by unsightly chunks of sediment; could light filtering have done that much damage to the character? Smells of old casks, butter cream, and oil in the first nosings after the pour; seven more minutes of aeration encourage the cream element to expand as

it almost turns cheese-like; a complex, multilayered calvados bouquet that's long on charm and depth. The palate entry is creamy in texture and tastewise it's a bit botanical, specifically bark-like and woodsy; the midpalate is hefty, slightly hot, and prickly, but displays lots of baked apple, tar, and oaky tastes. Worth a look for its atypical flavor phase and gritty aftertaste. Not your average calvados.

2003 Rating: ★★★/Recommended

Apreval Grande Réserve Pays d'Auge Calvados (France); 42% abv, $70.
Aged for ten years; attractive honey color; superb purity. The opening nosing passes come up against a reluctant, fabric-like bouquet that's closed down; swirling in the glass and an extra seven minutes of exposure to air assists the bouquet a bit, but basically leaves the aroma pretty much where it started right after the pour, nowhere; I detect mere hints of apple peel, cloth fiber, and oak; a ten year old calvados bouquet should offer much more than this. Better in the mouth than in the nose; the palate entry is short, mildly sweet/sour, and delicate; the midpalate point offers relatively evolved tastes of light caramel, baked apple, tea leaves, and fruit acid. The aftertaste is brief, so understated as to be hard to define. That's the problem with this calvados, it's so distant and meek that it's difficult to get a handle on it. Where is the lovely oily texture I liked so much in the Réserve? Drinkable, but strangely hollow and out-of-reach.

2003 Rating: ★★/Not Recommended

Apreval Réserve Pays d'Auge Calvados (France); 42% abv, $49.
A five year old calvados; medium amber color; very minor sediment seen, not a problem at all. Smells of freshly picked apples in the first two minutes of sniffing; several minutes in the glass allows for deeper scents to emerge including spice, apple peel, beeswax and oil. The palate entry is off-dry and caramel-like; by the midpalate stage the oily, silky texture forms a substantial base for the semisweet, toffee and apple and pear-like flavors. The finish is long, slightly woody, semisweet and acidic enough to counter to mild sweetness.

2003 Rating: ★★★/Recommended

Apreval XO Pays d'Auge Calvados (France); 42% abv, $125.
Matured for twenty years; gorgeous, bronze/topaz hue; excellent purity. The initial nosing passes offer similar fabric-like scents found in the Grande Réserve, but, thankfully, aeration helps this bouquet pick up the pace as mildly ripe and succulent aromas of light toffee, baked apple, poached pear, and honey make for intriguing sniffing. The palate entry is off-dry to sweet, very ripe, and apple-like; by the midpalate stage there's more than ample flavor impact, mostly in the forms of dried apple and oaky vanillin. The delicious finish is long, sweet, slightly honeyed, and nicely oily and textured. This is more like it; makes me wonder what happened to the timid ten year old Grande Réserve.

2003 Rating: ★★★★/Highly Recommended

Boulard Founder's Reserve 12 Year Old Pays d'Auge Calvados (France); 40% abv, $100.
The pretty topaz/bronze color shows a lot of fruit pulp-like sediment; is this really necessary? The initial couple of sniffings detect lovely, plump aromas of baked apple, stewed pear, and oaky vanilla; with several minutes of air contact the bouquet fully develops, emitting

creamy, ambrosial, and toasty fragrances of candied apple, holiday fruit cake, dried apricot, maple syrup, and toasty oak; a dazzling and mature calvados perfume. The palate entry is succulent, semisweet, and concentrated; by the time the midpalate rolls around the tastes are completely melded, roasted, and resiny, even showing the beginning touch of rancio. The aftertaste is luxurious, tight, integrated, and baked. Another sterling calvados from this esteemed distiller.

2001 Rating: ★★★★/Highly Recommended

Boulard Grande Solage Pays d'Auge Calvados (France); 40% abv, $46.

Brilliant topaz/amber/old gold color; flawless clarity. Offers toasted, bakery-like scents of brown butter, apple strudel, and melon; some of the toastiness fades following further air contact and is replaced by plumper aromas of oaky vanillin, sap, and resin. Entry is austere, nougaty, and almond-like; the midpalate phase features ripe, pleasingly sweet/sour apple and pear tastes that are wrapped in caramel and nougat. Finishes gracefully and more tart than sweet. The keen structural acidity is what makes this calvados so refreshing. Serve as a between course palate cleanser.

2007 Rating: ★★★/Recommended

Boulard Reserve du Chef Pays d'Auge Calvados (France); 40% abv, $12/200ml.

Sports a 14-carat gold/flax color; impeccable purity. Right out of the gate, it smells assertively of red apple juice and apple flesh; picks up a tangy note of vanilla after the additional aeration period as well as a nuance of pear; a simple, immature, juicy, no-nonsense calvados bouquet. Entry is lean, tinny, and a bit hollow after the multiple pleasures of the bouquet; the midpalate stage offers meager depth and superficial apple/pear presence, at best. Ends on a relatively high note as the spirit comes alive giving form to the last flavors of green apple and pear. Nothing special here.

2007 Rating: ★★/Not Recommended

Boulard XO Pays d'Auge Calvados (France); 40% abv, $95.

Breathtaking saffron/bronze/medium brown color; perfect purity. Smells of oak/teak, paraffin, spirit, and baked apple make for complex early-on sniffing; much of the woodiness fades with further exposure to air, leaving the door open for the fruit, which unfortunately fails to fill the aromatic void. Entry is lean, minerally/stony, slightly metallic/coin-like, and disappointing overall; the midpalate stage comes to the rescue of the flavor experience by finally opening up the treasure trove of apple/pear taste splendor in the tasty forms of baking spices (nutmeg, vanilla), tart red apple, under-ripe pear, black coffee, and dark caramel. Concludes well, deliciously lip-smacking, and suddenly toasty and oily. One of the best recoveries from the brink of disaster I've recently encountered, since after the entry I was fully prepared to bestow only two stars. Due to the lackluster bouquet and feeble entry, it doesn't deserve more than three stars.

2007 Rating: ★★★/Recommended

Busnel Hors d'Age 12 Year Old Pays d'Auge Calvados (France); 40% abv, $50.

Displays an old copper penny/auburn/henna color; good purity. The opening nosing passes offer concentrated oak, paraffin/melted candle, and baked apple aromas; following another seven minutes of air contact, the bouquet expands only incrementally as raisiny/pruny/dried red fruit and cocoa notes override the wood and wax base aromas. The palate entry is long, properly oily and textured, and full-bodied; at midpalate the flavor profile turns raisiny, chocolaty, and coffee-like, with just the slightest hint of seared beef/pork sausage. Finishes long, bittersweet, fat, buttery, and fruity.

2005 Rating: ★★★/Highly Recommended

Busnel Vieille Réserve VSOP Pays d'Auge Calvados (France); 40% abv, $33.

Pleasing bronze hue with orange/tawny core highlights; good purity. The first aroma is properly apple-like and nicely acidic and it isn't until past further aeration that huskier notes of oak, hard cheese, baked apple, baked pear, and beeswax appear. The palate entry is lean, off-dry, and alluringly baked and wax-like; at midpalate the taste profile turns drier, more caramel- and toffee-like, and even maple-like. Concludes bittersweet, refreshingly astringent, and resiny.

2005 Rating: ★★★/Recommended

Château du Breuil 15 Year Old Calvados (France); 41% abv, $50.

The lovely bronze/burnished orange hue is flawlessly clean. In the first whiffs, I pick up appetizingly toasty scents of baked apple and baked pear; later inhalations following seven minutes of aeration detect subtle aromas of brown sugar, marshmallow, and balled string; this is a temptress of a bouquet that, like a siren, keeps summoning you back. The palate entry is clean and rounded, emitting delicious tastes of ripe apple and pear; at midpalate the taste profile opens up to candied apple, cotton candy, and distant vanilla flavors that complete the flavor phase with panache. The aftertaste is toastier than the midpalate, but it works. This is a regal beauty of the first rank.

2005 Rating: ★★★★/Highest Recommendation

Chauffe Coeur Hors d'Age Calvados (France); 43% abv, $40.

Dark amber/saffron hue; flawless clarity. Opening inhalations encounter very toasty, baked apple, pie crust/pastry notes that are long, deep, and inviting; additional time allows spicy and resiny/rancio-like notes to emerge as well as walnut meat, butterscotch, and hard cheese; a complex bouquet that keeps unfolding long after the nosing stage is completed. Taste at entry is like caramel-covered apple, baked apple with cinnamon, and honey; the sweetness level rises at midpalate as the flavor profile grows more succulent, plump, and creamy/buttery. There are even hints of rancio in the finish, at which I find myself literally smacking my lips. Outstanding selection by Christine Cooney, whose palate never ceases to amaze me. A textbook hors d'age calvados.

2007 Rating: ★★★★/Highest Recommendation

Chauffe Coeur VSOP Calvados (France); 43% abv, $30.

Caramel brown/old gold color; ideal purity. Initial whiffs detect buttery/creamy scents that lie on top of the baked apple and wood structural aromas; further aeration adds enticing nuances of nutmeg, apple peel, flowers, and earth; a dazzlingly straightforward bouquet that could be nothing other than calvados. Entry taste is austere at first, then it explodes on the tip of the tongue in assertive waves of apple pastry, mineral/stone, and oaky vanilla; the

midpalate underscores all that's enjoyed at entry, but adds a layer of honey/light toffee that nearly makes me swoon. Finish is dusty dry to off-dry, wonderfully toffee-like, and elegant. A world-class brandy for $30 that I'd be happy to serve to anyone at anytime.
2007 Rating: ★★★★/Highly Recommended

Coeur de Lion 1963 Pays d'Auge Calvados (France); 42% abv, $310.
Impeccable clarity accents the brilliant old copper penny hue; really pretty. The first two passes in the nose find very peel-like scents like when you just slice an apple and your olfactory sense reacts to the acidity of the apple skin; further time in the glass reveals much deeper, more profound aromas that resemble milk chocolate, cream, and cotton fabric; a subtle temptress of a bouquet that teases as much as it pleases. The palate entry is clean, acidic, and sap-like; then at midpalate the flavor turns slightly sweeter and just under-ripe as if the apples were harvested a day before full ripeness. The aftertaste is very extended, juicy, and satiny. Simply one of the best vintage calvados I've sampled from Christian Drouhin or anyone else. A mature, stately marvel.
2003 Rating: ★★★★★/Highest Recommendation

Coeur de Lion 1966 Pays d'Auge Calvados (France); 42% abv, $310.
The bright deep amber/brown color is pretty and unblemished. The opening sniffs provide fruity, if reluctant aromas of tropical fruit, dried fruit, and refined sugar; another seven minutes of aeration releases moderately sweet, mildly honeyed and sherried aromas that have intriguing backnotes of marshmallow and pine. The palate entry is positively juicy and ripe; the midpalate features integrated, concentrated tastes of ripe apple, apple rind, baked apple strudel, and apple butter; in other words, it's intensely apple-like. The finish is long, sweet, oaky, seed-like, and bordering on being bittersweet. A masculine, yet elegant and focused style of calvados that I happen to love.
2003 Rating: ★★★★/Highly Recommended

Coeur de Lion 1981 Pays d'Auge Calvados (France); 42% abv, $155.
The dark bronze, almost tawny color shows no signs of sediment or flaws. In the first two minutes of inhalation, the sensuous bouquet offers buttery scents of old oak, dark toffee, and cola; seven more minutes of exposure to air sees the aroma expand two-fold into a top layer of cream/butter/caramel and a foundational layer comprised of oak, baked apple, baked pear, tobacco smoke, charcoal, and bacon fat. The palate entry is as bittersweet as brown sugar and dark honey; the midpalate stage is large, candied in an astringent manner, toasty, smoky, and warm. The aftertaste is long, oaky, intense, and silky. The bacon fat element reminds me of rancio and all the savory pleasures that introduces; lovely and borders on being decadently opulent.
2003 Rating: ★★★★/Highly Recommended

Coeur de Lion 800th Anniversary Pays d'Auge Calvados (France); 42% abv, $240.
Only 800 bottles offered. Brownish/amber in color; ideal purity. The initial nosing pass is brimming with spiced apple and baked pear scents; by the second whiff, the aroma becomes very apple pie-like, in that there's an added trace of pastry/dough scent; following

six minutes of air contact, the spice element takes charge in the third nosing pass; the fourth and final sniffing detects a seed-like or even pit-like bitterness that nicely counters the ripe pear/apple fruit; what's missing is any hint of wood, but aside from that this is a sleek, fruit-forward bouquet that's bound to please any lover of calvados. The palate entry is startlingly acidic and biting with nary a hint of smoothness; by the midpalate stage the lean, sinewy texture/taste broadens out slightly though it's still austere in the extreme when viewed in the context of other fleshier offerings from this esteemed distiller (think: the magnificent Hors d'Age, the 1973, or the 25 Year Old). The finish is raw and without an ounce of fat or flesh. I found this bottling too harsh and skeletal for my liking or recommendation.

2000 Rating: ★★/Not Recommended

Coeur de Lion Fine Pays d'Auge Calvados (France); 40% abv, $42.

Double distilled, made from fifteen apple varieties; golden yellow, with green core highlights; good purity. This bouquet is significantly more sophisticated than the paper thin Selection as layered scents of apple strudel, pastry, and ripe pear take the early lead; further aeration brings out off-dry to semisweet aromas of gentle oaky vanilla, nutmeg, citrus rind, and distant honey. On the tongue at palate entry there's a mild prickliness that doesn't distract my attention from the lightly smoked, tart apple opening flavor; at midpalate supplementary tastes of nutmeg, vanilla, new oak, and light honey make for tart sipping. The aftertaste is long, lean, woody, and ripely fruity. Another candidate for employment between courses of a meal; serve chilled.

2002 Rating: ★★★/Recommended

Coeur de Lion Selection Domfrontais Calvados (France); 40% abv, $25.

Single distilled, 3 years old. Straw yellow color of white wine; more sediment than I'd like to see. The opening nosing passes pick up richly fruity, gently sweet, and ripe scents of both apples and pears; seven more minutes of air contact releases enticing background traces of cinnamon, apple core, and sunflower seeds; a polite, elementary apple brandy bouquet. The palate entry is a bit sharp and totally acidic as it cleanses the tongue; by midpalate the sharpness retreats, leaving the door ajar for extremely tart and bittersweet apple and pear tastes to enter and take command through the finish. A drinkable, if ethereal and astringent, calvados that I would use as a palate cleaner in between dishes at a multicourse meal or in mixed drinks. Obviously a pup.

2002 Rating: ★★/Not Recommended

Comte Louis de Lauriston 20 Year Old Domfrantais Calvados (France); 42% abv, $139.

The topaz color is spoiled by transparent chunks of unsightly sediment. The initial inhalation uncovers a fat, juicy, and vanilla-like aroma; I am a bit concerned about the lack of evident acidity; further time in the glass adds notes of oak, butterscotch, and soft honey; there's nothing crisp or vigorous about this bouquet. While this brandy is lacking in acidity and, therefore, freshness, the palate entry does offer some pleasant woodiness and maple flavor; the midpalate showcases the fatty/oily and chunky flavor profile to the hilt. Finishes oily, buttery, and without a whisper of acid.

2006 Rating: ★★/Not Recommended

Comte Louis de Lauriston 40 Year Old Domfrontais Calvados (France); 42% abv, $300.
The chestnut color is pure, flawless, and very attractive. Following the pour, the nose emits tightly structured, close-knit scents of pear, apples, and wax; after additional aeration, the aroma evolves into a full-fledged brandy bouquet as lean scents of resin, baked apple, and vinyl take charge; not a voluptuous aroma but compelling all the same. The palate entry is a study of controlled sweetness/ripeness while the midpalate phase displays a more generous face in the forms of baked apple, fruit pastry, pipe tobacco, new honey, and oak. Ends crisp, properly acidic, and with baked flavors of fruit, nuts, and nougat.
2006 Rating: ★★★/Highly Recommended

Comte Louis de Lauriston Fine Domfrontais Calvados (France); 42% abv, $29.
The pale yellow color is sediment free and bright. The first sniffing finds light, perfumed, juicy, and ripe fruit smells of orchard fruit; the second round of inhalations offer considerably more peel-like aromas that don't have the succulence of the early nosings. The palate entry is pleasingly fruity and ripe; the midpalate stage features once again as much of the tart/astringent peel as it does the fruit flesh. While I understand that the concept here is to capture the freshness of the immature eau-de-vie, I actually wished for more wood impact. This one's a bit too harsh and crude for me.
2006 Rating: ★★/Not Recommended

Comte Louis de Lauriston Hors d'Age Domfrontais Calvados (France); 42% abv, $120.
The topaz color is completely brown, with no indication of orange, gold, or rust; good purity. The opening nosing passes detect mature scents of cooking spices (black pepper, allspice, marjoram), tobacco leaf, and spiced apple; following another six minutes in the glass, the aroma breaks open a bit more revealing traces of pear pulp, parchment, textile fibers, and oak. The palate entry is delightfully sweet, yet fruity and lean; the midpalate stage is where the acidity kicks in, giving this brandy a fine, lithe mouthfeel and a crisp taste. Concludes drier than the entry.
2006 Rating: ★★★/Recommended

Comte Louis de Lauriston VSOP Domfrontais Calvados (France); 42% abv, $49.
The inviting amber/honey color beams under the light; superb purity. The initial passes in the nose pick up curiously fabric-like scents right out of the gate, then with aeration the aroma settles down and offers more appropriate fragrances such as oaky vanilla, baked pear, and baked apple. The palate entry is lovely, elegant, semisweet, and fruity; at midpalate the spirit foundation emerges as the taste profile turns totally brandy-like, clean, refreshing, and mildly spicy. Finishes chewy, woody, and moderately oily.
2006 Rating: ★★★/Recommended

H. Menorval Prestige Calvados (France); 40% abv, $30.
Honey/gold hue; some black sediment, but not enough to detract from the overall appearance. The initial nosings pick up clean, snappy, tart aromas of crisp green apple; additional time in the glass stimulates a delightfully oily scent, not quite wood resin but more like nut butter or margarine. The palate entry is slightly prickly and hot, then at midpalate the taste profile turns dense, bittersweet, oily, and cocoa-like. The aftertaste is slender, resiny,

and very bitter. All right in the bouquet, then in the flavor phase this calvados begins to crumble under the weight of astringency and by the finish the taste totally succumbs to bitterness. My guess is that it's too immature and needs more time to round out in oak.
2003 Rating: ★★/Not Recommended

H. Menorval Réserve Calvados (France); 40% abv, $40.

The appealing harvest gold color is totally undercut by loads of yucky-looking gray/ white sediment; worse, both sample bottles displayed what looks like severe dandruff. The opening sniffs detect really nice, ripe apple scents that are fresh and clean; aeration serves to deepen the ripe red apple presence while adding a crisp, acidic trace of barely ripened pear and a deft touch of honey; very good job here, aromatically. The palate entry is pleasingly sweet/sour and mildly apple-like; at midpalate there are traces of cocoa bean, pear nectar, and apple rind. The finish is nicely focused on the sweet/sour apple taste and locates a late entry taste of apple crisp.
2003 Rating: ★★★/Recommended

H. Menroval Très Vieux Calvados (France); 40% abv, $50.

Amber/gold in color; the gray sediment quickly settles in the well of the copita. The first whiffs find unsweetened pear and barely ripe apple aromas; further minutes in the glass add alluring scents that include bread dough, tart apple peel, and apple butter. The palate entry is more tart than sweet and very true to apple flavor; by midpalate the taste profile turns sap-like, a bit honeyed, and apple pie-like (there's a trace of yeasty dough presence). The finish is tart, apple-like, and medium-long. Not a classic, but refreshing and properly crisp.
2003 Rating: ★★★/Recommended

Lecompte 12 Year Old Pays d'Auge Calvados (France); 42% abv, $60.

Beautiful honey/topaz color; superb purity. The opening nosing passes are met with spirity, mildly prickly sensations that also feature subtle scents of apple rind and baked pears; more time in the glass reveals multilayered, tart aromas of cinnamon/nutmeg, oak, and apple candy. The palate entry deals out toasty flavors of toffee, nougat, apple candy, and tobacco; the midpalate highlights a sweeter side of the taste stage as candied, caramel-like flavors feature honey, buttered candies, hard apple candy, and brown sugar. The finish is long, maple syrup-like, and honeyed. This calvados displays superb balance as well as maturity and vigor. Is 10 -12 years the ideal age for calvados? This Lecompte makes a strong case in favor of that argument; buy and enjoy in multiple ways.
2002 Rating: ★★★★★/Highest Recommendation

Lecompte 3 Year Old Pays d'Auge Calvados (France); 40% abv, $22.

Lovely medium amber/light honey hue; impeccable purity. The early sniffings within two minutes of the pour detect distant aromas of spice, apples, juniper, and mint; exposure to air stimulates further action in the bouquet as assertive, off-dry scents of baked apple, apple peel, and pears mingle with nuances of mint and cinnamon. The palate entry is highlighted by off-dry to sweet tastes of ripe apple, light caramel, and baked pears; by the midpalate point the addition of oak resin and vanilla flavors nicely support the ripe fruitiness. The aftertaste is medium long, more tart than the midpalate phase, and refreshing; solid, tight structure.
2002 Rating: ★★★/Recommended

Lecompte 5 Year Old Pays d'Auge Calvados (France); 40% abv, $30.

Very pretty amber/harvest gold color; excellent purity. The initial two nosing passes following the pour are treated to finely melded, mature aromas of apple butter, peaches, and pastry; eight more minutes of aeration arouse deeper off-dry scents of apple peel, light caramel, and tea leaves. The palate entry leaves no doubting the innate quality of this calvados as the first taste offers biscuity flavors of apple pastry, honey, and light toffee; by the midpalate stage the taste expands further to include semisweet flavors of slightly under-ripe apple and pear as well as cocoa and coffee. The finish is long, sap-like, and tart to off-dry. Lots going on here from layer to layer; delicious and baked.

2002 Rating: ★★★★/Highly Recommended

Lecompte Originel Pays d'Auge Calvados (France); 40% abv, $20.

The first bottled sampled had a horrific sediment problem with brown clouds and actual clumps of debris; luckily, I was in possession of a second bottle which showed a light amber color and better though hardly ideal purity. Smells of very crisp, slightly underripe apples in the first two nosings; aeration does little to expand the first impressions except to add nuances of holiday spices (cinnamon, nutmeg) and apple peel; fresh and inviting. The palate entry is tart, acidic, and remarkably appealing and fresh; the midpalate stage is softly ripe and is stone dry. The aftertaste continues the desert dry, extremely tart profile. A superb palate cleanser in between meal courses.

2002 Rating: ★★★/Recommended

Lemorton 10 Year Old Domfrontais Calvados (France); 40% abv, $55.

The bright amber/burnished orange tint pleases the eye as does the absolute purity. This nose shows a bit more depth than the Reserve in that the apple fragrance is more concentrated and layered; the second and third nosings over a span of three to four minutes pick up a leathery perfume that's seductive and atypical; the final nosing pass highlights the baked apple and a tony sweetness that's delightful, to say the least; not a power-packed bouquet, but one that offers plenty of grip and fruity impact. While this calvados is sweet and ripe in the nasal cavity, on the tongue it's dry, toffee-like, and resiny (as in wood) from entry to midpalate. The finish is chewy, textured, and toasty/resiny sweet. The flavor impact is delicious, especially in the aftertaste; a calvados at its peak.

2001 Rating: ★★★★/Highly Recommended

Lemorton 1970 Domfrontais Calvados (France); 40% abv, $115.

The burnished orange appearance is close to being full-out bronze; some minor sediment noted. This nose immediately following the pour is highly stylized with heightened scents of light caramel, green, immature vegetation (spring garden?), and beeswax; with time in the glass, the aroma breaks out the fruit as perfumy waves of apple and pear overshadow the candy and vegetation; by the final aromatic run-through, the nose starts to fade and dissipate, leaving behind spirit and tired apple notes. In the mouth, the taste displays plenty of grip, texture, and sweet, ripe apple flavor at entry; the midpalate stage shows a warmth and a candied apple taste that is appealing, sweet, and mildly oaky, but obviously on the downslope of evolution. The aftertaste is medium long, apple candy sweet, a touch baked, and buttery/resiny. This calvados still possesses some undeniable charm and is therefore recommended for seasoned mavens and collectors.

2001 Rating: ★★★/Recommended

Lemorton 1976 Domfrontais Calvados (France); 40% abv, $90.

The clean, pure appearance owns a very pretty amber/honey hue. The opening nosing leaps from the glass in spirited waves of fabric, fruit acid, apple perfume, and pear drop; the middle stage sniffings offer mature, dry scents of apple strudel, spiced pear, and leather; the last whiff, following over eight minutes of air contact, highlights the kid glove leathery scent more than the fruit. I respond far more favorably to the taste than to the lackluster bouquet; the entry is so sweet as to be succulent in a dark caramel, candied apple manner; the midpalate is savory, textured, and reeks of vanilla extract, baked pears, spiced apple, and oak. The aftertaste is long, luxurious, and owns an apple sauce taste that rounds out the flavor stages in style. While the bouquet failed to thrill me, the flavor and finish phases were impressive enough to warrant four stars.

2001 Rating: ★★★★/Highly Recommended

Lemorton Reserve Domfrontais Calvados (France); 40% abv, $39.

Pale amber/light honey hue; ideal purity. The opening nosing detects lovely spiced scents of baked apple with cinnamon and apple peel; middle stage whiffs pick up background notes of cocoa and pear; after sitting in the glass for over seven minutes, the aroma keeps its potency, perfume, and structural integrity admirably well. On the palate, the cocoa-like feature becomes more apparent, though the baked apple taste is the primary flavor at entry; at the midpalate stage sweetish tastes of ripe apple/pear and delicate spice mingle gracefully. The finish shows more spice than fruit and is medium long, significantly drier than the midpalate, and delectably elegant. Clearly a relatively young calvados that hasn't lost its youthful energy; SOLID VALUE ALL THE WAY.

2001 Rating: ★★★/Recommended

Père Magloire Fine Calvados (France); 40% abv, $24.

Pleasing harvest gold color; excellent purity. Smells of under-ripe apples and the bouquet is a bit sharp. Tastes sweeter than it smells; the hollow flavors include apple pastry, brown sugar. Finishes clean, lean, and toasty, if banal and totally ordinary.

2005 Rating: ★★/Not Recommended

Père Magloire VSOP Calvados (France); 40% abv, $35.

Attractive honey/amber hue; flawless clarity. Smells of baked apple, baked pear, light honey, and has a keen orchard fruit acidity that keeps the bouquet clean and tidy. Tastes of vanilla bean, light oak, tart red apples, pears, and honey. End well on an astringent note that cleanses the palate.

2005 Rating: ★★★/Recommended

Père Magloire XO Calvados (France); 40% abv, $70.

The deep amber color borders on being bronze/burnished orange. Sports a mature aroma of dried apple crisps, cinnamon, marshmallow, parchment, and old honey. Tastes of nougat, nutmeg, pastry, apple butter, and cinnamon. Concludes as gracefully as it begins. Terrific. One of the best calvados one could enjoy. Sublime and sensual.

2005 Rating: ★★★★/Highly Recommended

Roger Groult 15 Year Old Pays d'Auge Calvados (France); 41% abv, $65.

Attractive, deep amber/bronze color; impeccable purity. The nose is flat and mute in the opening sniffing; with aeration, the aroma stirs to life in the second pass as delicate scents of oak, ripe red apples, and spring forest emerge; in the third whiff a distant fragrance of crushed or mashed apple pulp gets added to the bouquet mix; in the fourth and final nosing pass nothing new comes on the scene except perhaps for a trace of spice; a reluctant, at-arms-length bouquet that's not the least bit welcoming or compelling. The palate entry is mildly sweet and full of texture; the midpalate stage is pleasantly round, almost chewy, and candy sweet. The aftertaste is caramel-like, sweet, and mildly oaky. I like the fleshy texture of this brandy, but the off-putting, flaccid bouquet doesn't supply a great first impression. Drinkable but average and, therefore, not recommended.

2000 Rating: ★★/Not Recommended

Roger Groult 8 Year Old Pays d'Auge Calvados (France); 41% abv, $50.

Yellow straw/honey/light amber color; perfect purity. The initial nosing pass reveals subtle hints of vanilla bean and apple peel; with aeration and a twist or two of the glass, the vanilla bean element makes a play for dominance, yet no other discernable aromas emerge; oddly, by the third whiff, nary a trace of apple can be found while the vanilla component rages on; after ten minutes of exposure to air, no expansion is noted in the fourth and final sniffing; a true one note aroma. The palate entry shows a bit of sweet candied apple plus a decent enough amount of acidity; the midpalate juncture sees some mildly pleasing flavor notes of oaky vanilla, baked apple, and distant spice. The aftertaste is medium long, moderately sweet, and a tad too resiny.

2000 Rating: ★★/Not Recommended

Roger Groult Age d'Or 30 Year Old Pays d'Auge Calvados (France); 41% abv, $126.

The brilliant bronze color carries orange core highlights and is perfectly clean. The initial nosing pass reveals a bit of spirity fire and rather hesitant scents of apple and wood; the second sniffing unearths distant spice and a trace of pear juice; the third whiff adds caramel, pepper, and wood resin; in the fourth nosing pass, following more than eight minutes of air contact, the aromas come together in a harmonious display of maturity and composure; not an overly expressive bouquet by any means, but a self-assured, steady, and even elegant one nonetheless. The palate entry is firm, sweet, and controlled; the midpalate stage is genuinely delicious as luxurious flavors of pepper, ripe apple, ripe pear, and pastry shine. The finish is long, appley sweet, and mildly oaky, with a honeyed tail end. This is a gorgeous calvados.

2000 Rating: ★★★/Highly Recommended

Roger Groult Doyen d'Age 40 Year Old Pays d'Auge Calvados (France); 41% abv, $169.

The color shines like a new copper penny; impeccable clarity; a truly beautiful brandy. The opening nose is stately, firm, acidic, yet ripe in a mature way; the second nosing pass reveals hints of pepper, brambles, and old oak; the brambly/viny aroma becomes pervasive in the third sniffing, edging out the apple and the wood; the fourth and last whiff, after eight minutes of aeration, turns more dry than sweet as the oakiness returns; the apple perfume never seemed to get enough momentum going. The flavors at palate entry are sweet and ripe with overtones of old oak and vanilla bean; the midpalate point is round, chewy, oaky sweet, and a touch baked and toasty. The aftertaste is long, round, chewy, and concentrated. Certainly, because of its age, the most imposing, but not more pleasing as a whole package than the 30 Year Old which is the pick of this litter in my opinion.

2000 Rating: ★★★/Recommended

Roger Groult Réserve 3 Year Old Pays d'Auge Calvados (France); 40% abv, $32.

The color is a light honey/straw hue; the purity level is superb. The opening nose is sweet and ripe, brimming with crisp apple richness; the second pass adds a nuance of spice that's more cinnamon than nutmeg; the third nosing, following seven minutes of air contact, turns slightly sappy, resiny, and baked; by the fourth and last sniffing much of the appealing acidy crispness is gone, being replaced by a flat/flabby pulpy/resiny aroma. The palate entry is very lean and spicy; the midpalate point features unpleasantly acidic, tart, and extremely resiny flavors that are more metallic than fruity. The finish is like varnish and leaves an highly undesirable taste in the mouth. The suspicious aroma ends up being capped by atrocious flavor and finish phases that come off as industrial (as in creosote) and manufactured rather than natural. An immature, misguided bomb.

2000 Rating: ★/Not Recommended

Roger Groult Reserve Ancestrale Pays d'Auge Calvados (France); 40% abv, $360.

The stunning color is like an old, worn copper penny; ideal purity. The opening nosing passes are greeted by voluptuous, fully integrated aromas of baked bread, baked apple, roasted chestnut, and old oak; air contact makes the bouquet plumper, more intense and focused on the apple perfume. The palate entry is leaner than I had anticipated and moderately sweet in a fruity rather than a woody way; the midpalate is stately, oaky sweet, but thinner than I'd like for the money. The finish is bittersweet, almost cocoa- and coffee-like. What began well, dissipated in the glass.

2001 Rating: ★★★/Recommended

Roger Groult Venerable 20 Year Old Pays d'Auge Calvados (France); 41% abv, $85.

Glimmering bronze/honey/amber hue; ideal clarity. The nose shows good apple presence in the first sniffing; in the second whiff, hints of old oak, sweet fruit, baked apple, and pastry make themselves known; with further aeration a savory element of baked pear gets added and very nearly steals the show; the fourth and last go-round offers toasty, oaky, roasted aromas of almonds, ripe red apples, moderately prickly spirit, and caramel. The polite palate entry is velvety, tart, and appley; the midpalate, however, gets revved up as flavors of oaky vanilla, baked apple, and dark caramel seize the chance and impress the taste buds with their sturdy structure and depth. The finish is medium long, sweet in a maple-like way, and clean.

2000 Rating: ★★★/Recommended

GRAPPA, EAU-DE-VIE, PISCO, ARAK, MARC, SLIVOVITZ & BRANDY—WORLD

The word brandy comes from the Dutch term, brandewijn, which means "burnt wine". Get it? Boiled or distilled wine. While the French dominate the worldwide brandy scene with cognac, armagnac, and calvados, there are many other wonderful brandies that are born in wine producing regions. Brandy is defined as a fruit or grape wine that's distilled in either a traditional pot still or a more modern column still. Not all brandies are aged in wood. Some, like grappa, marc, and eau-de-vie, are typically unaged.

Grappa (Italy) & Marc (France): Customary unaged village brandies make by winemakers from grape pomace. These are frequently very sophisticated spirits. Sometimes called Aqua Vitae, the Latin for "water of life".

Eau-de-vie (France, Austria, Switzerland): Top-notch, often world-class fruit brandies made for centuries by long-established European producers. These range from framboise (raspberry) to fraise (strawberry) to poire (pear) to kirsch (cherry) and many more.

Pisco (Peru & Chile): Pisco is a translucent and perfumed brandy made from the distilled wines of native grapes in Peru and Chile. Though both spirits are named pisco, they are strikingly different in production and character. The piscos from Chile are distilled mostly in towering column stills in large volumes and are usually allowed to mature in oak barrels. By contrast, Peru's piscos are distilled in small batches in copper pot stills and are not aged in wood barrels, making them wonderfully floral in aroma. Alcohol-by-volume percentages for each type of pisco range from 38% to 46%, depending on the producer. The best Peruvian piscos are identified by the words "Pisco Puro" that indicate that the pisco is the product of only one grape variety. Pisco Puros can be remarkably intense and elegant, clean and fragrant.

Arak/Arrack/Raki (International): Some of the oldest spirits known and are typically associated with the cultures of the eastern Mediterranean basin as well as Turkey and the Balkans nations. Usually clear, arak is made from aniseed while arrack/raki can be made from sugarcane, grain, plums, grapes or the sap of palm trees.

Slivowitz (Europe): A traditional blue plum brandy produced in central Europe nations, notably Hungary, that is known for its aromatic bouquet.

A.B. Pollentes Eau-de-Vie de Folle Blanche Fleur (France); 45% abv, $50.
Clear and clean as mineral water. The initial floral burst of aroma is like a spring garden after a shower; the second whiff exposes a minerally/slate-like odor that's dry and stony; in

the third sniffing after eight minutes of aeration a faint trace of cocoa bean is present in the background; the fourth and final pass reveals a strange maltiness that's quite atypical for an eau-de-vie, especially one made from folle blanche grapes; despite the oddness of it; I like this stone dry, minerally bouquet. The palate entry is tart, dry, and acidic; the midpalate, however, goes quickly sweet in a ripe grape manner and shows a flash of spirity fire. The minerally finish is long, sweet, and fiery. Very nice indeed.

2000 Rating: ★★★★/Highly Recommended

A.B. Pollentes Eau-de-vie de Poire Williams (France); 45% abv, $60.

Limpid, silvery clear, and very pure. In the opening nosing, I detect a wonderfully full and pure ripe pear perfume and by that I mean ideally ripe, not juicy or overly ripe; the second sniffing reveals a dry, seed or pit-like secondary scent that seems to underlie the surface fragrance of the ripe pear flesh; following over five minutes of exposure to air, the aroma advances in richness and depth without the faintest hint of the potent alcohol level and I find this feat astonishing; by the final whiff, some ten minutes into the evaluation, the depth of the pear scent is seductive, still dry, and unfailingly true to the fruit source; a superbly crafted bouquet in which the fruit is allowed to express itself without much human interference. The palate entry is lean, dry, and slightly acidic on the tip of the tongue; by midpalate the flavor of just-ripe pear flesh comes to full expression, but in a dry fashion except for a burst of sweetness at the very conclusion. The finish is pleasingly sweet, ripe, yet lean so as to be nearly austere; the spirit comes alive in the aftertaste as well as a slight searing occurs on the tongue. I prefer the bouquet more than the flavor.

2000 Rating: ★★★/Recommended

ABA Pisco (Chile); 40% abv, $20.

Clear as spring water, with very minor sediment. The opening whiffs detect delicate scents of slate, pomace, and minerals; aeration time of another six minutes releases the ripe grapiness and stemminess that deeply impress the olfactory sense with their harmony; a standout, top-notch pisco bouquet. The palate entry is whistle clean, off-dry to semisweet, and properly astringent; at midpalate the astringency cleanses the entire tongue while leaving behind fresh, ripe, fruity tastes of grapes, nectarines, and tangerines. The delicious aftertaste is lean, brief, and amply fruity and ripe. A superb pisco.

2003 Rating: ★★★★/Highly Recommended

Alexander Grappa di Cabernet (Italy); 40% abv, $27.

Limpid and pure. The opening two sniffings within three minutes of the pour find a round, must-like, red berry bouquet that's surprisingly well-developed for such an early stage; further time in the glass adds pronounced, medium-weighted scents of paraffin and wet stone; an understated bouquet that gets more subtle over time; does the aroma fade? yeah, but it's not a big concern. The palate entry shows a ripe, grapy richness right from the start that's just a hint sweet; the midpalate point is firmly structured, grapy, mildly sweet, and suitably fresh. It finishes off-dry, with tastes of ripe red grapes and acidic pomace. Hardly a great cabernet grappa, but a very solid one for the money.

2002 Rating: ★★★/Recommended

Alexander Grappa Distillato di Vinacce Pomace Distillate (Italy); 40% abv, $23.

Clear as rain water and totally free of sediment. In the initial couple of nosing passes I detect a lively freshness and a pleasant fruitiness that's more dry than sweet; air contact encourages further ethereal aromas to emerge, most prominently, unripened pear, grape pomace, and white raisins; this is a delightful bouquet with a light touch. The palate entry displays the first evidence of alcohol as a trace of spirity warmth greets the taste buds at the tip of the tongue; the midpalate juncture is soft, plump, ripe, and engagingly fruity. Aftertaste is moderately long, easy, and mildly fruity.

2002 Rating: ★★★/Recommended

Alexander Grappolo (Italy); 40% abv, $75.

Clean, clear, and sediment-free. The aroma right after the pour is a bit denser and oilier than its siblings; following seven minutes of additional aeration, the bouquet remains elegantly subtle, firm, mineral-like, grape seed-like, and even a touch banana-like; neither a powerhouse nor an assertive aroma, but pleasing and animated enough to be appreciated. It's obvious from the palate entry that this grappa shines brightest on the tongue as rich, grapy, and moderately oily tastes and textures enchant the taste buds; at the midpalate point the grapy richness turns grapy sweetness, but there's more than enough acid spine to support the fruity ripeness. The aftertaste is very extended, ripe, raisiny, light-bodied, and delightful.

2002 Rating: ★★★★/Highly Recommended

Alexander Platinum Aqua di Vita Grappa (Italy); 60% abv, $47.

Silvery clear purity in appearance. The powerful aroma at the pour is concentrated and grapy, but not in the least hot or overly spirity; following six minutes of exposure to air the bouquet turns intensely pumice-like yet clean and fresh. The palate entry is firmly structured, pleasingly spirity, grapy/musty, and quite acidic; at midpalate the ripeness of the pumice emerges as the taste profile turns sweeter/riper and marshmallow/cotton candy-like. Finishes cleanly, sweet, and grapy. Amazingly, the high level of alcohol never gets in the way of the enjoyment and indeed provides the solid foundation upon which the natural flavors play. Nicely done.

2005 Rating: ★★★★/Highly Recommended

Alita Brandy (Lithuania); 40% abv, $18.

Brilliant topaz/amber hue; superb purity. Smells of new leather in the first aromatic go-round; collects itself a bit more following seven minutes of undisturbed aeration as the bouquet profile expands marginally to include white grape juice, hard sour candy, and slightly sour unbaked cake batter. Enters very sweet and sugary on the palate; the midpalate stage offers unabashedly sweet flavors of toffee, caramel, and brown sugar. Ends up, well, sweet and simple. I wanted to recommend this by-the-numbers brandy but as it is, it is just too pedestrian and plain to score any higher than "average". There's no genuine depth or personality to it that makes it stand apart from scores of other common and nondescript brandies.

2007 Rating: ★★/Not Recommended

Asbach 8 Year Old (Germany); 38% abv, $100/3.

First of a gift set of three. Lovely copper/burnt orange hue; superb clarity. Smells of autumn leaves, maple, and fudge in the opening sniffs; displays more of a winey/grapy personality after seven minutes of aeration, leaving some of the sweetness behind. Entry is sweet, mildly woody, and a bit lacking in charm and dimension; the taste profile at midpalate doesn't change all that much as the emphasis remains on candied sweetness and wood. Finishes as it started out: predictably sweet and woody. What it sorely lacks is a fruit aspect. It's not terrible but it just tastes like wood-aged spirit and that flat, dull spirit could be anything, including neutral grain spirit.

2007 Rating: ★★/Not Recommended

Asbach 15 Year Old (Germany); 38% abv, $100/3.

Second of a gift set of three. Saffron/amber color; impeccable purity. This aroma is waxy and leathery, with distant scents of yellow fruits, especially nectarine in the first go-round; further air contact doesn't stimulate much more in the way of aromatic deepening or layering and while clean, the aroma seems to be running-in-place. Entry flavor is ripe, candied, and semisweet; by midpalate the wood aspect comes into play, but once again there's a dearth of base material presence. Drinkable, but without any clear character or direction.

2007 Rating: ★★/Not Recommended

Asbach 21 Year Old (Germany); 38% abv, $100/3.

Third of a gift set of three. The attractive color here is henna/old copper/auburn; perfect clarity. This aroma focuses on wood resin, cheese, and dried fruits, such as raisins, apricot, and quince; aeration features the spirit as much as the dried fruit, even a little nuttiness at the tail end of the sniffing phase. Entry is smooth, silky, and pleasantly sweet, with a resiny touch of wood; the taste profile at midpalate suffers from the identical problem as the 8 and 15 Year Olds and that is a general deficit of base material evidence which can give a brandy direction and charm; this is merely wood and indefinable spirit. It doesn't taste bad and therefore is drinkable, but the consuming pleasure is limited because the base spirit is so painfully neutral.

2007 Rating: ★★/Not Recommended

Badel Slivovitz 4 Year Old Plum Brandy (Croatia); 40% abv, $18.

Faint straw yellow tint; some floating debris noted. The initial two nosing passes pick up subtle and tart aromas of spiced plum and dried herbs; the last two sniffings, after several minutes of time in the glass, display little expansion and again feature the spiced plum; an altogether lackluster bouquet. The palate entry is savory, prickly, and off-dry; the midpalate shows considerable spunk and off-dry to moderately sweet presence after the frightfully meek aroma and offers satisfying flavors of ripe plum, cinnamon, and nutmeg. The finish is more spicy than fruity. A decent, if boring slivovitz.

2001 Rating: ★★/Not Recommended

Barsol Pisco Traditional Peruvian Acholado Grape Brandy (Peru); 40% abv, $20.

Silvery clear and positively pure in appearance. The first whiffs detect little in the way of assertive or solid aroma, just a faint grapy, blueberry-like scent; further aeration releases more of the blueberry scent than the grape, making for pleasantly simple sniffing. The palate entry is delightfully crisp, acidic, and fruity; at midpalate the taste profile focuses tightly on the blueberry-like character of the grape. Concludes fresh, fruity, and off-dry.

2005 Rating: ★★★/Recommended

Barsol Pisco Traditional Peruvian Italia Grape Brandy (Peru); 40% abv, $20.
Ideally clear and blemish-free appearance. The early-on aroma is as seductively fresh, floral, and alluring as a springtime garden; later inhalations add tropical fruit scents of banana, guava, and papaya, with a slight dash of sweet herbs. The palate entry is sweet, ripe, and silky in texture; at midpalate the tastes of ripe grapes and yellow watermelon are exhilarating. Concludes on a semisweet, fruity/acidic/melony note that complements the taste phases. Very elegant, classy stuff.
2005 Rating: ★★★★/Highly Recommended

Barsol Pisco Traditional Peruvian Quebranta Grape Brandy (Peru); 40% abv, $20.
Excellent clarity; flawless, limpid appearance. The first aroma after the pour is animated, juicy, concentrated, and even jammy; aeration calms down the bouquet, making it more subdued, grapy, and with a vinous/stemmy quality in the last minute that I like a lot. The palate entry is squeaky clean, more than adequately acidic, and intensely grapy; at midpalate the taste profile includes an odd flavor of chalk/limestone. Concludes with a ripe, grapy rush that's fully endowed, rich, and off-dry to semisweet.
2005 Rating: ★★★★/Highly Recommended

Barsol Pisco Traditional Peruvian Torontel Grape Brandy (Peru); 40% abv, $20.
Blemish-free, sediment-free, silvery/blue appearance. The initial sniffings pick up delightfully fruity, jammy, almost baked aromas, then in later passes following a six minute aeration period there's a medicinal/medicine cabinet aroma that over-rides the fruit preserves. The palate entry is sweet, ripe, and intensely grapy; at midpalate the spirit bestows a bit of welcome heat on the tongue, though it doesn't knock out the fruit element. Finishes grapy and ripe.
2005 Rating: ★★★/Recommended

Bocchino 10 Year Old Grappa Riserva della Cantina Privata (Italy); 45% abv, $115/375 ml.
The amber/autumnal gold hue is bright and flawlessly pure. The genuine grape must aroma during the first whiffs can only be grappa-based due to the intense earthiness and pulpy leaning; seven more minutes of air contact stimulates sour apple and yeast-like scents that go well with the assertive, but not aggressive alcohol/spirit. The zesty, but gracefully balanced palate entry is a toffee-like revelation of how elegantly grappa can age in oak for extended periods—this is luscious, period; by the midpalate stage the moscato element leaps ahead of the nebbiolo as incredibly tasty notes of orange peel and grapefruit take charge of the mouth phase. Finishes concentrated yet breezily fruity and citrusy. A marvel of freshness and youthful vigor, wrapped in a toffee/nougat glaze. Holy-moly. A brandy to be enjoyed only with the worthiest of friends.
2007 Rating: ★★★★★/Highest Recommendation

Bocchino 15 Year Old Grappa Riserva della Cantina Privata (Italy); 45% abv, $180/375 ml.
Solid amber/light honey/gold color; impeccable clarity. The musty/pulpy fragrance seems a touch deeper and more serious than the 10 Year Old's opening aroma as the scents

remind me of apple butter and hemp/textile/fiber; further aeration (six minutes) brings out a bread dough/yeasty quality that's more bakery-like (pastry/strudel) than fruit stand-like. The palate entry is focused on soy sauce, ginger, lanolin, and nut butter/nut paste; at the midpalate stage the taste profile turns resiny, heavily baked, and even a bit citrusy in its yeastiness/pulpiness/mustiness. Concludes astringent, yet sweet and sour. Very good and easily recommendable, but pales in comparison to the vital, off-the-charts 10 Year Old.
2007 Rating: ★★★/Recommended

Bocchino 16 Year Old Grappa Riserva della Cantina Privata (Italy); 45% abv, $240/375 ml.
Comes off a shade lighter than the 15 Year Old in its honey hue; excellent purity. The first sniffings detect pronounced smells of cardboard, parchment, fiber, and distant apple pie; additional exposure to air stimulates the fruit element which tends more towards dried varieties, especially apricot, pineapple, lemon, and pear, than bakery/dough/pastry odors. The palate entry is intensely nutty/nougaty and fruity (dried yellow fruit); at the midpalate stage the flavor profile is integrated, harmonious, and wonderfully fruity, with just a kiss of ripe sweetness in the form of light caramel. Ends up semisweet, correctly acidic, and elegant.
2007 Rating: ★★★★/Highly Recommended

Bocchino 22 Year Old Grappa Riserva della Cantina Privata (Italy); 45% abv, $270/375 ml.
The appearance is identical to that of the 15 Year Old's, the golden color of amontillado sherry. The initial inhalations pick up fiber-like notes of hemp, damp cloth, and cardboard; after another seven minutes in the glass, the bouquet stresses the cardboard component to the hilt; a disappointing aroma that's devoid of fruit and charm. The palate entry offers candied, even stale tastes that fall flat on the tongue; at the midpalate stage there's noticeable improvement as flavors of light toffee and chocolate emerge to rescue the mouth phase from oblivion. Finishes fruity, ripe, and very pleasant. The latter gains in the midpalate and finish aren't enough, however, to make this grappa recommendable.
2007 Rating: ★★/Not Recommended

Bocchino 29 Year Old Grappa Riserva della Cantina Privata (Italy); 45% abv, $300/375 ml.
The rich topaz color is bright and unblemished. The uninteresting opening aromas are stemmy, fibery, and vegetal; swirling and seven more minutes of aeration do virtually nothing to improve the bouquet; I expected to, at least, find some oak influence, but there was zero/zippo/nada. The palate entry displays a heavy dose of vanilla-like oak that eclipses the alcohol and masks the fruit components; at the midpalate stage the buttery oak continues its total domination of the taste phase, but in a more attractive fashion than at entry. Concludes waxy, creamy, concentrated. What this brandy lacks is balance and a sense of harmony. At nearly every stage one component or another lords over all others, making for mildly interesting drinking.
2007 Rating: ★★/Not Recommended

Bocchino 30 Year Old Grappa Riserva della Cantina Privata (Italy); 45% abv, $375/375 ml.

The lovely topaz/deep honey hue is flawlessly clean and very pretty. Like the 29, the first nosings pick up only ropy scents of fiber/textile/hemp and vegetation and nothing of the innate virtues of either nebbiolo or Moscato d'Asti; I'm sorry to report that further air contact has no impact on the aroma. The palate entry is flat, resiny, and hemp-like, with no evidence of wood (except for the resin) or fruit; the midpalate stage is mildly pineapple-like and even a bit grapefruity, but basically this grappa is dead in the bottle. Nothing more to say.

2007 Rating: ★/Not Recommended

Bonaventura Maschio Immature Brandy 1999 (Italy); 40% abv, $52.

Absolute clarity; not a single speck of sediment. The opening nosings display a full-throttle, evolved, and evocative bouquet that highlights nuances of pineapple, nectarine, white grapes, citrus zest, and new leather; aeration for an additional six minutes serves to deepen the bouquet's layers of aroma as the scents of leather and citrus zest take command; I like this bouquet for its pointed cleanness; it's sleek. The palate entry features astringent tastes of grape pomace and acid; the midpalate juncture shows a sweeter, grapier side as the flavor turns ripe, sweet, and black raisin juicy. The aftertaste is very long, moderate oily, and seed-like. A streamlined grappa that delivers the goods at all levels.

2002 Rating: ★★★★/Highly Recommended

Bonaventura Maschio Prime Arance Acquavitae d'Arancia Orange Brandy (Italy); 40% abv, $51.

As clean and pure as one could expect from a fine spirit. The initial sniffings confirm without a doubt that this spirit's base material is, in fact, oranges as the perfume is tart, citrusy, and zesty; time in the glass adds more subtle nuances of orange rind, citric acid, and orange pulp; a good perfume that's more astringent than ripe or sweet. The palate entry comes off rather neutral and it isn't until the midpalate point that the taste buds detect the attractively tart and authentic orange pulp character. The finish is astringent, clean, fresh, long, and intensely orangey. A revelation.

2002 Rating: ★★★★/Highly Recommended

Bonaventura Maschio Prime Uve Cru Chardonnay Harvest 2000 (Italy); 40% abv, $60.

Limpid, with minor sediment. The aroma is neutral throughout the first couple of sniffings after the pour; six minutes of additional exposure to air helps to marginally stimulate the bouquet, but not enough to get a genuine impression of the aromatics other than to cite very subdued scents of grape seed and pulp; the bouquet simply doesn't want to come out and play. The palate entry is very textured, as in oily, and the taste of ripe white grapes greets the taste buds; by the midpalate point the texture is very viscous and oily and the flavor is concentrated and sweet, indeed, almost (atypically) chocolaty and thick. The aftertaste is intensely ripe, bittersweet, and long. The taste and finish stages are so remarkably intense that they easily redeem the stonewall-prone aroma to the point of a four star rating.

2002 Rating: ★★★★/Highly Recommended

Bonaventura Maschio Prime Uve Cru di Moscato Giallo Harvest 2000 (Italy); 40% abv, $60.

Translucent, showing very minor, insignificant sediment. Right from the first whiff, the orangy/citrusy/tart aroma of lovely moscato (muscat) wafts up from the glass—is there a more ideal grape for grappa than moscato?; five minutes of further air contact solidifies and strengthens the mesmerizing citrus perfume that turns from orange/tangerine fruit/pulp to delicate orange blossom; enchanting and elegant. The palate entry is tart, oily, and piquant; by the midpalate juncture the taste/texture deepens into a full-weighted, citrusy, oily, and succulent flavor experience that is simultaneously profound and classy. The aftertaste is orangy/grapy sweet and perfectly balanced between grapiness/acid/alcohol. An outstanding grappa from start to finish.

2002 Rating: ★★★★★/Highest Recommendation

Bonaventura Maschio Prime Uve Nere Acquavite d'Uva Diluted Immature Grape Brandy (Italy); 38.5% abv, $62.

Owns the pale yellow/straw hue of a sauvignon blanc; clear of sediment. The aromas discovered in the opening nosing passes remind me a bit of olive brine, wet potting soil, and wood resin; another five to six minutes of exposure to air adds additional vegetal/garden-like scents to the aromatic mix, including pine needles and sap; it's an odd, but strangely pleasant bouquet of minor note. The palate entry is resiny sweet; the midpalate juncture features a deepening of the wood resin and a heightening of the sap-like sweetness. The aftertaste is delightfully woody and semisweet. Different and worth a try for serious grappa mavens.

2002 Rating: ★★★/Recommended

Bonollo Umberto Fior d'Uva (Italy); 40% abv, $33.

Mineral water clear, with some minor sediment spotted. The delicate, reluctant, peppery/citrusy bouquet barely shows itself in the first two nosing passes; with time in the glass, the bouquet develops by the third sniffing, offering elegant, if off-beat scents of green pepper, black pepper, and fat/lard; in the final whiff, the fat/buttermilk aroma dominates. The palate entry is intensely flowery/spicy sweet while the midpalate shows mild prickliness and juiciness. The aftertaste is long, pleasing, and juicy. Probably the best of an uninspiring lot.

2001 Rating: ★★★/Recommended

Bonollo Umberto Grappa di Amarone (Italy); 40% abv, $30.

Clear as spring water; pure. The opening bouquet is fresh, pulpy, and intensely grape must-like; the middle stage whiffs offer intriguing scents of cactus, green pepper, and parchment; the fourth and final inhalation adds a muted touch of rubber pencil eraser; something of a lumbering grappa perfume, devoid of elegance. The palate entry is mildly juicy/grapy but bland overall; the midpalate stage displays some finesse, mostly in the texture, but doesn't particularly satisfy on the flavor level; it seems strangely weedy on the palate. It's drinkably common, but lacking in charm and too rustic for what today is viewed as contemporary grappa.

2001 Rating: ★★/Not Recommended

Bonollo Umberto Grappa di Cabernet (Italy); 40% abv, $30.

Limpid and clean. The initial nosing pass right after the pour detects very ungrappa-like scents of cardboard and wet clothes; even after several minutes in the copita glass, the aroma just can't seem to shake the dull wet fabric odor that has absolutely nothing to do with pressed grapes; in the fourth and last whiff, following eight minutes in the glass, the aroma can't open up past the damp earth/wet fabric scent that's anything but fresh and inviting. The palate entry at last displays some grapiness in the form of ripe berries and juiciness; the midpalate shows even more grape/cabernet impact as the taste of sweet raisiny ripeness pleases the taste buds. The finish is clean, raisiny, sweet, and potent. It's not a fresh tasting grappa, but it does supply enough imbibing pleasure in the flavor and aftertaste stages to earn a third star.

2001 Rating: ★★★/Recommended

Bonollo Umberto Grappa di Moscato (Italy); 40% abv, $30.

Translucent, but quite a bit of floating sediment noted. When I think of moscato grappa, the alluring aromatic image is of orange blossom and citrus, this moscato, however, mysteriously smells of vegetables, vines, brambles, and sulphur; the middle stage sniffings do nothing to rescue the situation as the aroma starts to take on a rubbery, cabbage-like odor that's frightfully atypical and borderline nasty; following over eight minutes of contact with air, the aroma goes over completely to cabbage/cole slaw/raw vegetables in the dusty/musty final nosing pass; whither the usual orangey moscato perfume? Not here, matey. The palate entry finally offers some orange character along with an unfortunate spirity sting that stabs at the tongue; the midpalate phase settles down to offer some mildly impressive and juicy grapy/orangey moscato charm. The aftertaste is off-dry, musty, and the most typically moscato-like feature of the evaluation. Too erratic for a recommendation.

2001 Rating: ★★/Not Recommended

Bonollo Umberto Grappa di Prosecco (Italy); 40% abv, $30.

Rain water clean and pure. The first whiff picks up oddball aromas of fish fry, unbuttered popcorn, and chili pepper; in the second and third sniffings the fishiness becomes more pungent along with puzzling touches of soy sauce and bean curd; the fourth and final sniffing remains strangely fishy and unpleasant. Weirdly, the palate entry is plump, sweet, and very ripe; the midpalate shows some ripe grapy flavor, but overall comes off flat and flabby. The aftertaste is stale, attic-like, and rubbery; the kind of awkward taste and manner that for decades put consumers off grappa.

2001 Rating: ★/Not Recommended

Bortolo Nardini Bianca Aquavitae Grappa (Italy); 50% abv, $50/liter.

The appearance is translucent and blemish-free. The opening inhalations after the pour offer nicely fresh, grape pomace mustiness, and stemminess; following another seven minutes of aeration, the bouquet becomes intensely grapy and ripe, but with enough of an acidic foundation to remain fresh and clean. The palate entry is concentrated, grapy, and medium-sweet; at midpalate the flavor profile turns decidedly sweet and ripe. Concludes with a burst of spirity warmth that's welcome and not in the least burning or raw. Nice job.

2005 Rating: ★★★/Recommended

Bortolo Nardini Mandorla Almond Flavored Grappa (Italy); 50% abv, $50/liter.

Pale straw/lemon juice yellow/briny green in hue; absolute purity. The first whiffs pick up delectable scents of almonds, marshmallows, and honey; later sniffings after six minutes of aeration detect aromas that accent and isolate the almond element. The palate entry is medium-bodied in weight and moderately sweet, nutty, and toasty in taste; at midpalate a moderately fiery flash of spirit makes an impression as the sweetly nutty almond flavor dances lightly on the grappa base. Ends up zesty, nutty, mildly sweet, and clean.

2005 Rating: ★★★★/Highly Recommended

Bortolo Nardini Riserva Aquavitae Grappa (Italy); 50% abv, $60/liter.

Pretty gold/lemon juice yellow color; flawless purity. Lovely aromatic notes of seaweed, green olive brine, and musty pumice greet the olfactory sense; aeration brings out a pickling quality that's quite vinegar-like, but fresh. The palate entry is sweet, clean, and intensely grapy; at midpalate flavors of butter cream and green vegetable are added to the taste mix. Concludes sweet, grapy/must-like, and full-bodied. A big-hearted, generous, heady grappa that, while made more in the old-fashioned style, still wins over my palate.

2005 Rating: ★★★★/Highly Recommended

Bortolo Nardini Rue Flavored Aquavitae Grappa (Italy); 42.8% abv, $50/liter.

Unquestionable purity; the color is pale yellow/green and quite attractive. The first nosing passes pick up earthy/woodsy scents of damp soil, vegetation, and rubber pencil eraser; further air contact stirs other musky aromas of uncooked broccoli, mushrooms, and lead pencil. The palate entry is semisweet, intensely herbal, and very pleasurable; at midpalate the surface sweetness doesn't get in the way of the earthy/musky and spirity foundation flavors. Finishes sweet, very vegetal, and herbal. Not everyone's cup of grappa, but even though the aroma is weird, the overall experience is positive and unique. An old-fashioned type of flavored grappa that works.

2005 Rating: ★★★/Recommended

Caffo Very Italian Grappa (Italy); 40% abv, $21.

Clean as a whistle limpid appearance. Opening the aromatic phase is a pleasingly languid grapy/vinous scent that's got "grappa" plastered all over it; extra time in the glass brings out more focused scents of lead pencil, ripe grapes, and grape skins. The palate entry is a tad hot, but dry and like dried tropical fruit; at midpalate there's the lead pencil aspect once again as well as tastes of prunes and dates. Concludes warm, metallic, and just a bit grapy. Loses its way at palate entry and, while drinkable, doesn't display enough in the midpalate and finish to elevate it to recommended status.

2005 Rating: ★★/Not Recommended

Castello Banfi Aqua Vitae (Italy); 40% abv, $40.

The crystalline/silvery appearance shows inconsequential sediment beneath the examination lamp as many fine grappas/aqua vitaes do from Italy. The assertive aroma leaps from the glass in waves of fruity sweet ripe grapes, pears, and bubble gum; with time in the glass, the ripe grapy fruit component settles down, moving to the background, leaving the softly sweet scent of confectioner's sugar and tropical fruit; a seductive bouquet that ends on a dry note of lead pencil, fruit stone, and slate. The palate entry is sweet, fresh, and intensely grapy; at midpalate the fresh, almost raw grapiness turns more mellow and polished, offering multilayered flavors of dried red fruit, nickel, grape must, and orange zest. Finishes as amiably as it begins.

2004 Rating: ★★★★/Highly Recommended

Christian Drouin Blanche de Normandie Normandy Apple Brandy (France); 40% abv, $43.

Clear as rainwater; ideal purity. The smell of ripe, just-picked apple is mesmerizing, perfumed, slightly spicy, and genuine; the bouquet after further aeration stays the mildly sweet course enjoyed in the opening sniffs. The palate entry is crisp, tart, and firmly structured; the midpalate stage offers more intense and slightly baked tastes of apple fritter, apple peel, and baking spices (cinnamon, nutmeg especially). Concludes with a note of cocoa/dark chocolate and turns semisweet and luscious in the finish. This brandy never loses the apple eau-de-vie focus.

2006 Rating: ★★★★/Highly Recommended

Dettling Cuvée Schwarze Bergkirschen (Switzerland); 40% abv, $90/3.

One of gift set of three. Pure as rainwater. The cherry element in this eau-de-vie is markedly juice-like and ripe, especially black cherry juice in the initial sniffs; the amiable juiciness makes for delightful sniffing after further air contact and, though one-dimensional, this semisweet and tangy bouquet is disarming and compelling. Entry flavor highlights the innate juiciness but comes off drier in the mouth than in the nasal cavity; midpalate flavor is slightly mineral- and stone-like, but with plenty of dried cherry fruit to make its point with a high degree of elegance. Finishes sleek, clean, off-dry, and ripe.

2007 Rating: ★★★★/Highly Recommended

Dettling Kirsch Gift Set Dettling Réserve (Switzerland); 41% abv, $90/3.

Second of gift set of three. Shimmering clarity; silver color. First nosings encounter dry cherry pit stoniness and clean, crisp, leather-like spirit; the leather/vinyl aspect leaps ahead of the fruit stone with aeration. Entry is semisweet, a bit syrupy and sugary, but still keenly cherry-like; the taste profile at midpalate features the ripe sweetness of the fruit as the texture goes very silky. Ends up smooth, a bit brambly, and warming in the throat. Very nice.

2007 Rating: ★★★/Recommended

Dettling Wildkirsche 2000 (Switzerland); 40% abv, $90/3.

Third of gift set of three. Spring water crystalline and pure. Cherry pit/mineral scent all the way in the opening whiffs of this eau-de-vie; aeration dramatically alters the personality of this bouquet as the cherry pit fades, leaving behind full-throttle fresh cherry fruit ripeness with a hint of spice; my favorite bouquet of the three Dettling kirsches; gorgeous fragrance. Entry flavor is fully ripe, gently sweet, with enough acidity and stony fruit pit to keep it fresh and ultra-clean; by midpalate the cherry juice/fruit taste is in full flight, cleansing the palate while also scintillating the taste buds with authentic cherry taste. Concludes satiny smooth, nearly creamy, and real-deal cherry-like.

2007 Rating: ★★★★/Highly Recommended

Distillerie Paul Devoille Eau-de-Vie de Framboise (France); 45% abv, $15/375ml.
Crystal clear. The opening perfume is intensely raspberry preserves-like; in the second and third passes a bramble quality overtakes the raspberry fruit presence; the jammy fruit returns to dominance with further aeration, ending in a moderately sweet manner. It's surprisingly dry at palate entry, then turns brambly and viny at midpalate. The finish is short, mildly fruity, and off-dry. Very nice.
2001 Rating: ★★★/Recommended

Distillerie Paul Devoille Eau-de-Vie de Poire William (France); 45% abv, $15/375ml.
Clear as rain water. The initial nosing passes reveal fragrant and true-to-the-source aromas of ripe, juicy pear and pear skin; aeration stimulates the spirit as there's more of a spirity base on which the fruit perfume can develop; a comely, sturdy bouquet. In the mouth the pear flavor is first dry and acidic at entry, then turns succulent, ripe, and juicy sweet at midpalate. The aftertaste is beautifully textured, extended, ripe, and assertively fruity. A terrifically enchanting poire as only the European distillers can produce; excellent drinking.
2001 Rating: ★★★★/Highly Recommended

Distillerie Paul Devoille Kirsch Eau-de-Vie de Cerise (France); 45% abv, $15/375ml.
Properly clean and clear. The opening whiffs after the pour pick up very aggressive and pronounced cherry pit and cherry preserves aromas; following several minutes in the sampling glass the aroma remains solid, intensely spirity, almost heady, and pungent as the dry cherry perfume stays the course. In the mouth the power-packed spirit makes the tongue tingle at entry; the midpalate phase is alive with off-dry, ripe cherry flavor. The aftertaste is intense, long, and true.
2001 Rating: ★★★/Recommended

Domenis Kosher Grappa (Italy); 43% abv, $52.
Crystalline, clean appearance. The bouquet is lean yet ripe and fruity in the opening nosing stages; seven more minutes of air contact turns the aroma delicately plump, musty, and viny, even seed-like. The palate entry is tart, acidic, and very must-like; the midpalate phase displays delightful, balanced flavors of grape seed, must, grape pulp, and skins. It finishes gracefully, if a bit meekly, showing no spirity fire or prickliness. Elegant, composed, and eminently drinkable; contemporary and lovely; what it lacks in heft and profundity, it makes up for with integration and grace.
2003 Rating: ★★★★/Highly Recommended

Domenis Kosher Sliwovitz (Italy); 40% abv, $70.
About as close to perfection in terms of purity as any spirit could come. The nose immediately emits lovely, plummy scents that are delicate and ambrosial; time in the copita really makes a huge impact on the bouquet as intensely ripe and assertive aromatic waves dwell in the bowl of the glass; it's ripe but not necessarily sweet. The palate entry is off-dry, very soft in texture, hardly spirity at all, and very polite; by the midpalate stage there's a clear deepening in the plum ripe fruit flavor profile. The aftertaste is long, semisweet, acidic

enough to balance the rich fruit, and just plain nice. A pleasant, uncomplicated and quaffable brandy; greater gravity would have pushed into four star territory.

2003 Rating: ★★★/Recommended

Domenis Organic Kosher Grappa (Italy); 43% abv, $122.

Clear and pure as rainwater. The initial sniffings within two minutes of pour offer atypical aromas of fabric, especially cotton, plastic, and vinyl; what gives here? Additional aeration time finally stimulates some meager and distant traces of grapes, grape must, and stems; where is the raw grapiness that I look forward to when I inhale grappa aromas? The palate entry is off-dry to semisweet and slightly tropical fruit-like more than grapy; the midpalate stage at least displays a bit more in the way of true grapiness, but it still comes off as being reluctant and timid. The aftertaste shows some substance and grapiness but it's a little late and hardly enough to make up for the flaws, mostly lack of character or distinctive virtues, in the mediocre bouquet and flavor phases.

2003 Rating: ★★/Not Recommended

Etter Cuvée Anniversary Mixed Fruit Brandy (Switzerland); 41% abv, $50.

A fruit salad eau-de-vie distilled from pears, raspberries, grapes, apples, and cherries. Translucent and clean as mineral water. The initial two nosings after the pour find a ripe, gently sweet bouquet in which none of the fruit elements dominates; air contact seems to unleash the pear component more than the others as the later stages of the nosing tend toward slightly sour fruit peel. The palate entry is clean and pear-like; the midpalate sees the cherry and apple emerge. The finish is quick, tart, acidic, and lean.

2002 Rating: ★★★/Recommended

Etter Framboise Fine Eau-de-Vie (Raspberry) (Switzerland); 41% abv, $66.

Perfect clarity; silvery appearance. Fresh raspberries come screaming out of the glass as the first whiffs are treated to an ambrosial explosion of the grandest type; seven more minutes of exposure to air brings out a nuance of brambles/vines that wasn't apparent in the first nosing and therefore closes the circle on this how-to-do-it-right bouquet. Entry offers a surprisingly lean raspberry fruit flavor that's clearly tamped down by the high acidity; the midpalate stage boasts a gravelly/stony flavor underpinning that allows the fruit component all the opportunity to give us its best and juiciest, but it, to my disappointment, doesn't fully deliver on the immense promise found in the bouquet. Finishes smooth as silk, adequately raspberry flesh-like, and clean. Impeccable distilling and aroma are worth a recommendation, but some of the fruit got lost in the process.

2007 Rating: ★★★/Recommended

Etter Pomme Gravine (Apple) (Switzerland); 41% abv, $47.

Clear as rain water; absolute purity. The appley opening aroma after the pour is refreshing, tart, and green; further aeration stimulates the bouquet to become more assertive, intense, and round; the fresh off-the-tree apple perfume is delightfully delicate, even fey toward the end of the nosing phase. The palate entry is dry and spirity; at the midpalate phase the apple character shifts into fourth gear as the green apple taste coats the tongue. The finish is lean, almost austere, bone dry, and prickly.

2002 Rating: ★★★/Recommended

Etter Williams Fine Eau-de-Vie de Poire (Pear) (Switzerland); 42% abv, $72.
Limpid as spring water; ideal clarity. Initial sniffs detect a perfect balance between pear peel, pear flesh, subtle baking spice, and natural acidity, wrapped in a minerally/stony aroma that's a benchmark for the genre; further air contact stimulates the pear flesh/pulp more than the other elements, making for exquisite inhaling. Entry is so utterly pear juice/pear peel spot-on that it's scary in the most delightful of ways; the midpalate taste profile is properly and sharply acidic and clears the path for the mountain of pear flesh flavor that thrills the taste buds. Ends up dashingly clean, austere, razor crisp, and first-rate all the way. A classic and an iconic poire.
2007 Rating: ★★★★★/Highest Recommendation

Etter Zuger Kirsch Fine Eau-de-Vie (Cherry) (Switzerland); 41% abv, $72.
Impeccably pure; pewter appearance. Smells of fresh cherries as well as cherry pit, limestone/slate, and cooking spice (mace); additional minutes in the glass bring out a bigger fresh cherry presence as the slate/mineral component slides to the background; a dazzling clinic on authentic cherry perfume. Entry is ripe and seductively sweet, with touches of spice in the background; the midpalate stage explodes with juicy cherry and cherry compote tastes that are supported by a slaty/minerally foundation that keeps the sweetness/ripeness in check. Concludes with a rush of ripe cherry taste that's satisfying and fresh.
2007 Rating: ★★★★/Highly Recommended

F. Meyer Eau-de-Vie de Framboise Raspberry Brandy (France); 45% abv, $35.
Clean and pure as rainwater. Smells of big-hearted, sweet and jammy raspberry, and red currant run rampant in the opening sniffs; further air contact stimulates sweet, almost sugary aromas that are deficient in freshness. Entry is mildly pleasing, assertive in its ripeness, and a trace manufactured with sugar; the midpalate is concentrated, sweet, and bordering on top-heavy with ripeness. Ends on a spirity, sharp, sweet/sour note. Another case of supplying too much obvious sweetness and not enough delicacy (and acidity), therefore losing the base fruit to the over-sweetness.
2007 Rating: ★★/Not Recommended

F. Meyer Eau-de-Vie de Kirsch Cherry Brandy (France); 45% abv, $33.
Perfect clarity. Offers potent, vibrant, and stony cherry juice aromas right from the get-go; the assertiveness of the ripe cherry juice aroma continues into the latter stages following more aeration and the bouquet takes on a tarter/less ripe face in the final whiffs. Entry is sharply acidic, pleasingly tart, and adequately cherry-ripe; the midpalate is the best phase of the evaluation so far as the flavor profile turns viscous, full, intensely ripe but not in the least over-sweet. Finishes stony/minerally, still potent and spirity. What this eau-de-vie lacks in finesse it makes up for in exuberance.
2007 Rating: ★★★/Recommended

F. Meyer Eau-de-Vie de Mirabelle Mirabelle Plum Brandy (France); 45% abv, $30.
Pure as rainwater; sediment-free. Opening whiffs detect subtle scents of yellow plums and baking spices; the aroma turns more minerally/stony with additional time in the glass. Entry is sweet, ripe, and intensely plumy; the midpalate is long, medium-fat, and oily.

Concludes with a hit of spirit on the tongue and a delectable ripeness that's engaging and pleasingly sweet.
2007 Rating: ★★★★/Highly Recommended

F. Meyer Eau-de-Vie de Poire Williams Pear Williams Brandy (France); 45% abv, $32.
Silvery clear; unblemished. First inhalations encounter generous, but slightly dull aromas of pear skin; aeration doesn't stimulate much in the way of vivacity as the aroma seems a touch mossy/mushroom-like in the final moments of sniffing. Entry highlights the minerally pear peel element as the acidity drops in strength, leaving behind a rush of ripe fruit; the midpalate offers the best face of this eau-de-vie as the flavor profile fully evolves into a gently sweet, mildly spicy taste. Ends up more tart than at the midpalate stage and still a touch mossy/earthy.
2007 Rating: ★★★/Recommended

F. Meyer Eau-de-Vie de Quetsch Dark Red Plum Brandy (France); 45% abv, $26.
Transparent and flawlessly clean. Initially smells of sweet, ripe, dark yellow plums and even a little bit of honey; aeration brings down the ripeness/sweetness and features more of the earthy plumminess, with a judicious dash of baking spice. Entry features vibrant deep dark plum and blackcurrant acidity and fruity richness; the midpalate seems to lose a bit of momentum as the flavor profile, though superb, appears to be less vivid and more reined-in than the entry. Finishes well in a medium-weighted, slightly oily manner that displays good balance between the fruit and acid.
2007 Rating: ★★★★/Highly Recommended

Gaja Castello di Barbaresco Darmagi Grappa (Italy); 45% abv, $35/500 ml.
Clear, clean, with some minor sediment. The lovely, aromatic opening bouquet is pear-like and gently off-dry; six minutes of further aeration sees the unripened pear fruit base aroma expand only slightly as added delicate scents of nectarine and white raisins emerge; a fey, almost fragile, grappa bouquet that features fruit more than spirit. While the aroma stage may be dainty and feminine, the palate entry talks a far more assertive game as the fruitiness liked in the bouquet turns into an ambrosial banquet at entry; by the midpalate point the sexy oiliness of the texture comes into full play as it underpins the ripe and sweet pear/nectarine/white grape taste elements. The aftertaste features the tart, stone dry tastes of unripened pear and white grape components. A superbly satisfying grappa.
2002 Rating: ★★★★/Highly Recommended

Gaja Castello di Barbaresco Gaia & Rey Grappa (Italy); 45% abv, $35/500 ml.
Limpid, but with lots of black-gray sediment that looks like pomace. In the initial two nosing passes I detect inoffensive but puzzling smells of cardboard, fabric, and rubber pencil eraser, huh? allowing it another seven minutes of air contact doesn't assist in making this aroma more accessible and, in fact, what develop are distant hints of black pepper, metal, and minerals; not the bouquet I'd hoped for seeing the Gaia & Rey identification on the label. The palate entry is pleasantly sweet, quite oily in texture, and grapy; the midpalate flavor stage displays a flash of spirity warmth and sweetish tastes of ripe grapes and ripe red pears. The finish is a touch raw, heady, and fruity. The taste and aftertaste phases aren't strong

enough to pull this grappa into three star territory; certainly drinkable, but the flaws early-on are too much to surmount.

2002 Rating: ★★/Not Recommended

Gaja Castello di Barbaresco Magari Toscana Grappa (Italy); 45% abv, $35/500 ml.
Rain water clear and pure. The opening two nosing passes following the pour are piquant and spirity; the bouquet really comes alive after seven more minutes as punchy but complementary scents of ground black pepper, uncooked green vegetables (kale, spinach), gun powder, wet slate, fennel, and granite; with every nosing pass there's something else of interest popping up. While the aroma is intensely minerally, the palate entry is ripe, fruity, and concentrated; by the midpalate point the taste turns very sweet, grapy, and fat in texture. The finish is oily, viscous, fruity sweet, and extended.

2002 Rating: ★★★/Recommended

Gaja Castello di Barbaresco Rennina Brunello di Montalcino Grappa (Italy); 45% abv, $35/500 ml.
Pure and translucent; no sediment at all. The initial couple of sniffings after the pour detect peculiar but not offensive scents more akin to boiled vegetables and rubber tires than grape pomace or distilled spirit; further time in the glass doesn't stimulate aromatic expansion. The palate entry is fruity/grapy sweet and full-textured; the midpalate juncture highlights the natural oiliness of the spirit and the ripeness of the grape pomace. The aftertaste is long, a touch orangey (as in marmalade), and gently sweet. It displays a lot of finesse in the mouth.

2002 Rating: ★★★/Recommended

Gaja Castello di Barbaresco Sperss Grappa (Italy); 45% abv, $35.
The color is like the golden yellow of a barrel-fermented chardonnay. The first whiff speaks of fresh grape must, distillate, and damp cotton; the middle stage sniffings add nuances of linseed oil, chamomile, cardboard, and slate; the final nosing pass emits a subtle juiciness that's delicate and refined; a bouquet that starts out with the brass section and concludes with a single violin. The palate entry is piquant, intensely grapy, and almost jammy; advancing to the midpalate the heated spiritiness grows in intensity, then right before the finish succulent flavors of grape skin, ripe grapes, and vanilla crescendo on the tongue. It finishes softly, gently, and concentrated in its grapiness. A classic from the genius of Angelo Gaja.

2001 Rating: ★★★★★/Highest Recommendation

Imoya VSOP Fine Cape Alambic Brandy (South Africa); 40% abv, $35.
The bronze/burnished orange/rusty color dazzles the eye; fair-to-good purity. In the initial two minutes of sniffing toasty, almond-like scents greet the olfactory sense, then following another seven minutes of air contact delicate notes of oak, vanilla, and hard cheese are discerned; while enjoyable, the bouquet seems to be held back, meaning it's not in the least generous or expansive. The palate entry offers satisfying tastes of dark toffee, cocoa, and oak resin; the midpalate stage goes deeper and even sweeter as well-defined flavors of dark bittersweet chocolate, chocolate-covered cherries, butter cream, and honey vie for dominance. Ends up very sweet, silky, and oily in texture. Though not as sophisticated as the best grape brandies from Cognac, Armagnac, or the northern California alambic producers

(Germain-Robin, especially), a sound, very solid pot still brandy that would rate four stars if it eased up on the sweetness/caramel pedal.
2005 Rating: ★★★/Recommended

Jacopo Poli Arzente 10 Year Old Grape Brandy (Italy); 40% abv, $55/375 ml.

Distilled from trebbiano grapes harvested in the 1992 vintage. Dullish medium amber/topaz hue; large chunks of brown/gray sediment appear after the pour/same for the bottle when shaken; a picky consumer's visual nightmare. Smells alluringly of light caramel, nougat, brown butter, and marzipan in the first whiffs; following seven more minutes of aeration, the aroma turns mildly burnt/caramelized and even pipe or cigar tobacco-like. Entry is cocoa-like and seriously honeyed; the midpalate stage offers smoky, charred tastes of brown sugar, sweet oak, vanilla extract, and chocolate covered orange. Concludes semisweet, nutty, and medium-weighted. Absolutely recommendable as long as you don't look too closely at it. I suggest that you serve it in a completely blackened room.
2007 Rating: ★★★★/Highly Recommended

Jacopo Poli Barrique 1993 Single Vintage Grappa (Italy); 55% abv, $61.

Single vintage grappa matured in Allier 225-liter barriques for thirteen years. Sublime aromas of fruitcake, cinnamon, nutmeg, and honey greet and seduce the olfactory sense in the opening inhalations after the pour; aeration stimulates baked tropical fruit (banana, pineapple) and egg cream/vanilla soda smells that combine beautifully with the early fragrances, creating a stunningly classy and satisfying bouquet of the top rank. Entry is tight, concentrated, sherry- and honey-like, and moderately spiced; the midpalate stage couldn't be more spectacular as the taste profile expands to include baked fruit (nectarine, peach), clove, fruit pastry (Danish, prunes, black raisins)...this flavor experience just keeps unfolding. Finishes with flair and finesse as the focused and integrated flavors take the taste buds on a memorable journey to greatness. Could sell for $100 per bottle and still be worth every penny. Classic.
2007 Rating: ★★★★★/Highest Recommendation

Jacopo Poli Ciliegie di Poli Cherry Brandy (Italy); 40% abv, $51.

Translucent and flawlessly clear. Ohhhhh, Mama, this subtle, understated, cherry pit opening aroma has me on my knees with delight; seven minutes later, the low-key cherry fragrance notches up another degree to a delectable fruity ripeness that I could go on sniffing for the rest of the day...and right now it's only 8:34 AM. Entry is sublimely pitched on the ripe cherry flesh and cherry pit scale, with a dash of bittersweet juiciness that completes this phase with pizzazz; the midpalate features the juice more than the cherry flesh and is therefore eminently lip-smacking. Concludes clean, semisweet, intensely ripe, round, smooth as silk, and perfect. A clinic on cherry brandy.
2007 Rating: ★★★★★/Highest Recommendation

Jacopo Poli Lamponi di Poli Raspberry Brandy (Italy); 40% abv, $51.

Silvery clean and unblemished appearance. Strap me down, I'm going berserk over this one; as a raspberry fan, this first nosing takes me to raspberry heaven in strong, no-kidding waves of ripe, juicy, just-picked raspberries and vininess; with further aeration, the fresh

fruit element turns jammy and intensely concentrated while retaining some of the brambly quality that balances the ripeness so gracefully; a textbook on raspberry brandy bouquet. Entry highlights more of the ripe raspberry fruit than jamminess; the midpalate features solid, authentic raspberry flavor as much because of the high acidity. Ripe aftertaste works well. While I felt that the entry and midpalate phases didn't quite live up to the spectacular aroma, this remains a superlative raspberry brandy.
2007 Rating: ★★★★/Highly Recommended

Jacopo Poli Moscato Immature Grape Brandy (Italy); 40% abv, $55/375 ml.

Crystal clear and silvery; perfect purity. Mesmerizing perfume of orange blossom and honeysuckle waft from the port glass in leisurely waves; over time, the floral quality becomes more fruit-like in an orangy/citrusy/peachy/tangerine-like manner that's beguiling, lean, thrillingly aromatic, and deceptively potent and lasting; all one could desire from an unaged grape brandy. Entry is lusciously fruity, peachy, and orange marmalade-like; the midpalate stage soars with high-flying, gently sweet and ripe, fruit flavors that highlight the orange/citrus/tangerine component more than other tropical fruits (banana, casaba melon). Finishes with a riot of evolved fruit tastes and a succulent ripeness. Worth twice the price.
2007 Rating: ★★★★★/Highest Recommendation

Jacopo Poli Pere di Poli Pear Brandy (Italy); 40% abv, $51.

As clean and pure as rainwater. Scents of pear fruit, pear peel, and pear juice in the initial inhalations make it abundantly clear as to the source material and delightfully so; the pear-a-thon continues after further air contact with the welcome addition of delicate baking spice in the form of nutmeg; this is a genuinely sumptuous bouquet of the first rank. Entry is ripe, properly acidic, tart to off-dry, and balanced; the midpalate taste profile is pleasingly fruity, a touch baked, and a bit minerally, which pear flavor can be. Ends up medium-sweet and as much peel-like as fruit flesh-like. Elegant, true to the source, and concentrated.
2007 Rating: ★★★★/Highly Recommended

Jacopo Poli Po' Merlot di Poli Grappa (Italy); 40% abv, $38.

Rainwater clear and clean. Smells of musky/musty grape pomace in the initial nosings; then takes on a more focused and directed bouquet stance after seven minutes of aeration, becoming delightfully floral, summer garden-like, grapy, and minerally. Entry taste is ripe, sweet, grapy, and delicate; the midpalate taste profile is deliciously berry-like and ripe but not in the least cloying or sappy. Finishes elegantly, clean, and a touch drier than the midpalate. WOW.
2007 Rating: ★★★★/Highly Recommended

Jacopo Poli Po' Moscato di Poli Grappa (Italy); 40% abv, $34.

Mineral water clean and pure. Opening smells remind me of tropical fruits, especially guava, pineapple, and, most of all, banana; aeration releases a succulent baking spice note that mixes well with the tropical fruit component. Entry is minerally/chalky, pleasantly ripe, viscous in texture; the midpalate point is earthy, floral (since this is moscato, where has the floweriness been up to this point?), stony, and off-dry. Finishes gracefully, stony/minerally, and drier than the midpalate.
2007 Rating: ★★★★/Highly Recommended

Jacopo Poli Po' Pinot di Poli Grappa (Italy); 40% abv, $34.

Impeccably limpid and clear. First aromas include leather, candle wax, and textile/flax; further air contact unleashes a whole slew of intriguing earthy scents, from moss to grass to stone to damp soil. Entry is lusciously ripe and intensely grapy; the midpalate profile features the ripe grape element more than anything else and it works beautifully as the other tastes underpin the overriding grapiness, creating a sublime balance. Ends up keenly berry-like, medium-rich, satiny, and stone-like. My favorite of the Po' line.

2007 Rating: ★★★★/Highest Recommendation

Jacopo Poli Po' Traminer di Poli Grappa (Italy); 40% abv, $34.

Silvery clear; unblemished purity. The bit of elusive perfume that does expose itself after the pour reminds me of new cotton fabric or, better, compressed paper filter material; the delicacy of the aroma continues even following six more minutes in the glass as elements of paraffin and wax emerge. Entry is round, intensely floral (much like rose water), and off-dry; the midpalate is long, ripe, gently sweet, floral, and more than adequately acidic. Concludes on the richer side of the texture scale, lovely in its keen rose-like manner, and clean as a whistle.

2007 Rating: ★★★★/Highly Recommended

Jacopo Poli Sarpa di Poli Grappa (Italy); 40% abv, $29.

60% merlot/40% cabernet. Crystal clear; flawless purity. Smells of ripe grapes, grape harvest/grape must, and lead pencil in the initial whiffs after the pour; additional air contact stimulates added scents of baking spices, blackcurrants, jasmine, pepper, and paraffin; a clinic on proper grappa aromatics. Entry is crisp, tart, and intensely ripe in an overall red berry manner; the midpalate stage highlights the black grape fruit to the maximum concentration. Finishes elegantly, bittersweet to sweet, medium-weight in texture, seamless, totally integrated, perfect. Grappa doesn't come any finer.

2007 Rating: ★★★★★/Highest Recommendation

Jacopo Poli Sarpa Riserva di Poli Grappa (Italy); 40% abv, $37.

60% merlot/40% cabernet; aged in Allier 225-liter barriques for four years. Displays a bright golden flax/straw/silvery color; superb clarity. First sniffs discover unexpected and zesty aromas of green pepper, red pepper, and jalapeño pepper, all stacked together; swirling and aeration bring out woody/moderately resiny notes, as well as more subtle notes of parchment, coin, lead pencil, and paraffin. Entry is pleasingly oily, smooth, off-dry, and mildly peppery; the midpalate features battened down tastes of oak, vanilla, cream, cooking oil, and butter. Concludes clean, bittersweet, oily, with a trace of black pepper. My sole concern: it's devoid of fruit as the wood has come to completely dominate.

2007 Rating: ★★★/Highly Recommended

Jacopo Poli Torcolato Grape Brandy (Italy); 40% abv, $55/375 ml.

Rainwater clean and pewter in hue; unblemished clarity. Smells unappealingly of vinyl/plastic, shoe leather, and Styrofoam in the opening whiffs; further air contact time brings out viny/brambly scents that don't mesh with the plastic/textile aromas; one Poli bouquet that doesn't work for me. Entry features underwhelming flavors of wax/paraffin and fiber;

the midpalate, at least, sees a trace of fruitiness that's matched up with a mossy earthiness. Ends up moderately ripe, minimally grapy, tea-like, and austere. Simply lacks substance and charm. A misstep.

2007 Rating: ★★/Not Recommended

Jacopo Poli UvaViva Italiana di Poli Immature Grape Brandy (Italy); 40% abv, $34.

Flawlessly clean; translucent, colorless. The delicately sweet and ripe grapiness in the first whiffs is totally seductive; additional time in the glass brings about ethereal aromas of orange blossom, green melon, and peach stone. Entry is sweet, supple, and properly acidic; the midpalate point is accentuated by the earthy (flowers, grass) and fruity (orange peel, melon, white grapes) tastes that are seamlessly melded together in a showcase of integrated flavor. Ends gently sweet and delicately ripe. A textbook case of distillation understatement and finesse as created by a genius.

2007 Rating: ★★★★★/Highest Recommendation

Jacopo Poli Vespaiolo Grape Brandy (Italy); 40% abv, $55/375 ml.

Transparent; ideally pure. Not expressive at all in the initial sniffs; additional time in the glass and vigorous swirling fail to coax anything resembling a brandy aroma to appear; neutral, industrial, and disappointing. Entry shows far more animation than the mechanic/industrial distillate aroma as pleasing tastes of ripe grapes, raisins, marmalade, and even a touch of honey bring this brandy back from the brink of oblivion. Finishes elegantly, with ample viscosity, and a dried fruitiness that's pruny and bittersweet. Redeemed itself enough in the mouth and the aftertaste to merit three stars.

2007 Rating: ★★★/Recommended

KWV 10 Year Old Brandy (South Africa); 40% abv, $19.

Gorgeous amber/tawny hue; superb clarity. Smells of toasted almonds, toasted walnuts right out of the gate; after seven additional minutes of air contact, the bouquet adds white raisins, white peach, and marshmallow scents. Entry is semisweet, toffee-like, and more angular than round; the midpalate displays the toastiness of the first sniffs in the forms of pastry and toasted nuts. Concludes medium-weighted, semisweet, and better than average.

2007 Rating: ★★★/Recommended

La Botija Acholado Pisco (Peru); 41.5% abv, $16.

Clear as rain water. Highly perfumed right from the pour, the grapy nature of this pure brandy is enchanting and simple; contact with air stimulates subtle scents of grape pomace/pulp and freshly harvested grapes; a very pleasurable sniffing experience. In the mouth the very cleanness of the spirit impresses the taste buds at palate entry; the midpalate point features vibrant tastes of ripe grapes and, interestingly, cane sugar. The finish is soft, warming, and sweet. A delicious, textured, and intensely grapy pisco of the first rank.

2001 Rating: ★★★★/Highly Recommended

La Botija Italia Pisco (Peru); 41.5% abv, $17.

Some dark sediment spotted floating about in an otherwise clear appearance. The initial nosing passes detect an array of aromas from vegetable oil to cotton candy to popcorn to grape pomace to aniseed and that's just for openers; time in the glass smoothes out the rougher edges, leaving behind a biscuity, seed-like aroma that highlights caraway seed, cardboard, and allspice. The texture is like silk; in the mouth the palate entry is juicy, fruity, grapy, and nothing short of luscious; the midpalate is even more enjoyable as the creamy, grapy, and beautifully balanced flavor wraps around the tongue. The finish is lush, full-bodied, viscous, and remarkably fresh and vibrant. A great brandy and a great spirit.

2001 Rating: ★★★★★/Highest Recommendation

La Botija Quebranta Pisco (Peru); 41.5% abv, $16.

Translucent and pure. The opening nosing passes offer piquant, almost prickly aromas of fresh-off-the-still spirit, steamed white rice, and soy sauce; aeration encourages a slight odor of metal to mix with the spirity aroma; the bouquet's a little too industrial and oily for me. The flavor at palate entry is creamy and sweet, which surprised me; the midpalate point displays a sharply bitter note that tries to balance the ripe fruit but actually ends up clashing with it. The aftertaste is sweet, viscous, long, and amiable. Drinkable, but average.

2001 Rating: ★★/Not Recommended

Louis Dupré Napoleon VSOP French Brandy (France); 40% abv, $11.

Good medium amber color; insignificant debris spotted. The opening nosing passes detect a distant nuttiness; additional air contact unleashes more assertive scents of nougat, sautéed almonds, caramel, and oak. The palate entry is very sweet and sap-like; the midpalate stays the sweet, toffee candy course. The finish is medium long, sweet, and maple-like. No evidence of grapes or interior character; drinkable, almost like a liqueur, but as memorable and profound as a Steven Seagal movie; too "brandy by the numbers" to be taken seriously.

2002 Rating: ★★/Not Recommended

Maison Védrenne Burgundy Brandy (France); 45% abv, $90.

The autumnal gold/wheat harvest color shows far more floating debris than I like to see. The first whiffs detect pleasantly grapy/viney aromas; further air contact stimulates strangely compelling aromas of glue, gum, solvent, and marshmallow; I know the descriptors sound weird, but it's quite nice. The palate entry is intensely viny/leafy/vegetal and off-dry; at midpalate the flavor is remarkably sappy, green yet semisweet, and almost honeyed in a very mild way. Finishes clean, full-weighted, ripe, grapy, and satisfyingly rustic.

2006 Rating: ★★★/Recommended

Maison Védrenne Hospices de Beaune 1992 Eau-de-Vie de Marc (France); 45% abv, $100.

The harvest gold color is pretty and free of sediment. This intriguing perfume is as briny, salty, and pickled as it is grapy, pulpy, and musty in the first go-rounds; an additional seven minutes in the glass serve to bring out a concentrated stemminess that's almost chewy. The palate entry does not back away from the pickled quality found in the bouquet and as such the opening flavors are smoky and approach ripeness; at midpalate the taste profile detonates on the tongue, offering disparate yet somehow feasible flavors of soy bean, olive brine, green olive, ripe grapes, citric acid, and pine. Finishes lean, stringy, slightly hot, and incredibly tart and viny/leafy. Intense, unbridled, fiery marc. Possesses a completely different personality from the 1993 sibling.

2006 Rating: ★★★/Highly Recommended

Maison Védrenne Hospices de Beaune 1993 Eau-de-Vie de Marc (France); 45% abv, $100.

The hay/wheat field hue is burnished gold and pure. The pungent aroma in the opening nosings is intensely grapy and viny, astringent and pulpy; further aeration time does nothing to alter the direction of the bouquet, except to heighten the grape must intensity and add a touch of vinyl/plastic waxiness. The palate entry is stonily dry, cleansing, and acidic; at midpalate the acidic/minerally astringency gives way momentarily for a flash of ripe grapiness/pulpiness that's a pleasant respite from the mouth-puckering tartness. Finishes intensely grapy and musty, verging suddenly on being ripe and even raisiny. Now, this is marc.
2006 Rating: ★★★★/Highly Recommended

Maison Védrenne Très Vieux Marc de Bourgogne Égrappé (France); 45% abv, $72.

Made only from pinot noir grapes. The bright golden straw/pine sap color is gorgeous; perfect purity. There's a lovely marriage of ripe mustiness, prickly spirit, and tart acid in the initial sniffs; another six minutes of exposure to air stimulate an elegant vanilla-like oakiness that nicely complements the fruit, spirit, and natural acids; oddly, in the very tail end of the nosing stage I pick up an incongruous smell of rubber inner tube that nearly ruins the nosing stage. The palate entry is gently sweet and ripe; at midpalate the taste profile turns mildly oaky and honeyed. The aftertaste is full, smooth, satiny, and pleasingly tart. Weird, but nice enough for a recommendation. Not in the league as the two from the Hospices de Beaune, however.
2006 Rating: ★★★/Recommended

Mazzetti d'Altavilla Grappa di Arneis (Italy); 40.2% abv, $95.

Limpid, clear as rainwater; impeccably pure. The opening aroma is delicate, minerally, and only slightly floral; with aeration, the aroma expands into a bouquet in the second sniffing as a rich grapiness takes the helm; the third whiff exposes a stony/slate-like quality while the fourth and final nosing pass adds grape seed and must; not a standout grappa bouquet by any means. The palate entry is lean and sweet; the midpalate stage turns soft, ripe, grapy, and a touch candied. The finish is clean, intensely flowery, concentrated, and juicy sweet. Better than average and certainly recommendable.
2000 Rating: ★★★/Recommended

Mazzetti d'Altavilla Grappa di Nebbiolo da Barolo (Italy); 43% abv, $30.

Pale yellow/lemon juice hue; excellent purity. The initial nosings pick up intensely musty, ripe, and fruity pomace aromas; six more minutes of aeration release further succulent fruit notes including pear, banana, and peach. The palate entry is ripe and sweet, with a slight hint of spirity heat; by the midpalate the tastes of concentrated fruit, especially pears, white raisins, and yellow plums, take charge. The finish is full, fruity, moderately sweet, and very long. A superbly satisfying grappa experience from start to finish.
2002 Rating: ★★★★/Highly Recommended

Mendiola Pisco Select Peruvian Acholado Grape Brandy (Peru); 40% abv, $26.

Spotlessly clean and translucent. Nearly identical to the Barsol Acholado (are these the same spirits dressed up in different clothes?), the initial nosings unearth very little other than a delicate ripe grape and blueberry-like aroma; later inhalations find (almost exactly like the

Barsol) that the blueberry quality emerges significantly after aeration. The palate entry is fine, vinous, and off-dry; at midpalate the taste of ripe grapes dominates the flavor phase. Ends up light, off-dry to bitter, and appropriately fruity.
2005 Rating: ★★★/Recommended

Mendiola Pisco Select Peruvian Italia Grape Brandy (Peru); 40% abv, $26.
Textbook clarity and purity. The opening burst of aroma is fruity, if nondescript; then after another six minutes of air contact, the bouquet turns melony and banana-like. The palate entry is smooth, satiny, and properly fruity; at midpalate the taste goes sweeter than the entry and considerably more melon-like, but there's a flash of spirity heat that wasn't present in the Barsol Italia. That said, it finishes spirity, fruity, and refreshing.
2005 Rating: ★★★/Recommended

Mendiola Pisco Select Peruvian Quebranta Grape Brandy (Peru); 40% abv, $26.
Ideal appearance, clear and impeccably clean. The opening nosing passes are confronted with a low-key aroma that's borderline sweet/sour; further time in the glass brings out a mineral/slate quality that accents the fruit component nicely. The palate entry is long, lean, and vinous; at midpalate the mineral quality dominates the fruit and acidity. Ends up nicely with all the elements in harmony. Took me a while, but I really came around to it.
2005 Rating: ★★★★/Highly Recommended

Mendiola Pisco Select Peruvian Torontel Grape Brandy (Peru); 40% abv, $26.
Wonderfully clean appearance. The first nosings detect smoke that's more electrical than tobacco- or wood-like; more air contact turns the smoke into sulphur/burnt matchstick and seed/bean/pod, with nary a hint of grapes/fruit. The palate entry is firm, lean, and just a shade grapy; at midpalate the taste profile goes more towards earthy, woodsy, resiny/pod-like flavors. The finish which is seedy/pulpy attempts a redemption but just isn't enough to bring this pisco over the finish line with a recommendation.
2005 Rating: ★★/Not Recommended

Moletto Distillato d'Uva Immature Brandy (Italy); 40% abv, $29.
Limpid, with very slight slivers of sediment. The fresh grapy aroma is ripe, viny and just a delicate touch sweet; time in the glass reveals a slightly astringent, pear-like quality that reminds me of prosecco, the lightly fizzy wine made in northeast Italy; might this be made from the prosecco di conegliano grape type? Since the label doesn't identify the grape, I have to guess, guided by my nose. The palate entry displays far more grapy, peary, almost spicy ripeness than the bouquet; at midpalate the astringency noted in the aerated bouquet returns in the form of a refreshing, palate cleansing taste of pomace, grape skins, pulp, and light honey. Turns a bit citrusy in the finish. The teasing fragrance and the bouncy, fruity flavor win the day. Very nice aperitif-style brandy; serve it slightly chilled at between 55 to 60 degrees Fahrenheit.
2003 Rating: ★★★★/Highly Recommended

Nonino Cru Grappa di Monovitigno Picolit Colli Orientali del Friuli (Italy); 50% abv, $156.
Perfectly pure and clean, void of color. This aroma is immediately developed and stately, showing hints of delicate grapy perfume; the middle stage nosing passes offer elegant, but

deceptively powerful aromas of grapes, tropical fruit (pineapple especially), and pomace; the last sniffing displays the layered, concentrated, and focused aromatic features of a great grappa as the grapiness harmonizes with the alcohol and acid; a textbook grappa aroma that's different than anything I've experienced. While the bouquet is lovely, the flavor phase is a whole other universe of style and intensity; the palate entry is round, full-bodied, and textured with sweet, subtle ripe grape, and cocoa-like flavors; the midpalate is all about the viscous texture and ripe, almost jam-like, grapiness. The finish shows a bit of spirity fire; a truly remarkable spirit. Bravo.
2001 Rating: ★★★★★/Highest Recommendation

Nonino Cru Grappa di Monovitigno Verduzzo dei Colli Friulani (Italy); 45% abv, $95.

Absolutely clean and pure and clear as mineral water. The nose right after the bottle opening is reluctant to emerge, giving off a slightly stale/rubbery scent; the aroma doesn't seem to want to come out and play even by the middle stage nosing passes and after vigorous swirling and coaxing; the final pass sees just a hint of grapy pomace and dried fruit notes plus a curious waxiness; not the best Nonino bouquet. Much more expressive on the palate than in the nasal cavity; the palate entry is stony dry; then at midpalate the grapy, ripe, sweet flavor comes alive in seductive waves; the spirit doesn't get in the way of the flavor. The aftertaste is very long, keenly fruity/grapy, sweet but not overly so, and far more developed than the aroma. A well-made grappa that unfortunately gets off to a painfully deliberate start, but then picks up the pace once it gets in the mouth.
2001 Rating: ★★★/Recommended

Nonino Gioiello Nonino Distillato di Miele di Agrumi (Italy); 37% abv, $82.

Impeccably pure and clear as rain water. The first sniffs are pungent, stunningly citrus rind-like, moderately waxy, and zesty; seven more minutes in the glass affords the room needed for the bouquet to expand to include dazzling, agile scents of casaba melon, carnauba, light honey, and jasmine; like no spirit bouquet I've ever evaluated. The palate entry is balanced between fruit, acid, and honey flavor; the flavor shines brilliantly at midpalate as all the components unite for a harmonious grappa taste experience. The aftertaste is brief, fruity, and only moderately sweet. Easily one of the ten greatest spirits I've had the honor of knowing in the last five years.
2003 Rating: ★★★★★/Highest Recommendation

Nonino Gioiello Nonino Distillato di Miele di Castagno (Italy); 37% abv, $82.

Absolutely clear and spotless in appearance. The subtle nose after the pour is remarkably fresh, floral, and only slightly honey-like and it reminds me most of honeysuckle; further aeration stimulates incredibly seductive fragrances of ripe grapes still on the vine, very light honey, grape jam, and orange blossom; a magical aromatic ride. The palate entry is intensely wax-like, but delicate and softly sweet; at midpalate there's a flash of spirity warmth on the tongue. Then the feather-light tastes of honey and beeswax take command through the ethereal finish. Delicious, weightless, succulent, unusual enjoyment.
2003 Rating: ★★★★/Highly Recommended

Nonino Grappa il Chardonnay (Italy); 43% abv, $35.

Shows the yellow/gold color of a mature chardonnay; as pure as one could hope for. This nose is endowed and almost biscuity in the initial nosing pass; with time in the glass,

the aroma turns into a tangy, slightly piquant bouquet that adds a kind of desert cactus/dry/minerally scent that's delightfully different; in the last whiff, the dryness accelerates away from the grapiness/pulpiness and towards the minerally/stony/herbal quality; an atypical grappa bouquet that I find both intriguing and compelling. The palate entry is dry and minerally; the midpalate displays traces of herbs and stone, but the larger portion of taste goes to the grape pomace. The finish is long, sweeter than the midpalate, and tangy. Very good and recommendable, but not my favorite Nonino.
2001 Rating: ★★★/Recommended

Nonino Grappa il Merlot (Italy); 43% abv, $35.

Clear and pure in the glass. Now, here's a fourth-gear grappa aroma that features the undeniably pungent, pencil eraser perfume of grape pomace; the middle stage passes unearth additional scents of rose petals and cherry stones; the final sniffing, following over seven minutes of exposure to air, finds the aromatic elements in harmony; what's so attractive is the freshness of this bouquet. The palate entry is dry and grapy, then at midpalate the flavor turns succulently sweet and stunningly ripe and compelling. The aftertaste is seemingly infinite, never harsh, grapy, and concentrated. A svelte, sinewy grappa which is more elegant than powerful, but that's not to say that there isn't some fire in the hole.
2001 Rating: ★★★★/Highly Recommended

Nonino Quintessentia Amaro (Italy); 35% abv, $25.

The brilliant topaz/brown hue is akin to an oloroso or lighter cream sherry; ideal purity. The opening nosing pass is like an open market for mountain herbs, flowers, and spices; the middle stage passes offer hints of quinine, moss, caramel, rose petal, and cassia bark; the final pass is piquant and dry as the aromas swell with aeration in the glass, most notably rhubarb and litchi nuts; this is a veritable apothecary of earthy smells. The palate entry is surprisingly sweet and lithe on the tip of the tongue; the midpalate explodes with exotic herbal/rooty/floral tastes including dried fruit, fruit peel, quinine, cassia bark, and fruit stone. The finish is succulent, long, and intensely herbal and luscious.
2001 Rating: ★★★★/Highly Recommended

Nonino Ue (Italy); 43% abv, $43.

Rain water clean and pure. The ripe, fresh-picked, intensely grapy aroma enchants the olfactory sense from the very first moment of nosing; with time in the glass, the aroma transforms into a full-fledged bouquet that features fresh garden flowers, background charcoal, and a concentrated, almost jammy, grapiness; the final nosing pass, following eight minutes of aeration, focuses on the leafy/viney aspects of the grapes; in short, this is a dazzlingly fresh, nimble, and inviting perfume that I find irresistible. Absolutely no fire on the tongue at palate entry, just sweet grapiness; the midpalate is politely sweet and fruity with just a quick flash of embers warmth at the back of the tongue. The aftertaste is long, fruity, sweet in a ripe manner, and still incredibly agile and light, but polished and structurally sound. I can't think of a better starting point for anyone who wants to get to know grappa; delicious.
2001 Rating: ★★★★/Highly Recommended

Nonino Ue di Monovitigno il Fragolino (Italy); 38% abv, $114.

The bright, clean appearance is impeccably pure. This nose is more idiosyncratic than the standard Ue bottling and reminds me slightly of cherry stones; with air exposure, the cherry stone fades, leaving behind exotic, almost musty, aromatic notes of crushed violets in one's school yearbook and grape preserves; after a full eight minutes in the glass, the nose evolves into a jammy, delicately perfumed bouquet that's more dry than sweet; an understated gem. The palate entry is sublimely sweet and juicy, then at midpalate the taste turns concentrated and richly grapy. The finish is long, grapy, and ripe. While there doesn't exist endless layers of aroma or flavor in this mannered ue, the sheer simplicity and straightforward nature of it is immensely appealing; for anyone who still thinks that all grappa is "firewater", savor this exquisitely balanced beauty.

2001 Rating: ★★★★/Highly Recommended

Piave Grappa Selezione Cuore (Italy); 40% abv, $28.
    Silvery clear and flawlessly pure. The initial whiffs detect a strong musty/mushroomy aroma that, after aeration, turns remarkably rubbery, like the soles of new sneakers. Significantly more attractive in the mouth than in the nose; the palate entry is grapy, intense and semisweet; at midpalate the taste profile turns seed-like, bittersweet and very dried fruit-like (prunes? black raisins?). Ends up off-dry, bitter and musty. Not a top tier grappa, but better than average.

2004 Rating: ★★★/Recommended

Poyer & Sandri Acquavite di Ciliege Cherry Brandy (Italy); 45.5% abv, $33.
    Crystalline, with insignificant sediment. The initial nosing passes pick up fresh but not over-ripe scents of cherries and red fruit; more time in the glass sees the aroma mellow and soften; an elegant cherry eau-de-vie perfume. The palate entry is sweet, ripe, almost candied but fresh and firm; by midpalate there's a sense of moderate spirity heat on the tongue but that feature does not obstruct the fine fruit flavor that's sweet and plump. It finishes with a bit more just-manageable fire at the start of the aftertaste but it's the chocolate cherry profile that's really beguiling and on-the-money. Less than perfect due to the occasions of spirity heat, but very savory and easily recommendable.

2002 Rating: ★★★/Recommended

Poyer & Sandri Acquavite di Mele Cotogne Quince Brandy (Italy); 45.5% abv, $33.
    Clear, minor sediment. This nose is discreet and subtle, showing very little in the way of fruit or spirit in the initial three minute nosing span; aeration stirs some evidence of fruit, but the impression is mild. It's obvious from the palate entry that this eau-de-vie is all about taste as the first flavors of quince and guava are firm and assertive without being raw or flammable; the midpalate stage displays a touch of fire, but the emphasis is squarely on the interplay of quince and tropical fruit flavors. It finishes politely yet solidly in a fresh fruit flurry of taste that stays long on the tongue. I love it.

2002 Rating: ★★★★/Highly Recommended

Poyer & Sandri Acquavite di Prugne Prune Brandy (Italy); 45.5% abv, $33.
    Clear but with some widely-spaced white-gray sediment. The initial nosing pass detects vivacious, incredibly fresh, ambrosial scents of dark plum and wax; time in the glass allows the bouquet to develop a sweet succulence that is ripe and remarkably true to the fruit source; a dazzling aromatic display. The palate entry is keenly fresh, moderately hot but brimming with plummy flavor; by midpalate the spirity fire dies down enough for the rich plum taste to take command. The finish is concentrated, plummy, jammy, and long; except for the three-

alarm heat at palate entry which singes the taste buds. This is an explosive and aggressive but exciting eau-de-vie that deserves a close look.

2002 Rating: ★★★★/Highly Recommended

Poyer & Sandri Acquavite di Uva Fragolino Immature Grape Brandy (Italy); 45.5% abv, $33.

Limpid, but with way too much minuscule sediment that's actually cloudy. The opening bouquet is softly fruity but rather stale and metallic; aeration doesn't help this anemic aroma as it turns to wet fabric, damp cardboard, and mushrooms for its highlights; there's even distant echoes of cotton candy and cork; a weird and unpleasant nose. Shows some improvement once in the mouth as ripe and sweet tastes of white raisins and grapes nearly redeem the problems present in the bouquet; nice midpalate range of sweet, fruity flavors, but not concentrated or jammy. The aftertaste is medium-long, pleasantly sweet, and lean. The woolly/doggy bouquet is a real flaw but the flavor and finish together are fine enough to make this eau-de-vie drinkably ordinary.

2002 Rating: ★★/Not Recommended

Poyer & Sandri Acquavite Divino Brandy (Italy); 44.5% abv, $45.

This brandy is ten years old according to the data sent by the importer. Harvest gold hue, too much black floating debris which instantly spoils the visual impact of the otherwise lovely color. The nose displays a delightful toasty perfume in the opening stages; then with time it settles down into a sweet, lightly caramelized but not candied or honeyed bouquet which stresses softness and nuance rather than grit or robustness; definitely more pronounced and expressive in the mouth than in the nose. The entry is dry to off-dry and mildly nutty; the midpalate is more firmly caramel-like, offering pleasant but hardly deep or profound tastes of tea leaves, light toffee, and nougat. The finish is brief, off-dry, and simple. Not a complex brandy in the tradition of either cognac or armagnac, but certainly a brandy of virtue.

2002 Rating: ★★★/Recommended

Poyer & Sandri Grappa di Moscato Rosa (Italy); 47.5% abv, $55.

Limpid, but showing some chunky debris. The initial nosing passes after the pour find a nice, if reluctant, muscat/orange blossom scent; little seems to change after additional aeration time as the typical muscat/orange blossom fragrance stays the middle-of-the-road course in terms of intensity; what a shame since of all grapes muscat should show a full-throttle bouquet that keeps expanding and deepening—not so here—it's stuck in second gear. The palate entry is tart, astringent, and pleasantly orangy/citrusy; the midpalate is definitely its best stage as the tart orange pulp/orange peel taste starts to sweeten. The finish is off-dry to sweet, pulpy, and long. Were the anemic bouquet and sloppy appearance off-set by the better than average midpalate and pleasant aftertaste? No, they just didn't display enough quality to overcome the flaws.

2002 Rating: ★★/Not Recommended

Poyer & Sandri Grappa di Muller-Thurgau (Italy); 47.5% abv, $28.

Crystalline and spotless appearance. The aromatic nose is fruity, peel-like, and slightly tart in the initial nosing passes after the pour; subsequent sniffings reveal appetizing scents

of mildly sweet fruit, cardboard, pencil eraser, and pomace; it's a mild-mannered, lightly musty bouquet that reflects the inherently polite nature of the grape source. The palate entry is tart to off-dry, gently fruity, and focused; at midpalate the flavor profile gets its footing, displaying lovely, evolved tastes of ripe grapes, pears, and gum, all without incinerating the bejesus out of the taste buds. Finishes elegantly, with finely melded flavors of grapes, rubber, refined sugar, and pear peel. A delight.
2002 Rating: ★★★/Recommended

Poyer & Sandri Grappa di Rosso Faye (Italy); 47.5% abv, $28.
Translucent, but marred by clouds of unsightly sediment, both infinitesimal and chunk variety. The aroma at the pour is lively and delicately fruity; time in the glass stirs aromas of dried violets, gum, refined sugar, and ripe grapes; not a powerhouse bouquet but a fey, gently fragrant presence. Starts out firm but lean at palate entry, then at midpalate a searing, spirity burn torches the tongue until the finish when the flavors of ripe grapes, hard candy, and fruit peel emerge from beneath the blanket of spirity fire. An old-fashioned scorch-and-burn grappa style that's fine for old hands but difficult for newcomers. In the end, the unclean, blemished appearance, and high-octane, flammable midpalate phase work against it in my scoring; I reluctantly rate it two stars because underneath the flaws I can sense the potential for a good to very good spirit; three-word message to distillers Pojer Mario and Sandri Fiorentino: filter, filter, filter.
2002 Rating: ★★/Not Recommended

Poyer & Sandri Grappa di Sauvignon (Italy); 47.5% abv, $28.
Once again, the otherwise crystal appearance is ruined by black and gray chunks of god knows what. The nose is a bit mute at the outset; aeration brings out a slightly briny/saline quality that's odd for a grappa; basically, even after nearly ten minutes, this is a go-nowhere, do-nothing bouquet that offers very little in terms of aromatic depth or expression. The lackluster character of the aroma regrettably gets transferred to the palate entry; by midpalate there's evidence of some taste expansion, even if it's rather hollow. The moderately pleasant aftertaste is medium-long, somewhat sweet, ripe, and grapy, but frankly it's too little, too late for me. This is an under-developed spirit that comes off as though it was just thrown together as an after-thought.
2002 Rating: ★/Not Recommended

Poyer & Sandri Grappa di Schiava (Italy); 47.5% abv, $28.
Clear, but with what I've come to view as the usual purity problem of this distiller—too much sediment. The opening nose is mildly pleasing, grapy, and pulpy; aeration seems to channel the fruity/stemmy/pulpy aromas to form something of a mineral- and stone-like bouquet. The palate entry is sharp, tart, and razor-edged, offering less in the way of fruit flavor and more in the way of raw spirit-off-the-still; the midpalate phase doesn't see any improvement whatsoever as the taste is one-note, superficial harsh spirit. The finish is long, searing, and dull. Awkward and amateurish distilling.
2002 Rating: ★/Not Recommended

Raynal 10 Year Old Premium French Brandy (France); 40% abv, $15.

The deep copper/bay/auburn color displays perfect purity. The nutty/paraffin-like aroma impresses the olfactory sense right off the crack of the bat; aeration serves to change the direction of the bouquet slightly as it becomes more like dried fruit, brown rice, soy, and ginger; there are many layers to this invigorating aroma. The palate entry is lip-smacking sweet, bordering on being too sweet and sap-like, for me; at midpalate the intense core sweetness turns nutty/nougaty and maple-like. Finishes sweet, medium-to-thick in texture, and caramel-like. This brandy is easily recommendable but flirts with being a touch over-the-top on the sweetness/gooey texture front. I purposely sampled it next to the Raynal 5 Year Old (★★★★) and still preferred the younger one due to its lovely balance. That said, this is still a very nice brandy at a remarkable price.

2004 Rating: ★★★/Recommended

Razzouk Arak Distilled Grape Juice Flavored with Anis (Lebanon); 50% abv, $25.

Clear as rainwater; absolutely pure. The compelling first aromas emit intriguingly incongruous scents of rubber inner tube and unlighted charcoal; aeration encourages an aromatic expansion, including hints of fennel, cardboard, and steel wool; so weird that I can't wait to taste it just to see where it's heading. The initial burst at palate entry is all alcohol (it is 100-proof, don't forget), then at midpalate there's seed-like and dry-to-astringent evidence of aniseed and very faint licorice. The aftertaste is long, spirity, fiery, and yet strangely pleasant. Not for an American audience because of the concentrated bitterness and the elevated alcohol, but an interesting experience all the same.

2005 Rating: ★★★/Recommended

Rubi VSOP (France); 40% abv, $15.

The rusty/henna color is to die for; near flawless clarity; just a jaw-droppingly exquisite appearance. The opening aroma is pruny, ripe, floral (rose), and grapy; following another seven minute interval, the bouquet turns leathery and spicy (baking spices such as nutmeg, clove, cinnamon). The palate entry displays succulent tastes of melon, dried fruit, nuts, and pear; the midpalate point is focused, ripe, slightly woody, and definitely spicy. Finishes clean smooth, and elegant.

2007 Rating: ★★★/Recommended

Suvoborska Premium Slivowitz Natural Plum Brandy (Yugoslavia); 45% abv, $28.

Bright yellow hue; perfect purity. The opening sniffings right after the pour find zesty, mildly spiced aromas of yellow plums and chrysanthemum; later whiffs following six minutes of further exposure in the glass detect nectarine peel, slate, and minerals; what happened to the delightful yellow plum fragrance? The palate entry is keenly tart, almost astringent in its high acid levels, but refreshing, dry, and clean; by the midpalate point softly ripe, off-dry, and moderately ripe tastes of plum and bittersweet cocoa paste make for intriguing tasting. The aftertaste is bittersweet, bordering on austere, a trace nutty, and cleansing. Well-made, razor sharp, and engaging.

2002 Rating: ★★★/Recommended

T&W Grappa Di Muscatto (USA); 40% abv, $27.

Ideal transparency; pristine silvery appearance. The delightful opening aromas are ripe, juicy, grapy, and remind me of orange blossoms; later sniffs after further aeration bolster, but don't expand on, the aromatic impressions enjoyed in the first two minutes of inhaling. The palate entry is viny/leafy more than grapy/juicy and is therefore a touch too astringent; by the midpalate stage the muscat grapiness reemerges, offering simple tastes of orange rind and grapes that go far enough to redeem the raw entry. The aftertaste is plump, juicy, and semisweet. It works in its simplicity.

2006 Rating: ★★★/Recommended

Tacama Demonio de los Andes Pisco de Ica (Peru); 44% abv, $17.

Limpid, silvery clear, and pure. The pleasing nose is assertively dry and sooty in the initial nosing pass; in the second aromatic go-round I find nuances of pomace and bittersweet cocoa; following eight minutes of air contact, the grapy/pomace scent becomes intensely perfume-like and dominant; in the fourth and final sniffing, I detect a piquant, peppery quality that adds a counterpoint to the bittersweet pomace scent; I seriously like this concentrated, demanding bouquet. The palate entry is bitter in a dark cocoa/dark chocolate manner; the midpalate flavor offers tastes of pomace, prickly spirit, and black pepper. The finish is zesty enough to set the tongue tingling and is long, cleansing, and pomace-like. A very nice pisco indeed.

2000 Rating: ★★★★/Highly Recommended

Tacama Pisco Puro (Peru); 44% abv, $20.

Perfectly clean and as clear as mineral water. This nose is slightly more fabric/wet cotton-like in the first nosing pass after the pour; the second sniffing adds little other than a dry stone scent of slate/mineral; the third whiff, after seven minutes of aeration, finally introduces a subtle, mildly ripe and sweet scent of pomace; the fourth and last nosing pass expands to include background notes of bittersweet chocolate and ripe grapes. The palate entry is fuller than the Demonio and sweeter; by midpalate the sweetness becomes candy-like and intensely cocoa-like. The finish is luscious, rich, and long.

2000 Rating: ★★★★/Highly Recommended

Vendome Platinum VSOP Brandy (France); 40% abv, $13.

Very pretty medium amber/honey color; superb purity. The intriguing nose right after the pour emits expressive notes of light toffee, nougat, and grain-like (read: blended Scotch-like) sweetness; six minutes into further aeration, the bouquet turns fruity, especially apples, pears, cherries, and peaches. The palate entry is cocoa-like and smooth; at midpalate the flavor profile turns caramel- and toffee-like. The finish is long, sweet, satiny, and nutty. This uncomplicated brandy is well-made and easy to quaff.

2004 Rating: ★★★/Recommended

Viejo Tonel Pisco Acholado (Peru); 42% abv, $12.

Clear as rain water; unblemished purity. The enchanting first aroma is highly floral, pronounced, and fresh, with faint traces of citrus rind; later sniffings focus more on the flowery, fruity/grapy aspects. The palate entry is sweet, succulent, and balanced; at midpalate

the fruit/alcohol/acid balance is tight and integrated as sweet, grapy tastes bedazzle the taste buds. Concludes as sweet and elegant as it began. A major pisco find.
2005 Rating: ★★★★/Highly Recommended

Viejo Tonel Pisco Italia (Peru); 42% abv, $12.
Crystal clear and silvery pure appearance. The initial whiffs discover delicate, grappa-like scents of grape must, grape skin, and seeds; seven more minutes of air contact don't seem to open up the bouquet to any further degree. The palate entry is firm, semisweet, and concentrated; at midpalate the grapy flavor profile goes into passing gear as the acid element overshadows the fruit. Finishes in a stately manner, with the fruit returning to complement the acid and alcohol. Nice job.
2005 Rating: ★★★/Recommended

Viejo Tonel Pisco Mosto Verde (Peru); 42% abv, $12.
Flawless clarity and translucence. The first nosing passes detect faint hints of seeds, grape must, and green pepper; aeration has no impact upon this bouquet, as it remains steady in its seed/pomace/pepper mode. The palate entry is semisweet, delightfully grapy/musty, and nicely acidic/crisp; at midpalate the flavor profile edges towards the acid/crispness more than the grapiness/pomace. Concludes acidic, refreshing, and cleansing.
2005 Rating: ★★★/Recommended

Viejo Tonel Pisco Puro (Peru); 42% abv, $12.
Limpid and flawless appearance. The first whiffs pick up dry, seed-like aromas; six more minutes of air contact stimulate a subtle beaniness and a buttery quality. The palate entry is semisweet to bittersweet, beany, seedy, and full; at midpalate the taste profile stays the bean/seed course, leaving little room for fruit/grape. Ends up semidry, bean-like, and like very dark chocolate.
2005 Rating: ★★★/Recommended

Viejo Tonel Pisco Torontel (Peru); 42% abv, $12.
Ideal clarity, silvery and pure. The opening passes unearth a seductive floral/juniper/cedar aroma that entices the olfactory sense; further aeration turns the aroma into a perfumey bouquet that features far more of the floral side than the fruit/grape/pomace side of the base material. The palate entry is peppery, grapy, musty, and delicious; at midpalate the taste profile accentuates the pomace. Finishes refreshingly acidic, grapy, flowery, and musty. Lovely, understated, and savory.
2005 Rating: ★★★★/Highly Recommended

Villa Zarri Acquavitae di Vino Immature Chardonnay Brandy (Italy); 43% abv, $60.
Chardonnay brandy made from grapes grown in the Emilia-Romagna and Veneto grape growing regions. Very good clarity; silvery and transparent. The first aromatic impressions are of great delicacy; aeration time stirs only distant background notes of grape pomace/grape skins and a light herbaceousness. This elegant brandy gets cooking in the mouth at palate entry as the initial tastes are dry to off-dry and intensely grapy/plummy; at midpalate the flavor profile expands to add seductive tastes of cocoa butter, wood resin, paraffin, palm oil,

and grape jam. Concludes warm, chewy, grapy, and elegant. A dazzling display of power and finesse, all wrapped up in one package.

2005 Rating: ★★★★/Highly Recommended

Villa Zarri Acquavitae di Vino Trebbiano dei Collio Tosco-Romagnoli 10 Year Old Italian Brandy (Italy); 44% abv, $80.

An extra aged trebbiano brandy. Bright harvest amber/bronze color; flawless purity. The opening scents are of tobacco leaf, walnut butter, and oak; later sniffings following aeration find new aromas of ginger, cinnamon, and pipe tobacco. The palate entry is firm, oily, buttery, and semisweet; at midpalate the taste stays the course of oil/butter, adding delicious notes of vanilla and an early-budding rancio/blue cheese quality. Finishes classy, spirity warm, woody, and elegant.

2005 Rating: ★★★★/Highly Recommended

Zachlawi Fig Arak (USA); 40% abv, $38.

Deep straw/dusty gold color; some sediment seen floating about. The opening odor is keenly fig-like and a touch like plastic/vinyl sheeting; further time in the glass brings about added scents of pumpkin seed, macadamia nut, and floor wax. Entry is moderately sweet, intensely figgy and therefore minerally and bitter; at midpalate the fruit element of the fig comes more to the forefront, leaving behind much of the mineral/metallic quality. Concludes bittersweet, tangy, and piquant.

2007 Rating: ★★★/Recommended

Zachlawi Traditional Arak (USA); 40% abv, $38.

Silver color; average to good clarity. Smells deeply of aniseed and licorice right out of the gate; aeration introduces hints of mint, smoke, and rubber tire, but the aniseed maintains its hold. Entry is acutely anise-like, herbal, and mildly sweet; at midpalate there's a bit of gunmetal and minerals, but then in the finish the anise turns more licorice-like and pleasantly candied. Even though I'm not an avid fan of anything made with aniseed, I liked this well-made, not overly sweet arak.

2007 Rating: ★★★/Recommended

Brandy - USA

Once Prohibition was repealed in 1933, brandy production kicked into high gear in the western US, taking full advantage of the bounty of California's Central Valley. After World War II, cheap, big-volume brandy production catapulted forward creating a sweet style of everyday brandy that, in its own affable way, was palatable. Then, in the 1980s, a handful of artisanal distillers burst onto the scene, producing pot still, oak-aged, white collar brandies that forever changed the American brandy lanscape. Today, the US is a leading producer of fine, high-end brandies, eaux-de-vie, and grappas.

American Alembic (pot still) Brandy: High quality, small production, pot still fruit and grape brandies, vodkas, gins, rums, and whiskeys made by micro-producers, such as Germain-Robin, St. George Spirits, Clear Creek Distillery, Domaine Charbay, Jepson, Templeton Rye Distillery, Koenig Distillery, Rogue Distillery, Bonny Doon, and Prichard's Distillery.

American Brandy (continuous still): Big production distillers, like Gallo, Christian Brothers, make the lion's share of American brandy in enormous volumes. Sometimes they are surprisingly good.

Bierschnapps: Grain-based, distilled beers that in style land somewhere between immature whiskey and matured, fruit-based brandy.

At the moment, I'm not aware of any official classifications for American brandies, such as VS, VSOP, etc., even though some brandies are labeled as such.

American Fruits Pear Brandy (USA); 40% abv, $29/375 ml.

Too many bubbles that linger in the core before finally rising to the surface and dissipating; I know it's harmless but average, unsuspecting consumers might not. The opening aroma knocks me off my feet so divinely ripe and genuinely pear-like is it; following another seven minutes of air contact, the latter bouquet reinforces all the positives found in the first two minutes as the ripe pear fragrance dazzles the olfactory sense. The palate entry is too metallic and biting and, as such, is completely out of step with the lovely aroma; by the midpalate stage the astringency turns more severe and overshadows the fresh pear virtues. Unfortunately ends up on a nickel/coin-like note that quashes all the good qualities of the bouquet stage. There's authentic promise here, but this effort fails to get a recommendation.

2007 Rating: ★★/Not Recommended

Apple-Ation Eau-de-Vie de Pomme Dutton Ranch Sonoma County Bottle No. 60/1800 (USA); 40% abv, $35/375 ml.

The pale gold color shows some minor sediment and oiliness. The first nosing passes pick up odd notes of cotton, linen, and parchment, but nothing that resembles apples, at least to me; further air contact time of seven minutes brings out an acute waxiness (wax paper) that's not very pleasant. The palate entry is curiously more baked and burnt than fruity; the midpalate stage features a touch of buttery spirit that unfortunately is overshadowed by the excessive acidity and the burnt pastry/burnt toast character. Considering my Sonoma County background, it's not easy giving this product a poor rating. I urge the producer to pick up a bottle of Oregon-based Steve McCarthy's legendary Clear Creek Distillery Eau-de-Vie de Pomme Apple Brandy, which is not only the American benchmark, but one of the world's foremost fruit brandies of any kind.

2007 Rating: ★/Not Recommended

Aqua Perfecta Pear Eau-de-Vie (USA); 40% abv, $40.

Ideally clear as mineral water; impeccably pure. Opening scent reminds me of baked pear pastry because of the wonderful fruit and yeast/dough aromas; the pear perfume settles down a bit after further aeration, leaving behind alluring odors of pear peel and bread. Entry is intensely pear flesh-like, fresh, and genuine; the midpalate introduces a ripe sweetness that's countered by a rise in the acidity, making for a succulence that's keenly attractive, clean, and authentic. Finishes ripe yet austere, fruity yet minerally, and like liquid silk. Outstanding distilling.

2007 Rating: ★★★★★/Highest Recommendation

Christian Brothers Grand Reserve VSOP (USA); 40% abv, $12.

The autumnal color is medium amber/burnished gold; excellent purity. The opening aroma emits ripe fruit scents, specifically red berry, cherry and banana; the middle stage nosing passes add touches of marshmallow, light toffee, and nectarine; the fourth and last sniffing, following eight minutes of air contact, remains focused on fruit rather than wood; an undemanding, connect-the-dots brandy bouquet that's easy and benignly fruity. The palate entry is semisweet, medium bodied, and candied; the midpalate stage is mildly toasty and caramelized. The finish is gently sweet, candied, and very long. Let's be frank, at this price level you can't expect a profound brandy experience; this straightforward, unexceptional brandy delivers adequate satisfaction; it is the affable equal of Paul Masson Grande Amber (★★) and the better of E&J VSOP (★).

2001 Rating: ★★/Not Recommended

Christian Brothers Rare Reserve XO (USA); 40% abv, $16.

Topaz is the color; perfect purity. The bouquet after the pour is more sophisticated and less sweet than the CB VSOP; time in the sampling glass gives the aroma the opportunity to develop further into a friendly, mildly fruity, and seductively peppery perfume, one that could never be accused of being aggressive or awkward; the fourth whiff, after over nine minutes of aeration, adds a deft trace of oaky vanilla that completes the nosing with grace. In the mouth, an off-dry palate entry features the pepperiness while at midpalate hints of dried fruit, very mild oak, and light toffee round out the taste phase. The aftertaste is medium

sweet, balanced, and slightly woody. What's admirable about this brandy primarily is that it never attempts to hammer you with sweetness, wood, or fruit; it owns an attractive harmony that's understated; consequently, it's a good buy.
2001 Rating: ★★★/Recommended

Classick Bierschnaps 100% Barley Malt (USA); 40% abv $35.

Crystal clear; good purity. The nose after opening and pouring reminds me strikingly of whiskey right off the still; it's flowery, mildly sweet, and reminiscent of red cherries, especially in the third sniffing; the compellingly fresh and vigorous perfume continues on well into the fourth and final whiff. The palate entry is unlike that of any other distilled spirit I've tasted over the last fifteen years; I can absolutely taste beer and barley malt immediately, but then there's a peculiar stone dry flavor; I can only describe it as being leathery, velvety in texture, and cottony. The finish is moderately sweet, intensely grainy, and long. Kudos to the spirits adventurers at Classick for I believe that they're really onto something here.
2001 Rating: ★★★★/Highly Recommended

Clear Creek Distillery Sauvie Island Framboise Raspberry Brandy (USA); 40% abv, $50/375 ml.

Ideal clarity, as one would expect from such a skillful distiller. The opening nosing passes after the pour unearth a remarkably soft, polite, but firmly structured raspberry perfume that displays background traces of citrus and paraffin; air contact releases more juiciness and fresh fruit scents as detected six minutes into the nosing phase; this is an atypical framboise bouquet, but one that concentrates on the fruit source. In the mouth there's an intriguing bramble taste at the palate entry that's very leafy/viny and acts as a lovely balance to the succulent fruitiness; the midpalate stage offers ripe and sweet tastes of perfectly harvested red raspberry as well as a hint of tangerine peel and beeswax. The finish is long, comfortable, warming, and fruity. A dynamite spirit.
2001 Rating: ★★★★/Highly Recommended

E & J Patriarch 1979 Family Reserve 20 Year Old California Brandy (USA); 40% abv, $70.

Made from cabernet sauvignon; the medium topaz/bronze hue is very pretty and bright; impeccable purity. In the opening nosing pass, seductive scents of raisins and cotton candy lure the olfactory sense; the second whiff finds other layers of aroma, most notably roasted walnut, sugar cookies, and vanilla; following seven minutes of aeration, the third sniffing focuses on the oakiness of the latter stages of the bouquet; the fourth and final pass unearths further fruit, namely plums and baked pear; a multilayered bouquet that shows genuine depth of character and poise. The palate entry is sweet and spirity; the toasty, sublime midpalate flavors include oak resin, paraffin, and caramel. The finish is long and buttery. Clearly a benchmark for Gallo.
2000 Rating: ★★★★/Highly Recommended

E & J VS Very Special Brandy (USA); 40% abv, $9.

The gold/wheat/amber hue is ideally pure. The first sniffings detect lovely notes of butterscotch and walnuts; following six more minutes of exposure to air, the aroma goes very

nougat- and nut-like, almost like butter-brickle candy. The palate entry is concentrated and delightfully buttery; at midpalate the taste of ripe grapes overrides all other taste impressions, except for oak resin. Concludes semisweet, buttery/oily, and silky.
2004 Rating: ★★★/Recommended

E & J VSOP Superior Reserve Brandy (USA); 40% abv, $12.

The color is bright bronze; lots of minute black sediment seen under the examination lamp. The first nasal impressions include notes of buttered popcorn, butterscotch, and almond paste; seven more minutes of aeration add interesting notes of licorice and mince pie. The palate entry is intensely toffee-like and sweet; at midpalate the sweetness gets turned up a notch as all evidence of fruit or wood disappear. Finishes candy sweet, silky, and clean. The VS is a better overall brandy to my taste.
2004 Rating: ★★/Not Recommended

E & J XO Vintage Reserve 10 Year Old Brandy (USA); 40% abv, $35.

The soft amber/honey hue is marred by clouds of what resembles cork-like sediment; I held the bottle up to the examination lamp and found the same flaw; not the first E & J to suffer from cosmetic problems. The opening nosing passes are greeted by delicate and ripe scents of grapes and oaky spirit; additional aeration time of seven minutes doesn't stimulate further aromatic activity. It's very pleasing and easy at the palate entry; the midpalate stage though, is the point at which this brandy's real charm makes itself known in the forms of ripe but off-dry tastes of light caramel, resiny oak, vanilla frosting, and toffee. The finish is long, sweeter than the midpalate, and elegant. A very recommendable domestic brandy that would have scored higher had it been more assertive in the bouquet and the palate entry.
2003 Rating: ★★★/Recommended

E & J XO Vintage Reserve Brandy Limited Release Aged 7 Years (USA); 40% abv, $22.

A blend of pot still (alambic) brandy and column still brandy; the color is a bright tawny/copper hue that shows excellent purity. The first inhalations within two minutes of the pour reveal softly succulent aromas of butter, cream, and oak resin; following six more minutes of aeration time, the bouquet becomes fruitier, displaying alluring notes of baked apple and baked pear along with almond paste. The palate entry is engagingly sweet, slightly toffee-like, oily, and medium-bodied; by midpalate the taste profile takes on a more complex stature, offering layered notes of light caramel, candied pear, and maple. Concludes semisweet and silky, if a bit thinner than I would have liked; right up there with the lovely and svelte E & J 1992 Single Vintage 8 Year Old Brandy (★★★). Very nice job once again from the very talented distillers at Gallo.
2004 Rating: ★★★/Recommended

E & J 8 Year Old 1992 Single Vintage Brandy (USA); 40% abv, $30.

The pretty amber/autumnal gold color is marred by clouds of blackish sediment. Right after the pour; aromas of ripe grapes, white raisins, and gum start the nosing proceedings; with air contact the gumminess fades, allowing the grapy/raisiny quality the room it needs to expand by the fourth and last sniffing. The palate entry is off-dry and fruity, then by midpalate a mildly sweet, lightly oaked, but genuine brandy personality emerges.

The aftertaste is the best part of the experience as warm, soothing flavors coat the throat. Quaffable and solid but not as inspiring as the superb E & J Patriarch 1979 Family Reserve that was released in 2000.

2001 Rating: ★★★/Recommended

Germain-Robin Anno Domini 2001 Alambic Brandy (USA); 40% abv, $350.
Exceptionally pretty and brilliant bronze/burnished/topaz hue; ideal clarity; it shimmers in the glass. The nose at the pour is subtle, showing mere hints of sinewy oak and toasted almond; with a bit of swirling and aeration, this aroma begins to unfold in the second sniffing as more assertive scents of wood resin, grape must, and light toffee gain footing; yikes, by the third whiff this aroma is getting truly serious as further layers of pine, vanillin, and taffy come on board; after nine minutes of air contact, the various components meld into a singular aromatic thrust that's complex and muscular yet agile…kind of like Michael Jordan driving the lane in his prime; one of G-R's benchmark bouquets for me. The palate entry is sublimely full, assertive without being aggressive, and oaky; the midpalate stage focuses on the perfect balance between the alcohol, the dried, tangy fruit, and the soft, velvety, resiny oak influence. The aftertaste is very long, complex, layered, sweet, and woody. Yet another world-class effort for the dynamic duo at G-R; impressive by any brandy standards. A classic.

2000 Rating: ★★★★/Highest Recommendation

Germain-Robin Anno Domini 2002 Alambic Brandy (USA); 40% abv, $350.
Beguiling honey/amber hue. The first two nosing passes following the pour pick up lovely, married aromas of pears, nectarines, grapes, and light oak; aeration serves to stimulate deeper, mature aromas of fruit cake, cake frosting, pear nectar, and honey. In the mouth this alambic couldn't be more elegant as entry tastes of honey and ripe grapes enchant the taste buds; at the midpalate a savory, succulent, and sweet flavor of light caramel and milk chocolate sends this brandy into a whole other sphere of excellence. The finish is clean, sweet, ripe, and concentrated on toffee. Classic.

2001 Rating: ★★★★/Highest Recommendation

Germain-Robin Anno Domini 2004 Alambic Brandy (USA); 40% abv, $350.
Distillates of mostly pinot noir grapes (98%) from 1983 and 1984; 25 cases/300 bottles available. The deep amber/walnut color is dazzling and impeccably pure. The opening salvo of aromas come at you in waves, first, of saddle leather, then nougat, then old oak; another seven minutes in the glass helps to release further scents, including toasted almond, baked apple, tobacco leaf, and cigar box; a classic alambic brandy bouquet that alone should be bottled and sold as a perfume. The palate entry offers ripe, semisweet tastes of black raisins and oak resin; at midpalate there's a surge of warming spirit on the tongue that serves to accent the sap-like flavors of maple, butterscotch, and dark caramel. The lip-smacking aftertaste is long, crisp, clean, and deep. Utterly breathtaking and monumental.

2003 Rating: ★★★★/Highest Recommendation

Germain-Robin Anno Domini 2005 Alambic Brandy (USA); 40% abv, $350.
The pretty golden/autumnal amber color sparkles under the examination lamp. In the first couple of sniffs, the aroma is like yellow fruit and spice, then with another seven minutes

of air contact, the aroma turns itself into a bona fide pot still brandy bouquet and offers subtle and enticing notes of tobacco leaf, tea leaves, burnt orange rind, combed cotton, and grapefruit; a stunning bouquet. The palate entry is gently sweet, polite, composed, focused, linear, and grapy; by midpalate the taste profile becomes vertical, deep, intensely grapy/dried fruit-like (raisins), sap-like, and tropical fruit-like (especially guava). Concludes with incredible finesse, stately presence, and tropical fruit lushness; remarkably, the 2001, 2002, and 2004 Anno Domini versions all scored ★★★★★; say hello to the fourth ★★★★★ classic.
2004 Rating: ★★★★★/Highest Recommendation

Germain-Robin Apple Brandy (USA); 40.2% abv, $65.

Only 204 bottles available. Orange/bronze hue; superb clarity. The nose at opening is conspicuously mute and in need of air contact; the aroma explodes in the second sniffing in waves of tart apple, baked pear, and vanilla bean; the third whiff adds a judicious trace of mint; in the fourth and final nosing pass; following a full ten minutes of exposure to air, the baked fruit element surges ahead while the mint and vanilla fade to the background; there is a noticeable diminishment in aromatic strength by the last nosing. The palate entry is soft and very tart; the midpalate phase shows considerable potency and a flashing, perfectly acceptable flame of spirit on the back of the tongue as more dry than sweet flavors of baked apple and baked pear delight the taste buds. The aftertaste is lean, but not austere, moderately sweet, and medium long. An excellent apple brandy, to be sure, but not yet ready to run a dead-heat with Steve McCarthy's inspired Clear Creek Eau-de-Vie de Pomme which still ranks as America's foremost apple brandy.
2000 Rating: ★★★★/Highly Recommended

Germain-Robin Barrel Select XO Alambic Brandy (USA); 40% abv, $100.

Bottled in 2003; pure, golden/amber appearance. The upfront bouquet is a tad reluctant to come out and play and, as a result, only a distant scent of ripe grapes is detected; aeration time of seven minutes really allows the aroma to stretch and open properly as it emits seductive, integrated, and dry notes of oak resin, wood sap, cotton, and unsweetened coconut; a bouquet that whispers rather than shouts. The palate entry is very tart, resiny, and crisp, then at midpalate the flavors escape like a jail break, offering resiny, maple-like tastes of new oak, acidic spirit, and walnut. The finish is dry, almost bitter, but smooth and long. The understated, lean elegance of this brandy is what makes it so special and such a cornerstone of contemporary American distilling.
2003 Rating: ★★★★/Highly Recommended

Germain-Robin Grappa of Merlot (USA); 41.1% abv, $55/375ml.

Clear, but with some white sediment floating about. The opening bouquet is ripe, musty, pomace-like, and off-dry; time in the glass deepens the scents of fresh-off-the-still spirit, pomace, and ripe grapes. The palate entry is slightly tanky, minerally, and slate-like; the midpalate comes off a bit hot, but shows lots of stylish fresh spirit taste. The finish is long, sweet, and intensely musty. Not my favorite G-R grappa, but OK.
2001 Rating: ★★/Not Recommended

Germain-Robin Grappa Viognier (USA); 41.1% abv, $85/375 ml.

Crystal clear and 100% pure. The nose at opening offers some but not an abundance of the typical fresh flower perfume (rose petal especially) of viognier; the floral nature of the bouquet grows in intensity in the second whiff as orange blossom gets added to the mix; by the third pass, a seed-like quality enters the picture, but doesn't overshadow the flowery foundational scent; in the fourth and last sniffing, after almost nine minutes of exposure to air, the nose adds elements of mushroom, forest floor, and cedar; an exotic bouquet to say the least. The palate entry offers a sweet, fruity taste that grows by leaps and bounds on its way to the midpalate stage where it explodes with ripe, sweet, fruit flavors that dazzle and overwhelm my taste buds. The aftertaste is long, luxurious, intense, and fruity.Sure, I liked the bouquet, but I simply wasn't ready for the incredible, succulent rush of fruit on the palate. An eye-popper.

2000 Rating: ★★★★/Highly Recommended

Germain-Robin Grappa Zinfandel (USA); 40.9% abv, $65/375 ml.

Limpid as rain water and absolutely pure. The initial nosing pass is alive with fresh, ripe, grapy scents; the second sniffing picks up traces of rubber pencil eraser and cotton; the grape component comes back strong in the penultimate whiff, following over six minutes of air contact; by the fourth and last nosing pass; the ripe fruit scent is well established and all but unshakable; a clean, uncomplicated, and fruity bouquet right from the beginning. Clean, mildly sweet, and musty at the palate entry; then the flavor turns chalk-like, pulpy sweet, but lean at midpalate. The finish is medium long, pulpy/pomace-like, and sweet; rustic, unpolished, and delightful in a rough and ready manner.

2000 Rating: ★★★/Recommended

Germain-Robin Pinot Noir Single Barrel V199 & V200 Alambic Brandy (USA); 40.6% abv, $150.

Made from Mendocino County pinot noir that was harvested in the autumn of 1991; strikingly pale gold/straw color; excellent purity. The bouquet in the first two passes after the pour is shy, remote, and only slightly perfumed; exposure to air does little to encourage more aromatic expression or presence; the bouquet wanders without any focus. In the mouth there are signs of life at palate entry as delicate, if reluctant flavors of ripe grapes and honey mildly impress the taste buds; the midpalate stage is where this brandy finally appears to compose itself as tightly-knit, integrated tastes of honey, vanilla, and yellow raisins give cause for optimism. The aftertaste is medium-long, astringent, and pear-like. Is the pleasant midpalate worth waiting around for through the weak, lazy bouquet and anemic palate entry? Not for me, sorry—not when there are other Germain-Robin gems available.

2001 Rating: ★★/Not Recommended

Germain-Robin Single Barrel Viognier Brandy (USA); 40% abv, $140.

Amber/honey color; excellent purity. Opening aromas offer ripe, fruity, slightly toasted, and pleasingly sophisticated smells; additional air contact brings about scents of spice, orange rind, orange blossom, and black tea leaf. Entry is honeyed and remarkably fruity in a baked banana/baked peach/baked pear manner that's delicious; the midpalate is silky in texture, semisweet in dryness/sweetness degree, and bountifully tasty as evolved flavors of peach,

pear, grapefruit, and caramel merge into a splendid finish that's round, ripe, and savory in a chocolate covered fruit vein. Fabulously deep in character and expansive in flavor scope.
2007 Rating: ★★★★★/Highest Recommendation

Germain-Robin Syrah Grappa (USA); 41% abv, $55.
    Clear as rainwater. The pungent, musty, grapy opening aroma is a lusty charmer that gives its all right from the beginning; aeration deepens the aroma as it shifts from unfocused spirit to channeled grapiness/mustiness and moderately sweet charm; it's very floral and fruity. The palate entry is sweet, but lean and focused on the pulpy fruit; by midpalate there's an additional taste of seed-like bitterness that nicely offsets the ripe fruit. The aftertaste is generous, fruity, and semisweet. One of the nicest G-R grappas in years.
2003 Rating: ★★★★/Highly Recommended

Germain-Robin V45 Single Barrel Alambic Brandy 100% Colombard (USA); 42.1% abv, $150.
    The attractive medium amber hue is perfectly clean and clear. The opening aromatic salvo is resiny, dry and limber; in the second pass an intriguing, if fleeting, note of orange zest is noted almost as though there's a bit of muscat grape in it though I know after talking to G-R that there isn't; the third pass shows a regal, beautifully structured bouquet that showcases oak, nuts, grapes, and vanilla extract; the last whiff after ten minutes of aeration, brings the various elements together in a prickly, spirity, elegant, and toasty/roasted/oaky bouquet that's typically superb for this distiller. The palate entry is muscular, oaky sweet, and very, very toffee-like; by the midpalate stage the flavors got a bit hot and spirity, but the fundamental oaky/grapy taste remains steady and rich. The finish is long, compellingly oaky, almost resiny, and clean. G-R's single barrel bottling program continues to delight.
2000 Rating: ★★★★/Highly Recommended

Jepson Old Stock Mendocino Alambic Brandy (USA); 40% abv, $50.
    Made with colombard grapes from vines that are fifty years old. Pretty bronze/new copper penny tint; oily and clear of debris. The initial nosing pass reveals a toasty/biscuity aromatic quality that's very alluring; the second whiff offers a nuance of orange blossom that's almost muscat-like; in the third sniffing the orange blossom dissipates, leaving the door open for hints of oaky vanilla, kiwi fruit, and toffee; following nearly nine minutes of air contact, the fourth nosing adds pistachio nut; not necessarily a profound bouquet but one whose surface is evolving with every step. The palate entry is tart and lean, then at midpalate sinewy flavors of oak resin, spice, and light toffee abound on the tongue. The aftertaste is long, medium-bodied, sweet in a controlled manner, and oaky. A definite advance on the quality ladder from the Jepson pot still.
2000 Rating: ★★★/Recommended

Jepson Rare Mendocino Alambic Brandy (USA); 40% abv, $35.
    Invitingly sunny gold/wheat field/medium amber hue; excellent purity. Starts out smelling of toasted pine nuts and linseed oil in the initial two minutes of sniffing; adds heady notes of beeswax, burning rubber, rubber pencil eraser, and lard; I like this chunky, fatty and assertive bouquet. The palate entry displays subtle notes of cocoa oil and lignin; at midpalate

the flavor profile becomes raisiny/dried fruit-like and even a touch buttery. Finishes in-your-face, delectably oily, and uncomplicated. A three star brandy whose highlight virtues are its straight-ahead, simple character, and generous nature. Not a brandy to sit and ponder as much as it is one to enjoy many times over.
2004 Rating: ★★★/Recommended

Jepson Signature Reserve Mendocino Alambic Brandy (USA); 40% abv, $100.
Made from 100% French colombard from a single estate. Two shades deeper in color than the bright Rare; Signature is a brassy gold/orange tint, displaying flawless purity. Owns a forest floor, slightly burnt, ash-like opening aroma, then following seven minutes of undisturbed air contact the aromatic profile shifts to hot wax, smoldering campfire embers, toasted honey wheat bread, and pork rind. The palate entry is waxy and fatty; at midpalate there's a pleasing semi-sweetness that seems to be generated by the grapes more than the oak; I respond favorably to the veneer-like texture. Concludes on notes of light toffee and almond paste.
2004 Rating: ★★★/Recommended

Koenig Distillery Pear Brandy Williams Pear Northwest Eau-de-Vie (USA); 42% abv, $29/375 ml.
Good clarity; translucent. The first nosing passes detect properly accurate notes of pear and pear peel and, interestingly, the aroma is neither overly ripe nor sweet; in the sniffings that follow the seven minute aeration period, the aroma turns steely/metallic and intensely minerally; not what I had been hoping for aromatically. The palate entry is pinched, metallic, and peel-like, without any hint of ripe fruit; by the midpalate point the acids come to dominate, leaving in their wake any hope for fruitiness/peariness and, as a result, the entire mouth experience implodes. Raw, harsh, rough ending in the throat. Needs lots of work yet. Not even close to being market-worthy.
2007 Rating: ★/Not Recommended

Korbel Gold Reserve VSOP Brandy (USA); 45% abv, $19.
Attractive, deep honey/bronze color; minor sediment spotted. The initial two nosing passes detect very little after the pour; who's hiding the aroma?; five to eight minutes of aeration does virtually nothing to assist in stimulating any fragrance whatsoever. In the mouth the entry flavor is sweetly ripe and slightly toasted; at the midpalate juncture the flavor turns caramelized and pleasantly fruity, even honeyed. The aftertaste plays up the honey/fruit to the hilt. All-American and savory.
2001 Rating: ★★★/Recommended

Korbel Rich & Mellow Brandy (USA); 40% abv, $10.
The very pretty deep amber/honey brown color is flawlessly pure. Pleasant upfront aromas of grape spirit, tar, and mango work well; little change after seven more minutes of air contact. The palate entry is clean, grapy, and a touch toffee-like; at midpalate the flavor expands its range to include walnut butter, lanolin, and dried figs. Ends up on a mildly sweet and biscuity note. One of the best mass-produced standard class brandies one can find.
2004 Rating: ★★★/Recommended

Korbel XS Extra Smooth Brandy with Spices and Natural Flavors (USA); 40% abv, $15.

Pretty amber/light honey hue. The curious opening bouquet is herbal, mildly spiced, and very chocolate, as in candy bar milk chocolate; aeration encourages the addition of egg cream, root beer, and nutmeg scents. The palate entry is sweet, cola-like, and mapley on the tongue; the midpalate turns the egg cream/cola volume on high as most evidence of the brandy base is lost in the forest of added flavors; that's not to say it's not drinkable because it is for unsophisticated drinkers. It finishes like a cola, sweet and vanilla-like. Mix with Coke, maybe. Strange and ultimately a snore.

2001 Rating: ★★/Not Recommended

Laird's 12 Year Old Rare Apple Brandy, Batch No. 7 (USA); 44% abv, $50.

The bronze /copper color is dazzling; unblemished purity. Smells fetchingly of baked apple, nutmeg, oak, and pine. Tastes wonderfully of raisins, dates, apple pastry, pineapple, and maple. Finishes gracefully and assertively tart. A superb and elegant brandy.

2005 Rating: ★★★★/Highly Recommended

Laird's 7 1/2 Year Old Apple Brandy (USA); 40% abv, $26.

The honey brown color shows a little more sediment than I'd like to see, but the appearance is nonetheless appealing. The opening whiff is treated to toasty, baked apple smells that are pleasing tart, though not necessarily sour; seven more minutes allow the bouquet to incrementally expand, adding tightly wound aromas of wood resin, cedar, and apple pastry. The palate entry is angular, lean, appropriately astringent, and very clean on the tongue; the midpalate stage is where all the flavor impact takes place as tastes of apple peel, pears, pepper, and wood take charge. The finish is compact, refreshingly tart, and clean as a whistle.

2005 Rating: ★★★/Recommended

Monarch VS California Brandy (USA); 40% abv, $9.

The medium amber/honey hue is pretty and flawlessly clean. The first sniffings detect sweet aromas of light toffee and marzipan; after seven minutes of additional air contact a potent pruny/black raisin quality throws a dried fruit blanket over the whole bouquet. The palate entry is concentrated, simple, and unabashedly sweet; the midpalate stage puts a spotlight on the date-like pruniness, which while acceptable and drinkable, excludes all other flavors due to the sheer weight of the sweetness. Finishes intensely fig- and date-like and very sweet.

2007 Rating: ★★/Not Recommended

Osocalis Rare Alambic Brandy Fall 2003 Bottling (USA); 40% abv, $38.

Very pleasing harvest gold/autumnal amber hue; more sediment floating about than I'd like. The opening nosing passes encounter delicate, almost reluctant, acidic scents of grapes, green apple, and citrus; the additional seven minutes of aeration help this bouquet as the fruited aromas mingle with resiny wood, distant toffee, and beeswax; hardly a profound or deep bouquet, but a mildly interesting one all the same. This brandy comes together in the mouth at palate entry as the first taste of measured sweetness and light caramel please the taste buds; at midpalate the flavor range broadens to include charred marshmallow, dark toffee, nougat, and milk chocolate. Finishes well and composed. A California distiller to watch closely in the coming years.

2005 Rating: ★★★/Recommended

Paul Masson VSOP Grande Amber (USA); 40% abv, $15.

Very deep bronze/tawny color; excellent purity; quite lovely in appearance. The opening nosing right after the pour is a tad muted and closed off; by the second whiff, after three minutes of aeration, the first stirrings of aroma are noted in the forms of marshmallow and yellow fruit; three more minutes in the glass allows this tightly wound brandy to stretch out a little more as subtle scents of wood resin and caramel make themselves known; by the fourth and final sniffing the aroma still seems reluctant to cut loose; the meager scents of oak, dark caramel, and oil appear, in my opinion, to be making an attempt at rancio, but they don't make it since the real thing can't be manufactured in the laboratory; the implication here is just skip the aroma altogether. More expressive and pleasing in the mouth than in the nose; the palate entry offers a dry, dark caramel flavor while the midpalate goes oily to the taste, with background hints of dried fruit and old oak. The aftertaste is dry, medium long, and very caramel-like. To be sure, very drinkable and worth the price, but I feel that the cognac has been buried beneath a blanket of caramel, less than thrilling American brandy, and wood resin.

2000 Rating: ★★/Not Recommended

Sierra Nevada Bierschnaps Schnaps Distilled from Sierra Nevada Pale Ale (USA); 40% abv, $37.

Clear, limpid, with minor particles. The initial nosing pass following the pour displays an evergreen, minty, and cedar-like opening scent that's delightful; the second and third whiffs add fruit (ripe nectarine) and chewing gum while the fourth and last sniffing sees the sweet malt come alive. The palate entry is sweet and concentrated in a clearly ale-like way; the midpalate is toasty, slightly oily/grainy, mildly bitter, and drier than the entry. The aftertaste is bitter, malty, and hoppy. While I prefer the actual Pale Ale to this distilled version, it's nifty and cutting-edge just the same.

2001 Rating: ★★★/Recommended

BRANDY—SPAIN

The most prevalent variety of Spanish brandy is **Brandy de Jerez**, a robust style of grape brandy. Airen grapes are grown, fermented, and distilled in Spain's vast LaMancha region, then shipped via tanker trucks to Andalucia's famous sherry region, where the brandies are matured in the region's customary solera system that marries young brandies to old.

The solera system is an ingenious, gradual maturation method that is based on a pyramid formation of American oak barrels. Sherry is aged this way, often in the same warehouses as the Brandy de Jerez. The bottom row of barrels, that contain the oldest brandies, is the solera. The rows of barrels stacked on top of the solera are called criaderas. They contain younger brandies that get younger as you ascend in rows.

Here's how it works: When brandy is needed for bottling, the cellar masters withdraw brandy from the solera row, but no more than one-third of the barrel. That amount is replenished with brandy from the criadera row directly above the solera row. Then that criadera row is replenished with brandy from the criadera row directly above it and so on.

The solera system accomplishes two things. First, it marries older brandies with younger ones, creating a well-balanced brandy. Second, it keeps the flow of maturing brandy moving, thereby maintaining a freshness in barrel.

The three classifications for Brandy de Jerez are:
- *Brandy de Jerez Solera: matured in barrels for at least one year.*
- *Brandy de Jerez Solera Reserva: three year minimum.*
- *Brandy de Jerez Solera Gran Reserva: ten year minimum.*

Other grape brandies are produced around Spain to far lesser degrees than Brandy de Jerez, but they are worth searching for.

Cardenal Mendoza Sanchez Romate Solera Gran Reserva Brandy de Jerez (Spain); 40% abv, $43.
The prune juice-like chestnut/bay/brown color excites me; perfect purity. The nose upfront is all about intensely ripe grapes, especially Pedro Ximenez, and fruit-topped cheesecake; further sniffings after more air contact detect deep-seated aromas of prunes, dates, figs, coffee beans, and chocolate covered cherries; a massive bouquet of fathomless charm and aspects. The palate entry is long, sweet, cocoa-like, and rich; at midpalate, I find subtle bittersweet hints of citrus, black coffee, and caramel. Finishes as it begins, a huge, virile, sweet, concentrated brandy. Along with Gran Duque d'Alba defines what Spanish brandy from Jerez is all about.
2005 Rating: ★★★★/Highly Recommended

Conde de Osborne Brandy de Jerez Solera Gran Reserva (Spain); 40% abv, $44.
Chestnut/mahogany color; some sediment noted. Opening whiffs detect buttery/oily notes that are deep and wide; further aeration stimulates smells of beeswax, marzipan, burnt toast, honey, bacon fat, bacon rind, sulfur, and caramel. Entry is big, pruny, Danish pastry-like, and more bittersweet than sweet; the midpalate stage is engagingly toasted, dried fruit-like, fruitcake-like, honeyed, and even a touch smoky. Ends clean, and intensely bittersweet and pruny. A superb example of Brandy de Jerez in full form.
2007 Rating: ★★★★/Highly Recommended

Gran Duque d'Alba Brandy de Jerez Solera Gran Reserva (Spain); 40% abv, $45.
Old oak/mahogany/cream sherry brown color; excellent clarity. Smells of old leather, old books, toasted marshmallow,and pipe tobacco; additional time in the glass reveals fathomlessly deep scents of prune Danish, dried fruit/trail mix, salted butter, and caramel cream. Entry is hugely luscious, succulent, ripe, and sweet but hardly cloying or unctuous; the midpalate is concentrated, ripe, fruity, sherry-like, and caramelized. Concludes balanced yet sweet, honeyed, and with more than a hint of Pedro Ximenez sherry. A fat, glossy masterpiece that, for me, still defines Brandy de Jerez Solera Gran Reserva. Nothing is held back with this brandy; it's all in the glass.
2007 Rating: ★★★★★/Highest Recommendation

Miguel Torres Hors d'Age Imperial Brandy 20 Year Old Brandy (Spain); 40% abv, $34.
The nut brown/topaz/deep honey color is quintessential Spanish brandy; impeccable purity. In the initial whiffs, I detect all sorts of engaging dried and baked fruits, especially white raisins, banana, pineapple, and kiwi; after the additional aeration period, the bouquet becomes more wood influenced as notes of vanilla, baking spice (cinnamon), and caramel take charge. The palate entry is semisweet, toffee-like, and a touch burnt orange peel-like; by the midpalate point the taste profile turns woodier and more oily. Concludes on a little bit of a meek note as the flavors recede quickly; I wanted a longer finish. That said, this is a lovely, well-made brandy.
2007 Rating: ★★★/Recommended

Osborne Magno Solera Reserva Brandy de Jerez (Spain); 40% abv, $18.
The brown/honey color is more bronze than copper; excellent purity. The robust opening aroma is concentrated, intensely caramelized, and honeyed; further aeration time adds pungent aromas of roasted walnut, burning hemp, burning hay, tar, and cigar tobacco; not a bouquet for the timid. The palate entry is sweet, vanilla-like, and honeyed; at midpalate the honeyed sweetness turns to resiny/pomace-like bitterness. The aftertaste outshines both the entry and midpalate in terms of civility and appeal; too little, too late. As I've seen time and again once you go lower than Solera Gran Reserva with Brandy de Jerez, your senses go numb from the onslaught of over-the-top aromas and tastes; subtlety isn't the middle name of Jerez's brandy men.
2003 Rating: ★/Not Recommended

Sanchez Romate Uno en Mil Single Oak Cask Solera Gran Reserva Brandy de Jerez (Spain); 40% abv, $37.

Light gold/amber hue, with some sediment. The first nosings bring to light firm, biscuity scents of spice and bread dough, almost akin to cinnamon rolls; greater access to air allows the bouquet to expand into several layers of honey, sherry, sweet oak, salt water taffy, rubber, and burnt matches. The palate entry is delicate yet firm and integrated as flavors of pine, sage, and honey please the taste buds; at midpalate, the flavor profile commits to honey sweetness, light caramel, and oakiness to the point of exclusion. The aftertaste is chewy, sophisticated, toffee-like, and luscious. Creates a new, contemporary style of Brandy de Jerez, which needs a face lift as a category.

2003 Rating: ★★★★/Highly Recommended

Torres Jaime 1 Reserva de la Familia Brandy (Spain); 40% abv, $199.

Very deep mahogany/chestnut color. The initial nosing pass detects fourth-gear scents of dark caramel, butterscotch, cake batter, and soft, blue cheese; with aeration the bouquet builds in power in the second and third sniffings mostly in the form of concentrated butterscotch and nougat-like aromas; by the fourth and final whiff the nose reminds me of toasted honeywheat bread slathered in butter. The taste at palate entry is assertive, sweet, and prune-like; by the midpalate stage the flavor profile expands to include marzipan, dark chocolate, pralines, and roasted almond. It finishes sweet and thick. A top-heavy bruiser for those who like their brandies wicked, decadent, and sweet.

2001 Rating: ★★★/Recommended

LIQUEURS

LIQUEURS, SCHNAPPS & VERMOUTHS—WORLD

By definition liqueurs (please note that cordials is an out-of-date term that no longer applies to this ancient spirits category) are alcoholic beverages that have a spirits base of grape or other fruits, grain, or vegetables and are typically flavored with botanicals like herbs, roots, seeds, barks; fresh and dried fruits; nuts; dairy products (cream, in particular); and/or spices such as cinnamon, vanilla, nutmeg, allspice, coriander, and countless more.

Flavoring in liqueurs occurs through one of four methods:

1) *Percolation*, or flavor extraction through the circulating of spirits through containers holding flavoring agents.

2) *Infusion*, or steeping of mashed fruit/herbs in water or alcohol, filtering and mixing with spirits and sugar.

3) *Maceration*, or steeping of fruits/herbs in alcohol, filtering, and combining with spirits and sugar.

4) *Distillation*, or the mixing of low-level alcohol and flavorings before distillation.

Each method is effective and widely employed by the international distilling community.

Liqueurs have been around for at least six centuries. By 1100-1200 A.D. distillation was spreading rapidly throughout the European continent. During the era of plague, dirty water, and rampant pestilence, Christian monks were the most educated members of the social structure and frequently acted as community physicians as well as spiritual shepherds. The monks recognized the dire need for consumable antidotes to commonplace illnesses like influenza and colds. More than a few of the mysterious liquids created in the cellars of medieval monasteries led to libations that we still consume today, most typically, in the hour or two following a meal. The French label these comforting elixirs as *digestifs*. The Italians call them *digestivos*.

Popular herbal liqueurs, most notably, Chartreuse and Benedictine D.O.M., both French in origin, were invented centuries ago to assist in alleviating, among other maladies, the pains of dyspepsia. Other newer after-dinner libations, like Baileys Original Irish Cream and Carolans Finest Irish Cream, are popular, in part, because they are creamy, light and low in alcohol (less than 20% alcohol by volume). Some people believe that cream is desirable in proper digestion due primarily to the fact that it coats the esophagus and the stomach lining, lessening acid irritation and burning.

To this day, after-dinner liqueurs are viewed by millions of people the world over as one of the more civilized ways to bring down the curtain on the day and to ease a person's system into the restful evening. But, in reality, liqueurs are much more than "soothe operators" for one's turbulent tummy. They also are widely used in thousands of cocktail recipes.

Bitters/Amaros (Europe): concoctions made up of often secret recipes of roots, barks, plants, stems, seeds, and honey that are aimed at aiding digestion. Typically based in neutral grain spirits.

Schnapps (aka, snaps) (International): a widely used term that can cover types of liqueurs and brandies that originate in eastern Europe. Many are distilled from grain or potatoes and then flavored with fruit oils or essences.

Vermouth (International): an aromatized wine produced from grape juice that has been fortified with infusions of an astounding array of herbs, spices, or botanicals. Typically between 15% to 21% alcohol by volume, vermouths that are red are sweeter than clear vermouths, which are considered dry.

A.B. Pollentes Cassis à l'Armagnac (Blackcurrant) (France); 25% abv, $35.

Beautiful Bordeaux-like garnet/ruby sheen; absolute purity. The leafy/vegetal opening aroma is right on the mark; with aeration, the aroma turns into a full-fledged bouquet in the middle stage sniffings as the tart and viny/brambly blackcurrant perfume wafts from the sampling glass; in the fourth and last whiff, following almost nine minutes of exposure to air, the opulent and ripe cassis fruit takes flight in a jam-like manner that ends up being an impressive display of finesse and potency; a smashingly fine bouquet that builds steadily with aeration. The curranty palate entry is ripe yet refreshingly tart; by midpalate the taste shows genuine depth and elegance as the cassis concentration smoothes out on the tongue. The finish is long, satiny, and delicious. A dandy cassis by any measure and certainly one that rivals those from Dijon.
2000 Rating: ★★★★/Highly Recommended

A.B. Pollentes Crème de Fraise des Bois (Strawberry) (France); 25% abv, $35.

The brick red/tawny hue with copper core highlights is perfect for the type; impeccable clarity. The opening salvo of aromas reeks with freshness and vivacity, just like I've picked up a handful of strawberries in the field; the second and third nosing passes see the bouquet deepen into a preserves-like perfume that's totally irresistible; the fourth and final sniffing, after just under ten minutes of aeration, displays no lessening of power and indeed appears to grow in intensity; this is a classroom for strawberry liqueur aromas; superb and beguiling. The palate entry is sweet but not a bit cloying or syrupy; but it's the midpalate stage where this masterpiece comes to full fruition as the flavor becomes a dazzling showcase of chocolate covered strawberries; it's one of the four or five most brilliant liqueur midpalate experiences I've had. The finish is medium long, elegant, chocolaty, and ripe. Pure genius.
2000 Rating: ★★★★★/Highest Recommendation

A.B. Pollentes Framboise à l'Armagnac (Raspberry) (France); 25% abv, $35.

This ruby/crimson/blood red color is reminiscent of a southern Rhone red wine; ideally pure. The nose is intense right from the starting gate as jammy, concentrated, and ripe aromas of raspberry leap from the sampling glass; the middle stage passes only introduces a feeble brambly/viny note but that's hardly a match for the surging raspberry perfume which seems to know no bounds; the fourth and last sniffing merely reinforces the dominance of the raspberry monologue; a monster bouquet. The palate entry is ripe and raspberry sweet;

then the midpalate turns 180 degrees going incredibly tart and sour. The aftertaste is short and mildly sweet, not at all jammy or cloying. What I like about this masterfully crafted framboise is its non-reliance on sweetness and ripeness only; it leaves ample room for the cleansing quality of natural fruity tartness. Lovely.

2000 Rating: ★★★★/Highly Recommended

A.B. Pollentes Liqueur à la Mandarine (Orange) (France); 25% abv, $35.

The goldenrod/yellow honey color is very fetching; as pure as can be. The initial nosing pass is an ambrosial trek into an orange grove at harvest time as ripe, juicy scents envelop the nasal cavity; the middle stages experience an advance in the orange peel/orange zest area as the bouquet turns delightfully acidic and clean; the fourth and last sniffing, after eight minutes of air contact, brings the ripeness, tartness, and acidity together in a formidable aromatic display worthy just by itself of the price of the bottle; a supremely confident and definitive aroma. In the mouth, clearly the watchword is "delicacy" as the tart, acidic palate entry is followed by a fleshy/pulpy midpalate taste that accents the entry sensational beautifully. The finish is lean, ripe, and sweet in a governed way. A butterfly of a liqueur that offers a clinic in how to extract the essence of fruit without clubbing the drinker to death.

2000 Rating: ★★★★/Highly Recommended

A.B. Pollentes Mure à l'Armagnac (Plum) (France); 25% abv, $35.

Black, opaque, and as shiny as your old top hat; pure. The opening nosing doesn't pick up much in the way of aromatic expression other than a soft cotton fabric scent; the second and third whiffs following more than ample aeration time do no better as the strangely attractive cottony aroma persists; finally in the fourth and final nosing pass traces of additional aromas emerge, such as spice (black pepper especially), brambles, and flowers; a peculiar bouquet that seems, at least on the surface, to be inchoate yet it is mildly pleasing at the same time. The palate entry is dry, even tart; then the midpalate expands to include succulent but hardly flabby flavors of ripe black plums, cocoa, tea, and lead pencil. The aftertaste is long, luxurious but neither ropy nor syrupy, and ripe in its sweetness. Pleasant, better than average.

2000 Rating: ★★★/Recommended

Absente Liqueur (France); 55% abv, $35.

The fetching lime gelatin tint is seductive to the eye; absolute purity. The initial nosing pass detects nimble botanical scents of star anise, licorice, and wood resin; the second whiff picks up additional herbal/root fragrances of fennel and sunflower seed; the third sniffing, after over seven minutes of air contact, reveals for the first time an herbal sweetness that's borderline medicinal/botanical; following ten minutes of aeration, the fourth and last nosing pass adds lanolin and linseed oil to the aromatic mix; I favorably responded to this understated, poised perfume, which never loses its head of steam or its direction; absolutely lovely. I was expecting to have my taste buds blown up on the spot at palate entry, but that didn't occur until the taste reached the midpalate stage; the panorama of botanical/herbal flavors boggles the mind, but the tastes that do stand out for recognition include the wood resin, seed-like oil, licorice, and fennel. The aftertaste is hot, concentrated, intensely spirity, and extremely long in the mouth. Not something I'd choose to enjoy everyday, but every once in a while I could see savoring a glass of this supple, exotic stuff.

2000 Rating: ★★★★/Highly Recommended

Achaia Clauss Ouzo Traditional Anise Aperitif (Greece); 46% abv; $19.

Clear and ideally pure. The first whiffs are owned completely by the anise fragrance; aeration does little to expand on the anise theme, just supplementary notes of sweetness and rubber inner tube. The palate entry is shockingly soft and polite considering the alcohol level; by midpalate the sweetness becomes more pronounced as the anise settles back a bit; the texture is rich but not unctuous or ropy. The finish is sweet, slightly prickly on the tongue, and delightful. A smashing ouzo.

2003 Rating: ★★★★/Highly Recommended

Agavero El Original Licor de Tequila (Mexico); 32% abv, $30.

Has the amber/honey look of an añejo tequila. Smells enticingly of agave, flowers, and citrus rind. Tastes of honey, tequila, black pepper, citrus. Finishes cleanly, with delicately sweet notes of honey and sap. A delicious liqueur.

2005 Rating: ★★★★/Highly Recommended

Algarvinha Licor Almond Liqueur (Portugal); 20% abv, $10.

Very pale straw hue; superb clarity. The opening sniffing finds a nutshell-like aroma; with aeration, the nose is properly nutty/almondy with a sweet twist at the end of the nosing phase. The palate entry is smooth, medium-bodied, sweet, and almondy; by the midpalate stage the almondy sweetness almost takes on a background taste of cherry pit. The finish is medium long, mildly sweet, and correctly almond-like. Pleasant and quaffable; but hardly in the class of, say, Italy's Lazzaroni Amaretto or Luxardo Amaretto.

2002 Rating: ★★/Not Recommended

Alizé de France Bleu Premium French Vodka & Cognac with Natural Exotic Fruit Juices (France); 20% abv, $17.

Frosty blue, like a clear sky through fog appearance. The bouquet is properly snappy, tart, and tropical. The palate entry is pleasingly sour and refreshing; by midpalate a deft touch of sugary sweetness enters the picture. It wins rating points because it finishes sour, a bit sappy, fruity, delectable. The vodka, in particular, comes through at palate entry.

2005 Rating: ★★★/Recommended

Alizé Gold Passion Cognac with Passionfruit Juice Liqueur (France); 16% abv, $17.

The sunny, opaque orange/yellow color reminds me of apricot juice. The first whiffs detect engagingly tart aromas of ripe, fresh, tropical fruits, most notably, of course, is passionfruit, but there's also traces of citrus in the form of tangerine; aeration doesn't really affect this bouquet in the least, nor should it. The palate entry is frisky, tart, light, and wonderfully fruity; the midpalate phase is juicier than the entry and seems fuller in the mouth texturally. Refreshing and very pleasant because it retains the natural fruity tartness throughout the entire experience.

2006 Rating: ★★★/Recommended

Alizé Red Passion Cognac with Passionfruit, Cranberry, and Peach Juices (France); 16% abv, $17.

The rose pink color and opaque, chalky, juice-like appearance are typical for the

category. The aroma after the pour bursts with fresh, ripe but tart, tropical fruit perfume; further time in the glass serves to lessen the tartness and bring up the ripeness, in particular of the peach. The palate entry is lush, fruity, and berry ripe and shows just a hint of the spirit; the midpalate features the delightful interplay between the passionfruit and cranberry, with the peach taking a backseat. Ends well, fruity, and correctly acidic. A well-made product of the genre.
2006 Rating: ★★★/Recommended

Alizé Wild Passion Liqueur (France); 16% abv, $17.
Milky, opaque, pink lemonade hue. The bouquet is fetchingly tropical, exotic, and tart in the first two minute nosing span; a bit more time in the glass brings out the grapefruit and mango especially; I really like the intensely tart aroma profile. The citrusy/acidic palate entry forces my lips to purse; the midpalate features grapefruit juice and mango flavors which override all other taste elements. Finishes refreshingly tart, citrusy, light, and delicious. By quite a significant margin, the flat-out best Alizé flavored liqueur yet to come my way; bravo.
2002 Rating: ★★★★/Highly Recommended

Amaretto di Puglia Liqueur (Italy); 28% abv, $20.
The lovely tawny/bronze color is bright and pure. The assertive bouquet opens up with hearty, bittersweet scents of almond, and apricot stone; several more minutes in the glass go a long way in cementing the apricot stone scent as the lead aromatic component. The palate entry is lush, firm in texture, and richly sweet, but not in the least cloying or syrupy; the midpalate is toasty, warm, intensely nutty, and silky. The finish is medium-long, more nutty than apricot-like, and downright luscious.
2003 Rating: ★★★★/Highly Recommended

Amarula Marula Fruit Cream Liqueur (South Africa); 17% abv, $24.
Standard-issue milky brown, opaque appearance. The initial two inhalations after the pour detect pleasantly sweet, ripe, and fruity (almost banana-like or plum-like) and cream aromas; aeration adds a touch of light spice (nutmeg?) as a background scent, but the fruit and cream foundation bouquet is the unchallenged star. The palate entry flavor is delightfully off-dry to sweet but neither cloying nor heavy; the midpalate juncture displays a nicely balanced taste profile that's moderately fruity sweet, deftly spicy (now almost peppery/cinnamon), and mildly creamy. The aftertaste is long, more creamy than fruity, and a touch vanilla-like. A noteworthy and racy addition to the cream liqueur sweepstakes.
2002 Rating: ★★★★/Highly Recommended

American Fruits Apple Liqueur (USA); 19.5% abv, $15.
The color is flax-like and pale gold, almost like brut champagne; wonderfully clear and clean. The initial descent into the aroma finds muted scents of yellow fruit and fruit peel, but not much else; further air contact of seven minutes does zip to encourage any further aromatic expression of note. The palate entry is wayward, unfocused, and timid, offering but a scant trace of apple presence; the midpalate displays far more apple character as the taste profile suddenly pulls itself together and emits pleasing flavors of fresh and baked apple.

Finishes more like how it began, weakly and disorganized. There's a glimmer of potential here that clearly emerged in the midpalate.

2007 Rating: ★★/Not Recommended

American Fruits Blackcurrant Cordial (USA); 18% abv, $15.

The attractive ruby/crimson color is true to blackcurrant; flawless purity. The first nosing passes within two minutes after the pour discover tight, correctly astringent, near-ripe scents that are intensely vinous, berry-like, and vegetal; over the longer aromatic haul, the aroma transforms into a proper liqueur bouquet as the fruit drives the aroma forward. The palate entry is not in the least unctuous yet sweet more in a ripe fruit way than in a sugary/cloying manner; by the midpalate stage the flavor profile boasts a robust fruit/berry command and is delectably light and juicy. Ends well on a viny blackcurrant note that's both fresh and only moderately sweet. Not nearly as profound as many European blackcurrant liqueurs, but a nice job here and something to build upon for the future.

2007 Rating: ★★★/Recommended

American Fruits Sour Cherry Cordial (USA); 20% abv, $15.

Owns the genuine cherry/red brick look of black cherry juice; unblemished purity; a seriously fine looker. Right from the crack of the bat, my olfactory sense is treated to real-deal cherry scents that are ripe and mildly sweet, if quite vinous/bramble-like; after another seven minutes of sniffing and swirling, the aroma becomes more cherry compote-like, sour, and therefore lusciously appealing. The palate entry features a true-to-the-source sourness that's neither biting nor overly acidic, just intensely fruity and authentic; by the midpalate stage the taste delivers mildly tart/sour cherry flavor by the bucket-load, all while maintaining a keen acidity that makes for crisp and fresh drinking enjoyment. The pick of the American Fruits litter.

2007 Rating: ★★★★/Highly Recommended

Angostura Caribbean Rum Cream Liqueur (USA); 15% abv, $13.

The beige/sand color is typical for cream liqueurs. The opening nosing pass offers piquant aromas of holiday spices (cinnamon, nutmeg) and soft cream; aeration adds a bit of chocolate fragrance. The palate entry is delicately creamy and medium-rich; the midpalate flavors are mildly spicy, milk chocolaty, and easy on the tongue. It finishes moderately sweet and creamy. A nicely balanced dairy liqueur that doesn't go overboard with spice, cream, or sweetness. A very good quaff.

2002 Rating: ★★★/Recommended

Aperol Aperitivo Liqueur (Italy); 11% abv, $20.

The neon orange color is very pretty and ideally pure. Right out of the box the orange/tangerine/rhubarb aroma seduces the olfactory sense; more air contact stimulates the herbal/botanical aspects as the bouquet turns garden fresh, viny, grassy, and citrusy; this is a sophisticated and gentle aroma that I could sniff all day long. The palate entry is guardedly sweet and delightfully citrusy/fruity; the midpalate phase offers just enough herbal bitterness to balance the sweetness. Ends up refreshing, orangey sweet/ripe, and delectably herbal. A supremely mixable elixir (club soda, sparkling wine) that, if there is any justice, should

become a favored pre-dinner quaff in aware US households and restaurants.
2006 Rating: ★★★/Highly Recommended

Aqua Perfecta Raspberry Liqueur (USA); 20% abv, $20/375ml.

The attractive brick red/garnet color has "raspberry" written all over it. The first nosing passes conducted within two minutes of the pour reek of just-picked, ripe red raspberries; further time in the glass serves to bring out even deeper, juicier raspberry aromas and nuances; buy it if for nothing else then the mesmerizing bouquet. The palate entry is tart but juicy, reined in, but focused on red raspberry; the midpalate is so harmonious, so ideally integrated, and fruity that it's hard to think of this solely as a liqueur; I picture all sorts of uses, from an ice cream topping to a baking ingredient to a marvelous gift for raspberry loving friends. Concludes as stately and majestic as it begins. An American classic already and another benchmark from master distiller Jorg Rupf for domestic fruit liqueurs.
2005 Rating: ★★★★/Highest Recommendation

Artic Vodka & Thai Fruits Liqueur (Italy); 25% abv, $15.

Yet another blue Hypnotiq knock-off. The see-through sky blue/green color shows perfect clarity; the initial sniffings detect ripe, mildly sweet fruit notes similar to gooseberries, pineapple, and nectarine; the bouquet fades with time in the glass; no surprise since the aromas of all of this ilk do. The palate entry is sour yet appealing and deeply fruity; at midpalate the fruit presence is quite acidic and crisp which allows the vodka foundation to be appreciated. Ends well on the tongue.
2004 Rating: ★★★/Recommended

Ashbourne Irish Cream Liqueur (Ireland); 17% abv, $12.

Standard-issue, opaque milky brown color. In the first couple of whiffs after the pour there's a pleasant, snappy spiciness that sits atop the cream base; aeration serves to stimulate added scents of vanilla, cocoa, and butter cream; a better than average cream liqueur bouquet because it's more bittersweet than creamy/milky sweet. The palate entry is concentrated and creamy; but it's at the midpalate point where the taste phase displays its best stuff in the delectable, bittersweet forms of cinnamon, vanilla bean, and raisins. The finish is long, zesty (due to the spiciness), and semisweet.
2002 Rating: ★★★/Highly Recommended

Australian Herbal Liqueur (Australia); 35% abv, $30.

The neon green is exactly the color of lime-flavored gelatin; perfect purity. The initial sniffs detect assertive scents of peppermint and eucalyptus, the prime flavorings; after further aeration, the aroma loses some of the peppermint and, consequently, turns floor/furniture polish-like. The palate entry is reminiscent of mouthwash or cough lozenges, but it's clean and refreshing at the same time; by the midpalate point the taste profile hammers home the peppermint to the near-exclusion of the eucalyptus, though that aspect returns in the crisp, acidic, citrusy/lemony, and pleasant finish. While the potency of the flavorings excludes this liqueur from classic cocktails, it does possess an admitted charm that's probably better appreciated on its own over ice with a twist of lemon. Also, its texture is light and nimble, not oozy and thick.
2007 Rating: ★★★/Recommended

Averna Amaro Bitter Liqueur (Italy); 32% abv, $24.

Opaque, deep brown/black color. Smells tantalizingly of bittersweet dark chocolate, orange peel, and herbs in the first aromatic go-round; further air contact stimulates aromas of flowers, jasmine, bark, forest, honey, and very light quinine. The palate entry is intensely sweet and more floral than herbal; at midpalate the taste profile turns cocoa-like with other notes of citrus rind, molasses, brown sugar, and grass. Concludes sweet, thick, and luscious.
2005 Rating: ★★★★/Highly Recommended

Averna Lemoncello Lemon Liqueur (Italy); 27% abv, $20.

Predictable and appropriate frosty pale yellow appearance. The initial burst of aroma is fresh, concentrated, and extremely lemony/acidic/juicy; aeration settles down the aroma into a moderately juicy scent highlighted by lemon zest and lemon peel. The palate entry is clean, not in the least sugary, and tart; at midpalate the crisp tartness picks up the pace, accenting the fruit beautifully. Finishes acidic and clean, juicy and luscious. One of the better limoncellos out there. A perfect summertime treat served on ice.
2005 Rating: ★★★★/Highly Recommended

B & B Liqueur (France); 40% abv, $29.

A blend of original Benedictine and cognac. The auburn/bronze/burnt orange color is gorgeous and ideally sediment-free. Smells assertively of herbs (fennel, sage, licorice), honey, quinine, and baking spices (mace, allspice, cardamom) straight out of the starting gate; aeration stimulates further leafy vegetative aromas, most notably, black tea and tobacco. Entry tastes of tea, sage, fennel, and a deft touch of root-like quinine; at midpalate the cognac enters the equation and lends an obvious layer of elegance and genuine distillate presence. Finishes like a champion, long, semisweet, intensely herbal, mildly spicy, and satiny.
2007 Rating: ★★★★/Highly Recommended

Bailey's Mint Chocolate Irish Cream Liqueur (Ireland); 17% abv, $18.

A carbon copy look-a-like of Baileys Original and Baileys Caramel. A leafy spearmint perfume leaps from the glass in the initial sniffs after the pour; aeration stimulates the milk chocolate, cream, and spice, but the mint forges ahead, making for appealing inhaling. The palate entry is refreshingly minty, creamy, and mildly chocolaty; the midpalate features the mint/chocolate flavoring without eclipsing the cream and the spice. Finishes gracefully, silkily, and smooth.
2006 Rating: ★★★★/Highly Recommended

Bailey's Original Irish Cream Liqueur (Ireland); 17% abv, $18.

Milky khaki brown/wet sand color. The familiar nutty nose of Baileys is always welcome in these parts; aeration brings out some of the spice, but while the dairy element remains hidden, the nuttiness prevails until the end. The palate entry continues the nut-fest begun in the bouquet; it's in the midpalate where Baileys takes flight as full bodied flavors of cocoa bean, café au lait, Brazil nut, and Christmas spices pull the taste wagon in harmony. Concludes as chocolaty as any Irish cream in the marketplace. A superbly made product.
2006 Rating: ★★★★/Highly Recommended

Baileys Caramel Irish Cream Liqueur (Ireland); 17% abv, $18.

Owns the identical milky beige appearance of its parent, Baileys Original. The first nosing passes leave no doubt as to the flavoring agent since the dominant aromatic feature is caramel from beginning to end. The palate entry features the cream/dairy element as much as caramel and nuts; the midpalate stage highlights the alluring interplay of the cream, the caramel flavoring, the spirit, and the gentle spice. Concludes smooth, satiny, properly creamy, and with greater emphasis on the spice than the caramel. Well integrated; well made.

2006 Rating: ★★★★/Highly Recommended

Barenjager Honey Liqueur (Germany); 35% abv, $24.

Attractive golden honey color; absolute purity. I was expecting not to like this aroma but the first whiffs topple that expectation as delicate, lightly honeyed, and not overly sweet scents delight the olfactory sense; aeration encourages a really nice buttery/creamy quality to underpin the starring feature, the honey. The palate entry is gooey, concentrated to the point of being as chewy as honey, and numbingly sweet; the midpalate phase serves only to heighten the impressions of the entry. The aftertaste is scoop-out-with-spoon thick and tonsil-screamingly sweet. I can tell you flat out that the flavor and finish phases did live up to my expectations by being unabashedly unctuous; while I personally don't care for this type of icky-sticky stuff, from a technical standpoint I can't deny that it is well made and therefore better than average in its subcategory.

2003 Rating: ★★★/Recommended

Basilica CreamAretto Cream Amaretto Liqueur (Italy); 17% abv, $16.

Shows the typical pasty brown, opaque appearance of a cream liqueur. The first few inhalations find an utterly charming, sweet, nutty, and fruity (cherry? red plum?) bouquet; six more minutes in the glass stimulate the dairy element that somehow accentuates the fruit component more than the nut component; a sterling, understated aroma. The palate entry is intensely fruity and borders on being a bit too sweet and syrupy; by midpalate the taste profile includes chunky cherry-like fruit, milk chocolate, a faint hint of spice, and hardly any nuttiness at all. Finishes thickly and sweet, but still shows a touch of its early virtues; very drinkable and a borderline ★★/★★★ product; since I'm not completely convinced of its quality, I chose to go with a final ★★.

2004 Rating: ★★/Not Recommended

Bauchant Apple XO Liqueur (France); 24% abv, $40.

The color is neon pale green/yellow. The initial whiffs detect very tart and tight aromas of green apple and Jolly Rancher hard apple candy; with time, the bouquet levels out to a juicier fragrance that is actually more like spiced apple. The palate entry is clean, lean, green apple sweet/sour, and balanced; the midpalate highlights the sour apple aspect and sails off into the aftertaste which is bittersweet, properly apple-like, and even a touch oily in texture. A nicely rendered liqueur that doesn't try to be juicy/fruity, but concentrates more on the candy side of orchard fruit.

2006 Rating: ★★★/Recommended

Bauchant Napoleon Liqueur d'Orange au Cognac Brandy (France); 40% abv, $27.

Bright amber/topaz/bronze color; flawless purity. Smells of orange zest, tangerine juice, and Mandarin orange; additional time in the glass adds disarming notes of chocolate covered orange peel, distant honey, and orange bitters; a solid, captivating triple orange bouquet. Entry is off-dry and intensely orangy; the midpalate is this liqueur's best phase as the taste profile kicks up the orange concentration a notch, advancing from off-dry to bittersweet and intensely citrusy. Finishes with finesse, orange panache, and delicacy rather than aggression. A dandy of a triple sec that runs with France's leader, the youngest Grand Marnier.

2007 Rating: ★★★★/Highly Recommended

Bauchant Pear XO Liqueur (France); 24% abv, $40.

The dusty gold/wheat field color is attractive, pure, and translucent. The first inhalations encounter a pleasing pear scent that's one-step removed from the orchard, meaning the fruit fragrance isn't of just-picked pears as it is of processed pears; aeration brings out a delicate ripe fruitiness that's almost fragile, so whispered is it; I like this bouquet very much because of its focus on the core essence of pear perfume; like its Apple XO sibling, it's not trying to emulate fruit in the orchard. The palate entry is sweet, keenly pear-like, and sappy; the midpalate tastes tread lightly on the tongue and in the throat, emitting low-key but tightly structured flavors of baked pear pastry, spiced pear, and brown sugar. Finishes clean, juicy, and elegant.

2006 Rating: ★★★★/Highly Recommended

Bauchant Pomegranate XO Liqueur (France); 24% abv, $40.

The red brick/red cherry color is seriously pretty and perfectly clean. The opening sniffs discover alluringly tart and brambly/viny aromas that are a cross between wild berries, pomegranate, and wild vines; further air contact helps to accentuate and localize the natural pomegranate tartness/bitterness, making for very pleasant inhaling. The palate entry explodes in tart, then ripe tastes of red berries and pomegranate; the midpalate stage crescendos in a detonation of ripe, juicy, tart pomegranate flavor that is unbelievably powerful and authentic. Ends up clean, lean, refreshingly tart, and genuine. MIXOLOGIST ALERT: I have just found your new pomegranate liqueur for cocktails! This one is the benchmark for pomegranate-flavored libations.

2006 Rating: ★★★★★/Highest Recommendation

Bauchant Raspberry XO Liqueur (France); 24% abv, $40.

This liqueur's bright appearance is a crimson/pale ruby color; flawless purity. In the first two minutes of nosing, the aroma hides, for all intents and purposes, allowing only for a peculiar, but compelling scent of flowers/wet soil; finally after six more minutes of exposure to air, the bouquet shows some plump berry fruit perfume that is tart as it is ripe; this bouquet is a teaser. The palate entry is astringent, tart, and borderline bitter in its raspberry fruitiness; the midpalate features raspberry fruit head-on, not in a jammy/preserves manner but more in a candied way that isn't in the least cloying or over sweet. Concludes sweet, ripe, fruity, and, for the first time, juicy.

2006 Rating: ★★★★/Highly Recommended

Becherovka Carlsbad Liqueur (Czech Republic); 38% abv, $24.

Very pleasant harvest gold/amber color; superb purity. The opening inhalations detect extremely assertive and prickly-in-the-nose scents of rosewater, brambles, winter holiday spices (cinnamon, nutmeg, vanilla, ginger), root beer, and bitter herbs; additional exposure to air doesn't do much to change the aroma, except to turn down the volume on the prickliness. The palate entry offers highly bitter tastes of fruit peel, earth, rose petal, and ginger; the midpalate stage features heady flavors of keen root- and bark-like bitterness and a late-term sappy sweetness.

2006 Rating: ★★/Not Recommended

Beirao Liqueur Herb Liqueur (Portugal); 22% abv, $15.

The brown/dark amber color is pretty and pure. The nose at opening offers fresh garden-like scents of orange peel, honeysuckle, jasmine, and rose petal; time in the glass affords the opportunity for other herbal fragrances to emerge, among them anise, thyme, and rosemary. The palate entry is intensely sweet, almost red fruit ripe, and remarkably minty; the midpalate juncture features spicy tastes of peppermint, tangerine peel, and tea leaves. The finish is sweet but not cloying, herbal, and minty. Very nice.

2002 Rating: ★★★/Recommended

Belle de Brillet Extra Liqueur Poire Williams au Cognac (France); 30% abv, $35.

Very pretty medium amber/light honey color; perfect purity. The opening nosing pass unearths a rich, very ripe pear fragrance that's immediately enchanting; with air contact, the pear juice perfume deepens in the second sniffing; in the penultimate whiff, following six minutes of time in the glass, the bouquet enters a softer aromatic phase that goes in the direction of sweet pear nectar and away from the tarter side of pear pulp; by the fourth and final nosing pass, the perfume has lost no power or charm and, indeed, seems to have picked up spicy notes of citrus and cinnamon; a simply terrific bouquet. The palate entry is soft, mature, and reserved; the midpalate stage shows off the extra ripe pear fruit by the truckload as the texture turns borderline syrupy but retains enough acidity to keep it from going too thick. The finish is sweet, sinewy, and offers just a glimpse at the cognac component in the throat. All in all, a superbly crafted liqueur that's harmonious and remarkably focused; BRAVO!

2000 Rating: ★★★★★/Highest Recommendation

Benedictine Liqueur (France); 40% abv, $29.

More coppery /henna-like in color than B & B; excellent purity. The comely herbaceousness doesn't leap from the glass as much as it wafts in stately manner; aeration releases multiple layers of mesmerizing fragrance, including pine/cedar, quinine, fennel, white pepper, licorice, mace, allspice, sage, and rosemary; there is no other liqueur bouquet like it. What's missed in the aroma is the orange zest/tangerine that's evident in the palate entry; the flavor profile at midpalate is in full swing as layer after layer of appealing taste bobs up then ducks down, leaving room for the others; these exotic yet familiar flavors include orange zest, tangerine zest, multiple herbs and spices, honey, and pine. One of the ten best liqueurs in the world.

2007 Rating: ★★★★★/Highest Recommendation

Black 100 100 Proof Herbal Liqueur (USA); 50% abv, $14.

The jet-black, opaque appearance is like espresso. The opening sniffs encounter an array of forest-influenced scents, starting with cedar/pine and continuing, at varying strengths, with vines, spring leaves, grass, damp soil, chalk/limestone, and rosemary; after another six minutes of exposure to air, the bouquet turns sweeter, tobacco-like, and asphalt/tar-like, with subtle hints of mint; I like this bouquet. Regrettably, the palate entry is clumsily cloying, thick as molasses or fresh out of the ground petroleum, and totally awkward; the midpalate improves the situation slightly as the taste profile emphasizes the woodsy/minty flavors, downplaying the cumbersome texture. Finishes bittersweet, bark-like, and heavy. If the gooey texture could be thinned, this would have a chance for a third star. The basics are present; the execution is misguided.

2006 Rating: ★★/Not Recommended

Bols Anisette Liqueur (Holland); 25% abv, $19.

Pewter/gray color; superb clarity. Aniseed/licorice perfume comes roaring out of the tasting glass after the pour, making it both vegetal and spicy simultaneously; more time in the glass allows the aroma to expand into a creamy mode that's equal parts earthy, spicy, waxy, and vegetal. Entry is super-sweet, syrupy, yet brings enough aniseed bitterness to the dance that I don't feel overcome by the sugar; the midpalate stage continues what the entry began as the taste profile highlights the aniseed more than the sugary, sappy sweetness. Borderline in terms of the sweetness, but I liked it enough to look the other way.

2007 Rating: ★★★/Recommended

Bols Butterscotch Liqueur (Holland); 17% abv, $19.

Brandy-like, autumnal gold/amber hue; excellent purity. Smells engagingly of rich butterscotch and salted butter in the opening whiffs; following further air contact, the aroma turns mildly nutty/walnut-like as well as slightly minerally and parchment-like. Displays good, buttery, and sweet butterscotch flavor upfront at entry; the midpalate is candied (English toffee) and intensely caramel-like. Ends up moderately sweet and toffee-like. I like it because it comes through with real butterscotch taste. Just haven't a clue what to do with it.

2007 Rating: ★★★/Recommended

Bols Crème de Cassis Liqueur (Holland); 17% abv, $19.

Opaque purple/black. Smells immediately vinous/brambly, tart, yet sweet and unctuously ripe; following another seven minutes of air contact, much of the bramble recedes, allowing for a full-frontal attack by the intense and concentrated cassis. Entry is ultra-ripe and blackcurrant sweet; the midpalate stage features enveloping, creamy, tart/sweet tastes of blackberry and blackcurrant. Ends up off-the-charts sweet but with more than ample acidity to maintain the balance between sugar/tartness. An excellent cassis.

2007 Rating: ★★★★/Highly Recommended

Bols Ginger Flavored Brandy (Holland); 35% abv, $19.

Pale amber color; superb purity. Initial whiffs pick up assertive and piquant notes of tangy ginger and fennel; following an additional aeration period of seven minutes, the aroma stays the ginger/earthy/rooty course and, to its credit, never turns sweet. Entry is sweet, thick,

and gingery; the midpalate stage features high viscosity, a trace of brandy presence, and aggressive ginger tanginess. Good balance is featured in the finish, along with a rush of ginger piquancy. A tasty, substantial liqueur; not a brandy by any stretch of the imagination.
2007 Rating: ★★★/Recommended

Bols Hot Cinnamon Liqueur (Holland); 24% abv, $19.

Neon cherry red color; unblemished clarity. Waves of piquant cinnamon hit the olfactory sense like a fastball in the first minute, but it works; further aeration time doesn't typically apply to a beverage such as this, but this aroma turns rounder, sweeter, and subtler following seven more minutes of air contact; it's an engaging bouquet. Entry flaunts the cinnamon intensity and the sweetness degree is high, though it isn't cloying; the midpalate works better for me than the entry as the spice element cuts much of the sugary sweetness down to size. Concludes long, moderately cinnamony, slightly bitter (that's good), and suitably zesty/tangy.
2007 Rating: ★★★/Recommended

Bols Peppermint Schnapps Liqueur (Holland); 24% abv, $19.

Clear as rainwater; flawless purity. Peppermint leaps from the tasting glass after the pour, filling my SJ office with mouthwash-like perfume; additional time in the glass allows for the aroma to develop more of a stony/limestone/granite smell that underpins the topical peppermint fragrance; it's actually quite a nice, balanced bouquet once it settles down. Entry is sharply minty, yet pleasingly sweet in a candy cane manner; the midpalate is delightfully zesty and tangy as the über-mint flavor isn't too syrupy, too sweet, or too minty. Finishes cool, leafy, and keenly refreshing. Hits the peppermint nail on the head.
2007 Rating: ★★★★/Highly Recommended

Bols Pomegranate Liqueur (Holland); 17% abv, $19.

Neon cherry red color is clean and pure. Opening nose smells of wax paper, red fruits, and paraffin; further exposure to air brings out a trace of ripe sweetness, but not much else. Entry is berry/red fruit ripe and mildly sweet but the flavor profile doesn't say "pomegranate" to me; the midpalate shows a bit more pomegranate fruitiness. Concludes medium-sweet, moderately fruity. Problem is, I'd never know that this is pomegranate as opposed to some homogenous red–colored fruit liqueur. Hardly terrible, but just not individual enough to be recommended.
2007 Rating: ★★/Not Recommended

Bols Strawberry Liqueur (Holland); 22% abv, $19.

Neon strawberry red color; excellent purity. Smells of wax and plastic out of the gate; additional time in the glass achieves nothing in terms of stimulating any sense of strawberry perfume. Entry is moderately sweet and carries enough strawberry fruit to be able to identify the flavoring; the midpalate offers nothing but totally manufactured, faux strawberry (or some vague berry) taste that comes off like licking plastic. Horrible. Don't go there.
2007 Rating: ★/Not Recommended

Bols Triple Sec Liqueur (Holland); 15% abv, $19.
Translucent and impeccably clean. Opening whiffs pick up mildly zesty orange peel and orange candy scents; not much happens after further air contact. Entry is orangy sweet and candied; the midpalate stage displays some decent orange peel character, but gets blind-sided by the sugary sweetness in the aftertaste. Average, which means better than most standard brand triple secs which come off totally manufactured. Gets points for the pleasingly zesty upfront bouquet and the midpalate.
2007 Rating: ★★/Not Recommended

Borsci San Marzano Elisir Italian Liqueur (Italy); 34% abv, $18.
Has the exact look of opaque, midnight brown, black coffee. Smells of rubber inner tube, burning paper, window cleaner, vinegar, asphalt, and moss; seven more minutes of air contact doesn't affect the bouquet direction in the slightest, except to add a background note of chewing tobacco. Entry is delectably bittersweet, coffee bean-like, tar-like, even a touch cocoa-like, but not at all clumsy or cloying; the moderately sweet midpalate stage highlights cigar tobacco, cigar wrapper, prunes, figs, and black raisins. Finishes pleasantly bittersweet (this is not Amaro country) yet pruny/fruity and plump. My first exposure to this liqueur is a positive one.
2007 Rating: ★★★★/Highly Recommended

Borsci Succ'Agro Lemon Liqueur (Italy); 30% abv, $20.
Owns the right dusty, opaque yellow tint; shows good purity. The intensely lemony, sour initial bouquet is right on the mark in terms of acid/fruit/alcohol balance; the firm, highly delectable tightness/tartness prevails after six minutes of aeration; smells exactly like sour lemon-flavored hard candy; terrific. The palate entry features the squeaky clean, lemon juice sourness that remains unabated all through the excellent midpalate stretch. Finishes clean, sour, and tight as a drum. One of the top limoncellos I've tried.
2004 Rating: ★★★★/Highly Recommended

Bortolo Nardini Acqua di Cedro Liqueur (Italy); 29% abv, $56.
The appearance is thickly limpid and pure. The first inhalations pick up crisp aromas of lemon (cedro, pronounced CHAY-dro, is a pungent strain of lemon); aeration seems to settle down the aroma as it turns a touch fatter and sweeter, but it is always very true to the fruit source. The palate entry is sweet/sour, citrusy, properly lemony, and acidic; at midpalate there's a rush of lemony/zesty freshness that's irresistible and pure. Concludes fresh, lemony/citrusy, and suddenly tart. Different from limoncellos that are typically lighter and juicier.
2005 Rating: ★★★★/Highly Recommended

Bortolo Nardini Tagliatella Liqueur (Italy); 35% abv, $50/liter.
Nardini's amaro. The color is a lovely, deep auburn/henna hue that's perfectly pure. The first nosings remind me of cola, quinine, and dried orange peel; further air contact releases toasty/herbal notes of fennel and cassia bark. The palate entry is medium-sweet, earthy, and clean; at midpalate the flavor profile takes on more of the quinine and the orange peel. Ends up bittersweet to sweet, rustic/woodsy; a sophisticated, svelte, and lean amaro.
2005 Rating: ★★★/Recommended

Bottega Limoncino Sicilian Lemons and Grappa Liqueur (Italy); 30% abv, $26.

Not as opaque as many limoncellos tend to be. Shows a soft, luminescent yellow color. In the first few nosing passes, the aroma is on the sweeter side of the scale, but pleasantly lemony; following another six minutes, the aroma turns candied and firmly sweet. The palate entry is juicy, tart, and pleasing; at midpalate the taste profile turns a touch mineral- and metal-like, but is still delightfully citrusy. Concludes properly tart. Serve ice cold or on the rocks.

2005 Rating: ★★★/Recommended

Brady's Irish Cream Liqueur (Ireland); 17% abv, $10.

Standard issue, opaque milky beige/wet sand color. Shows some nice nutmeg-like spiciness in the opening aromatic passes; later sniffings detect nuts and, of course, the obvious cream element. Neither overly sweet nor creamy at palate entry, just pleasantly spicy; the midpalate offers more in the way of nuttiness/dairy presence than in the entry. Aftertaste is mellow, moderately sweet, and velvety. Excellent bargain that deserves some market share.

2005 Rating: ★★★/Recommended

Briscoes Irish Country Liqueur (Ireland); 17% abv, $20.

Color is appropriately of wet sand/beige. The first two whiffs pick up lots of cream and, suspiciously, little else; after allowing it to unwind in the glass for seven minutes, I'm disappointed that the aroma just simply can't reach past the cream and now even that component seems to be slipping away. The palate entry is horribly metallic to the point that it's akin to licking quarters; by midpalate it's clear that something has gone haywire here and I quickly open the second sample bottle but regrettably find the exact metallic, cream-gone-mad, utterly repugnant taste. Finishes irretrievably sour (and none too soon for me); the Titanic of cream liqueur disasters.

2004 Rating: ★/Not Recommended

Brogans Irish Cream Liqueur (Ireland); 17% abv, $22/liter.

Chalky tan color. The opening nosing is pleasingly, sharply spicy (nutmeg?) in the first pass, then the aroma drifts and fades in later sniffings becoming metallic and raw egg-like in the last inhalations; a bouquet that lost its way and unfortunately couldn't sustain its early virtues. The palate entry is meek, bland, and more milky than creamy; by the midpalate the taste profile gathers itself, presenting a more harmonious, creamy, lightly spiced, and milk chocolate face. Concludes with the spice complementing the cream in a pleasant fashion. Had the aroma not washed away and had the palate entry displayed more character, I might have bestowed a third rating star; as it is, this drinkable but lackluster Irish cream is nothing more than ordinary.

2004 Rating: ★★/Not Recommended

Bushmills Irish Cream Liqueur (Ireland); 17% abv, $19.

Deep beige, opaque appearance. The stately opening aroma rings with lovely, melded, sublimely sweet scents of cinnamon, candied walnut, and double cream; with time in the copita the bouquet begins to accentuate the nuttiness and the cream in the most pleasing, congruous manner imaginable, plus I detect the first evidence of whiskey. The palate entry is satiny smooth, delectably creamy, and properly spiced; at the midpalate point (which I don't

want to end), the creaminess takes on a bittersweet cocoa quality that's utterly spectacular. Concludes nutty, creamy, bittersweet, and spicy. Move over Baileys and Carolans, a new superstar has just ridden into town and is looking for a shoot-out. Without question, the finest, most sophisticated, most whiskey-centric Irish Cream in the marketplace, to date.
2004 Rating: ★★★★★/Highest Recommendation

Café Bohême Liqueur (France); 16% abv, $22.

The chocolate brown color is milky, but standard issue for a vodka and coffee liqueur. The overriding scent is black coffee in the opening inhalations; aeration releases other supplemental aromas, including cocoa butter, nuts, and dark chocolate. The palate entry delights the taste buds with succulent, creamy, and bittersweet tastes while the midpalate highlights the cream and the coffee bean components. Finishes creamy, lush, balanced, and delicious.
2004 Rating: ★★★★/Highly Recommended

Caffo Limoncino dell'Isola Infused Lemon Liqueur Calabria (Italy); 30% abv, $20.

Opaque, cloudy pale yellow appearance. The opening whiffs pick up sedate and very tart aromas of lemon peel and lemon pulp; extra time in the glass really brings out the zesty, bitter qualities of the dried lemon peel; this is the real deal. The palate entry is very tart, yet luscious lemony and juicy; at midpalate the flavor turns sweeter, though not candied, almost like proper iced lemon water with a teaspoon of sugar. Ends up deliciously tart, zesty, and pulpy. A superb juicy, true-to-the-fruit-source limoncello.
2005 Rating: ★★★★/Highly Recommended

Caffo Sambuca Secolare Aniseed Liqueur (Italy); 42% abv, $19.

Clear as mineral water, but viscous and oily in appearance. The intense aniseed aroma takes no prisoners right from the start; following some time in the glass a husky licorice scent drives the bouquet down Candy Lane. The palate entry is fat, oily, and concentrated; at midpalate the taste profile turns so intensely licorice-like that there's no room for anything else. Ends up sweet, generous, oily, and thick. The aniseed/licorice intensity is high on the feature scale.
2005 Rating: ★★★/Recommended

Caffo Vecchia Amaro del Capo Bitter Herb Liqueur (Italy); 35% abv, $24.

The bright bronze color has copper/henna core highlights. The opening salvo of aroma is pure, moderately herbal, woodsy, and medicinal; later sniffings after seven more minutes of aeration uncover pleasingly agile scents of bark, light quinine, damp earth, minerals, and cola nut. The palate entry is clean, intensely mineral-like, and modestly herbal; at midpalate the taste profile highlights the minerals, soil, and herbs, with a nifty background flavor of quinine. Concludes well, nimble, and clean.
2005 Rating: ★★★/Recommended

Calanes Anis Dulce Liqueur (Spain); 35% abv, $16/liter.

Crystal clear; some sediment. The opening nosing passes are treated to a fine display of snappy, mildly sweet, anise/licorice perfume; aeration serves to stir a bit more animation and assertiveness into the bouquet as the lead pencil quality of the anise takes charge of the

aroma. The palate entry is charged with a creamy, zesty anise taste that makes the tongue tingle slightly; the midpalate is gently sweet to the taste and velvety in texture. The aftertaste is deliciously herbal, correctly sweet, and just a dash spirity.
2002 Rating: ★★★★/Highly Recommended

Campari Bitter (Italy); 24% abv, $25.
The neon/cherry red color reminds me of cherry Kool-Aid; superb clarity. The opening whiffs immediately are treated to amazingly earthy/woodsy scents that could only be described as brambles/vines, moss, forest floor, and stones; further aeration, in this case, doesn't alter the direction of the aroma. The palate entry owns a unique tree bark-like taste that's oddly attractive to me; the midpalate stage features pungent flavors of ashes, roots, quinine, honey, citrus peels, and earth.
2007 Rating: ★★★/Recommended

Canton Ginger & Cognac Liqueur (France); 28% abv, $29.
Pale straw/ecru/oyster shell hue; impeccable clarity. Smells seductively of genuine snappy/zesty ginger root, with side notes of white pepper and aloe; after another seven minutes of air contact, the exotic, beautifully balanced aroma offers heightened and intensely earthy ginger/ginger snap cookie scents that are spot-on; a delicate, understated bouquet of the first rank and a must for ginger lovers. Entry is equal parts bittersweet ginger, firm spirit base, and earthy/mossy flavor; the midpalate point is blessed by the ideal balance of all prevailing components: spirit, acidity, bittersweet taste, peppery spice, and gingery tang. A perfect liqueur.
2007 Rating: ★★★★★/Highest Recommendation

Capella Liqueur (Italy); 25.4% abv, $23.
The amber/light honey hue is pretty and completely pure. The initial nosing after the pour unveils a bland nut meat scent that's more bitter than sweet; in the second pass, the nuttiness becomes more like walnut than any other type of nut; I find the aroma to go rather weedy and vegetal in the third sniffing, after six minutes of exposure to air; the fourth and final pass shell-like and bordering on being unpleasant. The palate entry is syrupy sweet and only mildly nutty; the midpalate stage reveals a pleasing nut/citrus peel dynamic that works. The aftertaste is ropy, sweet, only mildly nutty, and acceptable.
2000 Rating: ★★/Not Recommended

Capri Natura Limoncello (Italy); 36% abv, $25.
Cloudy corn yellow color. Charmingly and tartly smells of freshly sliced lemons; aeration serves to intensify the keenly fresh and acidic nature of this textbook bouquet. Entry is totally focused on the crisp, clean taste of lemon juice; at midpalate there's just enough sweetness to balance the lemony/citrusy character.
2007 Rating: ★★★★/Highly Recommended

Caravella Limoncello Originale d'Italia (Italy); 32% abv, $17.
Yellow/gray/green lemonade appearance; excellent purity. The initial nosing pass reveals a light, delightfully tart, lemon juice aroma; with time in the glass, the aroma takes on a

lemon peel bite in the second and third whiffs; the fourth and final blast is still fresh, citrusy tart, and intensely lemony; one of the cleaner, crisper limoncello bouquets I've come across lately. In the mouth, Caravella begins very tart but juicy at palate entry, then turns mildly sweet at midpalate. The aftertaste is concentrated, lemony, and more tart than sweet.
2001 Rating: ★★★★/Highly Recommended

Caravella Orangecello Liqueur (Italy); 30% abv, $17.

Sports the look of opaque orange soda pop; a faded orange color. The initial sniffings after the pour pick up a ripe, sweet orangy aroma that's pleasant and understated; further aeration fails to take this bouquet past the first impressions or to a higher stage of development; a mild aromatic disappointment since orange is one of my favorite flavors. The palate entry is delightfully tart and orangy; at the midpalate juncture, though, the flavor turns bittersweet and one-dimensional. It finishes medium-long, moderately tart, and low-key. Most certainly drinkable, in particular, for orange freaks, but it's clearly not in the class of its smashingly savory sibling, the much more flavorful and tangy Caravella Limoncello.
2002 Rating: ★★/Not Recommended

Carmichael's Heather Cream Liqueur (Scotland); 17% abv, $12.

Typical, beige/milky tan/wet sand color, creamy consistency. The opening odor is of steamed white rice and wet cotton fabric; the middle stage sniffings unearth a peanut-like creaminess that's pleasant, if slightly dull; the final nosing pass, after four minutes of aeration, reveals nothing new except for a distant smell of egg white or perhaps meringue is a more precise depiction; not a bad aroma, but just uninteresting; throughout the latter stages of the nosing phase I kept picking up a strong peanut scent that overrode the cream component. In the mouth the egginess makes itself known right from the palate entry and remains vigorous up until the midpalate stage; no sign of peanuts in the flavor phase. The aftertaste is long, moderately creamy, and a touch caramel-like.
2001 Rating: ★★/Not Recommended

Cask & Cream Caramel Temptation Liqueur (USA); 17% abv, $14.

Deep brown, opaque, milky appearance. The opening aroma is a tad flat and comes off as being "manufactured", meaning there's nothing here in the early stages that seems fresh or real; five more minutes doesn't seem to stimulate much more than a desultory caramel flavor. The mildly caramelly palate entry is more pleasant than the going-nowhere-but-that's-all right bouquet; by midpalate the caramel flavor component finally gets together with the cream and makes a decent, moderately sweet showing. Concludes sweet and candy-like. The taste stage saved this modest liqueur from the one star heap.
2005 Rating: ★★/Not Recommended

Cask & Cream Chocolate Temptation Liqueur (USA); 17% abv, $14.

This opaque liqueur is a dead-ringer for chocolate milk. Owns a sweet, slightly nutty opening scent; further aeration encourages a pleasing note of winter holiday spice, especially cinnamon. The palate entry is milk chocolate-like and only moderately sweet; at midpalate the spice element backs off, allowing the nutty chocolate flavor to take command. Ends well with the chocolate component seeming more like cocoa than watered down milk chocolate.

Nicely made for palates that have simple needs; give it a go.
2005 Rating: ★★★/Recommended

Casoni Limoncello di Sorrento Liqueur (Italy); 31% abv, $28.
Standard issue opaque, cloudy lemon juice yellow. Sports a keenly tart lemon juice fragrance in the first whiffs; after further aeration, the aroma turns on the lemon juice/ lemon zest spigot as the bouquet turns enticingly tart/astringent. Entry is sharply acidic (just as it should be for the category) and intensely lemony (more zest than juice or pulp); the midpalate stage features heightened lemon zest/peel concentration and a real sense of authenticity. Concludes wonderfully tart, astringent, and lemony. Bravo all the way.
2007 Rating: ★★★★/Highly Recommended

Castries Peanut Rum Creme (St. Lucia, West Indies); 16% abv, $30.
The color is milky beige/khaki/tan. Smells right upfront of roasted peanuts and, even more so, peanut butter; further time in the glass doesn't do anything in terms of aromatic expansion or change. Frothy to the feel at entry, the taste is milky and peanuty and not in the least chalky or cloying; the midpalate flavor displays a heightened roasted quality that's appealing. Finishes thick, milkshake-like, and properly peanuty. Not my cup of tea as a liqueur but it is good for what it is.
2007 Rating: ★★★/Recommended

Chambord Liqueur (France); 16.5% abv, $25.
Looks like a very young cabernet sauvignon in its ruby/crimson manner. The over-ripe aroma is concentrated, viny/seed-like, and intensely raspberry jam-like in both stages. Tastes of cassis, red raspberry syrup or, better, raspberry compote. Long, ripe, intense berry aftertaste.
2005 Rating: ★★★/Recommended

Chartreuse Green Liqueur Fabriquée par Les Pères Chartreux (France); 55% abv, $48.
The bright pale green color is crystal clear and attractive. The nose after the pour is vibrant, prickly, and completely integrated as layers of woods/barks (cedar), seeds (coriander, cardamom, aniseed), flowers (jasmine), herbs (rosemary, sage, basil), and other botanicals (fennel, kale) unite in this magical elixir; the bouquet after further aeration is even more harmonious than in the initial passes; a textbook bouquet that is unlike any other. The palate entry is lushly textured, herbal sweet, peppery, and minerally; the midpalate profile reinforces the entry impressions as the flavor goes on long, longer, longest into the sublime aftertaste. As many times over the course of every year that I taste this classic, it never becomes boring or routine. Each time, it's different, new, and brilliant.
2006 Rating: ★★★★★/Highest Recommendation

Chartreuse Green V.E.P. Liqueur Fabriquée par Les Pères Chartreux (France); 54% abv, $126/liter.
Extra-aged Green Chartreuse. The pale lime green color is eye-catching and flawlessly free of sediment. In the opening sniffs, the aroma is keenly botanical (anise, licorice, fennel) and seed-like (caraway, coriander); additional time in the copita stimulates more vegetal/ woodsy scents to emerge, especially sawdust, pine bark, cardamom, basil, and grass. The

palate entry is off-dry to bittersweet and concentrated on peppermint, citrus peel, and sage; the midpalate taste profile is harmonious as the various components of herbs, sweetness, alcohol, and woodsy botanicals meld perfectly into a single flavor thrust that is unforgettable. Concludes with finesse and power.
2006 Rating: ★★★★★/Highest Recommendation

Chartreuse Yellow Liqueur Fabriquée par Les Pères Chartreux (France); 40% abv, $48.
The yellow/green color is different from the all-gold V.E.P. version but lovely all the same; ideal clarity. The first nosing passes pick up loads of botanical treasures, most prominently, seeds (aniseed, cardamom), licorice, hay, and white pepper; aeration time and swirling help floral/viny scents to emerge along with coriander, sage, and thyme. The palate entry is sweet, floral, peppery, and viny; the midpalate profile features fennel, rosemary, allspice, and bark. Ends up regally and herbal sweet.
2006 Rating: ★★★★/Highly Recommended

Chartreuse Yellow V.E.P. Liqueur Fabriquée par Les Pères Chartreux (France); 42% abv, $126/liter.
Extra-aged Yellow Chartreuse. The color is sunshine gold; impeccable purity. The first inhalations encounter prickly scents of bramble/vines, fennel, and licorice; extra time in the glass brings out a supple sweetness that perfectly assimilates the herbal/brambly, saffron-like thrusts of the early-on aroma. The palate entry is sharply focused on a floral sweetness; the midpalate profile has so many layers of botanicals that it's hard to list them all, but they include sage, saffron, elderberry, anise, licorice, flowers, and thyme. Finishes elegantly, even stately as the sweetness of the entry becomes softer, more bittersweet, herbal, and divinely satisfying.
2006 Rating: ★★★★★/Highest Recommendation

Christian Brothers Amber Cream Brandy and Cream Liqueur (USA); 17% abv, $10.
Very milky beige and opaque. The initial nosing passes pick up a pleasing and very spicy (cinnamon, nutmeg, holiday spices), almost nut-like bouquet that's dairy-like and creamy but focused on the cinnamon; seven more minutes in the glass encourage deeper scents of chocolate, coffee bean, and cream to override the spice; very little evidence of brandy. The palate entry is very dairy-oriented, almost like half and half; at the midpalate point there's a surge in the brandy and spice tastes which dominate the creaminess. The aftertaste is semisweet, delightfully creamy, and properly thick. At this price, it's hard to beat.
2003 Rating: ★★★/Recommended

Cinzano Bianco Vermouth (Italy); 15% abv, $12.
The pale flax/oyster color is brilliant and unblemished. The first sniffs detect keenly herbal, minerally, and grassy notes that become waxy and lipstick/lip balm-like in the later inhalations after additional aeration. The palate entry is engagingly ripe, grapy, and sweet; at the midpalate point the acidity kicks in, keeping the ripe fruit from becoming too sweet and the stone/mineral flavor also accelerates, making for terrific warm weather quaffing. Heck, I'd enjoy this beauty simply served chilled on its own with a twist of lemon or orange. Absolutely delightful.
2007 Rating: ★★★★/Highly Recommended

Cinzano Extra Dry Vermouth (Italy); 18% abv, $14.

The appearance is riverstone/silver and bright; perfect clarity. The initial nosing passes pick up yeasty/doughy scents that are fresh, fabric-like, and dry; following further aeration not very much happens on the aroma side of the ledger. The palate entry is fresh, sinewy, lean, and acutely mineral-like; at the midpalate stage the flavor profile accelerates on the desert dry front, becoming even drier and more minerally. Squeaky dry and utterly refreshing.

2007 Rating: ★★★/Recommended

Cinzano Rosso Vermouth (Italy); 15% abv, $12.

The reddish/brown color is prune juice-like and clean. The opening whiffs pick up dried fruits, including prunes, dates, and black raisins; touches of herbs and spices get added to the aroma following the aeration period. The palate entry is more bittersweet than outright sweet and intensely fruity (stewed prunes); at the midpalate juncture the red fruit element really jumps out at you in mildly herbal/spicy tastes that include quinine, cinnamon, roots, and pepper.

2007 Rating: ★★★/Recommended

Clair's Cognac & Cream (France); 17% abv, $20.

Typical cream liqueur beige/wet sand/milky brown appearance. The opening nosing passes immediately following the pour detect little in the way of brandy/cream aromas; after seven minutes of additional aeration time, hints of brandy and fruit emerge along with nuances of bean-like spice; a limp, rather hollow bouquet. The palate entry is mildly creamy, but with no immediate brandy impact; by the midpalate an alluring flavor profile develops, one that's delicate, more creamy than brandy-like. A mild; soft, creamy, moderately spicy finish. Pleasant, elegant, walks softly.

2002 Rating: ★★★/Recommended

Cointreau Liqueur (France); 40% abv, $32.

Clear as mineral water; pure and viscous. The perfume of orange pulp is delicate, alluring, and tart in the first two minutes of sniffing; after aeration, the aroma turns much more dry peel-like, meaning oily and focused; fabulous, elegant, sophisticated bouquet. The palate entry is intensely orange peel-like yet more sweet than bittersweet; the midpalate stage is deeply orangey, brisk and crisp, sweet and sublimely juicy. Finishes ideally citrusy/tart/astringent, then turns lithe and sweet. The benchmark for all orange flavored liqueurs/triple secs. None better. State of the art, period. After tasting a whole slew of competing triple sec/orange liqueurs over the last decade, it is abundantly clear as to which brand is the gold standard. And I'm not even broaching the subject about using Cointreau as a necessary ingredient in margaritas.

2005 Rating: ★★★★/Highest Recommendation

Couprie Abricot au Cognac Liqueur (France); 21% abv, $32.

The shimmering, juice-like appearance is honey/gold; minor, as to be insignificant, suspended particles are noted. The opening nosing pass displays the firm, ripe scent of baked apricot and the leanness of eau-de-vie in perfect harmony; with the second sniffing coming after three minutes of air contact, the ripeness of the apricot picks up steam, becoming juicy sweet; in the third whiff a nuance of spice enters the scene, but at a distance; the fourth and final nosing pass displays the kind of sweet ripeness that one expects from a super-premium liqueur. The palate entry is intensely sweet and apricoty; the midpalate stage sees a minor reduction in fruit concentration as the brandy element kicks in. The aftertaste is full-bodied and thick, long and sweet. Handsome, well-crafted, and recommendable.

2000 Rating: ★★★/Recommended

Couprie Framboise au Cognac Liqueur (France); 21% abv, $32.

The fetching color is that soft orange/pink hue found especially in Tavel rosés; impeccable purity. The initial nosing pass reveals spare scents of brambles and berries; with three minutes of exposure to air, the aroma turns slightly sour in an unripened berry manner; by the third sniffing, the fruit perfume, admittedly fey to begin with, vanishes, leaving behind very delicate traces of seeds and pulp; the fourth pass sees all evidence of fruit totally gone and, as a result, a void is left and a flaw is exposed. The palate entry is light, tart, and lean; the midpalate phase is much more animated in terms of raspberry presence, but it will never be considered a blockbuster. The faint finish is too light for its own good. A wholly ordinary fruit liqueur whose biggest failing is its stingy nature.

2000 Rating: ★★/Not Recommended

Crème Boulard Cream Calvados Liqueur (France); 17% abv, $15.

Standard issue tan/beige color. The initial nosing passes are confronted with a curious aroma that's definitely one part apple and one part cream, but the combination at first blush seems awkward and ill-suited; time in the glass sees the bouquet develop a bit more roundness as the aroma takes on more of an apple streudel-with-cream perfume that's actually quite delightful. The palate entry is mildly apple-like, creamy, and comfortably sweet; the midpalate stage is comely, medium sweet, and pleasantly creamy. The aftertaste features more of the cream than the apple component. A different, distinctive twist on cream liqueurs that's fresh and well-made.

2002 Rating: ★★★/Recommended

Cruzan Rum Cream Liqueur (Ireland); 17% abv, $16.

Considerably whiter than most other cream liqueurs, very creamy texture. The initial nosing pass picks up snappy, zesty, almost cinnamon/nutmeg notes that stimulate the olfactory sense; by the third whiff, three to four minutes into aeration, the cream element really comes alive; by the final pass, the cream comes to dominate and stays strong for several minutes more along with appealing notes of caramel and low-key spice; a compelling cream liqueur bouquet. The palate entry is nimble, not overly creamy or sweet, and mildly spicy; the midpalate phase starts out rather dry in a light caramel fashion but then turns lip-smacking sweet and intensely creamy. The finish is long, lush, and crowd-pleasing. My only wish is that the tangy spiciness discerned in the early aroma stages would have continued throughout the midpalate and finish stages; other than that, an easily recommendable cream liqueur whose base spirit is rum.

2001 Rating: ★★★/Recommended

DeKuyper Original Blue Island Pucker Sweet & Sour Schnapps Imitation Liqueur (USA); 15% abv, $10.

Cobalt blue color; good purity. The initial whiffs unearth frisky, hard candy-like fruit scents of pineapple, mango, cherry, citrus, and banana; the fruit salad bouquet stays the course following six minutes of aeration. The palate entry is sweet and fruity; then at midpalate the sudden sourness makes my lips purse to at least a level four, well, pucker; got to admire the name/form aspect of this beverage. The aftertaste is intensely sour, then just as fast sweet, ripe, and, dare I say it, zesty and tasty. This type of tutti-frutti, neon-colored concoction is hardly my style of drink but doubtless much to the horror of long-time SJ subscribers I actually don't mind this Pucker edition (hence the rating), and can see its attraction to very young legal age drinkers (21-24) who were weaned on Mountain Dew, Pepsi-Cola, and Dr. Pepper.

2003 Rating: ★★★/Recommended

DeKuyper Pomegranate Liqueur (USA); 15% abv, $11.

Displays an excellent blood red/ruby color and impeccable clarity. Right out of the gate, the aroma rings moderately true with pomegranate, in that it's very fruity if a touch candied; ditto after the additional aeration period. The palate entry is delightfully tart, even sour, and therefore fresh and more genuine than the aroma; by the midpalate point the keen acidity heightens, making the fruit element that much more real. After the lackluster aroma, I was prepared not to like this liqueur, but the more than substantial gains made in the entry and midpalate make it unmistakably recommendable.

2007 Rating: ★★★/Recommended

DeKuyper Tropical Mango Imitation Liqueur (USA); 15% abv, $10.

Color of neon red cherry juice; very good clarity. The limp aroma after the pour reminds me of electrical wires that are about to go up in flames, meaning very metallic/coppery; aeration brings the aroma from burning wires to especially rank old sneakers…well, at least, there's some progression. The fruit component tastes nothing like mango and is basically all glyceriny and taste bud numbing; the midpalate is, well, oh forget it. The word "Imitation" on the neckband says it all. My biggest question: How do the people who make this pig swill sleep at night knowing that this is in the marketplace? Probable answer: Hey, they think it's delicious!

2007 Rating: ★/Not Recommended

DeKuyper Tropical Papaya Imitation Liqueur (USA); 15% abv, $10.

The pastel rose color is actually pretty; superb purity. Don't you dare say anything to anyone but I find the initial aroma ripe and pleasantly tropical and bubble gum-like; the ripeness accelerates somewhat after aeration. Entry taste is disappointingly but not surprisingly lame and sugary after a smidgen of promise in the aroma; midpalate doesn't exist except for a sugar water, hard candy flavor that's beyond simplistic. Rings up the cheap-o-meter with gusto. If my name was DeKuyper, I'd have it legally changed just because of this bomb.

2007 Rating: ★/Not Recommended

DeKuyper Tropical Pineapple Coconut Imitation Liqueur (USA); 15% abv, $10.

Neon yellow/gold appearance; excellent clarity. Smells peculiarly of wool blanket, floor wax, and pineapple candy in the opening round of sniffing; following aeration, the nose becomes gum-like, with the weird wool blanket thing kicking in again; very textile-like. The taste at entry is better than the oddball aroma, but is still completely artificial and not in the least authentic; midpalate reflects the entry to a tee, except for the out-of-left field flavor of butter cream candy. Leaps off the deep end of the weird imitation liqueur chart. "Cheap" doesn't begin to tell this story.

2007 Rating: ★/Not Recommended

Del Capo Liqueur of Calabrian Herbs (Italy); 35% abv, $26.

The appearance is a gorgeous nut brown/copper penny color that's clean and pure. The first inhalations discover tangy scents of orange zest, orange blossom, and mint; additional air contact brings out leafy/viny aromas of pine, cedar, jasmine, and flowers. The palate entry is citrusy, bittersweet, and medium-bodied; at midpalate the taste profile turns increasingly root-like and earthy, going away from the leaves/flowers and highlighting calamus and roots that make this liqueur distantly similar to American root beer. Concludes bittersweet.

2006 Rating: ★★★/Recommended

Der Lachs Original Danziger Goldwasser Herbal Liqueur (Germany); 40% abv, $28.

The pale straw color shows floating parchment-thin flakes of gold leaf. The first nosing is all about leafy herbs, such as parsley, sage, and thyme; later whiffs pick up more vegetal/ rooty scents like fennel, ginger, and rhubarb and the very final sniff detects anise. The palate entry highlights the leafy tastes of freshly cut herbs and ginger plus a pleasantly sugary base flavor; at midpalate the taste profile doesn't change that much. Finishes warm, tangy, and delightfully herbal.

2006 Rating: ★★★/Recommended

Destinee Ruby Liqueur (USA); 17% abv, $20.

A blend of cognac, vodka, grapefruit and "other" natural flavors. Shows the hazy, rosy appearance of pink lemonade. The opening inhalations pick up appealing, tart grapefruit pulp, waxy Crayola crayon notes; the extra seven minutes in the glass accomplish little, if anything. The palate entry is nicely tart, nearly sour, and appropriately acidic; at midpalate the fruit takes a backseat to the spirit, making for pleasing quaffing. Ends up fruity and light; grapefruit is a particularly hard flavor to include in any type of spirits, but the distillers got it right. Nice job here.

2004 Rating: ★★★/Recommended

Destinee Sapphire Liqueur (USA); 17% abv, $20.

This cloudy blue color has more yellow in it than, say, Alizé or Hpnotiq, but it's still pretty. The nose is barely fruity in the first sniffings, then in later passes a cotton candy scent takes charge. The palate entry is sweet/sour and ripe; the midpalate stage sees a touch of the vodka come through, but not enough to bolster the flabby fruit flavor. Concludes sour; drinkable, but simpler and less integrated in terms of the fruit/spirit when compared to its more dynamic peers, including its nicer sibling Destinee Ruby.

2005 Rating: ★★/Not Recommended

Di Amore Raspberry Liqueur (USA); 16.5% abv, $11.

Nearly opaque, deep purple appearance that's close to immature ruby port. The opening bouquet is fresh, ripe, and invitingly fruity in a garden-fresh, "hey, let's pick our own" berry manner; aeration encourages the aroma to dig a little deeper and the few extra minutes in the glass results in a sweet, almost sugary, dare I say with reluctance, soda pop-like, raspberry/cherry fragrance that's acceptably tutti-frutti and simple. The palate entry is clean, sweet but not cloying, and ripe; the midpalate point sees the volume turned up noticeably on the sugar-level, presenting a liqueur that comes off a mite too manufactured, sugar-prone, and no longer "field fresh". It's drinkable and, to its credit, not in the least unctuous or syrupy; but it doesn't reflect fresh fruit in the least. Use it in punches.

2002 Rating: ★★/Not Recommended

Domenis Kosher Amaro (Italy); 28% abv, $50.

Organic. The color of honey; absolute purity. As opposed to some other amaros in the marketplace, this amaro bouquet is delicate, lightly bitter and elegant and doesn't hammer one's olfactory sense into submission; in the first nosing go-round, there's evidence of gentle orange peel; aeration stirs subtle scents of orris root, anise, bark, and angelica; simply the classiest, best amaro bouquet I've ever evaluated; it's amazingly seductive. The palate entry is mellow, semisweet, not in the least bitter and botanical; the midpalate shows exceptional balance, with a taste emphasis on orange zest. It finishes gently on the tongue in soft tastes of orange peel, anise, and orris root. Divine and runs rings around every other amaro/bitter out there.

2002 Rating: ★★★★★/Highest Recommendation

Domenis Kosher Sambuca (Italy); 40% abv, $50.

Organic. Crystal clear and luminous under the lamp; perfect purity. The nose at opening is razor-sharp and totally focused on the anise; with time in the glass the aroma expands to include deep licorice and wet stone; a laser beam bouquet of directness and cleanness. The palate entry is sweet but not numbing as the anise concentration impresses the taste buds; strong, licorice/anise midpalate. The aftertaste is long, medium-viscous, semisweet, and luscious. One of the finest sambucas in the marketplace.

2002 Rating: ★★★★/Highly Recommended

Douce Provence Poire Williams and Cognac Liqueur (France); 30% abv, $25.

The pale flaxen color is ideally pure. The opening whiffs pick up lightly spiced fragrances of pears and white raisins; an extra seven minutes of air exposure assists in helping the cognac element emerge from behind the veil of ripe pear fruit perfume; together, the pear and cognac provide an elegant, delicate bouquet that's soft, fruity, and understated. The palate entry is tart immediately, then quickly turns semisweet as the pear influence overtakes the brandy component; by the midpalate stage the cognac returns to lend substance to the lithe, ambrosial surface flavors. The aftertaste is semisweet, ripely fruity, and intensely pear-like, but with that silent but firm structure provided by the cognac. A world-class liqueur.

2002 Rating: ★★★★/Highly Recommended

Dr. McGillicuddy's Cherry Schnapps Original Formula Liqueur (Canada); 15% abv, $15.

The bright cherry red color is gorgeous and clean. The first whiffs detect animated and

bitter scents of cherry stone and cherry fruit; after six minutes of additional aeration, the fruit component emerges more as the fruit stone bitterness recedes. The palate entry is ripe, sweet, moderately stony/mineral-like, and deeply cherry-flavored; by the midpalate stage the taste profile has gone over completely to the ripe cherry juice sweetness. Finishes gently sweet and concentrated without the slightest hint of overstatement. For its genre, very pleasing.
2007 Rating: ★★★/Recommended

Dr. McGillicuddy's French Kiss Vanilla Schnapps Liqueur (Canada); 24% abv, $13.
Transparent and clean. The first sniff picks up a firm, mildly sweet vanilla bean/vanilla extract perfume; time in the glass turns the bouquet more bean-like than sweet; a solid bouquet. The palate entry is pleasantly sweet and vanilla frosting-like; the midpalate displays a thick texture that supports the velvety vanilla frosting flavor. The finish is long, acceptably sweet, and actually lip-smacking. A vanilla flavored libation with a lower alcohol level that's fit ideally for a young, legal-age audience; worked for me.
2003 Rating: ★★★/Recommended

Drambuie Liqueur (Scotland); 40% abv, $35.
The old gold coin/deep straw/very old sauternes hue is beautiful and flawlessly pure. Smells of salty maritime single malt whisky right from the opening whiff; aeration plays to this great liqueur's strengths as the layers of aroma require some time to unfold; these layers offer succulent , integrated scents of honey, heather, pine needle, thyme, and most thrilling of all, salty single malt Scotch whisky. Entry is firm, thick, gently sweet but balanced by a fierce herbal quality that's fresh and dried at the same time; the flavor profile at midpalate features more of the whisky as the various herbs, spices, and honey make merry around their whisky core. One of the top five liqueurs ever produced in the history of distilled spirits.
2007 Rating: ★★★★★/Highest Recommendation

Echte Kroatzbeere Blackberry Liqueur (Germany); 30% abv, $30.
The blackberry jam/ruby/bay color is very attractive; excellent purity. The first whiffs detect viny/bramble-like, outdoorsy scents that are bitter; further aeration produces only meager aromatic progress as the bouquet offers intense bramble, but scant fruit. The palate entry is rich and concentrated with deep blackberry taste; by midpalate the taste profile gears up to be stony, ripe, preserves-like, and ripe-sweet. Finishes jammy and ripe. Displays potent and true blackberry character.
2006 Rating: ★★★/Recommended

Ecstasy Liqueur (USA); 35% abv, $32.
Clear and clean as spring water. I get a mélange of intriguing scents upfront, including tangerine, nectarine, red cherry, and Asian spice (ginger, ginseng, mace); seven more minutes doesn't alter the aromatic profile greatly, except for the gradual fading of the spices and the ramping up of the fruit components. Tastes of minerals/slate in the entry, then turns on the fruit at midpalate, but there's still a metallic/tinny/coin-like quality to the flavor profile that detracts from that stage. Concludes off-dry, tinny, and vaguely fruity.
2007 Rating: ★★/Not Recommended

Edmond Briottet Crème de Pêche Wild Peach Liqueur (France); 18% abv, $26.

The stunning appearance is an orange/topaz/bronze color; excellent purity. The opening nosing picks up tart notes of peach peel and bramble; the second pass turns more brambly than fruity; in the third sniffing nothing new is revealed; the fourth and final whiff, following eight minutes of aeration, unearths little new other than a keen ripeness that isn't part of the first three nosings; while true to the fruit source, overall a one-note aroma. The palate entry is peachy, sweet, ripe, and focused; the midpalate juncture shows some tartness/acidity to counter the ripeness. The finish is long, very clean, more tart than sweet, and tasty. While certainly good and recommendable, I didn't find myself swooning over this particular Briottet product like I have with his others.

2000 Rating: ★★★/Recommended

Eduardino Liqueur (Portugal); 25.5% abv, $11.

The brilliant topaz/bronze color is bright and relatively clean. The opening whiffs pick up sweetish scents of bubble gum, licorice, anise, fennel, and citrus rind; additional exposure to air sees the bouquet turn seriously minty (spearmint, especially) and fruity, as in tangerine peel; a singular, expressive bouquet that I like. The palate entry comes off a little too reminiscent of mouthwash in its sweet and minty bearing; the midpalate turns even sweeter, almost sugary, as the botanicals begin to fade in the face of the sugarcane sweetness. The finish is sweet, lackluster, and pedestrian.

2002 Rating: ★★/Not Recommended

Elisir du Dr. Roux Liqueur (France); 47% abv, $24/375 ml.

The medicinal color is pea green/yellow-green; perfectly pure. The perfume right after opening wafts up from the sampling glass in Oriental cooking-like waves of anise, angelica, and ginseng; in the second nosing pass the fennel element races to the forefront; by the penultimate sniffing, following nearly eight minutes of aeration, a concentrated bark-like/woodsy aroma takes command, leaving many of the discernable aromatic components by the wayside; the fourth and last whiff, after over ten minutes of air contact, focuses on the foresty/woodsy scents of balsam and bark; intriguing, ever-changing, and a medicinal blast for the nasal cavity. The palate entry is strangely neutral; but then by midpalate the flavors explode on the tongue in meteoric flashes of lemon peel, marjoram, and anise mostly, but hey, with so many botanical elements it's hard to clearly isolate them. The aftertaste is long, sweet, concentrated, herbal, woodsy, and most impressive of all, clean. After initially harboring some misgivings, I came around to this liqueur in a big way; but more than anything, I salute M. Roux for creating a beverage that's new and contemporary, but also tips its hat to past masters, i.e., Chartreuse, Benedictine.

2000 Rating: ★★★★/Highly Recommended

Elisir Gambrinus Wine Based Liqueur with Natural Aromatics (Italy); 27% abv, $25.

Appearance of dark brown/mahogany color, with a tawny core. The initial nosing passes after the pour discover an odd and unusual fig-like scent that's one part dried red fruit (black raisins, prune), one part brown butter, one part black truffles, and one part soft spirit; further aeration stimulates additional, if minor fragrances of wool, dates, and shale; I liked this bouquet a lot, even though I had trouble pinpointing all the aspects. The palate

entry is intensely fig-like, almost sherried, but sour enough to maintain a freshness that's beguiling; the midpalate juncture is sweeter than the entry; nicely viscous, but not cloying, with concentrated flavors of prunes, figs, dates, and raisins. Ends up moderately sweet, with a dash of bitterness just to keep the flavor moving forward. Like nothing I've ever tasted.
2007 Rating: ★★★★/Highly Recommended

Envy Liqueur (France); 17% abv, $25.
The cobalt blue appearance is pretty and as far as I can tell quite pure. The opening nosings find zesty but sweet aromas of pineapple, passion fruit, and guava headlining the early bouquet; with time in the glass the fruit element becomes rounder, less sweet, and quite succulent; there's hardly any trace of either vodka or cognac throughout the entire ten minute nosing phase. The palate entry is properly sweet/tart; then at midpalate the passionfruit jumps into the lead and remains there. The aftertaste is ripe, fruity, and shows just the slightest bit of vodka; as tasty and carefree as Hpnotiq.
2003 Rating: ★★★/Recommended

Envy Mango Melon Liqueur (France); 17% abv, $25.
Cloudy, medium green color. The fruity bouquet wastes no time exposing the melon and mango components; later nosings reveal a trace of spirit. The palate entry is more tart and acidic than sweet or ripe; the midpalate phase is less fruity and more spirity, offering a slightly dull backtaste. Ends neither sweet nor sour, just a bit fruity. Another drinkable, but ultimately ordinary liqueur that's deficient mostly in panache.
2005 Rating: ★★/Not Recommended

Escorial Liqueur (Germany); 56% abv, $33.
The faint green/silvery blue tint is very pretty and perfectly clear. Initial whiffs detect gently spiced and herbal scents that include barely discernible traces of peppermint and dried herbs; additional aeration time doesn't shake loose any other layers of fragrance. In the palate entry, a powerfully potent taste of mint grows in intensity on the tongue; at midpalate there's really nothing new except for an expanding bittersweet element. Finishes very cleanly and intensely pepperminty.
2006 Rating: ★★★/Recommended

Everglo Vodka-Tequila-Ginseng Liqueur (Holland); 24% abv, $24.
The foggy lime green Jello appearance doesn't do it for me; impeccable purity, though. The aroma is quite muted in the initial whiffs except for a way-in-the-background citrusy note; further aeration brings out the citrus, plus subtle notes of sweet/sour spice and crushed herbs; not an aroma to sit and ponder. The palate entry is light, fruity, and sweet/sour; at midpalate I keep wondering where the tequila is in the slick mass of citrusy sweet, sticky taste. Ends up sweet and limey, with little acknowledgement of the spirits. A kiddie-pop spirit that lacks the grace and sophistication of a fashionable liqueur like Hpnotiq.
2005 Rating: ★★/Not Recommended

Faretti Biscotti Famosi Biscotti Liqueur (Italy); 28% abv, $27.
The deep straw/old gold color is pretty and pure. The opening whiffs are true to what's described on the label as confectioner's sugar and cookie batter scents please the olfactory

sense in the first stages; aeration brings out a note of orange peel that mingles well with the sugar and batter. The palate entry is sweet, intense, and predictably biscuit-like; the orange aspect emerges in the midpalate taste which brings a pleasant citric acidity to the experience that balances the sugary sweetness. Ends well and elegantly.
2007 Rating: ★★★★/Highly Recommended

Frangelico Liqueur (Italy); 24% abv, $25.
Amber/burnished gold color; ideal clarity. Smells immediately of toasted hazelnut and peanut, with a slightly salty background scent; after another seven minutes in the glass, the aroma turns toastier and more buttery and nutty; an immediately identifiable bouquet. Entry is very sweet and borderline syrupy, but oh, that incredible toasted nut, slightly smoky, and altogether fruity opening taste salvo; the midpalate is long, silky, textured, and nutty sweet. Delicious from stem to stern.
2007 Rating: ★★★★/Highly Recommended

Germain-Robin Liqueur de Poète (USA); 25% abv, $45/375ml.
The attractive golden/amber hue is pretty and bright. The initial whiffs detect baked, toasted aromas; after another five minutes, subtle, caramelized notes of pear—baked pear—emerge in tiny increments; the unfolding of this reluctant bouquet demands patience but it's worth the wait. The palate entry flavor is soft, woody/resiny, and lightly fruited; the midpalate shows more layering as the baked pear, pruny, almost Madeira-like (sercial or verdelho) taste comes to the fore. Finishes sweet/sour, soft cheese-like (feta), and like dried fruit. Hubert Germain-Robin is a magician.
2005 Rating: ★★★★/Highly Recommended

Gilka Kaiser-Kümmel Liqueur (Germany); 38% abv, $33/liter.
The pale gray/yellow hay color is clean and clear. The initial inhalations detect the seed-like scent of caraway and nothing more; later sniffs pick up only the strong aroma of caraway seed and that's it. The palate entry is, well, intensely caraway seed-like and slightly coin-like; at midpalate the caraway seed taste blows away any sense of coins/metal, ending up nicely in a firm, oily finish that's concentrated and correctly seed-like.
2006 Rating: ★★★/Recommended

Ginja Sem Rival Cherry Liqueur (Portugal); 24.2% abv, $13.
Beautiful red wine-like, ruby/garnet/tawny color; superb purity. The aroma hits the ground running as concentrated, ripe, jammy scents of black cherry waft from the copita; several more minutes of air contact release deeper preserves-like aromas that are delectably bittersweet. The palate entry is bittersweet and ripe; by the midpalate point the taste goes slightly tannic but remains well true to the fruit and intensely fruity. The finish is medium long, tannic, and bitter. A "cherry" cherry liqueur.
2002 Rating: ★★★/Recommended

Gioia Luisa Lemoncello Lemon Liqueur (Italy); 30% abv, $10/375 ml.
The bright neon yellow color is spoiled by lots of floating debris; one hopes that the suspended particles are only bits of lemon pulp or peel. The nose is properly citrusy and

acidic in the opening sniffing, then in the second pass an artificial, as in manufactured, odor overshadows the lemon zest; following six minutes of aeration, the aroma can't seem to shake the metal-like scent and, as a result, the lemon perfume continues in a secondary role; the fourth and final pass sees no change at all, which is a shame because I can detect the makings of a decent liqueur here. The palate entry is lemony but strangely fabric-like at the same time; the midpalate stage is sweet, lemony, and seeming to come out of the funkiness found in the nose and the early mouth phase. The finish is rather short, thick, sweet, lemony, but somehow off. The unappetizing appearance is a serious turn-off.

2000 Rating: ★/Not Recommended

Giori Lemoncello Cream Liqueur (Italy); 17% abv, $17.
Yellowish, milky, canvas color. The nose right after opening is rich, heavily creamy, and a bit like egg nog; time in the glass brings out a deft touch of lemon by the second whiff, but in the third sniffing the bouquet reverts back to the deep creaminess; the fourth and last nosing pass, after a full nine minutes of aeration, sees the bouquet come off alluringly as the lemon and cream seem to have married successfully. The palate entry is moderately sweet and eggy; the midpalate stage is where the flavor displays its best stuff as the lemon and cream dance in sync on the tongue. The aftertaste shows far more lemon influence than either the aroma or the flavor phases. Very enjoyable and easily recommended.

2001 Rating: ★★★/Recommended

Giori Lemoncello Liqueur (Italy); 30% abv, $17.
Typical, opaque, cloudy yellow appearance. The nose at opening is zesty, piquant, and ideally bitter; in the middle stage nosings the bitter lemon peel scent picks up the pace, offering a lovely, fresh-squeezed lemon juice perfume; by the fourth and final sniffing, following nearly eight minutes in the glass, the juicy bitterness continues to accelerate; love this bouquet. The palate entry is sweet and lemony; then at midpalate the taste turns properly bitter and acidic as the lemon juice/lemon peel influence rises to the occasion. The finish is clean, bitter, lemony, and delicious. A superb lemoncello that never loses sight of its bitter by nature source. The problem with some lemoncellos is that they have too much sugar added which kills the premise; not so with this one.

2001 Rating: ★★★★/Highly Recommended

Girl By Necker Framboise, Litchi, Vodka & Cognac Liqueur (France); 25% abv, $25.
The pastel pink is a rose-colored visual pleasure; impeccable purity. Fragrant litchi dominates the opening aroma in the first couple of passes, then the ripe raspberry framboise bolts to the lead following further aeration. The palate entry is light, fruity (berry), and floral; at midpalate the taste profile turns off-dry and very floral. Finishes mildly sweet and engagingly fruity. Nice job here.

2007 Rating: ★★★/Recommended

Gozio Amaretto (Italy); 24% abv, $24.
Fantastically gorgeous deep copper/bordering on mahogany hue; ideal purity. The opening sniffings pick up lively and sweet aromas of almond and spice; more time in the glass allows the bouquet to rev up a bit and it blossoms into a multilayered, opulent perfume

that focused squarely on mildly bitter almond meat. The palate entry is delicate and lightly sweet, not in the least unctuous or thick; by the midpalate stage the flavor phase showcases the almond, but with less intensity than the entry. The aftertaste is long, creamy, and sublime in its bearing.

2003 Rating: ★★★★/Highly Recommended

Gozio Liquorice Liqueur (Italy); 26% abv, $33.

Dense, opaque nut brown/brown shoe polish color. The first whiffs pick up delicate scents of Brazil nuts and anise; aeration adds notes of burning rubber, black licorice, and paraffin. The palate entry is sharp and intensely aniseed-like; then at midpalate there's a huge, battering wave of black licorice that swamps all other taste possibilities. Concludes rich, but awkward and off balance. Not the slightest hint of subtlety here; only for the most extreme black licorice fanatics.

2004 Rating: ★★/Not Recommended

Gran Gala Triple Orange Liqueur (Italy); 40% abv, $19.

The color is a deep copper/bronze brandy-like hue; good purity. The first nosing pass detects intensely acidic notes of orange peel; with aeration, the aroma expands in the second sniffing to include scents of marzipan, candied orange rind, dried apricot, and almond oil; the third nosing pass returns to the tart citric acid/orange peel aroma that dominated the bouquet right after the pour; following ten minutes of air contact, the nose at last displays a hint of the brandy in the final whiff; a good, solid, but slightly too chunky orange liqueur bouquet. The palate entry is heavy and syrupy on the tongue texture-wise and very sweet to the taste; the midpalate stage is pleasantly fruity/orangey and sweet. The finish is long, thick, and similar to orange soda pop. I could envision where the Stock people wanted to go with this triple orange liqueur and if they would have been slightly less heavy-handed, Gran Gala would have been a potential four star product; as it is, I recommend it for mixing in cocktails, but not as a straight libation.

2000 Rating: ★★★/Recommended

Grand Marnier Cordon Rouge Triple Orange Liqueur (France); 40% abv, $40.

Bright copper color. Perhaps the most easily identifiable aroma in the greater liqueur category; sweet/sour, tangerine/mandarin orange perfume that never stops enchanting. Lovely, balanced in the mouth as the orange zest's acidity mingles gracefully with the cognac's alcohol, making for exquisite drinking. Finishes like satin. If this were the sole GM expression, I'd give it five stars, but because of the sublime existence of the Centenaire and the Cinquantenaire, it must be rated four.

2005 Rating: ★★★★/Highly Recommended

Grand Marnier Cuvée du Centenaire Triple Orange Liqueur (France); 40% abv, $100.

Looks very close to the coppery Cordon Rouge. Smells of cognac as much as it does of orange zest and that's the major difference with the Cordon Rouge. In the mouth, there's the ideal balance between the citric acid, alcohol, cognac, and wood, with the essence of the cognac always prevailing. Concludes with sheer finesse, sweet/sour presence, and that incredibly lush texture. Never ceases to amaze me for its perfection as a Grand Cru Classe liqueur.

2005 Rating: ★★★★★/Highest Recommendation

Grand Marnier Cuvée du Cent Cinquantenaire Triple Orange Liqueur (France); 40% abv, $190.
Dark amber/old copper penny color. The perfume is intense, but balanced through the ten minutes of sniffing; the triple orange acts as the ideal companion to the old cognac. Tastes wonderfully of orange zest and tangerine, as well as classic cognac. Ends up remarkably mellow and textured. Couldn't possibly be better than it already is.
2005 Rating: ★★★★★/Highest Recommendation

Hiram Walker Butternips Original Butterscotch Schnapps (USA); 15% abv, $16.
Medium amber, honey-like color; impeccable purity. Early aromas are toasty, candied aromas of butterscotch which then turn to light-colored caramel and salted English butter. Palate entry is alluringly off-dry to bittersweet, with delicate, on-the-money flavors of butter, caramel, saltwater taffy; at midpalate the core flavor profile is off-dry and intensely caramel-like, a touch nougat-like, and not the least bit syrupy, oily or cloying. Finish is medium-bodied, manageably bittersweet, and buttery.
2005 Rating: ★★★/Recommended

Hiram Walker Fruja Mango Exotic Fruit Liqueur (USA); 15% abv, $18.
Golden yellow color; limpid; absolute purity. Delicate, with soft fruity notes of mango, banana, and a judicious touch of spice in both initial and later aromatic passes. Palate entry is clean and properly sweet without being unctuous or heavy; at midpalate the solid fruit core is underpinned well by a crisp acidity that retains the natural freshness of the mango. Finish is satiny in the throat, clean, and appropriately sweet and ripe.
2005 Rating: ★★★/Recommended

Hiram Walker Original Peach Schnapps (USA); 15% abv, $16.
Translucent, egg white appearance. Luscious, yet understated bouquet of the juice of ripe yellow peaches; softly perfumed and off-dry; admirably genuine and true to the base flavor material. Off-dry, pleasantly peach-like, with seductive undertones of nectarine at palate entry; midpalate is gently ripe and sweet without being cloying; medium-bodied, silky texture. Finish is superb, round, with a fetchingly ripe aftertaste that's acidic enough to retain the freshness of the fruit.
2005 Rating: ★★★★/Highly Recommended

Hiram Walker Peppermint Schnapps (USA); 30% abv, $16.
Transparent as rainwater; flawlessly pure appearance. Concentrated, inviting, and appropriately peppermint-like aromas start off the nosing stages; later on, it's even a bit candied in the piquant bouquet and very similar to candy canes. Tastes of gently sweet peppermint candy canes in the first taste; the midpalate is more herbal/vegetal, reflecting the authentic pungent and oily flavor of crushed peppermint leaves. Finishes piquant and properly prickly in the throat, yet deliciously sweet and silky textured.
2005 Rating: ★★★★/Highly Recommended

Hiram Walker Pomegranate Schnapps (USA); 15% abv, $12.
The red cherry/raspberry hue is true to the source and flawless clean. Smells of pomegranate and green melon in the opening whiffs after the pour; following six minutes

of further air contact, the aroma settles down into a delightfully ripe fragrance that's just as much like berry and melon as it is about pomegranate. The palate entry is nicely sour and tart; the midpalate stage offers substantial acidic crispness that accentuates the freshness of the fruit. Tasty finish that's lean and tart. Not the equal of the more pomegranate-like PAMA (★★★★) or Bauchant XO (★★★★★) but very good and recommendable all the same.
2006 Rating: ★★★/Recommended

Hiram Walker Sour Apple Flavored Schnapps (USA); 15% abv, $16.

Transparent, pretty emerald green; clean. Assertive and similar to sweet/sour apple-flavored hard candy and freshly picked tart green apples in first nosing passes; perfumed, pleasing, and pure. At palate entry, mouth-puckeringly tart, clean, and intensely green apple-like; at midpalate flavors are crisp, properly astringent, and strikingly like the tart juice of green apples; refreshing and true to the fruit source. Finish is concentrated and delightfully acidic; the apple peel aftertaste cleanses the palate and tastes clean and tart in the throat.
2005 Rating: ★★★/Recommended

Hiram Walker Tangerine Schnapps (USA); 15% abv, $12.

Color is orange/bronze and unblemished. The first blast of aroma is pleasantly citrusy and tangerine/blood orange-like; the later sniffs detect true tangerine tartness and fruit pulp, ending up splendidly attractive. The palate entry is lusciously tangerine-like and sweet/sour; the midpalate takes a sweeter turn, sacrificing a portion of the citric acid to heighten the sweetness. Ends zestily and ripe.
2006 Rating: ★★★/Recommended

Hpnotiq Cognac, Vodka and Natural Tropical Fruit Juice Liqueur (France); 17% abv, $25.

The frosty sky blue color is opaque. Very tutti-frutti but tart in the first couple of passes after the pour, very tropical, citrusy, and mango-like; later nosing passes bring out a melon-like quality that's particularly pleasing; no traces of cognac or vodka, aromatically speaking. Light, acidic and very tart at palate entry; the midpalate stage is refreshing, intensely juicy, and almost sour. The aftertaste leans heavily on the tartness. The cognac and vodka are so well hidden beneath the draping of tropical fruit that you don't even know that they are present. Fun for youngish, legal age drinkers who aren't yet ready for complexity.
2003 Rating: ★★★/Recommended

Illy Espresso Liqueur (Italy); 28% abv, $25.

Jet black appearance. The first whiffs find an intensely bean-like aroma that's simultaneously bitter and cocoa-like; seven more minutes in the glass do nothing to alter the one-note bouquet whatsoever as the focused, concentrated coffee bean/espresso aromas rage on in the most positive sense of the word. The palate entry is startlingly bitter and intense, especially for someone who doesn't drink coffee; the midpalate sees the espresso intensity fade slightly, but definitely pick up in the cocoa end. The finish is brief, suitably bitter, and bean-like. My head swims at the thought of the caffeine level, but what an ideal and decadent topper for vanilla ice cream which is the way this well-made liqueur should be enjoyed.
2003 Rating: ★★★★/Highly Recommended

Intrigue Liqueur Premium French Vodka, Fine Cognac and Exotic Passion Fruits (France); 17% abv, $25.

Classiest package of the vodka-cognac-fruit from France set. The lime green/yellow color is less foggy than most of its peers. The bouquet is ripe yet neither sweet nor tart at first; the aroma goes nowhere even after another six minutes. The pleasant palate entry is nicely tart, with a backdrop of fruity sweetness missing in many other vodka-cognac-fruit offerings; the midpalate is lively, fruity tart, astringent, yet pleasantly spirity. Concludes zestily tart and delectably fruity. Runs with Hpnotiq and Alizé in drinking satisfaction.
2005 Rating: ★★★/Recommended

Jago's Vanilla Vodka Cream Liqueur (Scotland); 17% abv, $20.

Milky, eggshell color. The vanilla/egg cream bouquet at the outset reminds me strikingly of vanilla flavored diet drinks and therefore doesn't impress in a totally positive way; later whiffs, however, reveal more of the rich cream that eventually overrides the vanilla. The taste profile at the palate entry is incredibly rich and supple, featuring the vanilla element; it's at midpalate that this liqueur steps on the gas pedal and offers a luscious flavor, one that brings to mind a vanilla milk shake. Concludes velvety and thick on the tongue. The biggest asset is that this liqueur is never overly sweet or unctuous; it is rich, but it's never off-balance. I had my doubts as to whether or not I was going to like this liqueur, but as I worked my way through it, sense by sense, I realized what a gem it is.
2005 Rating: ★★★★/Highly Recommended

JdV Chocolate Cream with Tequila Liqueur (Mexico); 17% abv, $20.

Standard issue milky brown/beige appearance. The opening nosing passes following the pour pick up an admittedly interesting aroma of cream and herbal, dill-like agave; further time in the glass brings about a more pronounced agave presence as well as complementary notes of coconut and cocoa. The palate entry is off-dry, mildly creamy, and just a touch earthy/herbal; the midpalate stage is where the milk chocolate takes over, drowning out all other flavor aspects except for a trace of agave. The aftertaste is medium-long, semisweet, and creamy. Very good, in that it's nowhere near as sweet as many cream liqueurs and that, for me, is a huge plus because it allows the flavor to develop.
2003 Rating: ★★★★/Highly Recommended

JdV Coffee Cream with Tequila Liqueur (Mexico); 17% abv, $20.

Milky brown, opaque color. The initial sniffings detect mild, simple aromas of coffee bean and cream, nothing more; seven more minutes in the glass do nothing to stimulate further aromatic activity, leaving the cream and coffee latte on their own with no sense of tequila at all. The palate entry is soft, creamy, plush, and moderately sweet; by the midpalate stage the coffee bean taste gives way slightly to the herbal/dill taste of agave spirit. The finish is semisweet, delicate, and intensely creamy.
2003 Rating: ★★★/Recommended

JdV Mango Cream with Tequila Liqueur (Mexico); 17% abv, $20.

Opaque, bright milky yellow/banana color. The aroma after the pour is gently fruity, tropical, and easy; aeration sees the bouquet fade over six minutes, leaving a gum-like, Juicy

Fruity scent that's just a trace mango-like. The palate entry is ripe, mango-like, and properly creamy and semisweet; by the midpalate stage the taste profile shifts far more to the cream than either the mango or the tequila and in the process the point gets lost. The aftertaste is all cream. The dominance of one element plays against this liqueur.
2003 Rating: ★★/Not Recommended

John D. Taylor's Velvet Falernum Liqueur (Barbados); 11% abv, $14.
Made at the R.L. Seale Distillery in Barbados. A satiny, unctuous, syrupy textured mixer comprised of liquid sucrose, lime juice, almond and clove essences, and water; not to be consumed neat. Has the pale yellow color and consistency of canola oil. Leaves no doubt aromatically as to which is the dominant ingredients; the clove and lime juice dance around each other in each sniffing phase. Thick and sweet on the palate, but the lime juice acts as the perfect balance for the high-octane liquid sucrose. The finish highlights the lime juice, with the almond showing just a fleeting glimpse of itself. I liked it straight and at room temperature and can visualize scores of applications in cocktails that call for plain old simple syrup. Velvet Falernum could start a whole new cocktail revolution.
2003 Rating: ★★★★/Highly Recommended

Kahlua Especial Liqueur (USA); 35% abv, $20.
Has the dark cocoa, cola, inky look of black coffee. The opening sniffings are greeted by deep roasted, bitter, black coffee scents; the bouquet goes particularly beany after a few more minutes in the glass but that's as far as it travels aromatically; still, not too bad. This liqueur earns its stars in the taste; the palate entry is bitter and intensely black coffee-like; but the fireworks begin in earnest at midpalate when the deep-roasted flavor climbs to a whole new level of fresh-asphalt depth and semisweet intensity. It finishes bittersweet, smoky, tar-like, and beany. Even though I'm not a coffee fan, I still think this is a state-of-the-art coffee liqueur beauty.
2002 Rating: ★★★★/Highly Recommended

Kahlua Liqueur (Mexico); 20% abv, $19.
The dark brown/mahogany/cola color is gorgeous. Displays a concentrated, coffee bean, kernel-like aroma at the start; the aroma turns more cocoa/dark chocolate-like with aeration. The palate entry is creamy, thick, and intensely black coffee-like; at midpalate the sweetness accelerates and includes toasty flavors of roasted nuts and tar; ends sweetly, rich, and properly coffee-like. Hardly a great liqueur, but one that understandably has broad and sustained appeal.
2004 Rating: ★★★/Recommended

Ke Ke Key Lime Cream Liqueur (Holland); 15% abv, $n/a.
The sickly, milky lime green appearance is like something that's been vomited up after a very long night of bar hopping; doubtless the most unappealing liqueur color I've seen since the horrible Tequila Rose, about which I still have nightmares. The disgusting aroma mirrors the appearance as aromatic waves of rotten eggs, over-ripe limes, turned cream, and ancient foot locker combine to make a memorable and nauseating odor; the aroma is so foul that I refuse to run through my usual four stage nosing format; let's just say that this aroma doesn't

deserve even one star and leave it at that, hmmmmmmm? Who thinks up this stuff? Do they actually believe that they're offering something that the general public will favorably respond to? Lord almighty; the taste is abominable, awkward, cloyingly sweet, and putrid; green puke in a bottle…that's the kindest thing I can say about it; and, who cares what the price is; hurry and pass the water cos' I think I'm turning green.

2001 Rating: ★/Not Recommended

Killepitsch Kräuter Herbal Bitter Liqueur (Germany); 42% abv, $25.

The opaque, dense, cola brown color is like black coffee. The first inhalations discover a surprisingly delicate aroma that's fetchingly floral and fruity, anything but bitter; aeration releases subtle notes of black pepper, parchment, and kale. The palate entry is treated to a sweet, cherry cola-like, and root-like opening taste that's concentrated, syrupy sweet yet charming; at midpalate the berry/red fruit character takes charge as the herbal/earthy qualities back off. Finishes satiny smooth, ropey in texture, and almost like chocolate orange. Great stuff.

2006 Rating: ★★★★/Highly Recommended

Kirsberry Cherry Speciality Apple Wine with Molasses and Natural Flavors (Denmark); 17.5% abv, $17.

Lovely blood red color; excellent purity. Smells of tart cherry, even pear in the first go round; as it aerates in the glass, the bouquet turns more wine-like in its fruit demonstration than spirity or liqueur-like and that's a plus. The palate entry is nicely tart, even under-ripe, and pleasantly acidic; the midpalate stage features a solid fruit foundation flavor that supports the tartness and freshness. Finishes clean, medium-bodied, balanced, and extremely palatable.

2005 Rating: ★★★★/Highly Recommended

Knicker's Irish Cream Whiskey Liqueur (Ireland); 17% abv, $13.

Standard issue milky brown, opaque appearance. The aroma after the pour highlights the creaminess more than the spiciness; with aeration, the creaminess becomes richer and richer as the spice component fades; an appealing bouquet that's on par with those of Carolans and Baileys. In the mouth, Knicker's glides onto the tongue like silk and displays plenty of holiday spice that nicely complements the cream and the whiskey base; by the midpalate stage the flavor takes on a chocolaty personality that's long on pleasure and even opulence. The finish is chocolaty, slightly spiced, and lusciously creamy.

2003 Rating: ★★★★/Highly Recommended

KWV Van Der Hum the Original Cape Liqueur (South Africa); 25% abv, $19.

I've always admired the handsome henna/bay/chestnut color of this liqueur. The bouquet leaps from the glass in waves of perfectly ripe tangerine/blood orange, citrusy scents; with more time in the copita, the bouquet shifts slightly away from the citrus and highlights the mélange of fresh herbs and spices. The sweet/sour palate entry features the tangerine, but in a dried pulp, rind-like way; then at midpalate there are bitter traces of cardamom, bitter root, fennel, rose hip, and mustard seed; finishes sweet/sour.

2004 Rating: ★★★/Recommended

L'Amour des Trois Oranges Oranges Macerated in Sugar with Chateau de Briat Bas Armagnac (France); 36% abv, $60.

The color is honey-like; the clarity is superb. The opening aroma of ripe oranges is seductively sweet, but not candied; aeration opens up the fruit stand effect even more as the bouquet turns drier, more acidic and consequently more authentic than in the first whiffs (the real scent of orange is tart and biting) and I suspect that's because the oil from the orange peels come to life with air contact. The palate entry is lovely, round, and delightfully spirity; by the midpalate stage the taste profile includes judicious notes of caramel, armagnac, and honey that mix well with the heightened orange peel tartness. Finishes gracefully tart, oily, peel-like, and clean.

2006 Rating: ★★★★/Highly Recommended

La Mestiza Licor de Nance (Mexico); 30% abv, $34.

Pretty bronze color; flawless purity. The first whiffs detect intensely herbal/peppery aromas that can only be likened to asbestos, spoiled sap, burning straw or, better yet, burning vinyl; no amount of aeration could alter the course of the bouquet, so it remains chillingly unappealing and stunningly malodorous. The palate entry tastes of sickly sweet, over-ripened yellow fruit that's been cooked on Al Roker's barbeque for 3 days; the midpalate stage makes an attempt at a flavor of caramel corn but ends up unctuous, stale, and syrupy. Only the campy, kitschy bottle is worth anything…if nothing else for the howls of laughter from your friends.

2005 Rating: ★/Not Recommended

Lauria Alpensahne Alpine Cream Liqueur (Austria); 16% abv, $30.

First thing is the glutinous, thick-as-a-milkshake texture that clumps into the glass; second is the chocolate milk color that, like seeded or peppered Dijon mustard, has specks in it; not your typical cream liqueur appearance. The initial sniffs detect milk, yogurt, mild orchard fruit, and herbs; aeration doesn't seem to dent the ultra-thick consistency, but I do pick up aromatic nuances of soft cheese and eggs. The palate entry is thick as runny yogurt or melting ice cream and tastes of milk and pears; the midpalate showcases more of the Poire Williams influence as the taste profile actually becomes luscious and moderately sweet. Finishes viscous, pleasantly fruity, and creamy.

2006 Rating: ★★★/Recommended

Lejay-Lagoute Chocolate Liqueur (France); 25% abv, $20.

The black coffee appearance sports a cherry/ruby/tawny core color. The initial waves of aroma wash over the olfactory sense in kernel-like scents of cocoa bean and dark chocolate fudge; aeration serves to deepen the bean-like core aroma and turn the cocoa into dark chocolate shavings; a spectacular bouquet that captures the natural bitterness of cocoa and the bittersweetness of top drawer dark chocolate. The palate entry is opulently textured and sweetly flavored in an enthralling chocolate fudge manner; the midpalate is buttery, thick but not cloying, intensely chocolaty, and correctly bittersweet. Like the midpalate, the finish is long, decadent, and authentic in its rendering of the theme flavor. What's so great about this liqueur is how steadily it holds its concentration on true cocoa/dark chocolate flavor without becoming lumpy or syrupy. A masterpiece and a must buy for chocolate lovers.

2006 Rating: ★★★★★/Highest Recommendation

Lemonel Liqueur (Italy); 32% abv, $22.

The frosty pastel yellow color is pretty; very good purity. In the initial sniffs, the strong scent of just sliced ripe lemons is almost thrilling in its freshness and keen tartness; the sour candy lemon-a-thon continues vividly and pungently in the later inhalations after aeration. The palate entry is squeaky tart, rind-like, and refreshing; the midpalate holds up its end by offering zesty, tangy flavors of bitter lemon and lemon drop candy. Concludes tart, lean, and lovely. One of the better lemon liqueurs out there.

2006 Rating: ★★★★/Highly Recommended

Lichido Liqueur Blended Vodka and Cognac with Lichee, Guava and White Peach Juices (France); 18% abv, $23.

The frosty pink appearance is naturally foggy from the fruit juices. The intriguing opening aroma is an enticing blend of tropical fruit and litchi (I choose this spelling), with the white peach taking a back seat; additional time in the glass does compel the peach to emerge, adding a final piece to the aromatic puzzle, which is delightful. The palate entry is softly fruity, tart, and clean; the midpalate stage is fruit-fleshy in texture, rounded in taste, and has just the right amount of alcohol, acidity, and fruitiness to make for delicious quaffing. Ends peachy and guava-like. Racy, stylish, and fun.

2007 Rating: ★★★★/Highly Recommended

Licoro Coconut Liqueur (Dominican Republic); 28% abv, $17/200 ml.

The milky/cloudy/slightly yellowish appearance looks exactly like egg white, even in the gooey texture; way too much floating debris. The opening nosing passes discover a right-on-the-mark coconut meat aroma that's sweet and genuine; further time in the glass does little to alter the aroma in any way, except that it turns a bit skunky in the very last inhalation. The palate entry taste of fresh coconut is astoundingly authentic; the midpalate flavor profile is all sweetened coconut and nothing else. The finish is pleasantly sweet, fruity, and intensely coconut-ty. Though the taste phase especially was good, I'd be less than honest if I didn't say for the record that I'm concerned about the hygienic state of this product; it looks seriously awful, like swamp water in a coconut shaped bottle. That flaw alone could sink it in the finicky US marketplace.

2002 Rating: ★★/Not Recommended

Limoncello di Puglia Lemon Liqueur (Italy); 30% abv, $15.

Standard issue cloudy, lemon juice yellow appearance. Offers a no-nonsense, tart, lemon zest aroma in the opening sniffings; after a few more minutes in the glass, the bouquet turns as waxy as wax paper, but not at all unpleasant. The taste profile starts out bitter, citric acidy, and extremely tart in the palate entry but then turns richly lemony and hard candy-like in the midpalate stage providing a good balance between the lemon, the acid, and the alcohol. Ends up supremely lemony and astringent. Can't be beaten for the money.

2007 Rating: ★★★★/Highly Recommended

Limoncino dell'Isola Liqueur of Calabrian Lemons (Italy); 30% abv, $22.

The opaque, cloudy, silver/gray/yellow hue looks exactly like real lemon juice; excellent purity. The first sniffs are faint, mildly fruity, but true to the source; the bouquet goes a little

too flat after further exposure to air, losing some of its fey charm. What's lost in the latter stages of the aroma is somewhat regained in the palate entry in the form of a tart, rind-like, zesty taste; the midpalate offers even more in the way of juicy tartness and acidity. Ends up tart but not sour; zesty without being oily, and very clean on the tongue. Nice job.
2006 Rating: ★★★/Recommended

Limonice Liqueur (Italy); 30% abv, $25/liter.
Foggy lemon yellow appearance. The initial nosings after the pour pick up subtle and mildly juicy notes of lemon; aeration stimulates the tartness and the peel aspect of the bouquet, making for a very pleasing overall aromatic experience. The palate entry is viscous, thick, and off-dry; by the midpalate the peel element so admired in the bouquet is absent, leaving the taste profile to be dominated by the lemon pulp and juice. The aftertaste is zesty, full in the mouth, and correctly lemony. A quality product that would have garnered a fourth star had it been less husky/gooey in texture; very nice all the same.
2003 Rating: ★★★/Recommended

Luxardo Caffe Sport Espresso Liqueur (Italy); 27% abv, $20.
Opaque, inky, black/brown color. The forward nose is an inviting and bitter dark roasted coffee bean-a-thon in the first two sniffings; time in the glass, however, shows a softer, slightly sweeter side to this aroma in the form of traces of cocoa bean, tar, and black pepper; an intriguing bouquet that's aptly named. The palate entry is bittersweet and intensely bean-like; the midpalate stage is richly textured and tastes of espresso, bittersweet chocolate, and tar/ash. One of the better coffee liqueurs available.
2002 Rating: ★★★★/Highly Recommended

Luxardo Il Maraschino Originale Cherry Liqueur (Italy); 32% abv, $25.
Clear as rainwater appearance; impeccable purity. The first nosing is engagingly kirsch-like and very frisky in terms of spirit; later whiffs detect long, true-to-the-fruit scents of cherry stone and red cherry juice; the bouquet is balanced, properly astringent, ripe and juicy, and lovely. The palate entry is decadently sweet and textured; by the midpalate stage the flavor profile features vibrant tastes of cherry compote and cherry preserves. Finishes svelte, only moderately syrupy, and downright delicious. I suggest as one fabulous application for this outstanding liqueur: an AVIATION COCKTAIL!!
2007 Rating: ★★★★/Highly Recommended

Luxardo Limencello Liqueur (Italy); 27% abv, $24.
Neon yellow color and only slightly cloudy; more transparent than not. The opening sniffings detect an oily, skin-like zestiness that doesn't feature the fruit pulp nearly as much as the peel; seven more minutes in the glass serves to open up a keen astringency that's remarkably true to the fruit source. Light and nimble on the tongue at palate entry; by the midpalate stage the tart but not astringent flavor of authentic lemon enchants the taste buds; lovely, balanced, and smooth as silk. The finish is medium-long, properly juicy, and oily and in a word luscious. A superb, understated, and classy limencello.
2003 Rating: ★★★★/Highly Recommended

Luxardo Sambuca Cream (Italy); 17% abv, $20.

The wet sand-colored appearance looks a bit watery and thin at the edge; unusual for cream liqueurs, which typically are thick and viscous. The initial nosings pick up a solid scent of beany espresso that overrides the cream and sambuca elements; eight more minutes of air contact sees the cream take command as the espresso recedes. The palate entry deals with the creaminess; by the midpalate, though, the anise/licorice spirit base makes itself known as the espresso all but disappears, leaving the field open for the cream and anise to dominate the taste buds. The aftertaste is creamy and pleasant. More viscosity would earn it four stars.

2002 Rating: ★★★/Recommended

Maison des Futailles Amour en Cage Ground Cherry Liqueur (Canada); 23% abv, $25/375ml.

Bright golden/yellow color; good purity. The opening aroma is fusty, moldy, woodsy, and altogether unimpressive; the middle stage nosings add strange aromas like the glue that's on stamps, wet cotton, and pencil eraser; the fourth and final sniffing, following over seven minutes of aeration, smells remotely of white grape raisins, ripe banana, and yellow cherry; an aromatic mess devoid of focus that ultimately comes off as old, attic-like, and mushroomy. Slightly better in the mouth than in the nose, though that's not saying much; the palate entry is sweet, over-ripe, and very much like dried yellow fruit; the midpalate shows some mild raisiny appeal, but turns sap-like, bittersweet, and clumsy in the finish. The problems? How about undirected, never clear as to the fruit source, and awkward in the nose and the mouth? Really terrible and without any redeeming values whatsoever.

2001 Rating: ★/Not Recommended

Maison des Futailles Chicoutai Cloudberry Liqueur (Canada); 25% abv, $25/375ml.

Immensely appealing to the eye in its burnished copper-like hue and ideal purity. The nose at the pour is cloyingly sweet and syrupy, smelling of old foot locker; the stunningly unappetizing aroma picks up steam in the second and third sniffings as aeration seems to release more malodorous qualities including old sneakers, rotting vegetation, and chlorine; by the fourth and (gratefully) final whiff, the aroma turns unpleasantly medicinal and botanical; one of the rankest beverage alcohol aromas to come my sorry way in the last year. The palate entry is like rancid cough medicine, then the disgusting midpalate is sickly sweet and pulpy. The aftertaste can do nothing to salvage the putrid aroma and taste; Canada should be booted out of NAFTA for producing this debacle; truly horrible; looks aren't everything.

2001 Rating: ★/Not Recommended

Maison des Futailles Fine Sève Aged Maple Syrup Eau-de-Vie (Canada); 40% abv, $25/375ml.

The color is harvest gold/medium amber; excellent purity. The pleasantly zesty and perfumed nose at opening reminds me roughly of moderately sweet grain whisky from Scotland; in the second and third whiffs, following three and six minutes of aeration respectively, the aroma turns slightly candied, more in a nougat-like way than a toffee way, and stays remarkably attractive and compelling; in the final sniffing, after nine minutes in the glass, the raw aroma transforms into a full-fledged bouquet of delicacy and whisky-like presence. The palate entry is dry to off-dry and sap-like; the midpalate stage shows considerable elegance, toastiness, and restrained sweetness in a grain whisky manner. The aftertaste is long, whisky-like, and toasty; intriguing, savory, unique.

2001 Rating: ★★★/Recommended

Maison des Futailles l'Orléane Cassis d' IIle d'Orleans Blackcurrant Liqueur (Canada); 23% abv, $25/375ml.

Beautiful, ruby/blood red color; ideal purity. The opening aroma is supple, viny, and properly sweet/tart; with time in the glass, the aroma opens up further in the middle stages, adding bittersweet blackcurrant and blackberry scents in measured amounts; in the fourth and final sniffing, after seven minutes of air contact, the blackcurrant perfume is full, ripe, and lovely; an admirably correct and exhilarating cassis bouquet. The palate entry is sweet/sour and very ripe, but neither cloying nor viscous; the midpalate is pleasingly ripe, concentrated, and sweet. A better than average NA cassis, but still not in the league of France's Edmond Briottet or Lejay-Lagoute (both ★★★★★).

2001 Rating: ★★★/Recommended

Maison des Futailles Minaki Blueberry Liqueur (Canada); 18% abv, $25/375ml.

Striking crimson/ruby color that looks like an immature gamay; good purity. The opening aroma is very shy, offering only the bare minimum fruitiness; aeration doesn't seem to help release more aroma in the second and third passes; only after eight minutes of air contact does the bouquet at last emerge in anemic dried blueberry waves. The palate entry is dry, but almost muffled in flavor and very thin in texture; by midpalate only a hint of dry blueberry flavor entertains the taste buds. The finish is flat, lean, and moderately berry-like; below average drinkability; neither fresh nor layered; a mere distant echo of true blueberry intensity. So why'd they bother? I suggest that the distiller buys Lejay-Lagoute Crème de Myrtille (★★★) to find out what blueberry liqueur is all about.

2001 Rating: ★/Not Recommended

Maison des Futailles Sortilege Canadian Whisky and Maple Syrup Liqueur (Canada); 30% abv, $25/375ml.

The honey/amber color is pretty and bright; very good purity. The nose at opening is sappy/mapley more than whisky-like; with exposure to air, a mildly pleasant fragrance of butterscotch wafts up from the glass in the second pass; the third whiff shows a distant touch of grainy whisky; by the fourth pass, after more than eight minutes in the glass, the sweetness of the maple departs, leaving behind a grainy/caramel corn aroma that's nice. The palate entry is very sweet and intensely mapley, too much so for my taste; the midpalate tastes like caramel corn and maple candy. The finish is sweet, caramel-like, and medium long. Not my cup of liqueur, but for people who like maple/caramel tastes I could see some potential affinity.

2001 Rating: ★★/Not Recommended

Mandarine Impériale XO Limited Edition Liqueur (France); 40% abv, $110.

The pink/orange/salmon color is pretty and perfectly pure. The initial nosing pass displays a stately, bittersweet, citrus rind-like aroma of nectarine and tangerine; the second

and third sniffings offer mild spice and delicate, off-dry citrus peel scents; the final pass, following almost nine minutes of air contact, finds the spice component heightened while the zesty rind element recedes; a bouquet of nuance and understatement. The palate entry is dry, light, and bitter on the tip of the tongue, then at midpalate develops into a deeply flavorful and bitterly sweet and ripe taste of tangerine; a genuinely lovely flavor experience. The finish is medium long, moderately sweet, not the least bit thick or syrupy, and enchantingly polite. The gentle tangerine flavor and aftertaste are a joy to savor; a refined, sophisticated liqueur of grace and elegance, one that's European in style; superior quality and a classic.
2001 Rating: ★★★★/Highest Recommendation

Marchesa Anna Maria Toscano Limoncello Liqueur (USA); 35% abv, $17.

Yellow hue, moderately cloudy. The first two minutes of inhaling treats the olfactory sense to a fruity/citrusy and moderately tart perfume; by the six minute mark the juicy fruit still is the dominant aroma; usually I like a trace of oily, tangy lemon peel but this off-dry liqueur makes do with the pulp and juice. The palate entry is sweet/sour and intensely lemony; at the midpalate stage the acidity found in the peel or the zest overtakes the lemon fruit flavor in a way that is complementary and pleasing on the tongue. The finish is brief, concentrated, and citrusy.
2003 Rating: ★★★/Recommended

Marie Brizard Amaretto Liqueur (France); 28% abv, $19.

Beautiful, brilliant, light-catching amber/honey, brandy-like hue. The opening nosing passes take keen delight in the gently sweet, fragrant, floral, herbal, and nutty perfume; seven minutes of air contact releases the apricot scent more than the almond, making for a subtly sweet and ripe bouquet final impression. The palate entry is succulent, sweet, and smacks a little bit of toffee and marzipan; by the midpalate juncture the flavors remind me the most of almond pastry. The aftertaste is long, luxurious but not unctuous or cloying, mildly sweet, and intensely almondy. This French version is less intense and focused than the Italian models, but it's tasty, even savory, nonetheless; a more subtle amaretto style.
2002 Rating: ★★★/Recommended

Marie Brizard Anisette Liqueur (France); 25% abv, $24.

Clear as rain water. The initial two sniffings after the pour reveal a heightened licorice fragrance that's more herbal than sweet or candied; further time in the glass allows the earthy scent of anise to rise to the top of the aromatic chain; the textbook anisette bouquet. The palate entry is intensely herbal and only moderately sweet; it's at the midpalate point that the flavor takes off and defines what anisette should taste like; the flavor presence is defined, poised, mildly herbal, and succulently sweet at the midpalate; the texture is medium-bodied and not in the least cloying or syrupy. The aftertaste is long, gentle, softly sweet, and licorice-like. From now on, this is my anisette/anise gold standard. An authentically great liqueur that defines its sub-category.
2002 Rating: ★★★★/Highest Recommendation

Marie Brizard Apry Apricot Liqueur (France); 30% abv, $19.

Pretty topaz/bronze/caramel color; pure. The opening sniffs pick up heavy, syrupy sweet, mildly burnt scents of indistinguishable yellow fruit; even after seven more minutes of

mingling with air, the aroma still doesn't offer a clear-cut apricot perfume; the concentrated sweetness smothers any chance of the apricot emerging. The viscosity is such that it borders on being gel-like which doesn't win me over at the palate entry stage; by midpalate the flavor profile speaks softly of apricot candy and loudly of way too much sweetener. Ends cloying and awkward. With the exception of their genuinely horrible Banana Strawberry Liqueur, my least favorite offering from the normally reliable Marie Brizard.
2004 Rating: ★/Not Recommended

Marie Brizard Blackberry Liqueur (France); 30% abv, $17.
The ruby/crimson color allows some light to pass through the blood red core. The bramble- and currant-like opening snort is medium dry and intensely viny/leafy; further aeration brings about a greater sense of ripe blackberry, leaving the curranty/viny bitterness behind. The brambly palate entry is lovely and fruity without being overly sweet; the accelerated blackberry sweetness appears in the midpalate. It finishes more tart than ripe and very savory.
2003 Rating: ★★★/Recommended

Marie Brizard Blue Curaçao Liqueur (France); 30% abv, $19.
The cobalt blue appearance bedazzles the eye and has an aquamarine edge that I can't stop looking at and admiring; spectacular even if color additives are used. The initial nosing passes locate very little in the way of oranges, then after the liqueur is allowed to quietly sit for another six minutes, the presence of tart, acidic oranges peeks out; it's simply not a very expressive bouquet. The palate entry is sweet and only mildly orangy; at midpalate the piquant orange flavor is almost overcome by the sugary sweetness. The aftertaste is long, sweet, and moderately orangy. For sheer Curaçao orange taste go for the Marie Brizard Orange Curaçao, but when you want to make your cocktails ice blue, use this.
2004 Rating: ★★★/Recommended

Marie Brizard Cacao White Liqueur (France); 25% abv, $18.
Oily, thick, clear appearance; ideal purity. The opening whiffs pick up intense, concentrated, and squeezed-tight aromas of metal, brass, and fruit pit; more time affords the bouquet to become more roasted, green pea- and cocoa bean-like. This liqueur is not about the nose, it's about unbelievable taste power and expression on the tongue; the palate entry is tightly-wrapped and astringent, then at midpalate the cocoa flavor detonates on the tongue and WHAPP, it's a glorious and rewarding ride from there through the lip-smacking, tongue-blanketed, whip-cracking finish. What a rush, what a classic.
2004 Rating: ★★★★★/Highest Recommendation

Marie Brizard Cassis de Bordeaux Liqueur (France); 15% abv, $17.
The deep purple color is nearly opaque. The initial sniffings detect true-to-form blackcurrant perfume that's concentrated and properly brambly; time in the glass deepens the viny/brambly scent as the fruit turns ripe but bitter. The palate entry is soft, plush, sweet but not jammy, and focused; the midpalate point turns jammy, multilayered, and preserves-like as the blackcurrant taste crosses the finish line sweetly and with elegance. One of the best cassis products in the marketplace.
2003 Rating: ★★★★/Highly Recommended

Marie Brizard Crème de Banane Liqueur (France); 25% abv, $18.

The lovely golden/amber/pale honey color reminds me strikingly of a very old sauternes; impeccable purity. The first sniffs make me think that there's butterscotch flavoring as an underpinning, then seven minutes further on the aroma takes a turn into fried banana, honey, Graham cracker, and banana candy country. The palate entry is fruity tart to the point of almost being fruity sour; then at midpalate the flavor profile shifts into ripe banana dipped in honey mode and I'm a believer. Closes on a bittersweet, Graham cracker, and mildly toasty note.

2004 Rating: ★★★/Recommended

Marie Brizard Crème de Menthe Liqueur (France); 23% abv, $18.

Neon forest green appearance. Smells like Scope mouthwash or minty toothpaste in the opening whiffs, then with time a more nuanced leafy, minty core, totally dry and piquant, funnels into the nasal cavity; I didn't like the initial sniffs, but over time, the heightened mint bouquet grew on me. The palate entry is rich, intensely minty, and only moderately sweet; at midpalate the mint comes on strong, cleansing the tongue, and leaving behind a fresh taste. Concludes concentrated and properly minty. I admit that I'm not a fan of crème de menthes, but if you must buy one, here it is.

2004 Rating: ★★★/Recommended

Marie Brizard Grand Orange Liqueur (France); 38% abv, $19.

Displays the bright burnished orange/honey hue of a young brandy; superb purity. The sublimely fruity opening aroma is tart and orangy, not quite bittersweet Curaçao but more like fleshy Valencia oranges from Spain; additional time allows the bouquet to grow more focused on the heart of the orangy/citrusy acid. The palate entry is sweet to bittersweet and concentrated; the midpalate is orangy without being cloying or astringent, just gently fruited. The aftertaste is austere, acidic, and properly bittersweet.

2003 Rating: ★★★/Recommended

Marie Brizard Licor de Manzana Verde Green Apple Liqueur (France); 20% abv, $17.

Crystal clear appearance; excellent purity. The initial nosing pass discovers softly ripe but tart scents of green apple; further time in the glass brings about a gentle, delicate, almost cottony/flannel sweetness. The palate entry is juicy, tart, and true to the source; by the midpalate point there's a pleasantly acidic core flavor that balances the fruity ripeness perfectly. Ends on a softly sweet and juicy note. First-class all the way but with Marie Brizard, that's almost always a given.

2004 Rating: ★★★★/Highly Recommended

Marie Brizard Mango Passion Liqueur (France); 19.5% abv, $17.

Apple juice-like golden color. The opening bouquet is off-dry and shy, showing just a trace of tropical fruitiness; time in the glass allows the coconut component to take the lead; this liqueur is all about flavor, not bouquet. Palate entry is semisweet, fruity in a tropical manner, and not in the least unctuous or cloying; the midpalate stage features more discernible attributes, mostly mango with a hint of passionfruit. Aftertaste is medium-long, fresh, light, and subtle on the tongue. Ideal mixer for tropical cocktails.

2002 Rating: ★★★/Recommended

Marie Brizard Orange Curaçao Liqueur (France); 25% abv, $18.

The rich bronze/copper color is stunning and pure. The first couple of minutes offer citric scents of dried orange rind and lemon zest; six more minutes of air contact add subtle notes of white pepper, jasmine, and palm oil. The palate entry is luxuriously thick, oily, off-dry to bittersweet, and mildly orangy; by midpalate the flavor is deeply orangy, sweet/sour, and nearly pulpy. Ends sweetly and with just the right amount of rind.

2004 Rating: ★★★★/Highly Recommended

Marie Brizard Parfait Amour Liqueur (France); 25% abv, $19.

Spectacularly beautiful cobalt blue color. The delectably sweet, candied fruit initial bouquet is beguilingly reminiscent of baseball card bubble gum and powdered confectionery sugar; the sweet, berry fruit-like, bubble gum perfume only intensifies with aeration. The palate entry starts off mildly sweet, sugary, and light; then at midpalate turns concentrated and near-syrupy sweet and orangy, but not for a nanosecond cloying. The aftertaste is bubble gum, fruity orange sweet, yet slightly bittersweet. A fun, very good mixer for when you're showing off by making sweet blue margaritas.

2002 Rating: ★★★/Recommended

Marie Brizard Peach Liqueur (France); 18% abv, $17.

The orange/gold, honey-like appearance reminds me of an old sauternes; excellent purity. The scrumptious, ripe peach aroma right after the pour is enticing and welcoming; exposure to air over another seven minutes allows the bouquet to grow more concentrated and fruity as the ripe peach scent turns slightly baked and candied. The palate entry is surprisingly tart and acidic which gracefully balances the ripeness aspect, not allowing the taste to get too sweet; by the midpalate point the peach flavor is more baked than fresh but pleasant and true-to-the-source. The aftertaste is medium-long, pulpy, and medium-sweet.

2003 Rating: ★★★/Recommended

Marie Brizard Poire William Pear Liqueur (France); 25% abv, $18.

Looks precisely like a dry white wine in its pale yellow cloak; superb purity. The first whiffs pick up nice but not earth-shattering aromas of just-ripe pear; additional aeration makes no impact whatsoever on the bouquet; status quo. The palate entry is acceptably ripe but a dash too sweet; by midpalate the taste turns drier, more skin-like, and a bit manufactured rather than fresh and juicy. Concludes elegantly and nicely peary. An adequate, ordinary Poire William liqueur, nothing more, and a far cry from authentic Poire William eau-de-vie, or fruit brandy, which is the real deal.

2004 Rating: ★★/Not Recommended

Marie Brizard Raspberry de Bordeaux Liqueur (France); 16% abv, $25.

Deep, near-opaque, ruby/crimson/purple color. The nose at opening is concentrated, jammy, juicy, and tart; air contact releases more of the ripe fruit element and the intensity of the berry fruit almost pushes it into blackcurrant/cassis territory. The palate entry is like drinking raspberry juice so stunningly fresh and true-to-the-fruit source is this liqueur; at the midpalate point. The concentrated juiciness turns sweeter and ripe as the flavors become more vivid and fresh. The aftertaste is long, tart, juicy, and intensely raspberry-like. Top off vanilla ice cream with this luscious liqueur from Bordeaux; superlative.

2002 Rating: ★★★★/Highly Recommended

Marie Brizard Triple Sec Liqueur (France); 39% abv, $25.
Clear as spring water; very minor floating debris. The piquant, dry, almost sulphur-like/burnt match (I mean this in the positive) initial nosing passes speak eloquently about dried orange peels; aeration brings out the spiritiness a bit more as well as more of the Curaçao orange fruit. The palate entry is ultrasweet, orangy, and luscious; the midpalate stage highlights the ripe orange pulp taste that lies atop the thick, velvety texture. It finishes sweet, very long, with just a deft touch of citrusy tartness to balance the fruity sweetness. A fine triple sec.

2002 Rating: ★★★★/Highly Recommended

Mathilde Cassis Liqueur (France); 16% abv, $20.
Opaque, deep purple/nearly black color; ideal purity. The viny/bramble-like/green vegetation-like first sniffs instantly tell you what this liqueur is; further aeration time brings out the leafy/fruit skin scent of blackcurrant very nicely, without a great deal of fanfare, jamminess or sweetness; the perfect cassis bouquet. The palate entry is tart, concentrated, and intensely curranty; the midpalate is a bit more balanced in that the natural acids offset the intense jammy sweetness in just the right proportion. The aftertaste is long, more bittersweet than sweet, and luscious. A masterpiece of concentration and integration.

2003 Rating: ★★★★★/Highest Recommendation

Mathilde Framboise Liqueur (France); 18% abv, $20.
Pretty ruby/crimson color; ideal purity. The initial whiffs are treated to very ripe, intense aromas of fresh-off-the-vine raspberry perfume; a trace of welcome tartness brought on by acidity comes on the scene after six minutes of further aeration and counters the concentrated ripeness. The palate entry is sweet, ripe, and engagingly juicy; the midpalate stage is medium-bodied, ripe, sweet/sour, and juicy without being jammy or overbearing. The finish is long, exquisite, and intensely raspberry-like. An absolutely fantastic liqueur.

2003 Rating: ★★★★★/Highest Recommendation

Mathilde Pêches Liqueur (France); 18% abv, $20.
The pale gold color is pure and clean. The first couple of inhalations pick up nothing but sweet, ripe peach perfume that's true to the fruit source and beguiling; aeration serves to expand the aroma by adding tarter scents of peach skin and pit, however, the primary aromatic thrust still is the ripe, juicy peach scent. The palate entry is lean, very tart and acidic yet ripe; the midpalate flavor profile finds the acid underpinning gracefully balancing the sweet, peachy ripeness. The aftertaste is long, light-bodied, and appropriately juicy. Delicious.

2003 Rating: ★★★★/Highly Recommended

Mathilde Poires Liqueur (France); 18% abv, $20.
Looks like a new white wine with its light straw color; excellent purity. The perfume of fresh pears right off the tree is astounding in the opening whiffs; aeration means nothing to

this bouquet as it continues its ripe pear-a-thon unabated. The palate entry is delicately sweet and juicy; the midpalate taste is lusciously ambrosial and shows a hint of tartness through all the ripe pulp. The finish is clean, properly fruity, and fresh. What's so nice about this liqueur is its lightness and delicacy; it never falls into the lumbering, cloying mode that plagues so many other liqueurs. Excellent job here.
2003 Rating: ★★★★/Highly Recommended

Mathilde XO Liqueur d'Oranges au Cognac (France); 40% abv, $20.

The pretty orange/new copper penny color is bright and pure. The initial aromatic blast features the fetching perfume of grated orange and tangerine zests, with no evidence of cognac; aeration serves to arrest some of the orange/tangerine fragrance, allowing a tiny wedge of space for the cognac foundation. The palate entry is tart, refreshingly bitter, and eminently zest-like; the midpalate highlights the interplay between the orange zest and the cognac base as the taste profile turns bittersweet, razor-sharp, and acute. The finish mirrors the midpalate to a tee. A good, medium-bodied triple sec that's recommended because of its innate tartness.
2003 Rating: ★★★/Recommended

Mazetti d'Altavilla Frutti e Grappa - Grappa with Peach Juice (Italy); 16% abv, $13.

The muddy brown/beige color obviously reflects the dominant presence of the peach juice. The opening whiff picks up a rather dull, certainly overripe, scent of peach; the middle stage nosing passes add little except for a welcome trace of fruit acidity in the third sniffing, following over seven minutes of time in the glass; the final inhalation offers unexciting aromas of cotton fabric and peach skins; not a stellar example of a fruit liqueur bouquet with a grappa base. Mildly pleasant in the palate entry as the acidic peach taste greets the taste buds; the midpalate phase shows a bit of ripe sweetness but at the end of the day is hollow and flat. The aftertaste is brief, peachy, and boring; drinkable. Mixable to be sure, but wholly uninspiring, commonplace, and charmless.
2000 Rating: ★★/Not Recommended

Mazzetti d'Altavilla Frutti e Grappa - Grappa with Blackcurrant Juice (Italy); 16% abv, $13.

The red wine/purplish color is fine and seemingly pure. "Blackcurrant" is written all over the face of this initial nosing pass with no hint of grappa spirit at all; the more evolved, tart cassis aroma found in the second sniffing is a little more compelling, but not much; in the third whiff, after six minutes of aeration, the curranty quality turns ripe and pleasantly sweet; the fourth and last pass merely reinforces the third aromatic stage; there's no missing the blackcurrant at any step of the aromatic analysis, but this bouquet travels no deeper than that. The palate entry is quite inviting as the blackcurrant tartness cleanses the tongue; the midpalate stage is fruity, tart, and tasty, if simple. The finish is long and soda pop-like (remember Nehi Grape, anybody?). I liked this edition a bit more than the lackluster Peach but, frankly, not enough to bestow it with a third star and a recommendation.
2000 Rating: ★★/Not Recommended

Mazzetti d'Altavilla Frutti e Grappa - Grappa with Pineapple Juice (Italy); 16% abv, $13.
The appearance is of opaque grey dirty dish water; not a momentous beginning; frankly. Not a whole lot happening here aroma-wise except for a sickly pineapple odor in the first two sniffings; the third and fourth passes offer only a mildly sweet, pineapple pulp perfume that's devoid of charm, complexity, and the type of fruit intensity that one likes to see in a fruit liqueur; this bouquet is anemic. The palate entry is stunningly lacking in any type of virtue as gobs of dull fruit flavor blanket the tongue; the midpalate stage is sloppy, sweet, with no acid backbone to provide structure. The finish is, well, horrible; not even drinkable. A bland, directionless mess trying to pass itself off as a cheap fruit liqueur.
2000 Rating: ★/Not Recommended

Merry's Irish Cream Liqueur (Ireland); 17% abv, $10.
Correct, standard issue, milky brown, wet sand, beigey color; opaque. The opening sniffing picks up very flirtatious creamy/spicy notes that are alluring and rich; with aeration, the spice element recedes, leaving the creamy/milky aroma that somehow doesn't have the charm found and liked early-on. The palate entry is pleasantly sweet and not at all overbearing or chunky; at midpalate the taste goes bittersweet and chocolaty, more than either spicy or creamy. Concludes well and on a balanced aftertaste of cream, cinnamon stick, and milk chocolate. Nice job here.
2004 Rating: ★★★/Recommended

Montenegro Amaro (Italy); 23% abv; $22.
Exquisite, attractive appearance of deep bronze/topaz; perfect purity. The come-hither nose in the first passes entices with botanical scents of orange peel, fresh not dried coriander, and red cherry; seven more minutes in the copita allows the bouquet to add very delicate, almost indiscernible traces of pekoe tea, cucumber, and wet fern; a sexy bouquet that keeps you guessing and alert. The palate entry is sweet at first then it quickly turns mildly bitter and botanical; by the midpalate stage there's a slight sweetness that echoes citrus peel, could be tangerine, could be mandarin; the midpalate is excellent. The aftertaste is moderately bittersweet and citrusy. I normally despise amaro but this lovely liqueur has changed my mind; go and find.
2003 Rating: ★★★★/Highly Recommended

Navan Liqueur Vanille Noire de Madagascar Cognacs de France (France); 40% abv, $32.
Has the amber/golden straw look of an immature cognac; ideal purity. The aromatic profile is all about the bittersweet-to-sweet leaning Madagascar vanilla, gentle spiciness, and what I describe (from my childhood memories—all three of them) as cream soda or egg cream; further time in the glass heightens the sweetness and downplays the vanilla. The taste profile from entry through midpalate absolutely screams bittersweet vanilla extract and little more. Finishes on a spicy, lush, intensely honeyed note. A feast for sweet buffs and vanilla aficionados.
2005 Rating: ★★★/Recommended

Nocino della Cristina Walnut Liqueur, Napa Valley (USA); 30% abv, $60.
Made of northern California walnuts and spices from Africa, Asia, and the Americas. The dense, opaque look is of cocoa brown espresso. In the first nosings following the pour,

the mildly bitter, earthy scents remind me first of Italian amaro; after swirling and further air contact, the bouquet features intriguing scents of deep-roasted coffee bean (Columbian or Jamaican), black walnut, and chicory, with a faint hint of quinine. The palate entry is astonishingly tight-knit, semisweet, molasses-like, and walnuty; the midpalate features fifth-gear black walnut taste and buttery richness on top of the roasted coffee bean. Ends stately, elegant, concentrated, luxurious, and nuttily delicious. Who says that America can't make superb artisanal liqueurs?

2006 Rating: ★★★★/Highly Recommended

O'Reilly's Irish Cream Liqueur (Ireland); 17% abv, $20/1.75 liter.
Standard issue milky color of wet sand. The opening whiffs pick up fruity, cheesy scents of pineapple and cottage cheese; further exposure to air stimulates an all-dairy bouquet that's flecked lightly with spice (cinnamon) and rubber pencil eraser odors. The palate entry is pleasantly creamy and very spiced; the midpalate shows good staying power as the cinnamon taste overwhelms the cream and spirit, making for a zesty finish that's long, creamy, and vibrant.

2006 Rating: ★★★/Recommended

Opal Bianca White Sambuca Liqueur (Italy); 40% abv, $24.
Limpid, syrupy thick, and clean appearance. Displays pleasantly vibrant, earthy, and not overly sweet aniseed and licorice aromas at the start of the nosing phase; air contact does little to stimulate further aromatic expansion. The palate entry is soft, sweet, and ideally aniseed-like; at midpalate the taste profile focuses more on the aniseed/licorice foundation flavor than on the sweetness factor, which is a plus. The texture is very heavy and thick. Concludes elegantly and sweet. Very good, natural, and a skilled flavoring job here.

2005 Rating: ★★★/Recommended

Opal Nera Original Black Sambuca Liqueur (Italy); 40% abv, $24.
Jet black/black coffee appearance. The opening sniffings pick up beanier and drier aromas than the Bianca; by the latter stages of the second nosing phase the appealing scent of licorice is the dominant aroma. The palate entry is guardedly sweet but intensely licorice-like; at midpalate the aniseed component develops deliciously well within the licorice flavor frame. Finishes svelte, bittersweet, and pleasingly licorice-like. I like this liqueur very much; I think it tastes more nimble than the Opal Nera Bianca and, therefore, at least for me, is easier to drink. Delicious.

2005 Rating: ★★★★/Highly Recommended

Orangel Liqueur (Italy); 21% abv, $22.
The foggy orange color is like orange soda. The first sniffs pick up moderately pleasing scents of orange peel and zest; additional time in the glass goes more in the manner of orange soda rather than an orange version of limoncello. The palate entry is more serious in its approach, offering ripe yet bittersweet tastes of orange pulp and zest; the midpalate stays the course charted in the entry. Concludes orangy, drinkable, and ripe, but a bit too manufactured and bland. Not in the same league as its sibling Lemonel.

2006 Rating: ★★/Not Recommended

Ordoki Sloe Berry Liqueur (Spain); 25% abv, $20.

Transparent tawny/henna/auburn color; superb purity. Smells weirdly of brambles, cardboard, and wood in the opening sniffs; I hope that aeration assists in turning this unappealing fragrance around, but that doesn't happen as the brambly, viny, woody thing just keeps on a-comin'. Entry is thin, acidic, and remotely berry-like; the flavor profile at midpalate remains stuck in neutral as the viny/berry/brambly taste stays rustic, a tad raw, and unsophisticated; in short, the flavor hasn't a solid core of fruit even though the label says "Sloe Berry Liqueur." I will give it some points for its dried fruit aftertaste, but it's too little too late.

2007 Rating: ★★/Not Recommended

Original Italian Expresso by Mezzaluna Liqueur (Italy); 32% abv, $27.

Positively opaque and jet-black in color. Smells of burnt coffee beans, asphalt, charred wood, and, oh yes, espresso; with time, the burnt grain/roasted bean/extra well-done steak odor grows deeper and more charred; I mean, this bouquet comes off like your hibachi after a Fourth of July picnic where you've been barbecuing for twenty people. Entry is intensely bittersweet and espresso-like; by midpalate the bittersweet taste morphs into full-out bitter espresso that's over-the-top in its extreme bitterness. Ends heavily smoked and charred. Lacks the balance of other espresso liqueurs, like Illy Espresso or Luxardo Caffe Sport Espresso (both rated ★★★★).

2007 Rating: ★★/Not Recommended

Pagès Verveine Velay Extra (France); 40% abv, $60.

The color is deep amber/topaz; the purity level is highly questionable as way too much sediment is seen beneath the examination lamp. The opening whiffs pick up elegant, reined-in scents of dried herbs, flowers, and spices; another six minutes of air contact releases a mildly peppery/vegetal perfume that's understated and supplementary to the floral/herbal/root-like aroma. The palate entry is almost sour in its sweet/sour, herbal manner; at the midpalate there are finely woven flavors of mint, sage, fennel, quinine, thyme, and honey. Concludes more sweet than sour and delicately herbal/rooty. Lovely and elegant from beginning to end.

2006 Rating: ★★★★/Highly Recommended

Pagès Verveine Velay Jaune (France); 40% abv, $50.

The pretty, bright gold appearance shows more sediment than I like to see in any liqueur. The first nosing passes pick up tangy scents of dill, anise, and sage; further aeration doesn't appear to affect the bouquet positively or negatively; just remains finely herbal and viney. The palate entry is sweetly herbal and root-like; the midpalate stage brings out an intensely leafy taste that is halfway between rosemary and sage; there's also are dashes of fennel and quinine. Ends up concentrated, medicinal, and wildly herbal.

2006 Rating: ★★★/Recommended

Pagès Verveine Velay Verte (France); 55% abv, $50.

The neon/electric/green gelatin color is bright and pure. The initial sniffings are assaulted by the 110-proof spirit and therefore deep inhalations are out of the question; nipping at the edges of the bouquet after aeration, I discover nicely melded scents of green leaves, distant herbs, and mild spices, but nothing that is clearly identifiable. The palate entry is concentrated, herbal, leafy, vinous, and only mildly spiced; the midpalate is not in the least pungent or too spirity, but instead is round, gently sweet, and subtle. Finishes stately, with equal parts finesse and controlled power. Nowhere near the classical grandeur of Chartreuse Green, but a more than decent runner-up.

2006 Rating: ★★★/Recommended

Pallini Peachcello White Peach Liqueur (Italy); 26% abv, $24.

The orange/pale amber color is pristine and pretty. The first burst of aroma is wonderfully peachy as the perfume highlights fresh peach rather than juice, stone, peel, or concentrate; aeration serves to deepen the peach flesh presence as the delicate ripeness delights the olfactory sense. The palate entry offers a slightly tuned down peach component as the natural acidity deflects some of the juicy ripeness; at midpalate the emergence of the alcohol gives the flavor phase structure and direction. Finishes well, juicy, ripe, and suitably peach-like.

2006 Rating: ★★★/Recommended

Pallini Raspicello Raspberry Liqueur (Italy); 26% abv, $24.

The red brick/red cherry color is true to the source and clean. The initial whiffs are treated to succulent, concentrated aromas of raspberry preserves and raspberry compote; later inhalations find that the aromatic resolve doesn't diminish at all as the rich raspberry jam profile remains strong and purposeful. The palate entry features a near-syrupy texture that underpins the juicy, preserves-like red raspberry flavor; at midpalate the fruit's acidity helps to balance some of the jamminess/ripeness, making for pleasant quaffing. The aftertaste stage reverts back to the keen, sweet fruitiness found in the bouquet.

2006 Rating: ★★★/Recommended

Pallini Roma Limoncello Liqueur (Italy); 26% abv, $24.

The frosty pale yellow appearance is properly within what one expects for a limoncello. The snappy, zesty bouquet is clean, tart, and refreshing in the first sniffs, then in the latter stages the astringent presence of lemon peel really comes alive, successfully closing the aromatic circle. The taste at palate entry is like lemon drop hard candy, sweet but pleasantly tart; by midpalate the tartness accelerates becoming more astringent and refreshing with every sip. Concludes intensely lemony. One of the best, most authentic limoncellos to come my way in a year or two.

2005 Rating: ★★★★/Highly Recommended

PAMA Liqueur California Pomegranate Juice, Tequila and Vodka Liqueur (USA); 17% abv, $25.

The red cherry/cranberry color is striking and attractive; flawlessly clean. The aroma in the first whiffs is ripe, fruity, berry-like, and relatively true to the fruit source; with aeration the genuineness of the core bouquet develops an intensity that is both appealing and compelling. The palate entry is stunningly sour, acidic, and tart as the pomegranate taste is unmistakably obvious and true; the midpalate stage offers a flavor profile that's clean, less concentrated than the entry, but to my mind more enjoyable because it's less aggressive and riper. Finishes

tart, amazingly clean, and ripe. Another winner from the innovative distilling staff at Heaven Hill Distilleries in Bardstown, Kentucky. Great job on this fabulous cocktail ingredient.
2006 Rating: ★★★★/Highly Recommended

Paolucci Amaretto (Italy); 30% abv, $13.
The rich bronze/new copper penny color is gorgeous and unblemished by sediment. The opening aroma is properly nutty and kernel-like; aeration brings on a bit of a metallic/coin-like odor that nearly undercuts the nuttiness but, to my delight, doesn't succeed. The palate entry is nicely sweet and more pod-like than nut-like; at midpalate the pod- and seed-like flavor shows a flash of bitterness that's quickly covered by the sweetness. Finishes well in a silky way. Never comes off as cloying or ropey.
2006 Rating: ★★★/Recommended

Paolucci Amaro Ciociaro (Italy); 30% abv, $13.
Looks exactly like cola or even black coffee in its cloak of nut brown/mahogany color; excellent purity. The vibrant aroma after the pour is fresh, citrusy, and clean; aeration time of another seven minutes brings out a cola nut quality that nicely merges with the bittersweet bouquet that's as citrusy and peel-like as it is herbal, floral, and earthy. The palate entry is bittersweet, intensely herbal, and earthy but refreshingly citrusy (oranges mainly); the midpalate stage is marked by heightened sweetness and a more mineral-, seed-like core flavor that's really tasty. Savory, bittersweet finish.
2006 Rating: ★★★★/Highly Recommended

Paolucci Sambuca and Coffee (Italy); 40% abv, $13.
Very pretty tawny/auburn/mahogany color; superb purity. There's plenty of coffee bean bitterness in the opening whiffs; further exposure to air brings out only a small measure of the anise/licorice as the coffee influence remains dominant. The palate entry shows a nice balance between the sambuca and the coffee flavoring; at midpalate the taste profile continues to feature the black coffee flavor that, because of its richness and depth, is fine. The aftertaste is medium-long, bittersweet to sweet, cocoa-like, and very pleasing.
2006 Rating: ★★★/Recommended

Paolucci Sambuca (Italy); 42% abv, $13.
Silvery clear, but with lots of gray debris seen floating around. The first aromatic go-round is suitably aniseed-like and licorice-like; later sniffs detect additional scents including lead pencil and linseed oil. The palate entry is correctly licorice-like and syrupy; at midpalate the sweetness quotient accelerates, thereby accentuating the aniseed and waxy texture. Finishes long, mildly bittersweet, and even a touch quinine-like.
2006 Rating: ★★★/Recommended

Paul Masson Chocolate Hazelnut Cream Liqueur (USA); 17% abv, $13.
The color of wet sand, opaque, milky beige. Faint odors of milk chocolate and mild cream emerge in the opening two minutes of sniffing; after four minutes, the hazelnut/spice fragrance kicks in, providing a moderately pleasant bouquet experience. The palate entry is semisweet, mildly creamy, and a touch spicy; the midpalate taste is more developed

and defined as the hazelnut comes to the fore. Finishes plump, smooth, and nutty, with undertones of milk chocolate and nutmeg. Very good for the little amount of money.
2002 Rating: ★★★/Recommended

Paul Masson Mocha Caramel Cream Liqueur (USA); 17% abv, $13.
Darker and more brown than the Chocolate Hazelnut, opaque, looks like chocolate milk. The initial nosing passes pick up intensely milky, but not necessarily creamy, aromas, with a minor hint of caramel; later whiffs detect more of the caramel but not much of the mocha. The palate entry is fat, nicely creamy but with no definable flavor presence; the midpalate stage continues with the nondescript, bittersweet taste that's neither caramel nor mocha-like. The aftertaste is mildly sweet and creamy but lackluster and fat. Certainly drinkable, but ordinary and lacking in personality.
2002 Rating: ★★/Not Recommended

Pernod Spiriteaux Anis Liqueur (France); 40% abv, $25.
The neon yellow color is strikingly like Yellow Chartreuse; totally clean and blemish-free. The opening scent is slightly soapy and detergent-like, with only wispy trails of anise; further air contact stirs a more botanical lean to the aroma that is softly bittersweet but still soapy and perfume-like. The palate entry displays some pod-like trace of anise, but is basically meek and thin; at midpalate there's a better flavor thrust of licorice/anise/herbs. Ends up a bit timid and lean. I've tried to like this international brand, but after tasting Ricard, I've seen the light. Pernod is inferior to Ricard as an absinthe substitute, period.
2005 Rating: ★★/Not Recommended

Poison Wild Berry Schnapps Liqueur (USA); 40% abv, $20.
Silver/lavender color; transparent and clean. The initial whiffs detect pleasantly ripe and sweet notes of mixed berries, with strawberry and boysenberry standing out. The palate entry sensation is one tartness/bitterness in passing gear; by the midpalate stage the unripened berry taste dominates to the point of extreme bitterness. The finish lacks any type of berry presence. To the positive, Poison's not sweet or cloying in the least while to the negative the berry flavor gets lost amidst the bitterness; in other words the seed of a good liqueur is here and if the berry essence had been more pronounced, it likely would have earned a recommendation.
2003 Rating: ★★/Not Recommended

Poli Miele Honey Liqueur (Italy); 35% abv, $46.
The "Poli" is the legendary grappa distiller Jacopo Poli from Veneto. The slight pewter/gray tint is barely perceptible; flawless purity. Smells of pine cones, new rubber soles, candle wax, and dried flowers; more time in the glass stimulates notes of juniper, tree sap, and cedar. Entry is lusciously sweet, but not cloying, buttery, and gracefully honeyed; at midpalate the taste profile goes all creamy and ultra-sophisticated with not one flavor aspect dominating another as the honey, pine, juniper, flowers, and spirit integrate with precision and elegance. A perfect liqueur.
2007 Rating: ★★★★★/Highest Recommendation

Pontarlier Anis Liqueur (France); 45% abv, $35.

Pretty greenish/yellow hue; superb purity. The initial nosing passes detect lovely, lightly herbal aromas that highlight anise and lead pencil; with aeration the polite bouquet expands to include licorice and slate. The palate entry is green, unripe, acceptably bitter, and dry; by the midpalate point the taste profile deepens only slightly and becomes quite peppery, as in spicy green pepper. The finish is fresh, light-bodied, anisey, and bitter. What I admire the most about this anise liqueur is its vivacity and freshness; it isn't in the least heavy, ropy, or syrupy. A genuine find for anise liqueur aficionados.

2002 Rating: ★★★★/Highly Recommended

Prunier Liqueur d'Orange La Lieutenance (France); 40% abv, $21.

The bright orange/new copper penny hue is flawless in the glass. Right from the beginning sniffs, the cognac foundation is present and accounted for along with succulent scents of orange juice, orange zest, and orange pulp; the aroma grows substantially in the glass as the orange peel presence, in particular, expands and mingles perfectly with the cognac; a terrific liqueur bouquet. The palate entry is extremely zesty, piquant, peppery, spicy, and sublime; the midpalate makes the tongue glow with spirity warmth as the flavor profile takes the orange zest/peel to the edge of bitterness. The aftertaste is bittersweet, zesty, and drop-dead luscious. I've finally found the equal of Grand Marnier Cordon Rouge (★★★★); kudos.

2003 Rating: ★★★★/Highly Recommended

pXs Lively Green Passion in Excess Passion Fruit and Cognac Liqueur (France); 16% abv, $26.

Frosty lime green in color. The first sniffing detects a soft vegetal aroma that must be the cactus; aeration serves to bring out the citrus element aromatically; not bad but it's a bit Gatorade-like in the nose. The palate entry is clean, tart to off-dry, and more cactusy than citrusy; I prefer the midpalate stage because there's more evidence of spirit and citrus; cactus just isn't a very intriguing flavor. Finishes on a tart, astringent citrus note. Not as nice as the pXs Sweet Yellow.

2005 Rating: ★★/Not Recommended

pXs Spicy Red Passion in Excess Passion and Red Fruit and Cognac Liqueur (France); 16% abv, $26.

The opaque cherry red color strongly resembles typical fruit punch. The opening nosing passes pick up background traces of passion fruit and frontline aromas of moldering fruit—not an auspicious start; the stinkiness of the over-the-hill fruit lingers well into the next aromatic stage, wiping out any sense of freshness. The palate entry is tart to sour, mildly fruity, and a bit stale; the midpalate offers more fruit than the entry, but still not enough to make it a recommendable product. Concludes moderately fruity and sweet/sour. Alizé Red Passion and Remy Red needn't worry about this one eating into their marketshare.

2005 Rating: ★★/Not Recommended

pXs Sweet Yellow Passion in Excess Passion Fruit and Cognac Liqueur (France); 16% abv, $26.

The appearance is a dull, opaque orange. The smell of fresh passion fruit is unmistakable

and very, very charming; the fruit component is so powerful that any evidence of cognac is veiled. The palate entry is properly tart, fruity, and refreshing; the midpalate phase features the passion fruit to the hilt. Ends on a pleasantly fruity, light-bodied note. Good for its ilk.
2005 Rating: ★★★/Recommended

Rhum Clément Creole Shrubb Rum Liqueur (Martinique); 40% abv, $28.

Yellow/gold in color; impeccably pure. The first nosing is greeted by a delectably acidic and mildly sweet scent of orange peel (this is a smooth tasting concoction made from a maceration of rum, sugar cane syrup, and orange peel); further time in the glass reveals a deft touch of raw cocoa that rounds out the bouquet nicely. The palate entry is sweet, thick, and suitably orangey; at midpalate the orange peel zestiness kicks it up a notch in intensity, thereby countering the sugary sweetness. Ends up sweet, a bit intense, and appropriately orangey. If the sweetness level were turned down a bit, I'd make it four stars.
2005 Rating: ★★★/Recommended

Ricard 45 Pastis de Marseilles Aperitif Anis Liqueur (France); 45% abv, $28.

Very attractive amber/honey hue; superb purity. The first aromatic blast is seductively anise-like, even coming off as black licorice candy, only not as sweet; with aeration the aroma transforms into a bouquet as the anise/licorice tag team mellows out, turning softer, more herbal, and plumper with time; love this bouquet. The palate entry is all business, no nonsense or flapping around is allowed as the intensely bitter taste of anise both enlivens and cleanses the palate; at midpalate the pleasant sting of alcohol and the zest of rooty/woodsy botanicals make for memorable imbibing. Finishes elegantly and smooth, with just a trace of smoldering warmth deep in the throat. Special.
2005 Rating: ★★★★/Highly Recommended

Rinquinquin Peach Aperitif (France); 15% abv, $18.

The straw yellow color is like soft morning sunshine; regrettably, that beam of light has quite a lot of floating particles in it. The nose at opening is soft, dry, and fruity, with just a trace of peach pit bitterness; the second nosing pass shows a dash of ripeness and plenty of zest; in the third whiff, after six minutes of aeration, the dry, peach pit quality returns and nearly overtakes the ripe fruit element; in the last sniffing pass, the flesh of the fruit comes more into play, making for a very satisfying, though not exactly perfumed aromatic conclusion. Pleasant and light on the tongue at palate entry, the peach flavor is delicate, yet ripe; by midpalate the peach character comes alive and is in full control of the taste phase. The aftertaste is fruity, sweet, and ripe, but carries enough acidity to keep it fresh and lively. Though I sampled it neat at room temperature, I would suggest a slight chilling to 50 to 55 degrees Fahrenheit and I'd put in a splash of spumante to make it very special.
2000 Rating: ★★★/Recommended

Rumba Coffee Liqueur (Mexico); 26.5% abv, $18.

Nearly opaque, but pretty mahogany/nut brown color. A light, perfumed and beany aroma greets the olfactory sense in the first pass; nuances of cocoa, dark chocolate, espresso, and tobacco make for more interesting sniffing in the later stages. The palate entry is sweet

and beany; by the midpalate stage there's evidence of tobacco smoke, tar, dark cocoa, and dark-roasted coffee bean. The aftertaste is semisweet, intensely beany, and very pleasant. Not the greatest coffee liqueur in the world, but a darn good one.
2003 Rating: ★★★/Recommended

Rumba Coffee Liqueur Cream (Mexico); 17% abv, $20.

This liqueur is so thick it tumbles in lumps into the glass rather than pours—oh, oh—dark, milky brown and opaque. The opening nosing stage doesn't have a lot to analyze since the aromas of smoke and roasted coffee bean seem far off in the distance; additional aeration unlocks only a dash of coffee bean and a syrupy sweetness; no cream to speak of. The palate entry is chunky, thick and disconcertingly lumpy on the tongue; by the midpalate stage the flavor profile ekes out enough coffee bean taste to at least be identifiable. The finish is meek and semisweet, with little charm or character.
2003 Rating: ★/Not Recommended

Sambuca di Puglia Liqueur (Italy); 40% abv, $15.

Properly silvery clear and clean. The first inhalations out of the glass unearth mildly zesty, nearly dormant aromas of licorice and brambles; more time in the glass assists in composing the aniseed foundational aroma as suddenly richer, more muscular scents of black licorice, freshly ground black pepper, and fennel rise to the occasion. The palate entry is piquant, prickly, yet velvety and slightly stinging on the tongue; by midpalate the taste profile settles down and offers a viscous texture and spirity, heady flavors of anise and licorice. Ends up smooth and thick. Very good, but a bit uneven and lazy in the bouquet.
2004 Rating: ★★★/Recommended

Sambuca Latinae Extra Liqueur (Italy); 40% abv, $24/liter.

The pristine silver appearance is clear and sparkling under the examination lamp. The initial nosing passes pick up snappy, almost prickly scents of anise and black licorice that enliven the olfactory sense; added time in the glass release unexpected odors of vanilla, bark, and spice on top of the anise/licorice foundation. The palate entry reflects all the keenly appealing zestiness discovered in the first nosings; the midpalate offers creamy texture, tangy anise, and black licorice flavors, and a lovely mouthfeel that's warm and plump. Ends up elegant yet vigorous. Really pleasing.
2006 Rating: ★★★★/Highly Recommended

Sambuca Secolare (Italy); 42% abv, $16.

Good appearance; translucent and relatively debris free. In the first whiffs, the aroma is oily, fat, and pleasantly anise-like; aeration does little to enhance what's already there aromatically, but what's there is nice. The palate entry is a tad harsh and more minerally than botanical; the midpalate is pleasant, if indistinct from many other good but not great sambucas. Concludes well as the anise/licorice flavor finally steps up to the plate in the throat and hits a double off the wall; there's a lot of ground made up from midpalate through finish.
2006 Rating: ★★★/Recommended

Santa Teresa Rhum Orange Liqueur (Venezuela); 40% abv, $22.

As beautiful in color as its sibling the Santa Teresa 1796 Rhum; looks like an old vintage armagnac in its nut brown coloring; perfect purity. Smells immediately of brandied oranges, but not in an aggressive manner as much as a serene, self-assured way; later nosing passes find that the slightly bitter orange peel/orange zest scent starts to dominate the rum element; seductive. The palate entry is orangy/fruity and semisweet on the tip of the tongue; the midpalate taste is firmly structured in the rum base yet vibrant in a deeply orangy way. The aftertaste is softer than the flavor phase, long, and slightly syrupy. Superb for any type of mixed drink that calls for triple sec; I'd enjoy just by itself on-the-rocks.

2003 Rating: ★★★★/Highly Recommended

Schönauer Apfel German Apple Schnapps Liqueur (Germany); 21% abv, $18/liter.

The pale gold/straw color is pretty and impeccably clean. The initial nosing passes pick up strong and defined scents of apple strudel and baked apple with cinnamon; aeration doesn't really alter the aroma in a noticeable way; a pleasantly ripe and pastry-like bouquet. The palate entry is deliciously appley and more tart than sweet/ripe; the midpalate stage offers keen red apple tartness and enough acidity to maintain the impression of authentic apple crispness. Lovely all the way.

2006 Rating: ★★★★/Highly Recommended

Senior Chocolate and Curaçao (Curaçao); 25% abv, $39.

The deep coffee/cola brown appearance is pretty and nearly opaque. The opening whiffs discover vibrant scents of dark chocolate and orange zest, with the chocolate element dominant; another six minutes in the glass see the orange component come forth a little more, mixing very well with the candied, fudge-like chocolate perfume. The palate entry is sweet, full-textured, nutty, and alluringly chocolate-orange tasting; the midpalate stays the course as the chocolate and orange remain in balance. The texture in the finish approaches being syrupy; the taste profile concludes velvety rich, candied, and sweet. The chocolate definition is good and better than that of the orange, which seems over-matched at times.

2006 Rating: ★★★/Recommended

Senior Curaçao Blue Liqueur (Curaçao); 31% abv, $26.

The cobalt blue color leans towards green as much as blue. While I assume that the basic make-ups are identical between the Senior Curaçao Orange and the Blue, the Blue seems to possess greater definition in the opening inhalations; like the Orange sibling, further air contact doesn't do anything in terms of expansion. The palate entry is nicely citrusy and sour; at midpalate the orange taste is more pulpy and fruity than the orange which was zesty. Finishes well in cascades of orange pulp and orange rind flavors.

2004 Rating: ★★★/Recommended

Senior Curaçao Koffi Korsow Coffee Liqueur (Curaçao); 25% abv, $28.

The midnight black appearance is as dark as deep-roasted coffee beans. The initial inhalations offer bittersweet aromas of coffee, roasted chestnut, and chicory; an additional seven minutes in the glass stimulate deeper notes of espresso and molasses. The palate entry is heavily toasted, molasses-like, and sweet, with solidly authentic black coffee flavor;

the midpalate phase turns bitter, deeply coffee-like, and intensely beany. Finishes sweet/bittersweet, a bit syrupy, and correctly coffee-like. Very nice.
2006 Rating: ★★★/Recommended

Senior Curaçao Orange Liqueur (Curaçao); 31% abv, $26.
Moderately bright orange color; some sediment; The crisp, undeniable perfume of Curaçao oranges leaps from the glass; aeration doesn't particularly affect this liqueur one way or the other. The palate entry is tart, sour, and pleasantly orangy; at midpalate there's major thrust towards orange zest and dried rind. Ends sharp, delectably tart and concentrated.
2004 Rating: ★★★/Recommended

Senior Rumraisin and Curacao Liqueur (Curaçao); 25% abv, $28.
The amber/hay golden color is pretty and clean. Tantalizing notes of raisins, dates, and glazed orange tweak the olfactory sense; the bouquet turns more orangy/citrusy with further air contact. The palate entry is pleasingly simple, sweet, and orangy; the midpalate taste profile features rum, confectioner's sugar, orange marmalade, and figs. Ends up delightfully sweet but with enough acidity to balance the sugar. Not a profound liqueur by any stretch, but one with lots of simple charms and flavors.
2006 Rating: ★★★/Recommended

Shakers Winter Raspberry Honey Vodka Liqueur (USA); 26% abv, $33.
The pale pink/inner conch shell color reminds me of the Shakers Rose Vodka. The delicate bouquet shows soft, pillowy, moderately ripe scents of raspberry preserves more than fresh fruit; the elegance of the aroma doesn't particularly expand or deepen with more minutes in the glass, but the honey component does emerge to complement the raspberry. The palate entry is gently sweet, even stately as the honey presence clearly serves to underpin the raspberry element; by midpalate the three components—honey, vodka, raspberry—come together harmoniously. Finishes clean, fruity sweet; a hybrid vodka/liqueur mostly due to the honey element.
2005 Rating: ★★★★/Highly Recommended

Shakka Apple Eau-de-Vie (USA); 15% abv, $20.
Bright but transparent cherry/fire engine red color; ideal clarity. The robust, ripe, red apple perfume wafts up from the sampling glass and fills the entire office; a bit of aeration merely acts to accentuate the ripe, red apple scent. Clean, lithe, and more than adequately apple-like in the entry; the tartness, which I favorably respond to, really comes on strong at midpalate. Ends up pleasantly astringent, keenly tart, and just a whisper ripe and sweet. Hey, this lightweight stuff is remarkably tasty.
2005 Rating: ★★★/Recommended

Shakka Grape Eau-de-Vie (USA); 15% abv, $20.
The transparent purple/shiraz-syrah/dark gray appearance and the no-brainer, fruity grape juice-like aroma remind me strikingly of a soda pop—Nehi Grape—that was popular when I was a kid growing up in Chicago in the 1950s/1960s. Drank thousands of gallons of it in the hot and humid Chicago summers. This is a carbon copy of Nehi Grape, except

for the fact that it has a well-concealed 15% alcohol as its foundation. Like it enough to recommend it. Simple, straightforward, and as quaffable as anyone could hope for.
2005 Rating: ★★★/Recommended

Shakka Kiwi Eau-de-Vie (USA); 15% abv, $20.

The neon color is a see-through yellow/lime green; purity is excellent. Not much to report on the aroma front except for a faint green apple/kiwi pong which is kept at arm's length in the opening two minutes; the bouquet develops a bit further in the ensuing six minutes as it becomes a bit juicier. The palate entry is delightfully juicy and tart; the midpalate turns sweet/sour as the intense juiciness builds into a pleasing crescendo in the aftertaste. Nicely done.
2005 Rating: ★★★/Recommended

Soho Lychee Flavored Liqueur (France); 21% abv, $19.

Clear, limpid, with just the faintest gray tint; perfect clarity. The highly perfumed opening aroma is absolutely spot-on, emitting assertive, kernel- and nut-like scents that are completely true to the litchi fruit flavoring; additional time in the glass stimulates additional layers of fragrance, including parchment, palm oil, flowers, and sealing wax. The palate entry is gently sweet and properly fruity; the midpalate point displays a textured sweetness/ripeness that is delicious and light-to-medium weighted. Wraps up sweet, succulent, and genuinely tasty.
2006 Rating: ★★★★/Highly Recommended

Southern Comfort (USA); 35% abv, $14.

The burnished orange/topaz color suggests whiskey, but the label says that caramel has been added (most likely for color adjustment); otherwise clean and clear. The first aromas make me think peaches and blood oranges; later sniffings detect cotton candy and fabric. The compact and gently fruity entry taste pleases the taste buds; at midpalate the peach component becomes more apparent as the orange element recedes. Finishes herbal, slightly honeyed, and more bittersweet than flat out sweet. A deservedly popular liqueur that is frequently depicted as a bourbon-based liqueur when it is actually a neutral grain-based product. Bourbon was utilized in the original formula, but no longer.
2005 Rating: ★★★/Recommended

Southern Comfort (USA); 50% abv, $17.

This is the high strength version of the two Southern Comforts. Deep topaz/brandy brown color; superb purity. The early on aroma includes notes of buttered almond, baked peach cobbler, and herbs; aeration time of another six minutes allows the aroma to settle in and become a pleasantly fruity, toffee-like, caramel popcorn-like, even biscuity liqueur bouquet. The palate entry displays plenty of spirit structure but no fire or rawness; it's at midpalate that the flavor profile develops as toasty, semisweet, dried fruit tastes of raisins, peaches, orange peel, and nuts take command. Concludes semisweet, lip smacking, and peppery.
2005 Rating: ★★★/Recommended

St. Germain Liqueur Artisanale (France); 20% abv, $33.

The pale hay/yellow appearance is strikingly similar to manzanilla sherry; superb clarity. The opening inhalations pick up wonderfully floral, fruity, guava- and melon-like fragrances of elderflower; following an additional seven minute period of quiet aeration, the bouquet rounds out becoming richly pear- and quince-like, all the while maintaining its flowery and mildly viny/bramble-like integrity; a totally seductive bouquet of the first rank. The palate entry is soft, yet firm; flowery, yet neither oily nor cloying; by the midpalate point the flavor profile offers an ideal taste experience that's integrated, harmonious, and exquisitely balanced between alcohol level, sweetness, acidity, and floral impact. A perfect liqueur.

2007 Rating: ★★★★★/Highest Recommendation

Starbucks Coffee Liqueur (USA); 20% abv, $23.

Looks precisely like opaque black coffee. Even though I am not a coffee drinker, I must tell you that the opening aroma is stunningly luscious, spot on, and richly coffee-like; a further aeration period adds aromas of cocoa bean, cigarette tobacco, and sand/gravel. The palate entry is strong yet elegant, coffee-like, and bittersweet; at midpalate the bittersweet element gives way to an intense coffee bean flavor that's right on the money. Finishes more bitter than sweet and, therefore, genuinely coffee-like. A dazzling new entry into the coffee liqueur subcategory.

2005 Rating: ★★★★/Highly Recommended

Starbucks Cream Liqueur (USA); 15% abv, $23.

The milky brown color is opaque. The first burst of toasted aroma is all nuts, burnt toast, cashews, and cream; aeration time doesn't really affect the aroma at all as it stays the course set out in the initial nosing passes. The palate entry is divinely creamy and only moderately sweet, even a bit buttery; the midpalate stage highlights the sweet buttery cream and café au lait. Finishes satiny smooth, creamy, and luscious.

2006 Rating: ★★★★/Highly Recommended

Sting Sour Raspberry Schnapps Liqueur (USA); 40% abv, $20.

Sports the vivid red of cranberry juice; good purity. I like the opening bouquet of Sting since it offers better than average tart but juicy and ripe red raspberry perfume; air contact doesn't really affect a shooter's bouquet all that much; Sting is ultrasour like its mates Viper and Poison at palate entry, but I note a bit more fruit essence here; by the midpalate stage the sour raspberry flavor is borderline astringent, but it keeps walking the fence. The aftertaste is sour and mouth-puckering; keeping in mind what it is—a shooter—and which audience it's designed to attract—young, legal-age, frenetic, hormone-bursting. I can easily recommend this product even though it's not something I'd personally purchase.

2003 Rating: ★★★/Recommended

Super Punch Jannamico Liquore (Italy); 44% abv, $20.

Opaque, jet black/deep brown hue; owns a pleasing opening aroma of licorice and bark. Extended aeration has little effect on this bouquet and simple but reluctant traces of dried

herbs, roots and bark tease the olfactory sense. The palate entry is surprisingly sweet and syrupy; by the midpalate juncture there's all sorts of flavor bouncing in my mouth, including root beer, maple, dark caramel, ginger, road tar, tobacco leaf, and orris root. The aftertaste is long, fat, and chewy. A no-nonsense bitter that is terrific over ice with a thick slice of orange.
2003 Rating: ★★★★/Highly Recommended

Sylk Cream by Drambuie (Scotland); 17% abv, $22.

The opaque, egg cream color has the look of dry sand. The first nosings after the pour offer stunningly attractive scents of citrus rind, malt whisky, and light cream; aeration serves to highlight the fruity, gently honeyed, malty aroma of the whisky and adds extra aromatic dimensions including flowers, whipped egg white, and dry stone. While I genuinely admire the bouquet, it's the silky, balanced taste that wins me over totally; the palate entry speaks softly of malt whisky, always taking care not to overshadow the honey or cream; at midpalate the floral/blossom-like honey quality is more pronounced and becomes more of an equal partner with the whisky, making for exceptional drinking enjoyment. Finishes moderately sweet, very creamy, and just a tad malty. Only the Drambuie people could concoct such a liqueur marvel.
2004 Rating: ★★★★★/Highest Recommendation

T & W Limonela Liqueur Lime Liqueur (USA); 26% abv, $24.

Owns a barely discernable, pale green tint that exhibits unblemished clarity. The opening nosing passes detect strangely odd, if slightly stale aromas of fermented lime; another six minutes of aeration don't help the situation as the aroma becomes more "tanky" and industrial with each passing minute; it's kind of like a poor man's Rose's Lime Juice. The palate entry shows some progress as the sour lime flavor delivers minor joy; the midpalate stage advances the cause even more as the sour/bitter lime juice taste at last displays some authenticity. Finishes very tart and juicy. Could be employed with some success in a Gimlet cocktail, so the cause isn't totally lost. The primary problem is with the unappealing aroma.
2006 Rating: ★★/Not Recommended

T & W Orangela Liqueur Orange Liqueur (USA); 35% abv, $24.

Shows off a golden/pale yellow hue; good clarity. The aroma off the pour emits a pleasing orange peel bitterness that works well in the early stages; further exposure to air encourages more of the orange juiciness to come out and mingle with the zesty peel bitterness, thereby giving it the aura of triple sec though not as bitter. The palate entry is fruity and sweet yet with a background astringency that counters the sweetness; the midpalate stage is correctly bittersweet and juicy. Finishes with a nice orange zest thrust. Has clear mixing possibilities.
2006 Rating: ★★★/Recommended

Tao Liqueur by Raynal (France); 40% abv, $24.

A blend of Raynal French Brandy, French vodka and citrus flavorings; very pretty honey color; impeccable purity. The opening sniffings detect citrus peel and the oily trace of vodka; seven additional minutes in the copita serve to release more of the grapy/brandy character which I have to believe is the base spirit; curious yet compelling, this citrusy bouquet while not assertive is nevertheless delicately alluring. The palate entry is firmly structured and juicy sweet; at the midpalate point the brandy/vodka tag-team makes more of an effort to counter the citrusy surface taste. The aftertaste is medium-long, mildly fruity, and off-dry to semisweet. A pleasant quaff on its own on-the-rocks or as an ingredient in a cocktail; pushes the edge of the envelope in the most positive way by harmoniously combining spirit opposites.

2003 Rating: ★★★★/Highly Recommended

Tia Maria Liqueur Spirit (UK/Jamaica); 26.5% abv, $24.

Sports the color of coffee, except that it owns a ruby core color that's seriously attractive; excellent purity. Smells of fresh-brewed coffee, tobacco, and smoke; aeration brings about a distant scent of vanilla bean that's the perfect counter to the concentrated coffee aroma. Entry is sweet, coffee-like, beany, and caramelized; the midpalate offers a bit of relief from the sugary sweetness, but overall is pleasing due mostly to the bitterness of the coffee element. Ends up coffee bean-like, properly bitter, with the vanilla aspect coming back into play.

2007 Rating: ★★★/Recommended

TMD Banana Liqueur (Australia); 24% abv, $30/375 ml.

The pale yellow color reminds me of flax; impeccable clarity. The opening whiffs pick up painfully soft traces of banana scent and nothing more save for a light hit of spirit; nothing occurs aromatically following additional air contact. The palate entry offers ample acid and obvious alcohol, but the banana is MIA; by the midpalate juncture there's a smidgen more banana presence that peeks out from behind the acid curtain. Finishes clean, but I wished for more in the way of ripe banana. Drinkable, but ordinary.

2007 Rating: ★★/Not Recommended

TMD Chocolate Liqueur (Australia); 24% abv, $30/375 ml.

The straw/hay color reminds me of older vintage brut champagne; superb clarity. The initial whiffs pick up earthy, truffle-like aromas first, then behind those smells lies the chocolate; further aeration doesn't do a great deal to alter the aroma profile, which maintains its truffle/mushroom/root-like surface scent with milk chocolate fragrance underneath. The palate entry does, at last, see the chocolate component pushed forward ahead of the earthy/moss notes; by the midpalate stage the chocolate is in full charge and is borderline bitter/semisweet, but tasty. Finishes with a background fruitiness that's darn-near strawberry-like.

2007 Rating: ★★★/Recommended

TMD Honey Dew Melon Liqueur (Australia); 24% abv, $30/375 ml.

The pale color is a silvery/green hue; ideal clarity. The assertive and fresh fragrance of perfectly ripened honey dew melon bounds from the glass in agreeable waves; seven more minutes of exposure to air effect no change to the bouquet as it remains strong and true-to-the-source. The palate entry mirrors the aroma as the melony taste comes off genuine and fresh from the garden; at the midpalate stage the flavor profile punches up the natural acidity a bit which keeps the taste on course and in focus. Concludes clean, crisp, and very melon-like. Good because it doesn't overplay its hand with the flavoring and maintains its acid spine.

2007 Rating: ★★★/Recommended

TMD Macadamia Nut Liqueur (Australia); 24% abv, $30/375 ml.

The appearance is of deep straw/old gold coin and nearly topaz; excellent purity. The first sniffs cannot avoid the intense, freshly shelled macadamia aroma; another seven minutes of air contact stimulate a nutshell scent that's clean, almost fruity, and attractive. The palate entry is concentrated and properly nutty; in the midpalate the flavor profile is accurately macadamia-like and even a bit cocoa-like. By the finish, the cocoa element picks up steam and is appealing.

2007 Rating: ★★★/Recommended

TMD Mint Liqueur (Australia); 24% abv, $30/375 ml.

The appearance is of tarnished silver/oyster; ideal purity. The first inhalations are greeted by medium-potent peppermint stick aromas and little else (what could possibly compete with mint?); following seven minutes more of exposure to air, the mint fades substantially, becoming flaccid and flabby. The palate entry is surprisingly timid and flat, displaying just a hint of flabby mint; by the midpalate point the mint revives and lasts well into the finish. Simply skip this one and move straight to the Australian Herbal Liqueur.

2007 Rating: ★/Not Recommended

TMD Passionfruit Liqueur (Australia); 24% abv, $30/375 ml.

The pale tarnished gold color has a trace of orange in it; flawless purity. In the first inhalations, I detect enticing notes of spice tucked way behind the passionfruit scent; further aeration adds hints of beeswax and parchment as the passionfruit recedes a bit too much. The palate entry is meek and indistinct—this could be virtually any type of yellow fruit; once the midpalate comes around, there's a touch more evidence of passionfruit, but not enough to make this liqueur recommendable. I know that passionfruit is a subtle taste, but in this case, the subtlety is taken too far. Drinkable, but too timid.

2007 Rating: ★★/Not Recommended

Vedrenne Crème de Myrtille Blueberry Liqueur (France); 18% abv, $18.

Inky black with a purple rim. The aroma right after the pour from the bottle is fresh, but slightly reluctant to show itself; with time in the glass, the nose comes around eventually offering spirity scents of blueberries and vines; the fourth and final sniffing after eight minutes of air contact leans more to the leafy/viny side of the ledger than the fruit side; ends up a rather dull bouquet. While the aroma proved stingy and lackluster, the flavor at palate entry is vivid fruity, ripely sweet, and true to the fruit source; the midpalate is long and creamy texturewise and full of overripe blueberry taste. The finish is ultrasweet enough to be borderline cloying, but the fruit essence is true and pure and thereby deserves a recommendation.

2001 Rating: ★★★/Recommended

Vedrenne Crème de Pêche de Vigne Peach Liqueur (France); 18% abv, $18.

The pretty pale orange/dusty gold hue impresses the eye; ideal purity. The sweet, ripe peach opening aromatic salvo starts once the cork is popped and the pour begins; the room fills with the perfume of fresh picked peaches; the second and third sniffings unearth peachy scents that underscore other aromas that include wet cotton fabric, peach stone, and peach pie; the last nosing pass finds that the peach-o-rama calms down into a more modest and stately bouquet that's just as acidic as it is fruity; a superb aroma. On the palate the taste starts off rather flat and dull at entry; the midpalate doesn't find much improvement as the peach flavor comes off as being listless and weary, not fresh and vivacious as in the aroma. The finish is long, peach-like, and soft; very drinkable, indeed, but the flavor and finish only partially fulfilled the promise of the bouquet.

2001 Rating: ★★★/Recommended

Vedrenne Liqueur de Fraise Strawberry Liqueur (France); 20% abv, $18.

The brilliant appearance is of red cherry juice; excellent purity. The perfume of wild strawberries fills the SJ tasting office after the pour; following the initial aromatic burst, the nose settles down into a concentrated, strawberry preserves-like banquet in the second and third nosing passes; the last sniffing detects a lessening of the intense sweetness and a heightening of the fruity acid. On the palate the taste experience is surprisingly balanced between fruitiness, acidity, and texture from entry to midpalate. The finish is long, intensely berry-like, and only moderately sweet. The texture isn't even close to being lumpy or syrupy; a delicious fruit liqueur that does everything in its power to highlight the fresh-picked virtues of strawberries.

2001 Rating: ★★★★/Highly Recommended

Vedrenne Liqueur de Framboise Raspberry Liqueur (France); 18% abv, $18.

Very pretty, crimson/ruby hue; superb purity. The opening nosing pass immediately following the pour doesn't need lots of time to be bowled over by the jammy raspberry perfume; the second and third whiffs detect more fruit acid backbone than fleshy surface sweetness; the last sniffing finds the tart/viney fragrance of on-the-bramble raspberry totally enchanting. The palate entry is medium textured, sweet but not for a moment cloying, and intensely raspberry-like; the midpalate is very sophisticated, properly acidic, and roundly ripe and fruity. The aftertaste is medium long, ripe, and ideally sweet.

2001 Rating: ★★★★/Highly Recommended

Vedrenne Murelle Blackberry Liqueur (France); 18% abv, $18.

Opaque, deep purple color that resembles a young vintage port from a hot growing season. The opening nose on this liqueur is considerably heavier and fruit-driven than other Vedrenne offerings; the middle stage passes pick up outdoorsy aromas of brambles/vines more than fruit; the final pass, following nearly nine minutes of aeration, finds the brambly scent to be accelerating rather than receding. The palate entry is thick in texture and heavy on the blackberry jam taste; the midpalate is concentrated, sugary, and syrupy sweet, nearly cloying. The finish is better than the midpalate as the taste shows a bit of acidity to counter the ripe sweetness. Very tasty, but be aware of this liqueur's ropey/syrupy approach.

2001 Rating: ★★★/Recommended

Vedrenne Supercassis Crème de Cassis Blackcurrant Liqueur (France); 20% abv, $18.

This jet black, opaque liquid slowly flows out of the bottle like lava. The initial nosing pass shows a properly vinous/leafy/vegetal bouquet that frontally attacks the olfactory sense with vigor; the middle stage passes reveal a peppery (as in spicy black pepper) even pungent aroma that's perfectly in keeping with what crème de cassis should be; the last pass merely serves to reinforce the prickly/vinous bouquet found in the first three sniffings. The palate entry is tart to the point of being sour, but remarkably vivid in its fruit portrayal; the midpalate while tart and vinous, shows more sweetness in the form of very ripe blackcurrant fruit. The aftertaste is long, seductively creamy, and decadently luscious. Doubtless, one of the best crème de cassis one can find.

2001 Rating: ★★★★/Highest Recommendation

VeeV Açai Liqueur Blended with Prickly Pear, Acerola Cherry, Ginseng, and Other Exotic Ingredients (USA/Brazil); 30% abv, $35.

Tarnished silver appearance; perfect purity. Smells engagingly of fresh, ripe blueberries, bubble gum, and tangerine/blood orange in the opening sniffs; another seven minutes of air contact reinforces the blueberry and the tangerine aromatic notes; a fresh, vivacious bouquet that hits the right note of ripeness/sweetness. Entry is off-dry, metallic, and not as pleasing as the bouquet; the midpalate highlights a stony/limestone/chalky quality that doesn't work for me. Concludes earthy/minerally and too chalky for its own good. All the luster of the aroma gets quashed in the mouth. Too bad.

2007 Rating: ★★/Not Recommended

Vermeer Dutch Chocolate Cream Liqueur (Holland); 17% abv, $23.

Ingredients are vodka, dairy cream, and Dutch chocolate. Looks exactly like milky-brown chocolate milk. The opening nosing pass detects a strong almond-like aroma that had me wondering if some roasted almond or almond paste had been added; with time in the glass, the nose opens up slightly in the middle stage whiffs, offering more in the way of cream and bean-like aromas; the fourth and final sniffing, following a full nine minutes of aeration, finds the nuttiness/beaniness overtaking the cream; I missed the chocolate completely. The palate entry features the cream, both in taste and texture; the chocolate component makes itself known, at last, at the midpalate stage and does so handsomely. The finish is intensely creamy, concentrated, and only mildly chocolaty. While I was anticipating a bigger hit of Dutch chocolate, there's enough available to make this icky-sticky recommendable.

2001 Rating: ★★★/Recommended

Versinthe Liqueur Pays d'Aix en Provence (France); 45% abv, $25.

Owns the honey/green olive color so typical of herbal/botanically flavored liqueurs in the pastis/absinthe vein; quite a lot of floating debris noted. The pungent, prickly opening sniffing offers big-hearted aromas of anise, licorice, tree bark, and orris root; the middle stage nosing passes pick up cumin and coriander; the fourth and last whiff finds some diminishment in the spirity blast as the perfume goes vegetal, sappy, and pine-like. The palate entry is dry and intensely herbal; then at midpalate the flavor takes on a sweeter, but not syrupy, texture and tastes of licorice, anise, and orris root. The aftertaste is long, smooth, and concentrated totally on the botanicals rather than the sweetness. Very nice.

2001 Rating: ★★★★/Highly Recommended

Vesta Virgin Cranberry Liqueur (Hungary); 25% abv, $28.

Cherry/red brick color; perfect purity. To my surprise, the first two sniffings pick up little in the way of fruit; by the third whiff, there's at best a painfully faint tart berry aroma that's lurking way in the background; the final pass continues with the acidic, fruit peel-like scent that's neither fruity nor compelling. The palate entry is so tart as to be nearly bitter, but the midpalate phase displays minor ripeness/sweetness. The finish is short, bitter, austere. A vacuum.

2001 Rating: ★/Not Recommended

Villa Massa Crema di Limoni Liqueur (Italy); 17% abv, $25.

A yellowish, milky appearance that's opaque. The opening nosing passes detect notes of egg cream, citrus peel and meringue; further aeration doesn't change the aroma profile at all. Villa Massa Crema shows its best face in the mouth as lovely tastes of lemon, egg white, and cream combine beautifully from entry through midpalate. The aftertaste highlights the creaminess; balanced, gently sweet, and genuinely delicious.

2003 Rating: ★★★★/Highly Recommended

Villa Massa Mandarin Liqueur of Sorrento (Italy); 30% abv, $24.

The orange/straw appearance is cloudy, juice-like and shows lots of sediment; not the most appealing appearance, to be blunt. The opening whiffs pick up little in the way of citrus or mandarin orange since the aroma is limp and, at most, pulpy in the early stages; aeration doesn't release anything further in terms of aroma; a dud, bouquet-wise. The palate entry is acidic, tart, and only mildly orangy; the midpalate doesn't fare any better as the meek mandarin flavor limps along; the flavor profile suffers from a near total lack of personality. The finish is, well, timid and lithe. A disappointment after I seriously liked the new Crema and the frontline product, Villa Massa Liquore di Limoni (★★★★).

2003 Rating: ★/Not Recommended

Vincent van Gogh Rhapsody Dutch Chocolate Raspberry Liqueur (Holland); 15% abv, $n/a.

Packaged as part of a two-bottle gift set with Van Gogh Dutch Chocolate Vodka. Neon crimson/cherry Kool-Aid color; good purity. The nose features the espresso/cocoa bean/dark chocolate aroma more than the berry fruit. The palate entry displays some berry fruit, not sweet, but ripe; the midpalate highlights the cocoa bean and is mildly sweet. Designed specifically to be mixed with Van Gogh Dutch Chocolate and that marriage is extremely pleasant; on its own as a liqueur, this is very good and recommendable.

2002 Rating: ★★★/Recommended

Viper Sour Apple Schnapps Liqueur (USA); 40% abv, $20.

Neon green appearance; very good purity. The peculiar aroma initially smells of new carpeting, a kind of synthetic and rubber-like fragrance; with aeration the green apple makes an appearance from behind the screen of nylon and rubber pencil eraser; a strange carpet and flooring store bouquet. True to the label, Viper is extremely sour and astringent at palate entry and stays that way through the midpalate quashing the chance of any lasting flavor impact. My mouth puckers to the size of a pinhead by the finish, it's so ultrasour. I like it enough for a second star, but cannot recommend it except for very young legal age drinkers hunting for the quick "hit" of a shooter.

2003 Rating: ★★/Not Recommended

Vov Zabajone Liquore Egg Liqueur (Italy); 17% abv, $26/liter.

The opaque, milky, gold/yellow appearance resembles egg yolk, but isn't as golden. The first sniffings pick up aromas of sugary sweetness, almost like sugar cookies or cake batter; further aeration doesn't expand the aroma profile. The palate entry is sweet and biscuity; the midpalate is alarmingly starchy, thick, and cloyingly sweet. The aftertaste is mildly eggy and sweet. Not my cup of liqueur.

2003 Rating: ★★/Not Recommended

Voyant Chai Cream Liqueur (Holland); 12.5% abv, $24.

Dark, milky brown appearance. The eggnog-like first scents remind me of those sickly sweet, shake-like, nutritional supplement drinks that you're supposed to begin consuming the day you turn sixty; later whiffs find aromas of ginger, cinnamon, nutmeg, clove, and black leaf tea that all seem to dance on top of the sweet cream base. The palate entry is creamy and sweet, with just a touch of cinnamon spice, then at midpalate the ginger and clove really kick in making the mouth phase worth enduring the bouquet. Concludes pleasantly. Drinkable and nearly, but not quite, a three star product.

2005 Rating: ★★/Not Recommended

White Fang Peppermint Schnapps Liqueur (USA); 45% abv, $16.

Crystalline appearance; some very minor sediment, hardly worth mentioning. The aroma right off the crack of the bat is intensely minty and a touch herbal and woodsy; further aeration really brings out the cinnamon influence as the zesty spice starts to over-ride the mint; pleasant. The palate entry is thick, sweet, and very, very minty; once again the cinnamon comes on strong in the stretch at midpalate. The delightful finish is very sweet but not ooey-gooey, long, and more spicy than minty. Nicely crafted and, for what it is, far better than better than average.

2003 Rating: ★★★★/Highly Recommended

Wild Turkey American Honey Liqueur (USA); 35.5% abv, $22.

The honey/amber/goldenrod hue is pretty and unblemished. The first inhalations detect distant scents of honey, baked bread, and corn meal; as with most liqueurs, aeration doesn't particularly alter the aromatic profile, except in this case to add a citrus note. The palate entry is pleasingly balanced and not the least cloying; at the midpalate stage the flavor profile features integrated tastes of honey (natch), spice, and lemon zest. Finishes clean, balanced, and very enjoyable. The citrus element makes this liqueur recommendable because the citrus counters the honey and the bourbon.

2007 Rating: ★★★/Recommended

X Rated Fusion Liqueur (France); 17% abv, $28.

Served chilled. Foggy pink/rose color. Highly perfumed in the first whiffs, with ultra-tart scents of orange, passionfruit, and mango juices; following aeration, the tropical fruit concentration accelerates, adding exotic and wonderfully intense aromas of dried orange peel, passionfruit and mango pulp, with a backnote of spice. Entry is lusciously tart and fruity, displaying a perfect balance among alcohol base, acidity, and fruit; sweet at first then squeaky clean tart in the throat. Finishes impeccably balanced, clean, and juicy. The ideal

tropical fruit and vodka base liqueur that sets a new standard for this subcategory. Bravo!
2007 Rating: ★★★★★/Highest Recommendation

Zen Green Tea Liqueur (Japan); 20% abv, $30.

The green khaki/yellow/mint color is authentic and like green tea; excellent cleanness. The aroma out of the box is delicately herbal, sweet (more like honey than either sugar or corn syrup), and properly tea-like; aeration doesn't stimulate anything further and therefore is a non-factor. The palate entry is sweet, syrupy, and vaguely green tea-like, but then in the midpalate phase the green tea flavor emerges with greater authority, making for pleasing quaffing. Concludes softly herbal and sweet.
2007 Rating: ★★★/Recommended

Zirbenz Stone Pine Liqueur of the Alps (Austria); 35% abv, $42 ml.

The appearance is a very attractive new copper penny/burnished orange hue; excellent purity; the color is completely natural. The first nosing passes pick up appealing menthol, sap, and pine cone scents that are vibrant, clean, and inviting; following another seven minutes of aeration and swirling, this amazingly intriguing bouquet focuses on the pine cone/cedar /alpine forest perfume and little else. The palate entry is intensely piny/sappy and marginally sweet, but not bittersweet; the midpalate highlights the menthol aspect as the taste becomes bittersweet and woody/resiny/bark-like. Finishes bitter with waves of menthol/camphor and pinesap. Whether or not this type of idiosyncratic liqueur could ever hope to make appreciable in-roads in the North American marketplace is debatable. That said, the overall impression of this liqueur is one of superb quality and highly skilled distilling and blending craftsmanship in the tradition of employing one's nearby natural resources.
2006 Rating: ★★★★/Highly Recommended

Zwack Unicum Liqueur (Hungary); 40% abv, $23.

Very attractive, deep brown color. The initial nosing passes detect delicate odors of lead pencil, fennel, and orris root; seven minutes of further aeration really stimulate lots of intriguing and enticing herbal/vegetal/spice scents, including quinine, ginger, nutmeg, and allspice. The palate entry is keenly medicinal and astringent and deeply herbal; by the midpalate stage there's an underlying kernel/nut taste that's most reminiscent, at least for me, of cola nut. Finishes intensely herbal, root-like, and extremely bitter. Not something I'd buy because it's way too medicinal and relentlessly bitter; keeping Unicum in the context of other herbal liqueurs, however, I believe that it's more than safe to say that it's an acquired taste and is purely cultural.
2004 Rating: ★★/Not Recommended

APPENDIX A

CONSUMERS' FAQS

Q: After I buy whiskeys, brandies, gins, vodkas, liqueurs, tequilas, etc, do they need any further time in the bottle to mellow or mature?
A: No. The biochemical nature of distilled spirits is that they are ready to be enjoyed as soon as they are bottled and bought. Distillates do not require any further aging or "laying down" as many wines, heftier reds especially, do.

Q: Should I collect spirits?
A: Collecting, except for the most ardent mavens (read: arrested development geeks with nothing better to do), is pointless, in my opinion. I go by the belief that an asteroid is going to barrel into the Earth at any given moment and I'd never want my final thought to be, "Damn it. I didn't open The Glenlivet 40 Year Old." Consume because you're celebrating the present. Don't trust the future.

Q: Any special way that I should store my distilled spirits at home?
A: Most definitely. Similar to fine wine, all types of spirits should be stored in naturally dark, cool, moderately humid places, such as liquor cabinets, subterranean cellars/basements, or interior closets. THAT DOES NOT MEAN THAT THEY NEED REFRIGERATION. If stored in very warm and bright conditions, spirits will break down chemically. Once that happens, their taste goes flat because their acidity starts to erode. Once acidity collapses, the entire structure caves in. Gins, cream liqueurs, and vodkas can be refrigerated. All others should be served at room temperature.

Q: Once the bottle of spirits is opened, how long will it last?
A: One of the most asked questions of all. While wines and beers have virtually no shelf time once they are opened (24-48 hours max, but only if they are properly resealed and stored), uncorked spirits can last for many weeks, even months. Bear in mind that the moment that oxygen enters the bottle, the chemical constitution of any whiskey, brandy, white spirit, or liqueur starts to degrade. Also be aware that as the quantity of spirit lessens with use, more air is mixing with the remaining and dwindling spirit. Consequently, the spirit's crispness and vivacity diminish even quicker.

Here's my recommended timeframe for uncorked bottles of spirits, acknowledging that it's best to lean towards the shorter end of the scale:
- White rums, vodkas, gins, 100% agave blanco and reposado tequilas, marc, grappa, eau-de-vie: two to three months
- All variety of liqueurs: three to four months (author's note: cream liqueurs, of course, need to be refrigerated after opening)

- All whiskeys, oak-aged rums, and 100% agave añejo and extra añejo tequilas: three to four months
- All wood-matured brandies: three to four months

Q: Aside from using vodkas, gins, tequilas, and rums as pivotal cocktail base ingredients, how should I serve them?

A: By custom in Poland and Russia, vodka is served ice cold with food on its own in small shot glasses. I strongly urge the food part of the equation. Use a small 1 to 1 1/2-ounce shot glass for maximum impact. Chill the glass. Gin, for all intents and purposes, is flavored vodka and acutely displays all of its earthy charms when poured into a chilled, stemmed cordial glass that's been generously rinsed with lime juice. I'm a huge fan of enjoying room temperature super-premium 100% agave tequilas, in particular, blancos and reposados, straight in a small shot glass, chased by tangy, homemade sangrita. Rums that can be served unadulterated include the older oak-aged rums-rhums-rons from all around the Caribbean region (room temperature in an old-fashioned glass or a Spanish copita) and the over-proof white rums (150-proof) that should be served in shot glasses.

Q: Whiskey makes a terrific base for numerous cocktails. What about when served neat? Should they have a splash of water?

A: Single malt Scotch whiskies; single malt and pure pot still Irish whiskeys; small batch, single barrel, or older (ten plus years) straight bourbon or Tennessee sour mash whiskeys; and older (eight plus years) Canadian whiskies should, in my view, always be consumed on their own and not as part of a mixed drink. Whiskeys are best served at room temperature along with a carafe of room temperature mineral or spring water in case the drinker likes to dilute his/her whiskey. Water, for many people including most Scots, stimulates whiskey's natural scents, making the experience more satisfying. Which brings up ice cubes. If ice cubes are wanted, make certain to use ice made with mineral/spring water, not municipal tap water, which can contain lead, fluoride, and chlorine. Harsh chemicals, like these, can quickly alter the taste of any variety of fine whiskey to the detriment of the whiskey and the consumer.

Q: This is a no-brainer, right? Brandy should always be served in a large snifter?

A: First and foremost, brandies should always be served at slightly below room temperature (62-65 degrees Fahrenheit). Regrettably, for generations the custom has been to serve the world's finer brandies in short-stemmed, bulbous, 8 to 14-ounce snifters. The reasoning dictated that the brandy needed to warm up in order to become more aromatic. Hogwash. Balderdash. Hooey. Brandy producers themselves burst this balloon over a decade ago when they informally put the word out to the press that a better vessel is a smaller, tubular, fine crystal glass in the traditional shape of the stemmed Spanish copita or, just as good, a port glass. The smaller area directs the bouquet better and the tubular shape funnels the aroma straight up into the nasal cavity. In snifters the natural, often delicate aromas flatten out and dissipate too rapidly in the snifter bowl.

Q: What's the right way to spell the word whiskey? With the "e" or without?

A: Tradition dictates that when referring to Irish or American grain-based distillates that have been aged in wood, you employ the "e", whiskey (plural: whiskeys). For those grain-based, wood-matured spirits produced in Canada or Scotland, the "e" is dropped, whisky (plural: whiskies). When referring to the global category, whiskey is the spelling to use. For years, people have told me several cockeyed reasons for this weirdness, but I still think that it comes down to the spelling that's simply been used for decades, sometimes centuries and nothing more.

Q: You occasionally mention the odd word "rancio" in a review. What's rancio?

A: Rancio is not meant to imply "rancid", but rather an ethereal, very positive characteristic that applies mostly to grape brandies, such as cognac and armagnac, and, less frequently, older whiskeys. Difficult to describe and seemingly impossible to quantify, rancio reminds me mostly of hard cheese or truffles or dried mushrooms. Some distillers claim it is only a result of extended maturation in oak while others state that it's part of the base material make-up that emerges over time. I believe that it's the former.

APPENDIX B

F. PAUL PACULT'S 111 BEST WHISKEYS, BRANDIES, LIQUEURS, AND WHITE SPIRITS IN THE WORLD

The following is a highly personal list of my favorite libations that answers the question, at least for me, "What spirits do you want when/if stranded on an island for a long stretch of time?"

1. **Highland Park 18 Year Old** Orkneys Single Malt Whisky (Scotland); 43% abv, $79.
2. **Midleton Very Rare 2006** Irish Blended Whiskey (Ireland); 40% abv, $130.
3. **Darroze 1965 Domaine de Peyrot** Bas Armagnac (France); 49.2% abv, $290.
4. **Nonino Cru Grappa di Monovitigno Picolit** Colli Orientali del Friuli (Italy); 50% abv, $156.
5. **Neisson Rhum Agricole Blanc** Appelation d'Origine Controlée (Martinique); 50% abv, $30/liter.
6. **Partida Reposado** 100% Agave Tequila (Mexico); 40% abv, $55.
7. **Bowmore 18 Year Old** Islay Single Malt Whisky (Scotland); 43% abv, $85.
8. **Frapin Extra** Grande Champagne Cognac (France); 40% abv, $491.
9. **Four Roses Single Barrel** Warehouse No. CS Barrel No. 48-SP Kentucky Straight Bourbon Whiskey (USA); 50% abv, $43.
10. **Glenmorangie The Nectar D'Or** Extra Matured Range Sauternes Cask Non-Chill Filtered Northern Highlands Single Malt Whisky (Scotland); 46% abv, $75.
11. **La Favorite Rhum Agricole Ambre** Appelation d'Origine Controlée (Martinique); 50% abv, $36/liter.
12. **Jacopo Poli Sarpa di Poli** Grappa (Italy); 40% abv, $29.
13. **Wild Turkey** Kentucky Spirit Single Barrel Warehouse E/Rick No. 13/Barrel No. 22 Kentucky Straight Bourbon Whiskey (USA); 50.5% abv, $46.
14. **Xellent** Vodka (Switzerland); 40% abv, $35.
15. **Tanqueray** London Dry Gin (England); 47.3% abv, $22.
16. **Johnnie Walker Gold 18 Year Old** Blended Scotch Whisky (Scotland); 40% abv, $80
17. **Cointreau** Liqueur (France) 40% abv, $35.
18. **Gran Centenario "Leyenda"** 100% Agave Extra Añejo Tequila (Mexico); 40% abv, $250.
19. **Germain-Robin Single Barrel Viognier** Brandy (USA); 40% abv, $140.
20. **Macallan 30 Year Old** Fine Oak Speyside Single Malt Whisky (Scotland); 43% abv, $700.
21. **Parker's Heritage Collection Cask Strength** Kentucky Straight Bourbon Whiskey (USA); 61.3% abv, $80.
22. **Bushmills 16 Year Old** Irish Single Malt Whiskey (Ireland); 40% abv, $60.

23. **Jacopo Poli Moscato** Immature Grape Brandy (Italy); 40% abv, $55/375 ml.
24. **Aqua Perfecta Pear Eau-de-Vie** (USA); 40% abv, $40.
25. **Appleton Estate Extra** Rum (Jamaica); 40% abv, $35.
26. **Chinaco Extra Añejo** Lot No. 71 100% Agave Tequila (Mexico); 43% abv, $251.
27. **St. Germain** Liqueur Artisanale (France); 20% abv, $33.
28. **Highland Park 25 Year Old** Orkney Islands Single Malt Whisky (Scotland); 48.1% abv, $230.
29. **Rock Hill Farms Single Barrel** Kentucky Bourbon Whiskey (USA); 50% abv, $50.
30. **Chivas 18 Year Old** Blended Scotch Whisky (Scotland); 40% abv, $55.
31. **Partida "Elegante"** 100% Agave Extra Añejo Tequila (Mexico); 40% abv, $350.
32. **Gran Duque d'Alba** Brandy de Jerez Solera Gran Reserva (Spain); 40% abv, $45.
33. **Etter Williams Fine Eau-de-Vie de Poire** (Switzerland); 42% abv, $72.
34. **Pappy Van Winkle's Family Reserve 15 Year Old** KSBW (USA); 53.5% abv, $45.
35. **Delamain Reserve de la Famille** Grande Champagne Cognac (France); 43% abv, $473.
36. **BenRiach Pedro Ximenez Sherry Wood Finish 15 Year Old** Speyside Single Malt Whisky (Scotland); 46% abv, $95.
37. **Herradura Añejo** 100% Agave Tequila (Mexico); 40% abv, $65.
38. **Springbank Marsala Wood Expression 9 Year Old** Campbeltown Single Malt Whisky (Scotland); 58% abv, $110.
39. **Charbay** Rum (USA); 40% abv, $36.
40. **Duncan Taylor "Rarest of the Rare" 21 Year Old Linlithgow 1982** Cask No. 2214 Lowlands Single Malt Whisky (Scotland); 63.5% abv, $217.
41. **Rittenhouse 21 Year Old** Bottled-in-Bond Straight Rye Whiskey (USA); 50% abv, $150.
42. **Grand Marnier Cuvée du Centenaire** Triple Orange Liqueur (France); 40% abv, $100.
43. **Don Julio Blanco** 100% Agave Tequila (Mexico); 40% abv, $50.
44. **Domaine de Laubade 1978** Bas Armagnac (France); 40% abv, $135.
45. **Herb's Dill Leaf Herb** Infused Vodka (USA); 40% abv, $29.
46. **Trago Añejo** 100% Agave Tequila (Mexico); 40% abv, $60.
47. **Cold River** Vodka (USA); 40% abv, $35.
48. **Chauffe Coeur Hors d'Age** Armagnac (France); 40% abv, $45.
49. **Benedictine** Liqueur (France); 40% abv, $29.
50. **Absolut Pears** Pear Flavored Vodka (Sweden); 40% abv, $19.
51. **Drambuie** Liqueur (Scotland); 40% abv, $35.
52. **Four Roses Small Batch** Kentucky Straight Bourbon Whiskey (USA); 45% abv, $36.
53. **Cragganmore Rare Edition 10 Year Old Sherry Cask** Speyside Single Malt Whisky (Scotland); 60.1% abv, $150.
54. **A. Edmond Audry Exception** Fine Champagne Cognac (France); 43% abv, $250.
55. **El Tesoro de Don Felipe Añejo** 100% Agave Tequila (Mexico); 40% abv, $59.
56. **Ardbeg Airigh Nam Beist 1990** Non-Chill Filtered Islay Single Malt Whisky (Scotland); 46% abv, $110.
57. **Daniel Bouju Empereur XO** Grande Champagne Cognac (France); 40% abv, $78.

58. **Macallan 17 Year Old Fine Oak** Speyside Single Malt Whisky (Scotland); 43% abv, $120.
59. **Delamain Extra** de Grande Champagne Cognac (France); 40% abv, $319.
60. **Crown Royal XR** Extra Rare Blended Canadian Whisky (Canada); 40% abv, $150.
61. **Elijah Craig 18 Year Old Single Barrel** Kentucky Straight Bourbon Whiskey (USA); 45% abv, $36.
62. **Bocchino 10 Year Old Grappa Riserva** della Cantina Privata (Italy); 45% abv, $115/375 ml.
63. **Port Charlotte PC5 Evolution** Cask Strength Islay Single Malt Whisky/Distilled at Bruichladdich Distillery (Scotland); 63.5% abv, $110.
64. **Tanqueray No. Ten** Batch Distilled Gin (England); 47.3% abv, $27.
65. **Longrow 100-Proof 10 Year Old** Campbeltown Single Malt Whisky (Scotland); 50% abv, $130.
66. **Marcel Trépout 1925 80 Year Old** Armagnac (France); 40% abv, $833.
67. **Old Forester 2006 Birthday** Bourbon Kentucky Straight Bourbon Whiskey Distilled Spring 1993/Bottled 2006 (USA); 48% abv, $40.
68. **Château du Breuil 15 Year Old** Calvados (France); 41% abv, $50.
69. **Puriste No. 1** Premium Vodka (Austria); 40.2% abv, $40.
70. **Bruichladdich Rocks** Islay Single Malt Whisky (Scotland); 46% abv, $47.
71. **Vincent van Gogh** Gin (Holland); 47% abv, $25.
72. **Milagro Select Barrel Reserve Reposado** 100% Agave Tequila (Mexico); 40% abv, $70.
73. **Darroze 1988 Domaine du Martin** Bas Armagnac (France); 50.4% abv, $117.
74. **A. Hardy Noces de Diamant** 60 Year Old Grande Champagne Cognac (France); 40% abv, $500.
75. **Finlandia Grapefruit** Flavored Vodka (Finland); 40% abv, $18.
76. **Lysholm Linie** Aquavit (Norway); 41.5% abv, $25.
77. **Depaz Blue Cane** Rhum Agricole (Martinique); 45% abv, $42.
78. **Plymouth** Dry Gin (England); 41.2% abv, $30.
79. **Daniel Bouju Royal Brut de Fut** Grande Champagne Cognac (France); 60% abv, $65.
80. **Laphroaig 30 Year Old** Islay Single Malt Whisky (Scotland); 43% abv, $225.
81. **Balvenie "Thirty" 30 Year Old** Speyside Single Malt Whisky (Scotland); 47.3% abv, $499.
82. **Santa Teresa 1796** Ron Antiguo de Solera (Venezuela); 40% abv, $35.
83. **Cabo Wabo Reposado** 100% Agave Tequila (Mexico); 40% abv, $58.
84. **Chartreuse Green V.E.P.** Liqueur Fabriquée par Les Pères Chartreux (France); 54% abv, $126/liter.
85. **X Rated Fusion** Liqueur (France); 17% abv, $28.
86. **Flor de Caña Centenario 21 Year Old** Limited Edition Rum (Nicaragua); 40% abv, $60.
87. **Stolichnaya elit** Vodka(Russia); 40% abv, $60.
88. **Cadenhead's Old Raj** Dry Gin (Scotland); 55% abv, $50.
89. **Bowmore "Darkest" Sherry Cask** Islay Single Malt Whisky (Scotland); 43% abv, $65.

90. **Hangar One Kaffir Lime** Vodka (USA); 40% abv, $36.
91. **ZYR** Russian Vodka (Russia); 40% abv, $32.
92. **Richard Hennessy** Cognac (France); 40% abv, $1,500.
93. **Coeur de Lion Hors d'Age** Calvados Pays d'Auge (France); 42% abv, $95.
94. **Auchentoshan 18 Year Old** Oloroso Sherry Matured Lowlands Single Malt Whisky (Scotland); 55.8% abv, $1,000.
95. **La Botija** Italia Pisco (Peru); 41.5% abv, $17.
96. **Crown Royal Special Reserve** Blended Canadian Whisky (Canada); 40% abv, $40.
97. **Dalmore Cigar Malt** Northern Highlands Single Malt Whisky (Scotland); 43% abv, $37.
98. **Rhum Clemént Cuvée Homóre** Rhum Vieux Agricole (Martinique); 44% abv, $85.
99. **Domaine de Laubade 1967** Bas Armagnac (France); 40% abv, $175.
100. **Vincent van Gogh Dutch Chocolate** Vodka (Holland); 35% abv, $30.
101. **Pearl** Vodka (Canada); 40% abv, $25/liter.
102. **Marquis de Montesquiou 1971** Bas Armagnac (France); 44.9% abv, $100.
103. **Arran Malt Port Cask Finished** Single Cask Isle of Arran Single Malt Whisky (Scotland); 58.5% abv, $79.
104. **Appleton Estate Reserve** Jamaican Rum (Jamaica); 40% abv, $27.
105. **Chauffe Coeur Hors d'Age** Calvados (France); 43% abv, $40.
106. **Brillet Cognac Très Rare Heritage** Brut de Fut Grande Champagne Cognac (France); 50% abv, $300.
107. **Springbank 15 Year Old** Campbeltown Single Malt Whisky (Scotland); 46% abv, $116.
108. **Canton Ginger & Cognac** Liqueur (France); 28% abv, $29.
109. **Delord 25 Year Old Bas** Armagnac (France); 40% abv, $95.
110. **Grand Marnier Cuvée Spéciale Cent Cinquantenaire** Liqueur (France); 40% abv, $190.
111. **Shaker's Vodka** (USA); 40% abv, $33.

APPENDIX C

ABOUT *F. PAUL PACULT'S SPIRIT JOURNAL*

F. Paul Pacult's Spirit Journal: The Quarterly Independent Guide to Distilled Spirits, Beers, and Wines was established in the winter of 1991 by spirits and wine journalist F. Paul Pacult. After having worked in the California wine industry for a decade and after recognizing that wine was amply covered in newspapers, magazines and newsletters, Paul Pacult decided to give a voice to the world's distilled spirits through the vehicle of a subscription-only newsletter. Convinced that the only way to maintain critical and editorial impartiality, Paul made it the policy of the *F. Paul Pacult's Spirit Journal* not to accept advertising and not to charge fees for product submission for published reviews. Instead, the costs of publishing would be paid for by subscriptions. That policy has not changed.

Believing that it is virtually impossible to tell the difference between products rated closely on the 100-point scale, Paul decided instead to utilize a one-to-five star rating system, five being the highest.

A quarterly newsletter, *F. Paul Pacult's Spirit Journal* is mailed to US and overseas subscribers each March, June, September, and December. It is the supreme consumer buying guide giving Paul's unbiased opinions and keen insights on all types of spirits, wines, and beers available in the marketplace. The newsletter offers subscribers the latest, up-to-date reviews, usually numbering around 120-140 reviews per issue. *F. Paul Pacult's Spirit Journal* will assist you in exploring the myriad of beverage alcohol products that currently inhabit the marketplace. You won't find *F. Paul Pacult's Spirit Journal* on newsstands; readers receive it every quarter through paid subscription only.

http://www.spiritjournal.com

F. PAUL PACULT

F. PAUL PACULT is the founding editor and publisher of *F. Paul Pacult's Spirit Journal—The Quarterly Independent Guide to Distilled Spirits, Beers, and Wines* newsletter now in its 18th year of publication. He is the author of the critically acclaimed books *A Double Scotch: How Chivas Regal and The Glenlivet Became Global Icons* (John Wiley & Sons, 2005); *American Still Life: The Jim Beam Story and the Making of the World's #1 Bourbon* (John Wiley & Sons, 2003); as well as author of *Kindred Spirits* (Hyperion, 1997); and *The Beer Essentials* (Hyperion, 1997).

As well as being one of the most sought after consultants to the beverage alcohol industry through Spirit Journal, Inc., Paul is also the monthly wine and spirits columnist for *Sky*—the award-winning Delta Air Lines magazine; a columnist and the spirits tasting director for *Wine Enthusiast Magazine*; a contributing editor for *Beverage Dynamics Magazine*; the judging director at the annual San Francisco World Spirits Competition; and a founding member of Beverage Alcohol Resource, LLC (BAR) an educational company that focuses on spirits and mixology; BAR was the proud recipient of the 2007 *Cheers Magazine's* "Industry Innovator of the Year" award.

Paul won the "Award of Excellence for Wine Writing—2003" given by the Academy of Wine Writing. He is also honored to be the only journalist worldwide to concurrently be a life member of The Keepers of the Quaich Scotch Whisky Society (Edinburgh, Scotland), The Bourbon Hall of Fame (Bardstown, KY), as well as a member of the Armagnac Company of Musketeers (Gascony, France).

He lives ninety miles north of Manhattan in New York State's Hudson Valley with his wife and partner, Sue Woodley.

BIBLIOGRAPHY

IMPORTANT BOOKS TO HAVE CLOSE BY

Books: Spirits
Blue, Anthony Dias. *The Complete Book of Spirits: A Guide to Their History, Production, and Enjoyment*. New York, NY: HarperCollins, 2004.

Broom, Dave. *Rum*. San Francisco: Wine Appreciation Guild, 2003.

Coates, Geraldine. *Classic Gin*. London: Prion Books, 2000.

Dillon, Patrick. *Gin: The Much-Lamented Death of Madam Geneva*. Boston, MA, Justin, Charles & Co. 2002.

Emmons, Bob. *The Book of Gins & Vodkas*. Peru, IL: Open Court, 2000.

Emmons, Bob. *The Book of Tequila*. Peru, IL: Open Court, 1997.

Faith, Nicholas. *Cognac*. London: Mitchell Beazley, 2004.

Faith, Nicholas, and Ian Wisniewski. *Classic Vodka*. London: Prion Books, 1997.

Gabányi, Stefan. *Whisk(e)y*. New York: Abbeville Press, 1997.

Gregory, Conal R. *The Cognac Companion*. Philadelphia: Running Press, 1997.

Hamilton, Edward. *The Complete Guide to Rum*. Chicago: Triumph Books, 1997.

Jackson, Michael. *Michael Jackson's Complete Guide to Single Malt Scotch*. Philadelphia: Running Press, 1999.

Jones, Andrew. *The Aperitif Companion*. New York: Knickerbocker Press, 1998.

MacDonald, Aeneas. *Whisky*. Edinburgh, Scotland: Canongate Books, 1930/Reissue 2007.

MacLean, Charles. *malt whisky*. London: Mitchell Beazley, 1997.

MacLean, Charles. *MacLean's Miscellany of Whisky*. London: Little Books, Ltd, 2004.

Murray, Jim. *Classic Irish Whiskey.* London: Prion Books, 1997.

Neal, Charles. *Armagnac.* San Francisco: Flame Grape Press, 1998.

Pacult, F. Paul. *A Double Scotch: How Chivas Regal and The Glenlivet Became Global Icons.* Hoboken, NJ: John Wiley & Sons, 2005.

Pacult, F. Paul. *American Still Life: The Jim Beam Story and the Making of the World's #1 Bourbon.* Hoboken, NJ: John Wiley & Sons, 2003.

Pessey, Christian. *The Little Book of Cognac.* Paris: Flammarion, 2002.

Regan, Gary, and Mardee Haidin Regan. *The Bourbon Companion.* Philadelphia: Running Press, 1998.

Books: General
Ackerman, Diane. *A Natural History of the Senses.* New York, NY: Vintage Books – Random House, 1990.

Books: Cocktails
DeGroff, Dale. *The Craft of the Cocktail.* New York, NY: Clarkson Potter, 2002.

Felten, Eric. *How's Your Drink? Cocktails, Culture, and the Art of Drinking Well.* Chicago, IL: Surrey Books, 2007.

Grimes, William. *Straight Up or On the Rocks: A Cultural History of American Drink.* New York, NY: Simon & Schuster, 1993.

Haidin Regan, Mardee. *The Bartender's Best Friend: A Complete Guide to Cocktails, Martinis and Mixed Drinks.* Hoboken, NJ: John Wiley & Sons, 2003.

Haigh, Ted. *Vintage Spirits & Forgotten Cocktails.* Gloucester, MA: Quarry Books, 2004.

Hamilton, William L. *Shaken and Stirred.* New York, NY: HarperCollins, 2004.

Plotkin, Robert. *Secrets Revealed of America's Greatest Cocktails: The Hottest Spirits, Coolest Drinks and Freshest Places.* Tucson, AZ: BarMedia, 2007.

Regan, Gary. *The Joy of Mixology.* New York, NY: Clarkson Potter, 2003.

Wondrich, David. *Killer Cocktails.* New York, NY: HarperCollins, 2005.

Wondrich, David. *IMBIBE! From Absinthe Cocktail to Whiskey Smash, a Salute in Stories and Drinks to "Professor" Jerry Thomas, Pioneer of the American Bar.* New York, NY: Perigee Hardcover, 2007.

CPSIA information can be obtained at www.ICGtesting.com
Printed in the USA
LVOW11s0833040816

499005LV00002B/142/P